Southwest

Arizona, Colorado, New Mexico, and Utah

MACMILLAN • USA

Frommer's America on Wheels: Southwest
Regional Editors: Don and Barbara Laine
Inspections Coordinator: Laura Van Zee

Contributors: Mary Gail Brassard, Laura Bulkin, Alex Gray, Sean Pack, Eric Peterson, Keri Ross, Muriel Smedley, Anne Sullivan

Frommer's America on Wheels Staff
Project Director: Gretchen Henderson
Senior Editor: Christopher Hollander
Database Editor: Melissa Klurman
Assistant Editor: Marian Cole
Editorial Assistant: Tracy McNamara

Macmillan Travel
A Simon & Schuster Macmillan Company
1633 Broadway
New York, NY 10019-6785

Find us online at **http://www.mgr.com/travel** or on America Online at keyword **Frommer's**.

MACMILLAN is a registered trademark of Macmillan, Inc.

Manufactured in the United States of America

ISSN: 1087-0067
ISBN: 0-02-861112-8

SPECIAL SALES
Bulk purchases (10+ copies) of Frommer's and selected Macmillan travel guides are available to corporations, organizations, mail-order catalogs, institutions, and charities at special discounts, and can be customized to suit individual needs. For more information write to Special Sales, Macmillan General Reference, 1633 Broadway, New York, NY 10019.

Contents

Utah

Introduction

America on Wheels introduces a brand-new lodgings rating system—one that factors in the latest trends in travel preferences, technologies, and amenities and is based on thorough inspections by experienced travel professionals. We rate establishments from one to five flags, plus a unique rating we call Ultra, a special award reserved for only a handful of outstanding properties in each category. Our restaurant selections represent the ethnic diversity of today's dining scene and are categorized with symbols according to their special features, ambience, and services available. In addition, the series provides in-depth sightseeing information, including driving tours and best-of-the-state highlights.

State Introductions

Coverage of each state in the *America on Wheels* series begins with background information that will help familiarize you with your destination. Included is a summary of the state's history and an overview of its geography, followed by practical tips that we hope you will find useful in planning your trip—what kind of weather to expect, what to pack, sources of information within the state, driving rules and regulations, and other essentials.

The "Best of the State" section provides you with a rundown of the top sights and attractions and the most popular festivals and special events around the state. It also includes information on spectator sports and an A-to-Z list of recreational activities available to you.

Driving Tours

The scenic driving tours included guide you along some of the most popular sightseeing routes. Every tour is keyed to a map and includes mileage information and precise directions, refreshment stops, and, for longer tours, recommended places to stay.

The Listings

The city-by-city listings of lodgings, dining establishments, and attractions together make up the bulk of the book. Cities are organized alphabetically within each state. You will find a brief description or "profile" for most cities, including a source to contact for additional information. Any listings will follow.

Types of Lodgings

Here's how we define the lodging categories used in *America on Wheels*.

Hotel

A hotel usually has three or more floors with elevators. It may or may not have parking, but if it does, entry to the guest rooms is likely to be through the lobby rather than directly from the parking lot. A range of lodgings is available (such as standard rooms, deluxe rooms, and suites), and a range of services is available (such as bellhops, room service, and a concierge). Many hotels have a restaurant or coffee shop open for breakfast, lunch, and dinner; they may have a cocktail lounge/bar. Recreational facilities may be available (such as a swimming pool, fitness center, and tennis courts).

Motel

A motel usually has one to three floors, and many of the guest rooms have doors facing the parking lot or outdoor corridors. A motel may only have a small, serviceable lobby and usually offers only limited services; the nearest restaurant may be down the street. A motel is most likely to be located alongside a highway or in a resort area.

Inn

An inn is a small-scale hotel or lodge, usually in an older building that may or may not have been designed for lodgings, and it is often located in scenic surroundings. An inn should have a warm, welcoming atmosphere, with a more homelike quality to its furnishings and facilities. The guest rooms may be individually decorated in a style appropriate to the inn's age and location, and the rooms may or may not have telephones, televisions, or private bathrooms. An inn usually has a lounge or sitting room for guests (with parlor games and perhaps a television) and a small dining room that may or may not be open to the public. Breakfast, however, is almost always served.

Lodge

A lodge is essentially a small hotel in a rural, remote, or mountainous location. The atmosphere, service, and furniture may be more casual than you'd find in a regular hotel, and there may not be televisions or telephones in every guest room. The facilities usually include a coffee shop or restaurant, bar or cocktail lounge, games room, and indoor or outdoor swimming pool or hot tub. In ski areas, the lounge usually has a fireplace and facilities for storing ski gear.

Resort

A resort usually has more extensive facilities and recreational activities than a hotel, and offers three meals a day. The atmosphere is generally more informal than at comparable hotels.

How the Lodgings Are Rated

Every hotel, motel, resort, inn, and lodge rated in this series has been subjected to a thorough hands-on inspection by our team of accomplished travel professionals. We ask the kinds of questions that readers would ask if they could inspect the rooms in advance for themselves (How good is the soundproofing? How firm is the bed? What condition are the room furnishings in?). Then all of the inspection reports are reviewed by regional editors who are experts on their territories. The top-rated properties are then rechecked by a special consultant who has been reviewing and critiquing luxury hotels around the world for almost 25 years. *Establishments are not charged to be included in our series.*

Our ratings are based on *average* guest rooms—not lavish suites or concierge floors—so they're not artificially high. Therefore, in some cases a hotel rated four flags may indeed have individual rooms or suites that might fall into the five-flag category; conversely, a four-flag hotel may have a few rooms in its lowest price range that might otherwise warrant three flags.

The detailed ratings vary by category of lodgings—for example, the criteria imposed on a hotel are more rigorous than those for a motel—and some features that are considered essential in, for example, a four-flag city hotel are relaxed for a resort that offers alternative attractions, sporting facilities, and/or beautiful and spacious grounds. Likewise, amenities such as telephones and televisions—essential in hotels and motels—are not required in inns, whose guests are often seeking peace and quiet. Instead, the criteria take into account such features as individually decorated rooms and complimentary afternoon tea.

There are, of course, several basic attributes that apply to all lodgings across the board: the cleanliness and maintenance of the building as a whole; the housekeeping in individual rooms; safety, both indoors and out; the quality and practicality of the furnishings; the quality and availability of the amenities; the caliber of the facilities; the extent and/or condition of the grounds; the ambience and cleanliness in the dining rooms; and the caliber and professionalism of the service in relation to the rates and types of lodging. Since the *America on Wheels* rating system is highly rigorous, just because a property has garnered only one flag does not mean it is inadequate or substandard.

What the Individual Ratings Mean

One Flag

These properties have met or surpassed the minimum requirements of cleanliness, safety, convenience, and amenities. The staff may be limited, but guests can generally expect a friendly, hospitable greeting. Rooms will have basic amenities, such as air conditioning or heating where appropriate, telephones, and televisions. The bathrooms may have only showers rather than tubs, and just one towel for each guest, but showers and towels must be clean. The one-flag properties are by no means places to avoid, since they can represent exceptional value.

Two Flags

In addition to having all of the basic attributes of one-flag lodgings, these properties will have some extra amenities, such as bellhops to help with the luggage, ice buckets in each room, and better-quality furnishings. Some extra services may include availability of cribs and irons, and wake-up service.

Three Flags

These properties have all the basics noted above but also offer a more generous complement of amenities, such as firmer beds, larger desks, more drawer space, extra blankets and pillows, cable or satellite TV, alarm clock/radios, room service (although hours may be limited), and dry cleaning and/or laundry services.

Four Flags
This is the realm of luxury, with refinements in amenities, furnishings, and service—such as larger rooms, more dependable soundproofing, two telephones per room, in-room movies, in-room safes, thick towels, hair dryers, twice-daily maid service, turndown service, concierge service, and 24-hour room service.

Five Flags
These properties have everything the four-flag properties have, plus a more personal level of service and more sumptuous amenities, among them bathrobes, superior linens, and blackout drapes for lightproofing. Facilities normally include a business center and fitness center. Generally speaking, guests pay handsomely to stay in these properties.

Ultra
This crème-de-la-crème rating is reserved for those rare hotels and resorts, possibly also motels and inns, that are truly outstanding in every or almost every department—places with a "grand hotel" presence, an almost flawless level of service, and a standard of dining equal to that of the finest restaurants.

UNRATED

In the few cases where an inspector was not able to make a detailed inspection, the property is listed as unrated. Also, in some cases where a property was in the process of changing owners or managers, or if the property was undergoing the kind of major renovations that made formal evaluation impossible, then, again, it is listed as unrated.

Types of Dining

Restaurant
A restaurant serves complete meals and almost always offers seating.

Refreshment Stop
A refreshment stop serves drinks and/or snacks only (such as an ice cream parlor, bakery, or coffee bar) and may or may not have seating available.

How the Restaurants Were Evaluated

All of the restaurants reviewed in this series have been through the kind of thorough inspection described above for lodgings. Our inspectors have evaluated everything from freshness of ingredients to noise level and spacing of tables.

Unique to the *America on Wheels* series are the easy-to-read symbols that identify a restaurant's special features, its ambience, and special services. (See the inside front cover for the key to all symbols.) With them you can determine at a glance whether a place is a local favorite, offers exceptional value, or is "worth a splurge."

How to Read the Listings

LODGINGS

Introductory Information
The rating is followed by the establishment's name, address, neighborhood (if applicable), telephone number(s), and fax number (if there is one). Where appropriate, location information is provided. In the resort listings, the acreage of the property is indicated. Also included are our inspector's comments, which provide some description and discuss any outstanding features or special information about the establishment. You can also find out whether an inn is unsuitable for children, and if so, up to what age.

Rooms
Specifies the number and type of accommodations available. If a hotel has an "executive level," this will be noted here. (This level, sometimes called a "concierge floor," is a special area of a hotel. Usually priced higher than standard rooms, accommodations at this level are often larger and have additional amenities and services such as daily newspaper delivery and nightly turndown service. Guests staying in these rooms often have access to a private lounge where complimentary breakfasts or snacks may be served.) Check-in/check-out times will also appear in this section, followed by information on the establishment's smoking policy ("No smoking" for properties that are entirely nonsmoking, and "Nonsmoking rms avail" for those that permit smoking in some areas but have rooms available for nonsmokers). This information may be followed by comments, if the inspector noted anything in particular about the guest rooms, such as their size, decor, furnishings, or window views.

Amenities
If the following amenities are available in the majority of the guest rooms, they are indicated by symbols

(see inside front cover for key) or included in a list: telephone, alarm clock, coffeemaker, hair dryer, air conditioning, TV (including cable or satellite hookup, free or pay movies), refrigerator, dataport (for fax/modem communication), VCR, CD/tape player, voice mail, in-room safe, and bathrobes. If some or all rooms have minibars, terraces, fireplaces, or whirlpools, that will be indicated here. Because travelers usually expect air conditioning, telephones, and televisions in their guest rooms, we specifically note when those amenities are not available. If any additional amenities are available in the majority of the guest rooms, or if amenities are outstanding in any way, the inspector's comments will provide some elaboration at the end of this section.

Services

If the following services are available, they are indicated by symbols (see inside front cover for key) or included in a list: room service (24-hour or limited), concierge, valet parking, airport transportation, dry cleaning/laundry, cribs available, pets allowed (call ahead before bringing your pet; an establishment that accepts pets may nevertheless place restrictions on the types or size of pets allowed, or may require a deposit and/or charge a fee), twice-daily maid service, car-rental desk, social director, masseur, children's program, babysitting (that is, the establishment can put you in touch with local babysitters and/or agencies), and afternoon tea and/or wine or sherry served. If the establishment offers any special services, or if the inspector has commented on the quality of services offered, that information will appear at the end of this section. Please note that there may be a fee for some services.

Facilities

If the following facilities are on the premises, they are indicated by symbols (see inside front cover for key) or included in a list: pool(s), bike rentals, boat rentals (may include canoes, kayaks, sailboats, powerboats, jet-skis, paddleboats), fishing, golf course (with number of holes), horseback riding, jogging path/parcourse (fitness trail), unlighted tennis courts (number available), lighted tennis courts (number available), waterskiing, windsurfing, fitness center, meeting facilities (and number of people this space can accommodate), business center, restaurant(s), bar(s), beach(es), lifeguard (for beach, not pool), basketball, volleyball, board surfing, games room, lawn games, racquetball, snorkeling, squash, spa, sauna, steam room, whirlpool, beauty salon, day-care center, playground, washer/dryer, and guest lounge (for inns only). If cross-country and downhill skiing facilities are located within 10 miles of the property, then that is indicated by symbols here as well. Our "Accessible for People With Disabilities" symbol appears where establishments claim to have guest rooms with such accessibility. If an establishment has additional facilities that are worth noting, or if the inspector has commented about the facilities, that information appears at the end of this section.

Rates

If the establishment's rates vary throughout the year, then the rates given are for the peak season. The rates listed are EP (no meals included), unless otherwise noted. We'll tell you if there is a charge for an extra person to stay in a room; if children stay free, and if so, up to what age; if there are minimum stay requirements; and if AP (three meals) and/or MAP (breakfast and dinner) rates are also available. The parking rates (if the establishment has parking) are followed by any comments the inspector has provided about rates.

If the establishment has a seasonal closing, this information will be stated. A list of credit cards accepted ends the listing.

DINING

Introductory Information

If a restaurant is a local favorite, an exceptional value (one with a high quality-to-price ratio for the area), or "worth a splurge" (more expensive by area standards, but well worth it), the appropriate symbol will appear at the beginning of the listing (see inside front cover for key to symbols). Then the establishment's name, address, neighborhood (if applicable), and telephone number are listed, followed by location information when appropriate. The type of cuisine appears in boldface type and is followed by our inspectors' comments on everything from decor and ambience to menu highlights.

The "FYI" Heading

"For your information," this section tells you the reservations policy ("recommended," "accepted," or "not accepted"), and whether there is live entertainment, a children's menu, or a dress code (jacket required or other policy). If the restaurant does not have a full bar, you can find out what the liquor policy is ("beer and wine only," "beer only," "wine only," "BYO," or "no liquor license"). This is also where you can check to see if there's a no-smoking policy for the entire restaurant (please note that smoking policies are in flux throughout the country; if smoking—or avoiding smokers—is important to you, it's a good idea to call ahead to verify the policy). If the restaurant is part of a group or chain, address and phone information will be provided for additional locations in the area. This section does not appear in Refreshment Stop listings.

Hours of Operation
Under the "Open" heading, "Peak" indicates that the hours listed are for high season only (dates in parentheses); otherwise, the hours listed apply year-round. If an establishment has a seasonal closing, that information will follow. It's a good idea to call ahead to confirm the hours of operation, especially in the off-season.

Prices
Prices given are for dinner main courses (unless otherwise noted). If a prix-fixe dinner is offered throughout dinner hours, that price is listed here, too. This section ends with a list of credit cards accepted. Refreshment Stop listings do not include prices.

Symbols
The symbols that fall at the end of many restaurant listings can help you find restaurants with the features that are important to you. If a restaurant has romantic ambience, historic ambience, outdoor dining, a fireplace, a view, delivery service, early-bird specials, valet parking, or is family-oriented, open 24 hours, or accessible to people with disabilities (meaning it has a level entrance or an access ramp, a doorway at least 36 inches wide, and restrooms that are on the same floor as the dining room, with doorways at least 36 inches wide and properly outfitted stalls), then these symbols will appear (see inside front cover for key to symbols).

ATTRACTIONS

Introductory Information
The name, street address, neighborhood (if located in a major city), and telephone number are followed by a brief rundown of the attraction's high points and key attributes so you can quickly determine if it's worth a full day of exploration or just a brief detour.

Hours of Operation & Admission
Service information includes hours of operation ("Peak" indicates that the hours listed are for high season only) and the cost of admission. The cost is

ABBREVIATIONS

A/C	air conditioning
AE	American Express (charge card)
AP	American Plan (rates include breakfast, lunch, and dinner)
avail	available
BB	Bed-and-Breakfast Plan (rates include full breakfast)
bkfst	breakfast
BYO	bring your own (beer or wine)
CC	credit cards
CI	check-in time
CO	check-out time
CP	Continental Plan (rates include continental breakfast)
ctr	center
D	double (indicates room rate for two people in one room (one or two beds))
DC	Diners Club (credit card)
DISC	Discover (credit card)
EC	EuroCard (credit card)
effic	efficiency (unit with cooking facilities)
ER	En Route (credit card)
info	information
int'l	international
JCB	Japanese Credit Bureau (credit card)
ltd	limited
MAP	Modified American Plan (rates include breakfast and dinner)
MC	MasterCard (credit card)
Mem Day	Memorial Day
mi	mile(s)
min	minimum
MM	mile marker
refrig	refrigerator
rms	rooms
S	single (indicates room rate for one person)
satel	satellite
stes	suites (rooms with separate living and sleeping areas)
svce	service
tel	telephone
V	Visa (credit card)
w/	with
wknds	weekends

indicated by one to four dollar signs (see inside front cover for key to symbols). It's a good idea to call ahead to confirm the hours.

Special Information

DISABLED TRAVELER INFORMATION

The Americans with Disabilities Act (ADA) of 1990 required that all public facilities and commercial establishments be made accessible to disabled persons by January 26, 1992. Any property opened after that date must be built in accordance with the ADA Accessible Guidelines. Note, however, that not all establishments have completed their renovations to conform with the law; be sure to call ahead to determine if your specific needs can be met.

TAXES

State and city taxes vary widely and are not included in the prices in this book. Always ask about the taxes when you are making your reservations. State sales tax is given under "Essentials" in the introduction to each state.

A DISCLAIMER

Readers are advised that prices fluctuate in the course of time, and travel information changes under the impact of the varied and volatile factors that affect the travel industry. The publisher cannot be held responsible for the experiences of readers while traveling. Readers are invited to send ideas, comments, and suggestions for future editions to: *America on Wheels,* Macmillan Travel, 1633 Broadway, New York, NY 10019-6785.

TOLL-FREE NUMBERS/WORLD WIDE WEB SITES

The following toll-free telephone numbers and URLs for World Wide Web sites were accurate at press time; *America on Wheels* cannot be held responsible for any number or address that has changed. The "TDD" numbers are answered by a telecommunications service for the deaf and hard-of-hearing. Be sure to dial "1" before each number.

Lodgings

Best Western International, Inc
800/528-1234 North America
800/528-2222 TDD

Budgetel Inns
800/4-BUDGET Continental USA and Canada

Budget Host
800/BUD-HOST Continental USA

Clarion Hotels
800/CLARION Continental USA and Canada
800/228-3323 TDD
http://www.hotelchoice.com/cgi-bin/res/webres?clarion.html

Comfort Inns
800/228-5150 Continental USA and Canada
800/228-3323 TDD
http://www.hotelchoice.com/cgi-bin/res/webres?comfort.html

Courtyard by Marriott
800/321-2211 Continental USA and Canada
800/228-7014 TDD
http://www.marriott.com/lodging/courtyar.html

Days Inn
800/325-2525 Continental USA and Canada
800/325-3297 TDD
http://www.daysinn.com/daysinn.html

DoubleTree Hotels
800/222-TREE Continental USA and Canada
800/528-9898 TDD

Drury Inn
800/325-8300 Continental USA and Canada
800/325-0583 TDD

Econo Lodges
800/55-ECONO Continental USA and Canada
800/228-3323 TDD
http://www.hotelchoice.com/cgi-bin/res/webres?econo.html

Embassy Suites
800/362-2779 Continental USA and Canada
800/458-4708 TDD
http://www.embassy-suites.com

Exel Inns of America
800/356-8013 Continental USA and Canada

Fairfield Inn by Marriott
800/228-2800 Continental USA and Canada
800/228-7014 TDD
http://www.marriott.com/lodging/fairf.html

Fairmont Hotels
800/527-4727 Continental USA

Forte Hotels
800/225-5843 Continental USA and Canada

Four Seasons Hotels
800/332-3442 Continental USA
800/268-6282 Canada

Friendship Inns
800/453-4511 Continental USA
800/228-3323 TDD
http://www.hotelchoice.com/cgi-bin/res/webres?friendship.html

Guest Quarters Suites
800/424-2900 Continental USA

Hampton Inn
800/HAMPTON Continental USA and Canada
800/451-HTDD TDD
http://www.hampton-inn.com

Hilton Hotels Corporation
800/HILTONS Continental USA and Canada
800/368-1133 TDD
http://www.hilton.com

Holiday Inn
800/HOLIDAY Continental USA and Canada
800/238-5544 TDD
http://www.holiday-inn.com

Howard Johnson
800/654-2000 Continental USA and Canada
800/654-8442 TDD
http://www.hojo.com/hojo.html

Hyatt Hotels and Resorts
800/228-9000 Continental USA and Canada
800/228-9548 TDD
http://www.hyatt.com

Inns of America
800/826-0778 Continental USA and Canada

Intercontinental Hotels
800/327-0200 Continental USA and Canada

ITT Sheraton
800/325-3535 Continental USA and Canada
800/325-1717 TDD

La Quinta Motor Inns, Inc
800/531-5900 Continental USA and Canada
800/426-3101 TDD

Loews Hotels
800/223-0888 Continental USA and Canada
http://www.loewshotels.com

Marriott Hotels
800/228-9290 Continental USA and Canada
800/228-7014 TDD
http://www.marriott.com/MainPage.html

Master Hosts Inns
800/251-1962 Continental USA and Canada

Meridien
800/543-4300 Continental USA and Canada

Omni Hotels
800/843-6664 Continental USA and Canada

Park Inns International
800/437-PARK Continental USA and Canada
http://www.p-inns.com/parkinn.html

Quality Inns
800/228-5151 Continental USA and Canada
800/228-3323 TDD
http://www.hotelchoice.com/cgi-bin/res/webres?quality.html

Radisson Hotels International
800/333-3333 Continental USA and Canada

Ramada
800/2-RAMADA Continental USA and Canada
http://www.ramada.com/ramada.html

Red Carpet Inns
800/251-1962 Continental USA and Canada

Red Lion Hotels and Inns
800/547-8010 Continental USA and Canada

Red Roof Inns
800/843-7663 Continental USA and Canada
800/843-9999 TDD
http://www.redroof.com

Renaissance Hotels International
800/HOTELS-1 Continental USA and Canada
800/833-4747 TDD

Residence Inn by Marriott
800/331-3131 Continental USA and Canada
800/228-7014 TDD
http://www.marriott.com/lodging/resinn.html

Resinter
800/221-4542 Continental USA and Canada

Ritz-Carlton
800/241-3333 Continental USA and Canada

Rodeway Inns
800/228-2000 Continental USA and Canada
800/228-3323 TDD
http://www.hotelchoice.com/cgi-bin/res/webres?rodeway.html

Scottish Inns
800/251-1962 Continental USA and Canada

Shilo Inns
800/222-2244 Continental USA and Canada

Signature Inns
800/822-5252 Continental USA and Canada

Super 8 Motels
800/800-8000 Continental USA and Canada
800/533-6634 TDD
http://www.super8motels.com/super8.html

Susse Chalet Motor Lodges & Inns
800/258-1980 Continental USA and Canada

Travelodge
800/255-3050 Continental USA and Canada

Vagabond Hotels Inc
800/522-1555 Continental USA and Canada

Westin Hotels and Resorts
800/228-3000 Continental USA and Canada
800/254-5440 TDD
http://www.westin.com

Wyndham Hotels and Resorts
800/822-4200 Continental USA and Canada

Car Rental Agencies

Advantage Rent-A-Car
800/777-5500 Continental USA and Canada

Airways Rent A Car
800/952-9200 Continental USA

Alamo Rent A Car
800/327-9633 Continental USA and Canada
http://www.goalamo.com

Allstate Car Rental
800/634-6186 Continental USA and Canada

Avis
800/331-1212 Continental USA
800/TRY-AVIS Canada
800/331-2323 TDD
http://www.avis.com

Budget Rent A Car
800/527-0700 Continental USA and Canada
800/826-5510 TDD

Dollar Rent A Car
800/800-4000 Continental USA and Canada

Enterprise Rent-A-Car
800/325-8007 Continental USA and Canada

Hertz
800/654-3131 Continental USA and Canada
800/654-2280 TDD

National Car Rental
800/CAR-RENT Continental USA and Canada
800/328-6323 TDD
http://www.nationalcar.com

Payless Car Rental
800/PAYLESS Continental USA and Canada

Rent-A-Wreck
800/535-1391 Continental USA

Sears Rent A Car
800/527-0770 Continental USA and Canada

Thrifty Rent-A-Car
800/367-2277 Continental USA and Canada
800/358-5856 TDD

U-Save Auto Rental of America
800/272-USAV Continental USA and Canada

Value Rent-A Car
800/327-2501 Continental USA and Canada
http://www.go-value.com

Airlines

American Airlines
800/433-7300 Continental USA and Western Canada
800/543-1586 TDD
http://www.americanair.com/aahome/aahome.html

Canadian Airlines International
800/426-7000 Continental USA and Canada
http://www.cdair.ca

Continental Airlines
800/525-0280 Continental USA
800/343-9195 TDD
http://www.flycontinental.com

Delta Air Lines
800/221-1212 Continental USA
800/831-4488 TDD
http://www.delta-air.com

Northwest Airlines
800/225-2525 Continental USA and Canada
http://www.nwa.com

Southwest Airlines
800/435-9792 Continental USA and Canada
http://iflyswa.com

Trans World Airlines
800/221-2000 Continental USA
http://www2.twa.com/TWA/Airlines/home/home.html

United Airlines
800/241-6522 Continental USA and Canada
http://www.ual.com

USAir
800/428-4322 Continental USA and Canada
http://www.usair.com

Train

Amtrak
800/USA-RAIL Continental USA
http://amtrak.com

Bus

Greyhound
800/231-2222 Continental USA
http://greyhound.com

The Top-Rated Lodgings

Ultra

The Boulders, Carefree, AZ
The Phoenician, Scottsdale, AZ

Five Flags

The Broadmoor, Colorado Springs, CO
Loews Ventana Canyon Resort, Tucson, AZ

Four Flags

Arizona Biltmore, Phoenix, AZ
Arizona Inn, Tucson, AZ
The Armstrong Mansion Bed & Breakfast, Salt Lake City, UT
Aspen Club Lodge, Aspen, CO
Brigham Street Inn, Salt Lake City, UT
Brown Palace Hotel, Denver, CO
The Buttes, Tempe, AZ
C Lazy U Ranch, Granby, CO
Enchantment Resort, Sedona, AZ
Goldener Hirsch Inn, Deer Valley Resort, UT
Home Ranch, Steamboat Springs, CO
Homestead, Heber City, UT
Homewood Suites, Boulder, CO
Hotel Colorado, Glenwood Springs, CO
Hotel Jerome, Aspen, CO
Hyatt Regency Beaver Creek, Vail, CO
Hyatt Regency Scottsdale, Scottsdale, AZ
Inn at Temple Square, Salt Lake City, UT
Inn of the Anasazi, Santa Fe, NM
Inverness Hotel & Golf Club, Englewood, CO
Las Cruces Hilton Inn, Las Cruces, NM
L'Auberge de Sedona, Sedona, AZ
Little America Hotel & Towers, Salt Lake City, UT
Little Mountain Lodge B&B, Breckenridge, CO
The Little Nell, Aspen, CO
The Lodge at Cordillera, Vail, CO
Loews Giorgio Hotel, Denver, CO
Marriott's Camelback Inn Resort, Golf Club & Spa, Scottsdale, AZ
The Peaks at Telluride, Telluride, CO
Phoenix Hilton Suites, Phoenix, AZ
The Pointe Hilton at Squaw Peak, Phoenix, AZ
The Pointe Hilton Resort on South Mountain, Phoenix, AZ
Queen Anne B&B Inn, Denver, CO
The Ritz-Carlton, Aspen, CO
The Ritz-Carlton Phoenix, Phoenix, AZ
Riverside Condominiums, Telluride, CO
The Sardy House, Aspen, CO
Scottsdale Princess, Scottsdale, AZ
Sheraton San Marcos Resort, Chandler, AZ
Sheraton Steamboat Resort, Steamboat Springs, CO
The Snowmass Lodge & Club, Snowmass Village, CO
Sonnenalp Resort, Vail, CO
Stein Eriksen Lodge, Deer Valley Resort, UT
Tall Timber Resort, Durango, CO
The Westin La Paloma, Tucson, AZ
Westward Look Resort, Tucson, AZ
The Wigwam, Litchfield Park, AZ

ARIZONA

A Land of Extremes

Arizona is a land of extremes. "And today in Phoenix, the mercury topped 120°F for the fifth day in a row" is the sort of weather report that conjures up visions of a vast, baking desert and makes people sweat a thousand miles away. What many non-Arizonans don't realize is that when it's topping 100° in Phoenix, it can be snowing on the rim of the Grand Canyon, and when Phoenix is warm enough for sunbathing in January, skiers are hitting the slopes outside Flagstaff.

Arizona's elevation ranges from near sea level at Yuma to 12,760 feet on Humphreys Peak, producing a variety of landscapes that includes not only the familiar Sonoran Desert, which is home to the massive saguaro cactus, but also the ponderosa pine forests of the Mogollon Rim and the alpine meadows of the San Francisco Peaks. Nowhere are these contrasts more evident than in the Grand Canyon, which appears suddenly, full-blown and vertiginous, from the forests of the Kaibab Plateau.

Man has had a hand in creating Arizona's extremes. Except for where it flows through the Grand Canyon, most of the Colorado River has been dammed, creating huge mirage-like reservoirs in the desert or, at Lake Powell, an otherworldly landscape in which arches of red sandstone are reflected in quiet waters hundreds of feet deep. And in the cities, where high-tech and service industries foster an increasingly cosmopolitan atmosphere, glass-and-steel skyscrapers rise into the desert sky and Mercedes compete with BMWs for parking spaces at upscale shopping malls. However, away from the cities, the old Arizona of cattle ranches, copper mines, and cacti survives. In this "real" Arizona, pickup trucks are the vehicle of choice, Native Americans still shop at trading posts, and people still make a living riding the range and digging for gold.

At guest ranches all over the state, the Wild West comes alive as wranglers turn city slickers into cowpunchers for whom a night out means a chuck-wagon dinner under the stars and a cowboy singalong. But at the

STATE STATS

CAPITAL
Phoenix

AREA
114,000 square miles

BORDERS
New Mexico, Utah, Nevada, California, Mexico

POPULATION
4,220,000 (1995 estimate)

ENTERED UNION
February 14, 1912 (48th state)

NICKNAME
Grand Canyon State

STATE FLOWER
Blossom of the saguaro cactus

STATE BIRD
Cactus wren

FAMOUS NATIVES
Cesar Chavez, Linda Ronstadt, Sandra Day O'Connor, Barry Goldwater, William Rehnquist

resort hotels of Phoenix, Scottsdale, Tucson, and Sedona, manicured golf courses, health spas, elaborate swimming pools, and gourmet restaurants have created a new image for the state, one that is almost diametrically opposed to the rough-and-rugged life of the cowboy. In this new land of good living, two-pound steaks are replaced by smoked-duck tamales with mango-chilpotle sauce, and a night out might mean Pavarotti or the latest Broadway play.

The New West and the Old West ride side by side in the western art that is so prevalent in Arizona. This art captures on canvas and in bronze the none-too-glamorous real life of Arizona's cowboys. It also reflects the state's Indian heritage, although the works of the Indian craftspeople themselves are even more reflective of these cultures. Navajo rugs and sand paintings, Hopi kachinas and pottery, and Zuni silver-and-turquoise jewelry are quintessential Arizona, the crafts of people who were living on this land long before the first Spanish explorers marched north from Mexico in search of riches.

Ever since the Anasazi built their pueblos high on cliff walls, Arizonans have been coping with this region's extremes. The advent of air conditioning may have tempered the climatic excesses somewhat, allowing people to live year-round in the desert, but Arizona is still a place where the extremes are what give the state its unique character.

Fun Facts

- Spaniards were in Arizona 25 years before Spain established its colony at St Augustine, Florida, and 70 years before the English founded Jamestown.
- Arizona has more mountainous regions than Switzerland and more forested land than Minnesota.
- Strange as it seems, Arizona claims more boats per capita than any other state! (That's because of the abundance of lakes created to store water in the desert.)
- The city of Yuma enjoys the most days of sunshine—311 of them a year—of any spot in the United States.

A Brief History

Cliff Dwellings to Mission Churches Mammoth bones found in southeastern Arizona indicate that Paleo-Indians roamed this region more than 10,000 years ago. However, it was not until around the year AD 200 that the area's inhabitants began to leave permanent records of their presence. Early Indians lived in pit houses (houses partially dug into the ground), but by 700, they had begun building multistory pueblos (villages). The best preserved and most fascinating of these are the cliff dwellings of the Anasazi, who lived in the canyons of northeastern Arizona. Other tribes of the period were Sinagua, Mogollon, Hohokam, and Salado. Between 1250 and 1450, all of these early tribes abandoned their villages and disappeared; instead of an archeological forwarding address, they left behind one of the great mysteries of the Southwest.

In 1539, Marcos de Niza led the first European expedition into the area. He came in search of the fabled Seven Cities of Cíbola, and his claims to have seen them prompted Francisco Vásquez de Coronado to march northward from New Spain (Mexico). Rather than the riches he sought, Coronado found only primitive villages of stone and mud, but members of his expedition did make the first recorded sightings of both the Grand Canyon and the Hopi pueblos. Oraibi, the oldest of the latter, had by then been occupied for more than 400 years, and it is today one of the oldest continuously inhabited communities in the country.

More than 100 years went by before the Spanish again displayed an interest in this rugged region. In 1670 Franciscan friars founded missions among the Hopi, but the Pueblo Revolt of 1680 eliminated the Spanish presence. In 1691 Father Eusebio Francisco Kino, a Jesuit, visited the Pima Indian village of Tumacacori, south of present-day Tucson, but it was not until 1751 that a permanent mission and presidio (military post) were established at Tumacacori and nearby Tubac. These became the first permanent European settlements in Arizona.

In 1776, the presidio was moved to Tucson and in 1821, when Mexico won its independence from Spain, Tucson and the rest of Arizona became a part of Mexico. In 1848, in the wake of the Mexican-American War, most of northern Mexico was ceded to the United States, but because the Mexican-American border was then drawn just north of Tucson, it was not until the United States bought southern Arizona from Mexico as part of the Gadsden Purchase of 1853 that all of Arizona passed into US hands.

Territorial Times During the early years of the Civil War, Arizona sided with the Confederacy, partly because of US resistance to giving the region territorial status. However, Union troops quickly re-

claimed it, and Arizona was made a territory in 1863.

Because the Spanish had mistreated Arizona's Indian inhabitants, the Spanish occupation had not been peaceful, and when the United States acquired the territory, the new Americans found themselves facing Indian hostilities. In 1864, Colonel Kit Carson led a force against the Navajo, who had migrated into the region in the 1400s, and by destroying their winter food supply was able to bring about a Navajo surrender.

It was the Apache, living in the mountains of eastern Arizona, who put up the greatest resistance to white settlement, however. Led by Cochise and Geronimo, they attacked settlers, forts, and towns, forcing the United States to conduct a protracted war against them that did not end until Geronimo surrendered to US troops in 1886.

In the meantime, as the California gold rush got under way, miners making their way westward stopped in Arizona and eventually struck silver and gold throughout the state. It was on this mineral wealth that the territory's early fortunes were made, and mining towns such as Tombstone and Bisbee became the biggest, wildest boomtowns between New Orleans and San Francisco.

In 1867, the first white farmers to settle in Arizona began reusing the ancient system of canals that the Hohokam had dug centuries earlier. About this same time, cattle ranching was introduced in southeastern and northwestern Arizona. Life in the territory was changing, and when the railroads came in the 1880s, it began to change drastically. Previously, Spanish culture had dominated the region, but the railroads forged closer links with the east, and Arizona towns began to reflect the new influence.

DRIVING DISTANCES

Phoenix

116 miles NW of Tucson
125 miles SW of Sedona
141 miles SW of Flagstaff
180 miles NW of Nogales
226 miles S of the Grand Canyon
290 miles SE of Las Vegas, NV

Tucson

64 miles N of Nogales
70 miles NW of Tombstone
116 miles SE of Phoenix
129 miles SE of Ajo
156 miles SW of Lordsburg, NM
237 miles SE of Yuma

Flagstaff

63 miles NW of Winslow
84 miles SE of Grand Canyon Village
136 miles SW of Page
141 miles NE of Phoenix
204 miles SW of Canyon de Chelly
248 miles SE of Las Vegas, NV

The Desert Blossoms Just as the United States had resisted giving Arizona territorial status, so too did it resist giving the territory statehood. However, in 1911, with the construction of the Roosevelt Dam on the Salt River, eastern attitudes began to change. The reservoir behind this dam provided central Arizona with water for irrigation, and cotton fields and orange groves soon sprouted in the desert. On February 14, 1912, Arizona was granted statehood, the last of the 48 contiguous states to enter the Union.

Throughout the early part of the 20th century, copper mining dominated the Arizona economy, and with the onset of World War II, the state's mines gained greater importance. Fortunately, by the time many mines across the state shut down after the war, the economy had begun to diversify, with large-scale agriculture and cattle ranching gaining importance, and then manufacturing ultimately overtaking agriculture as the state's primary revenue earner. In the early 1980s, Arizona experienced rapid economic growth, with aerospace engineering, electronics, and other high-tech industries in the forefront.

However, it is tourism that has brought the state its greatest recognition. As early as the 1920s, cold-weary northerners had begun spending their winters in the Arizona desert. Guest ranches offered visitors a chance to relive the Wild West, and soon the word spread about the great Arizona vacations to be had. Guest ranches eventually gave way to more sophisticated resorts, and today Phoenix and Scottsdale together boast the nation's greatest resort concentration.

Although the economic boom of the early 1980s soon went bust (its demise aggravated by cutbacks in military spending that hurt the region's aerospace firms), the state is now recovering from the recession and Phoenix and Tucson are once again booming, their growth fueled in part by corporate confidence in the opportunities being created by the North American Free Trade Agreement (NAFTA).

Phoenix and Tucson today face many of the same problems that other cities around the nation are facing—smog, congestion, urban sprawl, gang violence, and water shortages. But urban planners are beginning to confront these problems, and urban renewal projects have begun luring people back into the Tucson and Phoenix downtown areas. As long as the water supply holds out, Arizona should have a sunny future.

A Closer Look

GEOGRAPHY

Although most people associate Arizona with the desert, the state encompasses far more than just cactus and mesquite. There are snow-capped mountain peaks, rolling grasslands, oak-shaded canyons, huge lakes busy with boats, and dense forests of tall pines. There are, in fact, more mountains in Arizona than in Switzerland and more forests than in Minnesota.

Northern Arizona, sometimes referred to as Canyon Country, encompasses arid, windswept plains as well as dense forests of ponderosa pine. It is dominated by the Colorado River's Grand Canyon, which carves its way through the Colorado Plateau for 277 twisted miles. The Grand Canyon is the state's top tourist attraction and the inspiration for its nickname—the Grand Canyon State. Flagstaff, a college and former railroad town, is the region's largest city. North of Flagstaff stand the San Francisco Peaks, the state's highest mountains. The Arizona Snowbowl ski area keeps people flocking up this way even during the dead of winter, when this is the coldest part of the state. South of Flagstaff is Oak Creek Canyon, a popular summer recreation area that offers a cool respite from the heat of the central Arizona desert. At its mouth lies Sedona, a retirement and arts community dominated by eroded red sandstone rock formations.

AVG HIGH/LOW TEMPS (°F)

	Phoenix	Flagstaff
Jan	65/39	42/15
Feb	68/43	45/17
Mar	75/47	49/20
Apr	83/53	57/26
May	92/62	67/33
June	102/71	78/41
July	105/80	82/50
Aug	102/78	79/49
Sept	98/71	74/41
Oct	88/59	64/31
Nov	74/47	51/26
Dec	66/40	44/16

Northeastern Arizona, known as the Four Corners region because of the four states (Arizona, New Mexico, Utah, and Colorado) that meet at a single point, is a high, windswept plain punctuated by mesas and buttes. This is the land of the Navajo and Hopi Indians and it is here that some of the state's most breathtaking landscapes are to be found. Sculpted by wind and water, the region's layers of colorful sandstone have been eroded into strange shapes.

Eastern Arizona, endowed with high mountains and snow-capped peaks, is where Phoenicians flee in the summer to beat the desert heat. The region's cool forests are dotted with lakes and laced with streams, which makes fishing and other outdoor activities particularly popular. However, the most prominent feature of eastern Arizona is the Mogollon Rim, a 1,000-foot-high escarpment that stretches for 200 miles. The Mogollon Rim was made famous years ago by the author Zane Grey, who for many years lived near the town of Payson. Much of this eastern region is today Apache reservation land.

The saguaro cactus is the quintessential symbol of Arizona's **Sonoran Desert,** and it is in the central region of the state that these cacti begin to dominate the landscape. The desert extends from north of Phoenix southward into Mexico and westward into California, and, surprisingly, it was in the midst of this harsh environment that early settlers chose to establish both Phoenix and Tucson, which today are the state's two largest cities.

Though there is no ocean, Arizona claims a **"West Coast"** along its border with California and Nevada. Lakes Havasu, Mohave, and Mead, the 3 long reservoirs that stretch along this border, were created by the damming of the Colorado River and offer vacationing Arizonans year-round water-sports activities. This region also happens to be the hottest part of the state, with Yuma and Bullhead City frequently registering the nation's highest summer temperatures.

Southern Arizona encompasses part of the Sonoran Desert and includes some of the state's most rugged and remote areas. It is here that the organ pipe cactus, which is similar to the saguaro, reaches the northern limits of its range. In the southeast corner, high plains are home to large cattle ranches. Rising above these plains are numerous small mountain ranges that were once Apache strongholds.

CLIMATE

Sure it's hot, but, as they like to say, "it's a dry heat." Arizona often claims the hottest spots in the nation during the summer, but because of the desert's low humidity, 100°F isn't nearly as uncomfortable here as it would be in other locales. Cold is also relative in Arizona. Tucson brags that it is usually 10° cooler than Phoenix, and Bullhead City is always considerably hotter than Phoenix. However, from October to May temperatures are generally moderate in Phoenix, Tucson, and the rest of the desert, with midwinter lows rarely dipping below freezing and highs in the 60°s. Winter or summer, the desert basks in the sun. Phoenix and Tucson each get more than 300 days of sunshine each year.

Arizona's many mountain ranges give the state its climatic diversity–as you climb into the mountains, the temperature drops, even in Arizona. Snow keeps the North Rim of the Grand Canyon closed from November through April each year and provides good skiing at the Sunrise and Arizona Snowbowl ski areas.

Any time of year and anywhere in the state, it's a good idea to wear a good sunscreen if you plan to spend much time outdoors. The desert sun is strong, even in winter. At higher elevations, the sunlight is even stronger and skin burns much faster.

WHAT TO PACK

The heat, the landscape, and western heritage dictate what to wear in Arizona. Though people here generally dress casually throughout the year, in the warmer months, dressing for the heat is paramount. Bring plenty of cool clothes, preferably cotton. Also be sure to bring a bathing suit. If you have them, don't forget your cowboy boots and jeans. In the winter a jacket or wool sweater is fine for the desert, but if you are heading up into the mountains, bring a heavy coat and plenty of warm clothes. A few restaurants in Phoenix and Tucson require jackets for men, and if you plan on attending the symphony or some other cultural event, you'll want to have some formal attire.

TOURIST INFORMATION

Contact the Arizona Office of Tourism, 2702 N Third St, Suite 4015, Phoenix, AZ 85004 (tel 602/230-7733 or toll free 800/842-8257), at least a month before you plan to visit and they'll send you a package of information on the state. The Arizona Office of Tourism also maintains a Web page (hhp://www.arizonaguide.com) with general information about the state. Nearly every Arizona town of any size also has a visitors bureau or chamber of commerce that can provide specific local or regional information. You'll find a list of these chambers of commerce and visitors bureaus in *Arizona Traveler,* a magazine available from the Arizona Office of Tourism. The Phoenix and Valley of the Sun Convention and Visitors Bureau, One Arizona Center, 400 E Van Buren St, Phoenix, AZ 85004-2290 (tel 602/254-6500), and the Metropolitan Tucson Convention and Visitors Bureau, 130 S Scott Ave, Tucson, AZ 85701 (tel 602/624-1817 or toll free 800/638-8350), are also good sources of information.

DRIVING RULES & REGULATIONS

The use of seat belts is required of drivers and front-seat passengers. Children 4 years old or younger or who weigh 40 pounds or less must be in a child's car seat. Unless posted otherwise, a right turn is permitted on red after you've come to a complete stop. General speed limits are 25 to 35 mph in towns and cities, 15 mph in school zones, and 55 mph on highways, except rural interstates, where the speed limit is 65 mph.

RENTING A CAR

Because they are major resort destinations, Phoenix and Tucson offer some of the lowest car rental rates in the country. Outside of these two cities, rates tend to be a bit higher. To get the best prices, make your reservation as far in advance as possible, because the fewer cars a company has available, the more it charges. Also call several companies, as rates vary considerably from one company to the next, and you might run across a special promotional rate in effect for the time of your visit. If you're a member of an organization such as AAA or AARP, you may be able to get a discount, and some credit card companies also offer discount rates to cardholders. Also, be sure to find out if your credit card or personal automobile insurance extends coverage to rental cars. Using existing insurance saves a bundle.

Major rental companies with offices in Arizona include:

- **Alamo** (tel toll free 800/327-9633)
- **Avis** (tel 800/331-1212)
- **Budget** (tel 800/527-0700)
- **Dollar** (tel 800/800-4000)
- **Hertz** (tel 800/654-3131)
- **National** (tel 800/227-7368)
- **Thrifty** (tel 800/367-2277)

ESSENTIALS

Area Code: The area code for all of Arizona outside the Phoenix metropolitan area is 520. The area code for the Phoenix area is 602.

Emergencies: For the police, an ambulance, or the fire department, dial **911.**

Liquor Laws: To purchase or consume alcoholic beverages, you must be 21 years old and have proper identification.

Taxes: Arizona's state sales tax is 5%; local sales taxes sometimes apply as well. Hotel taxes range from 6.5 to 8.5%. There is also a car-rental tax of 8.7 to 8.8%.

Time Zone: Arizona is in the Mountain time zone and does not switch to daylight saving time in summer, with the exception of the Navajo and Hopi reservations.

Best of the State

WHAT TO SEE AND DO

To find out more detailed information, look under "Attractions" for individual cities in the listings portion of this chapter.

Grand Canyon National Park A mile deep, 18 miles across at its widest, and 277 miles long, the Grand Canyon is one of the world's greatest natural wonders. More than 2 billion years of geologic time have been exposed by the weathering action of the Colorado River as it slices through the scrubland and forests of northern Arizona. However you choose to experience the Grand Canyon—from overlooks on the North and South rims; on a mule ride down into it; by hiking its trails; by helicopter or small plane; from a raft bouncing over the Colorado's many rapids—it will undoubtedly leave you awestruck. Keep in mind that the Grand Canyon is one of the most popular national parks in the United States, and a summertime visit requires some advance planning. If you want to stay at one of the Grand Canyon lodges, be sure to make your reservation six to 12 months in advance. The park's campgrounds also fill up nightly in summer.

Other Natural Wonders Arizona abounds in national monuments, state parks, and other preserves dedicated to natural wonders. The northeast part of the state, which is taken up almost entirely by the Navajo and Hopi reservations, offers the greatest concentration. Between Flagstaff and Winslow is **Meteor Crater,** a mile-wide, 570-foot-deep crater formed when a meteorite struck the earth 49,000 years ago. At **Petrified Forest National Park,** near Holbrook, you can see the country's greatest array of petrified wood. This park also protects the rainbow-hued hills of the **Painted Desert.** North of the Petrified Forest is **Canyon de Chelly National Monument,** a deep, narrow canyon with sandstone walls. Within the canyon are numerous cliff dwellings, as well as farms that are still worked by Navajo families. Northwest of here is **Monument Valley Navajo Tribal Park,** one of the most photographed spots in the entire Southwest. Its famous buttes have served as backdrops for countless films and television commercials. Nearby, within Glen Canyon National Recreation Area, stands **Rainbow Bridge,** a 290-foot-high arch that spans 275 feet.

East and west of Tucson are units of **Saguaro National Monument,** which preserves vast stands of huge saguaro cacti. About 120 miles west of Tucson is **Organ Pipe National Monument,** a preserve for a similar, large cactus that resembles a pipe organ. **Chiracahua National Monument,** 100 miles east of Tucson, is a fascinating landscape of naturally sculpted rock formations.

Manmade Wonders **Biosphere II,** a sort of giant terrarium for people rising out of the desert north of Tucson, has become one of Arizona's most impressive manmade wonders. Another surprising structure is **London Bridge,** which now spans the waters of Lake Havasu in western Arizona. Some distance up the Colorado from Lake Havasu is the **Hoover Dam,** the tallest concrete dam in the western hemisphere. Equally impressive is the **Glen Canyon Dam** in Page. This latter dam creates Lake Powell, which stretches for more than 180 miles.

Mission San Xavier del Bac, known as "The White Dove of the Desert" and located south of Tucson, is a beautiful mission church built by the Spanish in the 18th century. In the 20th century, the desert inspired architect Frank Lloyd Wright to build his **Taliesin West** school on the outskirts of Phoenix. Italian architect Paolo Soleri, after studying at Taliesin West, went out into the desert 60 miles north of Phoenix and began building the futuristic cast-concrete city of **Arcosanti,** which is still under construction.

Ruins Arizona has an abundance of ancient Indian ruins. By far the most impressive, though rather difficult-to-visit, ruins are the Anasazi cliff dwellings of Betatakin and Keet Seel in **Navajo National Monument.** Other Anasazi cliff dwellings can be seen at Canyon de Chelly National Monument. Near Flagstaff, there are the Sinagua Indian pueblo ruins at **Wupatki National Monument** and cliff dwellings at **Walnut Canyon National Monument.** South of Flagstaff, you'll find **Montezuma's Castle National Monument,** which preserves a Sinagua cliff dwelling. Not far from this monument is **Tuzigoot National Monument,** a hilltop pueblo ruin near the town of Clarkdale.

The Wild West Arizona can lay claim to some of the wildest western history. Southeast of Tucson is **Tombstone**—"the town too tough to die." However, if you're looking for something familiar from the movie *Tombstone,* you'll have to pay a visit to **Old Tucson Studios,** a western theme park that has served as a set for hundreds of film and television productions, including *Tombstone,* since 1939. One other setting that will be familiar to fans of Hollywood westerns is **Monument Valley,** on the Navajo Indian Reservation in northern Arizona. The valley and its stunningly picturesque sandstone buttes have served as a backdrop for countless films, television shows, commercials, and print ads. Throughout the state there are also dozens of genuine ghost towns, and while some are little more than foundations, others, such as Bisbee, Tombstone, Oatman, and Goldfield, have become regular tourist attractions and acquired a few too many residents to be proper ghost towns.

For a look at what pioneer life in Arizona was really like, stop in at the **Pioneer Arizona Living History Museum** north of Phoenix to see costumed interpreters practicing 19th-century crafts and skills. At the **Sharlot Hall Museum** in Prescott, you'll also find historic buildings and exhibits on pioneer life. At **Yuma Crossing Quartermaster Depot Historic Site,** a reconstructed military outpost brings the history of this important site to life, and at the **Fort Huachuca Museum,** a 19th-century military fort, you can learn the history of the fort and the buffalo soldiers, a troop of African-American soldiers that were once stationed here.

Museums Among the not-to-be-missed museums in Arizona are several that focus on Native American culture and history. These include the **Heard Museum** in Phoenix, the **Museum of Northern Arizona** in Flagstaff, and the **Amerind Foundation** in Texas Canyon, 60 miles east of Tucson. The smaller **Smoki Museum** in Prescott also features exhibits of Native American artifacts. To learn more about the state's cowboy history, visit the **Desert Caballeros Western Museum** in Wickenburg, and for a look at cowboy art, visit Prescott's **Phippen Museum of Western Art.** For an introduction to general statewide history, visit the **Arizona Historical Society Tucson Museum.**

The Phoenix Art Museum is strong on contemporary art, but it also has a display of miniature period rooms as well as an impressive collection of Spanish colonial furniture and religious art. The **Tucson Art Museum** also focuses on contemporary art. At the **Arizona State University Art Museum,** changing exhibits feature works by contemporary artists.

Parks & Zoos The **Arizona-Sonora Desert Museum** is a combination zoo and botanical garden that focuses on life in the Sonoran Desert and has some of the finest wildife displays in the country. To see animals from other parts of the world, go to the **Phoenix Zoo.** If you're interested in the plants of the desert, visit the **Desert Botanical Garden** in Phoenix, **Tucson Botanical Gardens,** or the **Boyce Thompson Southwestern Arboretum,** east of Phoenix.

Family Favorites Many of the attractions listed above will appeal to children of various ages. Particularly popular are **Old Tucson Studios** in Tucson, the real town of **Tombstone** southeast of Tucson, the **Arizona-Sonora Desert Museum,** and the **Phoenix Zoo.**

Wild West experiences that kids will probably enjoy are rodeos, horseback rides, and chuck-wagon cookouts. Around Phoenix and Tucson, you'll also find restaurants that are built to resemble old western towns and often offer cowboy shootouts, country music bands, hay rides, and other activities. Both Phoenix and Tucson have several miniature-golf courses that include other activities with kid appeal. Museums that children will enjoy include the **Tucson Children's Museum,** Phoenix's **Arizona Museum of Science and Technology,** and the **Mesa Southwest Museum** in Mesa. You'll also find planetariums in Tucson and Flagstaff. Most guest (dude) ranches specialize in family vacations and many of the state's big resorts have special children's programs during holidays and the summer months.

Art Communities The Arizona desert has attracted artists for years, and many of them have congregated in towns that were once nearly deserted. Among these artists' communities are **Bisbee,** a former copper-mining town (90 miles southeast of Tucson); **Tubac,** site of the first Spanish settlement in Arizona (60 miles south of Tucson); and **Jerome,** a former mining town high on a mountainside above Cottonwood (25 miles southwest of Sedona). Art galleries in Scottsdale and Sedona attract collectors from around the world.

EVENTS AND FESTIVALS

Phoenix and Central Arizona

- **Fiesta Bowl Football Classic,** Tempe. New Year's Day. Call 602/350-0900 for information.
- **Phoenix Open Golf Tournament,** Phoenix. Mid- to late January. Call 602/870-0163.
- **Heard Museum Guild Indian Fair,** Phoenix. Indian crafts sale. First weekend of March. Call 602/252-8840.
- **Scottsdale Arts Festival,** Scottsdale. Second weekend of March. Call 602/994-ARTS.
- **Phoenix Jaycee's Rodeo of Rodeo's,** Phoenix. Mid-March. Call 602/252-6771.
- **Arizona State Fair,** Phoenix. Mid- to late October. Call 602/252-6771.
- **George Phippen Memorial Day Western Art Show and Sale,** Prescott. Memorial Day weekend. Call 520/778-1385.
- **Prescott Frontier Days,** Prescott. Oldest rodeo in the United States. First week of July. Call 520/445-3103.
- **Annual Cowboy Artists of America Exhibition,** Phoenix. Late October to late November. Call 602/257-1880.

Tucson and Southern Arizona

- **Northern Telecom Open Golf Tournament,** Tucson. Mid-January. Call toll free 800/882-7660 for information.
- **Cinco de Mayo,** Tucson. Celebration of Mexican victory over the French. Parade, music, dancing. May 5. Call 602/623-8344.
- **Wyatt Earp Days,** Tombstone. Gunfight reenactments and Wild West entertainment. Memorial Day weekend. Call 602/457-2211.
- **Helldorado Days,** Tombstone. 1880s fashion show, tribal dances, street entertainment. Late October. Call 602/457-2211.

Flagstaff and Northern Arizona

- **Flagstaff Winterfest,** Flagstaff. Arts and crafts festival, sports events. Early to mid-February. Call 520/774-4505 for information.
- **Annual Festival of Native American Arts,** Flagstaff. Early July to early August. Call 520/779-6921.
- **Navajo Nation Fair,** Window Rock. Rodeo, dances, parade. Early September. Call 520/871-6659.
- **Grand Canyon Chamber Music Festival,** Grand Canyon Village. September. Call 520/638-9215.
- **Jazz on the Rocks,** Sedona. Late September. Call 520/282-1985.

SPECTATOR SPORTS

Baseball Because of the mild spring climate in Arizona's desert areas, the state is the site of **spring training** camps for numerous pro baseball teams. In the Phoenix area, you can catch games by the Oakland A's, the San Francisco Giants, the California Angels, the Chicago Cubs, the Milwaukee Brewers, the San Diego Padres, the Seattle Mariners, and the Colorado Rockies (who have their spring training camp in Tucson). During the summer, the AAA Pacific Coast League's **Phoenix Firebirds** (tel 602/275-0500) play at Scottsdale Stadium and the **Tucson Toros** (tel 602/325-2621) play at Hi Corbett Field.

Basketball The NBA's **Phoenix Suns** (tel 602/379-7867) play at the America West Arena in Phoenix. You can also see college basketball at **Arizona State University** in Tempe (tel 602/965-6592) and the **University of Arizona** in Tucson (tel 602/621-4163).

Football The **Arizona Cardinals** (tel 602/379-0101) play at Arizona State University's Sun Devil Stadium in Tempe, the same stadium where **Arizona State University** plays Pac-10 Conference football (tel 602/965-6592). More Pac-10 Conference college football action takes place in Tucson at the University of Arizona (tel 602/621-4163).

Greyhound Racing You can watch the greyhounds run at the **Phoenix Greyhound Park** (tel 602/273-7181) in Phoenix and the **Tucson Greyhound Park** (tel 602/884-7576) in Tucson.

Horse Racing The only permanent racetrack in Arizona is **Turf Paradise** (tel 602/942-1101) in

Phoenix. However, country fairs in Arizona often have horse races.

ACTIVITIES A TO Z

Ballooning The climate and wind conditions in the Arizona desert are ideal for hot-air ballooning, and more than a dozen companies offer trips. Companies to contact include A Aerozona Adventure (tel 602/991-4260 or toll free 800/421-3056) in Phoenix, Balloon America (tel 602/299-7744) in Tucson, and Northern Lights Balloon Expeditions (tel 520/282-2274) in Sedona.

Bird Watching Arizona is nationally renowned for its bird watching, particularly in the mountains and in the riparian (riverside) areas of the southern part of the state. Some top bird watching spots are Madera Canyon (south of Tucson), Ramsey Canyon (south of Sierra Vista), the San Pedro Riparian National Conservation Area (east of Tombstone), Patagonia Creek (between Nogales and Sierra Vista), and the South Fork of Cave Creek Canyon (in the Chiracahua Mountains near Portal).

Boating Thanks to the many lakes created to store water in the desert, Arizona has more boats per capita than any other state! Houseboating on Lakes Powell, Mead, Mohave, and Havasu are popular summer vacation activities, and motorboating and waterskiing are popular on bodies of water throughout the state. On Saguaro and Canyon lakes east of Phoenix there are paddlewheeler excursions.

Camping With more than a dozen national monuments and parks and numerous state parks, Arizona offers a wealth of campgrounds. Most are either in the mountains, where Arizona families go to escape the summer heat, or on lakes, which are popular both for fishing and powerboating. The *Arizona Campground Directory,* a free map and guide to the state's public campgrounds, is available from the **Arizona Office of Tourism,** 2702 N Third St, Suite 4015 Phoenix, AZ 85004 (tel 602/230-7733 or toll free 800/842-8257).

Fishing Arizona has great lake fishing for bass, perch, brown and rainbow trout, and northern pike, and some good trout fishing on rivers and streams in the White Mountains region. For more information, contact the **Arizona Game and Fish Department,** 2222 W Greenway Rd, Phoenix, AZ 85023 (tel 602/942-3000).

Golf The Phoenix area alone has more than 100 golf courses. The state's mild winters mean golfers can keep swinging all through the months when snow, ice, and freezing weather make golfing impossible in more northern latitudes. For more information, contact the **Arizona Golf Association** (tel 602/944-3035), or request a copy of *The Phoenix & Valley of the Sun Golf Guide* or *The Tucson & Southern Arizona Golf Guide* from one of the visitors bureaus mentioned above.

Guided Outdoor Adventures Among the most popular guided adventures in Arizona are the 1- to 3-day mule rides down into the Grand Canyon; for more information, contact **Grand Canyon National Park Lodges** (tel 520/638-2401). Also very popular are **desert jeep tours** in the Phoenix and Sedona areas; for more information, contact Desert/Mountain Jeep Tours (tel 602/860-1777) in Scottsdale or Pink Jeep Tours (tel 520/282-5000 or toll free 800/8-SEDONA) in Sedona. To lend a hand at an archaeological dig, contact the White Mountain Archaeological Center (tel 520/333-5857) or Casa Malpais Archaeological Project (tel 520/333-5375), both located near Springerville on the edge of the White Mountains.

Horseback Riding Arizona is cowboy country, and while there are still those who ride horses for a living, horseback riding for pleasure is one of the state's favorite activities. You'll find riding stables all over the state, and overnight horseback rides, wagon train rides, and cattle drives are all available. For more information, contact Don Donnelly Stables (tel 602/982-7822 or toll free 800/346-4403), Desert/Mountain Jeep Tours (tel 602/860-1777), or Double D Ranch and Wagon Train Company (tel 520/636-0418).

Snow Skiing Despite its image as a vast desert, Arizona does have several downhill ski areas, as well as cross-country ski trails. **Arizona Snowbowl** (tel 602/779-1951) outside of Flagstaff has the most reliable snowfall. **Sunrise** (tel 520/735-7669) on the White Mountain Apache Reservation near the town of McNary also offers good skiing. On Mount Lemmon just outside Tucson, you'll find the **Mount Lemmon Ski Valley** (tel 602/576-1321), the most southerly ski area in the United States.

Tennis In winter, tennis is nearly as popular in Arizona as golf. You'll find tennis courts at resorts and hotels—even some budget hotels—in Phoenix,

Tucson, and elsewhere. There are also numerous public tennis courts in Phoenix and Tucson.

Train Excursions Fans of rail travel won't want to miss the chance to travel by steam train from Williams to the Grand Canyon on the **Grand Canyon Railway** (tel toll free 800/843-8724). The Verde River Canyon Excursion Train (tel 602/639-0010) makes runs up a roadless canyon near Sedona.

White-Water Rafting Rafting through the Grand Canyon on the **Colorado River** is one of the world's premiere white-water trips. These trips range in length from three days to two weeks and can be done in wooden dories, huge rubber rafts with outboard motors, or in smaller rafts powered only by oars. Companies offering Grand Canyon raft trips include Arizona Raft Adventures (tel 520/526-8246 or toll free 800/786-RAFT), Grand Canyon Expeditions (tel 801/644-2691 or toll free 800/544-2691), and Western River Expeditions (tel 801/942-6669 or toll free 800/453-7450). Less demanding and less expensive white-water rafting takes place in the White Mountains northeast of Phoenix; contact Salt River Rafting (tel 602/577-1824 or toll free 800/242-6335) for more information.

For a more relaxing experience, there are half-day float trips from Glen Canyon Dam to Lee's Ferry. For more information, contact Wilderness River Adventures (tel 520/645-3279). Tubing (in inner tubes) down the Salt River east of Phoenix is another favorite summer activity; contact Salt River Recreation (tel 602/984-3305) for information.

Driving the State

PHOENIX, PRESCOTT, AND SEDONA

Start	Phoenix
Finish	Pioneer Arizona Living History Museum
Distance	362 miles
Time	3–5 days
Highlights	Rock formations, Victorian buildings, old mining towns, Native American ruins

From Phoenix's fine art museums to Sedona's red rocks, this tour of central Arizona's top attractions wanders through historic mining towns and the state's most sophisticated, modern communities, as well as past some of the most spectacular scenery in America. Mileages listed are from stop to stop only and do not include travel within a stop or side trips, which may easily add another hundred miles. Some mountain driving is included, and although most roads are paved and well-maintained, motorists should allow extra time. The section of AZ 89A north of Sedona, through spectacular Oak Creek Canyon, is not recommended for large trailers.

For additional information on lodgings, restaurants, and attractions in the region covered by the tour, refer to specific cities in the listings portion of this chapter.

1. **Phoenix.** When you hear people talking about the "New West," they're talking about Phoenix (elevation 1,132 feet), the eighth-largest US city. Although this metropolis is known for its fancy resorts, 117 golf courses, fine shopping, and urban sophistication, it has not forgotten its past. The area's first known inhabitants, the Hohokam, arrived about AD 300 and vanished in the 15th century, before Spanish conquistadors arrived in the mid-16th century. The present city of Phoenix began in the 1860s as a small settlement on the Salt River banks, named by an early settler who correctly predicted that a great city would grow from the ancient ruins, as the mythical phoenix rose from its own ashes.

   Phoenix and its surrounding cities—known collectively as the Valley of the Sun—attract both visitors and transplants with over 300 days of sunshine a year, mild temperatures, a robust economy, and an easy-going outdoor lifestyle. Although summers are hot, consistently topping 100 degrees, Phoenicians, as they like to call themselves, remind us that afternoon humidity averages a very low 17 percent, making the city far more comfortable than a number of other, cooler areas in the state. Although the Valley of the Sun actually includes 22 incorporated cities covering over 9,000 square miles, you're most likely to visit Phoenix, Scottsdale, Mesa, and Tempe.

   The Phoenix area has numerous fine lodging possibilities, and is particularly known for its luxurious resorts, such as **John Gardiner's Tennis Ranch, Safari Resort,** and **Scottsdale Hilton Resort & Villas,** all in Scottsdale. Besides resorts, you have a good variety of hotel choices, including **Fairfield Inn, Hampton Inn,** and **La Quinta Inn.**

   A good way to start your trip is by visiting some of the excellent museums in the area, where you may learn something about its past, people, and cultures. **Pueblo Grande Museum and Cultural Park,** 4619 E Washington St, Phoenix (tel 602/495-0900), contains ruins of an ancient Hohokam village. A "must stop" for anyone interested in Native American cultures is the **Heard Museum,** 22 E Monte Vista Rd, Phoenix (tel 602/252-8848), with extensive exhibits on Southwest tribes. Local artists and craftsworkers provide daily demonstrations here.

   The **Arizona State Capitol Museum,** 1700 W Washington St, Phoenix (tel 602/542-4675), which served as the territorial capitol from 1900 to 1912, has been restored to the way it looked in 1912, the year Arizona became a state; it contains historical exhibits. Although many of Phoenix's early buildings have disappeared, more than a half-dozen turn-of-the-century structures have been saved in the three-square-block area called **Heritage Square,** 115 N 6th St, at Monroe St, Phoenix (tel 602/262-5029), including **Rosson House,** which is open for tours; a 1912 school house that contains the **Arizona Doll and Toy Museum;** and an 1899 bungalow.

   Arizona's largest western theme park, **Rawhide 1880s Western Town,** 23023 N Scottsdale Rd, Scottsdale (tel 602/563-1880), is a replica Old West town, complete with gun fights, stagecoach and burro rides, a museum, and shops.

   Art lovers will enjoy the **Phoenix Art Museum,** 1625 N Central Ave, Phoenix (tel 602/257-1222), with works from the Renaissance to the present; and the **Arizona State University Art Museum,** Nelson Fine Arts Center, 10th St and Mill Ave, Tempe (tel 602/965-ARTS), showcases the work of contemporary American artists. An art museum just for kids is **Arizona Museum for Youth,** 35 N

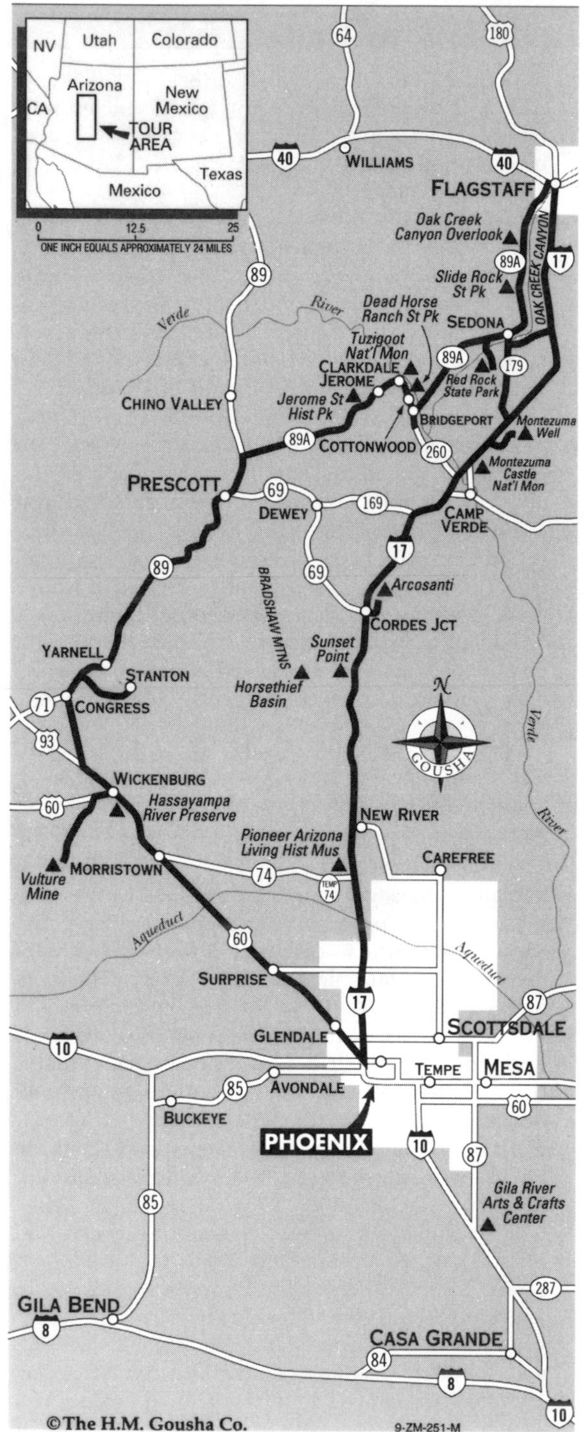

Robson St, Mesa (tel 602/644-2468), with interactive exhibits.

The **Desert Botanical Garden,** 1201 N Galvin Pkwy, in Papago Park, Phoenix (tel 602/941-1225), has more than 20,000 desert plants from around the world. Next door, also in Papago Park, you'll find more than 1,300 animals at **Phoenix Zoo,** 455 N Galvin Pkwy, Phoenix (tel 602/273-1341), along with a tropical rain forest and a children's zoo.

Architecture mavens should head for Scottsdale. **Cosanti,** 6433 Doubletree Ranch Rd, Scottsdale (tel 602/948-6145), a unique complex of cast-concrete structures, houses foundries where Paolo Soleri windbells are made and sold; there is also a model of Soleri's futuristic solar-powered city Arcosanti, under construction north of Phoenix

Take a Break

The popular **Christopher's,** 2398 E Camelback Rd in Phoenix's Biltmore area (tel 602/957-3214), may be the Valley of the Sun's most elegant restaurant, serving contemporary French cuisine; **Bistro,** next door in Suite 220 (tel 602/957-3214), and with the same owner/chef, is equally admired. For unusual Mexican dishes, try **Los Olivos,** 7328 Second St (tel 602/946-2256), a landmark Scottsdale dining spot. The **Hungry Hunter** chain of restaurants at 4455 S Rural Rd, Tempe (tel 602/820-2770), and other locations offers good medium-priced American meals.

Taliesin West, 108th St at Cactus Rd, Scottsdale (tel 602/860-2700), is architect Frank Lloyd Wright's former home and studio.

For beautifully crafted Pima Indian baskets, you can take a side trip 30 miles south from Phoenix on I-10 to the **Gila River Arts and Crafts Center** (tel 602/963-3981), exit 175 off I-10. The center has reconstructions of Native American villages, and a museum devoted to the history, arts, and crafts of more than two dozen tribes. The restaurant serves authentic Native American food.

After you've visited Phoenix, head northwest out of the city on US 60 (Grand Ave), and follow the railroad for 58 miles to:

2. **Wickenburg.** Founded in 1863 by Prussian immigrant Henry Wickenburg, who discovered what would become Arizona's richest gold and silver mine, this town is a good place to relive the Old West. As you enter Wickenburg on US 60, turn right (north) onto Tegner St, and then left (west) on Yavapai St, which takes you to Frontier St and the Chamber of Commerce, located in the old Santa Fe Depot; here you can pick up a historic walking tour map. On **Frontier Street,** you'll see false front buildings dating to the turn of the century. **Desert**

Caballeros Western Museum, 21 N Frontier St (tel 520/684-2272), displays a 1900 street scene, rooms from a Victorian home, minerals, and Native American artifacts. Don't miss the **Jail Tree,** near the corner of Wickenburg Way and Tegner St, where outlaws were once chained because no one wanted to take time out from mining to build a real jail.

About 12 miles south of town on Vulture Mine Rd, you'll find Wickenburg's original reason for existence, **Vulture Mine** (tel 602/377-0803), where you can take a self-guided, above-ground tour and explore some of the remaining 1884 buildings of Vulture City. About 3 miles south of Wickenburg on US 60 is the **Hassayampa River Preserve** (tel 520/684-2772), with self-guided nature walks along the Hassayampa River, Palm Lake, and through cottonwood-willow forests.

From Wickenburg, continue northwest on US 93 for 6 miles to AZ 89, which branches off to the north along the railroad tracks for 10 miles to Congress, and continue north about 2 miles on AZ 89 to a rough dirt road heading east onto the plain. Follow that about 7 miles to:

3. **Stanton.** Established in 1863 after gold nuggets reportedly the size of potatoes were discovered, Stanton (originally called Antelope Station) had 3,500 residents by 1868, but both its population and gold prospects had dwindled by the early 1900s. Today the town is owned by the **Lost Dutchman Mining Association** (tel 520/427-9908), which hosts "recreational" miners. Drop-in visitors are also welcome, and they can visit the 1870s Stanton Hotel, opera house, saloon, and other original buildings.

   From Stanton, drive back to AZ 89 and turn north. You'll soon climb Yarnell Hill, which presents a breathtaking valley view to the south. Follow AZ 89 north from the Stanton turn-off for 43 miles to:

4. **Prescott.** Another Arizona town (elevation 5,347 feet) born during the 1860s gold rush, Prescott was twice the capital of the Arizona Territory—from 1864 to 1867 and from 1877 to 1889. Today this pleasant small city is notable for its historic sites, museums, and arts and crafts. It also makes a good overnight stop. Among the local lodging choices are the historic 1927 **Hassayampa Inn;** the homey **Prescott Pines Inn;** and the economical **Super 8 Motel.**

   Upon your arrival, stop at the Chamber of Commerce, 117 W Goodwin St (tel 520/445-2000) for the **Historic Downtown Walking Tour Guide,** which describes close to three dozen historic buildings. Near the Chamber of Commerce, you can see the 1864 Governor's Mansion, built of logs, and a number of other historic edifices and exhibits at **Sharlot Hall Museum,** 415 W Gurley St (tel 520/445-3122). The **Smoki Museum,** 100 N Arizona St (tel 520/445-1230) contains baskets, rugs, pottery, and other artifacts from a variety of Native American tribes, as well as a collection of western art.

   Leaving Prescott, take AZ 89 north for 5 miles, passing through the beautiful, wild-looking red, pink, and gray rock formations of **Granite Dells.** Then branch off to the northeast on AZ 89A for 25 miles to:

> ## Take a Break
>
> For a trip back to the 1950s, head for **Kendall's Famous Burgers and Ice Cream,** 113 S Cortez St (tel 520/778-3658), or for a more formal dinner in an 1892 building, try the beef, ribs, or pasta at **Murphy's,** 201 N Cortez (tel 520/445-4044).

5. **Jerome.** Once upon a time the town of Jerome had 15,000 residents and was labeled "the wickedest town in the West" by a New York newspaper. But when the copper mines closed in 1950 after operating more than 70 years, the town was practically deserted until it was rediscovered in the 1960s by artists who were attracted by the Verde Valley's magnificent scenery. Much of the old town has been restored, and in addition to exploring its art galleries and crafts shops, you can delve into its past. **Gold King Mine, Museum and Ghost Town,** 1 mile west of Main St on Perkinsville Rd (tel 520/634-5477), has exhibits on Jerome's early mining days. **Jerome State Historic Park,** off AZ 89A (tel 520/634-5381), features a 1916 mansion built for mine owner James "Rawhide Jimmy" Douglas that reveals how rich miners lived during that time. The park has a spectacular view of the town and Verde Valley.

   From Jerome, continue north on AZ 89A about 4 miles, then leave AZ 89A and follow 11th St into:

6. **Clarkdale.** During copper-mining days Clarkdale was home to the smelter for copper mined at Jerome; when the mines closed, Clarkdale almost shut down, but it was revived by the establishment of a cement company in the 1950s. **Tuzigoot National Monument** (tel 520/634-5564), about 2 miles east of Clarkdale (turn east on Main St and follow the signs), contains remnants of a Sinaguan Indian village built of mud and rock between 1125 and 1400. For a good view of the beautiful Verde Valley, take a ride on the **Arizona Central Railroad,** 300 N Broadway (tel 520/639-0010), which passes areas inaccessible by car.

From Clarkdale, go east on Broadway about 2 miles into Cottonwood, where it becomes Main St; turn north onto 10th St and follow it to:

7. **Dead Horse Ranch State Park** (tel 520/634-5283). No dead horses here, this state park is best known for bird watching, but it also has opportunities for canoeing, stream and pond fishing, horseback riding, picnicking, camping, and leisurely walks along the Verde River.

   Leaving the park, drive east about 2 miles on Main St through Cottonwood, then follow AZ 89A north 20 miles to:

8. **Sedona.** Surrounded by huge red rocks and rugged terrain, and blessed by a mild climate, Sedona (elevation 4,400 feet) has become a haven for artists and other free spirits; more recently, it has attracted increasing numbers of retirees. The town boasts numerous art galleries, shops, and restaurants, and serves as a base for explorations into the back country on foot, horseback, or four-wheel drive vehicle. Sedona has a number of fine resorts and hotels, including **Best Western Arroyo Roble Hotel, Enchantment Resort, Quality Inn King's Ransom,** and **Sedona Motel.** However, local lodging is likely to fill up quickly, especially during the summer, and reservations are strongly recommended. An alternative is to drive on to Flagstaff (see stop #11 below), about 28 miles north, where there are many more lodging choices. Also, although the scenery in Flagstaff is not as pretty as in Sedona, the prices are lower.

   Scenery is one of the main reasons to visit Sedona. For a spectacular view, visit **Schnebly Hill Overlook.** To get there, head south from Sedona on AZ 179, crossing a bridge over Oak Creek, and turn east onto Schnebly Hill Rd, which you follow 12 miles to the top of the Mogollon Rim. It takes 40 to 60 minutes to drive this latter dirt road, but the view is well worth it. For another scenic perspective, drive south on AZ 89A about 4 miles from downtown Sedona, turn east onto Upper Red Rock Loop Rd, and follow it about 2 miles to the turnoff for **Red Rock Crossing.** About 1 mile down this dirt road you'll find a parking and picnic area, from where you can view Cathedral Rock and the gigantic red box canyon that surrounds you. This area is beautiful, tree-shaded, and serene when not too crowded, with several paths to explore, a few old buildings, and a number of huge fallen trees. Back on the Red Rock Loop Rd, which soon becomes a narrow and rough dirt thoroughfare, drive about 2 miles to return to paving and the entrance to **Red Rock State Park** (tel 520/282-6907), with hiking and horseback trails available during the day. From the park, follow Lower Red Rock Loop Rd about 3 miles back to AZ 89A and turn north, and go 5 miles back to Sedona. Just south of Sedona, high above AZ 179, you'll see the **Chapel of the Holy Cross** (tel 520/282-4069), a modern Roman Catholic chapel built from the canyon's red rock.

   Back in town, the **Sedona Arts Center,** at AZ 89A and Art Barn Rd (tel 520/282-3809), has exhibits of works by local and regional artists, as well as theater and music performance. Sedona's more than 40 local art galleries provides art lovers with hours of browsing.

   From Sedona, drive 7 miles farther north on AZ 89A to:

9. **Slide Rock State Park** (tel 520/282-3034). Especially popular on hot summer days, this park is named for its 30-foot water slide worn into rocks in Oak Creek. Swimmers often wear old cut-off blue jeans instead of bathing suits to protect themselves (and their suits) from the rough rocks.

   After cooling off at the park, continue north on AZ 89A for another 8 miles to:

10. **Oak Creek Canyon Overlook.** This stretch of highway through the inspirational red rocks and pine forests of Oak Creek Canyon is considered one of the most scenic in America, and the overlook provides an awesome view down the valley.

    Now, continue north on AZ 89A for another 13 miles to:

11. **Flagstaff.** Located at the junction of two interstate highways and within easy reach of **Grand Canyon National Park,** Flagstaff is an ideal overnight stop, with numerous lodging and dining choices. But even here, reservations are recommended.

    From Flagstaff, you can head south down I-17 for 47 miles to exit 293 and then north 4 miles to Montezuma Well (see directions to #12, below), or drive back to Sedona, 28 miles south on AZ 89A, for a different perspective on beautiful **Oak Creek Canyon.** Along the way you'll pass US Forest Service camp and picnic grounds, parking for hiking trails, and Slide Rock State Park, before finding yourself back in Sedona.

    From Sedona, go south past more magnificent red rock formations on AZ 179 for 15 miles to I-17 (exit 298), and then head south on the interstate for 5 miles to exit 293, and 4 miles north on an unmarked road, following signs to:

12. **Montezuma Well.** Actually a limestone sink formed by the collapse of an ancient underground cavern, Montezuma Well was home to first the Hohokam and then the Sinagua, who built irrigation ditches for growing corn, beans, squash, and cotton. You can see remnants of the ditches, an AD 1100 Hohokam pit house, and a variety of struc-

tures used by the Sinaguan between 1125 and 1400. Montezuma Well is managed as part of Montezuma Castle National Monument (see below).

Now go back to I-17 and drive 4 miles south to exit 289 for:

13. Montezuma Castle National Monument (tel 520/567-3322). Here you'll find a five-story 20-room cliff dwelling believed to have been constructed by the Sinagua some 800 years ago, plus the ruins of a larger, six-story pueblo built against the base of a cliff.

From here, head south 5 miles on Montezuma Castle Hwy, following signs into:

14. Camp Verde. East of I-17 exit 287, this area was established as a cavalry outpost in 1865 to protect settlers along the Verde River from raids by the Apache and Yavapai. **Fort Verde State Historic Park,** in the center of Camp Verde (tel 520/567-3275), includes five of the fort's original buildings, with exhibits depicting life in a late 19th-century fort.

Now, go west through town to I-17, head south about 23 miles to Cordes Junction (exit 262A), and go northeast about 3 miles on a dirt road, following signs to:

15. Arcosanti (tel 520/632-7135). This city of the future, designed by Paolo Soleri, remains under construction by Soleri's students. When it is eventually completed, it will be an ecologically friendly, 25-story-tall city of some 5,000 residents, with solar energy for both heating and cooling. At present, Arcosanti has a visitor's center, guest rooms, and a bakery, and guided tours.

Leaving Arcosanti, return to I-17 and continue south about 10 miles to:

16. Sunset Point. An interstate rest stop (between exits 256 and 248), Sunset Point sits on a promontory with a stunning view, taking in a ghost town site, an old stagecoach trail, Horsethief Basin, and the Bradshaw Mountains. It has photo displays and maps, as well as the usual rest stop facilities.

Now go south on I-17 about 26 more miles to Pioneer Rd (exit 225) and:

17. Pioneer Arizona Living History Museum (tel 602/993-0212). Costumed pioneers demonstrate life in Arizona's early days at this living history museum, with close to two dozen original and reconstructed buildings, including a stagecoach station, a Victorian mansion, a miner's cabin, a church, several farm houses, and carpenter's, blacksmith's, and wagon maker's shops. Melodramas and other performances are presented in the opera house, and each fall, there is a reenactment of Civil War events.

From the museum it's about 12 miles south on I-17 back to Phoenix.

TUCSON, SONORA DESERT, AND THE WILD WEST

Start	Tucson
Finish	Saguaro National Monument
Distance	386 miles
Time	3–4 days
Highlights	Old West and mining towns, rock formations, historic sites, early Spanish missions

This tour visits old Arizona, stopping at the Wild West town of Tombstone, the Spanish colonial Tumacacori mission, and the Arizona State Museum, with exhibits dealing with the area's first inhabitants, the Hohokam people. The route also takes in some of Arizona's most beautiful natural wonders, at Saguaro National Monument, Colossal Cave, and Chiricahua National Monument, as well as the desert life at the Arizona-Sonora Desert Museum. If possible, allow three days after leaving Tucson. Mileages listed are from stop to stop only, and do not include driving within a park or area or any side trips.

For additional information on lodgings, restaurants, and attractions in the region covered by the tour, refer to specific cities in the listings portion of this chapter.

1. **Tucson** (elevation 2,389 feet). If there is one city that epitomizes the American Southwest, it's Tucson. This appealing destination offers lovely year-round weather (though it gets quite hot in summer), impressive mountain and desert scenery, a rich Native American and Hispanic heritage, remnants of the Old West, a varied and exciting arts community, and numerous recreational opportunities.

   The Tuscon area was farmed by the Hohokam in the 1st century, and later became the home of Pima and Tohono O'odham tribes (formerly known as Papago). Europeans first discovered the region in 1687 with a visit by Spanish missionary Father Eusebio Francisco Kino. The city itself was founded in 1775 by Irishman Hugh O'Connor, who explored the region for Spain. Tuscon was under the Mexican flag from 1821, the year Mexico gained independence from Spain, until 1846, when it was taken over by US troops during the Mexican War. The 1854 Gadsden Purchase joined southern Arizona, including Tucson, with the rest of the Arizona Territory.

   Tucson has a broad selection of lodging choices, with posh resorts, comfortable hotels and motels, and historic inns. The luxurious **Loew's Ventana Canyon Resort** pampers its guests unmercifully; a more economical resort is **The Lodge on the Desert.** The historic **Arizona Inn** combines Old World charm with all the modern conveniences. Other attractive lodgings include **Hampton Inn, Econo Lodge,** and **Embassy Suites.**

   Start your visit to southern Arizona by visiting one or more of Tucson's fine historical museums. At the **Arizona State Museum,** on the University of Arizona campus at University Blvd and Park Ave (tel 520/621-6302), you learn about the state's first inhabitants, the Hohokam, and about tribes that lived here later, including the Pima, Tohono O'odham, Hopi, Navajo, and Apache. The **Arizona Historical Society Tucson Museum,** 949 E Second St (tel 520/628-5774), explores the state's fascinating past from Spanish colonial days to the Wild West period to the modern age.

   At the University of Arizona, be sure to visit **Flandrau Science Center & Planetarium,** at Cherry Ave and University Blvd (tel 520/621-STAR), where you can see a variety of programs and laser light shows. On clear nights, which most are, you can peruse the heavens through the planetarium's 16-inch telescope. Before leaving downtown, stop by the **University of Arizona Museum of Art,** at Park Ave and Speedway Blvd, with its excellent collection of European paintings dating back to the Renaissance and more recent American works. Nearby, also on the university campus, the **John P. Schaefer Center for Creative Photography,** just east of the Museum of Art, has one of the best and largest collections of works by the world's finest photographers.

   For Western art, visit the **Tucson Museum of Art,** 140 N Main Ave (tel 520/624-2333), which also features pre-Columbian art of Mexico and South and Central America. Also downtown, you'll find **Tucson Botanical Gardens,** 2150 N Alvernon Way (tel 520/326-9255); **Tucson Children's Museum,** 200 S Sixth Ave (tel 520/792-9985); and **Reid Park Zoo,** 1100 S Randolph Way (tel 520/791-4022).

   History and airplane buffs will enjoy the **Pima Air & Space Museum,** 6000 E Valencia Rd, south of Davis Monthan Air Force Base (tel 520/574-9658), which houses more than 180 aircraft, spanning over 90 years of aviation history.

   Mission San Xavier del Bac, 1950 W San Xavier Rd, 9 miles south of Tucson via I-19 to the Valencia Rd exit (tel 520/294-2624), is perhaps the finest

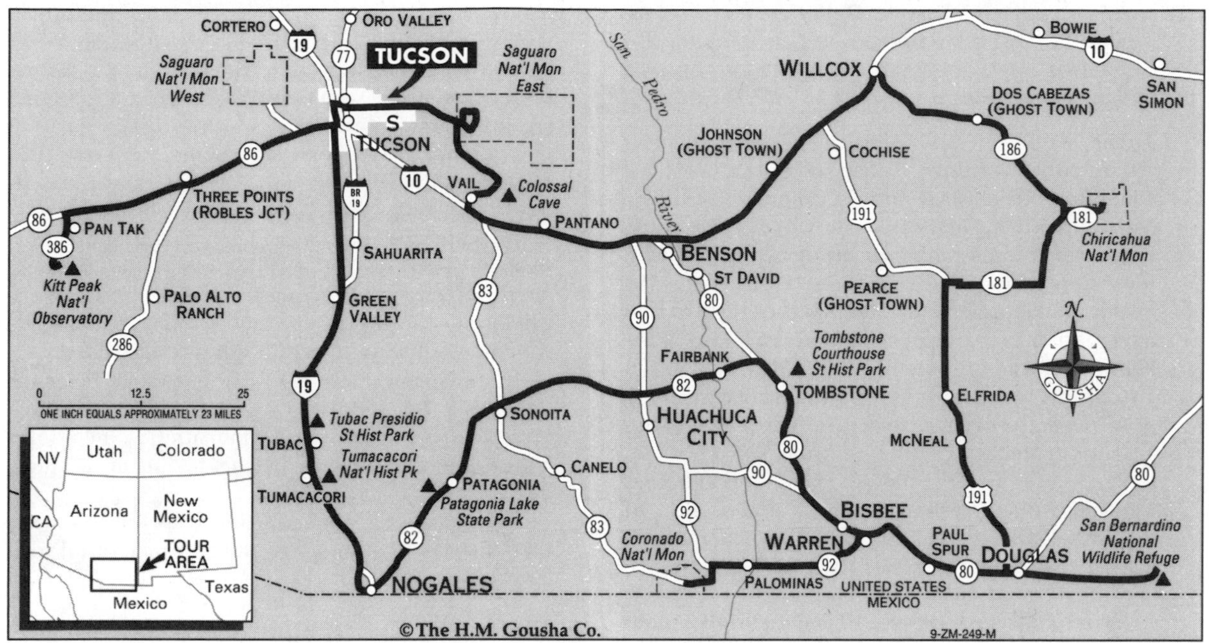

existing example of mission architecture in the United States; it incorporates Moorish, Byzantine, and Mexican Renaissance styles.

About a dozen miles west of the city, via Speedway Blvd, **Old Tucson Studios,** 201 S Kinney Rd (tel 520/883-0100), was created for the filming of the 1939 classic western *Arizona;* since then, the location has been used for more than 300 films (including *The Outlaw Josey Wales, Gunfight at the OK Corral,* and *Rio Bravo*) and for television shows and commercials. Old Tucson Studios is also a theme park, with gun fights, a steam railroad train, stagecoach rides, and behind-the-scenes tours and demonstrations of the making of western movies.

Two of Tucson's top attractions lie on the city's west side. Despite its name, the **Arizona-Sonora Desert Museum,** 2021 N Kinney Rd (tel 520/883-2702), is actually one of the finest zoos and botanical gardens in the country, with more than 200 species of animals and 1,200 species of plants indigenous to the Sonora Desert. Among animals you may see are mountain lions, black bears, otters, javelinas, birds, fish, scorpions, and tarantulas. There are also displays on prehistoric desert life, volcanos, and erosion. **Saguaro National Monument** (tel 520/733-5100), just north of the museum, is the home of the giant saguaro cactus, a symbol of the American West that can tower 50 feet above the desert, weigh more than eight tons, and drink some 200 gallons of water a year. The monument has two sections; one west and one east of Tucson. In the western section, called the Tucson Mountain District, an information center just inside the monument's boundary has brochures and exhibits describing the life cycle of the saguaro. You also have access to a 6-mile loop drive and hiking trails. See below for information on the eastern section.

About 35 miles west of Tucson, off AZ 86, is **Kitt Peak National Observatory** (tel 520/318-8600). Take Ajo Way, AZ 86, west for 35 miles, turn south onto AZ 386 and drive 11½ miles up a narrow and winding but well-maintained road to the conservatory. This part of the drive takes about 20 minutes, and there are stops at regular intervals for you to appreciate the view. This road is not recommended for those with a fear of heights or who suffer from high-altitude sickness. Perched atop 6,882-foot Kitt Peak, this observatory has close to two dozen telescopes, including the world's largest solar telescope and another telescope that contains a 30,000-pound quartz mirror. The site has a **Visitor Center**

Take a Break

If Tucson's Hispanic influences make you hungry for Mexican food, try **La Parilla Suiza,** in the center of Tucson at 5602 E Speedway Blvd (tel 520/747-4838), which specializes in Mexico City–style cuisine. **Pronto,** 2955 E Speedway (tel 520/326-9707), serves Italian specialties and has a gourmet bakery.

and Museum and **Visitor Galleries** for up-close views of the big telescopes, as well as tours.

From Tucson, go about 60 miles south on I-19 to the next stop at:

2. **Tubac,** exit 34. Considered the oldest European settlement in Arizona, Tubac today is a laid-back community of artists, who own galleries and shops, and retirees. But life was really more active in the 1750s when the Spanish government established a fort here to protect settlers from raids by hostile Native Americans. Remnants of the fort and days past may be seen at **Tubac Presidio State Historic Park,** Presidio Dr (tel 520/398-2252), a 10-acre area with an underground display showing portions of the original structure. The park also has a visitor center with exhibits tracing Tubac's sometimes-violent history and an 1885 schoolhouse. Modern Tubac is evident at the **Tubac Center of the Arts,** Plaza Rd (tel 520/398-2371), where you'll discover works by local artists, traveling exhibits, and theater and music performances.

From Tubac, return to I-19 and go south 3 miles to exit 29 for:

3. **Tumacacori National Historical Park** (tel 520/398-2341). The mission at Tumacacori, located just under 1 mile from I-19, was founded in 1691 by Father Eusebio Francisco Kino to convert the Pima Indians to Christianity. After a revolt in 1751 that left two priests and more than 100 settlers dead, the Spanish established a fort in nearby Tubac, and moved the mission across the Santa Cruz River. The handsome adobe ruins of this second Tumacacori mission church, a cemetery, and a mortuary chapel are what you see on a self-guided walking tour. The park also has a museum containing displays on mission life, and a garden with plants of the mission period. Nearby, within the boundaries of the park, you can see ruins of two other missions.

From Tumacacori, return to I-19 and go south for 18 miles to exit 1 and:

4. **Nogales.** Actually there are two Nogaleses—one in Arizona and a much larger one across the border in Mexico. Although definitely not Mexico at its best, this border town allows you a convenient opportunity to visit Mexico for some quick shopping and sightseeing. Most visitors park their cars on the Arizona side and walk across the border. If you do want to take your car into Mexico, you need to buy Mexican motor vehicle insurance before leaving the United States. You don't need a passport or tourist card to visit the Mexican Nogales, and you can bring back up to $400 worth of merchandise duty free, including one liter of liquor. The city has a variety of markets and shops where you can find leather goods, baskets, pottery, clothing, and other items, often at very attractive prices, although some visitors feel uncomfortable with the large number of beggars on the streets and the merchants' persistent efforts to lure shoppers into stores.

Back on the Arizona side is the **Pimeria Alta Historical Society Museum,** 136 N Grand Ave (tel 520/287-5402), which has exhibits on the history of this section of southern Arizona and northern Mexico. Two miles east of Nogales on AZ 82 is **Arizona Vineyard Winery** (tel 520/287-7972), where you can take a tour and try free samples of wine, including an interesting Rattlesnake Red.

From Nogales, take AZ 82 northeast 12 miles to **Patagonia Lake State Park** (tel 520/287-6965), with plenty of recreational opportunities, including a 250-acre lake, boating, fishing, hiking, and camping.

Back on AZ 82, continue northeast for 56 miles, then turn south onto AZ 80 and go 4 miles until you reach:

5. **Tombstone.** This town may be the most famous community of the Old West, thanks to numerous books and movies that have glorified its wild and wicked days, and particularly the famous "Gunfight at the OK Corral," during which Wyatt Earp and his brothers fought it out with the outlaw Clanton family. The town got its name from prospector Ed Schieffelin, who was warned that before he found any silver he'd find his own tombstone. When he made his first strike, Schieffelin gave the town its present name, probably to mock any doubters.

There's less shooting in Tombstone now, except for staged gunfights Sunday afternoons, but the place continues to live up to its nickname as "the town too tough to die" with a thriving tourist business. Historic Allen St has been beautifully restored, and you're likely to find film crews at work here. Half real and half make-believe, Tombstone is fun, especially if you don't take it too seriously.

At the **OK Corral,** on Allen St between 3rd and 4th Sts (tel 520/457-3456), you'll see where the famous 1881 gunfight took place. Next to the OK Corral's main entrance is **Historama** (tel 520/457-3456), with a program on Tombstone's past. **Boot Hill Graveyard,** off Ariz 80 on the north side of town (tel 520/457-9344), has a number of telling tombstones reflecting the town's genuinely violent history. Considered the West's wildest whorehouse and saloon, the **Bird Cage Theatre,** at 6th and Allen Sts (tel 520/457-3421), remains much like it was in 1881, when prostitutes were perched in cages hung from the ceiling. In contrast to the noisy shoot-em-up atmosphere in most of Tombstone in the 1880s, a sophisticated Victorian courthouse was built in 1882 at a cost of $50,000. Today it is the **Tombstone Courthouse State Historic Park,** 219 E Toughnut St (tel 520/457-3311), containing displays on the town's history. Another sign that Tombstone was home to more than gunslingers and ladies-of-the-night is **St Paul's Episcopal Church,** a handsome adobe structure built in 1882, at the corner of 3rd and Safford Sts.

Take a Break

For a variety of food choices in a historic building, stop at **The Nellie Cashman Restaurant,** 117 S 5th St (tel 520/457-2212).

Leaving Tombstone, take US 80 south 24 miles to the next stop:

6. **Bisbee** (elevation 5,490 feet). One of the region's best remaining examples of a turn-of-the-century town, Bisbee is another of the western boom towns that almost disappeared when the minerals—in this case copper—finally ran out. In 1919, Bisbee reportedly was the largest city between New Orleans and San Francisco, a wild place with 25,000 residents and close to 50 saloons and bordellos. Today, with a bit over 6,000 people, Bisbee is a fascinating mix of retired miners, artists, and transplanted city dwellers looking for a better life. Built on the exceedingly steep sides of Tombstone Canyon, the houses seem almost to grow out of one another.

   At the **Bisbee Chamber of Commerce,** Naco Rd (tel 520/432-5421), you'll find several brochures describing walking tours among the historic buildings. **Queen Mine,** 118 Arizona St (tel 520/432-2071), closed in 1975, but it offers underground tours as well as tours of the nearby **Lavender Pit** open mine. For a look at the history of mining and Bisbee, stop at the **Bisbee Mining and Historical Museum,** 5 Copper Queen Plaza (tel 520/432-7071). The **Muheim Heritage House Museum,** 207 Youngblood Hill (tel 520/432-7071), has been restored to its early 20th-century elegance, with period furnishings. Situated on a hill overlooking Old Bisbee, the museum site offers magnificent panoramic views of the surrounding countryside. For an interesting side trip from Bisbee, visit **Coronado National Memorial,** 30 miles west on AZ 92 and Montezuma Canyon Rd (tel 520/366-5515), which commemorates the first major European exploration of the Southwest, when Francisco Vásquez de Coronado of Spain arrived in 1540.

   If it's late in the day, you may want to consider spending the night here. In historic Old Bisbee, the **Bisbee Grand Hotel** and the **Copper Queen Hotel** offer a trip back to the turn of the century, while **High Desert Inn** has modern facilities in a historic building.

   From Bisbee, follow AZ 80 east for 23 miles to get to:

7. **Douglas.** Founded in 1901, Douglas (elevation 3,990 feet) began as the roundup site for the surrounding ranches. Today, with its convenient location on the US-Mexico border, Douglas's main industry is international commerce, with 15 manufacturing plants, and another 26 across the Mexican border in Agua Prieta. While in Douglas, stop at the historic **Gadsden Hotel,** 1046 G Ave. Built in 1907, this "last of the grand hotels" has a beautiful marble lobby, vaulted stained-glass skylights, and a Tiffany stained-glass window.

   From Douglas, take AZ 80 west for 2 miles, head north on US 191 for 37 miles, turn east onto AZ 181, and drive 22 miles to:

8. **Chiricahua National Monument** (tel 520/824-3560). Called "Land of the Standing-up Rocks" by the Chiricahua Apache for whom it is named, this monument is a wonderland of exotic and extraordinary rock sculptures, created by volcanic activity followed by millions of years of wind and water erosion. The park is a fantasy world of delicate spires, gigantic balanced rocks, massive columns, and intriguing rock grottos. A **visitor center** offers a slide show, exhibits, maps, and books. You can take a 16-mile scenic drive, and walk more than 20 miles of hiking trails past unusual rock formations such as Duck on a Rock. Also on the monument grounds is the turn-of-the-century **Faraway Ranch and Stafford Cabin,** with tours daily.

   From Chiricahua National Monument, follow AZ 186 northwest 32 miles to:

9. **Willcox,** at I-10 exit 340. Once called the "Cattle Capital of America," Willcox is still a major cattle shipping area, with the state's largest livestock auction. Lodging possibilities here include the modern, comfortable, and clean **Best Western Plaza Inn** and **Econo Lodge,** both just off the interstate highway.

   Fans of older-style country western music will want to stop at the **Rex Allen Arizona Cowboy Museum,** 155 N Railroad Ave (tel 520/384-4583), dedicated to hometown boy Allen, a popular country western singer and actor in the 1940s and 1950s. The **Cochise Visitor Center and Museum of the Southwest,** at I-10 exit 340, 1500 N Circle I Rd (tel 520/384-2272), contains exhibits on southeastern Arizona's Wild West days, cattle ranching, and geology.

From Willcox, take I-10 west 61 miles to exit 279 and:

10. Vail. The **RW Webb Winery** (tel 520/762-5777), on the frontage road, offers informal guided tours and wine tasting. Founded in 1980, this operation is said to be the first bonded winery in the state since Prohibition.

Next, follow the steep and winding Colossal Cave Rd on its roller coaster way north about 5 miles to:

11. Colossal Cave (tel 602/647-7275). Among the world's largest dry limestone caves, Colossal Cave was a favorite hideout for bandits in Arizona's Wild West days. The cave has a constant temperature of 72 degrees. There are lighted passageways among the numerous stalagmites and stalactites, and guided ½-mile tours are offered.

As you exit the cave property, the road becomes Old Spanish Trail, which you follow west 5 miles to the east section of:

12. Saguaro National Monument (tel 602/733-5100). Here you'll find an aging forest of giant saguaro cacti at the base of the Rincon Mountains. Stop first at the **visitor center** for hiking and driving guides, and to look at exhibits on saguaro and other desert life. You'll also learn about a fire that occurred on Mother's Day, 1994, destroying a number of giant saguaros. The monument area has an 8-mile **Cactus Forest Drive** winding through the saguaro forest, and close to 130 miles of hiking trails, including a short **Desert Ecology Trail** that shows the vital role of water in the desert.

From the monument, continue along Old Spanish Trail west about 12 miles to Broadway, which you follow about 8 miles into downtown Tucson.

GRAND CANYON AND NAVAJO AND HOPI COUNTRY

Start	Flagstaff
Finish	Meteor Crater Natural Landmark
Distance	535 miles
Time	2–5 days
Highlights	Grand Canyon, Native American trading posts, Painted Desert

This northeast Arizona tour includes some of the state's most stunning scenery as well as opportunities to see and buy beautiful Native American jewelry, rugs, baskets, and pottery. Early morning and late evening are best for viewing the canyons and Painted Desert. It's wise not to travel after dark in the remote reaches of the Hopi and Navajo reservations, where you might encounter sheep on the road. Highways in this tour are good, all-weather roads, but there can be great distances between services of any kind.

When traveling through the reservations keep in mind that these are considered sovereign nations, with their own laws. Also remember that although the Hopi and Navajo generally welcome visitors, these areas are made up of their homes and villages; you are asked to respect their privacy by only going inside buildings where you are obviously invited and by obeying all signs. Often, photography is prohibited, and even where it is permitted you're expected to ask for permission before photographing any individuals. Religious ceremonies are fascinating to watch, but keep in mind that these are serious services and behave accordingly.

For additional information on lodgings, restaurants, and attractions in the region covered by the tour, refer to specific cities in the listings portion of this chapter.

1. **Flagstaff.** Located at the base of the San Francisco Peaks, Flagstaff looks up at Mount Humphreys, the highest point in Arizona at an elevation of 12,633 feet. The combination of its 7,000-foot elevation and clear, dry air gives Flagstaff a mild climate year-round, with an average of 288 days of sunshine each year. You'll find recreational, cultural, and historical activities in and around the city, with opportunities for both downhill and cross-country skiing; and hiking, camping, hunting, and fishing in the Coconino National Forest, which surrounds Flagstaff and has the largest stand of ponderosa pine in the nation.

   A good place to begin your tour of northern Arizona, and possibly to use as a home base, Flagstaff has a variety of lodgings from which to choose, from basic to fancy. The historic **Monte Vista Hotel,** built in 1929, is located downtown. For a quiet, rustic retreat just outside the city try **Arizona Mountain Inn.** The **Best Western Woodlands Plaza Inn** is considered to be among Flagstaff's finest, and the attractive **Econo Lodge West,** in southwest Flagstaff, is a comfortable and economical choice.

   Downtown Flagstaff has several historical buildings; you can obtain a map for a self-guided walking tour at the visitors center at the corner of Route 66 and Beaver St (tel 520/774-9541 or toll free 800/842-7293). Highlights include the 1888 **McMillan Building,** now housing an art gallery; the 1889 **Weatherford Hotel,** now a youth hostel and nightclub; and the 1929 **Monte Vista Hotel,** with several specialty shops. The **Riordan State Historic Park,** 1300 Riordan Ranch St, has guided tours of the two-story mansion, built in 1904 for two Riordan brothers and their families.

   Lowell Observatory, 1400 W Mars Rd (tel 520/774-2096), about a mile from downtown Flagstaff on the top of Mars Hill, is one of the oldest astronomical observatories in the Southwest, founded in 1894. Early observations at this site supported the expanding universe theory, and it was here in 1930 that the ninth planet, Pluto, was discovered. The observatory welcomes visitors with daytime guided tours and nighttime astronomical programs.

   Northern Arizona University (tel 520/523-9011), off Old Route 66 via Riordan Rd in downtown Flagstaff, first opened in 1899 as a school for teacher preparation. The oldest of its several entries on the National Register of Historic Places is **Old Main,** built in 1894 and today housing a museum and art galleries. The university also has the **Richard E. Beasley Art Museum and Gallery** (tel 520/523-3471) with exhibits of contemporary art.

   Just northwest of downtown on US 180 (N Fort Valley Rd), you'll find three museums. Created in 1928, the **Museum of Northern Arizona,** N Fort Valley Rd (tel 520/774-5211), explores the cultural and natural history of the Colorado Plateau, a geographic area encompassing northern Arizona and the Four Corners region. It also exhibits work by Native American artists. **Pioneer Museum,** 2340 N Fort Valley Rd (tel 520/774-6272), opened in 1963. Here you can see Flagstaff's first fire engine, a sheepherder's wagon, and pioneer tools and artifacts. Also notable are photographs of the

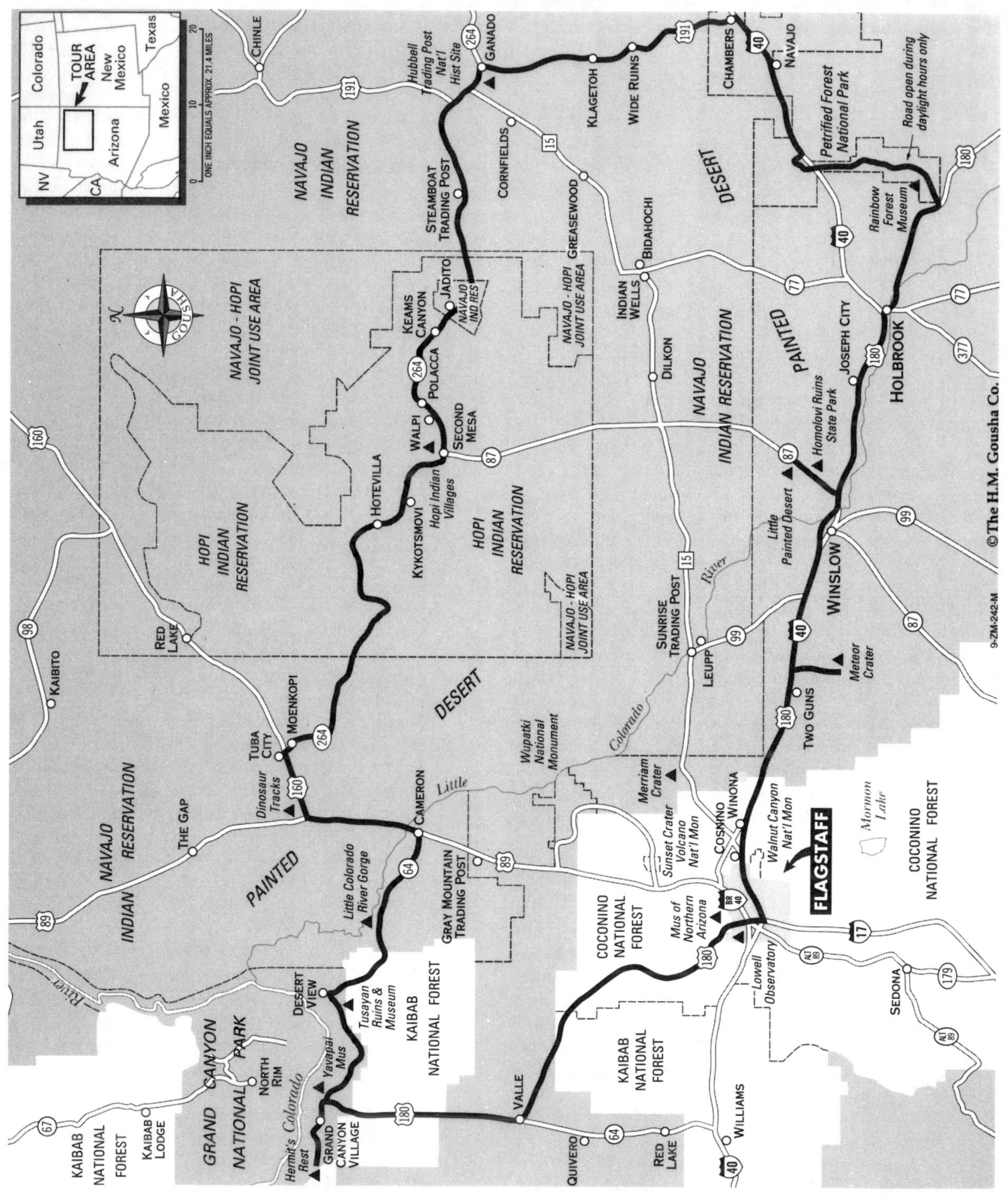

Grand Canyon taken between 1902 and 1906 by Emery Kolb. **Coconino Center for the Arts,** N Fort Valley Rd (tel 520/779-6921), is a regional art center with changing exhibits every five to six weeks, plus musical performances and workshops.

Head southwest about 4 miles from Flagstaff on

Woody Mountain Rd to the **Arboretum at Flagstaff** (tel 520/774-1441), the highest US botanical garden conducting horticultural research; it is located on 200 acres of ponderosa pine forest land.

Walnut Canyon National Monument, Walnut Canyon Rd (tel 520/526-3367), is on the east side of Flagstaff, about 10 minutes from downtown. Take Exit 204 off I-40. The 3-mile drive to the monument takes you through a beautiful ponderosa forest to the **visitor center.** Sometime before 1400, Sinagua Indians built over 300 rooms in the recesses of the high desert canyon walls. A steep foot trail takes you to 25 of the cliff dwelling ruins.

Sunset Crater Volcano and Wupatki National Monuments are on a loop road that takes off from US 89 about 13 miles north of Flagstaff. The Sunset Crater visitors center is 2 miles down the road, and there are numerous vistas and walking trails in the area. The visitors center for Wupatki is 22 miles north on the road; it features displays on the Indian ruins that comprise this monument, which were inhabited in the 12th and 13th centuries. Another 14 miles brings you back to US 89, and it's about 39 miles back to Flagstaff.

Take a Break

Flagstaff has lots of good eateries, including **Black Bart's,** 2760 E Butler Ave (tel 520/779-3142), with plenty of beef and a western motif; **Beaver Street Brewery and Whistle Stop Cafe,** 11 S Beaver St (tel 520/779-0079), where you'll find fresh beer, pizzas, sandwiches, and burgers; and **Kelly's Christmas Tree Restaurant,** 5200 E Cortland Blvd (tel 520/526-0776), with a variety of American and other specialties.

Once you've seen the sights of the Flagstaff area, head north on US 180 for 81 miles to:

2. **Grand Canyon National Park.** Considered the most popular natural attraction in the United States, the awe-inspiring Grand Canyon is some 2 billion years old. It is about 1 mile deep, 277 miles long, and 11 to 12 miles across. Elevation at the South Rim is 7,000 feet, and 8,200 feet at the North Rim. But the Grand Canyon's appeal consists of much more than numbers. Its quiet magnificence attains an almost spiritual beauty. It's not unusual to be standing at an overlook crowded with people and hear nothing but the sound of the wind. Sculpted by the Colorado River as it slices through layers of rock, the canyon is a maze of colorful and majestic towers, valleys, walls, and pinnacles.

   Because of the Grand Canyon's popularity, it is advisable to make reservations for lodging, camping, and especially mule rides as far in advance as possible. Call the park operator (tel 520/638-2631) to be connected with the proper offices.

   Once you're at the South Rim, stop first at the **visitor center** in Grand Canyon Village for helpful brochures and information on the free shuttle that operates during summer months. Then head out to see the canyon, either from the various overlooks, or by foot or mule into the canyon. On the 8-mile one-way **West Rim Drive** (only by shuttle and tour bus in summer), you get a fine canyon view and see a historic log and stone building at **Hermit's Rest,** named for an 1890s prospector. Then, the 25-mile **East Rim Drive** takes you out the park's east gate.

   Just east of Grand Canyon Village at **Yavapai Point,** you experience a different view; the **Yavapai Museum** has exhibits on the canyon's geological history. From here, continue east, stopping at the various overlooks. At **Tusayan Ruins,** you find the ruins of an ancient Anasazi village and a small museum. At **Desert View,** at the east end of East Rim Dr, climb to the top of the **Watchtower,** the highest point along the South Rim, for a spectacular view of the canyon, the Painted Desert to the east, and San Francisco Mountains to the south.

   From Desert View, drive east on AZ 64 for 15 miles to:

3. **Little Colorado River Gorge,** an awesome vista looking down into the Little Colorado River Canyon. Here you're also likely to find local Native Americans selling their crafts.

   From the overlook, continue east on AZ 64 another 17 miles, then go north 1 mile on US 89 until you reach:

4. **Cameron,** and the historic **Cameron Trading Post** (tel 520/679-2231 or toll free 800/338-7385). This genuine trading post, established in 1890, has a huge selection of rugs, pottery, textiles, beadwork, jewelry, and other Native American crafts, including museum-quality late 19th- and early 20th-century Navajo rugs. Still actively used by local Native Americans, the trading post also contains a general store with packaged foods and household goods.

   From Cameron, continue 15 miles north on US 89 through the Painted Desert to US 160, turn east and travel about 6 miles to an unpaved road heading north toward Moenave. Follow this dirt road about ¼ mile to find:

5. **Dinosaur Tracks.** Left in the mud flats over 200 million years ago, these dinosaur tracks and part of a dinosaur skeleton may be seen within about 200 feet of the unpaved road.

From the tracks, return to US 160, go east about 5 miles to AZ 264, and continue east on AZ 264, through the Painted Desert and red rock country for about 60 miles to:

6. **Second Mesa,** home of the Hopi Native Americans, who trace their ancestry to the ancient Anasazi. Visit the **Hopi Cultural Center** (tel 520/734-2401), with a fine museum telling the story of the Hopis through historic photos and artifacts. This is also a good place to find out what other parts of the reservation are open to visitors. Usually you can take a tour of **Walpi,** on First Mesa, about 10 miles east of Second Mesa, with its cliff homes. Most other Hopi villages are usually open to the public; the exception is Old Oraibi, a spiritual center, which is closed to all outsiders.

You'll find arts and crafts vendors at the cultural center, as well as next door at the **Hopi Arts and Crafts Silvercraft Cooperative Guild** (tel 520/734-2463), which offers excellent quality pottery, textiles, baskets, silver jewelry, paintings, and Kachina dolls. If you would like to spend the night, you'll find comfortable rooms at the **Hopi Cultural Center Restaurant and Motel.**

After exploring Hopi country, continue east on AZ 264 for 70 miles (from Second Mesa) to Ganado and:

7. **Hubbell Trading Post National Historic Site** (tel 520/755-3475). John Lorenzo Hubbell, who founded this trading post in 1878, was the foremost Navajo trader of the time, respected by both Navajos and whites. The site includes the original trading post, which still sells food, fabric, and household goods. You can look at Navajo rugs, silver and turquoise jewelry, baskets, and other crafts. A **visitor center and museum** covers the trading post's history, and you can watch Navajo weavers and jewelers at work.

From Ganado, head south on US 191 for 44 miles to I-40 at Chambers (exit 333), and take the I-40 west 22 miles to exit 311 for:

8. **Petrified Forest National Park** (tel 520/524-6228), which consists of six forests worth of petrified wood and some of the most colorful parts of the Painted Desert. Stop at the **Painted Desert Visitor Center** for orientation before driving 27 miles through the park, with some two dozen scenic overlooks and short walks. The **Painted Desert,** a pastel wonderland of colors and shapes, dominates the park's northern part, where you entered; most of the petrified logs are in the southern part. The area is particularly colorful at sunrise and sunset, and even better if you can catch it immediately after a rain shower has washed the dust away.

Heading south through the park you'll find the **Puerco Indian Ruins** and petroglyphs at **Newspaper Rock.** Other stops include **Jasper Forest Overlook,** where you'll see petrified roots as well as trunks, and **Agate House,** a partially restored pueblo. The **Giant Logs** self-guided trail passes by some of the park's largest petrified logs, and nearby, at the park's southern edge, you'll find **Rainbow Forest Museum,** with exhibits on the area's geological and human history, plus displays of petrified wood.

From the park's southern entrance, follow US 180 west for 21 miles into Holbrook, rejoining I-40 at exit 285. Then continue west on I-40 for 28 miles to exit 257 and head north on AZ 87 for 2 miles to:

9. **Homolovi Ruins State Park** (tel 520/289-4106), which includes ruins supposedly occupied between 1250 and 1600 by ancestors of today's Hopi tribe. (Homolovi is a Hopi word that means "place of the mounds.") Several hiking trails wind among pueblo ruins and petroglyphs, and another trail leads to **Sunset Cemetery,** all that remains of an 1870s Mormon settlement.

From the ruins, drive northeast 13 miles on AZ 87 to:

10. **Little Painted Desert.** This small country park is a wonderful place to have a picnic supper while watching the everchanging colors of the Painted Desert.

Return 15 miles to I-40 and drive 2 miles west to exit 253 for:

11. **Winslow.** A good place to spend the night, you'll find clean, attractive accommodations at **Best Western Town House Lodge.** Before leaving town, take time to stop at **Old Trails Museum,** 212 Kinsley Ave (tel 520/289-5861), in a 1916 bank building. The museum focuses on northeast Arizona history.

From Winslow, continue west on I-40 for 20 miles to exit 233, and then 6 miles south on Meteor Crater Rd to:

12. **Meteor Crater Natural Landmark** (tel 520/289-2362). A giant rock smashed into the earth here 49,000 years ago at more than 30,000 miles per hour. The meteor destroyed all plant and animal life within 100 miles, leaving this crater 570 feet deep and over 4,000 feet across; it has been used by US astronauts to train for moon walks. The **Museum of Astrogeology** has exhibits on the crater's creation, and there's also an **Astronaut Hall of Fame.**

Return 6 miles back to I-40, and continue west for 34 miles to return to Flagstaff.

Arizona Listings

Alpine

Named for its high elevation (8,030 feet), this small, picturesque community and the surrounding national forest are considered the Alps of Arizona. It's a year-round destination for hikers, fishermen, and hunters. **Information:** Alpine Chamber of Commerce, PO Box 410, Alpine 85920 (tel 520/339-4330).

LODGE

Tal-Wi-Wi Lodge
40 County Rd 2220, PO Box 169, 85920; tel 520/339-4319. 3 mi N of Alpine. County Rd 2220 exit off US 191. A lovely mountain setting, terrific for getting away from it all. **Rooms:** 20 rms. CI 3pm/CO 11am. Basic but comfortable rooms. **Amenities:** No A/C, phone, or TV. Some units w/terraces, some w/fireplaces, some w/whirlpools. **Services:** Twice-daily maid svce. **Facilities:** 1 restaurant (bkfst and dinner only), 1 bar (w/entertainment), whirlpool. **Rates:** Peak (June–Sept) $55–$95 S or D. Children under age 18 stay free. Min stay wknds. Lower rates off-season. Parking: Outdoor, free. MC, V.

Bisbee

A boomtown born in the 1870s with the discovery of vast amounts of gold, silver, and copper, Bisbee started as a wild mining camp but soon became known as the most refined city between New Orleans and San Francisco. Today the town, which retains much of its 19th-century charm, is home to artists, writers, and other creative types. **Information:** Greater Bisbee Chamber of Commerce, 7 Main St, PO Box BA, Bisbee 85603 (tel 520/432-5421).

HOTELS

The Bisbee Grand Hotel
61 Main St, PO Box 825, 85603; tel 520/432-5900 or toll free 800/421-1909. A charming, historic Old West hotel in the center of Old Bisbee. No smoking throughout. **Rooms:** 11 rms and stes. CI 1pm/CO 11am. Beautifully furnished turn-of-the-century rooms. The Victorian and Oriental suites are especially distinctive. **Amenities:** A/C. No phone or TV. **Services:** Twice-daily maid svce. **Facilities:** 75 1 bar (w/entertainment), games rm, washer/dryer. **Rates (BB):** $55–$78 S or D; $95–$110 ste. Special packages for Murder Mystery Weekends. AE, DISC, MC, V.

Copper Queen Hotel
11 Howell Ave, 85603; tel 520/432-2216 or toll free 800/247-5829 in AZ; fax 520/432-4298. Old Bisbee exit off US 80. This charming, historic hotel, built in 1902, offers a trip to Bisbee's glorious past. **Rooms:** 45 rms. CI 2pm/CO 11am. Nonsmoking rms avail. Comfortable, restored rooms are furnished with turn-of-the-century antiques. **Amenities:** A/C, cable TV. **Services:** Babysitting. **Facilities:** 50 1 restaurant, 1 bar (w/entertainment). **Rates:** $67–$88 S; $67–$95 D. Extra person $10. Children under age 12 stay free. AP and MAP rates avail. AE, DC, DISC, MC, V.

INN

Bisbee Inn
45 OK St, PO Box 1855, 85603; tel 520/432-5131. Comfortable inn located in a historic building. **Rooms:** 18 rms and stes (17 w/shared bath). CI 3pm/CO 11am. Rooms are furnished with antiques. Only the suite has private bath; other rooms share 7 toilets and 5 showers. **Amenities:** A/C. No phone or TV. **Services:** **Facilities:** Washer/dryer, guest lounge w/TV. **Rates (BB):** Peak (Jan–May) $35–$55 S or D w/shared bath; $71 ste. Extra person $13. Children under age 1 stay free. Lower rates off-season. Closed June–Sept. MC, V.

RESTAURANT

Cafe Roka
35 Main St (Old Bisbee); tel 520/432-5153. 24 mi S of Tombstone. **Italian.** An attractive, modern restaurant, with photographs on the walls. The somewhat limited menu features sea scallops and angel-hair pasta, and breast of chicken baked in phyllo. Soup, salad, and sorbet comes with every main course. The chef trained at the Biltmore Hotel in Phoenix. **FYI:** Reservations recommended. No smoking. **Open:** Tues–Sat 5–9pm. Closed Sept. **Prices:** Main courses $9–$16. MC, V.

ATTRACTIONS

Bisbee Mining and Historical Museum
5 Copper Queen Plaza; tel 520/432-7071. Housed in the 1897 Copper Queen Consolidated Mining Company office building, this small museum features several rooms of old mining equipment. In the mine tunnel room visitors learn how underground mines were blasted and "mucked" out. There's also an exhibit of minerals that are found in the ground beneath Bisbee. Other displays pertain to the history of the town itself. **Open:** Daily 10am–4pm. **$**

Queen Mine Tours
478 N Dart Rd; tel 520/432-2071. Copper built Bisbee, and between 1880 and 1975 the mines here produced $6.1 billion worth of metals. Though the mines are no longer productive, tours still take visitors into the tunnels. Go deep underground by train into the Queen Mine or travel by van to the Lavendar Pit to view a surface mine. Tours are conducted Mon–Fri at 9am, 10:30am, noon, 2pm, and 3:30pm. **$$$**

Muheim Heritage House
207 Youngblood Hill; tel 520/432-7071. Built in 1908 by local merchant Joseph Muheim, this restored home houses a small museum. Inside there is period furniture and old wine-making equipment used in the several saloons in town that Muheim owned. **Open:** Fri–Mon 10am–4pm. **$**

Bullhead City

Often registering the highest summer temperatures in the United States—regularly topping 120°F—Bullhead City is mainly known for its proximity to neighboring Laughlin, Nevada, a gambling mecca just across the Colorado River. Also nearby are boating and other outdoor recreation in Lake Mead National Recreation Area. **Information:** Bullhead Area Chamber of Commerce, 1251 AZ 95, Bullhead City 86429 (tel 520/754-4121).

HOTEL

Days Inn
2200 Karis Dr, 86442; tel 520/758-1711 or toll free 800/255-6903; fax 520/758-7937. Karis Dr exit off AZ 95. This attractive, basic hotel is centrally located. **Rooms:** 70 rms and stes. CI 2pm/CO noon. Nonsmoking rms avail. **Amenities:** A/C, cable TV, refrig. **Services:** **Facilities:** Whirlpool, washer/dryer. **Rates (CP):** Peak (Dec–Apr) $40–$60 S or D; $40–$75 ste. Extra person $5. Children under age 11 stay free. Min stay special events. Lower rates off-season. Parking: Outdoor, free. Senior discounts avail. AE, CB, DC, DISC, MC, V.

RESORT

Lake Mohave Resort
Katherine Landing, 86430-4016; tel 520/754-3245 or toll free 800/752-9669. 3 mi N of AZ 68 at Lake Mead Nat'l Rec Area. A complete resort for the boating enthusiast, with houseboats, ski boats, patio boats, fishing boats, plus facilities for personal watercraft. **Rooms:** 52 rms and effic. CI 2pm/CO 11am. Some rooms have fully equipped kitchenettes. **Amenities:** A/C, TV, refrig. Some units w/terraces. **Services:** **Facilities:** 1 restaurant, 1 bar, 1 beach (lake shore). There are a picnic area available for guests and an RV park on the property. **Rates:** Peak (Mar–Nov) $60–$69 S or D; $83–$89 effic. Extra person $6. Children under age 5 stay free. Min stay special events. Lower rates off-season. Parking: Outdoor, free. DISC, MC, V.

Camp Verde

ATTRACTIONS

Fort Verde State Historic Park
3 mi E of I-17; tel 520/567-3275. 35 miles SE of Sedona. Established in 1871, this was the third military post in the Verde Valley and was occupied until 1891, by which time tensions with the Native American population had subsided and made the fort unnecessary. Today the state park, which covers 10 acres, preserves 3 officers' quarters, an administration building, and some ruins. The buildings that have been fully restored house exhibits on the fort's history. **Open:** Daily 8am–4:30pm. **$**

Montezuma Castle National Monument
Exit 289 off I-17; tel 520/567-3322. This Sinagua cliff dwelling, perhaps the best preserved of all the cliff dwellings in Arizona, consists of 2 stone pueblos built in the early 12th century. Located a few miles north of Montezuma Castle is **Montezuma Well**, another prehistoric Indian site. Occupied by both the Hohokam and Sinagua at different times in the past, this desert oasis measures 368 feet across and 65 feet deep. **Open:** Daily 8am–5pm. **$**

Canyon de Chelly National Monument

See Chinle

Carefree

Situated about 25 miles north of Phoenix in the high Sonoran Desert, Carefree is cooler than the immediate Phoenix area. The area attracts outdoor enthusiasts drawn by the mountains and beautiful scenery. **Information:** Carefree/Cave Creek Chamber of Commerce, 748 Easy St, PO Box 734, Carefree 85377 (tel 602/488-3381).

RESORT

The Boulders

34631 N Tom Darlington Dr, PO Box 2090, 85377; tel 602/488-9009 or toll free 800/553-1717; fax 602/488-4118. 1,300 acres. One of America's most dramatically sited and masterfully conceived resorts. It is situated in the shadow of massive mounds of 12-million-year-old boulders, part of a 1,300-acre gated community located 2,500 feet up in the Sonora Desert. Navajo artifacts and art complement the regional styling of the beamed and vaulted public rooms. **Rooms:** 160 rms and stes; 20 cottages/villas. CI 4pm/CO noon. Clusters of pueblo-style, two-story casitas. Unique interiors skillfully combine southwestern architecture and earth tones with modern amenities. All rooms identical except for views: fairways and coyotes or arroyos and jackrabbits. **Amenities:** A/C, cable TV w/movies, dataport, in-rm safe, bathrobes. All units w/minibars, all w/terraces, all w/fireplaces. Wet bars and wood-burning fireplaces in each room; patios and terraces with loungers, tables, and chairs; roomy walk-in closets with stacks of drawers; carafes of iced water with slices of lemon for tennis players. **Services:** Twice-daily maid svce, car-rental desk, masseur, babysitting. Staff, primed for an urbane and pampered clientele, outnumber guests 2 to 1. **Facilities:** 36 6 550 5 restaurants (*see* "Restaurants" below), 2 bars (1 w/entertainment), lawn games, spa, sauna, steam rm, whirlpool. Two golf courses shared with 250 members of Boulders Club (one course for guests and one for members, rotating daily); dramatic pool beneath the boulders, second lap pool near the tennis courts; 3 jogging/hiking trails. Resort-supervised dining at the small, whimsical El Pedregal Festival Marketplace next door. **Rates:** Peak (Jan 19–May 4/Dec 25–31) $430 S; $465 D; $500 ste; $600–$1,000 cottage/villa. Extra person $25. Children under age 12 stay free. Lower rates off-season. MAP rates avail. Parking: Outdoor, free. A service charge of $16 per night is added to each room for tips to staff other than waiters and bartenders. Closed July–Aug. AE, CB, DC, MC, V.

RESTAURANTS

Latilla Room

In The Boulders, 34631 Tom Darlington Dr; tel 602/488-9009. 1 mi S of Carefree. **Regional American.** This dramatic dining room has tremendous views of huge, weather-beaten boulders. There are thick adobelike walls and wood-beam ceilings, and the mauve chairs and carpet are the color of the mountains just after sunset. Unusual offerings include appetizers like griddle Dungeness crab cakes with sun-dried tomato sauce, and entrees such as fresh pasta with lobster, andouille sausage, tomato, and sweet corn sauce. **FYI:** Reservations recommended. Jazz/singer. Children's menu. Jacket required. No smoking. **Open:** Breakfast Mon–Sat 6:30–10:30am; dinner daily 6–9:30pm; brunch Sun 11:30am–2pm. Closed July–Aug. **Prices:** Main courses $20–$36. AE, CB, DC, MC, V. VP

The Palo Verde

In The Boulders, 34631 N Tom Darlington Dr; tel 602/488-9009. Carefree Hwy exit off I-17; go east on Carefree to Scottsdale Rd, then left to the resort. **Southwestern.** Well worth a visit for creative southwestern cuisine presented in an adobe-style setting featuring wood latilla and viga ceilings, booths, banquettes, and glass doors that open to a circular terrace. Some specialties are pumpkinseed and sage-encrusted rack of lamb with dried fruit, cashew mashed potatoes, and wild mushrooms; southwestern bouillabaisse with Nepal cactus and corn crostini; and achiote-basted free-range veal chop with pumpkinseed cream and red pepper orzo. Meals are prepared in the exhibition kitchen under the guidance of celebrity chef Charles Wiley. **FYI:** Reservations recommended. Children's menu. No smoking. **Open:** Lunch daily 11:30am–2:30pm; dinner daily 6–9:30pm. Closed July–Aug. **Prices:** Main courses $22–$29. AE, CB, DC, DISC, MC, V. VP

Casa Grande

Originally a stop on the Southern Pacific Railroad, this town was named for nearby Casa Grande Ruins National Monument—all that remains of a community built by the Hohokam people in the 14th century. **Information:** Casa Grande Chamber of Commerce, 575 N Marshall, Casa Grande 85222 (tel 520/836-2125 or 800/916-1515).

HOTEL

Sunland Inn

7190 S Sunland Gin Rd, 85222; tel 520/836-5000. Sunland Gin Rd exit off I-10. Mid-sized hotel offering basic accommodations. **Rooms:** 100 rms. CI open/CO 11am. Nonsmoking rms avail. **Amenities:** A/C, satel TV. **Facilities:** 1 restaurant (bkfst and dinner only), 1 bar, washer/dryer. **Rates:** Peak (Jan–Mar) $24 S; $35 D. Extra person $6. Children under age 18 stay free. Lower rates off-season. Parking: Outdoor, free. AE, DISC, MC, V.

RESORT

Francisco Grande Resort & Golf Club

26000 Gila Bend Hwy, 85222; tel 520/836-6444 or toll free 800/237-4238; fax 520/836-6444. 5 mi W of town. Exit 185 off I-10, then AZ 387 S to AZ 84 W. 690 acres. This hotel/golf resort outside the small town of Casa Grande was originally built to house the San Francisco Giants baseball team during spring training. The resort claims to have the longest golf course in Arizona. **Rooms:** 112 rms and stes. Executive level. CI 3pm/CO noon. Nonsmoking rms avail. Rooms range from basic motel style to more luxurious tower rooms and executive suites, with large bathtubs and hide-a-beds. **Amenities:** A/C, cable TV w/movies, voice mail. Some units w/minibars, some w/terraces. Tower rooms and suites have coffeemakers. **Services:** **Facilities:** 1 restaurant, 1 bar (w/entertainment), volleyball, lawn games. **Rates:** Peak (Jan–Apr) $180 S; $200 D; $250 ste. Extra person $15. Children under age 18 stay free. Min stay special events. Lower rates off-season. Parking: Outdoor, free. AE, DC, MC, V.

Chandler

In the southeast corner of the Phoenix metropolitan area, this incorporated suburb is one of America's first master-planned communities, as well as an agricultural center. **Information:** Chandler Chamber of Commerce, 218 N Arizona Ave, Chandler 85224 (tel 602/963-4571 or 800/963-4571).

HOTEL

Wyndham Garden Hotel

7475 W Chandler Blvd, 85226; tel 602/961-4444 or toll free 800/822-4200 in the US, 800/631-4200 in Canada; fax 602/940-0269. Chandler Blvd exit off I-10. Open, partially sunken lobby is nicely furnished and has a fireplace. **Rooms:** 159 rms and stes. CI 3pm/CO noon. Nonsmoking rms avail. Simply furnished and comfortable. **Amenities:** A/C, satel TV w/movies, CD/tape player. **Services:** **Facilities:** 1 restaurant, 1 bar, spa, whirlpool, washer/dryer. **Rates:** Peak (Jan–May) $109 S; $119 D; $119 ste. Extra person $10. Children under age 10 stay free. Lower rates off-season. Parking: Outdoor, free. AE, DC, DISC, MC, V.

RESORT

Sheraton San Marcos Resort

1 San Marcos Place, 85224; tel 602/963-6655 or toll free 800/325-3535; fax 602/899-5441. Chandler Blvd exit off I-10. 123 acres. The original part of this historic hotel was built in 1912 and for years it was a playground for Hollywood celebrities. The property is well landscaped, with a trellis-shaded walkway and attractive pools. 250 rooms were added in 1986. **Rooms:** 295 rms and stes. Executive level. CI 3pm/CO noon. Nonsmoking rms avail. Very comfortable. **Amenities:** A/C, cable TV w/movies, dataport, in-rm safe. All units w/terraces, some w/whirlpools. **Services:** Babysitting. **Facilities:** 3 restaurants, 2 bars, volleyball, lawn games, whirlpool, beauty salon. **Rates:** Peak (Jan–Apr 2) $220–$245 S or D; $455–$610 ste. Extra person $10. Children under age 18 stay free. Lower rates off-season. Parking: Outdoor, free. AE, CB, DC, DISC, MC, V.

RESTAURANT

★ Guedo's Taco Shop

71 E Chandler Blvd; tel 602/899-7841. Exit Chandler Blvd off I-10 At corner of Arizona Blvd. **Mexican.** Everything is served à la carte at this informal eatery decorated with photos of sports figures and Mexican revolutionaries. Plastic food basket and cutlery. Choice of a variety of tacos, burritos, and quesadillas. **FYI:** Reservations not accepted. Beer only. No smoking. Additional location: 108 W Broadway, Mesa (tel 461-3660). **Open:** Tues–Sat 11am–9pm. **Prices:** Main courses $2–$5. No CC.

Chinle

Chinle is a small community and trading center on the Navajo reservation. Its name is the Navajo word for the location where water emerges from a canyon. **Information:** Navajo Nation, Navajo Tourism Dept, PO Box 663, Window Rock 86515 (tel 520/871-6436).

MOTELS

Best Western Canyon de Chelly Inn

Rte 7, PO Box 295, 86503; tel 520/674-5875 or toll free 800/327-0354. Rte 7 exit off US 191. One of only three hotels in Chinle, the gateway to Canyon de Chelly National Monument. **Rooms:** 102 rms. CI 2pm/CO 11am. Nonsmoking rms avail. All rooms have either two queen beds or one king. **Amenities:** A/C, cable TV. **Services:** **Facilities:** 1 restaurant. **Rates:** Peak (May 10–Oct) $104 S; $108 D. Extra person $4. Children under age 12 stay free. Lower rates off-season. Parking: Outdoor, free. AE, CB, DC, DISC, JCB, MC, V.

Holiday Inn Canyon de Chelly

Garcia Trading Post BIA Rte 7, PO Box 1889, 86503; tel 520/674-5000 or toll free 800/23-HOTEL; fax 520/674-8264. 2½ mi E of US 191. Opened in 1992, this is a pleasant addition to the accommodation choices in Chinle. **Rooms:** 108 rms. CI 3pm/CO noon. Nonsmoking rms avail. **Amenities:** A/C, cable TV. Some units w/terraces. **Services:** **Facilities:** 1 restaurant (*see* "Restaurants" below). Hiking and off-road vehicle tours of Canyon de Chelly are available. There are American Indian dance performances regularly. **Rates:** Peak (Apr–Sept) $95–$120 S or D. Extra person $10. Children under age 18 stay free. Lower rates off-season. Parking: Outdoor, free. AE, MC, V.

Thunderbird Lodge

Rte 7, PO Box 548, 86503; tel 520/674-5841. 3½ mi E of US 191. This motel is actually within the boundaries of Canyon de Chelly National Monument at the mouth of the canyon. The gift shop is located in the original Indian trading post. The entire motel is nonsmoking. **Rooms:** 72 rms and stes. CI 2pm/CO 11am. No smoking. **Amenities:** A/C, cable TV.

Services: **Facilities:** 1 restaurant. Jeep tours of Canyon de Chelly are run by the lodge, and full- and half-day tours of the Anasazi ruins are available; hiking tours are also available. **Rates:** Peak (Apr 1–Nov 15) $80–$85 S; $86–$90 D; $156–$160 ste. Extra person $4. Children under age 2 stay free. Lower rates off-season. Parking: Outdoor, free. AE, CB, DC, DISC, MC, V.

RESTAURANT

Garcia's Trading Post Restaurant
In Holiday Inn Canyon de Chelly, BIA Rte 7, Chinle; tel 520/674-5000. **American/Southwestern.** In addition to lamb chops, fish, steaks, and fajitas, there are such traditional dishes as Navajo fry bread and Navajo stew, a hardy mixture of lamb and vegetables in a tomato broth. **FYI:** Reservations not accepted. Children's menu. No liquor license. No smoking. **Open:** Breakfast daily 6:30–11am; lunch daily 11am–2pm; dinner daily 5–10pm. **Prices:** Main courses $8–$17. AE, DC, DISC, MC, V.

ATTRACTION

Canyon de Chelly National Monument
US 191; tel 520/674-5500. The park consists of two major canyons—**Canyon de Chelly** and **Canyon del Muerto**—as well as several smaller canyons. Together they extend for more than 100 miles through the rugged, slick-rock landscape of northeastern Arizona, draining the seasonal runoff from the snow melt of the Chuska Mountains. These streams have for centuries carved the canyons as they bring water for farming the fertile soils of the canyon bottoms. The smooth vertical sandstone walls of rich reds and yellows sharply contrast with the deep greens of corn, pasture, and cottonwood on the canyon floor.

A different view of the canyons is provided by the **North and South Rim drives**. Each drive is around 16 miles in each direction, and with stops it can easily take two hours to visit each rim.

The first stop on the **North Rim** is the Ledge Ruin Overlook, occupied by the Anasazi between 1050 and 1275. Nearby are Dekaa Kiva Viewpoint and Antelope House Overlook, which takes its name from the paintings of antelopes on a nearby cliff wall. Across the wash is the Tomb of the Weaver, where the well-preserved body of an old man wrapped in a blanket of golden eagle feathers was discovered in the 1920s. Visible from the overlook is Navajo Fortress, a red sandstone butte that the Navajo once used as a refuge from attackers. Continue on to Mummy Cave Overlook, named for two mummies found in burial urns, and then to Massacre Cave Overlook, the site of a mass slaying of Navajo by the Spanish military in 1805.

The **South Rim** drive begins at Tségi Overlook with a view of Chinle Wash. The second stop is Junction Overlook, where the view includes the junction of Canyon del Muerto and Canyon de Chelly. Next is White House Overlook, which provides the only opportunity for descending into Canyon de Chelly without a guide or ranger. The trail descends 600 feet to the canyon floor, crosses Chinle Wash, and then approaches the White House ruins (named after a long white wall in the upper ruin) and the best-known Anasazi cliff dwelling in the canyon. The ruins are located on both the canyon floor and 50 feet up the cliff wall in a small cave. (Note: Visitors cannot enter the ruins.) The 2½-mile round-trip hike takes about 2 hours; visitors should be sure to bring water for the trek.

Farther on is Sliding House Overlook, where Navajo ruins built on a narrow shelf appear to be sliding into the canyon. The drive finishes with stops at Wild Cherry Overlook, Face Rock Overlook, Spider Rock Overlook, and Speaking Rock, all providing glimpses of the ever-deepening canyon.

The visitor center, open daily 8am–5pm, is an essential first stop at Canyon de Chelly. Access to the canyons is restricted, and visitors must be accompanied by either a park ranger or an authorized guide; the only exception is on the White House Ruins trail. **Free**

Clarkdale

ATTRACTIONS

Tuzigoot National Monument
US 89A; tel 520/634-5564. Perched atop a hill overlooking the Verde River, this Sinagua ruin was inhabited between 1100 and 1400. Built of stones and mud, the village had 77 ground-floor rooms and may have housed as many as 200 people. Inside the visitor center is a small museum displaying many of the artifacts unearthed at Tuzigoot. Interpretive trail. **Open:** Daily 8am–5pm. **$**

Verde Canyon Railroad, LC
300 N Broadway; tel 520/639-0010 or toll free 800/293-7245. Once used to transport copper from the mining town of Jerome to the territorial capital of Prescott, the railroad today operates excursions from Clarkdale to Perkinsville. The route through the Verde River Canyon traverses unspoiled desert, inaccessible by car, that is part of Prescott National Forest. Call ahead for departure times. **$$$$**

Coolidge

ATTRACTION

Casa Grande Ruins National Monument
1100 Ruins Dr; tel 520/723-3172. An earth-walled ruin that was built 650 years ago by the Hohokam peoples. An amazing example of ancient architecture in the Southwest, it is built of shaped earth rather than adobe bricks. Casa Grande ruin had a four-foot-deep foundation and was three stories high. The

large ruin is surrounded by many smaller buildings, which were probably homes, and indicate that Casa Grande was not used as living quarters. **Open:** Daily 8am–5pm. **$**

Douglas

Originally part of a 19th-century cattle ranching area, Douglas became a town in 1901 with the arrival of the railroad and the construction of a smelting plant to serve the mining boomtown of Bisbee. Several historic buildings remain. **Information:** Douglas Chamber of Commerce, 1125 Pan American Ave, Douglas 85607 (tel 520/364-2477).

HOTEL

The Gadsden Hotel

1046 G Ave, 85607; tel 520/364-4481; fax 520/364-4005. This "last of the grand hotels," as the Gadsden calls itself, has a lovely art deco lobby with stained glass windows depicting western scenes; marble stairs leading to the mezzanine; art deco chandeliers; and stained glass skylights. It's listed on the National Register of Historic Places. **Rooms:** 150 rms, stes, and effic. Executive level. CI 3pm/CO 11am. Nonsmoking rms avail. Rooms are steeped in historic charm but are in need of renovation. **Amenities:** A/C, cable TV w/movies, dataport. 1 unit w/terrace. **Services:** **Facilities:** 100 1 restaurant, 1 bar, beauty salon, washer/dryer. **Rates:** $32–$36 S; $41–$65 D; $70–$85 ste; $85–$115 effic. Extra person $5. Children under age 18 stay free. Parking: Outdoor, free. AE, DC, MC, V.

ATTRACTION

Cochise Stronghold

Coronado National Forest; tel 520/826-3593. By the mid-1880s only Cochise and Geronimo and their Chiracahua Apaches were still fighting the US Army. Cochise used this rugged section of the Dragoon Mountains as his hideout and managed to elude capture for years because the granite boulders and dense forests made it impossible for the Army to track him. Cochise was buried at an unknown spot somewhere within the area. Hiking and equestrian trails, campground, picnic area. **Open:** Daily sunrise–sunset. **$$$**

Dragoon

ATTRACTION

Amerind Foundation Museum

Exit 318 off I-10; tel 520/586-3666. Established in 1937 and dedicated to the study, preservation, and interpretation of prehistoric and historic Native American cultures. To that end the foundation has compiled the nation's finest private collection of Native American archeological artifacts and contemporary items. The museum comprises two buildings, one containing the anthropology museum and the other the art gallery. Located 64 miles east of Tucson in the heart of Texas Canyon between Benson and Willcox. There is no museum sign on the highway. **Open:** Daily 10am–4pm. **$**

Elgin

ATTRACTION

Sonoita Vineyards Winery

Elgin exit off AZ 83; tel 520/455-5893. Produces a large variety of wines sold exclusively in Arizona. The success of the grape-growing here is the result of a "terra rossa"–type soil, most commonly found in France's Burgundy region. Tours include explanations of the wine-making process and tastings. **Open:** Daily 10am–4pm. **$**

Flagstaff

Northern Arizona's largest city—and at an elevation of 7,000 feet the state's coolest major city—Flagstaff is used as a base for visiting Grand Canyon National Park and other northern Arizona recreation areas. It is home to Northern Arizona University, which hosts a five-week Festival of the Arts each summer that features orchestra, chamber music, choral, dance, and theater performances. **Information:** Flagstaff Convention & Visitors Bureau, 211 W Aspen Ave, Flagstaff 86001 (tel 520/779-7611 or 800/556-1305).

HOTELS

AmeriSuites

2455 S Beulah Blvd, 86001; tel 520/774-5524 or toll free 800/833-1516; fax 520/774-5524. Exit 195B off I-40. Opened in 1993, this is an attractive offering in Flagstaff's mid- to upper-range accommodations. **Rooms:** 118 stes. CI 3pm/CO noon. Nonsmoking rms avail. **Amenities:** A/C, cable TV w/movies, refrig, VCR. Kitchenettes equipped with microwaves, coffee and tea. **Services:** Car-rental desk, babysitting. Unlimited free local phone calls. **Facilities:** 70 Whirlpool, washer/dryer. **Rates (CP):** Peak (June–Sept) $89–$95 ste. Extra person $8. Children under age 18 stay free. Lower rates off-season. Parking: Outdoor, free. AE, DC, DISC, MC, V.

Best Western Woodlands Plaza Hotel

1175 W US 66, 86001; tel 520/773-8888 or toll free 800/528-1234; fax 520/773-0597. Exit 195B off I-40. 1½ mi N to US 66, ¼ mi W. One of Flagstaff's better hotels. **Rooms:** 183 rms and stes. Executive level. CI 3pm/CO noon. Nonsmoking rms avail. **Amenities:** A/C, cable TV w/movies, refrig, dataport, bathrobes. Some units w/whirlpools. Toiletry kits are available. **Services:** Babysitting. **Facilities:** 350 2 restaurants (*see* "Restaurants" below), 1 bar, spa, sauna, steam rm, day-care ctr, washer/dryer. Two whirlpools. **Rates (CP):** Peak (May–Oct) $80–$119 S or D; $119–$129 ste. Extra person $8. Children under age 12 stay free. Lower rates off-season. Parking: Outdoor, free. AE, CB, DC, DISC, JCB, MC, V.

Embassy Suites
706 S Milton Rd, 86001; tel 520/774-4333 or toll free 800/228-5151. Exit 195B off I-40. An all-suites hotel for those wanting more space or staying several days. The lobby is luxurious and features a handsome stone fireplace. Close to Northern Arizona University. **Rooms:** 120 stes. CI 2pm/CO noon. Nonsmoking rms avail. All units have comfortable sitting rooms. **Amenities:** A/C, cable TV w/movies, refrig, VCR, CD/tape player. All suites have two TVs and a microwave. **Services:** Babysitting. Complimentary afternoon cocktails are served. **Facilities:** 35 1 restaurant (dinner only), whirlpool. **Rates (BB):** Peak (mid-June–mid-Sept) $100–$110 ste. Extra person $10. Children under age 12 stay free. Lower rates off-season. Parking: Outdoor, free. AE, DC, DISC, MC, V.

Little America Hotel
1-40 E at Butler Ave, PO Box 3900, 86003; tel 520/779-2741 or toll free 800/352-4386; fax 520/779-7983. Exit 198 off I-40. A pleasant, older hotel set on 400 acres. Easy freeway access. **Rooms:** 248 rms and stes. CI 4pm/CO 1pm. Nonsmoking rms avail. **Amenities:** A/C, cable TV w/movies. All units w/terraces, some w/fireplaces. Most rooms have refrigerators. **Services:** Car-rental desk, babysitting. **Facilities:** 800 2 restaurants, lawn games, washer/dryer. **Rates:** Peak (May 11–Oct 15) $109–$119 S or D. Extra person $10. Children under age 12 stay free. Lower rates off-season. Parking: Outdoor, free. AE, CB, DC, DISC, EC, ER, JCB, MC, V.

Monte Vista Hotel
100N San Francisco St, 86001; tel 520/779-6971 or toll free 800/545-3068. This downtown five-story brick hotel, built in 1929, is listed on the National Register of Historic Places. **Rooms:** 47 rms. CI 2pm/CO 11am. Each room is named for a famous actor or actress who supposedly stayed in that room. Most rooms have private baths. **Amenities:** Cable TV. No A/C. **Services:** Car-rental desk. **Facilities:** 20 2 restaurants, 1 bar (w/entertainment), games rm, beauty salon, washer/dryer. **Rates:** $25–$85 S or D. Parking: Outdoor, free. AE, DC, DISC, MC, V.

MOTELS

Econo Lodge West
2355 S Beulah Blvd, 86001; tel 520/774-2225 or toll free 800/424-4777; fax 520/774-2225 ext 250. Exit 195B off I-40 at I-17. An attractive motel in southwest Flagstaff, close to Sedona (21 miles) and other mountain and scenic areas. It's a good alternative to more expensive lodging in Sedona and other nearby resort communities. **Rooms:** 85 rms. CI 3pm/CO 11am. Nonsmoking rms avail. Pleasant, light-colored rooms with wood furnishings. **Amenities:** A/C, cable TV w/movies. **Services:** **Facilities:** Whirlpool, washer/dryer. **Rates:** Peak (May–Sept) $69–$89 S; $69–$99 D. Extra person $10. Children under age 18 stay free. Lower rates off-season. Parking: Outdoor, free. AE, CB, DC, DISC, JCB, MC, V.

InnSuites Hotel
1008 E Santa Fe Ave, 86001; tel 520/774-7356 or toll free 800/773-1262; fax 520/556-0130. Exit 198 off I-40. Pleasant, moderately priced establishment. **Rooms:** 128 stes. Executive level. CI 2pm/CO noon. Nonsmoking rms avail. Rooms are simply decorated with a southwestern flavor. Some have kitchenettes. **Amenities:** A/C, cable TV w/movies, refrig. Some units w/whirlpools. Nintendo video games. One suite has a whirlpool. **Services:** Babysitting. Free newspapers. **Facilities:** 30 Playground, washer/dryer. **Rates (BB):** Peak (June–Sept) $54–$110 ste. Extra person $10. Children under age 16 stay free. Min stay special events. Lower rates off-season. Parking: Outdoor, free. AE, CB, DC, DISC, MC, V.

Motel Dubeau
19 W Phoenix Ave, 86001; tel 520/774-6731 or toll free 800/332-1944; fax 520/774-4060. An unusual cross between a motel and hostel that caters to younger, international travelers. **Rooms:** 26 rms. CI open/CO 11am. Nonsmoking rms avail. Six campsites also available on the premises. **Amenities:** No A/C, phone, or TV. Community room has cable TV and a piano. **Services:** Complimentary coffee and tea all day long. **Facilities:** Free indoor-outdoor cooking facilities. **Rates (CP):** $25 S or D. Parking: Outdoor, free. Campsites are $6 per person. No CC.

Super 8 Flagstaff
3725 Kasper Ave, 86004; tel 520/526-0818 or toll free 800/800-8000. Exit 201 off I-40. A pleasant motel with easy freeway access. **Rooms:** 86 rms. CI 3pm/CO 11am. Nonsmoking rms avail. **Amenities:** A/C, cable TV w/movies. **Services:** **Facilities:** **Rates:** Peak (May–Sept) $59 S; $69 D. Extra person $5. Children under age 12 stay free. Lower rates off-season. Parking: Outdoor, free. AE, DC, DISC, MC, V.

RESORT

Arizona Mountain Inn
685 Lake Mary Rd, 86001; tel 520/774-8959. Lake Mary Rd exit off I-17. 13 acres. A rustic, quiet retreat in a wooded area on the outskirts of Flagstaff. Peace and quiet is the main attraction, although it's close to town and nearby activities. **Rooms:** 3 rms; 16 cottages/villas. CI 1pm/CO 11am. Nonsmoking rms avail. The three lodge rooms share bath. Cabins are self-catering and include fully furnished kitchenettes. **Amenities:** Refrig. No A/C, phone, or TV. Some units w/terraces, all w/fireplaces, some w/whirlpools. Cabins come with barbecues and some firewood. **Services:** Babysitting. Dogs allowed; no cats. **Facilities:** 25 Basketball, volleyball, games rm, playground, washer/dryer.

There's table tennis, horseshoes, and basketball, and hiking opportunities abound in the surrounding national forest. **Rates:** $90–$125 S or D; $75–$175 cottage/villa. Extra person $10. Children under age 3 stay free. Min stay wknds and special events. Parking: Outdoor, free. Cabin rates based on number of occupants. Lodge room rates include continental breakfast. DISC, MC, V.

RESTAURANTS

Beaver Street Brewery and Whistle Stop Cafe
11 S Beaver St (South Flagstaff); tel 520/779-0079. **American/Pizza.** Cafe popular with the college crowd and known locally for its wood-fired pizzas. Sandwiches and burgers are offered as well. The on-site brewery produces five handcrafted beers. **FYI:** Reservations not accepted. No smoking. **Open:** Daily 11:30am–midnight. **Prices:** Main courses $8–$15. AE, DISC, MC, V.

Black Bart's
2760 E Butler Ave; tel 520/779-3142. Exit 198 off I-40. **Seafood/Steak.** A large steak house, where local college students wait on tables and provide the musical entertainment. Decor is fittingly western, with cowhides and bull horns adorning the walls. Besides steak, there's also shrimp, swordfish, and salmon. **FYI:** Reservations recommended. Cabaret/Vaudeville. Children's menu. No smoking. **Open:** Peak (May–Sept) daily 5–10pm. **Prices:** Main courses $11–$24. AE, MC, V.

Cafe Espress
16 N San Francisco St (Downtown); tel 520/774-0541. **American/Vegetarian.** This comfortable, coffee house/bakery is particularly popular with students from nearby Northern Arizona University. It has wood floors and large original paintings. Offerings include vegetable dishes, pastas, various coffee drinks, and lots of muffins, cookies, and cakes. **FYI:** Reservations not accepted. Beer and wine only. No smoking. **Open:** Sun–Thurs 7am–10pm, Fri–Sat 7am–11pm. **Prices:** Main courses $6–$9. MC, V.

Cottage Place Restaurant
126 W Cottage Ave (South Flagstaff); tel 520/774-8431. **Continental.** Located in a small house, with an elegant and intimate atmosphere. The glassed-in front porch is filled with plants; original art by local artists adorns the walls. House specialties include veal regina (scallops of veal loin sautéed with sun-dried tomatoes and mushrooms), chateaubriand, and rack of lamb Provençale. Many dishes are prepared tableside, and over 130 wines are offered. **FYI:** Reservations recommended. Beer and wine only. No smoking. **Open:** Tues–Sun 5–9:30pm. **Prices:** Main courses $13–$21. AE, MC, V.

★ El Charro
409 S San Francisco St (Downtown); tel 520/779-0552. **American/Mexican.** A popular Mexican diner. Beer advertisements hang on the walls, and a mural of a rural Mexican scene separates the dining rooms. Traditional Mexican fare—tostadas, enchiladas, chile rellenos—as well as American dinners. **FYI:** Reservations accepted. Guitar. Children's menu. No smoking. **Open:** Mon–Thurs 11am–8:30pm, Fri–Sat 11am–10pm. **Prices:** Main courses $5–$10. MC, V.

Kelly's Christmas Tree Restaurant
In Continental Plaza Shopping Center, 5200 E Cortland Blvd (East Flagstaff); tel 520/526-0776. Exit 201 off I-40. **American/Continental.** For those who enjoy the holiday spirit all year round, this might be the perfect place. Christmas decorations are everywhere. There are several separate dining rooms, and a pleasant lounge with a fireplace. House specialties include chicken and dumplings, barbecued babyback ribs, curried chicken, and Black Angus cuts of beef. Daily pasta specials. **FYI:** Reservations recommended. Children's menu. No smoking. **Open:** Lunch Mon–Sat 11:30am–3pm; dinner Mon–Sat 5–10pm, Sun 4–10pm. **Prices:** Main courses $7–$23; prix fixe $14–$25. AE, MC, V.

Sakura Restaurant
In Best Western Woodlands Plaza Hotel, 1175 W US 66; tel 520/773-9118. Exit 195B off I-40. **Japanese.** A dimly lit restaurant decorated with Japanese lanterns and sake baskets. Teppan cooking (in which meats and fish are grilled right at the table) is the specialty. Extensive menu. **FYI:** Reservations recommended. Children's menu. No smoking. **Open:** Lunch Mon–Fri 11:30am–2pm; dinner daily 5–10pm; brunch Sun 10am–2pm. **Prices:** Main courses $12–$20. AE, DC, DISC, MC, V.

Woodlands Cafe
In Best Western Woodlands Plaza Hotel, 1175 W US 66; tel 520/773-9118. Exit 195B off I-40. **Southwestern.** A Southwestern cafe decorated with antler chandeliers and Native American pottery. One side of the dining room is an atrium. The ample menu includes seafood, chicken, lamb, duck, steaks, pasta, and a number of burgers. Specialties include trout Arizona and vegetable fettuccine. **FYI:** Reservations recommended. Children's menu. No smoking. **Open:** Daily 6am–10pm. **Prices:** Main courses $11–$18. AE, DC, DISC, MC, V.

ATTRACTIONS

Lowell Observatory
1400 W Mars Hill Rd; tel 520/774-2096. Located atop Mars Hill, this is one of the oldest observatories in the Southwest. Founded in 1894 by Percival Lowell, the observatory has played important roles in contemporary astronomy. Among the work carried out here was Lowell's study of the planet Mars and his calculations that led him to predict the existence of the planet Pluto. Call ahead for evening viewing hours. **Open:** Peak (Apr–Oct) daily 9am–5pm. Reduced hours off-season. **$**

Museum of Northern Arizona
3101 N Fort Valley Rd; tel 520/774-5213. State-of-the-art exhibits about the archeology, ethnology, geology, biology, and fine arts of the region. One exhibit is "Native Peoples of the Colorado Plateau," an exploration of both the archeology and cultural anthropology of the region from 15,000 BC to the present. Theater shows *Sacred Lands of the Southwest,* a sound and light show about regional history and culture. **Open:** Daily 9am–5pm. **$$**

The Arboretum at Flagstaff
S Woody Mountain Rd; tel 520/774-1441. Covering 200 acres of ponderosa pine forest, the arboretum includes a visitors center, children's garden, and wildflower meadows. In addition, there are displays on plants of the high desert, coniferous forests, and alpine tundra, all of which are environments found in the vicinity of Flagstaff. **Open:** Peak (May–Sept) Mon–Sat 10am–3pm, Sun noon–3pm. Reduced hours off-season. **$**

Coconino Center for the Arts
2300 N Fort Valley Rd; tel 520/779-6921. The center houses both a performance hall and a gallery space. The gallery exhibits contemporary and traditional arts and crafts from around northern Arizona. Performances in the 200-seat theater include music and dance, including Native American dances. **Open:** Tues–Sun 9am–5pm. **Free**

Arizona Historical Society Pioneer Museum
2340 N Fort Valley Rd; tel 520/774-6272. A historical collection from northern Arizona's pioneer days. The main museum building is a large stone structure that was built in 1908 as a hospital for the indigent. A 1929 Baldwin articulated locomotive and a Santa Fe caboose have been on the museum grounds since 1942. **Open:** Mon–Sat 9am–5pm. **Free**

Wupatki National Monument
US 89; tel 520/679-2365. 36 mi N of Flagstaff. The largest of the prehistoric pueblos in the area is Wupatki ruin in the southeastern part of the monument. Here the Sinagua people built a sprawling three-story pueblo containing nearly 100 rooms. The visitor center in this location has exhibits on the ancestral pueblo people who once inhabited the region.

An unusual feature of Wupatki is a natural phenomenon—a blowhole—that may have been the reason for building the pueblo on this site. A network of small underground tunnels and chambers acts as a giant barometer, blowing air when the underground air is under greater pressure than the outside air. **Open:** Peak (Mem Day–Sept) daily 8am–6pm. Reduced hours off-season. **$$**

Walnut Canyon National Monument
Walnut Canyon Rd; tel 520/526-3367. The remains of hundreds of 13th-century Sinagua cliff dwellings can be seen in this dry, wooded canyon 7 miles east of Flagstaff. The undercut layers of limestone in the 400-foot-deep canyon proved ideal for building dwellings well protected both from the elements and from enemies. A self-guided trail leads from the visitor center on the canyon rim down 185 feet to a section of the canyon wall where 25 cliff dwellings can be entered. **Open:** Daily 9am–5pm. **$$**

Sunset Crater Volcano National Monument
US 89; tel 520/556-7042. 15 mi N of Flagstaff. Taking its name from the sunset colors of the cinders near its summit, this volcanic crater, which began forming in 1064, stands 1,000 feet tall. Over a period of 100 years the volcano erupted repeatedly, creating the red-and-yellow cinder cone seen today and eventually covering an area of 800 square miles with ash, lava, and cinders. A mile-long interpretative trail passes through a desolate landscape of lava flows, cinders, and ash as it skirts the base. Visitor center, small campground. **Open:** Daily sunrise–sunset. **$$**

Riordan Mansion State Park
1300 Riordan Ranch St; tel 520/779-4395. Built in 1904 for local lumber merchants Michael and Timothy Riordan, this 13,000-square-foot mansion is actually two houses connected by a large central hall. The Riordans played important roles in the early history of Flagstaff: They built the first Roman Catholic church, the first library, the power company, and the phone company. **Open:** Peak (May–Sept) daily 8am–5pm. Reduced hours off-season. **$**

Arizona Snowbowl
AZ 180 and Snowbowl Rd; tel 520/779-1951. Located on the slopes of Mount Agassiz, this popular ski site has four chair lifts, 30 runs, 40 kms of cross-country terrain, and 2,300 vertical feet of slopes. In the summer the ski lift carries hikers and other visitors who want to enjoy the views. **Open:** Mid-Dec–mid-Apr, daily 9am–4pm. **$$$$**

Fredonia

This tiny northern Arizona town, just three miles from the Utah border, was settled in the late 1800s by Mormon polygamists from Kanab, Utah as an out-of-state hideout for extra wives. The name is said to be a combination of the words "free" and "doña," a Spanish title for a woman. **Information:** Fredonia Chamber of Commerce, 130 N Main, PO Box 547, Fredonia 86022 (tel 520/643-7241).

LODGE

Kaibab Lodge
AZ 67, PO Box 30, HC64, 86022; tel 520/638-2389. 18 mi N of the North Rim of Grand Canyon National Park. This rustic lodge, open in both summer and winter when the North Rim is generally closed, is popular with hunters because of easy access to the Kaibab National Forest. The lodge is inaccessible by car after the snows fall, however, so transportation is by special "snow vans." **Rooms:** 24 rms. CI 3pm/CO 10am. All bathrooms have showers only. **Amenities:** No A/C, phone, or TV. Some units w/terraces. The common room has

a fireplace, piano, and cable TV. At an altitude of 8,700 feet, air conditioning will not be missed. **Services:** **Facilities:** 1 restaurant (bkfst and dinner only), 1 bar, games rm, whirlpool. There's a store and a gas station with diesel fuel on the premises. Bag lunches are available. **Rates:** Peak (May–Oct) $70 S; $77 D. Extra person $10. Lower rates off-season. Parking: Outdoor, free. Cross-country ski packages are available. Closed Apr–Nov. DISC, MC, V.

Ganado

ATTRACTION

Hubbell Trading Post National Historic Site
AZ 264; tel 520/755-3475. The oldest continuously operating trading post on the Navajo Reservation. The trading post includes a small museum where visitors can watch Navajo weavers in the slow process of creating rugs. In the trading post visitors may encounter individuals trading jewelry or rugs for goods or cash. The rug room is filled with a variety of traditional and contemporary Navajo rugs for sale. There are also baskets, kachinas, and several cases of jewelry by Navajo, Hopi, and Zuni craftspeople in another room. In the general store there are basic foodstuffs and bolts of cloth used by Navajo women for sewing traditional clothing. **Open:** Peak (Apr–Oct) daily 8am–6pm. Reduced hours off-season. **Free**

Gila Bend

MOTEL

Best Western Space Age Lodge
401 E Pima St, PO Box C, 85337; tel 520/683-2273 or toll free 800/528-1234; fax 520/683-2273. Single-story modern motel in downtown Gila Bend. **Rooms:** 41 rms. CI 1pm/CO noon. Nonsmoking rms avail. **Amenities:** A/C, cable TV. Some rooms have refrigerators. **Services:** **Facilities:** 1 restaurant, whirlpool. 24-hour restaurant. **Rates:** Peak (Dec–Mar) $60–$82 S or D. Extra person $4. Children under age 17 stay free. Lower rates off-season. Parking: Outdoor, free. AE, CB, DC, DISC, ER, JCB, MC, V.

Glendale

A Phoenix suburb in the northwest metropolitan area, Glendale is Arizona's fourth-largest city. It is located in a rich agricultural region and is a shipping point for fruits and vegetables. Home to Luke Air Force Base, a jet fighter training center. **Information:** Glendale Chamber of Commerce, 7105 N 59th Ave, PO Box 249, Glendale 85311 (tel 602/937-4754 or 800/IDSUNNY).

RESTAURANT

★ **Portofino Ristorante**
In Gateway Village Shopping Center, 6020 W Bell Rd; tel 602/938-1902. At 59th Ave. **Italian.** Pleasant shopping center restaurant, with a fountain in the center of the dining room. **FYI:** Reservations recommended. Singer. No smoking. Additional location: 12851 W Bell Rd, Suite 115, Surprise (tel 583-1931). **Open:** Lunch daily 11am–2:30pm; dinner Mon–Sat 5–10:30pm, Sun 4–9pm. **Prices:** Main courses $6–$16. AE, CB, DC, DISC, MC, V.

ATTRACTION

Waterworld Safari
4243 West Pinnacle Peak Rd; tel 602/581-1947. A water park featuring a wave pool, nine water slides, and a special children's area. **Open:** June–Sept, Mon–Fri 10am–9pm, Sun 11am–7pm. **$$$$**

Globe

ATTRACTIONS

Besh-Ba-Gowah Archaeological Park
150 N Pine St; tel 520/425-0320. An excavation of this city park resulted in the discovery of the remains of a Salado pueblo. Built and occupied from about 1225 to 1400, this site once housed over 400 people in 300 rooms. Today visitors can view the ruins on an interpretive trail. A museum displays artifacts, models, and photographs relating to the site. Across from the dig is a park area with picnic facilities. **Open:** Daily 9am–5pm. $

Tonto National Monument
AZ 88; tel 520/467-2241. 30 mi NW of Globe. These cliff dwellings were built between 1100 and 1400 by the Salado peoples. The two cliff dwellings here are some of the only remaining pueblos of the Salado, who disappeared around 1450. They are built into the caves above the Salt River where they were protected from the elements and were thus well preserved. The largest, Upper Ruin, has 40 rooms and is 3 stories high in some places. Upper Ruin is accessible by guided tour only, November through April. It's a 3-mile round-trip hike and reservations are required. The Lower Ruin is open daily for self-guided tours; the trail is one mile round trip. **Open:** Daily 8am–5pm. **$$**

Grand Canyon National Park

Geologists believe that it has taken between 3 and 6 million years for the Colorado River to carve the Grand Canyon a mile deep and up to 18 miles wide. Banded layers of sandstone, limestone, shale, and schist give the canyon its color, and the interplays of shadows and light from dawn to dusk create an ever-changing palette of hues and textures.

The park is divided into three sections: the North Rim, the South Rim, and the inner canyon. Grand Canyon Village and Desert View on the South Rim are open year-round with full facilities, including lodging, dining, and entertainment. The North Rim is open mid-May to late October and has lodging, food, and camping facilities.

To view the Grand Canyon from the rim there are several scenic drives, including the 8-mile West Rim Drive from Grand Canyon Village to Hermits Rest, and the 25-mile East Rim Drive from Grand Canyon Village to Desert View. Popular ways to see the inner canyon are rafting down the Colorado River, taking a mule ride, flying over in a helicopter or small airplane, and hiking and backpacking. All trips into the inner canyon are physically exerting, but up close visitors can see fossils, old mines, petroglyphs, wildflowers, and extensive wildlife. Details about the canyon and inner canyon trips are available in the park's *Trip Planner*, a free newspaper available by calling the park (tel 520/638-7888). The Grand Canyon is located 80 miles northeast of Flagstaff and 60 miles north of Williams; take US 180 directly to the South Rim, or US 89 to AZ 64, which leads to the east entrance of the park.

HOTELS

El Tovar Hotel

South Rim, PO Box 699, Grand Canyon, 86023; tel 520/638-2401; fax 520/638-9247. A historic 1905 hotel perched on the South Rim of the Grand Canyon. **Rooms:** 78 rms and stes. CI 4pm/CO 11am. Nonsmoking rms avail. Standard rooms are comfortable but small. **Amenities:** TV. No A/C. Some units w/terraces. **Services:** Babysitting. **Facilities:** 1 restaurant (*see* "Restaurants" below), 1 bar (w/entertainment). The restaurant has a wonderful view. **Rates:** $111–$166 S or D; $182–$271 ste. Extra person $11. Children under age 16 stay free. Parking: Outdoor, free. AE, DC, DISC, JCB, MC, V.

Grand Canyon Squire Inn

AZ 64, PO Box 130, Grand Canyon, 86023; tel 520/638-2681 or toll free 800/622-6966; fax 520/638-0162. On the South Rim. A modern hotel just outside the entrance to Grand Canyon National Park, in the village of Tusayan. **Rooms:** 250 rms and stes. CI 3pm/CO noon. Nonsmoking rms avail. **Amenities:** A/C, satel TV, CD/tape player. Some units w/whirlpools. **Services:** **Facilities:** 250 2 restaurants, 2 bars, games rm, spa, whirlpool, washer/dryer. Bowling alley on premises. **Rates:** Peak (Mar 15–Oct 22) $145 S or D; $195 ste. Extra person $8. Children under age 12 stay free. Lower rates off-season. Parking: Outdoor, free. AE, CB, DC, DISC, JCB, MC, V.

Quality Inn Grand Canyon

AZ 64, PO Box 520, Grand Canyon, 86023; tel 520/638-2673 or toll free 800/221-2222; fax 520/638-9537. An attractive hotel 1 mile south of the entrance to Grand Canyon National Park, in Tusayan. **Rooms:** 176 rms. CI 3pm/CO 11am. Nonsmoking rms avail. **Amenities:** A/C, cable TV, refrig. Some units w/minibars, some w/terraces. **Services:** **Facilities:** 100 1 restaurant, 1 bar. There's an indoor Jacuzzi and an outdoor hot tub. **Rates:** Peak (Mar 25–Oct) $135 S or D. Extra person $10. Children under age 5 stay free. Lower rates off-season. Parking: Outdoor, free. AE, CB, DC, DISC, ER, JCB, MC, V.

MOTEL

Thunderbird & Kachina Lodges

South Rim, PO Box 699, Grand Canyon, 86023; tel 520/638-2631. On the South Rim. Pleasant, basic lodging. Registration for Thunderbird is at the Bright Angel Lodge, for Kachina at El Tovar Hotel. **Rooms:** 103 rms. CI 4pm/CO 11am. Nonsmoking rms avail. There are 48 rooms in Kachina, and 55 in Thunderbird. Some rooms face the canyon. **Amenities:** Cable TV. No A/C. **Services:** **Facilities:** 100 **Rates:** Peak (Apr–Oct) $98–$108 S or D. Extra person $9. Children under age 16 stay free. Lower rates off-season. Parking: Outdoor, free. AE, DISC, MC, V.

LODGES

Bright Angel Lodge and Cabins

W Rim Dr, PO Box 699, Grand Canyon, 86023; tel 520/638-2631. A rustic lodge on the South Rim of the park. **Rooms:** 44 rms; 43 cottages/villas. CI 4pm/CO 11am. Nonsmoking rms avail. There are a variety of accommodations, from motel-type rooms to historic cabins. Some have magnificent canyon views and some have access to Rim Walkway. **Amenities:** Cable TV, refrig, bathrobes. No A/C. 1 unit w/minibar, some w/terraces, some w/fireplaces. Air conditioning is rarely needed at the 7,000-foot elevation. **Services:** **Facilities:** 1 restaurant (*see* "Restaurants" below), 1 bar (w/entertainment), beauty salon. **Rates:** $38–$58 S or D; $64 cottage/villa. Extra person $8. Children under age 16 stay free. AP and MAP rates avail. Parking: Outdoor, free. AE, CB, DC, DISC, JCB, MC, V.

Moqui Lodge

AZ 64, PO Box 369, Grand Canyon, 86023 (Tusayan); tel 520/638-2424 or toll free 800/538-6267. On the South Rim. Rustic lodge with tall A-frame construction and motel-style rooms, located just south of the park in Kaibab National Forest. **Rooms:** 136 rms. CI 3pm/CO 11am. No smoking. **Amenities:** Cable TV. No A/C. **Services:** **Facilities:** 100 1 restaurant (bkfst and dinner only), 1 bar, games rm, beauty salon. Picnic and barbecue area; gas station. Wagon rides available. **Rates (BB):** Peak (Mar 16–Oct 19) $89–$99 S or D. Children under age 12 stay free. Lower rates off-season. Parking: Outdoor, free. Closed Dec–Feb 15. AE, CB, DC, DISC, MC, V.

RESTAURANTS

Arizona Steakhouse
In the Bright Angel Lodge and Cabins, South Rim, Grand Canyon; tel 520/638-2631 ext 6296. **American.** A simple steak house that features breathtaking views. The barbecue sampler lets you try pork ribs, beef ribs, and a chicken leg and thigh. **FYI:** Reservations not accepted. Children's menu. **Open:** Daily 5–10pm. Closed Jan–Feb. **Prices:** Main courses $12–$20. AE, DISC, MC, V.

Babbitt's Delicatessen
In Babbitt's General Store, South Rim, Grand Canyon; tel 520/638-2262. **Fast food.** Basic deli, located inside a grocery store. A good choice for a snack or light lunch. **FYI:** Reservations not accepted. No liquor license. No smoking. **Open:** Daily 8am–6pm. **Prices:** Lunch main courses $3–$6. No CC.

Canyon Cafe
In the Yavapai Lodge, South Rim, Grand Canyon; tel 520/638-2631. **American.** No-frills cafeteria dining, with traditional American fare. Additional seating in atrium room. **FYI:** Reservations not accepted. Beer and wine only. No smoking. **Open:** Daily 6am–9pm. Closed Jan–Feb. **Prices:** Main courses $5–$8. AE, DC, DISC, MC, V.

El Tovar Dining Room
In El Tovar Hotel, South Rim, Grand Canyon; tel 520/638-2631. **Southwestern.** Elegant dining in a historic setting. The lovely lodge-style dining room was built with Oregon pine and boasts a stone fireplace and high-beamed ceilings. Southwestern sauces and spices add punch to traditional dishes: Prickly-pear jalapeño honey is combined with roast duckling; smoked tomato pinenut sauce with chicken breast; and tomatillo salsa and chile-lime aioli with grilled salmon. During high season, lighter fare is served on the mezzanine between 2pm and 8pm. The private dining room, which seats up to eight people, is available with 48-hour advance reservation. **FYI:** Reservations accepted. Piano. Children's menu. No smoking. **Open:** Daily 6:30am–10pm. **Prices:** Main courses $15–$27. AE, CB, DC, DISC, MC.

Grand Canyon Lodge Dining Room
In Grand Canyon Lodge, North Rim, Grand Canyon; tel 520/638-2611 ext 160. **American.** The magnificent, lodge-style dining room provides spectacular views of the canyon. Open-beamed ceiling, chandeliers, and wall sconces. Seafood, beef, and vegetarian dishes; a specialty is the mountain red trout. **FYI:** Reservations recommended. Children's menu. **Open:** Breakfast daily 6:30–10am; lunch daily 11:30am–2:30pm; dinner daily 5–10pm. Closed end of Oct–mid-May, depending on snowfall. **Prices:** Main courses $10–$20. AE, DISC, MC, V.

Hermits Snack Bar
In Hermits Curio Shop, W Rim Dr, Grand Canyon; tel 520/638-2351. On the South Rim. **Fast food.** Simple snack bar, serving items like hot dogs, chicken nuggets, chips, cookies, and soft drinks. **FYI:** Reservations not accepted. No liquor license. No smoking. **Open:** Peak (May 27–Sept 30) daily 10am–4pm. **Prices:** Lunch main courses $1–$3. No CC.

Maswik Cafeteria
In the Maswik Lodge, South Rim, Grand Canyon; tel 520/638-2631. **American.** Basic cafeteria. Sandwiches, traditional hot American dishes, some Mexican plates. Half-price for children under age 12. **FYI:** Reservations not accepted. Children's menu. No smoking. **Open:** Daily 6am–10pm. **Prices:** Main courses $5–$7. AE, DC, DISC, MC, V.

ATTRACTIONS

GRAND CANYON NATIONAL PARK

Grand Canyon Visitor Center
Village Loop Dr, Grand Canyon; tel 520/638-7888. In addition to providing answers to questions about the Grand Canyon, the center also contains exhibits on its natural history and exploration. Throughout the day, slide and video programs are shown. **Open:** Peak (Mar–Nov) daily 8am–7pm. Reduced hours off-season. **Free**

Grand Canyon IMAX Theatre
South Rim, Tusayan; tel 520/638-2203. Located at the south entrance to the park. A huge seven-story screen completely fills the field of vision with incredibly realistic, high-definition film images. Every hour there is a 34-minute film about the canyon. **Open:** Peak (Mar–Nov) daily 8:30am–8:30pm. Reduced hours off-season. **$$$**

Over the Edge Theatres
Community Building, Village Loop Dr, Grand Canyon Village; tel 520/638-2224. This audiovisual program introduces the visitor to the geology and history of the canyon. The narration is given from the point of view of Capt John Hance, one of the canyon's first guides. **Open:** Daily 9am–9pm. **$$**

Yavapai Museum
Village Loop Dr, Grand Canyon; tel 520/638-7890. Located less than a mile east of the visitor center, with exhibits on the geologic history of the Grand Canyon. A panorama of the canyon is visible through the museum's large windows. **Open:** Peak (Mar–Nov) daily 8am–7pm. Reduced hours off-season. **Free**

Tusayan Museum
East Rim Dr, Grand Canyon; tel 520/638-2305. Provides insight into the Ancestral Pueblo (Anasazi) culture, and the lifestyle of tribes currently living near the Grand Canyon. A small museum displays authentic artifacts. A short, self-guided trail allows access to adjacent Ancestral Pueblo ruins. **Open:** Daily 9am–5pm. **Free**

The Watchtower
Desert View, East Rim Dr, Grand Canyon; tel 520/638-2736. Architect Mary Jane Colter, who is responsible for much of the Grand Canyon's historic architecture, designed this to resemble the prehistoric towers that dot the southwestern

landscape. Built as an observation post and rest stop for tourists, the watchtower incorporates Native American design and traditional art. **Open:** Peak (Mar–Nov) daily 8am–8pm. Reduced hours off-season. **$**

Kolb and Lookout Studios
South Rim, Grand Canyon Village; tel 520/638-2771 (Kolb) or 638-2631 ext 6087 (Lookout). Due to their location precariously close to the rim of the canyon, both of these buildings are listed on the National Register of Historic Places. **Kolb Studio** was built by the brothers Ellsworth and Emory Kolb, who used it as a photography studio beginning in 1904. Today it serves as a bookstore. **Lookout Studio,** built in 1914, was designed with native limestone and an uneven roofline to allow the studio to blend in with the canyon walls. Originally built by the Fred Harvey Company to compete with the Kolb brothers, it now houses a souvenir store and two lookout points. **Open:** Peak (June–Aug) daily 8am–7pm. Reduced hours off-season. **Free**

Greer

LODGE

Greer Lodge
AZ 373, PO Box 66, 85927; tel 520/735-7216. 5 mi E of jct AZ 260/AZ 373. A large log lodge set in a beautiful mountain setting, with three ponds and the Little Colorado River running directly behind the property. **Rooms:** 9 rms; 9 cottages/villas. CI open/CO 11am. No smoking. **Amenities:** No A/C, phone, or TV. Some units w/terraces, some w/fireplaces. **Services:** Babysitting. Hay rides and fly-fishing school in summer; sleigh rides and ice skating in winter. **Facilities:** 60 1 restaurant, 1 bar, volleyball, lawn games, washer/dryer. **Rates:** $120 S or D; $110 cottage/villa. Extra person $15. Children under age 2 stay free. Min stay wknds. Parking: Outdoor, free. AE, MC, V.

RESTAURANT

Cattle Kate's
80 N Main St; tel 520/735-7744. On AZ 373 5 mi E of AZ 260. **New American.** Inside this blond log building are enormous support beams, a high ceiling, an antler chandelier, western scenes and photos on the walls, and sturdy glass-topped tables. Great salads are available at lunch, while dinner brings chicken, pork, steaks, fish, and pasta. And there's always a vegetarian meal. Closed Monday and Tuesday Nov–Apr. **FYI:** Reservations recommended. No smoking. **Open:** Peak (May–Oct) daily 7am–9pm. **Prices:** Main courses $8–$17. MC, V.

Hereford

ATTRACTIONS

Ramsey Canyon Preserve
27 Ramsey Canyon Rd; tel 520/378-2785. Internationally known wildlife preserve recognized for its diversity of hummingbird species during migration—at least 14 species have been identified. Covering 300 acres, it is situated in a wooded gorge in the Huachuca Mountains. A nature trail leads through the canyon. Because there are only a few parking spaces, a parking reservation is strongly recommended. August is the best time to see hummingbirds. **Open:** Daily 8am–5pm. **$$**

Coronado National Memorial
4101 E Montezuma Canyon Rd; tel 520/366-5515. A visitor center tells the story of Francisco Vásquez de Coronado's fruitless quest for riches in the San Pedro River valley. The 5,000-acre memorial features a bird observation area where visitors might see some of the more than 140 species of birds that make their home here. **Open:** Daily 8am–5pm. **Free**

Holbrook

A gateway to Petrified Forest National Park and the Painted Desert, modern Holbrook took shape with the arrival of the railroad in the 1880s. It became the seat of Navajo County in 1895. There are several rock shops in town where visitors can buy petrified wood and other fascinating stones. **Information:** Holbrook Chamber of Commerce, 100 E Arizona St, Holbrook 86025 (tel 520/524-6558 or 800/524-2459).

MOTELS

Comfort Inn
2602 Navajo Blvd, 86025; tel 520/524-6131 or toll free 800/228-5150; fax 520/524-2281. Exit 289 off I-40. A good, basic motel. **Rooms:** 60 rms. CI noon/CO 11am. Nonsmoking rms avail. Simple, clean rooms. **Amenities:** A/C, cable TV w/movies. **Services:** **Facilities:** 1 restaurant, washer/dryer. **Rates (CP):** Peak (June–Sept) $48–$58 S; $50–$70 D. Extra person $5. Children under age 18 stay free. Lower rates off-season. Parking: Outdoor, free. AE, CB, DC, DISC, MC, V.

Days Inn
2601 Navajo Blvd, 86025; tel 520/524-6949 or toll free 800/325-2525; fax 520/524-6665. Exit 289 off I-40. One of the newest motels in the area. **Rooms:** 54 rms and stes. CI 11am/CO 11am. Nonsmoking rms avail. Rooms are simple but have some nice touches, especially the king suites, which have in-room whirlpool baths. **Amenities:** A/C, cable TV w/movies, voice mail. Some units w/whirlpools. **Services:** Twice-daily maid svce. **Facilities:** Spa, whirlpool, washer/dryer. **Rates (CP):** Peak (June–Aug) $49 S; $59 D;

$69 ste. Extra person $6. Children under age 12 stay free. Lower rates off-season. Parking: Outdoor, free. AE, DISC, MC, V.

Wigwam Motel
811 W Hopi Dr, PO Box 788, 86025; tel 520/524-3048. Exit 285 off I-40. Built in 1950, this motel is a must-see. Each room is designed as an Indian wigwam or teepee. **Rooms:** 15 rms. CI 2pm/CO noon. Nonsmoking rms avail. 1950s furnishings. **Amenities:** A/C, TV. No phone. **Services:** Twice-daily maid svce. **Rates:** Peak (May–Sept) $27 S; $32 D. Lower rates off-season. Parking: Outdoor, free. MC, V.

ATTRACTION

Petrified Forest National Park (Painted Desert)
I-40 or US 180; tel 520/524-6228. The petrified wood found here began its journey 225 million years ago as giant prehistoric trees. When the trees fell they were washed downstream and became preserved from decay by a layer of volcanic ash, silt, and mud. Silica later formed from the ash and filled the cells of the wood, eventually recrystallizing it into stone.

The Painted Desert is named for the vivid colors of the soil and stone that cover the barren expanses of eroded hills; these colors were created by minerals dissolved in the sandstone and clay soils that were deposited during different geologic periods.

The park's visitors centers both have maps and books about the region and both give out the free permits necessary to backpack and camp in the park. The **Painted Desert Visitor Center** is at the north end of the park and the **Rainbow Forest Museum** is at the south end. They are connected by a 27-mile scenic road with more than 20 overlooks. The petrified logs are concentrated in the southern part of the park, while the northern section overlooks the Painted Desert. At the north end, the Painted Desert Oasis provides a full-service cafeteria. **Open:** Peak (May–Sept) daily 7am–7pm. Reduced hours off-season. **$$**

Hopi Reservation

Completely surrounded by the Navajo Reservation in the Four Corners region of the state, the Hopi Reservation is a grouping of mesas that are home to the Hopi pueblos. This remote region of Arizona, with its flat-topped mesas and rugged, barren landscape, is the center of the universe for the Hopi people. The handful of villages here are ancient, independent communities that have today been brought together under the guidance of the Hopi Tribal Council. This land has been inhabited by the Hopi and their ancestors for nearly 1,000 years, and many aspects of the ancient pueblo culture remain intact. Photographing, sketching, and recording are all prohibited in the villages and at ceremonies, and kivas (ceremonial rooms) and ruins are off limits to visitors.

The reservation is divided into three mesas known simply as First, Second, and Third Mesa, which are numbered from east to west. Villages on First Mesa include Polacca, Walpi, Sichomovi, and Hano. Second Mesa is today the center of tourism in Hopiland, and the location of the **Hopi Cultural Center**. Second Mesa villages include Sungopavi, Mishongnovi, and Shipaulovi. **Oraibi,** which the Hopi claim is the oldest continuously occupied town in the United States, is located on Third Mesa, along with Hotevilla, Kykotsmovi, and Bacavi.

The Hopi have developed the most complex religious ceremonies of any of the southwestern tribes. **Masked kachina dances,** for which the Hopi are most famous, are held from January to July, while the **snake dances,** particularly popular with non-Hopis, are held from August through December. For more information about ceremonies or the reservation call the Hopi Tribal Council at 520/734-2441.

MOTEL

Hopi Cultural Center Restaurant and Motel
AZ 264, PO Box 67, Second Mesa, 86043; tel 520/734-2401. 22 mi W of Keams Canyon. In this very remote area accommodations are limited, so reservations are imperative in the summer. Although the exterior of the building has an "institutional" look, the motel rooms are very pleasant. **Rooms:** 33 rms. CI 3pm/CO 11am. No smoking. All rooms are nonsmoking. **Amenities:** A/C, cable TV. **Services:** **Facilities:** 50 1 restaurant. **Rates:** Peak (May–Sept) $75 S; $80 D. Extra person $5–$10. Children under age 12 stay free. Lower rates off-season. Parking: Outdoor, free. There is a $5 key deposit. AE, DC, DISC, MC, V.

ATTRACTION

Hopi Cultural Center
AZ 264; tel 520/734-6650. The tourism headquarters for the area. A museum has educational displays about Hopi culture and history. Signs indicate when villages are open to visitors. **Open:** Mon–Fri 8am–5pm. **$**

Jerome

ATTRACTION

Jerome State Historic Park
US 89A; tel 520/634-5381. Located in the former mining town of Jerome, a national historic landmark, the park contains the partially restored 1916 mansion of mine owner "Rawhide Jimmy" Douglas. The mansion's library has been restored as a period room, while other rooms contain exhibits on copper mining and the town's history, displays of colorful ores, and tools that were once used to extract the ore from the mountain. **Open:** Daily 8am–5pm. **$**

Kayenta

Located on the Navajo Reservation in northeastern Arizona, Kayenta was established in 1909 as an Indian trading post and today provides services for visitors to the reservation. **Information:** Navajo Nation, Navajo Tourism Dept, PO Box 663, Window Rock 86515 (tel 520/871-6436).

HOTEL

Holiday Inn Kayenta
Junction of US 160 and US 163, PO Box 307, 86033; tel 520/697-3221 or toll free 800/23-HOTEL. In a convenient location for visiting the Navajo National Monument and Monument Valley. **Rooms:** 164 rms. CI 3pm/CO noon. Nonsmoking rms avail. **Amenities:** A/C, cable TV w/movies. **Services:** **Facilities:** 1 restaurant. **Rates:** Peak (June–Sept) $110–$150 S or D. Extra person $10. Children under age 19 stay free. Lower rates off-season. Parking: Outdoor, free. AE, CB, DC, DISC, MC, V.

MOTELS

Anasazi Inn at Tsegi Canyon
US 160, PO Box 1543, 86033; tel 520/697-3793. 10 mi W of downtown Kayenta. In a remote location, with great views of Tsegi Canyon in all directions. **Rooms:** 59 rms. CI 2pm/CO 11am. Nonsmoking rms avail. **Amenities:** A/C, TV. No phone. **Services:** **Facilities:** 1 restaurant. Arts and crafts center on premises. **Rates:** Peak (May–Oct) $79–$89 S; $89–$109 D. Extra person $6. Children under age 12 stay free. Lower rates off-season. Parking: Outdoor, free. AE, DC, DISC, MC, V.

Wetherill Inn Motel
US 163, PO Box 175, 86033; tel 520/697-3231. US 163 exit off US 160. A pleasant, basic motel, close to the Navajo National Monument and Monument Valley. **Rooms:** 54 rms. CI 2pm/CO 11am. Nonsmoking rms avail. **Amenities:** A/C, cable TV. **Services:** **Facilities:** **Rates:** Peak (Apr 15–Oct 15) $82 S; $88 D. Extra person $6. Children under age 12 stay free. Lower rates off-season. Parking: Outdoor, free. AE, DC, DISC, MC, V.

ATTRACTION

Navajo National Monument
AZ 564; tel 520/672-2366. Located 30 mi W of Kayenta and 60 mi NE of Tuba City, it encompasses Tsegi Canyon and three of the best-preserved ancestral pueblo cliff dwellings in the region: Betatakin, Keet Seel, and the Inscription House. Fragile Inscription House has been closed to the public since 1968. **Betatakin**, which means "ledge house" in Navajo, is the only one of the 3 ruins that can be easily seen. The round-trip, ranger-led hike to Betatakin from the visitor center, conducted May–October, takes about 5 hours and involves descending more than 700 feet to the floor of Betatakin Canyon. **Keet Seel** was occupied beginning as early as AD 950 and continuing until 1300. The 17-mile round-trip hike to Keet Seel is strenuous and requires an overnight stay at a primitive campground. Open Mem Day–Labor Day, only 200 people per day may obtain permits to enter Keet Seel. The visitors center at the entrance to the monument has informative displays on native culture, including numerous artifacts from the area. **Open:** National monument, daily 24 hours; visitor center, daily 8am–5pm. **Free**

Kingman

Founded with the arrival of the railroad in the 1880s, Kingman was a successful gold and silver mining center until the 1920s. It took on new life as a stopover on Route 66 in the 1930s, and today attracts tourists seeking the nostalgia of that legendary highway. Each October the city celebrates Andy Devine Days, in memory of the hometown boy who found fame in early films and television. **Information:** Kingman Chamber of Commerce, 333 W Andy Devine Ave, PO Box 1150, Kingman 86402 (tel 520/753-6106).

HOTEL

Quality Inn Kingman
1400 E Andy Devine Ave, 86401; tel 520/753-4747 or toll free 800/4-CHOICE. 2 mi E of exit 48 / 2 mi W of exit 53 off I-40. Located on historic Route 66. The lobby is decorated with 1950s memorabilia, and the hotel sells Route 66 souvenirs. **Rooms:** 98 rms, stes, and effic. Executive level. CI noon/CO 1pm. Nonsmoking rms avail. Room 165 is the Wild Bill Hickok room. Actor Guy Madison, who played Hickok in the 1950s TV series, once stayed in this room; his photo is on the door. **Amenities:** A/C, cable TV, refrig, dataport. **Services:** Continental breakfast is served in Distillery Room, decorated with Route 66 memorabilia. **Facilities:** Sauna, beauty salon, washer/dryer. **Rates (CP):** Peak (May–Sept) $40–$64 S; $65–$69 D; $70–$95 ste; $70–$95 effic. Extra person $5. Children under age 18 stay free. Lower rates off-season. Parking: Outdoor, free. AE, CB, DC, DISC, JCB, MC, V.

MOTELS

Grand Canyon Caverns Inn and Campground
US 66, PO Box 180, Peach Springs, 86434; tel 520/422-3223. A rustic motel on old Route 66, halfway between Kingman and Seligman. The limestone Grand Canyon Caverns, located on the property, are the largest dry caverns in the United States. **Rooms:** 48 rms. CI 4pm/CO noon. Nonsmoking rms avail. Quaint rooms are partially pine-panelled and contain decorative rock collections under glass. **Amenities:** A/C, satel TV, refrig. Some rooms have rollout beds. **Services:** Guided tours of the caverns are available for a fee. **Facilities:** 1 restaurant, games rm. Picnic tables, barbecues, and a landing strip for small planes are on the premises; a gift shop and cafeteria are at the

caverns. **Rates:** Peak (Feb–Nov) $38 S; $45 D. Extra person $4. Lower rates off-season. Parking: Outdoor, free. AP rates available at certain times of the year. AE, MC, V.

Holiday Inn Kingman
3100 E Andy Devine Ave, 86401; tel 520/753-6262 or toll free 800/HOLIDAY; fax 520/753-7137. Exit 53 off I-40. A basic motel close to major highways. **Rooms:** 120 rms. CI 1pm/CO noon. Nonsmoking rms avail. **Amenities:** A/C, cable TV, dataport. **Services:** **Facilities:** 60 1 restaurant, 1 bar (w/entertainment), washer/dryer. **Rates (CP):** Peak (Feb–Sept) $49–$84 S or D. Extra person $5. Children under age 19 stay free. Lower rates off-season. Parking: Outdoor, free. Senior discounts avail. AE, CB, DC, DISC, JCB, MC, V.

Super 8 Motel
3401 E Andy Devine Ave, 86401; tel 520/757-4808 or toll free 800/800-8000; fax 520/757-4803 ext 324. Exit 53 off I-40. A clean, basic motel with good interstate access. **Rooms:** 61 rms and stes. CI open/CO 11am. Nonsmoking rms avail. **Amenities:** A/C, cable TV. Some rooms have waterbeds. **Services:** Free local calls. **Facilities:** 20 Large-vehicle parking available. **Rates (CP):** Peak (Apr–Sept) $30 S; $38 D; $43 ste. Extra person $6. Children under age 12 stay free. Lower rates off-season. Parking: Outdoor, free. AE, CB, DC, DISC, MC, V.

RESTAURANT

★ House of Chan
960 W Beale St; tel 520/753-3232. **American/Chinese.** A landmark Kingman restaurant serving up Chinese and traditional American food. Cantonese dishes include moo goo gai pan (sliced chicken, mushrooms, water chestnuts, bamboo shoots, and peas) and hot and spicy kung pao chicken. Seafood, beef—including prime rib and charbroiled steak—and chicken offerings fill out the American side of the menu. Chinese beer and wines and Japanese sake are available. During winter, call for Saturday lunch hours. **FYI:** Reservations accepted. Children's menu. **Open:** Mon–Fri 11am–10pm, Sat noon–10pm. **Prices:** Main courses $5–$26. AE, MC, V.

ATTRACTIONS

Chloride Historic District
US 93, Chloride; tel 520/565-3872. Located about 20 miles northwest of Kingman, the town was founded in 1862 when silver was discovered in the nearby Cerbat Mountains. By the 1920s there were 75 mines and 2,000 people, but when the mine shut down in 1944 the town lost most of its population. Much of the downtown area has been preserved as a historic district and includes the oldest continuously operating post office in Arizona, the old jail, and the Jim Fritz Museum. Melodramas are performed at the Silverbelle Playhouse on the first and third Saturday of each month.

Hoover Dam
US 93; tel 520/293-8367. Constructed between 1931 and 1935, this National Historic Landmark was the first major dam on the Colorado River. It is unique for several reasons. By providing the huge amounts of electricity and water needed by Arizona and California, it helped set the stage for the phenomenal growth the region has experienced this century. At 726 feet from bedrock to roadway, it was once the highest concrete dam in the western hemisphere. The 110-mile-long Lake Mead, which was created by damming the Colorado River, is the largest human-made reservoir in the United States. Guided tours begin in the Visitor Center on the Nevada side of the dam. **Open:** Daily 8:30am–5:40pm. **$**

Bonelli House
430 E Spring St; tel 520/753-3195. Two-story, territorial-style mansion built in 1915. It is constructed of locally quarried tufa stone to make it fire-resistant. Rooms are decorated in period style with many of the original furnishings. **Open:** Thurs–Mon 1–5pm. **Free**

Mohave Museum of History and Arts
400 W Beale St; tel 520/753-3195. Exhibits representing the history of Kingman fill this small museum. Dioramas and murals depict the history of the region, while an outdoor display contains wagons, railroad cars, and other large vehicles and machines that helped shape Kingman. **Open:** Mon–Fri 10am–5pm, Sat–Sun 1–5pm. **$**

Hualapai Mountain Park
Hualapai Mountain Rd; tel 520/757-0915. Located 7,000 feet up in the Hualapai Mountains, this park was developed in 1930 by the Civilian Conservation Corps as a pine-shaded escape from the desert. A popular spot for picnicking, hiking, and camping. **Open:** Daily 24 hours. **Free**

Oatman
Old US 66; tel 520/768-7400. Located 30 miles southwest of Kingman. Founded in 1906 when gold was discovered nearby, the town was home to 12,000 people in its heyday. In 1942, the US government closed down many of Arizona's gold-mining operations and Oatman's population plummeted. Today, the 250 inhabitants live amid the once-abandoned old buildings that have been preserved as a ghost town.

One of the biggest attractions of Oatman is its population of almost-wild **burros.** These animals, which roam the streets begging for handouts, are descendants of burros used by gold miners. The historic look of the town has also attracted filmmakers for years; among the movies filmed here was *How the West Was Won.* On weekends there are staged shootouts in the streets and dancing to western music in the evening.

Lake Havasu City

A resort development founded in 1963 on the edge of Lake Havasu, this hot desert community failed to catch on until developer Robert McCulloch bought London Bridge and had it shipped over from England. Today Lake Havasu City's bridge, plus excellent fishing and boating, make the city one of Arizona's most popular tourist stops. **Information:** Lake Havasu City Visitor & Convention Bureau, 1930 Mesquite Ave #3, Lake Havasu City 86403 (tel 520/453-3444 or 800/242-8278).

HOTEL

Holiday Inn Lake Havasu City

245 London Bridge Rd, 86403; tel 520/855-4071 or toll free 800/HOLIDAY; fax 520/855-2379. Exit 9 off I-40. A pleasant hotel set back from the lake, with lower rates than comparable area hotels. **Rooms:** 162 rms and stes. CI 3pm/CO noon. Nonsmoking rms avail. Rooms are spacious and comfortable. **Amenities:** A/C, satel TV w/movies, refrig. Some units w/terraces. **Services:** Children's program. **Facilities:** 200 1 restaurant, 1 bar (w/entertainment), games rm, whirlpool, beauty salon, washer/dryer. Discounts on greens fees are available for nearby PGA championship golf courses. **Rates:** Peak (Mar–Oct) $53–$89 S or D; $135–$135 ste. Extra person $8. Children under age 18 stay free. Min stay special events. Lower rates off-season. Parking: Outdoor, free. AE, CB, DC, DISC, JCB, MC, V.

RESORTS

London Bridge Resort

1477 Queens Bay, 86403; tel 520/855-0888 or toll free 800/624-7939; fax 520/855-9209. Swanson Ave exit off AZ 95. 110 acres. Large "theme park" hotel on the shores of Lake Havasu. Everything pertains to British royalty; a replica of the royal family's gold coronation coach is displayed in the lobby. **Rooms:** 183 rms and stes. Executive level. CI 4pm/CO 11am. Nonsmoking rms avail. A variety of accommodations are available, from deluxe rooms to two-bedroom suites. All are kept in impeccable condition. **Amenities:** A/C, cable TV, refrig. Some units w/terraces, some w/whirlpools. **Services:** Twice-daily maid svce, social director, masseur, children's program, babysitting. Complimentary shuttle to Laughlin, Nevada, casinos. **Facilities:** 500 3 restaurants, 3 bars (2 w/entertainment), 1 beach (lake shore), basketball, board surfing, whirlpool, beauty salon, day-care ctr, washer/dryer. 62 boat slips available. **Rates:** Peak (Apr–Oct) $59–$159 S or D; $99–$160 ste. Extra person $5. Children under age 18 stay free. Min stay special events. Lower rates off-season. Parking: Outdoor, free. Rates are increased on weekends. AE, CB, DC, DISC, JCB, MC, V.

Nautical Inn Resort & Conference Center

1000 McCulloch Blvd, 86403; tel 520/855-2141 or toll free 800/892-2141; fax 520/453-5808. Mesquite or Swanson exit off AZ 95. 50 acres. Popular with boaters. Somewhat rundown at time of inspection, though new owners plan complete renovation. **Rooms:** 120 rms and stes. CI 4pm/CO 11am. Some rooms have kitchenettes. **Amenities:** A/C, cable TV, refrig. Some units w/terraces. Some rooms have coffeemakers. **Services:** **Facilities:** 750 1 restaurant (*see* "Restaurants" below), 2 bars (1 w/entertainment), 1 beach (lake shore), volleyball, whirlpool, washer/dryer. Barbecues are available. Parasailing is offered. **Rates:** Peak (Mar–Oct) $90–$149 S or D; $150 ste. Children under age 18 stay free. Min stay special events. Lower rates off-season. Parking: Outdoor, free. AE, DC, DISC, MC, V.

RESTAURANTS

Captain's Table

In Nautical Inn Resort & Conference Center, 1000 McCulloch Blvd; tel 520/855-2141. Mesquite or Swanson Ave exit off AZ 95. **Continental/Seafood.** Lakefront restaurant offering diners pretty views. Seafood is prepared grilled, blackened, charbroiled, baked, or Provençale-style. Chicken and beef are served as well. **FYI:** Reservations recommended. Children's menu. **Open:** Sun–Thurs 7am–9pm, Fri–Sat 7am–10pm. **Prices:** Main courses $10–$26. AE, CB, DC, MC, V.

Shugrue's

1425 McCulloch Blvd; tel 520/453-1400. **Seafood/Steak.** Attractive, comfortable restaurant that features a solarium dining room with two large fishtanks and exceptional views of London Bridge. Primarily seafood and steak, but some Cajun, pasta, and wok dishes as well. House specialties include pan-fried Southwestern catfish. **FYI:** Reservations recommended. Children's menu. **Open:** Lunch Mon–Sat 11am–3pm, Sun 10am–3pm; dinner Sun–Thurs 5–10pm, Fri–Sat 5–11pm. **Prices:** Main courses $9–$22. AE, MC, V.

ATTRACTION

London Bridge

1550 London Bridge Rd; tel 520/855-4115. In the mid-1960s the British government decided to sell London Bridge, which was sinking into the Thames River, to Robert McCulloch, founder of Lake Havasu City. Reconstruction of the bridge began in 1968 and the grand reopening was held in 1971. When originally rebuilt, the bridge was located on a desert peninsula jutting into Lake Havasu, connecting desert to more desert. Since then a mile-long channel was dredged through the base of the peninsula, creating an island offshore from Lake Havasu City. Today the bridge is the second largest attraction in Arizona. Visitors can also explore the more than 50 British-style shops that comprise the **English Village** located near the bridge. **Open:** Daily 24 hours. **Free**

Lake Powell

See also Page

ATTRACTIONS

Glen Canyon Dam

US 89; tel 520/608-6404. Built across a section of Glen Canyon that's less than one-third mile wide, the dam impounds the waters of the Colorado River to form Lake Powell. Built to provide water for the desert communities of the Southwest and West, the dam also provides hydroelectric power. Self-guided tours of the dam take 30–45 minutes; guided tours available in summer. **Open:** Peak (May–Sept) daily 7am–7pm. Reduced hours off-season. **Free**

John Wesley Powell Memorial Museum

6 N Lake Powell Blvd; tel 520/645-9496. Lake Powell is named after John Wesley Powell, the one-armed Civil War hero who led the first expedition through the Grand Canyon in 1869. This small museum documents the Powell expedition with photographs, etchings, and artifacts. In addition, there are Native American artifacts ranging from Anasazi pottery to contemporary Navajo and Hopi crafts. Gift shop, information center. **Open:** Peak (May–Sept) Mon–Sat 8am–6pm, Sun 10am–6pm. Reduced hours off-season. **Free**

Lakeside

See Pinetop-Lakeside

Litchfield Park

A suburb just west of Phoenix, Litchfield Park is a planned community consisting of individual villages, each with its own businesses and recreation facilities. **Information:** Tri-City West Chamber of Commerce, 501 W Van Buren, Suite K, Avondale 85323 (tel 602/932-2260).

RESORT

The Wigwam

300 E Indian School Rd, 85340; tel 602/935-3811 or toll free 800/327-0396; fax 602/935-3737. Litchfield Rd exit off I-10. 75 acres. Dating from the 1920s, this resort retains much of its original casita-style ambience, though it is now less a desert hideaway than a suburban playground. Ideal for meetings in winter and congenial for families in summer, it's also perfect for golfers year-round. **Rooms:** 229 rms and stes; 2 cottages/villas. Executive level. CI 4pm/CO 1pm. Nonsmoking rms avail. Recent $44-million renovation restored original one-story casitas and added new two-story wings grouped around a second swimming pool complex. Original rooms (a tad smaller, less expensive) have more Southwestern flavor but their patios offer little shade and less privacy (the best bets are the casitas facing the first fairway). **Amenities:** A/C, cable TV w/movies, dataport, in-rm safe, bathrobes. All units w/minibars, all w/terraces, some w/fireplaces, some w/whirlpools. **Services:** Twice-daily maid svce, car-rental desk, social director, masseur, children's program, babysitting. Welcoming, responsive staff. **Facilities:** 54 1000 4 restaurants (*see* "Restaurants" below), 3 bars (2 w/entertainment), basketball, volleyball, games rm, lawn games, racquetball, spa, sauna, steam rm, whirlpool, beauty salon, playground. Golfers can use caddies rather than carts; golf facilities are shared with club members but guests get "first priority." Tennis courts include 500-seat stadium court. Trap and skeet shooting; day camp for kids. Live entertainment and dancing most evenings. **Rates:** Peak (Jan–Apr) $300–$350 S or D; $400–$500 ste; $400–$500 cottage/villa. Extra person $25. Children under age 18 stay free. Min stay special events. Lower rates off-season. AP and MAP rates avail. Parking: Outdoor, free. Given the resort's not-too-convenient location, the MAP rate of $48 extra per person (with choice of three restaurants, gratuities included) is worth considering. AE, CB, DC, DISC, MC, V.

RESTAURANT

Arizona Kitchen

In The Wigwam, 300 E Indian School Rd; tel 602/935-3811. Litchfield Rd exit off I-10. **Southwestern/Native American.** A cozy, informal setting for sampling innovative dishes. The inviting room is marked by timber-beamed ceilings, adobe walls, and sturdy wooden furniture—all dominated by a big, open kitchen with lots of tiles and copperware. The menu includes blue corn piki rolls (with shredded capon and jalapeño spinach); rattlesnake fritters; chilequiles pizza (with spiced chicken and tortillas); and roasted pheasant (with chipotle-pomegranate honey). **FYI:** Reservations recommended. Guitar. Children's menu. Dress code. **Open:** Mon–Sat 6–10:30pm. **Prices:** Main courses $12–$28; prix fixe $28–$32. AE, CB, DC, DISC, MC, V.

ATTRACTION

Wildlife World Zoo

16501 W Northern Ave; tel 602/935-9453. Features Arizona's largest collection of exotic animals housed in their natural surroundings on 45 acres, including 350 species and 1,400 individual animals such as dromedary camels, llamas, kangaroos, jaguars, and tigers. Unique attractions include four feeding areas where visitors can hand-feed parrots, giraffes, and other animals. **Open:** Daily 9am–5pm. **$$$**

Marble Canyon

See also Page

Colorado River explorer John Wesley Powell named the majestic river gorge here Marble Canyon as he floated through in 1869. Today the small community is a base for river rafters and explorations of the North Rim of Grand Canyon National Park. **Information:** Page/Lake Powell Chamber of Commerce, 106 S Lake Powell Blvd, PO Box 727, Page 86040 (tel 520/645-2741).

MOTEL

Cliff Dwellers Lodge

US 89A, PO Box 30, HC67, 86036; tel 520/355-2228 or toll free 800/433-2543. 9 mi W of Navajo Bridge. A serene escape in the remote high mesas of northern Arizona, with beautiful views of the Vermillion Cliffs. **Rooms:** 21 rms. CI 2pm/CO 11am. **Amenities:** A/C. No phone or TV. Some units w/terraces. **Services:** **Facilities:** 1 restaurant, 1 bar. Gas station, general store, and restaurant on premises. Landing strips for small planes nearby. **Rates:** Peak (May–Oct) $57–$67 D. Extra person $4. Lower rates off-season. Parking: Outdoor, free. DISC, MC, V.

LODGE

Marble Canyon Lodge

US 89A, 86036; tel 520/355-2225 or toll free 800/726-1789. 5 mi S of Lee's Ferry. An attractive lodge close to the Colorado River, particularly popular with rafters and fishermen. **Rooms:** 50 rms, stes, and effic. CI 2pm/CO 11am. **Amenities:** A/C, satel TV. **Services:** Airstrip directly across the highway from the lodge for fly-ins. **Facilities:** 40 1 restaurant, 1 bar, lawn games, washer/dryer. Several buildings have small sitting rooms with libraries. Gas station, store, and post office on site. **Rates:** Peak (Apr–Sept) $45 S; $60 D; $115 ste; $60 effic; $125 cottage/villa. Extra person $5. Children under age 14 stay free. Lower rates off-season. Parking: Outdoor, free. DISC, MC, V.

Mayer

ATTRACTION

Arcosanti

I-17 at Cordes Junction; tel 520/632-7135. Paolo Soleri, an Italian architect who came to Arizona to study with Frank Lloyd Wright, has a dream of merging architecture and ecology. He calls this merger *arcology*, and Arcosanti is the realization of his ideas. An experiment in urban living, the energy-efficient town (which is still under development) blends with the desert and preserves as much of the surrounding landscape as possible. Visitors cannot tour the grounds unescorted; guided tours are conducted on the hour from 10am–4pm. **Open:** Daily 9am–5pm. **$$**

McNary

ATTRACTION

Sunrise

AZ 273; tel 520/735-7669. The only ski area in the White Mountains, an area known for its ponderosa pine forests, lakes, and mountains. The resort is located on the Apache Reservation and is operated by the Apache people. Lots of winter sun, 11 lifts, and more than 60 trails make this a very popular spot for Arizonans. During the summer there is hiking and fishing. **Open:** Nov–Apr, daily 9am–4:30pm. **$$$$**

Mesa

The city of Mesa, whose name is the Spanish word for "table," rests on a plateau about 12 miles southeast of Phoenix. Among the fastest-growing communities in the state, it is the winter home of the Chicago Cubs. Large shopping malls and several inexpensive motels attract both locals and visitors. **Information:** Mesa Convention & Visitors Bureau, 120 N Center, Mesa 85201 (tel 602/827-4700 or 800/283-MESA).

HOTELS

Hampton Inn

1563 S Gilbert Rd, 85204; tel 602/926-3600 or toll free 800/HAMPTON; fax 602/926-4892. Gilbert Rd exit off US 60. A good choice for families. **Rooms:** 116 rms. CI 3pm/CO noon. Nonsmoking rms avail. **Amenities:** A/C, cable TV w/movies. All units w/minibars. King rooms have two phones, and some have sofa sleepers. **Services:** **Facilities:** 50 Whirlpool, washer/dryer. **Rates (CP):** Peak (Jan 1–Apr 15) $67–$92 S or D. Extra person $5. Children under age 18 stay free. Lower rates off-season. Parking: Outdoor, free. AE, DC, DISC, MC, V.

Holiday Inn

1600 S Country Club Dr, 85210; tel 602/964-7000 or toll free 800/HOLIDAY. Country Club Dr exit off US 60. Pleasant lobby, with lots of plants. **Rooms:** 248 rms and stes. CI 3pm/CO noon. Nonsmoking rms avail. Rooms are comfortable, with excellent views of the Superstition Mountains from the upper floors. **Amenities:** A/C, cable TV w/movies. Some units w/terraces. **Services:** Car-rental desk, children's program. **Facilities:** 700 1 restaurant, 3 bars (1 w/entertainment), sauna, steam rm, whirlpool, washer/dryer. Attractive indoor-outdoor pool with lots of trees. **Rates:** Peak (Jan–Apr) $109–$129 S or D; $139 ste. Extra person $10. Children under age 18 stay free.

Lower rates off-season. Parking: Outdoor, free. Reasonable rates considering the quality and location. AE, CB, DC, DISC, MC, V.

Holiday Inn Express
5750 E Main St, 85205; tel 602/985-3600 or toll free 800/888-3561; fax 602/832-1230. Exit Higley Rd off US 60. A no-frills suburban hotel. **Rooms:** 118 rms, stes, and effic. CI 3pm/CO 11am. Nonsmoking rms avail. Basic, comfortable rooms. **Amenities:** A/C, cable TV. All units w/terraces. **Services:** **Facilities:** 200 1 restaurant, 1 bar, whirlpool, washer/dryer. **Rates (CP):** Peak (Jan–Apr) $129 S or D; $139 ste. Extra person $10. Children under age 18 stay free. Lower rates off-season. Parking: Outdoor, free. AE, DC, DISC, MC, V.

Mesa Pavilion Hilton
1011 W Holmes Ave, 85210; tel 602/833-5555 or toll free 800/544-5866; fax 602/649-1886. Alma School Rd exit off US 60. Attractive eight-story atrium lobby, palm-filled with circular bar in center. **Rooms:** 263 rms and stes. Executive level. CI 3pm/CO noon. Nonsmoking rms avail. Some rooms for the disabled have roll-in showers. **Amenities:** A/C, cable TV w/movies, refrig. Some units w/minibars, all w/terraces, some w/whirlpools. **Services:** Car-rental desk, masseur, babysitting. **Facilities:** 700 1 restaurant, 2 bars (1 w/entertainment), spa, whirlpool, beauty salon. **Rates:** Peak (Jan 16–Apr 16) $135–$175 S; $145–$185 D; $160–$205 ste. Extra person $10. Children under age 18 stay free. Lower rates off-season. Parking: Outdoor, free. AE, DISC, MC, V.

Ramada Inn Suites
1410 S Country Club Dr, 85210; tel 602/964-2897 or toll free 800/53-SUITE. Country Club Dr exit off US 60. All-suite hotel popular with golfers; good for short or long stays. Attractively furnished lobby. **Rooms:** 120 stes. CI 4pm/CO noon. Nonsmoking rms avail. **Amenities:** A/C, cable TV w/movies, refrig, dataport, in-rm safe. Studios and one- and two-bedroom suites have ovens and cooking utensils. **Services:** Masseur, babysitting. **Facilities:** Spa, whirlpool, washer/dryer. Barbecue every Wednesday 5–7pm at no extra charge. **Rates (CP):** Peak (Jan 1–30) $149–$189 ste. Extra person $10. Children under age 16 stay free. Lower rates off-season. Parking: Outdoor, free. Extended-stay rates for studios. Rates are much less during off-season. AE, CB, DC, MC, V.

Sheraton Mesa Hotel
200 N Centennial Way, 85201; tel 602/898-8300; fax 602/964-9279. A large hotel in a quiet part of Mesa, featuring attractive landscaping and fountains. **Rooms:** 269 rms and stes. Executive level. CI 3pm/CO noon. Nonsmoking rms avail. Rooms are large and well appointed, with separate dressing areas. **Amenities:** A/C, cable TV w/movies, dataport, bathrobes. All units w/minibars, 1 w/whirlpool. **Services:** Twice-daily maid svce, social director, babysitting. Secretarial services available. **Facilities:** 5000 2 restaurants, 1 bar, spa, whirlpool. **Rates (CP):** Peak (Jan–Apr 15) $130–$150 S or D; $175–$175 ste. Extra person $10. Children under age 18 stay free. Lower rates off-season. Parking: Outdoor, free. AE, DISC, MC, V.

MOTEL

Days Inn
333 W Juanita Ave, 85210; tel 602/844-8900 or toll free 800/329-7466. Country Club Dr exit off US 60. Pleasant southwestern-style lobby with plants. **Rooms:** 124 rms. CI 2pm/CO noon. Nonsmoking rms avail. **Amenities:** A/C, satel TV w/movies, refrig. **Services:** **Facilities:** Spa, sauna, whirlpool, washer/dryer. **Rates (CP):** Peak (Feb–Mar) $91–$139 S or D. Extra person $6. Children under age 18 stay free. Lower rates off-season. Parking: Outdoor, free. AE, CB, DC, DISC, EC, ER, JCB, MC, V.

RESORTS

Arizona Golf Resort & Conference Center
425 S Power Rd, 85206; tel 602/832-3202 or toll free 800/528-8282; fax 602/981-0151. Power Rd exit off US 60. 160 acres. Set amid an 18-hole golf course on well-cared-for, spacious grounds. Recently added 26 casitas, with more planned. Convenient to shopping. **Rooms:** 186 rms and stes. CI 3pm/CO noon. Nonsmoking rms avail. Rooms are spacious and well designed, many with views of the golf course. **Amenities:** A/C, cable TV w/movies, refrig, in-rm safe. Some units w/terraces. VCRs available for fee. **Services:** Social director, babysitting. **Facilities:** 18 2 2 500 2 restaurants, 1 bar, basketball, volleyball, washer/dryer. Three whirlpool tubs. **Rates:** Peak (Jan 6–May 10) $119–$205 S; $205–$390 D; $119–$390 ste. Extra person $15. Children under age 16 stay free. Lower rates off-season. Parking: Outdoor, free. AE, CB, DC, DISC, JCB, MC, V.

Saguaro Lake Ranch Resort
13020 Bush Hwy, 85215; tel 602/984-2194; fax 602/380-1490. Bush Hwy exit off AZ 87. 20 acres. An older but very comfortable resort on the Salt River, a half-mile from Saguaro Lake. Built in 1927, this ranch has been a resort for over 60 years. **Rooms:** 24 rms. CI 2pm/CO noon. Nonsmoking rms avail. Some rooms sleep as many as 8; all have a homey feel with Southwestern prints on the walls, and many have Monterey furniture from the 1940s. **Amenities:** A/C. No phone or TV. All units w/terraces. **Services:** Social director, babysitting. **Facilities:** 80 Basketball, volleyball, games rm, lawn games, washer/dryer. Nearby activities include hiking, rafting, bird watching, waterskiing. **Rates:** $110 S; $190 D. Extra person $50. Children under age 6 stay free. AP rates avail. Parking: Outdoor, free. Five

rooms in the lodge offer the full American plan. $100 double, $85 single. Rates do not include fees for rafting or horseback riding. Closed July–Aug. AE, MC, V.

RESTAURANTS

Jade Empress
In K-mart Mall, 1840 W Broadway Rd; tel 602/833-3577. Exit Dobson Rd off US 60. **Chinese.** Low light, lots of plants, and Chinese prints. Specialties include Cantonese barbecue, subgum chop suey, and Szechuan chicken. **FYI:** Reservations recommended. Children's menu. **Open:** Mon–Sat 11am–10pm, Sun 11:30am–9pm. **Prices:** Main courses $5–$8; prix fixe $18–$24. AE, DC, DISC, MC, V.

The Landmark
809 W Main St; tel 602/962-4652. At Extension Rd. **American/Seafood.** Housed in a 1908 building that was formerly a Mormon church. The decor is early Americana, the cuisine is Midwestern homestyle cooking. Large soup and salad bar. **FYI:** Reservations not accepted. Children's menu. **Open:** Lunch Mon–Fri 11am–2pm; dinner Mon–Sat 4–9pm, Sun noon–7pm. **Prices:** Main courses $12–$15. AE, CB, DC, DISC, MC, V.

Raffaele's
In Dobbs Plaza Shopping Center, 2909 S Dobson Rd; tel 602/838-0090. **Italian.** A bright dining room, with soft colors and trompe l'oeil murals. Specialties include fettuccine Smirnoff—fettuccine topped with shallots, fresh tomatoes, basil, and vodka. **FYI:** Reservations accepted. No smoking. Additional location: 2999 N 44th St, Phoenix (tel 952-0063). **Open:** Lunch Mon–Fri 11:30am–3pm; dinner Sun–Thurs 5–10pm, Fri–Sat 5–11pm. **Prices:** Main courses $10–$30. AE, DC, DISC, MC, V.

Zur Kate
In Main St Plaza Shopping Center, 4815 E Main St; tel 602/830-4244. Between Higley and Greenfield Rds. **German.** Decorated in the style of a German inn, with steins, antlers, and German banners on the walls. Wide variety of German specialties, including homemade bratwurst. Call for holiday and summer hours. **FYI:** Reservations not accepted. **Open:** Peak (Sept–May) Mon–Thurs 11am–8pm, Fri–Sat 11am–close. **Prices:** Main courses $6–$10. MC, V.

ATTRACTIONS

Champlin Fighter Museum
4636 Fighter Aces Dr; tel 602/830-4540. Aeronautical museum dedicated exclusively to fighter planes and the men who flew them. Restored aircraft from World Wars I and II, the Korean War, and the Vietnam War are on display, with a strong emphasis on the wood-and-fabric biplanes and triplanes of World War I. Also memorabilia of famous flying fighter aces. **Open:** Daily 10am–5pm. **$$$**

Arizona Temple
525 E Main St; tel 602/964-7164. A Mormon Temple completed in 1927 from a plan based on classical Greek architecture. Visitor center, flower gardens, reflecting pool, guided tours. **Open:** Daily 9am–9pm. **Free**

Navajo Reservation

Roughly the size of West Virginia, the Navajo Reservation covers 25,000 square miles of northeastern Arizona, as well as parts of New Mexico, Colorado, and Utah. It is the largest Native American reservation in the United States and is home to nearly 200,000 Navajo. Though there are now modern towns with supermarkets, shopping malls, and hotels on the reservation, most Navajo still follow a pastoral life-style as herders. Flocks of sheep and goats, as well as herds of cattle and horses, have free range of the reservation and often graze beside the highways. Visitors should drive with care, especially at night.

A familiar sight on the reservation are the small hexagonal buildings with rounded roofs called **hogans,** the traditional homes of the Navajo. They are usually made of wood and earth. Hogans are on display at the Canyon de Chelly and Navajo National Monument visitor centers.

The Navajo are well known for their woven rugs, silverwork, and sandpaintings. The historic **Hubbell Trading Post** (see "Attractions" under Ganado) has an excellent selection of rugs and jewelry, and the **Cameron Trading Post,** at the crossroads of Cameron where AZ 64 branches off US 89 to Grand Canyon Village, specializes in museum-quality crafts including Navajo textiles from between 1860 and 1940.

The biggest event open to the public on the reservation is the **Navajo Nation Fair,** held in Window Rock every September featuring traditional dances, a rodeo, pow wow, parade, Miss Navajo Pageant, and arts and crafts exhibits and sales. For more information about the fair and the reservation contact the Navajoland Tourism Office at 520/871-6659.

Nogales

American bargain-hunters use this border town as a base for crossing into Mexico in search of hand-crafted Mexican items, while Mexicans enter the United States here to work or buy goods not available in their country. Nogales is also a major trade center for Mexican produce. **Information:** Nogales/Santa Cruz County Chamber of Commerce, Kino Park, Nogales 85621 (tel 520/287-3685).

MOTELS

Best Western Time Motel
921 N Grand Ave, 85621; tel 520/287-4627 or toll free 800/528-1234; fax 520/287-6949. Attractive, recently renovated

motel a little over a mile from the Mexican border. **Rooms:** 45 rms. CI open/CO noon. Nonsmoking rms avail. Rooms are small but adequate, with relatively new furnishings. **Amenities:** A/C, cable TV w/movies, VCR. **Services:** Car-rental desk, babysitting. **Facilities:** Whirlpool. **Rates (CP):** Peak (Nov–Apr) $40–$52 S or D. Extra person $4. Children under age 12 stay free. Lower rates off-season. Parking: Outdoor, free. AE, CB, DC, DISC, JCB, MC, V.

Super 8 Motel
547 W Mariposa Rd, 85621; tel 520/281-2242 or toll free 800/800-8000; fax 520/281-2242. Exit 4 off I-19. Close to shopping, this is a good choice for vacationers. **Rooms:** 117 rms and stes. CI 11am/CO noon. Nonsmoking rms avail. **Amenities:** A/C, cable TV, dataport. Some rooms have refrigerators. **Services:** Babysitting. **Facilities:** 220 1 restaurant, 1 bar, whirlpool, washer/dryer. **Rates:** Peak (Dec–May) $43–$46 S; $53–$57 D; $86–$88 ste. Extra person $2. Children under age 18 stay free. Lower rates off-season. Parking: Outdoor, free. AE, DC, DISC, MC, V.

RESORT

Rio Rico Resort and Country Club
1069 Camino Caralampi, Rio Rico, 85648; tel 520/281-1901 or toll free 800/288-4746; fax 520/281-7132. 10 mi N of Nogales, exit 17 off I-19. 23 acres. A lovely resort, fully remodeled recently, built on hill overlooking the Patagonia Mountains. **Rooms:** 180 rms and stes. Executive level. CI 4pm/CO noon. Nonsmoking rms avail. Rooms are extremely well appointed and very comfortable. Executive room, with four-poster bed, is particularly nice. **Amenities:** A/C, cable TV w/movies, dataport, voice mail. All units w/terraces. **Services:** Twice-daily maid svce, social director, masseur, babysitting. **Facilities:** 18 4 400 2 restaurants, 2 bars (1 w/entertainment), volleyball, sauna, steam rm, whirlpool, beauty salon. **Rates:** Peak (Jan–Apr) $120–$150 S or D; $175–$250 ste. Extra person $15. Children under age 12 stay free. Lower rates off-season. Parking: Outdoor, free. AE, CB, DC, DISC, ER, MC, V.

RESTAURANT

Mr C's Supper Club
282 W View Point Dr; tel 520/281-9000. Exit 4 off I-19. **Seafood/Steak.** Modern-looking restaurant considered by many locals to be Nogales's finest. With fresh fish prepared a variety of ways, steak and salad bar. **FYI:** Reservations accepted. Country music/rock. Children's menu. **Open:** Mon–Sat 11:30am–midnight. **Prices:** Main courses $10–$25; prix fixe $10–$20. DC, DISC, MC, V.

ATTRACTIONS

Pimeria Alta Historical Society
136 N Grand Ave; tel 520/287-4621. Located in the original City Hall building (1914), near the border-crossing in downtown Nogales. Maintains a small museum, library, and archives on this region from southern Arizona to northern Mexico. **Open:** Tues–Fri 10am–5pm, Sat 10am–4pm. **Free**

Arizona Vineyard Winery
1830 Patagonia Hwy; tel 520/287-7972. 19th-century-style winery produces 50,000 gallons a year of white burgundy, blanc de blanc, chablis, rosé, tino tinto, haute sauterne, mountain Rhine, and worker's red. The wine, produced in wood barrels, can be sampled in rooms filled with movie props that the owner rents out for the frequent filmings in the area. **Open:** Daily 10am–5pm. **Free**

Oak Creek Canyon

ATTRACTION

Slide Rock State Park
AZ 179; tel 520/282-3034. Located 7 miles north of Sedona on the site of an old homestead, this park preserves a natural water slide. A popular location for swimming and fishing. **Open:** Daily sunrise–sunset. **$**

Oracle

ATTRACTION

Biosphere 2
AZ 77, MM 96.5; tel 520/825-6400. On September 26, 1991, 4 men and 4 women were sealed inside a large and elaborate greenhouse to begin the first 2-year stint of what will be a 100-year experiment to attain a better understanding of the human role in the future of the planet. More than 4,000 species of plants and animals are part of the experiment, which includes a rain forest, desert, savannah, marsh, and even a tiny "ocean" complete with waves and tides. Facilities open to visitors include the orientation center, Biofair, test module, research and development center, and Biospherian Theater. Visitors cannot enter Biosphere 2. Arrive before 2pm to have time to see all exhibits. Cafe and snackbar. **Open:** Daily 9am–5pm. **$$$$**

Organ Pipe Cactus National Monument

Located 70 miles south of Gila Bend on AZ 5. A preserve for the rare organ pipe cactus and the plants and animals of the Sonoran Desert. The massive cactus forms many trunks, some 20 feet tall, that resemble organ pipes. It grows on south-facing slopes where it can absorb the most sun, and blooms in May, June, and July, showing its lavender-and-white flowers only at night.

Two scenic loop roads allow visitors to drive through the monument. The 21-mile **Ajo Mountain Drive** winds along the foothills of the Ajo Mountains, the highest range in the area. Desert landscapes and large groups of organ pipe cactus are among the highlights of this two-hour tour. The 53-mile **Puerto Blanco Drive** circles the colorful Puerto Blanco Mountains and passes **Quitobaquito Spring,** upon which Native Americans and pioneers once relied for the only source of water for miles around; the trip takes half a day. For more information contact the park information office, open daily 8am–5pm, at 602/387-6849.

Page

See also Marble Canyon

Created by the US Bureau of Reclamation in the 1960s as headquarters and housing during construction of Glen Canyon Dam, Page today provides lodging, food, and other services for vacationers at huge Lake Powell, created by the dam. **Information:** Page/Lake Powell Chamber, 106 S Lake Powell Blvd, PO Box 727, Page 86040 (tel 520/645-2741).

HOTEL

Best Western Arizona Inn

716 Rim View Dr, PO Box C, 86040; tel 520/645-2466 or toll free 800/826-2718; fax 520/645-2053. Rim View Dr exit off Lake Powell Blvd, ¾ mi E of US 89. Situated on a hilltop overlooking Lake Powell and Glen Canyon Dam. **Rooms:** 103 rms and stes. CI 3pm/CO noon. Nonsmoking rms avail. Half the rooms have views. **Amenities:** A/C, cable TV w/movies. **Services:** **Facilities:** 1 restaurant, 1 bar, whirlpool. Parking for RVs is available. **Rates:** Peak (May–Sept) $69–$89 S; $74–$99 D; $125–$155 ste. Extra person $10. Children under age 18 stay free. Lower rates off-season. Parking: Outdoor, free. AE, DC, DISC, MC, V.

MOTELS

Best Western Weston Inn

201 N Lake Powell Blvd, 86040; tel 520/645-2451 or toll free 800/637-9183. Page exit off US 89A. Located on a hill overlooking spectacular Glen Canyon Dam and Lake Powell. **Rooms:** 90 rms and effic. CI 2pm/CO 11am. Nonsmoking rms avail. Some rooms have views of the lake. **Amenities:** A/C, cable TV w/movies. Some units w/terraces. **Services:** **Facilities:** Washer/dryer. A golf course is two miles away, Lake Powell is six miles away, and shopping centers are within two blocks. **Rates (CP):** Peak (Apr–Oct) $58–$63 S; $76–$81 D; $145 effic. Extra person $5. Children under age 12 stay free. Lower rates off-season. Parking: Outdoor, free. AE, DC, DISC, MC, V.

Lake Powell Motel

US 89, PO Box 1597, 86040; tel 520/645-2477 or toll free 800/528-6154; fax 520/331-5258. 4 mi N of Glen Canyon Dam. Great views of Lake Powell from this motel set high on a hill away from Page and the marinas. **Rooms:** 25 rms. CI 3pm/CO 11am. Nonsmoking rms avail. All rooms have sliding glass doors giving access to lawn furniture out front. **Amenities:** A/C, cable TV. **Services:** **Rates:** Peak (Apr–Oct) $74 S or D. Extra person $6. Children under age 18 stay free. Lower rates off-season. Parking: Outdoor, free. Closed Nov–Mar. AE, DISC, MC, V.

LODGE

Wahweap Lodge

Lakeshore Dr, PO Box 1597, 86040; tel 520/645-2433 or toll free 800/528-6154. Lake Shore Dr exit off US 89. 4 mi N of Glen Canyon Dam. This large lodge is located at a marina on the shores of Lake Powell. **Rooms:** 375 rms and stes. CI 3pm/CO 11am. Nonsmoking rms avail. **Amenities:** A/C, cable TV w/movies. Some units w/terraces. **Services:** **Facilities:** 2 restaurants (*see* "Restaurants" below), 1 bar, whirlpool. Full boating facilities are available. **Rates:** Peak (Apr–Oct) $119–$130 S or D; $200 ste. Extra person $12. Children under age 18 stay free. Lower rates off-season. Parking: Outdoor, free. AE, DISC, MC, V.

RESTAURANTS

M Bar H Cafe

In Bar H Mercantile Center, 819 N Navajo Dr; tel 520/645-1420. **American.** A simple cafe done in a western motif. That famous western specialty, chicken-fried steak with mashed potatoes, gets top billing here. Homemade pies. **FYI:** Reservations accepted. No liquor license. **Open:** Mon–Sat 5am–3pm, Sun 5am–2pm. **Prices:** Main courses $5–$15. MC, V.

Rainbow Room

In Wahweap Lodge, Lakeshore Dr; tel 520/645-2433 ext 1017. 5 mi N of Page Lake Shore Dr exit off US 89. **Southwestern.** Sweeping, panoramic views of Lake Powell are visible through the curved glass wall of the dining room. Varied seafood and beef dishes offered. **FYI:** Reservations not accepted. Guitar. Children's menu. No smoking. **Open:** Peak (May 15–Oct 15) breakfast daily 6–11am; lunch daily 11am–3pm; dinner daily 5–10pm. **Prices:** Main courses $10–$22. AE, MC, V.

ATTRACTIONS

Glen Canyon National Recreation Area

US 89; tel 520/608-6200. One of the nation's most popular recreation areas. Lake Powell, a manmade lake, is the main attraction, set amid the slick-rock canyons of northern Arizona and southern Utah. It is more than 500 feet deep in some places and bounded by 1,960 miles of shoreline. Few roads penetrate the recreation area, so the only way to appreciate this rugged region is by boat; bring your own or rent one here. Houseboats, waterskiing, jet skiing, fishing, and camping. For more information write: PO Box 1507, Page 86040. **Open:** Daily 24 hours. **Free**

Rainbow Bridge National Monument
Glen Canyon National Recreation Area, off US 89; tel 520/608-6404. The world's largest natural bridge, this sandstone arch stands 290 feet high and spans 275 feet, a product of the powerful erosion that has sculpted the entire region. Located 50 miles from Glen Canyon Dam; accessible only by boat or on foot. **Open:** Daily 24 hours. **Free**

Parker

An outdoor recreation center for boaters and fishermen on the Colorado River below Lake Havasu, Parker is also a trade center for Native Americans on the Colorado River Indian Reservation. **Information:** Parker Area Chamber of Commerce, 1217 California Ave, Parker 85344 (tel 520/669-2174).

RESORT

Havasu Springs Resort
Rte 2, PO Box 624, 85344; tel 520/677-3361. 16 mi S of Lake Havasu City. 100 acres. There's a small motel in this resort at the south end of Lake Havasu, augmented by an RV park and houseboat rentals. **Rooms:** 44 rms and stes. CI 2pm/CO 11am. Some rooms have kitchenettes and half have lake views. **Amenities:** A/C, cable TV, refrig. **Services:** **Facilities:** 250 1 restaurant, 2 bars (1 w/entertainment), 1 beach (lake shore), games rm, washer/dryer. Full marina services are available. Barbecues and picnic tables are close by. **Rates:** Peak (Mar–Oct) $70–$80 S or D; $90 ste. Extra person $5. Children under age 3 stay free. Min stay special events. Lower rates off-season. Parking: Outdoor, free. MC, V.

ATTRACTION

Colorado River Indian Tribes Museum and Library
2nd Ave and Mohave Rd; tel 520/669-9211. Permanent and changing exhibits explain the history of the four tribes of the Colorado River area—the Mohave, the Chemehuevi, the Navajo, and the Hopi. Also on display are works by local artists, and Native American baskets and pottery. **Open:** Mon–Fri 8am–5pm, Sat 10am–3pm. **Free**

Patagonia

The site of one of the West's richest silver and lead mines in the 1860s, this mountain community has been a favorite of Hollywood filmmakers because of its classic western scenery. **Information:** Patagonia Community Association, PO Box 241, Patagonia 85624 (tel 520/394-0060).

MOTEL

Stage Stop Motel
303 McKeown Ave, PO Box 777, 85624; tel 520/394-2211. 18 mi N of Nogales. A comfortable motel, the only lodging available in Patagonia, a quiet town with several art galleries. The nearby Patagonia-Sonoita Creek Preserve, run by the Arizona chapter of the Nature Conservancy, is great for birdwatching. **Rooms:** 43 rms, stes, and effic. CI noon/CO noon. Rooms have sliding glass doors. **Amenities:** A/C, cable TV. **Services:** **Facilities:** 50 1 restaurant, 1 bar, washer/dryer. Pool undergoing repair. **Rates:** Peak (Mar–Aug) $40 S; $50 D; $80 ste; $60 effic. Extra person $10. Children under age 5 stay free. Lower rates off-season. Parking: Outdoor, free. AE, DISC, MC, V.

ATTRACTION

Patagonia-Sonoita Creek Preserve
Along AZ 82; tel 520/394-2400. A nature preserve owned by the Nature Conservancy that protects a mile and a half of Sonoita Creek riparian (riverside) habitat. More than 250 species of birds have been spotted on the preserve, making it a popular spot for bird watchers. Among the rare birds that may be seen here are 22 species of flycatchers, kingbirds, and phoebes, and the Montezuma quail. **Free**

Payson

Surrounded by national forest, this old mining and ranching community at an elevation of 5,000 feet offers an easy getaway from the summer heat of Phoenix for hikers, campers, and fishermen. The community hosts what it claims as the world's oldest continuous rodeo each August. Western novelist Zane Grey made his home in a cabin near the town. **Information:** Payson Chamber of Commerce, 100 W Main St, PO Box 1380, Payson 85547 (tel 520/474-4515 or 800/6-PAYSON).

MOTELS

Best Western Paysonglo Lodge
1005 S Beeline Hwy, 85541; tel 520/474-2382 or toll free 800/772-9766, 800/872-9766 in AZ; fax 520/474-1937. 1 mi S of jct with AZ 260. Pleasant motel catering to senior citizens; strictly enforced quiet hours. **Rooms:** 47 rms. CI 3pm/CO noon. Nonsmoking rms avail. **Amenities:** A/C, cable TV, refrig. Some units w/fireplaces. **Services:** **Facilities:** Whirlpool, washer/dryer. **Rates (CP):** Peak (Apr–Oct) $58–$108 S; $68–$108 D. Children under age 18

stay free. Min stay special events. Lower rates off-season. Parking: Outdoor, free. Senior discount. AE, DC, DISC, MC, V.

Majestic Mountain Inn
602 E AZ 260, 85541; tel 520/474-0185 or toll free 800/408-2442. AZ 260 exit off AZ 87. Opened in late 1993. One of the nicest in Payson. **Rooms:** 37 rms. CI 1pm/CO 11am. Nonsmoking rms avail. **Amenities:** A/C, cable TV w/movies, refrig. Some units w/terraces, some w/fireplaces, some w/whirlpools. Coffee cups and glasses are furnished in all rooms, and luxury rooms have VCR and hot tubs. **Services:** **Facilities:** **Rates:** Peak (May–Sept) $42–$80 S; $58–$85 D. Extra person $6. Min stay special events. Lower rates off-season. Parking: Outdoor, free. AE, CB, DC, DISC, MC, V.

Pueblo Inn
809 E AZ 260, 85541; tel 520/474-5241 or toll free 800/888-9828. ½ mi E of jct AZ 87/AZ 260. A modern pueblo-style motel, which is being expanded to include 6 suites with fireplaces and hot tubs. **Rooms:** 39 rms and stes. CI noon/CO 11am. Nonsmoking rms avail. Three of the suites have skylights over the hot tubs. **Amenities:** A/C, cable TV w/movies, refrig. Some units w/fireplaces, some w/whirlpools. Suites have coffeemakers, wet bars, and microwave ovens. **Services:** Free local calls. **Facilities:** **Rates:** Peak (May–Sept) $44–$59 S; $49–$69 D. Extra person $5. Children under age 3 stay free. Min stay wknds. Lower rates off-season. Parking: Outdoor, free. AE, CB, DC, DISC, MC, V.

RESORT

Kohl's Ranch Resort
E AZ 260, 85541; tel 520/478-4211 or toll free 800/331-5645 in AZ. 17 mi E of Payson. 12 acres. A lovely mountain resort on the banks of a stream. **Rooms:** 41 rms; 8 cottages/villas. CI 4pm/CO 11am. Nonsmoking rms avail. There are rooms in the main lodge, and one- and two-bedroom cabins, which sleep four to six adults. All cabins have full kitchens and a deck overlooking the stream. **Amenities:** A/C, cable TV. Some units w/terraces, some w/fireplaces. All cabins have fireplaces. **Services:** **Facilities:** 70 1 restaurant, 2 bars (1 w/entertainment), games rm, sauna. **Rates:** Peak (mid-May–mid-Oct) $75–$105 S; $85–$115 D; $150 cottage/villa. Extra person $5. Children under age 12 stay free. Min stay special events. Lower rates off-season. Parking: Outdoor, free. Specialized corporate retreats are offered. AE, DISC, MC, V.

RESTAURANTS

Heritage House Garden Tea Room
202 W Main St; tel 520/474-5501. **American.** Sandwich shop located inside a crafts and gift store. Wooden tables and chairs, lots of plants, and an old jukebox in the center of the room. Serving soups, salads, sandwiches, and desserts. **FYI:** Reservations accepted. No liquor license. **Open:** Mon–Sat 11am–3pm. **Prices:** Lunch main courses $4–$6. DISC, MC, V.

The Oaks Restaurant
302 W Main St; tel 520/474-1929. **American.** A cozy, comfortable restaurant with an early American look: wainscoted walls, patterned curtains, hurricane lamps, and a brick fireplace. The basic American menu includes prime rib, broiled salmon filets, lamb chops, roast cornish game hens, and a fresh vegetable platter. **FYI:** Reservations recommended. Children's menu. **Open:** Peak (May–Oct) lunch daily 11am–2pm; dinner daily 5–8pm; brunch Sun 11am–2pm. **Prices:** Main courses $13–$16. AE, CB, DC, DISC, MC, V.

ATTRACTION

Tonto Natural Bridge State Park
AZ 87; tel 520/476-4202. Located 15 miles north of Payson. The largest natural travertine bridge in the world. Discovered in 1877 by gold prospector David Gowan, who was being chased by Apaches, the bridge is 183 feet high and 150 feet across. There is also a restored historic lodge built in 1927 by Gowan's nephew. **Open:** Peak (Apr–Oct) daily 8am–6pm. Reduced hours off-season. **$**

Peach Springs

See Kingman

Phoenix

See also Carefree, Chandler, Glendale, Litchfield Park, Mesa, Scottsdale, Tempe

Arizona's capital and largest, most cosmopolitan city, Phoenix began in the 1860s as a small settlement on the banks of the Salt River. Constructed at the site of a prehistoric Hohokam Indian village, the new community was named by an early settler who correctly predicted that a great city would grow from the ancient ruins, just as the mythical phoenix rose from its own ashes. Today, Phoenix and its suburbs—known collectively as the Valley of the Sun—are famous for their luxurious resorts, fine restaurants, more than 100 golf courses, and over 300 days of sunshine each year. Summers are very hot (temperatures often exceed 100°F), ensuring fall, winter, and spring as the most popular times to visit. **Information:** Phoenix & Valley of the Sun Convention & Visitors Bureau, 400 E Van Buren, Suite 600, Phoenix 85004 (tel 602/252-5588).

PUBLIC TRANSPORTATION

The **Downtown Area Shuttle (DASH)** provides free bus service within the downtown area. Buses operate Mon–Fri, 6:30am–6pm, and make regular stops every 6–12 minutes.

HOTELS

Courtyard by Marriott

9631 N Black Canyon Hwy, 85021 (Metrocenter); tel 602/944-7373 or toll free 800/321-2211; fax 602/944-0079. This is a good choice for corporate travelers, as it's close to many Phoenix high-tech companies and just off I-17. **Rooms:** 146 rms and stes. CI 3pm/CO 1pm. Nonsmoking rms avail. **Amenities:** A/C, cable TV w/movies, dataport, voice mail. Some units w/terraces. Suites have refrigerators. **Services:** **Facilities:** 49 1 restaurant (bkfst and dinner only), 1 bar, games rm, whirlpool, washer/dryer. **Rates:** Peak (Jan–Apr) $110 S; $120 D; $130 ste. Extra person $10. Children under age 18 stay free. Min stay special events. Lower rates off-season. Parking: Outdoor, free. AE, DC, DISC, MC, V.

The Crescent Hotel

2620 W Dunlap Ave, 85021 (Metrocenter); tel 602/943-8200 or toll free 800/423-4126; fax 602/371-2857. Dunlap exit off I-17. A luxurious hotel, with particularly attractive public areas. There's a lovely fountain in the lobby, and outside dining under a tent. **Rooms:** 342 rms and stes. CI 3pm/CO noon. Nonsmoking rms avail. Rooms are large and well furnished. **Amenities:** A/C, satel TV, refrig, in-rm safe, bathrobes. All units w/minibars, all w/terraces, some w/whirlpools. **Services:** VP Social director, masseur, babysitting. **Facilities:** 2 1000 1 restaurant, 2 bars (1 w/entertainment), lawn games, racquetball, squash, spa, sauna, steam rm, whirlpool. Excellent recreational facilities. **Rates:** Peak (Oct–Apr) $125–$145 S; $125–$190 D; $200 ste. Extra person $15. Children under age 18 stay free. Lower rates off-season. Parking: Outdoor, free. A good value considering features and amenities. AE, CB, DC, DISC, MC, V.

Embassy Suites Hotel

2630 E Camelback Rd, 85016 (Biltmore); tel 602/955-3992 or toll free 800/362-2779; fax 602/955-6479. Good location in Phoenix's upscale shopping center, Biltmore Fashion Park. Perfect for those who wish to shop in the Park's clothing stores and bookstores or dine in one of the numerous fine restaurants. The five-story atrium lobby has huge fish ponds with large fish, and a piano bar. **Rooms:** 233 stes. Executive level. CI 3pm/CO noon. Nonsmoking rms avail. Rooms are attractively furnished and very comfortable. **Amenities:** A/C, cable TV w/movies, refrig, dataport, voice mail. Some units w/terraces. **Services:** Car-rental desk, masseur, babysitting. Complimentary cocktails. **Facilities:** 320 1 restaurant, 2 bars (1 w/entertainment), whirlpool, washer/dryer. 70 stores and 10 restaurants in Biltmore Fashion Park. **Rates (BB):** Peak (Jan–May) $215–$255 ste. Extra person $15. Children under age 12 stay free. Min stay special events. Lower rates off-season. Parking: Outdoor, free. AE, CB, DC, DISC, ER, MC, V.

Fairfield Inn

1241 N 53rd Ave, 85043; tel 602/269-1919 or toll free 800/228-2800; fax 602/269-1919. 51st Ave exit off I-10. Conveniently located, with easy freeway access. **Rooms:** 126 rms. CI 3pm/CO noon. Nonsmoking rms avail. All rooms have coded key-cards for security. **Amenities:** A/C, cable TV w/movies. **Services:** **Facilities:** 12 **Rates (CP):** Peak (Jan–mid-Apr) $73 S or D. Extra person $3–$6. Children under age 18 stay free. Lower rates off-season. Parking: Outdoor, free. AE, CB, DC, DISC, MC, V.

Fountain Suites

2577 W Greenway Rd, 85023 (Metrocenter); tel 602/375-1777 or toll free 800/338-1338; fax 602/375-1777 ext 5555. Greenway Rd off I-17. Spectacular landscaping. Large, airy lobby with lots of light. **Rooms:** 314 stes. CI 3pm/CO noon. Nonsmoking rms avail. The spacious, well-appointed rooms are a comfortable place to spend several days. **Amenities:** A/C, cable TV w/movies, refrig, dataport, voice mail, in-rm safe. Some units w/whirlpools. **Services:** Car-rental desk, children's program. **Facilities:** 2 300 1 restaurant, 1 bar, volleyball, racquetball, sauna, whirlpool, washer/dryer. Close to golf courses and horse racing. There's a very pleasant lounging area around the pool. **Rates:** Peak (Jan–Apr) $140 ste. Extra person $10. Children under age 18 stay free. Min stay special events. Lower rates off-season. AP and MAP rates avail. Parking: Outdoor, free. AE, CB, DC, DISC, ER, JCB, MC, V.

Hampton Inn Airport

4234 S 48th St, 85040; tel 602/428-8688 or toll free 800/HAMPTON; fax 602/431-8339. Exit 48th St off I-10. Easy airport access, good for business travelers. **Rooms:** 128 rms. CI 3pm/CO noon. Nonsmoking rms avail. **Amenities:** A/C, satel TV, VCR. **Services:** Free local calls and newspapers. **Facilities:** 50 1 restaurant, 1 bar, spa, whirlpool, washer/dryer. **Rates (CP):** Peak (Jan–Apr) $97–$117 S; $107–$127 D. Extra person $10. Children under age 18 stay free. Lower rates off-season. Parking: Outdoor, free. AE, DC, DISC, MC, V.

Holiday Inn

1500 N 51st Ave, 85043; tel 602/484-9009 or toll free 800/HOLIDAY; fax 602/484-9009 ext 505. 51st Ave exit off I-10. Conveniently located. Attractive atrium in the lobby. **Rooms:** 144 rms and stes. CI 2pm/CO noon. Nonsmoking rms avail. **Amenities:** A/C, satel TV w/movies. Some units w/minibars, some w/whirlpools. **Services:** **Facilities:** 250 1 restaurant, 1 bar, sauna, whirlpool. **Rates:** Peak (Jan–Apr) $139 S; $149 D; $150 ste. Extra person $10. Children under age 18 stay free. Lower rates off-season. Parking: Outdoor, free. Group rates avail. AE, DC, DISC, MC, V.

Holiday Inn Crowne Plaza

100 N 1st St, 85004 (Downtown); tel 602/257-1525 or toll free 800/359-7253; fax 602/253-9755. In the heart of downtown Phoenix, popular with convention attendees and

corporate travelers. **Rooms:** 532 rms and stes. Executive level. CI 4pm/CO noon. Nonsmoking rms avail. **Amenities:** A/C, satel TV w/movies. Some units w/minibars, some w/terraces. **Services:** **Facilities:** 1 restaurant, 2 bars, spa, sauna, beauty salon. Conveniently located for sports facilities. **Rates:** Peak (Nov–May) $159 S or D; $179 ste. Extra person $20. Children under age 18 stay free. Lower rates off-season. Parking: Indoor, $8/day. AE, CB, DC, DISC, MC, V.

Hyatt Regency Phoenix at Civic Plaza
122 N 2nd St, 85004 (Downtown); tel 602/252-1234 or toll free 800/223-1234; fax 602/254-9472. Popular with convention and business travelers, this Hyatt Regency claims to be the largest hotel in Arizona. **Rooms:** 712 rms and stes. Executive level. CI 3pm/CO noon. Nonsmoking rms avail. **Amenities:** A/C, satel TV w/movies, voice mail. Some units w/minibars, some w/terraces. **Services:** Car-rental desk, babysitting. **Facilities:** 2 restaurants, 2 bars, spa, whirlpool, beauty salon. The Compass Rose is a rooftop, revolving restaurant. The hotel is close to golf, tennis, and horseback riding. **Rates:** Peak (Jan–Apr) $175–$190 S; $200–$215 D; $350 ste. Extra person $25. Children under age 18 stay free. Lower rates off-season. Parking: Indoor, $6/day. AE, CB, DC, DISC, JCB, MC, V.

InnSuites Phoenix Best Western
1615 E Northern Ave, 85020; tel 602/997-6285 or toll free 800/752-2204; fax 602/943-1407. ¾ mi N of Glendale Ave. A lovely property nestled in Phoenix's Squaw Peak Mountain Preserve resort area. **Rooms:** 123 rms and stes. Executive level. CI 2pm/CO noon. Nonsmoking rms avail. Standard rooms, studio suites, and two-room suites available. **Amenities:** A/C, satel TV w/movies, refrig, dataport, voice mail. Some units w/whirlpools. All units have microwaves, free juices, and in-room coffee, tea, and microwave popcorn. King rooms have sofa sleepers. **Services:** Babysitting. Complimentary cocktails daily 5–6:30pm; free newspapers. Local calls are free, as is fax service within the United States. 24-hour front desk. **Facilities:** Whirlpool, playground, washer/dryer. Barbecue. **Rates (CP):** Peak (Jan–Apr) $119 S or D; $119–$189 ste. Children under age 18 stay free. Min stay special events. Lower rates off-season. Parking: Outdoor, free. AE, CB, DC, DISC, JCB, MC, V.

Lexington Hotel and City Square Sports Club
100 W Clarendon Ave, 85013; tel 602/279-9811 or toll free 800/53-SUITE; fax 602/631-9358. Exit 7th St off I-10. This midtown property is within walking distance of museums and other attractions. **Rooms:** 180 rms. CI 3pm/CO 11am. Nonsmoking rms avail. **Amenities:** A/C, cable TV, refrig. Some units w/minibars, some w/terraces. **Services:** Masseur. **Facilities:** 1 restaurant, 1 bar, racquetball, spa, sauna, steam rm, whirlpool, beauty salon. Use of adjacent health club included in rates. **Rates:** Peak (Mid-Jan–Apr) $109 S or D. Extra person $7. Children under age 18 stay free. Lower rates off-season. Parking: Indoor, free. AE, CB, DC, DISC, MC, V.

Marriott Residence Inn
8242 N Black Canyon Hwy, 85051 (Metrocenter); tel 602/864-1900 or toll free 800/331-3131; fax 602/995-8251. Dunlap Ave exit off I-17. Good freeway access. Popular for extended stays. **Rooms:** 128 stes. CI 3pm/CO noon. Nonsmoking rms avail. All suites have full-sized kitchens with appliances. **Amenities:** A/C, cable TV w/movies, refrig, dataport. Some units w/terraces, some w/fireplaces. VCR rentals available. **Services:** Social director, children's program, babysitting. Airport transportation free with four-day stay. Free shuttle for grocery shopping. Hospitality hour (Mon–Thurs) with soft drinks, beer, wine, and snacks. **Facilities:** Volleyball, lawn games, whirlpool, washer/dryer. Basketball and tennis available on a "sports court." Free daily membership to nearby fitness center. **Rates (CP):** Peak (Jan–May) $170–$215 ste. Children under age 18 stay free. Min stay special events. Lower rates off-season. Parking: Outdoor, free. AE, CB, DC, DISC, ER, JCB, MC, V.

Phoenix Hilton Suites
10 E Thomas Rd, 85012; tel 602/222-1111 or toll free 800/445-8667; fax 602/265-4811. Exit 7th St N off I-10. An all-suite hotel, especially attractive to business travelers. Suites surround central atrium with glass elevator. **Rooms:** 226 stes. Executive level. CI 3pm/CO noon. Nonsmoking rms avail. All rooms have sofabeds and dining tables. **Amenities:** A/C, cable TV, refrig, dataport, VCR, voice mail, bathrobes. Some units w/terraces. All units have microwaves. **Services:** Children's program, babysitting. Free photocopier, personal computer, and fax services within the United States. Complimentary beverage nightly 5:30–7:30pm. **Facilities:** 1 restaurant, 1 bar, games rm, sauna, whirlpool, washer/dryer. **Rates (BB):** Peak (Jan–May) $189–$195 ste. Extra person $15. Children under age 18 stay free. Min stay special events. Lower rates off-season. Parking: Indoor, free. Children stay free with parents. AE, CB, DC, DISC, ER, JCB, MC, V.

Premier Inn
10402 Black Canyon Hwy, 85051 (Metrocenter); tel 602/943-2371 or toll free 800/786-6835; fax 602/943-5847. Peoria exit off I-17. A good choice for those who like to shop, located in one of the Southwest's largest malls. Also close to almost 40 restaurants and several golf courses. **Rooms:** 252 rms and stes. Executive level. CI 3pm/CO noon. Nonsmoking rms avail. Rooms are clean, comfortable, and spacious. **Amenities:** A/C, satel TV. Some units w/terraces. Special business traveler rooms have extra-large work areas, refrigerators, and coffeemakers. **Services:** **Facilities:** Whirlpool, washer/dryer. **Rates:** Peak (Jan–Apr)

$64–$84 S or D; $129 ste. Extra person $6. Children under age 12 stay free. Min stay special events. Lower rates off-season. Parking: Outdoor, free. AE, CB, DC, DISC, MC, V.

Quality Inn South Mountain
5121 E LaPuente Ave, 85044; tel 602/893-3900 or toll free 800/562-3332; fax 602/496-0815. Elliot Rd exit off I-10. Comfortable and quiet, with good freeway access. Close to the airport, Tempe, and Mesa. **Rooms:** 193 rms and stes. CI 3pm/CO noon. Nonsmoking rms avail. **Amenities:** A/C, cable TV w/movies. Some units w/minibars. Microwaves and refrigerators available. **Services:** **Facilities:** 175 1 restaurant (bkfst and dinner only), 1 bar, whirlpool, washer/dryer. There are 5 golf courses within 5 miles. **Rates:** Peak (Dec–Apr) $109–$129 S; $119–$129 D; $129–$149 ste. Extra person $5. Children under age 16 stay free. Lower rates off-season. Parking: Outdoor, free. Discounts available for seniors and tours. AE, CB, DC, ER, JCB, MC, V.

Radisson Hotel Midtown
401 W Clarendon Ave, 85013; tel 602/234-2464 or toll free 800/333-3333. This is an older midtown hotel with a small but attractive lobby. **Rooms:** 106 rms and stes. CI 3pm/CO noon. Nonsmoking rms avail. **Amenities:** A/C, cable TV. All 37 suites have two telephones and a stocked minibar. **Services:** **Facilities:** 75 1 restaurant, 1 bar, whirlpool. **Rates (CP):** Peak (mid-Jan–Apr) $99–$120 S or D; $110–$125 ste. Extra person $10. Children under age 17 stay free. Lower rates off-season. Parking: Outdoor, free. AE, DC, DISC, MC, V.

Ramada Hotel Downtown
401 N 1st St, 85004; tel 602/258-3411 or toll free 800/2-RAMADA; fax 602/258-3171. Downtown hotel with good access to the convention center, Symphony Hall, and America West Arena. **Rooms:** 160 rms. CI 3pm/CO noon. Nonsmoking rms avail. Some rooms have a view of the pool. **Amenities:** A/C, cable TV. Some units w/terraces. **Services:** **Facilities:** 300 1 restaurant, 1 bar (w/entertainment). **Rates:** Peak (Jan 15–Apr 15) $79–$105 S or D. Extra person $10. Children under age 18 stay free. Lower rates off-season. Parking: Outdoor, free. AE, CB, DC, DISC, MC, V.

The Ritz-Carlton Phoenix
2401 E Camelback Rd, 85016 (Biltmore); tel 602/468-0700 or toll free 800/241-3333; fax 602/468-9883. Camelback Rd exit off I-17. In a city of resort hotels, this is 11 floors of no-nonsense, businesslike luxury, with only a pool, fitness center, and one tennis court. Close to major commercial center. **Rooms:** 281 rms and stes. Executive level. CI 3pm/CO noon. Nonsmoking rms avail. All the usual Ritz-Carlton refinements, including Italian marble bathrooms; but even in a climate where temperatures climb over 100°F, many guests might prefer windows that can be opened. **Amenities:** A/C, cable TV w/movies, in-rm safe, bathrobes. All units w/minibars, 1 w/fireplace, some w/whirlpools. Small closets, dataports, and two phones indicate that most guests are executives on overnight stays. Rosenthal china for room service. VCRs available. **Services:** Twice-daily maid svce, car-rental desk, masseur, babysitting. Smart, efficient, obliging staff. **Facilities:** 700 2 restaurants (*see* "Restaurants" below), 2 bars (1 w/entertainment), steam rm, washer/dryer. Second-floor sports roof with attractive pool, and poolside service; sun deck cooled by misting system. Complimentary transportation to nearby golf courses. Dancing with dinner in elegant Grill Room. **Rates:** Peak (Jan–May) $195–$250 S or D; $250–$375 ste. Children under age 18 stay free. Min stay special events. Lower rates off-season. Parking: Outdoor, $10/day. A bargain compared with the nearby resorts, and summer rates give everyone a chance to sample Ritz-Carlton swank. AE, CB, DC, DISC, JCB, MC, V.

Wyndham Metrocenter Hotel
10220 N Metro Pkwy E, 85021 (Metrocenter); tel 602/997-5900 or toll free 800/858-1033; fax 602/943-6156. Peoria Ave exit off I-17. Convenient to the freeway and Metrocenter, with 200 stores, 37 restaurants, and 17 theaters. **Rooms:** 284 rms and stes. Executive level. CI 3pm/CO noon. Nonsmoking rms avail. **Amenities:** A/C, cable TV w/movies, dataport. Some units w/terraces. **Services:** Car-rental desk, masseur, babysitting. **Facilities:** 500 1 restaurant, 1 bar (w/entertainment), sauna, steam rm, whirlpool. Golf nearby. **Rates (CP):** Peak (Jan–Apr) $78–$155 S or D; $349 ste. Extra person $10. Children under age 12 stay free. Min stay special events. Lower rates off-season. Parking: Outdoor, free. AE, CB, DC, DISC, ER, JCB, MC, V.

MOTELS

Hampton Inn
8101 N Black Canyon Hwy, 85021; tel 602/864-6233 or toll free 800/HAMPTON; fax 602/995-7503. Northern Ave exit off I-17. **Rooms:** 149 rms. CI 3pm/CO noon. Nonsmoking rms avail. Rooms are pleasant, comfortable, and quiet. **Amenities:** A/C, cable TV w/movies, dataport. **Services:** **Facilities:** 30 Whirlpool. Good family restaurant next door serves three meals daily. **Rates (CP):** Peak (Jan–Apr) $86–$100 S or D. Children under age 18 stay free. Min stay special events. Lower rates off-season. Parking: Outdoor, free. AE, CB, DC, DISC, MC, V.

La Quinta Inn
2510 W Greenway Rd, 85023 (Metrocenter); tel 602/993-0800 or toll free 800/531-5900; fax 602/789-9172. Greenway Rd exit off I-17. A good, basic motel for those who want to be on the north side of Phoenix. **Rooms:** 145 rms and stes. CI 3pm/CO noon. Nonsmoking rms avail. Comfortable rooms are attractively furnished. **Amenities:** A/C, cable TV w/movies, dataport. **Services:** Babysitting. **Facilities:** 200 1 bar, sauna, washer/dryer. Golf pro on premises. Complimentary pass to nearby fitness

center. **Rates (CP):** Peak (Jan–Apr) $95–$105 S or D; $165 ste. Extra person $10. Min stay special events. Lower rates off-season. Parking: Outdoor, free. AE, CB, DC, DISC, MC, V.

Travelodge Metrocenter
8617 N Black Canyon Hwy, 85021 (Metrocenter); tel 602/995-9500 or toll free 800/578-7878; fax 602/995-0150. Northern Ave exit off I-17. Close to the freeway and Metrocenter Mall. **Rooms:** 180 rms. CI 3pm/CO noon. Nonsmoking rms avail. **Amenities:** A/C, satel TV w/movies. **Services:** Free shuttle to the Metrocenter Mall. **Facilities:** Whirlpool, washer/dryer. **Rates (CP):** Peak (Jan–May) $60 S; $70 D. Extra person $7. Children under age 17 stay free. Lower rates off-season. Parking: Outdoor, free. AE, DISC, MC, V.

RESORTS

Arizona Biltmore
24th St and Missouri Ave, 85016; tel 602/955-6600 or toll free 800/950-0086; fax 602/381-7646. Camelback Rd exit off I-17. E on Camelback to 24th St then left to Missouri Ave. 39 acres. A multimillion-dollar renovation has enhanced the 65-year-old resort's one-of-a-kind architecture and appointments, inspired by Frank Lloyd Wright. New accommodations, completed in early 1995, are in keeping with the original style and ambience. **Rooms:** 500 rms and stes; 16 cottages/villas. Executive level. CI 3pm/CO noon. Nonsmoking rms avail. Deployed in four-story wings around main low-rise building, newly renovated to re-create the 1920s character of the resort's debut. Art deco styling gives them a special charm. Many patios face other patios (corner rooms on the fourth floor have extra-large terraces with more privacy). **Amenities:** A/C, cable TV w/movies, dataport, voice mail, bathrobes. All units w/minibars, some w/terraces, some w/fireplaces. Bathrobes and two-line phones provided on request. Energy-saving sensors adjust heat and air conditioning. **Services:** VP Twice-daily maid svce, car-rental desk, social director, masseur, children's program, babysitting. Turndown service on request. Regular shuttle to Biltmore Fashion Park. **Facilities:** 36 8 3000 3 restaurants (*see* "Restaurants" below), 2 bars (1 w/entertainment), basketball, volleyball, games rm, lawn games, spa, sauna, steam rm, whirlpool, beauty salon, day-care ctr, playground. The original Catalina pool has been relegated to the status of adjunct to a new $4 million, five-pool complex with waterslide, swim-up bar, and poolside cabanas with TV and phones. Athletic Club, tennis, and golf shared with 5,000 local members. **Rates:** Peak (Jan–Apr) $315–$420 S or D; $520 ste; $520 cottage/villa. Children under age 18 stay free. Lower rates off-season. AP and MAP rates avail. Parking: Outdoor, free. Cabanas cost an additional $30 to $150 a day. Incidental services fee of $4 added daily to include admission to health and fitness center and cover unlimited local phone calls and long-distance access. AE, CB, DC, DISC, EC, ER, JCB, MC, V.

Hermosa Inn
5532 N Palo Cristi Rd, 85253 (Paradise Valley); tel 602/955-8614 or toll free 800/241-1210; fax 602/955-8299. 6 acres. A unique resort, built in 1930 as the home of cowboy artist Lon Megargee. The lodge was rebuilt in 1994 after a fire. **Rooms:** 35 rms and stes; 4 cottages/villas. CI 3pm/CO noon. No smoking. There are a variety of individually decorated accommodations, from suites to casitas and villas, and many have kitchenettes or full kitchens. **Amenities:** A/C, cable TV, refrig. All units w/terraces, some w/fireplaces, some w/whirlpools. **Services:** **Facilities:** 3 110 1 restaurant, 1 bar, spa, whirlpool, washer/dryer. There's a barbecue on the grounds. **Rates:** Peak (Jan 14–Apr 17) $100–$130 S or D; $190 ste; $250 cottage/villa. Lower rates off-season. Parking: Outdoor, free. Weekly and monthly rates are available. AE, DC, DISC, MC, V.

The Pointe Hilton at Squaw Peak
7677 N 16th St, 85020; tel 602/997-2626 or toll free 800/876-4683; fax 602/943-4633. 300 acres. Another of Phoenix's plush Hilton resorts. **Rooms:** 497 stes; 78 cottages/villas. Executive level. CI 4pm/CO noon. Nonsmoking rms avail. Rooms are comfortable and well appointed. **Amenities:** A/C, cable TV w/movies, refrig, dataport, voice mail, bathrobes. All units w/minibars, all w/terraces, some w/fireplaces, 1 w/whirlpool. **Services:** Twice-daily maid svce, car-rental desk, social director, masseur, children's program, babysitting. Security guards patrol 24 hours. Pick-up and drop-off for horseback riding; hiking on nearby Squaw Peak. **Facilities:** 18 4 1000 3 restaurants, 6 bars (2 w/entertainment), volleyball, games rm, spa, sauna, steam rm, whirlpool, beauty salon, day-care ctr, playground, washer/dryer. Main swimming pool is flanked by swimming lagoon and man-made river for floating. **Rates:** Peak (Jan–May) $235–$265 ste; $350–$395 cottage/villa. Extra person $15. Children under age 18 stay free. Min stay special events. Lower rates off-season. Parking: Outdoor, free. Breakfast plan available. AE, CB, DC, DISC, ER, JCB, MC, V.

The Pointe Hilton at Tapatio Cliffs
11111 N 7th St, 85020 (North Phoenix); tel 602/866-7500 or toll free 800/876-4683; fax 602/993-0276. 2 mi N of Dunlap Ave. 650 acres. A large, plush resort on the side of Phoenix's North Mountain. Caters to both leisure and business travelers. **Rooms:** 585 stes. CI 4pm/CO noon. Nonsmoking rms avail. Rooms are comfortable and attractively furnished. **Amenities:** A/C, cable TV w/movies. All units w/minibars, all w/terraces, some w/fireplaces, some w/whirlpools. **Services:** Car-rental desk, social director, masseur, children's program, babysitting. Complimentary cocktails. **Facilities:** 18 15 1000 3 restaurants, 4 bars (2 w/entertainment), spa, sauna,

steam rm, whirlpool, beauty salon, day-care ctr, washer/dryer. **Rates (CP):** Peak (Jan–mid-May) $275 ste. Extra person $15. Children under age 18 stay free. Lower rates off-season. AP rates avail. Parking: Outdoor, free. AE, DC, DISC, MC, V.

The Pointe Hilton Resort on South Mountain
7777 S Pointe Pkwy, 85044; tel 602/438-9000 or toll free 800/572-7222; fax 602/431-6528. Baseline Rd exit off I-10. 700 acres. A large, luxurious resort, popular for conventions. **Rooms:** 638 stes. Executive level. CI 4pm/CO noon. Nonsmoking rms avail. **Amenities:** A/C, cable TV w/movies, dataport, voice mail. All units w/minibars, all w/terraces. **Services:** Twice-daily maid svce, car-rental desk, social director, masseur, children's program, babysitting. Complimentary cocktails are served daily from 4:30 to 6pm. Daily mall shuttle and 24-hour transportation around the resort. Free newspaper. **Facilities:** 18 10 2500 5 restaurants (*see* "Restaurants" below), 6 bars (3 w/entertainment), basketball, volleyball, lawn games, racquetball, spa, sauna, steam rm, whirlpool, beauty salon, day-care ctr, playground, washer/dryer. On-premise sports bar. Hiking and horseback riding available on adjacent South Mountain Preserve. **Rates:** Peak (Jan–May) $235–$285 ste. Extra person $15. Children under age 18 stay free. Min stay special events. Lower rates off-season. Parking: Outdoor, free. AE, CB, DC, DISC, ER, JCB, MC, V.

RESTAURANTS

Bistro
In the Biltmore Financial Center, 2398 E Camelback Rd, Suite 220 (Biltmore); tel 602/957-3214. **New American.** One of the most popular restaurants in Phoenix, this is a less formal version of Christopher's next door (see below), with the same owner/chef. As the name suggests, it is a bistro-style eatery, with tile floors and a marble bar. Innovative dinner specialties include braised lamb shank with lentils and wheatberries, and shallot steak with red wine sauce and pommes frites. Seafood dishes include ahi tuna, scallops, and grilled halibut. **FYI:** Reservations recommended. **Open:** Mon–Sat 11am–10:30pm, Sun 5–10:30pm. **Prices:** Main courses $16–$23. AE, CB, DC, DISC, MC, V. VP

Christopher's
In the Biltmore Financial Center, 2398 E Camelback Rd, Suite 180 (Biltmore); tel 602/957-3214. **French.** Considered by many to be Phoenix's premier dining experience, Christopher's has a small, elegant dining room with original country scenes and still-lifes on cream walls above wood-panelled wainscoting. A special appetizer is the house smoked salmon with ahi tuna and caviar. Dinner specialties include salad of foie gras with yams, smoked squab with tarragon and quinoa, and sautéed lamb with fried basil and curried potatoes. There's also a selection of tantalizing desserts. **FYI:** Reservations recommended. Jacket required. No smoking. **Open:** Tues–Sun 6–10pm. **Prices:** Main courses $29; prix fixe $70. AE, CB, DC, MC, V. VP

Christo's
6327 N 7th St (Midtown); tel 602/264-1784. **Continental/Italian.** A bright, modern restaurant with a sophisticated atmosphere. Art deco–style prints adorn the walls. Northern Italian cooking is the order of the day, with such specialties as scampi Christo's and shrimp Florentine. **FYI:** Reservations recommended. No smoking. **Open:** Lunch Mon–Fri 11:30am–2:30pm; dinner Mon–Sat 5:30–10pm. **Prices:** Main courses $9–$20. AE, DC, DISC, MC, V.

★ Ed Debevic's
2102 E Highland Ave; tel 602/956-2760. **American.** A trendy, 1950s-style diner where the waitresses dance with and for patrons. Sandwiches, hamburgers, and hot dogs are the main fare, but plates such as Ed's Mom's meatloaf, macaroni and cheese, and homemade pot roast are also offered. **FYI:** Reservations not accepted. Children's menu. No smoking. **Open:** Sun–Thurs 11am–9pm, Fri–Sat 11am–10pm. **Prices:** Main courses $4–$7. AE, DC, DISC, MC, V.

★ The Fish Market
1720 E Camelback Rd (East Phoenix); tel 602/277-FISH. **Pizza/Seafood.** A large seafood restaurant in a fashionable part of Phoenix, it's actually two restaurants in one: the simple downstairs restaurant with a sushi bar, and the fancier Top of the Market upstairs, open for dinner only (from 5 pm). A retail fish market also operates downstairs and provides the place with a "working" feel. Selections include mesquite-charbroiled fish, plus blackened, grilled, and fried fish. There are also pasta and seafood dishes. **FYI:** Reservations recommended. Children's menu. **Open:** Mon–Thurs 11am–9:30pm, Fri–Sat 11am–10pm, Sun noon–9:30pm. **Prices:** Main courses $7–$33. AE, CB, DC, DISC, MC, V.

$ Garcia's
4420 E Camelback Rd (Arcadia); tel 602/952-8031. **Mexican.** This large eatery offers basic Mexican fare: enchiladas, burritos, and chile rellenos, plus Olivia's Sampler, with mini tacos, flautas, chimichangas, and refried beans. **FYI:** Reservations accepted. Children's menu. Additional locations: 5509 N 7th St (tel 274-1176); 3301 W Peoria Ave (tel 886-1850). **Open:** Sun–Thurs 11am–10pm, Fri–Sat 11am–11pm. **Prices:** Main courses $5–$12; prix fixe $7–$12. AE, CB, DC, DISC, MC, V.

Gourmet House of Hong Kong
1438 E McDowell Rd (Midtown); tel 602/253-4859. **Chinese.** Basic Chinese food in a no-frills, diner atmosphere. Large variety of Canton/Hong Kong–style Chinese food. House specialties include orange-flavored duck, and scallops with ginger and onion. **FYI:** Reservations accepted. No liquor license. **Open:** Sun–Thurs 11am–10pm, Fri–Sat 11am–11pm. **Prices:** Main courses $5–$11. AE, MC, V.

Greekfest
In Greekfest Center, 1940 E Camelback Rd (Midtown); tel 602/265-2990. At 20th St. **Greek.** Archways, white-washed walls, Greek plates and artwork, and wood-beam ceiling give the feel of the Greek island of Chios, childhood home of owner-chef Tony Makridis. The menu is educational and enlightening, with detailed descriptions. Hot and cold appetizers and salads, mezethes, casseroles, souvlaki. **FYI:** Reservations recommended. **Open:** Lunch Mon–Sat 11am–2:30pm; dinner Mon–Thurs 5–10pm, Fri–Sat 5–11pm, Sun 5–9pm. **Prices:** Main courses $7–$18. AE, DC, DISC, MC, V.

The Grill
In the Ritz-Carlton Phoenix, 2401 E Camelback Rd (Biltmore); tel 602/468-0700. **American.** Fine dining in an English gentleman's club setting. Marble fireplace in the lounge, marble bar, soft chandelier lighting, dark paneling. Entrees include roast Colorado lamb (carved tableside), roast prime rib, veal chop, range chicken, Dover sole, Norwegian salmon, and yellowtail snapper. **FYI:** Reservations recommended. Piano. Children's menu. Jacket required. **Open:** Peak (Sept–May) daily 6–10:30pm. **Prices:** Main courses $10–$28. AE, CB, DC, DISC, MC, V. VP

Havana Cafe
4225 E Camelback Rd (East Phoenix); tel 602/952-1991. At 44th St. **Cuban/Spanish.** A small, cozy, yet modern cafe, popular with the Latino community and all lovers of Caribbean and Spanish food. Specialties include masas de puerco fritas, containing pork seasoned with a lime-cumin marinade and fried to a golden brown; pollo chilendron, boneless chicken sautéed with pork, onions, pimientos, herbs, white wine, and artichoke hearts; and zarzuela de mariscos, a medley of seafood in a spicy fresh tomato sauce. **FYI:** Reservations not accepted. No smoking. Additional location: 6245 E Bell Rd (tel 991-1496). **Open:** Mon–Sat 11:30am–10pm, Sun 4–9pm. **Prices:** Main courses $8–$23. AE, CB, DC, DISC, MC, V.

Houston's
In the Camelback Esplanade, 2425 E Camelback Rd (Biltmore); tel 602/957-9700. **New American.** Very comfortable restaurant with a Southwestern look. Tables have lamps, and the leather booths have sconce lighting. Offering unusual pizzas, burgers, salads, fish, chicken, beef, and ribs. **FYI:** Reservations not accepted. No smoking. Additional location: 6113 N Scottsdale Rd, Scottsdale (tel 922-7775). **Open:** Mon–Thurs 11am–11pm, Fri–Sat 11am–midnight, Sun 11am–10pm. **Prices:** Main courses $7–$17. AE, MC, V.

Indian Delhi Palace
5050 E McDowell Rd (Midtown); tel 602/244-8181. **Indian.** Simple, busy Indian restaurant in a commercial area of Phoenix. Chef's specialties include murg makhani, tandoori chicken cooked in butter in tomato gravy; vegetable korma, mixed vegetables and nuts cooked in cream and delicately spiced; and lamb boti kebab masala, boneless tandoori lamb in tomatoes and buttered gravy. **FYI:** Reservations recommended. **Open:** Lunch Mon–Fri 11:30am–2:30pm, Sat–Sun 11:30am–4:30pm; dinner daily 5–10pm. **Prices:** Main courses $7–$14. AE, DISC, MC, V.

Los Dos Molinos
8646 S Central Ave (South Phoenix); tel 602/243-9113. 1 mi S of Baseline Rd. **Southwestern.** Small, busy dining room with tiled floor, Mexican artifacts, posters, chile wreaths, murals, old license plates, and piñatas. Chef Victoria Chavez's specialties include chimichangas, enchiladas, chile rellenos, and pork ribs marinated in red chile. **FYI:** Reservations not accepted. Guitar/Spanish. Additional location: 260 S Alma School Rd, Mesa (tel 835-5356). **Open:** Daily 11am–9pm. **Prices:** Main courses $6–$9. DISC, MC, V.

Matador Restaurant
125 E Adams St (Downtown); tel 602/254-7563. **American/Greek/Mexican.** A spacious downtown eatery, with a dining room lit by large street lamps and bullfight prints decorating the walls. In addition to standard Mexican fare, the menu offers steaks and Greek dishes. The green corn tamales are especially popular. **FYI:** Reservations accepted. Children's menu. **Open:** Daily 7am–11pm. **Prices:** Main courses $7–$18. AE, CB, DC, DISC, MC, V.

★ Mrs White's Golden Rule Cafe
808 E Jefferson St (Downtown); tel 602/262-9256. At S 8th St. **Soul/Southern.** A southern soul food diner. Chicken-fried steak, catfish, pork chops, and barbecue head the entrees. Okra gumbo is also served up. Desserts include peach cobbler, and apple, sweet potato, and pecan pies. **FYI:** Reservations not accepted. Children's menu. No liquor license. No smoking. **Open:** Mon–Fri 11am–7:30pm, Sat noon–8pm. **Prices:** Main courses $6–$10. No CC.

The Olive Garden
10223 N Metro Pkwy E (Metrocenter); tel 602/943-4573. Peoria exit off I-17. **Italian.** A busy Italian chain restaurant offering basic fare, including a variety of pastas and meat and seafood dishes. **FYI:** Reservations not accepted. Children's menu. **Open:** Daily 11am–10pm. **Prices:** Main courses $7–$14; prix fixe $10–$13. AE, CB, DC, DISC, ER, MC, V.

Remington's
In The Scottsdale Plaza Resort, 7200 N Scottsdale Rd (Paradise Valley); tel 602/948-5000. **Regional American.** Low light and plants contribute to the ambience of this lovely restaurant. Specialties include Texas mixed grill and adobe chicken. **FYI:** Reservations recommended. Jazz/piano. **Open:** Lunch Mon–Fri 11am–2:30pm; dinner daily 5–10pm. **Prices:** Main courses $18–$21. AE, CB, DC, DISC, MC, V.

($) The Restaurant at the Ritz-Carlton
In the Ritz-Carlton Phoenix, 2401 E Camelback Rd (Biltmore); tel 602/468-0700. Camelback exit off I-17; go east on Camelback to Biltmore Fashion Park and the Camelback

Esplanade. **American/Continental.** Mansion decor, with original paintings and well-spaced tables. Popular for lunch with executives from the neighboring offices and with shoppers from Biltmore Fashion Park across the street, it is one of the classiest settings in America for a $7.50 sandwich or $8.50 plate of pasta. For dinner, the Grill Room offers a more expensive menu and live music. Specialties offered: tortilla soup with mini smoked chicken tamale; seared chicken breast with asparagus and cream cheese baked in phyllo; southwestern caesar salad with tortilla-crusted chicken strips; caramelized papaya tart with Midori sabayon. **FYI:** Reservations recommended. Piano. Children's menu. Dress code. No smoking. **Open:** Breakfast daily 6:30–11:30am; lunch Mon–Sat 11:30am–2:30pm; brunch Sun 11am–2:30pm. **Prices:** Lunch main courses $13–$16. AE, DISC, MC, V. VP

Richardson's
1582 E Bethany Home Rd; tel 602/265-5886. At 16th St. **Southwestern.** A busy southwestern-style bar and grill. New Mexico decor features chile ristras and wreaths, Indian wall blankets, and adobe booths surrounding a horseshoe-shaped bar. Among the specialties are grilled pork chop stuffed with chorizo with cilantro chutney sauce, and Chimayo chicken stuffed with spinach, sun-dried tomatoes, poblano chile, and asiago cheese. Daily specials and desserts. **FYI:** Reservations not accepted. **Open:** Daily 11am–midnight. **Prices:** Main courses $9–$18. AE, DC, MC, V.

Roxsand
2594 E Camelback Rd (Biltmore); tel 602/381-0444. **Eclectic.** The modernistic, high-tech look features a two-tiered dining room, track lighting, hanging lamps, and a huge metal pineapple suspended from the ceiling. The "fusion" cuisine (a blending of foods from different cultures) includes grilled New York steak with "Texas chain saw" chili sauce, polenta cake, and grilled vegetables; and air-dried duck with Szechuan black bean sauce, "evil jungle prince" sauce, plum sauce, and moo shu pancakes. **FYI:** Reservations recommended. **Open:** Mon–Thurs 11am–10pm, Fri–Sat 11am–10:30pm, Sun 5–9:30pm. **Prices:** Main courses $9–$24; prix fixe $15–$30. AE, DC, MC, V.

Rustler's Rooste
In the Pointe Hilton Resort on South Mountain, 7777 S Pointe Pkwy; tel 602/431-6474. Baseline Rd exit off I-10. **Southwestern/Steak.** A fun-filled raucous steak house: buffalo heads on the walls, sawdust on the floor, and a longhorn steer in a pen outside the entrance. There's a slide from the upstairs bar to the downstairs dining room for patrons' use. Beef is the chief offering, but the menu also includes mesquite-grilled catfish, marinated broiled swordfish, jumbo shrimp, barbecued or southern fried chicken, and even a vegetarian plate. Appetizers include deep-fried rattlesnake. A light menu is served until 11pm in the lounge. **FYI:** Reservations recommended. Big band. Children's menu. **Open:** Peak (Dec–Apr) Sun–Thurs 5–10pm, Fri–Sat 5–11pm. **Prices:** Main courses $9–$22. AE, DC, DISC, ER, MC, V. VP

The Rusty Pelican
9801 N Black Canyon Hwy (Metrocenter); tel 602/944-9646. Exit Dunlap off I-17. **Seafood/Steak.** Fresh fish dominates the menu, with many charbroiled specialties. Boat at anchor alongside dining room. **FYI:** Reservations recommended. Children's menu. Additional location: 1606 W Baseline Rd, Tempe (tel 345-0972). **Open:** Daily 11am–10pm. **Prices:** Main courses $12–$20. AE, CB, DC, DISC, MC, V.

Sam's Cafe
In Biltmore Fashion Park, 2566 E Camelback Rd, Suite 201; tel 602/954-7100. **Southwestern.** Located in a popular Phoenix mall. Decorated in Southwestern style with open beams and stucco walls. Selection of salads, pastas, and sandwiches, plus Southwestern fare including tamales, quesadillas, burritos, and tacos. Entrees may include chile-rubbed tuna and blue corn–fried catfish. **FYI:** Reservations recommended. Children's menu. No smoking. **Open:** Sun–Thurs 11am–10pm, Fri–Sat 11am–11pm. **Prices:** Main courses $10–$17; prix fixe $11–$20. AE, DC, DISC, MC, V.

Shogun
In Abco Shopping Center, 12615 N Tatum Blvd; tel 602/953-3264. At Cactus Rd. **Japanese.** A small, simple establishment with Japanese prints on the walls and wooden-shaded lamps hanging over the booths. Traditional Japanese fare, along with interesting appetizers such as ika panko, deep-fried, breaded squid strips. House specialties include tempura Alaskan codfish, chicken, and shrimp, all with tempura vegetables. Sushi bar. **FYI:** Reservations accepted. Beer and wine only. No smoking. **Open:** Lunch Mon–Sat 11am–2:30pm; dinner Mon 5–9pm, Tues–Sat 5–10pm. **Prices:** Main courses $8–$24. AE, CB, DC, DISC, MC, V.

Sing High Chop Suey House
27 W Madison (Downtown); tel 602/253-7848. **Chinese.** Specializes in Cantonese dishes. **FYI:** Reservations accepted. Children's menu. No liquor license. **Open:** Mon–Thurs 11am–9pm, Fri–Sat noon–11pm, Sun noon–9pm. **Prices:** Main courses $6–$10. AE, CB, DC, MC, V.

Steamer's Genuine Seafood
In Biltmore Fashion Park, 2576 E Camelback Rd (Biltmore); tel 602/956-3631. **Seafood.** A popular place for seafood. Extensive selection, including live Maine lobster. Smoking is allowed only in the bar. **FYI:** Reservations recommended. Children's menu. No smoking. **Open:** Mon–Thurs 11am–10pm, Fri–Sat 11am–11pm, Sun noon–10pm. **Prices:** Main courses $15–$25. AE, DC, DISC, MC, V. VP

Vincent Guerithault on Camelback
3930 E Camelback Rd; tel 602/224-0225. **Southwestern.** Decorated in French country style, with open beams, fresh and dried flower arrangements, arched windows, and still life studies on the walls. The large selection of appetizers includes spinach salad with wild boar bacon, and duck tamale with Anaheim green chile. Entrees are prepared with a southwest-

ern touch. **FYI:** Reservations recommended. **Open:** Lunch Mon–Fri 11:30am–2:30pm; dinner Sun–Fri 6–10:30pm, Sat 5:30–10:30pm. **Prices:** Main courses $20–$23. AE, DC, MC, V.

Wright's
In Arizona Biltmore, 24th St and Missouri; tel 602/955-6600. Camelback exit off I-17, E to 24th. **New American.** Fine dining in a setting of unique ambience. Intriguing art deco walls and spectacular chandeliers; contemporary southwestern art; an entire wall of conservatory-style windows. Knowledgeable wait staff in white tuxedos. The refined cuisine, served on Royal Doulton china, features seared scallops and roasted eggplant ravioli; butter-browned baby turbot with quinoa and braised fennel; cherry wood–smoked roast loin of venison with truffle-herb spaetzle; and warm apple tart with marionberry ice cream. 8,000-bottle wine cellar. **FYI:** Reservations recommended. No smoking. **Open:** Breakfast Mon–Fri 7–11am; lunch Mon–Fri 11am–2:30pm; dinner daily 6–10pm; brunch Sun 10am–2:30pm. **Prices:** Main courses $18–$33. AE, CB, DC, DISC, ER, MC, V.

ATTRACTIONS

MUSEUMS

Heard Museum
22 E Monte Vista Rd; tel 602/252-8848. One of the finest museums in the country that deals exclusively with Native American cultures. "Native Peoples of the Southwest" is an extensive exhibit that explores the culture of each of the major tribes of the region. "Our Voices, Our Land" is an audiovisual presentation in which contemporary Native Americans express their thoughts on their heritage. "Old Ways, New Ways" is an interactive exhibit where visitors can build a miniature tipi, step inside a Northwest Coast longhouse, or add designs to Zuni pottery. On weekends there are often artist demonstrations and performances by singers and dancers. The biggest event of the year is the **Annual Guild Indian Fair and Market**, which is held on the first weekend in March. Guided tours daily. **Open:** Mon–Sat 9:30am–5pm, Sun noon–5pm. **$$**

Phoenix Art Museum
1625 N Central Ave; tel 602/257-1222. The largest art museum in the Southwest, with a collection that spans the major artistic movements from the Renaissance to the present. The modern and contemporary art includes works by Diego Rivera, Frida Kahlo, Pablo Picasso, Karel Appel, Willem de Kooning, Henri Rousseau, Georgia O'Keeffe, and Auguste Rodin. The Thorne Miniature Collection is one of the museum's most popular exhibits and consists of tiny, exquisitely detailed rooms on a scale of 1 inch to 1 foot. **Open:** Tues and Thurs–Sat 10am–5pm, Wed 10am–9pm, Sun noon–5pm. **$$**

Arizona Museum of Science and Technology
600 E Washington St; tel 602/716-2000. The hands-on museum has more than 100 interactive exhibits on subjects such as psychology, weather, the human body, and aviation. In addition, visitors can travel to space via a state-of-the-art planetarium and large screen theater. **Open:** Mon–Sat 9am–5pm, Sun noon–5pm. **$$$**

Gila River Arts and Crafts Center
Exit 175 off I-10; tel 602/963-3981. Located on the Gila River Indian Reservation, the center provides visitors with an opportunity to learn more about the history and culture of the tribes that inhabit this region of the Arizona desert. In Heritage Park, there are replicas of villages of five different tribes, the Tohono O'odham, Pima, Maricopa, Apache, and Hohokam. Inside the museum there are historical photos, artifacts, and an excellent collection of Pima baskets. Other exhibits tell the story of the Gila River Basin. **Open:** Daily 8am–5pm. **Free**

Pueblo Grande Museum and Cultural Park
4619 E Washington St; tel 602/495-0900. The ruins of an ancient Hohokam tribal village, one of several villages located along the Salt River between AD 300 and 1400. Sometime around 1450, this and other villages were mysteriously abandoned. Small museum. **Open:** Mon–Sat 9am–4:45pm, Sun 1–4:45pm. **$**

Hall of Flame Firefighting Museum
6101 E Van Buren St; tel 602/275-3473. The world's largest firefighting museum. There are more than 90 vintage fire engines on display dating from 1725 to 1961. **Open:** Mon–Sat 9am–5pm, Sun noon–4pm. **$$**

HISTORIC BUILDINGS AND HOMES

Heritage Square
115 N 6th St; tel 602/262-5029. A collection of some of the few remaining houses in Phoenix that date to the last century and the original Phoenix townsite. All the buildings are listed on the National Register and most display Victorian architectural styles popular just before the turn of the century. Among the buildings located here are the ornate **Rosson House,** which is open for tours; the **Silva House,** a neoclassical-revival-style home that now houses historical exhibits on water and electricity use in the Valley of the Sun; the **Carriage House**; and the **Bouvier-Teeter House.** Also located here is the **Arizona Doll and Toy Museum**. Inside is a reproduction of a 1912 schoolroom in which all the children are antique dolls. Closed Aug. **Open:** Tues 1–4pm, Wed–Sat 10am–4pm, Sun noon–4pm. **$**

Pioneer Arizona Living History Museum
Pioneer Rd exit off I-17; tel 602/993-0212. A living-history museum with 28 original and reconstructed buildings from the 1890s. Costumed guides practice traditional pioneer occupations and create 19th-century crafts. The old Opera House hosts live melodramas every weekend. Each year in

October there are Civil War battle reenactments and a gathering of modern mountain men. **Open:** Oct–June; call ahead for hours. **$$$**

Arizona State Capitol Museum
1700 W Washington St; tel 602/542-4675. The former state capitol has recently been restored to its original 1912 appearance. Among the rooms on view are the Senate and House chambers, as well as the governor's office and historical exhbits. **Open:** Mon–Fri 8am–5pm, Sat 10am–3pm. **Free**

Arizona Biltmore
24th St and Missouri; tel toll free 800/950-0086. A landmark for 65 years, the resort's design was inspired by architect Frank Lloyd Wright, who collaborated with Albert Chase McArthur. One of the architectural points to look for is the detailed, patterned concrete blocks used in the building's structure. These were the first incidence of pre-cast concrete blocks in the history of architecture and are now known as Biltmore Blocks. All of the furnishings in the dining area are Wright-designed, as are several of the sculptures in the entrance and one of the stained-glass windows. Also see listing under "Resorts." **Free**

Mystery Castle
800 E Mineral Rd; tel 602/268-1581. A giant sand castle located on the edge of South Mountain Park, it was built over a period of 18 years by a single man for his daughter. The castle, which is on the National Historic Registry, contains 18 rooms, 13 fireplaces, and a small chapel where wedding ceremonies are often performed. **Open:** Oct–May, Tues–Sun 11am–4pm. **$$**

PARKS AND GARDENS

Desert Botanical Garden
1201 N Galvin Pkwy; tel 602/941-1225. Devoted exclusively to cacti and the more than 10,000 desert plants from all over the world that make their home here. The Plants and People of the Sonoran Desert trail explains the science of ethnobotany through interactive displays that demonstrate how the inhabitants of the Sonoran Desert once utilized wild and cultivated plants. **Open:** Peak (May–Sept) daily 7am–10pm. Reduced hours off-season. **$$$**

Phoenix Zoo
455 N Galvin Pkwy in Papago Park; tel 602/273-1341. Home to more than 1,300 animals, including 150 endangered or threatened birds, mammals, and reptiles from around the world. Each lives along one of five distinctive trails. Among the highlights are the Arizona Trail which features plants and animals of the American Southwest; the Africa Trail which presents meekrats, lions, and warthogs; the Children's Trail which brings young visitors together with a wide array of small mammals; and the Tropics Trail which highlights plants and animals from the rain forests of the world. **Open:** Peak (May–Labor Day) daily 7am–4pm. Reduced hours off-season. **$$$**

Salt River Recreation Area
Power Rd; tel 602/984-3305. Located 20 mi NE of Phoenix in Tonto National Forest. Visitors can take an inner tube trip down the river—a tame and relaxing ride and one of the best ways to see the desert. **Open:** Mid-Apr–Sept, daily 9am–4pm. **$$$**

ENTERTAINMENT VENUES

Desert Sky Pavilion
N 83rd Ave; tel 602/254-7200. An 18,500-seat amphitheater. Hosts a wide variety of entertainment from Broadway musicals to rock concerts. **Open:** Box office, Mon–Fri 8am–5pm. **$$$$**

Herberger Theater Center
222 E Monroe St; tel 602/252-TIXS. From the outside this theater resembles a colonial church. Inside, its 2 Broadway-style theaters host more than 600 performances each year by Arizona companies and traveling shows. **Open:** Box office, Mon–Fri 10am–5pm, Sat noon–5pm. **$$$$**

America West Arena
201 E Jefferson; tel 602/379-7800. Home of the NBA's Phoenix Suns, this arena also hosts a wide range of events throughout the year featuring everything from rodeos to rock music. **Open:** Box office, Mon–Fri 8:30am–5pm, Sat 10am–4pm. **$$$$**

Pinetop-Lakeside

Getaways in the cool forests of the White Mountains, Pinetop and its neighbor Lakeside are popular year-round destinations attracting hikers, anglers, hunters, skiers, and other winter sports enthusiasts. **Information:** Pinetop-Lakeside Chamber of Commerce, 592 W White Mountain Blvd, Lakeside 85929 (tel 520/367-4290).

MOTELS

Best Western Inn of Pinetop
404 White Mountain Blvd (AZ 260), PO Box 1006, Pinetop, 85935; tel 520/367-6667 or toll free 800/525-1234; fax 520/367-6672. Comfortable, modern motel. **Rooms:** 42 rms, stes, and effic. CI 3pm/CO 11am. Nonsmoking rms avail. **Amenities:** A/C, cable TV. Some units w/terraces. **Services:** **Facilities:** Sauna. **Rates (CP):** Peak (May–July/Nov–Feb) $74–$89 S or D; $175–$200 ste; $175–$200 effic. Extra person $5. Children under age 12 stay free. Lower rates off-season. Parking: Outdoor, free. AE, DC, DISC, MC, V.

Econo Lodge
458 White Mountain Blvd (AZ 260), PO Box 1226, Pinetop, 85935; tel 520/367-3636 or toll free 800/544-4444; fax 520/367-1543. Clean, comfortable motel centrally located to lakes, horseback riding, hiking, and other outdoor activities. **Rooms:** 43 rms and stes. CI open/CO 11am. Nonsmoking

rms avail. **Amenities:** A/C, cable TV w/movies. **Services:** Babysitting. Laptop computer jacks are available in the office. **Facilities:** Spa, whirlpool, washer/dryer. **Rates (CP):** Peak (Oct–Apr) $89–$99 S or D; $99–$199 ste. Extra person $5. Children under age 18 stay free. Lower rates off-season. Parking: Outdoor, free. AE, CB, DC, DISC, JCB, MC, V.

Lakeside Inn
1637 AZ 260, PO Box 1130-D, Lakeside, 85935; tel 520/368-6600 or toll free 800/843-4792; fax 520/368-6600. Attractive, comfortable motel. **Rooms:** 55 rms. CI 3pm/CO 11am. Nonsmoking rms avail. **Amenities:** A/C, cable TV w/movies, refrig. Some units w/fireplaces. VCRs available. **Services:** **Facilities:** Games rm, whirlpool. **Rates (CP):** Peak (Nov–Mar/July–Aug) $99–$139 S or D. Extra person $10. Children under age 12 stay free. Lower rates off-season. Parking: Outdoor, free. AE, CB, DC, DISC, MC, V.

LODGES

Lake of the Woods
2244 W White Mountain Blvd (AZ 260), PO Box 777, Lakeside, 85929; tel 520/368-5353. A pleasant get-away-from-it-all, cabin-in-the-woods kind of place, situated on a pretty lake. **Rooms:** 27 cottages/villas. CI 2pm/CO 11am. Old-fashioned-style cabins, with kitchens and lots of stone and wood. **Amenities:** Cable TV, refrig. No A/C or phone. All units w/terraces, all w/fireplaces. **Services:** Babysitting. **Facilities:** Games rm, lawn games, sauna, playground, washer/dryer. **Rates:** Peak (June–Aug) $75–$253 cottage/villa. Extra person $4. Children under age 1 stay free. Min stay peak. Lower rates off-season. Parking: Outdoor, free. DISC, MC, V.

The Place Resort
3179 White Mountain Rd (AZ 260), PO Box 2675, Lakeside, 85929; tel 520/368-6777. 5½ acres. Quiet retreat perfect for relaxing and enjoying the lovely surroundings or for use as base camp for fishing, hunting, skiing, golfing. **Rooms:** 19 cottages/villas. CI open/CO 10am. Simple one- and two-bedroom or studio cabins with kitchens. **Amenities:** Cable TV, refrig. No A/C or phone. All units w/terraces, all w/fireplaces. **Services:** **Facilities:** 20 Basketball, volleyball, lawn games. Groceries can be purchased nearby. **Rates:** Peak (June 15–Sept 15) $72–$103 cottage/villa. Extra person $6. Children under age 1 stay free. Min stay wknds. Lower rates off-season. Parking: Outdoor, free. MC, V.

Whispering Pines Resort
237 AZ 260, PO Box 1043, Pinetop, 85935; tel 520/367-4386 or toll free 800/840-3867. 12 acres. Quiet mountain retreat. **Rooms:** 4 rms; 29 cottages/villas. CI 1pm/CO 10am. A variety of cabins are offered, each with a kitchen. **Amenities:** Cable TV, refrig. No A/C or phone. All units w/terraces, some w/fireplaces. **Services:** Babysitting. **Facilities:** Volleyball, lawn games, whirlpool, playground, washer/dryer. **Rates:** $35–$45 S or D; $70–$110 cottage/villa. Extra person $10. Children under age 3 stay free. Parking: Outdoor, free. AE, MC, V.

Prescott

A gold mining boomtown in the 1860s, Prescott was the first capital of the Arizona Territory. With its well-preserved downtown business district featuring a number of handsome Victorian buildings, and outdoor recreation in the nearby national forest, Prescott supports a thriving tourism industry. **Information:** Prescott Chamber of Commerce, 117 W Goodwin, PO Box 1147, Prescott 86302 (tel 520/445-2000 or 800/266-7534).

HOTELS

Hassayampa Inn
122 E Gurley St, 86301 (Downtown); tel 520/778-9434 or toll free 800/322-1927; fax 520/778-9434. Built in 1927, this historic hotel is on the National Register of Historic Places. The lobby is done in art deco/pueblo style, with a huge painted mural above the fireplace, a tile floor, 2 pianos, and leather chairs. **Rooms:** 68 rms and stes. CI 3pm/CO noon. Nonsmoking rms avail. Each room is distinctly decorated, with original watercolors of local scenes, and period furnishings. **Amenities:** A/C, cable TV. 1 unit w/terrace, 1 w/whirlpool. Suites have hair dryers. **Services:** **Facilities:** 150 1 restaurant (*see* "Restaurants" below), 1 bar. Superbly decorated dining room. **Rates (BB):** Peak (Apr–Oct) $99–$129 S or D; $140–$190 ste. Extra person $10. Children under age 6 stay free. Lower rates off-season. Parking: Outdoor, free. AE, CB, DC, DISC, MC, V.

Hotel St Michael
205 W Gurley St, 86301; tel 520/776-1999 or toll free 800/678-3757; fax 520/776-7318. A historic downtown hotel located on Prescott's famous "Whiskey Row." **Rooms:** 72 rms and stes. CI 2pm/CO 11am. Nonsmoking rms avail. **Amenities:** A/C, cable TV. **Services:** Babysitting. **Facilities:** 1 restaurant (bkfst and lunch only). The Caffe St Michael in the hotel offers specialty coffee drinks. **Rates (CP):** $36–$52 S or D; $62–$72 ste. Extra person $8. Children under age 12 stay free. Parking: Outdoor, free. AE, CB, DC, DISC, MC, V.

Prescott Resort and Conference Center and Casino
1500 AZ 69, 86301; tel 520/776-1666 or toll free 800/967-4637. Located high on a hill above Prescott, this hotel has a commanding view, especially of the jagged San Francisco Peaks to the north. **Rooms:** 161 rms and stes. CI 3pm/CO noon. Nonsmoking rms avail. **Amenities:** A/C, satel TV, refrig. 1 unit w/minibar, all w/terraces. **Services:** Masseur, babysitting. **Facilities:** 2 800 1 restaurant, 2 bars (1 w/entertainment), racquetball, spa,

sauna, whirlpool, beauty salon. There's a slot machine casino on the premises. The swimming pool has retractable doors for indoor use during inclement weather. **Rates:** Peak (Apr–Sept) $140 S or D; $170 ste. Extra person $15. Children under age 18 stay free. Lower rates off-season. Parking: Outdoor, free. AE, DC, DISC, MC, V.

MOTEL

Super 8 Motel

1105 E Sheldon St, 86303; tel 520/776-1282 or toll free 800/800-8000; fax 520/778-6736. Sheldon St exit off AZ 89. This is a good, economical motel for vacationers or business travelers on a budget. Close to local colleges and the Veterans Administration hospital. **Rooms:** 70 rms. CI 3pm/CO 11am. Nonsmoking rms avail. **Amenities:** A/C, cable TV. **Services:** Fax and copy services are available, and there's a 24-hour front desk. Free local calls. **Facilities:** **Rates (CP):** Peak (Apr–Sept) $50–$70 S or D. Children under age 12 stay free. Lower rates off-season. Parking: Outdoor, free. AE, CB, DC, DISC, MC, V.

INNS

Prescott Country Inn

503 S Montezuma St (US 89), 86303; tel 520/445-7991. With comfortable cottages, a good choice for a romantic getaway. **Rooms:** 12 cottages/villas. CI 3pm/CO 11am. No smoking. Each unit is unique. **Amenities:** Cable TV, refrig. No A/C. Some units w/terraces, some w/fireplaces. **Services:** **Rates (CP):** Peak (May–Sept) $89 cottage/villa. Extra person $15. Children under age 6 stay free. Min stay special events. Lower rates off-season. Parking: Outdoor, free. AE, MC, V.

Prescott Pines Inn

901 White Spar Rd (US 89), 86303; tel 520/445-7270 or toll free 800/541-5374; fax 520/778-3665. A good choice for those who enjoy the atmosphere of a small bed-and-breakfast but prefer a bit more privacy. The main guest house dates from 1902. **Rooms:** 13 rms, stes, and effic. CI 3pm/CO noon. No smoking. The comfortable rooms are individually decorated. **Amenities:** A/C, cable TV, refrig. All units w/terraces, some w/fireplaces. **Services:** A full-service breakfast is available at $5 per person, if reserved by 7pm the previous evening. **Facilities:** Guest lounge. **Rates (BB):** $55–$95 S or D. Extra person $10. Higher rates for special events/hols. Parking: Outdoor, free. Rates are $4 to $10 higher Friday and Saturday nights than week nights. MC, V.

RESTAURANTS

★ El Charro

120 N Montezuma St; tel 520/445-7130. **Mexican.** Popular and affordable downtown eatery, with local artists' work for sale. **FYI:** Reservations accepted. No smoking. **Open:** Sun–Thurs 11am–8pm, Fri–Sat 11am–8:30pm. **Prices:** Main courses $3–$12; prix fixe $6–$8. MC, V.

Kendall's Famous Burgers and Ice Cream

113 S Cortez St; tel 520/778-3658. **Burgers/Ice cream.** A 1950s and '60s–style hamburger and ice cream joint, complete with pictures of Elvis, James Dean, and Corvettes. Flame-broiled burgers, fresh-cut fries, beer-batter onion rings, and old-fashioned ice cream sundaes fit the mood. **FYI:** Reservations not accepted. No liquor license. No smoking. **Open:** Mon–Sat 11am–8pm, Sun 11am–6pm. **Prices:** Main courses $4–$6. No CC.

★ Murphy's

201 N Cortez St; tel 520/445-4044. **American/Seafood.** The building housing this large restaurant dates from 1892 and is listed on the National Register of Historic Places. Historic photos are on the walls; a collection of antiques sits above the bar, which has the original tin ceiling. The menu includes prime rib, fresh fish, and selections from in-house bakery. With 60 bottled beers and 2 specialty beers on tap. **FYI:** Reservations accepted. Children's menu. No smoking. **Open:** Peak (June–Aug) lunch daily 11am–3pm; dinner daily 4:30–11pm. **Prices:** Main courses $11–$17. AE, DISC, MC, V.

The Peacock Room

In the Hassayampa Inn, 122 E Gurley St; tel 520/778-9434. **Continental.** Comfortable booths with art deco lamps, chandeliers, and soft music all contribute to the relaxed atmosphere. Specialties include shrimp scampi and chicken Venezia. **FYI:** Reservations recommended. Children's menu. Dress code. No smoking. **Open:** Breakfast Mon–Sat 6:30–11am, Sun 7am–1pm; lunch Mon–Sat 11am–2pm; dinner Sun–Thurs 5–9pm, Fri–Sat 5–9:30pm. **Prices:** Main courses $12–$24. AE, CB, DC, DISC, MC, V.

ATTRACTIONS

Sharlot Hall Museum

415 W Gurley St; tel 520/445-3122. A complex of historic buildings and gardens started by territorial historian Sharlot Hall. Restored buildings include the Old Governor's Mansion, built in 1864; the 1875 John C Frémont House; the William Bashford House, an example of Victorian architecture; and the Sharlot Hall Building, a museum. In addition, the grounds include a reproduction 1868 log schoolhouse, an early windmill, a steam locomotive, and a memorial rose garden. **Open:** Mon–Sat 10am–5pm, Sun 1–5pm. **Free**

The Smoki Museum

147 N Arizona St; tel 520/445-1230 or 778-7554. Houses a large collection of American Indian artifacts as well as a collection of western art. **Open:** May–Sept, Mon–Tues and Thurs–Sat 10am–4pm, Sun 1–4pm. **$**

Prescott's Phippen Museum of Western Art

4701 US 89 N; tel 520/778-1385. Exhibits works by both established western artists and newcomers. Throughout the year there are several one-person shows, as well as group exhibitions. The museum gift shop represents more than 100 Arizona artists. **Open:** Mon, Wed–Sat 10am–4pm, Sun 1–4pm. **$**

Prescott National Forest
344 S Cortez St; tel 520/721-4200. Pine forest containing hiking trails, several artificial lakes, and campgrounds. The Forest Service Office has maps and information about the area. **Free**

Rio Rico

See Nogales

Safford

On the banks of the Gila River, Safford was founded in 1872 by farmers who had lost their downstream properties in a flood. Today a center for outdoor recreation, including hiking, camping, and rock hounding. **Information:** Graham County Chamber of Commerce, 1111 Thatcher Blvd, Safford 85546 (tel 520/428-2511).

MOTEL

Best Western Desert Inn
1391 Thatcher Blvd, 85546; tel 520/428-0521 or toll free 800/528-1234; fax 520/428-7653. Pleasant, attractive motel. **Rooms:** 70 rms and stes. CI noon/CO 11am. Nonsmoking rms avail. **Amenities:** A/C, cable TV, refrig. **Services:** **Facilities:** 1 restaurant, 1 bar, washer/dryer. Sports bar in adjacent restaurant. **Rates:** $48–$50 S; $56–$58 D; $70 ste. Extra person $5. Children under age 12 stay free. Parking: Outdoor, free. AE, DC, DISC, MC, V.

ATTRACTION

Roper Lake State Park
I-10; tel 520/428-6760. Located in the foothills of Mount Graham, the 240-acre park features natural hot springs that are accessible in a continually flowing hot tub area. A man-made lake offers fishing and swimming; motor boats are not allowed on the lake. Camping, hiking, nature trails. **Open:** Daily 6am–10pm. **$**

Scottsdale

Among Phoenix's most luxurious suburbs, Scottsdale is known for its resorts, shopping, restaurants, scenic beauty, and abundant outdoor recreation facilities. And only New York and Santa Fe have more art galleries than Scottsdale, which has become one of the nation's centers for western and Native American art. **Information:** Scottsdale Chamber of Commerce, 7343 Scottsdale Mall, Scottsdale 85251 (tel 602/945-8481 or 800/877-1117).

HOTELS

Country Inn & Suites
10801 N 89th Place, 85260; tel 602/314-1200 or toll free 800/456-4000; fax 602/314-5868. At Shea Blvd, 1 block E of Pima Rd. A cozy inn conveniently located on the north side of town, near shopping, restaurants, golf courses, library, and Scottsdale Hospital. **Rooms:** 163 rms and stes. Executive level. CI 3pm/CO noon. Nonsmoking rms avail. Mid-sized rooms decorated in charming country style. **Amenities:** A/C, cable TV w/movies, refrig, dataport, voice mail. Some units w/terraces, some w/fireplaces, some w/whirlpools. **Services:** Babysitting. Breakfast includes yogurt and waffles. Complimentary newspaper, bedtime snacks. **Facilities:** 30 Whirlpool, washer/dryer. **Rates (CP):** Peak (Jan–May) $139 S or D; $159–$189 ste. Extra person $10. Children under age 18 stay free. Lower rates off-season. Parking: Outdoor, free. AE, DC, DISC, MC, V.

Courtyard by Marriott
13444 E Shea Blvd, 85259; tel 602/860-4000 or toll free 800/321-2211; fax 602/860-4308. Very quietly situated adjacent to Mayo Clinic. **Rooms:** 124 rms and stes. CI 3pm/CO noon. Nonsmoking rms avail. Rooms are well appointed; most overlook courtyard, some have view of McDowell Mountains. **Amenities:** A/C, cable TV w/movies, dataport. Some units w/terraces. **Services:** Twice-daily maid svce. Wheelchairs available for use in hotel. Free shuttle to Mayo Clinic. Smoking prohibited everywhere except in hotel lounge. **Facilities:** 50 1 restaurant, 1 bar, whirlpool, washer/dryer. All new exercise equipment, including treadmill. Small but very comfortable restaurant with fireplace. **Rates:** Peak (Jan–Apr) $129 S; $139 D; $165–$175 ste. Extra person $10. Children under age 5 stay free. Lower rates off-season. AP and MAP rates avail. Parking: Outdoor, free. AE, DC, DISC, MC, V.

Embassy Suites Resort Scottsdale
5001 N Scottsdale Rd, 85250; tel 602/949-1414 or toll free 800/528-1456; fax 602/947-2675. An attractive all-suites hotel, with fountains outside the lobby. **Rooms:** 310 stes. CI 3pm/CO noon. Nonsmoking rms avail. Rooms are spacious, particularly nice for those with children and for business travelers who need extra space. Handicapped-accessible room does not have roll-in shower, but bathroom floor has a drain for showering outside the tub. **Amenities:** A/C, satel TV w/movies. All units w/minibars, some w/whirlpools. **Services:** Car-rental desk, babysitting. Complimentary cocktails. **Facilities:** 2 1000 1 restaurant (lunch and dinner only), 1 bar, games rm, spa, whirlpool, washer/dryer. **Rates (BB):** Peak (Jan–Apr) $160–

$170 ste. Extra person $10. Children under age 12 stay free. Lower rates off-season. Parking: Outdoor, free. AE, DC, DISC, MC, V.

Fairfield Inn
13440 N Scottsdale Rd, 85254; tel 602/483-0042 or toll free 800/228-2800. 8 mi N of downtown. A step above the basic hotel/motel, recommended for both business travelers and vacationers. **Rooms:** 133 rms. CI 3pm/CO noon. Nonsmoking rms avail. Rooms are simple but very pleasant. **Amenities:** A/C, cable TV. **Services:** Free morning coffee and tea, and free local phone calls. Fax service available. **Facilities:** 10 Whirlpool. **Rates:** Peak (Jan–Apr) $85–$95 S or D. Children under age 18 stay free. Lower rates off-season. Parking: Outdoor, free. A particularly good value in off-season. AE, CB, DC, DISC, MC, V.

Howard Johnson
5101 N Scottsdale Rd, 85250; tel 602/945-4392 or toll free 800/446-4656. A handsome hotel, good for both business and pleasure travelers. Close to airports and shopping in old Scottsdale. **Rooms:** 216 rms and stes. CI 3pm/CO 1pm. Nonsmoking rms avail. Pleasant, comfortable rooms. **Amenities:** A/C, satel TV. **Services:** **Facilities:** 250 1 restaurant (bkfst only), 1 bar, whirlpool, washer/dryer. **Rates:** Peak (Jan 15–Apr 15) $95–$118 S or D; $153 ste. Extra person $10. Children under age 18 stay free. Lower rates off-season. Parking: Outdoor, free. A good value. AE, CB, DC, DISC, MC, V.

Scottsdale Manor Suites
4807 N Woodmere Fairway Dr, 85251; tel 602/994-5282 or toll free 800/523-5282. Ideal for longer, self-catering visits. **Rooms:** 72 stes. CI 3pm/CO 10am. Nonsmoking rms avail. All units have fully equipped kitchens, 2 bedrooms and 2 baths. Very spacious. **Amenities:** A/C, cable TV, refrig. Some units w/terraces. Linens, towels, vacuum cleaners, ironing boards, and irons are provided. **Services:** Daily maid service is available at an extra charge. Free local calls. **Facilities:** 2 Lawn games, whirlpool, washer/dryer. Putting green and 25 barbecue grills on premises. **Rates:** Peak (Jan 15–Apr 15) $200–$300 ste. Children under age 18 stay free. Min stay. Lower rates off-season. Parking: Outdoor, free. Each unit can house up to 4 persons for the base rate, and weekly and monthly rates are available. No CC.

Sunburst Resort
4925 N Scottsdale Rd, 85251 (Downtown); tel 602/945-7666 or toll free 800/528-7867; fax 602/946-4056. Centrally located hotel on lush grounds, close to shopping and sports facilities. Foyer and lobby completely remodeled, with central stone fireplace and waterfalls gracing one side of lobby. **Rooms:** 210 rms and stes. Executive level. CI 3pm/CO noon. Nonsmoking rms avail. Rooms very comfortably and attractively furnished. **Amenities:** A/C, cable TV w/movies, refrig, dataport, voice mail, bathrobes. All units w/minibars, all w/terraces, 1 w/whirlpool. Some rooms have coffeemakers. **Services:** Car-rental desk, social director, masseur, children's program, babysitting. **Facilities:** 1000 1 restaurant, 1 bar, spa, whirlpool. Swimming pool has sand beach plus lagoon, waterfall, and stream. **Rates:** Peak (Jan–Apr) $215–$225 S or D; $350–$675 ste. Extra person $15. Children under age 18 stay free. Min stay special events. Lower rates off-season. AP and MAP rates avail. Parking: Outdoor, free. AE, CB, DC, DISC, ER, JCB, MC, V.

MOTELS

Best Western Papago Inn and Resort
7017 E McDowell Rd, 85257; tel 602/947-7335 or toll free 800/528-1234; fax 602/994-0692. This pleasant, modern motel adjoins Papago Plaza Shopping Center and is close to Desert Botanical Gardens. **Rooms:** 56 rms and stes. CI 2pm/CO noon. Nonsmoking rms avail. **Amenities:** A/C, cable TV, refrig. 1 unit w/fireplace. Telephone adapts for machines for the hearing impaired. **Services:** Complimentary wine for guests. **Facilities:** 15 1 restaurant, 1 bar, sauna, washer/dryer. There's a bird aviary by the pool, and a large outdoor chess game. **Rates:** Peak (Jan–Apr) $108–$135 S or D; $165–$175 ste. Extra person $6. Children under age 12 stay free. Lower rates off-season. Parking: Outdoor, free. AE, DC, DISC, MC, V.

Rodeway Inn
7110 E Indian School Rd, 85251; tel 602/946-3456 or toll free 800/424-4777; fax 602/946-4248. Basic, centrally located lodging. **Rooms:** 65 rms and stes. CI 3pm/CO noon. Nonsmoking rms avail. Rooms are simply but comfortably furnished. **Amenities:** A/C, cable TV, refrig, dataport. **Services:** **Facilities:** Whirlpool. **Rates (CP):** Peak (Jan–Apr) $90–$130 S; $98–$140 D; $120–$140 ste. Extra person $8. Children under age 17 stay free. Lower rates off-season. Parking: Outdoor, free. AE, CB, DC, DISC, ER, JCB, MC, V.

Scottsdale Pima Motel
7330 N Pima Rd, 85258; tel 602/948-3800 or toll free 800/344-0262; fax 602/443-3374. This motel offers a wide range of accommodations and is good for long stays. Popular with golfers and business travelers. **Rooms:** 127 rms and stes. CI 3pm/CO noon. Nonsmoking rms avail. All suites have kitchens. **Amenities:** A/C, cable TV w/movies, refrig. Some units w/minibars, some w/terraces. **Services:** Complimentary 24-hour coffee bar. Free shuttle service within a 5-mile radius. **Facilities:** 250 1 bar, games rm, spa, sauna, steam rm, whirlpool, washer/dryer. Pool table. **Rates (CP):** Peak (Apr 17–May 21/Sept 9–Dec 29) $42–$99 S; $52–$109 D; $72–$149 ste. Extra person $10. Children under age 16 stay free. Lower rates off-season. Parking: Outdoor, free. Weekly and monthly rates avail. AE, CB, DC, DISC, JCB, MC, V.

Scottsdale's 5th Avenue Inn
6935 5th Ave, 85251 (Downtown); tel 602/994-9461 or toll free 800/528-7396; fax 602/947-1695. Located in the very

hub of Scottsdale; more than 250 shops and galleries are within walking distance. **Rooms:** 92 rms. CI 1pm/CO noon. Nonsmoking rms avail. **Amenities:** A/C, satel TV, refrig, dataport. **Services:** Car-rental desk. **Facilities:** Whirlpool. **Rates (CP):** Peak (Jan–Apr) $79–$95 S or D. Extra person $8. Children under age 12 stay free. Lower rates off-season. Parking: Outdoor, free. AE, CB, DC, DISC, EC, ER, MC, V.

RESORTS

DoubleTree Paradise Valley Resort
5401 N Scottsdale Rd, 85250 (Downtown); tel 602/947-5400 or toll free 800/222-TREE, 800/WYNDHAM in the US, 800/631-4200 in Canada; fax 602/481-0209. 22 acres. Beautiful and luxurious, with a large, open lobby with glass-enclosed aviary, palms, and skylights. **Rooms:** 387 rms and stes. Executive level. CI 3pm/CO noon. Nonsmoking rms avail. There are wood-beamed ceilings in the spacious rooms, which have individual climate controls. **Amenities:** A/C, satel TV w/movies, refrig, dataport, voice mail, bathrobes. All units w/minibars, all w/terraces, some w/fireplaces, some w/whirlpools. **Services:** Car-rental desk, social director, masseur, children's program, babysitting. Trolley transportation available to nearby shops. **Facilities:** 2000 1 restaurant, 3 bars (1 w/entertainment), lawn games, racquetball, squash, spa, sauna, steam rm, whirlpool, beauty salon. Waterfalls flow into the large swimming pools; poolside bar for beverages and snacks. Championship golf available at nearby courses. **Rates:** Peak (Jan–May 15) $205–$300 S or D; $300–$2,500 ste. Extra person $20. Children under age 18 stay free. Lower rates off-season. Parking: Outdoor, free. AE, CB, DC, DISC, EC, ER, JCB, MC, V.

Holiday Inn SunSpree Resort
7601 E Indian Bend Rd, 85250; tel 602/991-2400 or toll free 800/991-2400. 16 acres. A good, basic resort catering to golfers and tennis players. Recently renovated. **Rooms:** 200 rms and stes. Executive level. CI 3pm/CO noon. Nonsmoking rms avail. Well-appointed, comfortable rooms. **Amenities:** A/C, cable TV w/movies, refrig, dataport. Some units w/terraces. **Services:** Twice-daily maid svce, children's program, babysitting. **Facilities:** 2 600 1 restaurant, 1 bar, volleyball, games rm, lawn games, whirlpool, washer/dryer. **Rates:** Peak (Jan–Apr) $140–$150 S; $155–$165 D; $215–$275 ste. Extra person $10. Children under age 18 stay free. Min stay special events. Lower rates off-season. AP rates avail. Parking: Outdoor, free. AE, CB, DC, DISC, EC, ER, JCB, MC, V.

Hyatt Regency Scottsdale
7500 E Doubletree Ranch Rd, 85258 (Gainey Ranch); tel 602/991-3388 or toll free 800/233-1234; fax 602/483-5550. 15 mi E of Greenway Pkwy exit off I-17. Splendidly landscaped grounds covering 27 acres of a 560-acre spread known as the Gainey Ranch, with lagoons and fountains, tall stands of date palms, and stunning architecture incorporating textured concrete blocks à la Frank Lloyd Wright. **Rooms:** 486 stes; 7 cottages/villas. Executive level. CI 4pm/CO noon. Nonsmoking rms avail. Attractive decor with southwestern colors and artworks. Fireplaces and patios in casitas, larger-than-average rooms in Regency Club wing. **Amenities:** A/C, cable TV w/movies, refrig, dataport, voice mail, in-rm safe, bathrobes. All units w/minibars, all w/terraces, some w/fireplaces. **Services:** Car-rental desk, social director, masseur, children's program, babysitting. Free shuttle to nearby shopping malls. Young, cordial staff. **Facilities:** 27 8 1500 4 restaurants (*see* "Restaurants" below), 2 bars (w/entertainment), 1 beach (lake shore), lawn games, spa, sauna, steam rm, whirlpool, beauty salon, playground. 2.5-acre water playground with sandy beach; 10 interconnecting pools (including one for adults only); three-story waterslide; 25-foot-wide whirlpool (open until midnight); 14-foot waterfalls, floodlit at night; poolside bars. Boat rides on lagoons. Gainey Ranch golf courses shared with neighboring homeowners. Complimentary bicycles. Free spa features Mollen Clinic for health evaluations and exercise counseling. One restaurant has singing servers; the other overlooks a Japanese koi pond. **Rates:** Peak (Jan–June) $295–$1,565 ste; $1,175–$2,075 cottage/villa. Extra person $10. Children under age 18 stay free. Lower rates off-season. Parking: Outdoor, free. $40 premium for pool, fairway, or mountain views. Summer rates are less than half winter rates and are a bargain. AE, DC, DISC, JCB, MC, V.

Marriott's Camelback Inn Resort, Golf Club & Spa
5402 E Lincoln Dr, 85253 (Paradise Valley); tel 602/948-1700 or toll free 800/242-2635; fax 602/951-8469. Glendale Ave exit off I-17; continue east until Glendale becomes Lincoln. 125 acres. One of the original desert resorts and still a landmark, with its pueblo-style architecture. It's highly popular with people who organize business meetings, but individual vacationers may feel crowded out. Attractive, adobe-style lobby and lounge. **Rooms:** 424 rms and stes. CI 3pm/CO noon. Nonsmoking rms avail. Attractive, southwestern-style oak furniture, with seating areas in each 550-square-foot room, but balconies and patios often look out on walkways or other patios. Cramped bathrooms. **Amenities:** A/C, cable TV w/movies, refrig, dataport, voice mail, in-rm safe, bathrobes. All units w/minibars, all w/terraces, some w/fireplaces. In-room video services for messages and accounts review. Some suites with private pools. **Services:** Twice-daily maid svce, car-rental desk, social director, masseur, children's program, babysitting. Turndown service may be fastest on record, but in their rush housekeepers sometimes leave behind out-of-date activities list. **Facilities:** 2200 6 restaurants (*see* "Restaurants" below), 6 bars (1 w/entertainment), basketball, volleyball, lawn games, spa, sauna, steam rm, whirlpool,

beauty salon, playground, washer/dryer. Kokopelli Cafe offers southwestern nut coffees and baked goods. Striking circular swimming pool with tiered flower gardens, and handsome, 25,000-square-foot spa and wellness center (membership fee $22 per day) offering Adobe Clay Purification Treatments; the two championship courses are among the best bargains for golfers (but they are located several miles away at the Camelback Country Club Estates). Also Hopalong College for kids (seasonal), including cookouts and "camelhunts." **Rates (CP):** Peak (Jan–June) $309–$380 S or D; $500–$1,700 ste. Children under age 18 stay free. Min stay special events. Lower rates off-season. AP and MAP rates avail. Parking: Outdoor, free. AE, CB, DC, DISC, MC, V.

The Phoenician

6000 E Camelback Rd, 85251; tel 602/941-8200 or toll free 800/888-8234; fax 602/947-4311. Camelback Rd exit off I-17. 130 acres. Grand and affluent, filled with antiques and artworks and surrounded by estatelike gardens and ponds wedged between lush fairways and a hillside of cacti and ocotillos. But the extravagantly elegant lobby can be overwhelmed by business groups—60% of the clientele—and many rooms are a long hike from both the lobby and restaurants. **Rooms:** 580 rms and stes; 15 cottages/villas. CI 4pm/CO noon. Nonsmoking rms avail. Some have stunning views of the grounds and city lights, others have less-than-stunning views of other rooms and balconies. For some guests, the choicest (not the priciest) lodgings face the hillside at the rear; golfers and tennis players prefer the convenience of the casitas in a cluster of villas below the spectacular water playground. All rooms are distinguished by spaciousness (600 square feet and up) and refined appointments, down to brass doorknobs and hinges. Bathrooms, swathed in marble, are the size of most hotel rooms. **Amenities:** A/C, cable TV w/movies, dataport, voice mail, in-rm safe, bathrobes. All units w/minibars, all w/terraces, some w/fireplaces, some w/whirlpools. Balconies/patios large enough for proper tables, chairs and loungers; double walk-in closets; Nintendo and other playthings for kids; two-line speakerphones; TV message service and account reports. **Services:** Twice-daily maid svce, car-rental desk, social director, masseur, children's program, babysitting. Young and eager, if not always polished, staffers outnumber the guest rooms 2 to 1. **Facilities:** 9 restaurants (*see* "Restaurants" below), 4 bars (2 w/entertainment), games rm, lawn games, spa, sauna, steam rm, whirlpool, beauty salon, playground. Most resorts measure their pool areas in feet; here it's in acres, with 100-foot slides, lagoons, sundecks, and swim-up bars. Immaculate health spa and Center for Wellbeing with Meditation Atrium; first-rate tennis complex with automated practice court and pros who chill towels for perspiring players; golf course reserved exclusively for hotel guests. Delightful restaurants. **Rates:** Peak (Jan–June 15) $330–$465 S or D; $925–$1575 ste; $330–$465 cottage/villa. Extra person $50. Children under age 17 stay free. Min stay special events. Lower rates off-season. Parking: Indoor/outdoor, $6/day. Rates slightly higher than nearby Camelback and Princess resorts, but there's more to offer here than either. AE, CB, DC, DISC, JCB, MC, V.

Radisson Resort

7171 N Scottsdale Rd, 85253; tel 602/991-3800 or toll free 800/333-3333; fax 602/948-1381. 76 acres. A very attractive resort in the center of Scottsdale. **Rooms:** 116 rms and stes; 202 cottages/villas. CI 4pm/CO noon. Nonsmoking rms avail. Rooms are plush and finely decorated. **Amenities:** A/C, cable TV, refrig, voice mail, bathrobes. All units w/minibars, all w/terraces, some w/fireplaces, 1 w/whirlpool. **Services:** Twice-daily maid svce, car-rental desk, social director, masseur, children's program, babysitting. **Facilities:** 2 restaurants, 3 bars (2 w/entertainment), board surfing, games rm, lawn games, spa, sauna, steam rm, whirlpool, beauty salon, playground, washer/dryer. **Rates:** Peak (Jan–Apr) $205–$225 S or D; $325–$1,500 ste; $205–$530 cottage/villa. Extra person $10. Children under age 18 stay free. Min stay special events. Lower rates off-season. Parking: Outdoor, free. AE, CB, DC, DISC, MC, V.

Red Lion's La Posada Resort

4949 E Lincoln Dr, 85253; tel 602/952-0420 or toll free 800/547-8010; fax 602/852-0151. 30 acres. The hotel has an attractive arched adobe entrance and well-kept flower gardens. **Rooms:** 262 rms and stes. CI 4pm/CO noon. Nonsmoking rms avail. Rooms are large and well furnished. **Amenities:** A/C, satel TV w/movies. All units w/minibars, all w/terraces, some w/whirlpools. **Services:** Car-rental desk, masseur, children's program, babysitting. **Facilities:** 3 restaurants, 1 bar (w/entertainment), lawn games, racquetball, sauna, whirlpool, beauty salon. The main pool is divided by "Flintstone"-like man-made rocks, with cave and swim-through tunnel and waterfall. **Rates:** Peak (Jan 1–May 15) $219–$239 S or D; $400–$550 ste. Extra person $15. Children under age 18 stay free. Min stay wknds. Lower rates off-season. Parking: Outdoor, free. AE, CB, DC, DISC, MC, V.

Regal McCormick Ranch

7401 N Scottsdale Rd, 85253; tel 602/948-5050 or toll free 800/243-1332. 70 acres. Beautiful but unpretentious resort. Lobby is decorated in southwestern decor. **Rooms:** 125 rms and stes; 51 cottages/villas. Executive level. CI 3pm/CO noon. Nonsmoking rms avail. Rooms are especially well appointed. **Amenities:** A/C, satel TV w/movies, refrig, dataport, voice mail, bathrobes. Some units w/minibars, all w/terraces. Villas have full kitchens. **Services:** Car-rental desk, masseur, children's program, babysitting. **Facilities:** 1 restaurant, 1 bar (w/entertainment), volleyball, lawn games, whirlpool. Attractive lake. Additional golf courses nearby.

Rates: Peak (Jan–Apr) $175–$240 S or D; $295–$325 ste; $320–$650 cottage/villa. Extra person $10. Children under age 18 stay free. Lower rates off-season. Parking: Outdoor, free. AE, CB, DC, DISC, ER, MC, V.

Renaissance Cottonwoods Resort

6160 N Scottsdale Rd, 85253; tel 602/991-1414 or toll free 800/HOTELS-1; fax 602/951-3350. Near Lincoln Dr. 25 acres. This southwestern-style resort lies adjacent to the upscale Borgata of Scottsdale shopping center. **Rooms:** 170 rms and stes. CI 3pm/CO noon. Nonsmoking rms avail. **Amenities:** A/C, cable TV w/movies, refrig, in-rm safe. All units w/minibars, all w/terraces, some w/fireplaces, some w/whirlpools. **Services:** Social director, masseur, babysitting. There's an on-site tennis pro. **Facilities:** 2 2 250 1 restaurant, 1 bar, lawn games, whirlpool. Both swimming pools are open 24 hours. Putting green, tennis shop. **Rates (CP):** Peak (Jan–May) $235 S or D; $265–$305 ste. Extra person $10. Children under age 18 stay free. Min stay special events. Lower rates off-season. Parking: Outdoor, free. AE, CB, DC, DISC, MC, V.

Resort Suites of Scottsdale

7677 E Princess Blvd, 85255; tel 602/585-1234 or toll free 800/541-5203. 12 acres. Ideal for the golfer and those who want the conveniences and comforts of home while on vacation. **Rooms:** 287 stes. CI 3pm/CO 10am. No smoking. Condominium-style suites have full kitchens and walk-in closets, and a pool view. **Amenities:** A/C, cable TV w/movies, refrig. All units w/terraces. The two- and four-bedroom suites have their own washers and dryers. **Services:** Babysitting. Helicopter transport to area golf courses is available. **Facilities:** 3 36 150 1 restaurant, 1 bar (w/entertainment), spa, whirlpool, washer/dryer. The resort can arrange golf at any of 45 area courses. **Rates:** Peak (Jan–Apr) $195–$225 ste. Children under age 18 stay free. Lower rates off-season. Parking: Outdoor, free. Several golf packages are available. AE, MC, V.

Safari Resort

4611 N Scottsdale Rd, 85251; tel 602/945-0721 or toll free 800/845-4356; fax 602/946-4703. 12 acres. A landmark Scottsdale resort—the city's first—at the hub of downtown activities. **Rooms:** 188 rms and stes. CI 3pm/CO noon. Nonsmoking rms avail. Some units have kitchenettes. **Amenities:** A/C, cable TV w/movies. Some units w/terraces. Most rooms have refrigerators. **Services:** The lounge has complimentary appetizers during happy hour. **Facilities:** 2 600 2 restaurants, 1 bar (w/entertainment), lawn games, spa, whirlpool, beauty salon, playground, washer/dryer. The resort has a golf putting and pitching green, and is close to major shopping and dining districts. **Rates (CP):** Peak (Jan–mid-Apr) $92–$104 S; $102–$114 D; $150–$160 ste; $130–$140 effic. Extra person $10. Children under age 18 stay free. Lower rates off-season. Parking: Outdoor, free. AE, CB, DC, DISC, MC, V.

Scottsdale Conference Resort

7700 E McCormick Pkwy, 85258; tel 602/991-9000 or toll free 800/528-0293. 50 acres. This plush resort books mainly groups and corporate meetings. **Rooms:** 314 rms and stes; 12 cottages/villas. Executive level. CI 3pm/CO 1pm. **Amenities:** A/C, cable TV, dataport, bathrobes. All units w/minibars, some w/terraces, some w/fireplaces, 1 w/whirlpool. **Services:** VP Twice-daily maid svce, car-rental desk, social director, masseur. **Facilities:** 2 36 7 1000 2 restaurants, 1 bar, basketball, volleyball, games rm, spa, sauna, steam rm, whirlpool, beauty salon. **Rates (AP):** Peak (Jan–Mar) $375 S; $550 D; $655–$960 ste; $755 cottage/villa. Children under age 16 stay free. Lower rates off-season. MAP rates avail. Parking: Indoor/outdoor, free. AE, CB, DC, DISC, MC, V.

Scottsdale Hilton Resort and Villas

6333 N Scottsdale Rd, 85250; tel 602/948-7750 or toll free 800/528-3119; fax 602/948-2232. 20 acres. Lavish property, with a high-ceilinged lobby, southwestern-style carpets, and recorded background music. **Rooms:** 187 rms, stes, and effic; 45 cottages/villas. CI 4pm/CO 1pm. Nonsmoking rms avail. Rooms are unusually spacious. **Amenities:** A/C, cable TV w/movies. Some units w/terraces, some w/fireplaces, some w/whirlpools. **Services:** VP Car-rental desk, social director, masseur, children's program. **Facilities:** 2 4 500 1 restaurant, 1 bar (w/entertainment), spa, sauna, steam rm, whirlpool, beauty salon. Golf courses nearby, and numerous recreational opportunities on site. **Rates (CP):** Peak (Jan–May) $170 S; $180 D; $225 ste; $320 effic; $320 cottage/villa. Extra person $10. Children under age 10 stay free. Min stay special events. Lower rates off-season. Parking: Outdoor, free. An especially good value during the summer off-season. AE, CB, DC, DISC, MC, V.

Scottsdale Plaza Resort

7200 N Scottsdale Rd, 85253; tel 602/948-5000 or toll free 800/832-2025; fax 602/951-5100. 40 acres. A plush property in the center of the resort area. **Rooms:** 404 rms and stes. CI 3pm/CO noon. Rooms are attractively and comfortably furnished. **Amenities:** A/C, cable TV, refrig, in-rm safe, bathrobes. All units w/minibars, some w/terraces, some w/fireplaces. **Services:** Car-rental desk, masseur, babysitting. **Facilities:** 5 3 2 1000 3 restaurants, 3 bars (1 w/entertainment), lawn games, racquetball, spa, sauna, steam rm, whirlpool, beauty salon. **Rates:** Peak (Jan–Apr) $250–$275 S or D. Extra person $15. Children under age 18 stay free. Lower rates off-season. Parking: Outdoor, free. AE, DC, DISC, MC, V.

Scottsdale Princess

7575 E Princess Dr, 85255 (North Scottsdale); tel 602/585-4848 or toll free 800/344-4758; fax 602/585-0086. Bell Rd exit off I-170. 450 acres. Big and sprawling, with echoes of colonial Spain in its terra-cotta columns and red-tiled roofs, fountains and flagstone walkways, terraced lawns and gardens; but the sense of desert is eroded by surrounding subdivisions. A good value, given the wide range of activities and moderately priced dining options. **Rooms:** 650 rms and stes; 125 cottages/villas. CI 4pm/CO noon. Nonsmoking rms avail. Asymmetric configuration makes 525-square-foot rooms more interesting than usual cookie cutters, and they're comfortable and efficient. Oval bathtubs. Marginal views. **Amenities:** A/C, cable TV w/movies, dataport, voice mail, in-rm safe, bathrobes. All units w/minibars, all w/terraces, some w/fireplaces. In-room video services (telephone messages, accounts review, room-service orders); speakerphones with call-waiting, two extensions; swimsuit bags in closets; wood-burning fireplaces in casitas. **Services:** Twice-daily maid svce, car-rental desk, social director, masseur, children's program, babysitting. Genial, generally competent staff. **Facilities:** 36 1 7 2500 5 restaurants (*see* "Restaurants" below), 7 bars (2 w/entertainment), basketball, volleyball, lawn games, racquetball, squash, spa, sauna, steam rm, whirlpool, beauty salon. Golf courses, a short drive away, are operated by TPC (one of them is home of the Phoenix Open), owned by the city, and open to all, but Princess guests get priority tee times. 10-station fitness course; 10,000 square feet of workout space. Kids' Club activities include sand painting and Native American bead art. **Rates:** Peak (Jan–May 21) $300–$1,800 S or D; $480–$2,500 ste; $480–$2,500 cottage/villa. Extra person $30. Children under age 12 stay free. Min stay special events. Lower rates off-season. AP and MAP rates avail. Parking: Outdoor, free. AE, CB, DC, DISC, ER, JCB, MC, V.

RESTAURANTS

Baby Kay's Cajun Kitchen
7216 E Shoeman Lane; tel 602/990-9080. **Cajun.** A small Cajun diner and bar with funky New Orleans decor. The menu includes a spicy gumbo, catfish filets in sherry or crawfish sauce, barbecue shrimp, and red beans and rice. A specialty is chicken and sausage jambalaya. **FYI:** Reservations not accepted. Jazz. Additional location: 2119 E Camelback Rd, Phoenix (tel 955-6011). **Open:** Daily 4pm–1am. **Prices:** Main courses $8–$17. AE, DC, MC, V.

Bola's Grill
In the Holiday Inn Hotel and Conference Center, 7353 E Indian School Rd (Old Town); tel 602/994-9203. **New American.** A southwestern grill in the Scottsdale Civic Center Mall. The dining area is in a semi-circle around the exposed kitchen. Specialties include grilled lamb chops, baby back ribs, lemon oregano chicken, and southwestern duck. **FYI:** Reservations accepted. Guitar/piano/singer. Children's menu. No smoking. **Open:** Lunch Mon–Sat 11am–2pm; dinner Sun–Thurs 5–9pm, Fri–Sat 5–10pm; brunch Sun 11am–2pm. **Prices:** Main courses $9–$20. AE, CB, DC, DISC, MC, V.

Cantina del Pedregal
In El Pedregal Marketplace, 34505 N Scottsdale Rd; tel 602/488-0715. 1 mi S of Carefree. **Mexican.** This comfortable Mexican restaurant in the hills north of Phoenix offers patio dining and splendid views. Attractively decorated in folk art style, with "rock art" painted on the stucco walls. The Sonoran cuisine is highlighted by the Mexican Gulf shrimp with smoked red chile sauce. Also offered are hot pork tamales; chicken, beef, and shrimp fajitas; chiles rellenos; and chicken with mole sauce. The margaritas are very popular. **FYI:** Reservations recommended. Children's menu. No smoking. **Open:** Peak (Sept–July) lunch daily 11am–2:30pm; dinner daily 5–9:30pm. **Prices:** Main courses $9–$16. AE, CB, DC, MC, V.

Carver's
In Scottsdale Shopping Center, 10825 N Scottsdale Rd; tel 602/998-8777. Scottsdale Rd and Shea Blvd. **New American/Steak.** A warm, cozy restaurant offering top cuts of beef and seafood. Specialties include prime rib, whisky peppercorn steak, and roast duck in raspberry sauce. **FYI:** Reservations recommended. Children's menu. Additional location: 8172 W Bell Rd, Phoenix (tel 412-0787). **Open:** Lunch Mon–Fri 11am–2:30pm; dinner Mon–Thurs 5–9:30pm, Fri 5–10pm, Sat 4:30–10pm, Sun 4–9pm. **Prices:** Main courses $15–$19. AE, CB, DC, MC, V.

The Chaparral
In Marriott's Camelback Inn Resort, Golf Club & Spa, 5402 E Lincoln Dr (Paradise Valley); tel 602/948-1700. Glendale Ave exit off I-17; continue east until Glendale becomes Lincoln. **Continental/French.** Formal (but not stuffy) restaurant, with a well-informed staff and attentive, gracious service. Circular adobe rooms with Native American motifs, soft lighting, and picture windows for views of Camelback Mountain. Grilled eggplant with mascarpone cheese, pesto, and roasted tomato vinaigrette; veal medallions with crabmeat, lobster, and shrimp; grilled jumbo shrimp with corn fritters and melon salsa. **FYI:** Reservations recommended. Jacket required. **Open:** Daily 6–9pm. **Prices:** Main courses $21–$28. AE, DC, DISC, MC, V. VP

Chart House
7255 E McCormick Pkwy; tel 602/951-2550. 1/10 mi E of Scottsdale Road. **Seafood/Steak.** The large dining room (it seats 220) has a nautical theme and overlooks McCormick Lake. Menu changes frequently, but slow-roasted prime rib is always a specialty, and other beef, seafood, and pasta dishes are available. **FYI:** Reservations recommended. Children's menu. **Open:** Daily 5–10pm. **Prices:** Main courses $14–$25. AE, CB, DC, DISC, MC, V.

Don and Charlie's
7501 E Camelback Rd; tel 602/990-0900. At Scottsdale Rd. **American.** One word—sports—sums up the decor of this central Scottsdale eatery. With an emphasis on baseball, the restaurant is decorated with sports memorabilia, from photos to signed baseballs and footballs. The menu offers ribs,

steaks, barbecue, prime rib, seafood, and pasta. **FYI:** Reservations recommended. Children's menu. **Open:** Mon–Sat 5–10pm, Sun 4:30–9pm. **Prices:** Main courses $8–$24. AE, CB, DC, DISC, MC, V.

Eddie Chan's
In Mountain View Plaza, 9699 N Hayden Rd; tel 602/998-8188. **Chinese.** A pleasant, intimate, quiet spot in a Scottsdale shopping center. The walls and floor are dark green, and attractive carved wooden partitions separate dining areas. A large selection of Hunan and Cantonese specialties are featured. **FYI:** Reservations accepted. **Open:** Mon–Fri 11am–10pm, Sat noon–10pm, Sun 4:30–10pm. **Prices:** Main courses $6–$23. AE, DISC, MC, V.

8700
In the Citadel, 8700 E Pinnacle Peak Rd (Pinnacle Peak); tel 602/994-8700. At Pima Rd. **Continental.** This lovely restaurant is handsomely decorated with original paintings and sculpture, antiques, dried-flower arrangements, a travertine floor, and fireplace. Selections are continental with a Southwest flavor: roast rack of black buck antelope in jerk and juniper marinade; charbroiled veal chop with ancho chile-honey glaze; sautéed scallops with salmon and sole poached in cabbage. Variety of desserts prepared daily. **FYI:** Reservations recommended. No smoking. **Open:** Daily 6–10pm. **Prices:** Main courses $14–$30. AE, CB, DC, DISC, MC, V.

★ El Chorro Lodge
5550 E Lincoln Dr (Paradise Valley); tel 602/948-5170. **American.** Built in 1934 as a girls school, the building was converted to a lodge and restaurant in 1937. Today, the original schoolroom is the main bar. Decor is western, with numerous prints and sculptures. Traditional fare includes steaks, lamb chops, baby back ribs, and some seafood, as well as a few lighter options. **FYI:** Reservations recommended. Children's menu. **Open:** Lunch daily 11am–3pm; dinner daily 5:30–11pm; brunch Sun 9am–3pm. **Prices:** Main courses $15–$27. AE, CB, DC, DISC, MC, V. VP

Golden Swan
In the Hyatt Regency Scottsdale, 7500 E Doubletree Ranch Rd; tel 602/991-3388 ext 79. **Regional American.** The indoor dining area, decorated with etched glasswork, opens onto a patio and overlooks a duck pond. Traditional American dishes are prepared with an international flair. **FYI:** Reservations recommended. Piano. Children's menu. No smoking. **Open:** Dinner daily 6–10pm; brunch Sun 9:30am–2:30pm. **Prices:** Main courses $21–$33. AE, DC, DISC, MC, V. VP

The Grill
In the Scottsdale Princess, 7575 E Princess Dr; tel 602/585-4848. Bell Rd exit off I-17 head E to Scottsdale Rd. **American.** A relaxed, casual golf course restaurant offering great views of the course and nearby mountains. The ceiling is open-beamed, and caricatures of local personalities decorate the walls; there are TVs at the bar. The menu includes a variety of salads and sandwiches, plus full dinners of charbroiled meats and grilled fish. **FYI:** Reservations accepted. Children's menu. **Open:** Daily 6am–10pm. **Prices:** Main courses $15–$19. AE, CB, DC, DISC, ER, MC, V.

Jean-Claude's Petit Cafe
7340 E Shoeman Lane; tel 602/947-5288. **French.** Tucked away on a side street, this small French cafe has a faithful following. Hors d'oeuvres range from pâté to escargots in garlic butter to fresh seafood in a puff pastry. Entrees include duck cooked in a raspberry vinegar and grilled salmon with tarragon. The dessert soufflés are popular. **FYI:** Reservations recommended. **Open:** Lunch daily 11:30am–2pm; dinner daily 6–9pm. **Prices:** Main courses $13–$20. AE, CB, DC, DISC, MC, V.

Jewel of the Crown
In Financial Center 2, 4141 N Scottsdale Rd, Ste 110; tel 602/840-2412. At Indian School Rd. **Indian.** Delightful East Indian restaurant hidden away in the back of a business complex. Carved wooden elephants, urns, and screens. Tapestries adorn the walls. The tandoori and curry specialties feature chicken, shrimp, and fish. East Indian desserts served. **FYI:** Reservations recommended. **Open:** Lunch daily 11:30am–2pm; dinner daily 5–10pm. **Prices:** Main courses $6–$15. AE, DC, DISC, MC, V.

La Hacienda
In the Scottsdale Princess, 7575 E Princess Dr; tel 602/271-9000. Bell Rd exit of I-17, head E to Scottsdale Rd. **Mexican.** As the name might suggest, this is a Mexican hacienda-style restaurant, with thick stucco walls, two fireplaces, a stone floor in the lounge, and chile ristras throughout. The exotic Mexican menu includes cochinillo asado—suckling pig marinated in bitter orange, black pepper, and tamarind, carved at your table. Seafood entrees range from swordfish steamed in banana leaves to wood-grilled ahi tuna. Strolling mariachi musicians perform nightly. **FYI:** Reservations recommended. Children's menu. **Open:** Sun–Thurs 6–10pm, Fri–Sat 6–11pm. **Prices:** Main courses $17–$25. AE, CB, DC, DISC, ER, MC, V. VP

★ L'Ecole
In the Scottsdale Culinary Institute, 8100 E Camelback Rd; tel 602/990-7639. **International.** This locally popular restaurant is a training ground for students at the Scottsdale Culinary Institute. The menu includes veal, chicken, and fish dishes, some of which are prepared tableside. All meals include appetizer, salad, dessert, tea or coffee. **FYI:** Reservations recommended. Dress code. No smoking. **Open:** Lunch Mon–Fri 11:30am–1pm; dinner Mon–Fri 6:30–8pm. **Prices:** Prix fixe $14–$20. AE, DISC, MC, V.

★ Los Olivos
7328 2nd St (Downtown); tel 602/946-2256. **American/Mexican.** This Scottsdale landmark, opened in 1945, is well

known for its wonderful margaritas and live Latin music. Chef Juanita Recalde has been preparing unusual Mexican cuisine here for over 30 years. There are two large dining rooms and a dance floor. **FYI:** Reservations recommended. Jazz/Latin. Children's menu. **Open:** Sun–Thurs 11am–10pm, Fri–Sat 11am–11pm. **Prices:** Main courses $6–$14. AE, CB, DC, DISC, MC, V.

Malee's on Main Street
7131 E Main St (Old Town); tel 602/947-6042. **Thai.** Intimate restaurant with a small bar and lounge, soft sconce lighting, and muted watercolor paintings. A second dining room has a fireplace. The gourmet Thai dishes are rated for spiciness. **FYI:** Reservations recommended. **Open:** Lunch Mon–Fri 11:30am–2:30pm, Sat noon–2:30pm; dinner Mon–Thurs 5–9:30pm, Fri–Sat 5–10pm, Sun 5–9pm. **Prices:** Main courses $9–$19. AE, MC, V.

Mancuso's Restaurant
In the Borgata, 6166 N Scottsdale Rd; tel 602/948-9988. **French/Italian.** Set in an elegant château with chandeliers. The menu features about a dozen different pastas, plus veal saltimbocca, veal sweetbreads, and numerous beef, chicken, and seafood selections. **FYI:** Reservations recommended. Piano. Dress code. **Open:** Sun–Thurs 5–10pm, Fri–Sat 5–10:30pm. **Prices:** Main courses $15–$30. AE, DC, DISC, MC, V. VP

Marché Gourmet
4121 N Marshall Way (Old Town); tel 602/994-4568. **French.** Small, intimate French bistro. The main dining room has vine-covered windows. Specialties include cassoulet toulousain, Spanish paella, and merquez—spicy lamb sausages with fries. **FYI:** Reservations recommended. No smoking. **Open:** Breakfast daily 7:30–11am; lunch daily 11am–2pm; dinner Mon–Sat 5:30–8:30pm. **Prices:** Main courses $10–$20. AE, DC, DISC, MC, V.

Maria's When in Naples
In Scottsdale Promenade Shopping Center, 7000 E Shea Blvd; tel 602/991-6887. **Italian.** Authentic Italian food, with pastas made fresh on the premises, in the heart of Scottsdale. Murals and hanging garlic highlight the Italian peasant decor. Family owned. **FYI:** Reservations recommended. No smoking. **Open:** Lunch Mon–Fri 11:30am–2:30pm; dinner Mon–Fri 5–10pm. Closed Aug 1–14. **Prices:** Main courses $10–$20. AE, CB, DC, DISC, ER, MC, V. VP

$ The Market at the Citadel
In The Inn at the Citadel, 8700 E Pinnacle Peak Rd (North Scottsdale); tel 602/585-0635. **Southwestern.** A combination deli-restaurant, with a market-like dining room decorated with baskets, chile wreaths, and glassware. Wide variety of soups and salads, plus roast chicken, ribs, meatloaf, fajitas, enchiladas, and seafood. **FYI:** Reservations accepted. Children's menu. No smoking. **Open:** Daily 7am–10pm. **Prices:** Main courses $8–$18. AE, CB, DC, DISC, ER, MC, V.

Marquesa
In the Scottsdale Princess, 7575 E Princess Dr; tel 602/585-4848. Bell Rd continue east on Bell to Scottsdale Road. **Mediterranean/Spanish.** Catalan cuisine prepared and served in elegant surroundings. Stylish Estancia decor; tapas bar and patio with fireplace for outdoor dining. Among dishes offered are crabmeat and fontina cheese in baked sweet red peppers with garlic aioli; and veal tenderloin and breast of duckling with polenta and asparagus. Marquesa is also noted for its Sunday "marketplace" brunch—a buffet of some four dozen dishes, not including paellas and desserts. **FYI:** Reservations recommended. Dress code. **Open:** Dinner daily 6–10pm; brunch Sun 10:30am–2pm. Closed July–Aug. **Prices:** Main courses $24–$30. AE, CB, DC, DISC, MC, V. VP

Mary Elaine's
In The Phoenician, 6000 E Camelback Rd; tel 602/941-8200. Camelback exit off I-17. **French.** Opulent setting of softly lit gold-leaf accents, 18th-century paintings, and a wall-to-wall window looking out to the lights of Scottsdale. The custom-designed Mikasa china, Schott-Zwiessel crystal, and waiters dressed in formal attire enhance the air of elegance. Entrees include garlic-and-herb-crusted rack of Colorado lamb; seared duck breast with peppery apple glaze; and roasted sea scallops with curry-coconut sauce and mango chutney. Award-winning wine list, knowledgeable sommelier. The terrace is an romantic spot for after-dinner cognac. **FYI:** Reservations recommended. Singer. Children's menu. Jacket required. **Open:** Daily 6–10pm. **Prices:** Main courses $29–$34; prix fixe $75. AE, CB, DC, DISC, ER, MC, V. VP

Palm Court
In the Scottsdale Conference Resort, 7700 E McCormick Pkwy (McCormick Ranch); tel 602/991-3400. **Continental.** Elegant dining among palm trees and flowers; a glass-fronted wine cabinet is the centerpiece. The menu emphasizes seafood but also includes roast tenderloin, rack of lamb, duckling, and veal. **FYI:** Reservations recommended. Piano. Jacket required. No smoking. **Open:** Breakfast daily 7–10am; lunch daily 11am–2pm; dinner daily 5–10pm; brunch Sun 10:30am–2pm. **Prices:** Main courses $21–$30. AE, CB, DC, DISC, MC, V. VP

Pepin Restaurante Español
In Scottsdale Civic Center Mall, 7363 Scottsdale Mall; tel 602/990-9026. **Spanish.** Spanish atmosphere abounds: white stuccoed arches, bota wine flasks, and flamenco dancing and guitar music. The chef prepares dishes from the Spanish coastal province of Galicia, his homeland. Wide selection of tapas. **FYI:** Reservations accepted. Guitar/Flamenco. **Open:** Lunch Mon–Sat 11:30am–3pm; dinner daily 5–11pm. **Prices:** Main courses $10–$20. AE, DC, DISC, MC, V.

The Piñon Grill
In the Regal McCormick Ranch, 7401 N Scottsdale Rd; tel 602/948-5050. **Southwestern.** Offering innovative seafood

selections, as well as beef and chicken. A dessert specialty is the chocolate taco. **FYI:** Reservations recommended. Children's menu. **Open:** Daily 6:30am–10pm. **Prices:** Main courses $16–$26. AE, CB, DC, DISC, MC, V.

Reay's Cafe

In Reay's Ranch Market, 9689 N Hayden Rd (North Scottsdale); tel 602/596-9496. **Health/Spa.** Bright and cheery cafe located in a health food supermarket. There's patio dining under a large covered awning; a misting system keeps patrons cool. Limited entrees, mostly grilled fish and chicken. Good choice of gourmet coffees. **FYI:** Reservations not accepted. Beer and wine only. No smoking. **Open:** Daily 7am–8pm. **Prices:** Main courses $10–$15. DISC, MC, V.

Sfuzzi

In Fashion Square Shopping Center, 4720 N Scottsdale Rd; tel 602/946-9777. **Italian.** High-ceilinged bistro serving imaginative pastas and pizzas. **FYI:** Reservations recommended. Children's menu. **Open:** Mon–Sat 11am–10pm, Sun 10:30am–10pm. **Prices:** Main courses $8–$20; prix fixe $12. AE, DC, MC, V.

Sushi Ko

In Mercado Del Rancho Shopping Center, 9301 E Shea Blvd; tel 602/860-5605. **Japanese/Seafood.** Simply decorated eatery serving a broad range of traditional dishes. Sushi bar. **FYI:** Reservations accepted. No smoking. **Open:** Lunch Mon–Fri noon–2pm; dinner Mon–Sat 5:30–10pm, Sun 5:30–9pm. **Prices:** Main courses $7–$19. AE, CB, DC, DISC, MC, V.

Va Bene Trattoria

In Mountain View Plaza, 9619 N Hayden Rd (North Scottsdale); tel 602/922-3576. **Italian.** Small, intimate cafe specializing in Northern Italian cuisine. Specialties include nodino di vitello alla Valdostana, a veal chop sautéed with sage and baked with ham and cheese, and tris, or triple pasta. **FYI:** Reservations not accepted. No smoking. **Open:** Lunch Tues–Fri 11am–2pm; dinner Tues–Sun 5–10pm. **Prices:** Main courses $10–$22. AE, DC, MC, V.

Voltaire

8340 E MacDonald Dr; tel 602/948-1005. **Continental.** Red leather chairs, red carpet, and a mirrored wall give Voltaire a sophisticated, continental atmosphere. Some tables have their own chandeliers. Specialties include duckling in orange sauce, and calf sweetbreads sautéed in lemon butter with capers. **FYI:** Reservations recommended. Jacket required. No smoking. **Open:** Peak (Oct–May) Mon–Sat 5:30–10pm. Closed June–Sept. **Prices:** Main courses $16–$22. AE, MC, V.

Windows on the Green

In The Phoenician, 6000 E Camelback Rd; tel 602/941-8200. Camelback exit off I-17; continue east on Camelback to 44th Street. **Southwestern.** Golf course clubhouses don't come more stylish than this 120-seater, with its custom-designed china and original art. The airy, sunny room overlooks the fairways, and there is a striking collection of southwestern glass and pottery. The bar has a big-screen TV for major sporting events. The imaginative, refreshing cuisine ranges from lobster and roasted corn chili, to sugar and chile-cured venison chop with grits. **FYI:** Reservations recommended. Guitar. Children's menu. **Open:** Breakfast Sat–Sun 10am–3pm; lunch Tues–Sun 11am–3pm; dinner Tues–Sun 6–10pm. **Prices:** Main courses $17–$26. AE, CB, DC, DISC, MC, V. VP

ATTRACTIONS

Taliesin West

Frank Lloyd Wright Blvd and Cactus Rd; tel 602/860-2700. The headquarters of the Frank Lloyd Wright Foundation and School of Architecture. Tours offer background on Wright and an introduction to his theories of architecture. Wright believed in using local materials in his designs, which is evident here in the campus buildings. **Open:** Peak (June–Sept) daily 7:30am–3:30pm. Reduced hours off-season. **$$$**

Cosanti

6433 Doubletree Ranch Rd; tel 602/948-6145. This complex of cast-concrete structures served as a prototype and learning project for architect Paolo Soleri's much larger Arcosanti project, located north of Phoenix (see listing under "Mayer"). Soleri designs bronze wind bells, which are cast here and sold all over Arizona to finance his architecture projects. **Open:** Daily 9am–5pm. **$**

Fleischer Museum

17207 N Perimeter Dr; tel 602/585-3108. The permanent collection focuses on the California school of American impressionism. Other displays include Russian and Soviet impressionism during the cold war era. **Open:** Daily 10am–4pm. **Free**

Scottsdale Center for the Arts

7380 N 2nd St; tel 602/994-2301. Anchoring the Scottsdale Mall sculpture park at the heart of downtown Scottsdale, this cultural center hosts both visual-art exhibitions and performing-arts productions. The center includes three art galleries with rotating exhibits, an indoor theater, and an outdoor amphitheater. **Open:** Call for schedule. **$$$$**

Kerr Cultural Center

6110 N Scottsdale Rd; tel 602/965-5377. An adobe building that provides an intimate setting for an eclectic and diversified season. Offerings include everything from cowboy bands to classical music to jazz. **Open:** Box office: Mon–Fri 10am–5pm. **$$$**

Rawhide

23023 N Scottsdale Rd; tel 602/502-1880. A replica of an 1880s western town featuring a main street with 20 traditional craft shops, stagecoach rides, and a western stunt show every hour. New to the town is a Native American Village, built and staffed by Native Americans representing the seven local tribes of the area. Special events include rodeos and country music performances. **Open:** Peak (Oct–May) Mon–Thurs 5–10pm, Fri–Sun 11am–10pm. Reduced hours off-season. **Free**

Sedona

A haven for artists and practitioners of New Age philosophies, Sedona sits at the mouth of spectacularly beautiful Oak Creek Canyon. The city is an extremely popular tourist destination among lovers of the arts as well as outdoor recreationists, who use it as a base for exploring the surrounding red rock country on foot, mountain bike, or horseback, or by hot air balloon or four-wheel-drive vehicle. **Information:** Sedona–Oak Creek Canyon Chamber of Commerce, Corner 89A & Forest, PO Box 478, Sedona 86339 (tel 520/282-7722 or 800/288-7336).

HOTEL

Bell Rock Inn

6246 AZ 179, 86351; tel 520/282-4161 or toll free 800/881-7625; fax 520/284-0192. 8 mi W of I-17. A southwestern-style hotel in scenic Oak Creek, just south of Sedona. **Rooms:** 96 rms and stes. CI 3pm/CO 11am. Nonsmoking rms avail. Rooms are finished in rough wood and beamed ceilings and decorated with southwestern art. **Amenities:** A/C, cable TV. **Services:** Complimentary champagne provided. **Facilities:** 1 restaurant, 1 bar (w/entertainment), whirlpool. **Rates:** Peak (Apr–Nov) $59–$65 S; $79–$89 D; $109–$135 ste. Extra person $9. Lower rates off-season. Parking: Outdoor, free. AE, MC, V.

MOTELS

Best Western Arroyo Roble Hotel

400 N US 89A, PO Box NN, 86339; tel 520/282-4001 or toll free 800/528-1234; fax 520/282-4001. A striking five-story motel set above Oak Creek. Pleasant foyer. **Rooms:** 53 rms; 8 cottages/villas. CI 2pm/CO 11am. Nonsmoking rms avail. Some rooms have views of the canyon's spectacular red rock formations. **Amenities:** A/C, cable TV, refrig. All units w/terraces, some w/fireplaces, some w/whirlpools. **Services:** Babysitting. Complimentary coffee. **Facilities:** Games rm, spa, sauna, steam rm, whirlpool, washer/dryer. Close to golf, hiking trails, and horseback riding, and within walking distance of numerous restaurants. **Rates:** Peak (Feb 15–Nov) $105–$120 S; $115–$130 D; $155–$275 cottage/villa. Extra person $10. Children under age 12 stay free. Lower rates off-season. Parking: Outdoor, free. AE, CB, DC, DISC, MC, V.

Quality Inn King's Ransom

771 AZ 179, PO Box 180, 86339; tel 520/282-7151 or toll free 800/228-5151. A conveniently located motel, with peaceful and attractive rose gardens. **Rooms:** 101 rms. CI 3pm/CO 11am. Nonsmoking rms avail. Rooms have good lighting and southwestern furnishings. **Amenities:** A/C, cable TV. Some units w/terraces. **Services:** **Facilities:** 1 restaurant (*see* "Restaurants" below), 1 bar, whirlpool. **Rates:** Peak (Feb 15–Nov 30) $72–$125 S; $82–$125 D. Extra person $10. Children under age 18 stay free. Lower rates off-season. Parking: Outdoor, free. AE, CB, DC, DISC, ER, JCB, MC, V.

Sedona Motel

218 AZ 179, PO Box 1450, 86339 (Downtown); tel 520/282-7187. Economical lodging right in the heart of Sedona. **Rooms:** 16 rms and stes. CI 3pm/CO 10am. Nonsmoking rms avail. Many rooms offer spectacular views. **Amenities:** A/C, cable TV. **Services:** **Rates:** Peak (Mar–Nov) $69–$74 S; $69–$84 D; $89–$109 ste. Extra person $6. Lower rates off-season. Parking: Indoor, free. AE, DISC, MC, V.

INN

Canyon Villa Bed and Breakfast Inn

125 Canyon Circle Dr, 86351 (Oak Creek); tel 520/284-1226 or toll free 800/453-1166; fax 520/284-2114. A lovely inn, with marvelous furnishings and original art in the common areas. The inn adjoins national forest lands and has unobstructed views of Sedona's famous red rocks. Unsuitable for children under 10. **Rooms:** 11 rms. CI 3pm/CO 11am. No smoking. Each room is decorated in its own unique motif, some with handmade quilts and rocking chairs. **Amenities:** A/C, cable TV, bathrobes. All units w/terraces, some w/fireplaces, some w/whirlpools. **Services:** Afternoon tea served. **Facilities:** Guest lounge w/TV. The outdoor swimming pool is delightful. **Rates (BB):** Peak (Feb–Oct) $95–$155 S or D. Extra person $25. Min stay wknds and special events. Lower rates off-season. Parking: Outdoor, free. MC, V.

RESORTS

Enchantment Resort

525 Boynton Canyon Rd, 86336; tel 520/282-2900 or toll free 800/522-2282; fax 520/282-9249. 3 mi W of Sedona. Dry Creek Rd exit off US 89A. 70 acres. A secluded, tranquil pueblo-style resort offering some of the most spectacular views in Sedona. **Rooms:** 162 rms and stes; 56 cottages/villas. Executive level. CI 4pm/CO noon. Nonsmoking rms avail. Rooms are attractively decorated in Southwestern style. Can rent individual rooms in casitas, or entire casita. **Amenities:** A/C, cable TV w/movies, refrig, dataport, voice mail, bathrobes. All units w/minibars, all w/terraces, some w/fireplaces, some w/whirlpools. All casita studios have gas barbecues. **Services:** Twice-daily maid svce, social director, masseur, children's program, babysitting. Guests receive complimentary orange juice and faxed versions of *USA Today* each morning. **Facilities:** 2 restaurants (*see* "Restaurants" below), 1 bar (w/entertainment), volleyball, lawn games, spa, sauna, steam rm, whirlpool, playground, washer/dryer. Hiking and other

activities nearby. **Rates:** $225 S; $425 D; $375 ste; $595 cottage/villa. Extra person $20. Children under age 12 stay free. Min stay wknds and special events. Parking: Outdoor, free. AE, DISC, MC, V.

L'Auberge de Sedona
301 L'Auberge Lane, PO Box B, 86336; tel 520/282-7131 or toll free 800/272-6777; fax 520/282-2885. AZ 179 exit off AZ 89A. 11 acres. A resort with a diverse selection of accommodations. This is actually two resorts in one, with the Orchards at L'Auberge atop a hill above L'Auberge. The two are connected by a walkway and cable car. L'Auberge has rooms in the lodge and cottages; the Orchard has rooms only. Scenery along Oak Creek, which runs beside the cottages, is lovely. No smoking throughout. **Rooms:** 68 rms; 31 cottages/villas. Executive level. CI 3pm/CO 11am. No smoking. All rooms and cottages have canopy beds and are individually decorated. **Amenities:** A/C, cable TV, dataport, CD/tape player, in-rm safe, bathrobes. All units w/minibars, some w/terraces, some w/fireplaces, 1 w/whirlpool. Cottages have no TV. **Services:** Twice-daily maid svce, social director, masseur, babysitting. **Facilities:** 200 3 restaurants, 2 bars, whirlpool. **Rates:** Peak (Mar–Nov 14) $140–$210 S or D; $235–$335 cottage/villa. Extra person $20. Lower rates off-season. Parking: Outdoor, free. AE, DC, DISC, MC, V.

Los Abrigados
160 Portal Lane, 86336; tel 520/282-1777 or toll free 800/521-3131; fax 520/282-2614. Behind the Tlaquepaque Shopping Center. 22 acres. This Spanish revival–style resort, with red-tile roofs and brick and stucco walls, is reminiscent of Old Mexico. **Rooms:** 172 stes. CI 4pm/CO noon. Nonsmoking rms avail. **Amenities:** A/C, cable TV w/movies, refrig. All units w/minibars, all w/terraces, some w/fireplaces, some w/whirlpools. **Services:** Social director, masseur, babysitting. **Facilities:** 3 275 3 restaurants, lawn games, spa, sauna, steam rm, whirlpool, beauty salon, playground, washer/dryer. **Rates:** Peak (Feb–Dec) $210–$395 ste. Extra person $20. Children under age 16 stay free. Min stay special events. Lower rates off-season. Parking: Outdoor, free. AE, CB, DC, DISC, EC, ER, MC, V.

Poco Diablo Resort
1752 S AZ 179, PO Box 1709, 86336; tel 520/282-7333 or toll free 800/528-4275; fax 520/282-2090. 22 acres. Full-featured golf and tennis resort. **Rooms:** 109 rms and stes. CI 3pm/CO noon. Nonsmoking rms avail. Rooms are decorated with contemporary Southwestern art and furnishings; some offer splendid views of the surrounding canyon walls. **Amenities:** A/C, cable TV w/movies, bathrobes. All units w/minibars, some w/terraces, some w/fireplaces, some w/whirlpools. **Services:** Social director, masseur, babysitting. **Facilities:** 9 2 4 300 1 restaurant, 1 bar (w/entertainment), basketball, volleyball, racquetball, whirlpool, playground, washer/dryer. **Rates:** $135 S or D; $225–$360 ste. Extra person $20. Children under age 16 stay free. Min stay wknds. Parking: Outdoor, free. AE, CB, DC, DISC, JCB, MC, V.

RESTAURANTS

El Riñcon del Tlaquepaque
In Tlaquepaque Shopping Center, AZ 179; tel 520/282-4648. **Mexican.** Traditional Mexican decor with wrought iron, traditional Mexican food with some Navajo flavorings. **FYI:** Reservations recommended. Children's menu. No smoking. **Open:** Tues–Sat 11am–9pm, Sun noon–5pm. **Prices:** Main courses $5–$15. MC, V.

La Mediterranée de Sedona
In the Quality Inn Kings Ransom, 771 AZ 179; tel 520/282-7006. **Mediterranean/Middle Eastern.** Modern southwestern look, with a ten-foot-square window facing the red rocks to the north. There are two balconies for outdoor dining. Extensive menu contains many Mediterranean specialties as well as vegetarian dishes. **FYI:** Reservations recommended. No smoking. **Open:** Daily 7am–11pm. **Prices:** Main courses $6–$46. AE, DISC, MC, V.

L'Auberge
In L'Auberge de Sedona, 301 L'Auberge Lane; tel 520/282-2885. L'Auberge Lane exit off AZ 89. **French.** Offers a total dining experience for the connoisseur of French cuisine. The dining room, done in French country style, overlooks a shaded creek. **FYI:** Reservations recommended. Jacket required. No smoking. **Open:** Breakfast daily 7–11am; lunch daily 11:30am–2:30pm; dinner daily 5:30–10pm. **Prices:** Main courses $28–$36; prix fixe $55. AE, CB, DC, DISC, MC, V.

René at Tlaquepaque
In Tlaquepaque Shopping Center, AZ 179; tel 520/282-9225. **French.** Decorated with paintings by local artists and flowers and enhanced with soft light. Selection of relatively simple French dishes. Rack of lamb is a specialty. **FYI:** Reservations recommended. No smoking. **Open:** Lunch daily 11:30am–2pm; dinner Sun–Thurs 5:30–8:30pm, Fri–Sat 5:30–9pm. **Prices:** Main courses $15–$27; prix fixe $29. AE, MC, V.

★ **Sedona Swiss Restaurant & Cafe**
350 Jordan Rd; tel 520/282-7959. Jordan Rd exit off US 89A. **French/Swiss.** The Swiss owners fell in love with Sedona while vacationing here and never left. Most popular are the veal dishes, such as veal eminc Zurichois, which is veal sautéed in a cognac-mushroom sauce. Also on the menu are chicken, seafood, beef, and lamb. The pastries and chocolates are locally famous. **FYI:** Reservations recommended. Children's menu. No smoking. **Open:** Mon–Sat 7:30am–9:30pm. Closed Jan 1–21. **Prices:** Main courses $10–$22. MC, V.

Shugrue's Restaurant, Bakery & Bar
2250 W US 89A; tel 520/282-2943. **New American/Seafood.** A large, roomy restaurant, with three dining rooms, book-lined walls, and wood beams. One room holds a large fish tank. The prime rib is especially popular. Diners can create their own combinations, such as prime rib with shrimp scampi. **FYI:** Reservations recommended. Children's menu. No smoking. **Open:** Breakfast Tues–Sun 8–11:30am; lunch Tues–Sun 11:30am–3pm; dinner Mon–Fri 5–9pm, Sat–Sun 5–10pm; brunch Sat–Sun 8am–3pm. **Prices:** Main courses $10–$22; prix fixe $10–$14. AE, MC, V.

Yavapai Room
In the Enchantment Resort, 525 Boynton Canyon Rd; tel 520/282-2900. Dry Creek Rd exit off US 89A. **New American/Southwestern.** Two glass walls offer patrons at this top dining spot some terrific views of Sedona's famous red rock formations—especially beautiful at sunset. The kitchen offers innovative takes on standard dishes. Extensive wine list. **FYI:** Reservations recommended. Piano. Children's menu. Jacket required. No smoking. **Open:** Breakfast daily 7–11am; lunch daily 11:30am–2:30pm; dinner daily 6–10pm; brunch Sun 10:30am–2:30pm. **Prices:** Main courses $16–$33. AE, CB, DC, DISC, MC, V.

ATTRACTION

Sedona Arts Center
Art Barn Road exit off US 89A; tel 520/282-3809. Serves as both a gallery for artworks by local and regional artists and a theater for plays and music performances. Art classes offered year-round.

Sierra Vista

Site of both a historic fort and a modern military installation, Sierra Vista is a good base for nature lovers who want to explore nearby preserves and try to spot some of the 300 species of birds in the area. **Information:** Sierra Vista Chamber of Commerce/Tourist & Visitors' Center, 77 S Calle Portal, #A140, Sierra Vista 85635 (tel 520/458-6940 or 800/288-3861).

HOTEL

Wyndemere Hotel & Conference Center
2047 S AZ 92, 85635; tel 520/459-5900 or toll free 800/825-4656; fax 520/458-1347. 2 mi S of jct AZ 90/AZ 92. Modern three-story hotel. **Rooms:** 149 rms and stes. Executive level. CI 4pm/CO 11am. Nonsmoking rms avail. Rooms have large closets and contemporary furnishings. **Amenities:** A/C, cable TV w/movies. Some units w/whirlpools. Refrigerators available. **Services:** Social director, babysitting. **Facilities:** 1 restaurant, 1 bar (w/entertainment), whirlpool. Free use of adjacent health club. **Rates (BB):** $64–$86 S or D; $110 ste. Extra person $8. Children under age 12 stay free. AP rates avail. Parking: Outdoor, free. AE, CB, DC, DISC, MC, V.

ATTRACTIONS

Fort Huachuca
Jct AZ 90/92; tel 520/533-7536. This army base was established in 1877 and the buildings of the old post have been declared a National Historic Landmark. The Fort Huachuca Museum is dedicated to the many forts that dotted the Southwest in the latter part of the 19th century. Also on the base is one of Sierra Vista's most famous attractions, the **B Troop, 4th Regiment, US Cavalry Memorial**. This troop of about 30 members dress in the blue-and-gold uniforms of the 1880s cavalry and perform on horseback. Call 602/533-2714 for appearance schedule. **Open:** Mon–Fri 9am–4pm, Sat, Sun 1–4pm. **Free**

San Pedro Riparian National Conservation Area
AZ 90; tel 520/458-3559. A rare example of a natural riparian (riverside) habitat. Fossil findings indicate that people were living along this river 11,000 years ago. At that time the area was not a desert but a swamp, and the San Pedro River is all that remains of this ancient wetland. The conservation area is home to more than 300 species of birds, 80 species of mammals, 14 species of fish, and 40 species of amphibians and reptiles. The headquarters building has handouts and maps of the area. The San Pedro House, a 1930s ranch, operates as a visitor center and bookstore. **Open:** Daily sunrise–sunset. **Free**

Springerville

ATTRACTION

Apache-Sitgreaves National Forests
AZ 260; tel 520/333-4301. Over 800 miles of hiking trails are located on 2 million acres in these 2 connecting national forests. The many lakes provide excellent fishing opportunities, but the high elevation may make the water too cold for most swimmers. There are two visitor centers located at Mogollon Rim and Big Lake. **Open:** Daily 24 hours. **Free**

Superior

ATTRACTION

Boyce Thompson Southwestern Arboretum
37615 US 60; tel 520/689-2811. Built in the 1920s as an educational facility to promote the gardening of drought-tolerant plants, the arboretum's visitor center building is now on the National Register of Historic Places. Because of the presence of both a creek and a small lake, the arboretum has displays on the more water-demanding plants of the desert.

Though the cactus gardens are impressive, it's the two boojum trees from Baja California that visitors find most fascinating. Spring, when the desert wildflowers are in bloom, is the best time to visit. **Open:** Daily 8am–5pm. **$$**

Tempe

A Phoenix suburb in the southeast corner of the metropolitan area, Tempe is home to Arizona State University, with the largest university enrollment in the Southwest. The presence of so many young people keeps a very active nightlife going year-round. Mill Avenue, the center of activity both day and night, has dozens of unique shops along a stretch of about four blocks. **Information:** Tempe Convention & Visitors Bureau, 51 W 3rd St #105, Tempe 85281 (tel 602/894-8158 or 800/283-6734).

HOTELS

Embassy Suites

4400 S Rural Rd, 85282; tel 602/897-7444 or toll free 800/EMBASSY; fax 602/897-6112. Rural Rd exit off US 60. A good-quality, mid-range, all-suites hotel. **Rooms:** 224 stes. CI 3pm/CO 1pm. Nonsmoking rms avail. **Amenities:** A/C, satel TV w/movies, refrig, voice mail. Some units w/terraces. **Services:** Guest service information is in both English and Spanish. Complimentary cocktail hour nightly. **Facilities:** 400 1 restaurant (lunch and dinner only), 1 bar, games rm, spa, sauna, whirlpool, washer/dryer. **Rates (BB):** Peak (Jan–Apr) $165 ste. Extra person $10. Children under age 12 stay free. Lower rates off-season. Parking: Outdoor, free. AE, CB, DC, DISC, JCB, MC, V.

Fiesta Inn

2100 S Priest Dr, 85282; tel 602/967-1441 or toll free 800/528-6481; fax 602/967-0224. Broadway exit off I-10. Frank Lloyd Wright–inspired, partially sunken lobby. Beautiful landscaping. **Rooms:** 270 rms and stes. CI 1pm/CO 1pm. Nonsmoking rms avail. The 100 mini-suites have a pool view. **Amenities:** A/C, satel TV w/movies, refrig, dataport. **Services:** Twice-daily maid svce, car-rental desk, babysitting. Free local calls. **Facilities:** 3 250 1 restaurant, 1 bar, sauna, whirlpool. Guests have free use of bicycles, and there's a golf practice range. **Rates:** Peak (Jan–May) $145–$155 S; $119–$129 D; $225–$275 ste. Extra person $10. Children under age 16 stay free. Lower rates off-season. Parking: Outdoor, free. AE, CB, DC, DISC, MC, V.

La Quinta Inn

911 S 48th St, 85281; tel 602/967-4465 or toll free 800/531-5900; fax 602/921-9172. E of downtown near the airport. An attractive hotel with a pleasant lobby. A full renovation is nearing completion. **Rooms:** 129 rms and stes. CI 2pm/CO noon. Nonsmoking rms avail. Rooms are comfortable and nicely furnished. **Amenities:** A/C, satel TV w/movies, refrig, dataport. **Services:** **Facilities:** 25 Washer/dryer. Putting green in courtyard. **Rates (CP):** Peak (Jan–Apr) $95–$103 S or D; $115 ste. Extra person $10. Children under age 18 stay free. Min stay special events. Lower rates off-season. Parking: Outdoor, free. AE, CB, DC, DISC, MC, V.

Tempe Mission Palms Hotel

60 E 5th St, 85281 (Old Town); tel 602/894-1400 or toll free 800/547-8705. An attractive hotel close to Arizona State University. **Rooms:** 303 rms and stes. CI 3pm/CO noon. Nonsmoking rms avail. **Amenities:** A/C, cable TV w/movies. Some units w/terraces, some w/whirlpools. **Services:** Car-rental desk, babysitting. **Facilities:** 2 200 1 restaurant, 1 bar, spa, sauna, steam rm, whirlpool. **Rates:** Peak (Jan–May 27) $210–$230 S; $220–$240 D; $350–$750 ste. Extra person $10. Children under age 12 stay free. Lower rates off-season. Parking: Outdoor, free. AE, CB, DC, DISC, MC, V.

MOTELS

Comfort Inn

5300 S Priest St, 85283; tel 602/820-7500 or toll free 800/228-5150. Baseline Rd exit off I-10. A simple, comfortable motel, with reasonable rates for the area. **Rooms:** 160 rms. Executive level. CI open/CO noon. Nonsmoking rms avail. **Amenities:** A/C, satel TV w/movies, refrig, dataport. **Services:** **Facilities:** 65 Whirlpool. **Rates:** $69–$99 S or D. Extra person $10. Children under age 18 stay free. Min stay special events. Parking: Outdoor, free. AE, CB, DC, DISC, ER, JCB, MC, V.

Days Inn

1221 E Apache Blvd, 85281; tel 602/968-7793 or toll free 800/325-2525; fax 602/966-4450. Basic motel close to cultural activities at Gammage Center and to Arizona State University. **Rooms:** 100 rms. CI noon/CO 11am. Nonsmoking rms avail. **Amenities:** A/C, cable TV w/movies. **Services:** Free local calls. **Facilities:** 40 Whirlpool, washer/dryer. **Rates (CP):** Peak (Jan–May 30) $69–$89 S or D. Children under age 12 stay free. Lower rates off-season. Parking: Outdoor, free. AE, DC, DISC, MC, V.

Econo Lodge

2101 E Apache Blvd, 85281; tel 602/966-5832 or toll free 800/424-4777. A basic motel eight miles from Phoenix's Sky Harbor International Airport. **Rooms:** 39 rms. CI 11am/CO 11am. Nonsmoking rms avail. **Amenities:** A/C, cable TV w/movies. **Services:** Free local calls. **Facilities:** Washer/dryer. **Rates (CP):** Peak (Jan–Apr) $32–$85 S or D. Extra person $5. Children under age 18 stay free. Lower rates off-season. Parking: Outdoor, free. AE, DISC, MC, V.

RESORT

The Buttes

2000 Westcourt Way, 85282; tel 602/225-9000 or toll free 800/843-1986; fax 602/438-8622. 25 acres. This hilltop resort has commanding views of the area. There is a waterfall and fish pond in the lobby, and a desert garden behind the check-in desk. **Rooms:** 370 rms and stes. Executive level. CI 4pm/CO noon. Nonsmoking rms avail. Rooms are large, with shuttered, double French doors. **Amenities:** A/C, cable TV w/movies, dataport, voice mail. All units w/minibars, some w/terraces. **Services:** Car-rental desk, social director, masseur, children's program, babysitting. **Facilities:** 2 restaurants (*see* "Restaurants" below), 2 bars (1 w/entertainment), volleyball, spa, sauna. 4 whirlpools. **Rates:** Peak (Jan–May) $215–$260 S or D; $475 ste. Extra person $10. Children under age 18 stay free. Min stay special events. Lower rates off-season. Parking: Outdoor, free. AE, CB, DC, DISC, JCB, MC, V.

RESTAURANTS

House of Tricks

114 E 7 St (Old Town); tel 602/968-1114. **New American.** Located in a house with hardwood and tiled floors and a stone fireplace. The regularly changing menu offers innovative variations on American and international dishes. Gourmet food shop due to open adjacent to the restaurant. **FYI:** Reservations recommended. Beer and wine only. No smoking. **Open:** Mon–Thurs 11am–9pm, Fri–Sat 11am–10pm. Closed first 2 weeks of July. **Prices:** Main courses $12–$14. AE, CB, DC, DISC, MC, V.

Monti's La Casa Vieja

3 W 1st St (Old Town); tel 602/967-7594. **Steak.** A historic restaurant in the oldest building in Tempe, with beam and stone walls, animal heads and western paintings on the walls, and a fountain in one of its 13 dining rooms. Barbecued baby-back ribs, steak, deep-fried fish and seafood, and spaghetti and meatballs are among the offerings. **FYI:** Reservations recommended. Children's menu. **Open:** Sun–Thurs 11am–11pm, Fri–Sat 11am–midnight. **Prices:** Main courses $5–$25. AE, CB, DC, DISC, MC, V.

The Paradise Bar and Grill

401 S Mill Ave (Old Town); tel 602/829-0606. At 4th St. **American.** Original brick walls, lots of wood, and photos of old Tempe dominate this pub-type restaurant, located in an 1899 building that is listed on the National Register of Historic Places. Pastas, chicken, catch of the day, steak. **FYI:** Reservations not accepted. Children's menu. **Open:** Sun–Thurs 11am–10pm, Fri–Sat noon–11pm. **Prices:** Main courses $5–$15. AE, DC, DISC, MC, V.

Top of the Rock

In The Buttes, 2000 Westcourt Way; tel 602/225-9000. **Regional American.** Located in a modern, high-beamed circular building that affords diners stunning views of the valley. Creative Southwestern cuisine; specialties include pecan-crusted lamb chops. Pre-theater dinner specials offered in summer. **FYI:** Reservations recommended. Children's menu. **Open:** Dinner Sun–Thurs 5–10pm, Fri–Sat 5–11pm; brunch Sun 10am–2pm. **Prices:** Main courses $16–$28; prix fixe $30–$46. AE, CB, DC, DISC, MC, V.

ATTRACTIONS

Arizona State University Art Museum

At the Nelson Fine Arts Center, 10th St and Mill Ave; tel 602/965-ARTS. Inside are galleries for crafts, prints, contemporary art, American artists, a temporary exhibition gallery, and two outdoor sculpture courts. The museum's collection by American artists includes works by Georgia O'Keeffe, Edward Hopper, and Frederic Remington. **The Matthews Center**, at the corner of Cady and Taylor malls, is affiliated with the museum. It contains Latin American art, American ceramics, and South Pacific and African art. **Open:** Tues 10am–9pm, Wed–Sat 10am–5pm. **Free**

Grady Gammage Memorial Auditorium

Mill Ave and Apache Blvd; tel 602/965-3434. Designed by architect Frank Lloyd Wright, this venue is both graceful and massive. The auditorium, which is on the Arizona State University campus, hosts a wide variety of music and theater performances throughout the year. **Open:** Box office, Mon–Fri 10am–6pm, Sat 10am–4pm. **$$$$**

Sun Devil Stadium

6th St and Stadium Dr; tel 602/965-3434. Home of Arizona State University's Sun Devils football team, and the location of the Fiesta Bowl Football Classic. The stadium also hosts pro football's Arizona Cardinals. **Open:** Box office, Mon–Fri 10am–6pm, Sat 10am–4pm. **$$$$**

Big Surf

1500 N McClintock; tel 602/947-SURF. A water park with 10 waterslides, 2 children's areas, and a wave pool. Also on the premises are volleyball courts, an arcade, and a picnic area. **Open:** June–Sept, Mon–Sat 10am–6pm, Sun 11am–7pm. **$$$$**

Tombstone

A historic Wild West silver mining town, Tombstone was the site in 1881 of the celebrated gunfight at the OK Corral, commemorated each October during Helldorado Days. Many of the town's 19th-century buildings still remain. **Information:** Tombstone Chamber of Commerce & Visitor Center, 4th & Fremont, Box 995, Tombstone 85638 (tel 520/457-9317 or 520/457-3929).

MOTEL

Best Western Look-Out Lodge
US 80 W, PO Box 787, 85638; tel 520/457-2223 or toll free 800/652-6772; fax 520/457-3870. Popular with vacationers; offers splendid views of the Dragoon Mountains. **Rooms:** 40 rms. CI 2pm/CO 11am. Nonsmoking rms avail. Rooms feature king- or queen-size beds and large bathrooms decorated with pretty tile. **Amenities:** A/C, cable TV w/movies, dataport. **Services:** **Facilities:** **Rates (CP):** Peak (Dec–May) $58–$63 S; $68–$72 D. Extra person $5. Children under age 12 stay free. Min stay special events. Lower rates off-season. Parking: Outdoor, free. AE, CB, DC, DISC, MC, V.

RESTAURANT

The Nellie Cashman Restaurant
117 S 5th and Toughnut; tel 520/457-2212. 24 mi N of Bisbee. **American.** Located in a historic part of Tombstone and named for a legendary pioneer woman and philanthropist. Basic diner food, with several types of hamburgers plus hot sandwiches, salads, steaks, chicken, and fish. **FYI:** Reservations accepted. No liquor license. **Open:** Daily 7am–9pm. **Prices:** Main courses $7–$19. AE, DISC, MC, V.

ATTRACTION

Tombstone Historic District
US 80; tel 520/457-2211. Known as "the town too tough to die" and declared a National Historic Landmark in 1962, downtown Tombstone has come to epitomize the image of the Wild West for most people. The star attraction is the **OK Corral**, site of the gun battle between the Earps and the Clantons that has taken on mythic proportions. Each Sunday at 2pm there is a live reenactment of the famous shootout. Next door is Historama, a 30-minute audiovisual presentation on the history of Tombstone narrated by Vincent Price. Included in the price of a Tombstone pass is a four-page collection of the testimonies after the gun battle. This document is available at the office of the *Tombstone Epitaph*, the oldest newspaper in Arizona, begun in 1880.

Other Tombstone attractions include the **Rose Tree Inn Museum,** home of the world's largest rose bush, measuring over 8,000 square feet; the Crystal Palace, a restored 1879 saloon; and the Bird Cage Theater, named for the velvet-draped cages hanging from the ceiling that were used by prostitutes to ply their trade.

On the outskirts of town is the **Boot Hill Graveyard**. The cemetery is the final resting place of several members of the OK Corral shootout, as well as other notorious gunslingers. **Open:** Daily 9am–5pm. **$$**

Tubac

First visited by Spanish missionaries in 1691, Tubac was among the first European settlements in what is now Arizona. Deserted and reestablished several times, it has become known as the town with nine lives; today it is a popular haven for writers, artists, and retirees. Tubac's old buildings house more than 80 shops selling fine arts, crafts, and unusual gifts. **Information:** Tubac Chamber of Commerce, PO Box 1866, Tubac 85646 (tel 520/398-2704).

RESORT

Tubac Golf Resort
1 Otero Rd, PO Box 1297, 85646; tel 520/398-2211 or toll free 800/848-7893; fax 520/398-9261. Exit 34 or 40 off I-19. 400 acres. A golf resort on a restored historic ranch, with splendid views of the Santa Rita Mountains. **Rooms:** 17 stes; 16 cottages/villas. Executive level. CI 3pm/CO noon. Comfortable rooms have unusual brick interiors. **Amenities:** A/C, TV, refrig, bathrobes. All units w/terraces, some w/fireplaces. **Services:** Social director, babysitting. **Facilities:** 18 1 50 1 restaurant, 1 bar (w/entertainment), volleyball, lawn games, whirlpool, washer/dryer. **Rates:** Peak (Jan–Apr) $170 ste; $160 cottage/villa. Extra person $10. Children under age 12 stay free. Lower rates off-season. Parking: Outdoor, free. AE, MC, V.

ATTRACTIONS

Tubac Center of the Arts
9 Plaza Rd; tel 520/398-2371. The center of cultural activities in Tubac. Showcases rotating exhibits of artwork by members of the Santa Cruz Valley Art Association and also stages traveling exhibits, juried shows, an annual craft show, and theater and music performances. **Open:** Oct–May, Tues–Sat 10am–4:30pm, Sun 1–4:30pm. **Free**

Tubac Presidio State Historic Park
Presidio Dr; tel 520/398-2252. The park museum houses exhibits that explore the European background and Native American history of Tubac and Southern Arizona. On display is the 1859 press from Arizona's first newspaper. Park grounds feature an adobe schoolhouse built in 1885, and an archeological exhibit featuring a Spanish captain's house. **Open:** Daily 8am–5pm. **$**

Tucson

Arizona's second-largest city, Tucson was founded by Spanish colonists in 1775 and evolved into a major supply center for the US military and miners in the late 1800s. Today this modern American city retains elements of its Hispanic, Anglo, and Native American heritage. Its natural setting—four mountain ranges ring the city—makes Tucson an excellent home base for hiking, horseback riding, and other outdoor recreation. **Information:** Metropolitan Tucson Convention & Visitors Bureau, 130 S Scott Ave, Tucson 85701 (tel 520/624-1817 or 800/638-8350).

HOTELS

Arizona Inn

2200 E Elm St, 85719 (Midtown); tel 520/325-1541 or toll free 800/933-1093; fax 520/881-5830. Old-world charm combines with modern elegance in this historic Tucson hotel. Grounds are superbly manicured, with luxurious gardens and flowers. The bar, restaurant, and study in the main lodge are beautifully decorated. **Rooms:** 83 rms and stes. CI 3pm/CO noon. Each room is individually furnished with antiques and period furniture. **Amenities:** A/C, cable TV, dataport. Some units w/terraces, some w/fireplaces. **Services:** Twice-daily maid svce, babysitting. Complimentary afternoon tea is served Nov–Apr. **Facilities:** 225 1 restaurant (*see* "Restaurants" below), 1 bar (w/entertainment), lawn games. The 14-acre property includes a croquet court. The book-filled study with overstuffed chairs allows for comfortable reading. **Rates:** Peak (Jan–May) $132–$172 S; $165–$195 D; $210 ste. Extra person $15. Children under age 12 stay free. Lower rates off-season. AP and MAP rates avail. Parking: Outdoor, free. AE, MC, V.

Best Western–A Royal Sun Inn and Suites

1015 N Stone Ave, 85705; tel 520/622-8871 or toll free 800/545-8858; fax 520/623-2267. Attractive downtown hotel. **Rooms:** 79 rms and stes. CI 2pm/CO noon. Nonsmoking rms avail. **Amenities:** A/C, satel TV w/movies, refrig, VCR, CD/tape player. Some units w/minibars, some w/terraces. **Services:** **Facilities:** 25 1 restaurant, 1 bar, spa, sauna, whirlpool. **Rates:** Peak (Jan–Apr) $89 S; $99 D; $120 ste. Extra person $10. Lower rates off-season. Parking: Outdoor, free. AE, DC, DISC, MC, V.

Best Western Inn Suites Hotel

6201 N Oracle Rd, 85704; tel 520/297-8111 or toll free 800/554-4535; fax 520/297-2935. Exit 248 off I-10, 5½ mi E. Popular with both business and leisure travelers. **Rooms:** 159 rms and stes. Executive level. CI 2pm/CO noon. Nonsmoking rms avail. There are two types of suites: studio inn suites, with living rooms; and executive suites, with both living rooms and kitchenettes. **Amenities:** A/C, cable TV w/movies, refrig, dataport, voice mail, in-rm safe. Some units w/terraces, some w/whirlpools. **Services:** Complimentary barbecue Wednesday 5:30–6:30pm. **Facilities:** 150 1 restaurant (bkfst and lunch only), whirlpool, playground, washer/dryer. **Rates (CP):** Peak (Jan 15–Apr 5) $99 S or D; $145 ste. Extra person $10. Children under age 16 stay free. Min stay special events. Lower rates off-season. Parking: Outdoor, free. AE, CB, DC, DISC, MC, V.

Best Western Tanque Verde Inn Suites

7007 E Tanque Verde, 85715 (East Tucson); tel 520/298-2300 or toll free 800/882-8484; fax 520/298-6756. Well-appointed, mid-priced hotel featuring attractive courtyards and gardens. Recently redecorated. **Rooms:** 90 rms and stes. CI 3pm/CO 11am. Nonsmoking rms avail. 60 rooms have kitchenettes. **Amenities:** A/C, satel TV, refrig. Some units w/terraces. **Services:** Poolside happy hour daily 5:30–7:30pm (including two free drinks per guest). **Facilities:** 50 Whirlpool, washer/dryer. Free use of nearby health club. **Rates (CP):** Peak (Jan–Mar) $100–$125 S or D; $110–$130 ste. Extra person $8. Children under age 18 stay free. Lower rates off-season. Parking: Outdoor, free. Weekly and monthly rates available. AE, CB, DC, DISC, MC, V.

Clarion Hotel Tucson Airport

6801 S Tucson Blvd, 85706; tel 520/746-3932 or toll free 800/526-0550; fax 520/889-9934. 4 mi E from Valencia Rd exit off I-19. Better-than-average hotel close to the airport. **Rooms:** 191 rms and stes. CI 3pm/CO noon. Nonsmoking rms avail. Very attractively appointed with southwestern decor. **Amenities:** A/C, cable TV w/movies. Some units w/terraces. **Services:** Masseur, babysitting. In addition to full breakfast, guests receive complimentary cocktails and late-night snacks. 24-hour airport shuttle. **Facilities:** 200 1 restaurant, 1 bar, whirlpool, washer/dryer. **Rates (BB):** Peak (Jan–May) $85–$105 S; $95–$115 D; $125 ste. Extra person $10. Children under age 18 stay free. Lower rates off-season. Parking: Outdoor, free. AE, DC, DISC, MC, V.

Country Suites by Carlson

7411 N Oracle Rd, 85704; tel 520/575-9255 or toll free 800/456-4000; fax 520/575-8671. Exit 248 off I-10, E 5½ mi to AZ 77, N 2 mi. A fine, basic hotel, good for both business travelers and vacationers. **Rooms:** 157 stes. CI 3pm/CO noon. Nonsmoking rms avail. Rooms are attractively and comfortably furnished. **Amenities:** A/C, satel TV w/movies, refrig, voice mail. **Services:** Car-rental desk. Complimentary barbecue and beer Tuesday 5:30–6:30pm. **Facilities:** 30 Whirlpool, playground, washer/dryer. Putting green. **Rates (CP):** Peak (Jan–Apr) $79–$104 ste. Extra person $6. Children under age 18 stay free. Lower rates off-season. Parking: Outdoor, free. Long-term rates for six or more nights. AE, CB, DC, DISC, MC, V.

Courtyard by Marriott

2505 E Executive Dr, 85706; tel 520/573-0000 or toll free 800/321-2211; fax 520/573-0470. Conveniently located a half-mile from Tucson International Airport. **Rooms:** 149 rms and stes. CI 3pm/CO noon. Nonsmoking rms avail. Half the rooms look out at the pool. **Amenities:** A/C, cable TV w/movies, dataport, voice mail. Some units w/terraces, some w/whirlpools. All suites have wet bars and refrigerators, as well as two TVs. Most first- and second-floor king rooms have sofabeds. **Services:** Car-rental desk, social director, babysitting. **Facilities:** 40 1 restaurant (bkfst and dinner only), 1 bar, whirlpool, washer/dryer. **Rates:** Peak (Jan–May) $89–$120 S; $99–$130 D; $103–$149 ste. Extra person $10. Children under age 18 stay free. Lower rates off-season. Parking: Outdoor, free. AE, DC, DISC, MC, V.

The DoubleTree Hotel Tucson
445 S Alvernon Way, 85711 (Midtown); tel 520/881-4200 or toll free 800/222-8733; fax 520/323-5225. A centrally located and well-appointed high-rise hotel. **Rooms:** 295 rms and stes; 2 cottages/villas. Executive level. CI 3pm/CO noon. Nonsmoking rms avail. **Amenities:** A/C, cable TV w/movies, refrig, dataport. Some units w/minibars, some w/terraces. Rooms in the tower have minibars and coffeemakers. King rooms in the tower also have sofas. **Services:** Babysitting. Complimentary box of specialty cookies presented on arrival. **Facilities:** 1200 2 restaurants, 2 bars, whirlpool, beauty salon. **Rates:** Peak (Jan–Apr) $140–$160 S; $160–$180 D; $250 ste; $250 cottage/villa. Extra person $15. Children under age 18 stay free. Min stay special events. Lower rates off-season. Parking: Outdoor, free. AE, CB, DC, DISC, EC, ER, JCB, MC, V.

Embassy Suites Hotel
7051 S Tucson Blvd, 85706; tel 520/573-0700 or toll free 800/262-8866; fax 520/741-9645. All-suite hotel right next door to the airport; it's especially popular with corporate travelers. **Rooms:** 204 effic. Executive level. CI 1pm/CO 1pm. Nonsmoking rms avail. Six suites have adjoining conference suites. **Amenities:** A/C, cable TV w/movies, refrig, voice mail. Two TVs in every suite. **Services:** Car-rental desk. Complimentary cocktails served daily 5:30–7:30pm. **Facilities:** 450 1 restaurant (lunch and dinner only), 1 bar, whirlpool, washer/dryer. **Rates (BB):** Peak (Jan–May) $129 effic. Extra person $10. Children under age 12 stay free. Lower rates off-season. Parking: Outdoor, free. Special weekend rates available. AE, DC, DISC, EC, ER, MC, V.

Hampton Inn
6971 S Tucson Blvd, 85706; tel 520/889-5789 or toll free 800/HAMPTON; fax 520/889-4002. Located next to Tucson Int'l Airport. **Rooms:** 126 rms and stes. Executive level. CI 1pm/CO noon. Nonsmoking rms avail. **Amenities:** A/C, cable TV w/movies. Some units w/terraces. **Services:** Free local calls. The hotel has a "100% satisfaction guaranteed" program. **Facilities:** 45 Whirlpool, washer/dryer. **Rates (CP):** Peak (Jan–May) $85 S; $89 D; $99 ste. Children under age 18 stay free. Min stay special events. Lower rates off-season. Parking: Outdoor, free. AE, CB, DC, DISC, ER, MC, V.

Holiday Inn
181 W Broadway, 85701 (Downtown); tel 520/624-8711 or toll free 800/HOLIDAY; fax 520/623-8121. Exit W Congress St off I-10. A downtown hotel close to the convention center and oriented to the business traveler. **Rooms:** 309 rms and stes. CI 3pm/CO noon. Nonsmoking rms avail. Rooms are comfortable and attractive. **Amenities:** A/C, cable TV. **Services:** Car-rental desk. **Facilities:** 1000 1 restaurant, 1 bar (w/entertainment), games rm. Ample meeting space, and the exhibition area has space for 50 booths. **Rates (BB):** Peak (Jan–Apr) $115 S or D; $150 ste. Extra person $10. Children under age 19 stay free. Lower rates off-season. Parking: Indoor, free. AE, DC, DISC, MC, V.

Holiday Inn Express
750 W Starr Pass Blvd, 85713; tel 520/624-4455; fax 520/624-4455. 22nd St exit off I-10. Recently renovated. **Rooms:** 98 rms and stes. CI 3pm/CO noon. Nonsmoking rms avail. Some rooms have a pool view. **Amenities:** A/C, satel TV w/movies. All units w/terraces. **Services:** **Facilities:** 30 Sauna, whirlpool. **Rates (CP):** Peak (Jan–Apr) $85 S; $95 D; $130 ste. Extra person $10. Children under age 12 stay free. Lower rates off-season. Parking: Outdoor, free. AE, CB, DC, DISC, JCB, MC, V.

Hotel Park Tucson and Conference Center
5151 E Grant Rd, 85712 (Midtown); tel 520/323-6262 or toll free 800/257-7275; fax 520/325-2989. Midtown hotel suitable for both business and vacation travelers. **Rooms:** 216 rms and stes. CI 3pm/CO 1pm. No smoking. Many rooms have mountain views. **Amenities:** A/C, satel TV, refrig, CD/tape player, voice mail. Some units w/terraces. Suites have wet bars, two televisions, and two telephones. **Services:** Babysitting. **Facilities:** 325 2 restaurants (*see* "Restaurants" below), 2 bars (1 w/entertainment), spa, whirlpool, washer/dryer. 4,300-square-foot ballroom, executive board room, and smaller meeting rooms. **Rates (BB):** Peak (Jan 18–May 27) $155–$175 S; $165–$185 D; $165–$185 ste. Extra person $15. Children under age 12 stay free. Min stay special events. Lower rates off-season. Parking: Outdoor, free. AE, CB, DC, MC, V.

InnSuites Hotel at Randolph Park
102 N Alvernon Way, 85711 (Central Tucson); tel 520/795-0330 or toll free 800/227-6086; fax 520/326-2111. Exit 258 off I-10. Centrally located, older hotel awaiting renovation. **Rooms:** 157 rms, stes, and effic. Executive level. CI 3pm/CO noon. Nonsmoking rms avail. Rooms are attractive and comfortable. **Amenities:** A/C, cable TV, refrig, dataport. Some units w/terraces. **Services:** Complimentary barbecue Wednesday 5:30–6:30pm. **Facilities:** 250 1 bar, basketball, washer/dryer. **Rates (BB):** Peak (Feb–Apr) $109 S or D; $129–$139 ste; $109–$119 effic. Extra person $10. Children under age 17 stay free. Lower rates off-season. Parking: Outdoor, free. $10 charge for third and fourth person in a room. AE, CB, DC, DISC, MC, V.

Park Inn International
2803 E Valencia Rd, 85706; tel 520/294-2500 or toll free 800/864-2145; fax 520/741-0851. Valencia Rd exit off I-19 or I-10. This hotel close to the airport is good for business travelers. Management stresses personal service. **Rooms:** 95

rms and stes. CI noon/CO noon. Nonsmoking rms avail. Rooms have simple southwestern decor and good lighting. **Amenities:** A/C, cable TV w/movies. **Services:** Fax and copy services available. **Facilities:** 100 1 restaurant, 1 bar, whirlpool. **Rates:** Peak (Dec–Mar) $85–$95 S; $95–$105 D; $120–$135 ste. Extra person $5. Children under age 16 stay free. Lower rates off-season. Parking: Outdoor, free. AE, DC, DISC, MC, V.

Plaza Hotel and Conference Center

1900 E Speedway Blvd, 85719; tel 520/327-7341 or toll free 800/843-8052, 800/654-3010 in AZ; fax 520/327-0276. Exit 257 off I-10. Centrally located high-rise hotel close to the University of Arizona and University Medical Center. **Rooms:** 150 rms. Executive level. CI 2pm/CO noon. Nonsmoking rms avail. All rooms have mountain views. **Amenities:** A/C, cable TV w/movies. Some units w/terraces. Some rooms have refrigerators. **Services:** Twice-daily maid svce, babysitting. Complimentary newspapers, cocktails, and snacks. **Facilities:** 500 1 restaurant, 1 bar, whirlpool. **Rates:** Peak (Jan–Mar) $58–$83 S or D. Extra person $8. Children under age 16 stay free. Lower rates off-season. Parking: Indoor, free. AE, CB, DC, MC, V.

Quality Hotel and Suites

475 N Granada Rd, 85701; tel 520/622-3000 or toll free 800/228-2828; fax 520/623-8922. Exit St Mary's Rd off I-10. 12 acres. Downtown hotel with good freeway access. **Rooms:** 297 rms and stes. CI 3pm/CO noon. Nonsmoking rms avail. Rooms are simply and comfortably furnished. **Amenities:** A/C, satel TV w/movies, voice mail. Some units w/terraces. **Services:** Lifeguards at pool in summer. **Facilities:** 600 1 restaurant, 1 bar (w/entertainment), lawn games, washer/dryer. **Rates (BB):** Peak (Jan–Apr) $99 S or D; $135 ste. Extra person $10. Children under age 18 stay free. Min stay special events. Lower rates off-season. Parking: Outdoor, free. Summer rates available. AE, DC, DISC, MC, V.

Radisson Suite Hotel Tucson

6555 E Speedway Blvd, 85710 (Midtown); tel 520/721-7100 or toll free 800/333-3333. Exit Speedway Blvd off I-10. An all-suites hotel, good for long-term visitors and business travelers who need extra working space. **Rooms:** 304 stes. CI 3pm/CO noon. Nonsmoking rms avail. Second- to fifth-floor suites have balconies. Many rooms have mountain views. **Amenities:** A/C, satel TV w/movies, refrig. Some units w/terraces, some w/fireplaces, some w/whirlpools. Many standard suites have microwaves. **Services:** Twice-daily maid svce. Complimentary cocktails. **Facilities:** 400 1 restaurant, 2 bars, spa, whirlpool, washer/dryer. **Rates (BB):** Peak (Oct–May) $93–$185 ste. Extra person $10. Children under age 17 stay free. Lower rates off-season. Parking: Outdoor, free. AE, DC, DISC, MC, V.

Residence Inn by Marriott

6477 E Speedway Blvd, 85710 (Midtown); tel 520/721-0991 or toll free 800/331-3131; fax 520/290-8323. An attractive, comfortable hotel. Ideal for longer stays. **Rooms:** 128 stes. CI 4pm/CO noon. Nonsmoking rms avail. **Amenities:** A/C, satel TV w/movies, refrig. Some units w/fireplaces. All units have VCRs. **Services:** Complimentary afternoon snacks. **Facilities:** 50 Whirlpool, washer/dryer. Outdoor game court for volleyball, basketball, and paddle ball. **Rates (CP):** Peak (Jan–Apr) $160–$192 effic. Extra person $10. Children under age 13 stay free. Lower rates off-season. Parking: Outdoor, free. AE, CB, DC, DISC, MC, V.

Rodeway Inn

1365 W Grant Rd, 85745; tel 520/622-7791 or toll free 800/228-2000; fax 520/629-0201. Exit Grant Rd off I-10. An attractive, basic motel located close to downtown, with good freeway access. **Rooms:** 146 rms and stes. CI 3pm/CO noon. Nonsmoking rms avail. **Amenities:** A/C, satel TV w/movies. **Services:** **Facilities:** 150 1 restaurant, 1 bar, whirlpool, washer/dryer. **Rates (CP):** Peak (Mid-Jan–Apr) $50–$80 S or D; $125 ste. Children under age 18 stay free. Lower rates off-season. Parking: Outdoor, free. AE, DC, DISC, MC, V.

Tucson East Hilton

7600 E Broadway, 85710 (Eastside); tel 520/721-5600 or toll free 800/648-7177; fax 520/721-5696. Kolb Rd exit off I-10. A large eastside hotel popular with business travelers. The seven-story atrium lobby boasts a fountain. **Rooms:** 232 rms and stes. Executive level. CI 3pm/CO noon. Nonsmoking rms avail. **Amenities:** A/C, cable TV w/movies. All units w/minibars, some w/terraces. **Services:** Babysitting. **Facilities:** 500 1 restaurant, 1 bar, whirlpool. **Rates:** Peak (Feb–Apr) $164 S; $178 D; $225 ste. Extra person $13. Children under age 18 stay free. Lower rates off-season. Parking: Outdoor, free. Corporate rates are available. AE, CB, DC, DISC, JCB, MC, V.

Viscount Suite Hotel

4855 E Broadway, 85711; tel 520/745-6500 or toll free 800/527-9666; fax 520/790-5144. Located in the heart of the business district, four miles from downtown. A fountain graces the lobby. **Rooms:** 215 stes. Executive level. CI 3pm/CO noon. Nonsmoking rms avail. **Amenities:** A/C, satel TV w/movies. Suites have 2 TVs. **Services:** A complimentary cocktail reception runs from 5 to 7pm daily. The director of guest services can arrange tours and other activities. **Facilities:** 250 3 restaurants, 1 bar, sauna, whirlpool. There's a popular sports bar on premises. **Rates (BB):** Peak (Jan–Apr) $135–$145 ste. Extra person $10. Children under age 12 stay free. Lower rates off-season. Parking: Outdoor, free. AE, DC, DISC, MC, V.

MOTELS

Discovery Inn

1010 S Freeway, 85745; tel 520/622-5871 or toll free 800/622-5871; fax 520/620-0097. 22nd St exit off I-10. A pleasant, modern motel just off the interstate. **Rooms:** 146 rms and stes. CI open/CO 11am. Nonsmoking rms avail. Comfortable, although not all are well soundproofed. **Amenities:** A/C, cable TV w/movies. **Services:** **Facilities:** 40 1 restaurant (bkfst and dinner only), 1 bar, washer/dryer. **Rates:** Peak (Jan–Apr) $65–$70 S or D; $70 ste. Children under age 18 stay free. Lower rates off-season. Parking: Outdoor, free. All rooms are $35 in the off-season. AE, DC, DISC, MC, V.

Econo Lodge

3020 S 6th Ave, 85713; tel 520/623-5881 or toll free 800/623-5881. NW of airport. Basic, clean, comfortable accommodations. **Rooms:** 88 rms. CI noon/CO 11am. Nonsmoking rms avail. **Amenities:** A/C, cable TV. **Facilities:** Whirlpool, washer/dryer. **Rates:** Peak (Jan–Apr) $39 S; $49 D. Children under age 15 stay free. Lower rates off-season. Parking: Outdoor, free. AE, CB, DC, DISC, MC, V.

Motel 6

755 E Benson Hwy, 85713; tel 520/622-4614; fax 520/624-1584. Exit 262 off I-10. A clean, well-kept, no-frills motel on the east side of Tucson, with attractive cactus gardens on the property. **Rooms:** 120 rms. CI noon/CO noon. Nonsmoking rms avail. Simple, comfortable rooms. **Amenities:** A/C, cable TV. **Services:** **Facilities:** **Rates:** $37–$39 S; $43–$45 D. Extra person $3. Children under age 18 stay free. Parking: Outdoor, free. AE, CB, DC, DISC, MC, V.

Palm Court Inn

4425 E 22nd St, 85711 (Midtown); tel 520/745-1777 or toll free 800/288-1650. Popular with long-term visitors. **Rooms:** 201 rms and effic. CI 2pm/CO 11am. All rooms have full kitchenettes. **Amenities:** A/C, cable TV, refrig. Some units w/terraces. **Facilities:** Whirlpool, washer/dryer. **Rates:** Peak (Oct–Apr) $70 S or D; $140 effic. Lower rates off-season. Parking: Outdoor, free. Efficiency rates are weekly. MC, V.

Smuggler's Inn

6350 E Speedway Blvd, 85710 (Midtown); tel 520/296-3292 or toll free 800/525-8852; fax 520/722-3713. A nice mid-priced hotel with a lagoon. **Rooms:** 150 rms and stes. CI 4pm/CO 1pm. Nonsmoking rms avail. All rooms have easy chairs and views of the lake, pool, or garden. **Amenities:** A/C, cable TV, dataport. All units w/terraces, all w/fireplaces, all w/whirlpools. **Services:** Complimentary cocktail and snacks daily. **Facilities:** 7 1 200 1 restaurant, 1 bar, racquetball, whirlpool, washer/dryer. A putting green adjoins the lagoon. Complimentary membership in nearby fitness center. **Rates:** Peak (Jan–May) $109 S; $119 D; $135 ste. Extra person $10. Children under age 16 stay free. Lower rates off-season. Parking: Outdoor, free. AE, CB, DC, DISC, JCB, MC, V.

RESORTS

Best Western Ghost Ranch Lodge

801 W Miracle Mile, 85705; tel 520/791-7565 or toll free 800/456-7565; fax 520/791-3898. Exit Miracle Mile off I-10. 8 acres. This unusual resort, which dates from 1941, is steeped in history. The "Ghost Ranch" name was inspired by the original owner's friendship with New Mexico artist Georgia O'Keeffe. The lobby has a saltillo-tiled floor and Mexican furniture, and there are lovely cactus gardens. On the National Register of Historic Places. **Rooms:** 68 rms; 15 cottages/villas. Executive level. CI 2pm/CO noon. Nonsmoking rms avail. Cottages have private patios. **Amenities:** A/C, cable TV w/movies, refrig. Some units w/terraces. Cottages have fold-out sofas, microwaves, and cooking stoves. **Services:** Airport transportation free with five-day stay. **Facilities:** 35 1 restaurant, 1 bar, lawn games, sauna, whirlpool, washer/dryer. Outdoor, awning-covered dining. **Rates (CP):** Peak (Jan–Apr) $68–$92 S; $74–$98 D; $84–$98 cottage/villa. Extra person $6. Children under age 12 stay free. Lower rates off-season. Parking: Outdoor, free. AE, CB, DC, DISC, ER, JCB, MC, V.

Lazy K Bar Ranch

8401 N Scenic Dr, 85743; tel 520/744-3050 or toll free 800/321-7018; fax 520/744-7628. 160 acres. Although surrounded by wide-open spaces, this lovely ranch is only 17 miles from downtown. **Rooms:** 23 rms and stes. CI 2pm/CO 11am. **Amenities:** A/C. No phone or TV. All units w/terraces, 1 w/whirlpool. Deluxe king rooms have hide-a-beds; suites have fireplaces. Videos are available in the TV room. **Services:** Masseur, babysitting. **Facilities:** 2 50 Basketball, volleyball, games rm, lawn games, whirlpool, playground, washer/dryer. There's a pleasant library with a card table and piano. **Rates (AP):** Peak (Feb–Apr) $145–$175 S; $240–$270 D; $290 ste. Extra person $80. Lower rates off-season. AP rates avail. Parking: Outdoor, free. Minimum three-night stay; rates include daily horseback riding (except Sunday). Charge for third person in room varies according to age. AE, DISC, MC, V.

The Lodge on the Desert

306 N Alvernon Way, PO Box 42500, 85733 (Central Tucson); tel 520/325-3366 or toll free 800/456-5634; fax 520/327-5834. 5 acres. A quiet, centrally located old-style adobe resort dating from the 1930s. It feels and looks like a Mexican hacienda, and has lovely grounds. The original home is now a central lodge for the resort. **Rooms:** 40 rms and stes. Executive level. CI 3pm/CO noon. Four types of rooms: Standard, Deluxe, Luxury, and Elegant. All rooms are decorated differently, with furniture from the 1940s and '50s. Some rooms have separate tubs and showers. **Amenities:** A/C, TV w/movies. Some units w/terraces, some w/fire-

places. Some rooms have hide-a-beds; most have refrigerators and kiva fireplaces. VCRs available for rent. **Services:** Free airport transportation available for those staying at least seven days during peak season. **Facilities:** 1 restaurant (*see* "Restaurants" below), 1 bar, lawn games. The lodge has a good library with easy chairs. Outdoor dining by the fountain. **Rates (CP):** Peak (Nov–May) $80–$106 S; $92–$118 D; $118 ste. Extra person $10. Children under age 2 stay free. Min stay special events. Lower rates off-season. AP and MAP rates avail. Parking: Outdoor, free. AE, CB, DC, DISC, MC, V.

Loews Ventana Canyon Resort
7000 N Resort Dr, 85750; tel 520/299-2020 or toll free 800/234-5117; fax 520/299-6832. 20 mi NE of downtown Tucson. From I-10, take Ina Rd or Orange Grove Rd exits to Skyline Dr and turn left at Craycroft Rd. 93 acres. Located 3,000 feet up in the foothills of the Catalina Mountains, between desert slopes and Tom Fazio–designed fairways. Imposing, award-winning architecture fits 398 rooms into four stories of earth-toned wings with hints of Native American cliff dwellings and pueblos. Grand lobby/lounge echoes art deco of Arizona Biltmore in Phoenix, with artwork and sculpture and a wall of windows overlooking 1.5-acre tiered lake. Although two-thirds of guests are there for meetings, the resort has many romantic features. **Rooms:** 398 rms and stes. CI 3pm/CO noon. Nonsmoking rms avail. Roomy balconies—from some, guests can almost reach to touch the cactus and squawbrush, others have expansive views of the city below. Oversized bathtubs, southwestern art, attractive furniture of burnished pine. Avoid rooms overlooking west wing parking lot. **Amenities:** A/C, cable TV w/movies, dataport, voice mail, bathrobes. All units w/minibars, all w/terraces, some w/fireplaces, some w/whirlpools. In-room video for messages and accounts review; two-line phones. **Services:** Twice-daily maid svce, car-rental desk, masseur, children's program, babysitting. Young, alert staff; regular room service menu augmented by candlelight dinners catered by swank Ventana Room and served course by course. **Facilities:** 4 restaurants (*see* "Restaurants" below), 2 bars (w/entertainment), lawn games, spa, sauna, steam rm, whirlpool, beauty salon, playground. Beautiful freeform pool with heated whirlpool and waterfall-chilled plunge pool, surrounded by wispy palo verde and African sumac trees (open until 10pm); pathways to natural 80-foot-high waterfall. **Rates:** Peak (Jan–May 31) $295–$375 S or D; $700–$2,300 ste. Children under age 18 stay free. Min stay special events. Lower rates off-season. Parking: Outdoor, free. Room rates, in three categories, vary by floor and view. The special Celebration Packages are a good deal. AE, CB, DC, DISC, JCB, MC, V.

Omni Tucson National Golf Resort
2727 W Club Dr, 85741; tel 520/297-2271 or toll free 800/528-4856; fax 520/297-7544. 650 acres. Beautiful golf resort in a magnificent setting. Home of the PGA Northern Telecom Open. **Rooms:** 142 rms and stes; 25 cottages/villas. CI 3pm/CO noon. Nonsmoking rms avail. Minisuites have sofas and throw pillows on the beds. Some rooms have makeup tables. **Amenities:** A/C, cable TV w/movies, refrig, bathrobes. All units w/minibars, all w/terraces, some w/fireplaces. Each room has irons and ironing boards; minisuites have minibars. **Services:** Twice-daily maid svce, masseur, children's program, babysitting. **Facilities:** 3 restaurants, 5 bars, games rm, lawn games, spa, sauna, steam rm, whirlpool, beauty salon, playground, washer/dryer. **Rates:** Peak (Jan–May) $265 S or D; $275 ste; $350 cottage/villa. Extra person $10. Children under age 18 stay free. Lower rates off-season. MAP rates avail. Parking: Outdoor, free. AE, DC, DISC, MC, V.

Sheraton El Conquistador Resort and Country Club
10000 N Oracle Rd, 85737; tel 520/544-5000 or toll free 800/325-7832; fax 520/544-1228. Exit Ina Rd off I-10. 300 acres. Set at the base of Catalina State Park and National Park property, this resort has excellent views. **Rooms:** 428 rms and stes. CI 4pm/CO noon. Nonsmoking rms avail. Standard double rooms have queen beds; standard king rooms have king bed, couch, and coffee table. **Amenities:** A/C, cable TV w/movies, voice mail, in-rm safe. All units w/minibars, all w/terraces, some w/fireplaces, some w/whirlpools. **Services:** Twice-daily maid svce, car-rental desk, social director, masseur, children's program, babysitting. Complimentary morning newspapers. **Facilities:** 6 restaurants, 4 bars (2 w/entertainment), lawn games, racquetball, spa, sauna, whirlpool, beauty salon, day-care ctr. Hiking and bicycling opportunities available on the adjacent lands. **Rates:** Peak (Jan–May) $230–$315 S or D; $265–$1,200 ste. Extra person $15. Children under age 18 stay free. Lower rates off-season. Parking: Outdoor, free. AE, CB, DC, DISC, ER, JCB, MC, V.

Tanque Verde Ranch
14301 E Speedway Blvd, PO Box 66, 85748; tel 520/296-6275 or toll free 800/234-DUDE; fax 520/721-9426. 20 mi E of Tucson. 640 acres. Dude ranch in the Catalina foothills, popular with both European and American visitors. Magnificent views of the Catalina Mountains; not far from the Rincon Mountains and Saguaro National Monument. **Rooms:** 67 rms and stes. Executive level. CI 2pm/CO noon. Nonsmoking rms avail. **Amenities:** A/C, refrig. No TV. All units w/terraces, some w/fireplaces. TVs available. **Services:** Car-rental desk, social director, masseur, children's program, babysitting. Free airport transportation with stays of 4 nights or more. **Facilities:** 1 restaurant, 1 bar (w/entertainment), basketball, volleyball, games rm, sauna, steam rm, whirlpool, playground, washer/dryer. Fishing lake. Birdwatching and banding. Nature hikes. More than 130 horses available to ride. Golf nearby with complimentary temporary membership available. TV in

lodge. **Rates (AP):** Peak (Dec–Apr) $245–$295 S; $280–$350 D; $375–$395 ste. Extra person $85. Lower rates off-season. Parking: Outdoor, free. Rates include riding, tennis, sports, and all ranch activities. Add $65 to $75 (to double rate) for a third person in room. AE, DISC, MC, V.

Ventana Canyon Golf and Racquet Club
6200 N Clubhouse Lane, 85715 (Sabino Canyon); tel 520/577-1400 or toll free 800/828-5701; fax 520/299-0256. 1,100 acres. This small, intimate resort is good for corporate outings and retreats. **Rooms:** 49 rms and stes. CI 3pm/CO noon. No smoking. Rooms have picture-postcard scenic views. All suites have kitchens. **Amenities:** A/C, cable TV, refrig, bathrobes. All units w/terraces. **Services:** Masseur, babysitting. **Facilities:** 36 12 70 2 restaurants, 1 bar, lawn games, spa, sauna, steam rm, whirlpool, beauty salon, day-care ctr. **Rates:** Peak (Jan 15–Apr 30) $280–$384 S or D; $300 ste. Extra person $38. Children under age 17 stay free. Lower rates off-season. Parking: Outdoor, free. AE, MC, V.

The Westin La Paloma
3800 E Sunrise Dr, 85718 (La Paloma); tel 520/742-6000 or toll free 800/876-3683; fax 520/577-5878. 250 acres. A large, nicely appointed hotel at the base of the Catalina Mountains. The expansive lobby's 50-foot arched windows frame stunning mountain views. **Rooms:** 478 rms and stes. Executive level. CI 4pm/CO noon. Nonsmoking rms avail. **Amenities:** A/C, cable TV w/movies, VCR, voice mail, in-rm safe, bathrobes. All units w/minibars, all w/terraces, some w/whirlpools. Resort suites have whirlpools and barbecues on their patios. **Services:** Masseur, babysitting. **Facilities:** 27 1 10 2100 5 restaurants, 2 bars (1 w/entertainment), basketball, volleyball, games rm, lawn games, racquetball, spa, steam rm, beauty salon, day-care ctr, playground. Three whirlpools, lap pool, swim-up bar. **Rates:** Peak (Jan–May) $280–$340 S or D; $475–$1,000 ste. Extra person $20. Children under age 12 stay free. Lower rates off-season. AP rates avail. Parking: Indoor/outdoor, free. AE, CB, DC, DISC, ER, JCB, MC, V.

Westward Look Resort
245 E Ina Rd, 85704 (North Tucson); tel 520/297-1151 or toll free 800/722-2500; fax 520/297-9023. Exit Ina Rd off I-10. 80 acres. A lovely resort in the foothills of the Catalina Mountains. Large lobby with tile floor and fireplace. **Rooms:** 244 rms. CI 4pm/CO noon. Nonsmoking rms avail. **Amenities:** A/C, cable TV w/movies, refrig, dataport, voice mail, in-rm safe. All units w/minibars, all w/terraces. **Services:** Twice-daily maid svce, car rental desk, masseur, babysitting. Tennis lessons are available. **Facilities:** 3 5 300 2 restaurants (*see* "Restaurants" below), 1 bar (w/entertainment), basketball, volleyball, spa, whirlpool. There's a pro shop on the premises. **Rates:** Peak (Jan–Apr) $169–$269 S or D. Extra person $10. Children under age 16 stay free. Min stay special events. Lower rates off-season. MAP rates avail. Parking: Indoor, free. AE, CB, DC, DISC, MC, V.

White Stallion Ranch
9251 W Twin Peaks Rd, 85743; tel 520/297-0252 or toll free 800/782-5546; fax 520/744-2786. 17 mi N of downtown Tucson, exit Ina Rd off I-10. 3,000 acres. This sprawling guest ranch has beautiful mountain views, and a lobby that's homey and comfortable, with a fireplace. **Rooms:** 29 rms and stes. CI 2pm/CO 11am. Most rooms have western-style furniture. Rooms range in size from small (in the main lodge) to spacious suites. **Amenities:** A/C. No phone or TV. All units w/terraces, some w/fireplaces, some w/whirlpools. **Services:** Babysitting. Free airport pickup for stays of four days or more. **Facilities:** 2 1 restaurant, 1 bar, games rm, lawn games, whirlpool, playground, washer/dryer. The main lodge has a TV. There's a children's petting zoo, and about 80 horses for riding (no riding on Sunday). **Rates (AP):** Peak (Dec 18–Apr 29) $123–$150 S; $218–$266 D. Extra person $79. Children under age 2 stay free. Min stay peak. Lower rates off-season. Parking: Outdoor, free. Closed June–Aug. No CC.

RESTAURANTS

Anthony's in the Catalinas
6440 N Campbell Ave (Catalina Foothills); tel 520/299-1771. **Continental.** An elegant restaurant with terrific views of the Catalina Mountains and Tucson. The main dining room has a large fireplace, huge ceiling beams, and tapestries depicting scenes from the Middle Ages. Specialties include duck à l'orange with Grand Marnier sauce, lamb Wellington, and classic soufflés. **FYI:** Reservations recommended. Piano. **Open:** Lunch Mon–Fri 11:30am–2:30pm; dinner daily 5:30–10pm. **Prices:** Main courses $16–$26. AE, CB, DC, ER, MC, V.

Arizona Inn
In the Arizona Inn, 2200 E Elm St (Midtown); tel 520/325-1541. **Regional American/Continental.** Well-regarded restaurant located in a hotel steeped in tradition, with high, open-beamed ceilings, Indian blankets on the walls, a kiva fireplace, furniture from the 1920s, and soft lighting. A popular entree is chicken and shrimp in tequila with grilled red onion and prickly pear sauce. The menu also includes a daily pasta, venison, wild boar, duck, veal, chicken, and a number of grilled beef choices. **FYI:** Reservations recommended. Guitar. Children's menu. Dress code. No smoking. **Open:** Peak (Sept–May) breakfast daily 6:15–10am; lunch daily 11:30am–2pm; dinner daily 6–10pm; brunch Sun 11am–2pm. **Prices:** Main courses $16–$23; prix fixe $20. AE, CB, MC, V.

Boccata
In River Center, 5605 E River Rd; tel 520/577-9309. **Mediterranean.** Large second-floor restaurant offering balcony dining. Dark colors are set off prints by artist Miguel Marti-

nez and large flower arrangements. A variety of pastas are served in addition to pork, beef, and fresh fish. Specialties include Asian confit of duck, angel-hair pasta with lobster, mussels steamed in white wine and garlic, and profiteroles au chocolat. **FYI:** Reservations recommended. Children's menu. **Open:** Dinner Sun–Thurs 5:30–9pm, Fri–Sat 5–10pm; brunch Sun 10am–2pm. **Prices:** Main courses $12–$22. AE, DC, MC, V.

Cafe Magritte
254 E Congress (Downtown); tel 520/884-8004. At 6th Ave. **Eclectic.** Arty downtown cafe decorated with original artwork (available for purchase). A bar and lounge connect to the dining room, and there are sidewalk tables. High-carbohydrate foods are the specialty—numerous pasta, vegetable, and bean dishes. **FYI:** Reservations accepted. Cabaret/jazz. Beer and wine only. **Open:** Tues–Thurs 11am–11pm, Fri–Sat 11am–midnight, Sun 11am–11pm. **Prices:** Main courses $4–$11. AE, DISC, MC, V.

Cafe Terra Cotta
In St Philip's Plaza, 4310 N Campbell; tel 520/577-8100. **Southwestern.** A bright, modern-looking restaurant with a contemporary flair. Southwestern specialties, with lots of chiles and herbs, plus pizza and pastas. **FYI:** Reservations recommended. Children's menu. No smoking. **Open:** Sun–Thurs 11am–10pm, Fri–Sat 11am–11pm. **Prices:** Main courses $16–$22. AE, DC, DISC, MC, V.

Capriccio
4825 N 1st Ave; tel 520/887-2333. At River Rd. **Italian.** Elegant Italian dining, perfect for special occasions, with romantic candlelight and creamy walls with black tile borders, decorated with brass plates and artwork. Wide-ranging menu. House specialty is roast duckling with Grand Marnier and green peppercorn sauce. **FYI:** Reservations recommended. **Open:** Mon–Sat 5:30–9:30pm. Closed . **Prices:** Main courses $14–$22. AE, MC, V.

Carlos Murphy's
419 W Congress (Downtown); tel 520/628-1956. Exit W Congress off I-10. **Mexican.** Spacious restaurant housed in an old train station; a large model airplane hangs from the ceiling. Traditional Mexican fare, plus barbecued ribs, chicken, burgers, and salads. **FYI:** Reservations accepted. Children's menu. **Open:** Sun–Thurs 11am–10pm, Fri–Sat 11am–11pm. **Prices:** Main courses $8–$15. AE, DISC, MC, V.

★ Casa Molina
6225 E Speedway Blvd (Midtown); tel 520/866-5468. **Mexican.** A landmark Tucson restaurant, with a large statue of a bull standing guard outside. There are several dining rooms; an unusual one is the Redondo, or round, room, which has all-brick walls with beam spokes extending outward from a brick "hub." Variety of typical Mexican dishes. **FYI:** Reservations recommended. Guitar. Children's menu. **Open:** Daily 11am–10pm. **Prices:** Main courses $12–$17. AE, CB, DC, DISC, MC, V.

Daniel's Restaurant and Trattoria
In St Phillips Plaza, 4340 N Campbell Ave, Suite 107; tel 520/742-3200. **Italian.** Dark, plush, and elegant, with gold frond palm trees, etched glass partitions, mirrors, and vases of flowers. Food is prepared light with only "very natural, fresh ingredients." Entrees include grilled fish, seafood, and lamb. **FYI:** Reservations recommended. Dress code. **Open:** Daily 5–10pm. **Prices:** Main courses $15–$30. AE, DISC, MC, V. VP

Da Vinci
3535 E Fort Lowell Rd; tel 520/881-0947. **Italian.** A little slice of Italy in Tucson. Filled with statues and columns, plants, and murals. The menu includes a variety of Italian specialties and pizzas; desserts are all homemade. **FYI:** Reservations not accepted. Children's menu. **Open:** Mon–Sat 11:30am–10pm. **Prices:** Main courses $10–$16. AE, MC, V.

The Dining Room
In The Lodge on the Desert, 306 N Alvernon Way (Midtown); tel 520/325-3366. **American.** Features a Mexican hacienda look, emphasized by the fascinating collection of Mexican ceramic folk art, tin chandeliers, and tiled entryways. The menu includes simple, hearty, traditional fare, like charbroiled steaks and scallops with sharp sauce, plus three different nightly dinner specials. **FYI:** Reservations recommended. Dress code. **Open:** Breakfast Mon–Fri 7–9:30am, Sat–Sun 7:30am–9:30pm; lunch daily noon–1:30pm; dinner daily 6–8:30pm; brunch Sun 11am–2pm. **Prices:** Main courses $10–$21. AE, CB, DC, DISC, MC, V.

El Charro Cafe
311 N Court Ave; tel 520/622-1922. **Mexican.** A popular cafe located in a historic district. An extensive collection of old Mexican prints graces the walls. The dining patio has a fountain, and the bar is delightfully decorated with colorful folk art. Entrees range from seafood enchiladas to country-style spareribs to traditional Mexican combination plates. Spanish, Mexican, and Brazilian wines are served. **FYI:** Reservations recommended. Children's menu. **Open:** Sun–Thurs 11:30am–10pm, Fri–Sat 11:30am–11pm. **Prices:** Main courses $8–$18. AE, DISC, MC, V.

The Gold Room
In Westward Look Resort, 245 E Ina Rd (North Tucson); tel 520/297-1151. **Continental/Southwestern.** A spacious, elegant restaurant with exposed beams and lots of windows providing splendid views of Tucson. Beef, veal, and seafood are the main offerings. A specialty is seared ostrich in prickly pear sauce. **FYI:** Reservations recommended. Children's menu. **Open:** Breakfast daily 8–11am; lunch daily 11am–2pm; dinner daily 5:30–10pm; brunch Sun 11am–2pm. **Prices:** Main courses $16–$27. AE, CB, DC, DISC, MC, V. VP

Janos
150 N Main St (El Presidio District); tel 520/884-9426. **Southwestern.** Considered Tucson's best restaurant, located in one of the city's oldest homes. There are four dining rooms, including a porch at the rear of the house and several smaller rooms with fireplaces. Award-winning chef Janos Wilder makes generous use of cilantro, tomatillo salsa, and chile sauces in his southwestern dishes. The menu includes fish, meats, game, and vegetarian plates. **FYI:** Reservations recommended. **Open:** Peak (Oct–May) Mon–Sat 5:30–9:30pm. **Prices:** Main courses $19–$30. AE, CB, DC, MC, V.

Japanese Kitchen
8424 E Old Spanish Trail; tel 520/886-4131. **Japanese.** Japanese prints, paper lanterns, and indoor and outdoor fish ponds set the tone at this eatery, noted for its teppan cooking (in which meat is sliced and grilled on table-top stoves). Featuring a sushi bar, teriyaki seafood and meat dishes, and combination plates, including steak and sushi and steak and sashimi. **FYI:** Reservations recommended. Children's menu. **Open:** Lunch Mon–Fri 11:30am–2pm; dinner Sun–Thurs 5–9:30pm, Fri–Sat 5–10:30pm. **Prices:** Main courses $10–$19. AE, MC, V.

Keaton's
6464 E Tanque Verde Rd (East Tucson); tel 520/721-1299. **Regional American/Seafood.** Recently painted but still retaining the Old West look, with fringed stained-glass lamp shades, wood paneling, comfortable booths, and lots of memorabilia. Servers are dressed as Old West characters, from "school marms" to cowpunchers. The menu offers just about everything—chicken, steak, prime rib, seafood, pasta, and vegetarian dishes. **FYI:** Reservations recommended. Children's menu. Additional locations: 7401 N La Cholla (tel 297-1999); 2021 N Kinney Rd (tel 883-5705). **Open:** Mon–Sat 11am–10pm, Sun 10:30am–10pm. **Prices:** Main courses $10–$18. AE, CB, DC, DISC, MC, V.

La Parrilla Suiza
5602 E Speedway Blvd (Midtown); tel 520/747-4838. **Mexican.** A festive, bustling Mexican restaurant with a low ceiling, brick interior, and attractive tile-inlaid tables. Chile Christmas lights decorate the bar. Dishes feature traditional charro beans and homemade corn tortillas. Many items are charcoal-grilled. **FYI:** Reservations recommended. Additional location: 2720 N Oracle (tel 602/624-4311). **Open:** Mon–Thurs 11am–10pm, Fri–Sat 11am–11pm, Sun 11am–10pm. **Prices:** Main courses $4–$10. AE, CB, DC, DISC, MC, V.

★ **La Placita Cafe**
In Plaza Palomino Shopping Center, 2950 N Swan Rd; tel 520/881-1150. Swan Rd at Ft Lowell. **Mexican.** Located in a small, upscale shopping plaza. The interior dining area is adorned with Mexican folk art and Oaxacan black pottery, as well as a fireplace. The Oaxaca-born chef offers unusual and sometimes exotic Mexican fare. Dinners include escalopas callos de hacha (sautéed deep sea scallops), chiles rellenos de cangrejo (fresh green chiles stuffed with crab), and planta de hueva berenjena (fried eggplant filet). There are also steaks and carne seca (marinated dried beef). **FYI:** Reservations recommended. **Open:** Lunch Mon–Sat 11:30am–2:30pm; dinner daily 5–9pm. **Prices:** Main courses $6–$16. AE, CB, DC, DISC, MC, V.

Le Rendez-Vous
3844 E Fort Lowell Rd; tel 520/323-7373. **French.** A popular French bistro with plenty of atmosphere. There is an enclosed patio with a red canvas roof and tile floor throughout. French music plays in the background. The menu is small but select; the house specialty is duck à l'orange. **FYI:** Reservations recommended. **Open:** Lunch Tues–Fri 11:30am–2pm; dinner Tues–Sun 6–10pm. **Prices:** Main courses $14–$26. AE, CB, DC, DISC, MC, V.

Lotus Garden
5975 E Speedway Blvd (Central Tucson); tel 520/298-3351. **Chinese.** Decorated in subtle tones, this popular Chinese features an array of dishes, ranging from chop suey to house specialties like ying yang, whole shrimp and slices of beef in tomato and hot chile sauce. Chinese and Japanese wines are available. **FYI:** Reservations recommended. **Open:** Sun–Thurs 11:30am–11pm, Fri–Sat 11:30am–midnight. **Prices:** Main courses $8–$30; prix fixe $9–$20. AE, DC, MC, V.

Penelope's
3071 N Swan Rd (Downtown); tel 520/325-5080. **French.** Housed in an old adobe building in a residential area, with a stained-glass window/mural, ceiling fans, and original art. Entrees change regularly, but typical choices might be filet mignon with peppercorns, salmon with fruit relish, or rack of lamb. **FYI:** Reservations recommended. Beer and wine only. **Open:** Lunch Tues–Fri 11:30am–2pm; dinner Tues–Sun 5:30pm–close. Closed July–Aug. **Prices:** Main courses $12–$22; prix fixe $30. DC, MC, V.

Pinnacle Peak
In Trail Dust Town, 6541 E Tanque Verde Rd (East Tucson); tel 520/296-0911. **American/Steak.** This western-style steakhouse is famous for cutting off neckties—wearer beware—and hanging the ends from the ceiling. Besides a large selection of steaks, they offer chicken, trout, and salmon specialties. **FYI:** Reservations not accepted. Children's menu. **Open:** Daily 5–10pm. **Prices:** Main courses $4–$13. AE, DC, DISC, MC, V.

Presidio Grill
In Rancho Shopping Center, 3352 E Speedway Blvd (Downtown); tel 520/327-4667. **Southwestern.** A popular, modern grill in central Tucson, with a colonnade entrance and soft black leather booths. Pastas, salads, pizzas, meat, fish. **FYI:** Reservations recommended. Jazz. Children's menu. **Open:** Mon–Thurs 11am–10pm, Fri–Sat 11am–midnight, Sun 8am–10pm. **Prices:** Main courses $11–$20; prix fixe $40–$70. AE, MC, V.

Pronto
2955 E Speedway Blvd (Midtown); tel 520/326-9707. **Italian/Southwestern.** A bright, happy place with birthday cake and coffee cup designs—and the command "Mangia!" (eat!)—on the walls. There are soups, salads, regular and grilled sandwiches, burgers, pasta, pizzas, and several vegetarian dishes. Everything is made from scratch. The gourmet bakery produces innovative desserts. **FYI:** Reservations not accepted. Children's menu. Beer and wine only. No smoking. **Open:** Sun–Thurs 11am–9pm, Fri–Sat 11am–10pm. **Prices:** Main courses $2–$6. MC, V.

The Rancher's Club of Arizona
In Hotel Park Tucson and Conference Center, 5151 E Grant Rd (Midtown); tel 520/321-7621. **Southwestern.** Everything is western here, from the cowhide and leather chairs to the western paintings and photos to the cow horn chandelier and staring animal trophy heads. Steaks are grilled on a variety of aromatic woods. Seafood is also available. **FYI:** Reservations recommended. Harp. Dress code. **Open:** Lunch Mon–Fri 11:30am–2pm; dinner Mon–Sat 5:30–10pm. **Prices:** Main courses $17–$32. AE, CB, DC, MC, V.

Scordato's
4405 W Speedway Blvd; tel 520/792-3055. 6 mi W of Tucson. **Italian.** A Tucson landmark since 1972, Scordato's represents the epitome of fine dining. Decor is elegant, with a lovely glass wine storage unit in the entryway and soft chandelier lighting. The menu is extensive; veal is a house specialty. **FYI:** Reservations recommended. Children's menu. **Open:** Tues–Sat 5–10pm, Sun 4–10pm. **Prices:** Main courses $14–$24. AE, CB, DC, DISC, MC, V.

Solarium
6444 E Tanque Verde Rd (East Tucson); tel 520/886-8186. **Eclectic.** Designed by a group of artists, the restaurant has a bi-level dining room with lots of windows and plants, stone floors with inlaid tiles, and sculptured metal doors. The menu ranges from meat to fowl to pasta to seafood. Items are rated according to a "good for the heart" scale. **FYI:** Reservations recommended. Guitar. **Open:** Lunch Mon–Fri 11:30am–2:30pm; dinner Sun–Thurs 5–10pm, Fri–Sat 5–11pm. **Prices:** Main courses $7–$18. AE, DC, DISC, MC, V.

The Tack Room
2800 N Sabino Rd; tel 520/722-2800. **Regional American.** One of Tucson's premier restaurants occupies the main house of an old Spanish-style, 35-acre resort. Original art hangs between picture windows framing mountain views. Southwestern-style dishes are supplemented by a special summer grill menu. Standout dishes include roast duckling in Arizona pistachio crust glazed with jalapeño and lime, and Arizona four-pepper steak. All breads and desserts are made on premises. Closed Mondays May–Jan. **FYI:** Reservations recommended. Children's menu. Dress code. No smoking. **Open:** Peak (Feb–Apr) daily 6pm–close. Closed July 1–14. **Prices:** Main courses $25–$35; prix fixe $38–$45. AE, CB, DC, DISC, MC, V.

The Ventana Room
In Loews Ventana Canyon Resort, 7000 N Resort Dr; tel 520/299-2020 ext 5195. From I-10, take Ina Rd or Orange Grove Rd exits, then go east to Skyline Dr to Craycroft Rd. **French/Southwestern.** The ventanas (or windows) in question are filled with wall-to-wall, floor-to-ceiling panoramas of the flickering lights of Tucson below. The split-level room gives most diners a view, but in a short while the professional and courteous service and outstanding cuisine are of more interest than Tucson. Even the coffee service is special. Sample dishes include seared venison carpaccio; fillet of Hawaiian onaga, oven-braised with pappardelle of leeks; pepper-crusted veal chop with madeira truffle sauce; plum sorbet. **FYI:** Reservations recommended. Harp. Jacket required. **Open:** Daily 6–10:30pm. **Prices:** Main courses $18–$26. AE, CB, DC, DISC, MC, V.

ATTRACTIONS

MUSEUMS

Arizona State Museum
University of Arizona, University Blvd and Park Ave; tel 520/621-6302. Founded in 1892, the museum collects and preserves an extensive collection of artifacts from prehistoric and contemporary Native American cultures of the Southwest. Featured at the museum is *Paths of Life: American Indians of the Southwest,* a popular new exhibit which explores the origins, history, and life today of 10 Native American cultures of Arizona and northwest Mexico. **Open:** Mon–Sat 10am–5pm, Sun noon–5pm. **Free**

University of Arizona Museum of Art
Park Ave and Speedway Blvd; tel 520/621-7567. The museum is home to both an extensive permanent collection, featuring European works from the Renaissance to the 17th century, and a large group of 20th-century painting and sculpture, as well as 2 halls with changing exhibits. The star attraction is the *Retablo of the Cathedral of Ciudad Rodrigo,* which consists of 26 paintings from 15th-century Spain. **Open:** Peak (Sept–mid-May) Mon–Fri 9am–5pm, Sun noon–4pm. Reduced hours off-season. **Free**

Tucson Museum of Art and Historic Block
140 N Main Ave; tel 520/624-2333. The museum boasts a large collection of western and pre-Columbian art, most notably realistic and romantic portrayals of life in the Old West. Free guided tours of the restored homes that make up the historic block are conducted October–May, Wednesday at 11am and Thursday at 2pm. **Open:** Mon–Sat 10am–4pm, Sun noon–4pm. **$**

Arizona Historical Society Tucson Museum
949 E 2nd St; tel 520/628-5774. As Arizona's oldest historical museum, this repository of all things Arizonan is a

treasure trove for the history buff. A full-scale reproduction of an underground mine tunnel is on display that includes an assayer's office, miner's tent, blacksmith shop, and a stamp mill. A new interactive children's exhibit brings 1870s Tucson to life with a Mexican-American ranch, Tohono O'odham home, and a mercantile. **Open:** Mon–Sat 10am–4pm, Sun noon–4pm. **Free**

Frémont House Museum
151 S Granada Ave; tel 520/622-0956. Built in 1858 as a small adobe house, the structure was enlarged after 1866 and is a classic example of Sonoran Mexican adobe architecture. John C Frémont, the fifth territorial governor, rented the home in 1881. The house has been fully restored and is decorated with period antiques. **Open:** Wed–Sat 10am–4pm. **Free**

Center for Creative Photography
1030 N Olive Rd; tel 520/621-7968. Conceived by Ansel Adams, the research facility holds more than 500,000 negatives, 200,000 study prints, and 40,000 master prints by the world's greatest photographers, making it one of the best and largest collections in the world. Photography exhibits are mounted year-round; prints may be examined in a special room. It is suggested that visitors make an appointment and decide in advance whose works they would like to see. **Open:** Mon–Fri 10am–5pm, Sun noon–5pm. **Free**

Flandrau Science Center and Planetarium
Cherry and University Aves; tel 520/621-STAR. On the campus of the University of Arizona. Exhibits include a mineral museum and displays on the sun, moon, planets, asteroids, meteorites, and the exploration of space. Evening shows in the planetarium range from astronomy programs by guest lecturers to laser shows set to music. **Open:** Mon 8am–5pm, Tues 8am–9pm, Wed–Thurs 8am–10pm, Fri–Sat 8am–12:30am, Sun 1–5pm. **$$**

Pima Air and Space Museum
6000 E Valencia Rd; tel 520/574-9658. On display are more than 200 aircraft covering the evolution of American aviation. The collection includes replicas of the Wright Brothers' 1903 Wright Flyer and the X-15, the world's fastest aircraft. The museum also operates the Titan Missile Museum in nearby Green Valley. This is the only intercontinental ballistic missile (ICBM) complex in the world open to the public. **Open:** Daily 9am–5pm. **$$$**

Tucson Children's Museum
200 S 6th Ave; tel 520/792-9985. Hands-on children's museum. Touchable displays include a health and wellness exhibit called "Mind Your Own Business," and a firehouse where visitors learn about fire safety. **Open:** Hours vary, call ahead. **$$**

Old Tucson Studios
201 S Kinney Rd; tel 520/883-6457. Movie location and theme park used for more than 50 years to film western movies and television shows such as *Gunfight at the O K Corral* and *Little House on the Prairie*. There are shootout enactments on Main Street, rodeos, rides, and shows. **Open:** Daily 9am–8pm. **$$$$**

MONUMENTS AND LANDMARKS

El Tiradito
S Granada Ave at W Cushing St. Dedicated to a sinner who had been buried on unconsecrated ground at this spot, the now-crumbling shrine has long played an important role in local folklore and the life of Roman Catholic Tucsonans. Listed on the National Register of Historic Places. **Free**

Mission San Xavier del Bac
1950 W San Xavier Rd; tel 520/294-2624. Called the "White Dove of the Desert," the mission is considered to be the finest example of mission architecture in the United States. Masses are held Monday through Saturday at 8:30am and on Sunday at 8am, 9:30am, 11am, and 12:30 pm. **Open:** Daily 8am–5:30pm. **Free**

Saguaro National Park
3693 S Old Spanish Trail (east) or 2700 N Kinney Rd (west); tel 520/733-5100. The saguaro cactus has been called the monarch of the desert; it is the largest cactus native to the United States and can attain a height of 50 feet and a weight of more than 8 tons. Many species of bird live in holes in the cactus trunk. Coyotes, foxes, squirrels, and javelinas all eat the fruit and seeds.

Since 1933 the two sections of Saguaro National Park have protected the saguaro and all the other inhabitants of this section of the Sonoran Desert. The west section is more popular with vistiors and features a new visitors center with exhibits about the saguaro, the desert, and the Rincon Mountains. The east section of the park is popular with hikers because most of the area has no roads. Both sections of the park have loop roads, nature trails, hiking trails, and picnic grounds. **Open:** Daily 8:30am–5pm. **$**

Sabino Canyon
5900 N Sabino Canyon Rd; tel 520/749-2861. Located in the Santa Catalina Mountains of Coronado National Forest, this desert oasis has attracted people and animals for thousands of years. Along the length of the canyon are waterfalls and pools where vistiors can swim. Moonlight horseback rides are held three times each month April–December; call for reservations (602/749-2861). Narrated scenic tram ride through lower canyon. **Open:** Daily 24 hours. **Free**

Kitt Peak National Observatory
AZ 86; tel 520/325-9200. Located atop 6,882-foot Kitt Peak in the Quinlan Mountains, 40 miles southwest of Tucson, this is the largest of the astronomical observatories in Arizona. The world's largest solar telescope and four other major telescopes are located here. Guided tours are offered daily. People with medical problems are advised that the tour includes a great deal of walking, high altitudes, and steep mountain paths. **Open:** Daily 10am–4pm. **Free**

ZOOS AND GARDENS

Arizona-Sonora Desert Museum
2021 N Kinney Rd; tel 520/883-1380. Actually a zoo, and one of the best in the country. The Sonoran Desert encompasses much of central and southern Arizona as well as parts of northern Mexico. The region contains not only arid lands but also forested mountains, springs, rivers, and streams. The full spectrum of desert life is represented at the zoo, including black bears, mountain lions, beavers, tarantulas, fish, scorpions, prairie dogs, and javelinas. In addition, there is a simulated cave with exhibits on prehistoric desert life and more than 400 species of native plants, including the giant saguaro cactus. **Open:** Peak (May–Sept) Sun–Fri 7:30am–6pm, Sat 7:30am–10pm. Reduced hours off-season. **$$$**

Reid Park Zoo
Country Club Rd and 22nd St; tel 520/791-4022. The zoo is a breeding center for several endangered species. Among the animals in the zoo's programs are giant anteaters, white rhinoceroses, tigers, ruffed lemurs, and zebras. **Open:** Daily 9am–4pm. **$**

Hi Corbett Field
Randolph Way; tel 520/325-2621. This baseball field is located in the Reid Park complex. The **Colorado Rockies** pitch spring training camp here in March, and the **Tucson Toros**, the Houston Astros AAA team in the Pacific Coast League, play during the summer. **Open:** Feb–Sept. **$$**

Tucson Botanical Gardens
2150 N Alvernon Way; tel 520/326-9255. A five-acre oasis of greenery in downtown Tucson dedicated to demonstrating the variety of plants that can be grown in southern Arizona. **Open:** Daily 8:30am–4:30pm. **$**

PERFORMING ARTS

Tucson Convention Center Music Hall
Bounded by Church Ave, Broadway Blvd, Cushing St, and Granada Ave; tel 520/791-4101 or 791-4266. Large performing arts and convention complex. The Tucson Symphony Orchestra, the oldest continuously performing symphony in the Southwest, performs here October–May; concerts feature classics, pops, and chamber music. Also part of the complex is the the Arizona Opera Company, which stages four annual productions. **Open:** Box office, Mon–Sat 10am–6pm. **$$$$**

Temple of Music and Art
330 S Scott Ave; tel 520/884-8210 or 622-2823. Completely renovated in 1990, this landmark 1927 theater is the center of Tucsons's arts district. The Temple's main venue is the 605-seat Alice Hosclaw Theatre, which serves as a home for the Arizona Theatre Company. ATC presents six productions a year, from comedies and dramas to Broadway-style musicals. Other venues at the Temple include the 100-seat Cabaret Theatre and an art gallery. Tours available; restaurant. **Open:** Box office, Mon–Fri 10am–6pm, Sat 10am–5pm, Sun 10am–2pm. **$$$$**

Tumacacori

ATTRACTION

Tumacacori National Monument
Frontage Rd; tel 520/398-2341. Mission founded by Jesuit missionary and explorer Fr Eusebio Francisco Kino in 1691 to convert the Pima Indians. Much of the old brick-and-stucco mission church still stands, and Spanish architectural influence can easily be seen. On weekends, Native American and Mexican craftspeople give demonstrations of Native arts. The Tumacacori Fiesta is held in early December. Small museum. **Open:** Daily 8am–5pm. **$**

Wickenburg

Located on the northern edge of the Sonora Desert in central Arizona, Wickenburg was founded in the mid-1860s by Austrian miner Henry Wickenburg, who discovered gold and what would eventually become one of the richest mines in Arizona. The town likes to play up its Wild West heritage and has preserved one of its downtown streets much as it may have looked in 1900. There are several guest ranches (formerly known as dude ranches) in the area, ranging from the luxurious to the rustic. **Information:** Wickenburg Chamber of Commerce, 216 N Frontier St, PO Drawer CC, Wickenburg 85358 (tel 520/684-5479 or 800/WICKCHAMBER).

MOTEL

Best Western Rancho Grande
293 E Wickenburg Way, PO Box 1328, 85358; tel 520/684-5445 or toll free 800/854-7235; fax 520/684-7380. A Spanish-style, tile-roofed motel in the center of Wickenburg. **Rooms:** 80 rms and stes. CI 1pm/CO noon. Nonsmoking rms avail. Rooms are attractively furnished, with an Old West feel. **Amenities:** A/C, cable TV w/movies, refrig. Some units w/terraces. **Services:** Babysitting. **Facilities:** Playground. Two public golf courses are nearby. **Rates:** $55–$67 S; $65–$80 D; $80–$93 ste. Extra person $3. Min stay special events. Parking: Outdoor, free. AE, CB, DC, DISC, JCB, MC, V.

RESORTS

Flying E Ranch
2801 W Wickenburg Way, PO Box EEE, 85358; tel 520/684-2173; fax 520/684-5304. 2 mi N of town. 20,000 acres. This working ranch has accepted guests since the 1940s. There's plenty of room for horseback riding, but the cattle are not for guest use. **Rooms:** 17 rms, stes, and effic. CI

open/CO 11am. Nonsmoking rms avail. **Amenities:** A/C, TV, refrig. No phone. All units w/terraces. **Services:** Babysitting. **Facilities:** Basketball, volleyball, lawn games, sauna, whirlpool. Comfortable guest lounge with piano. Also, shuffleboard court and giant outdoor chess game. Livery stable for guests' horses. **Rates (AP):** $120–$160 S; $185–$250 D; $200–$250 ste; $200–$250 effic. Extra person $25–$75. Min stay special events. Parking: Outdoor, free. Closed May–Oct. No CC.

Kay El Bar Guest Ranch

Rincon Rd, PO Box 2480, 85358; tel 520/684-7593. Rincon Rd exit off US 89/93. 60 acres. The Kay El Bar has been a guest ranch since 1926, and a cattle ranch from about the turn of the century. It may not be fancy, but it has lots of charm, with buildings listed on the National Register of Historic Places. **Rooms:** 8 rms; 1 cottage/villa. CI open/CO open. **Amenities:** No A/C, phone, or TV. **Services:** Babysitting. **Facilities:** 1 bar, basketball, volleyball. Two horseback rides per day are included in rates. **Rates (AP):** $120 S; $225 D; $240–$455 cottage/villa. Extra person $35–$75. Children under age 2 stay free. Min stay. AP rates avail. Parking: Outdoor, free. Closed May–Sept. MC, V.

Rancho de los Caballeros

1551 S Vulture Mine Rd, PO Box 1148, 85390; tel 520/684-5484; fax 520/684-2267. 3 mi N of town; Vulture Mine Rd exit off US 60. 20,000 acres. This large, quiet, desert resort features a comfortable lobby with leather chairs, a billiard table, a piano, and a fireplace. Hummingbird feeders are placed throughout the property. **Rooms:** 77 rms and stes. Executive level. CI 4pm/CO 1pm. Nonsmoking rms avail. Some rooms have great views of the Bradshaw Mountains. **Amenities:** A/C, TV, refrig. All units w/terraces, some w/fireplaces, some w/whirlpools. **Services:** Twice-daily maid svce, social director, children's program, babysitting. **Facilities:** 18 275 2 restaurants, 2 bars (1 w/entertainment), volleyball, games rm, lawn games, playground, washer/dryer. **Rates (AP):** Peak (Feb–May) $160–$180 S; $254–$292 D; $175–$499 ste. Extra person $60–$70. Children under age 5 stay free. Min stay peak and special events. Lower rates off-season. AP rates avail. Parking: Outdoor, free. Closed June–Oct. No CC.

Wickenburg Inn

US 89, PO Box P, 85358; tel 520/684-7811 or toll free 800/942-5362; fax 520/684-2981. 8 mi N of town. 4,700 acres. A deluxe riding and tennis resort. **Rooms:** 6 rms and stes; 41 cottages/villas. CI 3pm/CO noon. Nonsmoking rms avail. Range of accommodations, from rooms in the lodge to three sizes of casitas, each with its own personality. Some casitas have spiral staircases to the roof. **Amenities:** A/C, refrig, voice mail. All units w/terraces, some w/fireplaces. **Services:** Social director, masseur, babysitting. Occasionally have visiting cowboy bands. **Facilities:** 9 75 1 restaurant, 2 bars, basketball, volleyball, lawn games, whirlpool, playground, washer/dryer. Nature and wildlife studies, arts and crafts center. About 85 horses, with plenty of space to ride. Golf is nearby. **Rates (AP):** Peak (Feb–Apr) $199 S; $279 D; $249–$349 ste; $229–$379 cottage/villa. Extra person $75. Children under age 3 stay free. Min stay special events. Lower rates off-season. Parking: Outdoor, free. Closed Aug. AE, DISC, MC, V.

ATTRACTIONS

Vulture Mine

Vulture Mine Rd; tel 602/377-0803. Wickenburg was founded as a mining town in 1863 when Henry Wickenburg struck gold. Today visitors can see the old mine where he struck his claim as well as the ghost town of Vulture City. Most of the buildings were built in 1884, including the assay office which was constructed with more than $600,000 worth of gold and silver ore. Visitors can also pan for gold. **Open:** Peak (Sept–Apr) daily 8am–4pm. Reduced hours off-season. **$$**

Hassayampa River Preserve

US 60; tel 520/684-2772. The riparian (riverside) habitat supports trees and plants that require more water than is usually available in the desert. This lush growth provides food and shelter for hundreds of species of birds, mammals, and reptiles. Nature trails lead along the river beneath cottonwoods and willows and past the spring-fed Palm Lake. Naturalist-guided walks; reservations are required. **Open:** Peak (May–Sept) Wed–Sun 6am–noon. Reduced hours off-season. **$$**

Desert Caballeros Western Museum

21 N Frontier St; tel 520/684-2272. Displays western art depicting life on the range in the days of "cowboys and Indians." Exhibits on the history of central Arizona include a branding and barbed-wire exhibit covering the ranching history of the area, and a re-created street from 1900. **Open:** Mon–Sat 10am–4pm, Sun 1–4pm. **$$**

Willcox

Once known as the Cattle Capital of America, Willcox continues as a major ranching center. It is also the hometown of singing cowboy Rex Allen, honored during Rex Allen Days each October. **Information:** Willcox Chamber of Commerce, 1500 North Circle I Rd, Willcox 85643 (tel 520/384-2272 or 800/200-2272).

MOTELS

Best Western Plaza Inn

1100 W Rex Allen Dr, 85643; tel 520/384-3556 or toll free 800/262-2645; fax 520/384-2679. Exit 340 off I 10. Pleasant, better-than-average motel, good for both vacationers and business travelers. **Rooms:** 92 rms and stes. CI open/CO noon. Nonsmoking rms avail. The attractive, comfortable rooms were renovated in 1993. **Amenities:** A/C, cable TV w/movies, refrig, dataport. Some units w/whirlpools.

Services: Babysitting. **Facilities:** 1 restaurant, 1 bar (w/entertainment), whirlpool, washer/dryer. **Rates (BB):** Peak (Feb–Apr) $70 S or D; $80 ste. Extra person $5. Children under age 12 stay free. Min stay special events. Lower rates off-season. Parking: Outdoor, free. AE, CB, DC, DISC, MC, V.

Econo Lodge
724 N Bisbee Ave, 85643; tel 520/384-4222 or toll free 800/424-4777; fax 520/384-3785. Exit 340 off I-10. Basic motel with easy access to area attractions. **Rooms:** 73 rms and stes. CI 2pm/CO 11am. Nonsmoking rms avail. **Amenities:** A/C, cable TV. **Services:** Video players and movies are available to rent. **Facilities:** Washer/dryer. **Rates:** $48–$70 S; $58–$80 D; $75–$85 ste. Extra person $5. Children under age 18 stay free. Min stay special events. Parking: Outdoor, free. AE, CB, DC, DISC, ER, JCB, MC, V.

ATTRACTIONS

Chiricahua National Monument
AZ 186; tel 520/824-3560. These gravity-defying rock formations sculpted by nature—called "the land of the standing-up rocks" by the Apaches and the "wonderland of rocks" by pioneers—are the equal of any of Arizona's many amazing rocky landmarks. Formed about 25 million years ago by a massive volcanic eruption, these rhyolite badlands were once the stronghold of renegade Apaches. Many species of birds, mammals, and plants now live in the mountains, taking advantage of a climate usually found farther to the south in Mexico. Campground, picnic area, visitor center. **Open:** Visitor center, daily 8am–5pm. **$$**

Fort Bowie National Historic Site
AZ 186; tel 520/847-2500. Fort Bowie was established in 1862 near the mile-high Apache Pass to protect the slow-moving Butterfield Stage, which carried mail, passengers, and freight, as it traversed this difficult region through the heart of Apache territory. It was from Fort Bowie that federal troops battled Geronimo until the Apache chief finally surrendered in 1886. Today there's little left of the fort but some crumbling adobe walls. It's a 1.5-mile hike to the ruins. **Open:** Ranger station, daily 8am–5pm; grounds, daily sunrise to sunset. **Free**

Museum of the Southwest
1500 N Circle I Rd; tel 520/384-2272. Exhibits on the geology of southeastern Arizona, the Apaches, settlement by pioneers, and cattle ranching. It also includes a cowboy hall of fame and an information center where visitors can find out more about Willcox and the surrounding region. **Open:** Mon–Sat 9am–5pm, Sun 1–5pm. **Free**

Rex Allen Museum
150 N Rail Road Ave; tel 520/384-4583. Rex Allen was a singing cowboy, famous for the song "Streets of Laredo" and the television program *Frontier Doctor*. The museum houses memorabilia from the entertainer's career. A life-size bronze statue is in the park across from the museum; Allen's horse, Koko, is buried beneath his statue. **Open:** Daily 10am–4pm. **$**

Williams

Williams is a center for hiking, fishing, hunting, and other outdoor recreation in the Kaibab National Forest and serves as a gateway to the South Rim of Grand Canyon National Park. **Information:** Williams-Grand Canyon Chamber of Commerce, 200 W Railroad Ave, Williams 86046 (tel 520/635-4061).

HOTEL

Ramada Inn Canyon Gateway
642 E Bill Williams Ave, 86046; tel 520/635-4431 or toll free 800/462-9381; fax 520/635-2292. Exit 161 off I-40. A large hotel set amidst 27 acres of pine forest at the eastern edge of Williams. **Rooms:** 96 rms. CI 2pm/CO noon. Nonsmoking rms avail. **Amenities:** A/C, cable TV. **Services:** **Facilities:** 2 restaurants, 1 bar, whirlpool. Both restaurants have live entertainment. Winter sports close by. **Rates:** Peak (Apr–Oct) $95–$125 S or D. Extra person $10. Children under age 18 stay free. Lower rates off-season. Parking: Outdoor, free. AE, CB, DC, DISC, MC, V.

MOTELS

Canyon Country Inn
442 W Bill Williams Ave, 86046; tel 520/635-2349 or toll free 800/643-1020; fax 520/635-9898. A comfortable motel located in an older home. **Rooms:** 13 rms and stes. CI 2pm/CO 11am. No smoking. **Amenities:** A/C, cable TV. **Services:** **Rates (CP):** Peak (May–Aug) $50–$60 S; $65–$75 D; $75–$95 ste. Extra person $10. Children under age 10 stay free. Lower rates off-season. Parking: Outdoor, free. Packages are available that include the steam train ride from Williams to Grand Canyon National Park. Closed Jan. AE, DISC, MC, V.

Comfort Inn
911 W Bill Williams Ave, 86046; tel 520/635-4045 or toll free 800/221-2222; fax 520/635-9060. Exit 161 off I-40. An attractive, basic motel located in Williams's historic district, with convenient access to Grand Canyon National Park and other area attractions. **Rooms:** 77 rms and stes. CI noon/CO 11am. Nonsmoking rms avail. Rooms are simply but comfortably furnished. **Amenities:** A/C, cable TV. Some units w/minibars. **Services:** **Facilities:** Games rm, whirlpool, washer/dryer. **Rates (CP):** Peak (Apr 16–Oct 15) $78–$108 S; $88–$118 D. Extra person $10. Children under age 12 stay free. Lower rates off-season. Parking: Outdoor, free. AE, CB, DC, DISC, MC, V.

Holiday Inn Express
831 W Bill Williams Ave, 86046; tel 520/635-9000 or toll free 800/HOLIDAY. Exit 161 off I-40. Built in 1992, this attractive hotel is a good addition to the range of accommodations in Williams. It has a large lobby with a fireplace. **Rooms:** 52 rms. CI 2pm/CO 11am. Nonsmoking rms avail. **Amenities:** A/C, cable TV. **Services:** **Facilities:** Whirlpool, washer/dryer. **Rates (CP):** Peak (Apr–Oct) $69–$119 S or D. Extra person $5. Children under age 18 stay free. Lower rates off-season. Parking: Outdoor, free. AE, CB, DC, DISC, MC, V.

Norris Motel
1001 W Bill Williams Ave, 86046; tel 520/635-2202 or toll free 800/341-8000; fax 520/635-2202. Exit 161 off I-40. Simple, comfortable motel; a good choice within this price range. Note that the newer wing has larger rooms, indoor corridors, and sprinklers. **Rooms:** 33 rms and stes. CI noon/CO 11am. Nonsmoking rms avail. Rooms are attractively furnished. **Amenities:** A/C, cable TV w/movies, refrig. **Services:** Complimentary bus service is provided to the historic downtown area and the Grand Canyon Railway Depot. **Facilities:** Whirlpool. There's a hot tub in a gazebo. **Rates:** Peak (May 18–Sept 7) $62 S; $62–$74 D; $107–$122 ste. Extra person $5. Children under age 3 stay free. Lower rates off-season. Parking: Outdoor, free. AE, DISC, MC, V.

Quality Inn Mountain Ranch
Rte 1, PO Box 35, 86046; tel 520/635-2693 or toll free 800/221-2222. 5 mi E of Williams, exit 171 off I-40. Set on 26 acres, this pleasant, clean motel offers a variety of outdoor activities for the vacationer. **Rooms:** 73 rms. CI 2pm/CO 11am. Nonsmoking rms avail. **Amenities:** A/C, cable TV. **Services:** **Facilities:** 2 1 restaurant (bkfst and dinner only), games rm, lawn games, whirlpool. **Rates:** Peak (Apr–Oct) $85–$102 S or D. Extra person $6. Children under age 6 stay free. Lower rates off-season. Parking: Outdoor, free. Closed Nov–Mar. AE, CB, DC, DISC, ER, JCB, MC, V.

Travelodge
430 E Bill Williams Ave, 86046; tel 520/635-2651 or toll free 800/578-7878; fax 520/635-2651. Exit 163 off I-40. A basic motel with easy access to I-40. **Rooms:** 41 rms and stes. CI 1pm/CO 11am. Nonsmoking rms avail. **Amenities:** A/C, cable TV w/movies. **Services:** **Facilities:** Whirlpool. **Rates:** Peak (May 15–Sept 15) $69 S; $74–$79 D; $89–$99 ste. Extra person $6. Children under age 17 stay free. Lower rates off-season. Parking: Outdoor, free. AE, DC, DISC, MC, V.

Window Rock

Named for a gigantic natural hole in a sandstone cliff, Window Rock is the capital of the sprawling Navajo Nation. **Information:** Navajo Nation, Navajo Tourism Dept, PO Box 663, Window Rock 86515 (tel 520/871-6436).

HOTEL

Navajo Nation Inn
48 W AZ 264, 86515; tel 520/871-4108 or toll free 800/662-6189; fax 520/871-5466. At jct AZ 264 & Rte 12. An attractive hotel, located in the capital of the Navajo Nation, the largest reservation in the United States. Close to many historical attractions, including Hubbell Trading Post, a National Historic Site. **Rooms:** 56 rms and stes. CI 2pm/CO 11am. Nonsmoking rms avail. **Amenities:** A/C, cable TV w/movies. **Services:** **Facilities:** 1 restaurant. **Rates:** Peak (May–Sept) $57–$72 S; $62–$72 D. Extra person $5. Children under age 12 stay free. Lower rates off-season. Parking: Outdoor, free. AE, DC, MC, V.

ATTRACTIONS

Window Rock
AZ 264; tel 520/871-6647. Named for a huge natural opening in a sandstone cliff wall on the Navajo Reservation, this has long been an important site to the Navajo. At one time there was a spring at the base of the rock, and water from it was used by medicine men performing the Tohee Ceremony, a water ceremony intended to bring rain. Another legend says that evil monsters were banished from the world through Window Rock during the time of creation. **Open:** Daily 24 hours. **Free**

Navajo Nation Zoological and Botanical Park
AZ 264; tel 520/871-6573. The only Native American–operated zoo in the country. On view are animals and plants that are part of the Navajo culture. Among the animals featured here are those considered to be "guardian animals" such as elk, deer, coyotes, black bears, and golden eagles. All animals on display have either been found injured, abandoned, or have been donated by other zoos. **Open:** Daily 8am–5pm. **Free**

St Michael's Mission Museum
24 Mission Rd; tel 520/871-4171. Exhibits explore the impact of the Franciscan Friars on the Navajo people, and life in Arizona in the late 1800s. The museum is housed in the original mission built in 1898. Inside are pottery, artifacts, and the first typewriter for the Navajo language. The new church is located nearby and is open year-round. **Open:** June–Sept, daily 9am–5pm. **Free**

Winslow

Established as a railroad diversion point, Winslow today is a stop along I-40 just outside the Navajo Indian Reservation. Though it's nearly 70 miles south of Second Mesa, this is the next-closest place to stay for visitors touring the Hopi pueblos. **Information:** Winslow Chamber of Commerce, 300 W North Rd, PO Box 460, Winslow 86047 (tel 520/289-2434).

MOTEL

Best Western Town House Lodge

1914 W 3rd St, 86047; tel 520/289-4611 or toll free 800/528-1234. Exit 252 off I-40. This is an attractive, older motel, with no surprises. **Rooms:** 68 rms and stes. CI 1pm/CO 11am. Nonsmoking rms avail. Rooms are simple, uncluttered, comfortable, and clean. **Amenities:** A/C, cable TV. **Services:** **Facilities:** 1 restaurant, 1 bar, playground, washer/dryer. **Rates:** Peak (May–Sept) $46–$52 S; $50–$54 D; $80 ste. Extra person $6. Children under age 12 stay free. Lower rates off-season. Parking: Outdoor, free. AE, CB, DC, DISC, MC, V.

ATTRACTION

Meteor Crater

Exit 233 off I-40; tel 520/289-2362. Nearly 50,000 years ago, a meteor estimated to be 100 feet in diameter slammed into the ground here at 45,000 miles per hour. It formed what is today the best-preserved crater in the world, measuring 570 feet deep and nearly a mile across. The resemblance of the crater landscape to the surface of the moon prompted NASA to use this as a training site for Apollo program astronauts. Part of the small museum at this site has a section dedicated to the exploration of space; the rest is devoted to exhibits on astrogeology, including a meteorite weighing nearly three quarters of a ton. **Open:** Peak (Mid-May–mid-Sept) daily 6am–6pm. Reduced hours off-season. **$$$**

Yuma

This narrow crossing of the Colorado River was visited by Spanish explorers in 1540. The town was established in the 1850s and became a stop during the California gold rush. Nineteenth-century buildings contribute to the old-west feel still evident today. Yuma is well known among rock hounds; within 80 miles of here are numerous gem fields. Among the hottest spots in America, the Yuma area endures summer temperatures that regularly top 120°F. **Information:** Yuma Convention & Visitors Bureau, 488 S Maiden Lane, PO Box 10831, Yuma 85366 (tel 520/783-0071).

HOTELS

Best Western Chilton Inn and Conference Center

300 E 32nd St, 85364; tel 520/344-1050 or toll free 800/528-1234; fax 520/344-4877. A centrally located hotel close to Yuma International Airport. **Rooms:** 121 rms. CI 3pm/CO noon. Nonsmoking rms avail. **Amenities:** A/C, satel TV, refrig, dataport, voice mail. **Services:** Free local phone calls. **Facilities:** 1 restaurant (bkfst and dinner only), 1 bar, whirlpool, washer/dryer. **Rates (BB):** Peak (Sept–Apr) $79 S; $84–$89 D. Extra person $5. Children under age 18 stay free. Min stay special events. Lower rates off-season. Parking: Outdoor, free. Weekly rates avail. AE, CB, DC, DISC, JCB, MC, V.

Best Western Coronado Motor Hotel

233 4th Ave, 85364; tel 520/783-4453 or toll free 800/528-1234; fax 520/782-7487. 4th Ave exit off I-8. An attractive, better-than-average hotel within walking distance of Yuma's major historic and cultural attractions. **Rooms:** 86 rms and stes. Executive level. CI 2pm/CO 11am. Nonsmoking rms avail. Large family suites are available. Some rooms have kitchenettes. **Amenities:** A/C, cable TV w/movies, refrig, dataport, VCR. Some units w/whirlpools. All rooms have microwaves. **Services:** **Facilities:** 1 restaurant (bkfst and lunch only), 1 bar, whirlpool, washer/dryer. A free video library is available for guest use. **Rates (CP):** Peak (Jan–Mar) $56–$72 S; $69–$84 D; $84–$99 ste. Extra person $5. Children under age 12 stay free. Lower rates off-season. Parking: Outdoor, free. AE, CB, DC, DISC, EC, ER, MC, V.

Best Western InnSuites Hotel Yuma

1450 S Castle Dome Ave, 85365; tel 520/783-8341 or toll free 800/922-2034; fax 520/783-1349. US 95 exit off I-8. Popular with both business travelers and vacationers, this upscale hotel is good for extended stays. **Rooms:** 166 rms and stes. Executive level. CI 2pm/CO noon. Nonsmoking rms avail. A variety of units are available, from the smaller Studio to the more luxurious Executive or Presidential Suites. **Amenities:** A/C, satel TV w/movies, refrig. Some units w/terraces, some w/whirlpools. **Services:** Free local phone calls and morning newspapers. Complimentary barbecue and cocktails Wednesday 5–6:30pm. **Facilities:** 1 restaurant, 1 bar, basketball, games rm, whirlpool, playground, washer/dryer. **Rates (CP):** Peak (Jan–Mar) $65–$149 S or D; $79–$149 ste. Children under age 18 stay free. Min stay special events. Lower rates off-season. Parking: Outdoor, free. AE, DC, DISC, MC, V.

UNRATED Radisson Inn Suites

2600 S 4th Ave, 85365; tel 520/726-4830 or toll free 800/333-3333; fax 520/341-1152. I-8 Business Loop exit off I-8. All-suite hotel popular for multi-night stays. **Rooms:** 164 stes. Executive level. CI 2pm/CO noon. Nonsmoking rms avail.

Every suite is decorated with Southwestern art. Many have sofabeds. **Amenities:** A/C, cable TV w/movies, refrig, dataport. Some units w/whirlpools. All suites have a microwave and two TVs. **Services:** Twice-daily maid svce. Complimentary cocktails served 5–7pm nightly. **Facilities:** Whirlpool, washer/dryer. **Rates (CP):** Peak (Sept–Apr) $99–$119 ste. Extra person $10. Children under age 18 stay free. Lower rates off-season. Parking: Outdoor, free. AE, DC, DISC, MC, V.

MOTELS

Yuma Cabana

2151 4th Ave, 85364; tel 520/783-8311 or toll free 800/874-0811. I-8 Business Loop exit off I-8. Exceptionally clean, attractive motel, centrally located. **Rooms:** 63 rms, stes, and effic. CI open/CO 11am. Nonsmoking rms avail. Kitchenettes are available. **Amenities:** A/C, satel TV, refrig, dataport. Some units w/terraces. **Services:** **Facilities:** Racquetball, washer/dryer. Shuffleboard court. Free use of adjacent gym. **Rates:** Peak (Jan–Mar) $38–$68 S or D; $72–$72 ste; $50–$80 effic. Extra person $6. Children under age 12 stay free. Min stay special events. Lower rates off-season. Parking: Outdoor, free. Senior discounts are available. AE, CB, DC, DISC, MC, V.

Yuma 4th Ave Travelodge

2050 4th Ave, 85364; tel 520/782-3831 or toll free 800/255-3050; fax 520/783-4616. I-8 Business Loop exit off I-8. Comfortable, standard motel on Yuma's "motel row." **Rooms:** 48 rms. CI open/CO 11am. Nonsmoking rms avail. **Amenities:** A/C, cable TV w/movies, refrig. **Services:** Free local phone calls and complimentary morning newspapers. Fax and photocopying services available. **Facilities:** Playground, washer/dryer. **Rates:** Peak (Jan–Mar) $42 S; $62–$72 D. Extra person $4. Children under age 17 stay free. Lower rates off-season. Parking: Outdoor, free. AE, CB, DC, DISC, JCB, MC, V.

RESTAURANTS

Garden Cafe and Coffee House

250 S Madison Ave; tel 520/783-1491. **Health/Spa.** This could be the coolest spot in what is often the hottest location in the United States. All seating is outdoors in the garden (which includes an aviary); a misting water system cools patrons. The menu includes homemade quiche and sweet basil chicken salad, plus sandwiches, soups, salads, and elegant desserts. A coffeehouse section offers espresso, cappuccino, and specialty drinks. **FYI:** Reservations recommended. Reservations accepted. Children's menu. BYO. No smoking. **Open:** Tues–Fri 9am–2:30pm, Sat–Sun 8am–2:30pm. Closed July–Sept. **Prices:** Lunch main courses $5–$8. AE, MC, V.

★ Lutes Casino

221 Main St; tel 520/782-2192. **American.** Built in 1901 as a general store with a hotel upstairs, Lute's became a pool hall in the 1920s and is now billed as the oldest continually operating pool hall in the state. Old photos, movie star posters, signs, and other memorabilia seem to be everywhere. Noted for its hamburgers and something called a "special," a cross between a hamburger and a hot dog. **FYI:** Reservations accepted. **Open:** Mon–Sat 9am–9pm, Sun 10am–6pm. **Prices:** Main courses $3–$5. No CC.

(\$) Yuma Landing

195 4th Ave; tel 520/782-7427. **American.** The first plane to land in Arizona touched down near this site in 1911. Burgers, steaks, pasta. **FYI:** Reservations accepted. **Open:** Daily 6am–2pm. **Prices:** Lunch main courses $4–$8. AE, CB, DC, DISC, MC, V.

ATTRACTIONS

Arizona Historical Society Century House Museum

240 S Madison St; tel 520/782-1841. Once the home of a prosperous Yuma merchant, today the old house is surrounded by palm trees and lush gardens. Inside the museum are historic photographs and artifacts from Arizona's past. **Open:** Tues–Sat 10am–4pm. **Free**

Yuma Territorial Prison State Historic Park

1 Prison Hill Rd; tel 520/783-4771. Yuma is one of the hottest places in the world, so it comes as no surprise that in 1876 the Arizona Territory chose this bleak spot for its first prison. The prison museum has some interesting displays, including photos of many of the 3,069 prisoners who were incarcerated at Yuma during its 33 years of operation. **Open:** Daily 8am–5pm. **$**

Quartermaster Depot State Historic Park

100 N 4th Ave; tel 520/329-0471. Yuma was a busy river port during the mid-19th century and a depot for military supplies shipped from California. Today, the large wooden buildings that comprised the port hold exhibits that tell the story of the people who lived and worked at Yuma Crossing. Costumed guides answer questions about the depot and its role in Arizona history. **Open:** Daily 10am–5pm. **$**

COLORADO

Heart of the Rocky Mountains

STATE STATS

CAPITAL
Denver

AREA
104,247 square miles

BORDERS
Wyoming, Nebraska, Kansas, New Mexico, and Utah

POPULATION
3,566,000 (1993 estimate)

ENTERED UNION
August 1, 1876 (38th state)

NICKNAME
Centennial State

STATE FLOWER
Rocky Mountain Columbine

STATE BIRD
Lark bunting

FAMOUS NATIVES
Scott Carpenter, Lon Chaney, Jack Dempsey, Anne Parrish, Douglas Fairbanks, Mamie Eisenhower

A mix of old and new, rough and refined, awaits you in Colorado. Here you're likely to see a grizzled cowboy, tanned and saddle-worn, sipping a cappuccino while using a cellular phone to consult his stockbroker. There are still echoes of the Old West, and visitors can still walk in the footsteps—perhaps over the same plank floors—where Bat Masterson, Buffalo Bill, Butch Cassidy, and Doc Holliday walked a century ago. Or go back further, and explore ancient stone and mud cities built by a civilization that disappeared near the end of the 13th century. To explore Colorado today is to step into its past, as well as to examine the science, technology, arts, and urban sophistication that characterize this state at the close of the 20th century.

You'll find rugged wilderness galore, untamed rivers, jagged mountain peaks soaring over 14,000 feet, and deep powder snow. But opportunities to experience the soft life also abound: to be pampered in luxurious hotels, to savor the cuisine of fine restaurants, to explore exotic and elegant shops. Colorado's larger cities have all the amenities you'd expect to find in any major American city. Transportation and communications systems are good, the weather is usually pleasant, and the people are mostly easy-going and friendly. In smaller towns you'll discover historic Victorian mansions, often beautifully restored, as well as working turn-of-the-century steam trains, living-history museums, old forts, ghost towns, Native American ruins, and 19th-century gold mines.

But visitors soon discover what the locals already know: Colorado is a place to be outdoors, to breathe the crisp mountain air, gaze upon sunrises and sunsets, lie in a field of wildflowers, and maybe even work up a sweat. You can go horseback riding, hiking, mountain biking, skiing, snowboarding, swimming, fishing, rock climbing, or simply

Frommer's #1

sit in the sun admiring the mountains. The scenery is spectacular, and much of the state—especially once you get away from the popular tourist destinations—is uncrowded.

Colorado is a land to explore, to discover. You could simply fly to Vail, spend a week skiing or hiking, and then fly home and say you've been to Colorado. But perhaps a better way is to bring or rent a car, spend a few days in one destination, and then move on, discovering Colorado's multiple personalities along the way.

A Brief History

Earliest Residents Nomadic hunters entered Colorado some 12,000 to 20,000 years ago via the Bering Strait, following the tracks of the woolly mammoth and bison. Then, about 2,000 years ago, the Anasazi people arrived, and made their homes in shallow caves in the Four Corners area (where the borders of modern-day Colorado, Utah, Arizona, and New Mexico meet). At first hunters, the Anasazi gradually learned farming and basket-making and pottery-making. They constructed pit houses and eventually built sophisticated villages, such as those at Mesa Verde National Park. Although the Anasazi had disappeared by the time Spanish explorers arrived in the mid-16th century, in their place were several groups of nomads—the Utes in the west, and the Arapahoe, Cheyenne, and Comanche across the eastern plains.

Fun Facts

- At one time Congress planned to name Colorado Jefferson, after Thomas Jefferson.
- Colorado's Highway 103 is the highest road in North America. You can drive right to the top of Mount Evans—14,260 feet high.
- During World War II, the 10th Mountain Division used the rugged terrain between Vail and Aspen as a training ground for alpine combat in Europe.
- The lowest elevation in the state is 3,350 feet above sea level—still over a half-mile high.

Rush to the West The Colorado area became part of the United States in 1803, when US President Thomas Jefferson paid $15 million for the vast Louisiana Territory, which included the lion's share of modern Colorado. As the West began to open up in the 1820s, the Santa Fe Trail was established, cutting through Colorado's southeast corner. Bent's Fort was built on the Arkansas River between 1828 and 1832; today you can visit the reconstructed fort, a National Historic Site, near La Junta.

The next boost occurred in 1858, when gold was discovered in what soon became the city of Denver. Additional strikes in the nearby mountains the following year added to the frenzy, and during the summer of 1859 some 50,000 would-be miners set out from the East for the Colorado gold fields. Congress created the Colorado Territory in 1861, and the Homestead Act the following year put much of the territory's public land into private ownership.

Controlling the native peoples was a priority of the territorial government, which frequently broke promises made to Native Americans. An 1851 treaty had guaranteed the entire Pikes Peak region to the Plains tribes, but the rush of gold-seekers in the late 1850s put an end to that. Then the Fort Wise Treaty of 1861 exchanged the Pikes Peak territory for five million acres of Arkansas Valley land, north of modern La Junta. However, the Arapahoe and Cheyenne continued to roam their old hunting grounds, and when conflicts arose the Colorado cavalry attacked a peaceful settlement of Cheyenne in 1864, killing several hundred people, many of them women and children. The Cheyenne and Arapahoe vowed revenge and launched a campaign to drive whites from their ancient hunting grounds; their biggest triumph was the destruction of the town of Julesburg in 1865. But the cavalry, bolstered by returning Civil War veterans, managed to force the two tribes onto reservations in what is now Oklahoma.

The Centennial State The Territory of Colorado had begun pushing for statehood during the Civil War, but it wasn't until August 1, 1876, that Colorado became the 38th state. Coming less than a month after the United States's 100th birthday, it was natural that Colorado should call itself the Centennial State. Colorado's new constitution gave the vote to blacks, but not to women, despite the strong efforts of the Colorado Women's Suffrage Association. The suffragettes finally succeeded in winning the vote in 1893, three years after Wyoming became the first state to offer universal suffrage.

At the time of statehood, most of Colorado's vast western region was still occupied by some 3,500 mountain and plateau dwellers of a half-dozen Ute tribes. Unlike the Plains tribes, their early relations with white explorers and settlers had been peaceful. Chief Ouray, leader of the Uncompahgre Utes, had negotiated treaties in 1863 and 1868 that guaranteed them 16 million acres, or most of western Colorado. In 1873, Ouray agreed to sell the United States one-fourth of that acreage in the mineral-rich San Juan Mountains in exchange for hunting rights and $25,000 in annuities. But a silver-mining boom that began in 1878 led to a flurry of intrusions into Ute territory, and in 1880 the Utes were forced to move to small reservations in southwestern Colorado and Utah; their lands were opened to settlement in 1882.

The silver market collapsed in 1893, but it was soon replaced by gold. In the fall of 1890, a cowboy named Bob Womack had found gold in Cripple Creek on the southwestern slope of Pikes Peak. He sold his claim to Winfield Scott Stratton, a carpenter and amateur geologist, and Stratton's mine earned him some $6 million by 1899. Cripple Creek turned out to be the richest gold field ever discovered, ultimately yielding $500 million of the precious metal.

Guardianship of the Land A turning point for Colorado occurred at the start of the 20th century. Theodore Roosevelt had visited the state in September 1900 as the Republican vice-presidential nominee. When he became president after the assassination of President McKinley in 1901, Roosevelt began to declare large chunks of the Rockies as forest reserves. By 1907, when an act of Congress stopped the president from creating any new reserves by proclamation, nearly one-fourth of Colorado—16 million acres—was national forest. Another project of the Roosevelt administration was the establishment in 1906 of Mesa Verde National Park.

Tourism grew hand-in-hand with the setting aside of public lands. Easterners had been visiting Colorado since the 1870s, when William Palmer founded his Colorado Springs resort and made the mountains accessible via his Denver & Rio Grande Railroad. Estes Park was among the first resort towns to emerge in the 20th century, spurred by the visit in 1903 by Freelan Stanley. With his brother Francis, Freelan had invented the Stanley Steamer, a kerosene-powered automobile. Freelan Stanley shipped one of his vehicles to Denver and drove the 40 miles to Estes Park in less than two hours, a remarkable speed for the day. Finding the climate conducive to his recovery from tuberculosis, he returned in 1907 with a fleet of a dozen Stanley Steamers and set up a shuttle service from Denver to Estes Park. Two years later he built the Stanley Hotel, which remains a landmark today.

Meanwhile, Enos Mills, an Estes Park innkeeper, nature writer, and lecturer, campaigned to have the national forest land around Longs Peak, outside of Estes Park, designated a national park. He finally succeeded, and in January 1915, 400-square-mile Rocky Mountain National Park was established.

DRIVING DISTANCES

Denver

65 miles S of Fort Collins
70 miles N of Colorado Springs
75 miles SE of Rocky Mountain National Park
98 miles E of Vail
110 miles S of Cheyenne, WY
163 miles W of Burlington
248 miles E of Grand Junction
332 miles NE of Durango

Colorado Springs

42 miles N of Pueblo
70 miles S of Denver
129 miles SE of Leadville
150 miles SW of Burlington
151 miles N of Raton, NM
159 miles NW of Lamar
166 miles E of Gunnison
347 miles NE of Cortez

Grand Junction

61 miles N of Montrose
89 miles W of Glenwood Springs
97 miles E of Green River, UT
150 miles W of Vail
169 miles N of Durango
194 miles SW of Steamboat Springs
197 miles N of Cortez
287 miles NW of Pueblo

Economic Gains In the early years of this century, Colorado's economic well-being was largely tied to the silver market. The Great Depression of the 1930s was a difficult time for many Coloradans, but it also had a positive side: the federal government raised the price of gold from $20 to $35 an ounce, reviving Cripple Creek and several other dying mining towns.

World War II was responsible for many of the defense installations that are now an integral part of the Colorado economy. The war also indirectly caused the other single greatest boon to Colorado's late 20th-century economy—the ski industry. Soldiers in the 10th Mountain Division, on leave from Camp Hale before heading off to fight in Europe, often crossed Independence Pass to relax in the lower altitude and milder climate of the 19th-century silver-mining town of Aspen. They tested their skiing skills, needed in the Italian Alps, against the slopes of Ajax Mountain, and liked what they saw. Aspen's first ski lifts began operating in January 1945.

Colorado has continued its steady economic growth, aided by tourism and the federal government. A brief oil boom in the 1970s was followed by a surge of high-tech businesses and more tourism and growth. Today Colorado has become one of the nation's top relocation destinations.

A Closer Look

GEOGRAPHY

Colorado measures about 385 miles east to west and 275 miles north to south, with the spiny ridge of the Continental Divide zigzagging more or less through its center. The basic topography of the 104,247-square-mile state, eighth-largest in the nation, can best be visualized by dividing Colorado into three vertical sections: the eastern plains, the high mountains, and the western mesa.

The central Rockies, though covering six times the mountain area of Switzerland, are not a single vast highland but a series of high ranges. Formed some 65 million years ago by pressures that forced hard Precambrian rock to the earth's surface, the Rockies broke through and pushed layers of earlier rock up on end. Then millions of years of erosion eliminated the soft surface material, producing the rugged Rockies we see today.

The Colorado River system dominates the western part of the state, with tributary networks including the Gunnison, Dolores, Yampa, and Green Rivers. East of the divide, the primary river systems are the South Platte, Arkansas, and Rio Grande, all flowing toward the Gulf of Mexico. Particularly in eastern Colorado, but also in the west, "rivers" are not broad bodies of water but more like rushing streams, heavy with spring snowmelt and reduced to mere trickles at other times.

Colorado's name—Spanish for "red"—derives from the state's red soil and rocks. Some of the sandstone agglomerates have become attractions in their own right, such as Red Rocks Amphitheatre west of Denver and the startling Garden of the Gods in Colorado Springs.

AVG HIGH/LOW TEMPS (°F)

	Denver	Colorado Springs
Jan	43/16	41/16
Feb	47/29	45/20
Mar	52/26	49/24
Apr	62/35	60/33
May	52/26	49/24
June	81/52	80/52
July	88/59	85/57
Aug	86/57	82/56
Sept	77/48	75/47
Oct	66/36	66/37
Nov	53/25	50/25
Dec	45/17	44/19

CLIMATE

Some say Colorado has only three seasons: winter, summer, and fall. Spring comes and goes fleetingly; one day, usually in April, the sun breaks through and the snow melts quickly.

Along the Front Range, including Denver and Colorado Springs, summer days are hot and dry while evenings are pleasantly mild. Relative humidity is low, and temperatures seldom rise above the 90s. Evenings start to get cooler by mid-September, but even as late as November, days often remain comfortably warm. Winters are surprisingly mild, and golf courses remain open year-round. However, below-zero temperatures and blowing snow are not unheard of.

Most of Colorado is considered semi-arid, and overall the state has an average of 296 sunny days a year (more than San Diego or Miami Beach). The rain, when it falls, is commonly a brief deluge. Snowfall, however, is a different story. If you want to see snow—and a lot of it—simply head to the mountains, where snowfall is measured in feet instead of inches, and mountain peaks may still be white in July. Most of the big resorts get at least 20 feet of snow every year.

WHAT TO PACK

Packing for a Colorado vacation is both easy and difficult. Easy because Colorado is casual, with perhaps only two or three restaurants in the entire state that require men to wear jackets and ties at dinner, but difficult because Colorado's weather can be extreme—so you'll need to carry clothing for a wide range of conditions. Even in summer, it can get cold at night (especially in the mountains), so you'll want a sweater or light jacket. Winter visitors discover that even when surrounded by snow, the Colorado sun is warm. In both cases, layering clothes is often best, so you can add or subtract garments as the temperature changes. No matter what your plans, a sturdy pair of walking shoes or hiking boots will be welcome. Sunglasses, hats, and sunscreen are essential at any time of year.

TOURIST INFORMATION

Contact the Colorado Travel & Tourism Authority, PO Box 22005, Denver 80222 (tel 800/COLORADO) for a free copy of the official state vacation guide, which describes attractions, activities, and lodgings throughout the state. The CTTA also maintains a Web page (http://www.colorado.com) with travel information about the state.

Contacts for information on lodgings include the Colorado Hotel and Lodging Association, 999 18th St, Suite 1240, Denver 80202 (tel 800/777-6880), which provides a reservation service for lodgings statewide. The Association of Historic Hotels of the Rocky Mountain West, 1002 Walnut St, Suite 201, Boulder 80302 (tel 303/546-9040) offers a free brochure describing about two dozen historic hotels in Colorado and other Rocky Mountain states. Another good information source is Colorado Dude & Guest Ranch Association, PO Box 300, Tabernash 80478 (tel 970/887-3128), which has information on more than three dozen dude and guest ranches.

To find out how to obtain tourist information for individual cities and parks in Colorado, refer to specific cities in the listings section of this chapter.

DRIVING RULES AND REGULATIONS

Drivers, front-seat passengers, and all passengers age 15 and younger are required to wear seat belts. All drivers must carry proof of motor vehicle insurance, as well as licenses and vehicle registration. Minimum age for drivers is 16, and teenagers under 16 with valid licenses from other states are prohibited from driving. Unless posted otherwise, drivers can make a right turn on a red signal after a complete stop. Maximum speed limit on interstate highways is 75 mph; 65 mph on non-interstates. Radar detectors are permitted, and motorcyclists are not required to wear helmets. Charges of driving while intoxicated are determined by a blood-alcohol content of 0.10%.

Snow tires or chains are often required when roads are snow-covered or icy, or during winter storms, particularly in mountain areas. Four-wheel-drive vehicles with adequate tires for existing conditions also are acceptable. Two notable highways are closed in winter: CO 82, over Independence Pass (elevation 12,000 feet) east of Aspen, which is the main route between Denver and Aspen in the summer months; and Mount Evans Road (CO 103 and CO 5) from Idaho Springs to the 14,000-foot summit of Mount Evans, open June to September only.

RENTING A CAR

Automobile rentals are readily available throughout Colorado, although you'll usually find the most competition—and therefore the best rates—in Denver and Colorado Springs. Those planning a winter trip to ski areas and other mountain destinations should consider spending the extra money for a four-wheel-drive vehicle, which usually handles better in snow.

- **Alamo** (tel 800/327-9633)
- **Avis** (tel 800/831-2847)
- **Budget** (tel 800/527-0700)
- **Dollar** (tel 800/800-4000)
- **Enterprise** (tel 800/325-8007)
- **Hertz** (tel 800/654-3131)
- **National** (tel 800/227-7368)
- **Thrifty** (tel 800/FOR-CARS)

ESSENTIALS

Area Codes: There are three area codes in use in Colorado. For the greater Denver metropolitan area, and north to Boulder, it is **303.** The southeast portion of the state, including Colorado Springs, is **719.** For the remainder of the state, it is **970.**

Emergencies: Throughout almost all of Colorado, dial **911** in an emergency. In some rural areas it may be necessary to dial "0" (zero, not the letter O) for an operator.

Liquor Laws: The minimum age to buy any alcoholic beverage in Colorado is 21. Bottled alcoholic beverages are sold in liquor stores Monday through Saturday, 8am to midnight; 3.2% beer is also available in supermarkets and convenience stores seven days a week, often from 5am to midnight.

Restaurants, lounges, and bars with proper licensing can sell alcoholic beverages until 2am.

Road Conditions: A statewide road conditions report is available by calling 303/639-1111. The Department of Transportation (tel 303/757-9228) can provide information on expected construction delays and general road conditions.

Smoking: There are no statewide smoking regulations, although municipalities may set their own rules. As of this writing, the strictest are in Boulder, where smoking is prohibited in all buildings open to the public. This includes restaurants and bars, except where a physically separated and independently ventilated smoking area is provided.

Taxes: Colorado state sales tax is 3%. Each county tacks an additional local tax on top of that, and many also charge a local hotel tax. Combined sales tax is usually 6% to 7%, and total tax on lodging is typically 8% to 12%.

Time Zone: Colorado is in the mountain time zone, two hours behind the East Coast and one hour ahead of the West Coast. Daylight saving time is in effect April through October.

Best of the State

WHAT TO SEE AND DO

National Parks & Monuments The crown jewel of Colorado's public lands is **Rocky Mountain National Park.** This spectacular park, with its snow-covered peaks, lush valleys, and icy alpine lakes, is a showcase of the West's best mountain scenery and outdoor recreation opportunities. More than 350 miles of hiking trails lead from ponderosa pine and juniper through stands of spruce and fir, and finally to the barren, wind-swept alpine tundra above tree-line. Park visitors are apt to see elk and mule deer, and even bighorn sheep at higher elevations. But one thing that makes Rocky Mountain National Park extra special is that these scenic wonders are not only available to the gung-ho backpacker. Trail Ridge Road, the highest-elevation continuous paved highway in the United States, offers much of the park's magnificent scenery to those who desire only short walks, and even to visitors who do not want to leave their cars.

The continent's tallest sand dunes are at **Great Dunes National Monument.** This wonderland of shifting sands is a favorite with hikers and off-road-vehicle enthusiasts, with some dunes as high as 700 feet. Many of the stone-and-mud cliff dwellings once home to the Anasazi tribe are now preserved in **Mesa Verde national Park,** where walking tours bring visitors right up to the ruins.

Natural Wonders Throughout the mountains of Colorado the visitor finds one scenic wonder after another, from tall snow-capped mountains to magnificent forests and rushing rivers. The **Black Canyon of the Gunnison,** near Montrose, is among the steepest and most narrow canyons in North America; **Colorado National Monument,** just west of Grand Junction, provides stunning panoramic vistas across its red-rock canyons and sandstone towers. **Dinosaur National Monument,** two-thirds of which is in Colorado, is known for its wealth of fossilized Jurassic-era dinosaur bones, as well as for great white-water rafting along the Green and Yampa Rivers.

Near Colorado Springs, **Garden of the Gods** is a superb rock garden of fanciful red sandstone formations, sculpted over hundreds of thousands of years by the relentless erosion of wind and water. The 238-mile **San Juan Skyway Scenic Drive,** in the Durango area, is among America's most spectacular scenic drives, with views of rugged mountains, fields of wildflowers, waterfalls and streams, and historic Old West mining and railroad camps.

Historic Sites Colorado is the heart of the Wild West, where towns were measured by the number of saloons and brothels they had, and dying of natural causes was considered a major accomplishment. Among the best places to experience this heritage are the historic towns of **Creede, Lake City, Telluride,** and **Leadville,** with well-preserved historic districts, stone jails, and false-fronted buildings from the late 1800s; and **Bent's Old Fort National Historic Site,** a reconstructed adobe, fort near La Junta, that was an important frontier outpost in the 1830s and 1840s. Among historic homes, of which there are many, you won't do better than the **Molly Brown House Museum** in Denver, the beautifully-restored 19th-century home of the woman who gained famed as the "unsinkable" Molly Brown for her heroic efforts during the sinking of the *Titanic* in 1912.

Museums Not surprisingly in a state so steeped in history, there are numerous historical museums. Among the top ones are the **Colorado Springs Pioneers Museum,** which shows in vivid exhibits the history of Colorado Springs, and also contains the Victorian home and furnishings of writer Helen Hunt Jackson, several art galleries, and an area devoted to the history of blacks in the region; and the unique **Colorado Territorial Prison Museum and Park** in Cañon City, with an actual gas chamber, hangman's noose, historic prison photos, and other reminders of what this land was like in its wilder days. In its gift shop the museum sells crafts made by inmates of the real prison next door.

Among other museums that easily qualify as being among the state's best are the **Denver Museum of Natural History,** one of the country's largest such museums, which has an exquisite "Prehistoric Journey" exhibit covering the history of life on earth for the past 3.5 billion years. Those who enjoy art should visit the **Denver Art Museum,** with an extensive collective of Native American and Western art; and **Koshare Indian Museum and Kiva** in La Junta, which contains a splendid collection of works both for and about Native Americans.

Family Favorites Not just for kids but a genuine favorite of the whole family is a trip on the **Durango & Silverton Narrow Gauge Railroad,** an 1880s steam train that not only provides an exciting trip into Colorado's Wild West days, but also is a relaxing way to see the beautiful San Juan Mountains. Another good bet for family fun is **Buckskin Joe Park and Railway,** a movie set and western theme park in Cañon City, where staged gunfights on dusty streets, as well as stagecoach and horseback rides, offer something for everyone. In Idaho Springs, kids of all ages can pan for gold, tour an old gold mine, and ride a half-scale steam train replica at **Argo Gold Mill and Museum.**

Shopping While most of Colorado is similar to the rest of America as far as shopping goes, with the same chain and specialty stores, shoppers will find particularly good selections of real Western wear throughout the state. But the best fashion Western wear, for the hip and rich, is in Aspen. Both Vail and Aspen are good choices for art, and Colorado wines will be found at the wineries near Grand Junction.

EVENTS AND FESTIVALS

- **Aspen/Snowmass Winterskol,** Aspen. This five-day event includes a parade, fireworks, torchlight ski descent, freestyle skiing and ice-skating, and more. Late January. Call 970/925-1940.
  International Snow Sculpture Championships, Breckenridge. Four-person teams transform 20-ton blocks of snow into works of art. Second week in January. Call 970/453-6018.
- **Boulder Bach Festival,** Boulder. Music of the master baroque composer. Last weekend in January. Call 303/494-3159.
- **Ullrfest,** Breckenridge. A week-long festival in honor of Ullr, Norse god of snow. Third week in January. Call 970/453-6018.
- **Cowboy Downhill,** Steamboat Springs. Professional rodeo cowboys tame a slalom course, lasso a resort employee, and saddle a horse before crossing the finish line. Mid-January. Call 970/879-0740.
- **National Western Stock Show And Rodeo,** Denver. World's largest livestock show and indoor rodeo. Second and third weeks in January. Call 303/297-1166.
- **Colorado Indian Market,** Denver. Members of more than 90 tribes display, sell, and demonstrate arts and crafts and perform traditional dances. Second and third weeks in January. Call 303/892-1112.
- **Steamboat Springs Winter Carnival,** Steamboat Springs. The longest continuously observed winter carnival west of the Mississippi River includes a week of downhill and cross-country ski races, jumping, broomball, and "ski joring" street events. First full week in February. Call 970/879-0740.
- **Pow Wow,** Denver. More than 700 dancers and musicians, representing some 70 tribes from 22 states. Arts and crafts are sold. Mid-March. Call 303/455-4575.
- **Mountain Man Rendezvous,** Kit Carson. Dressed in period costumes, mountain men engage in black powder shoots, cooking, and craft-making of the 19th century. Third weekend in April. Call 719/962-3249.
- **Telluride Mountain Film Festival,** Telluride. A festival of mountain and adventure films. Late May. Call 970/728-3041.
- **Territory Days,** Colorado Springs. Old Colorado City historic district hosts a carnival, games, contests, and gunfight. May. Call 719/577-4112.

- **Iron Horse Bicycle Classic,** Durango. Mountain bikers race the Durango & Silverton Railroad from Durango to Silverton. Memorial Day weekend. Call 800/525-8855.
- **Colorado Brewer's Festival,** Fort Collins. Sampling from Colorado's numerous microbreweries. Late June. Call 970/484-6500.
- **FIBArk Festival,** Salida. North America's longest and oldest down-river kayak race is the focus of a four-day festival. Mid-June. Call 719/539-7254.
- **Colorado Shakespeare Festival,** Boulder. Considered one of the top three Shakespeare festivals in the country. Late June through mid-August. Call 303/492-0554.
- **Telluride Bluegrass Festival,** Telluride. Country and acoustic music are also performed at this four-day event. Late June. Call 970/728-3041.
- **Pikes Peak Auto Hill Climb,** Colorado Springs. This "race to the clouds," held annually since 1916, takes drivers to the top of 14,110-foot Pikes Peak. July 4. Call 719/685-4400.
- **Brush Rodeo,** Brush. The world's largest amateur rodeo, with more than 400 participants, includes all the traditional rodeo events, plus wild cow milking, a parade, footrace, dance, and fireworks. Early July. Call 800/354-8659.
- **Colorado State Mining Championship,** Creede. Entrants from six states compete in old-style hand steeling, hand mucking, spike driving, and newer methods of machine drilling and machine mucking. July 4 weekend. Call 800/327-2102.
- **Pikes Peak Highland Games & Celtic Festival,** Colorado Springs. Sponsored by the Scottish Society of the Pikes Peak Region, with the caber toss and other traditional games, Celtic music, a Highland dance competition, and Scottish foods. Mid-July. Call 719/578-6777.
- **Denver Black Arts Festival,** Denver. Features the work of black artists and entertainers, plus a parade. Mid-July. Call 303/293-2559.
- **Rocky Mountain Wine and Food Festival,** Winter Park. Colorado's finest chefs and many of America's best-known vintners offer their creations to benefit the National Sports Center for the Disabled. Third weekend in August. Call 970/726-4118.
- **Colorado State Fair,** Pueblo. National professional rodeo, carnival rides, food booths, industrial displays, horse shows, animal exhibits, and entertainment by top-name performers. Mid-August through Labor Day. Call 800/876-4567.
- **A Taste Of Colorado,** Denver. Billed as "a festival of mountain and plain," this is Denver's largest celebration, with an annual attendance of about 500,000. Local restaurants serve house specialties; there are also crafts exhibits and free concerts. Labor Day weekend. Call 800/645-3446.
- **Steamboat Vintage Auto Race & Concours d'Elégance,** Steamboat Springs. More than 200 classic cars in a mountain course; vintage aircraft fly-in; rodeo series finals. Labor Day weekend. Call 970/879-0880.
- **Vail Fest,** Vail. An Oktoberfest-style weekend with street entertainment, yodeling contest, 5K and 10K runs, dancing, games, and sing-alongs. Second weekend in September. Call 970/476-1000.
- **Cowboy Gathering,** Durango. Cowboy poetry, western art, films, historical lectures, and demonstrations. Early October. Call 800/525-8855.
- **Christmas Mountain USA,** Salida. Over 3,000 lights outline a 700-foot tree on Tenderfoot Mountain; also a parade of lights and a visit from Santa Claus. Day after Thanksgiving. Call 719/539-2068.
- **World's Largest Christmas Lighting Display.** The Denver City and County Building is illuminated by some 40,000 colored floodlights. Throughout December.

SPECTATOR SPORTS

Auto Racing Motor racing is gaining in popularity in many parts of the state. The annual **Pikes Peak Auto Hill Climb** (tel 719/685-4400), known as "the Race to the Clouds," is held each July 4, when an international field of drivers negotiate the winding, harrowing Pikes Peak Highway to the top of the 14,110-foot mountain. In the Denver area, **Colorado National Speedway** (tel 303/665-4173), at I-25 exit 232, has NASCAR Winston Racing, superstocks, and RMMRA Midgets on a 3/8-mile asphalt oval track from April through September. Drag racing takes place from April through October at Bandimere Speedway, 3051 S Rooney Rd in Morrison (tel 303/697-6001 or 303/697-4870 for a 24-hour recording). In the Pueblo area, nationally sanctioned drag racing, motocross, quarter scale, quarter-midget racing, and Sportscar Club of America competitions take place April to September at **Pueblo Motor Sports Park,** US 50 and Pueblo Blvd (tel 719/547-9921), while stock-car races are held from mid-April through September on the quarter-mile paved oval track at **Beacon Hill Speedway,** 400 Gobatti Place (tel 719/545-6105). At Fort Morgan's **I-76 Speedway** (tel 970/867-2101), stocks, mini-sprints, dwarves, and IMCA modifieds race on a quarter-mile high-banked dirt oval track from April to October.

Baseball The **Colorado Rockies,** which began life as a National League expansion team in 1993, play at Coors Field, which opened in spring of 1995. The 50,000-seat stadium, with its red brick exterior, is designed in the style of baseball stadiums of old. For information and tickets, call ROCKIES (tel 303/762-5437 or toll free 800/388-7625). Meanwhile, the **Colorado Springs Sky Sox,** the Colorado Rockies AAA farm team, play 72 home games in Colorado Springs at Sky Sox Stadium, 4385 Tutt Ave (tel 719/597-3000). The season begins the second week of April and runs through Labor Day. Also in Colorado Springs, you can watch the **US Air Force Academy Falcons** (tel 719/472-1895 or 800/666-USAF). In Fort Collins, the team to watch is the **Colorado State University Rams** (tel 970/491-7267).

Basketball The **Denver Nuggets** (tel 303/893-3865) of the National Basketball Association play 41 home games a year at McNichols Sports Arena, 1635 Bryant St. The **University of Denver** (tel 303/871-2336) plays a competitive college basketball schedule from late November to March, as do the **US Air Force Academy** in Colorado Springs (tel 719/472-1895 or 800/666-USAF), the **University of Colorado in Boulder** (tel 303/492-8337), and **Colorado State University** in Fort Collins (tel 970/491-7267).

Football The **Denver Broncos** (tel 303/433-7466) of the National Football League make their home at Mile High Stadium, part of a sports complex off I-25 exit 210B. Tickets go on sale the third week of July and home games are sold out months in advance. It's easier to get into a college game. The **University of Colorado Buffaloes** in Boulder (tel 303/492-8337) play in the Big Eight Conference. The state's other top college football teams are the **Colorado State University Rams** in Fort Collins (tel 970/491-7267) and the **US Air Force Academy Falcons** in Colorado Springs (tel 719/472-1895 or 800/666-USAF).

Greyhound Racing The **Mile High Greyhound Park,** E 62nd Ave and Colorado Blvd in Commerce City (tel 303/288-1591), has pari-mutuel dog racing June through February. When the local dog-racing season ends, off-track betting from other Colorado greyhound tracks continues. In Colorado Springs, **Rocky Mountain Greyhound Park,** 3701 N Nevada Ave, at I-25 exit 148A (tel 719/632-1391 or 800/444-PAWS) has pari-mutuel dog races April to September and simulcast greyhound wagering October to March. There's live and simulcast dog racing and simulcast horse racing at **Pueblo Greyhound Park,** Lake Ave at Pueblo Blvd, off I-25 exit 94 (tel 719/566-0370).

Hockey Denver's new professional hockey team, the **Colorado Avalanche** (tel 303/893-6700), began playing in Denver for the 1995–96 season, with games at McNichols Arena, 1635 Bryant St. In Colorado Springs the team to watch is the **US Air Force Academy Falcons** (tel 719/472-1895 or 800/666-USAF).

Rodeo The **National Western Stock Show and Rodeo** (tel 303/295-1660) is held the second and third weeks of January at the Denver Coliseum, 46th and Humboldt. With more than $400,000 in prize money, it's one of the world's richest rodeos. The **Pikes Peak or Bust Rodeo,** held each August at Penrose Stadium, 1045 W Rio Grande Ave (tel 719/635-3547), is a major stop on the Professional Rodeo Cowboys Association circuit, with a purse of more than $150,000. The **Brush Rodeo** (tel 800/354-8659), the world's largest amateur rodeo, is held in the town of Brush, 10 miles east of Fort Morgan, each Independence Day weekend.

ACTIVITIES A TO Z

Bicycling Popular practically everywhere, especially in and around Denver and Boulder, but also (for mountain bikers) in the mountain communities of Crested Butte and Telluride. For a free copy of the annual magazine *Bicycle Colorado,* as well as other biking information, contact the magazine publisher (tel 800/997-2453). Information is also available from the not-for-profit group Bicycle Colorado, PO Box 698, Salida 81201 (tel 719/530-0051). Those planning to go mountain biking in western Colorado can receive a free trail map by sending a stamped self-addressed envelope to Colorado Plateau Mountain Bike Trail Association, PO Box 4602, Grand Junction 81502. The Colorado Trail, which runs some 500 miles from Denver to Durango, is also open to mountain bikers. For information contact the Colorado Trail Foundation, PO Box 260876, Lakewood 80226 (tel 303/526-0809).

Boating There are lakes throughout Colorado, from what is considered the world's highest-elevation anchorage at Grand Lake to large reservoirs perfect for water-skiing. Large craft take to Shadow Mountain, Granby, Dillon, Blue Mesa, and other lakes, while Navajo State Park in the southwest gives access to a 35-mile-long reservoir straddling the New Mexico border. For information on boating regulations and the state's parks, many on lakes, contact **Colorado State Parks,** 1313 Sherman St, #618, Denver 80203 (tel 303/866-3437).

Camping With vast areas of national forest and other public lands, Colorado offers practically unlimited opportunities for camping, especially in mountain areas. More than 400 public campgrounds are maintained in the national forests alone, and there is also camping in Bureau of Land Management areas, national parks, national monuments, and state parks. Most communities also have commercially-operated campgrounds with recreational vehicle hook-ups. Among information sources are **Colorado State Parks** (tel 303/866-3437), the Rocky Mountain Regional Office of the **US Forest Service** (tel 303/236-9431), and the **National Park Service** office in Denver (tel 303/969-2000).

Four-wheeling One of the best ways to explore Colorado's rugged mountains is on old mining and logging roads, accessible by four-wheel-drive vehicle. For information, contact the **Colorado Association of Four-Wheel-Drive Clubs,** PO Box 1413, Wheat Ridge 80034 (tel 303/343-0646). The association sells guides to four-wheel-drive roads throughout the state, and can help you find local off-road clubs.

Golf Clear, blue skies and a moderate climate in many areas of the state allow a long golfing season. For a directory of the state's major golf courses, contact the **Colorado Golf Resort Association,** 2110 S Ash St, Denver 80222 (tel 303/699-4653). Information is also available from the Colorado Golf Association, 5655 S Yosemite St, Suite 101, Englewood 80111 (tel 303/779-4653).

Hiking Colorado is literally crisscrossed with hiking trails, on national forests and other federal lands. Among the best trails are in Rocky Mountain National Park, and along the 500-mile Colorado Trail, which winds from Denver to Durango. For information, contact the **Colorado Trail Foundation,** PO Box 260876, Lakewood 80226 (tel 303/526-0809) or the **Colorado Llama Outfitters and Guides Association,** 30361 Rainbow Hill Rd, Golden 80401 (tel 303/526-0092).

Hunting & Fishing There are numerous opportunities for hunting and fishing throughout the state. In the small lakes and streams of the mountains you'll find numerous cold-water species of fish, including seven species of trout, while warm-water fish, such as catfish, crappie, and bass, are found in larger lakes and streams in eastern Colorado. Much of the big game hunting takes place in the state's mountain regions. For information on hunting and fishing regulations and seasons, contact the **Colorado Division of Wildlife,** 6060 Broadway, Denver 80216 (tel 303/297-1192). The division maintains various recorded messages on hunting and fishing. A recorded list is available (tel 303/291-7299). The information lines include one for general information on fishing (tel 303/291-7533), and another for up-to-date fishing reports, available April to September (tel 303/291-7534). Those who want to arrange a guided hunting or fishing trip can contact the Colorado Outfitters Association, PO Box 1304, Parker 80134 (tel 303/841-7760).

Rock Hounding & Gold Panning The state's mining heritage continues in many areas among rock hounders, who search for semiprecious gemstones, petrified woods, and agatized fossil bones. Gold is found in most major mining areas, and gold panning is a popular pastime. Information is available from the **Geology Museum at the Colorado School of Mines,** 1500 Illinois St, Golden 80401 (tel 303/273-3823). A number of publications, including several free brochures, are available from **Colorado Geological Survey,** 1313 Sherman St, #715, Denver 80203 (tel 303/866-2611 or 303/866-3340 for the publications office).

Skiing & Other Winter Activities Colorado racks up more than 11-million skier-days each year, more than any other state, at more than two dozen resorts. Contact **Colorado Ski Country USA,** 1560 Broadway, Suite 1440, Denver 80202 (tel 303/837-0793), for a free ski guide. The organization also provides a recorded ski condition report (tel 303/825-7669). A free directory is available from **Colo-**

Selected Parks & Recreation Areas

- **Rocky Mountain National Park,** Estes Park 80517 (tel 970/586-1206)
- **Mesa Verde National Park,** Mesa Verde National Park 81330 (tel 970/529-4465)
- **Great Sand Dunes National Monument,** 11500 CO 150, Mosca 81146 (tel 719/378-2312)
- **Black Canyon of the Gunnison National Monument,** 2233 E Main St, Montrose 81401 (tel 970/249-7036)
- **Curecanti National Recreation Area,** 102 Elk Creek, Gunnison 81230 (tel 970/641-237)
- **Dinosaur National Monument,** PO Box 210, Dinosaur 81610 (tel 970/374-2216)
- **Colorado National Monument,** Fruita 81521 (tel 970/858-3617)
- **Bent's Old Fort National Historic Site,** 35110 CO 194 E, La Junta 81050 (tel 719/384-2596)
- **Florissant Fossil Beds National Monument,** PO Box 185, Florissant 80816 (tel 719/748-3253)
- **Hovenweep National Monument,** c/o Mesa Verde National Park 81330 (tel 970/529-4465)
- **Arkansas Headwaters,** PO Box 126, Salida 81201 (tel 719/539-7289)
- **Bonny State Park,** 3010 Rd 3, Idalia 80735-9637 (tel 970/354-7306)
- **Boyd Lake State Park,** 3720 N County Rd 11-C, Loveland 80538 (tel 970/669-1739)
- **Colorado State Forest,** Star Rte Box 91, Walden 80480 (tel 970/723-8366)
- **Eldorado Canyon State Park,** PO Box B, Eldorado Springs 80025 (tel 303/494-3943)
- **Golden Gate Canyon State Park,** 3873 CO 46, Golden 80403 (tel 303/592-1502)

rado Cross Country Ski Association, Box 1292, Kremmling 80459 (tel 800/869-4560). For information on snowmobiling, contact the **Colorado Snowmobile Association,** PO Box 1260, Grand Lake 80447 (tel 800/235-4480).

White-Water Rafting Rivers swollen with winter snowmelt lure rafters and kayakers, especially from spring through mid-summer, when rivers are at their fullest. The towns of Salida and Buena Vista, both located on the upper Arkansas River, have become famous rafting centers, and other popular destinations include Fort Collins, Estes Park, Grand Junction, Glenwood Springs, and Dinosaur National Monument. For information, contact the **Colorado River Outfitters Association,** PO Box 1662, Buena Vista 81211 (tel 303/369-4632).

Wildlife & Bird Watching There are numerous locations in Colorado to see animals and birds in the wild, including some that are close to the state's major cities. The South Platte River Greenway near Denver is a good spot to see ducks and other waterfowl, songbirds, deer, and beaver; and the US Air Force Academy grounds in Colorado Springs offer good opportunities to see deer, an occasional elk, peregrine falcons, and golden eagles. Other top spots to see wildlife include areas near Durango, Glenwood Springs, Fort Collins, Vail, and in both Rocky Mountain National Park and Colorado National Monument.

BOULDER AND ROCKY MOUNTAIN NATIONAL PARK

Start	Boulder
Finish	Golden
Distance	186 miles
Time	1–3 days
Highlights	Spectacular mountain scenery, Victorian homes, gold mines, breweries, University of Colorado

This tour could alternatively be called "Classic Colorado," as it includes spectacularly beautiful Rocky Mountain National Park, plenty of the state's Old West flavor, and Colorado's largest university. It's a tour most suited to those who wish to leave their cars, hike a trail, explore a gold mine, or hop an old steam train, but there's plenty to see through the windshield, too, from snow-capped mountain peaks to handsome Victorian homes. There is, however, a catch: The entire tour can only be driven during summer, because snow usually closes the road through Rocky Mountain National Park from November until Memorial Day, and even in June it's not uncommon for a snowstorm to close the road for several hours at a time. Because of its high elevation (over 12,000 feet), the route through the park is not recommended for those with heart or breathing difficulties.

For additional information on lodgings, dining, and attractions in the region covered by the tour, refer to specific cities in the listings portion of this chapter.

1. **Boulder.** This sophisticated university town, a center for high-tech industries, is also one of America's outdoor-sports capitals. Sprawling at the base of the Rocky Mountains, Boulder, named for the large rocks in the area, was settled in 1858 by hopeful miners, who struck gold in the nearby hills the following year. By the 1870s Boulder had become a regional rail and trade center, but it was the University of Colorado (1877) that became the town's economic mainstay when the mining boom ended. Since the 1950s Boulder has grown as a center for scientific and environmental research. Residents spend a lot of time outdoors in the city's 56 parks and along its 150 miles of trails—there are an estimated 93,000 bicycles in the city, more than one per resident.

   Your first Boulder stop should be **Pearl Street Mall,** a four-block, tree-lined pedestrian mall along Pearl St from 11th to 15th Sts that offers shopping, dining, and people-watching. Musicians, mimes, jugglers, and other street entertainers perform, and you'll find malny of the city's best shops, galleries, and restaurants.

   In keeping with Boulderites' great love of the outdoors, visitors should make their next stop the **Boulder Creek Path,** from 55th St and Pearl Pkwy to Arapahoe Ave and Canyon Blvd. Following Boulder Creek, this nature corridor provides a nine-mile oasis for walkers, runners, bicyclists, and in-line skaters. Near the east end watch for prairie dog colonies and wetlands, the latter home to 150 species of birds, including geese, ducks, sandpipers, and owls. As you travel along the path, stop to feed the fish at the Boulder Creek Stream Observatory, and check out the restored steam locomotive. There's also a sculpture garden, kids' fishing ponds, and the Xeriscape Garden, where drought-tolerant plants test reduced water usage. Continuing west, Red Rocks Settlers' Park marks the beginning of the Boulder Canyon Pioneer Trail, with interpretive signs about the Missouri gold seekers who camped near here in 1858.

   The **University of Colorado**—called CU by locals—is the state's largest university, with 25,000 students. The CU Heritage Center, in Old Main, the oldest building on campus, is a museum dedicated to student life of long ago and to the university's work in space exploration. The University of Colorado Museum offers exhibits on the natural history and anthropology of the Rocky Mountains and the Southwest, and there are also three art galleries on campus. Tours are available at the university's Laboratory for Atmospheric and Space Physics (tel 303/492-6412) with at least one week's notice and the Sommers-Bausch Observatory (tel 303/492-5002) offers tours and Friday evening open-houses.

   After leaving the campus head for the **Boulder Museum of History,** 1206 Euclid Ave, housed in an 1899 French château-style sandstone mansion and featuring an impressive collection of turn-of-the-century memorabilia. Those traveling with kids may want to stop at **Collage Children's Museum,** 2065 30th St, where children can amuse themselves with numerous interactive exhibits and activities. The **National Center for Atmospheric Research,** 1850 Table Mesa Dr, is where scientists study the greenhouse effect, wind shear, and ozone deple-

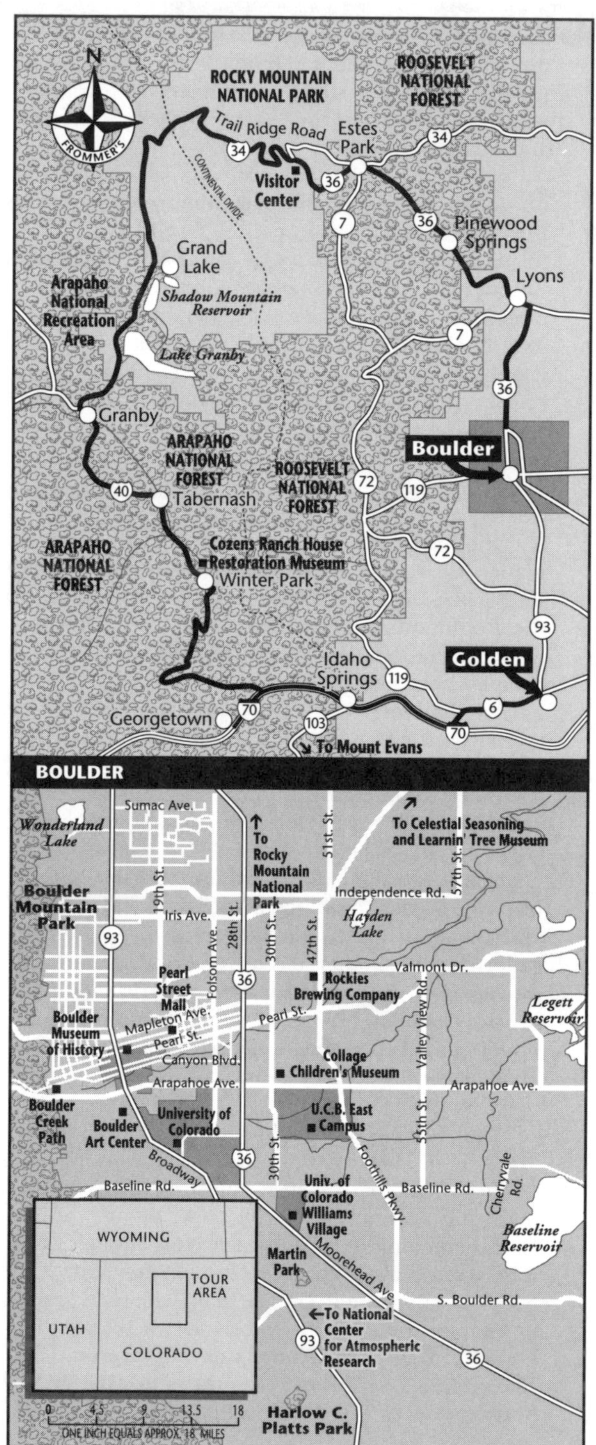

Take a Break

Those wanting a bite to eat have plenty of excellent choices. **Antica Roma,** 1308 Pearl St (tel 303/442-0378), is an Italian restaurant on the mall where dinner entrees range from $5 to $18. Also on Pearl Street Mall, you can get a burger and beer at **Tom's Tavern,** 1047 Pearl St (tel 303/443-3893). Unquestionably Boulder's finest dining establishment is **Flagstaff House Restaurant,** 1138 Flagstaff Rd (tel 303/442-4640), which offers not only an exquisite menu of game and seafood but among the best views of any Colorado restaurant. Entrees cost $23 to $43.

tion; visitors can see how satellites, weather balloons, robots, and supercomputers simulate the world's climates.

Guided tours are offered at **Celestial Seasonings,** 4600 Sleepytime Dr, among the nation's largest manufacturers of herbal teas; beer drinkers will want to stop for a tour at **Rockies Brewing Company,** 2880 Wilderness Place. The **Leanin' Tree Museum of Western Art,** 6055 Longbow Dr, contains almost 300 original works of Western art, many of which have been reproduced on the company's greeting cards.

From Boulder, take US 36 north for 35 miles to:

2. **Estes Park.** This resort town is a great home base for visiting Rocky Mountain National Park, but don't overlook what Estes Park itself has to offer. A good place to start is **Estes Park Area Historical Museum,** 200 4th St, where the lives of early homesteaders are depicted. The museum can also provide copies of historical walking-tour brochure for downtown Estes Park. Those interested in the Old West will also want to stop at **Macgregor Ranch Museum,** Devil's Gulch Rd, an 1873 ranch that not only shows what ranching was like in the late 1800s but offers spectacular views of the Rocky Mountains. **Prospect Mountain Aerial Tramway,** 420 E Riverside Dr, offers panoramic views of 14,255-foot Longs Peak, the Continental Divide, and Estes Park.

Late-19th-century innkeeper, conservationist, writer, and photographer Enos Mills was a leading advocate for the establishment of Rocky Mountain National Park. Today his daughter, Enda Mills Kiley, guides visitors down a short nature trail to **Enos Mills Cabin,** on CO 7 opposite Longs Peak Inn, and discusses her father's work. For a look and taste of the local brew, head to **Estes Park Brewery,** 470 Prospect Village Dr.

Those who want to make Estes Park their base while exploring the area have a number of lodging choices, such as the historic 1908 **Stanley Hotel,**

333 Wonderview Dr (tel 970/586-3371 or 800/976-1377), an impressive, luxurious hotel. Other possibilities include the moderately priced **Four Winds Travel Lodge,** 1120 Big Thompson Hwy (tel 970/586-3313), providing comfortable and homey accommodations; and the all-suite **Boulder Brook,** 1900 Fall River Rd (tel 970/586-0910 or 800/238-0910), a moderate-to-expensive property with condominium-style units in a woodsy setting along a stream.

Take a Break

For a good, quick meal, breakfast all day, and homemade pies, stop at the **Mountaineer Restaurant,** 540 S St Vrain St (tel 970/586-9001), serving traditional American fare priced from $3 to $8. For a romantic evening, try **The Dunraven Inn,** 2470 CO 66 (tel 970/586-6409), a fine Italian restaurant with entrees in the $8 to $20 range.

From Estes Park, head west on US 36 several miles to:

3. **Rocky Mountain National Park.** Straddling the Continental Divide, Rocky Mountain National Park is famous for its spectacular mountain scenery, with majestic snow-covered peaks towering over lush valleys and shimmering alpine lakes, fields of wild flowers, tall evergreens, and a vast array of wildlife. Within the 415 square miles of the park are 17 mountains above 13,000 feet.

   At the park's lower elevations, ponderosa pine and juniper cloak the sunny southern hillsides, while Douglas fir thrives on the cooler northern slopes; elk and mule deer are abundant. On higher slopes, forests of Engelmann spruce and sub-alpine fir take over, interspersed with wide meadows of wildflowers in spring and summer. Above 10,000 feet, trees become gnarled and stunted until they disappear altogether and alpine tundra—much like that found in the Arctic—takes over.

   Upon entering the park, it's a good idea to make your first stop the **Park Headquarters and Visitor Center** (tel 970/586-1206), with interpretive exhibits, books and maps, and general park information. You can also check road and trail conditions and obtain advice from rangers on how best to spend your time in the park. It's open daily in summer 8am–9pm and in winter 8am–5pm.

   From the Visitor Center, you'll be driving through the park on **Trail Ridge Road,** one of America's great alpine highways, which cuts west through the middle of the park from Estes Park then south down the park's western boundary to Grand Lake. Climbing to just under 12,200 feet, it's the highest continuous paved US highway. Depending on snowfall, the road is open from Memorial Day through October. The 48-mile scenic drive from Estes Park to Grand Lake takes about three hours, allowing for stops at scenic outlooks. Exhibits at the **Alpine Visitor Center** (open in summer only) at Fall River Pass (11,800 feet) explain life on the alpine tundra. Interpretive ranger programs are offered at visitor centers and campgrounds from June to September.

   Trail Ridge Rd through Rocky Mountain National Park has followed US 36 and US 34, so now follow US 34 west out of the park for a short distance to:

4. **Grand Lake.** This little village with board sidewalks is surrounded by the Arapahoe National Recreation Area, which includes Grand Lake, Shadow Mountain Reservoir, and Lake Granby. The area offers boating, fishing, hiking, horseback riding, picnicking, and camping. The historic log **Kaufman House,** on Pitkin Ave, serves as the museum of the Grand Lake Historical Society. There's an information center on US 34 at the turnoff into town.

   Grand Lake Yacht Club, the world's highest altitude yacht club, hosts the **Grand Lake Regatta** and **Lipton Cup Races** in August. The club was organized in 1902, when sails were added to rowboats; it began the regatta 10 years later. Sailboats from around the world compete to win the prestigious Lipton Cup, given to the club by Thomas Lipton in 1912. Grand Lake, which reaches a depth of 400 feet, is the largest glacial lake in the state—12 miles long and a mile wide.

   From Grand Lake, continue on US 34 west 14 miles to Granby, then go east on US 40 for 20 miles to:

5. **Winter Park.** Originally a Ute and Arapahoe hunting ground, the area was settled by whites in the 1850s and gradually became a timber center. In 1940, Winter Park ski area opened, and the community began a new life as a resort. While skiing is the main winter attraction, in summer visitors should stop at the **Rio Grande Caboose Museum,** housed in a 1945 railroad caboose at the Ski Train Terminal. The museum has exhibits on old-time skiing, and doubles as an information center. Nearby, **Amaze 'N Winter Park,** at the base of Winter Park Resort, is a human maze—a two-level labyrinth of twists and turns offering prizes to participants who can "beat the clock." Just north of town, on US 40, **Cozens Ranch House Restoration Museum** is a series of 1870s ranch buildings, plus the original Fraser Valley post office.

From Winter Park, drive east on US 40 for 24 miles to I-70. Go west for about 5 miles on I-70 to exit 228 and:

6. **Georgetown.** Among the best preserved of the area's 19th-century mining towns, Georgetown was named for an 1860 gold camp. Among the few old mining towns that did not suffer a major fire, its townspeople built eye-catching steeples on their firehouses instead of their churches.

Perhaps the first thing to do upon arrival is take a walk among the handsome Victorian-era homes and stores, starting at the **Old County Courthouse** at 6th and Argentine Sts, which serves as community center and tourist information office. Across Argentine Street is the Old Stone Jail, built in 1868. Those buildings open to the public include the **Hamill House,** 3rd and Argentine Sts, a handsome Gothic revival–style home built in 1867, and the French provincial **Hotel de Paris,** 6th and Taos Sts, which was opened in 1875 as an inn and is now a historical museum. It boasts many original furnishings, including diamond-dust mirrors, a large pendulum clock, and lace curtains.

For a trip back in time, hop aboard the **Georgetown Loop Railroad,** Loop Dr near 6th St, a restored narrow-gauge line making daily trips in summer between Georgetown and nearby Silver Plume. The 1884 steel railroad bridge, 300 feet long and 95 feet high, was considered an engineering miracle when it was built. Though the direct distance between the terminals is just over two miles, the track covers 4 ½ miles, climbing 638 feet in 14 sharp curves and switchbacks and culminating in a 360-degree spiral.

From Georgetown, head east on I-70 about 20 miles to:

7. **Idaho Springs,** site of a major gold strike in 1859. Mining is still active here at the **Phoenix mine** on Trail Creek Rd, where you can don a hard hat, follow a working miner through narrow tunnels, and dig your own ore sample. The **Argo Gold Mill and Museum,** 2350 Riverside Dr, offers tours of the Double Eagle Gold Mine, which remains relatively unchanged since early miners first worked it over 100 years ago. You can also ride the **Argo Express,** a one-half scale replica of a turn-of-the-century steam locomotive. The Colorado School of Mines in Golden uses the **Edgar Experimental Mine,** less than a mile north of Idaho Springs on Eighth Ave, as a research center and teaching facility for high-tech mining procedures. Underground walking tours are offered.

For a spectacular panoramic view, take a sidetrip on the 28-mile drive to the summit of 14,300-foot **Mount Evans**. CO 103 winds through Arapahoe National Forest, along Chicago Creek, to Echo Lake Park, with fire pits, hiking trails, and fishing. From there, CO 5 climbs to the mountain's summit. The road is usually open from Memorial Day to Labor Day.

Back in Idaho Springs, return to I-70 and continue east about 5 miles to exit 244, then follow US 6 east about 15 miles to:

8. **Golden.** This historic town, once the rival of mighty Denver, served as territorial capital from 1862 to 1867. Today visitors can see the old **Capitol** (1861) in the Loveland Building, 12th St and Washington Ave, which now houses offices and a restaurant. The **Astor House Hotel,** 822 12th St, a locally quarried stone structure built in 1867, offers guided tours; you can obtain a walking-tour to the Historic District here. The **Golden DAR Pioneer Museum,** 911 10th St, in the Golden Municipal Building, displays household articles and other historic items, including a re-created 19th-century parlor and boudoir.

Take a Break

Those hungry for Southwestern food or a thick steak can stop at **Silverheels Southwest Grill,** in the old Territorial Capitol at 1122 Washington Ave (tel 303/279-6390). Dinner prices from $10 to $15. For an elegant restaurant with great views of the mountains and city, drive up to **Chart House,** 25908 Genesee Trail (tel 303/526-9813), featuring steak and fresh seafood. Entrees range from $14 to $25.

Art enthusiasts may want to visit **Foothills Art Center,** 809 15th St. Housed in an 1872 Presbyterian church, the center features national and regional exhibits and sells crafts by local artisans. The changing exhibits at **Rocky Mountain Quilt Museum,** 1111 Washington Ave, include quilts from its permanent collection. Fans of old trains won't want to miss the **Colorado Railroad Museum,** 17155 W 44th Ave, housed in a replica of an 1880 railroad depot. On display are more than four dozen narrow- and standard-gauge locomotives and cars, historic equipment, numerous artifacts, photos, and model trains.

On Lookout Mountain, south of Golden, is the **Boettcher Mansion,** 900 Colorow Rd, a 1917 estate built as a summer home and hunting lodge and now offering art and history exhibits, plus a 1¼-mile nature trail. Also on Lookout Mountain, **Buffalo Bill Memorial Museum,** 987 ½ Lookout Mountain Rd, includes the legendary scout's grave and exhibits relating to his life as a Pony Express rider, buffalo hunter, and star of his own Wild West Show. **Mother Cabrini Shrine,** on Lookout Mountain near I-70 exit 259, is a 22-foot statue of Christ at the top of a 373-step stairway adorned by religious carvings.

At the **Colorado School of Mines Geology Museum,** 16th and Maple Sts, exhibits include a replica of a gold mine, minerals from around the world, and displays depicting Colorado's mining history. Visitors to the **National Earthquake Information Center,** 1711 Illinois St, can see how the US Geological Survey collects earthquake information, transmits warnings, and disseminates earthquake data. Tours are available by appointment (tel 303/273-8500).

Probably Golden's best-known resident, **Coors Brewing Company,** 13th and Ford Sts, is the world's largest single-site brewery, producing 1 ½-million gallons of beer each day. The company conducts free guided tours of its brewery, followed by free samples. Nearby, **Hakushika Sake USA,** 4414 Table Mountain Dr, produces sake—considered the national drink of Japan—for distribution throughout the United States and Europe. Guided tours, by reservation only (tel 303/279-7253), follow a glass-enclosed mezzanine providing an excellent view of the entire brewing and bottling process, plus an exhibit of Japanese art from the 19th and early 20th centuries.

The quickest and easiest route back to Boulder is to follow CO 93 (Foothills Rd) north for about 20 miles.

THE WESTERN SLOPE

Start	Grand Junction
Finish	Durango
Distance	213 miles
Time	1–3 days
Highlights	Spectacular mountain scenery, dinosaurs, historic Old West towns, a steam train

This tour covers some of Colorado's most spectacular scenery, particularly at Colorado National Monument at the beginning of the trip and along the drive from Ouray to Durango near the end. Although the route from Grand Junction to Durango is considered all-weather and is maintained year-round, it includes several mountain passes that are often closed for hours, and occasionally days, during winter snowstorms. Those who have severe fear of heights can avoid the steep and somewhat scary drive over Red Mountain by turning back at Ouray.

For additional information on lodgings, dining, and attractions in the region covered by the tour, refer to specific cities in the listings portion of this chapter.

1. **Grand Junction.** Founded in 1882 where the spike was driven to connect Denver and Salt Lake City by rail, Grand Junction quickly became the main trade center between the two state capitals. Its mild climate, together with fertile soil and irrigation from the Gunnison and Colorado Rivers, helped it grow into an important agricultural area producing soybeans, peaches, pears, and other fruits.

   The primary attraction here is **Colorado National Monument** (tel 970/858-3617). Although the east entrance is only 5 miles west of Grand Junction off Monument Rd, the best way to explore the monument is to begin at the west entrance, following signs off I-70 from the small community of Fruita, 15 miles west of Grand Junction. It's here that the 23-mile **Rim Rock Drive** begins, snaking up dramatic **Fruita Canyon** and offering panoramic views across the Colorado River valley to the Grand Mesa and Book Cliffs. Carved by millions of years of wind and water erosion, the park's spectacular landscape boasts red rock canyons and sandstone monoliths—some towering more than 1,000 feet high—plus a variety of fanciful and sometimes bizarre rock formations. Bighorn sheep, mountain lions, and golden eagles are among the wildlife inhabiting this semi-desert plateau. At the **Visitor Center** you'll find exhibits on the park's geology and history.

   While in Fruita you might want to stop at **Devil's Canyon Science & Learning Center,** 550 Crossroads Court. Just south of I-70 exit 19, the center is especially popular with kids, who can journey back to the Jurassic period to watch a mother *stegosaurus* defending her young, or visit the last Ice Age alongside a mighty mammoth. Interactive exhibits allow visitors to experience an earthquake, create a sandstorm, and feel the icy wall of a glacier. Nearby, **Rimrock Adventures,** on CO 340 about ½ mile S of I-70 exit 19, is home to exotic deer from around the world; you can also see goats, sheep, and elk, and visit a wildlife museum.

   Back in downtown Grand Junction, stop at the **Museum of Western Colorado,** 248 S 4th St, to learn about the geology, history, and culture of western Colorado. Inside is a pioneer room and kitchen. The museum also houses an extensive firearms collection, Native American artifacts, natural history exhibits, and Western art. Operated by the museum, **Cross Orchards Historic Site,** 3079 F Rd, is a re-creation of an early 20th-century farm, with a blacksmith shop, barn, workers' bunkhouse, and farm manager's home. Living-history demonstrations are offered daily in summer, and various events are held throughout the year.

   Dinosaur Valley, 362 Main St, contains animated replicas—complete with sound effects—of specimens such as stegosaurus, triceratops, and apatosaurus. Visitors can study regional paleontological history, examine a model of a dinosaur dig, and view plaster casts of dinosaur foot prints. At **Doo Zoo Children's Museum,** 635 Main St, children 12 and younger get hands-on experience in a variety of activities, from art to science to the almost-real world of adult work. The museum's toy store specializes in educational items.

   Before leaving Grand Junction, be sure to drive or walk by **Art on the Corner,** located along Main St between 1st and 7th Sts. This changing outdoor sculpture exhibit, featuring over four-dozen works, is part of a shopping park with wide tree-lined pedestrian walkways that also includes art galleries, antique shops, restaurants, and a variety of retail stores. The **Western Colorado Center for the Arts,** 1803 N 7th St, contains hundreds of works of art, many with Western themes, plus more than 50 Navajo weavings dating from the turn-of-the-

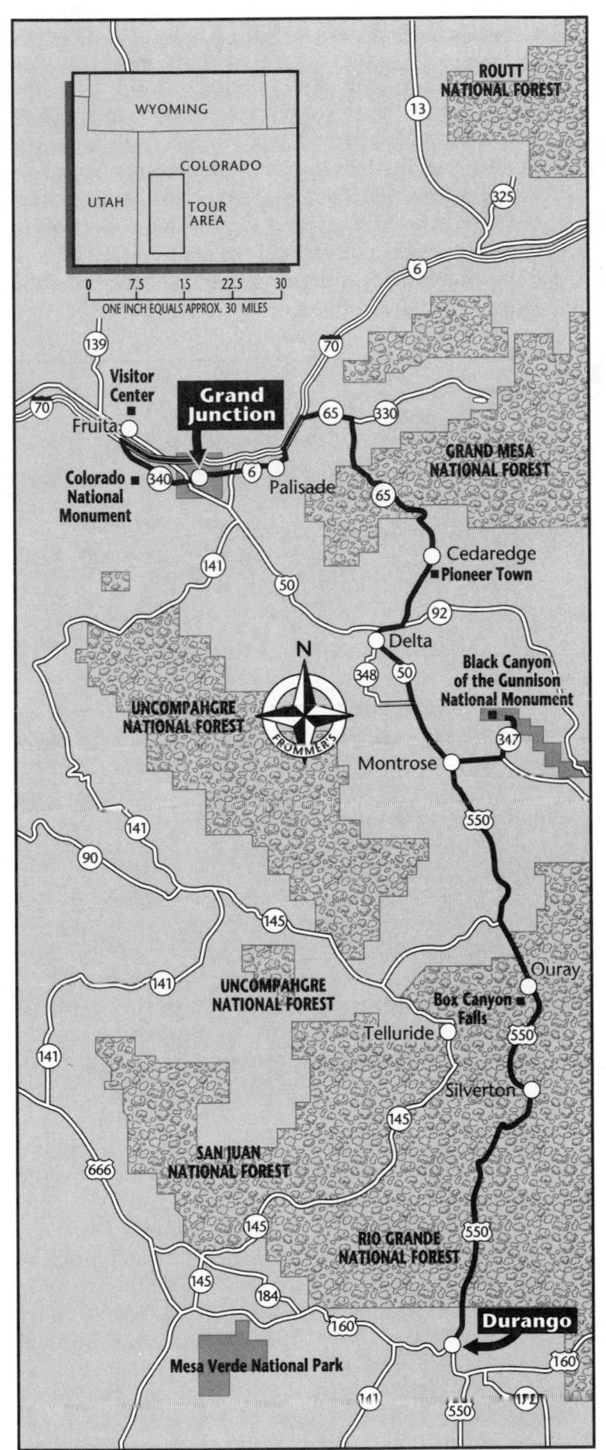

century, and a highly recommended gift shop featuring unique hand-crafted items.

Take A Break

As western Colorado's major center of business, you'll find numerous restaurants in Grand Junction, including **GB Gladstone's,** 2531 N 12th St (tel 970/241-6000), a quietly elegant, upscale restaurant that prepares interesting variations of beef, seafood, and pasta standards. Prices for dinner main courses are $5 to $18. For a quick sandwich, salad, or fresh pastry, stop at **Jitters Espresso Bar Cafe and Bakery,** 504 Main St (tel 970/245-5194), a coffeehouse-style cafe.

Heading east from Grand Junction, take US 6 about 12 miles up the Grand Valley to the farming community of:

2. **Palisade.** This self-proclaimed "Peach Capital of Colorado" is famous for its fruit orchards and vineyards. Most fruit is picked between late June and mid-September, when it's available at roadside stands, and there are about a half-dozen wineries that welcome visitors. The state's oldest existing winery, **Colorado Cellars,** 3553 E Rd (tel toll free 800/848-2812), produces an excellent selection of award-winning wines—chardonnay, cabernet, merlot, rieslings, fruit wines, and champagnes, plus more than 20 varieties of wine-based food products. **Carlson Vineyards,** 461 35 Rd, (tel 970/464-5554), is a winery with a sense of humor that has given its products names such as Prairie Dog White and Tyrannosaurus Red. And **Rocky Mountain Meadery/Confre Cellars,** 3701 G Rd (tel 970/464-7899), is Colorado's only producer of the Renaissance-era honey wine called mead. Tours and tastings are generally given year-round, but it's best to call ahead for hours.

   From Palisade, head E on I-70 for about 4 miles to exit 47, then take CO 65 about 52 miles southeast to:

3. **Cedaredge.** Stop in this quiet little residential community to see **Pioneer Town,** just south of the town's main intersection on CO 65. A re-creation of an early western town, complete with jail, saloon, bank, country store, and other period buildings, it also contains a Native American museum, country chapel that's available for weddings, an original railroad depot, and a blacksmith shop.

   Continue south 10 miles to CO 92 and head west 5 miles to:

4. **Fort Uncompahgre and the town of Delta.** The fort, off US 50 just north of Delta, is a living history museum in a reconstructed 1826 fur-trading post and fort. Hand-hewn log buildings—including a

trade room, storeroom, and living quarters—face a courtyard, and costumed traders, trappers, and laborers discuss the hard but exciting lives they would have led here more than 150 years ago. Just south of the fort is **Delta,** a town known for the colorful murals that adorn many of its historic buildings. Here you'll find the **Delta County Museum,** 251 Meeker St, and its world-class butterfly collection. Other exhibits here include the historic Delta County Jail, built in 1886, pioneer tools and machinery, a school room, and dinosaur bones.

From Delta, head south on US 50 about 21 miles to:

5. **Montrose.** Ute chief Ouray and his wife Chipeta ranched in the Uncompahgre Valley here until the government forced the tribe to migrate to Utah in 1881. Once the Utes were gone, white settlers moved in, and the area grew quickly with the arrival of the railroad the following year, which provided relatively reliable transport for the potatoes, beets, and other crops that were grown. Today Montrose continues its agricultural heritage with ranching and farming, but its main claim-to-fame is **Black Canyon of the Gunnison National Monument** (tel 970/249-7036), whose entrance is located 8 miles east on US 50 and 6 miles north on CO 347. Amazingly deep and narrow, this canyon of sheer granite walls ranges in depth from 1,730 to 2,700 feet. The width at its narrowest point is 1,100 feet at the rim and only 40 feet at the Gunnison River.

Although a summer-only access road winds to the bottom of the canyon at the East Portal dam in the adjoining Curecanti National Recreation Area, access to the canyon floor in the national monument itself is limited to hiking trails that wind down steep side canyons. Most visitors view the canyon from above, along the south rim, site of a visitor center, or along the lesser-used north rim. Short paths off both roads lead to viewpoints with signs explaining the canyon's unique geology. The visitor center is open daily in summer but has intermittent hours spring and fall; it is closed in winter. The road to the south rim is open 24 hours a day year-round, and the north rim is open around the clock except when closed by snow, usually between December and March.

Nearby, **Fort Eagle Tail,** 72291 US 50 E (5 miles east of Montrose), is a family-oriented living history museum that depicts the West from 1790 to 1860, with soldiers and other fort residents in period dress. Visitors can try their hands at tomahawk-throwing and other activities.

Once you're back in downtown Montrose, stop at the **Montrose County Historical Museum,** W Main St and Rio Grande Ave, in the historic Denver and Rio Grande Railroad Depot. The museum includes an 1890s homesteader's cabin, railroad memorabilia, farm equipment, antique dolls and toys, a country store, and Native American artifacts. **Ute Indian Museum,** 17253 Chipeta Dr, is on the site of the final home of Chief Ouray and wife Chipeta. Situated 2 miles south of downtown off US 550, this museum offers an extensive collection of Ute artifacts, including ceremonial items. Also on the grounds are Chipeta's grave and tiny, bubbling Ouray Springs.

Take a Break

Those looking for fresh baked goods and Southwestern dishes prepared over a mesquite grill will enjoy **Camp Robber Cafe,** 228 E Main St (tel 970/240-1590). Prices for dinner are in the $6 to $17 range. **The Whole Enchilada,** 44 S Grand Ave (tel 970/249-1881), offers Mexican dishes and burgers in a cheerful family-style atmosphere. Prices run $3 to $12.

Those planning to spend the night in Montrose have several good choices, including the **Best Western Red Arrow,** 1702 E Main St (tel 970/249-9641), a handsome, moderately priced modern motel with particularly attractive rooms, and the independent **Red Barn Motel,** 1417 E Main St (tel 970/249-4507), with clean, comfortable rooms in the budget price range.

From Montrose, continue south on US 550 for 37 miles to:

6. **Ouray.** Named for the great chief of the Southern Utes, who lived in this area, Ouray got its start in 1876 as a gold- and silver-mining camp. Within 10 years it had 1,200 residents, a school, several churches, a hospital, and dozens of saloons and brothels. Many of its original buildings still stand, and beautiful mountain scenery surrounds the town.

Begin your visit at the **Ouray County Museum,** 420 Sixth Ave, in the town's first hospital, built by the Sisters of Mercy in 1887. Exhibits include pioneer and mining era relics, memorabilia of Chief Ouray and the Utes, turn-of-the-century hospital equipment (including some truly frightening medical devices), and other historical items. The museum can also supply you with a copy of a walking-tour guide to Ouray's historic buildings. To really get a taste of the community's early days, take the **Bachelor-Syracuse Mine Tour,** 2 miles north of Ouray via County Rd 14. A mine train transports visitors deep inside an old mine, where over $100 million in gold, silver, and other minerals were mined after the first silver strike in 1884. Guides—many of them former miners—describe the mining process and relate various legends of the mine.

Next head to **Box Canyon Falls,** off Oak St above Third Ave. Among the most impressive falls in the Rockies, they are created as the Uncompahgre River tumbles almost 300 feet through an opening in a cliff. For a soothing soak, stop at the **Ouray Hot Springs Pool** along US 550 at the north end of town. The large pool contains nearly a million gallons of 80°F odorless mineral water, cooled from its ground temperature of 150°F. There's also a hot soak at 104°F.

The 23 miles on US 550 south from Ouray over 11,000-foot **Red Mountain Pass** to Silverton are part of a spectacular drive. It shimmies up the sheer sides of the Uncompahgre Gorge, through tunnels and past cascading waterfalls, then follows the route of a 19th-century toll road. Abandoned mining equipment and log cabins can be seen on the slopes of the steel-gray mountains, many of them over 14,000 feet in elevation. Along this route you'll also pass a monument to snow plow operators who died while trying to keep the road open during winter storms. Soon you'll arrive in:

7. **Silverton.** Perched at an altitude of 9,300 feet at the northern end of the Durango & Silverton Narrow Gauge Railroad, the entire town of Silverton is a National Historic Landmark District. A silver mining camp in 1871, the town was notorious for its row of saloons and brothels on Blair Street—so much so that famed lawman Bat Masterson, fresh from taming Dodge City, was called in to make Silverton suitable for decent folks. Today the original false-fronted buildings (which are sometimes used as movie sets) remain, but they now house restaurants and galleries.

   The **San Juan County Historical Society Museum,** in the turn-of-the-century jail at Greene and 15th Sts, displays memorabilia from Silverton's boom days. Other interesting buildings include the San Juan County Courthouse (next to the museum), with its gold-domed clock tower; and the recently restored Town Hall at 14th and Greene Sts.

   From Silverton continue 49 miles south on US 550 as it climbs over the 11,000-foot Molas Divide and follows the tracks of the Durango & Silverton Narrow Gauge Railroad into:

8. **Durango.** Born as a railroad town more than a century ago, Durango remains one—at least in summer, when thousands of visitors take a journey back in time aboard the **Durango & Silverton Narrow Gauge Railroad,** with a depot at 479 Main Ave. In continuous operation since 1881, this coal-fired steam train, with its string of Victorian coaches, puffs its way 45 miles up scenic Animas Canyon, past relics of 19th-century mining and railroad days, to Silverton, before heading back to Durango.

   A center for outdoor recreation, Durango is a good base for white-water rafting on the Animas River.

   Good lodging possibilities in Durango include the stately Victorian **Strater Hotel,** 699 Main Ave (tel 970/247-4431 or toll free 800/247-4431), with moderate-to-expensive rates, and, for those on a tight budget, the **Redwood Lodge,** 763 Animas View Dr (tel 970/247-3895), a clean and comfortable independent motel.

Take a Break

If you're seeking a meal, there are a number of good choices in Durango, including **Carver's Bakery/Cafe/Brewery,** 1022 Main Ave (tel 970/259-2545), a friendly neighborhood restaurant that offers good Southwestern cooking. Dinner main courses range from $5 to $7. The more upscale **Palace Grill,** 2 Depot Place (tel 970/247-2018), offers innovative steak and seafood dishes in an elegant, historic atmosphere. It's open for lunch and dinner; dinner prices are $12 to $24.

To return to Grand Junction, you can either re-trace your route or create a loop tour through more incredibly beautiful mountain scenery. Just follow US 160 west, past Mesa Verde National Park, to CO 145, which you can take north through the San Juan National Forest to the ski resort of Telluride. Then follow CO 145 and CO 141 north back to Grand Junction. This return route is 271 miles long.

Colorado Listings

Alamosa

Named for the cottonwood trees (*alamosa* in Spanish) that line the banks of the Rio Grande, the town was established in 1878 with the arrival of the railroad. Now, as then, it is primarily an agricultural center. **Information:** Alamosa County Chamber of Commerce, Cole Park, Alamosa 81101 (tel 719/589-3681 or 800/BLU-SKYS).

MOTELS

Alamosa Lamplighter Motel
425 Main St, 81101; tel 719/589-6636 or toll free 800/359-2138; fax 719/589-3831. 2 blocks E of courthouse. Rooms are larger than average in this motel located close to downtown. **Rooms:** 72 rms. CI 2pm/CO 11am. Nonsmoking rms avail. **Amenities:** A/C, cable TV w/movies. All units w/terraces. **Services:** **Facilities:** 1 restaurant, sauna, whirlpool. **Rates:** Peak (June–Sept) $42 S; $47 D. Extra person $6. Children under age 12 stay free. Lower rates off-season. Parking: Outdoor, free. AE, CB, DC, DISC, MC, V.

Best Western Alamosa Inn
1919 Main St, 81101; tel 719/589-2567 or toll free 800/528-1234; fax 719/589-0767. 1 mi W of jct US 285/US 160. Centrally located, standard Best Western. **Rooms:** 121 rms and stes. CI 3pm/CO 11am. Nonsmoking rms avail. **Amenities:** A/C, cable TV w/movies. **Services:** **Facilities:** 200 1 restaurant, 1 bar, whirlpool. **Rates:** Peak (May–Sept) $55–$74 S; $72–$82 D; $125 ste. Extra person $8. Children under age 12 stay free. Lower rates off-season. Parking: Outdoor, free. AE, CB, DC, DISC, MC, V.

INNS

The Cottonwood Inn & Gallery
123 San Juan Ave, 81101; tel 719/589-3882 or toll free 800/955-2623; fax 719/589-6437. 3 blocks N of Main St. This inn looks as though it was plucked from the hillsides of San Francisco and gently dropped in Alamosa. With short columns and scalloped shingles painted pink, purple, and blue-gray, it is one of the most strikingly colorful properties in town. Comfortably furnished with antiques, plus photos and artwork by local artists. **Rooms:** 7 rms and stes (2 w/shared bath). CI 4pm/CO 11am. No smoking. Each room has its own theme. The Rosa Room is filled with hand-painted florals and white wicker furniture, while the Blanca Room is a mix of art deco and southwestern decor. **Amenities:** Bathrobes. No A/C, phone, or TV. **Services:** Afternoon tea served. **Facilities:** Guest lounge w/TV. **Rates (BB):** $54 S w/shared bath, $75 S w/private bath; $58 D w/shared bath, $79 D w/private bath; $79 ste. Extra person $15. Min stay special events. AE, CB, DC, DISC, MC, V.

Great Sand Dunes Country Club & Inn
Zapata Ranch, 5303 CO 150, Mosca, 81146; tel 719/378-2356 or toll free 800/284-9213; fax 719/378-2428. 12 mi N of US 160. Nestled in an old cottonwood grove on the 110,000-acre Zapata Ranch on the east side of the San Luis Valley, this inn has magnificent views of the great Sand Dunes to the north with the Sangre de Cristo Mountains framing them. The old log cabin structure was recently renovated. Unsuitable for children under 10. **Rooms:** 15 rms and stes. CI 3pm/CO 11am. No smoking. Rooms are comfortably rustic; simple pine furniture. **Amenities:** Bathrobes. No A/C, phone, or TV. Some units w/terraces, 1 w/fireplace. **Services:** Children's program. Freshly baked oatmeal raisin cookies on arrival. Hunting trips can be arranged. **Facilities:** 18 35 1 restaurant (*see* "Restaurants" below), 1 bar (w/entertainment), spa, sauna, whirlpool, guest lounge w/TV. **Rates (BB):** Peak (June 30–Sept) $180 D; $250 ste. Extra person $25. Lower rates off-season. AP rates avail. Parking: Outdoor, free. AE, DISC, MC, V.

RESTAURANTS

Great Sand Dunes Country Club & Inn
In Zapata Ranch, 5303 CO 150, Mosca; tel 719/378-2356. 12 miles N of US 160. **American.** The dining room maintains a rustic ambience, with dark wooden tables and simple decor. Traditional American Indian ingredients and techniques are used to create dishes such as grilled San Luis Valley lamb chops and oven-baked trout. The nightly special is always a bison dish. **FYI:** Reservations recommended. Country music/

folk. Children's menu. No smoking. **Open:** Peak (June–Oct) daily 7am–9pm. Closed Jan. **Prices:** Main courses $12–$19. AE, DISC, MC, V.

Oscar's Restaurant
710 Main St; tel 719/589-9230. Just W of courthouse. **Mexican.** A friendly Mexican restaurant in downtown Alamosa. The interior is brightly lit and cheery, with stucco walls and a ceiling of large pine log beams. The walls are covered with hand-painted southwestern motifs, and chiles, plants, and colorful parrot statues hang from the beams. The menu offers a wide range of traditional Mexican entrees and appetizer plates. Although there's no full bar, you can order beer or margaritas. **FYI:** Reservations accepted. **Open:** Tues–Sun 11am–9pm. **Prices:** Main courses $3–$9. MC, V.

St Ives Pub & Eatery
719 Main St; tel 719/589-0711. Just W of courthouse. **American.** This little hole-in-the-wall pub is terrific for catching a beer and a burger or sandwich. The interior is dimly lit, and decorated with a few articles of sporting equipment. The atmosphere is casual, and the menu includes a good variety of inexpensive meals. Alternative rock groups often play here. Want to see some local color? Stop by on the weekend. **FYI:** Reservations accepted. Rock. **Open:** Mon–Sat 11am–midnight. **Prices:** Main courses $4–$6. DISC, MC, V.

True Grits Steak House
100 Santa Fe Ave; tel 719/589-9954. At Broadway. **American/Steak.** As you might expect, John Wayne portraits and memorabilia abound here. The interior is all wood, and western in every aspect, from food to music to ambience. The menu offers traditional western fare, including just about any steak one might want, as well as chicken-fried steak, plus lobster and shrimp entrees. It's a convenient roadside stop, right along US 160. **FYI:** Reservations recommended. **Open:** Peak (June–Oct) Mon–Sat 11am–10pm. **Prices:** Main courses $6–$13. DC, MC, V.

ATTRACTIONS

Great Sand Dunes National Monument
CO 150, Mosca; tel 719/378-2312. Located 38 mi NE of Alamosa. The park comprises a 55-square-mile expanse of sand, piled nearly 700 feet high against the western edge of the Sangre de Cristo Mountains. The tallest sand dunes in North America, they seem totally incongruous in this location, far from any sea or major desert.

The dunes were created over thousands of years by winds blowing southwesterly across the San Luis Valley. They began forming at the end of the last Ice Age, when streams of water from melting glaciers carried rocks, gravel, and silt from the mountains down into the valley. In addition, as the Rio Grande changed its course, it left behind sand, silt, and debris. Even today the winds are changing the face of the dunes, returning to the monument the sands that Medano Creek takes from the dunes' leading edge and carries into the valley.

Among the specialized animals that survive in this weird environment are the Ord kangaroo rat, a creature that never drinks water; and two insects found nowhere else on earth, the Great Sand Dunes tiger beetle and one type of darkling beetle. These animals and the flora of the adjacent mountain foothills are discussed in evening programs and guided walks during the summer season.

From Alamosa, there are two main routes to the national monument: east 14 miles on US 160, then north on CO 150; or north 14 miles on CO 17 to Mosca, then east on Six Mile Lane to the junction of CO 150. For more information contact Great Sand Dunes National Monument, 11500 CO 150, Mosca 81146. **Open:** Visitors center: peak (Mem Day–Labor Day) daily 8am–7pm. Reduced hours off-season. **$$**

Alamosa-Monte National Wildlife Refuge Complex
9383 El Rancho Lane; tel 719/589-4021. Nearly 25,000 acres of vital land for a variety of marsh birds and waterfowl have been preserved here, including habitat for many migrating and wintering species. Sandhill and whooping cranes visit in October and March; at other times of the year there may be egrets, herons, avocets, bitterns, and other avian species. A wide variety of ducks are year-round residents. Hiking and biking trails. **Open:** Daily sunrise–sunset. **Free**

Cole Park
425 4th St; tel 719/589-3681. The park is home to the Alamosa County Chamber of Commerce, which is housed in a replica 1880s railroad depot and displays a turn-of-the-century steam engine. The San Luis Valley History Center has exhibits depicting the lives of the area's early inhabitants, the coming of the railroad, the military, and mining. There are picnic tables and benches in the park, as well as a ¼-mile walking track. **Open:** Peak (June–Sept) daily 10am–4pm. Reduced hours off-season. **Free**

Allenspark

This tiny village is at the southeast corner of Rocky Mountain National Park, 16 miles south of Estes Park. **Information:** Estes Park Area Chamber of Commerce, PO Box 3050, Estes Park 80517 (tel 970/586-4431 or 800/44-ESTES).

INN

Allenspark Lodge
184 Main St, PO Box 247, 80510; tel 303/747-2552; fax 303/747-2552. 16 mi S of Estes Park on CO 7. Tucked away in a private little village at the southeast corner of Rocky Mountain National Park, this historic bed-and-breakfast, built in 1933, is a great place to get away from it all and enjoy a quiet mountain vacation. **Rooms:** 13 rms (8 w/shared bath); 3 cottages/villas. CI 2pm/CO 10am. No smoking. The all-

pine interior of the rooms gives them a genuinely rustic and comfortable feel. Great mountain views, including Long's Peak. **Amenities:** No A/C, phone, or TV. Some units w/terraces, some w/fireplaces. Humidifier. **Services:** Afternoon tea served. **Facilities:** 70 Games rm, whirlpool, guest lounge w/TV. Outdoor grill and picnic facilities. **Rates (CP):** $45 S w/shared bath, $70–$90 S or D w/private bath; $50–$60 D w/shared bath; $60–$70 cottage/villa. Extra person $5. Parking: Outdoor, free. MC, V.

Aspen

See also Snowmass Village

Aspen, founded in 1879, has twice been a boom town, first with the discovery of silver and later with the region's development into a mecca for skiers. The town's population mushroomed with the discovery of the world's largest silver nugget (1,840 pounds) but dwindled after the silver crash of 1893. The town blossomed again after World War II when a small ski area was established, and today Aspen is famous worldwide as a premier ski resort as well as a year-round playground for royalty, celebrities, and the very rich. **Information:** Aspen Chamber Resort Association, 425 Rio Grande Place, Aspen 81611 (tel 970/925-1940 or 800/26-ASPEN).

HOTELS

Aspen Club Lodge

709 E Durant Ave, 81611; tel 970/925-6760 or toll free 800/882-2582; fax 970/925-6778. 3 blocks E of Wagner Park. This luxury hotel, lying close to the lifts and downtown shopping and dining, offers a comfortable blend of Aspen hospitality and modern facilities. Perhaps the greatest asset is its link with the world-renowned Aspen Club. **Rooms:** 90 rms and stes. CI 3pm/CO 11am. Nonsmoking rms avail. Variety of rooms with different levels of luxury. All are clean and impressively comfortable. **Amenities:** Cable TV w/movies, refrig, dataport, bathrobes. No A/C. All units w/terraces, some w/fireplaces, some w/whirlpools. Humidifier. **Services:** VP Masseur, children's program, babysitting. Valet ski storage available. Lift ticket service. **Facilities:** 75 1 restaurant (bkfst only), 1 bar (w/entertainment), whirlpool. Complimentary passes available for Aspen's premier fitness/athletic/spa club, the Aspen Club. Ski shop. Pool facility includes overflowing hot tub. **Rates (BB):** Peak (Jan–Apr 15) $225–$360 S or D; $395–$525 ste. Extra person $15. Children under age 12 stay free. Min stay special events. Lower rates off-season. Parking: Indoor/outdoor, free. AE, DISC, MC, V.

Hotel Aspen

110 W Main St, 81611; tel 970/925-3441 or toll free 800/527-7369; fax 970/920-1379. Just NW of Paepcke Park. Within walking distance of downtown shopping and dining, this small hotel offers a lobby/lounge area with cozy fireplace and large picture windows commanding a fine view of Aspen Mountain. **Rooms:** 45 rms and stes. CI 4pm/CO 11am. Nonsmoking rms avail. Nice variety of well-maintained rooms, with Southwestern decor. **Amenities:** A/C, cable TV w/movies, refrig, voice mail, in-rm safe, bathrobes. Some units w/terraces, some w/whirlpools. **Services:** Babysitting. Après-ski in winter. **Facilities:** Whirlpool. **Rates (CP):** Peak (Feb 15–Mar) $169–$189 S or D; $219–$249 ste. Extra person $20. Children under age 12 stay free. Min stay special events. Lower rates off-season. Parking: Outdoor, $1/day. AE, CB, DC, DISC, MC, V.

Hotel Jerome

330 E Main St, 81611; tel 970/920-1000 or toll free 800/331-7213; fax 970/925-2784. Just W of Pitkin Co Library. Built in 1889 by Jerome B Wheeler, president of Macy's, this historic hotel was returned to the splendor of its silver boom days with a major renovation in 1985. The decor and furnishings are exquisitely reminiscent of the last century, yet the hotel has all the modern conveniences. **Rooms:** 93 rms and stes. CI 4pm/CO 11am. Nonsmoking rms avail. Each room is unique and attractively decorated with period antiques. Just over half the units are suites. **Amenities:** 2 A/C, cable TV w/movies, dataport, VCR, bathrobes. All units w/minibars, some w/terraces, some w/whirlpools. Humidifier, two-line phone. **Services:** VP Twice-daily maid svce, babysitting. Ski concierge will store your skis. **Facilities:** 400 2 restaurants, 1 bar (w/entertainment), whirlpool. Ski lockers, ski shop. **Rates:** Peak (Jan 2–Mar/July–Aug) $390–$520 S or D; $580–$1,525 ste. Min stay peak and special events. Lower rates off-season. Parking: Indoor, $10/day. AE, CB, DC, MC, V.

The Inn at Aspen

38750 CO 82, 81611; tel 970/925-1500 or toll free 800/952-1515; fax 970/925-9037. At foot of Summit Express lift, Buttermilk Mountain. This ski-in, ski-out hotel at the base of Buttermilk Mountain offers guests a modern accommodation away from the bustle of town. **Rooms:** 123 rms and stes. CI 4pm/CO 11am. Nonsmoking rms avail. Variety of condominium-style rooms, some with mountain views, others with a view of the valley. **Amenities:** A/C, cable TV w/movies, refrig, dataport, voice mail, bathrobes. Some units w/minibars, all w/terraces, some w/whirlpools. **Services:** Car-rental desk, masseur. Lift ticket services. **Facilities:** 220 1 restaurant, 1 bar, games rm, sauna, steam rm, whirlpool, washer/dryer. Ski shop and ski lockers. **Rates (CP):** Peak (Feb 16–Apr 7) $185–$270 S or D; $400–$450 ste. Children under age 12 stay free. Min stay special events. Lower rates off-season. Parking: Outdoor, free. AE, CB, DC, DISC, MC, V.

The Little Nell

675 E Durant Ave, 81611; tel 970/920-4600 or toll free 800/525-6200; fax 970/920-4670. Just E of Silver Queen Gandold. This elegant yet regionally rustic hotel has quickly become one of the area's most highly recommended. It offers

guests premier service just five minutes from the ski lifts. **Rooms:** 92 rms and stes. CI 4pm/CO noon. No two rooms are alike, but each is tastefully decorated. A variety of fine bird prints grace the walls. Exceedingly comfortable. **Amenities:** A/C, cable TV, refrig, dataport, VCR, in-rm safe, bathrobes. All units w/minibars, some w/terraces, all w/fireplaces, some w/whirlpools. **Services:** Masseur, babysitting. Ski concierge service includes complimentary storage, tuning, and waxing. **Facilities:** 2 restaurants (*see* "Restaurants" below), 1 bar (w/entertainment), steam rm, whirlpool. Signature shop and private boutiques on premises. **Rates:** Peak (Jan 5–Apr 8) $400–$780 S or D; $730–$2,400 ste. Children under age 18 stay free. Min stay wknds and special events. Lower rates off-season. Parking: Indoor, $10/day. AE, CB, DC, DISC, JCB, MC, V.

The Mountain Chalet

333 E Durant Ave, 81611; tel 970/925-7797 or toll free 800/321-7813; fax 970/925-7811. Just S of Wagner Park. One of Aspen's original ski lodgings, this little hotel has been catering to skiers on a budget for over 40 years. Return guests are common here. The owners cater to families, creating a very friendly atmosphere for everyone. **Rooms:** 47 rms; 4 cottages/villas. CI 4pm/CO 11am. No smoking. Each room is clean and well maintained and has small collection of books. **Amenities:** Cable TV, refrig. No A/C. Some units w/terraces, some w/fireplaces. **Services:** Babysitting. Coffee and tea available 24 hours. Après-ski cider. Spiced wine and cider parties every Monday evening. **Facilities:** 150 Games rm, sauna, steam rm, whirlpool, washer/dryer. Ski lockers available. Lounge has a large-screen TV with VCR. **Rates (BB):** Peak (Jan 26–Mar) $110–$220 S; $120–$230 D; $320 cottage/villa. Extra person $10. Min stay peak. Lower rates off-season. Parking: Indoor, free. Twelve bunks available for $40 per night. MC, V.

The Ritz-Carlton

315 E Dean St, 81611; tel 970/920-3300 or toll free 800/241-3333; fax 970/920-7353. Just S of Wagner Park. This red brick and sandstone hotel offers guests the best in visual surroundings and service. Regional 19th-century art is displayed throughout, accenting the fine furnishings and dried flower arrangements. The lobby area is quite spacious with a number of comfortably upholstered seating areas centered on large gas hearths. **Rooms:** 257 rms and stes. Executive level. CI 3pm/CO noon. Nonsmoking rms avail. Rooms are extremely comfortable and exquisitely furnished. **Amenities:** A/C, cable TV w/movies, dataport, in-rm safe, bathrobes. All units w/minibars, some w/terraces, some w/fireplaces, some w/whirlpools. **Services:** Masseur, children's program, babysitting. Morning newspapers; overnight shoe shines. **Facilities:** 1000 1 restaurant, 2 bars (w/entertainment), spa, sauna, steam rm, whirlpool, beauty salon. Ski shop. **Rates:** Peak (Jan–Apr 15) $295–$550 S or D; $595–$3,000 ste. Extra person $25. Children under age 18 stay free. Min stay peak. Lower rates off-season. Parking: Indoor, $17/day. AE, CB, DC, DISC, MC, V.

MOTELS

The Aspen Bed & Breakfast Lodge

311 W Main St, 81611; tel 970/925-7650 or toll free 800/36-ASPEN; fax 970/925-5744. 2½ blocks W of Paepcke Park. This modern and well-maintained property has an enormous floor-to-ceiling stone fireplace in its small lobby. **Rooms:** 38 rms. CI 4pm/CO 11am. Nonsmoking rms avail. Most rooms have a twin trundle bed or pull-out sofa. Decor is southwestern. **Amenities:** A/C, cable TV, dataport, voice mail, in-rm safe, bathrobes. All units w/minibars, some w/terraces, some w/whirlpools. Snacks in all rooms. **Services:** Masseur, babysitting. Traditional après-ski wine and cheese parties. **Facilities:** Whirlpool. Ski lockers. **Rates (CP):** Peak (Feb 16–Apr 1) $154–$200 S or D. Extra person $20. Children under age 12 stay free. Min stay peak and special events. Lower rates off-season. Parking: Outdoor, free. AE, CB, DC, DISC, MC, V.

Boomerang Lodge

500 W Hopkins St, 81611; tel 970/925-3416 or toll free 800/992-8852; fax 970/925-3314. 5 blocks W of Paepcke Park. Charles Paterson designed and built this ski lodge in the early 1950s, after studying with Frank Lloyd Wright at Taliesin. The unique decor and atmosphere are tasteful, timeless, extremely intimate, and somewhat secluded. **Rooms:** 29 rms; 5 cottages/villas. CI 4pm/CO 11am. Nonsmoking rms avail. **Amenities:** Cable TV. No A/C. All units w/terraces, some w/fireplaces. **Services:** Babysitting. Afternoon tea. **Facilities:** 50 Sauna, whirlpool, washer/dryer. Ski lockers. **Rates (CP):** Peak (Feb 15–Mar) $178–$250 S or D; $532 cottage/villa. Extra person $10. Children under age 12 stay free. Min stay peak and special events. Lower rates off-season. Parking: Outdoor, free. In winter, children are $10 extra. AE, CB, DC, DISC, MC, V.

Innsbruck Inn

233 W Main St, 81611; tel 970/925-2980; fax 970/925-6960. 2 blocks W of Paepcke Park. Neat little European chalet-style motel with intimate lobby, decorated in Tyrolean fashion, with moss rock hearth. **Rooms:** 29 rms. CI 3pm/CO 11am. Nonsmoking rms avail. **Amenities:** A/C, cable TV, dataport, bathrobes. Some units w/terraces. Ski racks; mini-refrigerator available on request. **Services:** Babysitting. Après-ski parties daily. **Facilities:** Sauna, whirlpool. **Rates (CP):** Peak (Feb 15–Mar 29) $160–$200 S or D. Extra person $15. Children under age 7 stay free. Min stay peak and special events. Lower rates off-season. Parking: Outdoor, free. Closed Apr 15–May 25. AE, CB, DC, DISC, MC, V.

Limelite Lodge
228 E Cooper Ave, 81611; tel 970/925-3025 or toll free 800/433-0832; fax 970/925-5120. Just W of Wagner Park. Large facility close to all downtown attractions and ski lifts. Lobby is spacious yet cozy. **Rooms:** 63 rms. CI open/CO 11am. Nonsmoking rms avail. **Amenities:** Cable TV w/movies, refrig. No A/C. 1 unit w/whirlpool. **Services:** 24-hour coffee, tea, and juice. Lift ticket service. **Facilities:** Sauna, whirlpool, washer/dryer. Ski lockers. **Rates (CP):** Peak (Feb 10–Mar) $148–$180 S or D. Extra person $10. Children under age 12 stay free. Min stay peak and special events. Lower rates off-season. Parking: Outdoor, $20/day. AE, CB, DC, DISC, MC, V.

St Moritz Lodge
334 W Hyman Ave, 81611; tel 970/925-3220 or toll free 800/817-2069; fax 970/920-4032. Near Paepcke Park. Friendly, European-style ski lodge, away from the center of town. The cozy lobby has a fireplace and small grand piano. **Rooms:** 25 rms; 5 cottages/villas. CI open/CO 10am. **Amenities:** Cable TV w/movies, refrig. No A/C. Some units w/terraces, some w/fireplaces. **Services:** Babysitting. **Facilities:** Sauna, whirlpool. Ski racks in hallway. **Rates (CP):** Peak (Jan 2–Mar 22) $125 S or D; $279 cottage/villa. Extra person $15. Children under age 18 stay free. Lower rates off-season. Parking: Outdoor, free. Dorm room bunks available at $35 per night in high season. AE, DISC, MC, V.

Snowflake Inn
221 E Hyman Ave, 81611; tel 970/925-3221 or toll free 800/247-2064; fax 970/925-8740. Just W of Wagner Park. Chalet-style building just a short walk from lifts and downtown shopping and dining. **Rooms:** 38 rms, stes, and effic. CI 4pm/CO 10am. Ski racks. **Amenities:** Cable TV w/movies, refrig, in-rm safe. No A/C. Some units w/fireplaces. **Services:** Babysitting. Guests can buy lift tickets at hotel. Tea and coffee available 7am–10pm. **Facilities:** Sauna, whirlpool, washer/dryer. **Rates (CP):** Peak (Feb 10–Mar 22) $180–$275 S or D; $210–$550 ste; $189–$250 effic. Extra person $20. Children under age 18 stay free. Min stay. Lower rates off-season. Parking: Outdoor, free. AE, CB, DC, DISC, MC, V.

INNS

Hearthstone House
134 E Hyman Ave, 81611; tel 970/925-7632; fax 970/920-4450. 1 block S of Paepcke Park. Very postmodern atmosphere in a European-style inn. Peaceful lounge area; leather and teak furnishings plus a library and stone fireplace make sitting area very comfortable and unique. Abstract artwork throughout. **Rooms:** 17 rms. CI open/CO 11am. No smoking. Very bright, clean, and contemporary. **Amenities:** Cable TV, bathrobes. No A/C. Some units w/whirlpools. **Services:** Afternoon teas are a treat. **Facilities:** Steam rm. **Rates (BB):** Peak (Dec 15–Apr 15) Min stay special events. Lower rates off-season. Parking: Outdoor, free. Closed Apr 16–Jun 10/Sept 30–Dec 15. AE, MC, V.

The Sardy House
128 E Main St, 81611; tel 970/920-2525 or toll free 800/321-3457; fax 970/920-4478. Just N of Paepcke Park. Built in 1892, with some more recent additions, this bed-and-breakfast is decorated with a nice blend of antiques and more contemporary pieces, all tastefully arranged. The interior is somewhat maze-like but has a nice, intimate feel. **Rooms:** 20 rms and stes. CI 4pm/CO noon. Rooms are comfortable, attractive, and well kept. **Amenities:** Cable TV, bathrobes. No A/C. 1 unit w/terrace, 1 w/fireplace, some w/whirlpools. **Services:** Babysitting. **Facilities:** 1 restaurant (bkfst and dinner only), 1 bar, sauna, whirlpool, guest lounge. Ski and boot storage. **Rates (BB):** Peak (Jan 3–Mar) $269–$369 D; $409–$609 ste. Min stay wknds and special events. Lower rates off-season. Higher rates for special events/hols. Parking: Indoor, free. AE, CB, DC, MC, V.

RESORT

Aspen Meadows
845 Meadows Rd, 81611; tel 970/925-4240 or toll free 800/452-4240; fax 970/925-7790. 40 acres. Part of the nonprofit Aspen Institute, the accommodations here are in the elegant Bauhaus style of Herbert Bayer. Located a short distance from town, the grounds offer fantastic views of surrounding valley, as well as plenty of space for exploration and meditation. **Rooms:** 98 rms and stes. Executive level. CI 4pm/CO 11am. Nonsmoking rms avail. Very bright and clean, with uniquely modern furnishings quite unlike anything else in the area. **Amenities:** Cable TV w/movies, refrig, dataport, VCR, CD/tape player. No A/C. Some units w/terraces, some w/fireplaces. **Services:** Masseur, babysitting. The Aspen Institute offers seminars based on the Socratic approach. **Facilities:** 6 1 restaurant, 1 bar, basketball, volleyball, spa, steam rm, whirlpool, washer/dryer. **Rates:** Peak (Feb–Mar/July–Sept 5) $195–$250 S or D; $265–$410 ste. Extra person $20. Children under age 16 stay free. Lower rates off-season. Parking: Indoor, $4/day. AE, CB, DC, DISC, MC, V.

RESTAURANTS

Benjamin's Deli
315 E Hyman Ave; tel 970/920-2955. Just N of Wagner Park. **Deli.** Late night meals are the main draw at this eatery, which feels more like a diner than a deli, with its half-oval counter with swivel stools. Choose from many deli-style sandwiches, both hot and cold, as well as bagels and a number of salads. Dinners consist entirely of nightly home-style specials, which might include meat loaf, lamb stew, macaroni and cheese, or

an open-face sandwich. **FYI:** Reservations not accepted. Children's menu. No liquor license. No smoking. **Open:** Daily 11am–3am. **Prices:** Main courses $5–$8. DISC, MC, V.

The Chart House
219 E Durant Ave; tel 970/925-3525. Just SW of Wagner Park. **Seafood/Steak.** The original restaurant of the large national chain, it is exceptionally spacious and was built entirely from wooden logs and beams. Decor includes sailing and other outdoor adventure photos, and charts and topographical maps covering some of the table tops. The menu is less adventuresome: prime rib is the signature offering, with seafood also available. Salad bar is included with all meals. **FYI:** Reservations recommended. Children's menu. No smoking. **Open:** Daily 5:30–10pm. **Prices:** Main courses $16–$25. AE, CB, DC, DISC, MC, V.

China Fun
132 W Main St; tel 970/925-5433. Just NW of Paepcke Park. **Chinese.** Occupying an old Victorian home, this restaurant's decor blends Victorian and Oriental influences. Hand-carved mermaids cavort over the mahogany bar, a relic from Liverpool, England. Overhead, an impressive stained-glass panel highlights one ceiling; the other ceilings are of pressed tin. Chinese photographs more than 120 years old decorate the walls. The menu offers an overwhelming array of Cantonese, Mandarin, Hunan, and Szechuan dishes, all created by Chef Greg Qin, who trained in China and worked in New York City for eight years. **FYI:** Reservations accepted. No smoking. **Open:** Daily 11:30am–11pm. **Prices:** Main courses $9–$33. AE, CB, DC, MC, V.

Flying Dog Brew Pub
424 E Cooper Ave; tel 970/925-7464. 1 block E of Wagner Park. **Pub.** This large, open brew pub is decorated with photos, drawings, posters, and memorabilia—all dog-related, of course. Standard pub fare is augmented by the special steaks and prime rib from Limousin beef. Several freshly brewed beers are always on tap. **FYI:** Reservations accepted. Bluegrass. Children's menu. No smoking. **Open:** Daily 11:30am–10pm. Closed Nov 1–14. **Prices:** Main courses $6–$17. AE, DISC, MC, V.

The Golden Horn
320 S Mill St; tel 970/925-3373. Just E of Wagner Park. **Swiss.** This basement restaurant with an alpine flavor has been an Aspen favorite since 1949. A large golden horn, the restaurant's namesake, occupies an illuminated nook on the far wall near the fireplace. The menu is an interesting blend of Swiss and game specialties, such as Wiener schnitzel and venison, but there are several pasta and seafood choices for lighter tastes. The extensive wine list, which exceeds 250 bottles, has been selected by the *Wine Spectator* as one of the top 100 in the United States. **FYI:** Reservations recommended. String quartet. No smoking. **Open:** Daily 5:30–10pm. Closed Apr 15–June/Sept 15–Nov 15. **Prices:** Main courses $15–$31. AE, MC, V.

Grill on the Park
307 S Mill St; tel 970/920-3700. Just N of Wagner Park. **New American.** This small, L-shaped restaurant overlooking Wagner Park features a contemporary, elegant style, a very attractive bar, and an open kitchen. Entrees are unique, and on the light side. Two of the most distinctive offerings are wasabi-crusted salmon and zinfandel-braised venison; traditionalists may prefer the New York strip steak or rotisserie chicken. Several salads are also offered. **FYI:** Reservations not accepted. No smoking. **Open:** Daily 11am–10pm. **Prices:** Main courses $16–$24. AE, DISC, MC, V.

★ La Cocina
308 E Hopkins Ave; tel 970/925-9714. Just E of Bass Park. **Mexican.** This great little Mexican restaurant has served locals and visitors for over 20 years. A pressed-tin ceiling and hand-painted country scenes decorate the intimate bar and lounge. The dining room is simpler, but still casual and friendly. Both the decor and menu have changed little over the years, which keeps the clientele returning for their favorites. The standard Mexican dishes have a slight regional twist, such as blue corn tortillas layered with cheese, onions, and red chile. **FYI:** Reservations not accepted. Children's menu. No smoking. **Open:** Daily 5–10pm. Closed Apr 15–June 10/Oct 15–Dec 5. **Prices:** Main courses $7–$11. No CC.

Little Annie's Eating House
517 E Hyman Ave; tel 970/925-1098. Near Wagner Park. **Regional American.** Named after the daughter of a miner who came to Aspen in the 1870s, Little Annie's was one of the first restaurants in town, and it has become popular with locals and visitors alike. The atmosphere is cheerful and festive, and in tune with the casual ski crowd in winter. Best picks are barbecue ribs, burgers, chicken-fried steak, Colorado veal chops, and the ever-popular spaghetti. **FYI:** Reservations not accepted. Children's menu. No smoking. **Open:** Daily 11:30am–11pm. **Prices:** Main courses $7–$21. AE, DISC, MC, V.

The Little Nell Restaurant
In the Little Nell Hotel, 675 E Durant Ave; tel 970/920-6330. Just E of the Silver Queen Gondola. **New American.** Large windows face the ski mountain in this bi-level restaurant, which is brightly lit and colorful during the day but very romantic in the evening. Paintings, oxidized copper chandeliers and lamps, and dried flower arrangements set the casually elegant scene. Unusual seafood dishes include grilled yellowtail with shiitake mushrooms and macadamia-crusted, poached halibut. Elk and New York steak are two beef options. **FYI:** Reservations recommended. Jazz. Children's menu. No smoking. **Open:** Breakfast daily 7–10:30am; lunch daily 11:30am–2:30pm; dinner daily 6–10pm; brunch Sun noon–2:30pm. **Prices:** Main courses $23–$31. AE, CB, DC, DISC, MC, V.

★ Main St Bakery & Cafe
201 E Main St; tel 970/925-6446. Just E of Paepeke Park. **Eclectic/Bakery.** In summer the line might stretch around the block for breakfast and lunch at this popular, down-to-earth eatery. The country decor and friendly service complement the hearty meals, all served with freshly baked bread. Dinner is served family style, with entrees ranging from pot roast and chunky chicken pot pie to pumpkin seed-crusted rainbow trout and several pasta dishes. **FYI:** Reservations not accepted. Beer and wine only. No smoking. **Open:** Breakfast Mon–Sat 7–11:30am, Sun 7am–2:30pm; lunch Mon–Sat 11:30am–4:30pm, Sun 11:30am–4pm; dinner Mon–Sat 5:30–9:30pm. **Prices:** Main courses $9–$15. AE, MC, V.

Piñons
105 S Mill St; tel 970/920-2021. 1½ block N of Wagner Park. **Regional American.** Woven leather railings adorn the stairwell at the entrance to this rustic western ranch-style restaurant. Aged stucco walls and large wooden beams, leather furnishings and pillows are some of the wonderful details of the dining area. Both service and food are very good. Sample entrees: sautéed Colorado pheasant breast, roasted Colorado striped bass. **FYI:** Reservations recommended. Children's menu. No smoking. **Open:** Daily 6–10pm. Closed Apr 15–June 15/Oct–Nov. **Prices:** Main courses $22–$33. AE, MC, V.

★ The Red Onion
420 E Cooper St; tel 970/925-9043. Just E of Wagner Park. **American/Mexican.** A casino and saloon during the silver boom, this eatery still sports the original bar and maintains a lively and friendly atmosphere. Located close to the ski mountain, it's a great après-ski spot. The menu offers a nice selection of sandwiches, burgers, and Mexican entrees, plus $6 daily lunch specials. **FYI:** Reservations not accepted. No smoking. **Open:** Daily 11:30am–10pm. Closed Apr 20–May 20/Oct 20–Oct 28. **Prices:** Main courses $5–$11. MC, V.

Renaissance
304 E Hopkins St; tel 970/925-2402. 2 blocks W of City Hall. **New American/French.** A thick glass panel etched with grapevines separates the entryway from this elegant and softly lit dining room. Modern ceramic art and paintings, and a ceiling made of small arches covered with billowing silk, create a lovely, intimate setting. Chef Charles Dale, awarded the 1995 Best New Chef in America by *Food & Wine* magazine, offers a constantly changing but always inspired menu. Specialties include spinach and crab tart with balsamic vinegar, tomato, and basil; fresh sautéed foie gras with caramelized pear and candied pecans; Thai bouillabaisse; and espresso-blackened tenderloin of beef. **FYI:** Reservations recommended. Rock. No smoking. **Open:** Daily 6–10:30pm. Closed Apr 15–June 1/Sept 30–Nov 25. **Prices:** Main courses $9–$36. AE, MC, V.

Takah Sushi
420 E Hyman Ave; tel 970/925-8588. ½ block E of Wagner Park. **Japanese.** The sushi bar is the heart of this basement restaurant, elegantly decorated with many Japanese prints and murals. With over 20 kinds of sushi—from halibut to octopus—it has been deemed one of the best sushi bars between the two coasts by the *New York Times*. There is also a variety of Asian and other dishes available, such as chicken and scallop stir-fry, grilled duck breast, and 18-oz beef rib steak. **FYI:** Reservations recommended. No smoking. **Open:** Daily 5:30–11pm. Closed Apr 15–May 20. **Prices:** Main courses $13–$20. AE, CB, DC, DISC, MC, V.

Wienerstube
633 E Hyman Ave; tel 970/925-3357. Near Wagner Park. **American/Austrian.** Skylights and many large leafy plants, international flags hanging from the ceiling, and German coats of arms in the entryway all make this lofty, light-filled place cheerful and inviting. Lunch ranges from traditional entrees such as French dip and Reuben sandwiches to Austrian dishes like Wiener schnitzel and special Scandinavian choices. Wonderful Viennese pastries are always available. **FYI:** Reservations not accepted. Children's menu. No smoking. **Open:** Tues–Sun 7am–2:30pm. **Prices:** Main courses $6–$19. AE, CB, DC, MC, V.

★ Woody Creek Tavern
Upper River Rd, Woody Creek; tel 970/923-4585. 2 mi N of CO 82. **Pub.** Somewhat off the beaten track, this rustic tavern has been a local favorite for years and is steadily becoming a refuge for visiting celebrities as well. Like the decor, the food is standard pub fare, with burgers, steaks, and ribs, plus a regional delight called buffalo bear sausage. **FYI:** Reservations not accepted. Children's menu. No smoking. **Open:** Daily 11:30am–10pm. **Prices:** Main courses $7–$15. No CC.

ATTRACTIONS

The Aspen Art Museum
590 N Mill St; tel 970/925-8050. Though it has no permanent collection, the Aspen Art Museum presents rotating exhibits highlighting the work of local and nationally known contemporary and progressive artists. Lectures and art education programs for adults and children are offered year-round, and there's a free reception every Thursday evening, 6–8pm. **Open:** Tues–Sat 10am–6pm, Sun noon–6pm. **$**

Aspen Historical Society Museum
620 W Bleeker St; tel 970/925-3721. Silver baron Jerome Wheeler had this three-story Victorian brick home built in 1888. Exhibits describe Aspen history from the Ute tribe's culture through the mining rush, from railroads and ranching to the founding of the ski industry. The Museum Annex presents changing exhibits, and the gift shop offers a variety of interesting souvenirs. Also offered are guided walking tours of historic Aspen during the summer. **Open:** Mid-June–Sept and Jan–mid-Apr, Tues–Sat 1–4pm. **$**

The Wheeler Opera House
320 E Hyman Ave; tel 970/920-5770. The focus of the performing arts in Aspen, the 1889 structure hosts a year-round program of music, theater, dance, film, and lectures. The building features brass wall sconces, crystal chandeliers, gold trim and stencils on the dark blue walls, rich wood, red carpeting, and red velvet covering on the seats. Guided tours by appointment. **Open:** Box Office, Mon–Sat 10am–5pm. **$$$**

Aspen Mountain
Durant Ave and Hunter St; tel 970/925-1220 or 925-1221 (snow report). Aspen Mountain—known to locals as "Ajax," for an old miner's claim—is not for the timid. It is the American West's original hard-core ski mountain, with no fewer than 23 of its named runs "double diamond"—for experts only. One-third of the mountain's runs are left forever ungroomed, ecstasy for bump runners. There are mountain-long runs for both intermediate and advanced skiers, but beginners should look to one of the other Aspen areas.

Aspen Mountain has a 3,267-foot vertical, with 75 trails on 631 skiable acres. Eight lifts—the high-speed Silver Queen gondola, three quad chairs, and four double chairs—serve up to 10,775 skiers per hour. Average annual snowfall at the summit is 300 inches (25 feet). Snowcats deliver advanced-and-expert skiers to an additional 1,500 acres of powder skiing in back bowls. **Open:** Thanksgiving–mid-Apr, daily 9am–3:30pm. **$$$$**

Aspen Highlands
Maroon Creek St; tel 970/925-1220. Highlands has the most balanced skiable terrain—novice to expert, with lots of intermediate slopes—in the Aspen valley. It takes two lifts to reach the 11,800-foot Loge Peak summit, where most of the advanced expert runs are found in the Steeplechase area and 199 acres of glades in the Olympic Bowl. Kandahar, Golden Horn, and Thunderbowl give the intermediate skier a long run from top to bottom, and novices are best served mid-mountain on trails like Red Onion and Apple Strudel. Highlands has 78 trails on 619 acres, served by nine lifts (two high speed quads, five double chairs and two surface lifts). **Open:** Thanksgiving–mid-Apr, daily 9am–4pm. **$$$$**

Buttermilk Mountain
W Buttermilk Rd at CO 82; tel 970/925-1220 or 925-1221 (snow report). Buttermilk is nominally a beginners' mountain, but there's plenty of intermediate and ample advanced terrain as well. The smallest of Aspen's four mountains has three segments: Main Buttermilk, rising from the Inn at Aspen, with a variety of intermediate trails and the long, easy, winding Homestead Road; Buttermilk West, a mountaintop (9,900 ft) novice area; and Tiehack, the intermediate-advanced section where Aspen town-league races are held. Seven lifts (one high-speed quad, five double chairs, and a platter-pull) serve 45 trails on 410 acres, with a 2,030-foot vertical. Average annual snowfall at the summit is 200 inches (16 feet, 8 inches).

Special features include the Vic Braden Ski College, which offers an intensive five-day adult learn-to-ski program; the Powder Pandas for 3-to-6-year-olds; and a 200-foot-long half-pipe for snowboarders, with a 23% grade. **Open:** Mid-Dec–early Apr, daily 9am–4pm. **$$$$**

Snowmass
Snowmelt Rd; tel 970/925-1220 or 925-1221 (snow report). A huge, ostensibly intermediate mountain with something for everyone, Snowmass has 33% more skiable acreage than the other three Aspen areas combined. Actually four distinct self-contained areas, each with its own lift system and restaurant, its terrain varies from easy beginner runs to the pitches of the Cirque and the Hanging Valley Wall, the steepest in the Aspen area.

Big Burn, site of a forest fire set by 19th-century Utes to discourage settlers, boasts wide-open advanced and intermediate slopes and the expert drops of the Cirque. Atop the intermediate Alpine Springs trails is the advanced High Alpine Lift, from which experts can traverse to the formidable Hanging Valley Wall. Elk Camp is ideal for early intermediates who prefer long cruising runs. Sam's Knob has advanced upper trails diving through trees, and a variety of intermediate and novice runs around its northeast face and base. All areas meet in the scattered condominium developments that surround Snowmass Village Mall.

All told, there are 2,500 skiable acres at Snowmass, with a 4,087-foot vertical drop. The mountain has 72 trails served by 15 lifts (five quad chairs, one triple chair, seven double chairs, and two platter-pulls). Average annual snowfall at the 12,310-foot summit is 300 inches (25 feet). **Open:** Thanksgiving–mid-Apr, daily 8:30am–3:30pm. **$$$$**

Avon

See Vail

Bayfield

See Durango

Beaver Creek

See Vail

Boulder

See also Longmont, Lyons

Situated at the base of a dramatic wall of tall jagged rocks, Boulder is just 30 miles northwest of downtown Denver at the foot of the Flatirons of the Rocky Mountains. It was settled in 1858 by miners searching for gold. The University of Colorado is a dominating presence in Boulder, but this sophisticated small city is also home to numerous high-tech companies and research concerns. Boulder residents are known for their love of the outdoors; it is estimated that there are 93,000 bicycles in the city—more than one per resident. **Information:** Boulder Convention & Visitors Bureau, 2440 Pearl St., Boulder 80302 (tel 303/442-2911 or 800/444-0447).

HOTELS

The Broker Inn

555 30th St, 80303; tel 303/444-3330 or toll free 800/338-5407; fax 303/444-6444. Just W of Williams Village housing complex. From the outside this looks like a typical small 1970s-style wood and brick structure, but the inside is gracefully decorated with elegantly crafted wooden fixtures adorned with leaded and stained glass. In need of minor renovation, but clean and comfortable. **Rooms:** 116 rms and stes. CI 4pm/CO noon. Nonsmoking rms avail. Brass beds and other antiques. **Amenities:** A/C, cable TV w/movies. 1 unit w/whirlpool. **Services:** Babysitting. **Facilities:** 1 restaurant, 2 bars (1 w/entertainment), whirlpool. Complimentary passes to nearby, state-of-the-art health club. **Rates (BB):** Peak (May–Oct) $99–$119 S or D; $185 ste. Extra person $10. Children under age 18 stay free. Lower rates off-season. Parking: Outdoor, free. AE, CB, DC, DISC, MC, V.

Clarion Harvest House

1345 28th St, 80302; tel 303/442-3850 or toll free 800/545-6285; fax 303/443-1480. 2 blocks E of Folsom Field. Not far from the university, this large hotel caters primarily to business travelers and conference groups, but is also convenient for families and tourists. It's adjacent to Boulder Creek Path, great for walking and biking, which offers an attractive alternative access to downtown. **Rooms:** 269 rms and stes. Executive level. CI 3pm/CO 11am. Nonsmoking rms avail. Wide variety of room sizes and luxury levels available. West side rooms have great views of university and Flatirons. **Amenities:** A/C, cable TV w/movies, voice mail. Some units w/terraces, 1 w/whirlpool. **Services:** Car-rental desk, social director, masseur, babysitting. **Facilities:** 10 5 200 1 restaurant, 2 bars, volleyball, whirlpool, washer/dryer. **Rates:** Peak (May–Oct) $128–$169 S or D; $175–$395 ste. Extra person $10. Min stay special events. Lower rates off-season. Parking: Outdoor, free. AE, CB, DC, DISC, MC, V.

Courtyard by Marriott

4710 Pearl East Circle, 80301; tel 303/440-4700 or toll free 800/321-2211; fax 303/440-8975. E of Pearl St exit off Foothills Pkwy. Stucco building with red tile roof in the style of many of the public buildings in Boulder. Easy access to Boulder Creek Path, popular for biking, jogging, and walking. **Rooms:** 149 rms and stes. CI 4pm/CO 1pm. Nonsmoking rms avail. Many units face attractive interior courtyard. Rooms on west side have great views of Boulder Flatirons and Front Range of the Rockies. **Amenities:** A/C, cable TV w/movies, voice mail. Some units w/terraces. **Services:** Babysitting. **Facilities:** 50 1 restaurant (bkfst and dinner only), 1 bar, whirlpool, washer/dryer. **Rates:** Peak (June–Sept) $64–$99 S; $74–$109 D; $104–$155 ste. Extra person $10. Min stay special events. Lower rates off-season. Parking: Outdoor, free. AE, DC, DISC, MC, V.

Days Inn Boulder

5397 S Boulder Rd, 80303; tel 303/499-4422 or toll free 800/329-7466; fax 303/494-0269. Just E of jct Foothills Pkwy. Newly renovated, modern hotel just a few miles from downtown and the university. **Rooms:** 76 rms and stes. CI 2pm/CO noon. Nonsmoking rms avail. Rooms on the west side have fantastic views of the Boulder Flatirons and some of the higher peaks of the Front Range of the Rockies. **Amenities:** A/C, cable TV w/movies. Some units w/terraces. **Services:** **Facilities:** 45 **Rates (CP):** Peak (May 31–Aug) $84 S; $89 D; $89 ste. Extra person $5. Children under age 17 stay free. Lower rates off-season. Parking: Outdoor, free. AE, CB, DC, DISC, MC, V.

Homewood Suites

4950 Baseline Rd, 80303; tel 303/499-9922 or toll free 800/225-5466; fax 303/499-6706. Near jct Foothills Pkwy. Built in 1991, this stylish hotel is surrounded with trees and manicured gardens. The lobby features large oak beams and houses a small dining room and lounge. Ideal for business travelers. **Rooms:** 112 stes. CI 3pm/CO noon. Nonsmoking rms avail. Suites are large and homelike. **Amenities:** A/C, cable TV w/movies, refrig, dataport, VCR, voice mail. Some units w/fireplaces. All suites have full kitchen facilities, two TVs. **Services:** Babysitting. **Facilities:** 30 Basketball, spa, whirlpool, washer/dryer. Complimentary use of equipment in business center. Nearby modern health club available for $5 on presentation of room key. **Rates (CP):** Peak (May 26–Sept 5) $139–$179 ste. Lower rates off-season. Parking: Outdoor, free. AE, CB, DC, DISC, MC, V.

Hotel Boulderado

2115 13th St, 80302; tel 303/442-4344 or toll free 800/433-4344; fax 303/442-4378. 1 block N of Pearl St. Located downtown, the Boulderado offers modern conveniences disguised with historic elegance. The beautiful lobby boasts a lovely leaded glass ceiling and cantilevered cherry wood staircase. During the Christmas season, you can admire the magnificent 24-foot Christmas tree from anywhere on the stairs. **Rooms:** 160 rms and stes. CI 4pm/CO 11am. Nonsmoking rms avail. Rooms are modern but retain historic flavor with fine antiques and period wallpapers. **Amenities:** A/C, cable TV w/movies. Some units w/terraces, some w/whirlpools. **Services:** Social director, babysitting. **Facilities:** 200 2 restaurants, 2 bars (1 w/entertainment). **Rates:** $135–$231 S or D; $177–$231 ste. Extra person $12. Children under age 12 stay free. Min stay special events. Parking: Indoor, free. AE, CB, DC, DISC, JCB, MC, V.

Residence Inn Boulder
3030 Center Green Dr, 80301; tel 303/449-5545 or toll free 800/331-3131; fax 303/449-2452. Just W of jct Foothills Pkwy/Valmont Rd. Located in a quiet part of Boulder about three miles from downtown and the university campus. Good choice for business people or families planning to be in area for several days. **Rooms:** 128 stes. CI 3pm/CO noon. Nonsmoking rms avail. **Amenities:** Cable TV w/movies, refrig, voice mail. No A/C. 1 unit w/minibar, all w/terraces, some w/fireplaces. Fully equipped kitchens. **Services:** Social director. Complimentary dinner on Wednesday with seating outside, weather permitting. **Facilities:** 40 1 bar, basketball, whirlpool. Paddle tennis court. Complimentary passes to local health club. **Rates (CP):** Peak (May–Oct) $99–$169 ste. Extra person $10. Min stay special events. Lower rates off-season. Parking: Outdoor, free. AE, DC, MC, V.

MOTELS

Arapahoe Lodge
2020 Arapahoe Ave, 80302; tel 303/449-7550; fax 303/449-1082. Just E of Boulder High School. No-frills motel with easy access to the university and downtown shopping. **Rooms:** 51 rms and effic. CI 2pm/CO 11am. Nonsmoking rms avail. **Amenities:** A/C, cable TV w/movies, refrig. All units w/terraces. **Services:** **Facilities:** Sauna, whirlpool, washer/dryer. **Rates:** Peak (May–Oct) $55–$70 S; $65–$90 D; $70–$90 effic. Extra person $5. Children under age 12 stay free. Lower rates off-season. Parking: Outdoor, free. AE, DC, DISC, MC, V.

Best Western Boulder Inn
770 28th St, 80303; tel 303/449-3800 or toll free 800/233-8469; fax 303/449-3800. Baseline Rd exit off US 36. Comfortable, basic establishment close to the university. **Rooms:** 95 rms and stes. CI 3pm/CO 11am. Nonsmoking rms avail. **Amenities:** A/C, cable TV w/movies, dataport. All units w/terraces. **Services:** **Facilities:** 70 1 restaurant (lunch and dinner only), 1 bar, sauna, whirlpool. Complimentary passes to local health club available. **Rates (CP):** Peak (May 15–Sept) $67–$83 S; $80–$95 D; $87–$97 ste. Extra person $5. Children under age 14 stay free. Min stay special events. Lower rates off-season. Parking: Outdoor, free. AE, DC, DISC, MC, V.

Best Western Golden Buff Lodge
1725 28th St, 80301; tel 303/442-7450 or toll free 800/999-BUFF; fax 303/442-8788. Located fairly close to the university and downtown, within easy walking distance of several restaurants and a magazine shop. Nice views of the Boulder Flatirons. **Rooms:** 112 rms and effic. CI 3pm/CO 11am. Nonsmoking rms avail. **Amenities:** A/C, cable TV w/movies. All units w/terraces. **Services:** **Facilities:** 55 1 restaurant (bkfst and lunch only), sauna, whirlpool. **Rates (CP):** Peak (May–Oct) $71 S; $83 D; $93 effic. Extra person $5. Children under age 12 stay free. Lower rates off-season. Parking: Outdoor, free. AE, CB, DC, DISC, JCB, MC, V.

Foot of the Mountain Motel
200 Arapahoe Ave, 80302; tel 303/442-5688. Next to Eben G Fine Park. As its name implies, this small motel is nestled up against the foot of the Front Range, at the western edge of town. Built in 1930, the motel feels like it's in the wilderness but is not too far from downtown. The park across the street has picnic space, plus a playground and the beginning of the Boulder Creek Path for hiking and biking. **Rooms:** 18 rms. CI noon/CO 10:30am. Nonsmoking rms avail. Each room is in its own little log cabin, rustically decorated and well suited to the surroundings. **Amenities:** A/C, cable TV, refrig. All units w/terraces. **Services:** **Facilities:** Acre of picnic grounds behind units. **Rates:** Peak (Apr–Oct) $50–$60 S; $65–$75 D. Extra person $5. Children under age 12 stay free. Min stay special events. Lower rates off-season. Parking: Outdoor, free. AE, DISC, MC, V.

Holiday Inn Boulder
800 28th St, 80303; tel 303/443-3322 or toll free 800/HOLIDAY; fax 303/443-0397. Just E of University of Colorado campus. With a rather nice atrium containing hot tub and fountain that feeds the pool. Proximity to the university makes it a good choice for anyone with business there. **Rooms:** 165 rms. CI 3pm/CO noon. Nonsmoking rms avail. **Amenities:** Cable TV w/movies, dataport. No A/C. Some units w/terraces. **Services:** **Facilities:** 200 1 restaurant, 1 bar, games rm, sauna, whirlpool. Children under 18 receive complimentary breakfast, lunch, and dinner daily. **Rates:** Peak (May–Sept) $89 S; $99 D. Extra person $10. Children under age 18 stay free. Lower rates off-season. Parking: Outdoor, free. AE, CB, DC, DISC, JCB, MC, V.

Super 8
970 28th St, 80303; tel 303/443-7800 or toll free 800/525-2149; fax 303/443-7800. Just E of University of Colorado campus. Recently renovated, basic motel convenient to both the university and downtown shopping. Nice mountain views. **Rooms:** 71 rms, stes, and effic. CI 4pm/CO noon. Nonsmoking rms avail. **Amenities:** A/C, cable TV w/movies, dataport. All units w/terraces. **Services:** VP **Facilities:** 50 Washer/dryer. **Rates:** Peak (May–Sept) $55–$85 S; $60–$95 D; $60–$94 ste; $71–$124 effic.

Extra person $5. Children under age 12 stay free. Lower rates off-season. Parking: Outdoor, free. AE, DC, DISC, MC, V.

University Inn
1632 Broadway, 80302; tel 303/442-3830 or toll free 800/258-7917; fax 303/442-1205. Between downtown and University of Colorado campus. Yellow brick building with blue trim, close to downtown shopping and university. **Rooms:** 39 rms. CI open/CO 11am. Nonsmoking rms avail. **Amenities:** A/C, cable TV w/movies, refrig. All units w/terraces. **Services:** **Facilities:** Washer/dryer. **Rates:** Peak (May 15–Aug) $67–$90 S; $77–$82 D. Extra person $7. Children under age 2 stay free. Lower rates off-season. Parking: Outdoor, free. AE, DC, DISC, MC, V.

INNS

The Alps
38619 Boulder Canyon Dr, PO Box 18298, 80302; tel 303/444-5445 or toll free 800/414-2577; fax 303/444-5522. 1 ¾ mi W of town on CO 119. 24½ acres. Combination of an old log cabin and a modern lodge, complete with giant stone fireplace. An intimate retreat. Unsuitable for children under 12. **Rooms:** 12 rms. CI 4pm/CO 11am. No smoking. Rooms individually decorated; variety of bathtubs and stained-glass windows. **Amenities:** Dataport. No A/C or TV. Some units w/terraces, all w/fireplaces, some w/whirlpools. **Services:** Afternoon tea served. **Facilities:** 30 Games rm, guest lounge w/TV. **Rates (BB):** $75–$200 S; $80–$205 D. Extra person $15. Min stay wknds and special events. Parking: Outdoor, free. AE, CB, DC, DISC, MC, V.

UNRATED **Boulder Victoria**
1305 Pine St, 80302; tel 303/938-1300; fax 303/938-1435. This colonial revival–style inn dates back to 1891, and has distinctively painted trim and beautifully maintained grounds. Within walking distance of downtown. Unsuitable for children under 12. **Rooms:** 7 rms and stes. CI 3pm/CO 11am. No smoking. Rooms are elegant and tastefully decorated, with spacious bathrooms; some have steam showers. **Amenities:** A/C, cable TV, bathrobes. Some units w/terraces. **Services:** Afternoon tea served. **Facilities:** Guest lounge. Complimentary use of fitness center three blocks away. **Rates (CP):** Peak (May–Oct) $114–$139 S; $129–$154 D; $149–$164 ste. Extra person $15. Min stay wknds. Lower rates off-season. AE, MC, V.

The Briar Rose
2151 Arapahoe Ave, 80302; tel 303/442-3007. Just E of Boulder High School. This beautiful brick and wood structure, built in 1897, is surrounded by well-manicured gardens. The only drawback is its location on a very busy street. **Rooms:** 9 rms. CI 3pm/CO noon. No smoking. Rooms individually decorated with antiques, floral prints, and hand-painted floral murals done by local artist. **Amenities:** No A/C or TV. Some units w/terraces, some w/fireplaces. **Services:** Afternoon tea served. **Facilities:** Guest lounge. Local health club passes $8. **Rates (CP):** Peak (May–Dec) $94–$124 S; $109–$139 D. Extra person $15. Children under age 6 stay free. Min stay special events. Lower rates off-season. Parking: Outdoor, free. AE, DC, MC, V.

RESTAURANTS

Antica Roma
In Pearl St Mall, 1308 Pearl St; tel 303/442-0378. Just E of 13th St. **Italian.** Located in the heart of the Pearl St shopping area, this restaurant is as Italian as they come, from the ambience to the food and wine. Large brick walls have wooden shutters and waitstaff stations with shingled roofs. Dining is at stout wooden tables, and plants hang from the beams above. The menu includes a wide range of fresh and unusual pastas, pizza, and calzones, as well as a few meat and fish dishes. It offers an extensive Italian wine list. **FYI:** Reservations accepted. Children's menu. No smoking. **Open:** Peak (May 31–Oct 15) lunch daily 11:30am–3:30pm; dinner Sun–Thurs 5–10pm, Fri–Sat 5–11pm. **Prices:** Main courses $5–$18. AE, CB, DC, DISC, MC, V.

Bangkok Cuisine
2017 13th St; tel 303/440-4830. Just N of Pearl St. **Thai.** Decorated with traditional Thai artwork and wall hangings, the atmosphere here is authentic, comfortable, intimate, and appealing. You can choose among the many and varied seafood, beef, poultry, pork, and vegetarian offerings. Virtually all can be spiced to your taste, and include ingredients such as wood-ear mushrooms, coconut milk, or peanut, curry, and chile sauces. **FYI:** Reservations accepted. Beer and wine only. No smoking. **Open:** Peak (May 15–Sept 15) lunch Mon–Fri 11:30am–2:30pm, Sat–Sun noon–4pm; dinner Mon–Fri 5–10pm, Sat–Sun 4–10pm. **Prices:** Main courses $6–$10. AE, DISC, MC, V.

Boulder Harvest Restaurant
In Harvest Commons, 1738 Pearl St; tel 303/449-6223. 3 blocks E of Pearl St Mall. **Continental/Vegetarian.** The staff prides itself on serving only the finest locally grown organic foods. The bright and airy, wood-and-brick interior is accented with many plants and affords a quiet and relaxed setting. Two specialties are Basque pie, featuring sautéed vegetables covered with mashed potatoes and baked cheeses, and the Indo-Ceylon stir-fry, a blend of curried vegetables with raisins, nuts, coconut, chutney, and multigrain pilaf. Kids under 12 eat free. **FYI:** Reservations accepted. Children's menu. Beer and wine only. No smoking. **Open:** Sun–Thurs 7am–9:30pm, Fri–Sat 7am–10pm. **Prices:** Main courses $5–$10. AE, CB, DC, DISC, MC, V.

Flagstaff House Restaurant
1138 Flagstaff Rd; tel 303/442-4640. 2 mi W of town. **Seafood/Game.** Chef-owned and operated, this restaurant offers one of the best dining views in all of Colorado—huge windows overlook all of Boulder (especially nice as the lights come on at sunset). The interior is luxuriously and tastefully decorated, and the food and service are exceptional. The

menu changes daily, offering a wonderful blend of seafood and game dishes, such as smoked and grilled Chilean sea bass or Australian elk fillet. The wine list is extensive. **FYI:** Reservations recommended. No smoking. **Open:** Sun–Fri 6–10pm, Sat 5–10pm. **Prices:** Main courses $23–$43; prix fixe $60–$65. AE, CB, DC, DISC, MC, V.

The Greenbriar Inn
8735 N Foothills Hwy; tel 303/440-7979. 6½ mi N of town on US 36. **New American/Continental.** Offering some of the best dining in Boulder, this dining room is set in a cottage surrounded by several patio gardens perfect for al fresco dining in summer. The interior is equally inviting, with wood paneling, wood and stained-glass dividers, and watercolors of freshwater fish. The menu might include items such as wild mushroom ravioli, lobster cardinal, or venison sirloin wrapped in phyllo. **FYI:** Reservations recommended. **Open:** Dinner Tues–Sun 5–10pm; brunch Sun 11am–2:30pm. **Prices:** Main courses $18–$34. AE, CB, DC, MC, V.

John's Restaurant
2328 Pearl St; tel 303/444-5232. 12 blocks E of Pearl St Mall. **Continental/Eclectic.** Located in a small but elegant house, this chef-owned and family-operated restaurant offers eclectic fare in a peaceful environment. Some of the unusual items on the menu include filet mignon with Stilton-ale sauce; mariscos Viscaina, a Basque dish of salmon, mussels, shrimp, scallops, and Chilean sea bass with red peppers and herbs in a saffron and shellfish stock; and Shrimp Nancy, pan-grilled shrimp dusted with southwestern spices and flamed in brandy. **FYI:** Reservations accepted. No smoking. **Open:** Daily 5:30pm–closing. **Prices:** Main courses $16–$23. AE, CB, DC, DISC, MC, V.

La Estrellita
2037 13th St; tel 303/939-8822. Just N of Pearl St. **Mexican.** Diners here are offered a wide range of good Mexican food in a warmly lit dining area. Wood beams and paneling, plus a large saltwater fish tank, create a comfortable, casual setting. Breakfast is served all day. **FYI:** Reservations accepted. Guitar. Children's menu. No smoking. Additional locations: 7617 W 88th St, Westminster (tel 422-3700); 45 N Main, Unit 9, Brighton (tel 654-9900). **Open:** Peak (May–Sept) Mon–Thurs 11am–10pm, Fri–Sat 11am–11pm, Sun noon–10pm. **Prices:** Main courses $3–$10. AE, DISC, MC, V.

Nancy's Restaurant
825 Walnut St; tel 303/449-8402. Near Pearl St Mall. **Continental/Eclectic.** This intimate, homey restaurant is renowned for its weekend breakfasts and afternoon tea. Located in a restored house in the downtown district, the dining area has flowered wallpaper and antique china plates decorating the walls. Specialties include filet mignon Malagasy, tenderloin seasoned with cracked pepper and fresh fruit chutney, and chicken breast Eubanks, chicken served with a delicate raspberry-champagne sauce. **FYI:** Reservations accepted. Children's menu. No smoking. **Open:** Breakfast daily 7:30am–2pm; lunch Mon–Fri 11:30am–2pm; dinner Tues–Sat 5:30–9pm. **Prices:** Main courses $8–$20. AE, MC, V.

The New York Delicatessen
In Pearl St Mall, 1117 Pearl St; tel 303/447-3354. 1 block W of Broadway. **Deli.** A small slice of New York City in Colorado. The brick interior is accented by posters and framed magazine articles describing the Big Apple, and a deli and takeout counter dominates the space. Enjoy specialty sandwiches and vegetarian dishes, as well as classic Jewish deli fare—knishes, latkes, lox, and kosher hot dogs. **FYI:** Reservations accepted. Children's menu. Beer and wine only. No smoking. Additional location: 900 Auraria Pkwy, Denver (tel 685-4904). **Open:** Peak (May 15–Oct 1) Fri–Sat 8am–11pm, Sun–Thurs 8am–10pm. **Prices:** Main courses $4–$14. AE, CB, DC, DISC, MC, V.

Pasta Jay's
925 Pearl St; tel 303/444-5800. Just W of Pearl St Mall. **Italian.** Old brick walls, hanging plants, and red-and-white checked tablecloths mark the interior, while an outside patio offers warm weather dining and people watching. Diners can order practically any Italian dish here, from pizza to eggplant parmigiana to gnocchi and baked rigatoni. Ice cream pies for dessert. **FYI:** Reservations accepted. Children's menu. Beer and wine only. No smoking. Additional locations: Old Town Sq, Fort Collins (tel 970/224-5800); 1435 Market St, Denver (tel 534-8800). **Open:** Mon–Thurs 11am–10:30pm, Fri–Sat 11am–11pm, Sun 11am–11pm. **Prices:** Main courses $6–$9. MC, V.

Pour la France
1001 Pearl St; tel 303/449-3929. Just W of Pearl St Mall. **French.** An attractive restaurant with open-air dining and a brick and wood interior that centers around a bar/espresso bar/bakery. Modern art adorns the brick walls, while large windows and fans give the place an airy, French cafe atmosphere. The kitchen prepares classics such as coq au vin and tourte de poulet, plus an Asian-inspired dish of ginger shrimp and chicken. A variety of salads and desserts round out the menu. **FYI:** Reservations not accepted. No smoking. **Open:** Mon–Wed 7am–10:30pm, Thurs–Sat 7am–midnight, Sun 8am–10pm. **Prices:** Main courses $7–$14. AE, MC, V.

Sushi Zanmai
1221 Spruce St; tel 303/440-0733. 1 block N of Pearl St. **Japanese.** The restaurant is done in traditional Japanese style, with awnings covering the ceiling; half the space is dedicated to the sushi bar and the other half to hibachi tables and booths. There is an extensive selection of chicken, steak, seafood, and vegetarian dishes (or combinations thereof), but it's the sushi—just about the best in the area—that draws most people. **FYI:** Reservations recommended. Karaoke. Children's menu. Beer and wine only. No smoking. **Open:** Lunch Mon–Fri 11:30am–2pm; dinner Sun–Fri 5–10pm, Sat 5pm–midnight. **Prices:** Main courses $10–$20. AE, MC, V.

$ Tom's Tavern
In Pearl St Mall, 1047 Pearl St; tel 303/443-3893. Just W of 11th St. **American/Burgers.** A mainstay in downtown Boulder since 1957, this typical tavern has a large bar and booths, and serves lots of burgers and sandwiches, plus a few dinner and barbecue platters. **FYI:** Reservations not accepted. Children's menu. No smoking. **Open:** Mon–Sat 11am–midnight, Sun 1–9:30pm. **Prices:** Main courses $5–$10. AE, CB, DC, DISC, MC, V.

Walnut Brewery
1123 Walnut St; tel 303/447-1345. 1 block S of Pearl St and 1 block W of Broadway. **Continental.** Within walking distance of downtown shops, this pub has lofty ceilings with exposed steel beams, booth and table seating, and plants atop the wooden dividers. The central feature is the brewing kettles and tanks above and behind the bar. In addition to the usual pub fare, menu items include smoked salmon fish-and-chips, unusual pastas, a mesquite-grilled chicken sandwich, and polenta with grilled zucchini. There are generally six microbrewed beers on tap. **FYI:** Reservations accepted. Blues/guitar/jazz. Children's menu. No smoking. **Open:** Sun–Thurs 11am–11pm, Fri–Sat 11am–midnight. **Prices:** Main courses $7–$18. AE, CB, DC, DISC, MC, V. ♿

ATTRACTIONS

University of Colorado at Boulder
Broadway and Baseline Rd; tel 303/492-6431. The largest university in the state, with 25,000 students on 786 acres. It's one of 12 universities with a NASA program. Visitor highlights include the CU Heritage Center; the University of Colorado Museum, which focuses on natural history; the Mary Rippon Outdoor Theatre, site of the annual Colorado Shakespeare Festival; the Fiske Planetarium and Science Center; and the Norlin Library, the largest research library in the state, with extensive holdings of American and English literature. Tours are available at the Laboratory for Atmospheric and Space Physics weekdays with at least one week's notice. **Open:** Mon–Fri 8am–5pm. **Free**

National Center for Atmospheric Research
1850 Table Mesa Dr; tel 303/497-1174. In this I M Pei–designed building scientists study the greenhouse effect, wind shear, and ozone depletion. Satellites, weather balloons, interactive computer monitors, robots, and supercomputers are among the technological tools on display. There are seven hands-on weather-oriented exhibits from the San Francisco Exploratorium Museum, now on permanent display. The center also hosts a changing art exhibit. Guided tours held at noon and by appointment. **Open:** Mon–Fri 8am–5pm, Sat–Sun 9am–3pm. **Free**

Boulder Museum of History
1206 Euclid Ave; tel 303/449-3464. The 1899 Harbeck House contains a museum with a collection of over 25,000 artifacts, 111,000 photographs, and 486,000 documents. Features include a Tiffany window on the stairway landing, a built-in buffet with leaded-glass doors, and hand-carved mantels throughout. The wardrobes in the upstairs bedrooms contain an extensive collection of Victorian and Edwardian clothing. **Open:** Tues–Sun noon–4pm. **$**

Leaning Tree Museum of Western Art
6055 Longbow Dr; tel 303/530-1442. Upstairs in the corporate headquarters of the world's largest publisher of western-art greeting cards is a collection of 200 original paintings and 75 bronze sculptures by contemporary artists. Represented are award-winning pieces from the National Academy of Western Art and Cowboy Artists of America. Many of the works have been reproduced on the company's greeting cards, for sale in the downstairs shop. **Open:** Mon–Fri 8am–4:30pm, Sat 10am–4pm. **Free**

Celestial Seasonings
4600 Sleepytime Dr; tel 303/581-1202. The company, which began in a Boulder garage in the 1970s, now produces more than 50 varieties of teas from more than 100 different herbs and spices, imported from 35 foreign countries. Visitors are invited to "see, taste, and smell the world of Celestial Seasonings" as they move from a consumer taste test in the lobby to marketing displays and into the production plant where the milling, mixing, packaging, and shipping takes place. The "mint room" is one of the highlights. Tours, which last one hour, are an experience for the senses. **Open:** Mon–Sat 10am–3pm. **Free**

Rockies Brewing Co
2880 Wilderness Pl; tel 303/444-8448. Visitors are led past copper vats that turn out 300 to 400 kegs of beer a day. The 25-minute tour of the microbrewery includes all steps from the grinding of the grain to the bottling of the beer, and ends with brew tastings. **Open:** Mon–Sat 11am–11pm. **Free**

Boulder Creek Path
55th St and Pearl Pkwy to Arapahoe Ave and Canyon Blvd; tel 303/441-3400. Following Boulder Creek, this nature corridor provides a nine-mile recreation area through the city and west into the mountains. The path hosts numerous walkers, runners, bicyclists, and in-line skaters. Visitors can see prairie dogs, Canadian geese, mallard ducks, spotted sandpipers, owls, and woodpeckers. At the Kids' Fishing Ponds children fish for free, keeping what they catch. The Whitewater Kayak Course has 20 slalom gates for kayakers and canoeists. **Open:** Daily 24 hours. **Free**

Chautauqua Park
9th St and Baseline Dr; tel 303/442-3282. During the late 19th and early 20th centuries more than 400 Chautauquas—adult education and cultural entertainment centers—sprang up around the United States. This 26-acre city park is one of the few remaining Chautauqua parks in the country. In summer, it hosts a wide-ranging program of music, dance, theater, and film, including the Colorado Music Festival. There are playgrounds, picnic grounds, tennis courts, and hiking trailheads. **Open:** Daily 24 hours. **Free**

Breckenridge

Many Victorian buildings remain from the late-19th-century boom days of gold and silver mining in this mountain community, perched 9,600 feet above sea level. Skiing, hiking, mountain biking, and fishing are some of the activities for which Breckenridge is known. It was here that a 13-pound, 7-ounce gold nugget—the largest ever found in Colorado—was uncovered in 1887. **Information:** Breckenridge Resort Chamber of Commerce, PO Box 1909, Breckenridge 80424 (tel 970/453-6018).

HOTELS

Breckenridge Resort Condominiums

465 4 O'Clock Rd, PO Box 2009, 80424; tel 970/453-2222 or toll free 800/525-2258; fax 970/453-0463. Near Quicksilver chair lift. These two complexes of privately owned condos are especially convenient for skiers and mountain bikers. **Rooms:** 67 cottages/villas. CI 4pm/CO 10am. Nonsmoking rms avail. **Amenities:** Cable TV, refrig, VCR. No A/C. All units w/terraces, all w/fireplaces, some w/whirlpools. Amenities vary from unit to unit; all units have steam showers. **Services:** Babysitting. **Facilities:** Whirlpool, washer/dryer. **Rates:** Peak (Dec 20–Mar) $170–$650 cottage/villa. Min stay. Lower rates off-season. Parking: Indoor, free. AE, DISC, MC, V.

River Mountain Lodge

100 S Park St, PO Box 1190, 80424; tel 970/453-4711 or toll free 800/627-3766. 4 blocks N of Quicksilver lift. Very modern, comfortable, and clean. Close to shopping, dining, and skiing. **Rooms:** 12 rms and effic. CI 4pm/CO 10am. Nonsmoking rms avail. **Amenities:** Cable TV, refrig, voice mail. No A/C. Some units w/terraces, some w/fireplaces, some w/whirlpools. Many rooms have laundry and cooking facilities. **Services:** Babysitting. **Facilities:** 96 1 restaurant, 1 bar (w/entertainment), sauna, steam rm, whirlpool. **Rates:** Peak (Mar 9–Mar 23/Dec 16–Jan 1) $109–$810 S or D; $169–$810 effic. Min stay. Lower rates off-season. Parking: Indoor, free. AE, CB, DC, DISC, MC, V.

The Village at Breckenridge

655 S Park St, PO Box 8329, 80424; tel 970/453-2000 or toll free 800/800-7829; fax 970/453-3116. At base of Peak 9. Perhaps the most conveniently located accommodations for skiers; guests have numerous dining and shopping choices both on the premises and nearby. **Rooms:** 350 rms. CI 4pm/CO 10am. Nonsmoking rms avail. Wide range of room sizes and luxuries. **Amenities:** Cable TV w/movies, voice mail. No A/C. Some units w/terraces, some w/fireplaces. **Services:** Car-rental desk, social director, children's program, babysitting. **Facilities:** 500 4 restaurants, 3 bars (2 w/entertainment), games rm, sauna, steam rm, whirlpool, beauty salon, day-care ctr, washer/dryer. **Rates:** Peak (Dec 16–Mar 23) $145–$620 S or D. Min stay. Lower rates off-season. Parking: Indoor, free. AE, CB, DC, DISC, MC, V.

INNS

Allaire Timbers Inn B&B

9511 CO 9, PO Box 4653, 80424; tel 970/453-7530 or toll free 800/624-4904; fax 970/453-8699. This attractive log and stone bed-and-breakfast is in a terrific location. Just a short walk along a meandering path through trees and fields to shopping, dining, and the ski lifts, it feels remote but is very accessible. Unsuitable for children under 13. **Rooms:** 10 rms. CI 3pm/CO 11am. No smoking. Rooms have fantastic views of ski area and town. **Amenities:** Voice mail, bathrobes. No A/C or TV. All units w/terraces, some w/fireplaces, some w/whirlpools. **Services:** Afternoon tea and wine/sherry served. **Facilities:** 30 Whirlpool, guest lounge w/TV. Ski storage and boot dryers available. **Rates (BB):** Peak (Dec 23–Mar) $180–$230 S or D. Min stay peak and special events. Lower rates off-season. Higher rates for special events/hols. Parking: Outdoor, free. AE, DISC, MC, V.

Little Mountain Lodge B&B

98 Sunbeam Dr, PO Box 2479, 80424; tel 970/453-1969 or toll free 800/468-7707; fax 970/453-1919. ½ mi E of Main St. 3 acres. Modern and spacious log-style inn tastefully decorated with western paintings and decor. Not far from the town and ski area. Unsuitable for children under 12. **Rooms:** 10 rms. CI 3pm/CO 11am. No smoking. Some have mountain views. **Amenities:** Cable TV w/movies, dataport, VCR, voice mail, bathrobes. No A/C. All units w/terraces, some w/fireplaces, some w/whirlpools. **Services:** Afternoon tea served. **Facilities:** 20 Games rm, whirlpool, guest lounge w/TV. Ski storage and boot dryer. **Rates (BB):** Peak (Dec 15–Jan 1) $185–$230 S or D. Min stay. Lower rates off-season. Higher rates for special events/hols. Parking: Outdoor, free. AE, MC, V.

RESTAURANTS

★ Breckenridge Brewery & Pub

600 S Main St; tel 970/453-1550. 3 blocks E of Quicksilver lift. **American/Pub.** A great place to relax after a day on the slopes, or a rough day shopping. Built around the rather large brewing paraphernalia, the main focus here is definitely the fresh beer, with the pleasant aroma of malt permeating the atmosphere. Such favorites as shepherd's pie and charbroiled fajitas, plus newer items such as Delmonico steak and Creole shrimp sauté, nicely complement the beer. **FYI:** Reservations not accepted. Blues/reggae/rock. Children's menu. No smoking. Additional location: 2220 Blake St, Denver (tel 303/297-3644). **Open:** Daily 11am–midnight. **Prices:** Main courses $6–$17. AE, DISC, MC, V.

Briar Rose Restaurant
109 E Lincoln St; tel 970/453-9948. Just E of Main St. **Seafood/Steak.** A fine dining establishment close to downtown, where a tone of sophistication and elegance is established with classical oil paintings and soft music. The adjoining lounge centers around a 100-year-old bar, and hunting trophies dot the walls. In addition to an array of steaks and seafood, the menu offers seasonal game (elk, moose, buffalo, caribou) and a few Italian dishes as well. Extensive wine list. **FYI:** Reservations recommended. Comedy/country music/guitar. Children's menu. No smoking. **Open:** Peak (Dec 15–Apr 15) daily 5–10pm. **Prices:** Main courses $15–$28. AE, DISC, MC, V.

Hearthstone Casual Dining
130 S Ridge St; tel 970/453-1148. **Seafood/Steak.** Simple yet elegant dining in a nice old Victorian building with white trim, a wrought-iron fence, and a fine view of the mountain. Steak, seafood, pasta, and vegetarian dishes are all prepared with a regional twist. Chicken Santa Fe is chicken breast served on a bed of tortilla strips and smothered in a garlic and chipotle pepper sauce; one version of the filet mignon arrives topped with crabmeat and béarnaise sauce. **FYI:** Reservations recommended. Children's menu. No smoking. **Open:** Daily 5pm–closing. **Prices:** Main courses $11–$25. AE, MC, V.

Horseshoe II Restaurant
115 S Main St; tel 970/453-7463. 2 blocks S of information center. **American.** Located in the heart of downtown in a historic 1880s building. The atmosphere in the parlorlike dining room is casual yet refined. Traditional fare, served all day long, includes items like chicken-fried steak, teriyaki steak, and charbroiled tuna. **FYI:** Reservations accepted. Children's menu. No smoking. **Open:** Peak (Nov 20–Apr 20) daily 7:30am–10pm. Closed Apr 25–May 25. **Prices:** Main courses $6–$18. AE, MC, V.

Mi Casa
600 Park Ave; tel 970/453-2071. Just N of The Village at Breckenridge. **Mexican.** Centrally located near the Quicksilver ski lift, this restaurant serves up traditional Mexican fare and is very popular for its happy hour and margaritas. The adobe and tile decor lends a festive atmosphere; one dining area, on a lower level, overlooks the river. **FYI:** Reservations not accepted. Children's menu. No smoking. **Open:** Peak (Dec–Apr) daily 11:30am–10pm. **Prices:** Main courses $8–$14. AE, MC, V.

Poirrier's Cajun Cafe
In Reliance Place, 224 S Main St; tel 970/453-1877. 2 blocks S of stop light. **Cajun/Creole.** Close to both downtown shopping and ski lifts, this brownstone restaurant has everything Cajun, from music to decor to terrific, flavorful food. For lunch, try one of the po'boy or muffuletta sandwiches, or New Orleans–style red beans and rice. Dinner specials include catfish fillet with crayfish étoufée, rib eye steak, and blackened fresh fish. And you probably won't want to miss the award-winning Lafayette bread pudding. **FYI:** Reservations accepted. Children's menu. No smoking. **Open:** Peak (Nov 15–Apr 15) lunch daily 11:30am–2:30pm; dinner daily 5:30–10pm. **Prices:** Main courses $13–$20. AE, CB, DC, DISC, MC, V.

ATTRACTIONS

Breckenridge National Historic District
105 W Adams Ave; tel 970/453-9022. The entire Victorian core of this 19th-century mining town has been carefully preserved. Colorfully painted shops and restaurants occupy the old businesses and homes, most of which date from the 1880s and 1890s. The main historic district focuses on Main St, and extends east on either side of Lincoln Ave. Among the 254 buildings in the district are the 1875 Edwin Carter Museum, 200 E Lincoln Ave; and the 1896 William Harrison Briggle House, 104 N Harris St, which houses the historical society's decorative-arts museum. The Summit Historical Society conducts guided two-hour walking tours from the Breckenridge Activity Center. **Open:** Tours: June–Aug, Mon–Sat 10am–4pm. **$**

Country Boy Mine
542 French Gulch Rd; tel 970/453-4405. The 100-year-old Country Boy Mine descends 1,000 feet underground. Visitors may gold pan in Eureka Creek and explore the mining exhibit and the five-story 75-year-old mill. Guided tours interpret the daily life and routine of a miner. **Open:** Daily 10am–5pm. **$$$$**

Amaze N Breckenridge
710 S Main St; tel 970/453-7262. Colorado's largest human maze, this two-level labyrinth of twists and turns offers prizes to participants who can "beat the clock." The maze is constructed in such a way that it can be easily changed, which the proprietors do weekly to maintain interest for repeat customers. The maze is quiet, clean, and wheelchair accessible. **Open:** Mem Day–Sept, call for schedule. **$$**

Brush

See Fort Morgan

Buena Vista

Spectacular views of some of Colorado's tallest mountains—more than 14,000 feet—earned this town its name. Buena Vista is a popular base camp for hikers, fishermen, and whitewater rafters. **Information:** Buena Vista Commerce of Commerce, PO Box 2021, Buena Vista 81211 (tel 719/395-6612 or 800/831-8594).

MOTELS

Alpine Lodge
12845 US 24, 81211; tel 719/395-2415. 1 mi E of US 285. Simple, no-frills motel with great views of Mount Princeton. **Rooms:** 20 rms and stes. CI open/CO 10am. Nonsmoking rms avail. **Amenities:** A/C, TV. **Services:** **Facilities:** **Rates:** Peak (May 15–Sept) $37–$70 S or D; $70 ste. Extra person $5. Lower rates off-season. Parking: Outdoor, free. AE, MC, V.

Super 8 Buena Vista
530 N US 24, 81211; tel 719/395-8888 or toll free 800/800-8000; fax 719/395-4090. ½ mi N of Chamber of Commerce. Modern, adobe-style motel within walking distance of town. **Rooms:** 38 rms. CI 1pm/CO 10am. Nonsmoking rms avail. Ground-floor rooms have both inside and outside entrances. Rooms on west side have great views of Collegiate Peaks. **Amenities:** A/C, cable TV w/movies, dataport. **Services:** **Facilities:** Whirlpool, washer/dryer. **Rates:** Peak (June–Oct 15) $69–$79 S or D. Extra person $5. Lower rates off-season. Parking: Outdoor, free. AE, CB, DC, DISC, MC, V.

Burlington

A wheat farming center located far out on Colorado's eastern plains, Burlington was established along a railroad line in the 1880s. The largest community in east-central Colorado, it has preserved its western heritage in its impressive Old Town district, where an old-west Christmas celebration is held every year. **Information:** Burlington Chamber of Commerce, 480 15th St, Burlington 80807 (tel 719/346-8070).

MOTELS

Burlington Inn
450 S Lincoln St, 80807; tel 719/346-5555; fax 719/346-5555. Just N of exit 437 off I-70. Convenient, basic motel with a friendly atmosphere. **Rooms:** 112 rms and stes. CI open/CO 11am. Nonsmoking rms avail. Rooms are spacious. **Amenities:** A/C, cable TV. **Services:** **Facilities:** 1 restaurant, 1 bar (w/entertainment). The Arena is a very large ballroom/meeting room used for dances, parties, and meetings. **Rates:** Peak (June–Sept 15) $36 S; $46 D; $51 ste. Extra person $5. Children under age 16 stay free. Lower rates off-season. Parking: Outdoor, free. AE, CB, DC, DISC, MC, V.

Sloan's Motel
1901 Rose Ave, 80807; tel 719/346-5333; fax 719/346-9536. ½ mi NE of exit 437 off I-70. Simple, no-frills motel that strives to meet the needs of travelers with disabilities. **Rooms:** 27 rms. CI open/CO 10:30am. Nonsmoking rms avail. **Amenities:** A/C, cable TV, voice mail. **Services:** Babysitting. **Facilities:** Playground. **Rates:** Peak (May–Sept) $29–$36 S; $30–$38 D. Extra person $4. Children under age 12 stay free. Lower rates off-season. Parking: Outdoor, free. AE, CB, DC, DISC, MC, V.

RESTAURANT

Mr A's Interstate House Restaurant
415 S Lincoln St; tel 719/346-8010. Just N of I-70. **American/Mexican.** A homey diner/truck stop serving standard Mexican and American fare, great as a quick stop for filling up both you and the car. Favorites are pork chops, chicken-fried steak, ground beef steak, and broiled or fried chicken; spaghetti is a specialty. **FYI:** Reservations accepted. Children's menu. No liquor license. No smoking. **Open:** Peak (June–Aug) daily 6am–10pm. **Prices:** Main courses $3–$15. AE, DC, DISC, MC, V.

ATTRACTIONS

Old Town
420 S 14th St; tel 719/346-7382. Close to two dozen turn-of-the-century-style old-west buildings make up this living-history museum, where visitors witness a gunfight, melodrama, or a can-can show in the Longhorn Saloon (summer months only). All furnished with turn-of-the-century artifacts, the buildings include a blacksmith shop, bank, law office, newspaper office, operating print shop, general store, schoolhouse, barn, and 1889 depot. Belgian draft horses pull the "Old Town Express" through the village, and special events and celebrations are scheduled throughout the year. **Open:** Mon–Sat 9am–6pm, Sun noon–6pm. **$$**

Kit Carson County Carousel
County Fairgrounds, 15th St at Colorado Ave; tel 719/346-8070. Carved in 1905 by the Philadelphia Toboggan Company, the carousel has been fully restored and is fully operational. It is one of the few wooden ones left in America that still wears its original coat of paint. The 46 stationary animals—mostly horses but also giraffes, zebras, camels, a hippocampus (sea horse), lion, tiger, and others—march counterclockwise around three tiers of oil paintings. A Wurlitzer Monster Military Band Organ, one of only two of that size and vintage in operation today, provides the music. **Open:** Mem Day–Labor Day, daily 1–8pm. **$**

Cañon City

Classic western scenery has attracted tourists to Cañon City since the late 1800s. Silent movie star Tom Mix launched his Hollywood career here, and the 1962 Oscar-winner *How the West Was Won* was filmed in the area. **Information:** Cañon City Chamber of Commerce, PO Bin 749, Cañon City 81215 (tel 719/275-2331 or 800/876-7922).

HOTEL

Canon Inn
3075 E US 50, 81212; tel 719/275-8676; fax 719/275-8675. 2 mi E of downtown. The hotel of choice for actors and crews of several movie companies. **Rooms:** 152 rms and stes. CI 3pm/CO 11am. Nonsmoking rms avail. **Amenities:** A/C, cable TV w/movies. **Services:** **Facilities:** 350 2 restaurants, 1 bar, games rm, whirlpool, washer/dryer. Lush indoor atrium houses six hot tubs, each secluded among large tropical plants. **Rates:** Peak (May 25–Sept 5) $85–$95 S; $80–$90 D; $125–$150 ste. Extra person $7. Children under age 12 stay free. Lower rates off-season. Parking: Outdoor, free. AE, CB, DC, DISC, MC, V.

ATTRACTIONS

Colorado Territorial Prison Museum
201 N 1st St; tel 719/269-3015. Housed in the state's former women's prison, just outside the walls of the original territorial prison opened in 1871, the museum contains an actual gas chamber, historic photos of life behind bars, confiscated inmates' weapons, the last hangman's noose used legally in the state, video programs, and other artifacts and exhibits. There's also a gift shop that sells arts and crafts made by inmates from the medium-security prison next door. **Open:** Peak (June–Aug) daily 8:30am–6pm. Reduced hours off-season. **$$**

Royal Gorge Country's Buckskin Joe Park and Railway
Royal Gorge Park; tel 719/275-5149. 8 mi W of Cañon City on US 50. An old-west town created from genuine 19th-century buildings relocated from around the state. Visitors can watch gunfights, pan for gold, see antique autos, and ride horseback or in a horse-drawn trolley. Train rides are available for a 30-minute trip to the Royal Gorge rim. **Open:** Daily 9am–6pm. **$$$$**

Colorado Springs

See also Manitou Springs

An exceptionally popular vacation destination at the base of 14,110-foot Pikes Peak, the growing city of Colorado Springs offers magnificent scenic beauty and vestiges of its old-west history. It is the site of the US Air Force Academy and attracts numerous military retirees; in recent years, the city has become a center for large nondenominational churches. Colorado Springs hosts the Pikes Peak Auto Hill Climb on the Fourth of July, the second-oldest auto race in America after the Indianapolis 500. **Information:** Colorado Springs Convention & Visitors Bureau, 104 S Cascade Ave, Suite 104, Colorado Springs 80903 (tel 719/635-7506 or 800/DO VISIT).

HOTELS

The Antlers Doubletree Hotel
4 S Cascade Ave, 80903; tel 719/473-5600 or toll free 800/222-8733; fax 719/444-0417. ½ block S of library. Large, modern hotel centrally located downtown with delicate marble floors and an elegant, contemporary decor. Spacious lobby offers plenty of comfortable, upholstered seating. **Rooms:** 290 rms and stes. CI 4pm/CO 11am. Nonsmoking rms avail. Tastefully decorated with wooden furniture and attractive details. West side rooms have great views of mountains; corner rooms are larger. **Amenities:** A/C, cable TV w/movies, voice mail. Some units w/terraces, some w/whirlpools. **Services:** Complimentary cookies at check-in. Guests can join hotel's Goldleaf frequent stay program. **Facilities:** 2000 2 restaurants, 2 bars (1 w/entertainment), whirlpool, beauty salon. **Rates:** Peak (May–Oct) $125–$180 S or D; $300–$700 ste. Extra person $10. Children under age 18 stay free. Lower rates off-season. Parking: Indoor, $5/day. AE, CB, DC, DISC, EC, ER, JCB, MC, V.

Colorado Springs Marriott
5580 Tech Center Dr, 80919; tel 719/260-1800 or toll free 800/962-6982; fax 719/260-1492. ½ mi W of exit 147 off I-25. Perched atop a bluff west of I-25, this large hotel offers a commanding view of the surrounding area. Clean, modern, and well maintained. **Rooms:** 310 rms and stes. CI 3pm/CO noon. Nonsmoking rms avail. Spectacular views of the mountains and in particular Pikes Peak. Rooms specially set up for business travelers are available. **Amenities:** A/C, cable TV w/movies, dataport, voice mail. Ironing board. **Services:** VP Babysitting. **Facilities:** 700 1 restaurant, 1 bar, sauna, whirlpool, washer/dryer. **Rates:** Peak (May 18–Oct 15) $109–$135 S or D; $149–$230 ste. Extra person $15. Children under age 18 stay free. Min stay special events. Lower rates off-season. Parking: Outdoor, free. AE, CB, DC, DISC, ER, JCB, MC, V.

UNRATED **Embassy Suites**
7290 Commerce Center Dr, 80919; tel 719/599-9100 or toll free 800/EMBASSY; fax 719/599-4644. Just N of exit 149 off I-25. A large atrium housing leafy palms, flowering plants, and an artificial stream (home to trout and goldfish) make this a unique and interesting accommodation. **Rooms:** 207 stes. CI 3pm/CO noon. Nonsmoking rms avail. **Amenities:** A/C, satel TV w/movies, refrig, dataport. All units w/terraces. Nintendo; ironing board. **Services:** Car-rental desk. Complimentary cocktails 5:30–7:30pm daily. Complimentary newspapers. **Facilities:** 250 1 restaurant (lunch and dinner only), 1 bar (w/entertainment), games rm, sauna, whirlpool, washer/dryer. **Rates (BB):** Peak (May 15–Sept 15) $129–$139 ste. Extra person $10. Children under age 12 stay free. Lower rates off-season. Parking: Outdoor, free. AE, CB, DC, DISC, MC, V.

Red Lion Hotel
1775 E Cheyenne Mountain Blvd, 80906; tel 719/576-8900 or toll free 800/RED-LION; fax 719/576-4450. Just W of exit 138 off I-25. Large outdoor courtyard is a signature of this modern hotel. **Rooms:** 299 rms and stes. CI 3pm/CO noon. Nonsmoking rms avail. Rooms considerably larger than most hotel rooms, and have double vanities. Many have nice views of mountains and Pikes Peak. **Amenities:** A/C, cable TV w/movies, dataport. All units w/terraces, some w/whirlpools. Ironing board. **Services:** **Facilities:** 1440 1 restaurant, 2 bars (1 w/entertainment), sauna, whirlpool. **Rates:** Peak (May 15–Oct) $119–$139 S; $134–$154 D; $375–$455 ste. Extra person $15. Children under age 19 stay free. Min stay special events. Lower rates off-season. Parking: Outdoor, free. AE, CB, DC, DISC, MC, V.

Residence Inn
3880 N Academy Blvd, 80917; tel 719/574-0370 or toll free 800/331-3131; fax 719/574-7821. ½ mi S of jct Austin Bluffs Pkwy. Great for families or extended stays. **Rooms:** 96 stes. CI 3pm/CO noon. Nonsmoking rms avail. Apartment-style units are very spacious and modern. **Amenities:** A/C, satel TV w/movies, refrig, dataport. Some units w/terraces, all w/fireplaces. **Services:** Complimentary shuttle within five-mile radius; happy hour Mon–Thurs; grocery shopping. **Facilities:** 50 Basketball, volleyball, lawn games, whirlpool, playground, washer/dryer. **Rates (CP):** Peak (May–Oct) $85–$165 ste. Extra person $10. Children under age 17 stay free. Min stay peak, wknds, and special events. Lower rates off-season. Parking: Outdoor, free. AE, CB, DC, DISC, JCB, MC, V.

UNRATED **Sheraton Colorado Springs Hotel**
2886 S Circle Dr, 80906; tel 719/576-5900 or toll free 800/576-5470; fax 719/576-7695. Just E of exit 138 off I-25. Modern hotel convenient to I-25 and the airport. **Rooms:** 500 rms and stes. Executive level. CI 3pm/CO 11am. Nonsmoking rms avail. **Amenities:** A/C, cable TV w/movies, dataport. Some units w/minibars, some w/terraces. **Services:** **Facilities:** 2 1700 2 restaurants, 1 bar (w/entertainment), games rm, sauna, whirlpool, playground. One of the three ballrooms has view of Pikes Peak. **Rates:** Peak (May–Sept) $88–$155 S or D; $310–$515 ste. Extra person $10. Children under age 18 stay free. Lower rates off-season. Parking: Outdoor, free. AE, CB, DC, DISC, MC, V.

MOTELS

Academy Inn
8280 CO 83, 80920; tel 719/598-6700; fax 719/598-3113. Just E of exit 150 off I-25. Just off I-25, convenient to Air Force Academy and nearby shopping. **Rooms:** 112 rms. CI 3pm/CO 11am. Nonsmoking rms avail. **Amenities:** A/C, cable TV w/movies, voice mail. Some units w/terraces, some w/whirlpools. **Services:** **Facilities:** 35 **Rates (CP):** Peak (May–Sept) $65–$70 S; $75–$80 D. Extra person $5. Children under age 18 stay free. Lower rates off-season. Parking: Outdoor, free. AE, CB, DC, DISC, MC, V.

Amarillo Motel
2801 W Colorado Ave, 80904; tel 719/635-8539 or toll free 800/216-8539; fax 719/473-2609. 2 blocks NW of jct 26th St. Clean, friendly, no-frills motel. Kitchenette units are good for families. **Rooms:** 30 rms and effic. CI 1pm/CO 11am. **Amenities:** A/C, cable TV, refrig. All units w/terraces. **Services:** **Facilities:** Washer/dryer. An antique and collectible shop within the motel offers eclectic collection of military memorabilia, firearms, stamps, coins, jewelry, and more. **Rates:** Peak (May 15–Sept 15) $30–$45 S or D; $30–$45 effic. Children under age 18 stay free. Lower rates off-season. Parking: Outdoor, free. MC, V.

Best Western Palmer House
3010 N Chestnut St, 80907; tel 719/636-5201 or toll free 800/223-9127; fax 719/636-3108. Just N of exit 145 off I-25. Clean, comfortable, and centrally located. **Rooms:** 150 rms. CI 3pm/CO 11am. Nonsmoking rms avail. All rooms have large bay windows. **Amenities:** Cable TV w/movies. No A/C. All units w/terraces. **Services:** **Facilities:** 125 1 restaurant, 1 bar. Putting green. **Rates:** Peak (May 16–Sept 15) $60–$85 S; $65–$95 D. Extra person $10. Children under age 18 stay free. Lower rates off-season. Parking: Outdoor, free. AE, CB, DC, DISC, MC, V.

Drury Inn
8155 N Academy Blvd, 80920; tel 719/589-2500 or toll free 800/325-8300; fax 719/589-2500. Just S of exit 150 off I-25. Basic accommodations with easy access to I-25 and Air Force Academy. **Rooms:** 118 rms. CI 3pm/CO noon. Nonsmoking rms avail. **Amenities:** A/C, cable TV w/movies, dataport. **Services:** Complimentary cocktails Mon–Thurs 5:30–7pm. **Facilities:** 50 Whirlpool, washer/dryer. **Rates (CP):** Peak (May 15–Sept 15) $74–$80 S; $84–$90 D. Extra person $10. Children under age 18 stay free. Lower rates off-season. Parking: Outdoor, free. AE, CB, DC, DISC, MC, V.

Garden of the Gods Motel
2922 W Colorado Ave, 80904; tel 719/636-5271 or toll free 800/637-0703. Just SE of jct 30th St. Modern, simple motel located near Old Colorado City and Garden of the Gods. **Rooms:** 32 rms; 2 cottages/villas. CI 2pm/CO 11am. Nonsmoking rms avail. **Amenities:** A/C, cable TV. All units w/terraces. **Services:** **Facilities:** Sauna. **Rates:** Peak (May 20–Sept 15) $50–$65 S; $70–$85 D; $99–$120 cottage/villa. Extra person $5. Children under age 16 stay free. Min stay special events. Lower rates off-season. Parking: Outdoor, free. AE, CB, DC, DISC, MC, V.

Quality Inn Garden of the Gods
555 W Garden of the Gods Rd, 80907; tel 719/593-9119 or toll free 800/221-2222; fax 719/260-0381. ¼ mi W of exit 146 off I-25. Modern yet homey motel very convenient to

I-25 and Garden of the Gods. **Rooms:** 157 rms. CI 4pm/CO 11am. Nonsmoking rms avail. Contemporary decor with comfortable seating. **Amenities:** A/C, cable TV w/movies. Some units w/terraces. **Services:** Complimentary coffee, tea, and juice 24 hours. Complimentary midnight snack. **Facilities:** 15 Washer/dryer. **Rates (CP):** Peak (May–Sept) $90–$140 S or D. Extra person $10. Children under age 18 stay free. Lower rates off-season. Parking: Outdoor, free. AE, CB, DC, DISC, MC, V.

Radisson Inn North

8110 N Academy Blvd, 80920; tel 719/598-5770 or toll free 800/333-3535; fax 719/598-3434. Just S of exit 150 off I-25. Modern motel at the north end of town, convenient to Air Force Academy. Spacious lobby atrium with fountains, large ficus trees, and pines. **Rooms:** 200 rms and stes. Executive level. CI 4pm/CO noon. Nonsmoking rms avail. **Amenities:** A/C, cable TV w/movies. Some units w/whirlpools. Iron and ironing board. **Services:** Car-rental desk. Complimentary shuttle service to nearby attractions. **Facilities:** 250 1 restaurant, 1 bar (w/entertainment), games rm, sauna, whirlpool, washer/dryer. Complimentary passes to Bally's Fitness Center. **Rates:** Peak (May–Sept) $80–$120 S or D; $149–$249 ste. Extra person $10. Children under age 18 stay free. Min stay special events. Lower rates off-season. Parking: Outdoor, free. AE, CB, DC, DISC, ER, JCB, MC, V.

Travel Inn

512 S Nevada, 80903; tel 719/636-3986; fax 719/636-3980. 2 blocks S of Pioneer Sq. Standard motel, with aqua trim. **Rooms:** 32 rms. CI open/CO 11am. Nonsmoking rms avail. **Amenities:** Cable TV. No A/C. All units w/terraces. **Services:** **Rates:** Peak (May–Oct) $47–$50 S; $50–$53 D. Extra person $5. Children under age 14 stay free. Lower rates off-season. Parking: Outdoor, free. AE, CB, DC, MC, V.

INNS

Hearthstone Inn

506 N Cascade Ave, 80903; tel 719/473-4413 or toll free 800/521-1885; fax 719/473-1322. 4½ blocks N of library. Two historic houses, one built in 1885 and the other in 1900, are connected by a carriage house; window frames, gables, pillars, and trim are painted in pinks, purples, and blues. Elegant, but no frills. Two front porches provide lovely space to sit and relax. **Rooms:** 25 rms and stes (2 w/shared bath). CI 2pm/CO 11am. No smoking. Rooms attractively decorated with period furnishings and wall hangings. **Amenities:** A/C. No phone or TV. Some units w/terraces, some w/fireplaces. **Services:** Afternoon tea served. **Facilities:** 40 Lawn games, guest lounge. **Rates (BB):** $62–$65 S or D w/shared bath, $78–$130 S or D w/private bath; $130–$148 ste. Extra person $15. Children under age 5 stay free. Min stay special events. Parking: Outdoor, free. AE, MC, V.

UNRATED **Holden House 1902 Bed & Breakfast**

1102 W Pikes Peak Ave, 80904; tel 719/471-3980. Near exit 141 off I-25. Tucked away from the heart of town, this inn is actually two adjacent historic homes carefully decorated with antiques and family heirlooms. Anyone allergic to cats should request the private and cat-free carriage house. Porches have swings. Unsuitable for children under 18. **Rooms:** 6 rms and stes. CI 4pm/CO 11am. No smoking. Rooms are named after Colorado mining towns. Suites have oversized bathtubs for two. **Amenities:** A/C, refrig, dataport. No TV. 1 unit w/terrace, some w/fireplaces. Bottled water in all rooms. **Services:** Afternoon tea served. Fax and copy services available for business guests. **Facilities:** Guest lounge w/TV. **Rates (BB):** $80 S or D; $105–$115 ste. Min stay peak and special events. Parking: Outdoor, free. AE, CB, DC, DISC, MC, V.

RESORT

The Broadmoor

Lake Ave, PO Box 1439, 80901-1439; tel 719/634-7711 or toll free 800/634-7711; fax 719/577-5700. Circle exit off I-25. 3,500 acres. A classic resort with the air of a grand hotel in the Alps, complete with art, antiques, and decorative ceilings. It dates from 1918, but constant updating has brought new attractions. Recently expanded today's Broadmoor is more a self-contained town than a country retreat—and highly prized by large groups of conventioneers. **Rooms:** 700 rms and stes. CI 4pm/CO noon. Nonsmoking rms avail. Rooms and suites are distributed throughout four buildings grouped around a small lake, with the larger rooms in the Broadmoor West wing, the most charming rooms in the original tower. Some rooms have mountain or fairway views, others overlook the parking lots. **Amenities:** A/C, cable TV w/movies, dataport, voice mail, in-rm safe, bathrobes. All units w/minibars, some w/terraces, some w/fireplaces, some w/whirlpools. Iron and ironing board. **Services:** VP Twice-daily maid svce, car-rental desk, masseur, children's program, babysitting. Service can sometimes be overwhelmed by the numbers. **Facilities:** 54 12 1200 9 restaurants (*see* "Restaurants" below), 6 bars (5 w/entertainment), spa, sauna, steam rm, whirlpool, beauty salon. If sports facilities were the sole yardstick, this would win the top rating: 54 holes of championship golf (walking allowed after 3pm), indoor and outdoor lap pools, mountain bikes, tennis courts headed by ex-champ Denis Ralston, paddleboats, and a spiffy new spa with 28 treatment rooms. Two business centers. Broadmoor Bee Bunch for kids includes outings to resort's zoo, wagon rides, nature walks, and tennis clinics. Most facilities (fitness center excepted) incur extra charge. **Rates:** Peak (May–Oct) $240–$355 S or D; $385–$1,950 ste. Children under age 18 stay free. Lower rates off-season. MAP rates avail. Parking: Outdoor, free. Automatic service charge of $12.50 per couple per night covers bellmen, maids, and valet parking, but not waiters. Special packages are worth looking into. AE, CB, DC, DISC, MC, V.

RESTAURANTS

Antonio's
301 Garden of the Gods Rd; tel 719/531-7177. Just E of exit 146 off I-25. **Italian.** The brightly lit interior, hanging plants, and lattice-work create a gardenlike atmosphere, while lead-ed-glass windows etched with grapevines plus a large mural add a touch of old Italy. There's an impressive selection of pasta, seafood, veal, and chicken dishes, plus specialties such as smoked salmon with green peppercorn sauce and baked California halibut with roasted garlic and a shrimp sauce. **FYI:** Reservations recommended. Opera. Children's menu. **Open:** Lunch Mon–Fri 11am–2pm; dinner daily 5–10pm. **Prices:** Main courses $9–$18. AE, CB, DC, DISC, MC, V.

Bon Ton's Cafe
In Old Colorado City, 2601 W Colorado Ave; tel 719/634-1007. At 26th St. **Cafe/Diner.** Bright, cheerful, and spacious inside, this cafe also has a large outdoor patio that's great for summer people watching. Breakfast is served all day, and there are a variety of sandwiches and special plates. Some of the paintings, which were done by local artists, are for sale. **FYI:** Reservations not accepted. Children's menu. **Open:** Mon–Wed 6:30am–3pm, Thurs–Sat 6:30am–9pm, Sun 8am–2pm. **Prices:** Lunch main courses $3–$6. AE, DISC, MC, V.

Charles Court
In The Broadmoor, Lake Ave; tel 719/634-7711. Circle exit off I-25. **New American/Continental.** Stylish, pleasant dining room in the resort's Broadmoor West wing, with large windows overlooking the lake and the new footbridge. Cuisine ranges from brown lentil and andouille soup to sautéed Colorado red trout fillet with Pernod cream sauce and grilled elk chop with onion risotto. Comprehensive wine list features 700 labels. **FYI:** Reservations recommended. Children's menu. **Open:** Breakfast daily 7–10:30am; dinner daily 6–9:30pm. **Prices:** Main courses $17–$34. AE, CB, DC, DISC, MC, V. VP

★ Corbett's
817 W Colorado Ave; tel 719/471-0004. Near exit 141 off I-25. **New American/International.** Located in a 1909 firehouse, this relatively small yet modern and elegant restaurant is tastefully decorated with photos, paintings, and ceramic art created by the chef's father. The menu, too, is elegant, with a number of unique dishes featuring unusual blends of fresh herbs and spices: mountain trout dredged in pistachios with dill butter; grilled portobello mushrooms served with wilted greens and garlic sauce. In addition to the extensive wine list, there are specialty microbrews available, plus regular wine, single-malt scotch, and even port tastings. **FYI:** Reservations recommended. Piano. No smoking. **Open:** Lunch Mon–Fri 11am–2pm; dinner Mon–Sat 5–10pm, Sun 5–9pm. **Prices:** Main courses $15–$28. AE, CB, DC, DISC, MC, V.

Dale Street Cafe
115 E Dale St; tel 719/578-9898. 2 blocks E of Fine Arts Center. **Italian.** This lively street-side cafe is modest but very welcoming and terrific for friendly conversation. All dishes are made from scratch with the freshest ingredients. Pastas and Mediterranean pizzas dominate the menu, but grilled choices such as barbecued shrimp, salmon, fresh trout, and chicken are also available. **FYI:** Reservations accepted. No smoking. **Open:** Mon–Thurs 11am–9pm, Fri–Sat 11am–9:30pm. **Prices:** Main courses $5–$11. MC, V.

Edelweiss Restaurant
34 E Ramona Ave; tel 719/633-2220. 4 blocks S of exit 140A off I-25. **Continental/German.** This quaint little Bavarian restaurant with a stone exterior has built its reputation on over 30 years of consistently good food. Try German specialties like jägerschnitzel and spiessbraten, or continental choices such as tournedos of beef and chicken provençale. **FYI:** Reservations accepted. Folk/guitar/accordian. Children's menu. No smoking. **Open:** Lunch Mon–Fri 11:30am–2pm; dinner Sun–Thurs 5–9pm, Fri–Sat 5–9:30pm. **Prices:** Main courses $8–$16. AE, CB, DC, DISC, MC, V.

Giuseppe's Old Depot Restaurant
In Old Depot Sq, 10 S Sierra Madre St; tel 719/635-3111. Just W of Antlers Park. **American/Italian.** Occupying the old Denver & Rio Grande train depot, this wonderfully large restaurant, which has been divided into more intimate areas, displays train travel memorabilia and photos on every inch of wall space. When a real train passes behind the restaurant, the pleasant sounds make it seem as though you're riding in an old Pullman dining car. The menu lists a wide range of standard Italian foods and stone-baked pizzas, plus such choices as chicken cordon bleu, shrimp Creole, and broiled twin lobster tails. **FYI:** Reservations accepted. Children's menu. **Open:** Sun–Thurs 11am–10pm, Fri–Sat 11am–midnight. **Prices:** Main courses $4–$20. AE, CB, DC, DISC, MC, V.

The Hungry Farmer
575 Garden of the Gods Rd; tel 719/598-7622. ¼ mi W of exit 146 off I-25. **American.** A true mainstay of the area for more than 20 years, this down-home family restaurant with farm decor (it sports bales of hay in season) is well known for its generous portions and its prime rib. The bar is encased in a library full of old books, and the sports lounge has inlaid wooden tables. Every entree includes "bottomless" soup, vegetable, salad, potato, homemade oatmeal muffins, and cinnamon rolls. And coffee brings with it a special sideshow called "high-pouring." **FYI:** Reservations recommended. Children's menu. **Open:** Lunch Mon–Fri 11:30am–2pm; dinner Mon–Sat 5–10pm, Sun noon–9pm. **Prices:** Main courses $8–$17. AE, CB, DC, DISC, MC, V.

La Petite Maison
1015 W Colorado Ave; tel 719/632-4887. Near exit 141 off I-25. **New American.** This small, beige and blue Victorian cottage houses an intimate, elegant restaurant offering very fine food and expert service. Recorded chamber music further enhances the delightful setting, a local favorite for celebrating special occasions. Dishes here are varied and unique, with many approved by the American Heart Association. Choices might include smoked salmon fettuccine with capers, dill, and a light cream sauce, or sautéed beef tenderloin with caramelized pearl onions. **FYI:** Reservations recommended. No smoking. **Open:** Tues–Sat 5–10pm. **Prices:** Main courses $15–$22. AE, CB, DC, DISC, MC, V.

The Margarita at Pine Creek
7350 Pine Creek Rd; tel 719/598-8667. ½ mi N of exit 149 off I-25. **Continental/Southwestern.** A small stucco restaurant with tile floors, tucked away among a little grove of pine trees. The interior is divided into smaller dining niches by angled and different-shaped walls, and decorated with plants and chile ristras. The prix fixe dinner includes appetizer, soup, salad, three choices of entrees with vegetable and fresh bread, plus dessert. Entrees are usually fresh fish, veal, steak, pasta, lamb, or duckling. A six-course Mexican dinner is offered Tues–Fri. **FYI:** Reservations recommended. Harpsichord. **Open:** Lunch Tues–Fri 11:30am–2pm; dinner Tues–Sat 6–8:30pm; brunch Sun 10:30am–1:30pm. **Prices:** Prix fixe $19–$23. AE, DISC, MC, V.

Meadow Muffins
In Old Colorado City, 2432 W Colorado Ave; tel 719/633-0583. Just NW of Bancroft Park. **Burgers.** Filled with an impressive blend of historic benches, bars, wagon wheels, and collectibles, this restaurant is part sports bar, part dance club, and part burger joint. Self-service lends a casual atmosphere. Burgers and sandwiches dominate the menu, with a few salads and lots of "munchies," but everything is well-prepared and reasonably priced. Look for the daily specials, which are even lighter on the wallet. Nightlife is lively and some of the best in town. **FYI:** Reservations accepted. Guitar. Children's menu. **Open:** Daily 11am–11pm. **Prices:** Main courses $3–$5. AE, DISC, MC, V.

Michelle's
122 N Tejon St; tel 719/633-5089. Just S of Acacia Park. **Cafe/Eclectic.** Animated Victorian scenes have been painted on the red walls of this restaurant, which also contains a gift and candy shop. The fare is standard but diverse, with everything from sandwiches and burgers to specialty salads and Greek favorites such as spanikopita and gyros. Three pages of the menu offer ice cream specialties, featuring hand-churned ice creams. For the truly adventuresome—and hungry—there's the 42-pound Believe It or Not Sundae, which includes every flavor Michelle's makes! **FYI:** Reservations not accepted. Children's menu. No liquor license. Additional location: Citadel Shopping Center (tel 597-9932). **Open:** Mon–Thurs 9am–11pm, Fri–Sat 9am–midnight, Sun 10am–11pm. **Prices:** Main courses $4–$7. AE, CB, DC, DISC, MC, V.

Phantom Canyon Brewing Co
2 E Pikes Peak Ave; tel 719/635-2800. ½ block S of library. **New American/Pub.** Located in the 1901 Cheyenne Building, this attractive brew pub has a lofty ceiling and wooden tables and trim. Beer may be the biggest draw, with five standard offerings always on tap and two seasonal specials, but the menu has some interesting and unusual items as well—like charbroiled top sirloin is stuffed with prosciutto and portobello mushrooms. Beer is an ingredient in many entrees, such as chipotle and porter-glazed pork tenderloin and beer-braised pot roast. Check out the fossils embedded in the stone slabs that make up the bar. **FYI:** Reservations accepted. Children's menu. **Open:** Mon–Thurs 11am–midnight, Fri–Sat 11am–2am, Sun 9am–midnight. **Prices:** Main courses $8–$14. AE, CB, DC, DISC, MC, V.

Steaksmith
In Maizeland Moors Centre, 3802 Maizeland Rd; tel 719/596-9300. Just N of jct Academy Blvd. **Seafood/Steak.** Well known in the area for its high-quality aged beef and fresh seafood (including Alaskan king crab and Australian lobster tails), this rustic restaurant offers top-notch food and service. A sign of its success, diners are warned that the prime rib and seafood specials often sell out early in the evening. Dessert specials might include caramel piñon nut ice cream. The restaurant features a rough-hewn wood interior accented with hand-carved panels. **FYI:** Reservations recommended. Children's menu. **Open:** Mon–Sat 5:30–10pm, Sun 4–9pm. **Prices:** Main courses $12–$35. AE, CB, DC, MC, V.

The Tavern
In The Broadmoor, 1 Lake Circle; tel 719/634-7711. At W end of Lake Ave. **Seafood/Steak.** A popular spot for late-night dining and entertainment. Each of the three dining rooms has its own atmosphere. The front room feels like a jazz bar, with original lithographs by Toulouse-Lautrec; the central Mayan Room is slightly darker, with hand-carved panels; and the rear Garden Room features a lush greenhouse atmosphere. Besides a wide range of steaks, the menu includes such items as cheese tortellini with breast of chicken and Mediterranean-style mahimahi. **FYI:** Reservations recommended. Jazz/piano/quartet. Children's menu. Dress code. **Open:** Lunch daily 11:30am–4pm; dinner daily 5–11pm. **Prices:** Main courses $10–$32. AE, CB, DC, DISC, MC, V. VP

ATTRACTIONS

MUSEUMS

Colorado Springs Fine Arts Center
30 W Dale St; tel 719/634-5581. Georgia O'Keeffe, John James Audubon, John Singer Sargent, Charles Russell, Albert Bierstadt, Nicolai Fechin, and other famed painters and

sculptors are represented in the permanent collection of the center's Taylor Museum for Southwestern Studies, which also includes a world-class collection of Native American and Hispanic works. There is a 450-seat performing arts theater, a 32,000-volume art research library, the Bemis Art School offering visual arts and drama classes, a tactile gallery for the blind, and a sculpture garden. Changing exhibits in the North and East Galleries showcase local collections, as well as touring international exhibits. **Open:** Tues–Fri 9am–5pm, Sat 10am–5pm, Sun 1–5pm. **$**

Colorado Springs Pioneers Museum
215 S Tejon St; tel 719/578-6650. Housed in the former El Paso County Courthouse (1903). Exhibits show the community's history including its beginning as a fashionable resort, the railroad and mining eras, and its growth and change into the 20th century. Visitors can ride an 80-plus-year-old Otis bird-cage elevator to the recently restored original courtroom, where several Perry Mason episodes were filmed. In addition, the museum contains the Victorian home and furnishings of writer Helen Hunt Jackson, several art galleries, a section on the history of African Americans in the region, plus Native American artifacts, turn-of-the-century toys, quilts, and clothing. **Open:** May–Sept, Tues–Sat 10am–5pm, Sun 1–5pm. **Free**

Western Museum of Mining and Industry
Exit 156A (Gleneagle Dr) off I-25; tel 719/488-0880. Historic hard-rock mining machinery and other equipment from Cripple Creek and other turn-of-the-century Colorado gold camps form the basis of this museum's 3,000-plus-item collection. There's an operating Corliss steam engine with a 17-ton flywheel, a life-size underground mine reconstruction, an actual 1890s mill, and an exhibit on mining-town life that shows how early western miners and their families lived. Visitors can also pan for gold and view an 18-minute multi-projector slide presentation on life in the early mining camps. **Open:** Mon–Sat 9am–4pm, Sun noon–4pm. **$$**

Peterson Air & Space Museum
Bldg 981, Peterson Air Force Base; tel 719/556-4915. Located 7 mi E of Colorado Springs. Through its exhibits this museum traces the history of Peterson Air Force Base, NORAD, the Air Defense Command, and Air Force Space Command. Of special interest are 17 historic aircraft, including P-47 Thunderbolt and P-40 Warhawk fighters from World War II, plus jets from the Korean War to the present. **Open:** Tues–Fri 8:30am–4:30pm, Sat 9:30am–4:30pm. **Free**

International Tesla Society
2220 E Bijou; tel 719/475-0918. Small but fascinating collection of early electronics and related gadgets. The museum's primary purpose is to display and demonstrate some of the many inventions of Nikola Tesla (1856–1943), who was awarded over 100 US patents and is credited with accidentally throwing all of Colorado Springs into darkness during one of his many experiments. Tesla, a contemporary of Thomas Edison's, perfected alternating current and invented the Tesla coil, a transformer used to produce high-frequency power. Guided tours. **Open:** Mon–Fri 10am–4pm, Sat 11am–4pm. **$$**

May Natural History Museum of the Tropics
710 Rock Creek Canyon; tel 719/576-0450 or toll free 800/666-3841. Located 4 mi S of the Colorado Springs city limits. One of the world's outstanding collections of giant insects and other tropical invertebrates is presented at this museum. James F May (1884–1956) spent more than a half-century exploring the world's jungles while compiling this illustrious collection of some 7,000 arthropods. **Open:** May–Oct, daily 8am–8pm. **$$**

Money Museum of the American Numismatic Association
818 N Cascade Ave; tel 719/632-2646. The largest collection of its kind west of the Smithsonian Institute consists of eight galleries of coins, tokens, medals, and paper money from around the world. There is also a collectors' library, a gallery for the visually impaired, and an authentication department. **Open:** Mon–Fri 8:30am–4pm. **Free**

Pro Rodeo Hall of Fame
101 Pro Rodeo Dr; tel 719/528-4764. Rodeo's development, from its origins in early ranch work to its evolution into a major professional sport, is featured in two multimedia presentations. Heritage Hall showcases cowboy and rodeo gear and clothing, and rodeo greats are honored in the Hall of Champions. The museum also displays western art and has a replica rodeo arena and live rodeo animals. **Open:** Daily 9am–5pm. **$$$**

World Figure Skating Museum and Hall of Fame
20 1st St; tel 719/635-5200. Said to be the only museum of its kind in the world, this is where visitors can see 1,200 years of ice skates, from early skates of bone to highly decorated cast-iron examples. There are skating costumes, medals, and other memorabilia; changing exhibits; films; a library; and a gift shop. A gallery exhibits skating-related paintings, including works by 17th-century Dutch artist Pieter Brueghel and Americans Winslow Homer and Andy Warhol. **Open:** Peak (June–Aug) Mon–Sat 10am–4pm. Reduced hours off-season. **Free**

HISTORIC BUILDINGS AND HOMES

McAllister House Museum
423 N Cascade Ave; tel 719/635-7925. This Gothic cottage, listed in the National Register of Historic Places, was constructed of brick in 1873 when the builder, an army major named Henry McAllister, learned that the local wind was of such force as to have blown a train off the tracks nearby. It contains many original furnishings, including three marble fireplaces. The house is now owned by the Colonial Dames of America, whose knowledgeable volunteers lead guided tours. **Open:** Peak (May–Aug) Wed–Sat 10am–4pm, Sun noon–4pm. Reduced hours off-season. **$**

Rock Ledge Ranch Historic Site
Gateway Rd; tel 719/578-6777. The history of three different pioneer eras comes to life at this living history farm at the east entrance to Garden of the Gods Park. Visitors can see how Coloradans lived during the homestead era (1867–1874), the working farm era (1874–1900), and the estate period (1900–1909). Guides in period clothing; working blacksmith shop; demonstrations of historical agricultural techniques; horse-drawn wagon rides. **Open:** June–Labor Day, Wed–Sun 10am–5pm. Reduced hours off-season. **$**

Ghost Town Museum
US 24 and 21st St; tel 719/634-0696. Comprised of authentic 19th-century buildings relocated from other parts of Colorado, this "town" is out of the elements and under cover in Old Colorado City. There's a sheriff's office, jail, saloon, general store, livery stable, blacksmith shop, rooming house, assayer's office, and more. Animated frontier characters tell stories of the Old West, while a shooting gallery, antique arcade machines, and nickelodeons provide additional entertainment. The Taming of the West Theater presents a short film on frontier ghost towns. **Open:** Peak (Mem Day–Labor Day) Mon–Sat 9am–6pm, Sun noon–6pm. Reduced hours off-season. **$$**

PARKS AND GARDENS

Monument Valley Park
170 W Cache La Poudre; tel 719/578-6640. This long, slender park follows Monument Creek through downtown Colorado Springs. At its south end are formal zinnia, begonia, and rose gardens, and in the middle are demonstration gardens of the Horticultural Art Society. There are softball/baseball fields, a swimming pool, volleyball and tennis courts, children's playgrounds, picnic shelters, and two trails—the 4¼-mile Monument Creek Trail for walkers, runners, and cyclists, and the one-mile Monument Valley Fitness Trail at the north end of the park, beside Bodington Field. **Open:** Peak (May–Oct) daily 5am–11pm. **Free**

Garden of the Gods
Exit 146 off I-25, Ridge Rd; tel 719/578-6933. One of the West's most unique geological sites, the park is a giant rock garden composed of red sandstone cliffs sculpted by rain and wind over millions of years. Hiking maps to the 1,300-acre, city-run park are available at the Visitor Center, which also offers an eight-minute geology show, displays on the history, geology, plants, and wildlife of the park, a cafeteria, and other conveniences. In summer park naturalists host 45-minute walks through the park and afternoon interpretive programs (call for schedules). **Open:** Peak (May–Oct) daily 5am–11pm. Reduced hours off-season. **Free**

North Cheyenne Cañon Park
2110 N Cheyenne Cañon Rd; tel 719/578-6640. Entirely within the city limits of Colorado Springs, this city park includes North Cheyenne Creek, which drops 1,800 feet in five miles in a series of cascades and waterfalls. There are picnic areas and hiking trails and a seasonal tram, while a visitor center at the foot of Helen Hunt Falls has exhibits on history, geology, flora, and fauna. The Starsmore Discovery Center, at the entrance to the park, has maps, information, tram tickets (fee), and interactive exhibits including audiovisual programs and a climbing wall. **Open:** Peak (May–Oct) daily 5am–11pm. Reduced hours off-season. **Free**

Seven Falls
South Cheyenne Cañon; tel 719/632-0752. A spectacular one-mile drive through a box canyon, through the Pillars of Hercules where the canyon narrows to just 42 feet, climaxes at these cascading falls. Seven separate waterfalls dance down a granite cliff illuminated during the summer months by colored lights. An elevator takes visitors to the Eagle Nest viewing platform. A mile-long trail atop the plateau passes the grave of 19th-century author Helen Hunt Jackson (*Ramona*) and ends at a panoramic view of Colorado Springs. **Open:** Peak (June–Aug) daily 8am–11pm. Reduced hours off-season. **$$$**

Palmer Park
3650 Maizeland Rd; tel 719/578-6640. Deeded to the city in 1899 by its founder, Gen William Jackson Palmer, this 722-acre preserve features hiking, biking, and horseback riding across a mesa overlooking the city. It boasts a variety of minerals (including quartz, topaz, jasper, and tourmaline), a rich vegetation (including a yucca preservation area), and considerable wildlife. The Edna Mae Bennet Nature Trail is a self-guided excursion; there are numerous other trails, including those shared with riders from the adjoining Mark Reyner Stables. The park also includes 12 separate picnic areas, softball/baseball fields, and volleyball courts. **Open:** Peak (May–Oct) daily 5am–11pm. Reduced hours off-season. **Free**

Cheyenne Mountain Zoo
Cheyenne Mountain Zoo Rd; tel 719/633-9925. The country's only mountain zoo, located 6,800 feet above sea level. Animals, many in "natural" environments, include Siberian tigers, lions, black leopards, elephants, hippos, otters, monkeys, giraffes, reptiles, and a variety of birds. Rocky cliffs have been created for the mountain goats; a pebbled beach for penguins; and a petting zoo for children. Three Mexican gray wolves—members of an endangered species—are at home in a mountainside "wolf woods." The zoo also has a colorful antique carousel. **Open:** Peak (June–Aug) daily 9am–6pm. Reduced hours off-season. **$$$**

OTHER ATTRACTIONS

United States Olympic Complex
1 Olympic Plaza, corner of Boulder St and Union Blvd; tel 719/578-4618. This 36-acre site houses a training center for Olympic sports, including swimming, basketball, and gymnastics, providing a training ground for some 17,000 athletes each year. The Visitor Center offers a guided tour starting every 30 minutes in summer and every hour during the

winter. Tours begin with a film on the US Olympic effort, and then take in the Sports Center with five gymnasiums and a weight-training room; Indoor Shooting Center with two 50-meter ranges; a new training gymnasium; and a swimming complex with a 50-meter 10-lane pool. **Open:** Peak (June–Aug) Mon–Sat 9am–5pm, Sun 10am–4pm. Reduced hours off-season. **Free**

United States Air Force Academy
Exit 156B off I-25; tel 719/472-2555. In 1954 Congress authorized the establishment of a US Air Force Academy and selected this 18,000-acre site—on a broad mesa buffered on the west by the Rockies—from among 400 other locations. Visitors can see an extensive outdoor B-52 bomber display; the Thunderbird Airmanship Overlook, where Thunderbirds cadets parachute, soar, and practice their takeoffs and landings; and the Parade Ground, where cadets can be spotted marching. The visitors center has a variety of exhibits and films on academy history and cadet life, extensive literature and self-guided tour maps, and the latest information and schedules on academy activities. **Open:** Daily 9am–5pm. **Free**

Pikes Peak Highway
PO Box 1575-MC # 451; tel 719/684-9383. There is perhaps no view in Colorado to equal that from the summit of Pikes Peak. Whether by cog railway or private vehicle, the ascent is a spectacular and exciting experience, although not for those with heart problems or a fear of heights. This 19-mile toll highway (paved for 7 miles, all-weather gravel thereafter) starts at 7,400 feet, some 4 miles west of Manitou Springs, and culminates at the 14,110-foot summit of the mountain. From the top, visitors have a spectacular 360° panoramic view of Colorado. There are numerous photo stops en route up the mountain, and restaurant/gift shops at the 11-mile point and the summit. Deer, mountain sheep, and other animals can often be seen on the slopes, especially above timberline (around 11,500 feet). **Open:** Peak (June–Aug) daily 7am–7pm. Reduced hours off-season. **$$**

Copper Mountain

See Frisco

Cortez

Settled in the late 1800s as a trade center for area ranchers, Cortez has become a base camp for visitors to numerous prehistoric Anasazi ruins. **Information:** Cortez Chamber of Commerce, PO Box 968, Cortez 81321 (tel 970/565-3414).

MOTELS

Anasazi Motor Inn
640 S Broadway, 81321; tel 970/565-3773 or toll free 800/972-6232; fax 970/565-1027. ½ mi S of jct US 160/US 666. Two-story, beige structure with a large, colorful Native American mural on one wall. **Rooms:** 87 rms. CI 2pm/CO noon. Nonsmoking rms avail. Rooms are clean, comfortable, and brightly decorated. **Amenities:** A/C, cable TV w/movies. All units w/terraces. **Services:** **Facilities:** 328 1 restaurant, 1 bar (w/entertainment), whirlpool. **Rates:** Peak (June–Sept) $55 S; $69 D. Extra person $6. Children under age 18 stay free. Lower rates off-season. Parking: Outdoor, free. AE, CB, DC, DISC, MC, V.

Arrow Motel
440 S Broadway, 81321; tel 970/565-7778 or toll free 800/727-7692; fax 970/565-7214. ¼ mi S of jct US 160/US 666. Nicely secluded, set back from the road. **Rooms:** 30 rms. CI 2pm/CO 11am. Nonsmoking rms avail. Some bathrooms have tubs. **Amenities:** A/C, cable TV. All units w/terraces. Some rooms have microwaves, refrigerators. **Services:** **Facilities:** Whirlpool, washer/dryer. **Rates:** Peak (May 23–Sept 3) $49–$58 S or D. Extra person $4. Children under age 12 stay free. Lower rates off-season. Parking: Outdoor, free. AE, CB, DC, DISC, MC, V.

Holiday Inn Express
2121 E Main St, 81321; tel 970/565-6000 or toll free 800/626-5652; fax 970/565-3438. ¾ mi E of Cortez Park. This modern motel is adobe-style with a red tile roof and has attractive views of Ute Mountain and Mesa Verde National Park. **Rooms:** 100 rms and stes. CI 3pm/CO 11am. Nonsmoking rms avail. **Amenities:** A/C, cable TV w/movies, dataport. Some units w/whirlpools. **Services:** Social director, children's program, babysitting. Friendly and helpful staff. **Facilities:** 200 1 bar (w/entertainment), sauna, whirlpool. **Rates (CP):** Peak (May 15–Sept 30) $90 S; $96 D; $125 ste. Extra person $6. Children under age 18 stay free. Lower rates off-season. Parking: Outdoor, free. AE, CB, DC, DISC, JCB, MC, V.

Ramada Limited
2020 E Main St, 81321; tel 970/565-3474 or toll free 800/272-6232; fax 970/565-0923. ¾ mi E of Cortez Park. Relatively large, modern, brick motel. **Rooms:** 70 rms. CI open/CO noon. Nonsmoking rms avail. **Amenities:** A/C, cable TV w/movies. All units w/terraces. **Services:** VCRs and video cassettes for rent. Friendly service. **Facilities:** Whirlpool, washer/dryer. **Rates (CP):** Peak (June 15–Sept 30) $65–$75 S; $75–$90 D. Extra person $5. Children under age 18 stay free. Lower rates off-season. Parking: Outdoor, free. AE, CB, DC, DISC, EC, MC, V.

RESTAURANTS

Homesteader's Restaurant
45 E Main St; tel 970/565-6253. 6 blocks W of Cortez Park. **American/Steak.** Entering this restaurant is like walking into a lofty barn after a hayride, an ambience reinforced by the license plates and implement relics nailed to the rafters. The fare is traditional, featuring hamburgers, steaks, and fried chicken. Try a teri-mushroom burger, chicken-fried steak, or

a Mexican plate. **FYI:** Reservations accepted. Guitar. Children's menu. **Open:** Breakfast Mon–Sat 7–11am; lunch Mon–Sat 11am–3pm; dinner Mon–Sat 5–9:30pm. **Prices:** Main courses $4–$14. AE, DISC, MC, V.

($) M&M Truck Stop & Family Restaurant
US 160 and 660; tel 970/565-6511. 1½ mi S of town. **Diner/Mexican.** Service is fast and friendly, and the food is very good. Breakfast is available 24 hours a day, and the specialty of the house is the Navajo taco—fry bread smothered with red and green chiles and topped with lettuce, tomatoes, and cheese. **FYI:** Reservations not accepted. Children's menu. No liquor license. **Open:** Daily 24 hrs. **Prices:** Main courses $3–$10. AE, CB, DC, DISC, MC, V.

Nero's
303 W Main St; tel 970/565-7366. At jct US 160/US 666. **Italian.** Perhaps Cortez's finest restaurant, the dining room is cozy and intimate, with southwestern furnishings. A secluded, street-side patio offers outdoor dining on summer evenings. The menu lists a wide range of pasta dishes plus shrimp, steak, veal, and steak entrees. **FYI:** Reservations recommended. Children's menu. **Open:** Peak (June–Oct) daily 5–10pm. **Prices:** Main courses $5–$15. AE, MC, V.

ATTRACTIONS

Hovenweep National Monument
Tel 970/529-4461. Entrance located 18 mi NW of Cortez via US 666 or McElmo Canyon Rd. This national monument is noted for its mysterious 20-foot-high sandstone towers, some of them square, others oval, circular, or D-shaped. Archeologists have suggested their possible function as everything from guard or signal towers, celestial observatories, ceremonial structures, water towers, or granaries. Headquarters are located at the Square Tower Site, the most impressive and best preserved of the sites; the Tower Point Loop Trail winds past the ruins and identifies desert plants used for food, clothing, medicine, and other purposes. **Open:** Daily 8am–sunset. **Free**

Ute Mountain Tribal Park
Jct US 666/160, Towaoc; tel 970/565-3751 ext 282 or toll free 800/847-5485. Located 19 mi S of Cortez. Set aside by Ute Mountain Indian Reservation to preserve its heritage, the 125,000-acre park—which abuts Mesa Verde National Park to the south and west—includes hundreds of surface ruins and cliff dwellings that compare in size and complexity with those in Mesa Verde, as well as wall paintings and ancient petroglyphs. Accessibility to the park is strictly limited to guided tours by confirmed reservation. Full and half-day tours begin at the **Ute Mountain Museum and Visitor Center** at the junction of US 666 and US 160. Mountain bike and backpacking trips are also offered. No food, lodging, gasoline, or other services are available within the park. **Open:** Mar–Nov, daily 8:30am–4pm. **$$$$**

Cortez Colorado University Center and Museum
25 N Market St; tel 970/565-1151. The center is a clearinghouse for information on various Anasazi sites and related activities in southwestern Colorado, and the museum features interpretive exhibits from the sites as well as the Ute reservation. Evening programs, including lectures and demonstrations, are presented Monday through Saturday in summer, and about once a week the rest of the year. **Open:** Peak (June–Aug) daily 10am–10pm. Reduced hours off-season. **Free**

Craig

The largest community in Colorado's northwest corner, Craig is a center for river rafting, hiking, fishing, and hunting. **Information:** Greater Craig Area Chamber of Commerce, 360 E Victory Way, Craig 81625 (tel 970/824-5689).

HOTEL

Holiday Inn Craig
300 S CO 13, 81625; tel 970/824-4000 or toll free 800/HOLIDAY; fax 970/824-3950. Just S of jct US 40. Clean, modern hotel. **Rooms:** 169 rms and stes. CI 2pm/CO noon. Nonsmoking rms avail. **Amenities:** A/C, cable TV w/movies, voice mail. **Services:** **Facilities:** 250 1 restaurant, 1 bar (w/entertainment), games rm, whirlpool, playground, washer/dryer. **Rates:** $50–$65 S; $50–$69 D; $65–$85 ste. Extra person $6. Children under age 18 stay free. Parking: Outdoor, free. Children 12 and under eat free. AE, CB, DC, DISC, MC, V.

MOTEL

Black Nugget Motel
2855 W Victory Way, 81625; tel 970/824-8161 or toll free 800/727-2088; fax 970/824-9446. Just W of jct CO 13/US 40. Set on a hillside outside of town, this quiet little motel overlooks Craig and the surrounding area. **Rooms:** 20 rms. CI 2pm/CO 11am. Nonsmoking rms avail. Rooms are clean and well maintained. **Amenities:** A/C, cable TV w/movies. **Services:** **Facilities:** Washer/dryer. **Rates (CP):** Peak (Oct–Nov 15) $47 S; $60 D. Extra person $4. Children under age 12 stay free. Min stay peak. Lower rates off-season. Parking: Outdoor, free. AE, CB, DC, DISC, MC, V.

Creede

See also Monte Vista, Pagosa Springs

Creede is among the best preserved of Colorado's 19th-century silver mining towns. At the peak of mining activity more than $1 million in silver was excavated every day. Bob Ford, who killed outlaw Jesse James, was gunned down in Creede in his very own saloon. Today tourism and outdoor recreation support the town. **Information:** Creede–Mineral County Chamber of Commerce, PO Box 580, Creede 81130 (tel 719/658-2374 or 800/327-2102).

LODGE

Wason Ranch

CO 149, 81130; tel 719/658-2413. 2 mi SE of town. Visitors entering the ranch will think they've just arrived at summer camp. Anyone who loves the outdoors will love coming here—for as long as possible. The Rio Grande runs right through the open bowl of the ranch, which is surrounded by mountains and forests. **Rooms:** 22 cottages/villas. CI open/CO 10am. Lodging is in spacious log cabins, rather rustic and simply furnished. **Amenities:** Refrig. No A/C, phone, or TV. All units w/terraces, some w/fireplaces. Each cabin has full kitchen. **Services:** **Facilities:** Basketball, volleyball, games rm. Ranch has access to four-mile stretch of river for fishing and swimming. **Rates:** Peak (June–Oct) $49–$129 cottage/villa. Extra person $3. Children under age 2 stay free. Lower rates off-season. Parking: Outdoor, free. No CC.

Crested Butte

Although started as a gold and silver mining town in 1880, Crested Butte actually made its money on coal, which was mined from the late 1880s until the early 1950s. Many of the original Victorian buildings have been restored, and the entire town has been designated a National Historic Landmark District. It is known for skiing in winter and for its wildflowers and mountain biking in summer. **Information:** Crested Butte/Mount Crested Butte Chamber of Commerce, PO Box 1288, Crested Butte 81224 (tel 970/349-6438 or 800/545-4505).

HOTEL

Grand Butte Hotel

500 Gothic Rd, PO Box A, Mount Crested Butte, 81225; tel 970/349-4000 or toll free 800/544-8448; fax 970/349-4466. Adjacent to Keystone Lift. The largest hotel in town, it is easy to recognize. Ski-in, ski-out access makes it an obvious choice for skiers. Plenty of comfortable seating and two fireplaces make the lobby a great place to gather for après-ski or conversation anytime. **Rooms:** 261 rms and stes. Executive level. CI 4pm/CO 11am. Nonsmoking rms avail. Rooms are spacious and comfortable, with views of Mount Crested Butte or surrounding valley. **Amenities:** Cable TV w/movies, dataport. No A/C. Some units w/minibars, all w/terraces, some w/fireplaces, all w/whirlpools. **Services:** VP Children's program, babysitting. Complimentary ski storage. Lift ticket desk. **Facilities:** 500 2 restaurants, 1 bar, games rm, sauna, whirlpool, washer/dryer. Ski shop. **Rates:** Peak (Nov 15–Apr 20) $87–$200 S or D; $139–$589 ste. Extra person $10. Children under age 12 stay free. Min stay peak. Lower rates off-season. Parking: Indoor/outdoor, free. AE, CB, DC, DISC, MC, V.

INNS

UNRATED The Claim Jumper

704 Whiterock Ave, PO Box 1181, 81224; tel 970/349-6471. Near Chamber of Commerce. This bed-and-breakfast has a fascinating and mind-boggling array of eclectic antiques, trinkets, and memorabilia on display—those with a sense of humor will love it. Within walking distance of town. A unique, interesting, and fun place to stay. Unsuitable for children under 12. **Rooms:** 7 rms. CI 2pm/CO noon. No smoking. Theme rooms range from nautical to cowboy to automotive. One of the most intriguing is the Sports Fan-attic, located in the attic and stuffed with a wild assortment of sports memorabilia. **Amenities:** Cable TV w/movies, VCR. No A/C or phone. 1 unit w/fireplace. **Services:** Ski lockers available at mountain for Claim Jumper guests. **Facilities:** Sauna, whirlpool, guest lounge w/TV. **Rates (BB):** Peak (Nov 15–Apr 21) $89–$129 S or D. Extra person $15. Min stay special events. Lower rates off-season. Parking: Outdoor, free. DISC, MC, V.

UNRATED Crested Butte Club

512 2nd St, PO Box 309, 81224; tel 970/349-6655 or toll free 800/815-CLUB; fax 970/349-7580. 4 blocks W and 2 blocks S of the Chamber of Commerce. This recently renovated historic inn is very classy and attractive. Within walking distance of downtown, it's great for skiers and couples. **Rooms:** 7 rms. CI 3pm/CO 11am. No smoking. Comfortable rooms decorated with eclectic antiques. Bathrooms equipped with smart copper claw-foot tubs. **Amenities:** Cable TV w/movies, bathrobes. No A/C. Some units w/terraces, all w/fireplaces. **Services:** Babysitting, afternoon tea and wine/sherry served. **Facilities:** 40 1 bar (w/entertainment), spa, steam rm, whirlpool, guest lounge w/TV. Climbing wall available. **Rates (CP):** Peak (Nov 15–Mar 20) $175–$230 D. Extra person $30. Min stay special events. Lower rates off-season. Parking: Outdoor, free. DISC, MC, V.

LODGES

Elk Mountain Lodge

Second and Gothic Sts, PO Box 148, 81224; tel 970/349-7533 or toll free 800/374-6521; fax 970/349-5114. Near Chamber of Commerce. Convenient to downtown and the ski slopes, this beautifully restored 1919 miner's hotel is very quiet and comfortable. The plush guest lounge has a wood-burning stove, baby grand piano, and small library. **Rooms:** 19 rms. CI 4pm/CO 10am. No smoking. Third-floor rooms have great views of surrounding mountains and town. **Amenities:** Cable TV w/movies. No A/C. Some units w/terraces. **Facilities:** Whirlpool. **Rates (BB):** Peak (Nov 17–Apr 21). Min stay peak. Lower rates off-season. Parking: Outdoor, free. AE, CB, DC, DISC, MC, V.

The Nordic Inn
14 Treasury Rd, Mount Crested Butte, PO Box 939, Crested Butte, 81224; tel 970/349-5542; fax 970/349-6487. 300 yds from ski lifts. The original lodging on the mountain, this is a comfortable lodge with great access to the ski area. **Rooms:** 27 rms and effic; 2 cottages/villas. CI 4pm/CO 11am. Nonsmoking rms avail. **Amenities:** Cable TV w/movies, dataport. No A/C. Some units w/terraces. **Services:** Babysitting. **Facilities:** Whirlpool. **Rates (CP):** Peak (Nov 15–Apr 20). Extra person $10. Min stay special events. Lower rates off-season. Parking: Outdoor, free. Closed Apr 15–May 30/Oct 15–31. AE, MC, V.

RESTAURANTS

The Bakery Cafe
302 Elk Ave; tel 970/349-7280. 3 blocks W of Chamber of Commerce. **Cafe/Bakery.** The pressed-tin ceiling, large windows, and stained glass give the cafe a very bright and welcoming atmosphere. A variety of sandwiches, freshly baked pastries, soups, and salads can make a light snack or a satisfying meal. A great stop for a break from skiing or biking. **FYI:** Reservations not accepted. Beer and wine only. No smoking. **Open:** Daily 7am–9pm. **Prices:** Main courses $4–$7. DISC, MC, V.

The Idle Spur
226 Elk Ave; tel 970/349-5026. 4 blocks W of Chamber of Commerce. **American/Mexican.** This restaurant/brewery resembles a huge mountain lodge, with giant log beams and supports, an impressive stone fireplace, and a variety of stuffed wildlife. The menu has burgers, steaks, and south-of-the-border entrees, all well matched to the freshly brewed beers. **FYI:** Reservations not accepted. Blues/reggae/rock. Children's menu. **Open:** Peak (Nov 20–Apr 15) daily 11am–10pm. Closed Apr 15–May 20. **Prices:** Main courses $6–$30. AE, MC, V.

($) Karolina's Kitchen
127 Elk Ave; tel 970/349-6756. 4½ blocks W of CO 135. **American.** The draw at this small rustic restaurant is authentic home cooking. Large wooden beams stacked one atop the other make up the walls; historic tools and sawmill apparatus are placed throughout. The adjoining saloon serves as a second dining room in the evenings, as well as a bar and gaming hall. **FYI:** Reservations not accepted. **Open:** Daily 11:30am–10pm. **Prices:** Main courses $4–$8. MC, V.

Le Bosquet
Elk Ave and 2nd St; tel 970/349-5808. 4 blocks W of CO 135. **French.** This small, sunny restaurant in the heart of town has large windows facing the street, and many hanging plants. The menu includes such items as hazelnut chicken, warm lobster and scallop salad, tenderloin of elk, and Colorado roast rack of lamb. **FYI:** Reservations recommended. Children's menu. No smoking. **Open:** Peak (July–Aug/Dec 15–Mar) lunch Mon–Sat 11:30am–2pm; dinner daily 5:30–10pm. Closed Apr 15–May 15/Nov 1–18. **Prices:** Main courses $15–$34. AE, DISC, MC, V.

The Slogar Bar & Restaurant
Second St at Whiterock Ave; tel 970/349-5765. 4 blocks W of CO 135. **American.** Located in the original 1882 Slogar Tavern, which catered to miners, this restaurant is characterized by a Victorian parlor and family-style seating. The set dinner is a choice of steak or flavorful skillet-fried chicken—the Slogar's claim to fame, made from the same recipe since 1915—plus relish, chutney, sweet-and-sour coleslaw, mashed potatoes, biscuits, corn, and ice cream. **FYI:** Reservations accepted. No smoking. **Open:** Daily 5–9pm. Closed Apr–June 15/Oct–Nov 15. **Prices:** Prix fixe $12–$17. MC, V.

ATTRACTIONS

Crested Butte Mountain Resort
500 Gothic Rd, Mount Created Butte; tel 970/349-2222 or toll free 800/544-8448. Situated at the intersection of two overlapping winter storm tracks, Crested Butte is guaranteed outstanding snow, and the average annual snowfall here is 229 inches. The resort has 1,160 acres of skiable terrain, plus 550 acres of "Extreme Limits" (double black diamond ungroomed terrain for experts only). There are 85 trails served by 13 lifts (three triples, two quads, four doubles, and four surface lifts) and the vertical drop is 2,775 feet from a summit of 12,162 feet. Special programs for children as well as people with disabilities; designated snowboarding area with snowboard rentals and lessons. **Open:** Late Nov–mid-Apr, daily 9am–4pm. **$$$$**

Crested Butte Mountain Heritage Museum
202 Sopris Ave; tel 970/349-1880. Located in the 1881 Denver & Rio Grande Railroad Station, this museum concentrates on the area's mining and ranching heritage, with a wide array of memorabilia from local settlers' cabins. The exhibits include a 1920 fire truck, used by the Crested Butte Fire Department, and other historic fire-fighting memorabilia. **Open:** Peak (Mem Day–Labor Day) daily 3–8pm. Reduced hours off-season. **$**

Cripple Creek

See Manitou Springs

Del Norte

See Monte Vista

Delta

The area was originally the home of the Utes, who were driven off by miners in the 1880s who were then joined by Anglo ranchers and farmers. The region produces apples, peaches, and cherries, and is known for the dinosaur bones that have been found nearby. **Information:** Delta Chamber of Commerce, 301 S Main St, Delta 81416 (tel 970/874-8616).

MOTEL

Best Western Sundance Motel
903 Main St, 81416; tel 970/874-9781 or toll free 800/626-1994; fax 970/874-5440. Near courthouse. Clean, comfortable, typical Best Western located on US 50. **Rooms:** 41 rms. CI 1pm/CO 11am. Nonsmoking rms avail. **Amenities:** Cable TV w/movies, dataport. No A/C. All units w/terraces. **Services:** **Facilities:** 1 restaurant, 1 bar (w/entertainment), whirlpool. **Rates (BB):** Peak (June–Aug) $44–$54 S or D. Extra person $5. Children under age 12 stay free. Lower rates off-season. Parking: Outdoor, free. AE, CB, DC, DISC, MC, V.

ATTRACTION

Fort Uncompahgre Living History Museum
205 Gunnison River Dr; tel 970/874-8349. The original fort was built in 1826 at the confluence of the Gunnison and Uncompahgre Rivers as a small fur-trading post; it was abandoned in 1844 after an attack by Ute Indians. Today it has been replicated as a living-history museum, with hand-hewn log buildings—a trade room, a storeroom, and living quarters—facing a courtyard. Costumed traders, trappers, and laborers describe life in the 19th century. **Open:** Peak (June–Aug) Tues–Sun 10am–5pm. Reduced hours off-season. **$$**

Denver

See also Englewood, Golden, Lakewood, Pine

Just another gold mining boomtown in the mid-1800s, Denver has done well for itself since then. When gold strikes in nearby mountains turned out to be richer than those found in the settlement itself, the community evolved into a shipping and trade center. The town was laid out in 1859—the first permanent building was a saloon—and in hopes of obtaining political favors was named after James Denver, governor of the Kansas Territory, which then included the area. Called the Mile High City (as it is about a mile above sea level), Denver is Colorado's capital, largest city, and center of commerce. It is a sprawling city noted for its dozens of tree-lined boulevards, its 200 city parks, and its architecture—from handsome Victorian mansions and cowboy-style saloons to sleek contemporary skyscapers. **Information:** Denver Metro Convention & Visitors Bureau, 225 W Colfax, Denver 80202 (tel 303/892-1112 or 800/645-3446).

PUBLIC TRANSPORTATION

The **Regional Transportation District (RTD)** calls itself "The Ride" for its bus routes and light rail system; free transfers are available. Local fares are $1 during peak hours, 50¢ during off-peak hours. Seniors pay 15¢ off-peak; children age 5 and younger ride free. **Free buses** run up and down the 16th Street Mall between the Civic Center and Market Street every 90 seconds, daily 6am–1am. Also popular among visitors is the **Cultural Connection Trolley** (tel 303/299-6000), which runs daily during the summer, with stops at Denver's most popular tourist attractions and almost all major downtown museums. Cost is $3 for a full-day pass (children 5 and younger ride free).

HOTELS

Adam's Mark
1550 Court Place, 80202 (Central Business District); tel 303/893-3333 or toll free 800/444-2326; fax 303/623-0303. Adjacent to 16th St Mall. Large, convention-style hotel within walking distance of major attractions, shopping, and dining. Undergoing major renovation. **Rooms:** 744 rms and stes. Executive level. CI 3pm/CO noon. Nonsmoking rms avail. **Amenities:** A/C, cable TV w/movies, dataport, voice mail. Some units w/minibars, some w/whirlpools. **Services:** Babysitting. **Facilities:** 2 restaurants, 1 bar (w/entertainment), sauna, steam rm, beauty salon, washer/dryer. **Rates (CP):** Peak (May 25–Sept 5) $75–$180 S or D; $200–$600 ste. Extra person $10. Children under age 14 stay free. Lower rates off-season. Parking: Indoor, free. Call for room rates. AE, CB, DC, DISC, MC, V.

Brown Palace Hotel
321 17th St, 80202 (Central Business District); tel 303/297-3111 or toll free 800/321-2599; fax 303/293-9204. 1 block NE of 16th St Mall. This historic hotel has never closed its doors since it began operating in 1892, and its charm and character have been maintained. A large atrium houses the lobby and reaches up through six tiers of balconies to a stained-glass ceiling. **Rooms:** 230 rms and stes. CI 4pm/CO noon. Nonsmoking rms avail. Rooms have historic ambience, although recently renovated and restored. **Amenities:** A/C, cable TV w/movies, dataport, voice mail, bathrobes. **Services:** Twice-daily maid svce, masseur, babysitting. Day passes to nearby International Wellness Center available for $10. Free tours of hotel. Traditional afternoon tea served in lobby. **Facilities:** 4 restaurants (*see* "Restaurants" below), 2 bars (1 w/entertainment), beauty salon. **Rates:** $185–$205 S or D; $245–$725 ste. Extra person $15. Parking: Indoor, $14/day. Attractive weekend packages avail. AE, CB, DC, DISC, ER, JCB, MC, V.

Burnsley All Suite Hotel
1000 Grant St, 80203 (Capitol Hill); tel 303/830-1000 or toll free 800/231-3915; fax 303/830-7676. Located a short distance from downtown attractions, this hotel offers slightly dated but very spacious rooms. **Rooms:** 82 stes. CI 2pm/CO noon. Nonsmoking rms avail. **Amenities:** A/C, satel TV, refrig, dataport, voice mail. All units w/terraces. **Services:** Babysitting. Complimentary newspapers and passes to nearby International Wellness Center. **Facilities:** 40 1 restaurant, 1 bar, washer/dryer. **Rates (BB):** $119–$150 ste. Extra person $10. Children under age 12 stay free. Min stay special events. Parking: Indoor/outdoor, free. AE, CB, DC, MC, V.

Cambridge Hotel
1560 Sherman St, 80203 (Downtown); tel 303/831-1252 or toll free 800/877-1252; fax 303/831-4724. Classy, older hotel, a little removed from the downtown bustle yet within walking distance of shops, restaurants, and attractions. **Rooms:** 30 stes. CI 3pm/CO noon. Nonsmoking rms avail. Clean, comfortable, and tastefully decorated. **Amenities:** Cable TV w/movies, refrig, dataport, bathrobes. No A/C. **Services:** VP Babysitting. **Facilities:** 25 1 restaurant (lunch and dinner only), 1 bar. **Rates (CP):** $125–$185 ste. Extra person $10. Children under age 10 stay free. Parking: Outdoor, $7/day. AE, CB, DC, DISC, MC, V.

Comfort Inn
401 17th St, 80202 (Central Business District); tel 303/296-0400 or toll free 800/237-7431; fax 303/297-0774. 1 block NE of 16th St Mall. Simple hotel with pleasant mix of historic ambience and modern amenities and services. A good deal considering the location. **Rooms:** 229 rms and stes. CI 4pm/CO noon. Nonsmoking rms avail. Rooms are relatively small. **Amenities:** A/C, cable TV w/movies, dataport, voice mail. **Services:** VP Babysitting. **Facilities:** 50 Beauty salon. Discounted YMCA passes available. **Rates (CP):** Peak (May–Oct) $75–$95 S; $80–$105 D; $119–$185 ste. Extra person $15. Children under age 18 stay free. Lower rates off-season. Parking: Indoor, $10/day. AE, CB, DC, DISC, JCB, MC, V.

UNRATED **Denver Marriott City Center**
1701 California St, 80202 (Central Business District); tel 303/297-1300 or toll free 800/228-9290; fax 303/298-7474. 2 blocks NE of 16th St Mall. Modern hotel in the business district. **Rooms:** 613 rms and stes. Executive level. CI 3pm/CO noon. Nonsmoking rms avail. **Amenities:** A/C, cable TV w/movies, dataport, voice mail. **Services:** VP Babysitting. **Facilities:** 2000 1 restaurant, 1 bar, games rm, whirlpool, washer/dryer. **Rates:** Peak (Feb–Nov) $139 S or D; $375–$800 ste. Extra person $10. Children under age 18 stay free. Lower rates off-season. Parking: Indoor, $15/day. AE, CB, DC, DISC, ER, MC, V.

Denver Marriott Tech Center
4900 S Syracuse St, 80237; tel 303/779-1100 or toll free 800/228-9290; fax 303/740-2523. Just NW of exit 199 off I-25. South of downtown Denver with easy access to both I-25 and I-225. Good location for business travelers. **Rooms:** 625 rms and stes. Executive level. CI 3pm/CO noon. Nonsmoking rms avail. Standard but very nice rooms. **Amenities:** A/C, cable TV w/movies, refrig, dataport, voice mail. Some units w/terraces, some w/whirlpools. **Services:** VP Car-rental desk, social director, babysitting. **Facilities:** 1300 2 restaurants, 1 bar, games rm, racquetball, sauna, whirlpool, beauty salon, washer/dryer. Large atrium banquet hall. **Rates:** Peak (June–Nov 9) $120–$130 S or D; $250–$350 ste. Children under age 16 stay free. Min stay. Lower rates off-season. Parking: Outdoor, free. Rates are usually lower for holidays. AE, CB, DC, DISC, JCB, MC, V.

Embassy Suites Denver Airport Hotel
4444 N Havana St, 80239; tel 303/375-0400 or toll free 800/345-0087; fax 303/371-4634. Just N of exit 280 off I-70. When you see the tropical atrium and fountain, tiled floors, and arched brick entryway, you might just think you're in Central America. Decor is Mexican, bright, and refreshing. **Rooms:** 212 stes. Executive level. CI 3pm/CO 1pm. Nonsmoking rms avail. Rooms are very spacious and modern. Pull-out couches. **Amenities:** A/C, cable TV w/movies, refrig, dataport, voice mail. Some units w/minibars. Microwave. **Services:** Complimentary cocktails served 5:30–7:30pm. **Facilities:** 700 1 restaurant (lunch and dinner only), 1 bar, sauna, steam rm, whirlpool, washer/dryer. **Rates (BB):** $96–$115 ste. Extra person $12. Children under age 18 stay free. Parking: Outdoor, free. AE, CB, DC, DISC, MC, V.

Embassy Suites Denver Southeast
7525 E Hampden Ave, 80231; tel 303/696-6644 or toll free 800/EMBASSY; fax 303/337-6202. 1½ mi E of exit 201 off I-25. Tropical indoor atrium with small waterfalls is a delightful addition to this quality hotel. **Rooms:** 206 stes. CI 3pm/CO 1pm. Nonsmoking rms avail. Spacious and comfortable. **Amenities:** A/C, cable TV w/movies, refrig, dataport, voice mail. All units w/terraces. Ironing board, microwave, Nintendo. **Services:** Babysitting. **Facilities:** 450 1 restaurant (lunch and dinner only), 1 bar (w/entertainment), sauna, steam rm, whirlpool. **Rates (BB):** Peak (May 31–Sept 5) $109–$139 ste. Extra person $10. Children under age 12 stay free. Lower rates off-season. Parking: Outdoor, free. AE, CB, DC, DISC, JCB, MC, V.

Embassy Suites Hotel
1881 Curtis St, 80202 (Central Business District); tel 303/297-8888 or toll free 800/733-3366; fax 303/298-1103. 3 blocks NE of 16th St Mall. Decorated with lots of mirrors, this modern hotel is spacious and bright. **Rooms:** 337 stes. Executive level. CI 4pm/CO noon. Nonsmoking rms avail. **Amenities:** A/C, cable TV w/movies, refrig, voice

mail. 1 unit w/whirlpool. **Services:** Masseur, babysitting. Complimentary cocktails served daily 5–7pm. **Facilities:** 1 restaurant, 2 bars, whirlpool, washer/dryer. Discounted passes for adjoining athletic club. **Rates (BB):** $146–$160 ste. Extra person $10. Children under age 12 stay free. Parking: Indoor, $8–$12/day. AE, CB, DC, DISC, JCB, MC, V.

Executive Tower Inn
1405 Curtis St, 80202; tel 303/571-0300 or toll free 800/525-6651; fax 303/825-4301. Just NE of Denver Performing Arts Complex. Well-maintained hotel convenient to convention centers and arts complex. Shopping and dining a short walk away. **Rooms:** 337 rms and stes. CI 4pm/CO noon. Nonsmoking rms avail. **Amenities:** A/C, cable TV w/movies, dataport. **Services:** Babysitting. **Facilities:** 1 restaurant, 1 bar, racquetball, squash, sauna, steam rm, whirlpool, washer/dryer. **Rates:** $137–$165 S; $147–$175 D; $257–$395 ste. Extra person $10. Children under age 18 stay free. Parking: Indoor, $8/day. AE, CB, DC, DISC, ER, JCB, MC, V.

Hampton Inn
4685 Quebec St, 80216; tel 303/388-8100 or toll free 800/HAMPTON; fax 303/333-7710. Just N of exit 278 off I-70. Modern accommodations convenient to airport and major highways. **Rooms:** 138 rms and stes. CI 2pm/CO noon. Nonsmoking rms avail. **Amenities:** A/C, cable TV w/movies, dataport. Some units w/terraces. **Services:** Babysitting. Complimentary newspapers. **Facilities:** Washer/dryer. **Rates (CP):** Peak (Jan–Sept) $68 S; $73 D; $85 ste. Extra person $5. Children under age 18 stay free. Lower rates off-season. Parking: Outdoor, free. AE, CB, DC, DISC, MC, V.

UNRATED **Holiday Inn Denver North/Coliseum**
4849 Bannock St, 80216; tel 303/292-9500 or toll free 800/638-8941; fax 303/295-3521. Just N of jct I-70/I-25. Standard hotel with easy access to I-25, the Coliseum, and other major sports venues. **Rooms:** 217 rms and stes. CI 3pm/CO noon. Nonsmoking rms avail. **Amenities:** A/C, cable TV w/movies, dataport, voice mail. **Services:** **Facilities:** 2 restaurants, 1 bar (w/entertainment), washer/dryer. **Rates:** Peak (June 15–Sept 15) $76–$99 S or D; $199 ste. Extra person $10. Children under age 18 stay free. Min stay special events. Lower rates off-season. Parking: Outdoor, free. AE, CB, DC, DISC, MC, V.

UNRATED **Holiday Inn DIA**
15500 E 40th St, 80239; tel 303/371-9494 or toll free 800/465-4329; fax 303/371-9528. Just N of exit 284 off I-70. Good, clean franchise hotel near Denver Int'l Airport. Efficient and friendly. **Rooms:** 256 rms and stes. CI 2pm/CO noon. Nonsmoking rms avail. **Amenities:** A/C, cable TV w/movies, dataport, voice mail. **Services:** Car-rental desk, social director, babysitting. **Facilities:** 1 restaurant, 1 bar (w/entertainment), sauna, whirlpool, beauty salon, washer/dryer. **Rates:** $105–$110 S; $115–$120 D; $250 ste. Extra person $10. Children under age 18 stay free. Parking: Outdoor, free. AE, CB, DC, DISC, MC, V.

Hyatt Regency Denver
1750 Welton St, 80202 (Central Business District); tel 303/295-1234 or toll free 800/233-1234; fax 303/292-2472. 2 blocks NE of 16th St Mall. Luxury hotel with a spacious and festive lobby tastefully decorated with many landscape paintings. Great location for business travelers. **Rooms:** 511 rms and stes. Executive level. CI 3pm/CO noon. Nonsmoking rms avail. Very modern and exceptionally comfortable. **Amenities:** A/C, cable TV w/movies, dataport, voice mail. All units w/minibars, some w/whirlpools. Some rooms equipped with fax machines. **Services:** Babysitting. **Facilities:** 1 restaurant, 1 bar, sauna, steam rm, whirlpool. **Rates (CP):** $140–$200 S or D; $310–$1,000 ste. Extra person $10. Parking: Indoor, $12/day. AE, CB, DC, DISC, MC, V.

Loews Giorgio Hotel
4150 E Mississippi Ave, 80222; tel 303/782-9300 or toll free 800/345-9172; fax 303/758-6542. Near exit 204 off I-25. This black, reflective high-rise hotel near Cherry Creek is the tallest building in this part of town. Inside is tasteful and elegant Italian Renaissance decor, including large faux marble pillars and ornate marble floors in the lobby. **Rooms:** 187 rms and stes. Executive level. CI 3pm/CO 11am. Nonsmoking rms avail. Marble washbasins grace bathrooms. Mountainside rooms are more expensive, but view is worth it. **Amenities:** A/C, cable TV w/movies, dataport, bathrobes. All units w/minibars. Iron and ironing board. Business-level rooms have fax machines. **Services:** Babysitting. Complimentary transportation to fitness center and Cherry Creek Mall. **Facilities:** 1 restaurant (*see* "Restaurants" below), 1 bar (w/entertainment). Complimentary passes to Bally's Fitness Center; passes to Cherry Creek Sports Club are $15. **Rates:** $175–$195 S; $195–$215 D; $250 ste. Extra person $20. Children under age 18 stay free. Parking: Outdoor, free. AE, CB, DC, DISC, MC, V.

Oxford Hotel
1600 17th St, 80202; tel 303/628-5400 or toll free 800/228-5838; fax 303/628-5413. Just NE of Union Station. Built in 1891, this hotel has maintained much of its historic ambience in an atmosphere of luxury. Many landscape paintings decorate the walls, and floors exhibit intricate tile work. Convenient to downtown. **Rooms:** 81 rms and stes. CI 3pm/CO 1pm. Nonsmoking rms avail. **Amenities:** TV. No A/C. All units w/minibars. **Services:** Masseur, babysitting. **Facilities:** 1 restaurant (*see* "Restaurants" below), 2 bars, spa, sauna, steam rm, whirlpool, beauty salon. **Rates:** Peak (Apr–Aug) $125–$150 S;

$135–$160 D; $180 ste. Extra person $10. Children under age 18 stay free. Lower rates off-season. Parking: Indoor/outdoor, $12/day. AE, CB, DC, DISC, MC, V.

Ramada Inn Denver Airport
3737 Quebec St, 80207; tel 303/388-6161 or toll free 800/999-8338; fax 303/388-0426. ½ mi S of exit 278 off I-70. Brick and stucco hotel ideal for business travelers. In need of some renovation. **Rooms:** 147 rms. CI 3pm/CO noon. Nonsmoking rms avail. **Amenities:** A/C, cable TV w/movies, dataport. **Services:** Car-rental desk. **Facilities:** **Rates:** $70–$88 S; $80–$98 D. Extra person $10. Children under age 12 stay free. Parking: Outdoor, free. AE, CB, DC, DISC, MC, V.

Ramada Inn Mile High Stadium
1975 Bryant St, 80204; tel 303/433-8331 or toll free 800/272-6232; fax 303/433-6294. Adjacent to Mile High Stadium. This column-shaped hotel is ideal for anyone in town to catch a game or performance at one of the sports and concert venues. Regarded as having the best night view of the downtown area. **Rooms:** 166 rms. CI 2pm/CO 11am. Nonsmoking rms avail. Rooms offer a variety of good views. **Amenities:** A/C, cable TV w/movies, dataport. **Services:** Babysitting. **Facilities:** 1 restaurant, 1 bar, games rm, washer/dryer. **Rates (BB):** Peak (May 25–Sept 15) $72–$80 S; $82–$90 D. Extra person $10. Children under age 18 stay free. Lower rates off-season. Parking: Outdoor, free. AE, CB, DC, DISC, EC, JCB, MC, V.

Red Lion Hotel
3203 Quebec St, 80207; tel 303/321-3333 or toll free 800/RED-LION; fax 303/329-5281. 1 mi S of exit 278 off I-70. Attractive and comfortable. **Rooms:** 573 rms and stes. CI 3pm/CO noon. Nonsmoking rms avail. **Amenities:** A/C, cable TV w/movies, dataport. Some units w/terraces. Ironing board, Nintendo. **Services:** Car-rental desk, babysitting. **Facilities:** 2 restaurants, 2 bars, sauna, whirlpool, washer/dryer. **Rates:** $134–$150 S or D; $200–$350 ste. Extra person $10. Children under age 18 stay free. Parking: Outdoor, free. AE, CB, DC, DISC, JCB, MC, V.

Stouffer Renaissance Denver Hotel
3801 Quebec St, 80207; tel 303/399-7500 or toll free 800/HOTELS-1; fax 303/321-1966. ½ mi S of exit 278 off I-70. Modern accommodations relatively close to airport. **Rooms:** 400 rms and stes. Executive level. CI 3pm/CO 1pm. Nonsmoking rms avail. **Amenities:** A/C, cable TV w/movies, dataport. All units w/minibars, some w/terraces, 1 w/whirlpool. **Services:** Car-rental desk, babysitting. Complimentary newspapers. **Facilities:** 1 restaurant, 1 bar (w/entertainment), spa, steam rm, whirlpool. **Rates:** $99–$215 S or D; $215–$600 ste. Extra person $10. Children under age 18 stay free. Parking: Indoor, $4/day. AE, CB, DC, DISC, ER, JCB, MC, V.

The Warwick
1776 Grant St, 80203; tel 303/861-2000 or toll free 800/525-2888; fax 303/839-8504. NE of State Capitol. Just a short distance from downtown, the Warwick offers convenience without the bustle of a major thoroughfare. The small lobby has the feel of a continental hotel, with marble and richly upholstered chairs and sofas. **Rooms:** 191 rms and stes. CI 3pm/CO 1pm. Nonsmoking rms avail. **Amenities:** A/C, cable TV w/movies, refrig, dataport, voice mail. Some units w/terraces. **Services:** Babysitting. **Facilities:** 1 restaurant, 1 bar. **Rates (CP):** $160 S; $170 D; $195–$810 ste. Extra person $10. Children under age 18 stay free. Parking: Indoor, $5/day. AE, CB, DC, DISC, JCB, MC, V.

Westin Hotel at Tabor Center
1672 Lawrence St, 80202 (Central Business District); tel 303/572-9100 or toll free 800/228-3000; fax 303/572-7288. 1 block NE of 16th St Mall. Deluxe, modern hotel with exceptionally large, comfortable lobby. Within easy walking distance of downtown and recently revitalized Lower Downtown, including Coors Field. **Rooms:** 420 rms and stes. Executive level. CI 3pm/CO 1pm. Nonsmoking rms avail. Rooms are spacious and luxurious. **Amenities:** A/C, cable TV w/movies, dataport, voice mail. All units w/minibars, some w/terraces, some w/whirlpools. **Services:** Masseur, babysitting. Westin Kids Club includes free meals in summer and free movies. **Facilities:** 1 restaurant (*see* "Restaurants" below), 2 bars (1 w/entertainment), volleyball, racquetball, spa, sauna, whirlpool, beauty salon. **Rates:** $114–$195 S or D; $150–$1,200 ste. Extra person $15. Children under age 18 stay free. Parking: Indoor, $12–$14/day. AE, CB, DC, DISC, EC, ER, JCB, MC, V.

Woodfield Suites Denver Tech Center
9009 E Arapahoe Rd, Greenwood Village, 80112; tel 303/799-4555 or toll free 800/338-0008; fax 303/792-3377. Just E of exit 197 off I-25. Attractive, spacious, modern units. Convenient to Denver Tech Center and I-25; ideal for business travelers. **Rooms:** 132 stes. CI 3pm/CO noon. Nonsmoking rms avail. Pull-out sofas. **Amenities:** A/C, cable TV w/movies, refrig, dataport, VCR, voice mail. Some units w/whirlpools. Iron, ironing board. Kitchenette or full kitchen. **Services:** Complimentary happy hour 5–7pm daily. **Facilities:** 1 bar, games rm, whirlpool, washer/dryer. **Rates (CP):** $100–$140 ste. Extra person $10. Children under age 18 stay free. Parking: Outdoor, free. AE, CB, DC, DISC, MC, V.

MOTELS

Cameron Motel
4500 E Evans Ave, 80222; tel 303/757-2100; fax 303/757-0974. Just W of exit 203 off I-25. Small, brick, mom-and-pop style motel. It's over 40 years old, but still very contemporary and well maintained. **Rooms:** 35 rms. CI open/CO

11am. Nonsmoking rms avail. **Amenities:** A/C, cable TV w/movies, refrig. All units w/terraces. **Services:** **Rates:** Peak (June–Sept 15) $42 S; $46 D. Extra person $5. Children under age 18 stay free. Lower rates off-season. Parking: Outdoor, free. AE, CB, DC, DISC, MC, V.

Central YMCA
25 E 16th Ave, 80202 (Downtown); tel 303/861-8300 or toll free 800/USA-YMCA; fax 303/830-7391. Close to the state capitol, this typical YMCA has no frills but is very clean and inexpensive. **Rooms:** 188 rms. CI 11am/CO 11am. Although dated, rooms are adequate; 30 have private bathrooms. **Amenities:** No A/C, phone, or TV. **Facilities:** 100 Basketball, volleyball, racquetball, squash, sauna, steam rm, whirlpool, washer/dryer. All facilities available for fee. **Rates:** $24–$30 S; $44–$47 D. MC, V.

Cherry Creek Inn
600 S Colorado Blvd, 80222 (Cherry Creek); tel 303/757-3341; fax 303/756-6670. Modern, well-maintained motel centrally located near Denver's attractions, about 45 minutes from Denver Int'l Airport. **Rooms:** 319 rms. CI 4pm/CO noon. Nonsmoking rms avail. West side rooms have great mountain views. **Amenities:** A/C, cable TV w/movies, refrig, dataport. Iron and ironing board. **Services:** VP Car-rental desk, masseur. Complimentary shuttle service within five-mile radius. **Facilities:** 100 1 restaurant, 1 bar, basketball, beauty salon, washer/dryer. Complimentary passes to Bally's Fitness Center next door. **Rates:** $88 S or D. Extra person $10. Children under age 18 stay free. Parking: Outdoor, free. AE, CB, DC, DISC, MC, V.

La Quinta Airport
3975 Peoria Way, 80239; tel 303/371-5640 or toll free 800/531-5900; fax 303/371-7015. Just S of exit 281 off I-70. Basic motel. **Rooms:** 112 rms and stes. CI 3pm/CO noon. Nonsmoking rms avail. **Amenities:** A/C, cable TV w/movies. All units w/terraces. **Services:** Free parking for up to 14 days. **Facilities:** Washer/dryer. **Rates (CP):** $65–$75 S or D; $90–$100 ste. Extra person $10. Children under age 18 stay free. Parking: Outdoor, free. AE, CB, DC, DISC, JCB, MC, V.

La Quinta Inn Central
3500 Park Ave W, 80216; tel 303/458-1222 or toll free 800/531-5900; fax 303/433-2246. Just S of exit 213 off I-25. Modern establishment with easy access to major highways. **Rooms:** 105 rms. CI open/CO noon. Nonsmoking rms avail. Excellently maintained and very contemporary. **Amenities:** A/C, satel TV w/movies. All units w/terraces. **Services:** **Facilities:** 35 Washer/dryer. **Rates (CP):** Peak (May 26–Sept 15) $75–$92 S or D. Extra person $10. Children under age 18 stay free. Lower rates off-season. Parking: Outdoor, free. AE, CB, DC, DISC, MC, V.

Motel 6
6 W 83rd Place, Thornton, 80221; tel 303/429-1550 or toll free 800/466-8356; fax 303/427-7513. Just W of exit 219 off I-25. Adobe-style, standard motel with no extras. **Rooms:** 121 rms. CI 2pm/CO noon. Nonsmoking rms avail. **Amenities:** A/C, cable TV w/movies. All units w/terraces. **Services:** **Facilities:** Washer/dryer. **Rates:** Peak (May 25–Oct 15) $32–$40 S or D. Extra person $3. Children under age 17 stay free. Lower rates off-season. Parking: Outdoor, free. AE, CB, DC, DISC, MC, V.

Quality Inn Denver South
6300 E Hampden Ave, 80222; tel 303/758-2211 or toll free 800/647-1986; fax 303/753-0156. Just E of exit 201 off I-25. Clean and comfortable motel with easy access to I-25. **Rooms:** 182 rms. CI 3pm/CO noon. Nonsmoking rms avail. Views are of the courtyard or the mountains. **Amenities:** A/C, cable TV w/movies, voice mail. All units w/terraces. **Services:** Complimentary newspapers. **Facilities:** 200 1 restaurant, 1 bar, whirlpool, washer/dryer. **Rates:** Peak (June–Sept) $65–$72 S; $72–$79 D. Extra person $7. Children under age 18 stay free. Lower rates off-season. Parking: Outdoor, free. AE, CB, DC, DISC, MC, V.

INNS

Castle Marne B&B
1572 Race St, 80206; tel 303/331-0621 or toll free 800/92-MARNE; fax 303/331-0623. Built in 1889 and later named for its similarity to castles on the Marne River in France, this beautiful stone structure with impressive carved details is a friendly getaway best suited for children over 10 years of age. **Rooms:** 10 rms and stes. CI 4pm/CO 11am. No smoking. **Amenities:** A/C, dataport, bathrobes. No TV. Some units w/terraces, some w/whirlpools. **Services:** Afternoon tea served. **Facilities:** 16 Games rm, guest lounge w/TV. **Rates (BB):** $70–$140 S; $85–$155 D; $180 ste. Extra person $15. Parking: Outdoor, free. AE, CB, DC, DISC, MC, V.

Queen Anne B&B Inn
2147-51 Tremont Place, 80205; tel 303/296-6666 or toll free 800/432-4667; fax 303/296-2151. NE of State Capitol. Just a short walk from downtown and 10 blocks from Coors Field, this bed-and-breakfast comprises two yellow Victorian cottages with green trim. Quiet and private, and ideal for romantic getaway. Unsuitable for children under 12. **Rooms:** 14 rms and stes. CI 3pm/CO noon. No smoking. All units are tastefully decorated and have fresh cut flowers. Chamber music available in each room. Four suites have been dedicated to and named for artists Alexander Calder, Norman Rockwell, Frederic Remington, and J J Audubon, and are decorated with representations of their work. **Amenities:** A/C. No TV. 1 unit w/terrace, 1 w/fireplace, some w/whirlpools. **Services:** Wine/sherry served. Complimentary local phone service. Fax service available. Evening wine service features Colorado wines. **Facilities:** 12 Guest

lounge. **Rates (BB):** $75–$135 D; $135–$165 ste. Extra person $15. Children under age 1 stay free. Min stay special events. Parking: Outdoor, free. AE, CB, DC, DISC, EC, MC, V.

Victoria Oaks Inn

1575 Race St, 80206; tel 303/355-1818 or toll free 800/662-6257. The owners of this quiet little retreat are continually upgrading and modernizing, while preserving the historic ambience. **Rooms:** 9 rms (2 w/shared bath). CI 3pm/CO noon. **Amenities:** Dataport. No A/C or TV. **Services:** Afternoon tea served. **Facilities:** Guest lounge w/TV. **Rates (CP):** $50 S w/shared bath, $75 S w/private bath; $60 D w/shared bath, $85 D w/private bath. Parking: Outdoor, free. AE, CB, DC, DISC, ER, MC, V.

RESTAURANTS

Al Fresco

1523 Market St (Lower Downtown); tel 303/534-0404. ½ block SW of 16th St Mall. **Italian.** Offering a nice variety of specialty pizzas, pastas, and meat dishes, this Italian restaurant has a very modern yet comfortable ambience. The original brick interior has been attractively enhanced with finely crafted wood trim and elegant table decor, and the open dining space is creatively separated into relatively private areas. Menu items include salmon calzone, pasta dishes, and grilled marinated swordfish. **FYI:** Reservations accepted. Additional locations: 2690 Baseline Rd, Boulder (tel 543-9090); I-25 Exit 269B at the Holiday Inn, Fort Collins (tel 970/493-6567). **Open:** Lunch Mon–Fri 11am–2pm; dinner Mon–Thurs 5–10pm, Fri–Sat 5–11pm, Sun 5–9pm. **Prices:** Main courses $8–$20. AE, CB, DC, DISC, MC, V. VP

Augusta

In Westin Hotel at Tabor Center, 1672 Lawrence St (Downtown); tel 303/572-9100. Just NE of 16th St Mall. **New American.** The etched glass and black walls of the entryway flow into the dining room of this small, elegant restaurant, and the long bowed wall of windows offers guests a great view of downtown. The menu might include a medley of sea scallops, salmon, crab claw, and New Zealand green-lipped mussels in a Dijon sauce or the roasted marinated duck breast in a Frangelica sauce. The extensive wine list complements both the elegant food and atmosphere. **FYI:** Reservations recommended. Piano. Children's menu. No smoking. **Open:** Daily 6:30am–11pm. **Prices:** Main courses $11–$27; prix fixe $40. AE, CB, DC, DISC, ER, MC, V. VP

The Broker Restaurant

821 17th St (Lower Downtown); tel 303/292-5065. 8½ blocks SE of Union Station. **Steak.** This elegant, intimate restaurant occupies a series of vaults in what was originally the Denver National Bank building. Much of the original structure has been preserved—for example, the vault door still rests in its original hinges. Large photographs of historic Denver line the walls of the various dining rooms and private chambers, ideally suited for both business lunches and romantic dinners. The menu lists a wide variety of traditional entrees plus daily seafood and game specials. Favorites include beef Wellington, prime rib, rack of lamb, Rocky Mountain trout, Alaskan king crab legs, and roast duck. **FYI:** Reservations recommended. Children's menu. Additional locations: I-70 and Peoria, Aurora (tel 371-6420); 5111 DTC Pkwy, Greenwood Village (tel 770-5111). **Open:** Lunch Mon–Fri 11am–2:30pm; dinner daily 5–11pm. **Prices:** Prix fixe $18–$34. AE, CB, DC, DISC, MC, V. VP

Buckhorn Exchange

1000 Osage St (Downtown); tel 303/534-9505. 1 block S of Lincoln Park. **Steak/Game.** This restaurant also serves as a natural history museum, as well as an exhibit hall for hunting trophies. Many varieties of birds have been mounted in glass cases along the walls, while a menagerie of game beasts adorn the walls and rafters. The rustic ambience suits the restaurant's history—the founder is said to have been a hunting scout for both Buffalo Bill and Theodore Roosevelt—and the hearty fare: no-frills steak and game dishes featuring the likes of buffalo, elk, pheasant, or quail. **FYI:** Reservations recommended. Folk. Children's menu. **Open:** Lunch Mon–Fri 11:30am–2pm; dinner Mon–Thurs 5:30–9:30pm, Fri–Sat 5–10pm, Sun 4–9pm. **Prices:** Main courses $17–$39. AE, CB, DC, DISC, MC, V.

City Spirit Cafe

1434 Blake St; tel 303/575-0022. 6 blocks SW of Coors Field. **Eclectic/Vegetarian.** This funky little cafe lies just a short walk from downtown. Inside, virtually everything that can be painted has been, from the ventilation ducts to the original mosaics on many of the tables and walls. The menu, too, is an eclectic and unusual blend of vegetarian, Mexican, Greek, and traditional sandwiches and entrees, from a home-style lamb sandwich to an organic tamale. Live music three nights a week and nightly tarot readings add to the offbeat character and unique local color. **FYI:** Reservations not accepted. Blues/folk/rock. Children's menu. **Open:** Mon–Thurs 11am–midnight, Fri–Sat 11am–2am. **Prices:** Main courses $5–$7. AE, CB, DC, DISC, MC, V.

Cliff Young's

700 E 17th Ave; tel 303/831-8900. Near State Capitol. **New American.** An elegant restaurant just east of the downtown district, with finely upholstered furnishings and crystal chandeliers setting a scene of luxurious comfort. Seafood, game, and regional specialties might include roasted Colorado rack of lamb with apricot mustard, pinwheel of Chilean sea bass and Atlantic salmon with saffron-scented tomato ragout, or marinated loin of wild boar. **FYI:** Reservations recommended. Piano/violin. **Open:** Lunch Mon–Fri 11:30am–2pm; dinner daily 6–9:30pm. **Prices:** Main courses $20–$33. AE, CB, DC, DISC, MC, V. VP

★ The Delectable Egg
1642 Market St (Lower Downtown); tel 303/572-8146. Just NE of 16th St Mall. **Cafe.** This bright brick-and-wood cafe close to the downtown district offers an exceptional variety of breakfast dishes, plus sandwiches and specials. Try a Mediterranean frittata—made with three eggs and a variety of fillings, and baked to perfection—or eggs Benedict, pancakes, waffles, or french toast. Even health-conscious diners can find something delicious by checking out the low-fat, low-cholesterol "Healthmark" selections. **FYI:** Reservations not accepted. Children's menu. No liquor license. Additional location: 1625 Court Place (tel 892-5720). **Open:** Mon–Fri 6:30am–2pm, Sat–Sun 7am–2pm. **Prices:** Lunch main courses $3–$6. AE, CB, DC, DISC, MC, V.

★ Duffy's Shamrock
1635 Court Place (Downtown); tel 303/534-4935. 1 block NE of 16th St Mall. **American.** This large, dark pub offers fast, friendly service and laid-back atmosphere. Irish coffees and beers are available along with steaks, sandwiches, and a few specialty items such as the Duffarito, an Irish take on the burrito. **FYI:** Reservations accepted. Children's menu. **Open:** Daily 7am–1:30am. **Prices:** Main courses $5–$12. AE, CB, DC, MC, V.

($) Healthy Habits
865 S Colorado Blvd; tel 303/733-2105. 10 blocks N of exit 204 off I-25. **Cafeteria/Health.** An upscale cafeteria catering to the health-conscious and anyone with a hearty appetite. Oxidized copper lamps hang above the tables, and large photos of sailboats and the outdoors decorate the space. Meals are prix fixe ($5 for lunch, $7 for dinner) and feature all-you-can-eat salad, soup, pasta, pizza, and baked goods. Perhaps the biggest draw is the stellar salad bar offering over 50 items, including marinated mushrooms, tabbouleh, pickled herring, jicama, and seasonal items. **FYI:** Reservations accepted. Beer and wine only. No smoking. Additional locations: 4760 Baseline Rd, Boulder (tel 494-9177); 14195 W Colfax Ave, Golden (tel 277-9293). **Open:** Daily 11am–9pm. **Prices:** Prix fixe $7. AE, CB, DC, DISC, MC, V.

Imperial Chinese Restaurant
431 S Broadway; tel 303/698-2800. 2½ blocks of exit 207A off I-25. **Chinese/Seafood.** A large sculpted golden Buddha greets guests at the entrance to this popular place. The elegant dining area, decorated with two large tropical fish tanks and a variety of Chinese ceramics, seems to be always filled to capacity. Both traditional and innovative fare is served—much of it seafood—and presentations are impeccable. Signature dishes include Nanking pork loin, seafood bird's nest, Dungeness crab stir-fry, and sesame chicken. **FYI:** Reservations recommended. **Open:** Mon–Thurs 11am–10pm, Fri 11am–10:30pm, Sat noon–10:30pm, Sun 4–10pm. **Prices:** Main courses $8–$28; prix fixe $15–$25. AE, CB, DC, MC, V.

Josephina's Ristorante
1433 Larimer St; tel 303/623-0166. 1½ blocks SW of 16th St Mall. **Italian.** The brick interior and historic decor lend an elegance to the comfortable surroundings. Carved Corinthian columns lend an old-world charm to the entrance. The menu offers traditional pizzas, pastas, and fish and meat dishes, many of which are healthfully prepared. There's also an award-winning specialty pizza. **FYI:** Reservations recommended. Blues/rock. Children's menu. **Open:** Sun–Thurs 11am–11pm, Fri–Sat 11am–midnight. **Prices:** Main courses $4–$18. AE, CB, DC, DISC, MC, V.

La Bonne Soupe
In Writer Sq, 1512 Larimer St (Downtown); tel 303/595-9169. Just SW of 16th St Mall. **French/Seafood.** Combining indoor and outdoor cafe-style dining, this sunlit space offers more than the usual cafe fare. Soups—barley, cream of asparagus, onion soup—can be meals in themselves, but there are also more substantial dishes available: Marseilles bouillabaisse, filet mignon au poivre, provençale shrimp. Chocolate fondue is tempting for dessert. **FYI:** Reservations accepted. Children's menu. **Open:** Mon–Thurs 11am–10pm, Fri–Sat 11am–11pm, Sun 11:30am–9:30pm. **Prices:** Main courses $7–$19. AE, CB, DC, MC, V.

Las Delicias
439 E 19th Ave; tel 303/839-5675. Near State Capitol. **Mexican.** The fine Mexican food at Las Delicias has won local acclaim and a loyal following. Chips and salsa accompany all meals, which cover most of the usual Mexican standards. The large dining area comprises half a dozen rooms; Mexican music enhances the casual atmosphere. **FYI:** Reservations accepted. Children's menu. Additional locations: 50 E Del Norte (tel 430-0422); 19553 Main St, Parker (tel 840-0325). **Open:** Mon–Sat 8am–9pm, Sun 9am–9pm. **Prices:** Main courses $3–$9. AE, DISC, MC, V.

Las Margaritas
1066 S Gaylord St (Washington Park); tel 303/777-0194. Just N of Mississippi Ave, near University Blvd exit off I-25. **Mexican.** An upscale Mexican restaurant in Washington Park, Las Margaritas is modern in decor but with hints of Old Mexico in murals and several art objects. The house specialties include snapper Veracruz, steak Azteca, and tamales. The bar stocks 56 brands of tequila. As might be expected, the margarita is the drink of choice here. **FYI:** Reservations accepted. **Open:** Sun–Thurs 11am–10pm, Fri–Sat 11am–11pm. **Prices:** Main courses $7–$11. AE, CB, DC, MC, V.

The Little Russian Cafe
1424 H Larimer St (Downtown); tel 303/595-8600. 1½ blocks SW of 16th St Mall. **Russian.** Set back in the Larimer Square courtyard, this intimate restaurant achieves its distinctive ambience with a red and white interior adorned with Russian paintings and prints. Several historic Russian mannequins stand in the entranceway, near the small but comfortable bar. Some diners like to start their meals with a shot of

ice-cold vodka—either plain or flavored with garlic, anisette, black currant, or other spices and herbs. Traditional dishes such as borscht, goulash, and beef Stroganoff are on the menu, as well as more unusual items like garlic-flavored minced chicken, shaped into patties and sautéed. **FYI:** Reservations accepted. Beer and wine only. No smoking. Additional location: 1430 Pearl St Mall, Boulder (tel 449-7696). **Open:** Lunch Mon–Thurs 11:30am–2:30pm, Fri 11:30am–4pm; dinner Mon–Thurs 5:30–9:30pm, Fri 4–10:30pm, Sat–Sun 5–10:30pm. **Prices:** Main courses $10–$15. AE, CB, DC, DISC, MC, V. ♿

Marlowe's
511 16th St (Downtown); tel 303/595-3700. Just SW of Republic Plaza. **New American.** This very popular eatery and saloon occupies a corner of the 1891 Kittredge building. Large windows, a vaulted ceiling, and plants make the interior bright and airy; an antique cherry bar and festive decorations further enhance the comfortable atmosphere. Unusual pasta dishes (some marked with a "Healthmark" on the menu) are featured along with signature items like chipotle-accented oysters Florentine and pan-seared beef tenderloin served with wild mushrooms and bordelaise sauce. **FYI:** Reservations recommended. **Open:** Lunch Mon–Fri 11am–4pm; dinner Mon–Thurs 4–11pm, Fri 4pm–midnight, Sat 5pm–midnight. **Prices:** Main courses $9–$22. AE, CB, DC, DISC, MC, V. ♿

McCormick's Fish & Oyster House
In Oxford Hotel, 1600 17th St; tel 303/825-1107. Just NE of Union Station. **Seafood.** Elegantly casual, with leaded and stained-glass panels decorating the bar and lounge area. The menu specializes in a wide variety of fresh seafood from both coasts and overseas; items change daily depending on market availability. This is the perfect choice if seafood is your preference. **FYI:** Reservations recommended. **Open:** Breakfast Mon–Fri 6:30–10am; lunch Mon–Fri 11am–2pm; dinner Sun–Thurs 5–10pm, Fri–Sat 5–11pm; brunch Sat–Sun 7am–2pm. **Prices:** Main courses $9–$24. AE, CB, DC, DISC, MC, V. ♿

Mike Berardi's
2115 E 17th Ave; tel 303/399-8800. 2 blocks W of City Park. **Italian.** This lively little Italian restaurant features crowd-drawing opera singers three nights a week. Photos of famous New Yorkers and Italians adorn the walls, while an expansive mural of the New York skyline and the Brooklyn Bridge beneath a luminous moon occupies one corner of the room. The menu is fairly standard, with many seafood and vegetarian options. The extensive wine list, predominantly Italian, contains some selections that can be sampled at the bar. **FYI:** Reservations recommended. Opera. Children's menu. **Open:** Lunch Mon–Fri 11:30am–2pm; dinner Mon–Thurs 5–10pm, Fri–Sat 5–11pm. **Prices:** Main courses $9–$16. AE, CB, DC, MC, V. ♿

The Old Spaghetti Factory
1215 18th St; tel 303/295-1864. Near Coors Field. **Italian.** Occupying the historic Tramway Building, which once served the longest continual cable system in the world, this restaurant is a good spot to take the family. Art deco lamps, stained-glass windows, and Victorian-style tables and chairs fill the dining areas, and there are tables available in an old cable car. The specialty is pasta with five different sauces, but also available are lasagna, oven-baked chicken, and ravioli. **FYI:** Reservations not accepted. Children's menu. Additional location: 10801 E Mississippi Ave, Aurora (tel 340-3400). **Open:** Lunch Mon–Fri 11:30am–2pm; dinner Mon–Thurs 5–10pm, Fri 5–11pm, Sat 4:45–11pm, Sun 4–10pm. **Prices:** Main courses $4–$8. DISC, MC, V.

Palace Arms
In Brown Palace Hotel, 321 17th St (Downtown); tel 303/297-3111. Just NE of 16th St Mall. **International.** Historic weapons, flags, and prints dominate the decor at this highly regarded hotel restaurant. The menu reflects a range of influences. Starters might include fresh lobster enchilada and wild rice soup with brandied almond cream, while rabbit terrine, beef Wellington, and miso-glazed yellowfin tuna might be offered as main courses. The wine list has garnered some prestigious awards. **FYI:** Reservations recommended. Jacket required. **Open:** Lunch Mon–Fri 11:30am–2:30pm; dinner daily 6–10pm. **Prices:** Main courses $19–$34. AE, CB, DC, DISC, MC, V. VP ♿

Paramount Cafe
511 16th St (Downtown); tel 303/893-2000. Just NW of Republic Plaza. **Burgers/Pub.** One of downtown Denver's original nightspots, this is the place for after-theater gatherings of patrons and actors from the Paramount Theatre. The very casual, upbeat dining area centers on the large rectangular bar. Photos and posters of celebrities deck the walls. Traditional pub fare is neatly rounded out by the plethora of beers on tap, including the house microbrew. **FYI:** Reservations accepted. Blues/cabaret/comedy/jazz/rock. Children's menu. **Open:** Mon–Sat 11am–midnight. **Prices:** Main courses $5–$8. AE, CB, DC, DISC, MC, V. ♿

★ Pete's Kitchen
1962 E Colfax Ave; tel 303/321-3139. 18 blocks E of capitol building. **Diner/Greek.** A local landmark for over 50 years, where the waitresses still call patrons "hon" and "doll." Weekend mornings are particularly busy, often with a waiting line out the door. And there's a small greenhouse dining room that's especially inviting on cold but sunny winter days. The food is standard but you can get breakfast all day long, and there are some Greek favorites such as gyros, chicken kabobs, and tzatziki sauce. **FYI:** Reservations not accepted. No liquor license. **Open:** Sun–Thurs 6–11pm, Fri–Sat 24 hrs. **Prices:** Main courses $2–$8. AE, MC, V. 24

Strings
1700 Humboldt St; tel 303/831-7310. **New American/Californian.** Popular with the 20-to-30-year-old set, this

contemporary restaurant offers several seating options, including a main dining area with a loft above, and a street-level "greenhouse." Show-biz memorabilia covers the walls, while large flower arrangements brighten the interior. Entrees include passion fruit–glazed roasted half duck and mesquite-grilled Atlantic salmon, and there are a variety of pastas. **FYI:** Reservations recommended. **Open:** Mon–Thurs 11am–11pm, Fri–Sat 11am–midnight, Sun 5–10pm. **Prices:** Main courses $11–$21. AE, CB, DC, DISC, MC, V.

Tante Louise

4900 E Colfax Ave; tel 303/355-4488. 10 blocks E of Colorado Ave. **New American/Seafood.** Occupying an old house east of the downtown district, this outwardly modest restaurant is quite elegant inside. Old hardwood floors, tasteful floral print wallpaper, art deco stained-glass windows, and classical prints and china add a touch of class. The dining area is spread over several rooms; each is intimate and ideal for quiet conversation. The menu offers a nice blend of seafood, pasta dishes, and game. It changes seasonally, but may include such choices as molasses-grilled Alaskan salmon, Summerfield Farms fallow deer medallions, or grilled portobello mushroom steak. **FYI:** Reservations recommended. **Open:** Mon–Sat 5:30–10pm. **Prices:** Main courses $17–$28. AE, CB, DC, DISC, MC, V.

Tuscany Restaurant

In Loews Giorgio Hotel, 4150 E Mississippi Ave; tel 303/782-9300. Near exit 204 off I-25. **New American/Italian.** The creative cuisine of chef Tim Fields together with an elegant, comfortable setting make this restaurant one of Denver's finest. Pillars and large, dried floral arrangements divide the dining room to provide diners intimacy; Tuscan-style still-lifes and landscapes adorn the walls. Enjoy a fine selection of Tuscan and new cuisine entrees: perhaps seafood tagliatelle (a blend of seafood, tomatoes, and crushed red-pepper olive oil), grilled duck pizza with wild mushrooms, or garlic-crusted lamb chops. Diners can retire to the lounge area after dinner for relaxing conversation at the marble bar or in one of the upholstered booths near an impressive Romanesque mural. **FYI:** Reservations recommended. Piano/violin. Children's menu. **Open:** Breakfast Mon–Sat 6:30–10:30am, Sun 7–10am; lunch Mon–Sat 11am–2pm; dinner daily 6–10:30pm; brunch Sun 11am–2pm. **Prices:** Main courses $15–$26. AE, CB, DC, DISC, MC, V.

T-Wa Inn

555 S Federal Blvd; tel 303/922-4584. 2 blocks S of jct Alameda Ave. **Vietnamese.** The oldest Vietnamese restaurant in town boasts an entryway dominated by a large fish tank with a large carp. Traditional Vietnamese carvings and wall hangings adorn the rest of the dining room. The exceptionally large and varied menu includes seafood, poultry, pork, beef, and vegetarian entrees, many of which can be requested extra spicy. **FYI:** Reservations accepted. Children's menu. **Open:** Daily 11am–10pm. **Prices:** Main courses $5–$14. AE, CB, DC, DISC, MC, V.

Washington Park Grille

1096 Gaylord St; tel 303/377-0707. University Blvd exit off I-25; just N of Mississippi Ave. **Californian.** This low-key, casual restaurant attracts a young crowd. It has an oak bar, brick walls, and leaded glass. Diners choose from a variety of salads, sandwiches, and pastas, plus steak, seafood, and chicken. The adjoining lounge serves as a smoking section and offers free pool. **FYI:** Reservations recommended. No smoking. **Open:** Mon noon–10pm, Tues–Thurs 11:30am–10pm, Fri–Sat 11:30am–11pm. **Prices:** Main courses $7–$15. AE, DC, MC, V.

Watson's

900 Lincoln St (Capitol Hill); tel 303/837-1366. Near State Capitol. **Diner.** Framed *Life* magazine covers and Coca-Cola memorabilia decorate this '50s-style malt shop, which also serves as a convenience store and post office. Servers wear the traditional white shirt, white hat, and red bow tie. Diner fare and luncheonette specials are available, but malts are the main draw, with at least 20 varieties to whet your whistle—just step up to the marble counter and name your choice. **FYI:** Reservations not accepted. No liquor license. **Open:** Mon–Thurs 8am–10pm, Fri 8am–11pm, Sat 10am–11pm, Sun noon–6pm. **Prices:** Lunch main courses $2–$5. AE, DISC, MC, V.

Wynkoop Brewing Co

1634 18th St (Lower Downtown); tel 303/297-2700. Across from Union Station. **Regional American/Pub.** Located in the heart of the LoDo district and not far from Coors Field, this is a hot spot on weekends and after Rockies baseball games. The brewery is decorated with the work of local artists, and a large room upstairs has several pool tables plus a bar. The menu offers pub food and sandwiches with a regional flair—elk medallions, brewer's burger, Pojoaque Valley green chile stew. A major draw is the freshly brewed beers (including home-brewed root beer), and there are several malts offered as well. **FYI:** Reservations accepted. Children's menu. **Open:** Mon–Sat 11am–midnight, Sun 10am–10pm. **Prices:** Main courses $5–$16. AE, CB, DC, DISC, MC, V.

ATTRACTIONS

MUSEUMS

Denver Art Museum

100 W 14th Ave (Downtown); tel 303/640-2793. Founded in 1893, this seven-story museum is wrapped by a thin 28-sided wall faced with one million sparkling tiles designed by Gio Ponti of Italy and James Sudler Associates of Denver. Inside is the largest and oldest collection of Native American art of any museum in the United States, as well as a large collection of western and American art, and four other curatorial departments. The Native American collection consists of 20,000 pieces from 150 tribes of North America, spanning

nearly 2,000 years. The collection is growing not only through the acquisition of historic pieces but through the commissioning of works by contemporary artists.

Other collections include African, Asian, oceanic, New World (pre-Columbian artifacts and Spanish colonial arts), painting and sculpture (featuring American and western art and a small collection of European art); and modern and contemporary art. The museum's newest collection, "Architecture, Design & Graphics," ranks as one of the largest modern design galleries in the United States. **Open:** Tues–Sat 10am–5pm, Sun noon–5pm. **$**

Denver Museum of Natural History

2001 Colorado Blvd; tel 303/322-7009 or TDD 370-8257. This rambling three-story museum is the fifth-largest natural history museum in the United States. Exhibits include more than 90 dioramas portraying ancient old-world cultures, Colorado wildlife, North American bears and sea life, Australian ecology, and South American wildlife. Also featured are hands-on exhibits, an IMAX Theater presenting science films with sense-surround sound on a multi-story screen, and a planetarium offering frequent multimedia star programs and laser light shows. **Open:** Daily 9am–5pm. **$$**

Black American West Museum and Heritage Center

3091 California St; tel 303/292-2566. Nearly one-third of the cowboys in the Old West were African American. Located in the heart of the Five Points neighborhood, this museum chronicles their little-known history along with that of black doctors, teachers, miners, farmers, newspaper reporters, and state legislators in the West. The museum is lodged in the Victorian home of Dr Justina Ford, the first African-American woman licensed to practice medicine in Denver. The 35,000-item collection has been acknowledged by the Smithsonian Institution for its great historical significance. **Open:** Mon–Fri 10am–5pm, Sat–Sun noon–5pm. **$**

Museum of Western Art

1727 Tremont Place; tel 303/296-1880. The museum occupies a three-story Victorian brick house that was originally Denver's most notorious brothel and gambling casino. Among the more than 125 paintings and sculptures are classic western scenes by Frederic Remington and Charles Russell, landscapes by Albert Bierstadt and Thomas Moran, and works by 20th-century masters such as Ernest Blumenschein and Georgia O'Keeffe. The gift shop sells hard-to-find art books and prints. **Open:** Tues–Sat 10am–4:30pm. **$**

Colorado History Museum

1300 Broadway; tel 303/866-3682. The Colorado Historical Society's permanent exhibits include "The Colorado Chronicle," an 1800–1949 time line that incorporates biographical plaques and a remarkable collection of photographs, news clippings, and various paraphernalia from Colorado's past. Dozens of dioramas portray various episodes in state history, from the medieval Anasazi cliff-dweller culture through early American settlement, including an intricate re-creation of 19th-century Denver. There's also a life-size display of early transportation and industry, including heavy mining equipment and exhibits of mining techniques. **Open:** Mon–Sat 10am–4:30pm, Sun noon–4:30pm. **$**

Turner Museum

773 Downing St; tel 303/832-0924. The Capitol Hill home of Douglas and Isis Graham houses one of the outstanding private art collections in the United States. Permanent exhibitions include watercolors and engravings of impressionist J M W Turner and numerous landscapes by Thomas Moran, whose work helped inspire the National Park Service. About 3,000 other works are shown on a revolving basis. There is a 30-minute personalized tour available. **Open:** Sun–Fri 2–5pm. **$$$**

Children's Museum of Denver

2121 Children's Museum Dr; tel 303/433-7444. Hands-on experience for children, with a computer lab where kids can log onto the Internet. Also in the Discovery Labs section are areas to explore light, sound, electronics, and biology. There's a woodworking shop, a TV weather forecasting studio, an exhibit where participants learn what it feels like to have various disabilities, and a gigantic mountain offering year-round ski lessons. Special events such as live theater are scheduled periodically; call for schedules. **Open:** Mon–Thurs and Sat 10am–5pm, Fri 10am–8pm, Sun noon–5pm. **$$**

Forney Transportation Museum

1416 Platte St; tel 303/433-3643. Housed in the former City of Denver streetcar powerhouse building. More than 100 antique and classic cars and trucks, plus some 350 other exhibits, fill the huge turn-of-the-century building and pour out onto the surrounding grounds. The collection includes a number of one-of-a-kind vehicles, including Amelia Earhart's "Gold Bug" roadster, a Rolls Royce that once belonged to Prince Aly Khan, and a 1909 French taxicab that transported World War I soldiers from Paris to the Battle of the Marne. Other displays include the world's largest steam locomotive—Big Boy No 4005—and wagons, music boxes, historic fashions, farm equipment, and a model-train display. **Open:** Mon–Sat 10am–5pm, Sun 11am–5pm. **$$**

HISTORIC BUILDINGS AND HOMES

Colorado State Capitol

Broadway and E Colfax Ave; tel 303/866-2604. Built to last 1,000 years, the building was constructed of granite from a Colorado quarry in 1886, its gold dome rising 272 feet above the ground. Murals depicting the history of water in the state cover walls of the first-floor rotunda. The west lobby has a case displaying dolls in miniature ball gowns as worn by various governors' wives. The **Colorado Hall of Fame** is located near the top of the dome, with stained-glass portraits of Colorado pioneers. Tours lasting 30 minutes are offered year-round (more frequently in summer). **Open:** Mon–Fri 9:15am–3:30pm. **Free**

Byers-Evans House
1310 Bannock St; tel 303/620-4933 8175. William N Byers, founder of the *Rocky Mountain News*, built this elaborate Victorian home in 1883. Restored to its 1912–24 appearance, the house contains original Evans family furnishings. In the renovated service wing and carriage house is the **Denver History Museum,** containing artifacts of early Denver life, from the gold rush to World War II. Guided tours. **Open:** Tues–Sun 11am–3pm. **$**

Molly Brown House Museum
1340 Pennsylvania St; tel 303/832-4092. Designed by Denver architect William Lang and built in 1889 of Colorado lava stone with sandstone trim. It was the residence from 1894 to 1932 of James and Margaret (Molly) Brown. The "unsinkable" Molly Brown became a national heroine in 1912 when the *Titanic* sank: she took charge of a group of immigrant women in a lifeboat and later raised money for their benefit. She was also the first preservationist of Denver, and in 1930 she bought the home of poet Eugene Field for the city. Today, the house has been restored to its 1910 appearance and features a large collection of turn-of-the-century furnishings and art objects, many the former possessions of the Brown family. A carriage house at the rear of the house is also open to visitors. **Open:** Peak (June–Aug) Mon–Sat 10am–4pm, Sun noon–4pm. **$$**

Pearce-McAllister Cottage
1880 Gaylord St; tel 303/322-3704. Whereas most of the historic homes in Denver are Victorian in architecture, this one is Dutch colonial revival. It was sold in 1907 to lawyer Henry McAllister Jr, whose wife Phebe decorated the home in the popular colonial revival style of the 1920s. All the furnishings, down to books and tiny knickknacks, were bequeathed to the Colorado Historical Society, which used them to re-create the McAllisters' lifestyle. The house also contains a gift shop and the Denver Museum of Miniatures, Dolls, and Toys. **Open:** Tues–Sat 10am–4pm, Sun 1–4pm. **$**

Larimer Square
1400 block of Larimer St; tel 303/534-2367 or 534-2367. This is where Denver began. Larimer Street between 14th and 15th Streets comprised the entire community of Denver City in 1858, with false-fronted stores, hotels, and saloons to serve gold seekers and other pioneers. In the mid-1870s it was the main street of the city and the site of Denver's first post office, bank, theater, and streetcar line. Today, visitors can tour all 16 of the block's renovated historic buildings. A free self-guided walking tour pamphlet is available at the Larimer Square information booth; visitors can call for an appointment and free guided tour. **Open:** Daily, call for schedule. **Free**

Four Mile Historic Park
715 S Forest St; tel 303/399-1859. Located 4 mi SE of downtown Denver. The oldest log home (1859) still standing in Denver is the centerpiece of a 14-acre living-history facility. Everything is authentic for the period 1859 to 1883—including the house (a former stagecoach stop) and its furnishings and outbuildings, and farm equipment. There are draft horses and chickens in the barn and crops in the garden. Weekend visitors can enjoy stagecoach rides or observe costumed volunteers engaged in different chores and crafts, from plowing and blacksmithing to quilting and cooking. **Open:** Peak (Apr–Sept) Wed–Sun 10am–4pm. Reduced hours off-season. **$$**

PARKS AND GARDENS

Denver Botanic Gardens
1005 York St; tel 303/331-4000. The 20-acre outdoor and indoor gardens display plants native to the desert, plains, mountain foothills, and alpine zones. There's also a traditional Japanese garden, scripture garden (tying plants to biblical history), herb garden, home demonstration garden, water garden, and "wingsong" garden to attract songbirds. The dome-shaped, concrete-and-Plexiglas Boettcher Memorial Conservatory houses 800 species of tropical and subtropical plants. **Open:** Daily 9am–5pm. **$$**

Denver Zoo
City Park (23rd Ave between York and Colorado Blvds); tel 303/331-4110. Four hundred species of animals, more than 3,500 animals total, live in this very spacious zoological park. Feeding times are posted near the zoo entrance so that visitors can time their visit to see the animals when they are at their most active. Highlights include **Northern Shores,** which allows underwater viewing of polar bears and sea lions, and **Tropical Discovery,** which re-creates an entire tropical ecosystem under glass, complete with leopards and crocodiles, piranhas and king cobras. Exotic waterfowl inhabit several ponds, and 300 avians live in **Bird World,** which includes a hummingbird forest and a tropical aviary. In August 1996, the zoo celebrated its 100th anniversary with the opening of the **Primate Panorama,** a five-acre facility whose displays simulate the natural environment of each species it houses. A miniature train circles the Children's Zoo near the zoo's west entrance. The rubber-tired Zooliner tours all zoo paths spring through fall. **Open:** Peak (June–Aug) daily 9am–6pm. Reduced hours off-season. **$$$**

City Park
E 17th to E 26th Ave, between York St and Colorado Blvd; tel 303/964-2500. Denver's largest urban park covers 314 acres—96 square blocks. Established in 1881, it retains Victorian touches, and it includes two lakes (with boat rentals), athletic fields, playgrounds, tennis courts, picnic areas, and an 18-hole municipal golf course. In the summertime there are band concerts. **Open:** Daily 24 hours. **Free**

AMUSEMENT PARKS

Elitch Gardens Amuseument Park
Speer Blvd at I-25; tel 303/595-4FUN or toll free 800/ELITCHS. A Denver tradition, established in 1889, this amusement park has close to two dozen rides, including

Twister II, a brand-new wooden roller coaster; Disaster Canyon, a raging river-rapids ride; the 300-foot Total Tower; and the newly renovated 1925 carousel with 67 hand-carved horses. The park also features musical revues and other entertainment, games, food, shopping, a "kiddieland," and beautiful flower gardens. **Open:** Mem Day–Labor Day, Sun–Thurs 10am–10pm, Fri–Sat 10am–11pm. **$$$$**

Lakeside Amusement Park

46th and Sheridan; tel 303/477-1621. Among the largest amusement parks in the Rocky Mountains, Lakeside has close to 30 major rides including a Cyclone Roller Coaster, a midway with carnival and arcade games, and a miniature train that circles the lake. There are also food stands and picnic facilities, and a separate Kiddies Playland with 15 children's rides. **Open:** Peak (June–Aug) daily, call for schedule. **$$$$**

ENTERTAINMENT VENUES

Denver Center for the Performing Arts

1245 Champa St; tel 303/893-4000 or 893-DCPA (recording). Components include the Helen G Bonfils Theatre Complex, with four theaters; the state-of-the-art Temple Hoyne Buell Theatre; the Auditorium Theatre; and the Galleria Theatre. It also contains the Boettcher Concert Hall, which presents music-in-the-round performances of symphony and opera. Free guided tours of the complex are offered by appointment. **Open:** Call for schedule. **$$$$**

Paramount Theatre

1621 Glenarm Pl; tel 303/534-8336. A historic-preservation group bought this impressive early 20th-century downtown theater in 1978 and returned its gilded columns and emblazoned walls to their former glory. Today the 2,054-seat theater is a place to enjoy jazz concerts, pop and folk performances, lectures, and films. **Open:** Call for schedule. **$$$$**

Red Rocks Amphitheater

Red Rocks Park, Morrison; tel 303/697-8935. Located 12 mi W on I-70. Denver's venue for top-name outdoor summer concerts is set in the Rocky Mountain foothills and flanked by 400-foot-high red sandstone rocks. The amphitheater seats 9,000; only 2,173 seats are reserved. The Red Rocks Trading Post/Visitor Center displays exhibits on the variety of performances that have taken place here since the opening in 1941. **Open:** Daily 9am–6pm. **Free**

Coors Field

2001 Blake St; tel 303/762-5437. Coors Field, which opened in 1995, is home to the Colorado Rockies of baseball's National League. The 50,000-seat stadium, with its red brick exterior, is designed in the style of baseball stadiums of old. **$$$$**

OTHER ATTRACTIONS

United States Mint

320 W Colfax; tel 303/844-3331 or 844-2770. The mint opened in 1863 and originally melted gold dust and nuggets into bars. In 1904 the office moved to the present site, and two years later began coinage operations in both gold and silver. Copper pennies began to be made a few years later. Silver dollars (containing 90% silver) were last manufactured in 1935; gold purchases were discontinued in 1968. In 1970 the coinage law changed and all silver was eliminated from dollars and half-dollars: today they are made of a copper-nickel alloy. The mint stamps more than 5 billion coins a year. A coin minted in Denver has a small *D* on it.

The mint has recently enclosed most of the coin-processing equipment for noise reduction, which limits visitors' viewing of actual coin operations. However, video monitors along the visitors' gallery provide a close view of the actual coin minting process. **Open:** Mon–Tues and Thurs–Fri 8am–2:45pm, Wed 9am–2:45pm. **Free**

Dillon

See also Frisco

This resort town provides food and lodging for skiers heading to Breckenridge, Copper Mountain, Keystone, and Arapahoe Basin ski resorts and for summer hikers, mountain bikers, and anglers. A planned community, Dillon was moved to its present location in the early 1960s when Dillon Reservoir flooded the original town. **Information:** Town of Dillon, PO Box 8, Dillon 80435 (tel 970/468-2403).

MOTELS

Best Western Ptarmigan Lodge

652 Lake Dillon Dr, PO Box 218, 80435; tel 970/468-2341 or toll free 800/842-5939; fax 970/468-6465. ¼ mi E of Lake Dillon Marina. Basic accommodations near Lake Dillon, within walking distance of restaurants and shops. Convenient to both Keystone and Silverthorne. **Rooms:** 69 rms; 7 cottages/villas. CI 3pm/CO 11am. Nonsmoking rms avail. **Amenities:** Cable TV w/movies. No A/C. All units w/terraces, some w/fireplaces. **Services:** Babysitting. **Facilities:** 1 restaurant, 1 bar (w/entertainment), sauna, whirlpool, washer/dryer. **Rates (CP):** Peak (Dec 15–30) $125–$150 S or D; $150–$160 cottage/villa. Extra person $10. Children under age 12 stay free. Min stay peak. Lower rates off-season. Parking: Outdoor, free. AE, CB, DC, DISC, MC, V.

Days Inn

580 Silverthorne Lane, Silverthorne, PO Box 1488, Dillon, 80435; tel 970/468-8661 or toll free 800/DAYS-INN; fax 970/468-5583. Just off I-70. No-frills motel convenient to local ski areas. **Rooms:** 73 rms, stes, and effic. CI 3pm/CO 10am. Nonsmoking rms avail. **Amenities:** Cable TV w/movies. No A/C. Some units w/terraces, some w/fireplaces. In-room ski lockers. **Services:** **Facilities:** Sauna, whirlpool, washer/dryer. **Rates (CP):** Peak (Dec 17–Jan 6) $55–$125 S; $70–$140 D; $70–$145 ste; $70–$140

effic. Extra person $10. Children under age 18 stay free. Min stay peak. Lower rates off-season. Parking: Indoor/outdoor, free. AE, CB, DC, DISC, MC, V.

Dillon Inn
708 Anemone Trail, 80435; tel 970/262-0801; fax 970/262-0803. ½ mi S of I-70. With convenient access to the highway and local ski areas, this comfortable motel is ideal for skiers. Within walking distance of local shops and outlets. **Rooms:** 30 rms. CI 3pm/CO 10am. Nonsmoking rms avail. **Amenities:** A/C, cable TV w/movies. **Services:** **Facilities:** Sauna, whirlpool. **Rates (CP):** Peak (Dec 15–Mar) $85 S; $120 D. Extra person $5. Children under age 12 stay free. Min stay special events. Lower rates off-season. Parking: Outdoor, free. AE, DISC, MC, V.

RESTAURANT

Keystone Ranch
Keystone Ranch Rd, Keystone; tel 970/468-4161. 3 mi off US 6. **New American/Regional American.** Offering perhaps the finest gourmet dining in this part of Colorado, this special restaurant occupies a historic 1940s ranch house that retains its warm coziness. Two seatings are available for dinner (5:45 and 8:15pm). The six-course dinner might include a main course featuring rack of lamb, elk or other regional game, or fresh seafood. Dessert is served in the living room around the original stone fireplace. **FYI:** Reservations recommended. Dress code. No smoking. **Open:** Peak (Nov 15–Apr 15) daily 5:45pm–closing. **Prices:** Prix fixe $62. AE, CB, DC, DISC, MC, V. VP

Dinosaur National Monument

For lodgings, see Craig, Grand Junction

Straddling the Colorado-Utah border, the national monument encompasses 325 square miles of stark canyon land at the confluence of the Yampa and Green Rivers. About 145 million years ago this region was a suitable habitat for dinosaurs, including vegetarians such as diplodocus, brontosaurus, and stegosaurus, and sharp-toothed carnivores such as allosaurus. In at least one spot floodwaters washed dinosaur carcasses onto a sandbar, where they were preserved in sand and covered with sediment. This Dinosaur Quarry, accessible only from the Utah side of the park, contains remains of many long-vanished species, including fossils of sea creatures two to three times older than any land dinosaurs. There's a visitors center at the quarry with exhibits and a short slide program. For more information, contact Dinosaur National Monument, Box 210, Dinosaur 81610 (tel 970/374-2216).

Durango

A former railroad town created in 1880 to haul gold and silver from nearby mines and provide the site for a smelter, Durango was known as a wide-open western town. Much of that flavor remains in its many historic landmarks, including the Durango and Silverton Narrow Gauge Railroad. In recent years Durango has also become a center for outdoor recreation, with offices for the San Juan National Forest and Bureau of Land Management. **Information:** Durango Resort Association, PO Box 2587, Durango 81302 (tel 970/247-0312 or 800/525-8855).

HOTELS

Hampton Inn
3777 Main Ave, 81301; tel 970/247-2600 or toll free 800/247-6885; fax 970/247-2600. Next to Durango Behavioral Center on US 550. Modern hotel conveniently located for skiers, or those just traveling through. Good views of Animas River plain to the south. **Rooms:** 76 rms and stes. CI 2pm/CO 11am. Nonsmoking rms avail. **Amenities:** A/C, cable TV w/movies, dataport. **Services:** Complimentary airport transportation in winter only. **Facilities:** 30 Whirlpool, washer/dryer. **Rates (CP):** Peak (June 19–Aug 20) $89–$99 S; $99–$109 D; $135 ste. Extra person $10. Children under age 18 stay free. Min stay special events. Lower rates off-season. Parking: Outdoor, free. AE, CB, DC, DISC, MC, V.

Jarvis Suite Hotel
125 W 10th St, 81301 (Historic District); tel 970/259-6190 or toll free 800/824-1024; fax 970/259-6190. This recently renovated modern hotel is located close to bars, restaurants, and the best shopping in town. Ideal for business travelers and those planning a stay of several days. **Rooms:** 22 stes. CI 3pm/CO noon. Nonsmoking rms avail. Suites vary in size and layout. Vaulted ceilings give a spacious feel, and some have lofts. **Amenities:** A/C, cable TV w/movies, refrig. All suites have full kitchens. **Services:** Babysitting. Small, eager-to-please staff. **Facilities:** Whirlpool, washer/dryer. **Rates:** Peak (May 16–Oct 16) $95–$155 ste. Extra person $10. Children under age 12 stay free. Min stay special events. Lower rates off-season. Parking: Outdoor, free. AE, CB, DC, DISC, MC, V.

Strater Hotel
699 Main Ave, 81302; tel 970/247-4431 or toll free 800/247-4431; fax 970/259-2208. 2 blocks N of train depot. Constructed in 1887 in downtown Durango, this four-story brick Victorian building with white wood trim has maintained its historic charm and western appeal. The interior is plushly carpeted and decorated with period antiques and fine upholstered furniture. Most suited for couples seeking modern comfort with the charm of the Wild West. **Rooms:** 93 rms. CI 4pm/CO noon. Nonsmoking rms avail. Rooms are elegantly furnished with upholstered furniture beautifully crafted from

a variety of hardwoods. Great views of Durango and surrounding mountains. **Amenities:** Cable TV w/movies, dataport. No A/C. **Services:** Car-rental desk, babysitting. **Facilities:** 1 restaurant (bkfst and dinner only), 2 bars (w/entertainment), whirlpool. In addition to fine restaurant, Henry's, and Diamond Belle Saloon, the Strater also offers theatrical performances during summer months in Diamond Circle Theatre. **Rates:** Peak (May 13–Oct 16) $95–$170 S; $115–$170 D. Min stay special events. Lower rates off-season. Parking: Outdoor, free. AE, CB, DC, DISC, MC, V.

MOTELS

Best Western Lodge at Purgatory
49617 US 550, 81301; tel 970/247-9669 or toll free 800/637-7727; fax 970/247-9681. 25 mi N of Durango. Conveniently located at base of Purgatory Ski Mountain with fantastic views of the surrounding mountains. **Rooms:** 31 rms, stes, and effic. CI 2pm/CO 11am. Nonsmoking rms avail. **Amenities:** Cable TV w/movies, refrig. No A/C. **Services:** **Facilities:** 1 restaurant (dinner only), 1 bar, whirlpool, washer/dryer. **Rates (CP):** Peak (June–Aug/Dec–Mar) $72 S; $70–$80 D; $75–$118 ste; $72–$118 effic. Extra person $5. Children under age 12 stay free. Min stay special events. Lower rates off-season. Parking: Outdoor, free. AE, CB, DC, DISC, MC, V.

Best Western Mountain Shadows
3255 N Main Ave, 81301; tel 970/247-5200 or toll free 800/521-5218; fax 970/247-5200. 1½ mi N of town on US 550. Part of the motel strip on the north end of town, this property is easily identifiable by the tinted geodesic dome over the pool and hot tub. **Rooms:** 65 rms, stes, and effic. CI 2pm/CO 11am. Nonsmoking rms avail. **Amenities:** A/C, cable TV w/movies. All units w/terraces. Some rooms have cooking facilities. **Services:** **Facilities:** Games rm, whirlpool, washer/dryer. **Rates (CP):** Peak (June 19–Sept 4) $81 S; $94 D; $107–$129 ste; $107–$129 effic. Extra person $5. Children under age 12 stay free. Lower rates off-season. Parking: Outdoor, free. AE, CB, DC, DISC, MC, V.

Comfort Inn
2930 Main Ave, 81301; tel 970/259-5373 or toll free 800/532-7112; fax 970/259-5373. 1½ mi N of the train station. Traditional southwestern stucco architecture. **Rooms:** 48 rms. CI 2pm/CO 11am. Nonsmoking rms avail. **Amenities:** A/C, cable TV w/movies. All units w/terraces. **Services:** **Facilities:** Whirlpool. **Rates (CP):** Peak (May 24–Oct 15) $60–$84 S; $74–$88 D. Extra person $5. Children under age 18 stay free. Min stay special events. Lower rates off-season. Parking: Outdoor, free. AE, CB, DC, DISC, ER, JCB, MC, V.

Iron Horse Inn
5800 N Main Ave, 81301; tel 970/259-1010 or toll free 800/748-2990; fax 970/385-4791. 4 mi N of town on US 550. Large motel and conference center complex in the Animas River Valley, within the southern San Juan Mountains. Vibrant red and white cliffs border the complex. **Rooms:** 144 stes. CI 3pm/CO 11am. Nonsmoking rms avail. All units are two-level suites: single suites have queen-size bed upstairs and small living area downstairs; double suites are slightly larger, with queen-size beds upstairs and downstairs. Although not totally contemporary, suites are clean and comfortable. **Amenities:** A/C, cable TV w/movies. All units w/fireplaces. **Services:** Car-rental desk. **Facilities:** 1 restaurant (bkfst and dinner only), 1 bar (w/entertainment), games rm, sauna, whirlpool, washer/dryer. Cross-country ski equipment available for rent. **Rates:** Peak (May 15–Oct 15) $85–$125 ste. Extra person $5. Children under age 12 stay free. Lower rates off-season. Parking: Outdoor, free. AE, CB, DC, DISC, MC, V.

Landmark Motel
3030 N Main Ave, 81301; tel 970/259-1333 or toll free 800/252-8853; fax 970/247-3854. 1 mi N of downtown on US 550. The brick construction and white metal fence give this motel a suburban look. Kept up-to-date and modern, it's a step above a basic motel. **Rooms:** 48 rms and stes. CI 2pm/CO 11am. Nonsmoking rms avail. Rooms are spacious and very nicely furnished. **Amenities:** A/C, cable TV w/movies. All units w/terraces. **Services:** **Facilities:** Sauna, whirlpool. **Rates (CP):** Peak (May 26–Sept 4) $74 S; $75–$89 D; $109–$120 ste. Extra person $5. Children under age 12 stay free. Min stay special events. Lower rates off-season. Parking: Outdoor, free. AE, CB, DC, DISC, MC, V.

Redwood Lodge
763 Animas View Dr, 81301; tel 970/247-3895. 2 mi N of town. Nice views of the surrounding cliffs and part of the Animas River plain. Fairly quiet and clean, but in need of some renovation. Good location for skiers. **Rooms:** 16 rms and effic. CI 2pm/CO 10am. Nonsmoking rms avail. **Amenities:** A/C, cable TV. All units w/terraces. **Services:** **Facilities:** Sauna, whirlpool, playground. **Rates:** Peak (June–Sept) $44 S or D; $56–$60 effic. Extra person $5. Children under age 5 stay free. Lower rates off-season. Parking: Outdoor, free. AE, DISC, MC, V.

Silver Spur Motel
3416 N Main Ave, 81301; tel 970/247-5552 or toll free 800/748-1715; fax 970/259-5559. 1½ mi N of downtown on US 550. Good choice for those traveling through. **Rooms:** 33 rms and stes. CI 2pm/CO 11am. Nonsmoking rms avail. Rooms are well maintained and relatively secluded. **Amenities:** A/C, cable TV w/movies. All units w/terraces. **Services:** **Facilities:** 1 restaurant, 1 bar (w/entertainment). **Rates:** Peak (July 4–Sept 5) $64–$89 S or D; $125 ste. Extra person $7. Children under age 12 stay free. Lower rates off-season. Parking: Outdoor, free. AE, CB, DC, DISC, MC, V.

INNS

General Palmer Hotel

567 Main Ave, 81301; tel 970/247-4747 or toll free 800/523-3358; fax 970/247-1332. Established in 1898, the Palmer still maintains its elegant Victorian atmosphere. All floors are served by an old gated elevator, and antiques adorn the narrow hallways and charming lobby. Conveniently located in the historic section of town, close to the Durango & Silverton Narrow Gauge Railroad Station. **Rooms:** 39 rms and stes. CI 4pm/CO noon. No smoking. Rooms tastefully furnished with large upholstered chairs and four-poster or brass beds. **Amenities:** Cable TV w/movies, bathrobes. No A/C. 1 unit w/whirlpool. **Services:** **Facilities:** 1 restaurant, 1 bar. **Rates (CP):** Peak (May 15–Oct) Extra person $10. Children under age 18 stay free. Lower rates off-season. Higher rates for special events/hols. Parking: Outdoor, free. AE, CB, DC, DISC, MC, V.

Lightner Creek Inn

999 County Rd 207, 81301; tel 970/259-1226; fax 970/259-0732. 3 mi W of town on US 160; 1 mi N of CO 207. 20 acres. Hidden away in the hills outside town, it's housed in a 1903 farmhouse reminiscent of an English countryside inn. Lightner Creek runs through the property, separating the inn from adjacent llama pasture. The quiet area is often visited by wildlife. The guest lounge has a baby grand player piano. Unsuitable for children under 10. **Rooms:** 8 rms (2 w/shared bath); 1 cottage/villa. CI 4pm/CO 11am. No smoking. Attractively decorated with traditional quilts. **Amenities:** No A/C, phone, or TV. Some units w/terraces. **Services:** Social director, masseur, afternoon tea and wine/sherry served. **Facilities:** Guest lounge w/TV. **Rates (BB):** Peak (May–Oct) $110 D w/shared bath, $95–$110 D w/private bath; $150 cottage/villa. Extra person $35. Lower rates off-season. Higher rates for special events/hols. Parking: Outdoor, free. DISC, MC, V.

RESORTS

Tall Timber Resort

SSR Box 90, 81301; tel 970/259-4813. 25 mi N of Durango. 180 acres. This unusual resort is set in a small valley along the Animas River, accessible only by the complimentary helicopter or the historic Durango & Silverton Narrow Gauge Railroad. The setting was chosen to offer a complete break from the fast pace and stress of today's world. It's not for everyone, but it's a good choice for anyone seeking solitude. **Rooms:** 10 cottages/villas. CI 2pm/CO 10am. No smoking. Hidden in an old aspen grove, cottages are spacious. Luxurious bathrooms. **Amenities:** Refrig, bathrobes. No A/C, phone, or TV. All units w/terraces, all w/fireplaces, some w/whirlpools. Cottages have huge handmade fireplaces. **Services:** Social director. Service is impeccable, individualized, and very flexible. Helicopter picnic in high alpine meadow and "heli-hike" available. Professional handgun safety course offered once a year. **Facilities:** 9 1 1 restaurant, sauna, whirlpool. Meals are of very high quality and are beautifully presented; resort-grown vegetables are used whenever possible. Large lodge serves as guest lounge and dining room, with each table set in a bay window. Pool is equipped to provide a current for guests seeking more exercise when swimming (although it's not a lap pool). Comfortable library has upwards of 3,000 volumes available. **Rates (AP):** Peak (July 7–Sept) $3,800 cottage/villa. Extra person $1,900. Lower rates off-season. Rates are for seven-day/six-night packages and include all facilities and services except helicopter picnic. Special children's rates avail. Closed Nov–May 15. No CC.

Tamarron Resort

40292 US 550 N, PO Box 3131, 81302; tel 970/259-2000 or toll free 800/456-2000; fax 970/259-0745. 18 mi N of Durango. 640 acres. Secluded in a nice hilly area overlooking the Animas River Valley, this resort is well laid out to take advantage of the natural habitat. It's a great place for conferences, and golfers who like mountain courses will feel right at home here. **Rooms:** 412 rms and effic. Executive level. CI 4pm/CO 11am. Nonsmoking rms avail. Traditional rooms in European-style main lodge; variety of condominiums in Gamble Oak, Pine Cone, and High Point complexes. **Amenities:** A/C, satel TV w/movies, refrig. Some units w/terraces, some w/whirlpools. **Services:** Twice-daily maid svce, social director, masseur, children's program, babysitting. **Facilities:** 18 3 500 2 restaurants, 1 bar, volleyball, games rm, spa, sauna, steam rm, whirlpool, day-care ctr, playground, washer/dryer. Rafting, jeep tours, and sleigh rides offered seasonally. Golf course intricately placed among and around accommodation complexes. **Rates:** Peak (June–Aug) $149–$179 S or D; $279–$409 effic. Extra person $20. Children under age 17 stay free. Lower rates off-season. AP and MAP rates avail. Parking: Outdoor, free. AE, CB, DC, DISC, MC, V.

The Wit's End Guest Ranch & Resort

254 County Rd 500, Bayfield, 81122; tel 970/884-4113; fax 970/884-3261. At N end of Vallecito Lake. 170 acres. Located outside of Durango in the majestic San Juan Mountains, the Wit's End is a one-of-a-kind place. The lodge is a three-story log barn with a full bar and pool table. **Rooms:** 16 cottages/villas. CI 4pm/CO 11am. Recently renovated cabins are spacious, quiet, and comfortable, with terrific views of surrounding mountains. **Amenities:** Cable TV w/movies, refrig, VCR, CD/tape player, bathrobes. No A/C. All units w/terraces, all w/fireplaces. Cabins have full kitchen facilities. **Services:** Social director, masseur, babysitting. **Facilities:** 2 50 1 restaurant, 1 bar (w/entertainment), volleyball, games rm, lawn games, whirlpool, playground, washer/dryer. Children's facility has games, toys, crafts. Teen center planned for near future will have pool and table tennis plus other recreational facilities. **Rates (AP):** Peak (June–Aug) $2,940–$3,380 cottage/villa.

Extra person $1,470. Children under age 4 stay free. Min stay peak. Lower rates off-season. Parking: Outdoor, free. Rates are for seven nights and include use of all facilities. One-night stays only in off-season. AE, MC, V.

RESTAURANTS

Ariano's

160 College Dr; tel 970/247-8146. Near train station. **Italian.** Cherry wood bar and tables, and still lifes and impressionist prints on the walls give this a friendly, pleasant atmosphere. The menu offers a wide range of pasta, poultry, meat, and fish dishes. Choose from fettuccine Napolitano, chicken in parchment paper, veal Zingara, or Italian baked trout. **FYI:** Reservations not accepted. Children's menu. No smoking. **Open:** Peak (May–Sept) daily 5–10:30pm. Closed Nov 1–7. **Prices:** Main courses $10–$23. AE, MC, V.

Carvers Bakery/Cafe/Brewery

1022 Main Ave; tel 970/259-2545. 5 blocks E of train station. **Cafe/Southwestern.** Somewhat quieter and less brightly lit than many cafes, this one is nicely accented with hardwood ceiling trim and booths, and tiled tables. Located in the historic district, the spacious entryway houses the bakery counter, the cafe is next, and the brewery with its small bar lies at the back. A great place for beer lovers—the beer is excellent—as well as vegetarians, the menu includes such items as garlic basil lasagna, Navajo tacos, and Thai pasta. They also serve terrific breakfasts. **FYI:** Reservations not accepted. Beer and wine only. No smoking. **Open:** Mon–Sat 6:30am–10pm, Sun 6:30am–1pm. **Prices:** Main courses $5–$7. MC, V.

Francisco's Restaurante Y Cantina

619 Main Ave; tel 970/247-4098. 2 blocks N of train station. **Mexican/Steak.** Wood pillars, carved in the style of ancient Mayan ruins, accent the stucco walls and heavy wood-beamed ceiling. A large tiled fountain graces the entrance to the cavernous dining room, which has been attractively divided into smaller spaces. Plants and ceramic plates and vessels decorate the walls; tables are inlaid wood. Food ranges from the simplest hamburger through beef and seafood to traditional Mexican plates. **FYI:** Reservations not accepted. Children's menu. **Open:** Peak (July 4–Oct) Mon–Sat 11am–10pm, Sun 9am–10pm. **Prices:** Main courses $5–$18. AE, CB, DC, DISC, MC, V.

Olde Tymer's Cafe

10th St and Main Ave; tel 970/259-2990. 5 blocks N of train depot. **American.** You can get sandwiches, homemade chili, salads, and what locals consider one of the best burgers around in this cafe in the heart of historic downtown Durango. Inside the historic building are brick walls and an old tiled ceiling, plus old photos of the town's early days and vintage medicine bottles, malted milk tins, and other memorabilia. In summer you can opt to sit on "Durango's favorite patio" out back. **FYI:** Reservations not accepted. **Open:** Daily 11am–10pm. **Prices:** Main courses $4–$8. MC, V.

The Palace Grill

2 Depot Place; tel 970/247-2018. Adjacent to train station. **Seafood/Steak.** Conveniently located next to the Durango & Silverton Narrow Gauge Railroad depot, this elegant restaurant is Victorian with solid oak trim and columns, and tiled floor alternating with plush carpets. Favorite menu items include the honey duck, topped with an almond sauce, and the McMahon, a New York steak set on hash browns and smothered with onions. The herb-crusted grouper and lemon-peppered salmon top the more unusual dishes. **FYI:** Reservations not accepted. Guitar. Children's menu. No smoking. **Open:** Lunch Mon–Fri 11:30am–2:30pm; dinner daily 5:30–10pm. **Prices:** Main courses $12–$24. AE, CB, DC, DISC, MC, V.

The Red Snapper

144 E 9th St; tel 970/259-3417. Near train depot. **Seafood/Steak.** The decor says "fish"—from the saltwater fish tanks dividing the dining room to the brass and wood models of sea creatures adorning the walls. The tables have fish-design inlays, and etched glass plates of nautical scenes separate the bar from the dining area. The menu is divided into seafood, "landfood," and "today's catch," which varies daily. There are four red snapper dishes, shrimp teriyaki, scallops dijonaise, filet mignon, and Hawaiian chicken; specials might include Hawaiian ahi or halibut Rosita. The salad bar has over 40 items. **FYI:** Reservations accepted. No smoking. **Open:** Daily 5–10pm. **Prices:** Main courses $13–$38. AE, MC, V.

ATTRACTIONS

Animas Museum

31st St and W 2nd Ave; tel 970/259-2402. This old stone schoolhouse features a turn-of-the-century classroom. An 1870s log home from the early days of Animas City (the town that predated Durango) has been restored, and there are exhibits depicting local history, Native Americans, and the West. Museum store. **Open:** May–Oct, Mon–Sat 10am–6pm. $

Durango & Silverton Narrow Gauge Railroad

479 Main Ave; tel 970/247-2733. In continuous operation since 1881, the railroad has never varied its route: up the Rio de las Animas Perdidas (the River of Lost Souls) and through 45 miles of mountain and San Juan National Forest wilderness to the tiny mining town of Silverton, and back. The coal-fired steam locomotives pull strings of Victorian coaches on the 3,000-foot climb past relics of mining and railroad activity from the last century. The trip takes 3¼ hours each way, with a two-hour stopover in the town of Silverton before the return trip. **Open:** Daily, call for schedule. **$$$$**

Edwards

See Vail

Englewood

A Denver suburb on the south side of the metropolitan area, Englewood is perhaps best known as the home of the Tech Center, which contains a number of technological industries and business parks and the headquarters of several major companies. **Information:** Greater Englewood Chamber of Commerce, 701 W Hampden, Suite G-34, Englewood 80154 (tel 303/789-4473).

HOTELS

Denver South Residence Inn

6565 S Yosemite St, 80111; tel 303/740-7177 or toll free 800/331-3131; fax 303/741-9426. Just W of exit 197 off I-25. Modern, spacious condominium units with an intimate feel. Close to Denver Tech Center. Ideal for long-term stays. **Rooms:** 128 cottages/villas. CI 4pm/CO noon. Nonsmoking rms avail. **Amenities:** A/C, cable TV w/movies, refrig, dataport. All units w/terraces, some w/fireplaces. All have fully equipped kitchens, including microwaves. **Services:** Complimentary happy hour Mon–Fri 5–7pm. **Facilities:** Basketball, lawn games, whirlpool, washer/dryer. **Rates (CP):** Peak (Apr–Sept) $115–$165 cottage/villa. Lower rates off-season. Parking: Outdoor, free. AE, CB, DC, DISC, JCB, MC, V.

Holiday Inn Denver South–Centennial Airport

7770 S Peoria St, 80112; tel 303/790-7770 or toll free 800/HOLIDAY; fax 303/799-6319. Across from Centennial Airport. Tucked away from much of the development, this more private hotel is relatively quiet except for the occasional jet. **Rooms:** 119 rms and stes. Executive level. CI 3pm/CO noon. Nonsmoking rms avail. Contemporary decor. **Amenities:** A/C, cable TV w/movies, dataport, voice mail, in-rm safe. Some units w/terraces, some w/fireplaces. **Services:** Complimentary van service within 10-mile radius. **Facilities:** 30 1 restaurant, 1 bar (w/entertainment), sauna, washer/dryer. **Rates (BB):** Peak (Apr–Sept) $94–$100 S or D; $104–$115 ste. Extra person $10. Children under age 18 stay free. Lower rates off-season. Parking: Outdoor, free. AE, CB, DC, DISC, JCB, MC, V.

RESORT

Inverness Hotel & Golf Club

200 Inverness Dr W, 80112; tel 303/799-5800 or toll free 800/346-4891; fax 303/799-5874. ¼ mi E of exit 194 off I-25. 25 acres. One of Denver's best overall hotels, this is a great choice for those wanting to be close to, but not in, downtown. Good for business travelers. **Rooms:** 302 rms and stes. Executive level. CI 3pm/CO noon. Nonsmoking rms avail. Attractive, contemporary Scandinavian furniture. Mountain or golf course views available. **Amenities:** A/C, cable TV w/movies, dataport. All units w/minibars, some w/terraces, 1 w/whirlpool. **Services:** VP **Facilities:** 18 3 1230 4 restaurants, 3 bars, volleyball, sauna, whirlpool. **Rates:** $70–$200 S; $80–$210 D; $130–$600 ste. Extra person $10. Children under age 13 stay free. Parking: Outdoor, free. AE, CB, DC, DISC, JCB, MC, V.

RESTAURANTS

Country Dinner Playhouse

6875 S Clinton St; tel 303/799-1410. Just SE of I-25 and Arapahoe Rd. **American.** At Colorado's only year-round Equity theater, featuring live Broadway shows like *Phantom of the Opera, Fiddler on the Roof,* and *South Pacific,* the ticket price includes an all-you-can-eat buffet served prior to each performance. The usual array includes fruits, vegetables, salads, North Atlantic turbot, oven-roasted chicken, and choice baron of beef. Bar service is available at the table or in the cocktail lounge. **FYI:** Reservations recommended. **Open:** Lunch Sat–Sun noon–4pm; dinner Tues–Sun 6–10pm. **Prices:** Prix fixe $21–$26. AE, DISC, MC, V.

Trail Dust Steak House

7101 S Clinton St; tel 303/790-2420. Just SE of exit 197 off I-25. **Steak.** Any customer who allows his necktie to be clipped from his chest gets a free drink, and the hundreds of ties hanging from the walls and rafters attest to the tradition's popularity. A large slide empties from the second-floor dining area onto the dance floor, which features dancing and country music nightly. The menu is somewhat limited, but there are non-steak offerings including ribs, chicken, swordfish, and a "vegetarian roundup." **FYI:** Reservations not accepted. Country music/dancing. Children's menu. Additional location: 9101 Benton St, Westminster (tel 427-1446). **Open:** Lunch Mon–Fri 11am–2pm; dinner Mon–Thurs 5–11pm, Fri 5pm–midnight, Sat 4pm–midnight, Sun noon–10pm. **Prices:** Main courses $8–$18. AE, CB, DC, DISC, MC, V.

Estes Park

See also Allenspark

The gateway to Rocky Mountain National Park, Estes Park has been a resort and vacation town since the 1860s. Long known by Utes and Arapahoes, the mountain park (7,522 feet) was discovered in 1859 by rancher Joel Estes. **Information:** Estes Park Area Chamber of Commerce, PO Box 3050, Estes Park 80517 (tel 970/586-4431 or 800/44-ESTES).

HOTELS

Holiday Inn of Estes Park

101 S St Vrain Ave, PO Box 1468, 80517; tel 970/586-2332 or toll free 800/803-7837; fax 970/586-2332. At jct US 36/CO 7. Conveniently located hotel with lovely views of the area. **Rooms:** 150 rms and stes. CI 3pm/CO 11am. Nonsmoking rms avail. **Amenities:** A/C, cable TV w/movies,

voice mail. Some units w/terraces. **Services:** Babysitting. **Facilities:** 1 restaurant, 1 bar (w/entertainment), games rm, whirlpool, washer/dryer. **Rates:** Peak (June–Sept) $59–$100 S or D; $100–$200 ste. Extra person $8. Children under age 19 stay free. Min stay special events. Lower rates off-season. Parking: Outdoor, free. AE, CB, DC, DISC, JCB, MC, V.

Stanley Hotel
333 Wonderview Dr, PO Box 1767, 80517; tel 970/586-3371 or toll free 800/976-1377; fax 970/586-3673. 2 blocks N of jct US 34/US 36. Opened in 1909 by FO Stanley, inventor of the Stanley Steamer, this large, white, historic hotel sits elegantly against the backdrop of the Rocky Mountains. Quality, luxury accommodations. **Rooms:** 129 rms and stes. CI 3pm/CO 11am. Nonsmoking rms avail. Rooms were being fully renovated. Wide range of sizes and luxury levels available; many units command excellent views of Longs Peak or Lake Estes. **Amenities:** Cable TV, voice mail. No A/C. Some units w/terraces. **Services:** **Facilities:** 2 restaurants, 1 bar (w/entertainment), volleyball, games rm, lawn games, spa, sauna, whirlpool. **Rates:** Peak (May 15–Oct 15) $99–$169 S or D; $159–$199 ste. Extra person $10. Children under age 12 stay free. Min stay special events. Lower rates off-season. Parking: Outdoor, free. AE, CB, DC, DISC, MC, V.

MOTELS

Best Western at Lake Estes Resort
1650 Big Thompson Ave, PO Box 1466, 80517; tel 970/586-3386 or toll free 800/292-VIEW; fax 970/586-9000. 1½ mi E of town. Modern, well-maintained motel overlooking Lake Estes; convenient to town and major highways. **Rooms:** 57 rms and stes; 1 cottage/villa. CI 3pm/CO 11am. Nonsmoking rms avail. **Amenities:** Cable TV w/movies, refrig, dataport. No A/C. Some units w/terraces, some w/fireplaces, some w/whirlpools. **Services:** Babysitting. **Facilities:** Lawn games, sauna, whirlpool, playground, washer/dryer. **Rates:** Peak (June 21–Sept 14) $92–$105 S; $105–$115 D; $145–$200 ste; $190–$210 cottage/villa. Extra person $9. Children under age 18 stay free. Min stay wknds and special events. Lower rates off-season. Parking: Outdoor, free. AE, CB, DC, DISC, JCB, MC, V.

Four Winds Travel Lodge
1120 Big Thompson Ave, PO Box 3460, 80517; tel 970/586-3313 or toll free 800/527-7509; fax 970/586-3313. ¾ mi E of jct US 36/US 34. Pine trees shade the entrance to this mom-and-pop motel, a comfortable resting spot. **Rooms:** 53 rms and stes. CI 3pm/CO 10am. Nonsmoking rms avail. **Amenities:** Cable TV w/movies, refrig. No A/C. All units w/terraces, some w/fireplaces, 1 w/whirlpool. **Services:** **Facilities:** Sauna, whirlpool, playground, washer/dryer. **Rates:** Peak (June 15–Sept 15) $56–$71 S; $70–$81 D; $100–$225 ste. Extra person $7. Lower rates off-season. Parking: Outdoor, free. AE, CB, DC, DISC, MC, V.

Miles Motel & Cottages
1250 S St Vrain Ave, 80517; tel 970/586-3185; fax 970/586-3185. 2 mi S of town on CO 7. A well-maintained motel on the outskirts of town. **Rooms:** 7 rms and effic; 12 cottages/villas. CI 2pm/CO 10am. No smoking. Units vary in size to accommodate different numbers of guests. Cottages are not separate units. **Amenities:** Cable TV, refrig. No A/C or phone. All units w/terraces, some w/fireplaces. **Services:** **Facilities:** **Rates:** Peak (June 15–Sept 15) $62–$72 S or D; $67 effic; $69–$175 cottage/villa. Extra person $10. Min stay special events. Lower rates off-season. Parking: Outdoor, free. DISC, MC, V.

Silver Moon Motel
175 Spruce Dr, PO Box 1879, 80517; tel 970/586-6006 or toll free 800/818-6006; fax 970/586-6007. Just W of downtown. Basic lodging within walking distance of town. **Rooms:** 36 rms; 4 cottages/villas. CI 2pm/CO 11am. Nonsmoking rms avail. **Amenities:** Cable TV. No A/C. All units w/terraces. **Services:** **Facilities:** Washer/dryer. **Rates:** Peak (May 15–Sept 15) $72 S or D; $65 cottage/villa. Children under age 12 stay free. Lower rates off-season. Parking: Outdoor, free. AE, CB, DC, DISC, MC, V.

Silver Saddle Motor Lodge
1260 Big Thompson Ave, PO Box 1747, 80517; tel 970/586-4476; fax 970/586-4476. 1 mi E of jct US 34/US 36. Very modern and well-maintained motel, with great south views. **Rooms:** 50 rms and stes. CI 3pm/CO 11am. No smoking. **Amenities:** A/C, cable TV w/movies, refrig. All units w/terraces, some w/fireplaces. **Services:** **Facilities:** Whirlpool, playground, washer/dryer. **Rates (CP):** Peak (June 15–Sept 15) $69–$120 S or D; $120–$160 ste. Extra person $5. Children under age 12 stay free. Min stay peak. Lower rates off-season. Parking: Outdoor, free. AE, CB, DC, DISC, MC, V.

Trappers Motor Inn
553 W Elkhorn Ave, PO Box 487, 80517; tel 970/586-2833 or toll free 800/552-2833. 3½ blocks W of downtown. Basic, no-frills motel within walking distance of shopping district. **Rooms:** 19 rms. CI 2pm/CO 10am. Nonsmoking rms avail. **Amenities:** Cable TV w/movies. No A/C or phone. All units w/terraces. **Services:** **Facilities:** Whirlpool. **Rates:** Peak (June 10–Sept 5) $46–$66 S or D. Extra person $5. Children under age 5 stay free. Min stay wknds and special events. Lower rates off-season. Parking: Outdoor, free. AE, MC, V.

INN

Riversong
1765 Lower Broadview Rd, PO Box 1910, 80517; tel 970/586-4666. 28 acres. Beautifully secluded inn tucked away in hills west of town along banks of Big Thompson River. Great

views of peaks along Continental Divide. Wildflowers cover grounds in spring and summer. Buildings set amid boulders, trees, and wildlife. Unsuitable for children under 12. **Rooms:** 9 rms and stes. CI 4pm/CO noon. No smoking. **Amenities:** Bathrobes. No A/C, phone, or TV. Some units w/terraces, all w/fireplaces, some w/whirlpools. **Services:** Afternoon tea served. Hosts are happy to prepare a candlelight gourmet dinner with prior arrangement. **Facilities:** Guest lounge. Mile-long path leads into surrounding hills. **Rates (BB):** $135–$205 D; $160–$205 ste. Extra person $50. Min stay. Parking: Outdoor, free. MC, V.

LODGES

Boulder Brook

1900 Fall River Rd, 80517; tel 970/586-0910 or toll free 800/238-0910; fax 970/586-8067. 1½ mi W of town on US 34. Condominium-style accommodations set back from the road, situated along river bank. **Rooms:** 16 stes. CI 2:30pm/CO 11am. Nonsmoking rms avail. Suites are individually decorated, very comfortable, luxurious, and intimate. **Amenities:** Cable TV w/movies, refrig, dataport, VCR, voice mail. No A/C. All units w/terraces, all w/fireplaces, all w/whirlpools. Some kitchenettes, some full kitchens. **Services:** Babysitting. **Facilities:** Whirlpool. **Rates:** Peak (June–Sept 15) $89–$179 ste. Extra person $10. Min stay wknds. Lower rates off-season. Parking: Outdoor, free. Special packages with lots of extras avail. AE, DISC, MC, V.

Castle Mountain Lodge

1520 Fall River Rd, Moraine Rte, 80517; tel 970/586-3664 or toll free 800/852-PINE; fax 970/586-6060. 1¼ mi W of town on US 34. Tucked back from the road on a slope overlooking the Fall River, this is a peaceful alternative to the usual motel and hotel. **Rooms:** 8 rms; 22 cottages/villas. CI 3pm/CO 11am. Nonsmoking rms avail. Rustic cabins come in a variety of sizes. **Amenities:** Cable TV w/movies, refrig. No A/C or phone. Some units w/terraces, some w/fireplaces, 1 w/whirlpool. Some have full kitchens, others kitchenettes. **Services:** Babysitting. **Facilities:** Lawn games. **Rates:** Peak (June 15–Sept 15) $83–$95 S or D; $115–$280 cottage/villa. Extra person $8. Min stay peak. Lower rates off-season. Parking: Outdoor, free. AE, CB, DC, DISC, MC, V.

Estes Park Center/YMCA of the Rockies

2515 Tunnel Rd, 80511; tel 970/586-3341; fax 970/586-6078. 5 mi SW of town on US 66. 860 acres. Beautiful setting close to Rocky Mountain National Park. Although it looks like a national forest, camping is not permitted anywhere on the property. **Rooms:** 565 rms; 210 cottages/villas. CI 3pm/CO 10am. No smoking. Variety of room sizes and amenity levels available. **Amenities:** No A/C or TV. Some units w/terraces, some w/fireplaces. Cabins with fully equipped kitchens available. **Services:** Social director, children's program, babysitting. **Facilities:** 3 2500 5 restaurants, basketball, volleyball, lawn games, day-care ctr, playground, washer/dryer. **Rates:** Peak (June–Nov) $45–$84 S or D; $51–$207 cottage/villa. Extra person $5. Min stay peak. Lower rates off-season. Parking: Outdoor, free. No CC.

Mountain Haven Inn and Cottages

690 Moraine Rte, 80517; tel 970/586-2864. ¾ mi SW of town on US 36. Nice setting on the Big Thompson River, convenient to downtown Estes Park. **Rooms:** 7 cottages/villas. CI 3pm/CO 10:30am. Modern and comfortable cabins. **Amenities:** Cable TV w/movies, refrig. No A/C or phone. All units w/terraces, all w/fireplaces. All cabins have full kitchens. **Services:** **Facilities:** 17 **Rates:** Peak (June 15–Sept) $149–$275 cottage/villa. Extra person $10. Min stay peak. Lower rates off-season. Parking: Outdoor, free. MC, V.

Streamside Cabins

1260 Fall River Rd, PO Box 2930, 80517; tel 970/586-6464 or toll free 800/321-3303; fax 970/586-6272. 1 mi W of town on US 34. Set back from the road in the woods along the Fall River, this establishment offers guests cottage-style accommodations ideal for extended stays. A lovely getaway spot. **Rooms:** 19 rms and stes. CI 3pm/CO 11am. Nonsmoking rms avail. Rooms come in a variety of sizes, but all are quite spacious and comfortably furnished. **Amenities:** Cable TV w/movies, refrig, VCR, bathrobes. No A/C or phone. All units w/terraces, all w/fireplaces, some w/whirlpools. All units have steam showers and gas grills. **Services:** **Facilities:** Lawn games, whirlpool, playground. **Rates:** Peak (May 20–Oct 15) $115–$165 S or D; $145–$175 ste. Extra person $15. Min stay peak, wknds, and special events. Lower rates off-season. Parking: Outdoor, free. Several multi-night packages avail. AE, DISC, MC, V.

Sunnyside Knoll Resort

1675 Fall River Rd, 80517; tel 970/586-5759. 1 mi W of town. Set back from the road, accommodations are modern yet comfortable and ideal for couples. **Rooms:** 15 rms; 2 cottages/villas. CI 2pm/CO 11am. Nonsmoking rms avail. Variety of room sizes available. **Amenities:** Cable TV, refrig, VCR. No A/C or phone. Some units w/terraces, all w/fireplaces, some w/whirlpools. **Facilities:** Games rm, lawn games, whirlpool. **Rates:** Peak (May 25–Sept) $92–$179 S or D; $150–$170 cottage/villa. Extra person $10. Min stay peak, wknds, and special events. Lower rates off-season. Parking: Outdoor, free. DISC, MC, V.

RESORTS

Aspen Lodge at Estes Park

6120 CO 7, Longs Peak Rte, 80517; tel 970/586-8133 or toll free 800/332-6867; fax 970/586-8133. 8 miles S of town. 80 acres. Nestled in the mountains south of town, this resort is easy to reach yet feels very secluded. The main buildings are large log lodges with huge warm fireplaces. Fantastic views of Longs Peak and the Continental Divide. In summer, the resort acts as a dude ranch. **Rooms:** 36 rms; 23 cottages/villas. CI 3pm/CO 11am. No smoking. Lodge rooms and various-sized cabins are comfortably rustic, yet modern. **Amenities:** No A/C or TV. All units w/terraces, some w/fireplaces. **Services:** Social director, children's program, babysitting. **Facilities:** 2 1 restaurant, 1 bar, basketball, volleyball, games rm, lawn games, racquetball, squash, spa, sauna, whirlpool, day-care ctr, playground, washer/dryer. A 3,000-acre ranch available for guided horse-packing trips. Snowmobiling, ice skating. **Rates (AP):** Peak (May 25–Sept 5) $450–$920 S; $920 cottage/villa. Children under age 2 stay free. Min stay peak. Lower rates off-season. Parking: Outdoor, free. Rates are for three, four, or seven-day summer packages; children's rates lower. Off-season, single-night rates avail. Children under 12 stay free. AE, CB, DC, DISC, MC, V.

Glacier Lodge
2166 Moraine Rte, PO Box 2656, 80517; tel 970/586-4401 or toll free 800/523-3920. 3 mi SW of town on CO 66. 15 acres. Spread over the hills southwest of town, this small resort on the Big Thompson River is a wonderful retreat for families or large groups. Wildlife abounds. **Rooms:** 29 cottages/villas. CI 2pm/CO 11am. Cabin-style units are spacious and modern. Three large lodges available for large groups. **Amenities:** TV, refrig. No A/C or phone. All units w/terraces, all w/fireplaces. Each unit has a full kitchen. **Services:** Babysitting. **Facilities:** 40 Basketball, volleyball, lawn games, playground. **Rates:** Peak (June–Sept 5) $92–$135 cottage/villa. Extra person $10. Children under age 2 stay free. Min stay peak. Lower rates off-season. MAP rates avail. Parking: Outdoor, free. MC, V.

RESTAURANTS

The Dunraven Inn
2470 CO 66; tel 970/586-6409. Just SW of YMCA. **Italian.** Guests will notice a couple of things when visiting this restaurant: the *Mona Lisa* and the dollar bill seem to be everywhere! The owners display prints and posters featuring every possible rendition of the portrait, while past customers have covered walls with their autographed greenbacks. The main dining room, rather dimly lit, has a quiet, intimate ambience. The menu lists traditional Italian entrees (linguine with clam sauce, chicken cacciatore) and combinations such as steak and lobster or shrimp. **FYI:** Reservations recommended. Children's menu. Dress code. **Open:** Sun–Thurs 5–10pm, Fri–Sat 5–11pm. **Prices:** Main courses $8–$20. AE, DISC, MC, V.

La Casa del Estorito
222 E Elkhorn Ave; tel 970/586-2807. W of town park. **Cajun/Mexican.** Conveniently located, this restaurant is bright, with wood-paneled walls and ceiling, and stained-glass ceiling lights. Food is hot and spicy—your choice of either Mexican or Cajun—with many seafood options. **FYI:** Reservations recommended. Guitar. Children's menu. No smoking. **Open:** Peak (May 15–Sept 15) daily 11am–10:30pm. **Prices:** Main courses $5–$15. AE, CB, DC, DISC, MC, V.

$ Mountaineer Restaurant
540 S St Vrain St; tel 970/586-9001. 1 mile S of town on CO 7. **American.** This bright and airy family restaurant is the place to come for breakfast anytime and for good homemade pies. There's also an impressive range of traditional lunches and dinners. **FYI:** Reservations accepted. Children's menu. No liquor license. **Open:** Peak (June–Sept) daily 6am–9:30pm. **Prices:** Main courses $3–$8. MC, V.

The Other Side
In National Park Village, 900 Moraine Ave; tel 970/586-2171. 1½ mi SW of town on US 36. **Seafood/Steak.** The large windows of this light- and plant-filled dining room offer patrons a pleasant view of the nearby small lake and any wildlife that might happen to stroll by. Several house specialties are offered in addition to the standard steak and seafood dishes, including beef tips Dijon, blackened buffalo steak, vegetable tetrazzini, and honey-baked bass. **FYI:** Reservations accepted. Children's menu. **Open:** Peak (May 25–Oct 15) daily 7am–10pm. **Prices:** Main courses $10–$20. AE, CB, DC, DISC, MC, V.

ATTRACTIONS

Enos Mills Cabin
CO 7; tel 970/586-4706. Enos Mills encouraged the appreciation of the Rocky Mountains and was a driving force behind the establishment of Rocky Mountain National Park. The cabin and 200-acre homestead of the late-19th-century conservationist is now open to the public as a museum. Memorabilia in the homestead cabin include copies of Mills's 15 books, and the cameras that took thousands of photographs. Visitors are asked to honk their car horns when they arrive at the parking area, and Enda Mills Kiley will guide them down a nature trail to the cabin while discussing her father's life and work. **Open:** Mem Day–Labor Day, Mon–Sat 10am–4pm. **Free**

Estes Park Area Historical Museum
200 4th St; tel 970/586-6256. The lives of early homesteaders in Estes Park are depicted in the museum, which includes a completely furnished turn-of-the-century log cabin, an old ranch wagon, an original Stanley Steamer automobile, and a changing exhibit gallery housed in the original headquarters of Rocky Mountain National Park. The museum also has a discovery room for kids, with hands-on activities, and the story behind the book *A Lady's Life in the Rocky Mountains*, written in the late 1800s by Englishwoman Isabella Bird. The museum distributes a historical walking tour brochure for downtown Estes Park and sponsors a variety of lectures and other programs. **Open:** Peak (May–Sept) Mon–Sat 10am–5pm, Sun 1–5pm. Reduced hours off-season. $

Prospect Mountain Aerial Tramway
420 E Riverside Dr; tel 970/586-3675. The lift provides panoramic views of Longs Peak, the Continental Divide, and Estes Park village to its riders. The lower terminal is one block south of the post office; the upper terminal has a gift shop and snack bar. Numerous hiking trails converge atop the mountain. **Open:** June–Aug, daily 9am–6:30pm. **$$$**

Estes Park Brewery
470 Prospect Village Dr; tel 970/586-5421. The only brewery in Estes Park produces 3,000 barrels per year using water from the Big Thompson River that is filtered through the moraines of Glacier Gorge. The brewery specializes in fresh beer and Belgian-style ales, the most popular being Longs Peak Raspberry Wheat. Free tours and samples are offered. Souvenir glasses, caps, and posters are sold, and there are billiard tables, darts, and other games. **Open:** Peak (June–Aug) Sun–Thurs 11am–10pm, Fri–Sat 11am–midnight. Reduced hours off-season. **Free**

Evans

See Greeley

Fort Collins

Home of Colorado State University, fast-growing Fort Collins is named for an army camp, commanded by Lieut Col William O Collins, that was established in the 1860s to protect area settlers from attack by hostile Native Americans. It is home to an Anheuser-Busch brewery plus several microbreweries, and hosts the Colorado Brewers' Festival each June. **Information:** Fort Collins Area Convention & Visitors Bureau, 420 S Howes, Suite 101, PO Box 1998, Fort Collins 80522 (tel 970/482-5821 or 800/274-FORT).

HOTELS

Fort Collins Marriott
350 E Horsetooth Rd, 80525; tel 970/226-5200 or toll free 800/548-2635; fax 970/282-0561. E of College Ave near Warren Lake. Easily distinguished by its tiered southwestern architecture, this Marriott is located less than five miles south of downtown and Colorado State University in a quiet, suburban area. **Rooms:** 230 rms and stes. Executive level. CI 4pm/CO noon. Nonsmoking rms avail. Rooms are slightly smaller than you might expect from the large exterior. **Amenities:** A/C, cable TV w/movies, voice mail. **Services:** Social director. **Facilities:** 1960 2 restaurants, 1 bar, games rm, whirlpool, washer/dryer. **Rates:** Peak (Feb 28–Nov) $99–$119 S; $109–$129 D; $119–$149 ste. Extra person $10. Children under age 10 stay free. Lower rates off-season. Parking: Outdoor, free. AE, CB, DC, DISC, EC, JCB, MC, V.

Holiday Inn University Park
425 W Prospect Rd, 80526; tel 970/482-2626 or toll free 800/HOLIDAY; fax 970/493-6265. Just S of Colorado State University. Located just south of the university and a few minutes from downtown. All rooms open onto the large indoor atrium and fountain. **Rooms:** 259 rms and stes. CI 3pm/CO 1pm. Nonsmoking rms avail. **Amenities:** A/C, cable TV w/movies. **Services:** Car-rental desk, social director. **Facilities:** 1200 1 restaurant, 1 bar (w/entertainment), sauna, whirlpool, beauty salon, washer/dryer. **Rates:** Peak (May–Oct) $89 S; $99 D; $99–$109 ste. Extra person $10. Children under age 18 stay free. Lower rates off-season. Parking: Outdoor, free. AE, CB, DC, DISC, JCB, MC, V.

MOTELS

Budget Host Inn
1513 N College Ave, 80524; tel 970/484-0870 or toll free 800/825-4678; fax 970/224-2998. N end of town on US 287. Owned and operated by Tom and Karen Weitkunat for some 20 years, the Budget Host is a well-maintained and very friendly hostelry. **Rooms:** 30 rms, stes, and effic. CI 1pm/CO 11am. Nonsmoking rms avail. **Amenities:** A/C, cable TV w/movies, refrig. All units w/terraces. **Services:** **Facilities:** Whirlpool. **Rates:** Peak (May 15–Sept 1) $42–$52 S; $52–$62 D; $72 ste; $47–$67 effic. Extra person $5. Children under age 3 stay free. Lower rates off-season. Parking: Outdoor, free. AE, DISC, MC, V.

Mulberry Inn
4333 E Mulberry St, 80524; tel 970/493-9000 or toll free 800/234-5548; fax 970/224-9636. E of exit 269A off I-25. Located about five miles east of Fort Collins, this inn is a step up from the usual roadside motel. **Rooms:** 122 rms and stes. CI 3pm/CO noon. Nonsmoking rms avail. Good views of Front Range from rooms on west side. **Amenities:** A/C, cable TV w/movies. Some units w/terraces, some w/whirlpools. **Services:** **Facilities:** 1 restaurant (dinner only), 1 bar. **Rates (CP):** Peak (May–Sept) $55–$65 S; $70–$85 D; $70–$120 ste. Extra person $5. Children under age 16 stay free. Lower rates off-season. Parking: Outdoor, free. AE, CB, DC, DISC, MC, V.

INN

Helmshire Inn B&B
1204 S College Ave, 80524; tel 970/493-4683; fax 970/493-4773. Just E of Colorado State University. Centrally located adjacent to the university and close to downtown, the Helmshire is tastefully decorated with antiques and reproductions. **Rooms:** 24 effic. CI 3pm/CO 11am. No smoking. Back rooms are quietest. **Amenities:** A/C, cable TV, refrig. **Services:** **Facilities:** 133 1 restaurant, 1 bar (w/entertainment), guest lounge. Access to nearby state-of-the-art health club for $5 fee. **Rates (BB):** $79 effic. Parking: Outdoor, free. AE, DISC, MC, V.

RESTAURANTS

Bisetti's
120 S College Ave; tel 970/493-0086. Near Old Town Sq. **Italian.** An amazing number of Chianti bottles hang from the ceiling and walls of this Italian restaurant. Together with the dim lighting, they give the place a certain old-world charm. Choices include a wide range of traditional dishes, from veal saltimbocca to lasagna and manicotti, and seafood dishes. Locals rave about the desserts. **FYI:** Reservations accepted. Children's menu. No smoking. **Open:** Lunch Mon–Fri 11am–2pm; dinner Sun–Thurs 5–9pm, Fri–Sat 5–10pm. **Prices:** Main courses $7–$16. AE, DISC, MC, V.

Coopersmith's Pub & Brewing Co
5 Old Town Sq; tel 970/498-0483. **British/Pub.** Large windows afford views of the brew kettles and tanks at this brew pub. In addition to a long list of standard and seasonal beers, there is handcrafted root beer, ginger ale, and cream soda. Pub fare covers burgers to fish-and-chips, plus some British specialties like bangers and mash and Highland cottage pie. **FYI:** Reservations accepted. **Open:** Sun–Thurs 11am–midnight, Fri–Sat 11am–2am. **Prices:** Main courses $6–$13. ER, MC, V.

Nico's Catacombs
115 S College Ave; tel 970/482-6426. Near Old Town Sq. **Continental.** Despite the unpretentious exterior, this below-ground, dimly lit restaurant is fairly elegant inside. Plants, flowers, wine bottles, distinctively framed artwork, and decorative wood panels make up the decor. Dining choices range from traditional continental fare to Australian rock lobster tail, New Zealand venison, and Rocky Mountain rainbow trout. **FYI:** Reservations recommended. Dress code. **Open:** Mon–Sat 5–10pm. **Prices:** Main courses $15–$28. AE, DC, MC, V.

★ Silver Grill Cafe
218 Walnut St; tel 970/484-4656. 1 block NW of Visitors Bureau. **Cafe/Bakery.** This pleasant, cozy cafe in the heart of old Fort Collins has had a faithful local clientele for all of its 60-plus years, and it still retains much of its 1950s-style diner decor. Standard American breakfast and lunch fare, with huge, delicious cinnamon rolls—a meal in themselves. **FYI:** Reservations not accepted. No liquor license. No smoking. **Open:** Mon–Sat 6am–2pm, Sun 7am–1pm. **Prices:** Lunch main courses $3–$8. DISC, MC, V.

ATTRACTIONS

Colorado State University
University and College Aves; tel 970/491-1101. Founded in 1870 as Colorado State Agricultural College, the university celebrated its 125th anniversary in 1995. The Administration Building houses a cafeteria, bar, bookstore, activities center, ballroom, and other facilities. Appointments can be made to visit the renowned Veterinary Teaching Hospital and the Equine Teaching Center at the Foothills Campus. The Art Department has five different galleries with revolving exhibits; and the University Theatre in Johnson Hall presents student productions year-round. **Free**

Fort Collins Museum
200 Mathews St; tel 970/221-6738. Located in the 1904 Carnegie Library Building, this museum boasts the largest collection of Folsom points of any western museum, military artifacts from Fort Collins, and pioneer and Victorian objects. There is an 1850s cabin, the 1864 log officers' mess known locally as "Auntie Stone's cabin," and a log one-room schoolhouse built in 1905. Events include Rendezvous, a fur-trading reenactment, in June; and Skookum Day, a living history day with an ice cream social and children's activities, held the third Saturday in July. **Open:** Tues–Sat 10am–5pm, Sun noon–5pm. **Free**

The Farm at Lee Martinez Park
600 N Sherwood; tel 970/221-6665. The museum has exhibits depicting farming techniques from the turn of the century. Early 20th-century farm machinery is on display, crafts are sold in the Silo Store, and oats are available to feed the animals. Special programs are scheduled year-round, and there are weekend pony rides in spring and summer. **Open:** Peak (June–Aug) Tues–Sat 10am–5:30pm, Sun noon–5:30pm. **Free**

Swetsville Zoo
4801 E Harmony Rd; tel 970/484-9509. This sculpture park is a menagerie of over 130 dinosaurs and other real and imaginary animals, flowers, and windmills—all constructed from car parts, farm machinery, and other scrap metal. There's also a miniature ¾-mile steam train that visitors can ride summer weekends and holidays, and an outdoor exhibit of old farm equipment and a 10-seat bicycle. **Open:** Daily sunrise–sunset. **Free**

Anheuser-Busch Brewery
2351 Busch Dr; tel 970/490-4691. Opened in mid-1988, the brewery has become one of Fort Collins's leading employers—and its top tourist attraction. Six million barrels of beer are produced here each year and distributed to 10 western states. Tours of the brewing facility leave from the visitors center, which includes exhibits on the Anheuser-Busch company, a gift shop, and a tasting room. The barn is home to the giant Clydesdale draft horses used to promote Budweiser and other Busch beers since 1933. **Open:** Peak (May–Oct) daily 9:30am–5pm. Reduced hours off-season. **Free**

HC Berger Brewery
1900 E Lincoln Ave; tel 970/493-9044. Produces German-style ales using a cold-maturation process. Among the beers offered in the tasting room are Whistlepin Wheat, Red Raspberry Wheat, Pale Ale, and Chocolate Stout. Brewery tours are offered Saturday 1–5pm and by appointment. **Open:** Mon–Fri 8am–5pm, Sat 1–5pm, Sun noon–4pm. **Free**

Odell Brewing Company
800 E Lincoln Ave; tel 970/498-9070. Specializing in English-style ales, Odell's produces only draft beers, which are available in restaurants and bars in Colorado and southern Wyoming. Tours and the tastings are offered; one gallon and half-gallon brewery jugs can be purchased. **Open:** Mon–Thurs 9am–6pm, Fri 9am–7pm, Sat 10am–7pm. **Free**

New Belgium Brewery
500 Linden St; tel 970/221-0524. Recently relocated to a state-of-the art, 100-barrel brewhouse. Among the selection of Belgian-style ales produced here are Sunshine Wheat, Old Cherry Ale, and Fat Tire Amber Ale. Fifteen-minute tours are available Saturday 1–5pm and by appointment. **Open:** Mon–Thurs 10am–6pm, Fri 10am–7pm, Sat 10am–5pm. **Free**

Fort Morgan

A military outpost in the 1860s, Fort Morgan owes its existence to sugar-beet processing, ranching, and oil. Its most famous citizen was big-band leader Glenn Miller, a 1921 graduate of Fort Morgan High School, who started his first band in the city. **Information:** Fort Morgan Area Chamber of Commerce, PO Box 971, Fort Morgan 80701 (tel 303/867-6702).

MOTELS

Best Western Park Terrace Inn
725 Main St, 80701; tel 970/867-8256 or toll free 800/528-1234; fax 970/867-8256. 1 block N of Chamber of Commerce. This typical Best Western offers quick access to downtown. **Rooms:** 24 rms. CI open/CO 11am. Nonsmoking rms avail. **Amenities:** A/C, cable TV w/movies. All units w/terraces. **Services:** **Facilities:** 1 restaurant. Memories Restaurant offers three "home-cooked" meals daily. **Rates:** Peak (May 15–Sept 15) $46–$52 S; $56–$59 D. Extra person $5. Lower rates off-season. Parking: Outdoor, free. AE, DISC, MC, V.

Budget Host Empire Motel
1408 Edison St, Brush, 80723; tel 970/842-2876 or toll free 800/283-4678. 1 mi W of downtown. Basic motel with few amenities or services, but clean and well maintained. **Rooms:** 18 rms. CI open/CO 10am. Nonsmoking rms avail. Rooms are on the small side. **Amenities:** A/C, cable TV. All units w/terraces. **Services:** **Rates:** $28–$32 S; $34–$43 D. Extra person $3. Children under age 2 stay free. Parking: Outdoor, free. AE, DISC, MC, V.

Central Motel
201 W Platte Ave, 80701; tel 970/867-2401; fax 970/867-2401. Close to the heart of town and locally owned and operated, the Central is well suited for families. Guests can swim free in the town pool. **Rooms:** 19 rms and stes. CI 2pm/CO 11am. Nonsmoking rms avail. Wide range of room sizes available, all clean and well maintained. **Amenities:** A/C, cable TV w/movies, refrig. All units w/terraces. **Services:** **Rates:** Peak (May 15–Sept 15) $39–$47 S; $49–$55 D; $65–$70 ste. Extra person $5. Children under age 10 stay free. Lower rates off-season. Parking: Outdoor, free. AE, DC, DISC, MC, V.

RESTAURANTS

Heinrich's Restaurant
In Madison Hotel, 14378 US 34; tel 970/867-8208. Exit 75 off I-76. **American/Continental.** A small restaurant in the style of an old German bar, with large wine casks, stained glass, decorative wood panels on the walls, and a low-beamed ceiling. Hearty salads and several seafood dishes round out a menu that also offers trout amandine, filet mignon, and buffalo burgers. **FYI:** Reservations accepted. Children's menu. **Open:** Breakfast daily 6–11am; lunch daily 11am–2pm; dinner Mon–Sat 5–10pm. **Prices:** Main courses $4–$16. AE, CB, DC, MC, V.

Stroh's Inn
901 W Platte Ave; tel 970/876-6654. 1 block W of bus depot. **American.** This family-run eatery offers generous portions of basic American fare—hamburgers, sandwiches, salads, roast chicken, and steaks, all served with few frills. Good for families. **FYI:** Reservations recommended. Children's menu. **Open:** Mon–Sat 6am–9pm, Sun 6am–2pm. **Prices:** Main courses $4–$13. AE, MC, V.

ATTRACTIONS

Fort Morgan Museum
414 Main St; tel 970/867-6331. An extensive collection of northeastern Colorado Native American artifacts, beginning with Clovis points 13,000 years old, is the highlight of this museum. Other permanent exhibits focus on farming, ranching, and the railroad history of Morgan County, including old Fort Morgan, and a display on the life of native son Glenn Miller. The 1920s Hillrose Drugstore soda fountain, a town social center, has been fully restored. **Open:** Mon and Fri 10am–5pm, Tues–Thurs 10am–8pm, Sat 11am–5pm. **Free**

Oasis on the Plains Museum
6877 County Rd 14; tel 970/432-5200. Located 15 mi SW of Fort Morgan. This working ranch displays artifacts, antiques, collectibles, and other items of interest from early homesteading in the northeastern Colorado plains. **Open:** Sun noon–4pm. **Free**

Fraser

See Winter Park

Frisco

See also Dillon

As a Wild West mining town in the late 19th century, Frisco was said to have been home to 3,500 miners, 19 dance halls, and 20 saloons. The city is decidedly more sedate these days as it serves the needs of Summit County skiers, hikers, mountain bikers, boaters, and anglers. **Information:** Summit County Chamber of Commerce, PO Box 214, Frisco 80443 (tel 970/668-5800).

HOTELS

UNRATED **Club Med Copper Mountain**

50 Beeler Place, PO Box 3337, Copper Mountain, 80443; tel 970/968-2161 or toll free 800/CLUB-MED; fax 970/968-2166. Between American Flyer and Union Creek. Modern facility characterized by a spacious yet cozy lounge that greets guests upon arrival. Known for its personalized service, Club Med caters to skiers of all ages and abilities. **Rooms:** 236 rms. CI 4pm/CO 10am. **Amenities:** A/C. No phone or TV. **Services:** Masseur, children's program. Extensive children's program. **Facilities:** 400 2 restaurants, 3 bars (1 w/entertainment), games rm, sauna, whirlpool, washer/dryer. Ski school with 40 instructors. **Rates (AP):** $195–$325 S; $300–$500 D. Parking: Outdoor, free. Rates include meals, lift ticket, ski lessons, and evening entertainment. Closed Apr 15–Nov. AE, MC, V.

Holiday Inn Summit County

1129 N Summit Blvd, PO Box 4310, 80443; tel 970/668-5000 or toll free 800/782-7669; fax 970/668-0718. S of exit 203 off I-70. Conveniently located just off I-70, close to Lake Dillon. Great for those traveling through and for skiers wishing to access several of the ski areas in Summit County. **Rooms:** 216 rms and stes. CI 3pm/CO noon. Nonsmoking rms avail. Many have great views of lake and surrounding mountains. **Amenities:** A/C, cable TV w/movies. Some units w/terraces, 1 w/whirlpool. **Services:** Social director, babysitting. Ski shuttle available. **Facilities:** 250 1 restaurant, 1 bar (w/entertainment), games rm, sauna, whirlpool, washer/dryer. **Rates:** Peak (Dec 15–Apr 15) $55–$195 S or D; $140–$205 ste. Extra person $10. Children under age 19 stay free. Min stay peak. Lower rates off-season. Parking: Outdoor, free. AE, CB, DC, DISC, JCB, MC, V.

INN

Twilight Inn

308 Main St, PO Box 397, 80443; tel 970/668-5009 or toll free 800/262-1002. 4 blocks W of Summit Blvd. This deceptively large inn provides comfortable lodgings within walking distance of restaurants and shops. Located in the heart of Frisco, not far from surrounding ski areas. **Rooms:** 12 rms (4 w/shared bath). CI 3pm/CO 10am. No smoking. Variety of sizes and luxury levels available. **Amenities:** No A/C, phone, or TV. All units w/terraces. **Services:** Babysitting, afternoon tea served. **Facilities:** Steam rm, whirlpool, washer/dryer, guest lounge w/TV. **Rates (CP):** Peak (Dec 9–Apr 15) $90 S or D w/shared bath, $103–$128 S or D w/private bath. Extra person $15. Min stay peak. Lower rates off-season. Parking: Outdoor, free. AE, DISC, MC, V.

RESTAURANTS

Charity's

307 Main St; tel 970/668-3644. 4 blocks W of Summit Blvd. **Regional American/Steak.** In the heart of town is this rustic, warm restaurant with a large stone fireplace, many hunting trophies, and comfortable, upholstered booths, semi-oval in shape. The traditional grilled fare has a regional touch, such as miner's stew served in a bread bowl, and pine nut–crusted chicken. **FYI:** Reservations not accepted. Children's menu. No smoking. **Open:** Daily 11:30am–10pm. **Prices:** Main courses $6–$15. AE, MC, V.

Golden Annie's

603 Main St; tel 970/668-0345. 2 blocks W of Summit Blvd. **Mexican.** Within walking distance of downtown shops, this festive restaurant is decorated with historic photos, hanging plants, and tile trim. In addition to unusual Mexican entrees, you can choose from a variety of seafood and steak cooked over a mesquite grill. The fajitas are excellent, but if you want something a little different, try the southwestern lime chicken or a mesquite-blackened tuna steak. **FYI:** Reservations not accepted. Children's menu. No smoking. **Open:** Daily 5–10pm. **Prices:** Main courses $10–$23. AE, MC, V.

O'Shea's Copper Bar

In Main Village, Copper Junction Bldg, Copper Mountain; tel 970/968-2882. Opposite Mountain Plaza. **American/Mexican.** A casual, rustic ski mountain cafe situated close to the ski lifts. Inside are lots of old wood paneling and historic photos. Diners can order huevos rancheros and other specialties at breakfast; a variety of sandwiches, salads, and Mexican dishes at lunch; and prime rib, mesquite-grilled chicken, and buffalo specialties in the evening. **FYI:** Reservations not accepted. Children's menu. **Open:** Daily 10:30am–midnight. Closed Apr 25–Nov 20. **Prices:** Main courses $7–$15. AE, CB, DC, MC, V.

ATTRACTION

Frisco Historic Park

120 Main St; tel 970/668-3428. This historic park comprises eight historic buildings, including the town's original 1881 jail, one-room schoolhouse, log chapel, and homes dating to the 1880s. The schoolhouse contains displays and artifacts on Frisco's early days, and a trapper's cabin has a hands-on exhibit of animal pelts. Artisans sell their wares in several of

the buildings, and special programs are scheduled during the summer. **Open:** Peak (June–Aug) Tues–Sun 11am–4pm. Reduced hours off-season. **Free**

Georgetown

For lodgings and restaurants, see Dillon, Frisco, Golden, Idaho Springs, Winter Park

ATTRACTIONS

Georgetown Loop Railroad
1106 Rose St; tel 303/569-2403 or toll free 800/691-4FUN. An 1884 railroad bridge serves this restored narrow-gauge line, which makes daily summertime runs between Georgetown and Silver Plume. The steel bridge is 300 feet long and 95 feet high, and was considered an engineering miracle a century ago. Though the direct distance between the terminals is 2.1 miles, the track covers 4.5 miles, climbing 638 feet in 14 sharp curves and switchbacks, crossing Clear Creek four times, and culminating with a 360° spiraling knot. The round trip takes about 2½ hours, including an optional walking tour of the Lebanon Mine and Mill, which can be reached only by train. Special meal car and mountain bike trips for additional fee. **Open:** Peaak (Mem Day–Labor Day) daily 9:20am–4pm. Reduced hours off-season. **$$$$**

Hamill House Museum
305 Argentine St; tel 303/569-2840. Built in country Gothic revival style, this house dates to 1867, when it was owned by silver speculator William Hamill and was the town's most ambitious residence. A carriage house and office occupy two stone structures behind the main house, and a delicately carved outhouse had two parts: one for the family with walnut seats; the other for servants with pine seats. Today the house maintains the original woodwork, fireplaces, and wallpaper. **Open:** Peak (Mem Day–Labor Day) daily 10am–5pm. Reduced hours off-season. **$**

Glenwood Springs

Glenwood Springs was discovered by members of the Ute tribe, who came to heal their wounds in the hot mineral springs and natural vapor caves. In 1860, three successful Aspen miners built what was then the largest hot springs pool in the world, and it attracted the elite of the day. A $490 million four-lane interstate highway completed in 1993 (among the most expensive roads ever built) runs 18 miles through spectacularly beautiful Glenwood Canyon. **Information:** Glenwood Springs Chamber Resort Association, 1102 Grand Ave, Glenwood Springs 81601 (tel 970/945-6589 or 800/221-0098).

HOTELS

Hotel Colorado
526 Pine St, 81601; tel 970/945-6511 or toll free 800/544-3998; fax 970/945-7030. Near exit 116 off I-70. This historic 1893 hotel, made of sandstone block and Roman brick, is a beautiful structure not to be missed, whether or not you stay the night. Facing south, its majestic facade and fountain piazza offer a wonderful space for guests to enjoy pleasant weather and views of the valley. Lobby and lower corridors have large windows and lots of plants. **Rooms:** 128 rms and stes. Executive level. CI 4pm/CO 11am. Nonsmoking rms avail. Rooms are individually decorated with tasteful antique furnishings and have lofty ceilings. Bell-tower suites are spectacular. **Amenities:** Cable TV, voice mail. No A/C. Some units w/terraces, some w/whirlpools. Ceiling fan. **Services:** Masseur. **Facilities:** 270 1 restaurant, 1 bar, games rm, spa, sauna, steam rm, whirlpool, beauty salon. Several small businesses on premises, including rafting outfitter in summer and ski rentals in winter. **Rates:** $62–$90 S; $70–$98 D; $110–$295 ste. Extra person $8. Children under age 18 stay free. Min stay wknds. Parking: Outdoor, free. AE, CB, DC, DISC, MC, V.

Hot Springs Lodge & Pool
415 6th St, 81601; tel 970/945-6571; fax 970/945-6571. Near exit 116 off I-70. Adobe style hotel offering clean modern accommodations with access to a hot springs pool and athletic club. **Rooms:** 107 rms. CI 4pm/CO noon. Nonsmoking rms avail. Rooms are tastefully decorated. **Amenities:** A/C, cable TV, in-rm safe. Some units w/terraces. **Services:** Masseur. **Facilities:** 45 1 restaurant, 1 bar, games rm, sauna, whirlpool, washer/dryer. Passes to athletic club cost $9 for hotel guests, and include pool usage. Rates for pool use only are lower. **Rates:** Peak (Mar 15–Sept) $70–$95 S or D. Extra person $5. Children under age 3 stay free. Min stay wknds. Lower rates off-season. Parking: Outdoor, free. AE, CB, DC, DISC, MC, V.

Ramada Inn
124 W 6th St, 81601; tel 970/945-2500 or toll free 800/332-1472; fax 970/945-2530. Just N of exit 116 off I-70. Full service hotel with easy access to I-70 and downtown. Centrally located for access to several of the area's ski resorts. **Rooms:** 123 rms and stes. Executive level. CI 3pm/CO 11am. Nonsmoking rms avail. **Amenities:** Cable TV w/movies. No A/C. Some units w/fireplaces, some w/whirlpools. **Services:** Car-rental desk. **Facilities:** 400 1 restaurant, 1 bar (w/entertainment), whirlpool, washer/dryer. **Rates:** Peak (Dec 15–Mar) $75 S; $85 D; $125–$155 ste. Extra person $10. Children under age 18 stay free. Lower rates off-season. Parking: Outdoor, free. AE, CB, DC, DISC, ER, JCB, MC, V.

INN

UNRATED **Adducci's Inn B&B**
1023 Grand Ave, 81601; tel 970/945-9341. 4 blocks S of Grand Ave bridge. Small Victorian-style bed-and-breakfast located close to the town's shopping district. **Rooms:** 5 rms (2 w/shared bath). CI noon/CO 11am. No smoking. Rooms are a little small, but clean and comfortable. **Amenities:** No A/C, phone, or TV. **Facilities:** 1 restaurant, 1 bar. **Rates (CP):** $28–$38 S w/shared bath, $45–$65 S w/private bath; $48–$55 D w/shared bath, $65 D w/private bath. Extra person $10. Min stay special events. Higher rates for special events/hols. Parking: Outdoor, free. MC, V.

RESTAURANTS

Andre's Restaurant
51753 US 6 and 24, West Glenwood Springs; tel 970/945-5367. Halfway between Exit 114 and 116 off I-70. **American/Italian.** This small, mom-and-pop place features model trains suspended from the ceiling and famous home-made desserts served in large portions. Comfort food like chicken pot pie and beef stew dominates the menu, but pizza and pasta are also available. Colorado candies and a small selection of gifts are available for sale. **FYI:** Reservations not accepted. Children's menu. No liquor license. No smoking. **Open:** Wed–Mon 11:30am–9pm. **Prices:** Main courses $5–$10. AE, DISC, MC, V.

The Bayou
52103 US 6, West Glenwood Springs; tel 970/945-1047. **Cajun/Creole.** A large green awning in the shape of a frog's head, complete with bulging eyes, shelters a small dining patio that gazes out across I-70 to a valley backed by sandstone mountains. The indoor dining room walls are camouflaged with a variety of Mardi Gras paraphernalia, including masks, beads, and "Mardi bras." The menu offers a variety of Cajun standards including blackened redfish, shrimp or chicken étoufée, po'boys, and the restaurant's signature "swamp and moo": rib eye, redfish, and rice. Levels of spiciness range from "spicy" to "hurt me"—and should be considered carefully before ordering. **FYI:** Reservations not accepted. Blues/reggae/rock. Children's menu. **Open:** Daily 4–10pm. Closed Nov 15–Dec 14. **Prices:** Main courses $6–$15. AE, DISC, MC, V.

★ Italian Underground
715 Grand Ave; tel 970/945-6422. Just S of Grand Ave bridge. **Italian.** Located in the basement of a building on the town's main street close to the river, this restaurant looks like a bistro in the old country, with brick floors, stone walls, Italian photos and wall hangings, and candles in Chianti bottles on the tables. Offerings are mainly pasta and pizza, both superbly done. Also on the menu are northern Italian rotisserie chicken and chicken cacciatore. **FYI:** Reservations not accepted. No smoking. **Open:** Daily 5–10pm. Closed Apr 15–30. **Prices:** Main courses $8–$10. AE, DISC, MC, V.

19th Street Diner
1908 Grand Ave; tel 970/945-9133. 12 blocks S of Grand Ave bridge. **Diner.** The black and white checked floor, stools and booths, and fast, friendly service give this spot an authentic diner feel. Breakfast, which offers many omelettes and other egg specialties, is served all day, and there's a wide selection of sandwiches and entrees, plus some vegetarian dishes. Three nights offer specials: Monday is Mexican, Wednesday is meat loaf, and Thursday is pasta. And, as one employee put it, "good music is always playing." **FYI:** Reservations not accepted. Children's menu. No smoking. **Open:** Mon–Sat 7am–10pm, Sun 7:30am–3pm. **Prices:** Main courses $4–$7. DISC, MC, V.

Restaurant Sopris
7215 CO 82; tel 970/945-7771. 7 mi S of downtown. **Continental.** Red walls and lighting give this Victorian-style restaurant a warm and soothing atmosphere. Reproductions of classic oil paintings and etched mirrors add to the elegant atmosphere. The menu ranges from standard steaks to Swiss veal, frogs' legs provençale, and chateaubriand. **FYI:** Reservations recommended. Guitar/jazz. Children's menu. **Open:** Daily 5–10pm. **Prices:** Main courses $8–$34. AE, DISC, MC, V.

ATTRACTIONS

Frontier Historical Society Museum
1001 Colorado Ave; tel 970/945-4448. The highlight of this museum, which occupies a late-Victorian home, is the original bedroom furniture of Colorado legends Horace and Baby Doe Tabor, brought here from Leadville. The collection also includes other pioneer home furnishings, antique dolls and toys, historic photos and maps, Native American artifacts, and minerals. **Open:** Peak (May–Sept) Mon–Sat 11am–4pm. Reduced hours off-season. **$**

Glenwood Hot Springs Pool
401 N River Rd; tel 970/945-7131. Created in 1888 by developers who diverted the course of the Colorado River and built a stone bathhouse. Fed by one of the world's hottest springs, the springs flow at a rate of 3.5 million gallons per day, with a temperature of 122°F. The two open-air pools together are nearly two city blocks in length. There's also a children's pool with a water slide and a miniature golf course. **Open:** Peak (June–Aug) daily 7:30am–10pm. Reduced hours off-season. **$$$**

Yampah Spa and Vapor Caves
709 E 6th St; tel 970/945-0667. The hot Yampah Spring water flows through the floor of nearby caves, creating natural underground steam baths. Utes once used the chambers to take advantage of their curative powers. Today the cave has an adjacent spa where such treatments as massages, facials, herbal wraps, and body muds are offered. There's also a full-service beauty salon on the premises. **Open:** Daily 9am–9pm. **$$$**

Doc Holliday's Grave
Linwood Cemetery. After the famous shoot-out at the OK Corral, Doc Holliday headed west seeking relief from his advanced tuberculosis. But even the mineral-rich waters of Glenwood Springs could not dissipate the ravages of hard drinking and disease, and Doc died in bed at the Glenwood Hotel. Visitors hike a ½-mile trail to find Doc's grave, marked with a flagpole. **Open:** Daily sunrise–sunset. **Free**

Golden

This early mining town once rivaled Denver in importance, and it was territorial capital from 1862 to 1867. Today Golden is best known as home of the huge Coors Brewery. The small city celebrates its old-west heritage with Buffalo Bill Days, held the third weekend in July. **Information:** Golden Area Chamber of Commerce, PO Box 1035, Golden 80402 (tel 303/279-3113 or 800/590-3113).

HOTELS

Denver Marriott West
1717 Denver West Blvd, 80401; tel 303/279-9100 or toll free 800/228-9290; fax 303/271-0205. Near exit 263 off I-70. This attractive hotel is a great base for those exploring the Rockies. Remodeled in early 1996. **Rooms:** 307 rms and stes. CI 3pm/CO noon. Nonsmoking rms avail. **Amenities:** A/C, cable TV w/movies, dataport, voice mail. Some units w/terraces. **Services:** Car-rental desk, social director, babysitting. **Facilities:** 1 restaurant, 1 bar, games rm, spa, sauna, whirlpool, washer/dryer. Ballroom. **Rates:** Peak (June–Oct 7) $105–$120 S or D; $225 ste. Children under age 18 stay free. Min stay. Lower rates off-season. Parking: Outdoor, free. AE, CB, DC, DISC, EC, ER, JCB, MC, V.

Table Mountain Inn
1310 Washington Ave, 80401 (Downtown); tel 303/277-9898 or toll free 800/762-9898; fax 303/271-0298. Just S of CO 58. Comfortable, new hotel in downtown Golden, decorated with southwestern style and pizzazz. Attractive alternative to chain motel. **Rooms:** 32 rms and stes. Executive level. CI 4pm/CO 11am. Nonsmoking rms avail. Rooms are individually decorated and meticulously maintained. **Amenities:** A/C, cable TV w/movies, refrig, dataport. Some units w/terraces, some w/whirlpools. **Services:** Car-rental desk. **Facilities:** 1 restaurant, 1 bar. Free recreation passes to Golden Community Center, which includes fitness center, pool, and children's area. **Rates:** $90–$110 S or D; $140 ste. Children under age 18 stay free. MAP rates avail. Parking: Outdoor, free. AE, DC, DISC, JCB, MC, V.

MOTEL

La Quinta Inn Golden
3301 Youngfield Service Rd, 80401; tel 303/279-5565 or toll free 800/531-5900; fax 303/279-5841. Exit 264 off I-70. Conveniently located between Golden and Denver, this hostelry is ideal for travelers desiring access to both city and mountains. **Rooms:** 129 rms and stes. CI open/CO noon. Nonsmoking rms avail. **Amenities:** A/C, cable TV w/movies, dataport. **Services:** Car-rental desk. **Facilities:** Washer/dryer. **Rates (CP):** Peak (May–Sept) $69–$79 S or D; $89–$99 ste. Extra person $8. Children under age 18 stay free. Lower rates off-season. Parking: Outdoor, free. AE, DC, DISC, MC, V.

RESTAURANTS

Chart House
25908 Genesee Trail; tel 303/526-9813. Just S of exit 254 off I-70. **Seafood/Steak.** This elegant yet unpretentious seafood and steak house has an incredible view of the mountains and the city below. The grill is open to view, surrounded by a terrific salad bar featuring caviar and hearts of palm. The menu changes nightly. **FYI:** Reservations recommended. Children's menu. **Open:** Mon–Sat 5–10pm, Sun 4:30–9pm. **Prices:** Main courses $14–$25. AE, CB, DC, DISC, MC, V.

Silverheels Southwest Grill
1122 Washington Ave; tel 303/279-6390. **Southwestern.** The Silverheels is decorated with relics of the Old West, including safes once possibly broken into by notorious villains. The traditional southwestern menu has been expanded to include steaks. This is an ideal refueling stop while exploring downtown Golden. **FYI:** Reservations recommended. Blues/guitar. Children's menu. Additional location: 81 Buffalo Dr, Silver Thorne (tel 970/468-2926). **Open:** Sun–Thurs 11:30am–9pm, Fri–Sat 11:30am–10pm. **Prices:** Main courses $10–$15. AE, MC, V.

ATTRACTIONS

Heritage Square
Exit 259 off I-70 W, CO 40; tel 303/279-2789. An entertainment village with a Wild West theme, Heritage Square features 50 Victorian specialty shops and a small museum. Warm weather highlights include go-carts, bumper boats, a water slide, a bungee tower, mountain bike rentals, white-water rafting, and a 2,350-foot alpine slide with bobsled-style carts. Heritage Square Music Hall offers theater with adult and children's shows. **Open:** Peak (June–Aug) Mon–Sat 10am–9pm, Sun noon–9pm. Reduced hours off season. **Free**

Historic Boettcher Mansion
900 Colorow Rd; tel 303/526-0855. This Jefferson County estate was built by Charles Boettcher in 1917 as a summer home and hunting lodge. The historic home now houses changing art and history exhibits. A 1¼-mile nature trail

winds through the 110-acre property among ponderosa pines and mountain meadows. Nature center. **Open:** Mon–Sat 8am–5pm. **Free**

Mother Cabrini Shrine
20189 Cabrini Blvd; tel 303/526-0758. A 22-foot statue of Christ stands at the top of a 373-step stairway, adorned by carvings representing the stations of the cross and mysteries of the rosary. Terra cotta benches provide respites along the way. The shrine is dedicated to America's first citizen saint, St Frances Xavier Cabrini, who founded the Order of the Missionary Sisters of the Sacred Heart. The order has a convent here with a gift shop. **Open:** Daily 7am–7pm. **Free**

The Rocky Mountain Quilt Museum
1111 Washington Ave; tel 303/277-0377. Changing bimonthly exhibits include examples from the permanent collection of more than 140 quilts. Local crafters' work can be purchased in the gift shop. Tours and classes offered. **Open:** Tues–Sat 10am–4pm. **$**

Coors Brewing Company
13th and Ford Sts; tel 303/277-BEER or toll free 800/443-8242. The world's largest single-site brewery, producing 1.5 million gallons of beer each day. Tours leave a central parking lot at 13th and Ford Sts, where visitors pile onto a bus for a short drive through historic Golden before arriving at the brewery. There, a 40-minute walking tour covers the history of the Coors family and their company, the barley-malting process, the 13,640-gallon gleaming copper kettles, and the entire process all the way to packaging. Tastings available. **Open:** Mon–Sat 10am–5pm. **Free**

Hakushika Sake USA
4414 Table Mountain Dr; tel 303/279-7253. Located in the Coors Technology Center. The Hakushika company, founded in 1662 and today one of Japan's foremost sake makers, has opened a brewery in Golden that produces sake for distribution throughout the United States and Europe. (Sake, considered the national drink of Japan, is made from fermented steamed rice.) Guided tours, by reservation only, follow a glass-enclosed mezzanine that provides an excellent view of the entire brewing and bottling process. Visitors also see displays of traditional sake brewing techniques, and an exhibit of fine Japanese art from the 19th and early 20th centuries. Tasting room. **Open:** Mon–Fri 10am–4pm. **Free**

Granby

This small mountain community is close to the western boundary of Rocky Mountain National Park and other outdoor recreation destinations. **Information:** Granby Chamber of Commerce, PO Box 35, Granby 80446 (tel 970/887-2311 or 800/325-1661).

HOTEL

The Inn at Silver Creek
62927 US 40, PO Box 4222, Silver Creek, 80446; tel 970/887-2131 or toll free 800/926-4386; fax 970/887-2350. 20 miles N of Winter Park. Located on a quiet plain surrounded by the Rocky Mountains, close to Silver Creek Ski Area. Hiking trails here go for miles and are great for mountain biking, too. Area activities include snowmobiling, sleigh rides, horseback riding. **Rooms:** 346 rms and stes. CI 4pm/CO 11am. Nonsmoking rms avail. Variety of condominium-type rooms available. **Amenities:** Cable TV w/movies, refrig. No A/C. All units w/terraces, some w/fireplaces, all w/whirlpools. **Services:** Babysitting. **Facilities:** 1 restaurant, 1 bar (w/entertainment), volleyball, games rm, lawn games, sauna, steam rm, whirlpool, playground, washer/dryer. **Rates:** Peak (Nov 20–Apr 15) $80–$155 S or D; $190–$240 ste. Extra person $10. Children under age 12 stay free. Min stay special events. Lower rates off-season. Parking: Outdoor, free. AE, CB, DC, DISC, MC, V.

RESORT

C Lazy U Ranch
3640 CO 125, PO Box 379, 80446; tel 970/887-3344; fax 970/887-3917. 3½ mi N of US 40 on CO 125. 5,000 acres. Located in a small valley with expansive views of the surrounding areas, this secluded ranch is a terrific retreat. **Rooms:** 41 rms. CI open/CO 10am. Rooms are spacious and comfortable, with several levels of luxury from which to choose. **Amenities:** In-rm safe, bathrobes. No A/C, phone, or TV. Some units w/minibars, some w/terraces, some w/fireplaces, some w/whirlpools. **Services:** Twice-daily maid svce, social director, masseur, children's program. **Facilities:** 2 bars (1 w/entertainment), basketball, volleyball, games rm, lawn games, racquetball, sauna, whirlpool, day-care ctr, playground, washer/dryer. 10,000-square-foot heated indoor riding arena available. **Rates (AP):** Peak (June–Sept 15) $1,500–$2,150 S. Min stay. Lower rates off-season. Parking: Outdoor, free. Rates are per person per week and include all meals, activities, and facility use. Seven-night minimum. Closed Oct 15–Dec 15/Apr–May 15. No CC.

Grand Junction

A major trade center since 1882, Grand Junction was founded at the site where a spike was driven connecting Denver and Salt Lake City by rail. Today it is the gateway to awe-inspiring Colorado National Monument and Dinosaur National Monument and the home to a half-dozen wineries offering tours and tastings. **Information:** Grand Junction Visitor & Convention Bureau, 740 Horizon Dr, Grand Junction 81506 (tel 970/244-1480 or 800/962-2547).

HOTELS

Grand Junction Hilton
743 Horizon Dr, 81506; tel 970/241-8888 or toll free 800/HILTONS; fax 970/242-7266. Just S of exit 31 off I-70. With its luxurious atmosphere, this modern, full-service hotel just might be the finest in the city. Regional artwork decorates the lobby. **Rooms:** 264 rms and stes. Executive level. CI 3pm/CO noon. Nonsmoking rms avail. Spacious, well-appointed rooms with nice views of the surrounding mesa country. **Amenities:** A/C, cable TV w/movies. Some units w/whirlpools. **Services:** Babysitting. **Facilities:** 2 restaurants, 2 bars (1 w/entertainment), volleyball, games rm, lawn games, whirlpool, playground. Travel agency on premises. **Rates:** Peak (May 15–Oct 15) $79–$129 S or D; $129–$225 ste. Children under age 12 stay free. Lower rates off-season. Parking: Outdoor, free. AE, CB, DC, DISC, MC, V.

Historic Hotel Melrose/International Hostel
337 Colorado Ave, 81501; tel 970/242-9636 or toll free 800/430-4555; fax 970/242-5613. Just N of Whitman Park. This historic brick building actually consists of three sections: the first built in 1908, the second in the 1920s, and the third in the 1950s. **Rooms:** 26 rms. CI open/CO 11am. Nonsmoking rms avail. Clean, well-maintained rooms are decorated with well-chosen antique furnishings. Private or shared bath. **Amenities:** A/C, cable TV w/movies. No phone. **Services:** Complimentary coffee and doughnuts. **Rates:** Peak (May 25–Sept 5) $23–$28 S; $26–$33 D. Extra person $5. Children under age 5 stay free. Lower rates off-season. Parking: Outdoor, free. Dorm room bunks available for $12.50. CB, DC, DISC, MC, V.

UNRATED **Holiday Inn**
755 Horizon Dr, PO Box 1725, 81502; tel 970/243-6790 or toll free 800/HOLIDAY; fax 970/243-6790. Just N of exit 31 off I-70. Conveniently located just off I-70, this hotel has an attractive central courtyard with the outdoor pool and skylit, gardenlike area housing the indoor pool. **Rooms:** 292 rms and stes. CI 2pm/CO 11am. Nonsmoking rms avail. Most rooms look out onto one of the pools. **Amenities:** A/C, cable TV w/movies, voice mail. Some units w/whirlpools. **Services:** **Facilities:** 1 restaurant, 1 bar (w/entertainment), games rm, sauna, whirlpool, washer/dryer. **Rates:** Peak (May 15–Sept 15) $65–$70 S; $70–$77 D; $77–$130 ste. Extra person $6. Children under age 18 stay free. Min stay special events. Lower rates off-season. Parking: Outdoor, free. AE, CB, DC, DISC, JCB, MC, V.

Ramada Inn
2790 Crossroads Blvd, 81506; tel 970/241-8411 or toll free 800/272-6232; fax 970/241-1077. ¼ mi N of exit 31 off I-70. Modern hotel decorated with reproduction antiques. **Rooms:** 156 rms and stes. CI 3pm/CO noon. Nonsmoking rms avail. Nice views of surrounding mesa country. **Amenities:** A/C, cable TV w/movies. Some units w/whirlpools. **Services:** **Facilities:** 1 restaurant, 1 bar (w/entertainment), sauna, whirlpool. **Rates:** Peak (May 15–Oct 15) $72 S; $79 D; $85–$210 ste. Extra person $7. Children under age 18 stay free. Lower rates off-season. Parking: Outdoor, free. AE, CB, DC, DISC, EC, JCB, MC, V.

MOTELS

Best Value Inn
718 Horizon Dr, 81506; tel 970/243-5080; fax 970/242-0600. ¼ mi S of exit 31 off I-70. Well-maintained brick motel surrounding private courtyard housing the pool. **Rooms:** 138 rms. CI 2pm/CO 11am. Nonsmoking rms avail. **Amenities:** A/C, cable TV w/movies. Some units w/terraces. **Services:** Complimentary local calls and coffee. **Facilities:** Washer/dryer. **Rates:** Peak (May 25–Sept 30) $35–$45 S or D. Extra person $5. Children under age 12 stay free. Lower rates off-season. Parking: Outdoor, free. AE, CB, DC, DISC, MC, V.

Budget Host Inn
721 Horizon Dr, 81506; tel 970/243-6050 or toll free 800/283-4678; fax 970/243-0310. ¼ mi S of exit 31 off I-70. Clean, attractive, and well-maintained motel located close to highway. **Rooms:** 54 rms. CI 2pm/CO 11am. Nonsmoking rms avail. Tastefully decorated. **Amenities:** A/C, cable TV w/movies. All units w/terraces. **Services:** Complimentary coffee 5am–noon. **Facilities:** Washer/dryer. **Rates:** Peak (May 25–Sept 30) $42–$47 S; $47–$52 D. Extra person $5. Children under age 12 stay free. Min stay peak. Lower rates off-season. Parking: Outdoor, free. AE, CB, DC, DISC, MC, V.

Peachtree Inn
1600 North Ave, 81501; tel 970/245-5770 or toll free 800/525-0030; fax 970/243-2955. Just N of Lincoln Park. A modest motel located close to the recreational activities in Lincoln Park. **Rooms:** 75 rms. CI 1pm/CO 10:30am. Nonsmoking rms avail. Attractive and comfortable. **Amenities:** A/C, cable TV w/movies. All units w/terraces. **Services:** Discount lift tickets to Powderhorn ski area available at front desk. **Facilities:** 1 restaurant (bkfst and lunch only), 1 bar, washer/dryer. **Rates:** Peak (May 15–Sept 15) $30–$40 S or D. Extra person $5. Children under age 12 stay free. Lower rates off-season. Parking: Outdoor, free. AE, DISC, MC, V.

RESTAURANTS

★ **G B Gladstone's**
In Village Fair Shopping Center, 2531 N 12th St; tel 970/241-6000. Just S of jct Patterson Rd. **Steak/Pasta.** An unusual and pleasing little restaurant featuring several distinct dining areas around a central bar. One area has skylights and hanging plants; another features old books and small booths for a more intimate meal. Throughout are memorabilia and collectibles, plus etched, leaded glass and art deco

stained glass. Favorite entrees include orange horseradish salmon and Thai pesto linguine with broiled chicken strips. **FYI:** Reservations accepted. Children's menu. **Open:** Mon–Sat 11am–10pm, Sun 11am–9pm. **Prices:** Main courses $5–$18. AE, CB, DC, DISC, MC, V.

Jitters Espresso Bar Cafe & Bakery
In Historic Downtown Shopping Park, 504 Main St; tel 970/245-5194. At 5th St. **Coffeehouse.** This unique and nonconformist coffeehouse-style cafe originated as a high-end dress shop in the 1950s. Tables front two horseshoe-shaped counters in back, all of which came from an old Woolworth's. Contemporary lighting blends with airbrush paintings and collectibles from the 1940s and '50s. The menu is dominated by sandwiches and salads, but also includes pastries and lattes, plus imaginative breakfasts. **FYI:** Reservations not accepted. Children's menu. No liquor license. No smoking. **Open:** Mon–Fri 7:30am–5:30pm, Sat 8am–5pm, Sun 8am–2pm. **Prices:** Lunch main courses $2–$6. DISC, MC, V.

Pantuso's Ristorante
2782 Crossroads Blvd; tel 970/243-0000. ¼ mi N of exit 31 off I-70 and just W of Horizon Dr. **Italian.** This small restaurant is inviting and friendly, with a smattering of houseplants and a mural on one wall depicting Roman columns and gardens. Pasta dishes and sandwiches are well represented on the menu, plus some entrees such as manicotti Florentine and braciola. **FYI:** Reservations not accepted. Children's menu. **Open:** Lunch Mon–Fri 11:30am–1:45pm; dinner Mon–Thurs 5–9:30pm, Fri–Sat 5–10pm. **Prices:** Main courses $5–$10. AE, CB, DC, DISC, MC, V.

ATTRACTIONS

Museum of Western Colorado
4th and Ute Sts; tel 970/242-0971. The geology, history, and culture of western Colorado are highlights of this worthwhile museum. Of special interest is the Western Colorado Timeline, with photos and exhibits from every decade since the 1880s, and the Pioneer Room, which contains mining and ranching displays, including a pioneer kitchen. The museum also has an extensive firearms collection, Native American artifacts, natural history, old-west-style paintings, and changing exhibits. **Open:** Mon–Sat 10am–5pm. $

Cross Orchards Historic Site
3073 F Rd; tel 970/434-9814. The original Cross Orchards Farm (1896–1923) covered 243 acres and contained 22,000 apple trees. Today the remaining 24-acre site (a division of the Museum of Western Colorado) shows what life was like during the early 20th century Grand Valley agricultural boom. Featured are a blacksmith shop, barn and packing shed, workers' bunkhouse, and former farm manager's residence, as well as an extensive collection of vintage farming and road building equipment, railway exhibit, farm activity area, and country store and gift shop. "Living history" demonstrations are offered daily in summer, and various special events are held throughout the year. **Open:** Mid-May–Oct, Tues–Sat 10am–5pm. $$

Colorado National Monument
CO 340, Fruita; tel 970/858-3617. Located 9 mi W of Grand Junction. Redrock canyons and sandstone monoliths, some towering more than 1,000 feet above the Colorado River and its intermittent tributaries, dominate a wilderness of 32 square miles. Bighorn sheep, mountain lions, and golden eagles are among the semidesert denizens of the monument. The Visitor Center near the Saddlehorn Campground offers exhibits on geology and history and a slide show to introduce the park year-round; guided walks and campfire talks are frequently scheduled. **Open:** Peak (Mem Day–Labor Day) daily 8am–8pm. Reduced hours off-season. $$

Dinosaur Valley
4th and Main Sts; tel 970/241-9210. The animated replicas (complete with sound effects) of such dinosaurs as stegosaurus, triceratops, and apatosaurus bring the distant past alive at Dinosaur Valley (the natural history division of the Museum of Western Colorado). Visitors can also study regional paleontological history, examine a model of a dinosaur dig, and look at plaster casts of dinosaur prints. On the premises are a working "paleo lab" and a gift shop. **Open:** Peak (June–Aug) 9am–5:30pm. Reduced hours off-season. $$

Grand Lake

The western gateway to Rocky Mountain National Park, Grand Lake is a village of board sidewalks and a place where horses are still sometimes ridden down the main drag. It is surrounded by Arapahoe National Recreation Area. The world's highest-altitude yacht club (8,370 feet) hosts the Grand Lake Regatta each August. **Information:** Grand Lake Area Chamber of Commerce, PO Box 57, Grand Lake 80447 (tel 970/627-3402 or 800/531-1014).

MOTELS

Daven Haven Lodge
604 Marina Dr, PO Box 1528, 80447; tel 970/627-8144; fax 970/627-5098. ½ mi S of town. Tucked back in a grove of pines at the south end of town, just a half block from the lake, this group of cabins surrounds a common area with a pool. Family oriented and secluded. **Rooms:** 12 cottages/villas. CI 4pm/CO 10am. Spacious cabins of different sizes. **Amenities:** Cable TV. No A/C or phone. All units w/terraces, some w/fireplaces. **Services:** Babysitting. **Facilities:** 1 restaurant (dinner only), 1 bar, volleyball, lawn games. **Rates:** $60–$112 cottage/villa. Extra person $10. Min stay wknds. Parking: Outdoor, free. DISC, MC, V.

Driftwood Lodge
12255 US 34, PO Box 609, 80447; tel 970/627-3654; fax 970/627-3654. 3 mi S of town. Across from Shadow Moun-

tain Reservoir, this pastel-green motel is hard to miss. Well maintained, very clean, comfortable. **Rooms:** 17 rms and stes. CI 2pm/CO 10am. Nonsmoking rms avail. **Amenities:** Cable TV, dataport. No A/C. All units w/terraces. **Services:** **Facilities:** Volleyball, lawn games, sauna, whirlpool, playground. **Rates:** Peak (May 20–Sept 15) $55–$67 S or D; $77 ste. Extra person $5. Children under age 2 stay free. Min stay wknds. Lower rates off-season. Parking: Outdoor, free. AE, CB, DC, MC, V.

The Inn at Grand Lake

1103 Grand Ave, PO Box 1590, 80447; tel 970/627-9234 or toll free 800/627-9234. Just E of city park. Originally the courthouse and jail for the town, the building has been renovated and reorganized into an attractive, western motel. Within walking distance of restaurants, lake, and park. **Rooms:** 16 rms. CI 3pm/CO 10am. Nonsmoking rms avail. Rooms modernized but retain historical ambience. **Amenities:** Cable TV. No A/C. All units w/terraces. **Services:** Babysitting. **Facilities:** **Rates:** Peak (May 25–June 15) $40–$90 S or D. Min stay special events. Lower rates off-season. Parking: Outdoor, free. DISC, MC, V.

RESTAURANTS

Chuck Hole Cafe

1131 Grand Ave; tel 970/627-3509. 2 blocks E of city park. **American.** A small cafe in the heart of Grand Lake, convenient for a quick meal. Western prints and historic photos adorn the walls. Traditional breakfasts with omelettes and pancakes; burgers and sandwiches for lunch. **FYI:** Reservations not accepted. Children's menu. No liquor license. **Open:** Peak (May 25–Sept 5) daily 6:30am–3pm. **Prices:** Lunch main courses $2–$6. No CC.

EG's Garden Grill

1000 Grand Ave; tel 970/627-8404. Across from city park. **New American/Seafood.** The trellised ceiling, large stone fireplace, and wood floor help create an atmosphere that's appealing, intimate, and warm while still welcoming children. Conveniently located downtown and close to the lake, this spot offers traditional dishes with a "new cuisine" flair, such as Iowa cut pork chops with Asian wild mushroom sauce or jumbo prawns stuffed with roasted red pepper and creamy havarti and wrapped in bacon. **FYI:** Reservations accepted. Folk/guitar. Children's menu. **Open:** Daily 11am–10pm. **Prices:** Main courses $7–$17. DISC, MC, V.

Great Sand Dunes National Monument

See Alamosa

Greeley

A farming and ranching center at the intersection of US 34 and US 85, Greeley is one of the few cities in the world that owes its existence to a newspaper. It was founded in 1870 as a sort of prairie Utopia by *New York Tribune* farm columnist Nathan Meeker, who named the city for his boss, publisher Horace Greeley. Through his widely read column, Meeker recruited more than 100 pioneers from all walks of life to populate his town, and Greeley has been growing streadily ever since. **Information:** Greeley Convention & Visitors Bureau, 1407 8th Ave, Greeley 80631 (tel 970/352-3566 or 800/449-3866).

HOTEL

Best Western Ramkota Inn & Conference Center

701 8th St, 80631; tel 970/353-8444 or toll free 800/528-1234; fax 970/353-4269. 2 blocks E of Lincoln Park. Located in downtown Greeley, this comfortable hotel caters to business travelers. **Rooms:** 148 rms and stes. CI 3pm/CO noon. Nonsmoking rms avail. **Amenities:** A/C, cable TV w/movies. Some units w/terraces, some w/whirlpools. **Services:** **Facilities:** 1 restaurant, 1 bar. **Rates:** Peak (May–Aug) $51–$59 S or D; $120–$150 ste. Extra person $8. Children under age 18 stay free. Lower rates off-season. Parking: Outdoor, free. AE, DC, DISC, MC, V.

MOTELS

Fairfield Inn

2401 W 29th St, 80631; tel 970/339-5030 or toll free 800/228-2800; fax 970/339-5030. Located just off US 34, close to several restaurants. **Rooms:** 64 rms and stes. CI 3pm/CO 11am. Nonsmoking rms avail. **Amenities:** A/C, cable TV w/movies, voice mail. **Services:** **Facilities:** Whirlpool. **Rates (CP):** Peak (Apr 15–Oct 15) $62 S; $69 D; $77 ste. Extra person $6. Children under age 12 stay free. Lower rates off-season. Parking: Outdoor, free. AE, DC, DISC, MC, V.

Greeley Inn

721 13th St, 80631; tel 970/353-3216. 1 block E of Meeker Home Museum. Simple inn close to university; few amenities. **Rooms:** 24 rms. CI 3pm/CO 11am. Nonsmoking rms avail. **Amenities:** A/C, cable TV w/movies. All units w/terraces. **Services:** **Rates:** Peak (June–Sept) $27–$35 S; $45–$51 D. Extra person $5. Children under age 12 stay free. Lower rates off-season. Parking: Outdoor, free. AE, CB, DISC, MC, V.

Winterset Inn

800 31st St, Evans, 80620; tel 970/339-2492 or toll free 800/777-5088; fax 970/330-1429. ½ mi S of US 34. Located in Greeley's industrial suburb of Evans, the Winterset is a traditional roadside motel. **Rooms:** 53 rms and stes. CI

noon/CO noon. Nonsmoking rms avail. **Amenities:** A/C, cable TV w/movies. All units w/terraces. **Services:** **Facilities:** Games rm, washer/dryer. **Rates:** Peak (May–Sept 15) $30–$35 S; $37–$45 D; $45–$80 ste. Extra person $7. Lower rates off-season. Parking: Outdoor, free. AE, DC, DISC, MC, V.

RESTAURANTS

Cable's End
In Market Sq Shopping Center, 3780 W 10th St; tel 970/356-4847. ¾ mi E of Greeley Country Club. **Italian.** Plenty of low-priced specials throughout the week make this find great for families with children. Offerings include pizzas, homemade pastas (including spaghetti and ravioli), chicken parmigiana, prime rib, burgers, and fresh seafood. **FYI:** Reservations accepted. Children's menu. **Open:** Mon–Sat 11am–1am, Sun 11am–11pm. **Prices:** Main courses $6–$14. AE, DISC, MC, V.

Potato Brumbaugh's Restaurant & Saloon
In Cottonwood Sq Shopping Center, 2400 17th St; tel 970/356-6340. **American/Continental.** A large fireplace and giant pine logs supporting the ceiling are part of the western decor at this casually elegant restaurant. The kitchen prepares both "lighter side" items and full-scale meals of Australian rock lobster tail, prime rib, or vegetarian Alfredo. **FYI:** Reservations recommended. No smoking. **Open:** Lunch Mon–Fri 11:15am–2pm; dinner Mon–Sat 5–10pm. **Prices:** Main courses $9–$21. AE, DC, DISC, MC, V.

ATTRACTIONS

Centennial Village Museum
1475 A St; tel 970/350-9220. This collection of buildings, depicting life on the High Plains of Colorado between 1860 and 1920, was established as a 1976 Bicentennial project. Set on a 5½-acre site are 28 structures representing the architectural and cultural life of the region. The buildings include a homesteader's shack, wagon house, adobe houses, one-room school, rural church, log cabin courthouse, blacksmith and print shops, and fully furnished elegant Victorian homes. **Open:** Apr–Oct, Tues–Sun 10am–5pm. **$$**

Meeker Home Museum
1324 9th Ave; tel 970/350-9221. This two-story adobe brick residence, built in 1870 for Greeley founder Nathan Cook Meeker, is on the National Register of Historic Places. The Union Colony era (1870–85) is interpreted through guided tours of the home, which is furnished with Meeker family belongings and 19th-century antiques. **Open:** Peak (Mem Day–Labor Day) Tues–Sat 10am–5pm, Sun 1–5pm. Reduced hours off-season. $

Greenwood Village

See Denver

Gunnison

From its roots as a 19th-century ranching and mining supply and transportation center, Gunnison has evolved into an outdoor recreation base camp for those exploring Curecanti National Recreation Area and the Gunnison National Forest. **Information:** Gunnison Country Chamber of Commerce, PO Box 36, Gunnison 81230 (tel 970/641-1501 or 800/274-7580).

MOTELS

ABC Motel Inc
212 E Tomichi Ave, 81230; tel 970/641-2400 or toll free 800/341-8000; fax 970/641-6342. Just E of jct US 50/CO 135. Attractive log-style motel convenient for skiers. **Rooms:** 24 rms. CI open/CO 10am. Nonsmoking rms avail. **Amenities:** A/C, cable TV w/movies. All units w/terraces. **Services:** **Facilities:** Whirlpool. **Rates:** Peak (May 15–Sept 15) $49 S; $59 D. Extra person $4. Lower rates off-season. Parking: Outdoor, free. AE, DISC, MC, V.

Best Western Tomichi Village Inn
US 50, PO Box 763, 81230; tel 970/641-1131 or toll free 800/641-1131; fax 970/641-9554. 2 miles E of town. Basic motel resembling a European chalet, situated slightly out of town amid rolling hills. **Rooms:** 50 rms. CI 2pm/CO 11am. Nonsmoking rms avail. **Amenities:** A/C, cable TV w/movies. All units w/terraces. **Services:** **Facilities:** 150 1 restaurant (lunch and dinner only), whirlpool, washer/dryer. Two-acre pasture available for guests traveling with horses. **Rates (CP):** Peak (June–Oct 3) $70–$78 S; $78–$82 D. Extra person $4. Min stay special events. Lower rates off-season. Parking: Outdoor, free. AE, CB, DC, DISC, MC, V.

Days Inn
701 US 50 W, 81230; tel 970/641-0608 or toll free 800/DAYS-INN; fax 970/641-2854. 1¼ mi W of jct CO 135. No-frills motel located on main highway through town. **Rooms:** 45 rms. CI 3pm/CO 11am. Nonsmoking rms avail. **Amenities:** A/C, cable TV w/movies. **Services:** **Facilities:** Whirlpool, washer/dryer. **Rates (CP):** Peak (June–Sept) $58 S; $68 D. Extra person $5. Children under age 12 stay free. Lower rates off-season. Parking: Outdoor, free. AE, CB, DC, DISC, MC, V.

Gunnison Super 8
411 E Tomichi Ave, 81230; tel 970/641-3068 or toll free 800/800-8000; fax 970/641-1332. Just E of jct US 50/CO 135. Economy motel located next to town park, within walking distance of town, close to Western State College. **Rooms:** 49 rms. CI 2pm/CO 11am. Nonsmoking rms avail. **Amenities:** A/C, cable TV w/movies. **Services:** **Facilities:** **Rates:** Peak (May–Oct) $55–$85 S or D. Extra person $5. Children under age 12 stay free. Lower rates off-season. Parking: Outdoor, free. AE, CB, DC, DISC, MC, V.

Holiday Inn Express
400 E Tomichi Ave, 81230; tel 970/641-1288 or toll free 800/GUNNISON; fax 970/641-1332. Just E of jct US 50/CO 135. Standard motel convenient for skiers. **Rooms:** 54 rms and stes. CI 2pm/CO noon. Nonsmoking rms avail. **Amenities:** A/C, cable TV w/movies. Some units w/whirlpools. **Services:** **Facilities:** Whirlpool, washer/dryer. **Rates (CP):** Peak (May–Oct) $60–$95 S or D; $75–$110 ste. Extra person $6. Children under age 19 stay free. Lower rates off-season. Parking: Outdoor, free. Ski packages avail. AE, CB, DC, DISC, MC, V.

Wildwood Motel
1312 W Tomichi Ave, 81230; tel 970/641-1663. 1 mile W of Main St. Simple but well-maintained motel set in an old grove of cottonwoods. **Rooms:** 18 effic. CI 2pm/CO 10am. **Amenities:** Cable TV, refrig. No A/C. All units w/terraces. **Services:** **Facilities:** **Rates:** $42–$49 effic. Extra person $5. Parking: Outdoor, free. Very good ski packages avail. DISC, MC, V.

INN

UNRATED **Mary Lawrence Inn**
601 N Taylor, 81230; tel 970/641-3343. Near jct US 50/CO 135. This comfortable bed-and-breakfast just north of Western State College dates back to 1885, when it served as a boardinghouse. Old photographs and antiques maintain the historic ambience. Unsuitable for children under 6. **Rooms:** 5 rms and stes. CI 4pm/CO 11am. No smoking. Sponge-painted walls and hand-stenciled floral patterns decorate rooms. **Amenities:** Bathrobes. No A/C, phone, or TV. **Services:** **Facilities:** Guest lounge. **Rates (BB):** $74 D; $90 ste. Extra person $15–$25. Parking: Outdoor, free. Seasonal packages avail. MC, V.

RESTAURANTS

Cattlemen Inn
301 W Tomichi Ave; tel 970/641-1061. 2 blocks W of jct US 50/CO 135. **American.** In business since the late 1940s, this down-home restaurant with an all-wood interior serves only the choicest cuts of steer. Most people come here to enjoy their favorite steak and salad, but diners can alternatively enjoy fish-and-chips, burritos, and sandwiches for lunch, and trout, chicken, and deep-fried shrimp for dinner. **FYI:** Reservations not accepted. Children's menu. **Open:** Daily 6:30am–11pm. **Prices:** Main courses $6–$23. CB, DC, MC, V.

★ **Farrells' Restaurant**
310 N Main St; tel 970/641-2655. 3 blocks N of jct US 50/CO 135. **Cafe/Bakery.** Located within walking distance of downtown, this cafe gets its character from lots of plants and artwork. The chalkboard menu, which changes daily, includes a variety of unique and tempting sandwiches, salads, and soups, plus freshly baked breads, pastries, and pies. **FYI:** Reservations not accepted. Children's menu. Beer and wine only. No smoking. **Open:** Mon–Fri 7am–3pm, Sat 7am–2pm. **Prices:** Lunch main courses $2–$5. DISC, MC, V.

Josef's Restaurant
US 50; tel 970/641-5032. 2 miles E of town. **Continental/German.** A European-style restaurant brightly decorated with large plants, and conveniently located close to town on the main thoroughfare. The menu lists a wide variety of dishes with a European flair, plus several seafood offerings. Specialties include Bavarian sauerbraten and Hungarian goulash. **FYI:** Reservations recommended. Children's menu. **Open:** Lunch Mon–Fri 11am–2pm; dinner daily 5–9pm. **Prices:** Main courses $6–$18. AE, CB, DC, DISC, MC, V.

ATTRACTIONS

Curecanti National Recreation Area
Visitors Center, 102 Elk Creek Rd (US 50); tel 970/641-2337. Three reservoirs extending 35 miles to the mouth of the Black Canyon of the Gunnison. Blue Mesa Lake (elevation 7,519 feet), the easternmost of the three, is the largest lake in Colorado when filled to capacity, and popular for fishing, motorboating, sailboating, board sailing, and other activities. Morrow Point Lake (elevation 7,160 feet) and Crystal Lake (elevation 6,755 feet) fill long, winding canyons accessible only by trails, and thus are limited to use by hand-carried boats. The Elk Creek Visitor Center presents numerous exhibits and audiovisual programs, as well as maps and publications. Nature hikes and evening campground programs are presented throughout the summer season. **Open:** Peak (mid-May–Sept) daily 8am–6pm. Reduced hours off-season. **Free**

Gunnison Pioneer Museum
S Adams St and US 50; tel 970/641-4530. Complex of eight buildings housing collections representing the history of Gunnison pioneers. A Denver & Rio Grande narrow gauge steam train and depot are among the machines and structures on display. Other exhibits include a rural schoolhouse, 19th-century furnishings, minerals and arrowheads, antique cars and wagons, dolls, and toys. Guided tours available. **Open:** Mem Day–Labor Day, Mon–Sat 9am–5pm. **$$**

Idaho Springs

Site of a major gold strike in 1859, Idaho Springs and the surrounding area remain an active mining center, where many visitors come to try their luck at panning for any gold that may still remain. A number of Victorian homes in Idaho Springs survive. **Information:** Idaho Springs Visitor Information Center, 2200 Miner St, PO Box 97, Idaho Springs 80452 (tel 303/567-4382 or 800/882-5278).

RESTAURANT

Beau Jo's Colorado Style Pizza
1517 Miner St; tel 303/567-4376. Exit 240 off I-70. **Pizza.** The aroma of Beau Jo's fresh-baked pizza, often rated the best in Colorado, permeates the entire restaurant. It's located in a historic downtown building, with a rustic and pleasant atmosphere. Specialty pizzas include Thai Pie, Cajun, and barbecue. Sandwiches and a soup and salad bar are also available. **FYI:** Reservations not accepted. No smoking. **Open:** Sun–Thurs 11am–9:30pm, Fri–Sat 11am–10pm. **Prices:** Main courses $6–$10. AE, DISC, MC, V.

Keystone

See Dillon

Kittredge

See Lakewood

La Junta

Once hunting grounds for the Cheyenne, Ute, and Arapahoe tribes, the town of La Junta (Spanish for "the junction") was founded as a railroad camp in 1875. Today it's a farming and ranching center. **Information:** La Junta Chamber of Commerce, PO Box 408, La Junta 81050 (tel 719/384-7411).

MOTELS

Best Western Bent's Fort Inn
10950 US 50, PO Box 108, Las Animas, 81054; tel 719/456-0011 or toll free 800/528-1231; fax 719/456-2550. 1 mi E of Las Animas on US 50. Small, cozy roadside motel just outside town. Good choice for hunters. **Rooms:** 38 rms. CI 2pm/CO 11am. Nonsmoking rms avail. **Amenities:** A/C, satel TV. **Services:** **Facilities:** 1 restaurant, 1 bar. **Rates:** $42–$46 S; $48–$52 D. Extra person $4. Children under age 12 stay free. Parking: Outdoor, free. AE, CB, DC, DISC, MC, V.

Mid-Town Motel
215 E 3rd St, 81050; tel 719/384-7741. 2 blocks S of US 50. Great little mom-and-pop motel off the main highway, offering pleasant, quiet stay. Owners Jack and PJ Culp are invaluable source of information for guests. **Rooms:** 26 rms. CI open/CO 11am. Nonsmoking rms avail. Recliners in single rooms. **Amenities:** A/C, cable TV. **Services:** **Rates:** $25–$28 S; $32–$36 D. Extra person $4. Children under age 2 stay free. Parking: Outdoor, free. AE, CB, DC, DISC, MC, V.

Quality Inn
1325 E 3rd St, PO Box 1180, 81050; tel 719/384-2571 or toll free 800/525-8682; fax 719/384-5655. Right off US 50 on 3rd St. Very pleasant franchise motel attractively decorated with original art. **Rooms:** 76 rms and stes. CI 4pm/CO 11am. Nonsmoking rms avail. Suites are very nice. **Amenities:** A/C, satel TV w/movies, dataport, VCR. 1 unit w/whirlpool. **Services:** Babysitting. **Facilities:** 1 restaurant, 1 bar, games rm, whirlpool. **Rates:** Peak (May–Sept) $49–$59 S; $54–$69 D; $59–$89 ste. Extra person $2. Children under age 18 stay free. Lower rates off-season. Parking: Outdoor, free. AE, CB, DC, DISC, EC, MC, V.

RESTAURANTS

Chiaramonte's Restaurant & Lounge
In Town Sq Mall, 208 Santa Fe Ave; tel 719/384-8909. N of 3rd St. **Seafood/Steak.** A locally owned restaurant, not fancy but cozy. The menu offers daily luncheon specials, prime rib on weekends, and a few Mexican dishes. **FYI:** Reservations accepted. Children's menu. **Open:** Lunch daily 11am–2pm; dinner Mon–Sat 5–9pm. **Prices:** Main courses $7–$15. DISC, MC, V.

Hog's Breath Saloon
808 E 3rd St; tel 719/384-7879. Off US 50. **Barbecue.** Reminiscent of an old road house, this rustic bar/restaurant with a western theme sports farming tools, guns—even a boar's head. A separate games room offers darts, pool, and pinball. **FYI:** Reservations accepted. Country music. **Open:** Daily 11am–10pm. **Prices:** Main courses $6–$14. AE, DISC, MC, V.

ATTRACTIONS

Bent's Old Fort National Historic Site
35110 CO 194 E; tel 719/384-2596. Bent's Old Fort has been reconstructed as it was during its reign as a major trading post, from 1833 to 1849. Reproductions furnish the 33 rooms, which include a kitchen with an adjoining pantry, a cook's room, and a dining room; a trade room with robes, pelts, and blankets in stock; blacksmith and carpenter shops; quarters for Mexican laborers, trappers, and soldiers; a billiard room; and the quarters of a merchant's wife who kept a meticulous diary. Hosts in period costume greet visitors during the summer. Demonstrations of frontier life, such as blacksmithing, adobe-making, trapping, cooking, and medical and survival skills are given. In summer, 45-minute guided tours begin on the hour daily. **Open:** Peak (Mem Day–Labor Day) daily 8am–5:30pm. Reduced hours off-season. $

Koshare Indian Museum
115 W 18th St; tel 719/384-4411. Native American art—featuring tribal members both as artists and as the subject of works of art—is the focus of this museum. Authentic clothing, jewelry, and basketry, along with western paintings and sculptures are displayed. One of the finest collections of

works by early Taos, New Mexico artists is presented as well. The Koshare Dancers, a nationally acclaimed troop of Boy Scout Explorers, performs primarily in their own great kiva, a circular chamber traditionally used for religious rites by southwestern tribes. Dances are held at least weekly in summer, and the Koshare Winter Ceremonials are a December tradition. **Open:** Peak (June–Aug) daily 10am–5pm. Reduced hours off-season. $

Lakewood

A Denver suburb on the western edge of the metropolitan area, Lakewood was where the elite of turn-of-the-century Denver built their summer homes. **Information:** West Chamber of Commerce, 10140 W Colfax Ave, Suite 1, Lakewood 80215 (tel 800/233-5555).

HOTELS

DoubleTree Hotel

137 Union Blvd, 80228; tel 303/969-9900 or toll free 800/222-TREE; fax 303/989-9847. 5 blocks S of US 6. In a good location on the west side of Denver, this comfortable hotel offers a quiet and tasteful club lounge available to all guests. **Rooms:** 170 rms and stes. CI 3pm/CO noon. Nonsmoking rms avail. Tastefully decorated, comfortable rooms. **Amenities:** A/C, cable TV w/movies, refrig. **Services:** Complimentary cookies upon check-in. **Facilities:** 100 1 restaurant (bkfst and dinner only), 1 bar, sauna, whirlpool. **Rates (BB):** Peak (Mar 15–Nov 15) $45–$139 S or D; $125 ste. Extra person $10. Children under age 18 stay free. Lower rates off-season. Parking: Outdoor, free. AE, CB, DC, DISC, MC, V.

Holiday Inn

7390 W Hampden Ave, 80227; tel 303/980-9200 or toll free 800/465-4329; fax 303/980-6423. Just SE of US 285/Wadsworth Blvd. Modern hotel with good access to both downtown Denver and mountains. **Rooms:** 190 rms and stes. CI 4pm/CO noon. Nonsmoking rms avail. **Amenities:** A/C, cable TV w/movies, dataport, voice mail. **Services:** **Facilities:** 300 1 restaurant, 1 bar, games rm, sauna, whirlpool, washer/dryer. Complimentary passes to local athletic club. **Rates:** $79 S; $89 D; $150 ste. Extra person $10. Children under age 18 stay free. Parking: Outdoor, free. AE, CB, DC, DISC, MC, V.

Sheraton Denver West

360 Union Blvd, 80228; tel 303/987-2000 or toll free 800/525-3966; fax 303/969-0263. 2½ blocks S of jct 6th Ave. A very high quality, business-class hotel within walking distance of numerous restaurants, and close to many attractions. **Rooms:** 242 rms and stes. Executive level. CI 3pm/CO 11am. Nonsmoking rms avail. Great views of either city or mountains. **Amenities:** A/C, cable TV w/movies, dataport, voice mail. Some units w/terraces, some w/whirlpools. Ironing board; Nintendo. **Services:** Car-rental desk, masseur, babysitting. Complimentary cocktails daily 4:30–6:30pm. **Facilities:** 700 1 restaurant, 1 bar (w/entertainment), sauna, steam rm, whirlpool, beauty salon. **Rates:** $69–$145 S or D; $295–$350 ste. Extra person $15. Children under age 18 stay free. Parking: Indoor/outdoor, free. AE, CB, DC, DISC, JCB, MC, V.

MOTEL

White Swan Motel

6060 W Colfax Ave, 80214; tel 303/238-1351 or toll free 800/257-9972; fax 303/238-0046. 9 blocks W of Sheridan Blvd. Small, modest, adobe-style mom-and-pop kind of motel. **Rooms:** 20 rms. CI 2pm/CO 11am. Simple rooms are comfortable and clean. **Amenities:** A/C, cable TV. All units w/terraces. **Rates:** Peak (June–Sept) $35–$55 S or D. Lower rates off-season. Parking: Outdoor, free. AE, CB, DC, DISC.

RESTAURANTS

Casa Bonita

In JCRS Shopping Center, 6715 W Colfax Ave; tel 303/232-5115. 6 blocks E of Wadsworth Blvd. **Mexican.** The pink bell tower on the restaurant sharply contrasts with the strip mall surrounding it. A further surprise is the atrium dining area, which is also the setting for unusual and varied entertainments. Fake palm trees and boulders create an amphitheater around a sparkling pool fed by a 40-foot waterfall where cliff divers perform. The service is cafeteria style and the food is primarily standard Mexican, although country-fried steak and fried chicken are available. **FYI:** Reservations not accepted. Mariachi. Children's menu. **Open:** Sun–Thurs 11am–9:30pm, Fri–Sat 11am–10pm. **Prices:** Main courses $5–$9. AE, CB, DC, DISC, MC, V.

The Fort

19192 CO 8, Morrison; tel 303/697-4771. Just N of US 285. **Steak/Game.** Set in a large adobe replica of a 19th-century fort just outside Morrison on the west side of Denver, this restaurant is decorated in southwestern motifs with lots of space. The grill area is open, so patrons can watch their food being prepared. Although specializing in game, particularly buffalo, ostrich, and elk, The Fort also offers southwestern foods. The extensive wine list includes Colorado wines. Open only for dinner except for special holidays, this is a great choice for a special meal, or for those seeking something a little bit different. **FYI:** Reservations recommended. Guitar. Children's menu. No smoking. **Open:** Mon–Fri 5:30–10pm, Sat 5–10pm, Sun 4–9pm. **Prices:** Main courses $17–$30. AE, CB, DC, DISC, MC, V.

Tivoli Deer

26295 Hilltop Dr, Kittredge; tel 303/670-0941. At jct CO 74. **Continental/Scandinavian.** This homey yet elegant restaurant is located in a small mountain town not far from downtown Denver. It's the perfect place to celebrate a special occasion. Stained glass and classical art decorate the dining room, and fresh flowers adorn the tables. The three-course specials for lunch or dinner are served in the Wine Garden, and the more formal prix fixe dinner, which includes wine, is served in the dining room. **FYI:** Reservations recommended. No smoking. **Open:** Wed–Mon 11am–10pm. Closed Jan 1–14. **Prices:** Main courses $12–$18; prix fixe $36. AE, CB, DC, DISC, MC, V.

White Fence Farm
6263 W Jewell Ave; tel 303/935-5945. **American.** A playground, country store, and farmhouse complete with farm animals make this a family restaurant in every sense. The chicken dinner is the specialty: it's served with potatoes, corn fritters, and coleslaw. Carriage rides are available. **FYI:** Reservations not accepted. Children's menu. No smoking. **Open:** Tues–Sat 5–9pm, Sun noon–8pm. Closed Jan. **Prices:** Main courses $10–$18. DISC, MC, V.

Lamar

Founded in 1886, Lamar was named for the US Secretary of the Interior at the time, who returned the favor by locating the regional land office in the town. Today it's a popular goose hunting locale in southeastern Colorado. **Information:** Lamar Chamber of Commerce, PO Box 860, Lamar 81052 (tel 719/336-4379).

MOTELS

Best Western Cow Palace Inn
1301 N Main St, 81052; tel 719/336-7753 or toll free 800/678-0344; fax 719/336-9598. At jct US 50/US 287. Pleasant motel with friendly personnel catering to hunters. Good choice for families. **Rooms:** 100 rms and stes. CI 2pm/CO 11am. Nonsmoking rms avail. Spacious and tastefully decorated. **Amenities:** A/C, satel TV, dataport, bathrobes. Some units w/terraces, 1 w/whirlpool. **Services:** Social director, babysitting. Special "two shot" goose hunting nights. **Facilities:** 500 1 restaurant, 1 bar (w/entertainment), sauna, whirlpool, beauty salon. Spacious banquet area. **Rates:** Peak (May 25–Sept 15) $80–$95 S; $85–$100 D; $100–$120 ste. Extra person $5. Lower rates off-season. Parking: Outdoor, free. AE, CB, DC, DISC, MC, V.

El Mar Budget Host Motel
1210 S Main St, 81502; tel 719/336-4431 or toll free 800/441-9831; fax 719/336-7931. 1 mi S of jct US 50/US 287. Budget motel on south side of town with plenty of wide open space. Good family stop. **Rooms:** 40 rms, stes, and effic. CI open/CO 11am. Nonsmoking rms avail. Plants decorate rooms. **Amenities:** A/C, cable TV. **Services:** **Facilities:** **Rates:** $29–$35 S; $37 D; $55–$65 ste; $55–$65 effic. Extra person $4. Parking: Outdoor, free. Special family rates avail. AE, CB, DC, DISC, MC, V.

Las Animas

See La Junta

Leadville

Believed to be the highest-altitude incorporated town in the country, at 10,152 feet, Leadville was a major gold and silver mining boomtown during the second half of the 19th century. With one of the best-preserved historic districts in Colorado, Leadville is a great place to explore the state's colorful frontier past. **Information:** Leadville Area Chamber of Commerce of Commerce, PO Box 861, Leadville 80461 (tel 719/486-3900 or 800/933-3901).

HOTEL

Delaware Hotel
700 Harrison Ave, 80461; tel 719/486-1418 or toll free 800/748-2004; fax 719/486-2214. At 7th St. The creaky floors remind you that you're in an old hotel. Renovation has modernized it without sacrificing the charm and historic appeal. **Rooms:** 36 rms and stes. CI 2pm/CO 11am. Rooms are furnished with antiques, and many have great mountain views. **Amenities:** Cable TV w/movies. No A/C or phone. **Services:** **Facilities:** 40 1 restaurant, 1 bar (w/entertainment), whirlpool. Small library on premises. **Rates (BB):** Peak (Dec 15–Mar/June 15–Sept) $65 S; $70 D; $105 ste. Extra person $5. Children under age 1 stay free. Lower rates off-season. Parking: Outdoor, free. AE, CB, DC, DISC, MC, V.

MOTELS

Club Lead
500 E 7th St, 80461; tel 719/486-2202 or toll free 800/349-2202. 5 blocks E of Harrison Ave. Outside the downtown district, this hostel-like accommodation offers a variety of sleeping choices, catering to large groups seeking outdoor adventures. **Rooms:** 8 rms. CI 4pm/CO noon. No smoking. Simple but clean rooms range from private to family-style bunk rooms with up to six beds. **Amenities:** No A/C, phone, or TV. **Services:** Dinner ($8 per person) can be arranged for groups. **Facilities:** 60 Games rm, whirlpool, washer/dryer. **Rates (BB):** $18 S. Children under age 5 stay free. MAP rates avail. Parking: Outdoor, free. Special skiing, biking, and rafting packages avail. DISC, MC, V.

Pan Ark Lodge
5827 US 24 S, 80461; tel 719/486-1063 or toll free 800/443-1063. 9 mi S of Leadville. Situated in the wide-open space of a flood plain near the headwaters of the Arkansas River, the lodge has tremendous views of the surrounding mountains, including Colorado's two highest: Mount Ebert and Mount Massive. A terrific getaway. **Rooms:** 48 rms and stes. CI 2pm/CO 10am. Nonsmoking rms avail. Rooms are

spacious and clean, with moss rock fireplaces and full kitchens. **Amenities:** Refrig. No A/C, phone, or TV. All units w/terraces, all w/fireplaces. **Facilities:** Lawn games, washer/dryer. **Rates:** $55–$59 S or D; $100–$120 ste. Extra person $6. Min stay special events. Parking: Outdoor, free. DISC, MC, V.

INNS

Apple Blossom Inn

120 W 4th St, 80461; tel 719/486-2141 or toll free 800/982-9279. Just W of Harrison Ave. The beautiful hardwood floors and walls of this 1879 inn sustain its historic atmosphere. **Rooms:** 6 rms and stes (4 w/shared bath). CI 4pm/CO 11am. No smoking. Rooms are festively decorated. **Amenities:** Bathrobes. No A/C, phone, or TV. 1 unit w/fireplace. **Services:** Babysitting, afternoon tea served. Complimentary 24-hour coffee and tea. Individual vacation and outdoor packages can be designed for guests upon request. **Facilities:** Games rm, guest lounge. Complimentary passes to local recreation center. Guest refrigerator. **Rates (BB):** $54 S w/shared bath, $74 S w/private bath; $59 D w/shared bath, $79 D w/private bath; $118 ste. Extra person $15. Children under age 1 stay free. AP rates avail. Parking: Outdoor, free. AE, MC, V.

The Leadville Country Inn

127 E 8th St, PO Box 1989, 80461; tel 719/486-2354 or toll free 800/748-2354; fax 719/486-0300. 1½ blocks E of Harrison Ave. Antiques furnish this 1893 structure. Rooms are in the main house and the adjacent carriage house. Children age 7 and over are welcome. **Rooms:** 9 rms and stes. CI 4pm/CO 11am. No smoking. Rooms are attractive and comfortable. **Amenities:** Cable TV w/movies, bathrobes. No A/C or phone. 1 unit w/minibar, 1 w/whirlpool. **Services:** Afternoon tea served. Six-course candlelit dinners are available with advance notice. **Facilities:** Whirlpool, guest lounge w/TV. **Rates (BB):** Peak (Feb 11–Mar) $69–$99 S or D; $109–$139 ste. Extra person $15. Lower rates off-season. Higher rates for special events/hols. MAP rates avail. Parking: Outdoor, free. AE, CB, DC, DISC, MC, V.

RESTAURANTS

The Prospector

2798 CO 91; tel 719/486-3955. 3 mi N of jct US 24. **Seafood/Steak.** The old wood paneling and mining equipment decorating the walls are a nice contrast with the elegance of the table appointments. The restaurant almost doubles as a museum, with many rock and mineral samples in a glass case on one wall, and over 2,000 ore samples above the bar. The main dining area surrounds an open, circular fireplace, ringed by windows affording attractive views of the surrounding mountains. The menu includes a wide selection of steaks, seafood, chicken, and pasta, and the well-stocked bar has a good selection of microbrews. **FYI:** Reservations accepted. Children's menu. **Open:** Tues–Sun 5–9pm. Closed Oct 16–Nov 17. **Prices:** Main courses $10–$24. MC, V.

$ Steph & Scott's Columbine Cafe

612 Harrison Ave; tel 719/486-3599. Between 6th and 7th Sts. **Diner.** Conveniently located downtown, this bright new cafe has old wooden skis and historic tools on its walls and friendly service. Breakfast includes traditional egg and pancake dishes plus more unusual items such as malted Belgian waffles and Steph's eggs Benedict, which substitutes avocado or tomato for the Canadian bacon. Lunch offers everything from home-style roast beef to Buddha's spicy Cajun burger—a secret recipe. Daily specials. **FYI:** Reservations not accepted. Children's menu. No liquor license. No smoking. **Open:** Daily 5:30am–3:30pm. **Prices:** Lunch main courses $3–$6. MC, V.

ATTRACTIONS

Leadville National Historic District

Chestnut St; tel 719/486-3900. A great many buildings—especially brick-and-masonry structures, but also some wood-frame houses—have survived from Leadville's heyday. Most of them line the seven blocks of Harrison Avenue, the main drag, or Chestnut Street, which intersects it at the south end of downtown. The chamber of commerce can provide self-guided driving-tour maps of the district. **Free**

Healy House and Dexter Cabin Museum

912 Harrison Ave; tel 719/486-0487. The semi-refined Victorian social and cultural life of the late 19th century is reflected in these two adjacent houses, which together make up a state historical museum. The three-story, wood-frame Healy House was built in 1878 by mining engineer August Meyer, who made it a center of social activity and escape from the rough and ready atmosphere of the mines. Daniel Healy purchased the house in 1888, and leased it out as a boarding-house. The adjacent Dexter Cabin was built of logs in 1879 by mining magnate James Dexter, who used the building as his Leadville residence. **Open:** Peak (Mem Day–Labor Day, daily 10am–4:30pm. **$**

The Tabor Opera House

308 Harrison Ave; tel 719/486-1147. Horace Tabor financed the construction of this handsome Victorian opera house in 1879. Over the next 75 years the acoustically outstanding theater hosted the great performers of the era, from the Ziegfeld Follies to stars of the New York Metropolitan Opera, and from prizefighter Jack Dempsey (a Colorado native) to magician Harry Houdini. Guided and self-guided tours of the 880-seat theater are available; visitors are encouraged to wander the aisles, visit the original dressing rooms, and study many of the original sets and scenery. **Open:** Mem Day–Sept, Sun–Fri 9am–5:30pm. **$$**

The Heritage Museum
102 E 9th St; tel 719/486-1878. Thirty miniature dioramas, along with displays of mining artifacts and a turn-of-the-century kitchen, depict various episodes of Leadville history. Visitors can pan for gold, learn about World War II's skiing soldiers, and see a model of Leadville's famous Ice Palace. An art gallery with rotating exhibits gives a taste of the cultural present. **Open:** May–Sept, daily 9am–5pm. **$**

H A W Tabor's Matchless Mine
7th St; tel 719/486-1899. Visitors can get a surface view of Horace Tabor's Matchless Mine, where Tabor's original purchase price of $117,000 paid back as much as $1 million per year during the peak years of its 14-year operation. Guided tour of the cabin where Tabor's widow, Baby Doe, spent the final 36 years of her life waiting to strike it rich once more before freezing to death in 1935. **Open:** Mem Day–Labor Day, daily 9am–5pm. **$**

National Mining Hall of Fame and Museum
120 W 9th St; tel 719/486-1229. Visitors to this museum can see what may be the finest survey of geology and the American mining industry in the country. Displays include descriptions of the mining of various ores, from silver and gold to copper, zinc, lead, and coal; working models of mining machinery; and 22 sequential dioramas illustrating the history of Colorado gold mining. Displays of crystals and luminescent minerals; life-size model of a blacksmith shop and hard-rock mine; priceless collection of gold nuggets. **Open:** Peak (May–Oct) daily 9am–5pm. Reduced hours off-season. **$$**

Limon

This old railroad town lies approximately 75 miles southeast of Denver. Its rail yards remain in use by several lines. **Information:** Limon Town Hall, PO Box 8, Limon 80828 (tel 719/775-2346).

HOTEL

Midwest Country Inn
795 Main St, PO Box 550, 80828; tel 719/775-2373. 2 mi E of exit 359 off I-70. Nice rustic setting in downtown Limon, perfect as weekend getaway for couples. Unique art and antiques in lobby—owners committed to local arts, history, and culture. **Rooms:** 32 rms and stes. CI 2pm/CO 10am. Nonsmoking rms avail. Individually decorated with original artwork and homey touches, such as candy on the desk. **Amenities:** A/C, cable TV. **Services:** **Rates:** Peak (June–Sept) $34–$38 S; $40–$44 D; $55–$65 ste. Extra person $4. Lower rates off-season. Parking: Outdoor, free. AE, CB, DC, DISC, MC, V.

MOTEL

Best Western Limon Inn
925 T Ave, PO Box 1361, 80208; tel 719/775-0277 or toll free 800/528-1234; fax 719/775-2921. At jct I-70/US 24. New motel right off I-70 at exit 359. Very clean, with friendly personnel. **Rooms:** 48 rms and stes. CI 3pm/CO 11am. Nonsmoking rms avail. **Amenities:** A/C, cable TV, dataport. 1 unit w/whirlpool. **Services:** **Facilities:** 30 Washer/dryer. **Rates (CP):** Peak (May–Sept 15) $60–$70 S; $70–$80 D; $75–$95 ste. Extra person $5. Children under age 12 stay free. Lower rates off-season. Parking: Outdoor, free. AE, CB, DC, DISC, JCB, MC, V.

Longmont

This city (founded 1871) just to the northeast of Boulder is a trade and processing center for a rich agricultural area irrigated by the Colorado–Big Thompson project. **Information:** Longmont Area Chamber of Commerce, 528 N Main St, Longmont 80501 (tel 303/776-5295).

HOTEL

Raintree Plaza Hotel & Conference Center
1900 Diagonal CO 119, 80501; tel 303/776-2000 or toll free 800/843-8240. A few miles southwest of town, the Raintree caters to business travelers. **Rooms:** 210 rms and stes. Executive level. CI noon/CO noon. Nonsmoking rms avail. Wide range of room styles and sizes. **Amenities:** A/C, cable TV w/movies, refrig, bathrobes. Some units w/whirlpools. **Services:** Car-rental desk. **Facilities:** 1340 1 restaurant, 2 bars, sauna, washer/dryer. **Rates (CP):** $89–$118 S; $99–$128 D; $130–$250 ste. Extra person $10. Children under age 18 stay free. Parking: Outdoor, free. AE, CB, DC, EC, ER, JCB, MC, V.

Loveland

Known as the "Sweetheart City" for its annual Valentine's Day re-mailing program, Loveland's name actually comes from W A H Loveland, president of the Colorado Central Railroad in the 1870s. Established as a trading post in the 1850s, the community remains a trading and transportation center, and is a growing arts center as well. **Information:** Loveland Chamber of Commerce, 114 E 5th St, Loveland 80537 (tel 970/667-6311).

HOTEL

Best Western Coach House Resort
5542 E US 34, 80537; tel 970/667-7810 or toll free 800/528-1234; fax 970/667-1047. Exit 257B off I-25. East of downtown in Loveland's agricultural sector. **Rooms:** 90 rms and stes. CI 2pm/CO noon. Nonsmoking rms avail. **Amenities:** A/C, cable TV w/movies, VCR, voice mail.

Some units w/whirlpools. **Services:** Facilities: 1 restaurant, 1 bar, whirlpool. **Rates:** Peak (June 17–Dec) $38–$65 S; $52–$91 D; $92 ste. Extra person $5. Children under age 12 stay free. Lower rates off-season. Parking: Outdoor, free. AE, CB, DC, DISC, ER, MC, V.

MOTEL

Budget Host Exit 254 Inn
2716 SE Frontage Rd, 80537; tel 970/667-5202 or toll free 800/825-4254. E of exit 254 off I-25. Comfortable, no-frills motel run by friendly locals. Fine for those traveling through. **Rooms:** 30 rms. CI 2pm/CO 11am. Nonsmoking rms avail. **Amenities:** A/C, cable TV. All units w/terraces. **Services:** **Facilities:** Washer/dryer. **Rates:** Peak (May 15–Oct 15) $28 S; $38 D. Extra person $4. Lower rates off-season. Parking: Outdoor, free. AE, DC, DISC, MC, V.

INN

Lovelander B&B Inn
217 W 4th St, 80537; tel 970/669-0798; fax 970/669-0798. Near City Hall. Situated in the heart of the old district of Loveland, the Lovelander occupies a 1902 brick and wood Victorian building with a beautiful garden courtyard in back. A great place for families with older children who can appreciate small-town charm. Unsuitable for children under 10. **Rooms:** 11 rms. CI 3pm/CO 11am. No smoking. Rooms individually decorated with hardwood beds and tables, and antique lamps and couches. The most luxurious, the Donnie B, sports a comfortable "jungle" motif. **Amenities:** No A/C, phone, or TV. Some units w/terraces, some w/fireplaces. **Services:** Afternoon tea served. **Facilities:** Guest lounge w/TV. **Rates (BB):** $69–$115 S; $79–$125 D. Parking: Outdoor, free. AE, DISC, MC, V.

RESORT

Sylvan Dale Guest Ranch
2939 N County Rd 31D, 80537; tel 970/667-3915; fax 970/635-9336. 7 mi W of Loveland on US 34. 3,000 acres. Situated along the Big Thompson River at the mouth of its canyon, about 20 miles from Estes Park, the ranch is nestled up against the Front Range of the Rockies. Best known for its horseback riding and fly fishing in the Big Thompson, the ranch also has wide-open spaces dotted with old shade trees that invite picnics and play. Guests come from around the world to enjoy the quality western experience offered by the Jessup family since 1946. **Rooms:** 14 rms; 11 cottages/villas. CI 3pm/CO 11am. No smoking. Rooms have neither names nor numbers, but range from single units to small, homey cottages. Each is individually decorated with wood trim and open beams. Some cottages have old-fashioned bathtubs and washbasins. **Amenities:** A/C, refrig. No phone or TV. All units w/terraces, some w/fireplaces. **Services:** Twice-daily maid svce, children's program, babysitting. **Facilities:** 2 Basketball, volleyball, games rm, lawn games, playground. **Rates (BB):** $75–$105 S or D; $85–$105 cottage/villa. Extra person $13. Children under age 1 stay free. AP rates avail. Parking: Outdoor, free. June 16–Aug 31, only six-night packages offered: $798 adults (ages 13 and older), $637 children ages 6–12, and $458 children ages 1–5. No CC.

RESTAURANTS

The Peaks Cafe
425 E 4th St; tel 970/669-6158. 4 blocks S of City Hall. **Cafe.** Located in the historic district of town, this brightly decorated cafe offers a wide variety of breakfast and lunch options (some healthful), from pancakes to falafel sandwiches. **FYI:** Reservations not accepted. No liquor license. No smoking. **Open:** Mon–Fri 7am–4pm. Closed Dec 25–Jan 1. **Prices:** Lunch main courses $3–$5. AE, MC, V.

The Summit
3208 W Eisenhower Blvd; tel 970/669-6648. **New American.** Located a little out of town, this wood and brick building with large wood beams offers a fine view of the Front Range. The remainder of the interior is rather dark, and the bar is minimal, but the menu offers a nice variety: three cuts of prime rib, New York strip steak, tenderloin of elk, chicken piccata, shrimp Diane, and Alaskan snow crab. Wines by the glass, homemade pies. **FYI:** Reservations recommended. Children's menu. **Open:** Peak (June–Aug/Dec) lunch Tues–Fri 11:30am–2pm; dinner Sun–Thurs 4:30–9:30pm, Fri–Sat 4:30–10pm; brunch Sun 10am–2pm. **Prices:** Main courses $8–$25. AE, DISC, MC, V.

ATTRACTION

Loveland Museum/Gallery
503 N Lincoln; tel 970/962-2410. Changing exhibits of local historical subjects and the work of regional, national, and international artists fill this museum. A "Life on Main Street" exhibit area depicts Loveland at the turn of the 20th century. The museum also sponsors programs on art and history, workshops, concerts, and poetry readings. **Open:** Tues–Fri 10am–5pm, Sat 10am–4pm, Sun noon–4pm. **Free**

Lyons

A particularly scenic town along the eastern route to Rocky Mountain National Park, Lyons was established in the late 1800s as a way station for tourists on their way to Estes Park. **Information:** Lyons Chamber of Commerce, 4th and Broadway, PO Box 426, Lyons 80540 (tel 303/823-5215).

RESORT

Peaceful Valley Lodge & Ranch Resort
475 Peaceful Valley Rd, 80540; tel 303/747-2881 or toll free 800/955-6343; fax 303/747-2167. On CO 72, 3½ mi S of jct CO 7. 350 acres. Built in the late 1950s, this secluded ranch

offers guests multiple-day packages for recreation in Colorado's back country. **Rooms:** 41 rms and stes; 11 cottages/villas. CI 2pm/CO 10am. Rooms are somewhat dated, but clean and comfortable. **Amenities:** No A/C or TV. Some units w/terraces, some w/fireplaces, some w/whirlpools. **Services:** Children's program, babysitting. **Facilities:** 1 restaurant, volleyball, games rm, lawn games, sauna, whirlpool, day-care ctr, playground, washer/dryer. Mountainside chapel for weddings. **Rates (AP):** Peak (June–Aug) $480–$1,353 S; $445–$1,285 D; $495–$1,353 ste; $545–$1,487 cottage/villa. Children under age 3 stay free. Min stay peak. Lower rates off-season. Parking: Outdoor, free. Rates are all-inclusive. AE, CB, DC, MC, V.

Mancos

See Mesa Verde National Park

MOTEL

Enchanted Mesa Motel

862 Grand Ave, PO Box 476, 81328; tel 970/533-7729. ½ mi W of town. No-frills motel with easy access to Mesa Verde National Park. **Rooms:** 10 rms, stes, and effic. CI noon/CO 10am. Nonsmoking rms avail. **Amenities:** Cable TV. No A/C or phone. All units w/terraces. **Services:** **Facilities:** **Rates:** Peak (May 25–Sept 6) $33 S; $43 D; $50 ste; $60 effic. Extra person $5. Lower rates off-season. Parking: Outdoor, free. AE, DISC, MC, V.

Manitou Springs

Legend has it that Ute Indians named the natural springs here Manitou, their word for "Great Spirit," because they believed the Great Spirit had breathed into the water to create the springs' effervescence. The town was established in 1872, and many of its stately Victorian homes remain, making Manitou Springs one of the largest National Historic Landmark Districts in the country. **Information:** Manitou Springs Chamber of Commerce, 354 Manitou Ave, Manitou Springs 80829 (tel 719/685-5089 or 800/642-2567).

MOTELS

El Colorado Lodge

23 Manitou Ave, 80829; tel 719/685-5485 or toll free 800/782-2246. Just W of jct Columbia Rd. Set back from the road, accommodations are separate adobe cottages with one to three rooms. Grassy slopes and old junipers provide a secluded feel. Ideal for families and larger groups. **Rooms:** 26 cottages/villas. CI 2pm/CO 10:30am. Nonsmoking rms avail. Rustic southwestern decor, complete with ceiling beams. **Amenities:** Cable TV. No A/C. All units w/terraces, some w/fireplaces. **Services:** **Facilities:** Basketball, playground. Claims to have the largest outdoor swimming pool in Manitou Springs. **Rates:** Peak (May 15–Sept 15) $50–$103 cottage/villa. Children under age 18 stay free. Lower rates off-season. Parking: Outdoor, free. AE, CB, DC, DISC, MC, V.

Holiday Inn Express

601 E Galena St, PO Box 1329, Cripple Creek, 80813; tel 719/689-2600 or toll free 800/445-3607; fax 719/689-3426. Just N of town. A typical motel in a great location—on a hill overlooking town with spectacular views of the magnificent Rocky Mountains to the south and west. **Rooms:** 67 rms and stes. CI 2pm/CO 11am. Nonsmoking rms avail. Virtually all rooms have good views of town and mountains. **Amenities:** A/C, cable TV w/movies. **Services:** **Facilities:** Sauna, whirlpool, washer/dryer. **Rates (CP):** Peak (May 15–Oct 15) $89–$99 S or D; $126 ste. Extra person $5. Children under age 18 stay free. Min stay special events. Lower rates off-season. Parking: Outdoor, free. AE, CB, DC, DISC, MC, V.

Silver Saddle Motel

215 Manitou Ave, 80829; tel 719/685-5611 or toll free 800/772-3353; fax 719/685-5611. Just S of Shriver Park. Basic motel with relatively easy access to I-25, though outside the city. **Rooms:** 54 rms. CI 3pm/CO 10:30am. Nonsmoking rms avail. Contemporary decor. Some rooms have views of Garden of the Gods to the northeast. **Amenities:** A/C, cable TV w/movies. All units w/terraces, some w/whirlpools. **Services:** **Facilities:** Whirlpool. **Rates:** Peak (May 15–Sept 10) $70–$110 S or D. Extra person $6–$10. Children under age 18 stay free. Lower rates off-season. Parking: Outdoor, free. AE, CB, DC, DISC, MC, V.

Villa Motel

481 Manitou Ave, 80829; tel 719/685-5492 or toll free 800/341-8000. Just S of Memorial Park. Centrally located, this two-story motel is a combination of adobe and mountain chalet architecture. Many sports facilities are about five minutes away. **Rooms:** 47 rms and effic. CI 2pm/CO 11am. Nonsmoking rms avail. Spacious rooms have contemporary decor. **Amenities:** A/C, cable TV w/movies. All units w/terraces. **Services:** Roll-away beds $8. **Facilities:** Whirlpool, washer/dryer. **Rates:** Peak (May–Sept 7) $72–$84 S or D; $86–$94 effic. Children under age 18 stay free. Lower rates off-season. Parking: Outdoor, free. AE, CB, DC, DISC, MC, V.

RESTAURANT

Craftwood Inn

404 El Paso Blvd; tel 719/685-9000. Just N of Buffalo Bill Wax Museum. **Regional American.** Originally built as a coppersmith shop in 1912, this small, intimate building was converted to a restaurant in 1940. Tucked away on a hillside above town, with great views of the Manitou area and magnificent Pikes Peak, its leaded windows, glass dividing panels, and Oriental carpets contribute to an elegant yet

casual atmosphere. A copper-headed fireplace hints at the building's origins. The menu is extensive, specializing in regional and game dishes—European red stag, elk, caribou, antelope, wild boar, rabbit, duck, pheasant, and quail. Seafood and chicken dishes add an extra dimension. **FYI:** Reservations recommended. No smoking. **Open:** Daily 5–10pm. **Prices:** Main courses $10–$30. DISC, MC, V.

ATTRACTIONS

Pikes Peak Cog Railway

515 Ruxton Ave; tel 719/685-5401. The first passenger train climbed 14,110-foot Pikes Peak on June 30, 1891. Four custom-built Swiss twin-unit rail cars, each seating 216 passengers, were put into service in 1989. It takes 75 minutes to ascend and to descend the 9-mile line, with grades up to 25°; including a stay of 40 minutes on top of the mountain, a round-trip requires 3¼ hours. The view from the summit takes in Denver, 75 miles to the north; New Mexico's Sangre de Cristo range; the Cripple Creek mining district, on the mountain's western flank, and wave after wave of Rocky Mountain subranges to the west; and the seemingly endless sea of Great Plains to the east. The Summit House has a restaurant and gift shop. **Open:** Apr–Oct, daily, call for schedule. **$$$$**

Pikes Peak Auto Hill Climb Educational Museum

135 Manitou Ave; tel 719/685-4400. Commemorating the nation's second-oldest auto race, after the Indianapolis 500, this museum displays memorabilia, historic photos, and close to two dozen race cars dating from the 1920s to today. Racing legends including Mario Andretti, Parnelli Jones, and Al and Bobby Unser have competed in the annual race—156 turns on a gravel highway, ending 14,110 feet above sea level. **Open:** Mon–Sat 9am–3pm. **$$**

Miramont Castle

9 Capitol Hill Ave; tel 719/685-1011. Built into a hillside by a wealthy French priest as a private home in 1895 and converted by the Sisters of Mercy into a sanatorium in 1907, this unique Victorian mansion has always inspired curiosity. At least nine identifiable architectural styles are incorporated into the structure, among them Gothic, Romanesque, Tudor, and Byzantine. The "castle" has 4 stories, 28 rooms, 14,000 square feet of floor space, and 2-foot-thick stone walls. One room is a miniature museum, and there's a model railroad museum in a separate building outside the castle. **Open:** Peak (June–Aug) daily 10am–5pm. Reduced hours off-season. **$**

Arcade Amusements

900 block of Manitou Ave; tel 719/685-9815. Among the West's oldest and largest amusement arcades, this game complex just might be considered a hands-on arcade museum, as well as a fun arcade for kids of all ages. There are some 250 machines, from original working penny pinball machines to modern video games, skee-ball, and 12-player horse racing. **Open:** May–Aug, daily 10am–midnight. **Free**

Cave of the Winds

CO 24; tel 719/685-5444. Discovered by two boys on a church outing in 1881, this impressive underground cavern has offered public tours for well over a century. The 40-minute Discovery Tour takes visitors along a well-lit three-quarter-mile trail through 20 subterranean chambers, complete with classic stalagmites, stalactites, crystal flowers, and limestone canopies. In the Adventure Room, modern lighting techniques return visitors to an era when spelunking was done by candle and lantern. There's also a physically demanding 2½-hour Wild Tour that's guaranteed to get participants dirty: armed only with flashlights and helmets, adventurers slither and scramble through remote tunnels of the Manitou Grand Caverns system. **Open:** Peak (June–Aug) daily 9am–9pm. Reduced hours off-season. **$$$$**

Mesa Junction

See Pueblo

Mesa Verde National Park

For lodgings and dining, see Cortez, Durango

The largest archeological preserve in the United States, with some 4,000 known sites dating from 600 to 1300, including cliff dwellings. The area was unknown until ranchers Charles and Richard Wetherill chanced upon it in 1888. More-or-less uncontrolled looting of artifacts followed their discovery until a Denver newspaper's stories aroused national interest in protecting the site. The 52,000-acre site was declared a National Park in 1906; it's the only one devoted entirely to the works of man.

The earliest known inhabitants of Mesa Verde (Spanish for "green plateau") built subterranean pit houses on the mesa tops. During the 13th century they moved into shallow caves and constructed complex cliff dwellings. These homes were obviously a massive construction project, yet they were only occupied for about a century; their residents left around 1300 for reasons as yet undetermined.

The **Cliff Palace** is a four-story apartment complex with stepped-back roofs forming porches for the dwellings above. Accessible by guided tour only (tickets are available at the Far View Visitor Center), it is reached by a quarter-mile downhill path. Its towers, walls, and kivas (large circular rooms used for spiritual ceremonies) are all set back beneath the rim of a cliff. Another ranger-led tour takes visitors up a 32-foot ladder to explore the interior of **Balcony House.**

In addition to the hidden cliff-side villages, the park's **Chapin Mesa Museum,** open daily year-round, houses artifacts and specimens related to the history of the area, including other nearby sites. In summer, rangers organize nightly campfire programs on various subjects. In winter, the Ruins Road and museum remain open, but most other facilities are closed. Call 970/533-7731 for more information.

Minturn

See Vail

Monte Vista

A stage stop in the 19th century, Monte Vista today is an agricultural center with easy access into the nearby Rio Grande and San Juan National Forests. **Information:** Monte Vista Chamber of Commerce, 1035 Park Ave, Monte Vista 81144 (tel 719/852-2731).

MOTELS

Best Western Movie Manor Motor Inn

2830 W US 160, 81144; tel 719/852-5921 or toll free 800/771-9468; fax 719/852-0122. 2 ½ mi W of town. Great panoramic views of the San Luis Valley and surrounding mountains. Known for its drive-in movie theater. Ideal for families. **Rooms:** 60 rms. CI open/CO 11am. Nonsmoking rms avail. All rooms look out on drive-in movie theater, providing "front row" seats for movies shown all summer. **Amenities:** A/C, cable TV w/movies, voice mail. All units w/terraces. **Services:** **Facilities:** 30 1 restaurant, 1 bar, playground. **Rates:** Peak (May 31–Aug 15) $55–$74 S; $72–$82 D. Extra person $5. Children under age 12 stay free. Lower rates off-season. Parking: Outdoor, free. AE, CB, DC, DISC, ER, MC, V.

Comfort Inn

1519 Grande Ave, 81144; tel 719/852-0612 or toll free 800/228-5150. Across from Fuller Park. Up-to-date motel that's a few years old. **Rooms:** 43 rms. CI noon/CO 11am. Nonsmoking rms avail. **Amenities:** A/C, cable TV w/movies. **Services:** **Facilities:** 20 Whirlpool. **Rates (CP):** Peak (May–Oct) $60–$65 S; $70–$80 D. Extra person $5. Children under age 18 stay free. Lower rates off-season. Parking: Outdoor, free. AE, DC, DISC, JCB, MC, V.

Rio Grande Motel

25 N Broadway, 81144; tel 719/852-3516 or toll free 800/998-7129. 1 block N of US 160 on US 285. Small, basic motel in a modern wooden building. **Rooms:** 15 rms. CI open/CO 11am. Nonsmoking rms avail. **Amenities:** Cable TV w/movies. No A/C. All units w/terraces. **Services:** **Rates:** Peak (June–Oct) $45 S; $58 D. Children under age 18 stay free. Lower rates off-season. Parking: Outdoor, free. AE, CB, DC, DISC, MC, V.

INN

Wild Iris Inn

La Garita Ranch, 38145 Rd E-39, Del Norte, 81132; tel 719/754-2533; fax 719/754-2533. 10 mi N of Del Norte. 155 acres. This warm, comfortable, log cabin–type building is on a ranch in the northwest corner of the beautiful San Luis Valley, with cliffs and rolling hills bounding it on the northwest and a terrific view of the Sangre de Cristo Mountains to the southeast. Inside is southwestern styling, with interesting articulated naval rope work for stair banisters and the railing around the mezzanine. **Rooms:** 8 rms (all w/shared bath); 3 cottages/villas. CI 2pm/CO 11am. Nonsmoking rms avail. Rooms in main building, plus three cottages, all very simply decorated. **Amenities:** No A/C, phone, or TV. Some units w/terraces, some w/fireplaces. **Services:** Afternoon tea and wine/sherry served. **Facilities:** 36 1 restaurant, 1 bar, lawn games, sauna, whirlpool, guest lounge w/TV. **Rates (BB):** $46 S w/shared bath; $56 D w/shared bath; $66–$114 cottage/villa. Extra person $5. Parking: Outdoor, free. AE, DISC, MC, V.

Montrose

Montrose, surrounded by national forests and within short drive of Black Canyon of the Gunnison National Monument and Curecanti National Recreation Area, is a popular staging area for hiking, fishing, and other outdoor activities. An agricultural center, it was originally named Pomona, for the Roman goddess of fruit, but the name was later changed to Montrose for a character in a novel by Sir Walter Scott. **Information:** Montrose Chamber of Commerce of Commerce, 1519 E Main St, Montrose 81401 (tel 970/249-5000 or 800/873-0244).

MOTELS

Best Western Red Arrow Motor Inn

1702 E Main St, PO Box 236, 81402; tel 970/249-9641 or toll free 800/468-9323; fax 970/249-8380. 13 blocks E of Townsend. Attractive motel with blue trim accenting the stucco and varnished wood walls. Easy access to major highways. **Rooms:** 60 rms and stes. CI open/CO noon. Nonsmoking rms avail. **Amenities:** A/C, cable TV w/movies, dataport, voice mail, bathrobes. All units w/terraces, some w/fireplaces, some w/whirlpools. **Services:** **Facilities:** 360 1 restaurant, whirlpool, playground, washer/dryer. **Rates:** Peak (July–Aug) $99 S or D; $109 ste. Extra person $8. Children under age 12 stay free. Lower rates off-season. Parking: Outdoor, free. AE, CB, DC, DISC, MC, V.

Red Barn Motel

1417 E Main St, 81401; tel 970/249-4507; fax 970/249-1828. 11 blocks E of Townsend. No-frills motel convenient to main highways. **Rooms:** 71 rms. CI noon/CO 11am.

Nonsmoking rms avail. **Amenities:** A/C, cable TV w/movies. All units w/terraces. **Services:** **Facilities:** 1 restaurant (lunch and dinner only), 1 bar, whirlpool, washer/dryer. **Rates:** Peak (June–Sept) $42–$60 S or D. Extra person $5. Children under age 12 stay free. Lower rates off-season. Parking: Outdoor, free. Bargain rates during holidays. AE, CB, DC, DISC, MC, V.

Western Motel
1200 E Main St, 81401; tel 970/249-3481 or toll free 800/445-7301. 9 blocks E of Townsend. Very comfortable, simple motel with friendly staff. **Rooms:** 28 rms. CI 2pm/CO 10am. Nonsmoking rms avail. Rooms also available for families and groups. **Amenities:** A/C, cable TV. All units w/terraces. **Services:** VCRs for rent. **Facilities:** **Rates:** Peak (May 24–Sept 2) $34–$58 S or D. Extra person $4. Lower rates off-season. Parking: Outdoor, free. AE, DISC, MC, V.

RESTAURANTS

Camp Robber Cafe
228 E Main St; tel 970/240-1590. Just W of Townsend. **Cafe/Southwestern.** This conveniently located cafe is bright and cheery, with large bay windows and a high ceiling. Work by local artists decorates the walls and is all for sale. The menu includes mesquite-grilled choices, freshly baked goods, and several interesting pasta dishes, such as spicy Chimayo shrimp pasta. Many dishes can be prepared to please vegetarians. **FYI:** Reservations recommended. Children's menu. Beer and wine only. No smoking. **Open:** Lunch Tues–Sat 11am–3pm; dinner Tues–Sat 5–9pm; brunch Sun 9am–2pm. **Prices:** Main courses $6–$17. AE, MC, V.

Sicily's
1135 E Main St; tel 970/240-9199. 8 blocks E of Townsend. **Italian.** The first of the two dining rooms, which caters to the lunch crowd, is light-filled and lofty, with hanging plants, sliding doors, and attractive green tiled tables. The second dining room—a great place for couples—is more elegant, with subdued lighting, cherry wood tables and chairs, and vineyard print wallpaper. Calzones, pizzas, and pasta are the main offerings here; the menu offers a few chicken and seafood choices, too. **FYI:** Reservations accepted. Guitar. Children's menu. Beer and wine only. No smoking. **Open:** Peak (May–Oct) daily 11am–10pm. **Prices:** Main courses $3–$15. AE, CB, DC, DISC, MC, V.

The Whole Enchilada
In Sampler Sq, 44 S Grand Ave; tel 970/249-1881. **Burgers/Mexican.** This family-style restaurant is given the expected southwestern atmosphere by stone walls and large wooden beams. Choose from a wide range of tacos, burritos, enchiladas, chimichangas, tostadas, and tamales, plus burgers. For something a little unusual, try the enchiladas Acapulco, stuffed with chicken, olives, almonds, and cheese. **FYI:** Reservations accepted. Children's menu. **Open:** Peak (May 15–Sept) Mon–Sat 11am–9pm, Sun noon–9pm. **Prices:** Main courses $3–$12. AE, MC, V.

ATTRACTIONS

Black Canyon of the Gunnison National Monument
US 50; tel 970/249-7036. The Black Canyon ranges in depth from 1,730 to 2,700 feet. Its width at its narrowest point (The Narrows) is only 1,100 feet at the rim and 40 feet at the river. The only access to the canyon floor is via hiking trails down steep side canyons, but most visitors view the canyon from the South Rim Road, site of a Visitor Center, or the lesser-used North Rim Road. Short paths branching off both roads lead to viewpoints with signs explaining the unique geology of the canyon. **Open:** Daily 24 hours. **$$**

Ute Indian Museum
17253 Chipern Dr, South Montrose; tel 970/249-3098. Located on the site of the final residence of southern Ute chief Ouray and his wife, Chipeta, the museum offers an exhibition of Ute traditional and ceremonial artifacts, including clothing. Several dioramas depict mid-19th-century lifestyles. Also on the grounds are Chipeta's grave and tiny, bubbling Ouray Springs. **Open:** Peak (mid-May–Sept) Mon–Sat 10am–5pm, Sun 1–5pm. Reduced hours off-season. **$**

Morrison

See Lakewood

Mosca

See Alamosa

Mount Crested Butte

See Crested Butte

Ouray

Named for the famed chief of the southern Ute tribe, Ouray began as a mining camp and developed into a prosperous and rowdy boomtown. Many historic buildings remain, and there is hiking, fishing, and camping in the area. **Information:** Ouray Chamber Resort Association, PO Box 145, Ouray 81427 (tel 970/325-4746 or 800/228-1876).

MOTELS

Box Canyon Lodge & Hot Springs
45 3rd Ave, PO Box 439, 81427; tel 970/325-4981 or toll free 800/327-5080; fax 970/325-0223. Next to trail to Box Canyon Falls. Off the main highway, yet within walking distance of downtown. Clean and quiet. Outdoor whirlpools are fed by mineral hot springs. **Rooms:** 38 rms and stes. CI 3pm/CO 11am. Nonsmoking rms avail. **Amenities:**

Cable TV w/movies. No A/C. All units w/terraces. **Services:** **Facilities:** Whirlpool. **Rates:** Peak (June 14–Sept) $75 S; $80 D; $103–$130 ste. Extra person $6. Children under age 2 stay free. Min stay special events. Lower rates off-season. Parking: Outdoor, free. AE, CB, DC, DISC, MC, V.

Cascade Falls Lodge
191 5th Ave, PO Box 771, 81427; tel 970/325-7203 or toll free 800/438-5713; fax 970/325-4840. Near post office. Conveniently located near downtown, yet not on the busy main thoroughfare. **Rooms:** 33 rms. CI 1pm/CO 11am. Nonsmoking rms avail. **Amenities:** A/C, cable TV w/movies. All units w/terraces. **Services:** **Facilities:** 28 Whirlpool, washer/dryer. **Rates (CP):** Peak (June 21–Sept) $52–$95 S or D. Extra person $6. Children under age 5 stay free. Lower rates off-season. Parking: Outdoor, free. CB, DC, DISC, MC, V.

Ouray Victorian Inn
50 3rd Ave, PO Box 1812, 81427; tel 970/325-7222 or toll free 800/846-8729; fax 970/325-7225. Next to trail to Box Canyon Falls. Modern motel set away from street yet within walking distance of downtown. **Rooms:** 38 rms and stes; 14 cottages/villas. CI 2pm/CO 11am. Nonsmoking rms avail. Sofa bed. **Amenities:** Cable TV w/movies. No A/C. Some units w/terraces. **Services:** Babysitting. **Facilities:** 30 Whirlpool, playground. **Rates (CP):** Peak (June 21–Sept) $75 S or D; $90 ste; $100–$120 cottage/villa. Extra person $6. Children under age 5 stay free. Lower rates off-season. Parking: Outdoor, free. AE, CB, DC, DISC, MC, V.

Wiesbaden Hot Springs Spa & Lodgings
6th Ave & 5th St, PO Box 349, 81427; tel 970/325-4347; fax 970/325-4358. 3 blocks E of post office. Very peaceful, set against sheer mountain walls, away from bustle of downtown. Natural caves serve as steam room and hot pool, fed by the natural mineral springs of the area. **Rooms:** 18 rms and stes; 5 cottages/villas. CI 2pm/CO 10:30am. No smoking. Each unit individually decorated; some quite large. **Amenities:** Cable TV w/movies. No A/C. Some units w/terraces, some w/fireplaces. Some units have cooking facilities. **Services:** Babysitting. **Facilities:** Spa, steam rm, whirlpool. **Rates:** Peak (June 15–Oct 15) $85–$100 S or D; $120 ste; $135–$145 cottage/villa. Extra person $12. Children under age 5 stay free. Min stay special events. Lower rates off-season. Parking: Outdoor, free. DISC, MC, V.

INNS

Damn Yankee Bed & Breakfast Inn
100 6th Ave, PO Box 709, 81427; tel 970/325-4219 or toll free 800/OURAY-CO; fax 970/325-0502. Near post office. Located along the Uncompahgre River, this modern bed-and-breakfast has terrific views of the jagged peaks surrounding the town. Luxuriously decorated with hardwood furniture and upholstered seating. Unsuitable for children under 12. **Rooms:** 10 rms and stes. CI 3pm/CO 11am. No smoking. **Amenities:** Cable TV w/movies, bathrobes. No A/C. All units w/terraces, some w/fireplaces, 1 w/whirlpool. **Services:** Afternoon tea served. **Facilities:** Whirlpool, guest lounge w/TV. Two guest lounges, one with a baby grand piano. **Rates (BB):** Peak (May 20–Oct 14) $92–$125 D; $145–$165 ste. Extra person $15. Min stay special events. Lower rates off-season. Higher rates for special events/hols. MAP rates avail. Parking: Outdoor, free. AE, DISC, MC, V.

St Elmo Hotel
426 Main St, PO Box 667, 81427; tel 970/325-4951; fax 970/325-0348. 2 blocks S of post office. Tastefully furnished, historic inn. This may be the finest hostelry in Ouray. **Rooms:** 9 rms and stes. CI 1pm/CO 11am. No smoking. **Amenities:** No A/C, phone, or TV. **Services:** Babysitting, wine/sherry served. **Facilities:** 25 1 restaurant (dinner only; *see* "Restaurants" below), 1 bar, sauna, whirlpool, guest lounge w/TV. **Rates (BB):** Peak (June–Sept) $62–$88 D; $69–$98 ste. Extra person $10. Min stay special events. Lower rates off-season. Higher rates for special events/hols. Parking: Outdoor, free. AE, DISC, MC, V.

RESTAURANTS

Bon Ton Restaurant
St Elmo Hotel; tel 970/325-4951. 2 blocks S of post office. **Italian/Seafood.** Rock walls and family-style wooden tables give this restaurant a warm atmosphere. In summer you can dine on the outdoor patio and watch the people go by on Main St. Choose from seafood specials plus a wide range of pasta dishes and unusual entrees. Try the Camp Bird miners' medley, consisting of veal, sausage, and chicken sautéed in olive oil, with garlic, mushrooms, peppers, herbs, spices, and port. **FYI:** Reservations recommended. Children's menu. No smoking. **Open:** Peak (June–Sept) dinner daily 5–10pm; brunch Sun 9:30am–1pm. **Prices:** Main courses $8–$22. AE, DISC, MC, V.

Mountain Garden Restaurant
520 Main St; tel 970/325-0449. 1 block S of post office. **Cafe.** This friendly restaurant is strictly for breakfast lovers. The menu offers a nice variety of breakfast fare, with huevos rancheros, eggs Benedict, and the Mountain Garden omelette. Freshly baked bread and freshly squeezed orange juice are the perfect accompaniments. **FYI:** Reservations not accepted. Children's menu. No liquor license. No smoking. **Open:** Daily 6:30am–12:30pm. **Prices:** Lunch main courses $4–$6. MC, V.

Silver Nugget Cafe
740 Main St; tel 970/325-4100. 1 block N of post office. **American/Cafe.** A clean, contemporary eatery set in a historic building at the north end of Ouray. Diners can try a Denver omelette or huevos rancheros for breakfast, and deli-style sandwiches at lunch. The dinner menu runs the gamut from liver and onions to fish-and-chips, rib eye steak to stuffed pork chops. Delicious homemade pies. **FYI:** Reservations

recommended. Children's menu. No liquor license. No smoking. **Open:** Peak (June–Sept) daily 7am–10pm. **Prices:** Main courses $5–$14. No CC.

ATTRACTIONS

Ouray County Museum
420 6th Ave; tel 970/325-4576. Lodged in the original Miners' Hospital, built in 1887 by the Sisters of Mercy, this three-story museum displays exhibits from Ouray's past. On display are pioneer and mining-era relics, memorabilia of Chief Ouray and the Utes, turn-of-the-century hospital equipment including medical devices, photographs, and other historic materials. **Open:** Peak (mid-June–early Sept) Mon–Fri 9am–6pm, Sat 9am–5pm, Sun 1–5pm. Reduced hours off-season. **$**

Bachelor-Syracuse Mine Tour
1222 County Rd 14; tel 970/325-0220. A mine train takes visitors 3,350 feet inside Gold Hill to see where some $8 million in gold, $90 million in silver, and $5 million in other minerals have been mined since the first silver strike was made by three men in 1884. Guides, many of them former miners, explain the mining process and equipment and recite the various legends of the mine. Also on the property is a working blacksmith shop, as well as streams where visitors can learn the technique of gold-panning. **Open:** Peak (June–Aug) daily 9am–5pm. Reduced hours off-season. **$$$**

Pagosa Springs

Hot mineral springs—*pagosa* is the Ute word for "boiling waters"—gave this town its name when it was founded as a lumber center in the late 1800s. The springs remain, and hot mineral baths (the water spurts from the ground at 146°F) are a favorite among visitors. The area is also the center for a wide variety of year-round outdoor recreation possibilities. **Information:** Pagosa Springs Area Chamber of Commerce, PO Box 787, Pagosa Springs 81147 (tel 970/264-2360 or 800/252-2204).

HOTEL

Pagosa Lodge
US 160, PO Box 2050, 81147; tel 970/731-4141 or toll free 800/523-7704; fax 970/731-4141. 3 mi W of town. Comfortable and convenient hotel in need of some renovation. **Rooms:** 100 rms, stes, and effic. CI 4pm/CO 11am. Nonsmoking rms avail. Rooms have excellent views of mountains north of town. **Amenities:** Cable TV, VCR. No A/C. Some units w/terraces. **Services:** Masseur. Passes for adjacent 18-hole golf course can be obtained at front desk. **Facilities:** 384 1 restaurant, 1 bar, basketball, volleyball, games rm, spa, sauna, whirlpool. **Rates:** Peak (Mem Day–Sept) $75–$95 S or D; $130 ste; $145 effic. Extra person $10. Children under age 18 stay free. Lower rates off-season. Parking: Outdoor, free. AE, CB, DC, DISC, MC, V.

MOTELS

The Spa Motel
317 Hot Springs Blvd, 81147; tel 970/264-5910 or toll free 800/832-5523; fax 970/264-2624. Located close to the hot springs, which heat the lap pool, hot tub, and therapeutic baths. **Rooms:** 18 rms and effic. CI 2pm/CO 11am. Nonsmoking rms avail. **Amenities:** Cable TV. No A/C. All units w/terraces. **Services:** Masseur. **Facilities:** Whirlpool. **Rates:** Peak (June–Oct 25) $40–$55 S or D; $60–$85 effic. Extra person $5. Children under age 5 stay free. Lower rates off-season. Parking: Outdoor, free. AE, CB, DC, DISC, MC, V.

The Spring Inn
165 Hot Springs Blvd, 81147; tel 970/264-4168 or toll free 800/225-0934; fax 970/264-4707. This standard one-story motel is in need of some renovation. It's easily recognizable from the steam and unmistakable sulfurous odor emanating from the surrounding hot springs. **Rooms:** 23 rms, stes, and effic. CI 3pm/CO noon. Nonsmoking rms avail. Rooms are geothermally heated. **Amenities:** A/C, cable TV w/movies, dataport, voice mail. All units w/terraces. **Services:** **Facilities:** Games rm, spa, whirlpool, washer/dryer. Hot pool and private bath facility in secluded area of motel adjacent to and overlooking San Juan River. Pools flow into and around each other, and entire facility is nicely accented with colorful and delicately textured travertine deposits and cone-shaped fountains surrounding it. Nonresidents can use facilities for $7.50. **Rates:** Peak (June 15–Sept) $54–$74 S or D; $84–$115 ste; $64–$94 effic. Extra person $5. Children under age 12 stay free. Lower rates off-season. Parking: Outdoor, free. CB, DC, DISC, MC, V.

Wolf Creek Ski Lodge
31042 US W 160, South Fork, 81154; tel 719/873-5547 or toll free 800/874-0416; fax 719/873-5547. 18 mi E of Wolf Creek Ski Area. Fairly typical, two-story roadside lodging. **Rooms:** 49 rms and effic. CI open/CO 10am. Nonsmoking rms avail. **Amenities:** Cable TV. No A/C. All units w/terraces. **Services:** Complimentary ski shuttle. **Facilities:** 125 1 restaurant (bkfst and dinner only), 1 bar, whirlpool, playground. **Rates:** Peak (Mar/July–Aug/Dec) $48 S; $57 D; $65 effic. Extra person $5. Children under age 12 stay free. Lower rates off-season. Parking: Outdoor, free. AE, CB, DC, DISC, MC, V.

INN

Echo Manor Inn
3366 US 84, 81147; tel 970/264-5646 or toll free 800/628-5004; fax 970/264-4617. 3 mi S of jct US 160. 6 acres. The interior of this charming and unusual English Tudor bed-and-breakfast is almost labyrinthine, with rooms and

corridors in the most unexpected places. The inn is deceptively large, decorated with hand-stenciled furniture, dolls, stuffed animals, and porcelain figurines. Unsuitable for children under 10. **Rooms:** 10 rms and stes. CI 4pm/CO 11am. No smoking. Rooms are rather small but quite comfortable; most have spectacular views of surrounding San Juan mountains. One suite accommodates up to 16 people. **Amenities:** No A/C, phone, or TV. 1 unit w/fireplace. **Services:** **Facilities:** Whirlpool, guest lounge w/TV. The spacious guest lounge has a full entertainment center, library, and baby grand piano. **Rates (BB):** $55–$85 S; $70–$100 D; $160–$280 ste. Extra person $10. Min stay special events. Parking: Outdoor, free. AE, MC, V.

RESTAURANTS

Riverside Restaurant
439 San Juan St; tel 970/264-2175. 1 block N of hot springs. **American/Mexican.** Located in the heart of town, this unpretentious restaurant with a delightful riverside patio is located in a hard-to-miss stucco building overlooking the San Juan River and the hot springs district. A limited menu includes a few Mexican entrees plus steaks and burgers. **FYI:** Reservations accepted. Children's menu. Beer and wine only. No smoking. **Open:** Peak (May 31–Oct) daily 7am–10pm. **Prices:** Main courses $4–$10. AE, DISC, MC, V.

★ Rolling Pin Bakery & Cafe
214 Pagosa St; tel 970/264-2255. 4 blocks E of downtown. **Cafe/Bakery.** This local favorite is a terrific place for a coffee break, and it offers a golden opportunity to assuage that sweet tooth. The wonderful aroma of freshly baked bread, cookies, muffins, turnovers, and danishes fills the air. Hearty lunch items include quiche, salad, soup, burgers, and subs. **FYI:** Reservations not accepted. No liquor license. No smoking. **Open:** Peak (May 31–Sept 5) Mon–Sat 7am–5:30pm. **Prices:** Lunch main courses $4–$6. No CC.

ATTRACTIONS

Chimney Rock Archaeological Area
3179 US 151; tel 970/264-2268. Home and sacred shrine to the Anasazi 1,000 years ago, this area comprises two developed trails leading to both excavated and undisturbed ruins of an ancient village perched on a high mesa. A Forest Service fire lookout tower offers an excellent view of the ruins. The site is open only to those who take two-hour guided tours, which are offered four times daily during the summer. Call for tour times. **Open:** Mid-May–mid-Sept, daily 9:30am–2pm. **$$**

Fred Harman Art Museum
2560 W CO 160; tel 970/731-5785. The original works of Fred Harman, one of five founders of the Cowboy Artists of America and creator of the "Red Ryder" and "Little Beaver" comic strips, are on display. Also featured are his collection of rodeo and western movie art and western memorabilia. **Open:** Mon–Sat 10am–5pm, Sun noon–4pm. **$**

Palisade

See also Grand Junction

ATTRACTIONS

Colorado Cellars Winery
3553 E Road; tel 970/464-7921 or toll free 800/848-2812. The state's oldest existing winery, Colorado Cellars produces a large selection of award-winning wines, including a few chardonnays, a cabernet, a merlot, rieslings, fruit wines, and several sparkling wines. The winery grows its own grapes and produces some 15,000 cases of wine annually, plus more than 20 varieties of wine-based food products. Tours, tastings, sales. **Open:** Mon–Fri 9am–4pm, Sat 11:30am–4pm. **Free**

Carlson Vineyards
461 35 Rd; tel 970/464-5554. This winery with a sense of humor offers bottles with names like Prairie Dog White and Tyrannosaurus Red. Wines are made with only Colorado grapes. Visitors are welcome for free tours and tastings. **Open:** Daily 11am–6pm. **Free**

Grande River Vineyards Winery
Exit 42 off I-70; tel 970/464-5867. Produces a large array of wines in traditional style including chardonnay, merlot, syrah, and viognier. Tastings and sales. **Open:** Peak (June–Aug) Mon–Sat 9am–7pm, Sun 10am–7pm. Reduced hours off-season. **Free**

Plum Creek Cellars
3708 G Rd; tel 970/464-7586. One of the two largest grape-growing farmers in the state, the winery produces chardonnay, merlot, sauvignon blanc, and cabernet sauvignon in addition to limited amounts of pinot noir, riesling, and gewürztraminer. Tastings and sales. **Open:** Mon–Sat 10am–5pm. **Free**

Pine

This picturesque mountain village is located in the forest southwest of Denver. **Information:** West Chamber of Commerce, 10140 W Colfax Ave, Suite 1, Lakewood 80215 (tel 800/233-5555).

RESTAURANT

★ Buck Snort Saloon
15921 S Elk Creek Rd; tel 303/838-0284. Located in Sphinx Park; follow signs from downtown. **American/Mexican.** Housed in a century-old building that was once a wagon stop, this traditional mountain bar and grill serves burgers, steaks, and Mexican food, and is known for its Buck burger and Philly cheese steak. Pictures from the past, tree stumps for bar stools, and graffiti-covered walls are reminiscent of a Wild West bar, and there's an old Coors beer sign in the front window. In winter call ahead, as the hours are very limited.

FYI: Reservations not accepted. Blues/folk/rock. Beer and wine only. **Open:** Peak (May–Oct) daily noon–9pm. **Prices:** Main courses $4–$8. No CC.

Pueblo

Site of a busy fur trading outpost founded by white settlers in the 1840s, it was abandoned after a massacre by Utes on Christmas Day 1854. The discovery of gold later that decade led to the town's rebirth, and the arrival of the railroad turned the southeastern Colorado community into a major trade and industrial center, which it remains today. The University of Southern Colorado is here. **Information:** Pueblo Chamber of Commerce Convention & Visitors Council, 302 N Santa Fe Ave, PO Box 697, Pueblo 81002 (tel 719/542-1704 or 800/233-3446).

HOTEL

Ramada Inn

2001 N Hudson, 81001; tel 719/542-3750 or toll free 800/272-6232; fax 719/542-6438. Modern adobe-style hotel, with easy access from I-25 and to town's attractions. **Rooms:** 186 rms and stes. CI 3pm/CO noon. Nonsmoking rms avail. Very contemporary decor. **Amenities:** A/C, cable TV w/movies, dataport. Some units w/terraces, some w/whirlpools. **Services:** **Facilities:** 400 1 restaurant, 1 bar (w/entertainment), whirlpool, beauty salon. **Rates:** Peak (May 15–Sept 5) $70–$85 S; $75–$90 D; $95–$115 ste. Extra person $5. Children under age 18 stay free. Lower rates off-season. Parking: Outdoor, free. AE, CB, DC, DISC, EC, ER, JCB, MC, V.

MOTELS

Best Western Inn at Pueblo West

201 S McCulloch Blvd, Pueblo West, 81007; tel 719/547-2111 or toll free 800/448-1972; fax 719/547-0385. 2 blocks S of US 50; 8 mi W of I-25. 15 acres. A small place with an expansive feel, this is a modern southwest hotel with tile roof and wide-open views. **Rooms:** 80 rms and stes. CI 3pm/CO noon. Nonsmoking rms avail. Rooms on west side have nice views of nearby rolling plains and distant mountains. **Amenities:** A/C, cable TV w/movies. Some units w/terraces. Stocked minibars available. **Services:** Babysitting. Complimentary newspapers delivered to rooms. Day trips arranged in season. **Facilities:** 18 2 150 1 restaurant, 1 bar (w/entertainment), sauna, whirlpool, washer/dryer. **Rates:** Peak (Apr 15–Aug) $69–$81 S; $72–$84 D; $84–$95 ste. Extra person $5. Children under age 12 stay free. Lower rates off-season. Parking: Outdoor, free. Reservations should be made well in advance for high season. AE, CB, DC, DISC, MC, V.

Hampton Inn

4703 N Freeway, 81008; tel 719/544-4700 or toll free 800/972-0165; fax 719/544-6526. Just W of exit 102 off I-25. Large adobe-style motel on north end of town right off I-25, about five minutes from university. **Rooms:** 112 rms. CI 3pm/CO noon. Nonsmoking rms avail. **Amenities:** A/C, cable TV w/movies. Some units have mini-kitchenettes with microwaves and refrigerators. **Services:** Babysitting. Mon–Thurs, complimentary newspapers delivered to rooms and complimentary happy hour 5:30–6:30pm. **Facilities:** 20 Washer/dryer. Complimentary passes to all university athletic facilities. **Rates (CP):** Peak (May 24–Sept 2) $75–$90 S; $85–$100 D. Children under age 18 stay free. Min stay special events. Lower rates off-season. Parking: Outdoor, free. AE, CB, DC, DISC, MC, V.

INN

Abriendo Inn

300 W Abriendo Ave, 81004; tel 719/544-2703; fax 719/542-6544. 3 blocks NW of library. Historic mansion built in 1906 and more recently converted to a bed-and-breakfast; old-world atmosphere with wood paneling, inlaid wood floors, stained-glass windows, and plethora of antiques and reproductions. Grounds are well kept and private. **Rooms:** 10 rms and stes. CI 3:30pm/CO 11am. No smoking. Rooms are decorous and festive. **Amenities:** A/C, TV, dataport. 1 unit w/fireplace, some w/whirlpools. Some rooms have refrigerator, cable TV, VCR. **Services:** Complimentary afternoon snack. **Facilities:** Guest lounge. **Rates (BB):** $60–$125 S or D; $85 ste. Extra person $15. Higher rates for special events/hols. Parking: Outdoor, free. AE, CB, DC, MC, V.

RESTAURANTS

Ianne's Whiskey Ridge

4333 Thatcher Ave; tel 719/564-8551. 3 blocks W of jct Pueblo Blvd. **Seafood/Steak.** The extensive menu at this relaxed, casual restaurant has something for everyone, but cooked-to-order pasta is what locals come for—especially the pasta primavera, lasagna, and ravioli. Family-run, the restaurant prides itself on its use of the freshest ingredients. **FYI:** Reservations recommended. Children's menu. **Open:** Mon–Sat 4–10pm, Sun 11am–10pm. **Prices:** Main courses $7–$21. AE, DISC, MC, V.

Irish Brewpub & Grille

108 W 3rd St; tel 719/542-9974. 1 block W of Chamber of Commerce. **Pub/Steak.** This is the place the locals flock to after work—a perfect spot for enjoying fresh-brewed beers. Standard pub fare includes Philly cheese steak, buffalo burger, and chicken club, and there are several salads and about 25 appetizers. Daily game specials are also offered. The bar is open until 2am. **FYI:** Reservations accepted. Children's menu. **Open:** Mon–Sat 9am–11pm. **Prices:** Main courses $5–$16. AE, CB, DC, DISC, MC, V.

La Renaissance
217 E Routt Ave; tel 719/543-6367. 2 blocks SW of Hose Company No 3 Fire Museum. **Seafood/Steak.** Located in a historic 1886 church, this restaurant offers elegant dining in a "come as you are" casual atmosphere. Old wooden pews provide some of the seating, and the vaulted ceilings and stained-glass windows give the dining area a lofty feel. The menu lists an all-inclusive three-course luncheon and five-course dinner as well as entrees such as baby back ribs, prime rib, New Zealand deep sea fillet, or Australian rock lobster tail. **FYI:** Reservations recommended. **Open:** Lunch Mon–Fri 11am–2pm; dinner Mon–Sat 5–9pm. **Prices:** Main courses $10–$30. AE, CB, DC, DISC, MC, V.

ATTRACTIONS

Rosemount Museum
419 W 14th St; tel 719/545-5290. This 37-room mansion is considered one of the finest surviving examples of turn-of-the-century architecture and decoration in North America. Built in 1891 for the pioneer Thatcher family, the three-story, 24,000-square-foot home is entirely of pink rhyolite stone in Richardsonian Romanesque style. Inside are exquisite oak, maple, and mahogany woodwork; remarkable works of stained glass; hand-decorated ceilings; exquisite Tiffany lighting fixtures; and 10 fireplaces, each with a unique character. All visitors join a guided tour. **Open:** Peak (June–Aug) Tues–Sat 10am–4pm, Sun 2–4pm. Reduced hours off-season. **$$**

Sangre de Cristo Arts Center and Children's Museum
210 N Santa Fe Ave; tel 719/543-0130. Pueblo's cultural hub is a two-building complex containing a 500-seat theater; two dance studios; four art galleries, one of which houses the Francis King Collection of Western Art; a spacious conference room; a gift shop; and the Pueblo Art Works Children's Museum, a hands-on participatory museum. **Open:** Mon–Sat 11am–4pm. **Free**

Fred E Weisbrod Aircraft/International B-24 Memorial Museum
31001 Magnuson Ave; tel 719/948-9219. About two dozen historic aircraft are on display here, as well as numerous exhibits on the B-24 and the bomber's role in World War II. **Open:** Mon–Fri 10am-4pm, Sat 10am–2pm, Sun 1–4pm. **Free**

Pueblo Zoo
City Park; tel 719/561-9664. More than 110 species of animals are exhibited at this zoo, which includes a tropical rain forest and the only underwater viewing of penguins in Colorado. Lion habitat features re-created South African grassland, and kangaroos, camels, lions, crocodiles, ostriches, and emus all reside in the zoo. In the Pioneer Ranch-at-the-Zoo, visitors can observe and feed a variety of rare domesticated animals. There are also botanical gardens and hands-on exhibits in the Discovery Room. **Open:** Peak (Mem Day–Labor Day) daily 10am–5pm. Reduced hours off-season. **$**

Greenway and Nature Center
5200 Nature Center Rd; tel 719/545-9114. A major recreation and education center, this area comprises more than 20 miles of biking and hiking trails along the Arkansas River, along with a fishing dock, volleyball courts, horseshoe pits, an amphitheater, a visitor center with exhibits, and picnic areas. At the Raptor Center of Pueblo, injured eagles, owls, hawks, and other birds of prey are nursed back to health and released to the wild. **Open:** Daily sunrise–10pm. **Free**

Rocky Mountain National Park

For lodgings and restaurants, see Allenspark, Estes Park, Granby, Grand Lake

The variety in ecological zones, which changes with elevation, is the park's most unique aspect. At lower elevations, about 7,500 to 9,000 feet, ponderosa pine and juniper cloak the sunny southern slopes, with Douglas fir on the cooler northern slopes. Blue spruce and lodgepole pine cling to streamsides, with occasional groves of aspen. Elk and mule deer thrive. On higher slopes, forests of Engelmann spruce and subalpine fir take over, interspersed with wide meadows alive with wildflowers in the spring and summer. This is also bighorn sheep country. Above about 10,500 feet the trees become increasingly gnarled and stunted, until they disappear altogether and alpine tundra takes over. Fully one-third of the park is in this bleak world, many of its plants identical to those found in the Arctic. Within the 415 square miles (265,726 acres) protected by the national park are 17 mountains above 13,000 feet. Longs Peak, at 14,255 feet, is the highest.

Trail Ridge Road, which cuts west through the middle of the park from Estes Park, then south down its western boundary to Grand Lake, is one of America's great alpine highways. Climbing to 12,183 feet near Fall River Pass, it's the highest continuous paved highway in the United States. Depending on snowfall, the road is open from Memorial Day to late September or early October. The 48-mile scenic drive from Estes Park to Grand Lake takes about three hours, allowing for stops at numerous scenic outlooks.

Exhibits at the **Alpine Visitor Center** at Fall River Pass, 11,796 feet above sea level, explain life on the alpine tundra. At **Park Headquarters,** an interpretive exhibit, books and maps for sale, and general park information are available. The **Kawuneeche Visitor Center** is located at the Grand Lake end of the Trail Ridge Road. The **Moraine Park Museum** also has full visitor facilities in addition to its excellent natural history exhibits. The **Lily Lake Visitors Center** offers nature walks and information on Roosevelt National Forest. Campfire talks and interpretive ranger programs are offered at each visitor center between June and September. Consult the biweekly *High Country Headlines* newsletter for scheduled activities, which vary from photo walks to fly-fishing and orienteering.

Visitors to the national park can avoid crowds by putting on a backpack or climbing onto a horse. Rocky Mountain has 355 miles of trails leading into all corners of the park. Backcountry permits are required for overnight hikes; these are obtained at park headquarters and ranger stations (in summer). Backcountry camping is limited to one week from June to September. The park also offers fishing and mountaineering, plus cross-country skiing in winter. Backcountry information can be obtained by calling 970/586-1242. For more information, write or phone Park Headquarters, Rocky Mountain National Park, Estes Park, CO 80517 (tel 970/586-1206).

Salida

Located on the upper Arkansas River, near the headwaters of the Colorado River and the Rio Grande, Salida is the whitewater rafting center of the Rockies. The area, which enjoys a pleasant climate, is especially popular with visitors during the annual FIBArk Whitewater Boat Race in mid-June. Salida, founded in 1880, has kept the historic ambience alive in its downtown core. **Information:** Heart of the Rockies Chamber of Commerce, 406 W Rainbow Blvd, Salida 81201 (tel 719/539-2068 or 800/831-8594).

MOTELS

Aspen Leaf Lodge

7350 W US 50, 81201; tel 719/539-6733 or toll free 800/759-0338. 1 mile W of town. Basic motel with lovely little garden area, filled with aspens, pines, and shrubs, where guests can relax in the hot tub or at the table and chairs. **Rooms:** 18 rms. CI 2pm/CO 10am. Nonsmoking rms avail. **Amenities:** A/C, cable TV w/movies. All units w/terraces. **Services:** **Facilities:** Whirlpool. **Rates:** Peak (May 15–Sept 15) $47–$53 S; $57–$63 D. Extra person $5. Children under age 17 stay free. Min stay special events. Lower rates off-season. Parking: Outdoor, free. AE, CB, DC, DISC, MC, V.

Redwood Lodge

7310 US 50, 81201; tel 719/539-2528 or toll free 800/234-1077; fax 719/539-2528. 1 mile W of town. Comfortable, simple motel built in adobe style but with redwood paneling. **Rooms:** 27 rms and stes. CI 3pm/CO 10am. Nonsmoking rms avail. **Amenities:** A/C, cable TV w/movies, dataport. Some units w/terraces, some w/whirlpools. **Services:** Babysitting. **Facilities:** Whirlpool. **Rates (CP):** Peak (June 11–Sept 6) $65 S or D; $59–$72 ste. Extra person $5. Children under age 9 stay free. Lower rates off-season. Parking: Outdoor, free. AE, CB, DC, DISC, MC, V.

RESTAURANTS

Country Bounty Restaurant & Gift Shoppe

413 W Rainbow Blvd (US 50); tel 719/539-3546. 1 mi W of town. **American/Mexican.** A family place catering to traditional tastes, with steak and chicken entrees dominating the dinner menu, plus a few seafood dishes. It's known for tasty homemade pies and cobblers. The shop offers jewelry and traditional arts and crafts. **FYI:** Reservations accepted. Children's menu. No liquor license. **Open:** Peak (June–Oct) daily 6:30am–9pm. **Prices:** Main courses $7–$13. DISC, MC, V.

★ First St Cafe

137 E 1st St; tel 719/539-4759. 1 block E of F St. **Cafe.** Located in a restored 1883 boarding house in the heart of historic downtown Salida, the cafe was partially constructed from wood paneling rescued from the Hotel Delphi and the Dewitt Hotel in Denver before they were razed. Historic photos and paintings lend a gallery feel. The kitchen turns out an eclectic selection of gourmet home-cooked meals: french toast stuffed with cream cheese and walnuts, vegetarian casseroles, Monte Cristo sandwich, Mexican dishes, steak, ribs, and halibut fillet. **FYI:** Reservations not accepted. Children's menu. Beer and wine only. **Open:** Peak (Apr 20–Oct 20) Mon–Sat 8am–10pm. **Prices:** Main courses $4–$18. AE, DISC, MC, V.

ATTRACTIONS

Salida Hot Springs Aquatic Center

410 W Rainbow Blvd; tel 719/539-6738. Colorado's largest indoor hot springs have been in commercial operation since 1937, when the Works Progress Administration built the pools as a Depression-era project. Ute tribes considered the mineral waters, rich in bicarbonate, sodium, and sulphate, to be sacred and medicinal. Today, the main 80-foot pool has two lap lanes available at all times; European-style private hot baths (114° to 120°F), are also available for adults. **Open:** Peak (Mem Day–Labor Day) daily 1–9pm. Reduced hours off-season. **$$**

Monarch Scenic Tram

23715 US 50, Garfield; tel 719/539-4789. Climbing from 11,312-foot Monarch Pass to the Continental Divide Observatory at an altitude of 11,921 feet, this tram offers views of five mountain ranges, up to 150 miles away when skies are clear. The tram includes six four-passenger gondolas. **Open:** Mid-May–late Sept, daily 9am–4pm. **$$$**

San Luis

The oldest town in Colorado, San Luis was founded by Spanish settlers who moved north from Taos, New Mexico in 1851. The Spanish influence and ties to northern New Mexico remain strong today. **Information:** San Luis Visitor Center, PO Box 9, San Luis 81152 (tel 719/672-3355).

RESTAURANT

Emma's Hacienda
355 Main St; tel 719/672-9902. **Mexican.** Emma's is a cozy, friendly roadside cafe serving enchiladas, burritos, tacos, and burgers. The decor is modest, with a southwest slant. The popular green chile and sopaipilla sundae with chokecherry syrup is homemade. A great place to stop on your way to Taos. **FYI:** Reservations accepted. Children's menu. **Open:** Peak (Apr–Sept) daily 10am–9pm. **Prices:** Main courses $4–$7. No CC.

Silver Creek

See Granby

Silverthorne

See Dillon

Silverton

A center of the silver boom in the 1870s, the entire town of Silverton is a National Historic Landmark District, and it occasionally serves as a western movie set. It is the northern terminus of the Durango & Silverton Narrow Gauge Railroad, a historic steam train that has also won fame in numerous films. **Information:** Silverton Chamber of Commerce, PO Box 565, Silverton 81433 (tel 970/387-5654 or 800/752-4494).

HOTEL

Grand Imperial Hotel
1219 Greene St, 81433; tel 970/387-5527; fax 970/387-5527. Near train depot. Historic yet comfortable 1882 hotel reminiscent of the mining history of this part of Colorado. Convenient to railroad depot and downtown. **Rooms:** 40 rms and stes. CI open/CO 11am. Nonsmoking rms avail. Rooms are lofty and bright, with many touches to reinforce the historic ambience. **Amenities:** No A/C, phone, or TV. **Services:** **Facilities:** 75 1 restaurant, 1 bar. **Rates:** Peak (June 15–Sept) $59–$125 S or D; $150 ste. Children under age 12 stay free. Lower rates off-season. DISC, MC, V.

INN

Teller House Hotel
1250 Greene St, PO Box 2, 81433; tel 970/387-5423 or toll free 800/342-4338. Near train depot. No-frills establishment located in downtown Silverton. **Rooms:** 13 rms and stes (5 w/shared bath). CI open/CO 11am. **Amenities:** No A/C, phone, or TV. **Services:** **Facilities:** 1 restaurant (bkfst and lunch only), 1 bar. **Rates (BB):** $25 S w/shared bath, $36 S w/private bath; $31 D w/shared bath, $47 D w/private bath; $43–$55 ste. Extra person $8. Children under age 12 stay free. DISC, MC, V.

Snowmass Village

See also Aspen

Snowmass Village contains lodgings, restaurants, and recreational and other facilities for vacationers at Snowmass Ski Resort. **Information:** Snowmass Resort Association, PO Box 5566, Snowmass Village 81615 (tel 970/923-2000 or 800/332-3245).

HOTELS

Mountain Chalet
115 Daly Lane, PO Box 5066, 81615; tel 970/923-3900 or toll free 800/843-1579; fax 970/923-3650. Just above Fanny Hill lift. This small, ski-in, ski-out European-style hotel is quite simple but very well kept and comfortable. Just a short walk to dining and shopping. **Rooms:** 64 rms. CI 5pm/CO 11am. Nonsmoking rms avail. Rooms have brick walls. **Amenities:** Cable TV w/movies, refrig. No A/C. Some units w/terraces, some w/fireplaces. **Services:** Babysitting. Complimentary soup lunch and 24-hour coffee and tea. Sunday après-ski parties. **Facilities:** 60 Whirlpool, washer/dryer. Ski storage. **Rates (BB):** Peak (Jan–Mar 28) $152–$230 S or D. Extra person $15. Children under age 3 stay free. Min stay special events. Lower rates off-season. Parking: Indoor, $8/day. Closed Apr 15–30/Sept 15–Nov 25. AE, DISC, MC, V.

Silvertree Hotel
100 Elbert Lane, PO Box 5009, 81615; tel 970/923-3520 or toll free 800/525-9402; fax 970/923-5192. Just above Fanny Hill lift. Snowmass's premier ski-in, ski-out property has an atrium lobby, nice for après-ski relaxing. Within walking distance of shopping and dining. **Rooms:** 262 rms and stes. CI 4pm/CO 10am. Nonsmoking rms avail. Rooms are modern, clean, and attractively decorated, with mountain views. Condos are also available. **Amenities:** Cable TV w/movies, refrig, dataport, voice mail. No A/C. Some units w/terraces, some w/whirlpools. Nintendo. **Services:** VP Masseur, children's program, babysitting. Valet ski storage. **Facilities:** 1000 3 restaurants, 3 bars (1 w/entertainment), games rm, spa,

sauna, steam rm, whirlpool, beauty salon, playground, washer/dryer. Ski shop. **Rates:** Peak (Jan 5–Mar 15) $205–$395 S or D; $595–$3,195 ste. Extra person $25. Children under age 12 stay free. Min stay peak. Lower rates off-season. Parking: Outdoor, free. AE, CB, DC, DISC, MC, V.

Wildwood Lodge
40 Elbert Lane, PO Box 5009, 81615; tel 970/923-3550 or toll free 800/525-9402; fax 970/923-4844. Just uphill from Fanny Hill lift. Although each room has an outside entrance, this facility feels like a full-service hotel. Within walking distance of ski lifts, shopping, dining. **Rooms:** 151 rms and stes. CI 4pm/CO 10am. Nonsmoking rms avail. **Amenities:** Cable TV w/movies, refrig, dataport, voice mail. No A/C. Some units w/terraces, some w/fireplaces, some w/whirlpools. Nintendo. **Services:** Masseur, children's program, babysitting. Valet ski storage. **Facilities:** 200 1 restaurant (bkfst and dinner only), 1 bar, games rm, spa, sauna, steam rm, whirlpool, beauty salon, washer/dryer. Ski shop. **Rates (CP):** Peak (Jan 5–Mar 15) $135–$235 S or D; $295–$795 ste. Extra person $25. Children under age 12 stay free. Lower rates off-season. Parking: Outdoor, free. AE, CB, DC, DISC, MC, V.

RESORT

The Snowmass Lodge & Club
0239 Snowmass Club Circle, PO Box G-2, 81615; tel 970/923-5600 or toll free 800/525-0710; fax 970/923-6944. ¾ mi E of village. 241 acres. Just a short distance from the village, this resort is slightly more intimate than other accommodations in the area. Stone and wooden beams accent the interior, decorated with an elegantly rustic, regional flair. **Rooms:** 76 rms and stes; 61 cottages/villas. CI 4pm/CO noon. Nonsmoking rms avail. Nice variety of rooms available with pull-out couches and views of mountains or valley. **Amenities:** Cable TV w/movies, refrig, dataport, in-rm safe, bathrobes. No A/C. All units w/terraces, some w/fireplaces. Fan; humidifier. **Services:** Masseur, children's program, babysitting. Complimentary shuttle to the lifts at Aspen and Snowmass Village. Lift tickets available on premises. Grocery shopping service. **Facilities:** 18 2 200 1 restaurant, 3 bars, spa, sauna, steam rm, whirlpool, day-care ctr. Ski shop. Golf and tennis pros and physical therapist on premises. **Rates:** Peak (Jan–Mar) $200–$330 S or D; $275–$360 ste; $240–$640 cottage/villa. Extra person $20. Children under age 12 stay free. Lower rates off-season. AP rates avail. Parking: Outdoor, free. AE, CB, DC, DISC, MC, V.

RESTAURANTS

Krabloonik
4250 Divide Rd; tel 970/923-3953. 1 mi W of center of village. **International/Game.** When it opened in 1981, the restaurant had one purpose: to help support the 200-plus sled dog community adjacent to it. This is the largest sled dog kennel in the lower 48 states, and diners can watch teams pulling sleds along the nearby trails. The building is a log cabin-type structure facing some of the more impressive peaks of the Rockies. Wild game from around the world dominates the menu, which changes every two weeks. A few of the favorites include noisettes of caribou, breast of pintelle pheasant, and Colorado lamb. **FYI:** Reservations recommended. No smoking. **Open:** Lunch daily 11am–2pm; dinner daily 5:30–9pm. Closed Apr 15–June 15/Oct–Nov 27. **Prices:** Main courses $21–$50. MC, V.

★ La Piñata
Daly Lane; tel 970/923-2153. Just uphill from Fanny Hill lift. **Mexican.** Free hot appetizers and margarita specials for après-ski make this is a favorite spot among locals and skiers. A large fireplace is the attraction in winter, while the outside deck is a summer favorite. Decor is somewhat simple, with—you guessed it—piñatas all around, and the service is also upbeat and friendly. There's a nice selection of not-so-standard Mexican entrees, such as seafood and vegetarian enchiladas, grilled pork crown in a southwestern cranberry chutney, and ahi tuna diablo. The nightlife continues until 2am. **FYI:** Reservations not accepted. Children's menu. **Open:** Daily 5–10pm. **Prices:** Main courses $13–$18. AE, MC, V.

South Fork

See Pagosa Springs

Steamboat Springs

Numerous mineral springs and abundant wild game made this a summer retreat for Utes for centuries before the arrival of the white man. Mid-19th-century trappers were reminded of the chugging of a steamboat upon first hearing the bubbling springs. Ranching and farming have been the mainstays of Steamboat Springs practically throughout its history. But the community has been better known as a premiere ski area ever since Norwegian ski-jumping and cross-country champion Carl Howelsen moved here in 1914, built the ski area that bears his name, and organized the first Winter Carnival. Steamboat Springs today is a somewhat odd but nonetheless successful mix of state-of-the-art ski village and western ranching town. **Information:** Steamboat Springs Chamber Resort Association, 1255 S Lincoln Ave, PO Box 774408, Steamboat Springs 80477 (tel 970/879-0880 or 800/922-2722).

HOTELS

Chateau Chamonix
2340 Apres Ski Way, 80487; tel 970/879-7511 or toll free 800/833-9877; fax 970/879-9321. Condominium-style accommodations just a short distance from Silver Bullet gondo-

la. **Rooms:** 27 cottages/villas. CI 4pm/CO 10am. Nonsmoking rms avail. Well-maintained and very spacious, with contemporary decor. All rooms have nice view of ski slopes. **Amenities:** Cable TV w/movies, refrig, VCR, CD/tape player. No A/C. All units w/terraces, all w/fireplaces, all w/whirlpools. **Services:** Babysitting. Ski shuttle. **Facilities:** 70 Sauna, whirlpool. Ski lockers available. **Rates:** Peak (Feb 24–Mar 22) $465–$700 cottage/villa. Min stay peak. Lower rates off-season. Parking: Outdoor, free. AE, MC, V.

Harbor Hotel
703 Lincoln Ave, PO Box 774109, 80477 (Downtown); tel 970/879-1522 or toll free 800/543-8888, 800/334-1012 in CO; fax 970/879-1737. Built in 1939, this European-style hotel maintains a historic atmosphere. Lobby is cozy and accommodations are homelike. **Rooms:** 86 rms and stes. CI 4pm/CO 11am. Nonsmoking rms avail. **Amenities:** Cable TV w/movies. No A/C. **Services:** Babysitting. Après-ski wine and cheese parties on Wednesday. **Facilities:** 40 Sauna, steam rm, whirlpool, washer/dryer. Ski lockers. **Rates (CP):** Peak (Feb 10–Mar) $125–$200 S or D; $165–$200 ste. Children under age 18 stay free. Lower rates off-season. Parking: Outdoor, free. AE, CB, DC, DISC, MC, V.

The Inn at Steamboat B&B
3070 Columbine Dr, PO Box 775084, 80477; tel 970/879-2600 or toll free 800/872-2601; fax 970/879-9270. Just S of Walton Creek Rd. Cozy, European-style ski chalet in residential district just south of the base of Silver Bullet gondola. **Rooms:** 32 rms. CI 3pm/CO 11am. No smoking. **Amenities:** Cable TV w/movies, VCR. No A/C. Some units w/terraces. Fan. **Services:** Twice-daily maid svce, babysitting. Full breakfast in winter; 24-hour coffee and tea year-round. Deli lunches, and beer and wine available. Après-ski hors d'oeuvres. Ski shuttle in winter. **Facilities:** 35 Games rm, sauna, steam rm, whirlpool, washer/dryer. Fax and copy machine available. **Rates (BB):** Peak (Jan–Mar 25) $120–$150 S or D. Extra person $10–$15. Children under age 12 stay free. Min stay special events. Lower rates off-season. Parking: Outdoor, free. Closed Apr 9–May 23/Oct 31–Dec 5. AE, DISC, MC, V.

The Ranch at Steamboat
1 Ranch Rd, 80487; tel 970/879-3000 or toll free 800/525-2002; fax 970/879-5409. Just N of ski area. Located on a hillside overlooking the Yampa Valley, these modern condominiums are private but close to the slopes. **Rooms:** 88 cottages/villas. CI 4pm/CO 10am. Nonsmoking rms avail. Individually decorated rooms are very spacious and contemporary, with full kitchens. **Amenities:** Cable TV w/movies, refrig. No A/C. All units w/terraces, all w/fireplaces. Washer/dryer. **Services:** Babysitting. Shuttle service to ski area and downtown. Children's movies available. **Facilities:** 4 200 Games rm, sauna, whirlpool. Ski lockers; private garages; barbecues. **Rates:** Peak (Feb 10–Mar) $250–$475 cottage/villa. Min stay. Lower rates off-season. Parking: Indoor, free. AE, MC, V.

Torian Plum at Steamboat
1855 Ski Time Square Dr, 80487; tel 970/879-8811 or toll free 800/228-2458; fax 970/879-8485. Adjacent to Silver Bullet Gondola. These condo-style accommodations offer ski-in and ski-out access, with access to the main village that's just as convenient. The festive lobby is very cozy. **Rooms:** 48 cottages/villas. CI 4pm/CO 11am. Nonsmoking rms avail. Units are individually and tastefully decorated. All have views of the slopes. **Amenities:** A/C, cable TV w/movies, refrig, VCR, CD/tape player, in-rm safe. All units w/terraces, all w/fireplaces, all w/whirlpools. Washer/dryer. **Services:** Babysitting. **Facilities:** 4 50 Sauna, steam rm, whirlpool. Ski lockers. **Rates:** Peak (Jan 4–Mar) $310–$800 cottage/villa. Children under age 18 stay free. Min stay peak and special events. Lower rates off-season. Parking: Indoor, free. Closed Apr 15–May 15/Oct 15–Nov 15. AE, MC, V.

MOTEL

Rabbit Ears Motel
201 Lincoln Ave, PO Box 770573, 80477; tel 970/879-1150 or toll free 800/828-7702; fax 970/870-0483. Just W of hot springs pool complex. Large, modern motel convenient to both mountain and downtown Steamboat Springs. **Rooms:** 65 rms. CI noon/CO 11am. Nonsmoking rms avail. **Amenities:** A/C, cable TV, refrig. Some units w/terraces. **Services:** Babysitting. **Facilities:** 45 Washer/dryer. Discounted passes available for hot springs. **Rates (CP):** Peak (Jan 5–Mar) $75–$100 S; $90–$115 D. Extra person $6. Children under age 12 stay free. Min stay special events. Lower rates off-season. Parking: Outdoor, free. AE, CB, DC, DISC, MC, V.

INN

Steamboat B&B
442 Pine St, PO Box 775888, 80477; tel 970/879-5724. Near hot springs. In season, lots of flowers brighten both the exterior and interior of this bed-and-breakfast, which occupies Steamboat's first church building (1891). Cozy guest lounge includes fireplace, wood stove, TV, VCR, and piano. Hosts are very friendly and helpful. **Rooms:** 7 rms. CI noon/CO 11am. No smoking. The clean, homelike rooms are furnished with antiques and reproduction beds. **Amenities:** No A/C, phone, or TV. **Services:** Babysitting, afternoon tea and wine/sherry served. **Facilities:** 14 Whirlpool, washer/dryer, guest lounge w/TV. **Rates (BB):** Peak (Feb 2–Mar/June–Oct) $115–$125 S or D. Extra person $15. Lower rates off-season. Higher rates for special events/hols. Parking: Outdoor, free. AE, DISC, MC, V.

LODGE

Sky Valley Lodge

31490 E US 40, PO Box 773132, 80477; tel 970/879-7749 or toll free 800/499-4759; fax 970/879-7752. 9 mi E of town. Located in an aspen grove below Rabbit Ears Pass, this secluded, European-style lodge has tremendous views down the Yampa Valley. **Rooms:** 24 rms. CI 4pm/CO 11am. No smoking. Rooms are on small side but comfortable and attractive. Only four have full bath; others have shower but no tub. **Amenities:** Cable TV w/movies. No A/C. Feather beds in winter. **Services:** Complimentary ski shuttle. **Facilities:** 1 restaurant (bkfst and dinner only), 1 bar, games rm, sauna, whirlpool. Ski lockers. Restaurant open only in ski season. **Rates (BB):** Peak (Feb 10–Mar) $85–$175 S or D. Extra person $10. Children under age 16 stay free. Min stay special events. Lower rates off-season. Parking: Outdoor, free. AE, CB, DC, DISC, MC, V.

RESORTS

Home Ranch

54880 RCR 129, PO Box 822-M, Clark, 80428; tel 970/879-1780; fax 970/879-1795. 18 mi N of Steamboat Springs. 1,500 acres. Set amid aspen groves in the Elk River Valley, this is a beautiful ranch surrounded by scenic mountains, in a very private location. The lodge is exceedingly cozy and well maintained. Children under 6 are not permitted. **Rooms:** 6 rms; 8 cottages/villas. CI 4pm/CO 10am. No smoking. Lodge rooms and cabins available. All are very comfortable and tastefully decorated. Two rooms have children's lofts. **Amenities:** Refrig, in-rm safe, bathrobes. No A/C, phone, or TV. All units w/terraces, all w/fireplaces, all w/whirlpools. Humidifiers, boot jacks, cookies, dried fruit, fresh flowers, and a *Far Side* comic at turndown are standard. **Services:** Social director, masseur, children's program, babysitting. Complimentary shuttle to Steamboat ski area. **Facilities:** Basketball, volleyball, games rm, lawn games, sauna, whirlpool, playground. Cross-country ski shop and 25 miles of groomed trails that double as walking trails in summer. Guided tours available in all seasons. Horseback riding area; full and half-day rides available. Afternoon sleigh rides in winter. **Rates (AP):** Peak (June–Oct 4) $3,010–$3,535 S or D; $3,360–$3,885 cottage/villa. Extra person $1,435. Min stay peak. Lower rates off-season. Parking: Outdoor, free. Rates are all-inclusive, except for alcohol, for two people for seven nights, which is the minimum stay in summer. Nightly rates available in winter. Closed Mar 15–May/Oct 5–Dec 20. AE, MC, V.

Sheraton Steamboat Resort

2200 Village Inn Court, 80477; tel 970/879-2220 or toll free 800/848-8878; fax 970/879-7686. Adjacent to Silver Bullet Gondola. 20 acres. Large, modern, well-maintained, ski-in ski-out resort centrally located for skiing, golfing, and other activities. **Rooms:** 270 rms and stes; 45 cottages/villas. Executive level. CI 5pm/CO 11am. Nonsmoking rms avail. Many rooms have nice views of ski slopes and surrounding Yampa Valley. **Amenities:** A/C, cable TV w/movies, refrig, dataport, voice mail. All units w/terraces, some w/fireplaces. Humidifier; Nintendo. **Services:** Masseur, children's program, babysitting. Complimentary ski valet and ski shuttle. **Facilities:** 18 4 600 2 restaurants, 2 bars (w/entertainment), volleyball, games rm, lawn games, sauna, steam rm, whirlpool, playground, washer/dryer. Ski shop, golf pro shop. Gourmet pastry shop. Resort is right next to Steamboat bike path. **Rates:** Peak (Jan 26–Mar) $195–$300 S or D; $289–$700 ste; $249–$625 cottage/villa. Extra person $15. Children under age 18 stay free. Min stay special events. Lower rates off-season. Parking: Indoor, free. Closed Apr 15–May 15/Oct 15–Nov 15. AE, CB, DC, DISC, ER, JCB, MC, V.

RESTAURANTS

Cugino's Pizzeria, Inc

825 Oak St; tel 970/879-5805. **Italian.** Large portions of good food make this modest restaurant popular with both locals and visitors. The lively atmosphere means it's a rare night that there's no wait for a table. Pizza, stromboli, calzones, and pasta make up the majority of the menu. But classic offerings such as chicken-eggplant parmigiana and pasta primavera also appear. **FYI:** Reservations not accepted. Beer and wine only. No smoking. **Open:** Daily 11am–10pm. **Prices:** Main courses $6–$14. No CC.

Hazie's

2305 Mount Werner Circle; tel 970/879-6111. At top of Silver Bullet Gondola. **New American.** A gondola ride (included in the cost of the prix fixe dinner) to the top of Thunderhead is the beginning of your dining experience at this unique restaurant. The incredible view of the Yampa Valley is the restaurant's greatest asset and one of its main draws. In daytime the panorama is spectacular; at night the lights of Steamboat Springs lend a feeling of old-world romance. The four-course prix fixe dinner might include chateaubriand, salmon with tomato basil salsa, lamb zingara, or penne jardiniere. **FYI:** Reservations recommended. Piano. No smoking. **Open:** Lunch daily 11:30am–2:30pm; dinner Tues–Sat 6–9:30pm. Closed Apr 15–June 1/Sept 15–Dec 1. **Prices:** Prix fixe $50. AE, CB, DC, DISC, MC, V.

Johnny B Good's Diner

738 Lincoln Ave (Downtown); tel 970/870-8400. **Diner.** Located in the downtown district of Steamboat Springs, this small diner is decorated with 1950s memorabilia, the traditional black-and-white checkered floor, and a bar with round stools that swivel. A giant mural on the back wall depicts James Dean, Marilyn Monroe, Elvis, and Humphrey Bogart. Standard diner fare, with breakfast available until 2pm. **FYI:**

Reservations not accepted. Children's menu. No smoking. **Open:** Mon–Sat 7am–10pm, Sun 7am–4pm. **Prices:** Main courses $4–$8. MC, V.

La Montana
Village Center Shopping Plaza; tel 970/879-5800. Just S of Silver Bullet Gondola. **Southwestern.** Close to the base village, this lively upstairs restaurant offers excellent Mexican cuisine in a casually elegant atmosphere. The seating is in booths upholstered with Mayan-style cloth, and the decor includes hanging plants and chiles. The menu is extensive, with standard southwestern and Mexican dishes. Some of the more unusual offerings include elk fajitas, chile-seared sea scallops, and Anasazi fillet of beef served with goat cheese and a red chile demiglacé. **FYI:** Reservations recommended. Children's menu. No smoking. **Open:** Daily 5–10pm. **Prices:** Main courses $9–$23. AE, DISC, MC, V.

★ Ore House at the Pine Grove
1465 Pine Grove Rd; tel 970/879-1190. Just S of Mount Werner Rd. **Seafood/Steak.** Almost as old as Steamboat Springs itself, the old barn of the Pine Grove Ranch was converted to a restaurant over 25 years ago. The original horse stalls now make up part of the seating in the main dining room. Chaps, wagon wheels, saddles, and other historic items lend an authentic barnlike atmosphere. Dim lighting lends intimacy to what is otherwise a lively and popular spot. Steak, ribs, game, and seafood are the most popular entrees. The Loft Bar upstairs is open Thurs–Sat. **FYI:** Reservations recommended. Children's menu. No smoking. **Open:** Daily 5–10pm. Closed Apr 15–May 15. **Prices:** Main courses $11–$30. AE, DISC, MC, V.

Steamboat Brewery & Tavern
435 Lincoln Ave; tel 970/879-2233. 2 blocks NW of hot springs. **Eclectic.** In the heart of downtown, this restaurant and brewery is a cheerful place to wind up a day of sking, biking, hiking, or rafting. Tastefully crafted wooden booths and trim give it a nicer tone than many brew pubs. A large buffalo trophy dominates the collection of beer collectibles on the walls. The menu is short but varied and changes every few months. Pizzas are a standby; other choices are gnocchi, grilled catfish, or red chile pepper linguine with breast of chicken. At least five fresh brews are always on tap. **FYI:** Reservations not accepted. Children's menu. No smoking. **Open:** Daily 11:30am–10pm. **Prices:** Main courses $9–$12. AE, CB, DC, DISC, MC, V.

The Tugboat Saloon & Eatery
Ski Time Sq; tel 970/879-7070. Just N of Silver Bullet Gondola. **American/Burgers.** A cherry bar dating from 1850s Wyoming is the centerpiece for this restaurant and sports bar. It's also a popular night spot. The room is spacious and lofty, almost barnlike, with a variety of hunting trophies, celebrity photos, and sporting memorabilia on the wooden walls. A wide selection of burgers complement standard entrees like New York steak and fried jumbo shrimp, or more adventurous items like basil chicken and chicken marsala. **FYI:** Reservations not accepted. Rock. Children's menu. **Open:** Daily 7:30am–10pm. Closed Apr 15–May. **Prices:** Main courses $5–$14. AE, MC, V.

ATTRACTIONS

Tread of Pioneers Museum
800 Oak St; tel 970/879-2214. Beautifully restored Victorian home features exhibits on pioneer ranch life, Colorado's Utes, and the history of skiing in Steamboat Springs. The museum also shows how a well-to-do family in Steamboat Springs would have lived about 1910. In addition, the museum offers video programs on local history, guided tours, and kids' activities. **Open:** Peak (June–Aug) daily 11am–5pm. Reduced hours off-season. **$**

Eleanor Bliss Center for the Arts at the Depot
13th and Stockbridge Rd; tel 970/879-4434 or 879-9008. The historic Steamboat Springs train depot, built in 1908, is now the home of the Steamboat Arts Council, which coordinates programs in music, dance, theater, and the visual arts in the upper Yampa Valley. The Depot Gallery here has changing exhibits and shows of local and regional artists. Performances take place in the community auditorium in the remodeled Baggage Room. **Open:** Mon–Fri 9am–5pm. **Free**

Steamboat Springs Health and Recreation Hot Springs
136 Lincoln Ave; tel 970/879-1828. More than 150 mineral springs are located in and around the Steamboat Springs area. Their healing and restorative qualities were recognized for centuries by Utes, and James Crawford, the area's first white settler, regularly bathed in Heart Spring (the center of the park) and helped build the first log bathhouse over it in 1884. In addition to the manmade pools into which the spring's waters flow, there's a lap pool, water slide, weight room, tennis courts, fitness classes, and massage therapy. Suits and towels can be rented. **Open:** Mon–Fri 7am–10pm, Sat–Sun 8am–10pm. **$$**

Howelsen Hill Park
River and 5th Sts; tel 970/879-4300. This park and recreation complex, Steamboat's original ski area, is still nationally important as a Nordic site. The Lodge at Howelsen Hill offers an exhibit on the history of local skiing. The park is also the location of the Romick Rodeo Arena, where the Professional Rodeo Cowboy Association holds a weekly series of rodeos (fee) from mid-June to Labor Day, as well as facilities for tennis, softball, soccer, volleyball, skateboarding, horseback riding, winter ice skating, summer roller skating, and hiking. **Open:** Daily 8am–10pm. **Free**

Sterling

Sterling, located on the South Platte River, is a trade center for farmers and ranchers in northeastern Colorado.

Throughout the town are whimsical carved living tree sculptures, including a mermaid, a golfer, and a family of giraffes. **Information:** Logan County Chamber of Commerce, PO Box 1683, Sterling 80751 (tel 970/522-5070 or 800/544-8609).

MOTELS

Best Western Sundowner
Overland Trail Rd, 80751; tel 970/522-6265 or toll free 800/528-1234; fax 970/522-6265. Next to Overland Trail Museum. This looks more like a home plucked out of a ski resort than a motel. It's modern, clean, and very comfortable. **Rooms:** 29 rms and stes. CI 2pm/CO 11am. Nonsmoking rms avail. Rooms are step above average motel, with hardwood floors in the entryway, attractive artwork, and fine linens. **Amenities:** A/C, cable TV w/movies, bathrobes. Some units w/terraces. **Services:** **Facilities:** Whirlpool, washer/dryer. Golf course two blocks away. **Rates (CP):** Peak (May–Sept) $57–$70 S; $64–$82 D; $80–$100 ste. Extra person $6. Children under age 12 stay free. Lower rates off-season. Parking: Outdoor, free. AE, CB, DC, DISC, MC, V.

Ramada Inn
I-76 and US 6 E, 80751; tel 303/522-2625 or toll free 800/272-6232; fax 303/522-1321. ½ mi E of exit 125 off I-76. Good-quality motel; two golf courses nearby. **Rooms:** 100 rms, stes, and effic. CI 2pm/CO noon. Nonsmoking rms avail. **Amenities:** A/C, cable TV w/movies. All units w/terraces. **Services:** **Facilities:** 400 1 restaurant, 1 bar, games rm, sauna, whirlpool, washer/dryer. **Rates:** Peak (May 20–Sept 15) $72–$83 S; $72–$76 D; $100 ste; $83 effic. Extra person $7. Children under age 18 stay free. Lower rates off-season. Parking: Outdoor, free.. Golf packages avail. AE, CB, DC, DISC, EC, JCB, MC, V.

Telluride

See also Ouray, Silverton

Among the wilder of the Wild West mining towns of the 1870s and 1880s, Telluride is where famed outlaw Butch Cassidy began his bank-robbing ways. Many charming 19th-century buildings have been preserved in this National Historic Landmark District, which underwent a transformation after the Telluride Ski Company opened its first runs in 1972. The following year brought the first of Telluride's many annual festivals. Among the most popular are the Bluegrass Festival in June and the noted Film Festival, held over Labor Day weekend. **Information:** Telluride Visitor Services, 666 W Colorado Ave, PO Box 653, Telluride 81435 (tel 800/525-3455).

HOTELS

Ice House Lodge
310 S Fir St, PO Box 2909, 81435; tel 970/728-6300 or toll free 800/544-3436; fax 970/728-6358. Near post office. Very modern accommodations within walking distance of ski lifts. **Rooms:** 42 rms and stes; 16 cottages/villas. CI 4pm/CO 10am. Nonsmoking rms avail. Southwestern-styled rooms are very comfortable and spacious. **Amenities:** Cable TV w/movies, refrig, voice mail, bathrobes. No A/C. All units w/minibars, all w/terraces, all w/whirlpools. **Services:** Social director, babysitting. **Facilities:** 25 1 bar, steam rm, whirlpool. **Rates (CP):** Peak (Feb 10–Mar 22) $200–$235 S or D; $260–$320 ste; $460–$500 cottage/villa. Extra person $15. Children under age 12 stay free. Min stay peak and special events. Lower rates off-season. Parking: Indoor, free. AE, CB, DC, DISC, JCB, MC, V.

New Sheridan Hotel
231 W Colorado Ave, PO Box 980, 81435; tel 970/728-4351 or toll free 800/200-1891; fax 970/728-5024. 2 blocks W of post office. This ultra-clean, bright, and luxurious hotel is located in the historic district. Built in 1895, it's thoroughly modern yet retains its historic flavor. **Rooms:** 32 rms; 6 cottages/villas. CI 2pm/CO 11am. No smoking. Rooms are very plush. **Amenities:** Cable TV w/movies, dataport, voice mail, bathrobes. No A/C. Some units w/whirlpools. **Services:** Social director, babysitting. **Facilities:** 10 1 restaurant (lunch and dinner only), 1 bar, washer/dryer. Ski lockers available. **Rates (BB):** Peak (Nov 22–Apr 14) $75–$195 S or D; $155–$285 cottage/villa. Extra person $15. Children under age 12 stay free. Min stay special events. Lower rates off-season. Parking: Outdoor, free. AE, CB, DC, JCB, MC, V.

Riverside Condominiums
450-460 S Pine St, PO Box 100, 81435; tel 970/728-6621 or toll free 800/538-7754; fax 970/728-6160. Near visitor's center. Located on south side of town, convenient to ski lifts and historic district. Great views of surrounding mountains. **Rooms:** 25 cottages/villas. CI 4pm/CO 10am. Nonsmoking rms avail. All units are spacious and very bright. **Amenities:** Cable TV w/movies, refrig, VCR, CD/tape player. No A/C. All units w/terraces, all w/fireplaces. Ski locker. **Services:** Social director, babysitting. **Facilities:** Steam rm, whirlpool, washer/dryer. **Rates:** Peak (Feb 10–Mar 23) $365–$555 cottage/villa. Extra person $10. Children under age 12 stay free. Min stay peak. Lower rates off-season. Parking: Outdoor, free. AE, DISC, JCB, MC, V.

Viking Lodge
651 W Pacific Ave, PO Box 100, 81435; tel 970/728-6621 or toll free 800/538-7754; fax 970/728-6160. Spacious, modern lodgings near visitor's center. **Rooms:** 45 stes and effic. CI 4pm/CO 10am. Nonsmoking rms avail. **Amenities:** Cable TV w/movies, refrig, VCR, CD/tape player, voice mail. No A/C. Some units w/terraces. **Services:** Social

director, babysitting. **Facilities:** Whirlpool. **Rates:** Peak (Feb 10–Mar 23) $160–$170 ste; $160–$170 effic. Extra person $10. Children under age 12 stay free. Min stay peak. Lower rates off-season. Parking: Outdoor, free. AE, DISC, JCB, MC, V.

MOTEL

The Victorian Inn

401 W Pacific Ave, PO Box 217, 81435; tel 970/728-6601; fax 970/728-3233. Just N of the Oak St ski lift. Very comfortable, modern motel. Convenient to shops and restaurants in historic district. **Rooms:** 26 rms. CI 4pm/CO 10am. No smoking. **Amenities:** Cable TV w/movies, refrig. No A/C. **Services:** **Facilities:** Sauna, whirlpool. **Rates (CP):** Peak (Dec 17–Mar) $110–$140 S or D. Extra person $8. Children under age 6 stay free. Min stay peak. Lower rates off-season. Parking: Outdoor, free. AE, CB, DC, DISC, MC, V.

INN

Pennington's Mountain Village Inn

100 Pennington Court, PO Box 2428, 81435; tel 970/728-5337 or toll free 800/543-1437; fax 970/728-5338. Just E of entrance to Mountain Village. 3½ acres. Very nice, modern bed-and-breakfast with spectacular views of surrounding mountains; convenient to ski lifts. Friendly and helpful staff. **Rooms:** 12 rms and stes. CI 2pm/CO noon. No smoking. **Amenities:** Cable TV w/movies, refrig, bathrobes. No A/C. All units w/minibars, all w/terraces, some w/whirlpools. **Services:** Babysitting, afternoon tea and wine/sherry served. **Facilities:** Games rm, steam rm, whirlpool, washer/dryer, guest lounge w/TV. Ski lockers available. **Rates (BB):** $275 S or D; $300 ste. Extra person $15. Children under age 11 stay free. Min stay peak and wknds. Higher rates for special events/hols. Parking: Outdoor, free. Closed May 1–22/Nov 1–17. AE, DISC, MC, V.

RESORT

The Peaks at Telluride

136 Country Club Dr, PO Box 2702, 81435; tel 970/728-6800 or toll free 800/789-2220; fax 970/728-6175. In the Mountain Village. 6 acres. Located in the mountain village above Telluride, this resort is surrounded by magnificent 8,000′–14,000′ peaks and tremendous views. The Great Room, or lobby, is large and lofty with rustic, leather couches; wooden tables and chairs; handwoven rugs; and a very nice floor-to-ceiling fireplace. Offers both ski-in/ski-out and golf-in/golf-out. **Rooms:** 177 rms and stes. CI 4pm/CO noon. Nonsmoking rms avail. Rooms are southwestern, with elegant bathrooms. **Amenities:** Cable TV w/movies, refrig, dataport, VCR, voice mail, in-rm safe, bathrobes. No A/C. All units w/minibars, some w/terraces. **Services:** Social director, masseur, children's program, babysitting. **Facilities:** 18 5 150 1 restaurant, 1 bar (w/entertainment), racquetball, squash, spa, sauna, steam rm, whirlpool, beauty salon, day-care ctr, playground. World-class spa, containing over 42,000 square feet on four floors, is one of the largest in the country. Rock-climbing wall on site. **Rates:** Peak (Dec 20–Jan 2) $130–$435 S or D; $235–$585 ste. Extra person $20. Children under age 18 stay free. Min stay peak and wknds. Lower rates off-season. AP rates avail. Parking: Indoor, free. Special spa/fitness/nutritional plans avail. Closed Apr 15–May. AE, DISC, MC, V.

RESTAURANTS

Eagles Bar & Grille

100 W Colorado Ave; tel 970/728-0886. Just SW of post office. **Continental/Italian.** Southwestern decor with lots of wood and wrought iron, sandstone columns and walls, kerosene-burning copper chandeliers and lamps, and three-foot-tall hand-carved eagles overlooking the bar. The menu includes a wide selection of pizza, pasta, and sandwiches. You might start with a hot spinach dip or romaine and watercress salad, then choose from such items as a Thai chicken pizza, orange roughy in parchment, or certified Angus steak. Artwork at the rear of the restaurant is available for purchase. **FYI:** Reservations not accepted. Blues/guitar/singer. No smoking. **Open:** Peak (Dec–Apr 10) daily 7am–midnight. **Prices:** Main courses $7–$20. AE, DISC, MC, V.

★ Eddie's

In Elk's Park, 300 W Colorado Ave; tel 970/728-5335. 3 blocks W of post office. **Italian/Pizza.** The first thing you'll see upon entering this eatery is the semicircular bar, which offers many of Colorado's microbrewery beers on tap. Some of the more unusual pizzas are the Dosie Doe and California Dreamin' Pizza, loaded with things like roasted garlic, sun-dried tomatoes, artichoke hearts, and gorgonzola cheese. Pasta offerings include a lot of seafood. **FYI:** Reservations not accepted. No smoking. **Open:** Peak (Nov 23–Apr 14) daily 10am–10pm. **Prices:** Main courses $8–$20. AE, MC, V.

Excelsior Cafe

200 W Colorado Ave; tel 970/728-4250. 1 block E of town hall. **Italian.** Located in the historic district, the lofty ceilings, brick walls, and wood trim of this cafe offer a warm atmosphere to tourists and skiers alike. On the lunch menu is possibly the best sandwich in town—the verdure sandwich on focaccia. The dinner menu includes a good selection of "new" Italian entrees such as grilled New Zealand green-lipped mussels in a saffron-shrimp broth with charred spinach or whole grilled portobello mushroom "pizza," filled with tomato, goat cheese, and basil. The wine list offers a wide range of California and Italian wines. **FYI:** Reservations accepted. Children's menu. No smoking. **Open:** Lunch daily 11am–3pm; dinner daily 6–10pm. **Prices:** Main courses $8–$19. AE, MC, V.

Maggie's Bakery & Cafe
217 E Colorado Ave; tel 970/728-3334. 2 blocks E of post office. **Cafe/Bakery.** A festive, hole-in-the-wall cafe with breads and pastries baked fresh daily. Sandwiches are available for lunch, but this eatery is best known for its pastries and carrot and chocolate cakes. The popular cinnamon rolls—made with croissant dough—are claimed by many locals to be the best anywhere. **FYI:** Reservations not accepted. Beer and wine only. No smoking. **Open:** Daily 6:30am–4pm. **Prices:** Lunch main courses $4–$5. No CC.

Swede-Finn Hall
472 W Pacific Ave; tel 970/728-2085. Near post office. **Continental.** Warm and open, and close to the ski lifts, the interior of this two-story restaurant and pool room looks like an old town hall, even down to the small stage. Tables are hardwood and the ceilings lofty. Choose from a variety of entrees such as pecan-crusted quail, trout paupiette, Jamaican jerk chicken, or the nightly game special, before playing a few games on the full-size pool tables. **FYI:** Reservations accepted. Comedy/guitar/jazz. No smoking. **Open:** Daily 3:30pm–2am. Closed Apr 15–31/Oct 31–Nov 15. **Prices:** Main courses $9–$20. MC, V.

T-Ride Country Club
333 W Colorado Ave; tel 970/728-6344. 3 blocks W of post office. **American.** This sports bar/restaurant, complete with banners and other sports paraphernalia, overlooks the town's main street and the ski mountain. It offers lots of steaks and sandwiches, plus a good variety of appetizers and beer. **FYI:** Reservations accepted. No smoking. **Open:** Daily 11:30am–10pm. **Prices:** Main courses $6–$19. AE, DISC, MC, V.

ATTRACTIONS

Telluride Historical Museum
400 N Fir St; tel 970/728-3344. The museum has 9,000 artifacts and 1,400 historic photos that show what Telluride was like in its Wild West days, when the likes of Butch Cassidy walked the streets. Exhibits include a very rare prehistoric Anasazi blanket, mining memorabilia, a turn-of-the-century schoolroom display, antique toys, and remembrances from Telluride's Victorian past. **Open:** Peak (May–Oct) Mon–Sat 10am–5pm, Sun noon–5pm. Reduced hours off-season. **$$**

Telluride Ski Resort
565 Mountain Village Blvd; tel 970/728-3856 or 728-3614 (snow report). The mountain's Front Face, which drops sharply from the summit to the town of Telluride, is characterized by steep moguls, tree-and-glade skiing, and challenging groomed pitches for experts and advanced intermediates. Gorrono Basin, which rises from the Mountain Village Resort, caters to intermediate skiers. The broad, gentle slopes of the Meadows stretch beneath Gorrono Basin to the foot of Sunshine Peak. This mountain, with trails over 2½ miles long devoted entirely to novice skiers, is served by a high-speed quad chair.

In all, Telluride offers 1,050 acres of skiable terrain. The vertical drop is an impressive 3,165 feet from the 11,890-foot summit. The mountain has 64 trails served by 10 lifts (one high-speed quad, two triples, six doubles, and a Poma). Twenty-one percent of the trails are rated for beginners, 47 percent for intermediates, and 32 percent for expert skiers. There are an additional 20 miles of Nordic trails, and helicopter skiing is also available. Average annual snowfall is 300 inches (25 feet). **Open:** Dec–early Apr, daily, call for schedule. **$$$$**

Thornton

See Denver

Trinidad

History and art make Trinidad a good place for those traveling along I-25 through southern Colorado. During the Wild West days Bat Masterson was sheriff and Wyatt Earp drove the stage; even Billy the Kid passed through. Many handsome buildings of brick and sandstone survive from the era. **Information:** Trinidad/Las Animas County Chamber of Commerce, 309 Nevada St, Trinidad 81082 (tel 719/846-9285).

HOTEL

Holiday Inn
9995 County Rd 69.1, 81082; tel 719/846-4491 or toll free 800/465-4329; fax 719/846-2440. Just W of exit 11 off I-25. Pleasant hotel on south side of town with beautiful surroundings. Well suited for couples and families. **Rooms:** 113 rms and stes. CI 2pm/CO noon. Nonsmoking rms avail. **Amenities:** A/C, cable TV, dataport. **Services:** Car-rental desk. Children's camp in summer; children's program and day-care center during peak season. **Facilities:** 1 restaurant, 1 bar, games rm, whirlpool, day-care ctr, washer/dryer. **Rates:** Peak (May 15–Sept 15) $79–$89 S; $89–$99 D; $105–$115 ste. Extra person $10. Children under age 19 stay free. Lower rates off-season. Parking: Outdoor, free. Special group rates for parties of five or more. AE, DISC, MC, V.

MOTELS

Best Western Country Club Inn
900 W Adams St, 81082; tel 719/846-2215 or toll free 800/955-2211, fax 719/846-2215. Just W of exit 13A off I-25. Standard motel just off I-25. **Rooms:** 55 rms and stes. CI 2pm/CO 11am. Nonsmoking rms avail. **Amenities:** A/C, cable TV. **Services:** Babysitting. **Facilities:** 1 restaurant, 1 bar, whirlpool, washer/dryer. **Rates:** Peak (May 15–Sept 15) $75–$89 S; $79–$95 D; $125–$155

ste. Extra person $10. Children under age 18 stay free. Lower rates off-season. AP rates avail. MAP rates avail. Parking: Outdoor, free. AE, CB, DC, DISC, MC, V.

Days Inn
702 W Main St, 81082; tel 719/846-2271 or toll free 800/329-7460; fax 719/846-2271. Near exit 13B off I-25. Basic roadside motel. **Rooms:** 61 rms and stes. CI 1pm/CO 11am. Nonsmoking rms avail. **Amenities:** A/C, cable TV. Refrigerators in suites. **Services:** **Facilities:** 250 1 restaurant, 1 bar, whirlpool, beauty salon, washer/dryer. **Rates (CP):** Peak (Apr–Sept) $50–$68 S; $65–$80 D; $65–$95 ste. Extra person $5. Children under age 16 stay free. Lower rates off-season. Parking: Outdoor, free. AE, CB, DC, DISC, MC, V.

RESTAURANTS

El Capitan Restaurant & Lounge
321 State St; tel 719/846-9903. Just W of exit 14A off I-25. **American/Italian/Mexican.** Family-owned and -operated for over 25 years, this roomy and inviting restaurant claims to serve the best margaritas in southern Colorado. In addition to Mexican and Italian dishes, you can get steak, seafood, burgers, and sandwiches. **FYI:** Reservations accepted. Children's menu. No smoking. **Open:** Peak (May–Sept) Mon–Fri 11am–10pm, Sat 4:30–10pm. **Prices:** Main courses $3–$10. AE, DISC, MC, V.

Nana & Nano's Pasta House
415 University St; tel 719/846-2696. Just W of exit 14A off I-25. **American/Italian.** A small, homelike restaurant where romantic music plays in the background. The menu features alla olio rigatoni, spaghetti, gnocchi, and ravioli, plus chicken, steak, and fish. The house specialty is lasagna, available on Friday and Saturday. All sauces are freshly made; some are sold over the counter. Monteleone Deli, which is attached to the restaurant, is open for lunch. **FYI:** Reservations accepted. Children's menu. No liquor license. No smoking. **Open:** Peak (May–Sept) Tues–Sat 4:30–8:30pm. **Prices:** Main courses $5–$12. AE, DISC, MC, V.

ATTRACTIONS

Trinidad History Museum
300 E Main St; tel 719/846-7217. Together, the Baca House, Bloom Mansion, Santa Fe Trail Museum, and Historic Gardens make up the History Museum and rank as Trinidad's principal attraction. The Baca House, built in 1870 along the mountain route of the Santa Fe Trail, is a two-story adobe in Greek revival style. Owned by sheep rancher Felipe Baca, the house contains some of the Baca family's original furnishings. Nearby stands the Bloom Mansion, a Second Empire–style Victorian manor embellished with fancy wood carving and ornate ironwork. Built in 1882 for cattleman Frank G Bloom and his family, it also contains period decor. The Colorado Historical Society operates both homes and the Santa Fe Trail Museum, in an outbuilding of the Baca House that was originally living quarters for ranch hands and sheepherders. Both the Baca House and Santa Fe Trail Museum are Certified Sites on the Santa Fe National Historic Trail. **Open:** May–Sept, daily 10am–4pm. **$**

A R Mitchell Memorial Museum of Western Art
150 E Main St; tel 719/846-4224. More than 250 paintings and illustrations by western artist Arthur Roy Mitchell (1889–1977) are displayed here, along with works by other nationally recognized artists and a collection of early Hispanic religious folk art. The building is 1906 western style with the original tin ceiling, wood floors, and a horseshoe-shaped mezzanine. The museum also contains the Aultman collection of photographs, taken by Oliver E Aultman and his son Glenn from the late 1800's through much of the 20th century. **Open:** Peak (June–Sept) Mon–Thurs 10am–4pm, Fri–Sat 10am–6pm. Reduced hours off-season. **Free**

Louden-Henritze Archaeology Museum
Trinidad State Junior College Library; tel 719/846-5508. Millions of years of history are displayed in this museum, from early geological formations, plant and animal fossils, casts of dinosaur tracks, arrowheads, baskets, pottery, petroglyphs, and other artifacts from prehistoric man discovered during area excavations. **Open:** Peak (May–Oct) Mon–Fri 10am–4pm. Reduced hours off-season. **Free**

Children's Museum
314 N Commercial St; tel 719/846-7721. A historic fire truck, Trinidad's original 1930s-era alarm system, and a restored turn-of-the-century schoolroom are exhibited. Another section of the museum has hands-on displays for children, including Grandma's trunk for dress-up. **Open:** June–Aug, Mon–Sat noon–4pm. **Free**

Vail

Consistently rated America's top ski resort, Vail is also gaining popularity as a summer vacation destination among hikers and mountain bikers. Off the slopes, Vail is an incredibly compact Tyrolean village of lodgings, restaurants, and trendy shops that is frequented by almost as many Europeans as Americans. **Information:** Vail Valley Tourism & Convention Bureau, 100 E Meadow Dr, Vail 81657 (tel 970/476-1000 or 800/525-3875).

HOTELS

Antlers at Vail
680 W Lionshead Place, 81657; tel 970/476-2471 or toll free 800/843-8245; fax 970/476-4146. Just W of gondola. Large complex of privately owned condos just a few minutes walk from the ski lifts, shops, and restaurants in West Vail. **Rooms:** 70 stes. CI 4pm/CO 11am. Nonsmoking rms avail. Many rooms have nice mountain and valley views. **Amenities:** Satel TV w/movies, refrig, dataport, VCR. No A/C. All units w/terraces, all w/fireplaces. **Services:**

Children's program, babysitting. **Facilities:** Sauna, whirlpool, washer/dryer. Ski lockers. **Rates:** Peak (Jan 27–Mar 30) $195–$735 ste. Extra person $15. Children under age 15 stay free. Lower rates off-season. Parking: Indoor/outdoor, free. AE, CB, DC, DISC, MC, V.

Beaver Creek Lodge

26 Avondale Lane, Beaver Creek, PO Box 2578, Avon, 81620; tel 970/845-9800 or toll free 800/732-6777; fax 970/845-8242. 50 yards from Centennial Lift. Adjacent to Beaver Creek, this classy establishment with dark wood trim is conveniently located in the center of town, just a short walk from most attractions and facilities. **Rooms:** 71 stes; 6 cottages/villas. CI 3pm/CO 11am. Nonsmoking rms avail. Each of the plush and spacious rooms has a large window alcove overlooking the hotel's interior. **Amenities:** Cable TV, refrig, VCR, bathrobes. No A/C. All units w/minibars, all w/fireplaces. **Services:** Masseur, babysitting. **Facilities:** 1 restaurant, 1 bar, spa, sauna, steam rm, whirlpool, beauty salon, washer/dryer. **Rates:** Peak (Nov 15–Apr 15) $195–$575 ste; $1,000–$1,800 cottage/villa. Min stay peak. Lower rates off-season. Parking: Indoor, $5/day. AE, CB, DC, DISC, MC, V.

Comfort Inn

161 W Beaver Creek Blvd, PO Box 5510, Avon, 81620; tel 970/949-5511 or toll free 800/423-4374; fax 970/949-7762. Just W of exit 167 off I-70. Stucco hotel in a great location for skiers and for those just stopping in town. **Rooms:** 146 rms. CI 3pm/CO 11am. Nonsmoking rms avail. Most of the spacious rooms have attractive views of surrounding mountains. **Amenities:** A/C, cable TV w/movies. Some units w/minibars, some w/terraces. **Services:** Babysitting. **Facilities:** Whirlpool, washer/dryer. Ski shop with ski storage. Access to new fitness/aquatic center 100 yards away for small fee. **Rates (CP):** Peak (Jan–Mar) $165–$185 S or D. Extra person $10. Children under age 18 stay free. Lower rates off-season. Parking: Outdoor, free. AE, CB, DC, DISC, MC, V.

Gasthof Gramshammer

231 E Gore Creek Dr, 81657; tel 970/476-5626 or toll free 800/610-7374; fax 970/476-8816. 2 blocks N of Vista Bahn Express. Conveniently located in the shopping and dining area not far from the ski lifts, this 30-year-old Tyrolean lodge has nice European atmosphere and charm; it's also quiet. **Rooms:** 28 rms and stes. CI 3pm/CO 11am. Nonsmoking rms avail. Rooms are tastefully decorated, with a wide variety of layout and bed choices. **Amenities:** Cable TV, in-rm safe. No A/C. Some units w/terraces, some w/fireplaces. **Services:** Babysitting. **Facilities:** 1 restaurant (lunch and dinner only), 1 bar (w/entertainment). Ski lockers on-site. **Rates (CP):** Peak (Dec–Mar) $195–$260 S or D; $270–$595 ste. Extra person $40. Children under age 9 stay free. Min stay peak. Lower rates off-season. Parking: Outdoor, free. AE, CB, DC, MC, V.

Holiday Inn Chateau Vail

13 Vail Rd, 81657; tel 970/476-5631 or toll free 800/HOLIDAY; fax 970/476-2508. Just S of exit 176 off I-70. Resembles a European chalet, complete with large hearth in lobby. Short walk to ski lifts, shopping, and dining. **Rooms:** 120 rms and stes. CI 3pm/CO 10am. Nonsmoking rms avail. **Amenities:** Cable TV w/movies, refrig. No A/C. Some units w/terraces, some w/fireplaces. **Services:** Babysitting. **Facilities:** 1 restaurant, 1 bar, games rm, sauna, whirlpool, washer/dryer. **Rates:** Peak (Nov 25–Mar) $125–$299 S or D; $200–$695 ste. Children under age 19 stay free. Min stay special events. Lower rates off-season. Parking: Outdoor, free. AE, CB, DC, DISC, MC, V.

The Inn at Beaver Creek

10 Elk Track Rd, Beaver Creek, PO Box 36, Avon, 81620; tel 970/845-7800 or toll free 800/859-8242; fax 970/845-5279. Next to Strawberry Park Express Lift. High quality ski-in, ski-out hotel with fine furniture, prints, and plush carpeting in a lovely alpine setting. Not large, it has an intimate atmosphere. **Rooms:** 45 rms and stes. CI 4pm/CO 10am. Nonsmoking rms avail. **Amenities:** Cable TV w/movies, refrig, dataport, bathrobes. No A/C. Some units w/terraces. **Services:** Masseur, children's program, babysitting. **Facilities:** 18 1 bar, volleyball, lawn games, sauna, steam rm, whirlpool, washer/dryer. **Rates (CP):** Peak (Jan 2–Apr 5) $250–$325 S or D; $500–$525 ste. Extra person $25. Children under age 12 stay free. Min stay peak and special events. Lower rates off-season. Parking: Indoor, free. AE, DISC, MC, V.

Lion Square Lodge

660 W Lionshead Place, 81657; tel 970/476-2281 or toll free 800/525-5788; fax 970/476-7423. Adjacent to gondola. Privately owned and decorated condos within walking distance of ski gondola and Born Free Express ski lift. **Rooms:** 108 rms and stes. CI 5pm/CO 10am. Nonsmoking rms avail. Large range of room choices. **Amenities:** Cable TV w/movies, refrig, voice mail. No A/C. Some units w/terraces, some w/fireplaces. Most units have barbecues. **Services:** Children's program, babysitting. Wine and cheese reception; grocery store shuttle; ski valet. **Facilities:** 1 restaurant (lunch and dinner only), sauna, whirlpool, washer/dryer. Ski shop. **Rates (CP):** Peak (Dec 20–Jan 6) $270–$315 S or D; $450–$1,100 ste. Extra person $25. Children under age 17 stay free. Min stay peak. Lower rates off-season. Parking: Indoor/outdoor, free. AE, CB, DC, DISC, MC, V.

The Lodge at Vail

174 E Gore Creek Rd, 81657; tel 970/476-5011 or toll free 800/331-5634; fax 970/476-7425. Next to Main Village lifts. The first hotel in Vail, this classy and comfortable property has terrific access to the ski lifts, shops, and restaurants. Lobby has delightful sitting area around a huge stone fireplace. **Rooms:** 100 rms and stes. CI 4pm/CO 11am.

Amenities: Cable TV w/movies, refrig, dataport, voice mail, bathrobes. No A/C. Some units w/terraces, some w/fireplaces. **Services:** Twice-daily maid svce, masseur, babysitting. **Facilities:** 250 2 restaurants, 1 bar (w/entertainment), sauna, whirlpool, washer/dryer. Ski shop on premises; ski lockers available for guests. **Rates (BB):** Peak (Dec 20–Jan 2) $300–$525 S or D; $550–$1,900 ste. Extra person $55. Min stay peak. Lower rates off-season. Parking: Indoor/outdoor, free. Closed Apr 15–May 25/Oct 15–Nov 15. AE, CB, DC, DISC, JCB, MC, V.

Mountain Haus at Vail

292 E Meadow Dr, 81657; tel 970/476-2434 or toll free 800/237-0922; fax 970/476-3007. Next to Vail Village covered bridge. Most units are condominiums individually owned and decorated with taste and style; a few hotel rooms available. **Rooms:** 70 rms and stes. CI 4pm/CO 10am. **Amenities:** Cable TV w/movies, refrig, VCR, bathrobes. No A/C. Some units w/terraces, all w/fireplaces, some w/whirlpools. **Services:** Masseur, babysitting. Lift tickets available on-site. **Facilities:** 75 1 restaurant (lunch and dinner only), spa, sauna, steam rm, whirlpool, washer/dryer. Ski lockers, boot dryers. **Rates (CP):** Peak (Feb 17–Apr 6) $185 S or D; $310–$1,000 ste. Min stay peak. Lower rates off-season. Closed Apr 20–May 25/Oct 14–Nov 14. AE, DISC, MC, V.

The Pines Lodge

141 Scott Hill Rd, Beaver Creek, PO Box 36, Avon, 81620; tel 970/845-7900 or toll free 800/529-8242; fax 970/845-7809. Just W of Village Rd. Tucked away on a hillside overlooking the village, this luxury hotel is a modern stucco structure with numerous gables, copper gutters, and an aqua-colored tile roof that's the town's trademark. **Rooms:** 60 rms and stes; 8 cottages/villas. CI 4pm/CO 10:30am. Nonsmoking rms avail. Rooms are spacious and bright, and many have fantastic views of the mountain or the village below. **Amenities:** Cable TV w/movies, refrig, VCR, bathrobes. No A/C. Some units w/terraces, some w/fireplaces, some w/whirlpools. **Services:** Masseur, children's program, babysitting. **Facilities:** 140 1 restaurant (bkfst and dinner only), 1 bar (w/entertainment), games rm, spa, steam rm, whirlpool, washer/dryer. **Rates:** Peak (Jan 2–Apr 5) $200–$310 S or D; $375–$700 ste; $575–$800 cottage/villa. Extra person $25. Children under age 12 stay free. Min stay peak. Lower rates off-season. Parking: Indoor, free. AE, CB, DC, DISC, MC, V.

MOTELS

Park Meadows Lodge

1472 Matterhorn Circle, 81657; tel 970/476-5598; fax 970/476-3056. ½ mi S of S Frontage Rd. This affordable motel is nicely tucked away in a small neighborhood on the west side of town, just a short walk from the Cascade ski lift. Clean, comfortable, and well maintained. **Rooms:** 28 rms and stes. CI 2pm/CO 10am. Nonsmoking rms avail. All rooms are privately owned and individually decorated. Six are studios. **Amenities:** Cable TV w/movies, refrig. No A/C. All units w/terraces. All units have full kitchens. **Services:** Babysitting. **Facilities:** 30 Games rm, whirlpool, washer/dryer. **Rates:** Peak (Dec 23–Apr 2) $104–$179 S or D; $104–$179 ste. Extra person $10. Children under age 13 stay free. Min stay special events. Lower rates off-season. Parking: Outdoor, free. MC, V.

The Roost Lodge

1783 N Frontage Rd W, 81657; tel 970/476-5451 or toll free 800/873-3065; fax 970/476-9158. ½ mi E of exit 173 off I-70. Comfortable motel on west end of town. **Rooms:** 74 rms and stes. CI 4pm/CO noon. Nonsmoking rms avail. **Amenities:** Cable TV w/movies. No A/C. All units w/terraces. **Services:** Babysitting. Ski shuttle to lifts. **Facilities:** Sauna, whirlpool. **Rates (CP):** Peak (Dec 20–Jan 8) $128–$142 S or D; $179 ste. Extra person $8. Children under age 13 stay free. Min stay peak. Lower rates off-season. Parking: Outdoor, free. AE, CB, DC, DISC, MC, V.

INNS

Black Bear Inn of Vail

2405 Elliott Rd, 81657; tel 970/476-1304; fax 970/476-0433. Just W of exit 173 off I-70. Very cozy, modern inn nestled against mountains on west side of town, close to I-70. Young children must be supervised at all times. Lounges are quite spacious. **Rooms:** 12 rms. CI 3pm/CO 11am. No smoking. Simple but attractive rooms with down comforters on beds. All have sofa sleepers. **Amenities:** No A/C or TV. **Services:** Babysitting, afternoon tea served. **Facilities:** 12 Games rm, lawn games, washer/dryer, guest lounge w/TV. **Rates (BB):** Peak (Feb–Mar) $95–$195 S or D. Extra person $25. Min stay peak. Lower rates off-season. Higher rates for special events/hols. Parking: Outdoor, free. Closes for 4–6 weeks after ski season. DISC, MC, V.

Christiania at Vail

356 E Hanson Ranch Rd, 81657; tel 970/476-5641 or toll free 800/530-3999; fax 970/476-0470. Just E of the Vista Bahn Express. European-style inn with attractive lounge and fireplace, festive hand-painted details on walls, and quite luxurious guest rooms. Within easy walking distance of ski lifts, dining, and shopping. **Rooms:** 22 rms, stes, and effic; 25 cottages/villas. CI 4pm/CO 11am. No smoking. **Amenities:** Cable TV w/movies, refrig, in-rm safe. No A/C. All units w/minibars, some w/terraces, some w/fireplaces. **Services:** **Facilities:** 40 1 bar (w/entertainment), games rm, sauna, washer/dryer, guest lounge w/TV. **Rates (CP):** Peak (Feb 11–Mar) $210–$315 S or D; $340–$420 ste; $365 effic; $325–$1,150 cottage/villa. Extra person $25. Children under age 18 stay free. Min stay peak. Lower rates off-season. Higher rates for special events/hols. Parking: Outdoor, $5/day. AE, MC, V.

Eagle River Inn
145 N Main St, PO Box 100, Minturn, 81645; tel 970/827-5761 or toll free 800/344-1750; fax 970/827-4020. 2 miles S of exit 171 off I-70. Located in a restored 1894 building, this red adobe bed-and-breakfast has an authentic Santa Fe atmosphere. The lounge is centered around a fireplace and has a traditional viga-and-latilla ceiling. The Eagle River flows through the backyard. Unsuitable for children under 12. **Rooms:** 12 rms. CI 3pm/CO 11am. No smoking. Walls in many of the rooms have old adobe-style texturing of mud and straw and are decorated with hand-painted plants and western motifs. **Amenities:** Cable TV. No A/C or phone. **Services:** Afternoon tea and wine/sherry served. **Facilities:** 15 Lawn games, whirlpool, guest lounge. Snowshoes. **Rates (BB):** Peak (Dec 20–Jan 5/Jan 28–Mar) $180–$200 S or D. Extra person $20. Min stay wknds. Lower rates off-season. Higher rates for special events/hols. Parking: Outdoor, free. Closes for 4–6 weeks after ski season. AE, MC, V.

RESORTS

Hyatt Regency Beaver Creek
136 E Thomas Pl, Beaver Creek, PO Box 1595, Avon, 81620; tel 970/949-1234 or toll free 800/233-1234; fax 970/949-4164. Just E of the Centennial Express Lift. 20 acres. Spectacular ski-in, ski-out resort hotel, built of native stone incorporating European alpine, Rocky Mountain, and modern styles. The lobby is made from beautiful woods and sandstone—a lofty space yet tremendously comfortable, with great views of the mountain just outside. **Rooms:** 295 rms and stes. CI 4pm/CO noon. Nonsmoking rms avail. Rooms are elegant and extremely tasteful; most have fantastic views. **Amenities:** Cable TV w/movies, dataport, voice mail, bathrobes. No A/C. All units w/minibars, some w/terraces, some w/fireplaces, some w/whirlpools. **Services:** VP Car-rental desk, social director, masseur, children's program, babysitting. Full range of spa treatments available for fee. **Facilities:** 18 6 1200 4 restaurants, 4 bars (3 w/entertainment), volleyball, lawn games, spa, sauna, steam rm, whirlpool, beauty salon, day-care ctr, playground, washer/dryer. Ski shop. **Rates:** Peak (Dec 26–Mar/June–Sept) $415–$585 S or D; $620 ste. Extra person $25. Children under age 18 stay free. Min stay peak. Lower rates off-season. Parking: Indoor, $6–$10/day. AE, CB, DC, DISC, MC, V.

The Lodge at Cordillera
2205 Cordillera Way, PO Box 1110, Edwards, 81632; tel 970/926-2200 or toll free 800/548-2721; fax 970/926-2486. 7¼ mi W of town. 4,100 acres. Reminiscent of an English country house with full slate roof, this peaceful getaway sits atop a hill at the west end of town and affords terrific views of surrounding mountains. Hallways and rooms are decorated with abundance of original artwork and hand-painted floral patterns. Very well maintained and private, with one of the top 10 spa facilities in the country. **Rooms:** 28 rms and stes. CI 4pm/CO noon. No smoking. All but one of the rooms have mountain views. **Amenities:** A/C, cable TV w/movies, bathrobes. Some units w/terraces, some w/fireplaces. **Services:** VP Twice-daily maid svce, masseur, babysitting. **Facilities:** 18 2 80 1 restaurant (*see* "Restaurants" below), 1 bar (w/entertainment), volleyball, lawn games, spa, sauna, steam rm, whirlpool, beauty salon, playground. **Rates:** Peak (June–Sept) $255–$450 S or D; $480–$600 ste. Extra person $20. Children under age 12 stay free. Min stay wknds and special events. Lower rates off-season. Parking: Outdoor, free. AE, CB, DC, MC, V.

Sonnenalp Resort
20 Vail Rd, 81657; tel 970/476-5656 or toll free 800/654-8312; fax 970/476-1639. Just S of jct W Meadow Dr. 20 acres. One of the finest accommodations in Vail, the Sonnenalp occupies three separate buildings, each displaying the charm of a small Bavarian inn. Amenities resemble those of a large resort complex. **Rooms:** 184 rms and stes. CI 4pm/CO 11am. Nonsmoking rms avail. Rooms vary in size and comfort, but all are spacious and attractive. **Amenities:** A/C, cable TV w/movies, dataport, VCR, voice mail, in-rm safe, bathrobes. Some units w/minibars, some w/terraces, some w/fireplaces, some w/whirlpools. Iron and ironing board. **Services:** VP 2 Twice daily maid svce, social director, masseur, children's program, babysitting. Lift ticket and complimentary shuttle service. **Facilities:** 18 4 200 5 restaurants, 5 bars (1 w/entertainment), games rm, racquetball, spa, sauna, steam rm, whirlpool, day-care ctr. Ski lockers and inexpensive ski rentals on premises. **Rates:** Peak (Jan 5–Apr 11/Nov 22–Dec 21) $225–$310 S or D; $330–$1,150 ste. Extra person $25–$75. Children under age 5 stay free. Min stay special events. Lower rates off-season. Parking: Outdoor, free. AE, CB, DC, MC, V.

RESTAURANTS

Beano's Cabin
Foot of Larkspur Lift, Beaver Creek; tel 970/949-9090. Adjacent to Larkspur Lift. **New American.** More than a dining experience, this is an adventure. The expansive cabin, with its massive stone fireplace, is on the ski mountain, accessible by snowcat-drawn sleigh in winter and by horseback or horse-drawn wagon in summer. The six-course prix fixe dinner always offers a choice of beef, chicken, seafood, or pasta. Items might include seared rare ahi tuna or crisp duck confit. **FYI:** Reservations recommended. Guitar. Children's menu. No smoking. **Open:** Daily 5–9:30pm. Closed Apr 16–June 14/Oct 2–Dec 1. **Prices:** Prix fixe $80. AE, DISC, MC, V.

★ Beaver Trap Tavern
In St James Place, 365 Beaver Creek Place, Beaver Creek; tel 970/845-8930. Just E of Centennial Lift. **Pub/Southwest-**

ern. The log interior, shaped and punched copper lamps, and the interesting bar surface, embedded with what look like beaver-chewed willows, make this a unique addition to the area's profusion of fine dining. The menu offers lots of traditional pub and grill fare but with a southwestern twist to it. During peak season, there are a number of nightly food and drink specials, and Thurs–Sun at dinner, a magician entertains diners. **FYI:** Reservations accepted. Children's menu. **Open:** Daily 11am–midnight. **Prices:** Main courses $8–$25. AE, MC, V.

Blu's
193 E Gore Creek Dr; tel 970/476-3113. Just W of covered bridge. **International.** Located next to the creek and just down the stairs from the Children's Fountain, this busy little restaurant has been a local favorite for some 15 years. Brick walls, track lighting, modern oil paintings, and large bay windows overlooking the creek complement the friendly atmosphere. Breakfast is served until 5pm. There are a number of rather unusual entrees including local favorites such as gypsy schnitzel and "Kick Ass California Chicken Relleno." Two of the chef's specialties are paella and farmhouse duck. **FYI:** Reservations not accepted. Children's menu. No smoking. **Open:** Daily 9am–11pm. Closed Apr 20–May 20. **Prices:** Main courses $9–$19. AE, CB, DC, MC, V.

The Bristol at Arrowhead
In Country Club of the Rockies, 676 Sawatch Dr, Edwards; tel 970/926-2111. Just N of base lift at Arrowhead Ski Area. **New American.** Large bay windows frame scenic views of the surrounding area while large wooden beams add a more rustic flavor to this lofty and elegant restaurant. Entrees are unique, drawing on international and regional influences, and include roasted red pepper and mozzarella ravioli and a mixed game grill that includes quail, buffalo, and venison. Horse-drawn sleigh rides make for memorable winter evenings. **FYI:** Reservations recommended. Children's menu. No smoking. **Open:** Lunch daily noon–3pm; dinner daily 6–9:30pm. Closed Apr 15–May 25. **Prices:** Main courses $18–$29. AE, MC, V. VP

Chanticler
In Vail Spa Condominiums, 710 W Lionshead Circle; tel 970/476-1441. 2 blocks W of gondola. **International.** The atrium-style dining room of this elegant restaurant is trimmed with fine mahogany woodwork and decorated with scenic impressionistic artwork of the Rockies. Incorporated into the creative cuisine are regional meats, fish, and fowl. Entrees include buffalo sausage with farfalle, and sautéed tiger shrimp and scallops pastry de mer. **FYI:** Reservations recommended. Children's menu. No smoking. **Open:** Daily 6–10pm. Closed May/Oct 15–Nov 15. **Prices:** Main courses $10–$29. AE, CB, DC, DISC, MC, V.

The Golden Eagle Inn
Village Hall, Beaver Creek; tel 970/949-1940. **New American/Game.** An elegant family-style restaurant with upholstered booths and country furnishings. A great place to stop for après-ski, or lunch year-round—enjoy the outdoor tables in summer. The signature dish is roast loin of elk, crusted with raspberry whole-grain mustard; but the menu also includes other regional items such as rainbow trout and unique choices like medallions of Australian kangaroo. **FYI:** Reservations accepted. Children's menu. No smoking. **Open:** Lunch daily 11:30am–4pm; dinner daily 5:30–10pm. **Prices:** Main courses $16–$28. AE, MC, V.

★ Hubcap Brewery & Kitchen
In Crossroads Shopping Center, 143 E Meadow Dr; tel 970/476-5757. Just W of Main Village parking plaza. **Burgers/Pub.** Patrons enter this lively, state-of-the-art brew pub through the area that houses the brewing kettles and tanks. Freshly brewed beer on tap awaits (as does a fine selection of single-malt scotch). Standard pub fare consists of sandwiches, chicken pot pie, meatloaf, barbecued chicken, burgers, and a vegetarian plate. During ski season, grilled quail and fresh seafood are also available. Beer can be purchased to go in everything from bottles to half-barrels. **FYI:** Reservations not accepted. Children's menu. **Open:** Daily 11:30am–10pm. **Prices:** Main courses $7–$19. AE, MC, V.

Imperial Fez
In The Vail Run, 1000 Lions Ridge Loop; tel 970/476-1948. 1¾ mi E of exit 173 off I-70 on N Frontage Rd. **Moroccan.** Berber carpets cover the floors and glittering fabrics adorn the walls of this unique restaurant, lending a tentlike atmosphere and making you feel as if you just left the Sahara Desert. Once seated on large, traditional pillows around circular tables, patrons are entertained by belly and sword dancers performing to Moroccan music. Moroccan dishes—including apricot lamb, fresh fish tagine, beef brochette, and couscous—are eaten in the traditional way: with your fingers (finger bowls are provided). All meals include soup, salad, appetizer, tea, and dessert. A fun experience for the adventuresome. **FYI:** Reservations recommended. No liquor license. No smoking. **Open:** Daily 5–10pm. **Prices:** Prix fixe $28–$33. AE, MC, V.

Montauk Seafood Grill
549 Lionshead Mall; tel 970/476-2601. Just N of Vail gondola. **Seafood.** The interior feels like a yacht, with gray wooden walls and copper mariner's lamps, while the bar resembles a ship's chart room with its varnished wood and brass fixtures. The wide variety of seafood comes from both the Atlantic and the Pacific, and there are a few steaks for diehard meat lovers. Choose from such items as Rocky Mountain cioppino, Chilean sea bass, and Hawaiian ahi; a good way to start off is with a big bowl of Manhattan clam chowder. The restaurant also boasts the town's only raw bar, offering shrimp, crab, and oysters. **FYI:** Reservations recommended. Children's menu. No smoking. **Open:** Peak (Nov 15–Apr 15) daily 5–10pm. Closed May 15–June 15. **Prices:** Main courses $15–$30. AE, MC, V.

The Red Lion
304 Bridge St; tel 970/476-7676. South end of Bridge St. **Barbecue/Pub.** Located close to the ski lifts, this is a great place to stop for lunch while skiing, or for dinner and drinks after a hard day on the slopes. Fourteen televisions and over 50 beers also make this a good choice for a sports evening. Standard pub fare includes lots of burgers, sandwiches, and hickory-smoked barbecue, plus a few traditional entrees. An extensive collection of Vail skiing memorabilia and photos adorn the brick walls. **FYI:** Reservations not accepted. Guitar/piano/singer. Children's menu. **Open:** Daily 11am–midnight. **Prices:** Main courses $7–$19. AE, DISC, MC, V.

Restaurant Picasso
In Lodge at Cordillera, 2205 Cordillera Way, Edwards; tel 970/926-2200. 7¼ mi W of town up Squaw Creek Rd. **New American/Continental.** Located high on a hillside west of Avon, this restaurant has great views of the surrounding mountains and a very intimate and serene atmosphere. A large lounge with fireplace provides a cozy spot for enjoying an après-ski drink, and Picasso's art is of course well represented. More unusual menu items include applewood-smoked tuna and vegetable and pasta papillote. **FYI:** Reservations recommended. Piano. Children's menu. Dress code. No smoking. **Open:** Breakfast daily 7–10am; lunch daily noon–2pm; dinner daily 6–10pm. **Prices:** Main courses $17–$37. AE, CB, DC, DISC, MC, V.

Sweet Basil
193 E Gore Creek Dr; tel 970/476-0125. Just N of Main Village lifts. **New American.** Located in the heart of the Main Village, this pleasant restaurant with simple, modern decor is quiet and casual. Several large bay windows on the north side of the dining area look out to the creek. The kitchen turns out unique dishes that draw from a variety of sources and ingredients; choices might include grilled squab with creamy spinach risotto and butternut squash, or dry-aged New York steak with potato strudel and grilled onion. **FYI:** Reservations recommended. Children's menu. No smoking. **Open:** Peak (Dec 15–Mar) lunch daily 11:30am–2:30pm; dinner daily 5:30–10pm. **Prices:** Main courses $22–$29. AE, MC, V.

Tyrolean Inn
400 E Meadow Dr; tel 970/476-2204. Just E of Main Vail Village parking complex. **Continental/Game.** This Swiss chalet–style restaurant has been a family-owned Vail landmark since 1972. The alpine dining room sports huge rustic ceiling beams from which an enormous sleigh is suspended. Hunting trophies and wildlife paintings decorate the walls. The spacious bar, with small hand-carved panels, has abundant old-world charm. Wild game is the house specialty here: venison sauerbraten, pheasant, wild boar, elk, and caribou are just some of the possibilities. Other choices include Athens grilled chicken, with artichokes, calamata olives, sun-dried tomatoes, asiago cheese, and pine nuts. The excellent desserts include Irish coffee crepes, napoleon of berries, and white chocolate mousse. **FYI:** Reservations accepted. No smoking. **Open:** Daily 6–10pm. Closed Apr 15–May 20. **Prices:** Main courses $14–$26. AE, MC, V.

Vendetta's
291 Bridge St; tel 970/476-5070. Halfway between covered bridge and Main Village lifts. **Italian.** A great place for lunch or après-ski relaxing. The dining area is comfortable and bright, with a gold metallic ceiling and modern prints on the walls, while the bar scene—one of the most popular in town—is lively and friendly. Fine Italian cuisine features dishes like manicotti Veneziana (baked with four cheeses), osso bucco, and Italian pepper steak; seafood specials are also served. Pizza is offered at lunch. **FYI:** Reservations not accepted. Children's menu. No smoking. **Open:** Daily 11am–10:30pm. **Prices:** Main courses $13–$20. AE, MC, V.

ATTRACTIONS

Betty Ford Alpine Gardens
Ford Park; tel 970/949-0721. Billed as "the highest public gardens in the world," this peaceful tract features more than 1,500 hardy perennials from around the world, along with an experimental rock garden and a meditation garden, employing elements of Chinese Zen and Japanese moss gardens. The gardens are wheelchair accessible. **Open:** Snowmelt–snowfall, daily sunrise–sunset. **Free**

Colorado Ski Museum and Ski Hall of Fame
231 S Frontage Rd E; tel 970/476-1876. The history of more than a century of Colorado skiing—from the boards that mountain miners first strapped on their feet, to the post–World War II resort boom, to Coloradans' success in international racing—is depicted in this popular showcase. Also included are the evolution of ski equipment and fashions and the role of the US Forest Service. One room is devoted to the 10th Mountain Division, the only division of the military trained in ski warfare. A theater presents historical and current ski videos. The museum incorporates the **Colorado Ski Hall of Fame,** with plaques and photographs honoring Vail founder Peter Seibert, filmmaker Lowell Thomas, Olympic skier Buddy Werner, and others. **Open:** Tues–Sun 10am–5pm. **Free**

Vail Ski Resort
Vail Rd; tel 970/476-5601 or toll free 800/525-2257. The area boundaries stretch seven miles from east to west along the ridge top, from Outer Mongolia to Game Creek Bowl, and the skiable terrain is measured at 3,834 acres. Virtually every lift on the front (north-facing) side of the mountain has runs for every level of skier, with a predominance of novice and intermediate terrain. (The longest run, 4½-mile Riva Ridge, is best for intermediate skiers.) The world-famous Back Bowls are decidedly not for beginners, and there are few options for intermediates. The seven bowls are, from west to east, Sun Down, Sun Up, Tea Cup, China, Siberia, Inner Mongolia, and Outer Mongolia; they are strictly for advanced and expert skiers. Snow and weather conditions determine

just how expert you ought to be. The bowls are served by only three lifts, one of them a short surface lift providing access to the Mongolias.

From Mongolia Summit, at 11,450 feet, Vail has a vertical drop on the front side of 3,250 feet; on the back side, 1,850 feet. Average annual snowfall is 334 inches (nearly 28 feet). All told, there are 120 named trails served by 20 lifts, a gondola, nine quad chairs, two triple chairs, six double chairs, and two surface lifts. **Open:** Thanksgiving–Apr, daily 8:30am–3:30pm. **$$$$**

Beaver Creek
I-70; tel 970/949-5750 or toll free 800/525-2257. Beaver Creek combines European château-style elegance in its base village with expansive slopes for novice and intermediate skiers. The Grouse Mountain lift reaches previously inaccessible expert terrain.

Beaver Creek's vertical is 3,340 feet, from the 8,100-foot base to the 11,400-foot summit. Currently, 10 lifts (two quad chairs, four triples, and four doubles) serve 59 trails. Average annual snowfall is 330 inches (27.5 feet). **Open:** Thanksgiving–mid-Apr, daily 8:30am–3:30pm. **$$$$**

Arrowhead
US 6; tel 970/926-3029 or toll free 800/525-2257. A small family-oriented area, with one high-speed quad chair lift and a beginners' surface lift serving 11 runs, nearly all of them for intermediates or novices. The mountain has a 1,700-foot vertical, from a base elevation of 7,400 feet to the summit of 9,100. With annual snowfall of just 115 inches (not quite 10 feet). **Open:** Mid-Dec–early Apr, daily 9am–3:30pm. **$$$$**

Vallecito

See Durango

Walsenburg

What began as the small Hispanic village of La Plaza de los Leones became Walsenburg, after a German merchant who arrived in the 1870s. Primarily a shopping area and a stop on the interstate, the town also provides a base for hiking, fishing, and other outdoor recreation in the area. **Information:** Huerfano County Chamber of Commerce, PO Box 493, Walsenburg 81089 (tel 719/738-1065).

MOTEL

Best Western Rambler
I-25, PO Box 48, 81089; tel 719/738-1121 or toll free 800/528-1234. Exit 52 off I-25. Nice roadside motel with comfortable, standard rooms. **Rooms:** 32 rms. CI 2pm/CO 11am. Nonsmoking rms avail. **Amenities:** A/C, satel TV. **Services:** Magazine lending library in lobby. **Facilities:** **Rates (CP):** Peak (Mem Day–Labor Day) $60–$70 S; $65–$85 D. Children under age 18 stay free. Lower rates off-season. Parking: Outdoor, free. AE, CB, DC, DISC, MC, V.

Westminster

See Denver

Winter Park

Opened in 1940, Winter Park is among Colorado's earliest ski resorts, and one of the few American ski towns with direct rail transportation (the Winter Park/Rio Grande Railroad leaves from Denver's Union Station). Though lodgings and restaurants are plentiful, shoppers will not find the bounty of opportunities available in Aspen; however, development of a major base village in the future should remedy that. **Information:** Winter Park/Fraser Valley Chamber of Commerce, PO Box 3236, Winter Park 80482 (tel 970/726-4118).

HOTELS

Gasthaus Eichler Hotel
78786 US 40, PO Box 3303, 80482; tel 970/726-5133 or toll free 800/543-3899; fax 970/726-5175. Just N of visitor's center. Centrally located, this small hotel offers very clean and tastefully decorated accommodations with a European ambience. Great for both skiers and summer explorers. **Rooms:** 15 rms. CI 3pm/CO 10am. Nonsmoking rms avail. **Amenities:** Cable TV w/movies. No A/C. All units w/whirlpools. **Services:** **Facilities:** 30 1 restaurant (*see* "Restaurants" below), 1 bar. **Rates (MAP):** Peak (Nov 15–Apr 21) $120–$160 S or D. Extra person $35. Min stay peak and special events. Lower rates off-season. AP rates avail. Parking: Outdoor, free. Extra person charge includes breakfast and dinner. Summer rates are lower but do not include meals. AE, MC, V.

Snowblaze
79114 US 40, PO Box 66, 80482; tel 970/726-5701 or toll free 800/525-2466; fax 970/726-5260. S end of town. Prestigious condominium development not far from downtown and just a couple miles from the ski resort. **Rooms:** 78 rms and stes. CI 4pm/CO 10am. Nonsmoking rms avail. Studios and one-, two-, and three-bedroom units available. **Amenities:** Cable TV, refrig. No A/C. Some units w/terraces, some w/fireplaces. **Services:** Social director, masseur, babysitting. Shuttle service to ski area. **Facilities:** 50 Basketball, volleyball, racquetball, sauna, steam rm, whirlpool, washer/dryer. Ski lockers. **Rates:** Peak (Mar 8–Apr 8/Dec 16–Jan 1) $77–$196 S or D; $145–$506 ste. Children under age 12 stay free. Min stay. Lower rates off-season. Parking: Indoor/outdoor, free. Peak-season rates vary. AE, MC, V.

The Vintage
100 Winter Park Dr, PO Box 1369, 80482; tel 970/726-8801 or toll free 800/472-7017; fax 970/726-9230. Adjacent to Winter Park Ski Area. Five-story, modern, château-style hotel very close to ski area. **Rooms:** 118 rms and stes. CI 4pm/CO 11am. Nonsmoking rms avail. Seven different room types available. **Amenities:** Cable TV w/movies, in-rm safe, bathrobes. No A/C. Some units w/fireplaces, some w/whirlpools. **Services:** Social director, masseur, babysitting. **Facilities:** 120 1 restaurant (bkfst and dinner only), 1 bar, games rm, sauna, whirlpool, washer/dryer. **Rates:** Peak (Dec 15–Jan 5) $85–$145 S or D; $275–$500 ste. Children under age 18 stay free. Min stay wknds and special events. Lower rates off-season. Parking: Outdoor, free. AE, CB, DC, DISC, MC, V.

INN

Engelmann Pines
1035 Cranmer Ave, PO Box 1305, 80482; tel 970/726-4632 or toll free 800/992-9512; fax 970/726-5458. 1 mi E of Fraser. Set amid the pines in a forest between Fraser and Winter Park, this redwood bed-and-breakfast feels secluded without being remote. The interior is filled with antiques and fine furniture. A great place to stay year-round. **Rooms:** 7 rms (2 w/shared bath). CI 4pm/CO 11am. No smoking. **Amenities:** No A/C, phone, or TV. Some units w/terraces, some w/fireplaces, all w/whirlpools. **Services:** Babysitting, afternoon tea and wine/sherry served. **Facilities:** 14 Guest lounge w/TV. Guest lounge stocked with refreshments and movies for evening entertainment. **Rates (BB):** Peak (Nov 15–Apr 15) $75–$85 S or D w/shared bath, $95–$115 S or D w/private bath. Extra person $10. Min stay peak. Lower rates off-season. Parking: Outdoor, free. AE, DISC, MC, V.

RESORTS

Devil's Thumb Ranch Resort
Grand County Rd 83, PO Box 750, 80478; tel 970/726-5632 or toll free 800/933-4339; fax 970/726-5632. 3 mi E of US 40. 395 acres. Set back from the highway, this rustic ranch is bordered by mountains on the east, with the ranch's namesake, the scenic Devil's Thumb, a distant rock formation. **Rooms:** 25 rms; 4 cottages/villas. CI 3pm/CO 11am. No smoking. **Amenities:** No A/C, phone, or TV. Some units w/terraces, some w/fireplaces. **Services:** Children's program, babysitting. Complimentary shuttle to Winter Park for downhill skiing. **Facilities:** 50 1 restaurant (*see* "Restaurants" below), 1 bar (w/entertainment), volleyball, games rm, lawn games, sauna, whirlpool, washer/dryer. One of the highest-rated Nordic centers in the country; 60 miles of trails surround the ranch, with more continually added. **Rates:** $22–$42 S; $32–$72 D; $40–$280 cottage/villa. Children under age 6 stay free. Min stay peak and special events. AP rates avail. Parking: Outdoor, free. 15% discount for children ages 6–12. MC, V.

Snow Mountain Ranch–YMCA of the Rockies
US 40, PO Box 169, 80482; tel 970/887-2152; fax 303/449-6781. 14 mi N of town. 4,950 acres. Located on expansive property in a secluded forest, this beautiful resort offers great privacy as well as a wide range of opportunity for exploration. Ideal for families and large groups. There are 52 campsites also available. **Rooms:** 248 rms; 45 cottages/villas. CI 3pm/CO 10am. No smoking. Extensive choice of rooms and spacious cabins. **Amenities:** No A/C or TV. Some units w/terraces, some w/fireplaces. **Services:** Social director, children's program, babysitting. **Facilities:** 2 1500 2 restaurants, basketball, volleyball, sauna, day-care ctr, playground, washer/dryer. **Rates:** Peak (June–Aug/Dec 13–Apr 7) $30–$87 S or D; $98–$242 cottage/villa. Extra person $5. Lower rates off-season. Parking: Outdoor, free. Campsites $14–$18. No CC.

RESTAURANTS

★ Crooked Creek Saloon & Eatery
US 40, Fraser; tel 970/726-9250. In town center. **American.** This restaurant/bar doubles as the natural history museum for the Fraser Valley: on the walls are a variety of historical items and photographs of the area, including photos of the Utes taken by John Wesley Powell on his first expedition into the western territory. The garden in back is made up of 80% native plants. The menu lists lots of sandwiches, some pasta and Mexican dishes, and a few types of steaks. **FYI:** Reservations not accepted. Blues/dancing/rock. Children's menu. No smoking. **Open:** Daily 7am–2am. **Prices:** Main courses $5–$14. DISC, MC, V.

Gasthaus Eichler
In Gasthaus Eichler Hotel, 78786 US 40; tel 970/726-5133. Just N of visitor's center. **German/Steak.** Rustic and festive, this restaurant located in the heart of town offers a mix of European and regional dishes. Venison is braised in burgundy and served with cranberries, spaetzle, and red cabbage; breast of chicken is wrapped around fresh basil and shrimp and served on a bed of fettuccine in a chardonnay sauce. **FYI:** Reservations accepted. Children's menu. No smoking. **Open:** Breakfast daily 7:30–10:30am; lunch daily 11am–2:30pm; dinner daily 5–9pm. **Prices:** Main courses $13–$23. AE, MC, V.

Ranch House Restaurant
In Devil's Thumb Ranch Resort, Grand County Rd 83; tel 970/726-5632. 3 mi E of US 40. **New American/Eclectic.** This small restaurant, located on a rather remote ranch north of town, offers guests a peaceful dining experience with great views of the ranch and surrounding mountains. The dining room is rustic, decorated with saddles and other ranch items, yet the large stone fireplace gives it a feeling of intimacy.

Specialties include lavender-blackened lamb chops, chicken "baklava," and wild "osso buco"—wild seasonal game cooked with grilled celery root and polenta. **FYI:** Reservations recommended. Blues/folk. Children's menu. No smoking. **Open:** Peak (Nov 23–May) breakfast Mon–Sat 8–11am; lunch Mon–Sat 11am–3pm; dinner daily 5–9pm; brunch Sun 8am–3pm. **Prices:** Main courses $10–$28. MC, V.

Woody Creek

See Aspen

NEW MEXICO

Land of Enchantment

Prickly pear cactus and tall evergreens, sun-baked desert and deep powder snow. New Mexico is a land of contrasts and contradictions. Its three dominant cultures—Native American, Hispanic, and Anglo—are unique but intertwined, each retaining its individual identity while influencing the other in a sometimes uneasy alliance. In many ways, a trip to New Mexico is an excursion to a foreign country, an exotic land of enchantment and excitement, yet no passport is needed.

When many people think of New Mexico they see American Indians, wrapped in blankets in their centuries-old adobe pueblos. And certainly many visitors come to experience the state's thriving Native American culture. But others are also curious to follow the trail of legendary gunslinger Billy the Kid or explore crumbling ghost towns where sage-brush and cactus have taken over once-busy streets. Railroad romantics can tour the depots from turn-of-the-century mining days that dot the state and climb aboard a historic steam train for a memorable trip into the past.

Besides being a treasure trove of Old West history, New Mexico is also a vibrant art center. There are hundreds of galleries, studios, and museums to explore. From ancient Indian petroglyphs to the most modern mediums, art lovers cannot only see and buy, but can join classes, tour studios, and watch many of today's artists at work.

Museums explore the cultural and historic, including beautiful Indian pottery and blankets, artifacts from the state's Spanish colonial days, Civil War and Old West memorabilia, and feats of science and engineering like the first atom bomb and the space shuttle.

A land of spectacular scenic beauty, New Mexico encompasses the towering Rocky Mountains, pristine desert sands, and vast underground caverns. Hunting, fishing, and camping are extremely popular, and

STATE STATS

CAPITAL
Santa Fe

AREA
121,666 square miles

BORDERS
Arizona, Colorado, Oklahoma, Texas, Mexico

POPULATION
1,653,521 (1994)

ENTERED UNION
January 6, 1912 (47th state)

NICKNAME
Land of Enchantment

STATE FLOWER
Yucca

STATE BIRD
Roadrunner

FAMOUS NATIVES
Peter Hurd, William "Billy the Kid" Bonney, Georgia O'Keeffe, Archbishop Jean-Baptiste Lamy

hikers revel in the state's unspoiled wilderness. Winter snows turn New Mexico into a skiers' paradise, with deep powder and plenty of sunshine. In addition to world-class downhill ski resorts, there are plenty of opportunities for cross-country skiing and snowmobiling.

In short, there are many reasons to visit New Mexico and a great variety of activities that are bound to satisfy almost every taste. Take time to explore the state's hidden treasures as well as its major attractions. See its mountains and deserts. Taste its foods. Meet its people. A New Mexico vacation really is like a trip to a distant land—without having to leave the country.

A Brief History

Prehistoric Peoples Somewhere between 20,000 and 25,000 years ago, Paleo-Indians roamed into the area we now know as New Mexico, following the mastodon, bison, and early forms of the camel and horse that provided the necessities of their nomadic life. The earliest evidence of their passage—a projectile point found in the Clovis area of southeast New Mexico—is about 12,000 years old.

As the glaciers receded and the climate became drier, man became more dependent on plants, and sometime in the first few centuries AD corn was introduced from Mexico. The people in the western two-thirds of New Mexico settled in villages, often located along river drainages, while those in the eastern third remained primarily nomadic. Those who settled in the northwestern corner of New Mexico are known as Anasazi; those in the southwestern part as Mogollon.

The Mogollon lived in pit houses, dug partially into the ground, and carried on a lively trade with the peoples to the south, in present-day Mexico. The Anasazi were more urbanized, living in complex houses usually built above ground. Discovering the increased strength of cluster-type construction, the Anasazi eventually created elaborate stone buildings of several stories and often hundreds of rooms, as well as ceremonial below-ground structures known as kivas. During this time, both the Mogollon and Anasazi began making pottery and baskets. The size of settlements increased, regional styles in architecture, ceramics, and other crafts developed, dependence on agriculture intensified, and trade networks expanded.

The Anasazi territory included nearly 40,000 square miles of the Four Corners area—northwestern New Mexico and adjacent corners of Colorado, Utah, and Arizona. In this area, archaeologists have located ruins of over 10,000 structures created between AD 400 and 1300, some half of them built between AD 950 and 1100. One of the largest is Chaco Canyon, an extremely complex and highly developed settlement in northwestern New Mexico, from which a great network of roads radiated to outlying settlements, the only known prehistoric planned transportation system north of Mexico.

Around AD 1200, the Anasazi left the Four Corners area, inexplicably abandoning their villages. Modern scientists hypothesize that although specific reasons may vary from area to area, the move probably was triggered by subtle changes in climate. The Mogollon also began moving northwards at this time, settling in smaller villages along rivers and often building with adobe.

Fun Facts

- The design of the state flag combines the ancient sun symbol of the Zuni Indians native to the state with the colors of the flag of Spain, which ruled the region for more than 250 years.
- In 1950, the town of Hot Springs, NM, became Truth or Consequences when it won a contest run by the legendary radio program of the same name. It was seeking an American town that was willing to change its name in honor of the show's 10-year anniversary.
- Taos is home to more artists per capita than Paris.
- The Acoma Pueblo is the oldest continually inhabited city in the United States: It can trace its occupation back to AD 1150. It's also famed as the "Sky City," because of its location 7,000 feet above sea level.
- It was in the town of Lincoln that Billy the Kid was to be hanged for cattle rustling and other crimes in 1878. The shackled and manacled Kid, however, managed to escape the hangman's noose at the final moment of truth. After a three-year manhunt, Sheriff Pat Garrett gunned down the outlaw at Fort Sumner in eastern New Mexico.

Conquistadors & Colonizers When Spanish conquistadors arrived in the 1500s, they called the people they found "Pueblo" Indians, because their buildings resembled Spanish villages, or pueblos. What they had hoped to find, however, was an area as rich in gold and silver as Aztec Mexico. Francisco Vásquez de Coronado, who set out from Mexico in 1540, and the leaders of later expeditions were among those who were sorely disappointed. Then in 1598, Don Juan de Oñate was appointed the Spanish governor of New Mexico and directed to colonize it.

With some 200 settlers, including soldiers, families, and priests, and 7,000 head of livestock in tow, Oñate established the first Spanish colony on the east bank of the Rio Grande near its confluence with the Rio Chama, close to Española, at present-day San Juan Pueblo.

He was succeeded by Pedro de Peralta, who, in 1610, when the King of Spain made New Mexico a royal colony, became the first royal governor of the province. Peralta promptly made Santa Fe the provincial capital. Thus, Santa Fe is not only the oldest capital in the nation, it also predates the English settlement at Plymouth, Massachusetts by a decade.

European settlements appeared all along the Rio Grande and its tributaries, from Taos to Socorro. Life was not altogether peaceful, however, with both civil and religious conflicts between settlers and Indians. In 1680, in an unprecedented demonstration of unity, the Pueblos revolted against Spanish oppression and forced conversion to Christianity and drove the hated Spanish conquerors south to El Paso. But only 13 years later, Captain General Diego de Vargas peacefully recaptured the province for Spain. To encourage increased settlement, he and his successors issued land grants for agriculture and grazing to Spanish colonists, and the communities that sprang up served as outposts against Indian attacks. Even so, life in New Mexico was defined by almost continuous warfare with marauding Indians, and an increasingly defensive posture.

The Frontier Period Begins In 1821, Spain's influence came to an end with the Mexican revolution, and under Mexican control New Mexico was encouraged to trade with its American neighbors. That same year, the Santa Fe Trail opened, linking Santa Fe with St Louis, an event that changed forever the course of New Mexican history. So many traders and settlers came over the Trail that the ruts from their wagon wheels are still visible in the northeastern part of the state. Santa Fe soon became a bustling hub of trade, through which caravans made their way onward to northern Mexico along the *Camino Real* (Royal Highway) and to California via the Old Spanish Trail.

Soon, not only traders were marching west. In 1841 the new Republic of Texas invaded New Mexico in an effort to control the trade route through the state. The Texans were defeated, but Mexico's inability to protect the province from attack led inevitably to its absorption by the United States.

DRIVING DISTANCES

Albuquerque

59 miles SW of Santa Fe
129 miles SW of Taos
138 miles E of Gallup
173 miles W of Tucumcari
223 miles N of Las Cruces
275 miles NW of Tucson, AZ
449 miles SW of Denver, CO

Las Cruces

47 miles NW of El Paso, TX
208 miles W of Carlsbad
223 miles S of Albuquerque
275 miles E of Tucson, AZ
282 miles SW of Santa Fe
352 miles SW of Taos
405 miles SE of Farmington

Santa Fe

59 miles NE of Albuquerque
70 miles SW of Taos
165 miles SW of Raton
199 miles SE of Farmington
268 miles NW of Carlsbad
282 miles NE of Las Cruces

In 1846, Brigadier General Stephen Watts Kearny led the US Army of the West from Fort Leavenworth, Kansas in a peaceful takeover of New Mexico. They walked into Santa Fe unopposed, just as Vargas had done 150 years earlier, and although they suffered a setback four months later when a group of New Mexicans rebelled, fearing their land rights would be invalidated by a new government, the revolt was quickly suppressed, and New Mexico was effectively claimed for the United States. The Treaty of Guadalupe Hidalgo officially ended the Mexican War in 1848 and made almost all of New Mexico, Arizona, and California part of the United States. The remainder came in 1853, when the Gadsden Purchase set the present-day Mexican-American boundary.

By this time gold had been discovered in the dusty mountains above San Francisco, and hundreds of thousands of people left their homes in the East and headed for the gold fields. Many of those who were unable to complete the journey settled in New Mexico, however, and in a mere 10 years between the 1850 and 1860 censuses, New Mexico's population increased over 30 percent.

With the advent of the Civil War, the South looked to the West for Colorado and California gold, and for military supplies from centers such as Fort Union, near Las Vegas, New Mexico. In July

1861, a Confederate army from Texas invaded New Mexico, and by early 1862 had captured both Albuquerque and Santa Fe. For two weeks, the Confederate flag flew over the territory's capitol. But in March 1862, hundreds of Union and Confederate troops fought the Battle of Glorieta, just east of Santa Fe. Afterwards, it was apparent that the Confederates had won, except that the Union troops had destroyed their supplies, forcing them to retreat to Texas and ending any further threat.

In the last decades of the 19th century, the Indians were confined to reservations around the territory, and there were dramatic changes in the way title to land was held. Theoretically protected by the Treaty of Guadalupe Hidalgo, Hispanic landowners found their land grants going to newcomers through crafty legal maneuvers. The Atchison, Topeka and Santa Fe Railroad arrived in 1880, and within 10 years, railroads had reached into every corner of the territory, bringing new residents and new ideas. The Santa Fe Trail closed, new towns sprang up along the rails, and the territory contributed to the folklore of the Wild West with William (Billy the Kid) Bonney, Clay Allison, and other notorious outlaws among its more infamous residents.

AVG HIGH/LOW TEMPS (°F)

	Albuquerque	Santa Fe
Jan	47/22	40/19
Feb	53/26	44/22
Mar	61/32	51/28
Apr	71/40	60/35
May	80/49	69/43
June	91/58	79/52
July	93/65	82/57
Aug	89/63	80/56
Sept	83/55	74/49
Oct	72/43	63/38
Nov	57/31	50/27
Dec	48/23	41/20

A Cloud in the Desert Sky On January 6, 1912, New Mexico became the 47th state in the Union. Farming and ranching flourished alongside a rapidly expanding mining industry in the early part of the century, and after Taos and Santa Fe gained national recognition as art colonies in the 1920s, tourism also became an important industry. The artists were drawn by such qualities as the purity of the New Mexico light and the serenity of the desert, and it is ironic that at least the latter characteristic also led to the selection of Los Alamos, a small town in the mountains northwest of Santa Fe, as the secret location of the top secret Manhattan Project, which developed the atom bomb. After 2 years of work, a team of scientists drove to the Trinity Test Site, and in the early hours of July 16, 1945, exploded their handiwork, ushering in the atomic age. New Mexico remains in the forefront of scientific research and development. White Sands Missile Range is an important site for the study of astrophysics; Albuquerque derives much economic support from aerospace research and defense contracts; the Air Force Special Weapons Center is located at Kirtland Air Force Base; and Los Alamos National Laboratory continues to work in nuclear research.

But even as the state moves toward the next century, shifting from a reliance on oil, gas, and minerals to high technology and manufacturing, it remains rooted in its past. The computer whiz may be telecommuting to some big city corporation, but Chimayo weavers still work at the looms their ancestors built a hundred years ago, and Pueblo potters quietly release the beauty hidden in a lump of clay.

A Closer Look

GEOGRAPHY

As America's fifth-largest state and the meeting ground for the Great Plains, the southern Rockies, and the Colorado Plateau, New Mexico offers a wide variety of terrain. Elevations range from 2,800 to over 13,000 feet and include six of the seven life zones found in the United States: Arctic-Alpine, Hudsonian, Canadian, Transition, Upper Sonoran, and Lower Sonoran. (The one you won't find is Tropical.)

Northeastern New Mexico encompasses the six counties of the Great Plains. There's ranching in this sparsely populated, wide-open country, with the railroad running north to south through the center and along the southern boundary. It's a fairly dry region, averaging about 14 to 18 inches of rain per year; the wettest season is summer.

North Central New Mexico includes the Sangre de Cristo Mountains of the southern Rockies and the northern valley of the Rio Grande and Rio Chama. Elevations are the highest in the state, and winters tend to be long, with much of the annual precipitation in the form of snow. Tourism supports the region, which contains some of New Mexico's most picturesque Indian pueblos, most of the state's ski areas, and the two major art centers of **Taos** and **Santa Fe.**

The mesas of **Northwestern New Mexico** were

home to the great Anasazi civilization of the first few centuries AD and are now part of the reservation of America's largest Native American tribe, the Navajo. The San Juan River flows through the northern part; much of the remainder is arid and stark. **Farmington,** the largest city in the area, has a mild climate that encouraged farming and ranching for many years, before the discovery of oil, coal, and gas.

Albuquerque dominates **Central New Mexico.** The Sandia Mountains border the eastern edge of the state's largest city (an estimated 398,492 people in 1992), and the Rio Grande wends its way south through the western part. Summer daytime temperatures can exceed 100°F, and winters are mild and sunny. The University of New Mexico is located here, and technology, including aerospace and defense research, is a major economic factor, along with light manufacturing and tourism.

Southwestern New Mexico has the San Mateo and Mogollon Mountains and the Black Range soaring above the desert, where temperatures also soar, often to over 100° during June, July, and August. Rainfall is low. The state's second largest city, **Las Cruces,** with 66,466 people (1992 estimate), is located here. The railroad was a major contributor to the growth of the area in the early part of the century. Mining remains important, since copper and gold are still coming out of the hills near Silver City. Ranching and farming are also key industries.

The landscape of **Southeastern New Mexico** is dominated by oil rigs and cattle ranches. **Roswell** is the area's largest city. Tourism is an important part of the economy; **Carlsbad Caverns National Park** receives almost 700,000 visitors per year. The climate is warm and dry, with little snow except in the Sacramento and Guadalupe Mountains in the west. Precipitation averages 8 to 14 inches yearly.

CLIMATE

Elevation and terrain have a tremendous influence on weather, and New Mexico, with mountains, deserts, canyons, and plains, experiences weather that is dramatic, exciting, and capricious. You may not like what it's doing, but it will never bore you. Be prepared for extreme changes in temperature at any time of year, and watch for summer afternoon thunderstorms that can leave you drenched and shivering in minutes. In winter, mountain temperatures can drop well below zero.

HEALTH AND SAFETY

Cities range in altitude from 3,030 feet at Jal in the southeast corner to 8,750 feet at Red River in the northern mountains. Santa Fe, Cloudcroft, and several other popular destinations are at 7,000 feet and above. These elevations can be taxing to lowlanders, so take things slow, especially at first, and drink plenty of water. Those with heart or respiratory problems should consult their doctors before planning a trip to the state's higher reaches. Because the sun's rays are more direct in New Mexico's thinner, clearer air, sunburn can be a real problem. Be sure to bring good-quality sun block, a hat, and sunglasses that protect against ultraviolet rays.

Always carry plenty of extra water in the desert, and be on the lookout for rattlesnakes and other poisonous creatures. If you're heading into the wilderness, let someone know where you're going and when you expect to return, and then stick to your schedule.

WHAT TO PACK

The bywords are comfortable and casual. Even the state's most elegant restaurants are more informal than those in New York or Chicago, and you'll be welcome almost everywhere wearing casual clothes.

You'll want comfortable walking shoes, a light jacket, preferably water resistant, and a sweater. Warm clothing is needed in mountain areas even in summer, as evenings cool down very quickly once the sun dips below the horizon. Layers are the best way to dress, since it tends to be cool at both ends of the day and temperatures can be delightfully warm when the sun is out, even in the middle of winter. Sunglasses, hats, and sunscreen are essential at any time of year.

TOURIST INFORMATION

For a copy of the *New Mexico Vacation Guide* and information on attractions statewide, contact the New Mexico Department of Tourism, PO Box 2003, Santa Fe, NM 87503-2003 (tel 505/827-7400 or toll free 800/545-2040). The New Mexico Department of Tourism also maintains a Web page at (http://www.nets.com:80/newmextourism) with general information about the state. When in Santa Fe, visit the Welcome Center in the historic Lamy Building at 491 Old Santa Fe Trail. There are also welcome centers distributing brochures and maps at both the Texas and Arizona ends of I-40 and I-10. Topographical maps are available from the US Geological Survey Distribution Section, Federal Center, Building 41, Denver, CO 80225 (tel 303/202-4700), and state and county maps are available from the New Mexico State Highway and Transportation Department, 1120 Cerrillos Rd, Santa Fe, NM 87501 (tel 505/827-5250).

For road conditions and closure information, call the state's Highway Hotline (tel toll free 800/432-4269).

DRIVING RULES AND REGULATIONS

The speed limit on interstate highways is 65 mph outside city limits, 55 mph within city limits. The statewide speed limit elsewhere is 55 mph outside city limits, unless otherwise posted. Seat belts are mandatory for all front-seat occupants in passenger cars and pickup trucks with a gross weight of 10,000 pounds or less, and approved child restraints or safety belts are required for all children under the age of 11. Motorcyclists under 18 must wear helmets. Charges of driving while intoxicated (DWI) are determined by minimum blood alcohol levels of 0.02% for those under age 21, and 0.08% for those 21 and over. Drivers convicted of a first offense can face up to 90 days in jail and a $500 fine, plus 90 days to 1-year license revocation.

Indian reservations are considered sovereign nations, and each enforces its own laws. For instance, many prohibit the transportation of alcoholic beverages and may require motorcyclists to wear helmets.

RENTING A CAR

Most major car rental agencies have outlets in Albuquerque, and some are also represented in Santa Fe, Las Cruces, and other cities. Among companies serving Albuquerque and Albuquerque International Airport are:

- **Advantage** (tel 800/777-5500)
- **Agency** (tel 800/321-1972)
- **Alamo** (tel 800/327-9633)
- **Avis** (tel 800/331-1212)
- **Budget** (tel 800/527-0700)
- **Dollar** (tel 800/800-4000)
- **Enterprise** (tel 800/325-8007)
- **Hertz** (tel 800/654-3131)
- **National** (tel 800/227-7368)
- **Payless** (tel 800/729-5377)
- **Rent-A-Wreck** (tel 800/247-9556)
- **Thrifty** (tel 800/367-2277)
- **Wheelchair Getaways of New Mexico** (wheelchair-accessible vans) (tel 800/367-2277)

ESSENTIALS

Area Code: The area code for all of New Mexico is 505.

Emergencies: Call 911.

Liquor Laws: The minimum legal age to drink any alcoholic beverage in New Mexico is 21. Liquor can be sold by the glass Monday through Saturday from 7am to 2am, and Sunday noon to midnight. Package liquor can be sold Monday through Saturday from 7am to midnight, and not at all on Sunday. Some counties are entirely dry on Sunday, and most Indian reservations are not only dry but forbid possession of alcoholic beverages.

Smoking: The New Mexico Clean Indoor Air Act requires designated smoking and non-smoking areas in all public (government-owned) buildings. Many counties and cities had passed their own antismoking ordinances. For instance, in Albuquerque, most restaurants are required to have nonsmoking areas.

Taxes: New Mexico has a gross receipts tax, administered as a sales tax, of 5% on goods and services. Additional county and city taxes bring the combined tax to about 6% in most communities. Most cities and counties also add a tax of 2 to 5% to lodging bills. For instance, the combined sales and lodgers tax in Albuquerque is about 10.8%. State and local taxes do not apply on Indian reservations.

Time Zone: New Mexico is in the Mountain time zone and observes daylight saving time from April through October.

Best of the State

WHAT TO SEE AND DO

Luring visitors for hundreds and perhaps thousands of years, New Mexico has scenic beauty and historical attractions, as well as a cultural mix—American

Indian, Hispanic, and Anglo—that flavors not only the cuisine, but also the activities, art and architecture, language, and customs. The best plan of attack may be to pick and choose, like at one of those all-you-can-eat buffets. Here's the menu.

To find out more detailed information, look under "Attractions" for individual cities in the listings portion of this chapter.

Art Attracted by clear mountain light and picturesque Indian and Hispanic villages, Anglo artists from the eastern United States "discovered" New Mexico about the beginning of the 20th century. Their work can be seen in the museums and galleries of **Taos, Santa Fe,** and **Albuquerque.** Check local newspapers for gallery openings, where you can talk with artists one-on-one about their work, often while sipping a glass of wine and nibbling cheese and crackers. Many communities also have annual or semi-annual arts festivals, such as the **Taos Arts Festival** each fall, with exhibits, tours of artists' studios, and arts-and-crafts markets. While there has been a long-time appreciation of Native American and Hispanic crafts, such as world-famous pottery made at **San Ildefonso Pueblo** and carved wooden *santos* (saints) by Hispanic artists, there is a growing awareness that there are also a number of Native American and Hispanic painters and sculptors. Check out the galleries in Albuquerque's **Old Town.**

Historic Sites & Buildings From prehistoric Indian pit houses to the **Kit Carson Home and Museum** in Taos to the spot where the world's first atomic bomb was assembled, New Mexico is covered with wonderful historic sites and buildings. Among them, you'll find the huge home of the ancient Anasazi Indians at **Chaco Culture National Historic Park,** ruins of an important military post at **Fort Union National Monument,** and the **Mission of San Miguel** in Santa Fe, one of the oldest surviving churches in the United States.

Guided tours of the ghost towns of **Shakespeare** and **Steins,** near Lordsburg, let you see the real thing, and in Chama the **Cumbres and Toltec Scenic Railroad** offers rides on a historic narrow-gauge steam train.

Museums From the most elaborate temperature and humidity-controlled buildings housing priceless works of art to funky small-town collections from grandma's attic, you'll find plenty to look at in New Mexico. Albuquerque, Santa Fe, and Taos have sophisticated museums housing extensive collections of American Indian and Spanish Colonial art and artifacts, like Taos's **Millicent Rogers Museum,** the **Albuquerque Museum,** and the **Museum of Indian Arts and Culture** in Santa Fe. But almost every small town has some sort of museum, and they're often fascinating, like the **Santa Fe Trail Museum** in Springer, with the only electric chair ever used in New Mexico.

Natural Wonders Simply put, New Mexico is a beautiful state. You'll find pristine lakes among tall pines near **Red River,** waves of gleaming gypsum at **White Sands National Monument,** and a spectacular fairyland of sculpture at the state's most popular national park, **Carlsbad Caverns.** The **Wild Rivers National Recreation Area,** near the state's northern border, offers spectacular views of the Rio Grande, and you'll find 400-foot tall rock formations at **Cimarron Canyon State Park.**

While most of us find it easy to appreciate the green, lush beauty of the mountains or an intricately carved rock formation, sometimes it's harder to appreciate the splendor of the desert. Take time to gaze across the vast expanses of seemingly nothing to distant peaks, and look for the red, purple, and yellow blooms of cactus, and the gnarled, weathered trunks of the sturdy piñon pine. Just watch where you step—there may be a rattler out there.

Wildlife The state's abundant wildlife ranges from elk, antelope, and deer that watch you drive by along US 64 near **Cimarron,** to the rare whooping crane at **Bosque del Apache National Wildlife Refuge.** You can see exotic and endangered fish at the **National Fish Hatchery** in Dexter and get up close to numerous desert dwellers at **Living Desert State Park** in Carlsbad.

Family Favorites New Mexico doesn't offer much in the way of pre-fab family fun—there are no major theme parks. But most children are fascinated by the vestiges of the real Old West in New Mexico, where you can count the bullet holes in the ceiling of the **St James Hotel** in Cimarron, or walk the same streets as outlaw Billy the Kid at **Lincoln State Monument.** And don't forget outer space, the new frontier, at Alamogordo's **Space Center** or the **UFO museums** in Roswell; and those state-of-the-art computers and science exhibits at Los Alamos's **Bradbury Science Museum.** Albuquerque has several attractions geared for families, including **Albuquerque Child-**

ren's Museum, with hands-on activities. Finally, head for a campsite along a pure mountain stream in one of the state's national forests.

Cuisine It isn't really Mexican, it isn't Tex-Mex, and it certainly isn't traditional American. New Mexicans have developed their own style of cooking. Travel the state from end-to-end and you'll find some subtle differences, but in general, New Mexicans like lots of green or red chile peppers, onion, garlic, cumin, and both Monterey jack and cheddar cheeses. The beans of choice are pinto, but don't expect any if you order a bowl of chile. In a true New Mexico restaurant a bowl of chile means chile stew —made from whole chile peppers, possibly with a bit of meat—and it's guaranteed to open your sinuses.

EVENTS AND FESTIVALS

Santa Fe, Taos and Northern New Mexico

- **New Year's Celebration,** Taos, Santo Domingo, San Felipe, Cochiti, Santa Ana, and Picuris pueblos. Turtle, matachines, and other traditional dances. January 1. Call 505/843-7270 for information.
- **Red River Winterfest,** Red River. Ski, sled dog, and snowmobile races, ice sculpture, country music, and dancing. Last weekend in January. Call 800/348-6444.
- **Taos Spring Arts Celebration,** Taos. Studio tours, gallery exhibits, poetry readings, and music. Second and third weeks in May. Call 800/732-8267.
- **Rails 'n' Trails Days,** Las Vegas. Old-time Atchison, Topeka, and Santa Fe Railroad exhibits, working-ranch tours, and a western dance. Late May. Call 505/425-8631 or 800/832-5947.
- **Spring Festival,** El Rancho de las Golondrinas, south of Santa Fe. Costumed villagers, Spanish colonial crafts, and festive Spanish music. Early June. Call 505/471-2261 or 800/777-CITY.
- **Summer Chamber Music Festival,** Taos. Concerts and seminars. Mid-June through early July. Call 505/776-2388.
- **Santa Fe Opera,** Santa Fe. Internationally acclaimed operatic productions with distinguished guest artists. Early July to late August. Call 505/986-5955 for schedule and information.
- **Nambe Waterfall Ceremonial,** Nambe Pueblo. Dance teams present all-afternoon buffalo, Comanche, corn, deer, and eagle dances. July 4. Call 505/455-2036.
- **Fiesta de Santiago y Santa Ana,** Taos. Live music, parades, a fiesta queen, food, and dancing. Late July. Call 505/758-4568.
- **Spanish Market,** Santa Fe. Top Hispanic artisans display and sell traditional Spanish colonial arts and crafts. Last weekend in July. Call 505/983-4038 or 800/777-CITY.
- **Fort Union Founder's Day,** Las Vegas. Living history groups recall military and pioneer life of the 1850s to 1870s. Last weekend in July. Call 505/425-8025 or 800/832-5947.
- **Inter-Tribal Indian Ceremonial,** Gallup. A nationwide gathering of tribes at Red Rock State Park for four days of parades, dances, arts-and-crafts demonstrations, fairs, and rodeo competition. MidAugust. Call 800/242-4282.
- **Indian Market,** Santa Fe. High-quality arts-and-crafts show, with competition for best Native American artisans. Second weekend before Labor Day. Call 505/983-5220 or 800/777-CITY.
- **La Fiesta de Santa Fe,** Santa Fe. Colorful celebration commemorating the reconquest of New Mexico by Don Diego de Vargas in 1692; Spanish music, dancing, and food vendors. First or second week after Labor Day. Call 505/984-6760 or 800/777-CITY.
- **Fall Arts Festival,** Taos. Tours of artists' homes and special exhibits of Taos art. Last two weeks of September and first week of October. Call 505/758-3873 or 800/732-8267.
- **San Geronimo Feast Day,** Taos Pueblo. Afternoon buffalo, Comanche, and corn dances; ceremonial foot races; and an arts-and-crafts fair. September 30. Call 505/758-9593 or 800/732-8267.
- **Harvest Festival,** El Rancho de las Golondrinas, south of Santa Fe. A traditional Spanish colonial fiesta. First weekend in October. Call 505/471-2261 or 800/777-CITY.
- **Annual Shiprock/Navajo Nation Fair,** Shiprock. A rodeo, carnival, mud bog, 10-kilometer run, country-western dancing, various Indian dances, a powwow, agricultural and arts-and-crafts exhibits, and the traditional nine-day chant called the Night Way or "Yeibichai." October. Call 602/871-6436.
- **Taos Mountain Balloon Rally,** Taos. Hot-air balloon rides, mass ascensions at dawn, an arts-and-crafts fair. Last weekend in October. Call 800/732-8267.

ALBUQUERQUE

- **Albuquerque Gem and Mineral Show,** Albuquerque. Geologists, mineralogists, and amateur rock hounds build competitive displays, demonstrate gold panning and mining techniques, and identify ore samples. Mid-March. Call 505/334-6174 for information.
- **San Felipe Fiesta,** Albuquerque. Three days of food and entertainment in Old Town in honor of Albuquerque's patron saint. Early June. Call 505/243-4628.
- **Aztec Dances,** Albuquerque. Dancers soar from the top of an 80-foot pole to the ground in a traditional Aztec ceremony. July. Call 505/843-7270.
- **New Mexico State Fair,** Albuquerque. A 17-day extravaganza with horse racing, a top rodeo event, living Indian and Spanish villages, nightly country-western concerts, livestock show, games, and rides. September. Call 505/265-1791 or 800/284-2282.
- **Kodak Albuquerque International Balloon Fiesta,** Albuquerque. More than 650 hot-air balloons in mass ascensions at daybreak; evening balloon "glows." Early October. Call 505/821-1000 or 800/284-2282.
- **Old Town Luminaria Tours,** Albuquerque. "Luminarias," candles in sand-weighted paper bags, decorate walls, walkways, and roof lines to light the way for the Santo Niño (Christ Child). Christmas Eve. Call 505/243-3696 or 800/284-2282.

SOUTHERN NEW MEXICO

- **Rock-Hound Roundup,** Deming. More than 500 hobbyists from 45 states attend this nationally famous informal tailgate-style convention. Includes a mineral-sample auction and guided field trips for semi-precious agate, jasper, and pink onyx. Second week in March. Call 505/546-2674 for information.
- **Trinity Site Tour,** Alamogordo. Open to the public only two days each year, this is where the world's first atomic bomb was detonated on July 16, 1945. First Saturday in April and October. Call 505/678-1134.
- **Wild Wild West Pro Rodeo,** Silver City. More than 300 contestants from surrounding states compete. May. Call 505/538-3229.
- **Pioneer Days Celebration and Balloon Fiesta,** Clovis. One of the top national rodeos, plus hot air balloon rally, parades, and western music. Early June. Call 505/763-3435.
- **Old Fort Days,** Fort Sumner. Reenactments of the death of outlaw Billy the Kid, Old West bank robberies, trials, and hangings. Early to mid-June. Call 505/355-7705.
- **National Standard-Class Glider and Soaring Championships,** Hobbs. Features the top pilots of high-performance sailplanes. Early July. Call 505/397-3202 or toll free 800/658-6291.
- **Frontier Days,** Silver City. Historic celebration with parades, a cowboy breakfast and barbecue, hot air balloon rally, art show, ice cream social, and junior rodeo. Early July. Call 505/538-3785 or toll free 800/548-9378.
- **Great American Duck Race,** Deming. Watch 500 ducks compete for $10,000 in prizes; with duck parade and duck dance. Last weekend in August. Call 505/546-2674.
- **Carlsbad Caverns Bat Flight Breakfast,** Carlsbad. Breakfast followed by an eerie, hour-long spectacle as some 500,000 Mexican freetail bats return at dawn to roost. Mid-August. Call 505/785-2232.
- **Hatch Chile Festival,** Hatch. Traditional and contemporary red and green chile dishes, chile ristras, and bushel baskets and sacks of chiles from the autumn harvest. September. Call 505/267-5216.
- **The Whole Enchilada Fiesta,** Las Cruces. The world's largest enchilada, Spanish music concerts, dances, and parades. Early October. Call toll free 800/FIESTAS.

SPECTATOR SPORTS

Auto Racing The season generally runs from late spring through early fall and concentrates on sprint cars, stocks and hobby stocks, and IMCA modifieds. In Albuquerque, check with **Duke City Raceway** (tel 505/873-7223); race fans in Las Cruces, head for **The Speedway,** at Southern New Mexico State Fairgrounds (tel 505/524-7913). In the Farmington area there's **Aztec Speedway,** south of the community of Aztec on Legion Rd (tel 505/334-6629). Drag race fans should check the schedule at **Albuquerque National Dragway** (tel 505/299-9478).

Baseball **Albuquerque Dukes,** the Triple-A farm team of the Los Angeles Dodgers, play at Albuquerque Sports Stadium (tel 505/243-1791) from mid-April through early September.

Basketball & Football The action is at the **University of New Mexico** in Albuquerque (tel 505/277-2116) and **New Mexico State University** in Las Cruces (tel 505/646-1420 or 505/646-NMSU for recorded information).

Horse Racing Some of the country's best quarter horses and thoroughbreds run at New Mexico's four tracks. The **Downs at Albuquerque** (tel 505/266-5555), in the State Fairgrounds, offers nearly $2 million in purses from January to mid-June and during the state fair in September. Racing takes place at the **Downs at Santa Fe,** just south of Santa Fe off I-25 (tel 505/471- 3311), from late June through Labor Day. **Ruidoso Downs** (tel 505/378-4431), considered the quarter horse capital of the world, has races from mid-May through Labor Day, when the All American Futurity takes place. Located on New Mexico's southern border, just 5 miles from El Paso, Texas, **Sunland Park** (tel 505/589-1131) has the state's longest season—from early October to early May.

Rodeo Many New Mexico communities have rodeo grounds and host regional events. Among major rodeos on the professional circuit are the **All-American Pro Rodeo** (tel toll free 800/235-FAIR), at the New Mexico State Fair in Albuquerque each September, and the **Clovis Rodeo** (tel 505/763-3435) in June during the Pioneer Days Celebration.

ACTIVITIES A TO Z

Ballooning Major hot-air balloon rallies take place in both Albuquerque and Taos each October, and companies throughout the state offer balloon rides. Among firms advertising that they are fully insured and certified by the FAA are Braden's Balloons Aloft (tel 505/281-2714) and Naturally High Balloon Company (tel 505/843-6888), both in Albuquerque.

Bicycling Popular throughout the state, although many roads in rural areas are narrow, with no shoulders or bike paths. Urban biking is best in Albuquerque, where information and bike maps are available from the **Albuquerque Cultural and Recreational Services Dept** (tel 505/768-3550). For information on mountain biking trails in New Mexico's national forests, contact the **USDA Forest Service Office** (tel 505/842-3292). For bike rentals try Recreational Equipment Inc (tel 505/247-1191) or Rio Mountain-sport (tel 505/766-9970), both in Albuquerque. Northeast Cyclery (tel 505/299-1210), also in Albuquerque, repairs all brands of bicycles.

Boating For information on lake boating, contact **New Mexico State Parks,** PO Box 1147, Santa Fe, NM 87504-1147 (tel 505/827-7173 or toll free 888/667-2757). Those interested in white-water rafting or kayaking on the Rio Grande or Rio Chama should contact the **Bureau of Land Management,** NM State Office, PO Box 27115, Santa Fe, NM 87502-0115 (tel 505/438-7400).

Camping & Hiking With 5 national forests, dozens of state and national parks, and vast tracts of other public land, there is no excuse to stay indoors. Information on state parks can be obtained from **New Mexico State Parks,** PO Box 1147, Santa Fe, NM 87504-1147 (tel 505/827-7173 or toll free 888/667-2757). National forest and wilderness maps are available from the USDA Forest Service Office, 517 Gold Ave SW, Albuquerque, NM 87102 (tel 505/842-3292). Topo-graphical maps can be obtained from the US Geological Survey Distribution Section, Federal Center, Building 41, Denver, CO 80225 (tel 303/202-4700). A variety of maps is also available from the Bureau of Land Management, NM State Office, PO Box 27115, Santa Fe, NM 87502-0115 (tel 505/438-7400); and a geologic highway map and rock-hound guide is available from the New Mexico Bureau of Mines and Mineral Resources, Campus Station, Socorro, NM 87801 (tel 505/835-5410).

Fishing & Hunting Opportunities for fishing and hunting are particularly numerous in the northern mountains. Licenses, information, and equipment can be obtained at sporting goods stores throughout the state. You can also contact the **New Mexico Department of Game and Fish,** PO Box 25112, Santa Fe, NM 87503 (tel 505/827-7911). The department maintains a 24-hour hotline (tel toll free 800/ASK-FISH), with information on the best places to fish, fishing conditions, licenses, and regulations. Those interested in guided trips can contact the **New Mexico Council of Outfitters and Guides,** 160 Washington St SE, No. 175, Albuquerque, NM 87108 (tel 505/243-4461), for a brochure and state outfitters' directory.

Golf Generally mild weather and more than 60 golf courses cater to golfers. Check with the **Sun Country Golf Association** (tel 505/897-0864) concerning private clubs throughout the state. For information on municipal courses in Albuquerque, contact the **Albuquerque Parks Division** (tel 505/888-8115).

Skiing New Mexico's mountains and an abundance of snow offer some of the best skiing in the country at the state's nine downhill and two cross-country ski areas. For information, contact **Ski New Mexico,** PO Box 1104, Santa Fe, NM 87504 (tel 505/982-5300); and for recorded daily snow conditions call the **Sno-Phone** (tel 505/984-0606).

SANTA FE, TAOS, AND BEYOND

Start	Santa Fe
Finish	Pecos National Historic Park
Distance	496 miles
Time	2–4 days
Highlights	Art galleries, museums, Native American pueblos, historic steam railroad, Spanish colonial churches, wildlife

A longtime favorite of ranchers, artists, writers, fortune hunters, and more than a few outlaws, north-central New Mexico claims some of the state's most impressive mountain scenery, a rich and exciting history, and a wide range of attractions. This tour visits the Santa Fe and Taos art centers, several Native American pueblos, an old fort, more than a dozen museums, several pristine lakes, and plenty of scenic beauty. Keep in mind that mountain driving can be slow. Mileage totals are from stop to stop only, and in-town and side trip travel may add several hundred miles. Those driving in winter should check on road conditions on US 64 between Chama and Taos before leaving Santa Fe by contacting the New Mexico Highway Department (tel toll free 800/432-4269). Snow storms often close a mountain section of this road for a day or more.

For additional information on accommodations, restaurants, and attractions in the region covered by the tour, refer to specific cities in the listings portion of this chapter.

1. **Santa Fe.** This "City Different" combines Old World charm with modern urban sophistication. Steeped in history, the city has a busy and prosperous artists' colony, excellent museums, an abundance of musical and theatrical events, and some of the state's most popular shops and restaurants.

   Originally inhabited by ancestors of present-day Pueblo Indians, Santa Fe (elevation 7,000 feet) was established in 1610 as Spain's New Mexico provincial capital. In the late 1600s, it was the site of a bloody Native American revolt and later reconquest. In the mid-19th century US troops invaded and secured the city without firing a shot.

   If you seek lodging, the downtown **Eldorado Hotel** (Santa Fe's largest) and **Hilton of Santa Fe** are close to Santa Fe Plaza and very convenient. The more economical **El Rey Inn** on Cerrillos Rd, southwest of downtown, is a favorite of New Mexicans visiting their capital city.

   Several of the city's main attractions are within easy walking distance of the **Plaza,** which makes it a good place to begin your sightseeing. On the plaza's north side, the **Palace of the Governors** (tel 505/827-6483), believed to be the oldest public US building, has a long "portal," or covered porch, where local Native Americans display and sell their jewelry, pottery, baskets, and other arts and crafts. Inside, there's a regional history museum, with exhibits on regional developments over the past 400 years. Across Lincoln St from the Palace of the Governors, off the northwest corner of the Plaza, the **Museum of Fine Arts** (tel 505/827-4455) showcases New Mexico's 20th-century artists. Just east of the Plaza, the **Institute of American Indian Arts Museum,** 108 Cathedral Place (tel 505/988-6281), has a Native American arts collection representing numerous US tribes. **St Francis Cathedral,** at Cathedral Place and San Francisco St (tel 505/982-5619), was constructed in the late 19th century to emulate the great cathedrals of Europe. The **Loretto Chapel,** 211 Old Santa Fe Trail, at Water St (tel 505/984-7971), by the same architects that built St Francis Cathedral, is famous for its "miraculous" spiral staircase, which appears to hang without visible support.

   Southwest of the Plaza area, **Santuario de Guadalupe,** 100 Guadalupe St (tel 505/988-2027), is reputedly the oldest existing US shrine to Mexico's patron saint, Our Lady of Guadalupe. Built in the late 1700s and extensively remodeled a century later, it is not used as a church today, but serves as a center for performing arts events and art exhibits. Southeast of the Plaza, the **Mission of San Miguel** (tel 505/983-3974) was built in the early 1600s on the site of a 12th-century pueblo. Inside the mission church is a bell considered to have been made in Spain in the 1350s.

   The **State Capitol,** commonly called the Roundhouse, on Old Santa Fe Trail at Paseo de Peralta (tel 505/986-4589), offers tours that include a visit to the art gallery in the governor's office, with works by New Mexican artists.

   Three museums are located on Camino Lejo, south of downtown. **Wheelwright Museum of the American Indian,** 704 Camino Lejo (tel 505/ 982-4636), contains both historic and contem- porary Native American arts and crafts, with an especially impressive collection of Navajo art. The **Museum of International Folk Art,** 706 Camino Lejo (tel 505/827-6350), has folk art from more than 100 coun-

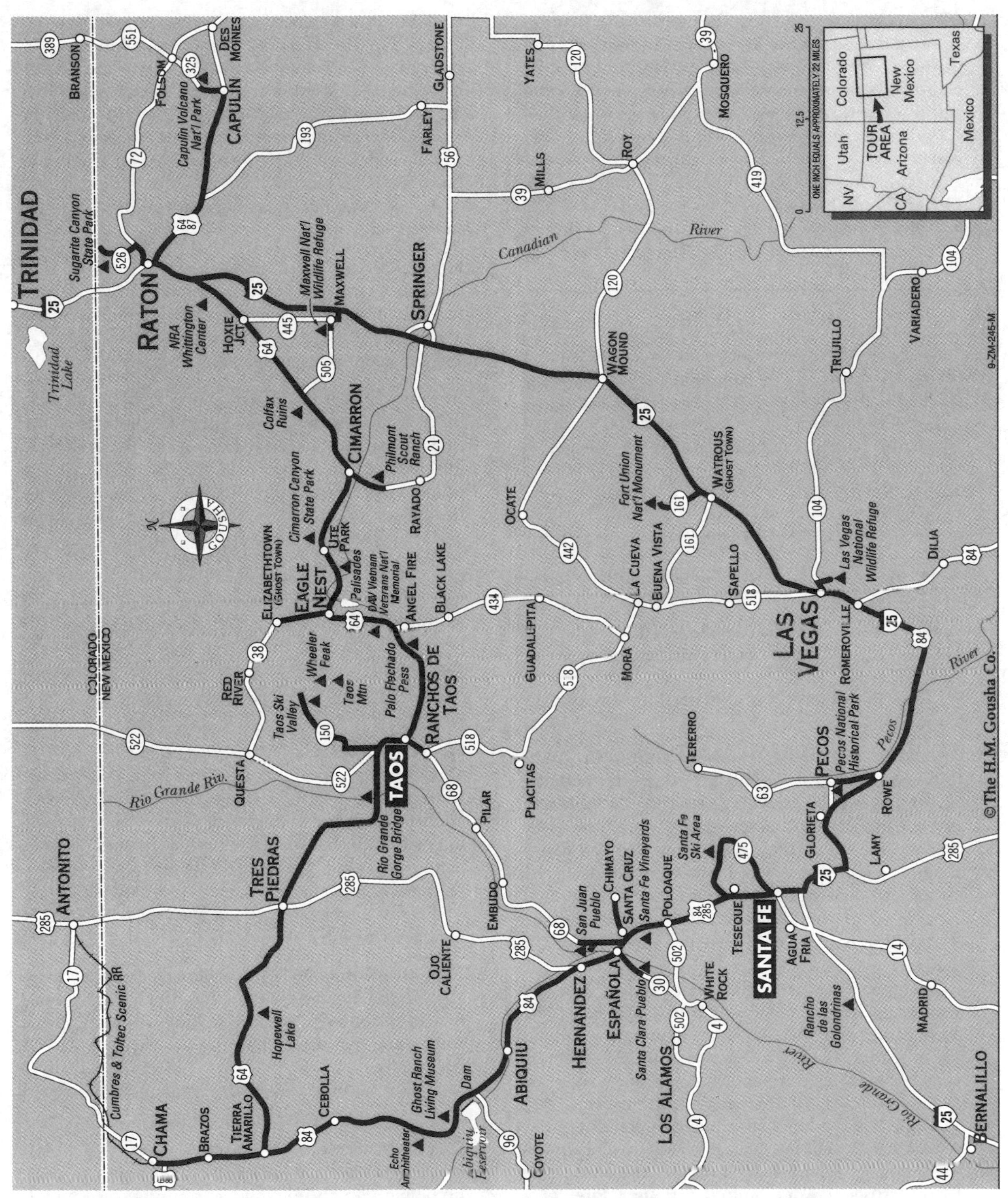
TRINIDAD
Trinidad Lake
Sugarite Canyon State Park
RATON
NRA Whittington Center
HOXIE JCT.
Maxwell Nat'l Wildlife Refuge
MAXWELL
SPRINGER
Capulin Volcano Nat'l Park
CAPULIN
FOLSOM
DES MOINES
BRANSON
GLADSTONE
FARLEY
YATES
MILLS
ROY
MOSQUERO
Canadian River
Colfax Ruins
CIMARRON
Philmont Scout Ranch
RAYADO
Cimarron Canyon State Park
UTE PARK
WAGON MOUND
OCATE
Fort Union Nat'l Monument
WATROUS (GHOST TOWN)
TRUJILLO
VARIADERO
ELIZABETHTOWN (GHOST TOWN)
EAGLE NEST
Palisades
DAV Vietnam Veterans Nat'l Memorial
ANGEL FIRE
BLACK LAKE
GUADALUPITA
LA CUEVA
BUENA VISTA
SAPELLO
Las Vegas National Wildlife Refuge
LAS VEGAS
DILIA
COLORADO
NEW MEXICO
RED RIVER
Wheeler Peak
Taos Mtn
Taos Ski Valley
Palo Flechado Pass
RANCHOS DE TAOS
MORA
ROMEROVILLE
Pecos River
QUESTA
Rio Grande Riv.
TAOS
PLACITAS
TERERRO
Pecos National Historical Park
PECOS
ROWE
ANTONITO
TRES PIEDRAS
Rio Grande Gorge Bridge
PILAR
CHIMAYO
Santa Fe Ski Area
GLORIETA
LAMY
EMBUDO
San Juan Pueblo
SANTA CRUZ
Santa Fe Vineyards
POLOAQUE
TESEQUE
SANTA FE
AGUA FRIA
OJO CALIENTE
HERNANDEZ
ESPAÑOLA
Santa Clara Pueblo
WHITE ROCK
Rancho de las Golondrinas
MADRID
Cumbres & Toltec Scenic RR
Hopewell Lake
Ghost Ranch Living Museum
Dam
ABIQUIU
LOS ALAMOS
Rio Grande River
BERNALILLO
CHAMA
BRAZOS
TIERRA AMARILLO
CEBOLLA
Echo Amphitheater
Abiquiu Reservoir
COYOTE
GOUSHA
NV
Utah
Colorado
TOUR AREA
New Mexico
CA
Arizona
Texas
Mexico
0 12.5 25
ONE INCH EQUALS APPROXIMATELY 22 MILES
9-ZM-245-M
©The H.M. Gousha Co.

tries, including one wing devoted to the Spanish colonial period. At the **Museum of Indian Arts and Culture,** 706 Camino Lejo (tel 505/827-6350), exhibits focus on the Apache, Navajo, and Pueblo cultures. Art lovers may also explore the more than 75 galleries, studios, and antique shops along **Canyon Road,** just a few blocks southeast of the Plaza.

About 15 miles south of Santa Fe Plaza via I-25, **El Rancho de las Golondrinas** (tel 505/471-2261) is a living history museum of restored buildings devoted to New Mexico's Spanish colonial period.

Take a Break

For a quick bite in downtown Santa Fe, stop at **The Burrito Co,** 111 Washington Ave (tel 505/982-4453). You'll find extremely elegant dining at **The Compound,** 653 Canyon Rd (tel 505/982-4253), which serves fine American cuisine, and a taste of old Santa Fe at **El Farol,** 808 Canyon Rd (tel 505/988-9912), a Mexican restaurant.

From Santa Fe, drive 20 miles north on US 84/285 to:

2. **Santa Fe Vineyards** (tel 505/753-8100), where you can take an informal winery tour and sample the local wines.

From the winery, continue north on US 84/285 for about 4 miles to:

3. **Española.** Settled by Spanish colonists in 1598, Española (elevation 5,590 feet) owes its modern-day importance as a trading center to the railroad, and specifically the narrow gauge "chili line," so-named because of the drying strings of red chiles hanging on the flat-roofed adobe homes along its route. The line ran from Antonito, Colorado, to Santa Fe from the 1880s to 1941, and a section of the line survives today as a scenic railroad based in Chama.

You can learn about the area's history and see work by local artists at **Bond House Museum,** 710 Bond St (tel 505/753-2377), a Victorian-style adobe home. **Santa Clara Pueblo** (tel 505/753-7326) is located about 2 miles south of Española via Los Alamos Ave (NM 30). Known for its distinctive, highly polished black pottery, the pueblo administers the **Puye Cliff Dwellings,** the impressive ruins of an ancient village where some 1,500 people once lived. To see artists at work, stop at **San Juan Pueblo,** 4 miles north of Española on NM 68 and then another mile west on NM 74 (tel 505/852-4400). At San Juan, arts and crafts from different northern New Mexico pueblos are for sale, and artists are often seen working, at **Oke-Oweenge Crafts Cooperative** (tel 505/852-2372). The tiny community of **Chimayo,** 10 miles east of Española on NM 76, is a worthwhile side trip where you can see traditional Rio Grande weaving at **Ortega's Weaving Shop** (tel 505/351-4215), or visit the beautiful **Santuario de Chimayo,** which contains dirt that believers say has miraculous healing powers.

From Española continue west for about 6 miles to the village of:

4. **Hernandez,** stopping along the road to try to find the exact spot where photographer Ansel Adams took his famous photo, *Moonrise, Hernandez, New Mexico,* in 1941.

Now, continue 16 miles west on US 84 to:

5. **Abiquiu.** Site of an ancient Native American pueblo, Abiquiu was settled by Spanish colonists in the mid-1700s, but became famous as the home of 20th-century artist Georgia O'Keeffe. Although the home is not open to the public, visitors can explore the village plaza and gaze at the sandstone bluffs and mesas that helped inspire the artist.

From Abiquiu, continue west on US 84 for 7 miles to:

6. **Abiquiu Dam and Lake.** (tel 505/685-4371). This large lake is a favorite of northern New Mexicans for boating, water skiing, fishing, swimming, camping, and picnicking.

Now continue 5 more miles west on US 84 to:

7. **Ghost Ranch Living Museum** (tel 505/685-4312). Operated by the US Forest Service and a private foundation, Ghost Ranch is a home for northern New Mexico wildlife creatures that have been severely injured or orphaned, or for other reasons are not able to survive in the wild. Residents include a bear, owls, eagles, skunks, foxes, and other animals.

From Ghost Ranch, head another 6 miles west on US 84 to:

8. **Echo Amphitheater.** This US Forest Service campground (tel 505/684-2486), at 6,600 feet elevation, is a pleasant stop to stretch your legs and spend some time exploring the high desert, with its red rock walls.

Now, continue west and north on US 84 for 40 miles to:

9. **Chama.** This isolated mountain village, at 7,860 feet elevation, is a delightful overnight stop, or home base for fishing, hiking, hunting, snowmobiling, or cross-country skiing jaunts. Most lodging here is a bit rustic, but you'll find all the modern conveniences. Especially recommended are **Chama Trails Inn** and **Elk Horn Lodge and Cafe.**

Take a Break

For homemade Mexican food and American burgers and sandwiches, stop at **Viva Vera's,** on Main St (tel 505/756-2557), 2/10 mile north of the "Y." You'll find an Old West atmosphere and good beef at **High Country Restaurant,** on Main St (tel 505/756-2384), 1/10 mile north of the "Y."

The number-one attraction is the **Cumbres and Toltec Scenic Railroad** (tel 505/756-2151), a narrow-gauge steam train line that runs from Chama into southern Colorado each summer and fall, passing through some of the region's most beautiful scenery.

From Chama, retrace your route 13 miles south on US 84, turn east onto US 64, and go 30 miles through spectacular mountain scenery to:

10. Hopewell Lake. This US Forest Service campground (tel 505/758-6200) has a popular fishing lake and is a good place to stretch your legs and perhaps have a picnic lunch.

From the lake, continue 35 miles east, through the tiny community of Tres Piedras (Spanish for "three rocks") to:

11. Rio Grande Gorge Bridge. Spanning the Rio Grande, this impressive bridge has fantastic views 650 feet down into the gorge, and both up and down the river.

From the bridge, continue east 15 miles on US 64 to:

12. Taos (elevation 6,965 ft). Already home to Native Americans for hundreds of years, Europeans arrived in 1615 with the establishment of Fernando de Taos village by Spanish colonists. Next came French-Canadian trappers, mountain men, artists, writers, and entrepreneurs. The end result is the Taos of today, a mixture of old and new, with some 100 art galleries, quaint adobe homes, historic haciendas, the ancient Taos Pueblo, and a world-class ski resort.

You have plenty of lodging choices. **Holiday Inn Don Fernando de Taos** and **Kachina Lodge** offer fine, modern rooms with a southwestern touch; the older but well-kept **El Monte Lodge** is cozy and economical; and **The Historic Taos Inn** is within easy walking distance of the main sights.

From most parts of town you can see **Taos Mountain,** most prominent as you look north down Paseo del Pueblo Norte; it has been painted and photographed countless times, and numerous variations on the landmark may be seen in local art galleries. Legend has it that this is a magic mountain, with its own mind. If the mountain likes you, you must return. But if you displease it, the mountain banishes you for life.

Most visits to Taos begin at **Taos Plaza,** with an abundance of art galleries, shops, and restaurants. Benches in the Plaza's center provide a shady break from sightseeing and provide good people-watching opportunities. Walking off the southwest corner of the plaza, watch for Ledoux St, where you'll find the **Blumenschein Home and Museum,** at #222 (tel 505/758-0505), with antique furnishings and paintings by Ernest Blumenschein, one of the East Coast artists who founded the Taos Society of Artists in 1915. The **Harwood Foundation Museum of Taos Art,** 238 Ledoux St (tel 505/758-9826), has changing displays of local artists' works.

Walking east of Taos Plaza about ½ block takes you to another era of Taos's heritage, the Old West, at **Kit Carson Home and Museum,** 113 Kit Carson Rd (tel 505/758-4741). The famous scout made Taos his headquarters for much of his life. His home, which he presented to his Mexican bride, Josefa Jaramillo, as a wedding present, has exhibits on Carson's career and New Mexico's mountain-man period. **Bent House Museum,** at 117 Bent St (tel 505/758-2376), just north of Taos Plaza, was the home of the first governor of the American territory of New Mexico, and the site where he was killed during the Taos Pueblo Rebellion of 1847.

Several blocks north of Taos Plaza at 227 Paseo el Pueblo Norte is the **Fechin Institute** (tel 505/758-1710). Nicolai Fechin was a Russian-born artist who painted in Taos and rebuilt an old adobe home, adding unique Russian-style carvings. His former house is open to the public during the summer and fall. Nearby, **Kit Carson Park** (tel 505/758-4160) contains a cemetery with the graves of Carson and his family and other prominent Taos citizens.

Taos's most popular attraction is **Taos Pueblo** (tel 505/758-9593), located 2 miles north of Taos Plaza via Paseo del Pueblo Norte and the pueblo access road. Home to Taos Indians since long before Columbus arrived in the so-called New World, this site is considered New Mexico's most beautiful pueblo. Visitors can watch Native American ceremonial dances, shop for handmade jewelry, pottery, and drums, and eat the traditional fried bread. The pueblo often closes to the public for about a month in late winter, so check before making the trip at this time.

Among Taos's best historic homes is the **Martinez Hacienda,** located 2 miles west of Taos Plaza on NM 240 (tel 505/758-1000). The fort-like building, with 21 rooms around two courtyards, contains Spanish colonial furniture and artifacts of the early 19th century, a working blacksmith shop, and exhibits on Spanish culture and Taos history.

Millicent Rogers Museum, 4 miles north of Taos Plaza via Paseo del Pueblo Norte/US 64 and Millicent Rogers Rd (tel 505/758-2462), has an excellent selection of Hispanic and Native American art and artifacts, including the best collection you'll see anywhere of San Ildefonso Pueblo pottery by famed artist Maria Martinez.

South of Taos about 4 miles on Paseo del Pueblo Sur/NM 68, in the community of Ranchos de Taos, is the much-photographed adobe **San Francisco de Asis Church** (tel 505/758-2754), which offers a glimpse into the religious past and present of northern New Mexico. The church houses a mystery painting of Christ; it contains a scientifically unexplained image of a cross that appears when viewed in total darkness.

Of course, if you're a skier, it will be hard to resist a day on the slopes at **Taos Ski Valley,** about 16 miles northeast of Taos via US 64 and NM 150 (tel 505/776-2291).

Take a Break

On Taos Plaza, a convenient stop for lunch is **The Garden Restaurant,** 127 N Plaza (tel 505/758-9483). Nearby, **Doc Martin's** at the Historic Taos Inn, 125 Paseo del Pueblo Norte (tel 505/758-1977), provides more formal dining, and the busy, somewhat noisy **Michael's Kitchen,** 305 Paseo del Pueblo Norte (tel 505/758-4178), is a local favorite, especially for breakfast.

From Taos, head east on US 64 for 22 miles, crossing 9,101-foot Palo Flechado Pass, to:

13. **DAV Vietnam Veterans National Memorial** (tel 505/377-6900). Built by Dr. Victor Westphall in memory of his son David, a US marine who died in the Vietnam War, this stunning structure has a visitor center and chapel, honoring all US soldiers who gave their lives in that war.

From the memorial, continue east on US 64, but look southwest to **Wheeler Peak,** New Mexico's highest mountain at 13,161 feet. From the DAV Memorial, it's 9 miles to:

14. **Eagle Nest.** Sitting at the junction of NM 38 and US 64, Eagle Nest is a favorite recreation spot, with boat and bank fishing at **Eagle Nest Lake** in warm weather, and ice fishing in winter. The lake is also popular for windsurfing.

From Eagle Nest, continue east on US 64 for about 8 miles into Cimarron Canyon and the:

15. **Palisades.** These spectacular cliffs with their striking rock formations were cut by the Cimarron River through igneous rock known as a sill, composed of the rock monzonite, left here some 40 million years ago when this section of the Rocky Mountains was uplifted. Popular with rock climbers, the cliffs are 800 feet high in some areas. **Cimarron Canyon State Park** is part of the 33,000-acre **Colin Neblett Wildlife Area.** Especially during early mornings and late evenings, watch for elk, mule deer, wild turkey, and maybe even a black bear as you drive carefully through the canyon.

From the Palisades it's about 16 miles east on US 64 to:

16. **Cimarron** (elevation 6,427 feet). This historic Old West town grew up in the mid-1800s as a Santa Fe Trail stop. It was the scene of the bloody Colfax County War over ownership of the gigantic Maxwell land grant, which covered much of north-central New Mexico. **St James Hotel,** opened as a saloon in 1873, counts 26 men killed within its thick adobe walls, and infamous gunman Clay Allison is said to have danced on the bar. The hotel, a National Historic Landmark, has been restored and offers tours. It's also a good place to eat or spend a night, with historic rooms decorated with antiques, and modern rooms in a motel annex. Visitors to Cimarron should also browse through the **Old Mill Museum,** on NM 21 south of US 64, a four-story building built as a grist mill in 1864 that now displays historic photos and memorabilia from Cimarron's past.

Philmont Scout Ranch, 4 miles southwest of Cimarron on NM 21 (tel 505/376-2281), hosts thousands of scouts from around the world each summer, and has three museums. **Kit Carson Museum,** furnished in 1850s style, includes part of a ranch house built by the famous scout; **Villa Philmonte** was once the lavish home of Oklahoma oil man Waite Phillips; and **Philmont Museum and Seton Memorial Library** houses the library, art, and natural history collections of Boy Scouts of America founder Ernest Thompson Seton. While driving to Philmont from Cimarron watch for bison, raised by the scout ranch, and deer and pronghorn antelope.

From Cimarron, follow US 64 east for 12 more miles to:

17. **Colfax Ruins.** Sitting along the northwest side of the road, these ruins and some abandoned railroad coaches are all that's left of an early 20th-century town.

From the ruins, continue east for about 20 miles to:

18. **NRA Whittington Center,** operated by the National Rifle Association, provides instruction in pistol, rifle, and shotgun shooting, as well as firearms safety.

From here, continue east on US 64 for about 4 miles to I-25 (exit 446), and take I-25 north about 3 miles to:

19. Raton (elevation 6,640 feet). First just a water hole on the Santa Fe Trail, the town was founded in 1879 as a railroad, mining, and ranching center. Start a self-guided walking tour of the city's historic district, described in a brochure available at the **Raton Museum,** 216 1st St (tel 505/445-8979). Housed in a 1906 brewery warehouse, the museum has a variety of memorabilia and displays depicting Raton's early days. Nearby, you'll see the 1903 **Santa Fe Railroad Depot,** the 1896 **Palace Hotel,** and the 1929 **Swastika Hotel,** which became the Yucca Hotel during World War II when the swastika symbol was adopted by the German Nazi Party. Also, don't miss the **Shuler Theater,** 131 N 2nd St (tel 505/445-5528), built in 1915 in European rococo style and recently restored to its former elegance.

Sugarite Canyon State Park, about 8 miles east of Raton via NM 72 and 2 miles north on US 526 (tel 505/445-5607), has hiking trails, picnicking, camping, and fishing in lakes stocked with trout. Watch for wild turkeys, mule deer, and beaver, as well as migratory waterfowl in the fall.

Capulin Volcano National Monument, 30 miles east of Raton via US 64/87 and north 3 miles on NM 325 (tel 505/278-2201), allows you to walk inside a volcano that erupted only a short 10,000 years ago.

For comfortable lodging in Raton, your best bets are the **Best Western Sands Motel** or **Harmony Manor Motel.**

Take a Break

Renowned for its margaritas, **Pappa's Sweet Shop Restaurant,** 1201 S 2nd St (tel 505/445-9811), also specializes in steak and prime rib. Locals recommend the Mexican food at **El Matador,** 1012 S 2nd St (tel 505/445-9575).

From Raton, go south for 24 miles on I-25 to exit 426 at Maxwell, go west off the interstate into Maxwell, and follow NM 445 north less than a mile and then NM 505 west about 2 miles to:

20. Maxwell National Wildlife Refuge (tel 505/375-2331). Fall is the best time to visit this refuge with three lakes, when you're likely to sight ducks, Canadian geese, bald eagles, and possibly American white pelicans and sandhill cranes. There's also a black-tailed prairie dog town, and you may see deer and antelope. Stop at the visitors center for a map.

From the refuge, return to I-25 and continue south about 13 miles to:

21. Springer (exits 414 and 412). Settled in 1879, Springer was the Colfax County seat from 1882 to 1897. The old courthouse, on Maxwell St, today houses the **Santa Fe Trail Museum** (tel 505/483-2341), with memorabilia and historic photographs, as well as the state's only electric chair, used in Santa Fe from 1933 to 1956, when seven convicted murderers were executed.

From Springer, continue south 48 miles on I-25 to exit 366, then travel 8 miles north on NM 161 to:

22. Fort Union National Monument (tel 505/425-8025). Opened in 1851 to protect Santa Fe Trail travelers from Native American attacks, the fort was expanded 10 years later to repel Confederate attacks during the Civil War. There's a self-guided walking trail among the fort's ruins.

From the fort, return 8 miles to I-25, and continue south 22 miles to:

23. Las Vegas. Founded in 1835 as a land grant from the Mexican government, Las Vegas has been a Santa Fe Trail stop, a military outpost, a railroad depot, a commerce center, and a Wild West town. You can view ornate Victorian buildings dating from the town's days of ranching prosperity in the late 1800s, as well as pre-Victorian Spanish Colonial adobes. Begin your visit at the **Rough Riders Museum,** 729 Grand Ave (tel 505/425-8726), with exhibits on Teddy Roosevelt's Rough Riders and area history. Next door at the **Las Vegas/San Miguel County Chamber of Commerce,** 727 Grand Ave (tel 505/425-8631 or toll free 800/832-5947), you can obtain a visitors' guide with a walking tour of the historic plaza and Bridge Street areas, with stops at late 18th- and early 19th-century buildings, including the handsome 1881 **Plaza Hotel,** 230 Old Town Plaza (tel 505/425-3591), beautifully restored in the 1980s. **Las Vegas National Wildlife Refuge,** 6 miles southeast of town via NM 104 and NM 281 (tel 505/425-3581), has opportunities to sight a variety of birds, including geese, bald eagles, and sandhill cranes. There's an overlook and a nature trail.

From Las Vegas, continue south on I-25 for 40 miles to exit 307. Take NM 63 north for 5 miles.

24. Pecos National Historical Park (tel 505/757-6414). This park has a 1¼ mile self guided trail through 13th-century pueblo ruins, a Spanish mission, and a visitors center with exhibits and brochures.

From the park, return 5 miles to I-25, and continue south for 26 miles back to Santa Fe.

ALBUQUERQUE AND THE GREAT NORTHWEST

Start	Albuquerque
Finish	Coronado State Monument, Bernalillo
Distance	611 miles
Time	2–5 days
Highlights	Native American ruins, pueblos, lava flows, museums

When travelers plan a vacation to New Mexico, their itinerary usually covers Santa Fe and Taos, while it overlooks Albuquerque; yet Albuquerque is also an enjoyable city to visit with a good choice of attractions. It's also a fine place to begin your trip before exploring the rest of the state. This tour takes you from Albuquerque to the northwest corner of the state, a sparsely populated, somewhat primitive area, with great distances between services and some of the state's worst roads. However, the tour also takes in Chaco Canyon, the biggest ancient Native American ruin in the Southwest, as well as other cultural, historic, and scenic sites worth visiting. Be advised before setting out that there is no way to get to Chaco Canyon without driving on 20 to 25 miles of dirt road; rain or snow can make the road impassable.

For additional information on lodgings, restaurants, and attractions in the region covered by the tour, refer to specific cities in the listings portion of this chapter.

1. **Albuquerque** (elevation 5,000 feet). New Mexico's largest city is a pleasant blend of cultures—Native American, Spanish, and Anglo. Ancient Native Americans lived in the Sandia Mountains near here some 10,000 years ago, followed by the Anasazi tribe around AD 1100. Next came Spanish conquistadors in the mid-16th century. The railroad brought Anglo-Americans to the region in the 1880s, and the automobile and Route 66 brought even more transplants in the 1930s. Visitors to Albuquerque today find it a comfortable city—just a big Western town, really–with excellent museums, a pleasant climate, and even its own baseball team.

   You'll probably want to spend a few days here, perhaps to allow your body to adapt to the elevation. The city has plenty of lodging choices, including most of the usual chain hotels and motels. In Old Town, you may enjoy the luxurious **Sheraton Old Town** or the historic charm of **Casas de Sueños.** Close to Old Town, off I-40, **Travelers Inn** is an economical choice. For an airport motel, you'll find **Best Western Airport Inn** surprisingly homey and quiet.

   Start your Albuquerque visit in **Old Town,** bounded by Rio Grande Blvd on the west and Central Ave on the south. Browse through some of the area's more than 100 art galleries and specialty shops, where you'll find art for practically any taste, and exquisite pottery, jewelry, weavings, and baskets created by New Mexico's Native American artisans. **San Felipe de Neri Church,** on the north side of Old Town Plaza (tel 505/243-4628), has been in almost continuous use since it was built in 1706. A brochure describing a self-guided Old Town walking tour is available from the **Albuquerque Museum,** 2000 Mountain Rd NW (tel 505/243-7255), which has a huge collection of Spanish colonial artifacts, including armor used by Spanish conquistadors, and historical exhibits.

   Also in Old Town is **Albuquerque Children's Museum,** 800 Rio Grande NW (tel 505/842-5525), with interactive exhibits and activities for ages 2 to 12. **American International Rattlesnake Museum,** 202 San Felipe St NW (tel 505/242-6569), displays just what you'd expect, including an albino rattler. The excellent **New Mexico Museum of Natural History and Science,** 1801 Mountain Rd (tel 505/841-2800), takes a participatory hands-on look at the natural world that's fun and educational for both adults and children; exhibits include an "active" volcano, dinosaurs, and an Ice Age cave. About a half-block west of Old Town, the **Turquoise Museum,** 2107 Central Ave NW (tel 505/247-8650), deals with the mining and uses of turquoise.

   Heading away from Old Town, but still on Albuquerque's west side, the 600-acre **Rio Grande Zoo,** 903 10th St SW (tel 505/843-7413), has more than 1,300 animals from around the world. **Rio Grande Nature Center State Park,** 2901 Candelaria Rd NW (tel 505/344-7240), contains a three-acre pond and marsh, and 2 miles of nature trails along the Rio Grande. Among New Mexico's newest parks, established in 1990, is **Petroglyph National Monument,** 4735 Unser Blvd NW (tel 505/839-4429). Still in development, the park has more than 15,000 prehistoric Native American petroglyphs in lava flows along Albuquerque's West Mesa. Guided tours are offered in summer. The **Indian Pueblo Cultural Center,** 2401 12th St NW, one block north of I-40 (tel 505/843-7270), has

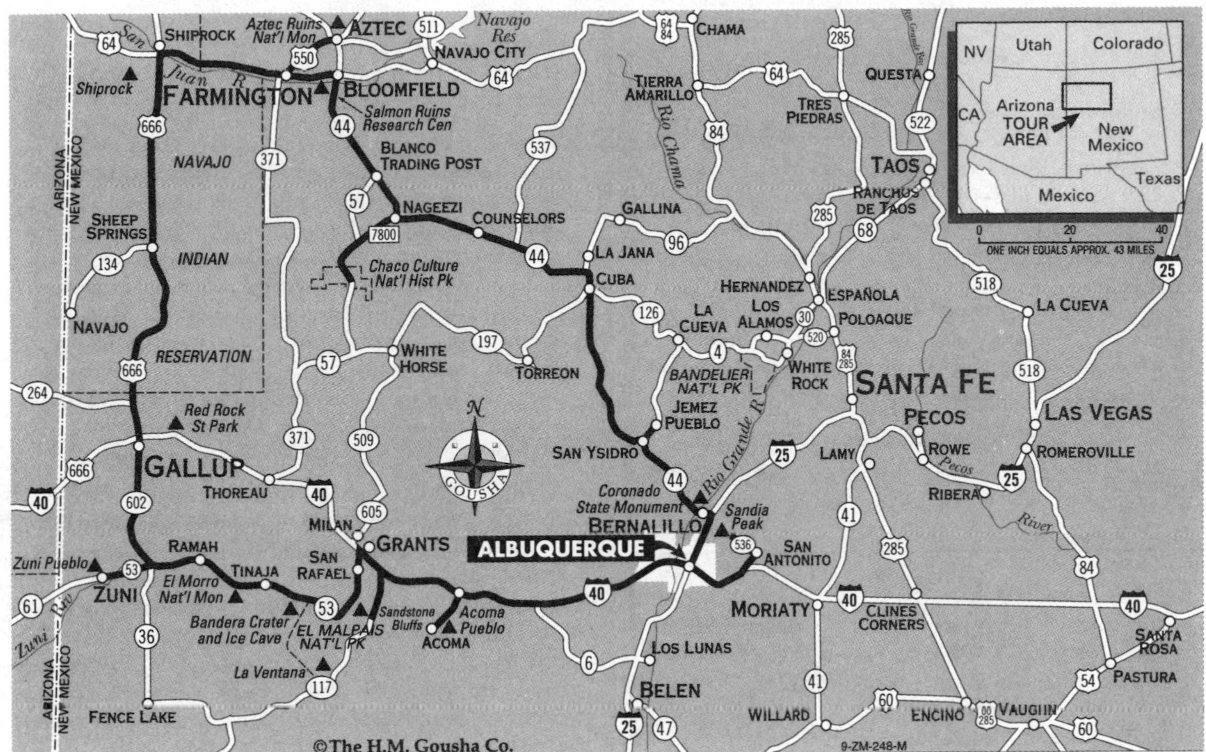

exhibits on New Mexico's 19 pueblos; Native American dance and craft demonstrations are held on weekends.

In southeast Albuquerque, on Kirtland Air Force Base at the corner of Wyoming Blvd and K St, you'll find the **National Atomic Museum** (tel 505/845-6670), with displays detailing the development of nuclear energy. The **University of New Mexico,** north of Central Ave and east of University Blvd (tel 505/277-0111), has five museums, including the acclaimed **Maxwell Museum of Anthropology** and **University Art Museum,** with works by 19th- and 20th-century American and European artists.

If you want a great view of Albuquerque, particularly at sunset, take the **Sandia Peak Aerial Tramway,** 10 Tramway Loop NE (tel 505/856-7325), 2.7 miles up to the summit of 10,378-foot Sandia Peak.

Take a Break

For the best malt in town, or a burger, sandwich, or blue-plate special, stop at **66 Diner,** 1405 Central Ave NE (tel 505/247-1421), west of the University of New Mexico. In Old Town, you can have a genuine New Mexico dining experience at **Maria Teresa,** 618 Rio Grande Blvd NW (tel 505/242-3900).

Those looking for a similar view at a different location might opt for the road to **Sandia Crest.** It's about a one-hour drive from downtown Albuquerque, taking I-40 east to NM 14, which you follow north to NM 536; the latter road takes you to the crest.

Albuquerque visitors may also want to take in an **Albuquerque Dukes** baseball game, 1601 Stadium Blvd SE (tel 505/243-1791), or tackle the slopes at **Sandia Peak Ski Area,** 20 miles northeast of the city (tel 505/242-9052).

Next head west 52 miles on I-40 to exit 108, the Acoma/Sky City turnoff, then 13 miles southwest to:

2. **Acoma Pueblo.** Perched on a high rock mesa, "Sky City," as it is called, is believed to be the oldest continuously occupied US city. Begin your tour at the **Visitor Center** (tel 505/252-1139 or toll free 800/747-0181), with a museum, a cafe, and shops, at the base of the mesa; then board the pueblo's tour bus for a ride to the top. You'll see a large mission church, built in 1629, containing numerous Spanish colonial artifacts, flat-roofed adobe homes; and members of the Acoma tribe selling fry-bread and distinctive white pottery with brown and black designs.

From Acoma, return 13 miles to I-40 and continue west for 19 miles to NM 117 (exit 89), then turn south and go 14 miles to:

3. **El Malpais National Monument** (tel 505/285-5406). El Malpais (which means "the badlands" in Spanish) is a seemingly endless lava-filled valley, produced by more than 3 million years of volcanic eruptions. **Sandstone Bluffs Overlook,** about 10 miles south of I-40, provides fine views of the lava flows, and several miles further south you can see **La Ventana,** one of the state's largest natural arches.

This is the eastern section of El Malpais; you'll see the west side later. Now return 14 miles north on NM 117 back to I-40 (exit 89), and go west 4 miles to exit 85 and:

4. **Grants.** Although Grants began some 100 years ago as a railroad and ranching center, it was not until 1950, with the discovery of uranium, that the town really boomed. Although there is little mining done here today, Grants keeps its short-lived mining tradition alive at **New Mexico Mining Museum,** 100 N Iron St at Santa Fe Ave (tel 505/287-4802 or toll free 800/748-2142), the only uranium mine museum in the world; it offers the experience of a simulated uranium mine, with authentic machinery and equipment.

Take a Break

You can get breakfast all day at **Grants Station Restaurant,** 200 W Santa Fe Ave (tel 505/287-2334), which displays railroad memorabilia, including a caboose. The menu has a variety of American and Mexican standard dishes.

From Grants, at I-40 exit 81, take NM 53 south and west, through the lava flows on the west side of **El Malpais National Monument,** about 25 miles to the next stop:

5. **Bandera Crater and Ice Cave** (tel 505/783-4303), where you can see a gigantic volcanic crater and its lava flows, and the ice cave, which is actually a lava tube that maintains a perpetual mass of ice year-round.

Now continue west on NM 53 for about 16 miles to:

6. **El Morro National Monument** (tel 505/783-4226). This fascinating national monument has something for everyone—spectacular scenery, Anasazi pueblo ruins, several self-guiding trails, and the famous **Inscription Rock,** where conquistadors, pioneers, and other travelers have left messages dating back to 1605. Much earlier Anasazi petroglyphs may be seen along the cliffs, including carvings of geometric designs and animals.

From the monument, drive west on NM 53 about 34 miles to:

7. **Zuni Pueblo** (tel 505/782-4481). Famous for its inlaid silver and turquoise jewelry, Zuni is among New Mexico's largest inhabited pueblos. Stop at **Zuni Arts and Crafts** (tel 505/782-5532), a tribal-owned arts and crafts market, and explore the exhibits at the **Zuni Museum Project** to learn about Zuni culture. **Our Lady of Guadalupe Mission** is decorated with murals by Zuni artist Alex Seowtewa.

From Zuni, return 10 miles east on NM 53 to the intersection with NM 602, and go north about 30 miles to:

8. **Gallup.** Traditionally a commerce center for Navajo, Zuni, and other tribes, Gallup has dozens of trading posts, galleries, and shops that specialize in Native American arts and crafts. Just east of town, **Red Rock State Park** (tel 505/722-3829) contains several archeological sites of the Anasazi, an 1888 trading post building, and a museum with exhibits on both prehistoric and modern Native Americans in the area and displays of Native American arts and crafts.

Also in Gallup, look for historic buildings along a remaining section of old US Route 66, here designated 66 Ave. Among these gems is **El Rancho Hotel & Motel,** built in 1937 and New Mexico and Arizona headquarters for film companies from the 1930s through the 1960s. El Rancho makes a fun stop for the night; for a more modern motel, try the economical **Blue Spruce Lodge** or one of the three **Best Westerns** in town.

From Gallup, take US 666 north through the Navajo Reservation 86 miles to:

9. **Ship Rock.** This prominent rock formation (1,700 feet tall), which you can see off to the west from several view points, is called "Rock with Wings" by the Navajos; others find it resembles a tall sailing ship. The rock is sacred to the Navajos and climbing it is prohibited.

From Ship Rock, continue about 7 miles to its namesake town of Shiprock, and take US 64 east for 29 miles to:

10. **Farmington** (elevation 5,395 feet). By far the biggest city in northwest New Mexico, this is a good home base for trips into the Navajo Reservation, Mesa Verde National Park in southeast Colorado, and Chaco Culture National Historical Park. Lodging choices here include **Holiday Inn of Farmington** and the **Anasazi Inn,** and the nostalgic 1950s-style **Enchantment Lodge** in nearby Aztec.

Aztec Ruins National Monument, about 15 miles northeast of Farmington and just past the town of Aztec on US 550 (tel 505/334-6174), includes the ruins of a 500-room pueblo, apparently abandoned by the Anasazi seven centuries ago. The monument contains the only reconstructed Anasazi great kiva (religious chamber) in existence. The visitors center has exhibits of baskets and pottery discovered in the ruins. Back in Farmington, visit the **Farmington Museum,** 302 N Orchard St (tel 505/599-1174), with exhibits on the area's history, including a replica of a 1930s trading post.

Take a Break

You'll find good Mexican food at **Señor Pepper's Restaurant,** Four Corners Regional Airport (tel 505/237-0436); and for those who enjoy a classic pub atmosphere there's **Clancy's Pub,** 2703 E 20th St (tel 505/325-8176).

From Farmington, go east 11 miles on US 64 until you reach:

11. **Salmon Ruin Research Center** (tel 505/632-2013). This large pueblo, built in the late 11th century, contains a rare elevated kiva, as well as a more traditional kiva. The center also has a museum displaying artifacts from the site, and **Heritage Park,** with reconstructed buildings representing different periods of the area's history.

From Salmon Ruin, continue east on US 64 for 2 miles to Bloomfield, take NM 44 south about 44 miles to Nageezi, go southwest on San Juan County Rd 7800 for 11 miles, then south on NM 57 for 15 miles to:

12. **Chaco Culture National Historical Park** (tel 505/-988-6727). This was once the New York City of the ancient Anasazi, when all roads led to Chaco. Occupied from about AD 900 to 1200, this historical park (elevation 6,300 feet), includes ruins of more than a dozen large Anasazi villages and hundreds of smaller sites. At its height in the 12th century, the oldest and largest village, Pueblo Bonito, towered four stories with some 600 rooms and 40 kivas. Although many parts of Chaco may be seen from roadways, some of the best views involve at least short hikes. A visitors center has exhibits and shows films on area history and cultures. *Warning:* In rainy or snowy weather the road from Nageezi into Chaco Culture National Historical Park may be impassable. Check with the park office before setting out.

From Chaco, return the 26 miles to Nageezi, turn east onto NM 44 and go 91 miles to San Ysidro, turn north onto NM 4 and drive 4 miles to:

13. **Jemez Pueblo.** Stop at the **Walatowa Visitor Center** (tel 505/834-7235) for information on this pueblo, known for its dances, pottery, and sculpture. In the **Red Rock Scenic Area,** you'll find roadside stands with traditional foods and arts and crafts. No photography is permitted.

From the Pueblo, return 4 miles to San Ysidro and continue southeast on NM 44 for about 23 miles to:

14. **Coronado State Monument** (tel 505/867-5351). This state monument preserves the ruins of a 15th-century Anasazi pueblo called Kuaua, with hundreds of excavated rooms and a reconstructed kiva ceremonial chamber. Anasazi murals with drawings of people and animals are also on display.

Continue on NM 44 about 2 miles into Bernalillo, then go south on I-25 for 12 miles to return to Albuquerque.

New Mexico Listings

Acoma Pueblo

The spectacular "Sky City," a walled adobe village perched high atop a sheer rock mesa 357 feet above the valley floor, Acoma Pueblo is said to have been inhabited since at least the 11th century. This makes it the longest continuously occupied community in the United States. Tour buses board at the visitor center at the base of the mesa and then climb through a rock garden of 50-foot sandstone monoliths to the mesa's summit. Transparent mica stone windows are prevalent among the 300-odd adobe structures.

Also located on the mesa is the mission church of **San Estevan del Rey.** Built in 1639, it contains numerous masterpieces of Spanish colonial art. The annual San Estevan del Rey feast day is held September 2, when the pueblo's patron saint is honored with a midmorning mass, a procession, an afternoon corn dance, and an arts-and-crafts fair. To reach Acoma from Grants, drive east 15 miles on I-40 to McCartys, then south 13 miles on paved tribal roads to the visitor center. For more information about Sky City contact Acoma Pueblo at 505/252-1139, or toll free at 800/747-0181.

Alamogordo

See also Cloudcroft, Mescalero

Known best for the world's first explosion of an atomic bomb at nearby Trinity Site on July 16, 1945, Alamogordo is home to a large air force base and missile test site. The city is popular with visitors to White Sands National Monument and Lincoln National Forest. **Information:** Alamogordo Chamber of Commerce, 1301 White Sands Blvd, ·PO Box 518, Alamogordo 88310 (tel 505/437-6120 or 800/545-4021).

MOTEL

Days Inn Alamogordo
907 S White Sands Blvd, 88310; tel 505/437-5090 or toll free 800/325-2525; fax 505/434-5667. A pleasant, standard motel, offering basic services and amenities. **Rooms:** 40 rms. CI 2pm/CO 11am. Nonsmoking rms avail. **Amenities:** A/C, cable TV w/movies. **Services:** **Facilities:** Washer/dryer. **Rates (CP):** $41–$48 S; $48–$55 D. Extra person $8. Children under age 13 stay free. Parking: Outdoor, free. AE, DC, DISC, MC, V.

RESTAURANTS

Kegs Brewery and Fine Dining
817 Scenic Dr; tel 505/437-9564. **American.** A friendly, dimly lit place, with ceiling fans, record albums, and movie and car posters on the walls. Offers steaks and fresh seafood, as well as ostrich fajitas and hamburgers, pasta, salads, and Mexican dishes. The bar is open until 2am. **FYI:** Reservations accepted. Big band/country music/rock. Children's menu. **Open:** Mon–Sat 11am–9pm. **Prices:** Main courses $8–$22. DISC, MC, V.

Ramona's
2913 N White Sands Blvd; tel 505/437-7616. **American/ Mexican.** Cheerful, open dining room. Specializes in Mexican food, but also serves steak, chicken, trout, hamburgers, and sandwiches. Favorites are the special Mexican plate and the chimichangas. Locally grown chile peppers are used. **FYI:** Reservations accepted. Children's menu. Beer and wine only. **Open:** Daily 6am–10pm. **Prices:** Main courses $6–$11. AE, MC, V.

ATTRACTIONS

White Sands National Monument
US 70/82; tel 505/479-6124. The park preserves the best part of the world's largest gypsum dune field, an area of 275 miles of pure white gypsum sand that reaches out over the floor of the Tularosa Basin in wavelike dunes. The 16-mile Dunes Drive loops through the "heart of sands" from the visitors center. Visitors can leave their cars at established parking areas to explore the area on foot. **Open:** Peak (Mem Day–Labor Day) dunes drive, daily 7am–10pm; visitors center, daily 8am–7pm. Reduced hours off-season. **$$**

Space Center
Scenic Dr and Indian Wells Rd; tel 505/437-2840 or toll free 800/545-4021. This is in two parts—the **International Space Hall of Fame** and the **Clyde W Tombaugh Space Theater.** The Space Hall of Fame occupies the Golden Cube, a five-story building with walls of golden glass. Exhibits recall the

accomplishments of the first astronauts and cosmonauts. Also on display are a spacecraft and a lunar exploration model, a space-station plan, a hands-on cutaway of a crew module called Space Station 2001, and explanations of life in space aboard Skylab and Salyut. On adjacent grounds is the Sonic Wind sled, which tested human endurance to speeds exceeding 600 mph in preparation for future space flights. At the Tombaugh Theater, Omnimax and Spitz 512 Planetarium Systems create earthly and cosmic experiences on a 2,700-square-foot screen. Twenty special-effects projectors can show 2,354 stars, the Milky Way, all the visible planets, and the sun and moon. Call ahead for show times. **Open:** Daily 9am–5pm. **$**

Alameda Park Zoo
1321 N White Sands Blvd; tel 505/439-4290. Established in 1898, it is the oldest zoo in the Southwest. Its collection includes hundreds of mammals and birds from around the world. **Open:** Daily 9am–5pm. **$**

Tularosa Basin Historical Society Museum
1301 N White Sands Blvd; tel 505/437-6120. Artifacts and photographs recall regional history. **Open:** Mon–Sat 10am–4pm. **Free**

Oliver Lee Memorial State Park
409 Dog Canyon Rd; tel 505/437-8284. Nestled at the mouth of Dog Canyon in a stunning break in the steep escarpment of the Sacramento Mountains, this site has drawn human visitors for thousands of years. Dog Canyon was one of the last strongholds of the Mescalero Apache, and was the site of battles between them and the US Cavalry in the 19th century. Today, springs and seeps support a variety of rare and endangered plant species, as well as a rich wildlife. Hiking trails into the foothills are well marked; the park also offers picnic and camping grounds. **Open:** Park: daily 7am–9pm. Visitors center: 9am–4pm. **$**

Albuquerque

See also Belen, Bernalillo, Los Lumas

Located on the upper Rio Grande in west-central New Mexico, Albuquerque is the state's largest city. It is popular for its sunny, moderate climate, nearby mountains, and quaint and artsy Old Town, founded by Spanish colonists in 1706. Though a new downtown, with a convention center, luxury hotels, financial district of glass skyscapers, and underground shopping mall, is emerging just to the north of the old center, Albuquerque retains strong elements of its original western spirit. Meanwhile, the University of New Mexico lends the city youthful energy as well as outstanding cultural programs and museums. Big events include the state fair in September and a huge hot air balloon rally in October. **Information:** Albuquerque Convention & Visitors Bureau, 121 Tijeras Ave NE, PO Box 26866, Albuquerque 87125-6866 (tel 505/243-3696 or 800/284-2282).

HOTELS

Albuquerque Hilton
1901 University Blvd NE, 87102; tel 505/884-2500 or toll free 800/821-1901; fax 505/889-9118. Menaul Blvd exit off I-25. A lovely, well-kept, and surprisingly quiet hotel just a block off I-25, with a gracious, comfortable atmosphere. **Rooms:** 264 rms and stes. Executive level. CI 3pm/CO noon. Nonsmoking rms avail. **Amenities:** A/C, cable TV w/movies, dataport, voice mail. All units w/terraces. Refrigerators are available; some rooms have bathroom telephones. **Services:** Twice-daily maid svce, car-rental desk, masseur, babysitting. **Facilities:** 1000 3 restaurants (*see* "Restaurants" below), 2 bars (1 w/entertainment), sauna, whirlpool. **Rates:** $109–$149 S; $119–$159 D; $325–$425 ste. Extra person $10. Children under age 18 stay free. Parking: Outdoor, free. AE, DC, DISC, MC, V.

Albuquerque Marriott Hotel
2101 Louisiana Blvd NE, 87110; tel 505/581-6800 or toll free 800/334-2086; fax 505/881-1780. This is a luxurious, full-service high-rise hotel close to Albuquerque's two major shopping centers and uptown businesses. **Rooms:** 410 rms and stes. CI 3pm/CO noon. Nonsmoking rms avail. **Amenities:** A/C, cable TV w/movies, refrig, voice mail. Some units w/minibars. **Services:** Babysitting. **Facilities:** 1100 1 restaurant, 1 bar, spa, sauna, whirlpool, washer/dryer. **Rates:** $140 S or D; $250 ste. Extra person $10. Parking: Outdoor, free. AE, DC, DISC, JCB, MC, V.

Best Western Fred Harvey
2910 Yale Blvd SE, 87106; tel 505/843-7000 or toll free 800/227-1117; fax 505/843-6307. Exit 222A (Gibson Ave) off I-25. In a good location for business travelers, right near the airport. **Rooms:** 266 rms and stes. Executive level. CI 1pm/CO noon. Nonsmoking rms avail. **Amenities:** A/C, cable TV w/movies. All units w/terraces. **Services:** **Facilities:** 2 400 2 restaurants, 1 bar, spa, sauna, washer/dryer. **Rates:** $93–$99 S; $103–$109 D; $150–$300 ste. Extra person $10. Children under age 18 stay free. Min stay special events. Parking: Outdoor, free. DISC, MC, V.

Holiday Inn Pyramid
5151 San Francisco Rd NE, 87109; tel 505/821-3333 or toll free 800/HOLIDAY; fax 505/828-0230. Exit 232 off I-25. A luxurious hotel on the north side of Albuquerque, especially suitable for business travelers and conventioneers. **Rooms:** 311 rms and stes. CI 3pm/CO noon. Nonsmoking rms avail. Rooms are well-appointed and very comfortable. **Amenities:** A/C, cable TV w/movies, refrig. Some units w/terraces. **Services:** Car-rental desk, children's program, babysitting. **Facilities:** 1300 2 restaurants, 2 bars (1 w/entertainment), spa, sauna, steam

rm, whirlpool, washer/dryer. **Rates:** $100–$130 S; $110–$140 D; $122 ste. Extra person $10. Children under age 17 stay free. Parking: Outdoor, free. AE, CB, DC, DISC, MC, V.

Hyatt Regency
330 Tijeras Ave NW, 87102; tel 505/842-1234 or toll free 800/233-1234; fax 505/766-6710. A luxurious high-rise hotel, catering to practically every need of the business or pleasure traveler. Next to the Albuquerque Convention Center. **Rooms:** 395 rms and stes. Executive level. CI 3pm/CO noon. Nonsmoking rms avail. **Amenities:** A/C, cable TV w/movies, voice mail. Some units w/whirlpools. **Services:** Car-rental desk, masseur. **Facilities:** 1 restaurant (*see* "Restaurants" below), 2 bars (1 w/entertainment), sauna. **Rates:** $145–$150 S; $160–$165 D; $325–$425 ste. Extra person $15. Children under age 13 stay free. Parking: Indoor, $8–$11/day. AE, DC, DISC, MC, V.

La Posada de Albuquerque
125 2nd St NW, 87102; tel 505/242-9090 or toll free 800/777-5732; fax 505/242-8664. 1 block N of Central Ave. Charming, historic hotel, built by Conrad Hilton in 1939. **Rooms:** 114 rms and stes. CI 3pm/CO 11am. Nonsmoking rms avail. Rooms have southwestern decor, with handmade furniture and Mexican tiles. **Amenities:** A/C, cable TV w/movies, refrig. **Services:** **Facilities:** 1 restaurant, 2 bars (1 w/entertainment), beauty salon. Guests have access to a health club next door. **Rates:** $102–$107 S; $112–$117 D; $195–$275 ste. Extra person $10. Children under age 18 stay free. Parking: Outdoor, free. AE, CB, DC, DISC, MC, V.

Ramada Plaza
6815 Menaul Blvd NE, 87110; tel 505/881-0000 or toll free 800/252-7772; fax 505/881-3736. Exit 162 off I-40. An attractive uptown hotel, adjacent to Albuquerque's largest shopping mall and close to the city's business and financial district. A good location for both business travelers and vacationers. **Rooms:** 297 rms and stes. Executive level. CI 2pm/CO noon. Nonsmoking rms avail. **Amenities:** A/C, cable TV w/movies, refrig, voice mail. Some units w/whirlpools. **Services:** American Airlines ticket counter in the lobby. **Facilities:** 2 restaurants, 1 bar (w/entertainment), spa, sauna, whirlpool, washer/dryer. Close to tennis, golf, and downhill skiing. The main ballroom has crystal chandeliers and a Wurlitzer organ. **Rates:** $99–$109 S; $109–$129 D; $175–$350 ste. Extra person $10. Children under age 12 stay free. Parking: Outdoor, free. AE, CB, DC, DISC, MC, V.

Residence Inn
3300 Prospect Ave NE, 87107; tel 505/881-2661 or toll free 800/331-3131; fax 505/884-5551. Exit 160 off I-40. Centrally located, and a good choice for those staying more than a night or two. **Rooms:** 112 stes. CI 2pm/CO noon. Nonsmoking rms avail. Condominium-like units have complete kitchens. **Amenities:** A/C, cable TV w/movies, refrig. Some units w/terraces, all w/fireplaces. **Services:** **Facilities:** 1 Spa, whirlpool, washer/dryer. **Rates (CP):** $75–$140 ste. Children under age 12 stay free. Parking: Outdoor, free. AE, DC, DISC, MC, V.

Sheraton Old Town
800 Rio Grande Blvd NW, 87104 (Old Town); tel 505/843-6300 or toll free 800/237-2133; fax 505/842-9863. A luxurious hotel in historic Old Town, within walking distance of numerous restaurants, shops, and attractions. **Rooms:** 190 rms and stes. Executive level. CI 3pm/CO noon. Nonsmoking rms avail. Rooms have new, locally crafted Southwestern furniture and new mattresses. **Amenities:** A/C, TV w/movies, refrig. All units w/minibars, some w/terraces. **Services:** Social director, masseur, babysitting. **Facilities:** 2 restaurants, 2 bars, whirlpool, beauty salon. **Rates:** Peak (Feb–Nov) $100–$110 S; $110–$120 D; $140 ste. Extra person $10. Children under age 19 stay free. Lower rates off-season. Parking: Outdoor, free. AE, CB, DC, DISC, MC, V.

Wyndam Garden Hotel
6000 Pan American Fwy NE, 87109; tel 505/821-9451 or toll free 800/544-9881; fax 505/858-0239. Handsome hotel in northeast part of town, close to I-25 access. Underwent major renovation in 1995. **Rooms:** 151 rms. CI 3pm/CO noon. Nonsmoking rms avail. **Amenities:** A/C, cable TV w/movies, VCR, in-rm safe. Some units w/terraces. Refrigerators available. **Services:** Twice-daily maid svce, babysitting. *USA Today* delivered to room Mon–Fri. **Facilities:** 1 restaurant, 1 bar, spa, sauna, washer/dryer. Small fitness room with machines but no weights. **Rates (BB):** $84–$79 S; $94–$89 D. Extra person $10. Children under age 19 stay free. Parking: Outdoor, free. AE, CB, DC, DISC, MC, V.

MOTELS

Amberly Suite Hotel
7620 Pan American NE, 87109; tel 505/823-1300 or toll free 800/333-9806; fax 505/823-2896. Exit 231 off I-25. These apartment-like units are excellent for families or business travelers who need extra room to work. **Rooms:** 170 rms, stes, and effic. CI 3pm/CO noon. Nonsmoking rms avail. Comfortable, homey rooms. **Amenities:** A/C, cable TV w/movies, refrig. **Services:** Babysitting. **Facilities:** 1 restaurant, 1 bar, spa, sauna, whirlpool, washer/dryer. The fitness center is open 24 hours. **Rates:** $103–$109 S; $122–$132 D; $122–$132 ste; $103–$109 effic. Extra person $10. Children under age 12 stay free. Parking: Outdoor, free. AE, CB, DC, DISC, MC, V.

American Inn
4501 Central Ave NE, 87108 (Nob Hill); tel 505/262-1681. Good, basic lodging near the University of New Mexico campus. **Rooms:** 130 rms and stes. CI open/CO 11am. Nonsmoking rms avail. **Amenities:** A/C, cable TV

w/movies. Some units w/terraces. **Services:** Babysitting. **Facilities:** **Rates:** $24 S; $28–$34 D; $35 ste. Extra person $10. Children under age 12 stay free. Parking: Outdoor, free. AE, DC, DISC, MC, V.

Best Western Airport Inn

2400 Yale Blvd SE, 87106; tel 505/242-7022 or toll free 800/528-1234; fax 505/243-0620. A Mexican hacienda–style motel, close to Albuquerque International Airport. **Rooms:** 120 rms. CI 1pm/CO noon. Nonsmoking rms avail. Pleasant, comfortable rooms, decorated with silk flowers, posters, and old photos. Surprisingly quiet. **Amenities:** A/C, cable TV w/movies. Some units w/terraces. **Services:** The adjacent Village Inn restaurant provides take-out and occasional room service. **Facilities:** Whirlpool. **Rates (CP):** Peak (Apr 15–Oct) $60–$70 S; $65 D. Extra person $5. Children under age 12 stay free. Lower rates off-season. Parking: Outdoor, free. AE, DC, DISC, MC, V.

Best Western Winrock Inn

18 Winrock Center NE, 87110; tel 505/883-5252 or toll free 800/866-5252; fax 505/889-3206. Louisiana Blvd exit off I-40. A conveniently located urban motel adjacent to a major shopping center. **Rooms:** 173 rms and stes. CI 3pm/CO noon. Nonsmoking rms avail. **Amenities:** A/C, cable TV w/movies. Some units w/terraces. Suites have refrigerators. **Services:** Rates include two evening cocktails per adult and soft drinks for children. **Facilities:** 1 bar, washer/dryer. **Rates (BB):** $59–$95 S; $66–$125 D; $105–$125 ste. Extra person $7. Children under age 17 stay free. Parking: Outdoor, free. AE, CB, DC, DISC, MC, V.

Clubhouse Inn

1315 Menaul Blvd NE, 87107; tel 505/345-0010 or toll free 800/258-2466; fax 505/344-3911. Lomas Ave exit off I-25. A homey, centrally located motel. **Rooms:** 154 rms and stes. CI 2pm/CO noon. Nonsmoking rms avail. Guest rooms have plenty of work space. **Amenities:** A/C, cable TV w/movies. Some units w/terraces, some w/whirlpools. Suites have refrigerators, microwaves, and wet bars. **Services:** Babysitting. Coffee, tea, and hot chocolate are available 24 hours. **Facilities:** Whirlpool, washer/dryer. Besides the pool, the patio has a sun deck and barbecue grills. **Rates (BB):** $66–$68 S; $68–$78 D; $83–$93 ste. Extra person $10. Children under age 16 stay free. Parking: Outdoor, free. AE, DC, DISC, MC, V.

Courtyard by Marriott

1920 Yale Blvd SE, 87106 (Albuquerque Int'l Airport); tel 505/843-6600 or toll free 800/321-2211; fax 505/843-8740. Gibson Blvd exit off I-25. Well-appointed motel, close to the airport. **Rooms:** 150 rms and stes. CI 4pm/CO 1pm. Nonsmoking rms avail. **Amenities:** A/C, cable TV w/movies, refrig, voice mail. There are extra-long phone cords, a large work desk, and shower massage. **Services:** Babysitting. In-room coffee and tea service provided. **Facilities:** 1 restaurant (bkfst and dinner only), 1 bar, spa, whirlpool, washer/dryer. **Rates:** $86 S; $96 D; $105–$115 ste. Children under age 16 stay free. Parking: Outdoor, free. AE, CB, DC, DISC, MC, V.

Fairfield Inn

1760 Menaul Rd NE, 87102; tel 505/889-4000 or toll free 800/228-2800; fax 505/889-4000. Exit 227A off I-25. This new Marriott-owned property has many of the amenities and services found at fancier hotels but at more economical rates. **Rooms:** 189 rms and stes. CI 3pm/CO noon. Nonsmoking rms avail. **Amenities:** A/C, cable TV w/movies. Some units w/terraces. **Services:** Coupons available for children's amusements in Albuquerque. **Facilities:** Sauna, whirlpool, washer/dryer. **Rates (CP):** $53 S; $63–$74 D; $125 ste. Extra person $10. Children under age 19 stay free. Parking: Outdoor, free. AE, DC, DISC, MC, V.

Hampton Inn

5101 Ellison NE, 87109; tel 505/344-1555 or toll free 800/426-7866; fax 505/345-2216. Exit 231 off I-25. A better-than-average motel on the north side of Albuquerque, a good location for those viewing the annual balloon fiesta in October, or planning day trips to Santa Fe. **Rooms:** 125 rms. CI 2pm/CO noon. Nonsmoking rms avail. **Amenities:** A/C, cable TV w/movies. **Services:** **Facilities:** **Rates (CP):** $58–$69 S or D. Children under age 18 stay free. Parking: Outdoor, free. AE, CB, DC, DISC, JCB, MC, V.

Holiday Inn Mountain View

2020 Menaul Blvd NE, 87107; tel 505/884-2511; fax 505/884-5720. An attractive motel conveniently located near both I-25 and I-40. **Rooms:** 363 rms. CI 2pm/CO noon. Nonsmoking rms avail. There are king leisure rooms designed for business travelers. **Amenities:** A/C, cable TV w/movies. Some units w/terraces, some w/whirlpools. **Services:** **Facilities:** 1 restaurant, 1 bar (w/entertainment), spa, sauna, whirlpool, washer/dryer. **Rates:** Peak (Mar–Oct) $95–$105 S; $100–$110 D. Extra person $10. Children under age 18 stay free. Lower rates off-season. Parking: Outdoor, free. AE, CB, DC, DISC, JCB, MC, V.

La Quinta Inn

2116 Yale Blvd SE, 87106; tel 505/243-5500 or toll free 800/531-5900; fax 505/247-8288. 1 mi E of I-25 Gibson/airport exit. Pleasant motel close to Albuquerque International Airport. **Rooms:** 105 rms and stes. CI 3pm/CO noon. Nonsmoking rms avail. Attractive, nicely furnished rooms. **Amenities:** A/C, cable TV w/movies. All units w/terraces. **Services:** **Facilities:** Washer/dryer. **Rates:** $61–$69 S; $70–$77 D; $85–$100 ste. Extra person $8. Children under age 18 stay free. Parking: Outdoor, free. AE, CB, DC, DISC, MC, V.

Le Baron Inn and Suites

2120 Menaul Blvd NE, 87107; tel 505/884-0250 or toll free 800/444-7378; fax 505/883-0594. Exit 160 off I-40. A well-appointed motel in the center of Albuquerque. **Rooms:** 200

rms and stes. CI 3pm/CO noon. Nonsmoking rms avail. Basic rooms are simply but nicely decorated; the suites are more plush. **Amenities:** A/C, cable TV w/movies. 1 unit w/whirlpool. Suites have refrigerators and microwaves. **Services:** Babysitting. **Facilities:** 50 Washer/dryer. **Rates (CP):** $55 S; $65 D; $75–$140 ste. Children under age 19 stay free. Parking: Outdoor, free. AE, CB, DC, DISC, MC, V.

Motel 6
1701 University Blvd NE, 87102; tel 505/843-9228. Exit 160 off I-40. A clean, basic motel for the budget-conscious. **Rooms:** 118 rms. CI 2pm/CO noon. Nonsmoking rms avail. Simple but quite adequate. **Amenities:** A/C, cable TV w/movies. **Services:** Babysitting. **Facilities:** **Rates:** $30 S; $36 D. Extra person $3. Children under age 17 stay free. Parking: Outdoor, free. AE, CB, DC, DISC, MC, V.

Plaza Inn
900 Medical Arts Ave NE, 87102; tel 505/243-5693 or toll free 800/237-1307; fax 505/843-6229. Located close to the University of New Mexico and the attractions and restaurants of historic Old Town. Offers similar services and amenities to larger, more expensive motels. **Rooms:** 120 rms. CI 3pm/CO noon. Nonsmoking rms avail. Pleasantly decorated rooms have large desks. **Amenities:** A/C, cable TV w/movies, refrig. Some units w/terraces. **Services:** Babysitting. **Facilities:** 50 1 restaurant, 1 bar, spa, washer/dryer. **Rates:** $70–$85 S or D. Extra person $5. Children under age 12 stay free. Parking: Outdoor, free. AE, CB, DC, DISC, MC, V.

Radisson Inn
1901 University Blvd SE, 87106 (Albuquerque Int'l Airport); tel 505/247-0512 or toll free 800/333-3333; fax 505/843-7148. A handsome property right near the airport. **Rooms:** 148 rms and stes. CI 3pm/CO noon. Nonsmoking rms avail. Spacious rooms have queen- or king-size beds. **Amenities:** A/C, cable TV w/movies. **Services:** Babysitting. **Facilities:** 200 1 restaurant, 1 bar (w/entertainment), whirlpool. **Rates:** $85 S; $95 D; $95 ste. Extra person $10. Children under age 17 stay free. Parking: Outdoor, free. AE, CB, DC, DISC, ER, MC, V.

Travelers Inn
411 McKnight Ave NW, 87102; tel 505/242-5228 or toll free 800/633-8300; fax 505/766-9218. Exit 159A off I-40. A well-kept motel built in 1991. Close to the shops, galleries, and attractions of historic Old Town. **Rooms:** 99 rms and stes. CI 2pm/CO 11am. Nonsmoking rms avail. The simple rooms are comfortable and furnished in wood tones, with stucco walls. **Amenities:** A/C, cable TV w/movies. **Services:** Complimentary coffee and tea available 24 hours in lobby. **Facilities:** 80 Whirlpool. **Rates (CP):** $41 S; $48 D; $62–$69 ste. Extra person $4. Children under age 12 stay free. Parking: Outdoor, free. AE, CB, DC, DISC, MC, V.

INNS

Casas de Suenos
310 Rio Grande Blvd SW, 87104 (Old Town); tel 505/247-4560 or toll free 800/CHAT-W/US; fax 505/842-8493. A delightful getaway in historic Old Town. Lovely shaded grounds. Unsuitable for children under 13. **Rooms:** 18 stes. CI 3–7pm/CO 11am. No smoking. Spanish-style decor; each unit follows individual theme. Some units have small waterfalls nearby. **Amenities:** A/C, cable TV w/movies, voice mail. All units w/terraces, some w/fireplaces, some w/whirlpools. **Services:** Afternoon tea and wine/sherry served. **Facilities:** Guest lounge. **Rates (BB):** $85–$245 ste. Extra person $15. Min stay special events. Parking: Outdoor, free. One-bedroom suite $85–$195, two-bedroom suite $175–$245. AE, DC, DISC, MC, V.

The WE Mauger Estate
701 Roma Ave NW, 87102; tel 505/242-8755. A delightful historic inn within walking distance of museums, Old Town, and several restaurants and night clubs. Close to nature center and new Albuquerque Aquarium. **Rooms:** 9 rms. CI 4–6pm/CO 11am. No smoking. Rooms are charmingly decorated in country Victorian; each with its own thermostat control; showers only. **Amenities:** A/C, refrig, bathrobes. No TV. 1 unit w/terrace, 1 w/fireplace. Guest lounge offers cable TV and about 200 recorded movies. **Services:** Babysitting, afternoon tea and wine/sherry served. **Facilities:** Whirlpool, guest lounge w/TV. **Rates (BB):** $65–$80 S; $115–$140 D. Extra person $1–$15. Min stay special events. Higher rates for special events/hols. Parking: Outdoor, free. AE, DC, DISC, MC, V.

RESTAURANTS

Artichoke Cafe
424 Central Ave SE; tel 505/243-0200. 1½ blocks E of Broadway. **New American/French.** Art deco dining room with modern art on the walls and tin ceilings. Imaginative variations on American and continental cuisine, including baked chicken stuffed with goat cheese, spinach and roasted red pepper, pumpkin ravioli, and New Zealand mussels with sweet Italian sausage in white wine. **FYI:** Reservations recommended. Beer and wine only. No smoking. **Open:** Lunch Mon–Fri 11am–2:30pm; dinner Mon–Sat 5:30–10pm. **Prices:** Main courses $10–$20. AE, DC, DISC, MC, V.

Bangkok Cafe
5901 Central Ave NE; tel 505/255-5036. 2 blocks E of San Mateo Blvd. **Thai.** Genuine Thai cuisine. Especially popular is Thai pad priew whan goong, which is Thai-style sweet-and-sour shrimp. **FYI:** Reservations not accepted. Beer and wine only. **Open:** Lunch Mon–Fri 11am–2pm; dinner Sun–Thurs 5–9pm, Fri–Sat 5–9:30pm. **Prices:** Main courses $5–$10. AE, CB, DC, DISC, MC, V.

Cafe Oceana
1414 Central Ave SE; tel 505/247-2233. **Seafood.** Located in a historic 1928 building featuring tin ceilings and hardwood floors, a nice patio, and a recently expanded bar/lounge area. Fresh seafood is this restaurant's calling: scallop and shrimp alfredo, Rocky Mountain trout, Duke City barbecued shrimp, and catch of the day. There's also a popular oyster bar. **FYI:** Reservations recommended. Children's menu. Jacket required. **Open:** Lunch Mon–Fri 11am–3pm; dinner Mon–Thurs 5–11pm, Fri–Sat 5–11:30pm. **Prices:** Main courses $12–$24. AE, CB, DC, DISC, MC, V.

Catalina's Mexican Restaurant
400 San Felipe St NW (Old Town); tel 505/842-6907. **Mexican.** Located in a historic adobe building. Traditional New Mexico–style Mexican food. Patio dining in warm weather. **FYI:** Reservations accepted. Children's menu. No liquor license. **Open:** Sun–Wed 8am–5pm, Thurs–Sat 8am–8pm. Closed Jan 15–Feb. **Prices:** Main courses $4–$7. AE, MC, V.

Cervante's
5801 Gibson Blvd SE; tel 505/262-2253. At San Pedro Blvd. **Mexican.** Classic Spanish decor. New Mexico–style Mexican food, including chiles rellenos, enchiladas, burritos, and stuffed sopaipillas. **FYI:** Reservations accepted. **Open:** Mon–Sat 11am–10pm, Sun noon–9pm. **Prices:** Main courses $6–$14. AE, CB, DC, DISC, MC, V.

Chili's Grill and Bar
6909 Menaul Blvd NE; tel 505/883-4321. **Burgers/Southwestern.** Casual bar atmosphere. Features burgers, available with or without green chiles or guacamole, and steaks, chicken, and Mexican dishes. **FYI:** Reservations not accepted. **Open:** Mon–Thurs 11am–11pm, Fri–Sun 11am–midnight. **Prices:** Main courses $6–$13. MC, V.

The Cooperage
7220 Lomas Blvd NE; tel 505/255-1657. 3 blocks E of NM State Fairgrounds. **Seafood/Steak.** The circular, wood-paneled dining room is decorated with reproductions of 19th-century art. There's a wide variety of beef, seafood, and chicken, plus buffalo steak. The house specialty is prime rib, and there's a popular soup and salad bar. **FYI:** Reservations recommended. Blues. Children's menu. Dress code. **Open:** Lunch Mon–Fri 11am–2:30pm, Sat noon–2:30; dinner Mon–Thurs 5–10pm, Fri–Sat 5–11pm, Sun noon–9pm. **Prices:** Main courses $10–$20. AE, CB, DC, DISC, MC, V.

The County Line Barbecue
9600 Tramway Blvd NE; tel 505/296-8822. Exit 234 off I-25. **Barbecue.** Generous portions of barbecued beef ribs, sausage, and brisket; plus chicken, smoked duck and pork, steaks, and salads. There's a spectacular view of the city, especially just after sunset as lights are coming on. **FYI:** Reservations not accepted. Children's menu. **Open:** Mon–Thurs 5–9pm, Fri–Sat 5–10pm, Sun 4–9pm. **Prices:** Main courses $9–$14. AE, CB, DC, DISC, MC, V.

ej's
2201 Silver Ave SE; tel 505/268-2233. 2 blocks S of Central Ave. **New American.** Classic college student hangout, serving up burgers, sandwiches, Mexican food, and salads. Entrees include sautéed snapper, stir-fried vegetables, and basil garlic pesto. **FYI:** Reservations not accepted. Big band/guitar/singer. No liquor license. No smoking. **Open:** Sun–Thurs 8am–11pm, Fri–Sat 8am–midnight. **Prices:** Main courses $4–$7. DISC, MC, V.

The Firehouse Restaurant at the Tram
38 Tramway Rd; tel 505/856-3473. **Seafood/Steak.** Located at the base of Sandia Tramway, the Firehouse offers a spectacular view of the city and Rio Grande Valley—especially from the outdoor balcony. Fresh fish and seafood, chicken, and beef dishes: grilled lime chicken, scallops with toasted piñons and white wine, and pepper steak. **FYI:** Reservations recommended. Children's menu. **Open:** Peak (June–Aug) lunch daily 11:30am–2:30pm; dinner daily 5–10pm. **Prices:** Main courses $9–$35. AE, DISC, MC, V.

Garduño's of Mexico
5400 Academy Rd NE; tel 505/821-3030. **Mexican.** Strolling musicians contribute to the noisy, festive atmosphere at this Mexican eatery, where the waitstaff dons Mexican dress and serves up large portions of chiles rellenos, chimichangas, carne adovada, and quesadillas. **FYI:** Reservations not accepted. Children's menu. **Open:** Mon–Thurs 11am–10pm, Fri–Sat 11am–10:30pm, Sun 10:30am–10pm. **Prices:** Main courses $15. AE, CB, DC, DISC, MC, V.

High Finance Restaurant and Tavern
40 Tramway Rd NE; tel 505/243-9742. Ride the train to the top of Sandia Peak. **Seafood/Steak.** Casually elegant mountain-top restaurant with a view of Albuquerque. Fresh seafood, prime rib, steaks, pasta, and chicken. Smoking is permitted only in the bar. The tram, which is necessary to get to the restaurant, is $13 per person without dinner reservations, $10 with reservations. **FYI:** Reservations recommended. **Open:** Lunch daily 11am–4pm; dinner daily 5–9:30pm. **Prices:** Main courses $14–$35. AE, DC, DISC, MC, V.

High Noon Restaurant and Saloon
425 San Felipe St NW (Old Town); tel 505/765-1455. **American/Mexican.** You'll find 19th-century saloon atmosphere inside this old (circa 1785) Albuquerque building, its stucco walls hung with historical photos. House specialties here include rib eye steak, red chile pasta, a mixed grill, and lamb chops. There are also chicken, seafood, and Mexican dishes, as well as game in season (venison, buffalo, caribou). **FYI:** Reservations recommended. **Open:** Peak (Mem Day–Labor Day) lunch Mon–Fri 11am–3pm, Sat 11am–3:30pm,

Sun noon–3:30pm; dinner Mon–Thurs 5–10pm, Fri–Sat 5–10:30pm, Sun 5–9pm. **Prices:** Main courses $14–$22. AE, DC, DISC, MC, V.

India Kitchen Restaurant
6910 Montgomery Blvd NE; tel 505/884-2333. **Indian.** A small, simple restaurant, decorated with Indian art. Both meat and vegetarian dishes are served. The menu provides spiciness ratings for individual dishes. **FYI:** Reservations accepted. Children's menu. Beer and wine only. No smoking. **Open:** Sun–Thurs 5–9pm, Fri–Sat 5–9:30pm. **Prices:** Main courses $7–$11. AE, CB, DC, DISC, MC, V.

La Hacienda Restaurant
302 San Felipe St NW (Old Town); tel 505/243-3131. **Mexican.** Decorated in Mexican motif, with chile ristras and hanging plants. Menu features fajitas (the house specialty), several seafood dishes, chiles rellenos, chimichangas, and enchiladas. Choose from more than a dozen varieties of margaritas. Small patio open in summer; singer performs occasionally. **FYI:** Reservations recommended. Children's menu. **Open:** Peak (Mem Day–Labor Day) daily 11am–10pm. **Prices:** Main courses $6–$10. AE, CB, DC, MC, V.

La Placita
208 San Felipe St NW (Old Town); tel 505/247-2204. **Regional American/Mexican.** This historic adobe hacienda dates back to 1706; it boasts hand-carved wooden doorways and fine regional art and furniture. A variety of Mexican specialties are offered—including a full Mexican dinner—in addition to steaks, chicken, and seafood. Wheelchair ramps are available on request. **FYI:** Reservations recommended. Children's menu. Beer and wine only. **Open:** Peak (Mem Day–Labor Day) daily 11am–9:30pm. **Prices:** Main courses $6–$13. AE, DISC, MC, V.

Le Marmiton
In Gourmet Plaza Shopping Center, 5415 Academy Blvd NE; tel 505/821-6279. **French.** Considered Albuquerque's best French restaurant. Intimate, French provincial atmosphere, with indirect lighting. The poulet au poivre is excellent. Early bird specials Tuesday through Thursday from 5–6:30pm. **FYI:** Reservations recommended. Beer and wine only. **Open:** Daily 5–9:30pm. **Prices:** Main courses $14–$20. AE, DC, DISC, MC, V.

Maria Teresa
618 Rio Grande Blvd NW (Old Town); tel 505/242-3900. **Continental.** Classic elegance in an 1840s adobe home distinguished by lovely wood paneling and tin ceilings, and Victorian antiques and paintings. A patio is available for warm-weather dining. Entrees include quail, tortilla soup, pork chops, pasta, duck, venison, rack of lamb, and salmon. **FYI:** Reservations recommended. Guitar. Children's menu. **Open:** Lunch Mon–Sat 11am–2:30pm; dinner daily 5–9pm; brunch Sun 10am–2pm. **Prices:** Main courses $17–$24. AE, CB, DC, MC, V.

Mario's Pizzeria & Ristorante
In Butterfield Plaza, 2401 San Pedro NE; tel 505/883-4414. ½ block S of Menaul Blvd across street from Coronado Center mall. **Italian/Pizza.** Family-owned and -operated for over 20 years, this restaurant has friendly, efficient service and generous portions. The open dining room with large arched windows is simply decorated with posters and other memorabilia of Italy. Manicotti, cannelloni, lasagna, ravioli, and other Italian dishes are served with a thick marinara sauce, and pizzas have a chewy crust. **FYI:** Reservations not accepted. Children's menu. Beer and wine only. **Open:** Mon–Sat 11am–10pm, Sun noon–10pm. **Prices:** Main courses $5–$12. AE, CB, DC, DISC, MC, V.

McGrath's Restaurant
In the Hyatt Regency, 330 Tijeras Ave NW; tel 505/766-6700. 1 block N of Central Ave at 3rd St. **Continental.** Plush yet casual setting. Gourmet dishes are prepared with a southwestern twist, such as filet mignon brushed with red chile butter, and southwest and chorizo confit. **FYI:** Reservations recommended. Children's menu. **Open:** Breakfast daily 6:30–11am; lunch daily 11am–2pm; dinner daily 5–10:30pm. **Prices:** Main courses $9–$21. AE, MC, V.

Monte Vista Fire Station
3201 Central Ave NE (Nob Hill); tel 505/255-2424. **Continental/Southwestern.** Housed in a 1936 art deco fire station. The kitchen does imaginative takes on classic dishes, offering a new menu every few weeks. Diners might start with grilled duck and pepper sausage with zinfandel sauce, then move on to yellowfin tuna, grilled sliced sirloin with forest mushroom sauce, or grilled marinated lamb chops with cucumber-yogurt sauce. Tiramisù for dessert. **FYI:** Reservations recommended. **Open:** Lunch Mon–Fri 11:30am–2:30pm; dinner Mon–Thurs 5–10:30pm, Fri–Sat 5–11pm. **Prices:** Main courses $14–$19. AE, DC, DISC, MC, V.

New Chinatown
5001 Central Avenue NE; tel 505/265-8859. 3 blocks W of San Mateo Blvd. **Chinese.** Statues of foo dogs guard the entrances. Walls are decorated with paintings of Chinese scenes and souvenirs from China; lighting is subdued and unobtrusive. Many Szechuan specialties are included on the mostly Cantonese menu. Sweet-and-sour shrimp and sweet-and-sour pork are two of the more than 40 dishes. Portions are large; there's a buffet lunch daily except Saturday. **FYI:** Reservations not accepted. No smoking. **Open:** Daily 11am–9:30pm. **Prices:** Main courses $6–$10. AE, CB, DC, DISC, MC, V.

Pelican's
9800 Montgomery Blvd NE; tel 505/298-7678. At Eubank Blvd. **Seafood/Steak.** Decorated in maritime motif; specializing in fresh fish, seafood, prime rib, and steaks. **FYI:** Reservations recommended. Children's menu. **Open:** Sun–Thurs 5–10:30pm, Fri–Sat 5–11:30pm. **Prices:** Main courses $8–$40. AE, DC, DISC, MC, V.

Prairie Star
1000 Jemez Canyon Dam Rd, Bernalillo; tel 505/867-3327. 2 mi W of Bernalillo; exit 242 off I-25. **Regional American.** A sprawling adobe home, with viga and latilla ceilings, decorated with original art. The menu features southwestern variations on standard dishes, such as trout with piñon nuts and shrimp margarita. The wine list has over 225 selections. **FYI:** Reservations recommended. Guitar. **Open:** Sun–Thurs 5–10pm, Fri–Sat 5–11pm. **Prices:** Main courses $17–$26. AE, DC, DISC, MC, V.

Rancher's Club
In the Albuquerque Hilton, 1901 University Blvd NE; tel 505/884-2500. Menaul Blvd exit off I-25. **Seafood/Steak.** Considered one of Albuquerque's finest restaurants. Styled in western elegance, with polished wood and a stone fireplace. Large steaks and a wide choice of poultry and seafood are grilled over hickory or mesquite, producing unique flavors. **FYI:** Reservations recommended. Piano. **Open:** Lunch Mon–Fri 11:30am–2:30pm; dinner daily 5:30–10:30pm; brunch Sun 10am–2pm. **Prices:** Main courses $15–$55. AE, DC, DISC, MC, V. VP

Rio Grande Yacht Club Restaurant and Lounge
2500 Yale Blvd SE; tel 505/243-6111. **Seafood/Steak.** Maritime-themed restaurant, with a tropical garden. Seafood is flown in fresh daily. Also steaks and seafood/beef combinations. **FYI:** Reservations recommended. Children's menu. **Open:** Lunch Mon–Fri 11am–2pm; dinner daily 5:30–10:30pm. **Prices:** Main courses $10–$33. AE, DC, DISC, MC, V.

Sadie's
6230 4th St NW; tel 505/345-5339. 1½ mi W on Montaño Rd. **Mexican/Southwestern.** A busy, no-frills restaurant specializing in burgers, steaks (some smothered in chiles), and such Mexican selections as stuffed sopaipillas, enchiladas, and carne adovada. **FYI:** Reservations not accepted. Children's menu. **Open:** Mon–Sat 11am–10pm, Sun 11am–9pm. **Prices:** Main courses $6–$15. AE, CB, DC, DISC, MC, V.

Scalo
In Nob Hill Center, 3500 Central Ave SE; tel 505/255-8781. **Northern Italian.** Bistro-style restaurant specializing in northern Italian cuisine, with homemade pastas as well as meat, chicken, and fish entrees. **FYI:** Reservations recommended. Jacket required. **Open:** Lunch Mon–Sat 11:30am–2:30pm; dinner Sun 5–9pm, Mon–Sat 5–11pm. **Prices:** Main courses $8–$17. AE, DC, MC, V.

Seagull Street Fish Market
5410 Academy Rd NE; tel 505/821-0020. Exit 230 off I-25. **Seafood.** An attractive seafood restaurant offering outdoor dining beside a freshwater lagoon. Fresh mesquite-grilled fish includes Pacific snapper Vera Cruz and skewered monkfish. Beef and pasta also available. Live blues and reggae in summer. **FYI:** Reservations recommended. Children's menu. **Open:** Lunch Mon–Fri 11am–2:30pm; dinner Fri–Sat 4:30–11pm, Sun noon–9pm, Mon–Thurs 4:30–10pm. **Prices:** Main courses $10–$30. AE, DC, MC, V.

66 Diner
1405 Central Ave NE; tel 505/247-1421. **Diner.** 1950s-style diner. Photos of Elvis and Marilyn Monroe. Burgers, sandwiches, and blue plate specials, including chicken pot pie and fried catfish. Old-fashioned malts and other fountain drinks. **FYI:** Reservations accepted. Children's menu. Beer and wine only. **Open:** Mon–Thurs 11am–11pm, Fri 11am–midnight, Sat 8am–midnight, Sun 8am–10pm. **Prices:** Main courses $4–$7. AE, DISC, MC, V.

Stephen's
1311 Tijeras Ave NW; tel 505/842-1773. At 14th St and Central Ave. **American/Continental.** An open, airy restaurant facing busy Central Avenue. Traditional American entrees are prepared in innovative ways. Specialties include rack of lamb, grilled salmon, filet mignon, Cajun mixed grill, and pork tenderloin scaloppine. The award-winning wine cellar has some 350 selections. **FYI:** Reservations recommended. **Open:** Lunch Mon–Fri 11am–2pm; dinner daily 5:30–9:30pm. **Prices:** Main courses $16–$24. AE, CB, DC, DISC, MC, V.

ATTRACTIONS

HISTORIC BUILDINGS AND MUSEUMS

Old Town
Central Ave and Rio Grande Blvd NW; tel 505/842-9100. A maze of cobbled courtyard walkways lead to hidden patios and gardens where many of Old Town's 150 galleries and shops are located. Adobe buildings, many refurbished in the pueblo revival style of the 1950s, ring the tree-shaded Old Town Plaza, created in 1780. Pueblo and Navajo artisans often display their wares on the sidewalks lining the plaza.

The first structure built when colonists established Albuquerque in 1706 was the **Church of San Felipe de Neri,** which faces the Plaza on its north side. The house of worship has been in almost continuous use for 285 years. The windows are 20 feet from the ground and its walls are 4 feet thick—structural details needed to make the church also serviceable as a fortress. A spiral stairway leading to the choir loft is built around the trunk of an ancient spruce.

Other notable structures include the 1877 **Our Lady of the Angels School,** 320 Romero St, the first public school in Albuquerque; **Antonio Vigil House,** 413 Romero St, an adobe-style residence with traditional viga ends sticking out over the entrance door; and **Casa Armijo,** at San Felipe St, a headquarters for both Union and Confederate troops during the Civil War. Guided walking tours are held Tuesday to Sunday during the summer.

National Atomic Museum
Wyoming Blvd and K St; tel 505/845-6670. Traces the history of nuclear-weapons development, beginning with the

top-secret Manhattan Project of the 1940s. A 50-minute film, *Ten Seconds That Shook the World,* is shown four times daily. There are full-scale models of the "Fat Man" and "Little Boy" bombs and displays and films on peaceful applications of nuclear technology and other alternative energy sources. Outdoor exhibits include missiles and bombers. The museum is located on Kirtland Air Force Base; visitors must obtain passes at the entry gates of the base. **Open:** Daily 9am–5pm. **Free**

Albuquerque Museum
2000 Mountain Rd NW; tel 505/243-7255. Exhibits chronicle the city's evolution from the earliest 16th-century forays of Coronado's conquistadores to its present-day status as a center for military research and high-technology industries. An object of special note is a 17th-century *repostero,* or tapestry, once belonging to the Spanish House of Albuquerque. Other highlights include *History Hopscotch,* an activity area for children, and the *Gem Theater,* where a multimedia audiovisual presentation explores the development of the city since 1875. **Open:** Tues–Sun 9am–5pm. **Free**

University Art Museum
Cornell St; tel 505/277-4001. Located on the University of New Mexico campus in the fine arts center, this collection focuses on 19th- and 20th-century American and European artists, Spanish Colonial artwork, and significant New Mexico artists. Also large photography collection.

The museum has opened two affiliate locations in Albuquerque: **University Art Museum Downtown,** 516 Central SW, which displays changing exhibitions drawn from the university's permanent collection; and the **Jonson Gallery,** 1909 Las Lomas NE, which was once the home of late modernist painter Raymond Jonson. **Open:** Tues–Fri 9am–4pm, Sun 1–4pm. **Free**

Indian Pueblo Cultural Center
2401 12th St NW; tel toll free 800/288-0721. Owned and operated as a nonprofit organization by the 19 pueblos of New Mexico, this is modeled after Pueblo Bonito, a spectacular 9th-century ruin (see under) Chaco Culture National Historical Park. A permanent exhibit depicts the evolution from prehistory to the present of the various pueblos, including displays of the distinctive handcrafts of each community. Local Native American dancers perform, and artisans demonstrate their crafts on weekends. Annual craft fair is held on July 4. **Open:** Daily 9am–5:30pm. **$**

New Mexico Museum of Natural History
1801 Mountain Rd NW; tel 505/841-2800. Permanent and changing exhibits on regional zoology, botany, geology, and paleontology. Innovative video displays, polarizing lenses, and black lighting enable visitors to stroll through geologic time. Visitors can walk a rocky path through the Hall of Giants, as dinosaurs fight and winged reptiles swoop overhead; step into a seemingly live volcano, complete with simulated magma flow; or share an Ice Age cave, festooned with stalagmites, with saber-toothed tigers and woolly mammoths. Hands-on exhibits in the Naturalist Center permit use of a video microscope, and viewing of an active beehive. **Open:** Daily 9am–5pm. **$$**

Geology Museum and Meteoritic Museum
200 Yale Blvd NE; tel 505/277-4204. Located in Northrop Hall on the University of New Mexico campus, these adjacent museums cover the gamut of recorded time from dinosaur bones to meteorites. A variety of minerals and fossils are also exhibited. **Open:** Mon–Fri 9am–5pm. **Free**

Maxwell Museum of Anthropology
Redondo Dr; tel 505/277-4405. A repository of southwestern anthropological finds located on the University of New Mexico campus. Permanent galleries include "Ancestors," describing 4 million years of human evolution, and "Peoples of the Southwest," a 10,000-year summary. Regional jewelry, basketry, and textiles are on display. **Open:** Mon–Sat 9am–4pm, Sun noon–4pm. **Free**

Spanish History Museum
2221 Lead St SE; tel 505/268-9981. This exclusive gallery features "From Kingdom to Statehood," an exhibit outlining Hispanics' role in New Mexico's pursuit of statehood from 1848 to 1912. **Open:** Peak (June–Aug) daily 10am–5pm. Reduced hours off-season. **$**

Ernie Pyle Memorial Library
900 Girard Blvd SE; tel 505/256-2065. Memorabilia and poignant exhibits recalling the Pulitzer Prize–winning war correspondent, killed in action during World War II, are displayed in his 1939 home. **Open:** Tues, Thurs 12:30–9pm; Wed, Fri–Sat 9am–5:30pm. **Free**

American International Rattlesnake Museum
202 San Felipe St NW; tel 505/242-6569. Live specimens in landscaped habitats. Featured are both common and very rare rattlesnakes of North, Central, and South America. Over 20 species can be seen, including such oddities as albinos and patternless rattlesnakes. **Open:** Daily 10am–6:30pm. **$**

OTHER ATTRACTIONS

Petroglyph National Monument
4735 Unser Blvd NW; tel 505/839-4429. These ancient lava flows were once hunting and gathering areas for prehistoric Native Americans, who chronicled their journeys with etched markings in the basalt. Today, 15,000 of these petroglyphs have been found in concentrated groups. Visitors may take any of the four levels of self-guiding hiking trails to see them. **Open:** Peak (June–Aug) daily 9am–6pm. Reduced hours off-season. **$**

Rio Grande Zoological Park
903 10th St SW; tel 505/843-7413. Open-motif exhibits, including sea lions, elephants, and koalas, are the highlights of this zoo. More than 1,200 animals of 300 species, among them endangered African hoofed animals, cats, elephants,

giraffes, and native southwestern species, share the 60 acres of riverside habitat among ancient cottonwoods. **Open:** Daily 9am–5pm. **$$**

Sandia Peak Tramway
10 Tramway Loop NE; tel 505/856-7325. The world's longest tramway extends 2.7 miles from Albuquerque's northeastern city limits to the summit of 10,360-foot Sandia Peak. The 15-minute ride takes visitors from urban desert at its base to lush mountain foliage in the Cibola National Forest at its peak. **Open:** Peak (Mem Day–Labor Day) daily 9am–10pm. Reduced hours off-season. **$$$$**

Sandia Peak Ski Area
10 Tramway Loop NE; tel 505/242-9052. There are 25 trails here, 14 of which are intermediate level. The mountain has a 10,360-foot summit and a 1,700-foot vertical drop. During the summer chair lifts are operational Thursday to Sunday and mountain bikes are available for rent. **Open:** Peak (mid-Dec–mid-Mar) daily 9am–4pm. Reduced hours off-season. **$$$$**

Cliff's Amusement Park
4800 Osuna Rd NE; tel 505/883-9063. New Mexico's largest amusement park, with 23 rides, including a roller coaster and log flume; video arcades; a recording studio; picnic grounds; and live entertainment. **Open:** Apr–early Oct; call ahead for hours. **$$$$**

Kimo Theatre
419 Central Ave NW; tel 505/764-1700. This showcase of the performing arts is designed as a tribute to the region's Native American cultures. Opened in 1927, the architecture is a colorful adaptation of the adobe pueblo and its interior decor emphasizes Native American motifs. Handmade tiles adorn the lobby; wall paintings simulate Navajo sand paintings; and murals of the legendary "Seven Cities of Cíbola" stand outside the balcony seating area. The 750-seat theater is home of the New Mexico Repertory Theatre, Opera Southwest, and La Compaña de Teatro de Albuquerque. **Open:** Daily 11am–5pm.

Popejoy Hall
Cornell St; tel 505/277-3121. The area's leading venue for major musical entertainment. Resident companies include the New Mexico Symphony Orchestra, the Albuquerque Civic Light Opera Association, and the New Mexico Ballet Company. **Open:** Ticket office, Mon–Sat 10am–6pm.

Artesia

Artesia, 30 miles north of Carlsbad on US 285, is named for the artesian wells that supply water for area farms. The quiet town is a center for oil and agriculture. **Information:** Greater Artesia Chamber of Commerce, 408 W Texas Ave, PO Box 99, Artesia 88211 (tel 505/746-2744 or 800/658-6251).

HOTEL

Pecos Inn Best Western Hotel
2209 W Main St, 88210; tel 505/748-3324 or toll free 800/528-1234; fax 505/748-2868. ½ mi W of US 285 on US 82. Simply but attractively decorated and landscaped. **Rooms:** 81 rms and stes. CI 4pm/CO 11am. Nonsmoking rms avail. **Amenities:** A/C, cable TV w/movies, refrig. Some units w/terraces. All regular rooms have wet bars. Hair dryers and microwave ovens are available. **Services:** **Facilities:** 200 1 restaurant, 1 bar, sauna, whirlpool. **Rates:** $52–$60 S; $58–$65 D; $65 ste. Extra person $7. Children under age 12 stay free. Parking: Outdoor, free. AE, DC, DISC, MC, V.

ATTRACTION

Artesia Historical Museum and Art Center
505 W Richardson Ave; tel 505/748-2390. Housed in an old Victorian home, with exhibits of Native Americans and pioneer artifacts, as well as works by local artists. **Open:** Tues–Sat 8am–5pm. **Free**

Aztec

See also Farmington

This town was misnamed by settlers who mistakenly believed that the Native American ruins they happened upon were those left by the Aztecs of Mexico (they were in fact remnants left by the Anasazi). The town's claim-to-fame today is Aztec Ruins National Monument. **Information:** Aztec Chamber of Commerce, 203 N Main Ave, Aztec 87410 (tel 505/334-9551).

MOTEL

Enchantment Lodge
1800 W Aztec Blvd, 87410; tel 505/334-6143 or toll free 800/847-2194; fax 505/334-6144. Nostalgic 1950s decor, with pink neon lights, and every room door a different color. **Rooms:** 20 rms. CI noon/CO 11am. Nonsmoking rms avail. **Amenities:** A/C, cable TV w/movies, refrig. **Services:** Babysitting. **Facilities:** Playground, washer/dryer. Pool-side umbrella tables and a fun, eclectic gift shop. **Rates:** Peak (May–Oct) $28–$34 S; $34–$40 D. Extra person $5–$7. Children under age 1 stay free. Lower rates off-season. Parking: Outdoor, free. DISC, MC, V.

ATTRACTIONS

Aztec Ruins National Monument
US 550; tel 505/334-6174. The ruins of a 500-room pueblo, abandoned by the Anasazi seven centuries ago and misnamed by pioneers who confused the Anasazi with the ancient Mexican Aztec people. The influence of the Chaco culture is strong at Aztec, as evidenced in the preplanned architecture,

the open plaza, and the fine stone masonry in the old walls. Aztec is best known for its Great Kiva, the only completely reconstructed Great Kiva in existence. The circular ceremonial room is 50 feet in diameter, with a main floor sunken 8 feet below the surface. The visitor center displays some outstanding examples of Anasazi ceramics and basketry found in the ruins. **Open:** Daily 8am–5pm. **$**

Navajo Lake State Park
NM 173; tel 505/632-2278. Three recreation sites—San Juan River, Pine River, and Sims Mesa—overlook Navajo Lake, the largest in northwestern New Mexico. Anglers can fish for trout, bass, crappie, catfish, and northern pike. Camping, hiking, boating, water sports. **Open:** Daily sunrise–sunset. **$**

Belen

Founded as a Spanish land grant in 1740, Belen was originally called *Nuestra Señora de Belén* (Our Lady of Bethlehem). Located south of Albuquerque along I-25, this agricultural and railroad center offers little for visitors except a quiet stop just a half-hour from the state's largest city. **Information:** Belen Chamber of Commerce, 712 Dalies Ave, Belen 87002 (tel 505/864-8091).

MOTEL

Best Western Belen
2101 Sasimo Padilla Blvd, 87002; tel 505/861-0980 or toll free 800/528-1234; fax 505/861-1395. Exit 191 off I-25. Located just off interstate, with view of surrounding hills. Used mainly by railroad personnel. **Rooms:** 70 rms. CI open/CO noon. Nonsmoking rms avail. **Amenities:** A/C, cable TV w/movies, dataport. **Services:** Old-fashioned diner on premises, open 24 hours. **Facilities:** 1 restaurant, whirlpool, washer/dryer. Very nice fitness center. **Rates:** $52–$70 S or D. Extra person $5. Children under age 14 stay free. Parking: Outdoor, free. AE, DISC, MC, V.

Bernalillo

Just north of Albuquerque, this farming community along the Rio Grande has been inhabited by the same Hispanic and Pueblo Indian families for generations. Nearby are several ancient pueblos, plus pueblo ruins at Coronado State Monument. **Information:** Greater Bernalillo Chamber of Commerce, PO Box 1776, Bernalillo 87004 (tel 505/888-7909).

ATTRACTIONS

Coronado State Monument
NM 44 (PO Box 95); tel 505/867-5351. When Coronado traveled through this region in 1540 to 1541, he wintered at a village located on the ruins of the ancient Anasazi pueblo known as Kuaua. Those excavated ruins have been preserved in this state monument. Hundreds of rooms can be seen, and a kiva has been restored so that visitors may descend a ladder into the enclosed space, once the site of sacred rites. There is also a small archeological museum. **Open:** Daily 9am–5pm. **$**

Sandia Pueblo
NM 313; tel 505/867-3317. Established about 1300, this was one of the few pueblos visited by Coronado's contingent in 1540. Remains of that village are still visible near the present church. The pueblo celebrates its St Anthony feast day on June 13 with a midmorning mass, procession, and afternoon corn dance. Photographs prohibited. **Open:** Daily sunrise–sunset. **Free**

Santa Ana Pueblo
2 Dove Rd; tel 505/867-3301. Guests are normally welcomed only on ceremonial days. Pueblo members perform the turtle and corn dances on January 1; the eagle, elk, buffalo, and deer dances on Three Kings Day, January 6; the spring corn basket dance at Easter; various dances for St Anthony's Day on June 29 and St Anne's Day on July 26; and several days of dances at Christmastime. Photographs prohibited. **Open:** Certain ceremonial days only. **Free**

Capitan

See also Lincoln

ATTRACTION

Smokey Bear Historical State Park
118 Smokey Bear Blvd; tel 505/354-2748. Smokey Bear was found here as a cub clinging to a tree after a forest fire in the Capitan Mountains in 1950. He lived a long life in the National Zoo in Washington, DC, and after his death was returned to his home for burial. Today, visitors can see his grave, walk nature paths, and view exhibits on Smokey and fire prevention in the museum (free). **Open:** Daily sunrise–sunset. **$**

Capulin

ATTRACTION

Capulin Volcano National Monument
NM 325; tel 505/278-2201. A 2-mile road spirals 1,000 feet to the summit of this 8,182-foot peak. Two self-guiding trails leave from the parking area permitting visitors to explore the inactive volcano: the 1-mile Crater Rim Trail, and the 1,000-foot descent to the ancient volcanic vent. The mountain was last active about 10,000 years ago when it sent out the last of three lava flows. **Open:** Peak (June–Aug) daily 7:30am–6pm. Reduced hours off-season. **$$**

Carlsbad

Originally called Eddy—for a pair of local ranching brothers—the town changed its name to Carlsbad after the discovery of nearby springs that were said to rival the famed mineral springs of Carlsbad in Bohemia. Besides a good tourist business from nearby Carlsbad Caverns National Park, the city thrives on irrigated farming and mines great quantities of potash. **Information:** Carlsbad Convention & Visitors Bureau, 302 S Canal St, PO Box 910, Carlsbad 88220 (tel 505/887-6516 or 800/221-1221).

MOTELS

Best Western Stevens Inn

1829 S Canal St, 88220; or toll free 800/730-2851; fax 505/887-6338. A full-service motel, recently renovated and very popular with business travelers. **Rooms:** 202 rms, stes, and effic. Executive level. CI open/CO noon. Nonsmoking rms avail. **Amenities:** A/C, cable TV w/movies, dataport, voice mail. Some units w/whirlpools. Microwave/refrigerator combination available for $5. **Services:** Car-rental desk, social director, babysitting. Free newspapers. **Facilities:** 400 1 restaurant (*see* "Restaurants" below), 1 bar (w/entertainment), games rm, playground, washer/dryer. **Rates:** $50–$55 S; $55–$60 D; $65–$85 ste; $65 effic. Extra person $5. Children under age 12 stay free. Parking: Outdoor, free. Long-term rates avail. AE, CB, DC, DISC, MC, V.

Carlsbad Super 8

3817 National Parks Hwy, 88220; tel 505/887-8888 or toll free 800/800-8000; fax 505/885-0126. Quiet accommodations at a good location on the south side of Carlsbad, 20 miles from the caverns and within 10 miles of Carlsbad's other attractions. **Rooms:** 60 rms. CI noon/CO 11am. Nonsmoking rms avail. Clean, well-appointed rooms. **Amenities:** A/C, cable TV. Refrigerators and microwave ovens are available. **Services:** **Facilities:** 20 Whirlpool. Patio area with grills for guest use. **Rates (CP):** Peak (June 3–Sept 3) $45–$49 S; $49–$57 D. Extra person $4. Children under age 12 stay free. Lower rates off-season. Parking: Outdoor, free. AE, CB, DC, DISC, MC, V.

Continental Inn

3820 National Parks Hwy, 88220; tel 505/887-0341; fax 505/885-1186. A pleasant, standard motel. **Rooms:** 60 rms and stes. CI 1pm/CO 11am. Nonsmoking rms avail. The honeymoon suite has a heart-shaped tub with mirrored ceiling and shower for two. **Amenities:** A/C, cable TV. Some units w/minibars. Suites have refrigerators. **Services:** **Facilities:** 24-hour restaurant within walking distance. **Rates:** Peak (Mar–Sept) $35 S; $40–$45 D; $50–$65 ste. Extra person $5. Children under age 14 stay free. Lower rates off-season. Parking: Outdoor, free. AE, CB, DC, DISC, MC, V.

Holiday Inn

601 S Canal St, PO Box 128, 88220; tel 505/885-8500 or toll free 800/742-9586; fax 505/887-5999. Attractive motel in downtown Carlsbad, in a striking New Mexico territorial-style building. **Rooms:** 100 rms and stes. Executive level. CI 2pm/CO 11am. Nonsmoking rms avail. **Amenities:** A/C, cable TV w/movies, dataport, voice mail. Some units w/whirlpools. **Services:** Car-rental desk, babysitting. **Facilities:** 200 2 restaurants, 1 bar, sauna, whirlpool, playground, washer/dryer. Close to two 18-hole golf courses. **Rates (BB):** Peak (Mar 15–Aug 15) $70–$80 S; $80–$90 D; $90–$100 ste. Extra person $6. Children under age 19 stay free. Lower rates off-season. Parking: Outdoor, free. AE, CB, DC, DISC, EC, JCB, MC, V.

Stagecoach Inn

1819 S Canal St, 88220; tel 505/887-1148; fax 505/887-1148. A modest, no-frills property that's undergoing gradual refurbishment. **Rooms:** 55 rms. CI open/CO 11am. Nonsmoking rms avail. **Amenities:** A/C, cable TV. **Services:** **Facilities:** 1 restaurant (*see* "Restaurants" below), whirlpool, playground, washer/dryer. **Rates:** Peak (Apr–Sept) $30–$35 S; $38–$44 D. Children under age 18 stay free. Lower rates off-season. Parking: Outdoor, free. AE, CB, DC, DISC, MC, V

RESTAURANTS

The Flume

In Best Western Stevens Inn, 1829 S Canal St; tel 505/887-2851. **Regional American.** Elegant restaurant done in hacienda style with chandeliers and wall sconces. The menu offers a variety of seafood, beef, and chicken selections. A house specialty is teriyaki chicken breast. **FYI:** Reservations recommended. Country music/dancing. Children's menu. Dress code. **Open:** Mon–Sat 6am–10pm, Sun 6am–9pm. **Prices:** Main courses $7–$16. AE, CB, DC, DISC, MC, V.

Lucy's

701 S Canal; tel 505/887-7714. **American/Mexican.** Busy cafe with partitioned areas for small family parties. Mexican dishes include burritos, enchiladas, fajitas, and tacos. Low-fat menu available. **FYI:** Reservations accepted. Children's menu. **Open:** Mon–Sat 11am–9:30pm. **Prices:** Main courses $4–$12. AE, CB, DC, DISC, MC, V.

Stagecoach Restaurant

In the Stagecoach Inn, 1801 S Canal St; tel 505/885-2862. **Regional American.** A southwestern cafe with ceiling fans and lights with a wagon wheel design. Specializes in steaks, burgers, barbecue, and Mexican plates. A breakfast buffet is available Saturday and Sunday from 11am to 2pm. **FYI:** Reservations not accepted. Children's menu. No liquor license. **Open:** Mon–Fri 5am–9pm, Sat–Sun 6am–8pm. **Prices:** Main courses $4–$15. MC, V.

ATTRACTIONS

Carlsbad Caverns National Park

3225 National Parks Hwy; tel 505/785-2232. One of the largest and most spectacular cave systems in the world, the caverns comprise some 80 caves that snake through the porous limestone reef of the Guadalupe Mountains. Two caves, Carlsbad Cavern and Slaughter Canyon Cave, are open to the public. At the lowest point in the trail the caverns reach 830 feet below the surface. They are filled with stalactites and stalagmites that create fantastic and grotesque formations resembling everything from waterfalls to castles. At sunset during summer, a crowd gathers at the cavern entrance to watch nearly one million bats take off for the night. Visitors are advised to wear flat shoes with rubber soles and heels to avoid falls on the slippery paths. **Open:** Peak (June–Aug) daily 8:30am–5pm. Reduced hours off-season. **$$**

Living Desert State Park

1504 Miehls Dr; tel 505/887-5516. A 45-acre stretch of Chihuahuan Desert preserved with all its flora and fauna. There are more than 50 species of mammals, birds, and reptiles in the open-air park, and hundreds of varieties of plants, including cactus. Animals arrive through a rehabilitation program that cares for sick or injured creatures. Golden eagles and great horned owls are among the birds of prey; larger mammals such as deer, antelope, elk, javelina, buffalo, and bobcat also share the area. **Open:** Peak (Mem Day–Labor Day) daily 8am–8pm. Reduced hours off-season. **$**

Chaco Culture National Historical Park

Chaco represents the high point of pre-Columbian pueblo civilization. It includes more than a dozen large Anasazi ruins occupied from the early 900s to about 1200, and hundreds of smaller sites in the wide streambed of the normally dry Chaco Wash. Most of the ruins are located on the north side of the canyon, including the largest, **Pueblo Bonito,** constructed over 3 acres of land in the 11th century. It comprises four stories, 600 rooms, and 40 kivas and may have housed as many as 1,200 people. The Anasazi also engineered a network of 300 miles of roads, best seen from the canyon rim 100 feet above the ruins.

The visitor center houses a small museum and provides self-guided trail maps and permits for the overnight campground. Chaco is fairly isolated; Farmington is the closest city and is a two-hour, 75-mile drive down NM 44. Nageezi Trading Post, the closest location for gas, food, and lodging, is 26 miles by way of graded dirt road. This final stretch becomes flooded and dangerous when it rains; inquire about road conditions before leaving the paved roadway. For more information contact the park at 505/988-6727, daily 8am–5pm.

Chama

At an elevation of 8,000 feet, this isolated northern New Mexico town is a favorite base for hunters, fishermen, snowmobilers, cross-country skiers, and hikers seeking the rugged beauty of the surrounding mountains. **Information:** Chama Valley Chamber of Commerce, PO Box 306, Chama 87520 (tel 505/756-2306 or 800/477-0149).

MOTELS

Branding Iron Motel

W Main St, PO Box 557, 87520; tel 505/756-2162 or toll free 800/446-2650. A standard motel. **Rooms:** 41 rms. CI 2pm/CO 11am. Nonsmoking rms avail. **Amenities:** A/C, cable TV. All units w/terraces. **Facilities:** 1 restaurant. **Rates:** Peak (May 27–Oct 20) $62–$70 S; $69–$95 D. Lower rates off-season. Parking: Outdoor, free. AE, DISC, MC, V.

Chama Trails Inn

W Main St, PO Box 975, 87520; tel 505/756-2156 or toll free 800/289-1421. At the "Y". Chile ristras adorn the white stucco facade of this handsome property. Far above the usual small-town motel. The owners are friendly and knowledgeable. **Rooms:** 16 rms and stes. CI noon/CO 11am. Nonsmoking rms avail. Custom-made pine furnishings and hand-carved wood beams. **Amenities:** Cable TV, refrig. No A/C. All units w/terraces, some w/fireplaces, 1 w/whirlpool. **Services:** **Facilities:** 15 An art gallery with local artists' work is on the premises. **Rates:** Peak (late May–Oct) $37–$43 S; $43–$51 D; $80 ste. Extra person $6. Lower rates off-season. Parking: Outdoor, free. AE, DISC, MC, V.

Elkhorn Lodge and Cafe

US 84, Rte 1, PO Box 45, 87520; tel 505/756-2105 or toll free 800/532-8874; fax 505/756-2638. A charming, somewhat rustic motel, reminiscent of a mountain lodge, set beside a stream. **Rooms:** 22 rms; 11 cottages/villas. CI 2pm/CO 11am. Clean, spacious rooms, with solid wood paneling. **Amenities:** Cable TV. No A/C. **Services:** **Facilities:** 1 restaurant, lawn games, playground. Barbecue pits on the grounds. **Rates:** Peak (May–Oct) $48–$56 S; $56–$76 D; $70–$120 cottage/villa. Extra person $6. Children under age 5 stay free. Lower rates off-season. Parking: Outdoor, free. DISC, MC, V.

RESTAURANTS

★ High Country Restaurant

Main St; tel 505/756-2384. **Seafood/Steak.** A friendly, comfortable eatery, decorated with western art and knick-knacks. Selection of steak, fish, seafood, chicken, pork, and sandwiches. **FYI:** Reservations accepted. Country music. **Open:** Daily 7am–11pm. **Prices:** Main courses $8–$14. AE, DISC, MC, V.

Viva Vera's
Main St; tel 505/756-2557. **Regional American/Mexican.** Comfortable restaurant with Spanish touches. Basic Mexican and American food, including enchiladas, chile stew, burritos, hamburgers, and sandwiches. **FYI:** Reservations accepted. Beer and wine only. **Open:** Peak (May–Oct) daily 7am–9:30pm. **Prices:** Main courses $6–$11. AE, DISC, MC, V.

ATTRACTIONS

Cumbres and Toltec Scenic Railroad
US 64; tel 505/756-2151. American's longest and highest narrow-gauge steam railroad operates on a 64-mile track between Chama and Antonito, Colorado. Built in 1880 as an extension of the Denver and Rio Grande Line to serve the mining camps of the San Juan Mountains, it is perhaps the finest surviving example of what once was a vast network of remote Rocky Mountain railways. The C&T passes through forests of pine and aspen, past striking rock formations, and through the magnificent Toltec Gorge of the Rio de los Pinos. It crests at the 10,105-foot Cumbres Pass, the highest in the United States used by passenger trains. Reservations are recommended. **Open:** Mem Day–mid-Oct, daily departure 10:30am. **$$$$**

Jicarilla Apache Indian Reservation
Off US 64, Dulce; tel 505/759-3242. About 3,200 Apache live on this 768,000-acre reservation. The tribal craftspeople are noted for their basket-weaving and both contemporary and museum-quality examples can be seen at **Jicarilla Apache Arts and Crafts Shop and Museum**. Two isolated pueblo ruins are found on the reservation: the **Cordova Canyon** ruins on Tribal Road 13 and the **Honolulu** ruin on Road 63. **Open:** Daily sunrise–sunset. **Free**

Cimarron

Once you get past the gas stations and modern motels, this is one of New Mexico's few genuine historic towns left intact, with 100-year-old bullet holes still to be found in the St James Hotel, a testament to Cimarron's wilder days. The town is also home to 140,000-acre Philmont Scout Ranch, and makes a good base for hikers, hunters, and fishermen. **Information:** Cimarron Chamber of Commerce, PO Box 604, Cimarron 87714 (tel 505/376-2417 or 800/700-4298).

HOTEL

St James Hotel
Rte 1 Box 2, 87714; tel 505/376-2664; fax 505/376-2623. At 17th and Collinson Sts. This handsome historic hotel, opened in 1890, was popular with many of the legends of the Old West, including Buffalo Bill Cody, Annie Oakley, train robber Blackjack Ketchum, and gunfighter Clay Allison, who reportedly once danced on the bar. Restored to its original Victorian grandeur in 1985, the lobby and rooms are furnished with turn-of-the-century antiques. The original tin ceiling of the hotel's dining room shows off bullet holes left from its wilder days. **Rooms:** 25 rms and stes. CI 3pm/CO noon. Restored rooms in the original building are very much like they were in the 1890s, many with the original marble sinks. Room 18 is not rented because its resident ghost, TJ Wright, does not welcome visitors. Rooms in the annex, built in the 1950s, are standard motel rooms. **Amenities:** No A/C, phone, or TV. Annex rooms have TVs and telephones. **Services:** Masseur. The St James offers tours during summer months ($2 per person) and shows a 20-minute video on the history of the hotel. **Facilities:** 2 restaurants (*see* "Restaurants" below), 1 bar, games rm. Coffee shop serves three meals a day. Close to hiking, fishing, hunting, and horseback riding. **Rates:** $50–$85 S; $60–$90 D; $105 ste. Extra person $5. Children under age 18 stay free. Min stay special events. Parking: Outdoor, free. Mystery Weekend packages are available; reservations are suggested at least six months in advance. AE, DISC, MC, V.

RESTAURANT

Lambert's
In St James Hotel, 17th and Collinson Sts; tel 505/376-2664. 1 block S of US 64 on NM 21. **Continental.** A delightful, historic dining room built in 1873 by Henri Lambert, personal chef to President Lincoln and General Grant. The room is decorated with Victorian antiques, and patrons can pass time counting the numerous bullet holes in the tin ceiling. There is also a painting on display depicting one of the shootings that took place here. The menu includes steak, seafood, and continental dishes. **FYI:** Reservations recommended. Children's menu. **Open:** Dinner Mon–Sat 5pm–close, Sun noon–close. **Prices:** Main courses $13–$25. AE, DC, DISC, MC, V.

ATTRACTIONS

Philmont Scout Ranch
I-25; tel 505/376-2281. This 137,000-acre property was donated to the Boy Scouts of America in 1938 by Texas oilman Waite Phillips. There are three museums located on the property that are open to the public: The **Villa Philmonte** is a Mediterranean-style summer home built in 1927 for Phillips and is furnished with the family's European antiques. The **Philmont Museum and Seton Memorial Library** commemorates the art and taxidermy of Ernest Thompson Seton, the naturalist and author who founded the Boy Scouts of America. The **Kit Carson Museum**, located 7 miles south of Philmont headquarters in Rayado, is a period hacienda furnished in 1850s style. Tours are led by staff in historical costumes. **Open:** Daily 8am–5pm. **Free**

Old Mill Museum
NM 21; tel 505/376-2913. Land baron Lucien Maxwell founded the town of Cimarron in 1848 as base of operations for his 1.7-million-acre empire. In 1857 he built the Maxwell

Ranch, which he furnished opulently with heavy draperies, gold-framed paintings, and two grand pianos. The ranch isn't open for inspection today, but Maxwell's 1864 stone grist mill, built to supply flour to Fort Union, is. It houses an interesting collection of early photos and memorabilia of the ranch. **Open:** May–Oct, Mon–Wed and Fri–Sat 9am–5pm, Sun 1–5pm. **$**

Cimarron Canyon State Park
US 64; tel 505/377-6271. This designated state wildlife area lies at the foot of crenellated granite formations known as the Palisades. Covering 32,000 acres, the park is a popular spot for hunting, fishing, and hiking. **Open:** Daily 24 hours. **$**

Clayton

Founded as a railroad town and rest stop for cattle drives in the 1880s, Clayton remains a cattle ranching and feedlot center. Although isolated and quiet today, its Wild West heritage is remembered in the 1901 hanging of notorious train robber Black Jack Ketchum, captured while attempting to single-handedly stop and rob a moving train. **Information:** Clayton/Union County Chamber of Commerce, PO Box 476, Clayton 88415 (tel 505/374-9253).

ATTRACTIONS

Clayton State Park
NM 370, Seneca; tel 505/374-8808. Located 25 mi N of Clayton. The 170-acre park offers picnicking, camping, and excellent fishing amongst rolling grasslands, volcanic rocks, and sandstone bluffs. However, the main attraction here is the more than 500 preserved dinosaur footprints estimated to be at least 100 million years old. The dinosaur tracks are located on the dam spillway, at the end of an easy ½-mile trail, and descriptive information at the site helps to identify the eight different types of tracks. Visitors center, playground, shelters, boat dock. **Open:** Daily sunrise–sunset. **Free**

Kiowa National Grasslands
714 Main St; tel 505/374-9652. This area provides food, cover, and water for a wide variety of wildlife such as antelope, quail, barbary sheep, and mule deer. Also located at Kiowa are the Canadian River and the Canadian River Canyon. The variety of recreational options available include warm water fishing, hunting, picnicking, and camping. **Open:** Office: daily 8am–4:30pm. Grasslands: daily 24 hours. **Free**

Cloudcroft

High in southern New Mexico's Sacramento Mountains, Cloudcroft is primarily a resort community frequented by Texans seeking escape from the heat. Cloudcroft Lodge has one of the highest-elevation golf courses in North America, where golfers are asked to refrain from feeding the bears. **Information:** Cloudcroft Chamber of Commerce, PO Box 1290, Cloudcroft 88317 (tel 505/682-2733).

LODGE

The Lodge at Cloudcroft
1 Corona Place, PO Box 497, 88317; tel 505/682-2566 or toll free 800/395-6343; fax 505/682-2715. From US 82, turn S at USFS office. Beautiful, historic mountain lodge with six-story tower; highly recommended for a vacation getaway. The lobby is elegantly and comfortably furnished with plush seating around a brick fireplace. **Rooms:** 60 rms and stes; 1 cottage/villa. CI 4pm/CO noon. Nonsmoking rms avail. Rooms are uniquely furnished in turn-of-the-century style, cozy and comfortable. Deluxe and luxury guest rooms available, including the more formal Governor's Suite. **Amenities:** Cable TV. No A/C. Some units w/fireplaces, some w/whirlpools. **Services:** Social director, masseur, babysitting. Fax and photocopying services are available. **Facilities:** 18 200 1 restaurant (*see* "Restaurants" below), 1 bar (w/entertainment), volleyball, games rm, lawn games, sauna, whirlpool. The mezzanine has tables and chairs for board games. There are lots of hiking trails in the surrounding forest, and tennis at nearby public courts. The gift shop has homemade fudge. **Rates:** Peak (May–Sept) $79–$115 S or D; $119–$199 ste; $299–$309 cottage/villa. Extra person $10. Children under age 12 stay free. Min stay special events. Lower rates off-season. MAP rates avail. Parking: Outdoor, free. AE, DC, DISC, MC, V.

RESTAURANTS

★ Ray's Western Cafe
Burro Ave; tel 505/682-2445. **American/Mexican.** Old West–style cafe with exposed wood ceiling beams and wood and stucco walls. The cashier is behind bars like a bank teller of old. Burgers, sandwiches, and a variety of homestyle dinners, plus standard Mexican plates. Pool tables in adjoining bar. **FYI:** Reservations not accepted. Country music/rock. Children's menu. **Open:** Peak (June–Aug) Thurs–Sun 7am–9pm, Fri–Sat 7am–10pm. **Prices:** Main courses $4–$15. DISC, MC, V.

Rebecca's at the Lodge
In The Lodge at Cloudcroft, 1 Corona Place; tel 505/682-2566. **Regional American.** An elegant yet unpretentious restaurant. There are two dining rooms: one with a wall of windows facing west that allows diners to look out over the trees to White Sands; the other a bit cozier with a large fireplace. A grand piano is on a slowly revolving dais centered between the two. The award-winning chef prepares innovative variations of American and continental cuisine, including sliced pork tenderloin sautéed in a creamy apple brandy sauce. The bartender proudly offers 100-year-old brandy, brought to the table in beautiful hand-painted decanters and warmed just before serving. **FYI:** Reservations recommend-

ed. Piano. Children's menu. Dress code. No smoking. **Open:** Peak (June–Sept) breakfast daily 7–10:30am; lunch Mon–Sat 11:30am–2:30pm; dinner daily 5:30–9:30pm; brunch Sun 11am–2:30pm. **Prices:** Main courses $13–$24. AE, CB, DC, DISC, MC, V.

Clovis

Santa Fe Railroad officials created Clovis in 1907 when landowners in nearby Portales grew too greedy. The town was named by a railroad official's daughter who had been reading French history and became captivated with Clovis, the first Christian king of France. An agricultural and ranching center today, the town holds a livestock auction each Wednesday. **Information:** Clovis/Curry County Chamber of Commerce, 215 N Main St, Clovis 88101 (tel 505/763-3435).

MOTELS

Best Western La Vista Inn

1516 Mabry Dr (US 60/70/84), 88101; tel 505/762-3808 or toll free 800/524-1234; fax 505/762-1422. A pleasant, basic motel. **Rooms:** 47 rms. CI 1pm/CO 11am. Nonsmoking rms avail. **Amenities:** A/C, cable TV. **Services:** 24-hour desk and maid service. **Facilities:** Games rm, washer/dryer. **Rates (CP):** $30–$40 S; $36–$46 D. Extra person $4. Children under age 12 stay free. Parking: Outdoor, free. AE, CB, DC, DISC, MC, V.

Clovis Inn

2912 Mabry Dr (US 60/70/84), 88101; tel 505/762-5600 or toll free 800/535-3440. Pleasant accommodations. **Rooms:** 97 rms and stes. CI open/CO noon. Nonsmoking rms avail. **Amenities:** A/C, cable TV w/movies. Refrigerators and microwaves are available. **Services:** Coffee is available in the lobby all day. **Facilities:** 135 Whirlpool, washer/dryer. Outdoor basketball court; barbecue pit and shaded picnic tables near the pool. **Rates (CP):** Peak (Feb–Nov) $41 S; $43 D; $50–$55 ste. Extra person $3–$6. Children under age 12 stay free. Lower rates off-season. Parking: Outdoor, free. AE, DC, DISC, MC, V.

RESTAURANT

Poor Boy's Steakhouse

2115 N Prince; tel 505/763-5222. **Seafood/Steak.** Early American decor, with Tiffany lamps, booths, and seating on a raised center section. Steaks, seafood, chicken dishes, and sandwiches; large salad bar. **FYI:** Reservations not accepted. Children's menu. No liquor license. **Open:** Sun–Thurs 11am–9pm, Fri–Sat 11am–10pm. **Prices:** Main courses $4–$19. AE, DISC, MC, V.

ATTRACTIONS

Hillcrest Park Zoo

10th and Sycamore Sts; tel 505/769-7873. Located in Hillcrest Park, the 22-acre zoo displays a full range of animals from native swamp deer to zebras. **Open:** Peak (June–Aug) Tues–Sun 9am–5pm. Reduced hours off-season. **$**

Lyceum Theatre

411 Main St; tel 505/763-6085. A restored and refurbished vaudeville theater, now the city's center for performing arts. **$$$$**

Blackwater Draw Archeological Site and Museum

US 70, Portales; tel 505/562-2202. Located 15 mi S of Clovis. This site contains the first well-documented evidence of man in North America, dating back approximately 11,000 years. On display are artifacts uncovered at the dig, including stone tools believed to be used by the Clovis people to hunt for mammoth. **Open:** Peak (June–Aug) Mon–Sat 10am–5pm, Sun noon–5pm. Reduced hours off-season. **$**

Cochiti Pueblo

Occupied continuously since the 14th century, this is the northernmost of the Keresan-speaking pueblos, stretching along the Rio Grande. Cochiti is well known for its pottery, especially the famous storyteller figures created by Helen Cordero. The San Buenaventura Feast Day is July 14, when the corn dance and rain dance are performed. Fishing and bird hunting on pueblo grounds is allowed with a permit from the pueblo governor. Water sports are available at Cochiti Lake. Photographs are prohibited. The pueblo is approximately 40 miles north of Albuquerque via US 85, then north on NM 22 and NM 16. For more information contact the Cochiti Pueblo at 505/465-2244.

Deming

Billing itself the "City of Pure Water and Fast Ducks," this agricultural center is best known for its annual August duck races. The surrounding mountains are popular with hunters. It was just south of Deming in 1916 that Mexican revolutionary and bandit Pancho Villa led some 1,000 men in a cross-border raid on the United States before being chased back into Mexico by American troops. **Information:** Deming/Luna County Chamber of Commerce, 800 E Pine St, PO Box 8, Deming 88031 (tel 505/546-2674 or 800/848-4955).

HOTEL

Grand Hotel

1721 E Motel Dr, PO Box 309, 88031; tel 505/546-2631; fax 505/546-4446. Exit 81 off I-10. Located east of downtown. Attractive motel with colonial-style entrance and a large lobby. **Rooms:** 62 rms and stes. CI open/CO noon. Nonsmoking rms avail. Rooms are decorated in French provincial style and look out on the pool and lawn. **Amenities:** A/C, cable TV. Refrigerators available. **Services:** **Facilities:** 1 restaurant, 1 bar. **Rates:** $35–$40 S; $40–$48 D; $65 ste. Extra person $6. Children under age 12 stay free. Parking: Outdoor, free. AE, CB, DC, DISC, MC, V.

MOTELS

Best Western Mimbres Valley Inn
Frontage Rd, I-10 W, PO Box 1159, 88030; tel 505/546-4544 or toll free 800/528-1234. Exit 81 off I-10. Located on the west side of town. Opened in 1993. **Rooms:** 40 rms. CI 8am/CO 11am. Nonsmoking rms avail. Pleasant, pastel-colored rooms, with wood furnishings and southwestern art. **Amenities:** A/C, cable TV. **Services:** 24-hour front desk. **Facilities:** 18-hole public golf course three miles away. **Rates (CP):** $44 S; $49 D. Extra person $5. Children under age 12 stay free. Parking: Outdoor, free. AE, CB, DC, DISC, MC, V.

Days Inn
1709 E Spruce St, PO Box 790, 88030; tel 505/546-8813 or toll free 800/DAYS-INN; fax 505/546-7095. Conveniently located, western-style hotel. **Rooms:** 57 rms. CI open/CO 11am. Nonsmoking rms avail. **Amenities:** A/C, cable TV. **Services:** Photocopying and fax services available. **Facilities:** 1 restaurant. **Rates (CP):** $35 S; $45 D. Extra person $6. Children under age 12 stay free. Parking: Outdoor, free. AE, CB, DC, DISC, MC, V.

Holiday Inn
I-10 E, PO Box 1138, 88031; tel 505/546-2661 or toll free 800/HOLIDAY; fax 505/546-6308. Exit 85 off I-10. Built in the 1970s, this meticulously maintained motel has been completely renovated and is rated one of the top Holiday Inns in the country. **Rooms:** 117 rms and stes. CI open/CO 11am. Nonsmoking rms avail. Rooms have an elegant decor, with comfortable chairs and Southwestern art. **Amenities:** A/C, cable TV, dataport. Some units w/whirlpools. **Services:** **Facilities:** 1 restaurant (*see* "Restaurants" below), 1 bar, whirlpool, washer/dryer. **Rates:** $50–$55 S; $55–$60 D; $110 ste. Extra person $6. Children under age 19 stay free. Parking: Outdoor, free. Rate includes discount on breakfast in Fat Eddie's restaurant. AE, CB, DC, DISC, JCB, MC, V.

Wagon Wheel Motel
1109 W Pine, 88030; tel 505/546-2681. A clean, comfortable mom-and-pop motel within walking distance of several restaurants. Much renovation recently completed; more underway. **Rooms:** 19 rms. CI open/CO 11am. Nonsmoking rms avail. Basic but homey rooms. **Amenities:** A/C, cable TV, dataport. **Services:** **Facilities:** Washer/dryer. Heated swimming pool open in summer only. Within walking distance of several restaurants. **Rates:** $23 S; $24 D. Extra person $2. Children under age 12 stay free. Parking: Outdoor, free. DISC, MC, V.

RESTAURANTS

Cactus Cafe
218 W Cedar St; tel 505/546-2458. Exit 82A off I-10. **Mexican/Southwestern.** The $5.95 Mexican buffet at this cafe is very popular, as are the chiles rellenos and shrimp fajitas. **FYI:** Reservations accepted. Children's menu. Beer and wine only. **Open:** Daily 7am–9pm. **Prices:** Main courses $4–$10. AE, CB, DC, DISC, MC, V.

Fat Eddie's at the Inn
In the Holiday Inn, PO Box 1138; tel 505/546-2661. Exit 85 off I-10. **American/Mexican.** Choice of standard American and Mexican entrees; specialties include baby-back pork ribs and pepper steak. Buffet offered three times a week. **FYI:** Reservations accepted. Children's menu. **Open:** Breakfast daily 6–11am; lunch daily 11am–2pm; dinner Sun–Thurs 4–9pm, Fri–Sat 4–10pm. **Prices:** Main courses $4–$16. AE, CB, DC, DISC, MC, V.

K-Bob's
316 E Cedar St; tel 505/546-8883. Exit 82 off I-10. **Steak.** A family steak place with old guns and brands on the walls. Besides steak, K-Bob's offers catfish, trout, chicken, and sandwiches. **FYI:** Reservations accepted. Children's menu. Beer and wine only. **Open:** Daily 10:30am–10pm. **Prices:** Main courses $3–$16. AE, DISC, MC, V.

ATTRACTIONS

Deming Luna Mimbres Museum
301 S Silver St; tel 505/546-2382. Deming was the meeting place of the second east-west railroad to connect the Pacific and Atlantic Coasts, and that heritage is recalled here. Collections include pioneer-era quilts and laces, military mementos of 19th-century forts and raids, over 800 dolls, and a gem and mineral display. **Open:** Mon–Sat 9am–4pm, Sun 1:30–4pm. **Free**

Rockhound State Park
NM 11; tel 505/546-6182. Located at the base of the wild Florida Mountains, this arid, cactus-covered land is traversed by trails leading down into dry gullies and canyons. Visitors are encouraged to pick and take home with them as much as 15 pounds of minerals—jasper, agate, quartz crystal, and flow-banded rhyolite—from these trails. Hunting, playgrounds, camping. **Open:** Daily sunrise–sunset. **Free**

Pancho Villa State Park
NM 11; tel 505/531-2711. Located 32 miles south of Deming in the tiny border town of Columbus, looking across to Mexico. The state park here marks the last foreign invasion of American soil. A temporary fort at this site was attacked in 1916 by Mexican revolutionaries led by Pancho Villa, who cut through the boundary fence at Columbus. The Mexicans retreated across the border, and an American punitive expedition, headed by Gen John J Pershing, was launched in Mexico, but Villa was never captured. Today ruins of the border fort, called Camp Furlong, can be seen at the park.

Other features include a desert botanical garden, visitors center, playground, and campsites with shelters. **Open:** Daily 6am–9pm. **$**

Elephant Butte

See also Truth or Consequences

The small community, lake, and state park here are named for a rock formation that to some resembles an elephant. New Mexico's largest lake was created when a dam was built across the Rio Grande in 1916; extremely popular, it attracts thousands of boaters and fishermen. **Information:** Elephant Butte State Park, PO Box 13, Elephant Butte 87935 (tel 505/744-5421).

MOTEL

Elephant Butte Inn
NM 195, PO Box E, 87935; tel 505/744-5431. 5 mi N of Truth or Consequences, exit 83 or 79 off I-25. Popular with boaters, fishermen, and other water lovers. **Rooms:** 48 rms. CI 2pm/CO 11am. Nonsmoking rms avail. Beautiful views of the lake from the rooms at the back. **Amenities:** A/C, cable TV. **Services:** **Facilities:** 2 120 1 restaurant, 1 bar (w/entertainment), volleyball, playground. Within walking distance of the public beach at Elephant Butte Lake. **Rates:** Peak (Apr–Sept) $49–$62 S or D. Extra person $5. Children under age 18 stay free. Min stay special events. Lower rates off-season. Parking: Outdoor, free. Rates include up to four persons in room; $5 charge for each additional person. Higher rates on weekends. AE, DC, DISC, MC, V.

RESTAURANT

Dam Site Restaurant
In Elephant Butte State Park, NM 177; tel 505/894-2073. 5 mi E of Truth or Consequences; exit 83 off I-25. **American.** This simple dining room has white walls and Mexican touches. One side offers a lovely view of Elephant Butte Lake, while the other looks over a cactus garden. Steak, seafood, chicken, and several Mexican dishes are offered. Separate patio menu. Closed Tues–Wed Nov–Mar. **FYI:** Reservations accepted. Children's menu. **Open:** Peak (Mar–Oct) Sun–Thurs 11am–9pm, Fri–Sat 11am–10pm. **Prices:** Main courses $6–$13. AE, DC, DISC, MC, V.

ATTRACTION

Elephant Butte Lake State Park
NM 85; tel 505/744-5421. The park contains the largest lake in New Mexico, covering 38,000 acres. Fishing, swimming, boating, sailing, waterskiing, and camping. **Open:** Daily 24 hours. **$**

El Morro National Monument

Located on NM 53, "Inscription Rock" looms up out of the sand and sagebrush, a bluff 200 feet high holding some of the most captivating messages in North America. Between 1605 and 1906, nearly every explorer, conquistador, missionary, army officer, surveyor, and pioneer emigrant who passed the rock left a written record of their journey. Early Native Americans also left their mark in the form of petroglyph carvings. A paved walkway makes it easy to walk to the writings, and there is a stone stairway leading up to other markings.

Atop Inscription Rock via a short, steep trail are ruins of an Anasazi pueblo occupying an area 200 by 300 feet. The visitor center (tel 505/783-4226), open (peak Mem Day–Labor Day) daily 9am–7pm, distributes self-guided trail booklets.

Española

A good home base for exploring northern New Mexico Indian pueblos, Española is close to Santa Fe, Los Alamos, and Taos. It is well known for its abundance of low riders—often elaborately painted cars that have been dramatically lowered—which can be seen slowly cruising through town evenings and weekends. **Information:** Española Valley Chamber of Commerce, 417 Big Rock Center, Española 87532 (tel 505/753-2831).

MOTEL

Chamisa Inn
920 N Riverside Dr, 87532; tel 505/753-7291 or toll free 800/766-7943; fax 505/753-1218. Take US 84 to NM 68. A good, basic motel. **Rooms:** 51 rms. CI 11am/CO 11am. Nonsmoking rms avail. Standard motel rooms. **Amenities:** A/C, cable TV. **Services:** **Facilities:** 250 The pool is in a nice grassy area, with rose bushes about. **Rates (CP):** Peak (May 25–Oct 12) $30–$65 S; $38–$70 D. Extra person $5. Children under age 16 stay free. Lower rates off-season. Parking: Outdoor, free. AE, CB, DC, DISC, JCB, MC, V.

ATTRACTIONS

Santa Clara Pueblo
NM 30, tel 505/753-7326. This is one of the larger pueblos in the area, with a population of about 1,600. Driving and walking tours are offered weekdays, with a week's notice, and include visits to the pueblo's historic church and artists' studios. The Puye Cliff Dwellings (see below) are on the Santa Clara reservation. **Open:** Daily sunrise–sunset. **Free**

Puye Cliff Dwellings
NM 30; tel 505/753-7326. Thought to have been occupied from about 1250 to 1577 by the Santa Clara people, this site at the mouth of the Santa Clara Canyon is a national landmark. Visitors can descend the volcanic tuff via staircases and ladders from the 7,000-foot mesa top into the 740-room pueblo ruin, which includes a ceremonial chamber and community house. Petroglyphs are evident in many of the rocky cliff walls. **Open:** Peak (June–Aug) daily 8am–8pm. Reduced hours off-season. **$$**

Farmington

See also Aztec

Called a "farming town" by 19th-century ranchers who bought fresh vegetables and grain here, it was formally named when a post office was established in 1879. The largest community in northwest New Mexico, Farmington remains a supply center for ranchers, farmers, the oil and gas industry, and the adjacent Navajo Nation. **Information:** Farmington Convention & Visitors Bureau, 203 W Main St, Suite 401, Farmington 87401 (tel 505/326-7602 or 800/448-1240).

HOTELS

Anasazi Inn
903 W Main St, 87401; tel 505/325-4564; fax 505/326-0732. A pueblo-style hotel with friendly personnel. **Rooms:** 64 rms and stes. CI noon/CO 11am. Nonsmoking rms avail. Rooms are comfortable, with one king- or two queen-size beds and wood furnishings. **Amenities:** A/C, cable TV, refrig. **Services:** **Facilities:** 80 2 restaurants, 1 bar. **Rates:** Peak (July–Aug) $40 S; $48 D; $60 ste. Extra person $8. Lower rates off-season. Parking: Outdoor, free. AE, DC, DISC, MC, V.

Best Western Inn and Suites
700 Scott Ave, 87401; tel 505/327-5221 or toll free 800/600-5221; fax 505/327-1565. Conveniently located, with a sky-lit central courtyard. **Rooms:** 192 rms and stes. CI 1pm/CO noon. Nonsmoking rms avail. Well-appointed rooms have one king- or two queen-size beds, and 2 sinks. **Amenities:** A/C, cable TV, refrig. **Services:** Children's program. **Facilities:** 500 1 restaurant, 1 bar, games rm, sauna, whirlpool, washer/dryer. **Rates:** Peak (May–Sept) $64–$86 S; $74–$96 D; $82–$102 ste. Extra person $10. Children under age 12 stay free. Lower rates off-season. AP rates avail. Parking: Outdoor, free. AE, CB, DC, DISC, JCB, MC, V.

MOTELS

Holiday Inn of Farmington
600 E Broadway, 87401; tel 505/327-9811 or toll free 800/HOLIDAY; fax 505/325-2288. The recently renovated lobby is attractively furnished in an Aztec motif. **Rooms:** 149 rms. CI 3pm/CO noon. Nonsmoking rms avail. All king rooms have sofa beds. Some rooms open onto the pool and a grassy area with trees. **Amenities:** Cable TV w/movies. No A/C. Some units w/whirlpools. **Services:** Children's program. **Facilities:** 300 1 restaurant (*see* "Restaurants" below), 1 bar, sauna, whirlpool. **Rates:** $64 S; $70 D. Extra person $6. Children under age 19 stay free. Parking: Outdoor, free. AE, DC, DISC, MC, V.

La Quinta
675 Scott Ave, 87401; tel 505/327-4706 or toll free 800/531-5900; fax 505/325-6583. N of Broadway. Pleasant mid-size motel. **Rooms:** 106 rms and stes. CI noon/CO noon. Nonsmoking rms avail. **Amenities:** A/C, cable TV w/movies. **Services:** **Facilities:** **Rates (CP):** Peak (May 27–Sept) $54–$60 S; $54–$68 D; $74–$82 ste. Extra person $8. Children under age 18 stay free. Lower rates off-season. Parking: Outdoor, free. AE, CB, DC, DISC, MC, V.

Motel 6
1600 Bloomfield Hwy, 87401; tel 505/326-4501; fax 505/326-3883. Adequate lodging for the cost-conscious. **Rooms:** 134 rms. CI 7am/CO noon. Nonsmoking rms avail. **Amenities:** A/C, TV. **Services:** **Facilities:** Washer/dryer. **Rates:** $25 S; $31 D. Extra person $6. Children under age 17 stay free. Parking: Outdoor, free. AE, CB, DC, DISC, MC, V.

Super 8 Motel
1601 Bloomfield Hwy, 87401; tel 505/325-1813 or toll free 800/800-8000; fax 505/325-1813. An attractive, newer motel. **Rooms:** 60 rms and stes. CI 6am/CO 11am. Nonsmoking rms avail. Clean, comfortable rooms with attractive bedspreads and art. **Amenities:** A/C, cable TV w/movies. **Services:** **Facilities:** Games rm. **Rates (CP):** Peak (May–Sept) $34 S; $40 D; $55 ste. Extra person $7. Children under age 13 stay free. Lower rates off-season. Parking: Outdoor, free. AE, CB, DC, DISC, MC, V.

RESTAURANTS

Brass Apple
In Holiday Inn of Farmington, 600 E Broadway; tel 505/327-9811. **Continental/Southwestern.** Modern dining room with large windows and lots of plants. Specialties include seafood chiles rellenos, pork asada, chicken dijonaise, Cajun barbecued shrimp, filet mignon, and prime rib. **FYI:** Reservations accepted. Children's menu. **Open:** Daily 6am–10pm. **Prices:** Main courses $6–$15. AE, CB, DC, DISC, MC, V.

★ **Clancy's Pub**
2701 E 20th St; tel 505/325-8176. At Hutton Rd. **Eclectic.** A classic pub, reminiscent of television's *Cheers,* with dark-green decor and an enclosed patio with lattice-work umbrella tables. There's a number of sandwiches, burgers, and southwestern dishes to choose from. Specialties include steak

Clancy's, tenderloin steak with Swiss cheese, ham, and green chiles; fish and chips; and barbecued ribs. **FYI:** Reservations accepted. Blues/singer. **Open:** Mon–Sat 11am–2am, Sun noon–midnight. **Prices:** Main courses $5–$10. AE, DC, DISC, MC, V.

K B Dillon's
101 W Broadway; tel 505/325-0222. **Southwestern/Steak.** A comfortable, fun pub. Decorated with lots of plants and sports memorabilia. Fish, chicken, beef, and seafood. **FYI:** Reservations recommended. Blues/rock. Dress code. **Open:** Lunch Mon–Fri 11am–2pm; dinner Mon–Sat 5:30–10pm. **Prices:** Main courses $11–$21. AE, MC, V.

Señor Pepper's Restaurant
In Four Corners Regional Airport, Navajo St; tel 505/327-0436. **Mexican.** Mexican fiesta-style decor. All food is prepared from fresh ingredients. Stacked and rolled enchiladas, a variety of burritos, tostadas, tacos, chiles rellenos, and combination plates. Southwestern-style steak, chicken, and seafood dishes also served. Items labeled "Life Course" contain no cheese or sour cream. **FYI:** Reservations accepted. Comedy. Children's menu. **Open:** Sun–Thurs 6am–10pm, Fri–Sat 6am–10:30pm. **Prices:** Main courses $5–$30. AE, DC, DISC, MC, V.

ATTRACTIONS

Salmon Ruin & San Juan County Archaeological Research Center
6131 US 64, Bloomfield; tel 505/632-2013. This massive C-shaped pueblo overlooking the San Juan River was built in the 11th century as a Chacoan colony and is one of the most recently excavated ruins in the West. In 1990, **Heritage Park** was established on an adjoining plot of land. It comprises a series of reconstructed ancient and historic dwellings representing the area's cultures, from a paleoarchaic sand-dune site to an Anasazi pit house. Visitor center, small museum. **Open:** Peak (Apr–Oct) daily 9am–5pm. Reduced hours off-season. **$**

Angel Peak Recreation Area
NM 44; tel 505/599-8900. At the foot of the distinctive 6,800-foot pinnacle of Angel Peak is a variety of unusual, colorful geological formations and canyons to explore on foot. The Bureau of Land Management has developed two campgrounds and a picnic area, however there is no water and no on-site personnel. **Open:** Daily 24 hours. **Free**

Ship Rock
US 64, Shiprock. This distinctive landmark is known to the Navajo as *Tes be dahi*, "Rock With Wings." Composed of igneous rock flanked by long upright walls of solidified lava, it rises 1,700 feet off the desert floor to an elevation of 7,178 feet. There are viewpoints off US 666, 6 to 7 miles south of the town of Shiprock. You can get closer by taking the tribal road to the community of Red Rock; but to get any nearer this sacred Navajo rock, you must have permission from the Navajo Tribal Council. Climbing is not permitted.

Bisti Badlands
Old NM 371; tel 505/599-8900. A federally protected area of strange rock formations, petrified logs, and prehistoric fossils. Visitors can walk among the huge turrets, buttes, spires, and pinnacles. The site is administered by the Bureau of Land Management, however there are no facilities on the premises. **Open:** Daily 24 hours. **Free**

Flora Vista

See Aztec, Farmington

Gallup

See also Ramah

Situated along I-40 just 22 miles from the Arizona state line, Gallup is a trade center for the huge Navajo Nation and nearby Zuni Pueblo and is a popular stop for visitors seeking Native American crafts. Each August the Intertribal Indian Ceremonial attracts tribes from throughout North America. **Information:** Gallup Convention & Visitors Bureau, 701 Montoya Blvd, PO Box 600, Gallup 87305 (tel 505/863-3841 or 800/242-4282).

HOTEL

El Rancho Hotel and Motel
1000 E 66 Ave, 87301; tel 505/863-9311 or toll free 800/543-6351; fax 505/722-5917. Exit 22 off I-40. This historic 1937 hotel was headquarters for numerous film crews and movie stars on location in the Southwest from the 1940s to the 1960s. There's an unmanned shoe shine stand in the lobby, and stills from movies shot in Gallup on the mezzanine level. **Rooms:** 98 rms, stes, and effic. CI 1pm/CO noon. Nonsmoking rms avail. All rooms have ceiling fans and artwork on the walls and are all named for movie stars. The Presidential Suite (Ronald Reagan stayed here when he was an actor) has a king bed, sofa, chairs, and an incredibly large bathroom with a whirlpool and bidet. The Marx Brothers Suite has three beds. **Amenities:** Cable TV. No A/C. Some units w/terraces, 1 w/whirlpool. **Services:** Babysitting. 24-hour front desk. **Facilities:** 120 1 restaurant, 1 bar, washer/dryer. **Rates:** $33–$39 S; $49–$54 D; $68–$75 ste; $49–$54 effic. Extra person $5. Children under age 2 stay free. Parking: Outdoor, free. AE, DC, DISC, MC, V.

MOTELS

Best Western Gallup Inn
3009 W US 66, 87301; tel 505/772-2221 or toll free 800/528-1234; fax 505/722-7442. Exit 16 off I-40. A mid-size Best Western, noted for its large atrium courtyard containing a swimming pool and cafe. **Rooms:** 126 rms and stes. Executive level. CI open/CO noon. Nonsmoking rms avail. Rooms are attractively decorated with an American Indian motif. **Amenities:** A/C, cable TV, refrig, dataport. **Services:** **Facilities:** 1 restaurant (bkfst and dinner only), 1 bar (w/entertainment), games rm, sauna, steam rm, whirlpool, playground, washer/dryer. **Rates:** Peak (May–Sept) $52–$69 S; $62–$79 D; $69–$102 ste. Extra person $10. Children under age 12 stay free. Lower rates off-season. Parking: Outdoor, free. AE, CB, DC, DISC, MC, V.

Best Western Red Rock Inn
3010 E US 66, 87301; tel 505/722-7600 or toll free 800/528-1234; fax 505/722-9770. Exit 26 off I-40. Features a high-ceilinged lobby with comfortable furniture and Native American pictures. **Rooms:** 70 rms and stes. CI 3pm/CO 11am. Nonsmoking rms avail. Early American–style beds and overstuffed wing chairs; furnishings are of good quality. **Amenities:** A/C, cable TV. Some units w/terraces, some w/whirlpools. Some rooms have refrigerators. **Services:** **Facilities:** Sauna, whirlpool, washer/dryer. **Rates (CP):** Peak (May–Oct) $75–$90 S; $80–$95 D; $90–$125 ste. Extra person $7. Children under age 11 stay free. Lower rates off-season. Parking: Outdoor, free. AE, CB, DC, DISC, MC, V.

Best Western Royal Holiday Motel
1903 W US 66, 87301; tel 505/722-4900 or toll free 800/528-1234; fax 505/722-5100. Exit 16 off I-40. Conveniently located, Spanish-style motel. **Rooms:** 50 rms. CI open/CO 11am. Nonsmoking rms avail. Recently renovated and refurnished rooms are handsome and unusually spacious, with Early American–style beds, American Indian paintings, and deep-green carpeting. **Amenities:** A/C, cable TV. Some rooms have refrigerators. **Services:** **Facilities:** Sauna, whirlpool, playground. **Rates (CP):** Peak (May–Oct) $58–$84 S; $62–$88 D. Extra person $7. Children under age 12 stay free. Lower rates off-season. Parking: Outdoor, free. AE, CB, DC, DISC, MC, V.

Blue Spruce Lodge
1119 E US 66, 87301; tel 505/863-5211. Exit 22 off I-40. A friendly, clean, small motel. Good value. **Rooms:** 20 rms. CI noon/CO 11am. Nonsmoking rms avail. Rooms face either the highway or railroad tracks. Comfortable furnishings. **Amenities:** A/C, cable TV. **Services:** **Rates:** $22–$26 S; $24–$32 D. Extra person $3. Children under age 6 stay free. Parking: Outdoor, free. AE, DISC, MC, V.

El Capitan Motel
1300 E US 66, 87301; tel 505/863-6828. Exit 22 off I-40. Pleasant, one-story, adobe-style motel. **Rooms:** 42 rms and stes. CI noon/CO 11am. Nonsmoking rms avail. Southwestern decor, with prints on the walls and tile bathrooms. **Amenities:** A/C, cable TV. **Services:** **Rates:** Peak (Apr–Oct) $36–$38 S or D; $40–$45 ste. Extra person $5. Children under age 5 stay free. Lower rates off-season. Parking: Outdoor, free. AE, DISC, MC, V.

Holiday Inn
2915 W US 66, 87301; tel 505/722-2201 or toll free 800/432-2211; fax 505/722-9616. Exit 16 off I-40. A large, comfortable lobby and a patio area with welcoming green grass are hallmarks of this fine Holiday Inn. **Rooms:** 212 rms. CI 3pm/CO noon. Nonsmoking rms avail. Rooms are comfortable and quiet. **Amenities:** A/C, cable TV. **Services:** **Facilities:** 2 restaurants, 1 bar (w/entertainment), games rm, sauna, whirlpool, washer/dryer. Putting area in games room; sun deck outside the indoor pool. Equipment for the hearing impaired is available. **Rates:** Peak (Mar–Oct) $56–$80 S; $61–$90 D. Extra person $5. Children under age 12 stay free. Lower rates off-season. Parking: Outdoor, free. AE, CB, DC, DISC, JCB, MC, V.

RESTAURANTS

Panz Alegra
1201 E 66 Ave; tel 505/722-7229. Exit 22 off I-40. **Mexican/Steak.** Brick walls and Tiffany lamps, booths and tables. Steaks, seafood, burgers, salads, a few Italian items, and a variety of Mexican dishes, including posole, combination plates, fajitas, and burritos. **FYI:** Reservations accepted. Children's menu. **Open:** Mon–Thurs 11am–10pm, Fri–Sat 11am–10:30pm. **Prices:** Main courses $8–$11. AE, CB, DC, DISC, MC, V.

The Ranch Kitchen
3001 W US 66; tel 505/722-2537. Exit 16 off I-40. **Mexican/Southwestern.** Features two large, attractive dining rooms with blond tables, white walls, corner fireplaces, low ceilings with vigas, wagon wheel chandeliers, and local art. An open-pit barbecue is outside. The menu includes New Mexican dishes, Navajo tacos, steaks, pork, and chicken; there's also a salad bar. Summer outdoor dining is offered after 5pm. A Navajo gift shop is on the premises. **FYI:** Reservations accepted. Children's menu. Beer and wine only. **Open:** Peak (Mar–Oct) daily 6am–10pm. **Prices:** Main courses $8–$13. AE, CB, DC, DISC, MC, V.

ATTRACTION

Red Rock State Park
NM 566; tel 505/722-3839. The park is best known as the site of the Marland Aitson Amphitheater, a large outdoor venue situated in a natural setting amidst red sandstone buttes. This arena is the site of numerous annual events, including the Inter-Tribal Indian Ceremonial held in mid-August. The **Red**

Rock Museum has displays on prehistoric Anasazi and modern Zuni, Hopi, and Navajo culture, as well as changing art gallery exhibits. **Open:** Park, daily sunrise–sunset; museum, Mon–Fri 8am–4:30pm. $

Grants

See also Acoma Pueblo, Ramah

A true boomtown, Grants first prospered as a railroad stop, then as a logging center, and finally as a uranium mining town in the 1950s. With that last boom gone bust, Grants is today attracting tourists to the two nearby national monuments and the Acoma and Laguna pueblos. **Information:** Grants/Cibola County Chamber of Commerce, 100 Iron Ave, PO Box 297, Grants 87020 (tel 505/287-4802 or 800/748-2142).

MOTELS

Best Western Grants Inn

1501 E Santa Fe Ave, 87020; tel 505/287-7901 or toll free 800/600-5221; fax 505/285-5751. Exit 85 off I-40. A good-looking motel featuring a central courtyard and pool surrounded by lush tropical plants. **Rooms:** 126 rms and stes. CI 1pm/CO noon. Nonsmoking rms avail. Rooms are quiet and spacious, with attractive artwork. **Amenities:** A/C, cable TV, dataport. Some suites have microwaves, refrigerators. **Services:** **Facilities:** 1 restaurant, 1 bar (w/entertainment), games rm, spa, sauna, whirlpool, washer/dryer. Fitness center planned for 1997. **Rates:** Peak (May–Oct 15) $63–$73 S; $71–$79 D; $73–$79 ste. Extra person $10. Children under age 18 stay free. Lower rates off-season. Parking: Outdoor, free. AE, CB, DC, DISC, MC, V.

Sands Motel

112 McArthur St, PO Box 1437, 87020; tel 505/287-2996 or toll free 800/424-7679. Exit 85 off I-40. Pleasant family-style motel. A very good value. **Rooms:** 24 rms. CI 2pm/CO 11am. Nonsmoking rms avail. Some rooms have separate dressing areas. **Amenities:** A/C, cable TV, refrig. **Services:** Babysitting. **Facilities:** Close to several restaurants; coffee shop within walking distance. **Rates:** Peak (May–Dec) $33 S; $44–$47 D. Extra person $5. Children under age 12 stay free. Lower rates off-season. Parking: Outdoor, free. AE, CB, DC, DISC, MC, V.

RESTAURANTS

El Jardin Palacio's

319 W Santa Fe Ave; tel 505/285-5231. Exit 81 off I-40. **Southwestern.** Mexican family-owned restaurant decorated with original oil paintings; located in a building that formerly housed the city hall, jail, and firehouse. Most selections are favorite family recipes. The menu offers Mexican combination plates, fajitas, burritos, chiles rellenos, and chimichangas. Also rainbow trout and several shrimp dishes. **FYI:** Reservations accepted. Children's menu. Beer and wine only. **Open:** Lunch Mon–Sat 11am–2:30pm, Sun 11am–4pm; dinner Mon–Sat 5–9pm. **Prices:** Main courses $3–$8. AE, MC, V.

Grants Station Restaurant

200 W Santa Fe Ave; tel 505/287-2334. Exit 85 or 81 off I-40. **Regional American.** A fun place for kids and railroad buffs. Railroad memorabilia is everywhere; even the waitstaff sports railroad uniforms, and the children's menu can be folded into a railroad engineer's cap. A caboose outside is used as a private dining room. Steaks, fish, pork chops, chicken, shrimp, Mexican dishes, and sandwiches, plus salad bar. Breakfast is served all day. **FYI:** Reservations accepted. Children's menu. No liquor license. **Open:** Peak (June–Sept) daily 6am–11:30pm. **Prices:** Main courses $5–$12. AE, DC, DISC, MC, V.

La Ventana

110½ Geis St; tel 505/287-9393. Exit 81 off I-40. **Seafood/Steak.** Attractive, dimly lit restaurant with southwestern decor and separate rooms for meetings and special events. Steaks, seafood, ribs, chicken, and a few Mexican dishes. **FYI:** Reservations recommended. **Open:** Mon–Sat 11am–11pm. **Prices:** Main courses $5–$13. AE, CB, DC, DISC, MC, V.

Monte Carlo Restaurant and Lounge

721 W Santa Fe Ave; tel 505/287-9250. Exit 81 or 85 off I-40. **Steak/New Mexican.** A historical landmark on old Route 66, this adobe restaurant opened in 1947. Specialties are steak Marie (topped with green chile and melted cheese), chile rellenos del mar (with shrimp and crabmeat), burritos, fajitas, and Navajo tacos and Mexican pizza. **FYI:** Reservations accepted. Children's menu. **Open:** Daily 11am–10pm. **Prices:** Main courses $7–$13. AE, DISC, MC, V.

ATTRACTIONS

The New Mexico Museum of Mining

100 N Iron St; tel 505/287-4802. The world's only uranium-mining museum is structured over a re-creation of an actual underground mine, complete with original machinery and equipment. Once underground, visitors can touch and feel the mining tools, equipment, and cement walls. Retired miners often lead tours. **Open:** Peak (June–Aug) Mon–Sat 9am–6pm, Sun noon–6pm. Reduced hours off-season. $

El Malpais National Monument

620 E Santa Fe Ave; tel 505/285-5406. One of America's newest national monuments, it is one of the outstanding examples of volcanic landscape in the United States. The area covers 115,000 acres of cinder cones, vast lava flows, hundreds of lava tubes and ice caves, sandstone cliffs, and natural bridges and arches. Anasazi ruins, ancient Indian trails, and Spanish and Anglo homesteads are located throughout.

From **Sandstone Bluffs Overlook** (NM 117), many craters are visible in the lava flow. From NM 53 visitors have access to the **Zuni-Acoma Trail**, an ancient trade route that crosses 4 major lava flows in a 7½-mile (one-way) hike. **El Calderon**, 20 miles south of I-40, is a trailhead for exploration of a cinder cone, lava tubes, and a bat cave. **Open:** Daily 8am–4:30pm. **Free**

Cibola National Forest
1800 Lobo Canyon Rd; tel 505/287-8833. Two major parcels of the forest flank I-40 on either side of Grants. To the southeast, NM 547 leads some 20 miles into the San Mateo Mountains. The range's high point, 11,301-foot Mount Taylor, is home of the annual Mount Taylor Winter Quadrathlon in February. The route passes two campgrounds, Lobo Canyon and Coal Mine Canyon. Hiking and elk hunting are popular in summer, cross-country skiing in winter. **Open:** Daily 24 hours. **Free**

Hobbs

An oil town just three miles from Texas, Hobbs is also a ranching and farming center and has two small colleges. **Information:** Hobbs Chamber of Commerce, 400 N Marland Blvd, Hobbs 88240 (tel 505/397-3202 or 800/658-6291).

MOTELS

Econo Lodge
619 N Marland St, 88240; tel 505/397-3591. A clean and comfortable, basic no-frills motel. Very popular with business travelers. **Rooms:** 38 rms. CI 5am/CO 11am. Nonsmoking rms avail. **Amenities:** A/C, cable TV w/movies. Some units w/terraces. **Services:** Babysitting. Complimentary morning coffee. **Facilities:** **Rates:** $30–$35 S; $35–$40 D. Extra person $3. Children under age 12 stay free. Parking: Outdoor, free. Weekly rates are available. AE, DISC, MC, V.

Ramada Inn
501 N Marland St, 88240; tel 505/397-3251 or toll free 800/635-6635; fax 800/635-6635. A pleasant full-service motel, popular with business travelers and tour groups. **Rooms:** 76 rms and stes. CI 2pm/CO 1pm. Nonsmoking rms avail. **Amenities:** A/C, cable TV w/movies. 1 unit w/minibar. Refrigerators are available. **Services:** **Facilities:** 100 2 restaurants, 1 bar (w/entertainment). Ten percent discount for guests in the motel restaurants. **Rates:** $41–$50 S; $55–$60 D; $95 ste. Extra person $7. Children under age 16 stay free. Parking: Outdoor, free. AE, CB, DC, DISC, MC, V.

RESTAURANT

Cattle Baron Steak and Seafood Restaurant
1930 N Grimes St; tel 505/393-2800. **Seafood/Steak.** Tastefully appointed with handsome polished wood and parquet tables. Etched-glass dividers separate booths. Three sizes of prime rib are offered. Entrees include salad bar, fresh-baked bread, and choice of baked potato, fries, rice pilaf, or steamed fresh vegetable. Happy hour weekdays 4-7pm; meals can be served in the bar. **FYI:** Reservations accepted. Children's menu. **Open:** Sun 11am–9pm, Mon–Thurs 11am–9:30pm, Fri–Sat 11am–10pm. **Prices:** Main courses $7–$21. AE, DC, DISC, MC, V.

ATTRACTION

Lea County Cowboy Hall of Fame and Western Heritage Center
5317 Lovington Hwy; tel 505/392-5518. Honors the area's ranchers and rodeo performers with displays of memorabilia and artifacts; as well as a chronological history of Lea County. **Open:** Mon–Fri 10am–5pm, Sat 1–5pm. **Free**

Jemez Pueblo

The 2,400 Jemez natives are the only remaining people to speak the Towa dialect of the Tanoan group. Famous for their dancing, Jemez feast days attract residents from many other pueblos. Celebration days include the Feast of Our Lady of Angels on August 12; the Feast of San Diego on November 12, when the Pecos bull dance is performed; and the Feast of Our Lady of Guadalupe on December 12, featuring the Matachines dance, based on a Spanish morality play.

There is fishing and picnicking along the Jemez River on government forest lands, and camping at the Dragonfly Recreation Area. Pueblo stores sell fishing permits, and permits for game hunting may be bought from the pueblo governor's office. The pueblo is 42 miles northwest of Albuquerque via I-25 to Bernalillo, NM 44 to San Ysidro, and NM 43 to the pueblo. Photographs prohibited. For more information contact the pueblo at 505/834-7359.

Jemez Springs

ATTRACTION

Jemez State Monument
NM 4; tel 505/829-3530. All that is left of the Mission of San Jose de los Jemez, founded by Franciscan missionaries in 1621, is preserved at this site. The mission was excavated between 1921 and 1937, along with portions of a prehistoric Jemez pueblo. Artifacts found during the excavation are housed in a small museum. **Open:** Peak (May–mid-Sept) daily 9:30am–5:30pm. Reduced hours off-season. **$**

Laguna Pueblo

The pueblo consists of a central settlement and five smaller villages some 32 miles east of Grants, and 50 miles west of Albuquerque. It is the youngest of New Mexico's pueblos. Located here is the **Mission of San Jose de los Lagunas,** famous for its interior artwork. Pueblo and Navajo people from throughout the region attend the Fiesta de San Jose, held September 19, at the Laguna mission. The fair kicks off with a mass and procession, followed by a harvest dance, sports events, and a carnival. Photographs, sketches, and tape recordings of pueblo ceremonies are striclty forbidden. For more information contact the Laguna Pueblo at 505/552-6654.

Lamy

See Santa Fe

Las Cruces

The state's second-largest city, Las Cruces is named for the crosses planted in an impromptu cemetery where a group of Spanish travelers were buried after a massacre at the hands of Native Americans in the 1800s. Today the city is an agricultural center (known for its pecans and chiles) and regional transportation hub at the intersection of I-25 and I-10. Although Las Cruces itself wasn't established until 1849, the adjacent community of La Mesilla was settled by Spanish-Mexican colonists in the late 1500s; many historic buildings still remain. **Information:** Las Cruces Convention & Visitors Bureau, 311 N Downtown Mall, Las Cruces 88001 (tel 505/524-8521 or 800/FIESTAS).

HOTEL

Las Cruces Hilton Inn

705 S Telshor Blvd, 88011; tel 505/522-4300 or toll free 800/288-1784; fax 505/522-4300. Exit 2 off I-25. A luxurious downtown hotel, convenient to all Las Cruces attractions and activities, and adjacent to the city's largest shopping mall. **Rooms:** 206 rms and stes. Executive level. CI 1pm/CO 1pm. Nonsmoking rms avail. Accommodations range from deluxe guest rooms to executive suites. **Amenities:** A/C, cable TV w/movies, dataport, voice mail. Some units w/minibars, some w/whirlpools. **Services:** Car-rental desk. **Facilities:** 572 1 restaurant, 1 bar (w/entertainment), whirlpool. Access to Picacho Hills private 18-hole golf course. **Rates (CP):** $89–$109 S or D; $115–$220 ste. Extra person $10. Children under age 18 stay free. Parking: Outdoor, free. Golf packages avail. AE, CB, DC, DISC, EC, ER, JCB, MC, V.

MOTELS

Best Western Mesilla Valley Inn

901 Avenida de Mesilla, 88005; tel 505/524-8603 or toll free 800/327-3314; fax 505/526-8437. Exit 140 off I-10. This modern, southwestern-style motel is close to Old Mesilla's galleries, shops, and restaurants, and to downtown Las Cruces. **Rooms:** 166 rms and effic. CI 2pm/CO 11am. Nonsmoking rms avail. **Amenities:** A/C, cable TV w/movies. 1 unit w/terrace. Executive rooms have refrigerators and clock radios. **Services:** Babysitting. **Facilities:** 350 1 restaurant, 1 bar (w/entertainment), games rm, whirlpool, washer/dryer. Golf and tennis within three miles. **Rates:** $56–$64 S; $62–$70 D; $80–$100 effic. Extra person $7. Children under age 13 stay free. Parking: Outdoor, free. Rates include discount on restaurant meals, and children under 13 eat free. AE, CB, DC, DISC, MC, V.

Best Western Mission Inn

1765 S Main St, 88005; tel 505/524-8591 or toll free 800/528-1234; fax 505/523-4740. An attractive Mexican mission-style building with stucco walls and a red tile roof. **Rooms:** 68 rms and stes. CI 2pm/CO noon. Nonsmoking rms avail. Rooms are adorned with Mexican tiles and western art. **Amenities:** A/C, satel TV w/movies. **Services:** **Facilities:** 150 1 restaurant, 1 bar, playground. The restaurant serves a daily breakfast buffet only. **Rates (BB):** $50–$70 S or D; $70–$90 ste. Extra person $4. Children under age 12 stay free. Parking: Outdoor, free. AE, CB, DC, DISC, MC, V.

Hampton Inn

755 Avenida de Mesilla, 88005; tel 505/526-8311 or toll free 800/426-7866; fax 505/527-2015. Exit 140 off I-10. Well-maintained, better-than-average motel at a convenient location on the southwest side of town, near historic Old Mesilla's shops, galleries, and restaurants. **Rooms:** 118 rms. CI 3pm/CO noon. Nonsmoking rms avail. **Amenities:** A/C, cable TV w/movies. **Services:** Free local calls. **Facilities:** 33 **Rates (CP):** $57–$59 S; $62–$64 D. Children under age 19 stay free. Parking: Outdoor, free. AE, CB, DC, DISC, MC, V.

INNS

Lundeen's Inn of the Arts

618 S Alameda Blvd, 88005 (Downtown); tel 505/526-3327; fax 505/647-1334. A historic and comfortable yet elegantly furnished inn, with wonderful artwork. Unsuitable for children under 12. **Rooms:** 18 rms, stes, and effic; 2 cottages/villas. CI 4pm/CO noon. No smoking. The rooms have no numbers, but each is named for a well-known artist and decorated in a motif recalling the artist's work. **Amenities:** A/C, cable TV, dataport. Some units w/terraces, some w/fireplaces. Many rooms have bidets. **Services:** Afternoon tea served. The innkeepers often provide refreshments in the afternoon. **Facilities:** 30 Beauty salon, guest lounge w/TV. The innkeepers' Academy of the Arts program presents week-long programs on silversmithing, coil pottery, painting, and other art forms. Nearby tennis, golf, and ballroom dancing. **Rates (BB):** $60 S; $67 D; $85 ste; $67–$85 effic; $85 cottage/villa. Extra person $10. Higher rates for special events/hols. Parking: Outdoor, free. Weekly rates avail. AE, CB, DC, DISC, MC, V.

Meson de Mesilla
1803 Avenida de Mesilla, PO Box 1212, 88046; tel 505/525-9212 or toll free 800/732-6025. A lovely adobe inn on the east side of Old Mesilla, this is a bed-and-breakfast in the European tradition. **Rooms:** 15 rms and stes. CI 1:30pm/CO 11am. No smoking. Southwestern decor is uncluttered, comfortable, open and airy, with brass beds, antiques, and tile bathrooms. All rooms, except three on the ground floor, open onto an attractive second-floor veranda. **Amenities:** A/C, cable TV. No phone. Some units w/terraces, some w/fireplaces, 1 w/whirlpool. **Services:** Babysitting. Full gourmet breakfast, including such items as orange yogurt pancakes or eggs Benedict. **Facilities:** 1 restaurant (*see* "Restaurants" below), 1 bar. **Rates (BB):** $50–$92 S or D; $140 ste. Extra person $10. Parking: Outdoor, free. CB, DC, DISC, EC, MC, V.

RESTAURANTS

Cattle Baron Steak and Seafood Restaurant
790 S Telshor Blvd; tel 505/522-7533. E of Mesilla Valley Mall. **Seafood/Steak.** Open and airy dining room with polished wood, off-white stucco walls, and lots of plants. Specializes in steak, prime rib, and fresh seafood, but grilled chicken, burgers, soups, and salads also available. **FYI:** Reservations accepted. Children's menu. **Open:** Sun–Thurs 11am–9:30pm, Fri–Sat 11am–10pm. **Prices:** Main courses $9–$21. AE, DC, DISC, MC, V.

Double Eagle
308 Calle Guadalupe; tel 505/523-6700. **Continental.** An elegant restaurant in an old building, sporting a gold-leaf tin ceiling and furnished with antiques. Especially popular are chateaubriand, filet mignon, salmon with orange-chile sauce, ostrich fillet, and lamb chops. Several entrees are prepared tableside. Homemade desserts. **FYI:** Reservations recommended. Dress code. **Open:** Mon–Sat 11am–10pm, Sun 5–9pm. **Prices:** Main courses $11–$25. AE, CB, DC, DISC, ER, MC, V.

La Posta
Old Mesilla Plaza; tel 505/524-3524. SE corner of Old Mesilla Plaza. **Southwestern.** Housed in a historic 150-year-old adobe building with viga ceilings, rough wood, and white stucco walls. The menu features New Mexico–style Mexican food and charbroiled steaks. A house specialty is tostadas compuestas (which originated at the restaurant in 1939, the year it opened): a toasted corn tortilla cup filled with chile con carne and frijoles, topped with chopped lettuce, diced tomato, and grated cheese. Sunday brunch available. **FYI:** Reservations recommended. Children's menu. Beer and wine only. **Open:** Sun 11am–9pm, Tues–Thurs 11am–9pm, Fri–Sat 11am–9:30pm. **Prices:** Main courses $3–$12. AE, CB, DC, DISC, MC, V.

Meson de Mesilla
1803 Avenida de Mesilla, Mesilla; tel 505/525-2380. Exit 140 off I-10. **Continental.** Southwestern decor complimented by stained-glass windows and tile floors. Entrees include duck breast, veal, salmon, quail, and the house specialty—chateaubriand for two, flamed in cognac and prepared tableside. **FYI:** Reservations recommended. Guitar. No smoking. **Open:** Lunch Wed–Fri 11:30am–1:45pm; dinner Tues–Sat 5:30–9pm; brunch Sun 11am–1:45pm. **Prices:** Main courses $19–$26. CB, DC, DISC, MC, V.

Peppers
306 Calle Guadalupe; tel 505/523-4999. **Southwestern.** Located in a 150-year-old adobe, with viga and latilla ceilings, handmade Mexican-style chairs, and colorful southwestern furnishings. Unusual fare is offered, such as green chile wontons with pineapple salsa, shark fajitas, and crab enchiladas. **FYI:** Reservations recommended. **Open:** Mon–Sat 11am–10pm, Sun noon–9pm. **Prices:** Main courses $8–$14. AE, CB, DC, DISC, ER, MC, V.

Santa Fe Restaurant
1410 S Solano Dr; tel 505/522-0466. **Southwestern.** Wood and white-block walls, inlaid tile tables. Innovative Mexican dishes, steak, chicken, and shrimp. **FYI:** Reservations recommended. Guitar. Children's menu. Beer and wine only. No smoking. **Open:** Lunch Mon–Fri 11:30am–2pm, Sat 11:30am–4pm, Sun 11:30am–4pm; dinner Mon–Fri 5–10pm, Sat 4–10pm, Sun 4–9pm. **Prices:** Main courses $5–$12. AE, CB, DC, DISC, MC, V.

ATTRACTIONS

Aguirre Springs Recreation Area
US 70; tel 505/525-4300. Located on the western slope of the Organ Mountains, so called because the peaks resemble the pipes of a church organ. Hiking, camping, picnicking, horse trails. **Open:** Daily 8am–8pm. **$**

San Albino Church
Calle de Santiago and Calle Principal; tel 505/526-9349. The parish was founded in 1852, and the church was constructed in 1907, making this is one of the oldest churches in the Mesilla Valley. It was named for St Albin, a mid-sixth century bishop of Angiers, France. The church bells date from the early 1870s; the pews were made in Taos of Philippine mahogany. Tours, Tues–Sun 1–3pm. **Free**

Las Vegas

A stop-over on the Santa Fe Trail in the mid-1800s, Las Vegas boomed in 1879 with the arrival of the railroad. Many of the lavish Victorian homes erected in those days remain today. **Information:** Las Vegas/San Miguel County Chamber of Commerce, 727 Grand Ave, PO Box 148, Las Vegas 87701 (tel 505/425-8631 or 800/832-5947).

HOTEL

Plaza Hotel

230 Old Town Plaza, 87701; tel 505/425-3591 or toll free 800/328-1882; fax 505/425-9659. Exit 343 off I-25. A handsome, historic hotel right on Las Vegas Plaza, renovated to offer modern comforts in an 1880s setting. **Rooms:** 36 rms and stes. CI 3pm/CO 11am. Nonsmoking rms avail. Each room is uniquely decorated, with period furnishings, high ceilings, and distinctive moldings. **Amenities:** A/C, cable TV. **Services:** **Facilities:** 1 restaurant, 1 bar (w/entertainment). **Rates:** Peak (May–Nov) $59–$92 S; $65–$98 D; $110 ste. Extra person $6. Children under age 12 stay free. Lower rates off-season. Parking: Outdoor, free. AE, DC, DISC, MC, V.

MOTELS

Comfort Inn

2500 N Grand Ave, 87701; tel 505/425-1100 or toll free 800/716-1103; fax 505/454-8404. Exit 347 off I-25. A new motel on the outskirts of the city. **Rooms:** 101 rms. CI 2pm/CO 11am. Nonsmoking rms avail. **Amenities:** A/C, cable TV. **Services:** Babysitting. **Facilities:** Whirlpool, washer/dryer. **Rates (CP):** $38–$53 S; $42–$59 D. Children under age 18 stay free. Lower rates off-season. Parking: Outdoor, free. AE, DC, DISC, MC, V.

Inn on the Santa Fe Trail

1133 Grand Ave, 87701; tel 505/425-6791 or toll free 800/425-6791; fax 505/425-0417. Exit 345 off I-25. An attractively updated hacienda-style motel, close to the downtown plaza. **Rooms:** 42 rms and stes. CI 1pm/CO 11am. Nonsmoking rms avail. All overlook a central courtyard. The furniture was designed and hand-crafted by local artisans. **Amenities:** A/C, cable TV. Refrigerators are available in some rooms. **Services:** Masseur, babysitting. **Facilities:** Whirlpool, washer/dryer. **Rates (CP):** Peak (May 15–Oct 15) $54–$64 S; $59–$69 D; $80 ste. Extra person $5. Children under age 12 stay free. Lower rates off-season. Parking: Outdoor, free. AE, CB, DC, DISC, MC, V.

RESTAURANTS

El Alto Supper Club

Sapello St off New Mexico Ave; tel 505/454-0808. Exit 343 off I-25. **Seafood/Steak.** Situated on a hill overlooking the city, the El Alto has been run by the same family for over 50 years. It's known for its steaks, which are cut fresh daily. Some seafood and a few New Mexican combination dinners are offered as well. **FYI:** Reservations accepted. Children's menu. **Open:** Peak (May–Oct) daily 6–9pm. **Prices:** Main courses $11–$25. MC, V.

El Rialto Restaurant

141 Bridge St; tel 505/454-0037. ½ block S of the Plaza. **Mexican/Seafood/Steak.** Located in an old building with a tin ceiling; offers a good range of enchiladas, tacos, and sopaipillas, plus steak, chicken, and seafood dinners. **FYI:** Reservations accepted. Children's menu. **Open:** Mon–Sat 11am–9pm. **Prices:** Main courses $7–$23. AE, DISC, MC, V. 

Hillcrest Restaurant

1106 Grand Ave; tel 505/425-7211. Exit 347 off I-25. **Regional American.** Run by the same family since the 1940s. There are two dining areas—one a more formal dining room serving lunch and dinner, and the other a coffee shop. The homestyle cooking includes classic American fare from chicken-fried steak to hamburgers. Lunch buffet on Sunday with roast turkey and all the trimmings. **FYI:** Reservations recommended. Children's menu. **Open:** Lunch daily noon–5pm; dinner daily 5–8pm; brunch Sun 9am–2pm. **Prices:** Main courses $5–$12. MC, V.

ATTRACTIONS

Fort Union National Monument

Exit 366 off I-25; tel 505/425-8025. Although this was the largest military installation in the 19th-century Southwest, today it is in ruins. There's little to see but adobe walls and chimneys, but the very scope of the fort is impressive. The visitor center has interpreted the fort's history through exhibits, booklets, and a walking trail. **Open:** Daily 8am–5pm. **$**

Rough Riders Memorial and City Museum

Grand Ave; tel 505/425-8726. About 40% of Teddy Roosevelt's Spanish-American War campaigners in 1898 came from New Mexico—many from this frontier town. The museum chronicles their contribution to US history. **Open:** Mon–Sat 9am–4pm. **Free**

Las Vegas National Wildlife Refuge

NM 281; tel 505/425-3581. More than 270 species of birds and animals make their home here on 8,670 acres of native grasslands, croplands, marshlands, ponds, timbered canyons, and streams. **Open:** Mon–Fri 8am–4:30. **Free**

Lemitar

See Socorro

Lincoln

See also Capitan

ATTRACTION

Lincoln State Monument

US 380 W; tel 505/653-4372. Lincoln is one of the last historic yet uncommercialized 19th-century towns remaining in the West. The entire town is a National Historic Landmark.

Billy the Kid shot his way out of the **Old Courthouse** located here, now a state museum. A hole made by a bullet from the Kid's gun still exists.

At the Lincoln County Heritage Trust's **Historical Center**, exhibits explain the role of Apaches, Hispanics, Anglo cowboys, and Buffalo Soldiers in Lincoln's history and provide details of the Lincoln County War. **Open:** Peak (May–Sept) daily 9am–6pm. Reduced hours off-season. **$$**

Lordsburg

A small town in dusty southwest New Mexico, Lordsburg was named for an engineer of the Southern Pacific Railroad, which created the town in 1880. Usually just an overnight stop along I-10, Lordsburg is noteworthy for two well-preserved ghost towns and for rock-hounding opportunities. **Information:** Lordsburg/San Miguel County Chamber of Commerce, 208 W Motel Dr, PO Box 699, Lordsburg 88045 (tel 505/542-9864).

MOTELS

Best Western American Motor Inn

944 E Motel Dr, 88045; tel 505/542-3591 or toll free 800/528-1234. Exit 24 off I-10. 1 mi W on I-10 business loop. This better-than-average motel is a good choice for either business or vacation travelers. **Rooms:** 88 rms and stes. CI 11am/CO 11am. Nonsmoking rms avail. **Amenities:** A/C, satel TV w/movies. 24-hour lobby. **Services:** Fax service available. **Facilities:** 1 restaurant, 1 bar (w/entertainment). **Rates (BB):** $39–$49 S; $44–$49 D; $86–$90 ste. Extra person $5. Parking: Outdoor, free. AE, CB, DC, DISC, EC, MC, V.

Best Western Western Skies Inn

1303 S Main St, 88045; tel 505/542-8807 or toll free 800/528-1234; fax 505/542-8895. Exit 22 off I-10. A popular travelers' stopover, halfway between El Paso and Tucson. Reservations are highly recommended. **Rooms:** 40 rms. CI open/CO 11am. Nonsmoking rms avail. **Amenities:** A/C, cable TV. **Services:** **Facilities:** Lawn games, washer/dryer. **Rates:** $48–$53 S; $53–$58 D. Extra person $5. Children under age 12 stay free. Parking: Outdoor, free. AE, CB, DC, DISC, MC, V.

RESTAURANT

Kranberry's Family Restaurant

1405 S Main St; tel 505/542-9400. Exit 22 off I-10. **American/Mexican.** A friendly, casual family restaurant with large windows and southwestern art. Variety of homestyle family favorites, including burgers, sandwiches, chicken and beef entrees, and salads. Baked goods are made on the premises. **FYI:** Reservations accepted. No liquor license. **Open:** Daily 6am–9:30pm. **Prices:** Main courses $3–$14. AE, CB, DC, DISC, MC, V.

ATTRACTIONS

Shakespeare Ghost Town

I-10 exit 22; tel 542-9034. A National Historic Site, this was once the home of 3,000 miners, promoters, and dealers of various kinds. Since 1935, it's been privately owned by the Hill family, who have kept it uncommercialized with no souvenir hype or gift shop. They offer two-hour guided tours on a limited basis, and reenactments and special events four times a year. Six original buildings and two reconstructed buildings survive in various stages of repair or disrepair. **Open:** 10am and 2pm second and fourth weekends of every month. **$**

Steins Railroad Ghost Town

I-10 exit 3; tel 505/542-9791. This settlement 19 miles west of Lordsburg started as a Butterfield Stage stop, then was a railroad town of about 1,000 residents from 1905 to 1945. Today there are 10 buildings with 16 rooms filled with 19th- and 20th-century artifacts and furnishings. There's also the Steins Mercantile shop and a petting zoo for kids. **Open:** Daily 9am–5pm. **$**

Los Alamos

Los Alamos, the birthplace of the atom bomb, was created in secret by the US government in 1942 as a development site for the bombs that would be dropped on Japan three years later. Nuclear research continues to drive this community, which is spread on craggy, fingerlike mesas 33 miles northwest of Santa Fe. It is said that Los Alamos has among the highest concentrations of PhDs in the world. **Information:** Los Alamos Chamber of Commerce, 2132 Central Ave, PO Box 460, Los Alamos 87544 (tel 505/662-8105 or 800/444-0707).

HOTEL

Hilltop House Hotel

400 Trinity, 87544; tel 505/662-2441 or toll free 800/462-0936; fax 505/662-5913. Basic hotel, with some magnificent views of the Sangre de Cristo Mountains. **Rooms:** 108 rms, stes, and effic. Executive level. CI 3pm/CO 11am. Nonsmoking rms avail. **Amenities:** A/C, cable TV w/movies, voice mail. Some units w/terraces. **Services:** Twice-daily maid svce, car-rental desk, masseur. **Facilities:** 150 1 restaurant, 1 bar, washer/dryer. **Rates (CP):** Peak (Mem Day–Labor Day) $77–$87 S; $87–$92 D; $100–$225 ste; $82–$92 effic. Extra person $10. Children under age 12 stay free. Lower rates off-season. Parking: Outdoor, free. AE, DC, DISC, MC, V.

ATTRACTIONS

Bradbury Science Museum

1309 15th St; tel 505/667-4444. Offers a glimpse into World War II's historic Manhattan Project as well as today's advanced science and technology. There are more than 35 hands-on exhibits for visitors to explore lasers and computers and view laboratory research in energy, defense, the environment, and health. **Open:** Tues–Fri 9am–5pm, Sat–Mon 1–5pm. **Free**

Bandelier National Monument
NM 4; tel 505/672-3861. Combines the extensive ruins of an ancient cliff-dwelling Anasazi pueblo culture with 46 square miles of canyon-and-mesa wilderness. A cottonwood-shaded 1½-mile trail along Frijoles Creek heads to the principal ruins; 70 miles of maintained trails lead to more ruins and ceremonial sites, waterfalls, and wildlife habitats. The separate Tsankawi section of the monument, reached by an ancient 2-mile trail close to White Rock, contains a large unexcavated ruin on a high mesa overlooking the Rio Grande Valley. Visitor center and museum near entrance. **Open:** Daily sunrise–sunset. **$$**

Los Alamos Historical Museum
1921 Juniper St; tel 505/662-6272. Recounts area history, from prehistoric cliff dwellers to the present, with exhibits ranging from Native American artifacts to school memorabilia and wartime displays. **Open:** Peak (June–Aug) Mon–Sat 9:30am–4:30pm, Sun 11am–5pm. Reduced hours off-season. **Free**

Fuller Lodge Art Center
2132 Central Ave; tel 505/662-9331. The massive log building that once housed the dining and recreation hall for the Los Alamos Ranch School for boys is now a National Historic Landmark known as the Fuller Lodge. Besides the art center, its current occupants include the Los Alamos Historical Museum (see above) and the Los Alamos Cultural Arts Center. The art center has works of northern New Mexico artists and stages traveling exhibitions of regional and national importance. **Open:** Peak (Apr–Oct) Mon–Sat 10am–4pm, Sun 1–4pm. Reduced hours off-season. **Free**

Los Lunas

See Albuquerque, Belen

RESTAURANT

The Luna Mansion
NM 6 and NM 85; tel 505/865-7333. Exit 203 off I-25. **New American/Steak.** Located in a National Historic Landmark building dating from 1881. The menu features a variety of steaks, prime rib, game, chicken, and seafood. Specialties include lamb loin medallions with two sauces. **FYI:** Reservations recommended. **Open:** Dinner Sun–Thurs 5–9pm, Fri–Sat 5–9:30pm; brunch Sun 11am–2pm. **Prices:** Main courses $10–$21; prix fixe $8–$10. AE, DC, DISC, MC, V.

Mescalero

See also Ruidoso

This small town serves as headquarters for the 2,800-member Mescalero Apache Reservation. A beautiful resort here offers numerous outdoor recreation opportunities, including golf, horseback riding, hiking, fishing, and skiing. **Information:** Mescalero Apache Indian Reservation, PO Box 176, Mescalero 88340 (tel 505/671-4494).

RESORT

Inn of the Mountain Gods
Carrizo Canyon Rd, PO Box 269, 88340; tel 505/257-4431 or toll free 800/545-6040; fax 505/257-6173. 3 mi SW of Ruidoso. 700 acres. A luxurious mountain resort operated by the Mescalero Apaches on the tribe's 460,000-acre reservation. The spectacular multi-story building has a tall copper fireplace in the center of the lobby. **Rooms:** 253 rms and stes. CI 4pm/CO noon. Nonsmoking rms avail. Beautifully decorated in a Native American motif; most have views of the pool area and Lake Mescalero. **Amenities:** A/C, cable TV. All units w/terraces, 1 w/fireplace. Each has a wet bar and some have refrigerators. **Services:** Babysitting. **Facilities:** 18 6 600 3 restaurants, 5 bars (1 w/entertainment), 1 beach (lake shore), basketball, volleyball, games rm, lawn games, sauna, whirlpool, playground. Championship golf course designed by Ted Robinson. Mescalero Café serves Southwestern/Mexican food. **Rates:** Peak (May–Sept) $120–$125 S or D; $130–$150 ste. Extra person $12. Children under age 12 stay free. Lower rates off-season. Parking: Outdoor, free. AE, CB, DC, DISC, MC, V.

ATTRACTION

Mescalero Apache Indian Reservation
US 70; tel 505/671-4495. Immediately south and west of Ruidoso, it covers 460,000 acres and is home to about 3,500 members of the Mescalero, Chiricahua, and Lipan bands of Apache. The Mescalero Cultural Center has photos, artifacts, clothing, craftwork, and other exhibits that demonstrate the history and culture of the people.

St Joseph's Mission, just off US 70 on a hill overlooking the reservation, is a Gothic-style structure with walls 8 feet thick that was built by the Apache between the two World Wars. Symbols of Apache mountain gods and Roman Catholic saints appear in paintings and carvings inside. **Open:** Mon–Fri 8am–4:30pm. **Free**

Mesilla

See Las Cruces

Mora

ATTRACTIONS

Cleveland Mill Historical Museum
NM 518, Cleveland; tel 505/387-2645. From 1901 to 1947, this two-story adobe mill ground out 50 barrels of wheat flour a day. Today, it's been converted into a museum with exhibits on regional history and culture. **Open:** Mem Day–Oct, Fri–Sun 10am–5pm. **$**

Morphy Lake State Park
NM 518; tel 505/387-2328. Located 4 miles south of Mora down a dirt road. The pine forest offers primitive camping, and the lake is known for its trout fishing. **Open:** Daily sunrise–sunset. **$**

Pinos Altos

See Silver City

Radium Springs

ATTRACTION

Fort Selden State Monument
I-25; tel 505/526-8911. Founded in 1865, the fort housed the famous African-American cavalry, the "Buffalo Soldiers," who protected settlers from marauding Apaches. Today there are only eroding ruins remaining; displays in the visitor center tell the fort's story. Adjacent to the state monument is **Leasburg Dam State Park** where visitors can picnic, camp, boat, and swim. **Open:** Daily 9am–6pm. **$**

Ramah

This small farming community was settled by Mormon pioneers in 1874 and named for an individual in the Book of Mormon.

RESTAURANT

($) Blue Corn Restaurant
NM 53; tel 505/783-4671. 1 mi W of town. **Eclectic/Southwestern.** Located 12 miles west of El Morro and 20 miles east of Zuni, this restaurant has a warm atmosphere, with southwestern style wooden tables and chairs, a corner fireplace (nonworking), and paintings by local artists. People come from all over the state to dine on the international dishes creatively prepared with a southwestern flair. Several specials are offered each day, perhaps including roasted yellow bell pepper and pecan enchilada, marinated New York strip steak, or tiger shrimp. The regular menu includes crab enchiladas, beef Normandy, beef sambre et mousse, and vegetarian meals. **FYI:** Reservations recommended. Blues/folk/guitar. No liquor license. **Open:** Wed–Sun 11am–9pm. Closed 1 week at Christmas. **Prices:** Main courses $9–$12. No CC.

Raton

Raton (Spanish for "rat") was named for the numerous rodents that thrive on the piñon nuts that grow in the area. First a water stop on the Santa Fe Trail, the town became a ranching, mining, and railroad center in the late 1800s. Today it boasts a small but well-preserved historic district. **Information:** Raton Chamber of Commerce, 100 Clayton Hwy, PO Box 1211, Raton 87740 (tel 505/445-3689 or 800/638-6161).

MOTELS

Best Western Sands Motel
300 Clayton Rd, 87740; tel 505/445-2737 or toll free 800/518-2581; fax 505/445-4053. Exit 451 off I-25. An attractive motel, with a fenced, tree-shaded area for relaxing in lawn chairs. **Rooms:** 50 rms and stes. CI noon/CO 11am. Nonsmoking rms avail. Custom-made furniture and southwestern art. The family room sleeps up to 8. **Amenities:** A/C, cable TV w/movies. All rooms in the luxury wing have refrigerators, reclining, overstuffed lounge chairs, 25-inch TVs, coffeemakers, and clock radios. VCRs and videotapes are available for rent. **Services:** **Facilities:** 50 1 restaurant (*see* "Restaurants" below), whirlpool, playground. The restaurant is open April to October only. **Rates:** Peak (June 16–Sept 6) $67–$87 S; $70–$90 D; $70–$94 ste. Extra person $3. Children under age 12 stay free. Min stay special events. Lower rates off-season. Parking: Outdoor, free. AE, CB, DC, DISC, MC, V.

Harmony Manor Motel
351 Clayton Rd, 87740; tel 505/445-2763 or toll free 800/922-0347. Exit 451 off I-25. Very clean, pleasant motel offering basic lodging. **Rooms:** 18 rms. CI 6am/CO 11am. Nonsmoking rms avail. **Amenities:** A/C, cable TV. **Services:** Babysitting. **Facilities:** Playground. **Rates:** Peak (May 10–Sept 4) $40–$48 S; $48–$58 D. Extra person $4. Children under age 18 stay free. Lower rates off-season. Parking: Outdoor, free. AE, CB, DC, DISC, MC, V.

Melody Lane Motel
136 Canyon Dr, 87740; tel 505/445-3655 or toll free 800/421-5210; fax 505/445-3641. Exit 454 off I-25. A quiet motel on the north side of downtown. **Rooms:** 27 rms. CI 1pm/CO 11am. Nonsmoking rms avail. Rooms are pleasant and well-appointed, with pine ceilings, southwestern art, and solid furnishings. **Amenities:** A/C, cable TV w/movies. Roll-a-way beds are available. There are some in-room steam baths. **Services:** **Facilities:** 30 **Rates (CP):** Peak

(mid-May–Labor Day) $36–$46 S; $41–$51 D. Extra person $5. Lower rates off-season. Parking: Outdoor, free. AE, CB, DC, DISC, MC, V.

RESTAURANTS

Capri Restaurant
304 Canyon Dr; tel 505/445-9755. **American/Italian/Mexican.** A small, simple cafe. Pasta specials offered Friday and Saturday evenings cost $6 and include salad, garlic bread, and a glass of wine. (Reservations are recommended for those evenings, and for large parties.) At other times there's American fare, including steak sandwiches, burgers, pork chops, fish, and chicken; plus several Mexican dishes. The restaurant has a packaged liquor store. **FYI:** Reservations accepted. **Open:** Peak (May–Sept) breakfast daily 8am–1pm; dinner daily 5–8:30pm. **Prices:** Main courses $6–$13. AE, CB, DC, MC, V.

★ El Matador
1012 S 2nd St; tel 505/445-9575. **Southwestern.** Bright, diner-like restaurant. Recommended for its Mexican food: enchiladas, tamales, tacos, burritos, and bowls of red or green chile. Burgers, sandwiches, steak, and seafood are also available. **FYI:** Reservations accepted. Children's menu. No liquor license. **Open:** Tues–Sun 7am–8:30pm. **Prices:** Main courses $5–$13. MC, V.

Pappas' Sweet Shop Restaurant
1201 S 2nd St; tel 505/445-9811. **American.** Upscale, well-established restaurant. Decorated with antiques and collectibles; furnishings include tiles and other items from the family's original 1925 candy and ice cream shop, plus old photos of the Raton area. Steak and prime rib is the specialty, and Pappas' is noted for its margaritas. Sandwiches are made on homemade breads. There's an attached gift shop, and parking for RVs and other large vehicles in back. **FYI:** Reservations recommended. Piano. Children's menu. **Open:** Peak (June–Sept) breakfast daily 9–11am; lunch daily 11am–2pm; dinner daily 5–9pm. **Prices:** Main courses $10–$25. AE, CB, DC, DISC, MC, V.

Sands Restaurant
In Best Western Sands Motel, 300 Clayton Rd; tel 505/445-8041. Exit 451 off I-25. **Regional American.** Traditional American cooking in an open and spacious dining room with large picture windows. The turkey and chicken casseroles are popular. **FYI:** Reservations accepted. Children's menu. No liquor license. **Open:** Daily 6:30am–9pm. Closed Nov–Mar. **Prices:** Main courses $6–$16. AE, DISC, MC, V.

ATTRACTIONS

Dorsey Mansion
US 56; tel 505/375-2222. A two-story log-and-stone home built in the 1880s by cattleman/senator Stephen Dorsey. It features 36 rooms, hardwood floors, Italian marble fireplaces, a hand-carved cherry wood staircase, and a dining room that seats 60. Visitation by appointment only. **$**

Raton Museum
216 S First St; tel 505/455-8979. Displays a wide variety of mining, railroad, and ranching items from the early days of the town. Walking tour maps available. **Open:** Peak (June–Aug) Tues–Sat 9am–5pm. Reduced hours off-season. **Free**

Red River

A small mountain tourist town surrounded by national forest, Red River was a mining camp at the turn of the century. Its Wild West character lives on with false-front buildings, "shoot-outs" on Main Street, and guided trips to old mines. Red River is a popular destination for square dancing as well as for hiking, hunting, fishing, and both cross-country and downhill skiing. **Information:** Red River Chamber of Commerce, PO Box 1020, Red River 87558 (tel 505/754-2366 or 800/348-6444).

HOTEL

Lifts West Condominium Resort Hotel
Main St, PO Box 330, 87558; tel 505/754-2778 or toll free 800/221-1859; fax 505/754-6617. The dramatic lobby is three stories high, with a large stone fireplace at one end and a glass elevator at the other. It's the site of classical music concerts, square dancing, and lectures, plus cozy after-ski chats around the blazing fire. **Rooms:** 86 rms and effic. CI 2pm/CO 10am. Accommodations are large and beautifully furnished, with fully equipped kitchens and dining areas. **Amenities:** Cable TV, refrig, VCR. No A/C. Some units w/terraces, some w/fireplaces. **Services:** Babysitting. **Facilities:** 150 1 restaurant, sauna, whirlpool, washer/dryer. **Rates:** Peak (Nov–Mar) $76–$99 S; $108–$262 D; $109–$198 effic. Extra person $10. Children under age 12 stay free. Min stay special events. Lower rates off-season. Parking: Indoor/outdoor, free. Rates are reasonable, considering the quality. AE, CB, DC, DISC, MC, V.

MOTEL

Ponderosa Lodge
200 W Main St, PO Box 528, 87558; tel 505/754-2988 or toll free 800/336-RSVP. A conveniently located motel in the center of town, close to all of Red River's attractions and activities. **Rooms:** 36 rms, stes, and effic. CI 1pm/CO 10am. Nonsmoking rms avail. Standard rooms with modest furnishings. **Amenities:** Cable TV, refrig. No A/C. All units w/terraces, some w/fireplaces. **Services:** **Facilities:** 25 Washer/dryer. **Rates:** Peak (Dec–Mar) $65 S or D; $77 ste; $120–$220 effic. Extra person $10. Children under age 12 stay free. Min stay special events. Lower rates off-season. Parking: Outdoor, free. Closed Apr. AE, DISC, MC, V.

LODGES

Alpine Lodge

Main St, PO Box 67, 87558; tel 505/754-2952 or toll free 800/252-2333. An attractive lodge, conveniently located, with a view of the river. A park along the river has picnic tables, grills, and benches, and a bridge connecting the property to the main ski lift. **Rooms:** 45 rms, stes, and effic; 1 cottage/villa. CI 2pm/CO 10am. Rooms are well-appointed and comfortable. Many overlook the river; others have a view of the ski slopes. **Amenities:** Satel TV w/movies, refrig. No A/C. All units w/terraces, some w/fireplaces. **Services:** Babysitting. **Facilities:** 40 1 restaurant (bkfst and lunch only), 1 bar (w/entertainment), playground, washer/dryer. **Rates:** Peak (July–Sept/Nov–Mar) $32–$54 S; $37–$54 D; $56–$64 ste; $49–$72 effic; $98–$132 cottage/villa. Extra person $8. Children under age 12 stay free. Min stay special events. Lower rates off-season. Parking: Outdoor, free. AE, MC, V.

The Riverside

201 E Main St, PO Box 249, 87558; tel 505/754-2252 or toll free 800/432-9999; fax 505/754-2495. Located on a full city block in the center of town. The grounds are spacious and well-kept. **Rooms:** 41 rms, stes, and effic. CI 3pm/CO 10am. Nonsmoking rms avail. Rooms are simple but large, good for families. Duplexes sleep five. **Amenities:** Cable TV, refrig. No A/C. All units w/terraces, some w/fireplaces. **Services:** **Facilities:** 35 Lawn games, playground. **Rates:** Peak (Dec–Mar/June–Sept) $55–$90 S or D; $95 ste; $95 effic. Extra person $10. Lower rates off-season. Parking: Outdoor, free. DISC, MC, V.

RESTAURANT

Texas Red's Steakhouse and Saloon

111 E Main St; tel 505/754-2964. **Steak.** Down-home, Old West–style eatery. The menu is mostly steak, with some salads and chicken. There's usually a wait, but patrons can call the "waiting list hot line" at 754-2922 to check on seating availability. **FYI:** Reservations not accepted. **Open:** Daily 5–9:30pm. Closed Nov. **Prices:** Main courses $12–$30. AE, CB, DC, MC, V.

ATTRACTION

Red River Ski Area

Pioneer Rd; tel 505/754-2223. The 58 trails on the mountain are geared toward the intermediate skier. There's a 1,600-foot vertical drop here to a base elevation of 8,750 feet. **Open:** Nov–Mar, daily 9am–4pm. **$$$$**

Roswell

Once a Native American campsite, Roswell today is the home of New Mexico Military Institute and a center for agriculture, ranching, oil production, and industry. But its real claim-to-fame is the alleged crash of a UFO near here in 1947. The US Air Force asserts it was a top-secret spy balloon being tested; UFO fans claim a cover-up. **Information:** Roswell Chamber of Commerce, 131 W 2nd St, PO Box 70, Roswell 88202 (tel 505/623-5695).

MOTELS

Days Inn

1310 N Main St, 88201; tel 505/623-4021 or toll free 800/329-7466; fax 505/623-0079. 1 mi N of US 70/380 on US 285. No-frills, standard motel. **Rooms:** 62 rms. CI noon/CO 11am. Nonsmoking rms avail. **Amenities:** A/C, cable TV w/movies. **Services:** **Facilities:** 60 1 restaurant (bkfst and dinner only), 1 bar, whirlpool. **Rates (CP):** $38–$44 S; $46–$56 D. Extra person $5. Children under age 12 stay free. Parking: Outdoor, free. DISC, MC, V.

Frontier Motel

3010 N Main St, 88201; tel 505/622-1400 or toll free 800/678-1401; fax 505/622-1405. 1 mi N of center of town on US 285. A well-kept "mom and pop" motel, friendly and welcoming. **Rooms:** 38 rms. CI 11am/CO 11am. Nonsmoking rms avail. Simple, clean, standard motel rooms. Some smaller, less expensive rooms have showers only; larger rooms have shower/bath combinations. **Amenities:** A/C, cable TV w/movies, refrig. **Services:** **Facilities:** 1 restaurant. **Rates (CP):** $35–$44 S; $39–$48 D. Extra person $3. Parking: Outdoor, free. AE, CB, DC, DISC, MC, V.

National 9 Inn

2001 N Main St, 88201; tel 505/622-0110 or toll free 800/423-3106; fax 505/622-6011. ½ mi N of center of town on US 285. A small, no-frills motel. **Rooms:** 67 rms and effic. CI noon/CO 11am. Nonsmoking rms avail. **Amenities:** A/C, cable TV w/movies. **Facilities:** **Rates:** $30–$32 S; $34–$37 D; $34–$37 effic. Extra person $4. Children under age 13 stay free. Parking: Outdoor, free. AE, CB, DC, DISC, EC, ER, JCB, MC, V.

Sally Port Inn

2000 N Main St, 88201; tel 505/622-6430 or toll free 800/600-5221; fax 505/623-7631. ½ mi N of downtown on US 285. Attractively decorated and well maintained. **Rooms:** 124 rms. CI noon/CO noon. No smoking. **Amenities:** A/C, cable TV w/movies. **Services:** Twice-daily maid svce, car-rental desk. **Facilities:** 450 1 restaurant, 1 bar, sauna, whirlpool, beauty salon, washer/dryer. There's an 18-hole golf course adjacent to the property. **Rates:** $52–$54 S; $62–$64 D. Extra person $10. Children under age 18 stay free. Parking: Outdoor, free. AE, CB, DC, DISC, MC, V.

RESTAURANTS

Keuken Dutch Restaurant

1208 N Main St; tel 505/624-2040. **American/Dutch.** Decorated in blue and white, with prints of Holland on the walls and Delft china (which is for sale). Choice of basic American dishes and several Dutch entrees. **FYI:** Reservations accepted. No liquor license. **Open:** Daily 6–10pm. **Prices:** Main courses $6–$11. AE, CB, DC, DISC, MC, V.

Mario's
200 E 2nd St; tel 505/623-1740. 1 block E of US 285. **American/Mexican.** Southwestern steakhouse decor, with ceiling fans, painted brick walls, plants. Intimate bar. Mexican and American specialties, including steak, catfish, a number of "heart smart" dishes, and a salad bar. **FYI:** Reservations accepted. Children's menu. **Open:** Mon–Thurs 11am–9pm, Fri–Sat 11am–10pm. **Prices:** Main courses $7–$13. AE, MC, V.

($) Nuthin' Fancy Cafe
2103 N Main St; tel 505/623-4098. ½ mi N of downtown Roswell on US 285. **American.** An open and airy cafe with chile ristras, neon cactus, and western prints. Seating at both booths and tables. Burgers, sandwiches, and diner-type favorites such as meat loaf, chicken-fried steak, and fried catfish. Also grilled chicken and fish, and nightly specials. **FYI:** Reservations accepted. Beer and wine only. **Open:** Daily 6am–9pm. **Prices:** Main courses $4–$8. AE, DISC, MC, V.

Peppers Grill and Bar
In Sunwest Centre, 500 N Main St; tel 505/623-1700. **Mexican/Southwestern.** Delightful cartoon chile characters decorate the walls in this fun restaurant and bar. There are big, comfortable booths, as well as tables. The menu has many southwestern dinners, plus beef, chicken, and seafood entrees. Specialties include steak or chicken fajitas, mesquite-smoked baby-back ribs, and, on Friday and Saturday nights, prime rib. **FYI:** Reservations accepted. Blues/guitar. Children's menu. **Open:** Mon–Thurs 11am–9pm, Fri–Sat 11am–10pm. **Prices:** Main courses $4–$12. AE, DISC, MC, V.

ATTRACTIONS

UFO Museum and Research Center
400-406 North Main; tel 505/625-9495. The museum features displays and videos about extraterrestrials and UFOs, and is a popular stop for visitors interested in the purported 1947 crash of a UFO in the New Mexico desert. Highlights include an extensive collection of tabloid news clips, a model of an alien body on a hospital gurney, and "private research rooms" where visitors who claim to have been abducted by aliens can be debriefed. **Open:** Daily 11am–5pm. **Free**

Historical Center for Southeast New Mexico
200 N Lea Ave; tel 505/622-8333. On the National Register of Historic Places, this 1910 mansion built by rancher J P White is a monument to turn-of-the-century style. The house is fully restored and furnished with early 20th-century antiques; there is also a gallery of changing historical exhibits. **Open:** Fri–Sun 1–4pm. **$**

Roswell Museum and Art Center
100 W 11th St; tel 505/624-6744. The museum proclaims the city's role as a center for the arts and a cradle of America's space industry. The art center contains the world's finest collection of works by Peter Hurd and his wife, Henriette Wyeth, as well as representative works by Georgia O'Keeffe, Ernest Blumenschein, Joseph Sharp, and other famed members of the early 20th-century Taos and Santa Fe art colonies. The Robert Goddard Collection presents actual engines, rocket assemblies, and specialized parts developed by the rocket scientist in the 1930s, when he lived and worked in Roswell. **Open:** Mon–Sat 9am–5pm, Sun 1–5pm. **Free**

New Mexico Military Institute
101 W College Blvd; tel 505/624-8100. Considered the "West Point of the West," the military school celebrated its centennial in 1991. The **General Douglas L McBride Military Museum** on campus houses a collection of artillery and artifacts that document New Mexico's role in America's wars. **Open:** Daily 8am–4pm. **Free**

Spring River Park and Zoo
1400 E College Blvd; tel 505/624-6760. The park covers 48 acres and features a miniature train, an antique carousel, a large prairie dog town, a children's fishing pond, a picnic ground, and playgrounds. The zoo contains regional animals displayed in their natural habitats as well as a children's petting zoo, and a Texas longhorn ranch. **Open:** Daily 10am–sunset. **Free**

Bitter Lake National Wildlife Refuge
US 70; tel 505/622-6755. A great variety of waterfowl—including cormorants, herons, pelicans, sandhill cranes, and snow geese—find a winter home on these 24,000 acres of river bottomland, marsh, stands of salt cedar, and open range. **Open:** Daily sunrise–sunset. **Free**

Bottomless Lakes State Park
NM 409; tel 505/624-6058. This chain of seven lakes, surrounded by rock bluffs, is a popular recreation site for Roswell residents. Rainbow trout fishing, swimming and windsurfing, campsites. **Open:** Daily 6am–9pm. **$**

Ruidoso

See also Mescalero

This southern New Mexico mountain resort community provides food, lodging, and other services for those exploring the mountains of Lincoln National Forest or betting on the horses at Ruidoso Downs. The city's name, Spanish for "noisy," comes from the babbling Ruidoso Creek. **Information:** Ruidoso Valley Chamber of Commerce, 720 Sudderth Dr, PO Box 698, Ruidoso 88345 (tel 505/257-7395 or 800/253-2255).

MOTELS

Best Western Swiss Chalet Inn

1451 Mechem Dr, PO Box 759, 88345; tel 505/258-3333 or toll free 800/477-9477; fax 505/258-5325. 5 mi N of downtown. In an attractive white and blue chalet-style building located in a mountain setting. **Rooms:** 81 rms and stes. CI 4pm/CO noon. Nonsmoking rms avail. Rooms are modern and comfortable. **Amenities:** A/C, cable TV w/movies, dataport. Some units w/terraces, 1 w/whirlpool. **Services:** Car-rental desk. **Facilities:** 140 1 restaurant (bkfst and dinner only), 1 bar (w/entertainment), sauna, whirlpool, washer/dryer. Downhill skiing is 12 miles away at Ski Apache. **Rates:** Peak (June–Aug) $70–$90 S or D; $96–$135 ste. Extra person $6. Children under age 12 stay free. Min stay special events. Lower rates off-season. Parking: Outdoor, free. AE, CB, DC, DISC, JCB, MC, V.

Dan Dee Cabins

310 Main Rd Upper Canyon, PO Box 844, 88345; tel 505/257-2165 or toll free 800/345-4848. Go to the end of Sudderth Dr and head into Upper Canyon on Main Rd. Built in the 1930s as a retreat from the Texas heat, this property has plenty of space and privacy. **Rooms:** 12 cottages/villas. CI 4pm/CO 11am. Each cabin is unique, finished in wood with handsome stone fireplaces, and nestled among tall pine trees. All have full kitchens. **Amenities:** Cable TV, refrig. No A/C or phone. All units w/terraces, all w/fireplaces. **Services:** **Facilities:** Basketball, playground. Lots of hiking trails in the national forest just ½ mile up the creek. Good fishing nearby. **Rates:** Peak (June 15–Labor Day) $82 cottage/villa. Extra person $8. Children under age 1 stay free. Min stay special events. Lower rates off-season. Parking: Outdoor, free. DISC, MC, V.

Enchantment Inn

307 US 70 W, PO Box 4210 HS, 88345; or toll free 800/435-0280; fax 505/378-5427. ¼ mi W of US 70 and Suddereth Jct. Recently renovated. Lots of wood and glass; Mexican-tiled floor. **Rooms:** 80 rms, stes, and effic. CI 1pm/CO 11am. Nonsmoking rms avail. **Amenities:** A/C, cable TV. Some units w/whirlpools. **Services:** **Facilities:** 90 1 restaurant, 1 bar (w/entertainment), games rm, whirlpool, washer/dryer. Patio with barbecue grills. A major downhill ski resort is about 20 miles away. **Rates:** Peak (May–Sept) $65–$80 S or D; $80–$185 ste; $65–$75 effic. Children under age 18 stay free. Min stay special events. Lower rates off-season. Parking: Outdoor, free. AE, CB, DC, DISC, MC, V.

Inn at Pine Springs

Off US 70, PO Box 2100, Ruidoso Downs, 88346; tel 505/378-8100 or toll free 800/237-3607; fax 505/378-8215. Across from Ruidoso Downs Race Track. Just outside Ruidoso, this better-than-average standard motel is in a delightful mountain setting, surrounded by pine trees. **Rooms:** 100 rms and stes. CI 2:30pm/CO noon. Nonsmoking rms avail. Rooms are uncluttered and spacious; many have great views of the surrounding hillsides. **Amenities:** A/C, cable TV. Some units w/terraces. **Services:** **Facilities:** 125 Whirlpool. Hiking, fishing, golfing, and horse racing are nearby, and downhill skiing is within 20 miles. **Rates (CP):** Peak (Mem Day–Labor Day) $66–$73 S; $76–$83 D; $140–$160 ste. Extra person $10. Children under age 13 stay free. Min stay special events. Lower rates off-season. Parking: Outdoor, free. AE, CB, DC, DISC, MC, V.

Pines Motel

620 Sudderth Dr, 88345; tel 505/257-4334 or toll free 800/257-4334. A handsome, meticulously maintained motel, with six older, completely refurbished rooms, and four new, more luxurious units. Owners live on premises. A very good value. **Rooms:** 10 rms and stes. CI 2pm/CO 11am. No smoking. Rooms in the new section overlook the Rio Ruidoso. **Amenities:** Satel TV, refrig. No A/C. All units w/terraces. **Services:** Babysitting. **Facilities:** 10 Lawn games, playground, washer/dryer. Horseshoes and a gazebo in the tree-shaded area along the river. Trout fishing in the Rio Ruidoso. **Rates:** Peak (Nov 15–Mar 30) $40–$45 S or D; $75–$85 ste. Children under age 18 stay free. Min stay special events. Lower rates off-season. Parking: Outdoor, free. Ski packages avail. AE, DISC, MC, V.

Shadow Mountain Lodge

107 Main Rd Upper Canyon, PO Box 1427, 88345; tel 505/257-4886 or toll free 800/441-4331. A beautifully landscaped adult complex, with lots of trees and a nearby stream. Perfect for couples. **Rooms:** 19 stes. CI 4pm/CO 11am. Nonsmoking rms avail. Units are comfortable and airy, with stone fireplaces, attractive wood panelling, and kitchenettes. **Amenities:** A/C, cable TV. All units w/terraces, all w/fireplaces. **Facilities:** Whirlpool. Located close to good fishing streams; plenty of hiking trails nearby. **Rates:** Peak (May–Sept) $70–$95 ste. Extra person $10. Min stay special events. Lower rates off-season. Parking: Outdoor, free. AE, CB, DC, DISC, MC, V.

LODGE

Carrizo Lodge

Carrizo Canyon Rd, PO Box Drawer A, 88345; tel 505/257-9131 or toll free 800/227-1224; fax 505/257-5621. Turn south off Sudderth Dr across from the Chamber of Commerce and go about 1 mile to Lodge. Located on 7½ acres of lovely wooded mountain property in a tranquil setting along Lincoln National Forest. Beautiful Carrizo Creek runs through the property. Adjacent to casino, restaurant, and nightclub. **Rooms:** 66 rms and stes; 9 cottages/villas. CI 4pm/CO noon. Nonsmoking rms avail. **Amenities:** A/C, cable TV w/movies, refrig. All units w/terraces, some w/fireplaces. Condominium units have wood-burning fireplaces. **Services:** **Facilities:** Washer/dryer. The Carrizo Art School operates from May through October. **Rates:** Peak (May–Sept) $59–$89 S or D; $69–$100 ste; $59–

$79 cottage/villa. Extra person $8. Children under age 12 stay free. Lower rates off-season. Parking: Outdoor, free. AE, CB, DC, DISC, MC, V.

RESTAURANTS

★ Cafe Rio

2547 Sudderth Dr; tel 505/257-7746. **International/Pizza.** Decorated with red-and-white checked tablecloths and rough wood walls, this unpretentious restaurant offers a vast selection of unique foods from around the world, including pizza. The owners/chefs were trained in New York and have cooked on both the Gulf and West Coasts. The large selection of beers includes several seasonal varieties. **FYI:** Reservations not accepted. Beer and wine only. **Open:** Daily 11am–8:30pm. Closed Dec 1–21/3 weeks after Easter. **Prices:** Main courses $4–$14. No CC.

Casa Blanca

501 Mechem Dr; tel 505/257-2495. **Southwestern.** The simple, attractive decor features solid wood furnishings and white adobe walls displaying works by local artists. Basic Mexican dishes and some southwestern variations, plus charbroiled chicken, burgers, sandwiches, and salads. The most popular item is the fresh green chile chicken enchilada. **FYI:** Reservations accepted. Children's menu. **Open:** Daily 11am–10pm. **Prices:** Main courses $5–$10. AE, MC, V.

Cattle Baron Steak and Seafood Restaurant

657 Sudderth Dr; tel 505/622-3311. **Seafood/Steak.** A handsome dining room, with low, adobe-style dividers and wood furnishings. The atmosphere is elegant and upscale, but still friendly. Specialties are steak, prime rib, and fresh seafood. In summer, diners in the waterfall room can watch a lovely, manmade waterfall cascading just outside a wall of windows. **FYI:** Reservations accepted. Children's menu. **Open:** Sun–Thurs 11am–9:30pm, Fri–Sat 11am–10:30pm. **Prices:** Main courses $5–$18. AE, CB, DC, DISC, MC, V.

Flying J Ranch

NM 48 N; tel 505/336-4330. 8 mi N of Ruidoso. **Regional American.** A western-style "dinner theater," located in a large barnlike building with a high, rough wood ceiling and rough wood walls, and large windows. There's only one seating, at 6pm; a fast-paced western music stage show follows. Diners share long picnic tables after going through the chuck wagon–style chow line. The choice of beef or chicken, simmered for several hours in barbecue sauce, comes with baked potato, ranch beans, biscuit, applesauce, and spice cake. **FYI:** Reservations recommended. Children's menu. No liquor license. No smoking. **Open:** Mon–Sat 6–9:30pm. Closed Labor Day–Mem Day. **Prices:** Prix fixe $14. DISC, MC, V.

The Hummingbird Tearoom

In Village Plaza, 2306 Sudderth Dr; tel 505/257-5100. **American.** The dining room is small but airy and simply furnished. Classical music enhances the tearoom atmosphere. The menu features homemade soups, salads, and sandwiches; plus exotic desserts, which are served until 5pm during the summer in the adjoining dessert shop. Smoking is permitted only on the patio (open summer only). **FYI:** Reservations accepted. No liquor license. No smoking. **Open:** Mon–Sat 11am–2:30pm. **Prices:** Lunch main courses $4–$6. MC, V.

La Lorraine

2523 Sudderth Dr; tel 505/257-2954. **French.** An elegant French restaurant with plush seating, attractive artwork, and a brick fireplace. Specialties include beef chateaubriand with béarnaise sauce for two; gourmet French rack of lamb; duck à l'orange; and chicken provençal. **FYI:** Reservations recommended. Beer and wine only. **Open:** Lunch Tues–Sat 11:30am–2pm; dinner Mon–Sat 5:30–9pm. Closed Dec 1–19/3 weeks after Easter. **Prices:** Main courses $14–$22. AE, MC, V.

ATTRACTION

Museum of the Horse

US 70 E; tel 505/378-4142. A collection of more than 10,000 horse-related items, including saddles from all over the world, a Russian sleigh, a horse-drawn fire engine, and an 1860 stagecoach. The museum also has original works by American artists Frederic Remington, Charles M Russell, Frank Tenney Johnson, and Henry Alkins. Site of *Free Spirits at Noisy Water,* a large equine monument. **Open:** Tues–Sun 10am–5pm. **$$**

Salinas Pueblo Missions National Monument

For lodgings and restaurants, see Belen, Socorro

The Spanish conquistadors' Salinas Jurisdiction, on the east side of the Manzano Mountains, was an important 17th-century trade center because of salt extracted by Native Americans from nearby salt lakes. Franciscan priests, utilizing local labor, constructed missions of adobe, sandstone, and limestone for the native converts. The ruins of some of the most durable—along with evidence of preexisting Anasazi and Mongollon cultures—are on display here.

The monument headquarters, on US 60 in Mountainair, serves as the information center, museum, and bookstore. The monument consists of three separate units: the ruins of Abo, Quarai, and Gran Quivira. **Abo,** located 8 miles west of Mountainair on US 60, boasts the 40-foot-high ruins of the Mission of San Gregorio de Abo, a rare example of medieval architecture in the United States. **Quarai,** 9 miles north of

Mountainair on NM 55, preserves the largely intact remains of the Mission of La Purisima Concepcion de Cuarac (1630). **Gran Quivira,** 25 miles south of Mountainair on NM 55, maintains the ruins of 300 rooms, six kivas, and two churches (800–1300). The visitor center has a museum with artifacts from the site, an audiovisual presentation, and an art exhibit. For more information about the monument contact the headquarters at 505/847-2585.

San Antonio

See Socorro

San Juan Pueblo

The largest and northernmost of the Tewa-speaking pueblos, this is also the headquarters of the **Eight Northern Indian Pueblos Council,** which serves as a chamber of commerce and social-service agency. The pueblo is reached via NM 74, 1 mile off NM 68, 4 miles north of Española.

The **O'ke Oweenge Arts and Crafts Cooperative** focuses on the works of San Juan artists, who are known for their distinctive red pottery incised with traditional geometric symbols, silver jewelry, wood and stone carvings, embroidery, and paintings. Located on the main road through the pueblo is the **Tewa Indian Restaurant,** serving traditional pueblo food such as chiles, blue-corn, and posole. The **San Juan Tribal Lakes** are open to visitors for water sports and trout fishing. For more information call 505/852-4400.

Santa Fe

New Mexico's capital—the longest continuously occupied US capital city—charming Santa Fe is brimming with art, culture, and history. Founded by Spanish conquistadors in 1610, the city sits high and dry at the foot of the Sangre de Christo range. Its 18th-century look is achieved through the preservation and perpetuation of Spanish colonial–style architecture of thick adobe walls and flat roofs. Most of the state's best museums—celebrating the region's three cultures (Native American, Hispanic, and Anglo)—are in Santa Fe, and there is the famous, thriving art colony. Major events include the Indian Market in late August and Fiesta in September. **Information:** Santa Fe Convention & Visitors Bureau, PO Box 909, Santa Fe 87501 (tel 505/984-6760 or 800/777-CITY).

HOTELS

DoubleTree Hotel Santa Fe
3347 Cerrillos Rd, 87501; tel 505/473-2800 or toll free 800/777-3347; fax 505/473-4905. Exit 278 off I-25. A pleasant, basic hotel. **Rooms:** 213 rms and stes. CI 3pm/CO 11am. Nonsmoking rms avail. **Amenities:** A/C, cable TV, refrig. Some units w/terraces. Coffeemakers in suites. **Services:** Car-rental desk, masseur, babysitting. **Facilities:** 400 2 restaurants, 1 bar (w/entertainment), spa, whirlpool, washer/dryer. **Rates (CP):** Peak (May–Oct) $115–$165 S; $125–$175 D; $140–$185 ste. Extra person $12. Children under age 12 stay free. Lower rates off-season. Parking: Outdoor, free. AE, CB, DC, DISC, MC, V.

Eldorado Hotel
309 W San Francisco St, 87501; tel 505/988-4455 or toll free 800/955-4455; fax 505/988-5376. Exit 282 off I-25. Santa Fe's largest hotel is located a few blocks from the plaza. The lobby is quite large, with an impressive entrance and some compelling art. **Rooms:** 219 rms and stes; 8 cottages/villas. CI 4pm/CO 11am. Nonsmoking rms avail. Rooms are spacious with a well-coordinated Santa Fe decor. There are a variety of sizes, shapes, and options. The Presidential Suite is especially fine. **Amenities:** A/C, cable TV w/movies, refrig, VCR, bathrobes. All units w/minibars, some w/terraces, some w/fireplaces, 1 w/whirlpool. **Services:** VP Twice-daily maid svce, masseur, babysitting. Butler service for rooms on the fifth floor and a few special rooms elsewhere. **Facilities:** 1000 2 restaurants, 2 bars (1 w/entertainment), spa, sauna, whirlpool, beauty salon. **Rates:** Peak (June 29–Sept 5) $234 S or D; $414–$955 ste; $309–$429 cottage/villa. Children under age 16 stay free. Min stay special events. Lower rates off-season. Parking: Indoor, $5.95/day. AE, CB, DC, DISC, MC, V.

Hilton of Santa Fe
100 Sandoval St, PO Box 25104, 87504; tel 505/988-2811 or toll free 800/336-3676; fax 502/986-6435. Take St Francis Dr to Cerillos Rd; E on Cerillos then W on Sandoval. The territorial architecture and Southwestern decor makes the lobby very inviting and comfortable. Just two blocks from Santa Fe Plaza, the hotel is within easy walking distance of shops, galleries, restaurants, historical sites, cultural events, and museums. **Rooms:** 155 rms and stes; 3 cottages/villas. Executive level. CI 4pm/CO noon. Nonsmoking rms avail. Rooms are done in Southwestern style, very attractive and comfortable. **Amenities:** A/C, cable TV w/movies, dataport, voice mail, in-rm safe. All units w/minibars, some w/terraces, 1 w/fireplace. **Services:** VP Car-rental desk, children's program, babysitting. **Facilities:** 600 2 restaurants (bkfst and dinner only), 1 bar, whirlpool. Guests have access to Club International for use of exercise and spa facilities. **Rates:** Peak (May–Oct 28) $149–$249 S; $169–$269 D; $300–$700 ste; $300–$550 cottage/villa. Extra person $20. Children under age 18 stay free. Lower rates off-season. Parking: Outdoor, free. AE, CB, DC, DISC, EC, ER, JCB, MC, V.

Hotel Plaza Real
125 Washington Ave, 87501; tel 505/988-4900 or toll free 800/297-7325; fax 505/988-4900. Exit 284 off I-25. In a convenient location within easy walking distance of Santa Fe

Plaza. The territorial-style hotel contains both Indian and Spanish influences in the decor. **Rooms:** 56 rms and stes. CI 3pm/CO noon. Nonsmoking rms avail. Rooms are attractively decorated in southwestern style. **Amenities:** A/C, cable TV. Some units w/terraces, some w/fireplaces, some w/whirlpools. VCRs are available. **Services:** Masseur, babysitting. **Facilities:** 1 bar. **Rates (CP):** Peak (July–Oct) $149 S or D; $199 ste. Min stay special events. Lower rates off-season. Parking: Indoor, AE, DC, DISC, MC, V.

Hotel St Francis

210 Don Gaspar Ave, 87501; tel 505/983-5700 or toll free 800/529-5700; fax 505/989-7690. Exit 284 off I-25. This historic hotel, close to the plaza, has a large old-fashioned lobby with a beautiful fireplace. It offers casual elegance and 1920s romance with a comfortable European ambience. **Rooms:** 83 rms, stes, and effic. CI 3pm/CO 11am. Nonsmoking rms avail. Rooms are quaint and charming, with old photographs on the walls, and furnished with a mixture of antiques and period reproductions. **Amenities:** A/C, cable TV, refrig, in-rm safe. 1 unit w/terrace. **Services:** Babysitting. Afternoon tea is served daily in the lobby. Free local phone calls. **Facilities:** 1 restaurant, 1 bar. **Rates:** Peak (May–Oct) $98 S; $118–$188 D; $353 ste; $228 effic. Extra person $15. Children under age 12 stay free. Min stay special events. Lower rates off-season. Parking: Outdoor, free. AE, CB, DC, DISC, JCB, MC, V.

Hotel Santa Fe

1501 Paseo de Peralta, 87501; tel 505/982-1200 or toll free 800/825-9876; fax 505/984-2211. Exit 282 off I-25. Close to Santa Fe Plaza, with sculpture on the grounds, heavy-beamed ceilings, a kiva fireplace, and warm ambience. **Rooms:** 131 rms and stes. CI 4pm/CO noon. Nonsmoking rms avail. **Amenities:** A/C, cable TV w/movies. All units w/minibars, some w/terraces. Suites have in-room safes, microwaves, and two telephones. **Services:** Masseur. **Facilities:** 1 bar (w/entertainment), whirlpool, washer/dryer. There's a small sandwich and breakfast bar on premises. Guests have use of Club International's fitness center. **Rates:** Peak (May–Oct 15) $109–$159 S or D; $139–$219 ste. Extra person $20. Children under age 18 stay free. Lower rates off-season. Parking: Outdoor, free. AE, CB, DC, DISC, JCB, MC, V.

The Inn at Loretto

211 Old Santa Fe Trail, 87501; tel 505/988-5531 or toll free 800/727-5531; fax 505/984-7988. 1 block S of the plaza. Within easy walking distance of Santa Fe Plaza. The Loretto Chapel, with its famous "miraculous staircase," is here, and there are several shops and galleries located on the premises. **Rooms:** 136 rms and stes. CI 3pm/CO noon. Nonsmoking rms avail. Rooms are spacious, and handsomely decorated in Santa Fe style. **Amenities:** A/C, cable TV, refrig, voice mail. Some units w/terraces, 1 w/fireplace. **Services:** Car-rental desk, babysitting. **Facilities:** 1 restaurant, 1 bar, beauty salon, washer/dryer. Tennis and golf can be arranged by the hotel. **Rates:** Peak (July–Oct 21) $175–$195 S; $185–$205 D; $350 ste. Extra person $15. Children under age 17 stay free. Lower rates off-season. Parking: Outdoor, free. AE, CB, DC, DISC, JCB, MC, V.

Inn of the Anasazi

113 Washington Ave, 87501; tel 505/988-3030 or toll free 800/688-8100; fax 505/988-3277. Exit 284 off I-25. An elegant hotel in the heart of downtown. **Rooms:** 59 rms. CI 3pm/CO noon. Nonsmoking rms avail. Rooms are beautifully appointed, with great attention to detail. **Amenities:** A/C, cable TV, refrig, dataport, VCR, in-rm safe, bathrobes. All units w/minibars, some w/terraces, all w/fireplaces. **Services:** Twice-daily maid svce, masseur, babysitting. The service-oriented staff can fulfill practically any request. **Facilities:** 1 restaurant (*see* "Restaurants" below), 1 bar (w/entertainment). **Rates:** Peak (Apr–Oct) $240–$400 S or D. Extra person $20. Children under age 12 stay free. Min stay special events. Lower rates off-season. Parking: Indoor, $10/day. AE, CB, DC, DISC, JCB, MC, V.

Inn of the Governors

234 Don Gaspar Ave, 87501; tel 505/982-4333 or toll free 800/234-4534; fax 505/989-9149. Exit 284 off I-25. A lovely property in downtown Santa Fe, with fresh flowers in the open and airy tiled-floor lobby. **Rooms:** 100 rms and stes. Executive level. CI 4pm/CO noon. Nonsmoking rms avail. Attractive rooms are decorated in Santa Fe style. **Amenities:** A/C, cable TV w/movies, refrig, voice mail. Some units w/minibars, some w/terraces, some w/fireplaces. Stereos are available in some rooms. **Services:** Complimentary coffee and newspaper daily. **Facilities:** 1 restaurant, 1 bar (w/entertainment). Pleasant al fresco dining in the courtyard. **Rates:** Peak (June 27–Dec 2) $109–$159 S or D; $219–$269 ste. Extra person $10. Children under age 18 stay free. Lower rates off-season. Parking: Indoor/outdoor, free. AE, CB, DC, MC, V.

Inn on the Alameda

303 E Alameda St, 87501; tel 505/984-2121 or toll free 800/289-2122; fax 505/986-8325. Exit 282 off I-25. Has a cozy, attractively furnished lobby with library. **Rooms:** 66 rms and stes. CI 4pm/CO noon. Nonsmoking rms avail. Furnished with Southwestern pizzazz. **Amenities:** A/C, cable TV, dataport, voice mail, bathrobes. All units w/terraces, some w/fireplaces. One-third of the rooms have refrigerators. **Services:** Masseur, babysitting. Complimentary breakfast can be delivered to room. The hotel offers a Pet Program, with pet amenities and a walking map. **Facilities:** 1 bar, whirlpool, washer/dryer. **Rates (CP):** Peak (July–Oct) $170–$225 S or D; $260–$350 ste. Extra person $15. Children under age 18 stay free. Lower rates off-season. Parking: Outdoor, free. AE, CB, DC, DISC, MC, V.

La Fonda
100 E San Francisco St, PO Box 1209, 87501; tel 505/982-5511 or toll free 800/523-5002; fax 505/988-2952. Exit 284 off I-25. This is the "Inn at the End of the Santa Fe Trail" in the oldest capital in the United States. When Santa Fe was founded in 1610, it already had a "fonda," or inn, and when the first successful trading expedition from Missouri arrived in 1821, the fonda welcomed the members. The name stuck, and this soon became the destination for trappers, traders, mountain men, merchants, soldiers, politicians, and all who followed. **Rooms:** 153 rms and stes. Executive level. CI 3pm/CO noon. Nonsmoking rms avail. Each room uniquely decorated in New Mexico style. Flowers in the hallways. **Amenities:** A/C, cable TV w/movies, dataport, voice mail, in-rm safe. Some units w/terraces, some w/fireplaces. Refrigerators available in some rooms. **Services:** Twice-daily maid svce, masseur, babysitting. Santa Fe Detours Desk in the lobby can arrange excursions, from white-water raft trips to city tours. **Facilities:** 600 2 restaurants, 2 bars (1 w/entertainment), whirlpool. The Bell Tower Bar, at the top of the hotel, is a great place to watch sunsets. Several shops are located on premises. **Rates:** $160–$170 S; $170 D; $250–$450 ste. Extra person $15. Children under age 12 stay free. Parking: Indoor, $2/day. AE, CB, DC, DISC, EC, JCB, MC, V.

La Posada de Santa Fe
330 E Palace Ave, 87501 (Downtown/Plaza area); tel 505/986-0000 or toll free 800/727-5276; fax 505/982-6850. Exit 287 off I-25. A lovely old hotel on six acres, just two blocks from the Plaza. The grounds are a delight to stroll through. **Rooms:** 119 rms and stes. CI 3pm/CO noon. No smoking. A wide variety of rooms are offered, each unique and individually decorated in Santa Fe style. **Amenities:** A/C, cable TV w/movies, refrig. Some units w/minibars, some w/terraces, some w/fireplaces, 1 w/whirlpool. **Services:** Masseur, babysitting. **Facilities:** 150 1 restaurant, 1 bar, beauty salon. Guests have use of Santa Fe Spa and Fort Marcy Public Sports Complex. **Rates (AP):** Peak (May–Oct) $95–$185 S; $105–$195 D; $165–$395 ste. Extra person $10. Children under age 12 stay free. Lower rates off-season. Parking: Outdoor, free. AE, DC, DISC, MC, V.

Radisson Picacho
750 N St Francis Dr, 87501; tel 505/982-5591 or toll free 800/441-5591; fax 505/988-2821. Exit 282 off I-25. An attractive hotel. Well-known flamenco dancer Maria Benitez performs here several nights a week in the summer. **Rooms:** 159 rms, stes, and effic. CI 4pm/CO noon. Nonsmoking rms avail. Condos are also available. **Amenities:** A/C, cable TV. Some units w/terraces, some w/fireplaces, some w/whirlpools. Refrigerators and hair dryers available. **Services:** Babysitting. Complimentary shuttle service to downtown Santa Fe. **Facilities:** 150 1 restaurant, 1 bar (w/entertainment), whirlpool, washer/dryer. Guests have access to the Santa Fe Spa next door with its indoor pool, weights, exercise equipment, and racquetball courts. **Rates (CP):** Peak (May–Oct) $128–$133 S or D; $178–$183 ste; $170–$200 effic. Extra person $20. Children under age 17 stay free. Min stay special events. Lower rates off-season. Parking: Outdoor, free. AE, CB, DC, DISC, JCB, MC, V.

MOTELS

El Rey Inn
1862 Cerrillos Rd, PO Box 4759, 87502; tel 505/982-1931 or toll free 800/521-1349; fax 505/989-9249. Exit 278 off I-25. Take Cerrillos Rd exit into town; El Rey will be on the east side of street. One of the nicest choices on Cerrillos Rd, this motel has an old, classic, "Route 66" feel. **Rooms:** 85 rms and stes. CI 2pm/CO noon. Nonsmoking rms avail. Each room is unique, with a personal touch. There is a full range of choices from simple rooms to suites to efficiencies with kitchen, two bedrooms, and a fold-out bed in the living room. **Amenities:** A/C, cable TV. Some units w/terraces, some w/fireplaces. **Services:** **Facilities:** 30 Whirlpool, playground, washer/dryer. **Rates (CP):** $56–$115 S or D; $98–$207 ste. Children under age 18 stay free. Parking: Outdoor, free. AE, CB, DC, DISC, MC, V.

Fort Marcy Compound Hotel Suites
320 Artist Rd, 87501; tel 505/982-6636 or toll free 800/795-9910; fax 505/984-8682. Exit 282 off I-25. Take St Francis Dr north through town. Drive east on Paseo de Peralta to Washington Ave and north on Washington to Artist Rd. A lovely complex just four blocks from Santa Fe Plaza and set on nine acres of piñon tree–covered hills. **Rooms:** 145 cottages/villas. CI 4pm/CO 10am. Nonsmoking rms avail. All units are full condos and are individually owned and decorated. **Amenities:** A/C, cable TV, refrig, VCR, CD/tape player, voice mail. All units w/terraces, some w/fireplaces. **Services:** Babysitting. Pets are permitted in twelve units. Although there's no daily maid service, there is a daily towel exchange. **Facilities:** 150 Whirlpool, washer/dryer. Guests have use of the Fort Marcy Sports Complex, a public facility with a pool, racquetball courts, and weight and exercise equipment. **Rates (CP):** Peak (July 1–Sept 14) $69–$334 cottage/villa. Extra person $20. Children under age 18 stay free. Min stay. Lower rates off-season. Parking: Outdoor, free. AE, MC, V.

Garrett's Desert Inn
311 Old Santa Fe Trail, 87501; tel 505/982-1851 or toll free 800/888-2145; fax 505/989-1647. Exit 284 off I-25. A pleasant, basic motel. **Rooms:** 82 rms and stes. CI 3pm/CO noon. Rooms are simple but attractively decorated in a southwestern style. **Amenities:** A/C, cable TV. Some units w/terraces. **Services:** Car-rental desk, babysitting. **Facilities:** 40 2 restaurants (*see* "Restaurants" below), 1 bar, games rm. A new restaurant, Le Café on the Trail, recently opened in the hotel, serving excellent and

French food and pastries. **Rates:** Peak (May–Oct) $95–$105 S or D; $115 ste. Children under age 12 stay free. Lower rates off-season. Parking: Outdoor, free. AE, CB, DC, DISC, MC, V.

Howard Johnson
4044 Cerrillos Rd, 87502; tel 505/438-8950 or toll free 800/446-4656; fax 505/471-9129. Exit 278 off I-25. Modest motel at the south end of Cerrillos Rd. **Rooms:** 47 rms and stes. CI noon/CO noon. Nonsmoking rms avail. Simple, basic rooms. **Amenities:** A/C, cable TV w/movies. **Services:** Babysitting. **Facilities:** Spa. **Rates (CP):** Peak (Mem Day–Aug) $59–$69 S; $89–$99 D; $120 ste. Extra person $6. Children under age 18 stay free. Lower rates off-season. Parking: Outdoor, free. AE, CB, DC, DISC, MC, V.

La Quinta Inn
4298 Cerrillos Rd, 87505; tel 505/471-1142 or toll free 800/531-5900; fax 505/438-7219. Exit 278 off I-25. An attractive motel located close to an outlet mall and the city's largest shopping center. **Rooms:** 130 rms and stes. CI 2pm/CO noon. Nonsmoking rms avail. Newly renovated. **Amenities:** A/C, satel TV w/movies. **Services:** Babysitting. **Facilities:** Washer/dryer. A 24-hour restaurant is next door. **Rates (CP):** Peak (May–Oct) $80–$87 S or D; $120–$128 ste. Extra person $8. Children under age 18 stay free. Lower rates off-season. Parking: Outdoor, free. AE, CB, DC, DISC, ER, MC, V.

Santa Fe Budget Inn
725 Cerrillos Rd, 87501; tel 505/982-5952 or toll free 800/288-7600; fax 505/984-8879. Exit 282 off I-25. Take St Francis Dr to US 85 (Cerrillos Rd). Located close to Santa Fe Plaza. The small lobby has a rack of brochures for visitors. **Rooms:** 160 rms. CI 11am/CO 11am. Clean, basic motel rooms. **Amenities:** A/C, cable TV w/movies. **Services:** Babysitting. **Facilities:** There's a restaurant next door. **Rates:** Peak (July 4–Oct 25) $64–$75 S; $72–$86 D. Extra person $9. Children under age 12 stay free. Min stay special events. Lower rates off-season. Parking: Outdoor, free. AE, CB, DC, MC, V.

Santa Fe Motel
510 Cerrillos Rd, 87501; tel 505/982-1039 or toll free 800/999-1039; fax 505/986-1275. Exit 282 off I-25. Take St Francis Dr to US 85 (Cerrillos Rd); go east on Cerrillos to motel. Clean and basic, close to Santa Fe Plaza. **Rooms:** 22 rms; 1 cottage/villa. CI 2pm/CO noon. Nonsmoking rms avail. There are standard motel rooms in the main motel; rooms in two 75-year-old adobe houses; and the Thomas House, a historic house that sleeps six and comes with a fully equipped kitchen, one bath, dining room, living room with fireplace, private garden, and breakfast patio. **Amenities:** A/C, cable TV. Some units w/terraces, some w/fireplaces. **Services:** Babysitting. **Rates:** Peak (May–Oct) $80–$90 S; $85–$95 D; $180 cottage/villa. Extra person $5. Children under age 12 stay free. Lower rates off-season. Parking: Outdoor, free. AE, MC, V.

Santa Fe Plaza Travelodge
646 Cerrillos Rd, 87501; tel 505/982-3551 or toll free 800/255-3050; fax 505/983-8624. Exit 284 off I-25. A decent, basic motel. **Rooms:** 45 rms. CI 2pm/CO 11am. No smoking. **Amenities:** A/C, cable TV. **Services:** **Facilities:** **Rates:** Peak (June 25–Aug 28) $71 S; $77 D. Extra person $6. Children under age 18 stay free. Min stay special events. Lower rates off-season. Parking: Outdoor, free. AE, DC, DISC, MC, V.

Super 8 Motel
3358 Cerrillos Rd, 87501; tel 505/471-8811 or toll free 800/800-8000; fax 505/471-3239. Exit 278 off I-25. A pleasant, standard motel with a large lobby, located south of town. **Rooms:** 96 rms and stes. Executive level. CI 4pm/CO 11am. Nonsmoking rms avail. Basic motel rooms with no frills. **Amenities:** A/C, cable TV. **Facilities:** **Rates (CP):** Peak (May–Oct) $40–$45 S; $47–$52 D; $55–$65 ste. Extra person $3. Lower rates off-season. Parking: Outdoor, free. AE, CB, DC, DISC, MC, V.

INNS

El Paradero
220 W Manhattan Ave, 87501; tel 505/988-1177. An attractive bed-and-breakfast in an old Spanish farmhouse built between 1800 and 1820. Territorial details were added in the 1880s, and in 1912 the Victorian doors and windows appeared. The present owners have encouraged the eccentric look of the house in their renovations. Unsuitable for children under 4. **Rooms:** 14 rms and stes (4 w/shared bath). CI 2pm/CO 11am. No smoking. A wide variety of rooms, from simple to luxurious. Downstairs rooms front the courtyard, and the upstairs rooms have tile floors and baths. One room has a lovely view of the Sangre de Cristo Mountains. **Amenities:** No A/C or TV. Some units w/terraces, some w/fireplaces. Two units have small kitchenettes, TVs, and A/C. **Services:** Babysitting, afternoon tea served. Full breakfasts include different dishes rotating throughout the week, such as pancakes, eggs Benedict, huevos tostados, and huevos rancheros. Fruit is included. **Facilities:** 15 Guest lounge w/TV. **Rates (BB):** $50–$60 S w/shared bath, $65–$70 S w/private bath; $60–$70 D w/shared bath, $70–$110 D w/private bath; $120–$130 ste. Extra person $15. Min stay wknds and special events. Parking: Outdoor, free. Three-day minimum stay required for suites. MC, V.

Grant Corner Inn
122 Grant Ave, 87501; tel 505/983-6678. A charming, colonial manor bed-and-breakfast inn in downtown Santa Fe, decorated with antiques and historic photos. Unsuitable for children under 8. **Rooms:** 12 rms (2 w/shared bath); 2 cottages/villas. CI 2–6pm/CO noon. No smoking. Rooms are charmingly decorated with antique quilts, brass, four-poster

beds, armoires, and artwork. **Amenities:** No A/C or TV. Some units w/terraces, 1 w/fireplace. **Services:** Twice-daily maid svce, masseur, babysitting, afternoon tea and wine/sherry served. Breakfast is served by a crackling fire, or on the front veranda in the summer. **Facilities:** 1 restaurant (bkfst only), guest lounge. **Rates (BB):** $90–$95 S w/shared bath, $90–$95 S w/private bath; $100–$105 D w/shared bath, $100–$160 D w/private bath; $140–$145 cottage/villa. Extra person $20. Min stay special events. Higher rates for special events/hols. Parking: Outdoor, free. MC, V.

UNRATED **The Preston House**
106 Faithway St, 87501; tel 505/982-3465. A lovely bed-and-breakfast in a turn-of-the-century home close to the plaza, with a resident cat. Unsuitable for children under 10. **Rooms:** 15 rms and stes (2 w/shared bath). CI 3pm/CO 11am. No smoking. **Amenities:** A/C, TV, bathrobes. 1 unit w/terrace, some w/fireplaces. **Services:** Babysitting, afternoon tea and wine/sherry served. The friendly and helpful staff can supply information on local attractions, and are happy to assist with tickets, dinner reservations, and other visitor needs. **Facilities:** 30 Guest lounge. **Rates (CP):** Peak (Mar–Oct) $48–$138 D w/shared bath; $115–$160 ste. Extra person $20. Lower rates off-season. Parking: Outdoor, free. AE, MC, V.

Pueblo Bonita
138 W Manhattan St, 87501; tel 505/984-8001 or toll free 800/461-4599; fax 505/984-3155. Adobe bed-and-breakfast is conveniently located close to Santa Fe's downtown attractions. The property has beautiful private courtyards, narrow brick paths, adobe archways, and shady gardens sheltered by huge trees. The second floor offers splendid views of downtown and the Sangre de Cristo Mountains. **Rooms:** 18 rms and stes. CI 2pm/CO noon. Nonsmoking rms avail. Each room is cozily furnished with Navajo rugs, baskets, and sand paintings; Pueblo and Mexican pottery; antiques; Spanish santos; and works by local artists. **Amenities:** Cable TV. No A/C. Some units w/terraces, all w/fireplaces. Suites have coffeemakers and refrigerators. Hair dryers are available on request. **Services:** Afternoon tea and wine/sherry served. **Facilities:** Washer/dryer, guest lounge. **Rates (CP):** Peak (May–Oct) $65–$90 S; $70–$105 D; $110–$140 ste. Lower rates off-season. Parking: Outdoor, free. MC, V.

Territorial Inn
215 Washington Ave, 87501; tel 505/989-7737; fax 505/986-9212. Located just two blocks from the Plaza in an 1890s stone-and-adobe territorial-style house, this bed-and-breakfast has a cozy sitting room and a small patio area for pleasant summer relaxation. Unsuitable for children under 10. **Rooms:** 10 rms (3 w/shared bath). CI 3pm/CO 11am. No smoking. Rooms are individually decorated, light and airy. Many feature Early American antiques. **Amenities:** Cable TV. No A/C. 1 unit w/terrace, 1 w/fireplace. **Services:** Babysitting, afternoon tea served. **Facilities:** 20 Whirlpool, washer/dryer, guest lounge. **Rates (CP):** Peak (May–Oct) $95 S or D w/shared bath, $90–$150 S or D w/private bath. Extra person $15. Min stay special events. Lower rates off-season. Higher rates for special events/hols. Parking: Outdoor, free. MC, V.

RESORTS

The Bishop's Lodge
Bishop's Lodge Rd, PO Box 2367, 87504; tel 505/983-6377 or toll free 800/732-2240; fax 505/989-8739. 3 mi N of Plaza. 1,000 acres. Originally a retreat for the first bishop of Santa Fe, Bishop Jean Baptiste Lamy, and later a vacation home for the Pulitzer publishing family of St Louis, Bishop's Lodge is now a magnificent resort adjoining the national forest, just a few miles from downtown Santa Fe. The Bishop's chapel is still used for weddings. **Rooms:** 88 rms and stes. CI 3pm/CO noon. Rooms have an old New Mexican atmosphere and are beautifully furnished with art and old photos. **Amenities:** A/C, satel TV w/movies, dataport, voice mail, in-rm safe, bathrobes. Some units w/terraces, some w/fireplaces. Hair dryers, VCRs, and computer/fax hookups are available. **Services:** Twice-daily maid svce, masseur, children's program, babysitting. **Facilities:** 4 150 1 restaurant, 1 bar, volleyball, lawn games, sauna, whirlpool, playground. **Rates:** Peak (July–Labor Day) $195–$300 S; $210–$315 D; $260–$375 ste. Extra person $15. Children under age 4 stay free. Min stay special events. Lower rates off-season. MAP rates avail. Parking: Outdoor, free. AE, DISC, MC, V.

Rancho Encantado
Route 4, PO Box 57C, 87501; tel 505/982-3537 or toll free 800/722-9339; fax 505/983-8269. 8 mi N of downtown; exit 282 off I-25. 168 acres. This fun resort 15 minutes north of downtown Santa Fe is especially popular for horseback riding and enjoying the wide open spaces of the West. **Rooms:** 26 rms and stes; 62 cottages/villas. CI 3pm/CO 11am. Nonsmoking rms avail. There is a wide range of accommodations, from individually owned villas in Pueblo Encantado to simple rooms and spacious casitas; all are attractive and comfortable. **Amenities:** A/C, cable TV, voice mail, bathrobes. Some units w/terraces, some w/fireplaces. Hair dryers, VCRs, and refrigerators are available. Villas have washers and dryers. **Services:** Social director, masseur, children's program, babysitting. **Facilities:** 1 1 200 1 restaurant, 2 bars, basketball, volleyball, lawn games, whirlpool. **Rates:** Peak (May 24–Oct 14) $175–$250 S or D; $210–$375 ste; $210–$1,000 cottage/villa. Children under age 18 stay free. Lower rates off-season. Parking: Outdoor, free. AE, CB, DC, DISC, MC, V.

RESTAURANTS

Bobcat Bite
Old Las Vegas Highway; tel 505/983-5319. 8 mi SE of Santa Fe via Old Las Vegas Hwy. **Burgers/Steak.** Atmosphere

reminiscent of a 1950s roadside hamburger joint. Locally popular for steaks and huge hamburgers, including a green chile cheeseburger. **FYI:** Reservations not accepted. No liquor license. **Open:** Wed–Sat 11am–7:50pm. **Prices:** Main courses $4–$12. No CC.

The Burrito Co
111 Washington Ave; tel 505/982-4453. ½ block NE of the Plaza. **Southwestern.** A popular place to stop for a quick bite, and a step above most fast food restaurants. Breakfasts include huevos rancheros and breakfast burritos, in addition to the usual bacon and eggs. Mexican fare includes blue corn chicken enchiladas smothered in red or green chiles and topped with cheese and beans, or posole. **FYI:** Reservations not accepted. Children's menu. No liquor license. No smoking. **Open:** Mon–Sat 7:30am–7pm, Sun 10am–5pm. **Prices:** Main courses $3–$5. No CC.

Cafe Escalera
130 Lincoln Ave; tel 505/989-8188. ½ block N of Plaza. **New American.** This spacious second-floor cafe has an bright and airy atmosphere. The menu, which changes nightly, places an emphasis on fresh ingredients. Known for homemade breads and desserts. **FYI:** Reservations recommended. **Open:** Mon–Sat 11:30am–10pm. **Prices:** Main courses $10–$25. AE, MC, V.

Cafe Pasqual's
121 Don Gaspar Ave; tel 505/983-9340. 1 block S of the Plaza. **International/Southwestern.** The menu features imaginative variations on both American and southwestern dishes. Specialties include chile-rubbed grilled salmon with corn pudding and grilled vegetables; roasted whole garlic with tomatillo salsa and warm brie; chicken mole enchiladas; and New Mexico lamb chops with fresh tomato mint salsa. There's a community table for single diners. **FYI:** Reservations accepted. Beer and wine only. No smoking. **Open:** Peak (May–Oct) breakfast Mon–Sat 7am–3pm, Sun 8am–3pm; dinner daily 6–10:30pm. **Prices:** Main courses $16–$25. AE, MC, V.

(\$) Carlos' Gosp'l Cafe
In First Interstate Bank Building Courtyard, 125 Lincoln Ave; tel 505/983-1841. 1 block N of the Plaza. **Deli.** A popular place for summer outdoor dining and for families seeking a filling, inexpensive lunch. Basic deli fare: sandwiches, soups, salads, homemade desserts. **FYI:** Reservations not accepted. No liquor license. **Open:** Mon–Fri 11am–4pm, Sat 11am–3pm. **Prices:** Lunch main courses $3–$7. No CC.

The Compound
653 Canyon Rd; tel 505/982-4253. **Continental.** Located in an old adobe home, this elegant restaurant is noted for superb service. The specialty of the house is roast rack of prime lamb with mint sauce. Also on the menu are beef, veal, chicken, trout, and seafood. Entrees are served with saffron rice or braised potatoes, vegetables of the day, and fresh baked rolls. **FYI:** Reservations recommended. No smoking. **Open:** Tues–Sat 6pm–close. Closed Jan. **Prices:** Main courses $18–$25. AE.

Cowgirl Hall of Fame
319 S Guadalupe St; tel 505/982-2565. Exit 282 off I-25. **Regional American/Barbecue.** Decked out in cowgirl memorabilia, this is a fun place and a smart choice for families with young children. A "kid's corral" has horseshoes, a play area, pin-the-tail-on-the-cow, and other activities to keep kids entertained. The menu includes sandwiches and a variety of chicken dishes as well as fish, beef, and vegetarian plates. Brisket and ribs and salmon tacos are house specialties. The specialty dessert is the "cowgirl's original ice cream baked potato," which is ice cream molded into a potato shape, rolled in spices, and topped with whipped cream and green pecans. The bar has a happy hour 3–6pm weekdays and is open until 2am; a wide variety of entertainment is available. **FYI:** Reservations recommended. Children's menu. **Open:** Daily 11am–11pm. **Prices:** Main courses $7–$14. AE, DISC, MC, V.

Coyote Cafe
132 W Water St; tel 505/983-1615. 1 block S and 1 block W of the Plaza. **Southwestern.** Decor is chic California/southwest, with painted tabletops and multicolored china. The menu changes seasonally, but includes a wide variety of southwestern appetizers and a variety of innovative fish, poultry, and meat entrees. The rooftop cantina is open daily 11:30am–10pm from April through September. **FYI:** Reservations recommended. No smoking. **Open:** Peak (May–Oct) lunch daily 11:30am–1:45pm; dinner daily 5:30–9:45pm. **Prices:** Prix fixe $40. AE, CB, DC, DISC, MC, V.

★ El Farol
808 Canyon Rd (Historic East Side); tel 505/988-9912. **Spanish.** The original bar is classic New Mexico; here patrons can enjoy live entertaiment each evening at 9:30. One of the house specialties is tapas, and there is a wide variety of these small appetizers, both hot and cold, featuring seafood, meats, chicken, or vegetables. Diners often make a meal of them. **FYI:** Reservations recommended. Blues/folk/flamenco. **Open:** Daily 11am–10pm. **Prices:** Main courses $11–$23. DC, DISC, MC, V.

El Nido
NM 22, Tesuque; tel 505/988-4340. 5 mi N of Santa Fe Tesuque exit off US 84/285 N. **Seafood/Steak.** Located in a delightful old building adorned with fascinating murals and possessing an Old Santa Fe ambience. Close to the Santa Fe Opera, it is a good spot for a pre-opera dinner. Salmon, prime rib, and sirloin are specialties, and beef, seafood, and chicken are also served. **FYI:** Reservations recommended. **Open:** Mon–Thurs 6–9:30pm, Fri–Sat 6–10pm. **Prices:** Main courses $10–$27. AE, MC, V.

Geronimo
724 Canyon Rd; tel 505/982-1500. Exit 282 off I-25. **Southwestern.** Housed in a lovely old Canyon Road adobe home, with attractively furnished, intimate dining rooms, and a front porch and side patio for outdoor dining. The innovative menu includes southwestern variations on a variety of classic dishes, such as ravioli stuffed with smoked chicken, mascarpone cheese, chile-dusted pecans, and green onion with a chipotle chile cream sauce. **FYI:** Reservations recommended. **Open:** Lunch Tues–Sun 11:30am–2:30pm; dinner daily 6–10:30pm. **Prices:** Main courses $17–$24. AE, MC, V.

Green Onion
1851 St Michael's Dr; tel 505/983-5198. Exit 278 off I-25. **Burgers/Southwestern.** A locally popular sports bar, serving salads, burgers and hot dogs, a variety of sandwiches, and the usual Mexican plates. **FYI:** Reservations not accepted. Children's menu. **Open:** Mon–Sat 11am–2am, Sun 11am–midnight. **Prices:** Main courses $5–$9. AE, DISC, MC, V.

($) Guadalupe Cafe
422 Old Santa Fe Trail (Downtown); tel 505/982-9762. 5 blocks SE of the Plaza. **Southwestern.** A casual cafe in an attractive old building. New Mexico–style Mexican dishes, with a wide choice of enchiladas and burritos. Reservations accepted for parties of six or more. **FYI:** Reservations not accepted. Children's menu. Beer and wine only. No smoking. **Open:** Breakfast Tues–Fri 7–11am, Sat–Sun 8am–2pm; lunch Tues–Sun 11am–2pm; dinner Tues–Sat 5:30–9pm. **Prices:** Main courses $6–$12. DISC, MC, V.

India Palace
227 Don Gaspar Ave; tel 505/986-5859. 2 blocks S of the Plaza. **Indian.** Quiet and serene atmosphere. Large choice of tandoori dishes; chicken, lamb, beef, seafood and vegetarian dishes; and Indian breads. **FYI:** Reservations recommended. Beer and wine only. **Open:** Lunch daily 11:30am–2:30pm; dinner daily 5–10pm. **Prices:** Main courses $7–$27. AE, DISC, MC, V.

Inn of the Anasazi Restaurant
In the Inn of the Anasazi, 113 Washington Ave; tel 505/988-3236. 1 block N of the Plaza. **Southwestern.** Elegant southwestern-style restaurant features handpainted tables and walls and lovely custom-made china. The menu, which changes several times each year, features natural beef, lamb, and chicken as well as organically grown fruits and vegetables. **FYI:** Reservations recommended. Guitar. Children's menu. No smoking. **Open:** Breakfast Mon–Sat 7–10:30am; lunch daily 11:30am–2:30pm; dinner daily 5:30–10pm; brunch Sun 7am–2:30pm. **Prices:** Main courses $17–$29; prix fixe $35–$50. AE, CB, DC, DISC, MC, V. VP

Julian's
221 Shelby St; tel 505/988-2355. 2 blocks S of the Plaza. **Italian.** An elegantly simple restaurant with a central kiva fireplace, located in a historic building. The northern Italian fare features such specialties as saltimbocca alla Romana, veal sauteed with herbs, white wine, and marsala and topped with prosciutto, mozzarella, and Fontina cheese. **FYI:** Reservations recommended. No smoking. **Open:** Daily 6–10pm. **Prices:** Main courses $13–$26. AE, CB, DC, DISC, MC, V.

Le Café on the Trail
In Garrett's Desert Inn, 311 Old Santa Fe Trail; tel 505/982-7302. 3 blocks S of the Plaza. **French.** A French-style restaurant, the menu includes fresh pastas like linguini fisherman (scallops, shrimp, mussels, fish, garlic, tomato, and basil), angel-hair pasta with chicken (garlic, basil, parmesan, and cream sauce), and fettucine venitienne (julienne of mushrooms, chicken, and ham with velouté tomato). Hamburgers, poultry, fish, and veal dishes are also offered. **FYI:** Reservations recommended. Beer and wine only. **Open:** Daily 7am–9pm. **Prices:** Main courses $6–$15. AE, MC, V.

Le Tertulia
416 Agua Fria St; tel 505/988-2769. Exit 282 off I-25 St Francis Dr N to Agua Fria St. **Southwestern/Steak.** Located in a former convent, this elegant restaurant with a large dining room has a timeless feel. Classic New Mexico cuisine. House specialties include carne adovada and chiles rellenos. Also steaks and chops. **FYI:** Reservations recommended. Dress code. **Open:** Lunch Tues–Sun 11:30am–2pm; dinner Tues–Sun 5–9pm. Closed Dec 1–7. **Prices:** Main courses $8–$19; prix fixe $20. AE, DC, DISC, MC, V.

★ Maria's
555 W Cordova Rd; tel 505/983-7929. Exit 282 off I-25. **Southwestern.** A delightful restaurant with authentic Old New Mexico ambience. The floor is covered with Mexican tile, and there are old wooden tables and carved chairs. Fajitas—beef and chicken—are the specialty. Soups and salads are also served, and there is a daily lunch special. The margaritas, touted as the best in town, come in 41 varieties. **FYI:** Reservations recommended. Guitar. Children's menu. No smoking. **Open:** Mon–Fri 11am–10pm, Sat–Sun noon–10pm. **Prices:** Main courses $8–$15. AE, CB, DC, DISC, MC, V.

The Natural Cafe
1494 Cerrillos Rd; tel 505/983-1411. Exit 278 off I-25. **International/Vegetarian.** A simple cafe with polished wood tables and an attractive flagstone patio for warm-weather dining. There are usually four or five specials in addition to innovative international vegetarian dishes, fresh fish, and free-range chicken. Organically grown produce; whole wheat french bread baked daily. **FYI:** Reservations recommended. Guitar. Beer and wine only. No smoking. **Open:** Peak (May–Sept) lunch Tues–Fri 11am–2:30pm; dinner Tues–Sun 5–9:30pm. **Prices:** Main courses $6–$16. DISC, MC, V.

★ Old Mexico Grill
In College Plaza South, 2434 Cerrillos Rd; tel 505/473-0338. Exit 278 off I-25. **Mexican.** Authentic Mexican decor to go along with authentic Mexican cuisine. Mole, tacos, and fajitas, plus dishes with chicken, salmon, beef tenderloin, and baby back ribs. **FYI:** Reservations accepted. **Open:** Lunch Mon–Fri 11:30am–2:30pm; dinner Sun–Thurs 5:30–9pm, Fri–Sat 5:30–9:30pm. **Prices:** Main courses $8–$18. DISC, MC, V.

The Palace Restaurant and Saloon
142 W Palace Ave; tel 505/982-9891. 1 block W of the Plaza. **Continental/Italian.** Located in a historic building close to the plaza, this restaurant is known for its caesar salad and escargot portobello bruschetta appetizer. Also popular are baked shrimp and crab, pan-seared New Mexico lamb chops, and fettuccine pomodoro. All pastas, breads, and desserts are made on premises. The menu also includes chicken, sweetbreads, veal, salmon, and steak. **FYI:** Reservations recommended. Piano. **Open:** Lunch Mon–Sat 11:30am–3pm; dinner daily 5:45–10pm. **Prices:** Main courses $10–$24. AE, CB, DC, DISC, MC, V.

Paul's
72 W Marcy St; tel 505/982-8738. 1 block N of the Plaza. **International.** An intimate restaurant where screens separating tables and low lighting help make for a romantic evening. The menu changes seasonally and depends on the availability of fresh ingredients. Paul's won the Taste of Santa Fe for best entree in 1992 and best dessert in 1994. **FYI:** Reservations recommended. Beer and wine only. No smoking. **Open:** Lunch Mon–Sat 11:30am–2pm; dinner daily 5:30–9:30pm. **Prices:** Main courses $13–$18. AE, DISC, MC, V.

The Pink Adobe
406 Old Santa Fe Trail; tel 505/983-7712. Exit 284 off I-25. **Continental/Southwestern.** Cozy, warm, intimate atmosphere, set in an old adobe home. Entrees include spaghetti, baked chicken, beef tournedos, lamb curry, pork Napoleon, lamb chops, grilled tuna, and fried shrimp Louisianne, plus several Mexican dishes. Especially popular is steak Dunigan—charred sirloin with fresh mushrooms and green chile, served with browned potatoes and Creole salad. **FYI:** Reservations recommended. Children's menu. No smoking. **Open:** Lunch Mon–Fri 11:30am–2:30pm; dinner daily 5:30–10pm. **Prices:** Main courses $11–$23. AE, CB, DC, DISC, MC, V.

Poulet Patate
106 N Guadalupe St (2 blocks W of Plaza); tel 505/820-2929. Exit 282 off I-25. **French/Rotisserie.** The specialty at this stylish cafe is gourmet rotisserie chicken prepared in the French manner. Diners enjoy full views of the open kitchen, where the chickens turn on their spits. **FYI:** Reservations recommended. Children's menu. Beer and wine only. No smoking. **Open:** Lunch Mon–Fri 11:30am–2:30pm; dinner daily 5:30–10pm; brunch Sun 10am–2:30pm. **Prices:** Main courses $11–$18. AE, CB, DC, DISC, MC, V.

Pranzo Italia Grill
In Sanbusco Center, 540 Montezuma St; tel 505/984-2645. Exit 282 off I-25. **Italian.** This sleek, attractive Italian bistro-style restaurant has an open grill as its centerpiece. Choose from among homemade soups, salads, creative pizzas (like the Mediterranea, with shrimp, zucchini, and roasted garlic), and dinner entrees of steak, veal, and chicken, as well as fresh, garlicky seafood grills. There's a modified menu available for late at night. **FYI:** Reservations recommended. No smoking. **Open:** Lunch Mon–Sat 11:30am–3pm; dinner Sun–Thurs 5–10pm, Fri–Sat 5–11pm. **Prices:** Main courses $9–$19. AE, CB, DC, DISC, MC, V.

Saigon Cafe
In Cordova Rd Shopping Center, 501 W Cordova Rd; tel 505/988-4951. Exit 282 off I-25. **Chinese.** A simple Chinese restaurant with a luncheon and dinner buffet. **FYI:** Reservations not accepted. No liquor license. **Open:** Lunch Mon–Sat 11am–2:30pm; dinner Mon–Sat 5–8:30pm. **Prices:** Prix fixe $15–$42. AE, MC, V.

San Francisco Street Bar and Grill
In Plaza Mercado, 114 W San Francisco St; tel 505/982-2044. 1½ blocks W of the Plaza. **New American.** A modern grill with tile floor, wood tables, rush-seated chairs, and photographs on the walls. Sandwiches, hamburgers, steak, fresh fish, soups, salads, and homemade pasta. **FYI:** Reservations not accepted. Children's menu. No smoking. **Open:** Daily 11am–11pm. **Prices:** Main courses $6–$13. AE, DISC, MC, V.

Santacafé
231 Washington Ave; tel 505/984-1788. 2 blocks N of the Plaza. **New American.** A cozy, intimate restaurant located in a historic house. The menu changes often but generally includes chicken, fish, lamb, steak, and one or two vegetarian dishes. **FYI:** Reservations recommended. **Open:** Lunch Mon–Fri 11:30am–2pm; dinner daily 6–10pm. **Prices:** Main courses $17–$25. AE, MC, V.

Sergio's Ristorante
In St Michael's Village West, 1620 St Michael's Dr; tel 505/471-7107. Exit 278 off I-25. **Italian.** Bistro-style restaurant featuring homemade sauces and fresh pastries, as well as a popular salad bar. **FYI:** Reservations not accepted. Beer and wine only. No smoking. **Open:** Lunch Mon–Sat 11am–2:30pm; dinner Mon–Thurs 5–9pm, Fri–Sat 5–10pm. **Prices:** Main courses $7–$13. AE, DISC, MC, V.

★ The Shed
In Sena Plaza, 113 ½ E Palace Ave; tel 505/982-9030. ½ block E of the Plaza. **Southwestern.** Popular eatery that takes up several rooms of a rambling hacienda built in the late 1600s. Decorated with murals and lace curtains. New Mexican cuisine, with a few burgers and salads offered. Blue corn enchiladas and green chile soup are very popular. **FYI:** Reservations not accepted. Beer and wine only. No smoking.

Open: Lunch Mon–Sat 11am–2:30pm; dinner Thurs–Sat 5:30–9pm. **Prices:** Main courses $7–$14. DISC, MC, V.

Shohko-Cafe
321 Johnson St; tel 505/983-7288. 3 blocks W of the Plaza. **Chinese/Japanese.** A sushi bar that also offers some Chinese dishes and seafood specials. **FYI:** Reservations recommended. Beer and wine only. **Open:** Peak (July–Aug) lunch Mon–Fri 11:30am–2pm; dinner Mon–Thurs 6–9:30pm, Fri–Sat 6–10pm. **Prices:** Main courses $8–$18. AE, DISC, MC, V.

Steaksmith at El Gancho
In El Gancho Club, Old Las Vegas Hwy; tel 505/988-3333. 2½ mi E of Santa Fe; exit 284 off I-25. **Seafood/Steak.** Done in the style of an English pub, this restaurant serves steak and seafood, barbecue ribs, chicken, and New Mexican dishes. **FYI:** Reservations recommended. Children's menu. **Open:** Mon–Sat 5:30–10pm, Sun 5–9pm. **Prices:** Main courses $9–$25. AE, DC, DISC, MC, V.

Szechwan Chinese Cuisine
1965 Cerrillos Rd; tel 505/983-1558. Exit 278 off I-25. **Chinese.** Basic Chinese, with a popular luncheon buffet. One specialty is tangerine delight: chunks of chicken, beef, and shrimp, with broccoli in a hot and spicy tangerine sauce. The menu lists over 80 items. **FYI:** Reservations accepted. Beer and wine only. **Open:** Daily 11am–9:30pm. **Prices:** Main courses $6–$13; prix fixe $9–$12. DISC, MC, V.

($) Tecolote Cafe
1203 Cerrillos Rd; tel 505/988-1362. Exit 278 off I-25. **American/Southwestern.** Breakfast is served until 2 pm in this New Mexican–style cafe. Items include carne adovada burrito, shirred eggs tecolote, corned beef hash, and sheepherder's breakfast. For lunch there's both New Mexican and standard American fare. **FYI:** Reservations not accepted. No liquor license. **Open:** Tues–Sun 7am–2pm. **Prices:** Lunch main courses $5–$8. AE, DISC, MC, V.

Tia Sophias
210 W San Francisco St; tel 505/983-9880. 2 blocks W of the Plaza. **Southwestern.** Casual restaurant, with seating available at large wooden booths. Standard New Mexican fare includes daily breakfast specials like eggs with blue corn enchiladas and burritos with chorizo, potatoes, chile, and cheese. Salads and sandwiches, too. **FYI:** Reservations not accepted. Children's menu. No liquor license. **Open:** Mon–Sat 7am–2pm. **Prices:** Lunch main courses $4–$8. MC, V.

★ Tiny's Restaurant & Lounge
In Penn Rd Shopping Center, 1015 Penn Rd; tel 505/983-9817. Exit 282 off I-25. **Seafood/Southwestern/Steak.** A favorite with locals since it opened in 1948. There are two dining rooms: one in an older part of the building with a bar-like atmosphere; the other newer and curved around an outdoor patio. Tiny's specialty is its award-winning fajitas. Also a variety of other New Mexican dishes, plus steak, seafood, burgers, and salads. **FYI:** Reservations recommended. Cabaret/guitar. Children's menu. **Open:** Lunch Mon–Fri 11:30am–2pm; dinner Mon–Sat 6–10pm. **Prices:** Main courses $6–$14. AE, CB, DC, DISC, MC, V.

★ Tomasitas Santa Fe Station
500 S Guadalupe St; tel 505/988-5721. Exit 282 off I-25. **Southwestern.** Located in a former railway depot. Known for its chiles rellenos and enchiladas. Also served here are burritos, stuffed sopaipillas, chalupas, tacos, burgers, steak, and several vegetarian dishes. **FYI:** Reservations not accepted. Children's menu. No smoking. **Open:** Mon–Sat 11am–10pm. **Prices:** Main courses $6–$11. MC, V.

Tortilla Flats
3139 Cerrillos Rd; tel 505/471-8685. Exit 278 off I-25. **Southwestern.** Southwestern-style restaurant with fast service. The usual New Mexican dishes are offered—enchiladas, chiles rellenos, tacos, quesadillas—plus Santa Fe trail steak (rib eye steak smothered with red or green chiles and topped with grilled onions) and green chile chops (two pork chops smothered with green chile and topped with grilled tomatoes and onions). **FYI:** Reservations not accepted. Children's menu. **Open:** Peak (May–Sept) daily 7am–10pm. **Prices:** Main courses $5–$10. DISC, MC, V.

Toushie's
4220 Airport Rd; tel 505/473-4159. Exit 278 off I-25. **American/Mexican.** A simple restaurant and bar, with entertainment on weekends. Steak, seafood, and New Mexican dishes. **FYI:** Reservations accepted. Children's menu. **Open:** Mon–Fri 11am–9:30pm, Sat–Sun 4–9:30pm. **Prices:** Main courses $5–$17. AE, MC, V.

($) Zia Diner
326 S Guadalupe St; tel 505/988-7008. 3 blocks E of Plaza. **American.** A popular, busy diner done in Santa Fe art deco style, with a nice outdoor patio for summer dining. Traditional all-American cuisine, including chicken-fried steak, meatloaf, mashed potatoes, and daily specials. The pies and cakes are well regarded. **FYI:** Reservations accepted. **Open:** Peak (June–Sept) daily 11:30am–11pm. **Prices:** Main courses $5–$15. AE, MC, V.

ATTRACTIONS

HISTORIC BUILDINGS AND MUSEUMS

Palace of the Governors
North Plaza; tel 505/827-6483. Built in 1610, the original capitol building has been in continuous public use longer than any other structure in the United States. Today it is a state history museum with a series of exhibits chronicling the four centuries of New Mexico's Hispanic and Anglo history, from the 16th century Spanish explorations through the frontier era to modern times. The museum also contains several period reprodcution rooms including a Mexican Governor's office (ca 1846), a Territorial Parlor (ca 1883), and a mid-19th century chapel. The bookstore has one of the

finest selections of art, history, and anthropology books in the Southwest. There is also a print shop and bindery, in which limited edition works are produced on hand presses.

Outside the museum, beneath the long covered portal facing the Plaza, colorfully dressed Native American artisans sit shoulder-to-shoulder selling jewelry, pottery, beadwork, and paintings. **Open:** Daily 10am–5pm. **$$**

State Capitol
Paseo de Peralta and Old Santa Fe Trail; tel 505/986-4589. The only round capitol building in America, it derives its shape from a Native American *zia* emblem, which symbolizes the Circle of Life: four winds, four seasons, four directions, and four sacred obligations. Surrounding the capitol is a lush, 6½-acre garden containing dozens of varieties of plants—roses, plums, almonds, nectarines, and sequoias among them. **Open:** Mon–Fri 6am–7pm. **Free**

Museum of Fine Arts
107 W Palace Ave; tel 505/827-4452. The museum's permanent collection of more than 8,000 works emphasizes regional art, including numerous Georgia O'Keeffe paintings, landscapes and portraits by all the Taos masters, and more recent works by such contemporary greats as Luis Jimenez and Fritz Scholder. There is also a collection of Ansel Adams photography. **Open:** Peak (June–Dec) daily 10am–5pm. Reduced hours off-season. **$$**

Center for Contemporary Arts
291 E Barcelona Rd; tel 505/982-1338. Presents the work of internationally, nationally, and regionally known artists through gallery exhibitions, contemporary dance and new music concerts, poetry readings, performance-art events, theater, and video and film screenings. **Open:** Mon–Fri 9am–5pm, Sat noon–4pm. **Free**

Museum of International Folk Art
706 Camino Lejo; tel 505/827-6350. Over 200,000 objects from more than 100 countries. Special collections include Spanish Colonial silver, traditional and contemporary New Mexican religious art, tribal costumes, Brazilian folk art, European glass, African sculptures, and East Indian textiles. In addition, the Hispanic Heritage Wing often presents art demonstrations, performances, and workshops. **Open:** Daily 10am–5pm. **$$**

Museum of Indian Arts and Culture
710 Camino Lejo; tel 505/827-6344. Interpretive displays detail tribal history and contemporary lifestyles of New Mexico's Pueblo, Navajo, and Apache cultures. More than 50,000 pieces of basketry, pottery, clothing, carpets, and jewelry is on continual rotating display. There are daily demonstrations of traditional skills, as well as regular performances of Native American music and dancing. **Open:** Daily 10am–5pm. **$$**

Wheelwright Museum of the American Indian
704 Camino Lejo; tel 505/982-4636. Navajo medicine man Hastiin Klah took the designs of sand paintings used in healing ceremonies and adapted them into the textiles that are a major part of the museum's treasure. There are rotating single-subject shows of silverwork, jewelry, tapestry, pottery, basketry, and paintings. Outdoor sculpture garden. **Open:** Mon–Sat 10am–5pm, Sun 1–5pm. **$**

Institute of American Indian Arts Museum
108 Cathedral Place; tel 505/988-6281. Operated by the federal Bureau of Indian Affairs, the institute encourages Native American artists to create out of their own traditions and experiences. Representatives from 70 tribes display their current work in four to five major exhibitions a year. **Open:** Mon–Fri 8am–5pm, Sat–Sun 10am–5pm. **$$**

Indian Art Research Center
660 Garcia St; tel 505/982-3584. One of the world's finest collections of southwestern tribal art. Admission is highly restricted, but tours are given most Fridays at 2pm. Entrance is free for Native Americans. **$$$$**

Santa Fe Children's Museum
1050 Old Pecos Trail; tel 505/989-8359. Offers interactive exhibits in the arts, humanities, science, and technology. Special art and science activities and family performances are regularly scheduled. **Open:** Peak (June–Aug) Wed–Sat 10am–5pm, Sun noon–5pm. Reduced hours off-season. **$**

Footsteps Across New Mexico
211 Old Santa Fe Trail; tel 505/982-9297. This multimedia presentation provides an impressive introduction to the state. Slides, music, and a sculpted, three-dimensional map combine to tell the New Mexico story, from pre-Hispanic Pueblo culture to the landing of the space shuttle at White Sands. **Open:** Mon–Sat 9:30am–5pm, Sun 9:30am–4pm. **$$**

El Rancho de las Golondrinas
334 Los Pinos Rd; tel 505/471-2261. This 200-acre ranch was once the last stopping place on the 1,000-mile El Camino Real from Mexico City to Santa Fe. Today, it is a living 18th- and 19th-century Spanish village comprising a hacienda, a village store, a schoolhouse, and several chapels and kitchens. There's also a working molasses mill, a wheelwright and blacksmith shops, weaving rooms, a threshing ground, winery and vineyards, and four water mills. **Open:** June–Sept, Wed–Sun 10am–4pm. **$$**

CHURCHES AND SHRINES

St Francis Cathedral
Cathedral Place at San Francisco St; tel 505/982-5619. An architectural anomaly in Santa Fe, this Romanesque building was built between 1869 and 1886 by Archbishop Jean-Baptiste Lamy to resemble the great cathedrals of Europe. The small adobe Our Lady of the Rosary chapel on the northeast side of the cathedral is the only parcel remaining from Our Lady of Assumption Church, founded with Santa Fe in 1610. The new cathedral was built over and around the old church.

A wooden icon set in a niche in the wall of the north chapel, *La Conquistadora,* Our Lady of Conquering Love, is the oldest representation of the Madonna in the United States. Around the cathedral's exterior are doors featuring 16 bronze panels of historic note and a plaque memorializing the 38 Franciscan friars who were martyred in New Mexico's early years. There is also a large bronze statue of Bishop Lamy, and his grave lies under the main altar of the cathedral. **Open:** Daylight hours daily. **Free**

Loretto Chapel
211 Old Santa Fe Trail; tel 502/982-0092. Patterned after the famous Sainte-Chapelle church in Paris, it was constructed in 1873. The chapel is especially notable for its remarkable spiral staircase that makes two complete 360°-turns with no central or other visible support. Entrance is through The Inn at Loretto. **Open:** Daily 9am–4:30pm. **$**

Santuario de Nuestra Señora de Guadalupe
100 S Guadalupe St; tel 505/988-2027. Built between 1776 and 1796 at the end of El Camino Real by Franciscan missionaries, this is believed to be the oldest shrine in the United States honoring the Virgin of Guadalupe, patroness of Mexico. Inside is the famous oil painting, *Our Lady of Guadalupe*, created in 1783 by renowned Mexican artist Jose de Alzibar. **Open:** Peak (May–Oct) Mon–Sat 9am–4pm. Reduced hours off-season. **Free**

Cristo Rey Church
1120 Canyon Rd; tel 505/983-8528. Huge adobe structure built in 1940 to commemorate the 400th anniversary of Coronado's exploration of the Southwest. **Open:** Daily 7am–7pm. **Free**

Mission of San Miguel
401 Old Santa Fe Trail; tel 505/983-3974. One of the oldest churches in America, it was built within a few years of the 1610 founding of Santa Fe. Severely damaged in the 1680 Pueblo revolt, the church was almost completely rebuilt in 1710. Among the highlights of the mission are San Jose Bell, reputedly cast in Spain in 1356, and a series of buffalo hides and deerskins decorated with Bible stories. **Open:** Mon–Sat 10am–4pm, Sun 1:30-4pm. **Free**

PUEBLOS

Nambe Pueblo
Rte 1; tel 505/455-2036. The 700-year-old Tewa-speaking pueblo is located at the foot of the Sangre de Cristo range. A few of the original pueblo buildings still exist, including a large round kiva, used today in ceremonies. Pueblo artisans make woven belts, beadwork, and brown micaceous pottery.

Nambe Falls make a three-tier drop through a cleft in a rockface 4 miles beyond the pueblo, tumbling into Nambe Reservoir. A recreational site offers fishing, boating, hiking, camping, and picnicking. **Open:** Daily 8am–5pm. **Free**

Pojoaque Pueblo
NM 11; tel 505/455-3460. The Poajaque Pueblo Visitor Information Center offers maps, brochures, and free tourist information, making this an important center for traveler services. Indigenous pottery, embroidery, silverwork, and beadwork are available for sale at the **Poeh Cultural Center and Museum.** There are also exhibits here that present the tribe's history and culture, as well as paintings by Tewa artists. Traditional dances are performed Saturday and Sunday at 11am and 1pm. **Open:** Daily 8:30am–5:30pm. **Free**

San Ildefonso Pueblo
NM 5; tel 505/455-3549. This pueblo is nationally famous for the matte-finish black-on-black pottery developed by resident Maria Martinez. At the **San Ildefonso Pueblo Museum** the pottery-making process is explained; it also maintains exhibits on pueblo history. Tours of the pueblo are offered from the visitor center. San Ildefonso Feast Day, January 22–23, is a good time to observe the social and religious traditions of the pueblo, when buffalo, deer, and Comanche dances are presented. **Open:** Peak (June–Aug) Mon–Fri 8am–5pm, Sat–Sun 9am–6pm. Reduced hours off-season. **$**

Tesuque Pueblo
US 84/285; tel 505/983-2667. Despite some concessions to the late 20th century, the 400 pueblo dwellers here are faithful to traditional religion, ritual, and ceremony. Excavations confirm that there was a pueblo at the site in 1250. A mission church and adobe houses surround the plaza. **Open:** Daily 9am–5pm. **Free**

PERFORMANCE VENUES

Santa Fe Opera
Old Taos Hwy; tel toll free 800/280-4654. Located on a wooded hilltop 7 miles north of the city, the sweeping curves of this serene structure seem perfectly attuned to the contour of the surrounding terrain. At night, the lights of Los Alamos can be seen in the distance from the open-air amphitheater. The opera company is noted for its performances of great classics, little-known works by classical European composers, and American premieres of 20th-century works. **Open:** June–Aug, call for schedule. **$$$$**

Paolo Soleri Amphitheatre
1501 Cerrillos Rd; tel 505/989-6318. This outdoor arena is the locale of many warm-weather events. More than one dozen concerts are presented here each summer, including the Santa Fe Summer Concert Series. **Open:** Call for schedule.

St Francis Auditorium
Lincoln and Palace Aves; tel 505/827-4455. This music hall, patterned after the interiors of traditional Hispanic mission churches, is noted for its acoustics. It hosts a wide variety of musical events, including the Santa Fe Chamber Music Festival in July and August. Call for fees and schedule.

Sweeney Convention Center
20 W Marcy; tel 505/984-6760. Santa Fe's largest indoor arena hosts a wide variety of trade expositions and other events during the year. It's also the home of the Santa Fe Symphony Orchestra. **$$$$**

PARKS

Randall Davey Audubon Center
1800 Upper Canyon Rd; tel 505/983-4609. This wildlife refuge occupies 135 acres at the mouth of Santa Fe Canyon. More than 100 species of birds and 120 types of plants live here, and a variety of mammals have been spotted, including black bears, mountain lions, and coyotes. The Randall Davey houses museum exhibits (Mem Day–Labor Day). **Open:** Daily 9am–5pm. **$**

Old Fort Marcy Park
Artist Rd. Marks the site of the first US military reservation in the Southwest. The Cross of the Martyrs, at the top of a winding brick walkway from Paseo de Peralta near Otero Street, is a popular spot for bird's-eye photographs. **Free**

Santa Rosa

Located along I-40 in New Mexico's eastern plains, Santa Rosa lies in a semi-desert area that is nearly surrounded by lakes, including one warm-water spring popular with scuba divers. **Information:** Santa Rosa Chamber of Commerce, 486 Parker Ave, Santa Rosa 88435 (tel 505/472-3763).

MOTELS

Best Western Adobe Inn
Business Loop 40 at I-40, PO Box 410, 88435; tel 505/472-3446 or toll free 800/528-1234; fax 505/472-3446 ext 100. Exit 275 off I-40. A pleasant, roadside motel. **Rooms:** 59 rms. CI 4pm/CO 11am. Nonsmoking rms avail. Rooms are clean and comfortable, with queen-size beds. **Amenities:** A/C, cable TV w/movies. **Services:** Babysitting. **Facilities:** **Rates:** Peak (May 15–Aug) $50 S; $54 D. Extra person $6. Children under age 12 stay free. Lower rates off-season. Parking: Outdoor, free. AE, DC, DISC, MC, V.

Motel 6
3400 Will Rogers Dr, 88435; tel 505/472-3045. Exit 277 off I-40. Basic lodging, perfectly adequate for an overnight stay. **Rooms:** 90 rms. CI 4pm/CO noon. Nonsmoking rms avail. Rooms are clean and functional. **Amenities:** A/C, cable TV w/movies. **Services:** Babysitting. **Facilities:** **Rates:** $32 S; $38 D. Extra person $3. Children under age 17 stay free. Parking: Outdoor, free. AE, DC, DISC, MC, V.

Super 8 Motel
1201 Will Rogers Dr, 88435; tel 505/472-5388 or toll free 800/800-8000; fax 505/472-5388. Exit 275 off I-40. A pleasant, basic motel, similar to others in the chain. **Rooms:** 88 rms. CI 4pm/CO 11am. Nonsmoking rms avail. **Amenities:** A/C, cable TV. **Services:** Babysitting. **Facilities:** 20 Washer/dryer. **Rates:** $36 S; $45 D. Extra person $6. Children under age 12 stay free. Parking: Outdoor, free. DISC, MC, V.

ATTRACTIONS

Fort Sumner
US 84; tel 505/355-7705. Located on US 84, 44 miles southeast of Santa Rosa. In the early 1860s the US Army, under the command of Col Kit Carson, invaded the Mescalero Apache and Navajo homelands and forced the residents to march over 400 miles to Fort Sumner where they hoped to create a self-sustaining agricultural colony for captive Native Americans. The forced reservation experiment was a disaster, and in 1865 the entire group of Apache and Navajo escaped. Today, there is a museum that tells the story of the fort through artifacts, pictures, and documents; a Navajo shrine is maintained at the monument.

Behind the museum is the **Grave of Billy the Kid**, with a six-foot tombstone engraved "William H Bonney, alias Billy the Kid, died July 16, 1881." Two previously slain comrades are buried with the outlaw. **Open:** Thurs–Mon 9am–5pm. **$**

Santa Rosa Lake State Park
2nd St; tel 505/472-3110. Located on a dammed portion of the Pecos River, the park has camping, hiking, excellent fishing, and a visitor information center. **Open:** Daily 24 hours. **$**

Santo Domingo

ATTRACTION

Santo Domingo Pueblo
NM 22; tel 505/465-2214. One of New Mexico's largest pueblos, this farming community on the east bank of the Rio Grande is also one of the state's most traditional. Dramatic Santo Domingo Pueblo feast day, held on August 4, hosts an incredibly lavish corn dance featuring over 500 dancers. Other ceremonies include Three Kings Day, January 6, with elk, eagle, buffalo, and deer dances; Candelaria Day, February 2, with the buffalo dance; the Easter spring corn dance and basket dance; the San Pedro's Day corn dance, June 29; and many traditional dances in the Christmas season. Photographs prohibited. **Open:** Daily sunrise–sunset. **Free**

San Ysidro

ATTRACTION

Zia Pueblo
135 Capitol Square Dr; tel 505/867-3304. The pueblo is best known for its famous sun symbol, which is now the official

symbol of the state of New Mexico. Zia has a reputation for excellence in pottery making; examples can be seen and purchased at the Zia Cultural Center. Photographs prohibited. **Open:** Daily sunrise–sunset. **Free**

Silver City

Not surprisingly, Silver City was named for its abundant silver mines in the late 1800s, when it attracted its share of gamblers, "loose women," and outlaws. Today there's a well-preserved downtown historic district to explore; visitors can also use the town as a base for exploring the Mogollon Mountains and Gila Cliff Dwellings National Monument. **Information:** Silver City/Grant County Chamber of Commerce, 1103 N Hudson St, Silver City 88061 (tel 505/538-3785 or 800/548-9378).

HOTEL

Palace Hotel

106 W Broadway, PO Box 5093, 88061; tel 505/388-1811. Built in 1890 and restored to its original elegance in 1990. Wonderful Victorian atmosphere. **Rooms:** 18 rms and stes. CI 2pm/CO 11am. All rooms are on the second floor and all are slightly different. Victorian furniture. Some rooms have transoms. **Amenities:** Cable TV. No A/C. Breakfast is served in the upstairs, sky-lit garden room, which can also be used by guests as a lounge. **Services:** Babysitting. **Facilities:** Access may be difficult for guests with disabilities. **Rates (CP):** $30–$42 S or D; $48–$56 ste. Children under age 18 stay free. Parking: Outdoor, free. AE, DC, DISC, MC, V.

MOTELS

Copper Manor Motel

710 Silver Heights Blvd (US 180), PO Box 1405, 88062; tel 505/538-5392 or toll free 800/853-2916. A clean, comfortable motel. **Rooms:** 68 rms. CI open/CO 11am. Nonsmoking rms avail. **Amenities:** A/C, cable TV. **Services:** Security person makes the rounds all night. **Facilities:** 1 restaurant (lunch and dinner only; *see* "Restaurants" below), 1 bar, whirlpool. **Rates:** $42 S; $49 D. Extra person $8. Children under age 10 stay free. Parking: Outdoor, free. AE, CB, DC, DISC, MC, V.

Holiday Motor Hotel

3420 E US 180, 88061; tel 505/538-3711 or toll free 800/828-8291. A quiet, pleasant motel, where guests can hear birds singing. **Rooms:** 78 rms and stes. CI 2pm/CO noon. Nonsmoking rms avail. Rooms are attractive and restful, with an integrated decor. **Amenities:** A/C, cable TV, refrig. 1 unit w/minibar. **Services:** Babysitting. Phone attachment for the hard-of-hearing available. A security guard patrols all night. **Facilities:** 250 1 restaurant, washer/dryer. **Rates:** $44–$55 S; $55–$68 D; $75–$120 ste. Extra person $6. Children under age 12 stay free. Parking: Outdoor, free. Weekly rates avail. AE, CB, DC, DISC, JCB, MC, V.

INN

Bear Mountain Guest Ranch

Bear Mountain Rd, PO Box 1163, 88062; tel 505/538-2538 or toll free 800/880-2538. 4 mi NW of downtown. 160 acres. Featuring a large, comfortable lobby with two stone fireplaces in a lovely, rustic setting. The area is a haven for bird watchers, with over 200 species in the vicinity. **Rooms:** 8 rms; 2 cottages/villas. CI open/CO noon. Rooms are individually decorated and have lots of windows. **Amenities:** No A/C, phone, or TV. Some units w/terraces. **Services:** Babysitting. Bird-watching guide books and classes are available. Tours can also be arranged. **Facilities:** 40 Guest lounge. Stargazing facilities are in the works. **Rates (AP):** $60–$100 S; $100 D; $70–$110 cottage/villa. Extra person $30. Parking: Outdoor, free. Commercial and senior citizen rates avail. No CC.

RESTAURANTS

Buckhorn Saloon

NM 15, Pinos Altos; tel 505/538-9911. 7 mi N of Silver City. **Seafood/Steak.** Old West atmosphere; viga ceiling, white-washed brick walls, large brick fireplaces. Steaks, seafood, chicken, and burgers. Specialties are prime rib and filet mignon. A loaf of fresh-baked bread is taken to each table. **FYI:** Reservations recommended. Blues/country music/folk. **Open:** Mon–Sat 6–10pm. **Prices:** Main courses $11–$27. MC, V.

The Red Barn Family Steakhouse

In Copper Manor Motel, 708 Silver Heights Blvd; tel 505/538-5666. **Regional American/Steak.** This big red barn holds two spacious dining areas with atmospheric wagon wheel lamps overhead. Hearty fare consists of 20-oz T-bones, steak Oscar, beef teriyaki, seafood, chicken, and Mexican plates, as well as a salad bar. **FYI:** Reservations recommended. Children's menu. **Open:** Daily 11am–10pm. **Prices:** Main courses $8–$17. AE, CB, DC, MC, V.

ATTRACTIONS

Silver City Museum

312 W Broadway; tel 505/538-5921. The museum is lodged in the 1881 H B Ailman House, a former city hall and fire station remarkable for its cupola and Victorian mansard roof. Displays include early commerce and mining exhibits and an 1880s parlor. A local history research library is open to the public and includes photographs from the museum's extensive photoarchive. **Open:** Tues–Fri 9am–4:30pm, Sat–Sun 10am–4pm. **Free**

Western New Mexico University Museum

1000 W College Ave; tel 505/538-6386. Contains the largest exhibit of prehistoric Mimbres pottery in the United States.

Also displayed are Casas Grandes Indian pottery, stone tools, ancient jewelry, historical photographs, and mining and military artifacts. **Open:** Mon–Fri 9am–4:30pm, Sat–Sun 10am–4pm. **Free**

Gila National Forest
2610 N Silver St; tel 505/388-8201. Covers 3.3 million acres in four counties. The Gila, Aldo, Leopold, and Blue Range wildernesses make up nearly one fourth of the acreage. Within the forest are 1,490 miles of trails for hiking and horseback riding. **Open:** Daily sunrise–sunset. **Free**

Gila Cliff Dwellings National Monument
NM 15; tel 505/536-9461. A two-hour drive north from Silver City, the ruins can be found in six of the seven natural caves in the southeast-facing cliff on the side of Cliff Dweller Canyon. In total there are about 42 rooms. The dwellings allow a rare glimpse inside the homes and lives of prehistoric Native Americans; about 75% of what is seen is original. A 1-mile loop trail, rising 175 feet from the canyon floor, provides access. Camping and picnicking are encouraged in the national forest. **Open:** Peak (Mem Day–Labor Day) daily 8am–6pm. Reduced hours off-season. **Free**

Socorro

Socorro was among the first stops made by the Spanish upon entering the region in the late 16th century. Colonizers built a church here for the local Native American residents and planted what are believed to be the first grapes to be grown in New Mexico. An interesting historic district survives. **Information:** Socorro County Chamber of Commerce, 103 Francisco de Avondo, PO Box 743, Socorro 87801 (tel 505/835-0424).

MOTELS

Econo Lodge
713 California St, PO Box 977, 87801; tel 505/835-1500 or toll free 800/528-3118; fax 505/835-3261. Exit 150 off I-25. In a good location in the center of town, yet quiet. An easy walk to several restaurants. **Rooms:** 44 rms and stes. CI 1pm/CO 11am. Nonsmoking rms avail. **Amenities:** A/C, cable TV, refrig. Some units w/terraces. Microwave. **Services:** Twice-daily maid svce. **Facilities:** Whirlpool. **Rates (CP):** $36 S; $44 D; $80 ste. Extra person $3. Children under age 17 stay free. Parking: Outdoor, free. AE, DC, DISC, MC, V.

Holiday Inn Express
1100 California NE, 87801; tel 505/838-0556 or toll free 800/HOLIDAY; fax 505/838-0598. Exit 150 off I-25; N end of town. Possibly the nicest motel in Socorro, with a very friendly, helpful staff. Lobby is very attractive and comfortable and features a fireplace and several tables and loveseats. **Rooms:** 80 rms and stes. CI 1pm/CO noon. Nonsmoking rms avail. Rooms are pleasantly decorated with Southwestern colors and pictures. **Amenities:** A/C, cable TV, refrig, dataport. Microwave. **Services:** **Facilities:** Whirlpool, washer/dryer. **Rates (CP):** $56–$59 S or D; $65–$100 ste. Extra person $3. Children under age 19 stay free. Parking: Outdoor, free. AE, CB, DC, DISC, EC, ER, JCB, MC, V.

Sands Motel
205 California St NW, 87801; tel 505/835-1130. Exit 150 off I-25. A modest, well-kept motel in the center of town. Within easy walking distance of restaurants. **Rooms:** 25 rms. CI open/CO 11am. Rooms are basic and cheerful. **Amenities:** A/C, cable TV. **Services:** Babysitting. **Rates:** $21–$23 S; $24–$36 D. Extra person $5. Children under age 12 stay free. Parking: Outdoor, free. AE, CB, DC, DISC, MC, V.

Super 8 Motel
1121 Frontage Road NW, 87801; tel 505/835-4626 or toll free 800/800-8000; fax 505/835-3988. Exit 150 off I-25. Standard motel featuring helpful, bilingual staff. **Rooms:** 88 rms and stes. CI 1pm/CO 11am. Nonsmoking rms avail. **Amenities:** A/C, cable TV, refrig. **Services:** **Facilities:** 1 restaurant (*see* "Restaurants" below), washer/dryer. **Rates (CP):** $43 S; $50 D; $67–$75 ste. Extra person $6. Children under age 12 stay free. Parking: Outdoor, free. AE, CB, DC, DISC, MC, V.

RESTAURANTS

Coyote Moon Cafe
W Frontage Rd, Lemitar; tel 505/835-2536. 7 mi N of Socorro; exit 156 off I-25. **American/Mexican.** Situated in what was originally a chile processing plant, this large restaurant decorated with original paintings from a local gallery and chile ristras has a casual "cowboy" atmosphere. Generous portions of Mexican fare are served, along with beef, chicken, sandwiches, burgers, and salads. Specialties include carnitas con papas, chunks of lean beef fried with potatoes and onions; and papa llena, a baked potato stuffed with taco meat, beans, cheese, lettuce, tomato, and either chile or salsa. **FYI:** Reservations accepted. Children's menu. No liquor license. **Open:** Peak (late Apr–late Oct) Wed–Mon 11am–10pm. Closed 3rd week in Mar. **Prices:** Main courses $6–$11. DISC, MC, V.

Don Juan's Cocina
118 Manzanares Ave; tel 505/835-9967. **Mexican.** Located in the 1885 Knights of Pythias Hall, this standard eatery has a simply decorated main dining room, but the festive outdoor patio features some extraordinary murals. Breakfast, served all day, might consist of huevos rancheros or a breakfast burrito; lunch and dinner appetizers include taquitos, chile cheese fries, and sopaipillas. Main courses can be ordered à la carte or as part of a full plate with beans and rice. **FYI:** Reservations accepted. No liquor license. **Open:** Peak (May–Oct) Mon–Fri 9am–5pm, Sat 9am–3pm. **Prices:** Lunch main courses $2–$7. AE, DC, DISC, MC, V.

Frank and Lupe's El Sombrero
210 Mesquite St NE; tel 505/835-3945. Exit 150 off I-25. **Mexican.** Cheerful and very attractive restaurant containing a charming atrium with water fountains as well as a fireplace. Homestyle Mexican cooking. **FYI:** Reservations accepted. Children's menu. Beer and wine only. **Open:** Peak (May–Sept) daily 11am–9pm. **Prices:** Main courses $4–$11. DC, MC, V.

K-Bob's
In Super 8 Motel, 1123 NW Frontage Rd; tel 505/835-2900. Exit 150 off I-25. **American/Steak.** Three large dining rooms, with stone fireplaces, are decorated with old photos of Socorro, plus an attractive southwestern mural in the main room. Service is very friendly. The menu features steak, ribs, and chicken. The salad bar is large and well stocked. **FYI:** Reservations not accepted. Children's menu. Beer and wine only. **Open:** Mon–Thurs 7am–9pm, Fri–Sat 7am–10pm. **Prices:** Main courses $5–$14. AE, DISC, MC, V.

Owl Bar and Cafe
NM 1 and US 380, San Antonio; tel 505/835-9946. 8 mi S of Socorro 1 mi E of exit 139 off I-25. **Burgers/Steak.** This authentic western cafe has the original bar from a saloon and boarding house once owned by Augustus Hilton, the father of Conrad Hilton, who founded the successful hotel chain. Its green chile cheeseburgers and onion rings are well regarded. Other burgers and sandwiches, plus a few dinners, are also offered. Attached to the cafe is a steakhouse, open only Friday and Saturday, 5–9:30pm, serving T-bones, filet mignon, and catfish. **FYI:** Reservations accepted. **Open:** Mon–Sat 8am–9:30pm. **Prices:** Main courses $3–$11. DISC, MC, V.

Val Verde Steak House
203 Manzanares Ave; tel 505/835-3380. **Southwestern/Steak.** Located in the original dining room of the 1919 Val Verde Hotel, this beautifully restored restaurant displays paintings by local artists. The menu features a wide selection of steaks and seafood. House specialties include pepper steak, beef stroganoff, and the Val Verde enchilada. Weekday lunch specials, at $4.75, are a bargain. Meals are served at the full bar 11am–10pm. **FYI:** Reservations accepted. Blues/jazz. Children's menu. **Open:** Sun 11am–9pm, Mon–Sat 11am–10pm. **Prices:** Main courses $7–$22. AE, CB, DC, DISC, MC, V.

ATTRACTIONS

Bosque del Apache National Wildlife Refuge
NM 1; tel 505/835-1828. An estimated 300 species of permanent and migratory birds and more than 100 species of amphibians, reptiles, and mammals make their homes in the 57,000-acre reserve. Photographers and nature watchers can start the 15-mile driving tour, or one of five trails, at the visitor center at the refuge entrance. **Open:** Daily sunrise–sunset. **$**

Old San Miguel Mission
403 El Camino Real, NW; tel 505/835-1620. Completed in 1626 but abandoned during the Pueblo Revolt of 1680, this church was subsequently restored and a new wing was built in 1853. It boasts thick adobe walls, large carved vigas, and supporting corbel arches. Masses are held Saturday at 6pm, and Sunday at 8am, 10am, and noon. **Open:** Daily 7am–6pm. **Free**

Mineral Museum
Campus Rd; tel 505/835-5420. Located on the New Mexico Institute of Mining and Technology campus, this museum houses the largest geological collection in the state. Its more than 10,000 specimens include mineral samples from all over the world, fossils, mining artifacts, and photographs. **Open:** Mon–Fri 8am–5pm, Sat–Sun 10am–3pm. **Free**

Taos

With some 100 art galleries and studios listed in the local phone book, the small town of Taos rightfully claims the title as the West's leading center for the arts. Three distinct cultures—Taos Pueblo, Hispanic, and Anglo—coexist (almost) peacefully, creating a fascinating cultural soup that influences everything from the local cuisine to gift and clothing boutiques. The big event is Fiesta, held in late July; also popular are Taos Pueblo celebrations on San Geronimo Day in late September and on Christmas Eve and Christmas Day. **Information:** Taos County Chamber of Commerce, 1139 Paseo del Pueblo Sur, PO Drawer I, Taos 87571 (tel 505/758-3873 or 800/732-8267).

HOTELS

Holiday Inn Don Fernando de Taos
1005 Paseo del Pueblo Sur, PO Drawer V, 87571; tel 505/758-4444 or toll free 800/759-2736; fax 505/758-0055. 1½ mi S of Taos Plaza on NM 68. The decor sets this above the usual Holiday Inn. The lobby has white stucco adobe-like walls, a kiva-style fireplace, and a heavy-beamed, high ceiling. **Rooms:** 126 rms and stes. CI 2pm/CO 11am. Nonsmoking rms avail. Pleasant, spotless rooms are decorated with local art. **Amenities:** A/C, cable TV. Some units w/fireplaces. **Services:** Twice-daily maid svce, babysitting. **Facilities:** 1 150 1 restaurant, 1 bar (w/entertainment), whirlpool. The lobby bar has locally popular karaoke nights and a large-screen TV for sports events. **Rates:** Peak (Jan 19–Mar 31/May 28–Oct 16) $100 S; $110 D; $130–$140 ste. Extra person $10. Children under age 19 stay free. Lower rates off-season. Parking: Outdoor, free. AE, CB, DC, DISC, JCB, MC, V.

The Inn at Snakedance
Hwy 150, PO Box 89, Taos Ski Valley, 87525; tel 505/776-2277 or toll free 800/322-9815; fax 505/776-1410. Combines old-world ambience and modern conveniences.

Rooms: 60 rms. CI 3pm/CO 10:30AM. No smoking. Rooms furnished with locally built pine furniture and Taos art. **Amenities:** Cable TV, refrig. No A/C. Some units w/fireplaces. **Services:** Masseur. **Facilities:** 1 restaurant, 1 bar (w/entertainment), spa. The fitness center boasts state-of-the-art workout machines, separate massage room, and huge whirlpools. **Rates (BB):** Peak (Dec–Mar) $175–$270 S or D. Extra person $20. Lower rates off-season. Parking: Outdoor, free. Closed Apr 6–June 15 and Oct 1–Nov 27. MC, V.

La Fonda de Taos
South Plaza, PO Box 1447, 87571 (Taos Plaza); tel 505/758-2211 or toll free 800/883-2211; fax 505/758-8508. A historic, quaint hotel, unusual and a bit funky. There are few modern amenities. The lobby, with its outstanding collection of local art, crafts, and furniture, is alone worth a visit. Hidden away in an office, but available for viewing for a fee, are the somewhat infamous paintings of the author D H Lawrence, a one-time Taos area resident. **Rooms:** 24 rms and stes. CI open/CO noon. Basic, comfortable rooms with hand-painted window glass, doors, and furniture. **Amenities:** No A/C or TV. 1 unit w/terrace. Few modern amenities are provided. **Services:** Babysitting. **Facilities:** Washer/dryer. **Rates:** Peak (May–Sept) $65–$85 S or D; $120 ste. Min stay special events. Lower rates off-season. Parking: Outdoor, free. AE, MC, V.

Sagebrush Inn
Paseo del Pueblo Sur, PO Box 557, 87571; tel 505/758-2254 or toll free 800/428-3626; fax 505/758-5077. 3 mi S of Taos. Historic adobe hotel with well-kept grounds. The original building is distinguished by arched doorways, heavy ceiling beams, and kiva fireplaces. **Rooms:** 100 rms and stes. CI 2pm/CO 11am. Nonsmoking rms avail. Many rooms have lovely views of the mountains and surrounding valley. **Amenities:** A/C, satel TV. Some units w/terraces, some w/fireplaces. **Services:** Babysitting. **Facilities:** 2 900 2 restaurants (bkfst and dinner only), 1 bar (w/entertainment), whirlpool. Guests have use of lawn chairs in a quiet, grassy courtyard. The lobby bar is a popular gathering spot for local residents, with frequent live country-and-western music. **Rates (BB):** $80–$110 S or D; $115–$130 ste. Extra person $10. Children under age 12 stay free. Parking: Outdoor, free. AE, CB, DC, DISC, MC, V.

MOTELS

El Monte Lodge
317 Kit Carson Rd, PO Box 22, 87571; tel 505/758-3171 or toll free 800/808-8267; fax 505/758-1536. 2 blocks E of Taos Plaza. Within walking distance of Taos Plaza, this 1932 property is in a quiet, residential area. All units face a lovely grassy picnic area with tall cottonwoods and a terrific view of Taos Mountain. **Rooms:** 13 rms and effic. CI 2pm/CO 11am. Nonsmoking rms avail. **Amenities:** Cable TV, refrig. No A/C. Some units w/fireplaces. **Services:** There's a $5 pet fee. **Facilities:** Washer/dryer. **Rates:** Peak (Thanksgiving–Easter) $55–$95 S; $75–$135 D; $85–$135 effic. Extra person $10. Lower rates off-season. Parking: Outdoor, free. AE, DISC, MC, V.

El Pueblo Lodge
412 Paseo del Pueblo Norte, PO Box 92, 87571; tel 505/758-8700 or toll free 800/433-9612; fax 505/758-7321. ½ mi N of Taos Plaza. A friendly place, good for families. Convenient to town attractions, yet quiet. **Rooms:** 60 rms, stes, and effic. CI 3pm/CO 11:30am. Rooms are in southwest style, with wood-beamed ceilings and American Indian motif decorations. Especially nice wheelchair-accessible rooms. **Amenities:** A/C, cable TV w/movies, refrig. All units w/terraces, some w/fireplaces. **Services:** Babysitting. **Facilities:** 40 Whirlpool, washer/dryer. **Rates (CP):** Peak (June 18–Oct/Jan 3–Apr 2) $63–$75 S or D; $68–$75 ste; $73–$75 effic. Extra person $7. Lower rates off-season. Parking: Outdoor, free. AE, DISC, MC, V.

Indian Hills Inn
233 Paseo del Pueblo Sur, PO Box 1229, 87571; tel 505/758-4293 or toll free 800/444-2346. 2 blocks S of Taos Plaza. This basic, comfortable motel is within walking distance of Taos Plaza and its shops and restaurants. Recently renovated and generally spruced up. **Rooms:** 55 rms. CI 2pm/CO 11am. Nonsmoking rms avail. The rooms have above-average artwork and framed antique maps and wall tiles. Room quality is much nicer than expected for the rates. **Amenities:** A/C, cable TV, dataport. Some units w/fireplaces. **Services:** Babysitting. **Facilities:** **Rates (CP):** Peak (Nov 24–Mar) $99 S or D. Extra person $5. Lower rates off-season. Parking: Outdoor, free. AE, DISC, MC, V.

Kachina Lodge de Taos
413 Paseo del Pueblo Norte, PO Box NN, 87571; tel 505/758-2275 or toll free 800/522-4462; fax 505/758-9207. ½ mi N of Taos Plaza traffic light. A pleasant, modern motel within walking distance of most Taos tourist attractions and several good restaurants. **Rooms:** 118 rms and stes. CI 2pm/CO 11am. Nonsmoking rms avail. Recently renovated rooms. **Amenities:** A/C, cable TV. Some units w/terraces. **Services:** A guest services desk in the lobby provides tourist and other information in the summer. **Facilities:** 400 2 restaurants, 1 bar (w/entertainment), whirlpool, beauty salon, washer/dryer. A Taos Pueblo Indian family performs dances nightly, May through October. **Rates:** $100–$115 S or D; $145 ste. Children under age 13 stay free. Parking: Outdoor, free. AE, DC, DISC, MC, V.

Quality Inn
1043 Paseo del Pueblo Sur, PO Box 2319, 87571; tel 505/758-2200 or toll free 800/845-0648; fax 505/758-9009. 2 mi S of Taos Plaza. A clean, pleasant motel, with a friendly and helpful staff. **Rooms:** 99 rms and stes. CI 2pm/CO 11am. Nonsmoking rms avail. Some rooms have nice local touches, such as copperwork-framed mirrors or RC Gorman prints on

the walls. **Amenities:** A/C, cable TV, CD/tape player, in-rm safe. Some units w/terraces. **Services:** Breakfast included in the low season. **Facilities:** 350 1 restaurant, 1 bar, whirlpool. **Rates:** Peak (Dec 20–Jan 3/July–Aug) $55–$109 S or D; $150 ste. Extra person $7. Children under age 18 stay free. Lower rates off-season. Parking: Outdoor, free. AE, DC, DISC, MC, V.

Rancho Ramada
615 Paseo del Pueblo Sur, 87571; tel 505/758-2900 or toll free 800/2-RAMADA; fax 505/758-1662. 1½ mi S of Taos Plaza. An attractive, modern motel. The lobby has several cozy sitting areas with local art and handcrafted furnishings. **Rooms:** 124 rms and stes. CI 3pm/CO noon. Nonsmoking rms avail. Clean, comfortable rooms. **Amenities:** A/C, cable TV. All units w/terraces, some w/fireplaces. **Services:** Twice-daily maid svce. **Facilities:** 200 1 restaurant (lunch only), 1 bar (w/entertainment), games rm, whirlpool. **Rates:** Peak (Mar 1–Mar 19/Nov 15–Feb 28) $95 S; $113 D; $207 ste. Extra person $15. Children under age 18 stay free. Lower rates off-season. Parking: Outdoor, free. AE, DC, DISC, MC, V.

INNS

Amizette Inn
Taos Ski Valley Rd, PO Box 756, Taos Ski Valley, 87525; tel 505/776-2451 or toll free 800/446-TAOS. A charming hostelry, perfect for a romantic getaway or an enchanting escape for the skier. **Rooms:** 12 rms and stes. CI 2pm/CO 11am. Nonsmoking rms avail. Rooms are spacious, with separate sitting areas, lovely wood furniture, and panoramic views of the river and mountains. **Amenities:** Satel TV. No A/C. Some units w/terraces. **Services:** Twice-daily maid svce. **Facilities:** 1 restaurant. **Rates (BB):** Peak (Dec–Apr) $110–$143 S or D; $132 ste. Extra person $20. Children under age 5 stay free. Min stay peak. Lower rates off-season. AP and MAP rates avail. Parking: Outdoor, free. AE, CB, DC, DISC, MC, V.

Austing Haus
Taos Ski Valley Rd, PO Box 8, Taos Ski Valley, 87525; or toll free 800/748-2932. A clean, comfortable place, with interesting construction and beautiful woodwork. **Rooms:** 42 rms and stes. CI 2pm/CO 11am. Nonsmoking rms avail. **Amenities:** Satel TV. No A/C. Some units w/terraces, some w/fireplaces. **Services:** **Facilities:** 1 restaurant (bkfst and dinner only), washer/dryer. **Rates (BB):** Peak (Nov 24–Jan 2/Feb–Mar) $45–$108 S; $49–$120 D; $85–$160 ste. Extra person $25. Children under age 5 stay free. Lower rates off-season. Parking: Outdoor, free. CB, DC, DISC, MC, V.

The Historic Taos Inn
125 Paseo del Pueblo Norte, PO Drawer N, 87571; tel 505/758-2233 or toll free 800/TAOS INN; fax 505/758-5776. ½ block N of Taos Plaza. A lovely combination of historic charm and modern convenience. The lobby/bar is popular with locals, with live entertainment, a central fountain under a skylight, and beautiful decor and ambience. **Rooms:** 37 rms and stes. CI 3pm/CO 11am. Nonsmoking rms avail. Comfortable rooms exhibit a wonderful use of local art and designs and are furnished with standing armoires, built-in love seats, and kiva fireplaces. **Amenities:** A/C, cable TV, voice mail. Some units w/terraces, some w/fireplaces. **Services:** Babysitting. Refreshments served in courtyard near pool in summer. **Facilities:** 1 restaurant (*see* "Restaurants" below), 2 bars (1 w/entertainment), whirlpool. Wheelchair access is from rear parking lot. **Rates (BB):** Peak (July–Oct) Children under age 16 stay free. Min stay special events. Lower rates off-season. Parking: Outdoor, free. AE, DC, MC, V.

RESORT

Quail Ridge Inn
NM 150, PO Box 707, 87571; tel 505/776-2211 or toll free 800/624-4448; fax 505/776-2949. 5 mi N of Taos. Turn right at blinking light. 37 acres. A pleasant family resort, with the best on-premise sports facilities in the area. It's out in the country yet convenient to town, skiing, and historic sites. **Rooms:** 110 rms, stes, and effic. CI 4pm/CO 11am. Nonsmoking rms avail. Rooms are spacious and modern, with southwestern touches. **Amenities:** Satel TV w/movies, VCR. No A/C. Some units w/terraces, all w/fireplaces. **Services:** Masseur, children's program, babysitting. **Facilities:** 6 2 120 1 restaurant, 1 bar (w/entertainment), basketball, volleyball, racquetball, squash, spa, sauna, whirlpool, day-care ctr, washer/dryer. Indoor and outdoor tennis. **Rates:** Peak (Feb 15–Mar 30) $138 S or D; $385 ste; $160 effic. Extra person $10. Children under age 18 stay free. Min stay peak. Lower rates off-season. Parking: Outdoor, free. DISC, MC, V.

RESTAURANTS

The Apple Tree
123 Bent St; tel 505/758-1900. 1 block N of Taos Plaza. **Southwestern.** Located in an old adobe building that just oozes southwest charm. There are several small dining rooms, some with fireplaces, all decorated with attractive art. The menu has variations on southwestern cuisine, with beef, lamb, chicken, seafood, and vegetarian offerings. Specialties include velarde carnitas enchiladas—lean pork layered between blue corn tortillas with apple chutney, sour cream, and white cheddar cheese, and smothered in red or green chiles. All desserts and baked goods are made on premises. Chef will modify dishes to suit specific dietary needs whenever possible. **FYI:** Reservations recommended. Guitar/singer. Children's menu. Beer and wine only. No smoking. **Open:** Lunch Mon–Fri 11:30am–3pm; dinner daily 5:30–9pm; brunch Sat 11:30am–3pm, Sun 10am–3pm. **Prices:** Main courses $11–$19. CB, DC, DISC, MC, V.

Bent Street Deli and Cafe
120 Bent St; tel 505/758-5787. **Eclectic.** Busy cafe atmosphere inside; pleasant patio outside, heated in winter. The menu consists of usual deli fare, with seafood and Italian specialties added for dinner. **FYI:** Reservations accepted. Beer and wine only. No smoking. **Open:** Mon–Sat 8am–9pm. **Prices:** Main courses $10–$16. MC, V.

Casa Cordova
NM 150; tel 505/776-2500. 8 mi N of Taos. **Continental.** This elegant restaurant in a charming old adobe building has a spacious courtyard with fountain, several dining rooms, and a cozy bar where patrons can relax and enjoy piano music along with their desserts or after-dinner drinks. The gourmet menu includes fish, seafood, chicken, quail, pork, lamb, veal, and steaks. There's also a wide selection of pastas. **FYI:** Reservations recommended. Piano. Children's menu. **Open:** Mon–Sat 4pm–close. **Prices:** Main courses $15–$25. AE, DISC, MC, V.

Doc Martin's
In The Historic Taos Inn, 125 Paseo del Pueblo Norte; tel 505/758-1977. ½ block N of Taos Plaza. **New American/Southwestern.** Widely acclaimed cuisine and an award-winning wine list are the big reasons to dine here, but the changing art exhibits and historic atmosphere at this adobe hotel certainly add to the experience. The contemporary American cooking has a pronounced southwestern emphasis, whether it's the huevos rancheros at breakfast or the southwest lacquered duck—roasted and grilled with red chile broth, posole, and mango relish—at dinner. **FYI:** Reservations recommended. No smoking. **Open:** Breakfast daily 8–11am; lunch daily 11:30am–2:30pm; dinner daily 5:30–9:30pm. **Prices:** Main courses $13–$22. AE, DC, MC, V.

Dori's Bakery and Café
402 Paseo del Pueblo Norte; tel 505/758-9222. 3 blocks N of Taos Plaza. **Cafe/Bakery.** Very popular for breakfast, this casual and friendly cafe decorated with posters and original art has seating available inside or out. Basic meals, southwestern specialties, and healthy dishes are offered during the day, and a full bakery offers fresh baked goods. Full espresso and juice bar. **FYI:** Reservations not accepted. Guitar/piano. Children's menu. No liquor license. No smoking. **Open:** Mon–Sat 7am–2:30pm, Sun 8am–1pm. **Prices:** Lunch main courses $4–$7. MC, V.

El Taoseño Restaurant
819 Paseo del Pueblo Sur; tel 505/758-4142. **American/Mexican.** A busy, local gathering place that's a favorite among many in the Taos community. The dining room is large and open, with paintings by local artists on display (and for sale). The breakfast burrito, served anytime, is locally famous. Mexican food, steaks, chicken, fish, burgers, and sandwiches can also be had. A separate lowfat menu is available. **FYI:** Reservations not accepted. **Open:** Mon–Sat 6am–9pm, Sun 6:30am–3pm. **Prices:** Main courses $6–$12. AE, MC, V.

The Garden Restaurant
In Taos Plaza, 127 N Plaza; tel 505/758-9483. **New American/Southwestern.** A casual, busy eatery offering a variety of beef, chicken, pasta, sandwiches, and burgers. Pollo de Taos is grilled chicken breast served on warm sour cream and green chile sauce and topped with avocado slices; trout à la pecan is pan-fried with pecans toasted in butter. **FYI:** Reservations accepted. Folk/guitar/singer. Children's menu. No liquor license. **Open:** Daily 7:30am–9pm. **Prices:** Main courses $7–$10. AE, DISC, MC, V.

Lambert's of Taos
309 Paseo del Pueblo Sur; tel 505/758-1009. 2½ blocks S of Taos Plaza. **New American.** Very attractive, combining southwestern decor and modern, casual elegance. Traditional American dishes are given a twist, like the pepper-crusted lamb with red wine demiglace and garlic pasta, and fresh Dungeness crab cakes with dipping sauce and pickled vegetables. All dinner entrees are offered in two sizes to suit different appetites. Lunch is a good opportunity to try quality food at lower prices. **FYI:** Reservations recommended. Children's menu. Beer and wine only. **Open:** Lunch Mon–Fri 11:30am–2pm; dinner Sun–Thurs 6–9pm, Fri–Sat 6–9:30pm. **Prices:** Main courses $8–$19. AE, DC, MC, V.

Mainstreet Bakery and Cafe
Guadalupe Plaza, Camino de la Placita; tel 505/758-9610. 1 block W of Taos Plaza. **International.** A casual cafe popular with locals and visitors alike. Several picnic-style tables are out front. Locally well-known chef John Maestas, who recently joined the staff, has introduced new specialties. New Mexico trout is prepared with Dos Equis beer and lime, while braised chicken breast is served with mushroom-hazelnut cream sauce and Frangelico; there are also numerous vegetarian and pasta dishes. Full bakery with variety of breads and pastries. **FYI:** Reservations accepted. Children's menu. No liquor license. No smoking. **Open:** Sun–Mon 7:30am–2pm, Tues–Sat 7:30am–9pm. **Prices:** Main courses $7–$12. No CC.

★ Michael's Kitchen
305 Paseo del Pueblo Norte; tel 505/758-4178. **Southwestern.** Cheerful and casual, with simple western decor and solid wood tables. The hearty fare is accented with southwestern and western flavors. The menu includes sandwiches and burgers, beef, chicken, fish, and Mexican items. Portions are ample, and breakfast is served all day. **FYI:** Reservations not accepted. Children's menu. No liquor license. **Open:** Daily 6am–8:30pm. Closed Apr and Nov. **Prices:** Main courses $6–$12. AE, DISC, MC, V.

Stakeout Grill and Bar
Stakeout Dr; tel 505/758-2042. 8 mi S of Taos Stakeout Dr exit off NM 68. **Seafood/Steak.** The Stakeout is located on a mountain slope south of Taos and offers incredible views of the Sangre de Cristo Mountains, Taos Valley, Rio Grande Gorge, and lovely sunsets. There are several dining rooms, and the outdoor patio is very popular in the summer months. Specialties include prime rib, grilled fillet of salmon, fresh rainbow trout baked with vegetables and herbs, veal, and roasted duck. **FYI:** Reservations recommended. Guitar/harp/jazz/piano. Children's menu. **Open:** Daily 5–10pm. **Prices:** Main courses $12–$27. AE, CB, DC, DISC, MC, V.

Villa Fontana
NM 522; tel 505/758-5800. 5½ mi N of Taos. **Italian.** Elegant, romantic atmosphere abounds in this adobe house decorated to feel like an Italian country home, with a few southwestern touches. Art by the owner/chef is displayed, and summertime outdoor dining offers terrific views of the mountains and surrounding valley. The northern Italian cuisine features freshly picked wild mushrooms. **FYI:** Reservations recommended. **Open:** Lunch Tues–Fri 11:30am–2pm; dinner Mon–Sat 5:30pm–close. Closed June–Oct. **Prices:** Main courses $20–$27. AE, CB, DC, DISC, MC, V.

ATTRACTIONS

Angel Fire Resort
N Angel Fire Rd; tel 800/633-7463. The 30 miles of ski runs are heavily oriented toward beginning and intermediate skiers. There is a vertical drop of 2,180 feet to a base elevation of 8,500 feet. In summer the resort operates an 18-hole, 6,600-yard, PGA rated championship golf course. **Open:** Dec–Apr, daily 9am–4:30pm. **$$$$**

Taos Pueblo
Tel 505/758-9593. The northernmost of New Mexico's 19 pueblos, located 2½ miles north of the Plaza, it has been the home of the Tiwa tribe for more than 900 years. Two massive, multi-story adobe apartment buildings appear much the same today as when a regiment from Coronado's expedition first saw them in 1540. Houses are built one upon another to form porches, balconies, and roofs accessed by ancient ladders.

San Geronimo is the patron saint of the Taos pueblo, and his feast day on September 30 combines Catholic and pre-Hispanic traditions. Taos Pueblo Pow Wow, a dance competition and parade drawing tribes from throughout North America, is held in mid-July. Ask permission before taking photographs of individuals. **Open:** Daily, summer 8am–5pm, winter 9am–4pm. **$**

Millicent Rogers Museum
NM 522; tel 505/758-2462. Rogers was a wealthy art patron and Taos émigré who, in 1947, began to assemble a magnificent array of beautiful Native American arts and crafts. Included in the collection are Navajo and Pueblo jewelry, Pueblo pottery, and paintings from the Rio Grande Pueblo people. The scope of the museum's permanent collection has been expanded to include Hispanic, religious, and secular arts and crafts, from Spanish and Mexican colonial times to the present. **Open:** Peak (Apr–Oct) daily 9am–5pm. Reduced hours off-season. **$$**

Martinez Hacienda
Lower Ranchitos Rd; tel 505/758-1000. This Spanish colonial-style, 21-room hacienda was built around two interior courtyards. It was the home of merchant and trader Don Antonio Martinez. Today many of the rooms are decorated with period furnishings; the rest of the hacienda has been turned into a "living museum" with weavers, blacksmiths, and wood carvers demonstrating their crafts. **Open:** Daily 9am–5pm. **$$**

Kit Carson Home and Museum of the West
E Kit Carson Rd; tel 505/758-4741. A general museum of Taos history. The 12-room adobe home was built in 1825 and purchased in 1843 by Carson, the famous mountain man, Indian agent, and scout. A living room, bedroom, and kitchen are furnished as they might have been when occupied by the Carsons. An array of pioneer items are on display including antique firearms and trappers' implements. **Open:** Peak (Mem Day–Labor Day) daily 8am–6pm. Reduced hours off-season. **$$**

Ernest L Blumenschein Home and Museum
222 Ledoux St; tel 505/758-0505. An adobe home with garden walls and a courtyard, parts of which date to the 1790s. It was the home and studio of Ernest Blumenschein and his family beginning in 1919. Period furnishings include European antiques and handmade Taos furniture in Spanish colonial style. Blumenschein was one of the founders of the Taos Society of Artists and an extensive collection of work by early 20th-century Taos masters is on display in several rooms of the home. **Open:** Daily 9am–5pm. **$$**

The Fechin Institute
227 Paseo del Pueblo Norte; tel 505/758-1710. Special exhibitions, concerts, and art workshops are offered in the former home of Russian artist Nicolai Fechin, who died in 1955. The adobe building is embellished with hand-carved doors, windows, gates, posts, fireplaces, and other features of a Russian country home. The house and adjacent studio are the location of Fechin Institute educational activities, as well as concerts and lectures. **Open:** June–Oct, Wed–Sun 1–5:30pm. **$**

Harwood Foundation Museum
238 Ledoux St; tel 505/758-3063. This pueblo-style museum complex holds paintings, drawings, prints, sculpture, and photographs by the artists of the Taos area from 1800 to the present. Featured are paintings from the early days of the art colony by members of the Taos Society of Artists, including Oscar Berninghaus, Ernest Blumenschein, and Herbert Dun-

ton. Also on display are 19th-century *retablos,* religious paintings of saints. In addition, the museum houses a large collection of wood sculpture by Taos artist Patrociño Barela. **Open:** Mon–Fri 10am–5pm, Sat 10am–4pm. **Free**

Governor Bent House Museum
117 Bent St; tel 505/758-2376. The residence of Charles Bent, the New Mexico Territory's first American governor. Bent was killed in the 1847 Indian and Hispanic rebellion; his wife and children escaped by digging a hole through an adobe wall. The hole is still visible today. Period art and artifacts are displayed. **Open:** Daily 10am–5pm. **$**

Taos Volunteer Fire Department
323 Placitas Rd; tel 505/758-3386. An excellent collection of the work of early Taos artists is on display here. The collection was started in the 1950s when volunteer Taos firemen asked their artist friends to decorate the station's recreation room. **Open:** Mon–Fri 8am–4:30pm. **Free**

San Francisco de Asis Church
NM 68; tel 505/758-2754. This famous church resembles a modernesque adobe sculpture. It has been photographed by Ansel Adams and painted by Georgia O'Keeffe. Displayed in an adjacent building is the painting *The Shadow of the Cross* (1896) by Henri Ault; in the dark, the painting mysteriously becomes luminescent, and the shadow of a cross forms over the left shoulder of Jesus's silhouette.

The history of the church and of the painting is explored in a video presentation presented in the parish hall across the street from the church. **Open:** Mon–Sat 9am–4pm. **$**

D H Lawrence Memorial
NM 522; tel 505/776-2245. This shrine to the controversial early 20th-century author is a pilgrimage site for literary devotees. The short uphill walk is littered with various mementos—photos, coins, messages from fortune cookies—placed by visitors. Lawrence lived in Taos off and on between 1922 and 1925. His ashes were returned here for burial. **Open:** Daily 8am–6pm. **Free**

Kit Carson Park and Cemetery
Paseo del Pueblo Norte; tel 505/758-4160. Major community events are held in the park in summer. The cemetery, established in 1847, contains the graves of Carson and his wife; Charles Bent, the New Mexico Territory's first American governor; the Don Antonio Martinez family; and other noted historical figures and artists. **Open:** Daily sunrise–sunset. **Free**

Rio Grande Gorge Bridge
US 64. This impressive bridge spanning the Southwest's greatest river rises 650 feet above the canyon floor. At different times of day the changing light plays tricks with the colors of the cliff walls.

Taos Ski Valley
NM 150, Taos Ski Valley; tel 505/776-2291. The preeminent ski resort in the southern Rocky Mountains. There are 73 trails and bowls, and between the 11,800-foot summit and the 9,200-foot base, 323 inches of light, dry powder fall annually. **Open:** Peak (Nov–Apr) daily 9am–4pm. Reduced hours off-season. **$$$$**

Sipapu Ski Area
NM 518, Vadito; tel 505/587-2240. The oldest ski area in the Taos region, located 25 miles southeast in Tres Rios canyon. Half of the 18 trails are classified as intermediate. **Open:** Dec–Mar, daily 9am–4pm. **$$$$**

Tesuque

See Santa Fe

Truth or Consequences

See also Elephant Butte

It was originally known as Hot Springs—so named for the nearby mineral springs—but citizens voted in 1950 to change the town's name as part of a contest held by the popular radio and television show of the era. Known locally as T or C, the community continues to celebrate the show at its fiesta each May. Geronimo Days (first weekend in October) is another popular annual festival. **Information:** Truth or Consequences/Sierra County Chamber of Commerce, 201 S Foch St, PO Drawer 31, Truth or Consequences 87901 (tel 505/894-3536 or 800/831-9487).

MOTELS

Best Western Hot Springs Inn
2270 N Date St, 87901; tel 505/894-6665 or toll free 800/528-1234. Exit 79 off I-25. A basic motel in a pleasant setting. Personnel are friendly and helpful. **Rooms:** 40 rms. CI 1pm/CO noon. Nonsmoking rms avail. Inviting rooms with framed western scenes on walls; not large but more than adequate space. **Amenities:** A/C, satel TV. **Services:** K-Bob's restaurant (on premises) will deliver food to room. **Facilities:** 1 restaurant (*see* "Restaurants" below). **Rates:** Peak (Apr–Oct) $47 S; $55 D. Extra person $7. Children under age 12 stay free. Lower rates off-season. Parking: Outdoor, free. AE, CB, DC, DISC, MC, V.

Rio Grande Motel
720 Broadway, PO Box 67, Williamsburg, 87942; tel 505/894-9769. 4 mi S of Truth or Consequences, exit 75 off I-25. Attractive motel close to Elephant Butte and Caballo Lakes. The best rates in the area. **Rooms:** 50 rms. CI open/CO 11am. Nonsmoking rms avail. Rooms are surprisingly pleasant; one, two, or three beds available. **Amenities:** A/C, cable TV. Kitchenette units have refrigerators, 2-burner hot plates, and dishes. Electric hookups to charge boat batteries are in every room. **Services:** **Facilities:** Washer/dryer. Picnic ground and tennis and basketball courts are

next door. **Rates:** $26 S; $36 D. Extra person $4. Children under age 12 stay free. Parking: Outdoor, free. Best rates around. DISC, MC, V.

RESTAURANTS

K-Bob's Steakhouse

In Best Western Hot Springs Inn, 2260 N Date St; tel 505/894-2127. Exit 79 off I-25. **Burgers/Steak.** A spacious, comfortable, and attractive restaurant, part of a state-wide chain of family steak houses. The menu features steaks, burgers, seafood, chicken, and Mexican dishes, plus daily specials. Extensive salad bar. Patio dining. **FYI:** Reservations accepted. Children's menu. Beer and wine only. **Open:** Peak (Apr–Sept) Sun–Thurs 7am–9pm, Fri–Sat 7am–10pm. **Prices:** Main courses $6–$15. AE, CB, DISC, ER, MC, V.

La Cocina

280 Date St; tel 505/894-6499. Exit 79 off I-25. **Mexican.** This traditional restaurant has an unusual southwestern decor with inlaid tile tables and local art. Service here is very swift, cheerful, and friendly. Popular for Mexican combination plates and burritos, La Cocina also offers chicken, steaks, sandwiches, and enchiladas. The sopaipillas are positively huge. Takeout available. **FYI:** Reservations accepted. Children's menu. No liquor license. **Open:** Peak (May–Oct) daily 10:30am–10pm. **Prices:** Main courses $4–$15. No CC.

Los Arcos

1400 N Date St; tel 505/894-6200. Exit 79 off I-25. **Seafood/Steak.** There's an attractive, restful ambience—aided by subdued lighting, wrought iron tables, and friendly, attentive service—in the dining rooms of this hacienda-style restaurant. Steaks here are well regarded, and the fish includes fresh local catches like walleye pike and catfish. Shish kabob, ribs, and chicken are also available, as is a salad bar. **FYI:** Reservations accepted. Children's menu. **Open:** Sun–Thurs 5–10:30pm, Fri–Sat 5–11pm. **Prices:** Main courses $6–$20. AE, CB, DC, DISC, MC, V.

ATTRACTION

Geronimo Springs Museum

211 Main St; tel 505/894-6600. Exhibits of prehistoric Mimbres pottery, Spanish colonial artifacts, and historical murals. Outside is **Geronimo's Spring,** where the great Chiricahua Apache war chief is said to have taken his warriors to bathe their battle wounds. **Open:** Mon–Sat 9am–5pm, Sun 1–4pm. $

Tucumcari

A busy overnight stop on historic Route 66 in the 1940s and 1950s, Tucumcari grew quieter when I-40 replaced the legendary highway and travelers found it easier to keep rolling onward to Albuquerque or Amarillo. Several area lakes provide boating and fishing opportunities, and the Piñata Festival in late June features sporting events, a parade, and a rodeo. **Information:** Tucumcari/Quay County Chamber of Commerce, 404 W Tucumcari Blvd, PO Drawer E, Tucumcari 88401 (tel 505/461-1694).

MOTELS

Best Western Discovery Motor Inn

200 E Estrella Ave, 88401; tel 505/461-4884 or toll free 800/528-1234; fax 505/461-2463. Exit 332 off I-40. Stresses service. **Rooms:** 107 rms and stes. CI 4pm/CO 11am. Nonsmoking rms avail. Pleasant, modern, and comfortable furnishings. One king-size or two queen-size beds. **Amenities:** A/C, satel TV w/movies, refrig, VCR. Some units w/terraces, 1 w/whirlpool. **Services:** Babysitting. 24-hour front desk. **Facilities:** 1 restaurant (lunch and dinner only), games rm, spa, sauna, whirlpool, washer/dryer. **Rates:** Peak (May 16–Sept 16) $44–$50 S; $50–$56 D; $60 ste. Extra person $4. Children under age 12 stay free. Lower rates off-season. Parking: Outdoor, free. AE, DC, DISC, MC, V.

Best Western Pow Wow Inn

801 W Tucumcari Blvd, 88401; tel 505/461-0500 or toll free 800/527-6996; fax 505/461-0135. Recently underwent complete renovation. **Rooms:** 93 rms and effic. CI 4pm/CO noon. Nonsmoking rms avail. All rooms and suites are at ground level. **Amenities:** A/C, cable TV w/movies, refrig. **Services:** Babysitting. 24-hour desk. **Facilities:** 1 restaurant, 1 bar (w/entertainment), washer/dryer. **Rates:** Peak (Apr–June) $50–$65 S or D; $75 ste. Extra person $6. Children under age 12 stay free. Lower rates off-season. Parking: Outdoor, free. MC, V.

Comfort Inn

2800 E Tucumcari Blvd, 88401; tel 941/461-4094 or toll free 800/221-2222; fax 941/461-4099. Exit 335 off I-40. A well-maintained motel, east of the main business district. **Rooms:** 59 rms. CI 4pm/CO 11am. Nonsmoking rms avail. Rooms are exceptionally light, clean, and airy. **Amenities:** A/C, cable TV w/movies. **Services:** Babysitting. **Facilities:** **Rates:** Peak (June–Sept) $52–$60 S; $58–$80 D. Extra person $6. Lower rates off-season. Parking: Outdoor, free. AE, CB, DC, DISC, JCB, MC, V.

Friendship Inn

315 E Tucumcari Blvd, 88401; tel 505/461-0330 or toll free 800/537-3893; fax 505/461-0330. Exit 332 off I-40. Completely acceptable lodging for the economy-minded. **Rooms:** 31 rms. CI 4pm/CO 11am. **Amenities:** A/C, cable TV w/movies. **Services:** Babysitting. **Facilities:** 1 restaurant. **Rates:** Peak (June–Sept) $25–$30 S; $32–$40 D. Extra person $4. Children under age 12 stay free. Lower rates off-season. Parking: Outdoor, free. AE, DISC, MC, V.

Safari Motel
722 E Tucumcari Blvd, 88401; tel 505/461-3642. A small, well-maintained mom-and-pop motel. **Rooms:** 23 rms. CI 4pm/CO 11am. Nonsmoking rms avail. **Amenities:** A/C, cable TV. **Facilities:** Washer/dryer. **Rates:** $23–$26 S; $30–$33 D. Extra person $3. Children under age 12 stay free. Parking: Outdoor, free. MC, V.

RESTAURANTS

Del's
1202 E Tucumcari Blvd; tel 505/461-1740. Exit 332 off I-40. **Mexican.** Authentic dishes south-of-the-border. **FYI:** Reservations not accepted. Children's menu. No liquor license. **Open:** Mon–Sat 6am–9pm. **Prices:** Main courses $5–$14. MC, V.

La Cita
812 S 1st St; tel 505/461-0949. **Mexican.** Variety of Mexican dishes. Specialties include fajitas and green chile chicken enchiladas. **FYI:** Reservations accepted. Children's menu. No liquor license. **Open:** Mon–Sat 11am–8pm, Sun 11am–2pm. **Prices:** Main courses $3–$7. AE, MC, V.

ATTRACTIONS

Tucumcari Historical Museum
416 S Adams; tel 505/461-4201. On view are an early sheriff's office, an authentic western schoolroom, a hospital room of the early West, a real chuck wagon, a historic windmill, and a barbed-wire collection. **Open:** Peak (June–Aug) Mon–Sat 9am–6pm, Sun 1–6pm. Reduced hours off-season. **$**

Conchas Lake State Park
NM 104; tel 505/868-2270. The reservoir here is 25 miles long and has two modern marinas that provide facilities for boating, fishing, and waterskiing. The south side of the lake offers camping, picnic areas, and a nine-hole golf course. **Open:** Daily 6am–9pm. **$**

Williamsburg

See Truth or Consequences

Zuni Pueblo

Located 38 miles south of Gallup on NM 53. The largest and westernmost of New Mexico's 19 pueblos, Zuni is home to 8,084 members of the tribe. Zuni was built upon the ruins of the ancient site of Halona, an early pueblo destroyed by the conquistadors. Built in the early 1600s, the Zuni Mission was razed during the 1680 Pueblo revolt, rebuilt, and then destroyed yet again in 1849. Finally, in 1968, after 119 years, it was reconstructed as **Our Lady of Guadalupe Church.**

Thirteen miles southwest of Zuni are the ruins of **Hawikuh.** In all probability this is the famed "city of gold" spied in 1539 by the friar who incited the rush for the fabled **Seven Cities of Cíbola.** It was the largest Zuni pueblo of its day, until conquered by the Spanish. Though traditionally farmers, the Zuni are best known for their turquoise-and-silver inlay jewelry and other handcrafts, including stone animal fetishes. For camping, fishing, and hunting permits or for more information about the pueblo, call 505/782-4481.

UTAH

An Untamed Land

STATE STATS

Salt Lake City

AREA

84,990 square miles

Idaho, Wyoming, Colorado, Arizona, Nevada

860,000 (1993 estimate)

January 4, 1896 (45th state)

NICKNAMES

Beehive State, Mormon State

Sego lily

Seagull

Merlin Olsen, Loretta Young, Maude Adams, John Moses Browning

The word about Utah is getting around, as more and more visitors marvel at the scenic beauty of its national parks, bike its slickrock trails, explore its pristine wilderness, visit its historic sites, and discover its cities, towns, and villages—then go home to tell their friends about it. What today's visitors to Utah find is some of the West's most beautiful scenery: rugged wilderness and spectacular red rocks, some of America's most magnificent national parks, and opportunities to see this country the way the pioneers saw it when they arrived some 150 years ago.

Settled by members of the Church of Jesus Christ of Latter-Day Saints, also known as Mormons, Utah continues to be strongly influenced by the LDS church, with its emphasis on work, strong family ties, and abstinence from tobacco and alcoholic beverages. Don't expect to find the level of restaurants, nightlife, and lodging that is commonplace in New York, Dallas, San Francisco, or even Denver and Albuquerque. With a few notable exceptions, it doesn't exist here, although that's changing as more and more outsiders, including many from California, decide to make Utah their home.

This is a land for the do-it-yourselfer who wants to explore the region by car, motorhome, boat, bike, or horse; to get outside and hike the trails of the state's five national parks, raft the rapids of the Colorado and Green Rivers, or lounge on the deck of a houseboat on Lakes Powell or Flaming Gorge. There are beautiful temples with soaring spires built by Mormon pioneers more than 100 years ago, 19th-century railroads, and reminders of early mountain men and even earlier Native American cultures that are now gone.

In many ways, a walk through Utah is a walk through the Old West, where you can see the land through the eyes of the pioneers, miners, outlaws, and missionaries who built the Utah we see today. Utah isn't perfect, but it does possess many of the qualities that Americans seek in the 1990s: a wide-open country with plenty of room to roam, relatively little crime, and out-going, hard-working people.

A Brief History

First Inhabitants Archeological evidence shows that the area now known as Utah was inhabited as early as 9000 BC. We know little about these people today, although their ancestors, Native Americans that we call the Desert Gatherers, left behind a substantial record of paintings in the caves and cliffs along the Colorado River. The Anasazi arrived sometime around AD 9000, and by 1200 their villages were scattered throughout present-day Utah. For some reason—possibly drought—those villages were abandoned by 1250, leaving the ruins we see today at Hovenweep National Monument.

European Settlement Some of Spanish conquistador Francisco Coronado's men may have wandered into Utah as early as 1540. The first definite European settlement occurred in July 1776, when a group of Franciscan priests from Spain passed through on their way from New Mexico to California. This route, known as the Old Spanish Trail, went largely unused until fur trappers moved into the area during the 1820s. In 1824, trappers discovered the Great Salt Lake, which they believed to be part of the Pacific Ocean.

The Mormons To a large extent, the history of modern Utah is the history of the Church of Jesus Christ of Latter-Day Saints, who arrived seeking an escape from religious persecution. The area was chosen by church leader Brigham Young specifically because it was primarily a barren land, where Young believed the Mormons would be left alone.

Mormonism began in the 1820s in New York, when Joseph Smith claimed to have received golden tablets containing the *Book of Mormon,* which he translated into English and used as the foundation of the new sect. The church preached the values of family, hard work, and community, traits that helped its followers succeed in colonizing and building cities where others saw wasteland. This success bred jealousy and suspicion, and eventually persecution. Forced to leave New York, Smith and his followers settled in Ohio and Missouri, then in Illinois. Also during these years, the practice of polygamy grew slowly among church leaders. In 1844, Joseph Smith and his brother Hyrum were murdered by a mob in Carthage, IL, and the Latter-Day Saints decided they must abandon their homes.

Brigham Young, a confidant of Smith, became the second leader of the church and the Mormons headed west again, reaching the Salt Lake Valley in July 1847. Young reportedly looked out on the great wasteland of sand and salt, decided that no one would bother the Mormons here, and declared, "This is the right place." Within hours the pioneers had begun building an irrigation system and establishing fields for growing food. Young chose the site of the temple and laid out the new city with streets 132 feet wide—to allow a team of four oxen and a covered wagon to turn around. By the end of 1848, almost 3,000 Mormons had arrived in the Salt Lake Valley.

Young was wrong, however, about no one else being interested in Utah. A year after the Mormons arrived, the United States gained the area from Mexico as part of the Treaty of Guadalupe Hidalgo, and the territory of Utah, named for the Ute tribe, was created, with Brigham Young as territorial governor. Although not officially run by the LDS church, the territory was assured of the church's continued influence; the vast majority of voters were Mormons, who elected church leaders to positions of authority in the civic government as well.

The War for Utah As non-Mormons passed through Utah on their way to California, word spread about the new residents' beliefs, particularly their practice of polygamy, and soon another wave of persecution began. This time with the US government, in 1857, sent in a new governor to replace Young, along with federal troops in case of rebellion. Thus began the "Utah War," in which Mor-

Fun Facts

- The nation's first solar cell plant was dedicated on June 7, 1980, at Natural Bridges Monument.
- Brigham Young University in Provo is the nation's largest privately owned institution of higher learning.
- The seagull monument in Salt Lake City was erected by grateful Mormons to commemorate the gulls that devoured a swarm of locusts in 1848. The locusts were attacking the fields of early Mormon settlers.
- More Jurassic Period dinosaur bones have been found near Dinosaur National Monument in Utah than in any other place in the world.

mons harassed the troops by driving off livestock and attacking their supply trains, forcing them to winter in western Wyoming. As the new governor entered Salt Lake City, the Mormons fled to avoid confrontation, moving south and leaving the capital virtually deserted. The exodus drew national and international attention. An uneasy truce was finally established, the Mormons returned to their homes, and the two groups lived side-by-side until the outbreak of the Civil War, when the army was called back East.

A milestone occurred on May 10, 1869, with the completion of the transcontinental railroad at Promontory Point, Utah. This not only eased the migration of more Latter-Day Saints, but increased the numbers of non-Mormons entering the territory. At the end of the Civil War, attention was again directed toward the enforcement of anti-polygamy laws, and many Mormons were imprisoned. Finally, in 1890, church leaders issued a statement that the church was no longer permitting polygamy.

Statehood & Growth Finally, on January 4, 1896, Utah became the nation's 45th state. Like the rest of America, the Great Depression hit Utah hard, with unemployment reaching 35%. The economy improved, however, with the United States's entry into World War II, when several military bases were established and missile plants were built.

After the war, steel companies reopened, the mining industry boomed, and high-tech businesses moved in. Dams were also built—Glen Canyon Dam, which created Lake Powell, and Flaming Gorge Dam, which created Lake Flaming Gorge, among many others—ensuring water supplies and providing recreational opportunities, and tourism grew. And the first artificial heart was designed and built at the state university during the 1970s.

Into the Future As Utah moves into the latter years of the 1990s, it's facing questions of how to deal with population growth, air pollution and traffic congestion, and the impact of hosting the 2002 Winter Olympics. The new Utah pioneers are likely to work in the aerospace or computer industries; some are even show business refugees inspired by the example of part-time Utah resident Robert Redford. And given that approximately 70% of the statewide population remains Mormon, the Church of Jesus Christ of Latter-Day Saints still plays a significant role.

DRIVING DISTANCES

Salt Lake City

31 miles W of Park City
35 miles S of Ogden
45 miles N of Provo
81 miles S of Logan
152 miles S of Pocatello, ID
194 miles W of Flaming Gorge National Recreation Area
303 miles NE of St George

St George

43 miles W of Zion National Park
53 miles S of Cedar City
83 miles W of Kanab
112 miles NE of Las Vegas, NV
126 miles SW of Bryce Canyon National Park
148 miles W of Page, AZ
161 miles NW of Grand Canyon National Park, North Rim

Moab

5 miles S of Arches National Park
53 miles S of Green River
31 miles E of Canyonlands National Park, north entrance
100 miles SW of Grand Junction, CO
145 miles NE of Capitol Reef National Park
150 miles N of Monument Valley Navajo Tribal Park
166 miles NE of Glen Canyon National Recreation Area, Bullfrog Basin

A Closer Look

GEOGRAPHY

Much of Utah's scenic beauty is the result of uplifting and erosion on the **Colorado Plateau,** which extends along the state's southern border halfway up the east side. Millions of years ago rock strata were created from different materials—or different combinations of the same materials—resulting in layers of varying densities. As wind and water began their inevitable erosion, softer rock wore down faster, leaving the intricate and sometimes bizarre shapes prevalent throughout southern Utah, and particularly at Bryce Canyon National Park. The myriad of colors come from minerals, mostly iron.

The **Rocky Mountain region,** which covers northeast Utah, is the most populated section of the state, claiming Salt Lake City, Ogden, Provo, and almost all of the state's ski resorts. Salt Lake City offers numerous cultural activities and historic sites, including famous Temple Square, the international headquarters of the Church of Jesus Christ of Latter-Day Saints and the most-visited site in Utah. Skiers love Salt Lake City for its location—within one hour you can be at any of seven downhill resorts, and in not much more time you can be on the slopes at four others.

The western side of Utah, ending in a point at the southwest corner, is dominated by the **Great Basin Desert,** which might be described as a whole lot of flat land covered with salt. The Great Salt Lake—eight times saltier than most oceans—and the Bonneville Salt Flats cover much of this region, and it's not the sort of place to go for a picnic. Much of the basin is used by the US military as testing grounds.

CLIMATE

Utah has four seasons, but because of the vast range in elevations—from 2,200 feet to 13,528 feet—conditions vary considerably across the state. Generally, summer days are hot but nights are cool. Winters are cold and snowy, except in southwest Utah's "Dixie," where it seldom gets very cold and snow is rare. Mountain temperatures are always pleasantly cool, and can be very cold at night, even in summer.

AVG HIGH/LOW TEMPS (°F)

	St George	Salt Lake City
Jan	54/27	37/20
Feb	61/32	44/24
Mar	67/37	52/30
Apr	76/44	61/32
May	86/52	72/45
June	96/61	83/53
July	102/68	93/62
Aug	99/66	90/60
Sept	93/57	80/50
Oct	81/45	67/39
Nov	65/38	50/29
Dec	55/27	39/22

WHAT TO PACK

Like much of the West, Utah is a casual state, and even in Salt Lake City you won't need fancy clothes. Remember that even in summer, evenings at higher elevations can be cool, and even chilly if it should rain. A light, water-resistant jacket, sweater, and comfortable walking shoes are standard. Dressing in layers is best any time of year. Sunglasses, hats, and sunscreen are essential.

TOURIST INFORMATION

For the state's official visitor guide and map contact the **Utah Travel Council,** Council Hall, Salt Lake City 84115 (tel 801/538-1030 or 800/220-1160). The Council also maintains a Web page (http://www.utah.com) with links to tourist information. For state park information contact **Utah Parks and Recreation,** 1636 W North Temple, Suite 116, Salt Lake City 84116 (tel 801/538-7220; for campground reservations, 801/322-3770 or 800/322-3770).

To find out how to obtain tourist information for individual cities and parks in Utah, refer to specific cities in the listings section of this chapter.

DRIVING RULES AND REGULATIONS

Safety belts are required for drivers and all front-seat passengers; restraints are required for all children under 8, regardless of where they are sitting. Drivers must carry proof of insurance, vehicle registration, and a valid driver's license at all times, and minimum age for drivers is 16. Radar detectors are permitted. Right turns are allowed at red signal lights after a full stop, unless otherwise posted. Maximum speed limit is 75 mph.

Tires rated for mud and snow are needed in most areas in winter, and are required on roads leading to most major ski areas from November through March. Studded snow tires are permitted on state roads only between October 15 and April 15.

RENTING A CAR

Salt Lake City, Ogden, and St George will usually have the best selections and rates on car rentals, and inexpensive rentals are usually available in Las Vegas, NV, which is particularly convenient for those planning to visit southern Utah's national parks. Visitors who plan to drive in mountain areas during the winter should consider renting four-wheel-drive or front-wheel-drive vehicles, which handle better in snow.

- **Avis** (tel 800/831-2847)
- **Budget** (tel 800/527-0700)
- **Dollar** (tel 800/800-4000)
- **Hertz** (tel 800/654-3131)
- **National** (tel 800/227-7368)
- **Payless** (tel 800/729-5377)
- **Thrifty** (tel 800/367-2277)

ESSENTIALS

Area Code: All of Utah is in the **801** area code.

Emergencies: Throughout most of Utah, dial 911 in an emergency. In a few rural areas, it will be necessary to dial "0" (zero, not the letter O) for an operator.

Liquor Laws: Utah's drinking laws are a bit unusual, but alcoholic beverages can be purchased practically everywhere in the state. The legal drinking age is 21. Supermarkets and convenience stores sell 3.2% beer and wine coolers seven days a week; but full-strength beer, wine, and hard liquor are available only at state-owned liquor stores and package agencies, which are closed Sundays and state holidays.

Buying liquor, beer, or wine by the drink is a bit more complicated. Most better restaurants serve alcoholic beverages with meals, starting at noon—though patrons usually must ask, as servers will not offer an alcoholic drink. Establishments that are licensed as taverns can sell 3.2% beer only. There are also private clubs, which are essentially bars, and may or may not be attached to restaurants. Patrons must be members to enter, but two-week memberships are available, usually for $5. Private clubs can be open 10am to 1am Monday through Saturday and noon to midnight Sunday.

Road Info: For a 24-hour recording giving road conditions in the Salt Lake City area, call 801/964-6000. For roads in the rest of the state, call 800/492-2400.

Smoking Laws: The Utah Indoor Clean Air Act prohibits smoking in any publicly owned building or office, and in all enclosed indoor places of public access. This includes restaurants, but not private clubs and taverns.

Taxes: State sales tax is just under 6%, but local sales taxes add another 1% in most areas. Local lodging taxes usually add an additional 3% or 4%. There are no sales taxes collected on Indian reservations.

Time Zone: Utah is in the mountain time zone, and observes daylight saving time from April through October.

Best of the State

WHAT TO SEE AND DO

Below is a general overview of some of the top sights and attractions in Utah. To find out more detailed information, look under "Attractions" for individual cities in the listings portion of this chapter.

National Parks, Recreation Areas & Monuments One thing that distinguishes Utah from the rest of the United States is its spectacular national parks, recreation areas, and monuments. **Zion National Park,** in southwest Utah, is the state's most popular national park, known for its towering multicolored walls of stone, narrow canyons, and cascading waterfalls. Nearby, it's easy to be enchanted by the fantasyland created by **Bryce Canyon National Park's** delicately sculpted rock hoodoos; or marvel at the peculiar geologic formations and spectacular colors at **Capitol Reef National Park** to the east, called "Land of the Sleeping Rainbow" by the Navajo. Farther east, Utah's two remaining national parks are more arid, giving them a particularly rugged, wild, and stark beauty. **Arches National Park** is the most accessible, with a splendid scenic drive and several fairly easy hikes; **Canyonlands National Park** requires longer and more difficult hikes to explore its deep canyons, steep cliffs, and tall, red spires of stone.

While Utah is generally dry, man has created two spectacular water recreation areas by the damming of major rivers. Crossing from southern Utah into northern Arizona, **Glen Canyon National Recreation Area's** Lake Powell stretches 186 miles, with almost 100 major side canyons that give it a shoreline of almost 2,000 miles. Created by the damming of the Colorado River, it's an area of stark contrasts—with baking desert, deep blue water, brilliant red rocks, and rich greenery. To the north, spreading from northeastern Utah into southern Wyoming, **Flaming Gorge National Recreation Area** was formed when a dam was built across the Green River, producing a lake 91 miles long with more than 350 miles of coastline. In addition to boating, both recreation areas have hiking and mountain biking trails, camping, and picnicking.

Often less crowded than national parks and recreation areas, national monuments are little-known gems. Beautiful rock bridges are easily accessible at **Natural Bridges National Monument,** in southeast Utah. And at **Dinosaur National Monument,** in the state's northeast corner, visitors can see the West's best display of dinosaur bones. Just a bit south of Salt Lake City is **Timpanogos Cave National Monument,** where ranger-led hikes lead through eerie limestone caverns. Those interested in Native American ruins will be rewarded at the end of the long, tedious drive to **Hovenweep National Monument,** in southeast Utah and southwest Colorado, where the unique stone towers are reminiscent of European castles.

State Parks A number of Utah's state parks are so beautiful they would probably be national parks or monuments if the state didn't already have so many. Of particular interest are **Snow Canyon State Park** in the state's southwest corner, with imposing red rock cliffs and walls of Navajo sandstone; and **Coral Pink Sand Dunes State Park,** also in southwest Utah, with huge, shifting sand dunes. **Kodachrome Basin State Park,** near Bryce Canyon National Park, was named for the photogenic qualities of its colorful rock spires, and **Bear Lake State Park,** along the Utah-Idaho border, offers beautiful turquoise-colored water and a delightful beach. Finally, **Monument Valley Navajo Tribal Park,** in southeast Utah and northeast Arizona, is a land of stark rock sentinels of deep red and brown that have become a symbol of the American West through numerous Western movies filmed there.

Historic & Cultural Sites Because the Mormon Church dominated the settlement of modern Utah, a majority of the state's historic sites are also religious sites. Receiving the most visitors of any Utah attraction is **Temple Square,** a 10-acre area in the center of Salt Lake City. Here you can gaze up at the soaring spires of the Salt Lake LDS Temple, visit the Tabernacle (home of the famed Mormon Tabernacle Choir), and take a guided tour. Nearby, the stately **Beehive House,** built in 1854, gives you an idea of how Mormon leader Brigham Young and his large family lived. Young designed the home in the style he remembered from his New England youth, complete with a widow's walk. Several other important Mormon Church sites are in St George, in the southwest corner of the state. The red stone **St George Tabernacle** is a magnificent example of old-world craftsmanship, with pine detailing finished to look like fine hardwoods and marble. The **Jacob Hamblin Home,** which was owned by a 19th-century Mormon Church official, looks like a typical 19th-century pioneer home until you notice that there are two identical bedrooms, one for each of Hamblin's wives.

Not directly related to the Mormon Church, **Fort Buenaventura State Park** in Ogden is a reconstructed 1846 fort and trading post, with exhibits on the history of the mountain men and fur trade of northern Utah back to the 1820s. Fans of old trains will want to stop at **Golden Spike National Historic Site,** near the north edge of the Great Salt Lake, where the East and West Coasts were joined by rail in 1869. Reproductions of those colorful steam locomotives are fired up each summer.

Native American Sites Long before fur traders and Mormon pioneers discovered Utah in the 1800s, Native Americans called this land home. Ruins of the villages they built and the rock art they painted can be seen at **Hovenweep National Monument** in the state's southeast corner, **Anasazi Indian Village State Park** near Boulder, **Edge of the Cedars State Park** in Blanding, **Fremont Indian State Park** in Richfield, and in the Horseshoe Canyon section of **Canyonlands National Park,** where you'll find an 80-foot-long panel of rock art that contains numerous larger-than-life figures dating back several thousand years.

Museums Utah is dotted with interesting little museums run by the **Daughters of Utah Pioneers,** which generally have exhibits of local memorabilia and 19th-century artifacts, plus information on prominent Mormon pioneer families. Other museums of note include those in **Union Station** in Ogden. Inside this historic railroad depot are **Utah State Railroad Museum,** with a variety of railroading exhibits plus an extensive HO-gauge layout of the first transcontinental route; the **Browning Firearms Museum,** which displays Browning guns from 1878 to modern times and has a replica of an 1880s gun shop; and the **Browning-Kimball Car Collection,** which includes beautiful examples of classic cars, mostly pre–World War II luxury models. Outside the depot is a pavilion containing several historic locomotives, cabooses, and other rolling stock.

The University of Utah in Salt Lake City is home to what is likely the state's best art museum, the **Utah Museum of Fine Arts,** with exhibits of ancient Egyptian objects, Italian Renaissance paintings, European and American art from the 17th century to the present, and art from Southeast Asia, China, Japan, and African and pre-Columbian cultures. The university also runs the **Utah Museum of Natural History,** with over 200 exhibits. Also in Salt Lake City, the **Utah State Historical Society Museum,** housed in the waiting room of the 1910 Denver & Rio Grande Depot, displays pioneer artifacts, historic photos, and paintings. Highlights include an artificial heart developed in 1976 by Dr Robert K Jarvik of the University of Utah.

Family Favorites There are a number of attractions in Utah for those interested in dinosaurs, including **Dinosaur National Monument** in the state's northeast corner, where fossilized dinosaur bones are preserved in sand and sediment in one of the world's most concentrated and accessible deposits. Utah's only passenger-carrying turn-of-the-century steam train is the **Heber Valley Historic Railroad,** in Heber City, which makes a 16-mile run through a spectacularly beautiful canyon. In the town of Kaysville, near Ogden, the **Cherry Hill Family Campground & Resort** is a fun-packed, privately run outdoor activity center that has a water park with slides, pools, and even a pirate ship. In Kanab, the **Johnson Canyon Movie Set,** where numerous Western TV shows and movies were shot, is being restored. Guided tours take visitors to the well-weathered buildings, including the Long Branch Saloon and Doc's office from *Gunsmoke,* and others constructed for films such as the 1979 epic *How the West Was Won.*

EVENTS AND FESTIVALS

- **Utah Winter Games,** Salt Lake City, Park City, and other locations. Amateur athletes compete in downhill and Nordic skiing, figure skating, and hockey. January. Call 801/975-4515.
- **Sundance Film Festival,** Park City. Screenings of the best independent films, along with seminars. Late January. Call 801/328-3456.
- **Hostler Model Railroad Festival,** Ogden. Model train fans gather at historic Union Station, where collectors can locate hard-to-find items. First week in March. Call 801/629-8446.
- **Snowshine Festival,** Park City. Fun-in-the-snow events, including ski races and snow softball. Late March through early April. Call 801/649-8111.
- **Mountain Man Rendezvous,** Ogden. Black powder shooting contests and other early-1800s activities at Fort Buenaventura State Park. Easter weekend. Call 801/621-4808.
- **Golden Spike Anniversary,** Golden Spike National Historic Site. Commemorates the day in 1869 when the final spike connected rail lines from the East and West Coasts. May 10. Call 801/471-2209.
- **Living Traditions Festival,** Salt Lake City. Food, music, and traditional activities demonstrate Utah's ethnic diversity. Mid-May. Call 801/533-5760.
- **America's Freedom Festival,** Provo. Sporting events, concerts of patriotic music, art festivals, parades, and fireworks. Mid-June through July 4. Call 801/345-2008.
- **Utah Shakespearean Festival,** Cedar City. Professional theater production of works by the Bard plus contemporary offerings. Late June through August. Call 801/586-7878.
- **Utah Arts Festival,** Salt Lake City. Music and dance performances, and art and craft exhibits. Late June. Call 801/322-2428.
- ***Utah!,*** St. George. Utah's early Mormon history comes to life, using music, comedy, drama, and special effects. Mid-June through mid-Oct. Call 800/746-9882.
- **Music in the Mountains,** Park City. A series of outdoor concerts, including some by the Utah Symphony. June through September. Call 801/649-6100.
- **Dinosaur Roundup Rodeo,** Vernal. Bull riding, calf roping, barrel racing, steer racing, a western dance, and parade. Mid-July. Call 801/789-1352 or 800/421-9635.
- **Pioneer Day,** statewide. Utah residents celebrate the day in 1847 when Brigham Young led the first group of Mormon pioneers into the Salt Lake Valley. July 24.
- **Utah Jazz and Blues Festival,** Snowbird. One of Utah's premier music events boasting big-name musicians. Late July. Call 801/355-2200 or 801/521-6040.
- **Festival of the American West,** Logan. Traditional Old West fair including medicine man shows and square dancing, plus a multimedia historical pageant. Late July through early August. Call 800/225-FEST.
- **Utah State Fair,** Salt Lake City. A horse show, rodeo, live entertainment, and arts and crafts exhibits. Early September. Call 801/538-FAIR.
- **Mountain Man Rendezvous,** Ogden. A gathering of mountain men at Fort Buenaventura State Park, with early 1800s activities. Early September. Call 801/621-4808.
- **Moab Music Festival,** Moab. Live music from classical to jazz and bluegrass, presented in a beautiful red-rock amphitheater and other locations. Mid-September. Call 801/259-8431.

- **Red Rock Gem and Mineral Show,** Moab. Rockhounders display exotic rocks, gems, and minerals. Mid-October. Call 801/259-5904.
- **Christmas Parade and Lighting of the Dinosaur Gardens,** Vernal. Life-size replicas of dinosaurs are illuminated for the holidays. Late November. Call 801/789-6932.
- **Parade of Christmas Lights,** Lake Powell. Boats decorated for Christmas, led by the *Canyon King* paddle wheeler, are reflected in the waters of Lake Powell. Late November or early December. Call 801/684-3046.

SPECTATOR SPORTS

Auto Racing Drag racing fans head to **St George Raceway Park** (tel 801/635-2447) during its March through November season for two to three racing days per month. The raceway is located on the north side of St George, off I-15 exit 8.

Baseball The **Salt Lake Buzz** (tel 801/485-3800) of the Pacific Coast League plays at Franklin Quest Field in Salt Lake City. The **Ogden Raptors** (tel 801/393-2400) play professional ball in the Pioneer League. In St George, the **Dixie College Rebels** (tel 801/652-7525) compete in men's baseball and women's softball in 5,000-seat Hansen Stadium.

Basketball Salt Lake City's **Utah Jazz** (tel 801/355-3865) usually packs the house at Delta Center in Salt Lake City. At **Brigham Young University** in Provo, Cougar basketball is played in the Marriott Center (tel 801/378-4418). The **University of Utah** Runnin' Utes compete in the NCAA and Western Athletic Conference, with games at Salt Lake City's Jon M Huntsman Arena (tel 801/581-8849). In Logan, the team to watch is at **Utah State University** (tel 801/797-0305). **Weber State University's** Wildcats in Ogden play in the Big Sky Athletic Conference for men's sports and Mountain West Athletic Conference for women, with games for both at Dee Events Center (tel 801/626-8500). The **Dixie College Rebels** (tel 801/652-7525) are the team to root for in St George, with games at Burns Arena.

Football The popular **Brigham Young University** Cougars play at 65,000-seat Cougar Stadium (tel 801/378-4418) in Provo, and the **University of Utah** Runnin' Utes in Salt Lake City play at Rice Stadium (tel 801/581-8849). In Ogden, **Weber State University's** games take place at Dee Events Center (tel 801/626-8500). **Utah State University** (tel 801/797-0305) in Logan is a member of the Big West Athletic Conference, with games at Romney Stadium. The **Dixie College Rebels** (tel 801/652-7525) in St George play at Hansen Stadium.

Gymnastics The women's gymnastics team at the **University of Utah** in Salt Lake City, which competes at Jon M Huntsman Arena (tel 801/581-8849), has been national champion nine out of the last fifteen years. Another good team is at **Utah State University** (tel 801/797-0305) in Logan.

Hockey The **Utah Grizzlies** (tel 801/325-7328) of the International Hockey League, currently play in Delta Center in Salt Lake City, although a new arena is expected to be completed by fall 1997.

Volleyball Salt Lake City's **Utah Predators** (tel 801/485-9799) are members of the National Volleyball Association. Colleges with volleyball teams include Provo's **Brigham Young University** (tel 801/378-4418), **University of Utah** (tel 801/581-8849) in Salt Lake City, **Utah State University** (tel 801/797-0305) in Logan, and in Ogden, **Weber State University** (tel 801/626-8500).

ACTIVITIES A TO Z

Bicycling Although you'll see road bikes around cities such as Ogden and Provo, Utah really belongs to mountain bikers, who have numerous established trails over the slickrock terrain in the Moab area and through the mountains at Brian Head Ski Resort. Be aware, though, that bikes are not permitted on trails in national parks, although they're welcome in most areas administered by the Bureau of Land Management and US Forest Service, which are often adjacent to national parks. There are excellent trails at Flaming Gorge National Recreation Area in northern Utah, under the jurisdiction of the US Forest Service. For additional information, contact **Bicycle Utah,** PO Box 738, Park City 74060 (tel 801/649-5806).

Boating For a state that most people think of as desert, Utah has a lot of water, in large part because of its numerous man-made lakes. Perhaps the very best boating in the state is at Lake Powell, in Glen

Canyon National Recreation Area, a huge and incredibly beautiful lake in southern Utah's red rock country, and at Flaming Gorge Lake in Flaming Gorge National Recreation Area in far northern Utah. For a brochure on boating regulations as well as information on boating at the state's parks, contact **Utah Parks and Recreation** (tel 801/538-7220).

Camping Practically all of Utah's public lands are available for camping. Camping in the national parks is extremely popular, but don't miss camping opportunities in state parks, national forests, and Bureau of Land Management areas. Information is available from the individual national parks, the **US Forest Service** (tel 801/524-5030, or 800/280-2267 for campground reservations), the **US Bureau of Land Management** (tel 801/539-4001), and **Utah Parks and Recreation** (tel 801/538-7220, or 801/322-3770 or 800/322-3770 for campground reservations).

Cattle Drives Several outfitters offer opportunities to return to the West's roots and participate in a cattle drive, where you can ride and rope, and get a feel for what it was like to be a working cowboy 100 years ago. For information, contact **Utah Guides & Outfitters,**153 E 7200 South, Midvale 84047 (tel 801/566-2662).

Fishing & Hunting Fishing and hunting opportunities abound in Utah, particularly in the mountain areas. Fishermen head to the numerous reservoirs at state parks, plus Flaming Gorge National Recreation Area along the Utah-Idaho border and Strawberry Reservoir, southeast of Heber City. Contact the **Utah Division of Wildlife Resources,** 1596 W North Temple, Salt Lake City 84116 (tel 801/538-4700).

Four-wheeling There are numerous old mining and logging roads throughout the state that are ideal for the off-roader, with a number of particularly popular areas around Moab and Escalante. Those with dune buggies head for Coral Pink Sand Dunes State Park near Kanab. For information contact the **US Forest Service** (tel 801/524-5030), the **US Bureau of Land Management** (tel 801/539-4001), or **Utah Parks and Recreation** (tel 801/538-7220).

Golf Beautiful scenery, year-round golf weather, and a variety of challenging terrain are what golfers find in Utah, particularly in the St George area, home of the state's best courses and mildest climate. A free directory of the state's more than 80 courses is available from the Utah Travel Council.

Hiking Absolutely the best way to see the national parks and monuments and many of Utah's state parks is on foot. Be aware that weather conditions can be extreme, and summer hikers should always carry at least one gallon of water per day. Also, pets are not permitted on trails in national parks, but are allowed in state parks, national forests, and Bureau of Land Management areas. For information, contact individual national parks, the **US Forest Service,** (tel 801/524-5030), the **US Bureau of Land Management** (tel 801/539-4001), or **Utah Parks and Recreation** (tel 801/538-7220).

Horseback Riding At Bryce and Zion National Parks, and other areas throughout the state you'll find stables and outfitters who lead rides lasting from one hour to several days. For information, contact **Utah Guides & Outfitters,** 153 E 7200 South, Midvale 84047 (tel 801/566-2662).

Rock Climbing This sport is growing in popularity in Utah, particularly at Zion National Park, where it is as much a spectator sport as participatory activity, at Snow Canyon State Park near St George, and in Logan Canyon northeast of Ogden.

White-Water Rafting Both the Colorado and Green Rivers are top destinations for serious white-water rafters, as well as kayakers and canoeists, with Moab a major staging area for the Colorado, and Dinosaur National Monument a popular spot for tackling the Green. A recorded report on statewide river flows and reservoir information is available from the **Colorado Basin River Forecast Center** (tel 801/539-1311). The Utah Travel Council (see address above) will provide a free copy of *Raft Utah,* and additional information is available from **Utah Guides & Outfitters** (tel 801/566-2662) and the **US Bureau of Land Management** (tel 801/539-4001).

Wildlife With its abundance of open space, forests, and rugged wilderness, Utah offers plenty of opportunities to see wildlife, from bighorn sheep along the cliffs above Flaming Gorge Lake to elk and antelope in the Wasatch Mountains, lizards and snakes in the red rock country of the south, and

Selected Parks & Recreation Areas

- **Arches National Park,** PO Box 907, Moab 84532-0907 (tel 801/259-8161)
- **Bryce Canyon National Park,** Bryce Canyon 84717 (tel 801/834-5322)
- **Canyonlands National Park,** 2282 South West Resource Blvd, Moab 84532-8000 (tel 801/259-7164)
- **Capitol Reef National Park,** Torrey 84775 (tel 801/425-3791)
- **Zion National Park,** Springdale 84767-1099 (tel 801/772-3256)
- **Cedar Breaks National Monument,** 82 N 100 East, Cedar City 84720-2606 (tel 801/586-9451)
- **Dinosaur National Monument,** 4545 US 40, Dinosaur, CO 81610 (tel 970/374-3000 or 801/789-2115)
- **Natural Bridges National Monument,** PO Box 1, Lake Powell 84533 (tel 801/692-1234)
- **Timpanogos Cave National Monument,** RR 3, Box 200, American Fork 84003-9800 (tel 801/756-5239)
- **Flaming Gorge National Recreation Area,** USDA Forest Service, PO Box 279, Manila 84046 (tel 801/784-3445)
- **Glen Canyon National Recreation Area,** PO Box 1507, Page, AZ 86040 (tel 520/608-6404)
- **Golden Spike National Historic Site,** PO Box 897, Brigham City 84302 (tel 801/471-2209)
- **Antelope Island State Park,** 4528 W 1700 South, Syracuse 84075-6861 (tel 801/773-2941)
- **Bear Lake State Park,** PO Box 184, Garden City 84028-0184 (tel 801/946-3343)
- **Coral Pink Sand Dunes State Park,** PO Box 95, Kanab 84741-0095 (tel 801/874-2408)
- **Dead Horse State Park,** PO Box 609, Moab 84532-0609 (tel 801/259-2614)
- **Escalante State Park,** PO Box 350, Escalante 84726-0350 (tel 801/826-4466)
- **Fort Buenaventura State Park,** 2450 A Ave, Ogden 84401-2203 (tel 801/621-4808)
- **Goblin Valley State Park,** PO Box 637, Green River 84525-0637 (tel 801/564-3633)
- **Jordanelle State Park,** PO Box 309, Heber City 84032-0309 (tel 801/645-8036)
- **Kodachrome Basin State Park,** PO Box 238, Cannonville 84718-0238 (tel 801/679-8562)
- **Snow Canyon State Park,** PO Box 140, Santa Clara 84765-0140 (tel 801/628-2255)
- **Wasatch Mountain State Park,** PO Box 10, Midway 84049-0010 (801/654-1791)

wetland birds at the state's numerous lakes and reservoirs. Contact the **Utah Division of Wildlife Resources** (tel 801/538-4700) for more information.

Winter Sports Utah's geography and climate produce some of the best powder snow in North America, and more than a dozen ski resorts provide numerous opportunities for those who want to experience it. In addition, there is ample terrain for cross country skiers and snowmobilers in both developed resorts and on US Forest Service and other public lands. For information, contact **Ski Utah, Inc,** 150 W 500 South, Salt Lake City 84101 (tel 801/534-1779).

PARK CITY, OGDEN, AND NORTH TO BEAR LAKE

Start	Park City
Finish	Bear Lake State Park
Distance	224 miles
Time	2–5 days
Highlights	A silver mine, steam trains, beautiful mountain scenery, swimming and boating, wildlife, jet planes

From the intriguing Old West charm of Park City to modern missiles and jet fighters housed in the barren Utah desert, this tour of northern Utah covers a wide range of attractions and activities. You can descend into the blackness of a genuine silver mine, admire the gleaming brass of antique firearms and luxury automobiles, see through the eyes of Utah's finest artists, and gaze upon towering monuments created by Mormon pioneers more than 100 years ago. But this is mostly a land of vast open spaces and tall, evergreen-covered mountains. On this route you can walk along the shore of a turquoise-colored lake, canoe across a quiet pond, fish, swim, hike, ski, or watch for eagles, deer, and raccoons.

The drive begins in the mountains of Park City, travels north past farms and orchards, touches briefly on the desert around the Great Salt Lake, and then heads back into the rugged and beautiful mountains as you approach Utah's northern border. Roads here are generally paved and well maintained, although there are some stretches where you'll go a long way between services. Most of the attractions, especially in Park City and Ogden, are open year-round, but some do close or limit hours in winter. Those traveling between October and May should call first if there are specific attractions they especially want to see.

For additional information on lodgings, dining, and attractions in the region covered by the tour, refer to specific cities in the listings portion of this chapter.

1. **Park City.** Famous for its champagne powder skiing each winter, this historic mining town is worth a visit any time of year for its splendid mountain scenery and Old West charm, evident today along its well-preserved Main Street. Founded as a silver camp in the late 1800s, Park City soon exploded, with a population that soared to 10,000, over 30 saloons, and a flourishing red-light district. Today Park City is known for its impressive galleries and shops, excellent performing arts, some of the liveliest nightlife in the state, and as a base for year-round outdoor recreation in the surrounding mountains.

   A good place to start your visit is the **Park City Museum of History & Territorial Jail,** 528 Main St. The damp and tiny stone cells of this, the town's original jail, were considered state-of-the-art in 1886. The museum also houses a restored assay office, 19th-century mining equipment, historic photos, early skiing equipment, and the Park City Visitor Center. Those interested in the West's mining days will want to visit the **Park City Silver Mine Adventure,** 1½ miles south of town on UT 224, which takes visitors down into a genuine silver mine, the Ontario, source of some $400 million in silver during its 100-year lifespan.

   The arts are well-represented, too, with a number of Main Street galleries and **Kimball Art Center,** 638 Park Ave.

Take a Break

For a quick bite to eat, stop at **Burgie's,** 570 Main St (tel 801/649-0011). Not surprisingly, this cafe specializes in burgers, but the menu also includes homemade soups, chicken sandwiches, and locally famous onion rings, all in the $4 to $8 range. If you enjoy a picnic, you'll find especially good sandwiches—to eat in or take out—at **Main Street Deli,** 525 Main St (tel 801/649-1110). Bagels are baked fresh, and there are homemade cakes, cookies, and pies. Prices run from $4 to $6.

From Park City, head east on I-80 about 15 miles to exit 156 for:

2. **Rockport State Park.** Only a half-mile wide, this picturesque man-made lake (tel 801/336-2241) is about three miles long, and offers boating, windsurfing, water skiing, sailing, kayaking, fishing, hiking, swimming, and camping. It's a great spot for a picnic and perhaps a short walk where you might see mule deer, yellow-belly marmots, badgers, raccoons, weasels, and ground squirrels. Birds also abound, and golden and bald eagles can sometimes be spotted.

   From the park, continue east on I-80 for 12 miles to I-84, follow that 32 miles west to exit 87, then go north on US 89 about 5 miles to:

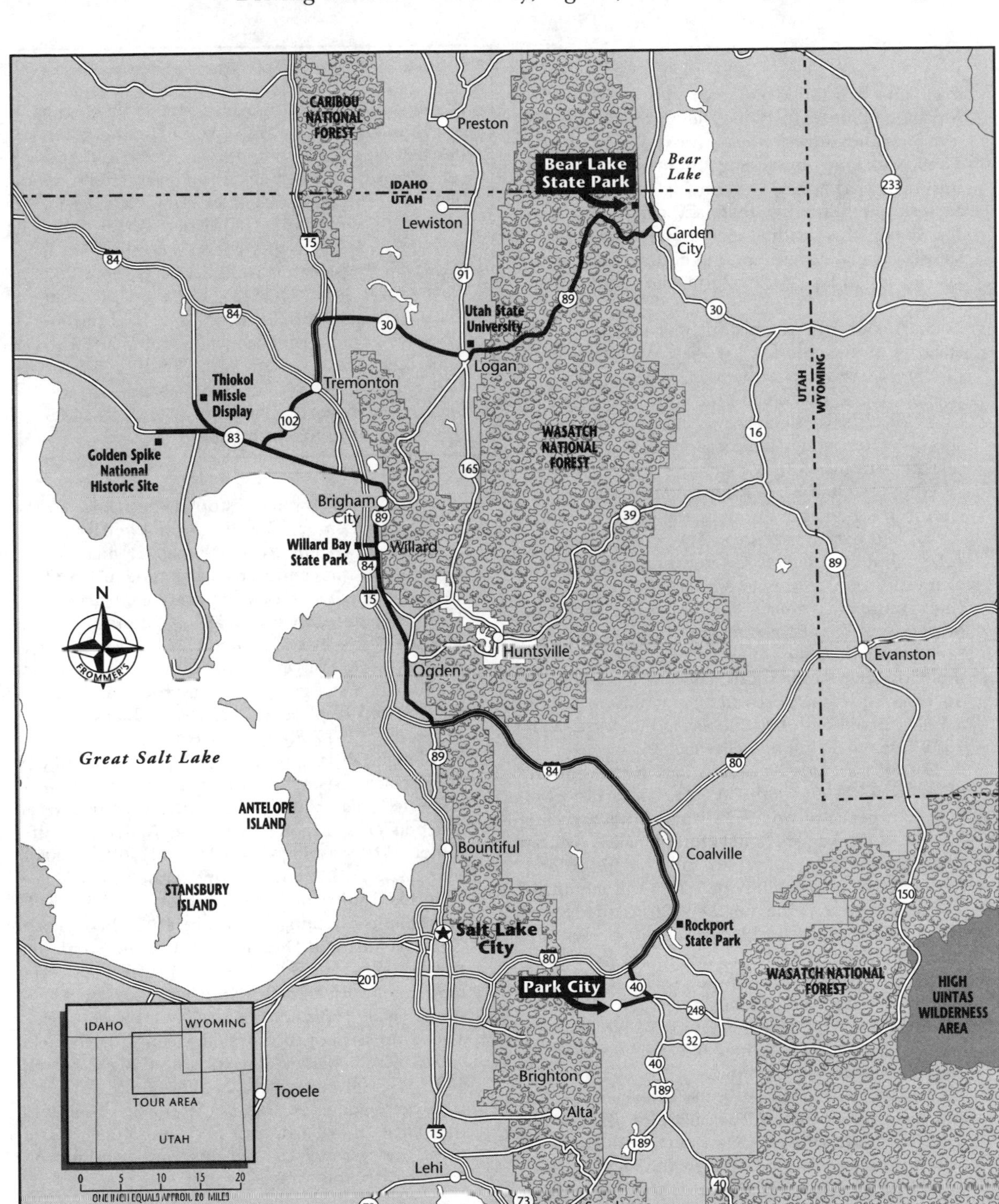
CARIBOU NATIONAL FOREST
Preston
Bear Lake State Park
Bear Lake
IDAHO
UTAH
Lewiston
Garden City
Utah State University
Logan
Thiokol Missle Display
Tremonton
Golden Spike National Historic Site
WASATCH NATIONAL FOREST
UTAH
WYOMING
Brigham City
Willard Bay State Park
Willard
N
FROMMER'S
Huntsville
Ogden
Evanston
Great Salt Lake
ANTELOPE ISLAND
Bountiful
Coalville
STANSBURY ISLAND
Rockport State Park
Salt Lake City
Park City
WASATCH NATIONAL FOREST
HIGH UINTAS WILDERNESS AREA
IDAHO
WYOMING
TOUR AREA
UTAH
Tooele
Brighton
Alta
Lehi
Sundance
0 5 10 15 20
ONE INCH EQUALS APPROX. 20 MILES

3. **Ogden.** Popular as a rendezvous site for mountain men and fur trappers in the 1820s, the settlement grew into a full-fledged town with the arrival of Mormon pioneers in 1849. The city quickly became a major junction with the arrival of the railroad in 1869, with lines branching throughout Utah and into neighboring states. Soon Ogden was a manufacturing, milling, livestock, and agricultural center. Today, this bustling city of over 60,000 offers the visitor good museums and historic sites, and is also a popular base for exploring the nearby mountains.

Start your visit at a historic railroad depot. The stately **Union Station,** 2501 Wall Ave, at the head of 25th Street, was built in 1924 to replace the original depot, which had been destroyed by fire. It now houses several museums, an art gallery, gift shop, theater, restaurant, visitor information center, and Amtrak ticket office.

Here the **Utah State Railroad Museum** displays gas turbine locomotive designs, shows a video about trains, and has an extensive HO-gauge model railroad layout that depicts the construction and geography of the 1,776-mile western portion of the transcontinental route. The **Browning Firearms Museum** exhibits Browning guns from 1878 to the present, plus a replica of an 1880s gun shop. Inside the **Browning-Kimball Car Collection** are about a dozen classic cars, mostly luxury models, including a 1901 curved-dash Oldsmobile and an ultra-fancy 1932 Lincoln 12-cylinder Berline.

On the west side of town is **Fort Buenaventura State Park,** 2450 South "A" Ave. This historical park in a peaceful wooded setting shows what life was like in this rugged land before so-called civilization arrived. There's a replica of an 1846 fort and trading post, and exhibits depicting the mountain men and fur trade era from the 1820s to the 1850s. There are several small ponds, and canoes are available for rent. Another place to get away from city life is **Ogden Nature Center,** 966 W 12th St, an animal hospital and wildlife sanctuary where injured animals are treated before being released back to the wild. The center has trails and a small museum with wildlife exhibits.

A favorite of children is the **George S Eccles Dinosaur Park,** 1544 E Park Blvd, on the Ogden River Parkway, which has life-size reproductions of over 40 prehistoric monsters from the Cretaceous, Jurassic, and Triassic periods. There's also a shop with interactive displays and activities. Kids also enjoy the **Treehouse Children's Museum,** 2255 B Ogden City Mall, a hands-on entertainment and learning center where children can climb into a giant treehouse. A print shop lets them make their own books, cards, and stationery.

Take a Break

If you landed here at lunch or dinner time, stop at **Union Grill,** 2501 Wall Ave in Union Station (tel 801/621-2830), an historic railroad-theme cafe that offers diners a view of the trains rumbling by. The menu includes fresh fish, pasta, homemade soups, and sandwiches. Prices range from $6 to $13. Another good choice for a meal is just up the street at **Delights of Ogden,** 258 25th St (tel 801/394-1111), a classy restaurant that offers innovative selections such as phyllo-wrapped salmon with spinach, and marinated game hen with roasted garlic, plus generous deli-style sandwiches and homemade soups, breads, and desserts. Main courses cost $4 to $5 at lunch, $10 to $20 at dinner.

Art lovers will want to stop at the **Eccles Community Art Center,** 2580 Jefferson Ave. Housed in a handsome, 1893 Richardsonian Romanesque–style house, the center hosts changing art exhibits with an emphasis on contemporary Utah artists. At **Hill Aerospace Museum,** 7961 Wardleigh Rd at Hill Air Force Base (I-15 exit 341), visitors get a close-up view of over 50 planes, plus missiles and bombs, on a self-guided walking tour. Among the most prized displays are the SR-71 Blackbird spy plane and a B-17 Flying Fortress.

If nightfall is approaching, Ogden would be a good place to stay. It offers a number of well-respected chain and franchise lodgings, plus several independents. Among them, the **Radisson Suite Hotel,** 2510 Washington Blvd (tel 801/627-1900 or 800/333-3333), offers moderate-to-expensive rooms and suites in a stately, historic building with hand-painted ceilings and graceful chandeliers. **Comfort Suites of Ogden,** 1150 W 2150 South (tel 801/621-2545 or 800/228-5150), offers modern, moderately priced suites with large-screen televisions, small refrigerators, and microwave ovens. Those on a budget will find clean, comfortable rooms with a homey atmosphere at **Big Z Motel,** 1123 W 2100 South (tel 801/394-6632).

From Ogden, take old US 89 north 12 miles to the village of Willard, turn west onto 4000 North, drive under the I-15 overpass, and continue on 4000 North, following signs, to:

4. **Willard Bay State Park.** This state park (tel 801/734-9494), with almost 10,000 acres of fresh water and an abundance of trees, is a good choice for a leisurely picnic and walk along the shore, or an afternoon of boating, swimming, or fishing. An important habitat for over 200 species of birds,

you'll have a good chance of spotting gulls, sandpipers, ducks, geese, herons, eagles, and falcons.

From the park, return to the village of Willard and follow US 89 about 7 miles north, past orchards and fruit stands, to:

5. **Brigham City.** Named for early Mormon Church leader Brigham Young, Brigham City is a friendly little town with a tree-lined Main Street and well-preserved 19th-century architecture. Recommended stops include the beautiful stone and brick **Box Elder Tabernacle,** 251 S Main St, with its numerous soaring spires; and the **Brigham City Museum/Gallery,** 24 N 300 West, featuring works by Utah artists and exhibits of pioneer life. Also worth a look is the historic **Union Pacific Depot,** 833 W Forest St, built in 1907.

From Brigham City, head north on I-15 4 miles to exit 368, and go west on UT 83 for 29 miles to the sign and turn-off (south 7½ miles) to:

6. **Golden Spike National Historic Site.** This is the spot where, on May 10, 1869, rails from America's east and west coasts were joined, as the Central Pacific met the Union Pacific at Promontory Summit. Today there's about 1¾ miles of track, re-laid on the original roadbed, where you can observe exact replicas of the two colorfully painted engines, the Central Pacific's "Jupiter" and Union Pacific's "119." From the end of April into early October, the magnificent machines are on display and make short daily runs. At the Visitor Center you can view slide programs, films, and museum exhibits explaining the significance of the linking of the nation by rail.

Train buffs can drive the self-guiding Promontory Trail along nine miles of the historic railroad grades to see the two parallel grades laid by the competing railroad construction companies, clearings for sidings, original rock culverts, and many cuts and fills. Allow about 1¼ hours.

From Golden Spike, drive the 7½ miles back to UT 83, turn west, and go just under 2 miles to:

7. **Thiokol Missile Display.** Here, in Thiokol Corporation's (tel 801/863-3511) front yard, is an extensive display of missiles, missile motors, rockets, and booster rockets used by NASA, the US Navy, and the Air Force. You can wander among the outdoor exhibits, reading descriptive signs and getting a close-up look at these tools of exploration and war, including a 60-foot-long Minuteman ICBM.

From Thiokol, head back east about 7 miles on UT 83 to UT 102, turn north onto UT 102 and follow as it winds about 15 miles through farmland to I-84. Take I-84 east a mile to I-15 and head north for about 5 miles to exit 387, where you take UT 30 about 23 miles east to:

8. **Logan.** Nestled in the fertile Cache Valley between the Wasatch and Bear River mountains, this area was a favorite of mountain men, who came here in the 1820s to trap beaver in the Logan River. Now in a rich farming area famous for its cheeses, Logan is a compact city with a number of attractions, including historical buildings, art galleries, and outdoor recreation opportunities.

Those planning to overnight in Logan have several good choices, including the attractively landscaped **Best Western Baugh Motel,** 153 S Main St (tel 801/752-5220 or 800/462-4154). This moderately priced motel offers spacious rooms and all the usual amenities. For something a bit different, try the intriguing **Center Street Bed & Breakfast Inn,** 169 E Center St (tel 801/752-3443), a moderate-to-expensive inn located in a three-story Victorian mansion built in 1879. Rooms are imaginatively decorated in various themes, such as the western decor of the Jesse James room and the fantasy-like Castle of the Purple Dragon.

The center of much activity in Logan—especially performing arts and sporting events—is **Utah State University,** 102 Old Main (the 400-acre campus lies north of US 89 and mostly east of 800 East). Founded in 1888, USU was established as an agricultural college through the federal land-grant program, and now, with an enrollment of more than 20,000, offers undergraduate and graduate degrees in a variety of specialties that include business, education, engineering, and the humanities.

Old Main, on University Hill, was the first USU building, begun just one year after the college was established, and is the oldest building in continuous use on any Utah college campus. Its tall bell tower is a campus landmark. The **Nora Eccles Harrison Museum of Art,** 650 N 1100 East, has a fine collection of ceramics on display, and offers changing exhibits in a variety of media.

Operated by USU graduate students, the **Ronald V Jensen Living Historical Farm,** 4025 S US 89/91, 6 miles SW of Logan in Wellsville (tel 801/245-4064), is an authentic re-creation of a 1917 dairy farm, a 120-acre interpretive center where guides in period costume discuss life on the farm. Although not open on a regular basis, there are a number of events each year, such as a turn-of-the-century wedding, sheep shearing, quilting bees, and an old-fashioned Christmas celebration.

The **Cache Valley Historical Museum,** 160 N Main St, is housed in the same building as the Logan Information Center. This small museum has displays of 19th-century pioneer artifacts of the area, including guns, musical instruments, unique

Mormon-style sofas, fashions, and kitchen utensils. There are several pieces of furniture made by Mormon leader Brigham Young for his daughter, Luna Young Thatcher, who lived in Logan. Nearby, the local **Church of Jesus Christ of Latter-day Saints Tabernacle,** 50 N Main St, is a majestic 19th-century building that combines Greek, Roman, Gothic, and Byzantine architectural styles, made of locally quarried stone. Its pillars of wood are expertly painted to simulate marble, a technique widely used throughout pioneer Utah. Although the **LDS Temple,** 175 N 300 East, is not open to the public, it's well worth driving or walking by. Completed in 1884, its octagonal towers give the four-story solid limestone temple the appearance of a medieval castle.

Take a Break

To eat where the locals have been eating for generations, stop at **The Bluebird,** 19 N Main St (tel 801/752-3155). Decor is reminiscent of the 1920s, with the original marble back of the soda fountain, and a mural depicting Logan from 1856 to modern times. The menu includes a wide variety of hot and cold sandwiches, plus traditional American-style meals such as steak, chicken, and fish, and the very popular slow-roasted prime rib. Prices are in the $4 to $13 range. Since you'll likely be hitting the road again soon, you might want to visit **Old Grist Mill Bread Co,** 78 E 400 North (tel 801/753-6463), a bakery and delicatessen offering a variety of deli-style sandwiches, all prepared with fresh baked-on-the-premises breads and bagels. Sandwiches cost $3 to $4 and are prepared to take out. The bakery is open by 7:30am for those who want only the freshest baked bread.

Before leaving town, take a stroll through the **Willow Park Zoo,** 419 W 700 South, where you'll see and hear a variety of animals, including monkeys, macaws, condors, raccoons, swans, and Amazon parrots. Attractive and shady grounds include a play and picnic area.

From Logan follow US 89 for 40 miles east through narrow, winding, and beautiful Logan Canyon to:

9. Bear Lake State Park. High in the Rocky Mountains along the Utah-Idaho border, this state park (tel 801/946-3343) is a splendid stop for anyone who enjoys the outdoors. Covering 112 square miles, Bear Lake is Utah's second-largest freshwater lake, and when the light is right, suspended calcium carbonate particles give the water an incredible turquoise cast.

You can easily spend a few hours or a few days here. Activities include fishing for lake trout and the native Bear Lake cutthroat, plus several rare species including Bonneville whitefish and Bear Lake sculpin. Visitors can also go boating (small craft are available for rent), scuba diving, swimming, hiking, camping, or just relax in the sun on the sandy beach. This is also a prime bird-watching location, where you're apt to see numerous waterfowl, including loons, herons, ducks, geese, white pelicans, and sandhill cranes. It isn't unusual to spot deer and several species of squirrels in the park, as well. Those with bikes strapped to their cars might want to spend a few hours on the loop trail that circles the lake, providing excellent views of the lake and surrounding mountains.

Those visiting in mid-to-late summer will want to stop at one of the nearby roadside stands for a pint or two of fresh raspberries, a specialty of local farms. The peak of the season is in early August, when local residents celebrate the harvest with a festival that includes a rodeo, fireworks, and buckets of raspberry milk shakes.

To return to Park City from Bear Lake, follow UT 30 for 25 miles east to UT 16, turn south and go 42 miles to I-80, which you take west and continue about 53 miles to Park City (exit 145).

Utah Listings

Alta

See also Salt Lake City

A seriously rowdy silver mining town in the 1860s and 1870s, when it had 26 saloons, 6 breweries, and almost daily shootings. Alta practically died with the end of the silver boom. It gained renewed life when the ski resort opened in 1937. **Information:** Alta Travel, Alta 84092 (tel 801/942-0404).

LODGE

Alta Lodge
PO Box 8040, 84092; tel 801/742-3500 or toll free 800/707-2582; fax 801/742-3504. At top of Little Cottonwood Canyon. A lovely 40-year-old lodge resting at the base of the ski slopes, the Alta proudly boasts an 80% guest return rate. The entire atmosphere is friendly and welcoming. **Rooms:** 57 rms. Executive level. CI 1pm/CO 11am. Nonsmoking rms avail. Rooms are simple but comfortable and have great views of the mountain or ski slopes. **Amenities:** A/C, voice mail. No TV. Some units w/terraces, some w/fireplaces. Daycare/ski lessons for children 3 months to 12 years. **Services:** Masseur, children's program, babysitting. **Facilities:** 1 restaurant, 1 bar, sauna, steam rm, whirlpool, washer/dryer. **Rates (MAP):** Peak (Nov 15–Apr 7) $141–$240 S; $205–$305 D. Extra person $78. Children under age 4 stay free. Lower rates off-season. Parking: Outdoor, free. One condo available at $290–$395. Room discount (20%) available after April 7. Closed Apr 15–June 1/Oct 3–Nov 15. No CC.

ATTRACTION

Alta Ski Area
UT 210; tel 801/742-3333. Although famous for its expert runs, Alta also has fine beginner and intermediate trails. The breakdown is 25% beginner, 40% intermediate, and 35% advanced, with a base elevation of 8,550 feet rising to 10,650 feet at the top, yielding a vertical drop of 2,100 feet. There are six double and two triple lifts servicing 39 runs on 2,200 skiable acres making use of the more than 500 inches (over 40 feet) of snow per year. **Open:** Mid-Nov–mid-Apr, daily 9:15am–4:30pm. **$$$$**

Arches National Park

For lodgings and restaurants, see Moab

Sitting next to Canyonlands National Park in eastern Utah, Arches is much more visitor-friendly, with relatively short, well-maintained trails leading to most of the park's major attractions. Natural stone arches and fantastic rock formations, sculpted as if by an artist's hand, are the defining feature of this park, and they exist in remarkable numbers and variety. Bridges are formed when a river cuts a channel, while the often bizarre and beautiful contours of arches result from the erosive force of rain and snow freezing and thawing as it dissolves the "glue" that holds sand grains together, and chips away at the stone.

The **Visitors Center,** located just inside the entrance gate, has maps, brochures on hiking trails, and a short slide show. During the summer, rangers lead guided hikes on the Fiery Furnace Trail twice daily, as well as daily nature walks from various park locations. Evening campfire programs, also in summer only, are on topics such as rock art, geological processes, and wildlife.

Visitors can see many of the park's most famous rock formations without even getting out of their car. An 18-mile (one-way) **scenic drive** offers splendid views of countless natural rock arches and other formations, and several easy hikes open up additional scenery. Allow 1½ hours for the 36-mile round-trip drive, adding time for the optional hikes.

From the Devil's Garden Trail visitors may see up to 60 arches, on a fairly long, strenuous, and difficult hike. There is an easy-to-moderate 1.6-mile round-trip hike to Landscape Arch, a long, thin ribbon of stone that is one of the most beautiful arches in the park. Considered by many as the park's best and most scenic hike, the three-mile round-trip **Delicate Arch Trail** is a moderate-to-difficult hike, with slippery slickrock and some steep drop-offs along a narrow cliff, but it rewards hikers with a dramatic and spectacular view of Delicate Arch and other great scenes along the way.

For more information, contact: Superintendent, Arches National Park, PO Box 907, Moab, UT 84532 (tel 801/259-8161).

Beaver

Beaver was settled by Mormon pioneers in 1856 and named for the beaver dams in the area. The historic district contains some 30 interesting 19th-century buildings of pink stone. Notorious train and bank robber Butch Cassidy (Robert LeRoy Parker) was born here in 1866. **Information:** Beaver County Travel Council, 105 E Center St, PO Box 272, Beaver 84713 (tel 801/438-2975).

MOTELS

Best Western Paice Inn

161 S Main St, PO Box 897, 84713; tel 801/438-2438 or toll free 800/528-1234; fax 801/438-1053. Exit 109 off I-15. Attractive building located south of the main hub of Beaver but within walking distance of a shopping center. Well-appointed rooms. **Rooms:** 24 rms and stes. CI noon/CO 11am. Nonsmoking rms avail. **Amenities:** A/C, cable TV. **Services:** **Facilities:** 1 restaurant, sauna, whirlpool. Some units have covered parking. Picnic area behind building. **Rates:** Peak (May 15–Oct) $44–$46 S; $46–$52 D; $60–$70 ste. Extra person $2. Children under age 8 stay free. Lower rates off-season. Parking: Indoor/outdoor, free. AE, CB, DC, DISC, MC, V.

Delano Motel

480 N Main St, PO Box 1488, 84713; tel 801/438-2418 or toll free 800/288-3171; fax 801/438-2115. E of exit 109 or 112 off I-15. Older motel, unprepossessing from the outside but spacious and comfortable inside. **Rooms:** 11 rms. CI open/CO 11am. Nonsmoking rms avail. Rooms are clean, bright, spacious. Two lawn chairs in front of each unit. **Amenities:** A/C, cable TV. Some units have refrigerators. **Services:** Small pets only ($5 fee). **Facilities:** Washer/dryer. Outside covered parking. **Rates:** Peak (Apr–Oct) $32–$36 S; $39–$45 D. Extra person $3. Children under age 12 stay free. Lower rates off-season. Parking: Indoor/outdoor, free. AE, DISC, MC, V.

Quality Inn

1540 S 450 West, PO Box 1461, 84713; tel 801/438-5426 or toll free 800/228-5151; fax 801/438-2493. 2 mi S of exit 109 off I-15. Modern motel on south side of town overlooking Beaver and surrounding countryside. Large lobby has high beamed ceiling and floor-to-ceiling windows. **Rooms:** 52 rms and stes. CI 2pm/CO 11am. Nonsmoking rms avail. Moderately spacious rooms; east windows have nice view of mountains. King and queen beds available. **Amenities:** A/C, cable TV. Some units w/whirlpools. **Services:** Car-rental desk. Fax machine available for fee. **Facilities:** 1 restaurant, whirlpool. **Rates:** Peak (Apr–Sept) $40–$54 S; $48–$60 D; $50–$60 ste. Extra person $6. Children under age 16 stay free. Lower rates off-season. Parking: Outdoor, free. AE, DC, DISC, MC, V.

RESTAURANTS

The Cottage Inn

171 S Main St; tel 801/438-5855. **American/Southwestern.** A cozy, intimate dining establishment with a friendly atmosphere and a collection of dolls, handmade by the owner. The extensive menu includes burgers, hot sandwiches, soups, salads, and Tex-Mex selections. **FYI:** Reservations accepted. Children's menu. No liquor license. No smoking. **Open:** Peak (Apr–Jan) daily 7am–10pm. **Prices:** Main courses $9–$13. MC, V.

Kan Kun Mexican Restaurant

1474 S 450 West; tel 801/438-5908. Near exit 109 off I-15. **Mexican.** The Kan Kun satisfies those seeking authentic, tasty, home-cooked Mexican food. The white building with red tile roof and an old Mexican-style gate is hard to miss—just look for the cartoonlike mural on the wall by the front door. Inside, the motif is continued with bold Mexican cartoon figures on just about every wall. After one of the burritos or enchiladas, be sure to try the deep-fried ice cream for dessert. **FYI:** Reservations accepted. Children's menu. Beer only. No smoking. **Open:** Daily 10:45am–10pm. **Prices:** Main courses $4–$8. DISC, MC, V.

Bluff

In 1880 Mormon pioneers, too exhausted to proceed any further on their arduous wagon train journey, chose this location along the San Juan River to build a settlement. Visitors can see the historic rock homes from Bluff's early days, and marvel at ruins and rock art left by the prehistoric Anasazi people. **Information:** San Juan County Travel Council, 117 S Main St, PO Box 490, Monticello 84535 (tel 801/587-3235 or 800/574-4FUN).

MOTEL

Recapture Lodge

US 191, PO Box 309, 84512; tel 801/672-2281; fax 801/672-2284. In town center. Nestled amongst trees in the tiny oasis of Bluff along the San Juan River, this rustic older lodge is a good choice for the outdoor aficionado and leisure traveler. **Rooms:** 28 rms, stes, and effic. CI noon/CO 11am. Nonsmoking rms avail. Charming rooms are decorated in western style with Native American rugs on walls; all have a view of mountains. Several budget rooms available with shower only and one double bed. **Amenities:** A/C, TV w/movies. No phone. **Services:** Babysitting. Guided tours and overnight llama trips available. Coffee and tea available 24 hours in lobby. **Facilities:** Basketball, lawn games, whirlpool, washer/dryer. Nature trail follows San Juan River along back of property. Picnic tables. Shuttle available for river runners, bicyclists. **Rates:** Peak (May–Sept) $32–$42 S; $34–$48 D; $42–$52 ste; $38–$52 effic. Extra person $4. Lower rates off-season. Parking: Outdoor, free. DISC, MC, V.

RESTAURANT

★ Sunbonnet Cafe

Historic Loop; tel 801/672-2201. Off US 191. **Vegetarian/Navajo.** Located in a nearly century-old family home, this restaurant offers hearty fare in its two dining rooms: Navajo tacos and Indian fry bread, burgers and sandwiches, and dinners of country fried steak, fried chicken, and pork chops. The vegetarian side of the menu includes a veggie version of the Navajo taco plus chili, salads, and sandwiches. **FYI:** Reservations accepted. Children's menu. No liquor license. No smoking. **Open:** Peak (Mar–Oct) Mon–Sat 7am–9pm. **Prices:** Main courses $6–$9. MC, V.

Brigham City

Founded as Box Elder and renamed for 19th-century Mormon leader Brigham Young, the city is the center of a large farm area. The first major business was an orchard, started in 1855 with 100 peach pits brought in from Salt Lake City. Peach Days, with a parade and other festivities, takes place each September. **Information:** Brigham City Chamber of Commerce, 6 N Main St, Brigham City 84302 (tel 801/723-3931).

MOTEL

Howard Johnson

1167 S Main St, 84302; tel 801/723-8511 or toll free 800/446-4656; fax 801/723-8511. Two-story plain motel with basic facilities. **Rooms:** 44 rms and stes. CI noon/CO noon. Nonsmoking rms avail. Rooms are comfortable with eclectic furnishings. Second-floor has nice view of valley or Wasatch Mountains to the east. Each has a 25″ TV in cabinet. **Amenities:** A/C, cable TV. Free coffee 24 hours. **Services:** **Facilities:** 1 restaurant (*see* "Restaurants" below), whirlpool. **Rates (CP):** $40 S; $46 D; $63–$130 ste. Children under age 17 stay free. Parking: Outdoor, free. AE, CB, DC, DISC, MC, V.

RESTAURANTS

Maddox Ranch House

1900 S US 89, Perry; tel 801/723-8545. 1 mi S of exit 364 off I-15. **Steak.** Located south of Brigham City, the Maddox is a family-owned restaurant offering good homemade meals and fast service. It's famous for steak and fried chicken, and is developing a reputation for shrimp and other seafood. The decor is rustic inside and out, with wagon wheel chandeliers. Entrees come with homemade soup, fresh salad or seafood cocktail, and homemade rolls. **FYI:** Reservations recommended. Children's menu. No liquor license. No smoking. **Open:** Tues–Sat 11am–9:30pm. **Prices:** Main courses $11–$16. AE, DISC, MC, V.

★ Red Baron Restaurant

In the Howard Johnson, 1167 S Main St; tel 801/723-3100. 2 mi E of exit 364 off I-15. **American.** A popular spot for down-home American food, promptly served. Seating is either at tables or a counter overlooking a large mural showing a tiny Red Baron airplane. Lunches and dinners feature sandwiches, chicken, and steak. A complimentary salad bar is included with all entrees. Homemade pies for dessert. **FYI:** Reservations accepted. Children's menu. No liquor license. No smoking. **Open:** Peak (June–Aug) Mon 7am–9pm, Wed–Sat 7am–10pm, Sun 8am–8pm. **Prices:** Main courses $5–$12. AE, DISC, MC, V.

ATTRACTIONS

Brigham City Museum-Gallery

24 N 300 West; tel 801/723-6769. Founded in 1970, the museum sponsors 11 rotating art or history exhibits per year and has a permanent collection of artifacts representing the early history of the community from 1855 to 1885. Temporary exhibits focus on regional and national art and regional history, including exhibits from the Smithsonian, Exhibits USA, or other national touring companies. A regional quilt show is held each July. **Open:** Tues–Fri 11am–6pm, Sat 1–5pm. **Free**

Golden Spike National Historic Site

UT 83; tel 801/471-2209. 32 mi W of Brigham City. On May 10, 1869, the Central Pacific met the Union Pacific, joining America's east and west coasts. Today 1.7 miles of track have been re-layed on the original roadbed, where visitors can see exact replicas of the two engines, the Central Pacific's Jupiter and Union Pacific's 119. From the end of April into early October, the engines make short runs. Presentations are given track-side, sometimes in period dress. There are picnic areas, hiking trails, a visitor center with bookstore, slide programs, films, and museum exhibits. Special events: on May 10, a reenactment of the original Golden Spike Ceremony with hot food, souvenirs, and handicrafts; in mid-August, the Annual Railroader's Festival with reenactments of the ceremony, a spike driving contest, handcar races and rides, hot food, handicraft booths, and live music; Christmas season, the Annual Railroader's Film Festival and Winter Steam Demonstration. **Open:** Peak (Mem Day–Labor Day) daily 8am–6pm. Reduced hours off-season. **$**

Bryce

See Bryce Canyon National Park

Bryce Canyon National Park

The main highlight of Bryce Canyon is the thousands of intricately shaped hoodoos, large and colorful rock formations that define the park's landscape. Hoodoos are pinnacles of rock, often oddly shaped, left standing by the forces of millions of years of water and wind erosion. After the colorful hoodoos, one notices the deep amphitheaters that are their home, with their cliffs, windows, and arches, all colored in shades of red, brown, orange, yellow, and white. The park sustains three separate life zones, each with its own unique vegetation, changing with elevation.

The **Visitor Center,** at the north end of the entrance to the park, has exhibits on the geology and history of the area and presents a short introductory slide show on the park. Rangers answer questions, provide backcountry permits, and present a variety of free programs and activities.

One of the best facets of Bryce Canyon is the number of hiking trails offered at all levels. The **Rim Trail,** which does not drop into the canyon but offers splendid views from above, meanders along the rim for over five miles. Visitors' choice for descending into the canyon and seeing the most with the least amount of physical exertion is to combine two popular trails—the **Navajo Loop** and **Queen's Garden.** The total distance is just under three miles, with a 521-foot elevation change, and most hikers take from two to three hours.

The park has a variety of wildlife, ranging from mule deer to the commonly seen mountain short-horned lizard, often spotted while hiking down into the canyon. Occasionally a mountain lion comes into view, most likely on the prowl in the park in search of mule deer; elk and pronghorn antelope may also be seen at higher elevations.

To see Bryce Canyon the way early pioneers did, visitors ride on horseback. **Canyon Trail Rides** (tel 801/834-5219; 679-8665 off-season), with a desk inside Bryce Lodge, offers a close-up view of Bryce's spectacular rock formations from the relative comfort of a saddle; first-time riders are welcomed. Guided rides are also provided by Ruby's Outlaw Trail Rides (tel 801/679-8761 or 800/679-5859), at Ruby's Inn. Reservations are recommended for both companies. Cross-country skiers will find several marked and ungroomed trails in the park. A limited number of snowshoes are loaned free of charge at the visitor center and may be used anywhere in the park except on cross-country ski tracks (all above the rim).

For more information on what to see, hiking trails, camping, and lodging, write: Superintendent, Bryce Canyon National Park, Bryce Canyon, UT 84717 (tel 801/834-5322).

MOTELS

Bryce Canyon Pines

UT 12, PO Box 43, Bryce, 84764; tel 801/834-5441 or toll free 800/892-7923; fax 801/834-5330. 6 mi NW of park entrance. Modern motel set among pine trees, combining western charm with comfort and convenience. Lobby has large rock fireplace, high beamed ceiling, 36″ TV, and oversize wagon wheel chandeliers. **Rooms:** 50 rms, stes, and effic; 4 cottages/villas. CI 3pm/CO 11am. Nonsmoking rms avail. Rooms are modern with individually controlled cooling and heating. **Amenities:** A/C, satel TV. Some units w/fireplaces. **Services:** **Facilities:** 1 restaurant, whirlpool. **Rates:** Peak (May–Oct) $50–$60 S; $70–$75 D; $90–$110 ste; $80–$90 effic; $70–$75 cottage/villa. Extra person $5. Children under age 12 stay free. Lower rates off-season. Parking: Outdoor, free. AE, DC, DISC, MC, V.

Bryce Pioneer Village

UT 12, PO Box 119, Tropic, 84776; tel 801/679-8546 or toll free 800/222-0381; fax 801/679-8607. 9 mi E of park entrance. Old-west-style village with units in log cabin–like structures on 14 acres. Ebenezer Bryce's original cabin sits on adjacent lot. Extensive lawn area with large shade trees. Tent and RV camping also available. **Rooms:** 48 rms and effic. CI 3pm/CO 11am. Nonsmoking rms avail. Rooms are small but adequate; mismatched furniture. Views of Bryce Canyon and Escalante Mountain. **Amenities:** A/C, TV. **Services:** **Facilities:** Picnic tables on lawn. **Rates:** Peak (May–Oct 15) $55–$65 S or D; $75 effic. Children under age 12 stay free. Lower rates off-season. Parking: Outdoor, free. Closed Nov–Feb. DISC, MC, V.

Foster's Motel

UT 12, PO Box 64101, Bryce, 84764; tel 801/834-5227; fax 801/834-5304. 5 mi SW of park entrance. Located right on the highway, this modest but clean motel is convenient for visitors to the park. **Rooms:** 40 rms. CI open/CO 11am. Nonsmoking rms avail. **Amenities:** A/C. **Services:** Horseback riding nearby. **Facilities:** 20 1 restaurant (*see* "Restaurants" below). Restaurant on premises will make box lunches; grocery store and bakery nearby. **Rates:** Peak (Apr–Nov) $60 S or D. Extra person $8. Children under age 18 stay free. Lower rates off-season. Parking: Outdoor, free. AE, DISC, MC, V.

World Host Bryce Valley Inn

200 N Main St, PO Box A, Tropic, 84776; tel 801/679-8811 or toll free 800/462-7923; fax 801/679-8846. 10 mi E of park entrance. Rustic motel with spacious, attractive rooms. **Rooms:** 65 rms and stes. CI 4pm/CO 11am. No smoking. Some rooms offer views of Powell Point and other parts of the park. Some three- and four-bedroom units available. **Amenities:** A/C, TV. **Services:** **Facilities:** 30

1 restaurant (*see* "Restaurants" below), washer/dryer. Restaurant serves American and Mexican cuisine and offers patio dining. **Rates:** Peak (Apr–Oct) $57–$75 S or D; $80–$85 ste. Extra person $5. Children under age 12 stay free. Lower rates off-season. Parking: Outdoor, free. AE, MC, V.

LODGE

UNRATED **Bryce Canyon Lodge**
UT 63, PO Box 400, 84721; tel 801/586-7686; fax 801/586-3157. 3 mi S of UT 12. The only lodging inside the park offers lovely rustic cabins and several lodge rooms, plus basic motel units. Surrounded by tall pines, the handsome sandstone and ponderosa pine lodge was built in 1924. The busy lobby has service desks for horseback riding, tram tours, and other activities. **Rooms:** 121 rms and stes; 40 cottages/villas. CI 4pm/CO 11am. Nonsmoking rms avail. Motel building looks like a hunting lodge; rooms here are pleasant and quite spacious. Cabins, decorated in "rustic luxury," are fairly small, but tall ceilings give feeling of spaciousness and there are gas-burning fireplaces, pine board walls, and log beams. **Amenities:** TV. No A/C. All units w/terraces, some w/fireplaces. **Services:** Children's program, babysitting. **Facilities:** 100 1 restaurant (*see* "Restaurants" below). Hiking trails abound. Gift shop. **Rates:** $75–$80 S or D; $112–$115 ste; $87–$95 cottage/villa. Children under age 16 stay free. Parking: Outdoor, free. Closed Nov–Mar. AE, MC, V.

RESORT

Best Western Ruby's Inn
UT 63, Bryce, 84764; tel 801/834-5341 or toll free 800/528-1234; fax 801/834-5265. Just outside park entrance. 3,000 acres. Imposing western-style resort offering the closest lodging to Bryce Canyon National Park. Exceptionally well maintained and continually upgraded. Spacious lobby has several service desks offering variety of tours of the park and environs. **Rooms:** 369 rms and stes. CI open/CO 11am. Nonsmoking rms avail. Attractive southwestern-style rooms in variety of sizes, from basic to family units to king spa suites. Many units have views of the park. **Amenities:** A/C, cable TV w/movies. Some units w/whirlpools. VCRs, some refrigerators and microwaves available. **Services:** Helicopter rides. Cross-country ski trails go into surrounding national forest. Area van transport. **Facilities:** 350 2 restaurants (*see* "Restaurants" below), games rm, whirlpool, beauty salon, washer/dryer. New large indoor pool. General store, post office, gas station, state liquor store, art gallery. Fast food cafe. **Rates:** Peak (May–Oct) $83–$98 S or D; $125 ste. Extra person $5. Lower rates off-season. Parking: Outdoor, free. AE, DC, DISC, MC, V.

RESTAURANTS

Bryce Canyon Lodge
In Bryce Canyon Lodge, UT 63; tel 801/834-5361. 3 mi S of UT 12. **Regional American.** The dining room, located in a handsome sandstone and ponderosa pine lodge that opened in 1924, boasts two large stone fireplaces and large windows looking out to the park. Native American weavings and baskets and a huge, 45-star American flag from 1897 are some of the decorations. House specialties at dinner include an excellent slow-roasted prime rib, slow-roasted pork ribs, and fresh mountain trout. There are several vegetarian items as well. Lunch offerings include trout and barbecued pork plus burgers, sandwiches, and salads; lunches-to-go are also available. Breakfasts offer all the usual American selections. Be sure to ask about the lodge's specialty ice creams, such as exotic wild berry crunch. **FYI:** Reservations recommended. Children's menu. No smoking. **Open:** Breakfast daily 6:30–10am; lunch daily 11:30am–2:30pm; dinner daily 5:30–9:30pm. Closed Nov–mid-Apr. **Prices:** Main courses $11–$16. AE, DC, DISC, MC, V.

Canyon Diner
In Best Western Ruby's Inn, UT 63, Bryce; tel 801/834-5341. Just outside park entrance. **Fast food.** A neat, clean, fast-food kind of place serving burgers, sandwiches, and salads. Take it to go or sit at one of the tables or booths. **FYI:** Reservations not accepted. Children's menu. No liquor license. No smoking. **Open:** Daily 7am–10pm. Closed Nov–Mar. **Prices:** Main courses $4–$8. AE, CB, DC, DISC, MC, V.

Foster's Family Steakhouse
In Foster's Motel, UT 12, Bryce; tel 801/834-5227. 5 mi SW of park entrance. **Seafood/Steak.** A bright and airy family steak house in a large modern building adjacent to a motel and supermarket, Foster's offers steak, seafood, prime rib, and chicken plus sandwiches, salads, and homemade soups. Serves three meals daily in summer, but dinner only Thursday, Friday, and Saturday from November through February. **FYI:** Reservations accepted. Children's menu. Beer only. No smoking. **Open:** Peak (May–Oct) daily 6am–10pm. **Prices:** Main courses $9–$19. AE, DISC, MC, V.

Hungry Coyote Restaurant & Saloon
In World Host Bryce Valley Inn, 200 N Main St, Tropic; tel 801/679-8822. In town center on UT 12. **Southwestern.** A friendly western-style restaurant with knotty pine walls and old-west memorabilia scattered about. Specialties are steaks, Mexican dinners, and the ever-popular, all-you-can-eat barbecued beef ribs. Other choices: crisp fish-and-chips and a variety of sandwiches and burgers. **FYI:** Reservations not accepted. Children's menu. No smoking. **Open:** Peak (May–Oct) breakfast daily 6:30–10am; dinner daily 5–11pm. Closed Jan–Mar. **Prices:** Main courses $9–$16. AE, MC, V.

Ruby's Inn Cowboy's Buffet & Steak Room
In Best Western Ruby's Inn, UT 63, Bryce; tel 801/834-5341. Just outside park entrance. **Regional American.** This pleasant restaurant with a rustic wood-sided exterior offers an all-you-can-eat buffet at every meal. Choose from hamburgers, soups, salads, fish sandwiches, prime rib, steak, and ribs. Pictures depicting the region's early days decorate the walls. **FYI:** Reservations not accepted. Children's menu. No smoking. **Open:** Daily 6:30am–10pm. **Prices:** Main courses $7–$18. AE, CB, DC, DISC, MC, V.

Canyonlands National Park

For lodgings and restaurants, see Moab, Monticello

Utah's largest national park rewards those with time and energy to explore the rugged backcountry. Sliced into districts by the Colorado and Green Rivers, this is a land of extremes: vast panoramas, deep canyons, steep cliffs, broad mesas, and red spires.

The most accessible part of Canyonlands is the **Island in the Sky District,** in the northern section of the park, where a paved road leads to viewpoints such as Grand View Point, overlooking 10,000 square miles of rugged wilderness. Island in the Sky also has several easy to moderate trails, offering sweeping vistas of the park. A short walk offers views of Upheaval Dome, which resembles a large volcanic crater but may actually be a meteorite crater. For the more adventurous, the 100-mile White Rim Trail takes experienced mountain bikers and those with high-clearance four-wheel-drive vehicles on a winding loop tour through a vast array of scenery.

The **Needles District,** in the park's southeast corner, offers only a few viewpoints along the paved road, but numerous possibilities for hikers, backpackers, and those with high-clearance four-wheel-drive vehicles. Named for its tall, red-and-white striped rock pinnacles, it is a diverse area of arches, including the 150-foot-tall Angel Arch, as well as grassy meadows and the confluence of the Green and Colorado Rivers. Backcountry visitors to the Needles District will also find ruins and rock art left by the ancient Anasazi some 800 years ago.

A mixture of mountain and desert animals are found in Canyonlands, depending on the time of year and particular location within the park. The best times to see most wildlife is early and late in the day, especially in summer when the midday sun drives all Canyonlands residents in search of shade. Throughout the park visitors hear, if not see, the coyote. The elusive bighorn sheep graze along isolated cliffs, where visitors may also see a golden eagle or turkey vulture soaring above the rocks in search of food. The best chances of seeing deer, beaver, and other mammals are along riverbanks and the few natural springs in the park.

Canyonlands National Park operates two visitor centers: **Island of the Sky Visitor Center,** in the northern part of the park, and **Needles Visitor Center,** in the southern section. Visitors can pick up maps and free brochures on hiking trails and most important, talk with rangers about their plans. For advance information on what to see in the park, plus hiking and four-wheel drive trails and camping, contact: Superintendent, Canyonlands National Park, 2282 S West Resource Blvd, Moab, UT 84532 (tel 801/259-7164).

Capitol Reef National Park

Capitol Reef offers spectacular southern Utah scenery with a unique twist and a personality of its own. The area's geologic formations are downright peculiar, such as the appropriately named Hamburger Rocks, sitting atop a white sandstone table; the tall, bright red Chimney Rock; the silent and eerie Temple of the Moon; and the commanding Castle. The colors of Capitol Reef's canyon walls are draw from a spectacular palette, which is why the Navajos called the area "Land of the Sleeping Rainbow."

Throughout the park is evidence of man's presence throughout the centuries. The Fremont people lived along the river as early as AD 700. Many of their petroglyphs (images carved into rock) and some pictographs (images painted on rock) are still visible on the canyon walls. Prospectors and other travelers passed through the Capitol Gorge section of the park in the late 1800s, leaving their names on the Pioneer Register. Mormon pioneers established the aptly-named community of Fruita when it was discovered that this was a good locale for growing fruit. The tiny **Fruita Schoolhouse,** built in 1896, was a church, social hall, and community meeting hall in addition to a one-room schoolhouse. The orchards those Mormon settlers planted continue to flourish.

Hiking trails through Capitol Reef National Park offer sweeping panoramas of colorful cliffs and soaring spires, eerie journeys through desolate, steep-walled canyons, and cool oases along the tree-shaded Fremont River. This is also the real Wild West, little changed from the way cowboys, bank robbers, settlers, and gold miners found it in the late 1800s, and one of the best things about hiking here is the combination of scenic beauty, Native American art, and western history to be discovered.

The **Visitors Center,** located on the park access road at its intersection with UT 24, has exhibits on the geology and history of the area and presents a short introductory slide show on the park. Park rangers can provide backcountry permits. For advance information on what to see in the park, hiking trails, and camping, write: Superintendent, Capitol Reef National Park, Torrey, UT 84775 (tel 801/425-3791).

MOTELS

Best Western Capitol Reef Resort
2600 E UT 24, PO Box 750160, Torrey, 84775; tel 801/425-3761 or toll free 800/528-1234; fax 801/425-3300. 1 mi W of park entrance. Pleasant two-story motel just outside the park's western entrance. **Rooms:** 30 rms and stes. CI 3pm/CO 11am. Nonsmoking rms avail. Rooms are comfortable and attractively decorated; some have great park view. Some suites have private patios overlooking the red cliffs. **Amenities:** A/C, satel TV. Some units w/terraces. **Services:** **Facilities:** 1 restaurant, basketball, whirlpool, washer/dryer. **Rates:** Peak (June–Sept) $76–$81 S or D; $110–$125 ste. Extra person $5. Children under age 1 stay free. Lower rates off-season. Parking: Outdoor, free. AE, CB, DC, DISC, MC, V.

Boulder View Inn
385 W Main St, PO Box 750237, Torrey, 84775; tel 801/425-3800 or toll free 800/444-3980. 1 mi W of jct UT 12/UT 24. Attractive motel built in 1994; nice guestroom views of surrounding red rock cliffs. Restaurant across street. **Rooms:** 12 rms and effic. CI 2pm/CO 11am. No smoking. **Amenities:** A/C, cable TV. **Services:** Car-rental desk. Complimentary coffee. **Facilities:** Basketball. **Rates:** Peak (Apr–Oct) $49 S; $52 D; $65 effic. Extra person $4. Children under age 12 stay free. Lower rates off-season. Parking: Outdoor, free. AE, DISC, MC, V.

Wonderland Inn
Jct UT 24/UT 12, PO Box 750067, Torrey, 84775; tel 801/425-3775 or toll free 800/458-0216; fax 801/425-3212. Modern white building with beautiful landscaping; located on a hill offering a panoramic view of the surrounding countryside. **Rooms:** 50 rms. CI 2pm/CO 11am. Nonsmoking rms avail. **Amenities:** A/C, satel TV w/movies. Some units w/terraces, some w/whirlpools. **Services:** Masseur, babysitting. **Facilities:** 1 restaurant, volleyball, sauna, whirlpool, beauty salon, washer/dryer. Sundeck; tanning room. **Rates:** Peak (Apr–Oct) $45–$55 S; $54–$64 D. Extra person $6. Lower rates off-season. Parking: Outdoor, free. AE, CB, DC, DISC, JCB, MC, V.

RESTAURANTS

Brink's Burgers Drive-In
165 E Main St, Torrey; tel 801/425-3710. In town center on UT 24. **Fast food.** Burgers, fish-and-chips, chicken sandwiches, milk shakes, and ice cream cones are some of the basic offerings at this sparkling clean fast food eatery. There are munchies too: cheese sticks, onion rings, zucchini sticks, spicy potato wedges. Picnic tables are set up outside in warm weather. **FYI:** Reservations not accepted. No liquor license. No smoking. **Open:** Peak (Apr–Sept) daily 11am–9pm. Closed Nov–Mar. **Prices:** Main courses $3–$7. MC, V.

Capitol Reef Cafe
360 W Main St, Torrey; tel 801/425-3271. W side of Torrey on UT 24. **Health/Spa/Vegetarian.** One wall contains a dramatic mural of red rock canyon country, while an abstract representation of the heavens—with stars and swirling comets in brilliant colors—covers the ceiling. The cuisine is as bold as the decor, featuring creative use of herbs and spices and local fresh fruit, vegetables, cheese, and rainbow trout. Rolls, bread, and pies and other desserts are homemade. Beverages include espresso and fresh juices. **FYI:** Reservations accepted. Children's menu. Beer and wine only. No smoking. **Open:** Breakfast daily 7–11am; dinner daily 5–9pm. Closed Oct–May. **Prices:** Main courses $8–$13. DISC, MC, V.

Cedar City

The southern Utah community of Cedar City is the site each summer of the internationally acclaimed Utah Shakespearean Festival, which runs from early July through the first week of September. Proximity to major national parks, monuments, and forests also draws tourists to the city, which offers a surprising number of modern motels, restaurants, and other facilities geared toward vacationers. America's first iron refinery west of the Mississippi River was established in Cedar City shortly after the community was founded in 1851. **Information:** Cedar City Chamber of Commerce Visitor Center, 286 N Main St, Cedar City 84720 (tel 801/586-4484).

HOTEL

Holiday Inn Convention Center
1575 W 200 North, 84720; tel 801/586-8888 or toll free 800/HOLIDAY; fax 801/586-1010. W of exit 59 off I-15. Modern hotel with a spacious, skylit lobby with fireplace and front wall of glass. **Rooms:** 100 rms and stes. CI 3pm/CO noon. Nonsmoking rms avail. Spacious, attractive rooms with metal doors for extra security. **Amenities:** A/C, cable TV w/movies, refrig, dataport. **Services:** VCRs and movies for rent. **Facilities:** 1 restaurant, sauna, whirlpool. Mail center with FedEx and UPS pick-up; fax available (fee). **Rates:** Peak (May–Oct) $72 S or D; $155 ste. Extra person $10. Children under age 18 stay free. Lower rates off-season. Parking: Outdoor, free. AE, CB, DC, DISC, JCB, MC, V.

MOTELS

Abbey Inn
940 W 200 North, 84720; tel 801/586-9966 or toll free 800/325-5411; fax 801/586-6522. Exit 59 off I-15. Attractive

brick motel with large columns in front. Lobby has fireplace, tall windows, and western memorabilia. **Rooms:** 81 rms and effic. CI 2pm/CO 11am. Nonsmoking rms avail. Rooms are spacious and attractively furnished. Poster beds. **Amenities:** A/C, cable TV w/movies, refrig, dataport. 1 unit w/whirlpool. Continental breakfast is at nearby Shoney's, with coupon. **Services:** Babysitting. **Facilities:** 1 restaurant, whirlpool, washer/dryer. Pool area is very nicely done, with greenery and pool furniture, all-glass south wall, and adjoining sundeck. **Rates (CP):** Peak (May 29–Sept 15) $68 S; $72 D; $90–$110 effic. Extra person $4. Children under age 12 stay free. Lower rates off-season. Parking: Outdoor, free. AE, CB, DC, DISC, MC, V.

Best Western El Rey Inn
80 S Main St, 84720; tel 801/586-6518 or toll free 800/586-6518; fax 801/586-7257. Closest accommodations to Shakespearean Festival; short walking distance to Southern Utah University. Two-story stone fireplace in lobby. **Rooms:** 75 rms, stes, and effic. CI 2pm/CO 11am. Nonsmoking rms avail. Large, elegantly furnished rooms look out at pool and stately pine trees. Family units and honeymoon suite available. **Amenities:** A/C, cable TV, refrig, dataport. Some units w/terraces. Microwave. **Services:** Car-rental desk, babysitting. Coffee and hot chocolate available all day. **Facilities:** 100 1 restaurant, games rm, sauna, whirlpool. **Rates (CP):** Peak (Mem Day–Labor Day) $56–$79 S; $60–$79 D; $90–$125 ste; $80–$115 effic. Extra person $4. Children under age 18 stay free. Lower rates off-season. Parking: Outdoor, free. Ski and Shakespearean Festival packages avail. AE, CB, DC, DISC, EC, ER, JCB, MC, V.

Quality Inn City Center
18 S Main St, 84720; tel 801/586-2433 or toll free 800/228-5150; fax 801/586-7257. Attractive, modern three-story motel just one block from the university. **Rooms:** 50 rms. CI 2pm/CO 11am. Nonsmoking rms avail. Rooms have a king or two queen beds, cherry wood furniture. Some have balconies that overlook pool; others have view of mountains or city. **Amenities:** A/C, cable TV, refrig, dataport. Some units w/terraces. Microwave. **Services:** Babysitting. **Facilities:** 25 1 restaurant, sauna, whirlpool. **Rates (CP):** Peak (Mem Day–Labor Day) $59–$78 S; $65–$78 D. Extra person $4. Children under age 18 stay free. Lower rates off-season. Parking: Outdoor, free. AE, CB, DC, DISC, JCB, MC, V.

RESTAURANT

Sulli's Steakhouse
301 S Main St; tel 801/586-6761. Downtown. **American/Steak.** Situated in the busy downtown area, Sulli's has two seating areas—a country-style dining room in front and a more rustic one in back. Menu staples are prime rib, steak, and seafood. **FYI:** Reservations accepted. Children's menu. No smoking. **Open:** Daily 6am–10pm. **Prices:** Main courses $6–$16. AE, DISC, MC, V.

ATTRACTIONS

Cedar Breaks National Monument
UT 148; tel 801/586-9451. At more than 10,000 feet elevation, it's always cool at Cedar Breaks. The visitor center, open daily from June to Labor Day, displays exhibits on the geology, flora, and fauna of the area. Rangers offer guided hikes as well as nightly campfire talks at the campground and talks on the area's geology. Activities include hiking and wildlife watching—mule deer, marmots, Clark's nutcracker, swallows, blue grouse, and both golden and bald eagles. The Wildflowers of Cedar Breaks is a wildflower show held in summer with mountain bluebells, spring beauty, beardtongue, and fleabane early in the season; later columbine, larkspur, Indian paintbrush, wild roses, and other varieties bloom. **Open:** Visitors center, daily 8am–5pm. **$**

Dixie National Forest
UT 14 or I-15; tel 801/865-3200. Hiking, biking, and fishing are available in this forest to the north of St George operated by the Bureau of Land Management. There are 200 miles of trails for hiking and plenty of small lakes and hidden streams for fishing. The old mining and logging roads are used for biking and four-wheel exploring. Rangers answer questions, recommend trails, and supply backcountry permits. For more information contact the Dixie National Forest's Pine Valley Ranger District office, 345 E Riverside Dr, St George, UT 84770 (tel 801/652-3100); or the BLM's Dixie Resource Area office, 225 N Bluff St, St George, UT 84770 (tel 801/673-4654). **Open:** Daily 24 hours. **Free**

Iron Mission State Park
585 N Main St; tel 801/586-9290. Founded by Mormon pioneers in search of much-needed iron in 1851, the small blast furnace closed seven years later in the face of hardships posed by Native Americans, floods, heavy freezes, and impending starvation. The park contains picnic grounds plus a museum featuring a horse-drawn vehicle collection, including a bullet-scarred overland stagecoach from Butch Cassidy's era. Also on display here are more than 500 Indian artifacts once used by the Paiutes. **Open:** Peak (June–Aug) daily 9am–7pm. Reduced hours off-season. **$**

Dinosaur National Monument

See Colorado listings

Escalante

Called Potato Valley when it was settled in 1875—for the wild potatoes growing in the area—Escalante today is a base camp for hiking, fishing, and other outdoor recreation on nearby public lands. **Information:** Garfield County Tourism Office, 55 S Main St, Panguitch 84074 (tel 801/676-8826 or 800/444-6689).

MOTELS

Circle D Motel

475 W Main St, PO Box 305, 84726; tel 801/826-4297; fax 801/826-4402. Basic motel in a long building. **Rooms:** 29 rms and stes. CI 2pm/CO 11am. Nonsmoking rms avail. Newer units have extra-long double beds. Four large units have two queen beds. **Amenities:** A/C, cable TV. **Services:** **Facilities:** **Rates:** Peak (Apr–Oct) $30 S; $35 D; $50 ste. Extra person $5. Lower rates off-season. Parking: Outdoor, free. AE, MC, V.

Prospector Inn

380 W Main St, PO Box 93, 84726; tel 801/826-4653; fax 801/826-4285. You can't miss this distinctive two-story motel with its vertically set red brick and metal roof. **Rooms:** 51 rms. CI open/CO 11am. Nonsmoking rms avail. Rooms are particularly quiet and spacious and decorated with framed photos of the area. **Amenities:** A/C, cable TV, dataport. **Services:** Car-rental desk. Free morning coffee in lobby. **Facilities:** 80 1 restaurant (lunch and dinner only; *see* "Restaurants" below), 1 bar. Jeep rentals; tours of Anasazi cliff dwellings; trail rides. **Rates:** Peak (Apr–Dec) $45 S; $50 D. Extra person $5. Children under age 12 stay free. Lower rates off-season. Parking: Outdoor, free. AE, MC, V.

RESTAURANTS

Cowboy Blues Diner

530 W Main St; tel 801/826-4251. Downtown on UT 12. **American/Mexican.** This down-home, folksy eatery, which features an old-style juke box, specializes in southwestern foods. It is known especially for its chile verde. Also popular are the hamburgers, roast beef sandwich, and grilled chicken sandwich. An all-you-can-eat salad bar is also available for just $5. Country music on summer weekends. **FYI:** Reservations not accepted. Singer. No liquor license. No smoking. **Open:** Peak (Mar–Nov) daily 6am–10pm. **Prices:** Main courses $7–$14. DISC, MC, V.

Prospector Restaurant

In Prospector Inn, 380 W Main St; tel 801/826-4653. W side of Escalante on UT 12. **American/Steak.** This large log and knotty pine restaurant topped with a red roof has an interior of high arched ceilings with huge beams and antler wall mountings. The windows frame the view of Escalante Canyon. The menu offers hamburgers, sandwiches, steaks, prime rib, and trout, plus bread and rolls made fresh daily. **FYI:** Reservations accepted. Children's menu. No smoking. **Open:** Peak (May–Nov) lunch daily 11:30am–1:30pm; dinner daily 4–10pm. **Prices:** Main courses $7–$9. AE, MC, V.

Flaming Gorge National Recreation Area

Tucked away in the far northeast corner of Utah and stretching up into Wyoming, Flaming Gorge National Recreation Area features a huge, gorgeous manmade lake that has become one of the prime fishing and boating destinations of the region. Named by Maj John Wesley Powell during his exploration of the Green and Colorado Rivers in 1869, Flaming Gorge has a rugged, wild beauty that comes alive when the rising or setting sun paints the red rocks around the lake with a fiery, brilliant palette. It is a land of clear blue water, colorful rocks, tall cliffs, and dark forests, where the summer sun is hot and the winter wind is cold.

Visitors will find some of the best fishing in the West, well over 100 miles of hiking and mountain biking trails, and hundreds of camp and picnic sites. Out on the water is everything from kayaks and canoes to personal watercraft, ski and fishing boats, pontoons, and gigantic houseboats. Other activities available include horseback riding and swimming in summer, and ice fishing, cross-country skiing, and snowmobiling in winter. For more information contact the District Ranger, Flaming Gorge National Recreation Area, USDA Forest Service, Box 279, Manila, UT 84046 (tel 801/784-3445).

Glen Canyon National Recreation Area

See Page in Arizona

Green River

A mail relay station when it was founded in 1878, Green River is a popular starting point for raft and canoe trips. As an agricultural center, it's the place to come in late summer to buy watermelons. **Information:** Green River Information Center, 885 E Main St, Green River 84525 (tel 801/564-3526).

MOTELS

Best Western River Terrace

880 E Main St, PO Box 420, 84525; tel 801/564-3401 or toll free 800/528-1234; fax 801/564-3403. Exits 158 and 162 off US 70. This three-story, well-maintained motel has a quiet location on the banks of the Green River at the east end of town. A spacious lawn leads down to the river. **Rooms:** 51 rms. CI 2pm/CO 11am. Nonsmoking rms avail. Rooms are beautifully decorated and comfortable, with views of the nearby river. **Amenities:** A/C, cable TV w/movies. Some units w/terraces. **Services:** **Facilities:** 1

restaurant, whirlpool. Restaurant next door gives 10% discount with motel key. **Rates (CP):** Peak (May–Oct 15) $70–$98 S or D. Extra person $2. Lower rates off-season. Parking: Outdoor, free. AE, CB, DC, DISC, MC, V.

Budget Host Bookcliff Lodge
395 E Main St, PO Box 545, 84525; tel 801/564-3406 or toll free 800/493-4699; fax 801/564-8359. Off I-70 Business Loop. Older building on large lot with lots of grassy areas where children can play. **Rooms:** 78 rms. CI 2pm/CO 11am. Nonsmoking rms avail. Rooms overlook grassy areas, flower beds, and pool. Large comfortable chair. **Amenities:** A/C, cable TV. **Services:** **Facilities:** 1 restaurant. **Rates:** Peak (May–Sept) $38–$50 S; $50–$80 D. Extra person $5. Lower rates off-season. Parking: Outdoor, free. AE, CB, DC, DISC, MC, V.

RESTAURANT

Lemieux Cafe & Lounge
135 Main St; tel 801/584-9698. ½ block E of city park. **American.** This partially self-serve cafe—great for families—offers home-cooking to eat in or take to go. At breakfast, patrons help themselves to juice and coffee while waiting for bacon and eggs or hot cakes; lunch and dinner includes sandwiches, pizza, chicken, pork chops, steak, and seafood. The lounge, which is totally separate from the cafe, offers beer and food and has pool tables. **FYI:** Reservations not accepted. No liquor license. No smoking. **Open:** Peak (May 15–Oct) daily 5am–10pm. **Prices:** Main courses $7–$12. No CC.

Heber City

Heber City, the tiny seat of Wasatch County in north-central Utah, was founded in 1859 by 11 determined men who, when confronted by a snow slide on their way to settle Heber Valley, simply dismantled their wagons, carried them piece by piece through the snow, and reassembled them to continue their trek. Today the town is a base for hunting, fishing, and other outdoor activities. **Information:** Heber Valley Chamber of Commerce, 475 N Main St, PO Box 427, Heber City 80432 (tel 801/654-3666).

MOTELS

Danish Viking Lodge
989 S Main St, 84032 (Downtown); tel 801/654-2202 or toll free 800/544-4066; fax 801/654-2770. One of Heber's most popular motels boasts European-style architecture. A good choice for families. Full renovation planned for 1997. **Rooms:** 34 rms, stes, and effic. CI open/CO 11am. Nonsmoking rms avail. Doors to the comfortable rooms are beautifully painted in individual floral designs. Most rooms overlook playground. **Amenities:** A/C, cable TV w/movies, refrig, dataport, voice mail. Some units w/terraces, 1 w/whirlpool. **Services:** Masseur. **Facilities:** Games rm, sauna, whirlpool, washer/dryer. Large, well-equipped playground. **Rates:** Peak (Dec–Mar/May 15–Sept) $40–$49 S; $50–$65 D; $55–$200 ste; $75–$95 effic. Extra person $10. Children under age 18 stay free. Lower rates off-season. Parking: Outdoor, free. Ski and snowmobiling packages available. Special rates for stays over three days when Sunday is included. AE, DC, DISC, MC, V.

Swiss Alps Inn
167 S Main St, 84032 (Downtown); tel 801/654-0722. On US 40; exit 148 off I-80. Just 15 minutes from Park City, this alpine chalet–style motel is great for families and anyone seeking outdoor recreation in any season. Rooms have views of Mount Timpanogos and surrounding Wasatch Mountains. **Rooms:** 14 rms and stes. CI open/CO noon. Nonsmoking rms avail. **Amenities:** A/C, cable TV. Some units have refrigerators. **Services:** Free coffee in small lobby. **Facilities:** Basketball, sauna, whirlpool. Playground adjoins large pool with slide. **Rates:** Peak (Mem–Labor Day) $49 S or D; $69 ste. Extra person $5. Lower rates off-season. Parking: Outdoor, free. AE, DC, DISC, MC, V.

RESORT

Homestead
700 N Homestead Dr, PO Box 99, Midway, 84049; tel 801/654-1102 or toll free 800/327-7220; fax 801/654-5087. 40 acres. This lovely resort tucked away on the east side of the Wasatch Mountains is a perfect spot for a retreat from the hustle and bustle of the city. The Virginia House dates back to 1886, when natural mineral springs were discovered in the area, and the springs are still used for medicinal purposes. The atrium, filled with luscious green plants, is a great place to relax after a day of hiking, riding, or skiing. **Rooms:** 122 rms, stes, and effic. CI 3pm/CO 11am. Nonsmoking rms avail. Rooms have great view of the beautifully manicured grounds; each is individually decorated in themes ranging from New England to Southwest to classic traditional. **Amenities:** A/C, cable TV w/movies. All units w/terraces, some w/fireplaces, some w/whirlpools. **Services:** Babysitting. Complimentary homemade fudge. **Facilities:** 18 2 restaurants, 2 bars (1 w/entertainment), basketball, volleyball, games rm, lawn games, sauna, whirlpool. Mineral baths; buggy or sleigh rides; snowmobiling. **Rates (BB):** $85–$129 S or D; $155–$225 ste; $210–$400 effic. Children under age 12 stay free. Min stay special events. Parking: Outdoor, free. Variety of sports/activity packages avail. AE, CB, DC, DISC, JCB, MC, V.

ATTRACTIONS

Heber Valley Historic Railroad
450 S 600 West; tel 801/654-5601. For 70 years this train, affectionately known "The Heber Creeper," carried people, livestock, and general freight up and down Provo Canyon. But in the late 1960s, the trains stopped running; the

automobile and truck had usurped its function. Then, in 1971, the first excursion train rolled out of Heber City. The diversity of the landscape on this short trip is unparalleled. On its hour-and-a-half run, the train passes through a rich, lush valley, along the shore of a fair-sized lake, and between towering canyon walls before reaching Vivian Park. After a half-hour stay there, the engine starts the slow haul back up the 2% grade out of the canyon. Special excursions are scheduled periodically throughout the year, such as fall foliage tours and the Santa Claus Express. **Open:** Peak (July–Sept) 8:30am–4pm. Reduced hours off-season. **$$$$**

Strawberry Reservoir
US 40; tel 801/548-2321. Located 21 mi SE of Heber City in the eastern portion of the Uinta National Forest. The reservoir and surrounding area offers Utah's premier trout fishing, boating, hiking, camping, and mountain biking opportunities. In winter, it is used for cross-country skiing, ice fishing, and snowmobiling. Its four marinas provide restrooms, convenience stores, boat and slip rentals, gas, and guide service, plus dry boat storage and deep moorage rentals. **Open:** May–Oct, daily sunrise–sunset. **Free**

Jordanelle State Park
711 UT 319; tel 801/649-9540. Approximately 10 mi from Heber City on UT 40. The Perimeter Trail connects the highly developed Hailstone Recreation Site to the more primitive Rock Cliff. Hailstone's camping and picnicking areas face the widest part of the reservoir, which is used for speed boats, water skiing, and jet skiing. Above Hailstone is a wakeless water area, used for sailboats and quiet fishing. The 27 miles of trails that encircle the reservoir and connect to other trails in the region are open to hikers, joggers, mountain bikers, horseback riders, and cross-country skiers. The exhibit room in the visitor center at Hailstone presents an overview of human history in the area. **Open:** Peak (June–Aug) daily 6am–10pm. Reduced hours off-season. **$$**

Huntsville

RESTAURANTS

Jackson Fork Inn
7345 E 900 South; tel 801/745-0051. 9 mi E of Ogden on UT 39. **Continental.** This is a quaint country inn in a renovated dairy barn, with lodging upstairs. The menu features filet mignon, T-bone, prime rib, chicken, seafood, and the ever-popular vegetable chicken fettuccine. Mud pie is the preferred dessert. **FYI:** Reservations accepted. No smoking. **Open:** Peak (Mem Day–Labor Day) dinner Mon–Sat 5–9:30pm; brunch Sat–Sun 9am–2pm. **Prices:** Main courses $10–$13. AE, DISC, MC, V.

Shooting Star Saloon
7340 E 200 South; tel 801/745-2002. Downtown on UT 29. **Burgers.** A visit to the Shooting Star is like stepping back into the old west—the saloon, after all, dates back to 1879. It even retains the original bar and cash register. Dollar bills cover the ceiling, and you could spend hours reading the graffiti in the bathrooms (really). There are many burgers to choose from; the specialty is the "Star Burger," with two beef patties, Polish knockwurst, cheese, and all the trimmings. Also on the menu are sandwiches and other typical bar fare. **FYI:** Reservations accepted. Beer only. **Open:** Daily noon–10pm. **Prices:** Main courses $4–$5. No CC.

Hurricane

See Zion National Park

Kanab

Surrounded by rugged red cliffs and other classic western scenery, Kanab has been popular with movie makers since 1927. The pretty town lies near the Arizona border and is close to both Lake Powell and Grand Canyon. Its name comes from the Paiute Indian word for willow, which grew along Kanab Creek. **Information:** Kanab Area Chamber of Commerce, 41 S 100 East, PO Box 369, Kanab 84741 (tel 801/644-5033).

MOTELS

Best Western Red Hills
125 W Center St, 84741; tel 801/644-2675 or toll free 800/830-2675; fax 801/644-5919. Comfortable two-story red rock motel located downtown. **Rooms:** 72 rms and stes. CI 3pm/CO 11am. Nonsmoking rms avail. Extra-large rooms; some overlook pool. Upstairs northeast facing rooms have good view of coral hills. **Amenities:** A/C, cable TV. Some units w/terraces. Some rooms have refrigerators. **Services:** 24-hour front desk. Coffee and cocoa in lobby until 11am. **Facilities:** 200 Whirlpool, washer/dryer. Covered picnic area near pool. **Rates:** Peak (May 15–Oct) $76 S or D; $100–$110 ste. Extra person $5. Lower rates off-season. Parking: Outdoor, free. AE, CB, DC, DISC, MC, V.

Holiday Inn Express
815 E US 89, 84741; tel 801/644-8888 or toll free 800/574-4061; fax 801/644-8880. 1 mi E of downtown. This new building of Spanish architecture is attractively framed by coral cliffs. Adjacent to majestic Coral Cliffs Golf Course. **Rooms:** 17 rms and stes. CI 2pm/CO 11am. Nonsmoking rms avail. Rooms have great views of valley or coral cliffs. **Amenities:** A/C, cable TV, dataport. **Services:** Car-rental desk. Fax service. **Facilities:** 75 Whirlpool. 10% discount for golf; one free golf pass per room. Spacious "great room" with large-screen TV. **Rates (CP):** Peak (May 16–Oct) $49–$79 S or D; $75–$125 ste. Extra person $6. Children under age 18 stay free. Lower rates off-season. Parking: Outdoor, free. AE, DC, DISC, MC, V.

Parry Lodge
89 E Center St, 84741; tel 801/644-2601 or toll free 800/748-4104; fax 801/644-2605. This historic white colonial-style building has long been a place for movie actors to stay while filming in the region. Many of their autographed photos are displayed in the public areas. **Rooms:** 89 rms and effic. CI 11am/CO 11am. Nonsmoking rms avail. Wide variety of rooms available, including 12 two-bedroom units and an efficiency. Above each door of the hotel's original guestrooms is the name of a movie star who stayed there. **Amenities:** A/C, cable TV w/movies. Some units w/whirlpools. **Services:** Pet fee $5. **Facilities:** 2 restaurants (*see* "Restaurants" below), washer/dryer. **Rates:** Peak (May–Oct) $47–$57 S; $56–$65 D; $73 effic. Extra person $6. Children under age 14 stay free. Min stay special events. Lower rates off-season. Parking: Outdoor, free. AE, DISC, MC, V.

Shilo Inn
296 W 100 North, 84741; tel 801/644-2562 or toll free 800/222-2244; fax 801/644-5333. North edge of town on US 89. Attractive modern motel with southwestern flair, offering all mini-suites. **Rooms:** 119 rms, stes, and effic. CI 2pm/CO noon. Nonsmoking rms avail. All units are spacious and attractively furnished. Many rooms overlook pool, others red rock cliffs. **Amenities:** A/C, cable TV w/movies, refrig. Microwave. **Services:** Free *USA Today*. Pet fee $6. **Facilities:** 100 Whirlpool, washer/dryer. **Rates (CP):** Peak (May–Oct) $86–$102 S; $98–$105 D; $105–$144 ste; $105–$144 effic. Extra person $6. Lower rates off-season. Parking: Outdoor, free. AE, CB, DC, DISC, MC, V.

RESTAURANTS

Houston's Trail's End Restaurant & Mobile Catering
32 E Center St; tel 801/644-2488. **Regional American/Barbecue.** This restaurant combines good old western hospitality with good food. The decor is strictly western, with knotty pine and wallpaper walls and pictures of gunslingers and cowboys and Indians. The waitresses wear sidearms, and the salad bar is in a covered wagon. Specialties include chicken fried steak, shrimp, and cream gravy. Besides a variety of beef offerings there are soups and salads. **FYI:** Reservations not accepted. Children's menu. No liquor license. No smoking. **Open:** Peak (Apr–Oct) daily 6am–10pm. Closed Jan–Feb. **Prices:** Main courses $6–$13. AE, DISC, MC, V. VP

Parry Lodge
89 E Center St; tel 801/644-2601. UT 89, S of business district. **American.** Elegant yet cozy restaurant in a historic colonial-style building, the Parry has been the choice of Hollywood types and tourists since 1929. Stars who dined here while filming in the area include John Wayne, Charlton Heston, and Barbara Stanwyck—their photos and many others are on the walls. Home-style cooking means prime rib, chicken and dumplings, poached salmon, trout, and breaded veal. Box lunches available. **FYI:** Reservations accepted. Children's menu. Beer and wine only. No smoking. **Open:** Peak (May 31–Sept 1) breakfast daily 7am–noon; lunch daily 11:30am–3pm; dinner daily 6–10pm. Closed Nov–Mar. **Prices:** Main courses $8–$17. AE, DISC, MC, V.

Rose's Country Inn
625 E 300 South; tel 801/644-8411. UT 89 on SE edge of town. **American.** On the outskirts of Kanab, this simple restaurant has a coffee shop on one side and a red-carpeted dining room on the other that caters to parties. It specializes in good home-cooking, with everything made from scratch, from the french fries to the Italian sauces. German and domestic beer available. **FYI:** Reservations accepted. Children's menu. Beer only. No smoking. **Open:** Peak (May–Oct) daily 7am–10pm. **Prices:** Main courses $6–$13. V.

The Wok Inn
86 S 200 West; tel 801/644-5400. 1 block W of US 89. **Chinese.** Located in a century-old building, the owners have added many Chinese furnishings—a rickshaw, parasols, fans, and hanging lamps—to camouflage the western look. Exotic and delicious Hunan and Szechuan meals feature beef, chicken, shrimp, and lobster. A "twilight special" is offered 3–6pm daily for $4.95. Free delivery to Kanab motels with a minimum purchase of $15. **FYI:** Reservations recommended. Children's menu. No smoking. **Open:** Peak (Apr–Oct) Mon–Fri 11:30am–10pm, Sat–Sun 3–10pm. **Prices:** Main courses $6–$16. AE, DISC, MC, V. VP

Lake Powell

See Lake Powell in Arizona

Loa

Tiny Loa, in south-central Utah, was named for Mauna Loa in Hawaii by a Mormon missionary who was reminded of the volcano when he saw a nearby mountain. The area is popular for fishing, hunting, hiking, and other outdoor recreation. **Information:** Panoramaland Travel Region, PO Box 820, Richfield 84701 (tel 801/896-9222 or 800/748-4361).

INN

Road Creek Inn
90 S Main St, PO Box 310, 84747; tel 801/836-2485 or toll free 800/388-7688. On UT 24. 2,100 acres. This two-story historic inn is beautifully appointed and elegantly furnished, and there's a grand piano on the mezzanine. **Rooms:** 14 rms, stes, and effic. CI open/CO 11am. No smoking. Each room is individually decorated with antiques and period furniture; TVs are hidden away in armoires. Some rooms have poster

beds. **Amenities:** A/C, cable TV w/movies. **Services:** Social director, babysitting. **Facilities:** 1 restaurant (bkfst and dinner only), games rm, spa, sauna, whirlpool, guest lounge. Sunken hot tub is particularly large and beautifully tiled. Private trout fishing nearby. **Rates (BB):** Peak (Apr–Sept) $65 S; $75 D; $98 ste; $250 effic. Extra person $6. Lower rates off-season. Parking: Outdoor, free. Seasonal fishing and hunting packages avail. AE, DISC, MC, V.

Logan

Home of Utah State University, this small city is a good base for year-round outdoor recreation in the surrounding mountains. The Festival of the American West, a historical pageant featuring medicine man shows and square dancing, is held annually from late July through early August. **Information:** Bridgerland Travel Region & Cache County Chamber of Commerce, 160 N Main St, Logan 84321 (tel 801/752-2161 or 800/882-4433).

MOTEL

Best Western Baugh Motel

153 S Main St, 84321 (Downtown); tel 801/752-5220 or toll free 800/462-4154; fax 801/752-3251. This red brick building with white trim and a red tile roof is attractively landscaped with large shade trees, grass, and flowers. The lobby boasts a beautiful mountain view. **Rooms:** 78 rms and stes. CI 2pm/CO noon. Nonsmoking rms avail. Spacious rooms are tastefully furnished with king or queen beds; pillows are part down and very soft. **Amenities:** A/C, cable TV w/movies, dataport, VCR, CD/tape player. Some units w/fireplaces, some w/whirlpools. **Services:** Babysitting. Movies available to rent. Free beverages in lobby. **Facilities:** 1 restaurant. Free passes to city recreational center a half-block away, with exercise machines, racquetball, and basketball. Fishing stream and small fishing pool for kids. **Rates:** Peak (Apr–Sept) $44–$84 S; $48–$84 D; $74–$78 ste. Extra person $4. Children under age 12 stay free. Lower rates off-season. Parking: Outdoor, free. AE, DC, DISC, MC, V.

INNS

Alta Manor Suites

45 E 500 North, 84321; tel 801/752-0808; fax 801/752-2445. 1 mi W of Utah State University. Elegant, two-story inn with old English Tudor charm. Lobby is in an old church nearby. **Rooms:** 8 stes. CI 2pm/CO 11am. No smoking. Large rooms are beautifully decorated with Queen Anne reproductions. Suites have full kitchens and pull-out couches. **Amenities:** A/C, cable TV, refrig, dataport. 1 unit w/terrace, all w/fireplaces, all w/whirlpools. Variety of gourmet coffees and teas available in each room. **Services:** **Facilities:** Guest lounge. **Rates (CP):** $75–$85 ste. Parking: Outdoor, free. Discount of $20 for stays of seven days or longer. AE, DC, DISC, MC, V.

Center Street Bed & Breakfast

169 E Center St, 84321 (Downtown); tel 801/752-3443. Located in a Victorian mansion listed on the National Register of Historic Places. The parlor boasts the original staircase and inlaid walnut floor and a ceiling covered with lovely murals. The music rooms and dining room are decorated with antiques and Renaissance paintings. Three additional buildings house individual theme-oriented rooms and suites. **Rooms:** 18 rms and stes (2 w/shared bath). CI 3pm/CO 11am. No smoking. All rooms are unusual and delightfully decorated in keeping with some theme. The Space Odyssey has exotic smoke and sound effects to convey the feeling of space travel. The Empire Room sports a large hot tub with faux-marble steps surrounding it and a four-poster bed with canopy. **Amenities:** Cable TV w/movies, VCR. No A/C. Some units w/terraces, some w/fireplaces, some w/whirlpools. One suite has a refrigerator and microwave. Some units have swamp coolers. **Services:** Continental breakfast delivered to room in basket. **Facilities:** Sauna, whirlpool, guest lounge. Indoor pool available only to guests in the three larger suites. **Rates (CP):** $55 S or D w/shared bath, $85–$110 S or D w/private bath; $130–$180 ste. Children under age 1 stay free. Higher rates for special events/hols. Parking: Outdoor, free. AE, DISC, MC, V.

LODGE

Beaver Creek Lodge

11808 N US 89, PO Box 263, 84323; tel 801/753-1076. 25 mi E of downtown. Located in beautiful Logan Canyon not far from Beaver Mountain Ski Resort, this lovely log and stone structure has a casual atmosphere. The lobby, with vaulted ceiling, features a large-screen TV and comfortable log furniture. Terrific view of valley and surrounding mountains. **Rooms:** 11 rms and stes. CI 3pm/CO 11am. No smoking. Rooms are modest but adequate and have that great view. Log furniture with Navajo-design coverings. **Amenities:** Satel TV w/movies, VCR. No A/C or phone. All units w/terraces, some w/fireplaces, all w/whirlpools. **Services:** Breakfast and dinner can be arranged. Snowmobiling (rentals available); guided tours available. **Facilities:** Whirlpool. **Rates:** Peak (Dec–Apr/June–Sept) $59–$79 S; $75–$85 D; $115–$125 ste. Extra person $5. Children under age 2 stay free. Lower rates off-season. Parking: Outdoor, free. Ski packages avail. MC, V.

RESTAURANTS

★ Angie's Restaurant

690 N Main St; tel 801/752-9252. 6 blocks N of Tabernacle Sq. **American/Coffeehouse.** A popular cafe in a modern building with windows all around. For especially fast service, sit at the counter. Breakfast is served all day. The freshly

prepared food includes a large variety of burgers, sandwiches, and salads, with sundaes for dessert. Dinner options include chicken, turkey, steak, seafood, and prime rib. **FYI:** Reservations accepted. No liquor license. No smoking. **Open:** Sun–Thurs 6am–10pm, Fri–Sat 6am–11pm. **Prices:** Main courses $6–$10. AE, DISC, MC, V.

★ The Bluebird
19 N Main St (Downtown); tel 801/752-3155. **American.** The Bluebird is a landmark in Logan, starting out as a candy, ice cream, and soda fountain in 1914, then adding some lunch items, moving to its present location in 1923, and expanding its menu to include dinner. Today it continues to offer good food along with fountain treats. Menu items include fresh salads, sandwiches, steak, fish, and chicken. The restaurant has its original counter, tables and chairs, and tile floor. **FYI:** Reservations recommended. Children's menu. No liquor license. No smoking. **Open:** Daily 11am–9pm. **Prices:** Main courses $6–$12. AE, CB, DC, DISC, MC, V.

Copper Mill Restaurant
In The Emporium Mini-Mall, 55 N Main St (Downtown); tel 801/752-0647. **American/Steak.** Located in the former JC Penney store on the third floor of the 1940s Emporium, the Copper Mill offers great views of the historic Logan Tabernacle across the street. Light and airy, with brick floors and walls, the dining room is decorated with pioneer relics such as an old washing machine, plus copper wall hangings and stained glass. The menu features great steaks, pasta, seafood, and turtle cake. A special treat: the freshly baked rolls come with raspberry preserves. **FYI:** Reservations recommended. Children's menu. Beer and wine only. No smoking. **Open:** Mon–Thurs 11am–9:30pm, Fri–Sat 11am–10:30pm. **Prices:** Main courses $9–$12. AE, CB, DC, DISC, MC, V.

Grapevine
129 N 100 East (Downtown); tel 801/752-1977. 1 block E of Main St. **Continental.** The Grapevine is situated in a pristine gray and white Victorian-style house with a bright, cheery atmosphere. Some of the paintings that decorate the walls are by local artists. Entrees include baked chicken pomegranate, Minnesota-style duck, and peppercorn steak, plus fresh seafood, game, and Italian offerings. Bread is baked on premises daily. Patio dining in summer. **FYI:** Reservations recommended. No smoking. **Open:** Wed–Sat 5:30–10pm. Closed 2 weeks at end of summer. **Prices:** Main courses $13–$29. AE, DISC, MC, V.

(\$) Kate's Kitchen
71½ 1200 South; tel 801/753-5733. Just E of US 89. **American/Barbecue.** A cozy dining room with pink table decor and basketsful of artificial flowers on the walls, Kate's offers home-cooking served family style. Entrees include pot roast, country fried steak, country-style barbecued ribs, and roast chicken. Accompaniments usually include mashed potatoes and gravy; for dessert there's homemade ice cream. Children can eat for $1 on their birthday. **FYI:** Reservations accepted. Children's menu. No liquor license. No smoking. **Open:** Tues–Sat 4–10pm. **Prices:** Main courses $9–$11. MC, V.

Old Grist Mill Bread Co
78 E 400 North; tel 801/753-6463. 4 blocks N and 1 block E of jct Center/Main Sts. **Deli.** This bakery, which produces about a half-dozen types of bread and bagels, also prepares take-out sandwiches with a variety of deli meats, cheeses, and cream cheese spreads. Breads are of the healthy variety, like golden honey wheat and whole-wheat sourdough. More exotic varieties, including cinnamon-raisin-walnut wheat and cranberry-pecan white, are sometimes available. Bread and bagels are available from 7am. **FYI:** Reservations not accepted. No liquor license. No smoking. **Open:** Mon–Sat 10:30am–7pm. **Prices:** Main courses $3–$4. No CC.

ATTRACTIONS

Roanld V Jensen Living Historical Farm
4025 S US 89/91; tel 801/245-4064. 6 mi SW of Logan. This authentic 1917 dairy farm is a 120-acre interpretive center operated by Utah State University graduate students. Guides in period costume discuss life on the farm and explain the farm equipment and implements. There are usually about two special events planned each month, which might include a turn-of-the-century wedding, sheep shearing, quilting bee, hay threshing, or an old-fashioned Christmas celebration complete with horse-drawn sleigh and caroling; call for schedule. **Open:** June–Aug, Tues–Sat 10am–4pm. **$$**

Cache County Daughters of Utah Pioneers
160 N Main St; tel 801/752-5139. Housed in the same building as the information center, this small museum displays pioneer artifacts from 1859 to 1899. Guns, musical instruments (including the first organ used in the Mormon Tabernacle), Mormon-style sofas, clothing, and kitchen items are on view, along with several pieces of furniture made by Brigham Young for his daughter Luna Young Thatcher, who lived in Logan. Also on display are dresses made by Mary Ann Weston Maugham, the area's first white woman settler, who arrived in 1859. **Open:** June–Aug, Mon–Fri 10am–4pm. **Free**

Midway

See Heber City

Moab

See also Arches National Park, Canyonlands National Park

Gateway to both Arches and Canyonlands National Parks, Moab is also a major mountain biking, rafting, and jeeping destination. With its dramatic location in a green valley among striking red sandstone cliffs, Moab has lured Hollywood film makers over the years. Hit movies shot in the area have included *The Comancheros, The Greatest Story Ever Told,* and *Indiana Jones and the Last Crusade.* **Information:** Grand County Travel Council, PO Box 550, Moab 84532 (tel 801/259-8825 or 800/635-MOAB).

MOTELS

Best Western Canyonlands Inn

16 S Main St, PO Box 66, 84532; tel 801/259-2300 or toll free 800/528-1234; fax 801/259-2301. Modern building in the center of town has a large lobby with floor-to-ceiling windows and a fun water fountain. **Rooms:** 77 rms, stes, and effic. CI 4pm/CO 11am. Nonsmoking rms avail. Many rooms look out onto pool and patio area. TV is housed in a large armoire. **Amenities:** A/C, cable TV, refrig. 1 unit w/whirlpool. **Services:** Free coffee. **Facilities:** 35 1 restaurant (lunch and dinner only), games rm, whirlpool, playground, washer/dryer. Bicycle storage. **Rates (CP):** Peak (Mar–Oct) $89–$96 S or D; $96–$160 ste; $98–$121 effic. Extra person $8. Children under age 6 stay free. Lower rates off-season. Parking: Outdoor, free. AE, DC, DISC, MC, V.

Red Stone Inn

535 S Main St, 84532; tel 801/259-3500 or toll free 800/772-1972; fax 801/259-2717. **Rooms:** 50 rms. CI 2pm/CO 11am. Nonsmoking rms avail. **Amenities:** A/C, cable TV w/movies, refrig. **Services:** **Facilities:** Washer/dryer. **Rates:** Peak (Apr–Sept) $55 S; $60 D. Extra person $5. Children under age 3 stay free. Lower rates off-season. Parking: Outdoor, free. AE, DISC, MC, V.

Super 8 Motel

889 N Main St, 84532; tel 801/259-8868 or toll free 800/800-8000; fax 801/259-8968. On US 191 on N edge of town. Basic motel, the largest in town. **Rooms:** 146 rms and stes. CI 3:30pm/CO 11am. Nonsmoking rms avail. Rooms are spacious, many with views of surrounding red rock country. **Amenities:** A/C, cable TV. Suites have microwaves and refrigerators. **Services:** Copy machine available. **Facilities:** 1 restaurant, whirlpool, washer/dryer. Bicycle storage. **Rates:** Peak (Mar–Nov) $53–$77 S or D; $74–$108 ste. Extra person $6. Children under age 6 stay free. Lower rates off-season. Parking: Outdoor, free. AE, CB, DC, DISC, MC, V.

INNS

Lazy Lizard Int'l (Not-Just-for-Youth) Hostel

1213 S US 91, 84532; tel 801/259-6057. 1 mi S of downtown. Located behind a bowling alley and self-storage units, this hostel offers exceptionally clean, comfortable lodging at bargain rates for those willing to share. In the main building is a kitchen and living room with TV, VCR, and collection of movies. **Rooms:** 10 rms (all w/shared bath); 4 cottages/villas (4 w/shared bath). CI open/CO 11am. No smoking. Private rooms are small but serviceable; dormitory rooms have four to seven beds. There are four cabins for families. Everyone shares the bath houses. **Amenities:** A/C. No phone or TV. Main building is air conditioned but second one has only fans in rooms. **Services:** **Facilities:** Whirlpool, washer/dryer, guest lounge w/TV. Gas barbecue grill, picnic tables. Bicycle rack. **Rates:** Peak (Mar–Nov) $20 S or D w/shared bath; $25 cottage/villa w/shared bath. Extra person $4. Children under age 4 stay free. Lower rates off-season. Parking: Outdoor, free. Tent space available for $5 per person. No CC.

Pack Creek Ranch

La Sal Mountain Loop Rd, PO Box 1270, 84532; tel 801/259-5505; fax 801/259-8879. 14 mi S of downtown via US 191 and La Sal Mountain Loop Rd. 298 acres. Quiet, peaceful retreat cradled in the foothills of the La Sal Mountains. The rustic structures are old but comfortable, and the surroundings are green and welcoming. A creek runs nearby, and the lodge is surrounded by public lands. **Rooms:** 2 effic; 10 cottages/villas. CI 11am/CO 2pm. Nonsmoking rms avail. Rooms have terrific views in just about all directions. Decor is modest, with knotty pine paneling and front porches. Each unit has full kitchen. **Amenities:** Refrig. No A/C, phone, or TV. Some units w/fireplaces. **Services:** Masseur, afternoon tea served. **Facilities:** 50 1 restaurant, spa, sauna, whirlpool, guest lounge. Will prepare take-out meals. Trail rides, overnight pack trips, wilderness hiking. **Rates (BB):** Peak (Apr–Oct) $125 effic; $125 cottage/villa. Children under age 1 stay free. Lower rates off-season. Parking: Outdoor, free. Children under 12 stay for half-price. AE, MC, V.

Sunflower Hill Bed & Breakfast Inn

185 N 300 East, 84532; tel 801/259-2974; fax 801/259-2470. This lovely B&B is quiet and serene yet just three blocks from town. In a beautifully renovated, nearly century-old adobe building surrounded by lovely flower gardens and delightful paths and seating areas. Unsuitable for children under 8. **Rooms:** 11 rms and stes. CI 4pm/CO 11am. No smoking. Rooms are individually decorated in 19th-century country style, with some antiques, and stenciling and hand-painting on some walls. Some afford lovely views. **Amenities:** A/C, cable TV w/movies, bathrobes. Some units w/terraces, some w/whirlpools. **Services:** Afternoon lemonade, hot herbal teas, and other beverages available. **Facilities:** 10 Games rm, whirlpool, washer/dryer, guest lounge w/TV. Bicycle storage. **Rates (BB):** Peak (Mar–Nov 15) $70–$140 S; $95–$140 D; $110 ste. Extra person $15. Lower rates off-season. Parking: Outdoor, free. MC, V.

RESTAURANTS

Center Cafe

In Center Square Bldg, 92 E Center St; tel 801/259-4295. ½ block E of Main St. **International.** An intimate, elegant restaurant in downtown Moab, with a large picture window in front and lovely photographs, which are signed and numbered and offered for sale. Fare consists of steak, lasagna, shrimp, salmon, roast duck, and barbecued chicken, plus salads, pizzas, and pasta. Locally grown produce is used whenever possible, and breads and pastries are made fresh on premises. Nice selection of wines. **FYI:** Reservations recommended. Folk/guitar/singer. No smoking. **Open:** Daily 5:30–10pm. Closed Dec–Jan. **Prices:** Main courses $10–$22. DISC, MC, V.

Eddie McStiff's Restaurant & Brew Pub
In Western Plaza, 57 S Main St; tel 801/259-2337. Just S of Center St. **Pizza/Southwestern.** This adobe restaurant in the heart of downtown is popular with young and old alike, and very much alive with the sound of enjoyment. All three dining rooms are decorated with southwestern artifacts and items; there's a patio downstairs and a game room upstairs. The newsletter-style menu has pages of burgers, sandwiches, pizza specials, and pasta choices interspersed with cartoons. House specials include steaks, vegetarian dishes, and homemade desserts. McStiff's serves its own rootbeer as well as alcoholic beers, and offers Utah wines. **FYI:** Reservations not accepted. Children's menu. No smoking. **Open:** Peak (Apr–Oct) daily 3pm–midnight. Closed Dec 15–Feb. **Prices:** Main courses $8–$12. DISC, MC, V.

Fat City Smokehouse
36 S 100 West; tel 801/259-4302. 1 block W of Main St. **Barbecue.** Located in a 100-year-old building, this plain but comfortable restaurant is famous for its flame-grilled and smoke-pit meats, but you can also order vegetarian and "big dude" sandwiches. In summer tables are set up outside. **FYI:** Reservations not accepted. Blues/guitar. Beer only. No smoking. **Open:** Peak (Feb–Nov) daily 11am–10pm. Closed Jan 1–15. **Prices:** Main courses $8–$15. AE, MC, V.

★ Moab Diner & Ice Cream Shoppe
189 S Main St; tel 801/259-4006. Downtown. **Diner.** A typical diner, with lots of activity and friendly chatter. The owners claim to have the best green chili in Utah, and they sell sandwiches, full dinners (such as Kokopelli chicken), and "heart healthy" meals. Fresh fruit is used in many of the ice cream flavors. **FYI:** Reservations not accepted. Children's menu. No liquor license. No smoking. **Open:** Peak (Apr–Oct) daily 6am–10pm. **Prices:** Main courses $5–$16. MC, V. VP

Rio Colorado Restaurant & Bar
2 S 100 West; tel 801/259-6666. 1 block W of Main St. **Southwestern.** This large southwestern dining room features natural wood bar, counters, and table tops. Everything here is made from scratch, including the salsa, enchilada sauce, and desserts. A popular item is the Sonoran steak, seasoned with "Rio Spices" and topped with grilled onions and peppers and melted cheese. Other choices are shrimp, catfish, and vegetarian dishes. **FYI:** Reservations not accepted. Blues/reggae/rock. Children's menu. No smoking. **Open:** Mon–Sat 11:30am–10pm, Sun 10am–2pm. Closed Dec–Jan. **Prices:** Main courses $8–$14. AE, MC, V.

Monticello

So named because the terrain, much greener than many areas of southern Utah, reminded settlers of Thomas Jefferson's plantation home in Virginia, Monticello is often used as a base camp for hikers, mountain bikers, cross-country skiers, and other recreationists making trips into the nearby national forests and national parks. **Information:** San Juan County Travel Council, 117 S Main St, PO Box 490, Monticello 84535 (tel 801/587-3235 or 800/574-4FUN).

MOTELS

Best Western Wayside Inn
197 E Central St, PO Box 669, 84535; tel 801/587-2261 or toll free 800/587-2261. 2 blocks E of US 191 on US 666. Newly rebuilt modern motel off the main thoroughfare. **Rooms:** 38 rms. CI 2pm/CO 11am. Nonsmoking rms avail. Rooms are large yet cozy and overlook pool, flower beds, and lawn. **Amenities:** A/C, cable TV, dataport. **Services:** **Facilities:** Whirlpool. Picnic tables. **Rates:** Peak (May–Sept) $64–$85 S or D. Extra person $5. Children under age 12 stay free. Lower rates off-season. Parking: Outdoor, free. AE, CB, DC, DISC, MC, V.

Monticello Days Inn
549 N Main St, PO Box 759, 84535; tel 801/587-2458 or toll free 800/DAYS-INN; fax 801/587-2191. ½ mi N of jct US 191/US 666. Modern, attractive, two-story motel on north side of town. **Rooms:** 43 rms. CI 2pm/CO 11am. Nonsmoking rms avail. Some rooms have great views of the mountains. **Amenities:** A/C, cable TV w/movies. **Services:** Fax available. Free coffee 6–11am. **Facilities:** Whirlpool. **Rates (CP):** Peak (Apr–Oct) $45–$55 S; $55–$66 D. Extra person $6. Children under age 12 stay free. Lower rates off-season. Parking: Outdoor, free. AE, CB, DC, DISC, MC, V.

Monument Valley

MOTEL

Goulding's Lodge
Monument Valley Access Rd, PO Box 360001, 84536; tel 801/727-3231; fax 801/727-3344. 2 mi W of US 163. Historic lodge nestled against towering cliffs and looking toward awe-inspiring Monument Valley. John Ford and John Wayne stayed here often while filming their westerns. **Rooms:** 62 rms. CI 2pm/CO 11am. No smoking. Views of Monument Valley from balconies. **Amenities:** A/C, cable TV w/movies, refrig, VCR. All units w/terraces. **Services:** Babysitting. VCRs, movies for rent. Guided half- and full-day tours of Monument Valley available. Shuttle to nearby shopping. **Facilities:** 70 1 restaurant (*see* "Restaurants" below). Earth Spirit multimedia

shows in theater nightly. **Rates:** Peak (May–Oct) $98–$118 S or D. Extra person $6. Lower rates off-season. Parking: Outdoor, free. AE, CB, DC, DISC, EC, ER, JCB, MC, V.

RESTAURANT

Goulding's Restaurant
In Goulding's Lodge, Monument Valley Access Rd; tel 801/727-3231. 2 mi W of US 163. **Eclectic/Navajo.** Every window of this restaurant, which is nestled against a towering cliff of rock, frames a breathtaking view of the valley. In operation since 1940, it is decorated with American Indian curios and baskets and enjoys a bit of fame for its Navajo taco. In addition to native foods, diners can order lamb, beef, chicken, pork, fish, and seafood, plus soups, salads, and hot and cold sandwiches. **FYI:** Reservations not accepted. Children's menu. No liquor license. No smoking. **Open:** Peak (Apr 15–Oct 15) daily 6:30am–8:30pm. **Prices:** Main courses $10–$23. AE, CB, DC, DISC, MC, V.

Nephi

Settled in 1851, Nephi lies 38 miles south of Provo on the southern boundary of the Wasatch Front. Each July the town celebrates its western roots with the Ute Stampede, a three-day event that includes a professional rodeo. **Information:** Nephi City Hall, 153 N 100 East, Nephi 84648 (tel 801/768-7100).

MOTELS

Roberta's Cove
2250 S Main St, PO Box 268, 84648; tel 801/623-2629 or toll free 800/456-6460. Exit 222 off I-15. Two-story modern motel on south side of town. **Rooms:** 43 rms. CI 2pm/CO 11am. Nonsmoking rms avail. Rooms are attractive, clean, and modern. **Amenities:** A/C, satel TV. Some units w/whirlpools. **Services:** **Facilities:** Washer/dryer. Picnic area. **Rates:** Peak (July) $32–$45 S; $40–$55 D. Extra person $5. Children under age 5 stay free. Lower rates off-season. Parking: Outdoor, free. AE, DC, DISC, MC, V.

Safari Hotel
413 S Main St, PO Box 81, 84648; tel 801/623-1071. 3 mi NW of exit 222 off I-15. Pleasant standard motel with small rooms. **Rooms:** 28 rms. CI open/CO 11am. Nonsmoking rms avail. **Amenities:** A/C, cable TV w/movies. **Services:** **Facilities:** Outdoor fireplace with grill, picnic tables. **Rates:** Peak (May–Oct) $25–$28 S; $32–$36 D. Extra person $3. Children under age 6 stay free. Lower rates off-season. Parking: Outdoor, free. AE, MC, V.

Ogden

See also Salt Lake City

A rendezvous site for mountain men in the early 1800s, Ogden was settled about 1850 at the confluence of the Ogden and Weber Rivers. The city became a major transportation center for the West with the arrival of the transcontinental railroad in 1869. Although laid out by Mormon leader Brigham Young and settled by Mormons, the coming of the railroad and other non-Mormon influences (including the city's numerous saloons and gambling halls) set it apart from the rest of the state—much to the chagrin of church leaders. Modern Ogden serves as a base camp for winter and summer recreation in the surrounding mountains, and several parks line the Ogden River as it winds its way through the city. Weber State University is a center for cultural activities. **Information:** Ogden/Weber County Convention & Visitors Bureau, 2501 Wall Ave, Ogden 84401 (tel 801/627-8288 or 800/255-8824).

HOTELS

Best Western Ogden Park Hotel
247 24th St, 84401 (Downtown); tel 801/627-1190 or toll free 800/421-7599; fax 801/394-6312. Near Union Station. This modern red brick building is within easy walking distance of historic 25th St. The lobby has a sunken area with comfortable seating, a central planter with lovely greenery, and a beautifully landscaped inner courtyard for relaxing. Good for business travelers and tourists alike. Worth a splurge. **Rooms:** 288 rms and stes. CI 3pm/CO noon. Nonsmoking rms avail. Rooms are elegantly decorated. A two-level penthouse with loft is available. **Amenities:** A/C, cable TV w/movies, refrig, dataport. Some units w/terraces. **Services:** Car-rental desk, masseur. Complimentary cocktails and hors d'oeuvres poolside weekdays. **Facilities:** 1000 1 restaurant, 1 bar, games rm, spa, whirlpool, beauty salon, washer/dryer. Kidney-shaped pool with many tables, chairs, and live trees. State liquor store on premises. **Rates (BB):** $77 S; $87 D; $115–$180 ste. Children under age 18 stay free. Parking: Outdoor, free. AE, DC, MC, V.

Comfort Suites of Ogden
1150 W 2150 South, 84401; tel 801/621-2545 or toll free 800/228-5150; fax 801/627-4782. Near exit 346 off I-15. This attractive new hotel opened in January 1995. It's a good choice for families and business travelers. **Rooms:** 142 stes and effic. CI 2pm/CO noon. Nonsmoking rms avail. Rooms are attractively and comfortably furnished in a modern southwestern style. **Amenities:** A/C, cable TV w/movies, refrig, dataport, voice mail, bathrobes. Some units w/whirlpools. VCRs in suites. **Services:** **Facilities:** 300 1 restaurant (*see* "Restaurants" below), 1 bar, games rm, spa, whirlpool, playground, washer/

dryer. Well-equipped business center. Water slide within walking distance. **Rates (BB):** $65–$150 ste; $65–$150 effic. Extra person $5. Children under age 16 stay free. Parking: Outdoor, free. AE, CB, DC, DISC, JCB, MC, V.

MOTELS

Big Z Motel

1123 W 2100 South, 84401; tel 801/394-6632. Exit 346 off I-15. Basic motel just five minutes from downtown, near pool and water slide. Lobby is small. **Rooms:** 33 rms and effic. CI noon/CO 11am. Rooms are homey but have tiny baths. Four family units sleep up to six comfortably, with separate bedroom and complete kitchen. **Amenities:** A/C, cable TV. **Services:** **Facilities:** Washer/dryer. **Rates:** $32 S; $35–$40 D; $42 effic. Extra person $3. Children under age 10 stay free. Parking: Outdoor, free. AE, DISC, MC, V.

Holiday Inn Ogden

3306 Washington Blvd, 84401 (Downtown); tel 801/399-5671 or toll free 800/999-6841; fax 801/621-0321. Exit 344A off I-15. Unpretentious two-story motel with friendly staff. Small lobby with adjoining lounge. Renovation nearing completion. **Rooms:** 109 rms. CI 2pm/CO 11am. Nonsmoking rms avail. Rooms are not large but are clean and efficient, with both a small table and desk. Most have view of pool or mountains. **Amenities:** A/C, cable TV, dataport. **Services:** Car-rental desk. **Facilities:** 240 1 restaurant (bkfst and dinner only), 1 bar, games rm, whirlpool, washer/dryer. Olympic-size pool has abundant seating and plants. **Rates (CP):** $74 S or D. Extra person $8. Children under age 18 stay free. Parking: Outdoor, free. Priority Club members ($10 annually) receive special rates and full breakfast. AE, CB, DC, DISC, ER, JCB, MC, V.

Super 8 Motel

1508 W 2100 South, 84401; tel 801/731-7100 or toll free 800/800-8000; fax 801/731-2627. Exit 346 off I-15. Nondescript motel offering economy lodgings in quiet surroundings. **Rooms:** 60 rms. CI open/CO 11am. Nonsmoking rms avail. **Amenities:** A/C, cable TV. **Services:** Car-rental desk. Free local calls. **Facilities:** Washer/dryer. Convenience store; gas station with diesel fuel. **Rates:** Peak (Apr–Sept) $34 S; $38–$42 D. Extra person $2. Lower rates off-season. Parking: Outdoor, free. Ski packages avail. AE, CB, DC, DISC, ER, JCB, MC, V.

RESTAURANTS

ABC Mandarin

5260 S 1900 West, Roy; tel 801/776-6361. **Chinese.** Attractive and comfortable, this eatery offers sweet-and-sour shrimp, cashew chicken, Hunan-style lamb, tangerine beef, pork chops in Peking sauce, crispy duck, and many other items. **FYI:** Reservations accepted. Dulcimer. Beer only. No smoking. **Open:** Sun–Thurs 11am–9:45pm, Fri–Sat 11am–10:45pm. **Prices:** Main courses $4–$10. DISC, MC, V.

$ Berconi's Pasta House

4850 Harrison Blvd; tel 801/479-4414. **Italian/Pizza.** This cozy restaurant serves great Italian food. It's decorated in red and green, with an atrium that's a special delight in winter. All menu items—including Sicilian-style pizza, soups, salads, seafood, and pasta—are prepared individually, so don't expect speed. But the quality is worth the wait. **FYI:** Reservations accepted. Children's menu. No smoking. **Open:** Mon–Thurs 4–10pm, Fri–Sat 4–11pm, Sun 4:30–9:30pm. **Prices:** Main courses $6–$17. AE, CB, DC, DISC, MC, V.

Cactus Reds Restaurant

In Comfort Suites of Ogden, 1150 W 2150 South; tel 801/621-1560. Near exit 346 off I-15. **Southwestern.** This charming restaurant features innovative southwestern cuisine in an atmosphere to match. It's light and airy, with light wood, stained glass, and cactuses everywhere. Specialties include barbecued pork ribs, fajitas, T-bone steaks, and prime rib. The bar and lounge are quite comfortable and feature popular microbrews and wines from the mountain west. **FYI:** Reservations recommended. Children's menu. No smoking. **Open:** Peak (June–Aug) daily 6am–11pm. **Prices:** Main courses $6–$15. AE, DISC, MC, V.

Delights of Ogden

258 25th St (Historic District); tel 801/394-1111. 1 block from Convention Center. **New American/Coffeehouse.** Excellent food is the hallmark of Delights, located in a historic building with a lovely glassed-in dining area added at the rear, plus outdoor seating in warm weather. The polished hardwood floors, a mirrored wall, plenty of green plants, and attractive table decor give it an elegant yet casual atmosphere. The menu features innovative sandwiches, soups, salads, and burgers. **FYI:** Reservations accepted. Children's menu. No smoking. **Open:** Peak (May–Sept) Mon–Thurs 11am–8pm, Fri–Sat 11am–9:30pm, Sun 10am–2pm. **Prices:** Main courses $5–$17. AE, DC, MC, V.

★ The Greenery Restaurant

1875 Valley Dr; tel 801/392-1777. At mouth of Ogden Canyon. **American.** A bright, friendly, modern restaurant with a terrific view of the mountains through the seeming acres of glass. The green and white decor, augmented by wrought iron "ice cream" chairs, is refreshing. Choose from among salads, sandwiches, and tantalizing desserts. **FYI:** Reservations accepted. Children's menu. Beer and wine only. No smoking. **Open:** Mon–Thurs 11am–10pm, Fri–Sat 11am–11pm, Sun 11am–9pm. **Prices:** Main courses $7–$9. AE, DISC, MC, V.

Prairie Schooner Steak House

445 Park Blvd; tel 801/621-5511. 6 blocks N of Union Station, just off Washington Blvd. **Seafood/Steak.** An Ogden tradition for some 20 years, this steak house is a step back into Utah's colorful past. Guests dine in covered wagons in an outdoor prairie setting "under the stars." Prairie animals, such as the wolf and fox (preserved by taxidermy) are scattered about. Steak, prime rib, crab, and grilled salmon are

popular entrees. The music of the Sons of the Pioneers, Patsy Cline, and the Bar J Wranglers from Jackson Hole adds to the ambience. **FYI:** Reservations accepted. Children's menu. No smoking. **Open:** Lunch Mon–Fri 11am–2pm; dinner Mon–Thurs 5–10pm, Fri–Sat 5–11pm, Sun 4–9pm. **Prices:** Main courses $10–$27. AE, DC, DISC, MC, V.

Roosters 25th Street Brewing Co
253 25th St; tel 801/627-6171. 1 block E of Union Station. **New American.** A friendly pub atmosphere pervades this century-old building on historic 25th St, where old-style wooden tables and lots of greenery join the original brick walls and window. The menu is varied and includes burgers, pizzas, pasta, soups, salads, and sandwiches. Dinner specials might include barbecued beef, lamb chops, chicken, and Alaskan or king crab. On Sunday afternoons the three house beers plus three rotating seasonal flavors are available for just $1. And you can get "Pub Grub to Go." **FYI:** Reservations not accepted. Guitar. No smoking. **Open:** Peak (May–Sept) Mon–Thurs 11:30am–10pm, Fri–Sat 11:30am–midnight, Sun 10am–9pm. **Prices:** Main courses $6–$15. AE, CB, DC, DISC, MC, V.

Timbermine
1701 Park Blvd; tel 801/393-2155. At mouth of Ogden Canyon, NE of downtown. **American.** Located on the Ogden River parkway near Dinosaur Park, this big barnlike building with rustic cedar and old barn-wood siding has five dining rooms, one with a dance floor and stage. There's also an old mine with a lifelike prospector and other historic figures, plus a waterfall, old stove, Victrola, elk and moose heads, wagon wheels, and countless other relics of pioneer Utah. The menu features steak, prime rib, and seafood. Patio dining is a summer treat. **FYI:** Reservations accepted. Children's menu. No smoking. **Open:** Mon–Thurs 5–10pm, Fri–Sat 5–11pm, Sun 5–9pm. **Prices:** Main courses $11–$27. AE, DC, MC, V.

Union Grill
In Union Station, 2501 Wall Ave; tel 801/621-2830. At 25th St. **New American.** This attractive but informal restaurant is located in historic Union Station. Candles and fresh flowers brighten the space. Fare consists of homemade soups, sandwiches, fresh seafood, pasta, and steak, plus desserts from the Grill's own bakery. Everything is homemade and tastefully presented. **FYI:** Reservations not accepted. No smoking. **Open:** Mon–Thurs 11:30am–10pm, Fri–Sat 11:30am–10:30pm. **Prices:** Main courses $6–$13. AE, DC, DISC, MC, V.

ATTRACTIONS

Weber County Daughters of Utah Pioneer Museum and the Miles Goodyear Cabin
2148 Grant Ave; tel 801/393-4460. The 1902 Gothic-style brick Relief Society Building houses the museum, containing pioneer photographs, artifacts, and memorabilia. On display in the authentically furnished rooms are a harp once belonging to the royal family of France and brought to Utah in 1875; an 1868 handmade lounge of native pine; and a doll carriage made of native willows. **Open:** Mon–Sat 10am–5pm. **Free**

Union Station
2501 Wall Ave; tel 801/629-8444. Built in 1924 to replace the original depot that was destroyed by fire, the station now houses several museums, an art gallery, a gift shop, a theater, a visitor information center, and the Ogden/Weber Convention and Visitors Bureau. The Utah State Railroad Museum displays gas turbine locomotive designs and has an extensive HO-gauge layout that depicts the construction and geography of the 1,776-mile transcontinental route. The Browning Firearms Museum displays Browning guns from 1878 to modern weapons. The Browning-Kimball Car Collection has examples of classic cars, mostly luxury models from the early 1900s. The Myra Powell Gallery exhibits a variety of art through invitational and competitive shows. **Open:** Mon–Sat 10am–6pm. **$**

Fort Buenaventura State Park
2450 A Ave; tel 801/621-4808. A replica of an 1846 fort and trading post and exhibits depicting the mountain men and fur trade of the area back to the 1820s show what life was like in this rugged land before "civilization" arrived. Ranger-guided tours are available. The visitor center has exhibits of Native American artifacts typical of the area. Activities include canoeing, hiking, and fishing with a current license. Several traditional mountain man rendezvous are scheduled on Easter and Labor Day weekend, with music, food, and a variety of contests, including a tomahawk throw, canoe race, shooting competition, and foot races, with all competitors in pre-1840s dress. There's also a Pioneer Skills Festival on July 24th. **Open:** Apr–Nov, daily 8am–sunset. **$**

Panguitch

A base for vacationers heading to Bryce Canyon National Park and other southwestern Utah attractions. Panguitch is the Paiute word for "big fish," chosen because of the excellent fishing in nearby Panguitch Lake. **Information:** Garfield County Travel Council, 55 S Main St, Panguitch 84074 (tel 801/676-8826 or 800/444-6689).

Park City

See also Salt Lake City

This popular year-round resort dates back to 1868 when two soldiers struck silver, inaugurating what was soon to become the country's largest silver mining camp. It was dubbed Park City because a local boardinghouse owner thought the green mountain setting resembled a park. Today the resort lures visitors with three ski areas, some of Utah's best hotels, lively nightlife, and an authentic old-west atmosphere. **Information:** Park City Chamber Bureau, PO Box 1630, Park City 84060 (tel 801/649-6100 or 800/453-1360).

HOTELS

Goldener Hirsch Inn

Deer Valley Resort, PO Box 859, 84060; tel 801/649-7770 or toll free 800/252-3373; fax 801/649-7901. Located in prestigious Silver Lake Village at the foot of Deer Valley's Bald Mountain, the Goldener Hirsch combines the warm hospitality and charm of an Alpine country inn with the personalized professional service for which European hotels are renowned. Authentic Austrian antiques and architecture faithfully reflect the proud tradition and 500-year heritage of Hirsch's sister hotel, the world-famous Hotel Goldener Hirsch in Salzburg, Austria. The warm, cozy lobby has a full-service fireside lounge. **Rooms:** 20 rms and stes. CI 4pm/CO 11am. No smoking. Twenty spacious rooms and suites are elegantly furnished with hand-painted and carved furniture imported from Austria and king-size beds with luxurious down comforters. **Amenities:** Cable TV w/movies, refrig, dataport, bathrobes. No A/C. All units w/minibars, all w/terraces, some w/fireplaces. Most rooms have VCRs. **Services:** Twice-daily maid svce, car-rental desk, masseur, babysitting. Après-ski entertainment. **Facilities:** 20 1 restaurant, 1 bar (w/entertainment), sauna, whirlpool. Heated underground parking. **Rates (CP):** Peak (Dec–Apr) $300–$450 S or D; $440–$600 ste. Extra person $25. Children under age 2 stay free. Min stay peak and special events. Lower rates off-season. Parking: Indoor, free. Closed Apr–June 15/Nov. AE, MC, V.

Horne's Best Western Landmark Inn

6560 N Landmark Dr, 84098; tel 801/649-7300 or toll free 800/548-8824; fax 801/649-1760. Exit 145 off I-80. Modern hotel right next door to factory outlet stores and only 15 minutes from downtown Park City. Lobby is on three levels, with view of indoor pool and large spa and exercise room on lower level. **Rooms:** 106 rms and stes. CI 3pm/CO 11am. Nonsmoking rms avail. Most rooms have view of mountains. **Amenities:** A/C, cable TV w/movies. Some units w/fireplaces, some w/whirlpools. Ski racks. **Services:** Car-rental desk, masseur, babysitting. Complimentary beverage bar in lobby. Free shuttle to ski resorts and historic Main St. $25 refundable pet fee. **Facilities:** 250 1 restaurant, games rm, whirlpool, washer/dryer. Liquor store; 24-hour restaurant. **Rates:** Peak (Dec 15–Feb 18) $109–$144 S or D; $220–$320 ste. Children under age 18 stay free. Lower rates off-season. Parking: Outdoor, free. Four-day minimum stay (but with discounted rates) in peak season. AE, CB, DC, DISC, MC, V.

Radisson Inn Park City

2121 Park Ave, PO Box 1778, 84060; tel 801/649-5000 or toll free 800/333-3333; fax 801/649-2122. Across from Park City Municipal Golf Course. The newest full-service hotel in Park City boasts a large lobby and a fireplace in the cozy lounge area. **Rooms:** 131 rms and stes. Executive level. CI 2pm/CO 11am. Nonsmoking rms avail. Rooms are attractively decorated with textured white walls and colorful bedspreads. Many overlook two nearby golf courses; some have spectacular views of surrounding mountains. **Amenities:** A/C, cable TV w/movies, voice mail, bathrobes. Some units w/minibars, 1 w/fireplace, some w/whirlpools. **Services:** Babysitting. **Facilities:** 70 1 restaurant, 1 bar, volleyball, games rm, lawn games, sauna, whirlpool, washer/dryer. State liquor store, lounge, private club, driving range, and playground on premises. **Rates (BB):** Peak (Dec–Mar) $95–$169 S or D; $150–$200 ste. Extra person $10. Children under age 17 stay free. Min stay peak. Lower rates off-season. Parking: Indoor/outdoor, free. AE, DISC, MC, V.

Silver King Hotel

1485 Empire Ave, PO Box 2818, 84060 (Historic District); tel 801/649-5500 or toll free 800/331-8652; fax 801/649-6647. Just a short distance from historic Main Street, this charming hotel has a lovely atrium of beams and glass. **Rooms:** 64 rms, stes, and effic. CI 4pm/CO 11am. Nonsmoking rms avail. Rooms have dramatic views of ski slopes, elegant furniture, and comfortable, homey atmosphere. **Amenities:** A/C, cable TV w/movies, refrig, dataport, VCR, CD/tape player. All units w/fireplaces, all w/whirlpools. Basket filled with wood for fireplace. **Services:** Car-rental desk, social director, masseur, babysitting. **Facilities:** 200 Sauna, steam rm, whirlpool, washer/dryer. Pool surrounded by lovely greenery. 18-hole golf course nearby. **Rates:** Peak (Dec 18–Apr 15) $95–$120 S or D; $160–$290 ste; $160–$200 effic. Min stay peak. Lower rates off-season. Parking: Indoor/outdoor, free. AE, DISC, MC, V.

The Yarrow

1800 Park Ave, PO Box 1840, 84060; tel 801/649-7000 or toll free 800/927-7694; fax 801/649-4819. ½ mi N of Main St. Located just a half-mile from the ski lifts is this multistory, full-service hotel with a tan facade, offering attractive and comfortable rooms. **Rooms:** 181 rms, stes, and effic. CI 4pm/CO 11am. Nonsmoking rms avail. Views of pool and the surrounding mountains. Armoires house refrigerator and TV. **Amenities:** A/C, cable TV w/movies, refrig, dataport, voice mail. Some units w/terraces, some w/fireplaces, some w/whirlpools. **Services:** Masseur, babysitting. Free Park City bus stops here. Après-ski refreshment offered in the Pub. **Facilities:** 600 1 restaurant, 1 bar, whirlpool, washer/dryer. Ski rental and repair shop. Hotel sells lift tickets. **Rates:** Peak (Jan–Mar) $189–$209 S or D; $249–$419 ste; $219–$239 effic. Extra person $30. Children under age 12 stay free. Min stay peak. Lower rates off-season. Parking: Outdoor, free. Charge for extra person in off-season is $10. For stays of at least six nights, breakfast is included for two adults. AE, CB, DC, DISC, MC, V.

MOTEL

Chateau Apres Lodge

1299 Norfolk Ave, PO Box 579, 84060; tel 801/649-9372 or toll free 800/357-3556; fax 801/649-5963. N of Historic Main St. Family-run motel in older building with charm of a Swiss chalet, complete with balcony along the front. Not far from ski area. **Rooms:** 32 rms. CI 1pm/CO 10am. Nonsmoking rms avail. Rooms are basic but have great views of mountains. **Amenities:** TV. No A/C or phone. **Services:** **Facilities:** 90 **Rates (CP):** $70 S or D. Extra person $10. Min stay peak. Parking: Outdoor, free. Closed Apr 15–Nov 22. AE, DISC, MC, V.

INNS

The Old Miner's Lodge

615 Woodside Ave, 84060; tel 801/645-7420 or toll free 800/648-8068; fax 801/645-7420. Recently restored property originally built in 1889 as a boarding house for miners. Its location, one block west of historic Main Street, has easy access to shopping, dining, and skiing. **Rooms:** 10 rms and stes. CI 2pm/CO noon. No smoking. Furnished in antiques; down pillows and comforters. Rooms on the front have beautiful view of mountains and valley. Upstairs front rooms have sun porch. One room has a rather unique entryway—it simulates a mine. **Amenities:** No A/C, phone, or TV. **Services:** Babysitting, afternoon tea served. Complimentary refreshments in the evening. **Facilities:** 20 Whirlpool, guest lounge. Homey lounge area has comfortable seating and a variety of reading materials. Ski and bicycle storage available. **Rates (BB):** Peak (Nov 15–Apr 15) $95–$135 S; $115–$160 D; $170–$180 ste. Extra person $15. Min stay special events. Lower rates off-season. Higher rates for special events/hols. Parking: Outdoor, free. AE, DISC, MC, V.

Washington School Inn

543 Park Ave, PO Box 536, 84060; tel 801/649-3808 or toll free 800/824-1672; fax 801/649-3802. On hill overlooking Historic Main St. Beautifully refurbished property located in charming 1884 stone school building high on hill overlooking Main St. It still sports the building's original bell tower. Decorated with antiques but with modern comforts. Unsuitable for children under 12. **Rooms:** 15 rms and stes. CI 3pm/CO 10am. No smoking. Rooms are spacious and attractive. Rooms on the east have view of Main St. Some overlook wildflower gardens, some look out at the mountains. **Amenities:** TV, bathrobes. No A/C. Some units w/fireplaces. A few rooms have TVs. **Services:** Afternoon tea served. Après-ski beverages and snacks in parlor. **Facilities:** 25 Sauna, whirlpool, guest lounge w/TV. Basement exercise room has direct access from outside for easy entry with ski equipment. **Rates (BB):** Peak (Dec 20–Apr) $200–$235 S or D; $300–$350 ste. Extra person $20. Min stay peak. Lower rates off-season. Parking: Outdoor, free. Four-night minimum stay peak season. AE, DC, DISC, MC, V.

RESORT

Stein Eriksen Lodge

Deer Valley Resort, PO Box 3177, 84060; tel 801/649-3700 or toll free 800/453-1302; fax 801/649-5825. Park City exit off I-80. 20 acres. A touch of the fjords in the Rockies, this stylish resort was created by and named for a legendary Norwegian Olympic skier—still a presence at the lodge and on the slopes. The elegant lobby and foyer is entered via a heated but utilitarian parking garage with direct access to most rooms. With its doorstep ski lifts, the resort is an outstanding venue for avid skiers; others may consider it overpriced in winter. But it's certainly a steal other times of year (rooms that cost jetsetters $485 in winter go for just $159 the other eight months or so)—and there are plenty of diversions in the surrounding hills and dales to make the resort a worthwhile destination any time. **Rooms:** 130 rms, stes, and effic. CI 4pm/CO 11am. Nonsmoking rms avail. Lodgings are individually owned, each unit consisting of a sumptuous suite with two smaller rooms attached (all rentable separately). Some patios afford stunning views of mountains; others, views of condos and villas. Separate dressing and bath areas. Suites have full kitchens, two full baths. **Amenities:** Cable TV w/movies, refrig, VCR, in-rm safe, bathrobes. No A/C. All units w/terraces, some w/fireplaces, all w/whirlpools. Large stone fireplaces in living rooms and bedrooms. **Services:** VP Twice-daily maid svce, masseur, babysitting. Brisk, efficient concierge desk; gung-ho staffers give the impression they're pros looking after guests' needs rather than ski bums just waiting to get to the slopes themselves. **Facilities:** 150 2 restaurants (*see* "Restaurants" below), 1 bar (w/entertainment), sauna, whirlpool, washer/dryer. Two distinguished dining rooms plus casual heated terrace for snowbirds. Fitness center has panoramic view of mountains; year-round outdoor pool and hot tub. Fur storage and ski tuning facilities. **Rates (CP):** Peak (Dec–Apr 7) $400–$525 S or D; $900–$950 ste; $900–$950 effic. Extra person $25. Children under age 12 stay free. Min stay wknds. Lower rates off-season. Parking: Indoor, free. AE, DC, DISC, JCB, MC, V.

RESTAURANTS

Barking Frog

368 Main St; tel 801/649-6222. **Southwestern.** A popular eatery in a mid-1800s building, with the pressed metal ceiling, brick walls, and large front windows typical of mining towns of the era. Brightly colored posters enliven the walls. Menu specialties include the Barking Frog pistachio meat loaf, chicken adobe, high mesa lamb, and southwest noodles with

lime-tequila chicken. Soups and salads are also available. **FYI:** Reservations recommended. No smoking. **Open:** Daily 5:30–10pm. **Prices:** Main courses $17–$24. AE, DISC, MC, V.

Burgie's
570 Main St; tel 801/649-0011. **American/Burgers.** Burgie's is famous for—you guessed it—burgers. This is a fast food kind of place with better-than-average fare. A clean, light cafe offers homemade soups, onion rings, and grilled gourmet burgers. Upstairs there are video games, two pool tables, foosball, and a large-screen TV. A small balcony overlooks historic Main Street. **FYI:** Reservations not accepted. Children's menu. Beer and wine only. No smoking. **Open:** Daily 11am–10pm. **Prices:** Main courses $3–$7. AE, DISC, MC, V.

Cafe Terigo
424 Main St; tel 801/645-9555. **Italian.** This contemporary Italian restaurant has a sophisticated modern, bright decor, and patio dining in summer. Entrees include pan-seared duck breast, ginger coconut prawns, grilled flank steak, and fresh Atlantic salmon, plus a variety of pizzas, salads, and pastas. There's a boutique in the front. **FYI:** Reservations accepted. Children's menu. No smoking. **Open:** Peak (Apr 8–Dec) lunch Mon–Sat 11:30am–2:30pm; dinner daily 5:30–10pm. Closed Apr 1–7. **Prices:** Main courses $9–$20. AE, MC, V.

Claimjumper Restaurant
573 Main St; tel 801/649-8051. **American/Steak.** Located in the turn-of-the-century Park Hotel building, the dining room retains the elegant and friendly atmosphere of the old-west hotel it once was. Available are huge Alaskan king crab legs, Utah trout, and a wide selection of tender steaks. Desserts standouts include mud pie, brownie sundae, and cheesecake. The downstairs saloon, a private club (with two-week memberships available for visitors), offers the same menu as the restaurant, plus a smoking area. **FYI:** Reservations accepted. Children's menu. No smoking. **Open:** Daily 5:30–10pm. **Prices:** Main courses $10–$25. AE, DISC, MC, V.

Glitretind
In Stein Eriksen Lodge, Deer Valley Resort; tel 801/649-3700. Park City exit off I-80. **New American/Continental.** Stylish Norwegian rustic decor with two wood-burning fireplaces and views of the slopes. Casual dress code belies the polished service and sophisticated cuisine—appetizers of crisp potato lasagne and barbecued pork tamale, entrees of mustard-crusted rack of lamb with grilled vegetable tabbouleh, and seared yellowfin tuna with shrimp dumplings and ponzu sauce. There is also an outstanding wine list. In winter, the adjoining Forest Room becomes one of America's outstanding game restaurants —the place to go to sample grilled buffalo Rossini, marinated Alaskan caribou, and Utah ostrich. **FYI:** Reservations recommended. Children's menu. No smoking. **Open:** Breakfast daily 7–10am; lunch daily 11:30am–2:30pm; dinner daily 6–10pm; brunch Sun 11am–2:30pm. **Prices:** Main courses $22–$35. AE, DC, DISC, MC, V.

Grappa Italian Restaurant
151 Main St; tel 801/645-0636. At top of Main St. **Italian.** This lovely three-story historic building at the top of the hill houses a fine restaurant specializing in northern Italian cuisine. All three floors have dining rooms, simply furnished with hand-carved chairs, locally hand-made and hand-painted stoneware, and decks for outdoor dining under umbrellas. Buckets of fresh fruit and vegetables surround the kitchen area near the entrance. The menu features exotic dishes such as spit-roasted game hens and grilled spareribs of wild boar with balsamic vinegar and garlic glaze. Classical music plays in the background. **FYI:** Reservations recommended. No smoking. **Open:** Daily 5–10pm. Closed Apr 15–June 1. **Prices:** Main courses $24–$32. AE, DISC, MC, V.

Main Street Deli
525 Main St; tel 801/649-1110. **Burgers/Deli.** A typical self-serve deli, with friendly atmosphere and speedy service. The burger with all the trimmings is the most popular offering, but sandwiches and salads are available too. **FYI:** Reservations not accepted. Children's menu. BYO. No smoking. **Open:** Daily 7:30am–9:10pm. **Prices:** Main courses $4–$6. AE, MC, V.

Morning Ray
268 Main St; tel 801/649-5686. **Deli/Vegetarian.** The aroma of fresh-baked breads and pastries fills the bright, cheerful dining area of this cozy deli catering to the health-conscious. The owners use organically grown ingredients whenever possible; they specialize in freshly squeezed vegetable and fruit juices. Breakfast is a big draw, particularly the house specialty: "Morning Ray," a large plate of fries topped with sautéed vegetables, melted jack cheese, sour cream, and guacamole. Numerous tasty and unusual sandwiches and salads are on the lunch menu. **FYI:** Reservations not accepted. Folk. Beer only. No smoking. **Open:** Daily 7am–3pm. **Prices:** Lunch main courses $4–$7. AE, MC, V.

Texas Red's Pit Barbecue & Chili Parlor
440 Main St; tel 801/649-7337. **Barbecue.** Park City's busiest chili stop is also known for its authentic pit barbecue, with six different meats slow cooked over apple wood. The unusual decor features three-dimensional murals with buffalo and elk heads emerging from Wild West paintings. Soup and sandwich specials are available daily. **FYI:** Reservations not accepted. Children's menu. No smoking. **Open:** Daily 11:30am–10pm. **Prices:** Main courses $8–$11. AE, DISC, MC, V.

Wasatch Brew Pub
250 Main St; tel 801/649-9500. **New American.** Utah's oldest and largest microbrewery serves award-winning fresh beer daily. The varied dinner menu offers such items as a pub burger, shrimp pesto, rack of lamb, and Utah trout. If you sit

at the bar, you have a full view of the brewery vats below. The atmosphere is casual and friendly, with pool tables and large-screen TV in the upstairs sports bar, and sports memorabilia on the walls. **FYI:** Reservations not accepted. Children's menu. No smoking. **Open:** Lunch daily 11am–4pm; dinner daily 5–10pm. **Prices:** Main courses $7–$16. AE, MC, V.

ATTRACTIONS

Kimball Art Center
638 Park Ave; tel 801/649-8882. This center for visual arts has two galleries offering changing exhibits that include regional and national traveling shows as well as exhibits by local artists. Art classes, workshops, and seminars are offered throughout the year, and the gift shop sells local and regional art. The Northwest Rendezvous Art Exhibition in July attracts art lovers, collectors, and media representatives from all over the United States. The Park City Art Festival in early August displays the work of national artists in the streets of downtown. **Open:** Mon–Sat 10am–6pm, Sun noon–6pm. **Free**

Park City Museum
528 Main St; tel 801/645-5135. The original territorial jail downstairs includes tiny cells that were state-of-the-art in 1886. Upstairs are an assay office, 19th-century mining equipment, historic photographs, early ski gear, and several beautifully tooled door knobs and locks. There are also a variety of personal items that immigrants to Park City brought with them, ranging from a Dutch hymnal to a tin lunch bucket. **Open:** Mon–Sat 10am–7pm, Sun noon–6pm. **Free**

Deer Valley Resort
2250 Deer Valley Dr S; tel 801/649-1000. Deer Valley offers 67 runs and three bowls spread over Flagstaff, Bald, and Bald Eagle Mountains. There are two high-speed quad lifts, nine triple, and two double chairs for a total of 13 chairlifts. The base is at 7,200 feet and the summit at 9,400 feet, yielding a 2,200-foot vertical drop. With 1,100 skiable acres, the terrain is rated as 15% beginner, 50% intermediate, and 35% advanced. **Open:** Dec–mid-Apr, daily, call for schedule. **$$$$**

Park City Ski Area
Empire Ave; tel 801/649-8111. Facilities include a four-passenger gondola, plus three quad, six triple, and four double chairs servicing 89 runs on 2,200 skiable acres; there's even a triple-chair access lift directly from the Old Town onto the mountain, and two runs (Quit'n' Time and Creole) on which visitors can ski back into town. Trails are rated 16% beginner, 45% intermediate, and 39% expert. With a base elevation of 6,900 feet and summit of 10,000 feet, the vertical drop is 3,100 feet. **Open:** Mid-Nov–Apr, daily, call for hours. **$$$$**

Wolf Mountain Resort
4000 Park West Dr; tel 801/649-5400 or toll free 800/754-1636. Facilities include 62 runs on 1,400 skiable acres, serviced by seven double chairlifts. It receives over 300 inches of snow a year, and has 20 acres of snowmaking capabilities. The vertical drop is 2,200 feet, with a summit elevation of 9,000 feet and base of 6,800 feet. Runs are rated 22% beginner, 30% intermediate, and 48% advanced. Night skiing is available. The only area resort that welcomes snowboarders, it has a lighted snowboard park where lessons are given. **Open:** Dec–early Apr, daily 9am–9pm. **$$$$**

Payson

Located 15 miles south of Provo, Payson was founded by Mormon settlers in 1850. The town, an agriculture center, celebrates its livelihood each September with Onion Days. **Information:** Payson City Hall, 439 W Utah Ave, Payson 84651 (tel 801/465-9226).

HOTEL

Comfort Inn
830 N Main St, 84651; tel 801/465-4861 or toll free 800/228-5150; fax 801/465-4861. Exit 254 off I-15. Large, modern hotel featuring spacious, southwestern-style lobby with high, beamed ceiling and fireplace with comfortable seating. Restaurant nearby; golf course five miles away. **Rooms:** 62 rms, stes, and effic. CI 2pm/CO 11am. Nonsmoking rms avail. Average size rooms have light, southwestern decor and modern wood furniture. Most have view of countryside. **Amenities:** A/C, satel TV w/movies. Some units w/whirlpools. **Services:** VCRs for rent. **Facilities:** Spa, sauna, whirlpool, washer/dryer. **Rates (CP):** Peak (Apr–Sept) $55 S; $68 D; $99 ste; $55–$68 effic. Children under age 18 stay free. Lower rates off-season. Parking: Outdoor, free. AE, CB, DC, DISC, ER, JCB, MC, V.

Perry

See Brigham City

Price

Home of the College of Eastern Utah, Price is becoming known as the place to go to learn about dinosaurs and ancient Native American cultures. It is also a base for outdoor recreation in the Manti–La Sal National Forest and a gateway to the Canyonlands region to the southeast. **Information:** Price Visitor Information, 155 E Main St, Price 84501 (tel 801/637-3009 or 800/842-0789).

MOTELS

Carriage House Inn

590 E Main St, 84501; tel 801/637-5660 or toll free 800/228-5732. Off US 6 and US 191. White colonial-style building with black shutters, fronted by four pillars. **Rooms:** 41 rms. CI noon/CO noon. Nonsmoking rms avail. **Amenities:** A/C, cable TV, dataport. Some rooms have microwaves and refrigerators. **Services:** Free coffee and other beverages 6:30–11am. **Facilities:** Whirlpool. Pool has retractable roof. **Rates:** Peak (Mar–Sept) $35–$55 S; $45–$65 D. Extra person $5. Lower rates off-season. Parking: Indoor/outdoor, free. AE, CB, DC, DISC, MC, V.

Days Inn Price

838 Westwood Blvd, 84501; tel 801/637-8880 or toll free 800/DAYS-INN; fax 801/637-7707. At exit 240 off US 6. Modern motel on outskirts of Price with large, attractive lobby. **Rooms:** 148 rms and stes. CI 3pm/CO 11am. Nonsmoking rms avail. Wildlife pictures on the walls. **Amenities:** A/C, cable TV, voice mail. Some units w/terraces. Ironing board. **Services:** Fax service. **Facilities:** 200 1 restaurant, 1 bar (w/entertainment), games rm, spa, sauna, steam rm, whirlpool. **Rates:** Peak (Apr–Sept) $45–$51 S; $49–$55 D; $53–$98 ste. Extra person $6. Children under age 16 stay free. Lower rates off-season. Parking: Outdoor, free. Golf packages avail. AE, CB, DC, DISC, JCB, MC, V.

Green Well Motel

655 E Main St, 84501; tel 801/637-3520; fax 801/631-4858. Older, comfortable motel. Convenient to shopping. **Rooms:** 125 rms. CI 2pm/CO 11am. Nonsmoking rms avail. Appealing and cozy rooms with southwestern decor. **Amenities:** A/C, cable TV w/movies, dataport. Refrigerators available. **Services:** $10 pet fee. **Facilities:** 1 restaurant, 1 bar. **Rates (CP):** $28–$37 S; $32–$40 D. Extra person $5. Children under age 12 stay free. Parking: Outdoor, free. AE, CB, DC, DISC, MC, V.

RESTAURANT

Luito's

86 E 100 South; tel 801/637-8224. **Mexican.** Located in an unassuming 1950s building, Luito's has a large mural on one wall, and a few serapes and other southwestern articles complete the decor. Fare consists of traditional Mexican dishes, such as enchiladas, tacos, and burritos. **FYI:** Reservations accepted. Children's menu. No liquor license. No smoking. **Open:** Peak (Nov–Jan) lunch daily 11am–2pm; dinner daily 5–9pm. **Prices:** Main courses $5–$11. AE, MC, V.

Provo

See also Payson, Salt Lake City

Brigham Young University and its 30,000-plus students dominate life in this conservative, family-oriented city, the seat of Utah County in a mining and irrigated farm area. Provo was settled in 1849 by Mormons, who to this day greatly influence everyday life and culture in the city. Utah Lake, the state's largest natural freshwater lake, lies just west of Provo. Each Independence Day is celebrated with the huge America's Freedom Festival. **Information:** Utah County Travel Council, Historic County Courthouse, 51 S University Ave, Suite 110, Provo 84604 (tel 801/370-8393 or 800/222-8824).

HOTELS

Fairfield Inn Provo

1515 S University Ave, 84601 (East Bay Business Park); tel 801/377-9500 or toll free 800/228-2800; fax 801/377-9591. 1 block E of exit 266 off I-15. This three-story modern hotel is one of the newest in Provo, and a good choice for the business traveler. **Rooms:** 72 rms. CI 3pm/CO noon. Nonsmoking rms avail. Some rooms feature wonderful views of the towering Wasatch Mountains to the east. Mini-suites have two bedrooms, extra sofa, two sinks. **Amenities:** A/C, cable TV, dataport. Mini-suites have refrigerators and microwaves. **Services:** Car-rental desk. Juice bar and snacks in hall; free coffee. **Facilities:** 50 Whirlpool. **Rates (CP):** Peak (Apr–Sept 15) $49–$55 S; $65–$70 D. Extra person $4. Children under age 18 stay free. Min stay special events. Lower rates off-season. Parking: Outdoor, free. AE, CB, DC, DISC, MC, V.

Provo Holiday Inn

1460 University Ave, 84601; tel 801/374-9750 or toll free 800/HOLIDAY; fax 801/377-1615. Exit 266 off I-15. Modern hotel with spacious, well-appointed rooms, near Brigham Young University. Lobby features unusual fountain. **Rooms:** 78 rms. CI 3pm/CO noon. Nonsmoking rms avail. Comfortable seating, mahogany furniture, brightly colored bed spreads. East-facing rooms have fine view of Mount Timpanogos. **Amenities:** A/C, cable TV. **Services:** Fax and copier at front desk; *Wall Street Journal* and *USA Today* available on request. **Facilities:** 100 1 restaurant (lunch and dinner only), 1 bar, washer/dryer. **Rates (CP):** Peak (May–Sept) $79–$89 S or D. Extra person $10. Children under age 16 stay free. Min stay special events. Lower rates off-season. Parking: Outdoor, free. AE, DC, DISC, MC, V.

Provo Park Hotel

101 W 100 North, 84601 (Downtown); tel 801/377-4700 or toll free 800/777-7144; fax 801/377-4708. Nine-story, full-service hotel in the heart of Provo; very popular with business travelers. High-ceilinged lobby has impressive fireplace and comfortable sitting areas. **Rooms:** 232 rms and stes. Execu-

tive level. CI 3pm/CO noon. Nonsmoking rms avail. Attractive rooms are quiet and spacious. **Amenities:** A/C, cable TV w/movies, voice mail. Some rooms have dataports. **Services:** Car-rental desk, babysitting. Free shuttle around valley. **Facilities:** 1 restaurant, 1 bar, sauna, whirlpool. Large-screen TV in bar and lounge. State liquor store on premises. **Rates:** Peak (May–Sept) $85–$95 S or D; $130–$415 ste. Extra person $15. Children under age 18 stay free. Lower rates off-season. Parking: Indoor/outdoor, free. AE, CB, DC, DISC, MC, V.

MOTELS

Best Western Rome Inn Motel

50 W 1200 South, 84601; tel 801/375-7500 or toll free 800/528-1234; fax 801/373-9700. Exit 266 off I-15, 2 blocks N on University Ave. A great choice for families. Lobby has a fountain, Roman-style architecture, and picture windows facing the mountains. **Rooms:** 55 rms. CI noon/CO noon. Nonsmoking rms avail. Rooms are fairly spacious, comfortable, and attractive. **Amenities:** A/C, cable TV. **Services:** Free local calls. **Facilities:** **Rates (CP):** $44–$54 S; $49–$56 D. Extra person $7. Children under age 12 stay free. Parking: Outdoor, free. AE, DISC, MC, V.

Travelodge

124 S University Ave, 84601; tel 801/373-1974 or toll free 800/578-7878; fax 801/373-1974. Located downtown across from the LDS Tabernacle. Picture windows in lobby offer nice view of the mountains, plus a collection of costumed teddy bears. **Rooms:** 60 rms. CI 3pm/CO noon. Nonsmoking rms avail. Some units are very large with three queen beds. Some rooms have shower only. **Amenities:** A/C, cable TV. **Services:** **Facilities:** **Rates:** Peak (June–Aug) $42–$65 S or D. Extra person $2. Children under age 18 stay free. Lower rates off-season. Parking: Outdoor, free. AE, DISC, MC, V.

UNRATED Uptown Motel

469 W Center St, 84601 (Downtown); tel 801/373-8248. Basic, clean motel located across the street from a park and within walking distance of restaurants and supermarket. Good choice for families. **Rooms:** 28 rms, stes, and effic. CI open/CO 11am. Nonsmoking rms avail. Some of upper rooms overlook the park. **Amenities:** A/C, TV w/movies, refrig. Some units w/terraces. **Services:** Pet fee $4. **Facilities:** **Rates:** Peak (July–Aug) $26–$36 S; $34–$54 D; $42–$64 ste; $34–$54 effic. Extra person $4. Children under age 12 stay free. Lower rates off-season. Parking: Outdoor, free. AE, DISC, MC, V.

INN

Victorian Inn Bed & Breakfast

94 W 200 South, Springville, 84663; tel 801/489-0737; fax 801/489-0075. Located in the historic Kearn's Hotel, which has been faithfully restored to its Victorian elegance and is listed on the National Resister of Historic Places. A lovely mix of historic ambience with modern amenities. The parlor still has the original stained-glass windows. **Rooms:** 8 rms. CI 4pm/CO 11am. No smoking. Rooms are individually decorated in lavish Victorian style with mixture of antiques and reproductions; most have queen beds. **Amenities:** A/C, cable TV w/movies, refrig, VCR. Some units w/terraces, some w/whirlpools. **Services:** Babysitting, afternoon tea served. **Facilities:** Whirlpool, guest lounge. **Rates (BB):** $65–$105 S or D. Children under age 5 stay free. Parking: Outdoor, free. Bridal and anniversary packages avail. AE, DISC, MC, V.

RESORT

Sundance Resort

UT 92, Sundance, 84604; tel 801/225-4107 or toll free 800/892-1600; fax 801/226-1937. 2 mi N of jct US 189. Nestled among the pines on 5,000 acres of near-wilderness, Sundance combines outdoor activities with the visual and performing arts. **Rooms:** 105 rms and stes; 65 cottages/villas. CI 3pm/CO 11am. No smoking. Accommodations include standard rooms, junior and full suites, and mountain homes. Most units have views of the stream meandering through the property, or the mountains surrounding it. **Amenities:** Cable TV w/movies, refrig, voice mail, bathrobes. No A/C. Some units w/terraces, some w/fireplaces, some w/whirlpools. Some rooms have VCRs. Videos available. **Services:** Car-rental desk, social director, masseur, children's program, babysitting. **Facilities:** 3 restaurants, 1 bar, washer/dryer. General store; theater. Ski lessons. **Rates (BB):** Peak (Jan–Mar) $115–$175 S or D; $150–$295 ste; $315–$425 cottage/villa. Children under age 18 stay free. Min stay peak. Lower rates off-season. AP and MAP rates avail. Parking: Outdoor, free. AE, MC, V.

RESTAURANTS

Magleby's

In Village Green Professional Plaza, 1675 N 200 West; tel 801/374-6249. At jct Freedom Blvd/University Pkwy. **New American/Seafood.** A delightful and popular restaurant in the Village Green, a small business and professional plaza near BYU. The modern building has a charming Mediterranean appearance, and the several dining rooms are light and airy. Its breadsticks and mint truffles are famous. Lunch items include chicken à la Roma, catch-of-the-day, and a "lighter side" salad with chicken or halibut; dinner entrees include steak, prime rib, chicken, and seafood. **FYI:** Reservations accepted. Children's menu. No liquor license. No smoking. **Open:** Mon–Thurs 11am–10pm, Fri 11am–11pm, Sat 11am–4pm. **Prices:** Main courses $9–$22. AE, DC, DISC, MC, V.

★ The Malt Shoppe

1290 N University Ave; tel 801/375-1906. **American/Burgers.** This burger and fast food restaurant and drive-in specializes in malts, shakes, freezes, and yogurt. The plain building has windows along the west side and Tiffany-style lamps over the booths. Old records decorate the walls, including two gold records by Elvis and one by the Beatles. A Wurlitzer jukebox plays hits from the 1940s and '50s. Menu items include burgers, hot pastrami on rye with fries, and gourmet fish and chips. Patio dining is a summer treat. **FYI:** Reservations not accepted. No liquor license. No smoking. **Open:** Mon–Thurs 10am–midnight, Fri–Sat 10am–1am, Sun noon–10pm. **Prices:** Main courses $2–$5. No CC.

The Underground Restaurant
59 N University Ave (Provo Town Sq); tel 801/337-5044. Basement of 50 N University Ave. **New American.** This basement restaurant is decorated with art deco posters and collectibles, plus a moose head and polar bear. But the real highlight is two classic cars outfitted with table and chairs so patrons can dine inside. The specialty is charbroiled beef, chicken, and seafood. **FYI:** Reservations accepted. Guitar/piano. Children's menu. No liquor license. No smoking. **Open:** Mon–Thurs 11am–9pm, Fri–Sat 11am–11pm. **Prices:** Main courses $8–$15. AE, DISC, MC, V.

ATTRACTIONS

Brigham Young University Earth Science Museum
1683 N Canyon Rd; tel 801/378-3680. The museum offers one of Utah's largest collections of dinosaur bones from the Jurassic period. Exhibits include a nine-foot shoulder blade of ultrasaurus; a 150-million-year-old Jurassic dinosaur egg with an X-ray revealing the embryo; two fully mounted skeletons of camptosaurus and allosaurus; and a touch-table featuring real fossils. A window offers the chance to see museum personnel preparing fossils in the lab. **Open:** Mon 9am–9pm, Tues–Fri 9am–5pm, Sat noon–4pm. **Free**

Monte L Bean Life Science Museum
1430 N University Ave, east of the Marriott Center; tel 801/378-5051. Located on the Brigham Young University campus, this museum houses a large collection of dioramas that contain insects, plants, reptiles, fish, shells, and mounted animals and birds from around the world. An emphasis is given on Utah's wildlife. **Open:** Mon 10am–9pm, Tues–Sat 10am–5pm. **Free**

McCurdy Historical Doll Museum
246 N 100 E St; tel 801/377-9935. Laura McCurdy Clark began collecting dolls from around the world in 1910; in 1979 the museum was founded to exhibit her collection and others. Today, over 4,000 dolls are on display in this restored carriage house, including antique dolls crafted in Germany, France, and England; 40 dolls of American presidential First Ladies; priceless antique dolls representing historical figures; and many dolls depicting fashions throughout history. The museum offers storytelling, lectures, craft classes, and a doll "hospital," which provides repair services. An Academy Award–winning documentary about dolls and toys is shown as part of the tour. **Open:** Peak (Apr–Dec) Tues–Sat noon–5pm. Reduced hours off-season. **$**

Museum of Art
492 E Campus Dr; tel 801/378-2787. The state-of-the-art museum located on the Brigham Young University campus is one of the largest in the West. Its 14,000-piece collection is quite varied, including ceramics, sculptures, paintings, and pottery. Also on exhibit are etchings by Rembrandt and Monet and jade and ivory from Asia. A bookstore and gift shop are on the premises. **Open:** Mon–Fri 9am–5pm. **Free**

Utah Stake Tabernacle
100 S University Ave; tel 801/370-6655. This two-story brick edifice seats 2,000 and is still used for LDS Stake Conferences. Built in 1883, it was partly condemned when the roof started sagging under the weight of the central tower. Around 1916, stained-glass windows were installed, the tower was removed, and the structure was again declared sound. **Open:** Call for schedule of events. **Free**

Timpanogos Cave National Monument
UT 144, American Fork; tel 801/756-5239. Located 15 mi N of Provo. This national monument comprises three caves—Hansen, Middle, and Timpanogos—linked together by manmade tunnels. Martin Hansen discovered the first cavern in 1887 while tracking a mountain lion. The other two were reported in the early 1920s, and the connecting tunnels were constructed in the 1930s. The caves are filled with every type of formation, from stalactites and stalagmites to draperies and helictites. They are not easy to reach, but the beauty and variety of the caves make them well worth the climb. **Open:** Mem Day–Labor Day, daily 7am–5:30pm. **$$**

Sundance Resort and Institute
UT 92, Sundance; tel 801/225-4107 or toll free 800/892-1600. Situated in beautiful Provo Canyon at the base of 12,000-foot Mount Timpanogos, Sundance is a year-round resort that emphasizes its arts programs as much as its skiing and other outdoor activities. The retreat is a full-service ski resort in winter, with downhill slopes offering 20% beginner, 40% intermediate, and 40% advanced terrain, with a total of 41 runs over 450 acres. There are cross-country trails, equipment rentals, a ski school, and a children's program. Hiking and nature trails are open in summer; fly fishing and horseback riding are available.

The Sundance Institute, which actor Robert Redford founded in 1980 to support and encourage independent American filmmaking and playwriting, plays host to the Sundance Film Festival in the first week in January. For more information, contact Sundance Resort and Institute, RR 3 Box A-1, Sundance, UT 84604. **Open:** Peak (mid-Dec–Apr) daily 9am–4:30pm. Reduced hours off-season. **$$$$**

Rainbow Bridge National Monument

See Page, AZ

Richfield

Richfield has been an agricultural center since its founding in 1864, when pioneers named the community for the richness of its soil. Hunting, fishing, hiking, and other outdoor recreation is available in nearby Fishlake National Forest. **Information:** Panoramaland Travel Region, PO Box 820, Richfield 84701 (tel 801/896-9222 or 800/748-4361).

MOTELS

Best Western Appletree Inn

145 S Main St, 84701; tel 801/896-5481 or toll free 800/528-1234; fax 801/896-9465. Exit 37 or 40 off I-70. Modern building of sand-colored brick; large windows in the lobby. **Rooms:** 62 rms. Executive level. CI 2pm/CO noon. Nonsmoking rms avail. Attractively decorated in southwestern motif. **Amenities:** A/C, cable TV, dataport. **Services:** Fax available ($4). Pet fee $6. **Facilities:** Washer/dryer. **Rates (CP):** Peak (May–Sept) $47–$59 S; $51–$73 D. Extra person $5. Children under age 18 stay free. Lower rates off-season. Parking: Outdoor, free. AE, CB, DC, DISC, MC, V.

Budget Host Knights Inn

69 S Main St, 84701; tel 801/896-8228 or toll free 800/525-9024; fax 801/896-8228. On US 89, S of exit 37 or exit 40 off I-70. Two-story, red variegated brick building with white shutters. Comfortable, inviting lobby. **Rooms:** 50 rms and stes. CI 2pm/CO noon. Nonsmoking rms avail. Well-maintained rooms. **Amenities:** A/C, cable TV w/movies. Some rooms have refrigerators and microwaves. **Services:** **Facilities:** 150 1 restaurant (*see* "Restaurants" below). **Rates:** Peak (May–Sept) $32–$44 S; $36–$60 D; $75 ste. Extra person $4. Children under age 12 stay free. Lower rates off-season. Parking: Outdoor, free. AE, CB, DC, DISC, MC, V.

Days Inn

333 N Main St, 84701; tel 801/896-6476 or toll free 800/DAYS-INN; fax 801/896-6476. S of exit 40 off I-70. Modern motel across from park in downtown. Lobby is English Tudor style with high ceilings. **Rooms:** 51 rms and stes. CI open/CO 11am. Nonsmoking rms avail. Some rooms look out on the park. **Amenities:** A/C, cable TV w/movies, refrig, dataport. **Services:** **Facilities:** 100 3 restaurants, sauna, whirlpool. **Rates:** Peak (Apr–Sept) $52–$69 S; $70–$85 D; $75–$95 ste. Extra person $5. Children under age 12 stay free. Lower rates off-season. Parking: Outdoor, free. AE, DC, DISC, JCB, MC, V.

Quality Inn

540 S Main St, 84701; tel 801/896-5465 or toll free 800/228-5151; fax 801/896-5465. S of exit 37 or exit 40 off I-70. Modern two-story motel with spacious lobby. **Rooms:** 58 rms. CI 2pm/CO noon. Nonsmoking rms avail. Rooms are attractive and efficient; some have view of pool. **Amenities:** A/C, cable TV, dataport. Some units w/whirlpools. **Services:** Free coffee. **Facilities:** 250 Spa, whirlpool. Microwave in lobby. **Rates:** Peak (May–Sept) $49–$54 S; $75 D. Extra person $6. Children under age 18 stay free. Lower rates off-season. Parking: Outdoor, free. AE, DC, DISC, MC, V.

RESTAURANT

Anderson's BHC–Knight's Family Restaurant

In Budget Host Knights Inn, 89 S Main St; tel 801/896-4330. **Greek/Italian.** Located in a 50-year-old building, this restaurant comprises four cozy dining areas, one of which showcases the nature paintings of a local artist. The extensive menu specializes in traditional Greek and Italian dishes; all soups are homemade. **FYI:** Reservations not accepted. Children's menu. No liquor license. No smoking. **Open:** Daily 6am–10pm. **Prices:** Main courses $7–$10. AE, CB, DC, DISC, MC, V.

ATTRACTION

Territorial Statehouse State Park

50 W Capitol, Fillmore; tel 801/743-5316. 25 miles NW of Richfield. Before statehood, Utah's lawmakers met here once in 1855. Today, the Territorial Statehouse displays Utah pioneer artifacts and paintings. The collection includes butter churns, spinning wheels, firearms, farming equipment, woodworking tools, kitchen implements, clothing, and formal portraits. Furniture from pioneer homes is arranged in a variety of settings. Upstairs in the legislative hall are paintings by pioneer and contemporary Utah artists. On the museum grounds are an All-American Rose Society Garden, picnic area, two restored pioneer cabins, and an 1867 rock schoolhouse. **Open:** Daily 9am–5pm. **$**

Roy

See Odgen

St George

By far the largest community in southern Utah, St George is the trade center for Utah's Dixie, so called because of its hot summers and the cotton that was grown here when supplies from the real Dixie were cut off during the Civil War. The state's best golf courses are here—and the warm weather allows for year-round play. St George is the site of Dixie

College. **Information:** St George Area Chamber of Commerce, 97 E St George Blvd, St George 84770 (tel 801/628-1658).

HOTELS

Hilton Inn of St George
1450 S Hilton Dr, 84770; tel 801/628-0463 or toll free 800/662-2525; fax 801/628-1501. W of exit 6 off I-15. A 20-year-old hotel adjacent to Southgate Golf Course. Lobby features a beautiful mural of a pink-and-orange-hued canyon. **Rooms:** 100 rms and stes. Executive level. CI 3pm/CO noon. Nonsmoking rms avail. Most rooms overlook pool. **Amenities:** A/C, cable TV w/movies, dataport, voice mail. Some units w/terraces. **Services:** Fax available. **Facilities:** 500 1 restaurant, 1 bar, sauna, steam rm, whirlpool. Privileges at nearby health club and indoor pool. Horseback riding and hiking nearby. **Rates:** Peak (Mar–Oct) $75–$95 S; $85–$110 D; $100–$155 ste. Extra person $10. Children under age 18 stay free. Min stay special events. Lower rates off-season. Parking: Outdoor, free. AE, CB, DC, DISC, MC, V.

Holiday Inn Resort Hotel
850 S Bluff St, 84770; tel 801/628-4235 or toll free 800/457-9800; fax 801/628-8157. 5 blocks W of exit 6 off I-15. Located in a striking, rust-colored, columned building. Its impressive lobby contains a massive fireplace in one corner, a skylit, arched ceiling, and an indoor/outdoor pool surrounded by a large patio. **Rooms:** 164 rms and stes. CI 3pm/CO 11am. Nonsmoking rms avail. Rooms are spacious and bright. **Amenities:** A/C, cable TV, dataport. Some units w/terraces, some w/whirlpools. Four conference suites have a Murphy bed and wet bar. **Services:** Babysitting. **Facilities:** 500 2 restaurants, games rm, whirlpool, playground, washer/dryer. Putting green. **Rates:** Peak (Feb–May/Sept–Oct) $71–$81 S; $79–$89 D; $79–$90 ste. Extra person $8. Children under age 18 stay free. Min stay special events. Lower rates off-season. Parking: Outdoor, free. AE, CB, DC, DISC, JCB, MC, V.

MOTELS

Best Western Coral Hills
125 E St George Blvd, 84770; tel 801/673-4844 or toll free 800/542-7733; fax 801/673-5352. 10 blocks W of exit 8 off I-15. Exceptionally well-kept facility in heart of St George; the inviting lobby has a three-tiered chandelier. **Rooms:** 98 rms and stes. CI 2pm/CO 11am. Nonsmoking rms avail. Rooms are pleasant and cheery. Family suites have two bedrooms. **Amenities:** A/C, cable TV, refrig. Some units w/terraces, some w/whirlpools. **Services:** Masseur. **Facilities:** 50 Spa, whirlpool. **Rates (CP):** Peak (Jan–Nov 23) $51–$60 S; $54–$62 D; $69–$100 ste. Extra person $4. Children under age 12 stay free. Min stay special events. Lower rates off-season. Parking: Outdoor, free. AE, CB, DC, DISC, MC, V.

Budget Royal
1165 S Bluff St, 84770; tel 801/628-4482 or toll free 800/231-4488; fax 801/673-0992. 2 blocks W of exit 6 off I-15. Pleasant modern-looking stucco structure with a touch of southwestern styling. **Rooms:** 96 rms and stes. CI 2pm/CO 11am. Nonsmoking rms avail. **Amenities:** A/C, cable TV w/movies, refrig, dataport. 1 unit w/whirlpool. **Services:** Car-rental desk. **Facilities:** Whirlpool, washer/dryer. **Rates (CP):** $32–$44 S; $35–$49 D; $135 ste. Children under age 18 stay free. Parking: Outdoor, free. AE, DC, DISC, MC, V.

Dixie Palms Motel
185 E St George Blvd, 84770; tel 801/673-3531. Modest motel with small but comfortable rooms. In center of town, within walking distance of several restaurants. **Rooms:** 15 rms, stes, and effic. CI open/CO 11am. Nonsmoking rms avail. **Amenities:** A/C, cable TV. **Services:** Pet fee $5. **Rates:** Peak (Mar–Oct) $28–$40 S or D; $40–$60 ste; $25–$40 effic. Extra person $5. Children under age 12 stay free. Lower rates off-season. Parking: Outdoor, free. MC, V.

Econo Lodge
460 E St George Blvd, 84770; tel 801/673-4861 or toll free 800/55-ECONO; fax 801/673-4878. Well-maintained older property in heart of downtown. **Rooms:** 54 rms and stes. CI 2pm/CO 11am. Nonsmoking rms avail. Most rooms have grand view of red rock cliffs to the west. **Amenities:** A/C, cable TV. Some units w/terraces. **Services:** Car-rental desk. **Facilities:** 50 1 restaurant, whirlpool. **Rates:** Peak (Nov–Jan) $42–$57 S or D; $72 ste. Extra person $5. Children under age 12 stay free. Lower rates off-season. Parking: Outdoor, free. AE, CB, DISC, JCB, MC, V.

Singletree Inn
260 E St George Blvd, 84770; tel 801/673-6161 or toll free 800/528-8890; fax 801/674-2406. Two-story shingled motel built around an attractively landscaped pool area. Restaurants within walking distance; some offer discounts to guests. **Rooms:** 47 rms. CI 2pm/CO 11am. Nonsmoking rms avail. Spacious rooms have been recently remodeled. **Amenities:** A/C, cable TV w/movies. Some rooms have microwaves and refrigerators. **Services:** Small pets accepted with $4 fee. **Facilities:** 25 Whirlpool, washer/dryer. **Rates (CP):** Peak (Feb–Apr) $46–$56 S; $50–$60 D. Extra person $4. Children under age 18 stay free. Lower rates off-season. Parking: Outdoor, free. AE, DISC, MC, V.

INNS

Greene Gate Village
76 W Tabernacle St, 84770; tel 801/628-6999 or toll free 800/350-6999; fax 801/628-6989. Across from LDS Tabernacle. 4 acres. Nine beautifully restored homes from the late 1800s make up B&B in downtown St George. Grounds are beautifully landscaped to resemble a small village, with trees and flowers, walkways, a gazebo, and a 100-year-old green gate. **Rooms:** 16 rms, stes, and effic. CI 3pm/CO 11am. No

smoking. Rooms are attractively furnished with antiques and reproductions, mostly Victorian style. Views of the grounds. **Amenities:** A/C, cable TV. Some units w/terraces, some w/fireplaces, some w/whirlpools. **Services:** Car-rental desk, babysitting. **Facilities:** 1 restaurant (bkfst only), whirlpool, guest lounge. **Rates (BB):** $60–$125 S or D; $85–$125 ste; $75–$125 effic. Extra person $10. Children under age 2 stay free. Min stay special events. Higher rates for special events/hols. Parking: Outdoor, free. AE, DC, MC, V.

Seven Wives Inn Bed & Breakfast
217 N 100 West, 84770 (Historic District); tel 801/628-3737 or toll free 800/600-3737. Two two-story Victorian homes, both on the National Register of Historic Places. The spacious parlor, furnished with period antiques, serves as a gathering place. **Rooms:** 12 rms and stes. CI 3pm/CO 11am. No smoking. Rooms are individually decorated with Victorian and Eastlake antiques. One has a French ceramic stove and a Murphy bed; honeymoon suite has a two-person whirlpool tub. A two-bedroom family room is available. **Amenities:** A/C, cable TV. Some units w/terraces, some w/fireplaces, some w/whirlpools. **Facilities:** Guest lounge. **Rates (BB):** $55–$125 S or D; $125 ste. Extra person $15. Min stay wknds. Parking: Outdoor, free. AE, CB, DC, DISC, MC, V.

RESTAURANTS

Andelin's Gable House Restaurant
290 E St George Blvd; tel 801/673-6796. **Regional American.** High-beamed ceilings, flower wallpaper, and lovely paintings all combine to offer an elegant backdrop for the fine food served here. For lunch there are croissant sandwiches, a nice selection of salads, and chicken pot pie. Dinner entrees include such specialties as slow-cooked beef brisket, and mountain trout lightly floured and sautéed in butter. Prix-fixe dinners offer a choice of prime rib, roast rack of pork, or the fish of the day. **FYI:** Reservations accepted. Children's menu. No liquor license. No smoking. **Open:** Mon–Sat 11:30am–10pm. **Prices:** Main courses $8–$17; prix fixe $22–$26. AE, DISC, MC, V.

★ Basila's Greek & Italian Cafe
In Ancestor Sq, 2 W St George Blvd; tel 801/673-7671. At Main St. **Greek/Italian.** Located in a quaint, rambling one-story brick building, Basila's is simply decorated with lush green plants and Mediterranean objets d'art. To start, your server will bring to your table crusty homemade bread and "Greek butter"—a light mixture of olive oil and balsamic vinegar. Everything is made from scratch and well-seasoned. Choose from pasta dishes such as four-cheese ravioli in marinara sauce, numerous gyros, vegetarian items, and a Greek meat loaf made with sirloin and lamb and Greek seasonings and topped with tzatziki sauce. The spanakopita spinach pie is a favorite at both lunch and dinner. Small outdoor patio. **FYI:** Reservations accepted. No smoking. **Open:** Lunch Mon–Sat 10:30am–2:30pm; dinner Mon–Sat 5–10pm. **Prices:** Main courses $9–$24. AE, CB, DC, DISC, MC, V.

Dick's Cafe
114 E St George Blvd; tel 801/673-3841. **American/Southwestern.** Dick's has been serving basic American fare ever since its opening in 1935. Dinners here include roast beef with mashed potatoes and gravy, fried chicken, spaghetti, and hamburgers, plus soups and salads. Over the years several Mexican items have been added for variety. Pies are fresh-baked on the premises. A senior citizen's menu is available. **FYI:** Reservations accepted. Children's menu. No liquor license. No smoking. **Open:** Daily 6am–9:30pm. **Prices:** Main courses $4–$11. AE, DC, MC, V.

Sullivan's Rococo Steakhouse
511 S Airport Rd; tel 801/673-3305. Across from airport on bluff on W side of town. **Seafood/Steak.** Perched on the bluff on the west side of downtown, this elegant restaurant affords a breathtaking panoramic view of the city and surrounding red rock country. The specialties of the house are prime rib, a variety of steaks, and some of the best lobster available in southwest Utah. Lunch features several sandwiches, including an extra-special prime rib sandwich, as well as burgers, salads, and a daily special. Try to save some room for a slice of the homemade pie—the shredded apple with caramel sauce and ice cream is spectacular. **FYI:** Reservations not accepted. Children's menu. No smoking. **Open:** Lunch Mon–Fri 11am–4pm; dinner daily 5–10pm. **Prices:** Main courses $7–$36. AE, DC, DISC, MC, V.

Tom's Delicatessen
In Holiday Inn Shopping Center, 175 W Bluff St; tel 801/628-1822. **Deli.** Tom's offers hot and cold sandwiches of just about every imaginable kind, plus side dishes of pepperoncino, sauerkraut, and the popular potato salad. Tasty desserts include German chocolate cake and cheesecake. **FYI:** Reservations not accepted. No liquor license. No smoking. **Open:** Tues–Sat 11am–6pm. **Prices:** Lunch main courses $4–$7. No CC.

ATTRACTIONS

Brigham Young Winter Home Historical Site
67 W 200 North; tel 801/673-2517. Church leader Brigham Young was one of St George's first snowbirds. He escaped the Salt Lake City cold during the last few winters of his life by coming south to this house. In addition to its obvious religious importance to the Church of Jesus Christ of Latter-Day Saints, it is a handsome example of how the well-to-do of the late 19th century lived. Guided ½-hour tours. **Open:** Peak (Mem Day–Labor Day) daily 8:30am–8:30pm. Reduced hours off-season. **Free**

Jacob Hamblin Home
Main St; tel 801/673-5181. Located 3 mi W of St George on US 91. This stone and pine house, built in the 1860s, is

typical of pioneer homes throughout the West, except that is definitively Mormon: It has two identical bedrooms, one for each of Hamblin's wives. The dining table is set in the typical Mormon fashion, with plates upside down and chairs facing away from the table to facilitate kneeling for before-meal prayers. Guided half-hour tours. **Open:** Peak (Mem Day–Labor Day) daily 8:30am–8pm. Reduced hours off-season. **Free**

Daughters of Utah Pioneers Museum
145 N 100 East; tel 801/628-7274. This "Grandma's attic" contains an eclectic collection of items belonging to the pioneers who settled this area more than 100 years ago. There is some furniture, including a bed used by Brigham Young, spinning wheels, an 1894 loom, guns, tools, musical instruments, and other relics from bygone days. Historic photos, mostly of pioneer families, are on display and can be purchased. Guided tours are given. **Open:** Mon–Sat 10am–5pm. **Free**

St George Tabernacle
440 S 300 East; tel 801/628-4072. An example of old-world craftsmanship, from the hand-quarried red stone walls to the intricate interior woodwork. Completed in 1876 after 13 years of work, the tabernacle served as a house of worship and town meeting hall. Today it functions as a community center and presents free weekly concerts and other cultural events. Half-hour guided tours. **Open:** Daily 9am–6pm. **Free**

St George Temple
250 E 400 South; tel 801/673-3533. Completed in 1877, the St George Temple was the first LDS temple in Utah, and it remains the oldest still in use in the world today. The majestic white temple is not open to the general public, but visitors can walk among the beautiful gardens. **Open:** Daily 9am–9pm. **Free**

Salina

Named for its salt deposits and mines, Salina is popular with hunters and fishermen venturing into nearby Fishlake National Forest. **Information:** Chamber of Commerce, 60 E Main, Salina 84654 (tel 801/529-7839).

MOTELS

Safari Motel
1425 S State St, 84654; tel 801/529-7447; fax 801/529-7447 ext 250. 1 block N of exit 54 off I-70. This two-story, honey-colored brick motel has a nice lobby with floor-to-ceiling windows and a large, circular, sunken gas fireplace. Small petting zoo with chickens, ducks, sheep, and rabbits. **Rooms:** 27 rms. CI open/CO 11am. Nonsmoking rms avail. **Amenities:** A/C, cable TV. **Services:** **Facilities:** 40 1 restaurant, playground. **Rates:** Peak (May–Oct) $44 S; $48–$52 D. Extra person $6. Children under age 12 stay free. Lower rates off-season. Parking: Outdoor, free. AE, CB, DC, DISC, MC, V.

Shaheen's Best Western Motel
1225 S State St, 84654; tel 801/529-7455 or toll free 800/528-1234; fax 801/529-7257. 2 blocks N of exit 54 off I-70. Simple modern red brick motel with tile roof. Stables and rodeo arena nearby. **Rooms:** 40 rms. CI 2pm/CO 11am. Nonsmoking rms avail. **Amenities:** A/C, cable TV. **Services:** **Facilities:** 25 1 restaurant, washer/dryer. **Rates:** Peak (May–Sept) $50 S; $56 D. Extra person $4. Children under age 12 stay free. Lower rates off-season. Parking: Outdoor, free. AE, CB, DC, DISC, MC, V.

Salt Lake City

See also Heber City, Ogden, Park City, Provo

At the foot of the Wasatch Range and near the Great Salt Lake, Salt Lake City is Utah's capital and largest city, and world headquarters for the Church of Jesus Christ of Latter-Day Saints. When Mormon leader Brigham Young arrived here with a group of his followers on July 24, 1847, he declared, "This is the place." Fleeing religious persecution, Young had said he was seeking a place that nobody else wanted. Salt Lake City is known for its wide streets, laid out so a team of oxen could turn around without backing up, as well as for its proximity to a half-dozen ski resorts and year-round recreational opportunities. At the heart of the city center is Temple Square, a stone-walled complex of historic buildings and gardens, all dominated by the gigantic, majestic Salt Lake Temple. Several colleges, including the University of Utah, are in the city. **Information:** Salt Lake City Convention & Visitors Bureau, 180 S West Temple, Salt Lake City 84101 (tel 801/521-2822 or 800/541-4955).

HOTELS

Best Western Olympus
161 W 600 South, 84101 (City Center); tel 801/521-7373 or toll free 800/426-0722; fax 801/524-0354. Exit 310 off I-15A. 13-story, full-service hotel with an outstanding rooftop restaurant. Close to all downtown attractions. Good choice for business travelers, skiers, and families. **Rooms:** 393 rms and stes. CI 2pm/CO noon. Nonsmoking rms avail. East rooms have spectacular views of towering Wasatch Mountains. Some have good views of Temple Square and Capitol. **Amenities:** A/C, cable TV w/movies. All units w/terraces, some w/whirlpools. **Services:** Car-rental desk. Complimentary shuttles to ski areas, airport, and Amtrak. City bus stops at hotel's front door. **Facilities:** 500 2 restaurants, 1 bar, spa, whirlpool, beauty salon, washer/dryer. State liquor store on premises. **Rates:** Peak

(June–Oct/Feb–Mar) $85–$99 S; $95–$119 D; $250 ste. Children under age 18 stay free. Lower rates off-season. Parking: Outdoor, free. AE, CB, DC, DISC, ER, JCB, MC, V.

Courtyard by Marriott
130 W 400 South St, 84101 (Downtown); tel 801/531-6000 or toll free 800/321-2211; fax 801/531-1273. 2 blocks N of I-15/I-80 exit 310. Comfortable, modern property well suited to both business travelers and families. **Rooms:** 121 rms and stes. CI 3pm/CO 1pm. Nonsmoking rms avail. Rooms are spacious, with great city views. Some have views of Capitol and Temple Square; others look out to towering Wasatch Mountains. **Amenities:** A/C, cable TV, dataport, voice mail. Some units w/terraces, some w/whirlpools. **Services:** Babysitting. Excellent security. Convenient to buses heading to ski area. **Facilities:** 100 1 restaurant, whirlpool, washer/dryer. Magleby's restaurant is famous for its pies and breadsticks. **Rates:** $89–$109 S or D; $140 ste. Extra person $10. Parking: Outdoor, free. AE, DC, DISC, MC, V.

Crystal Inn
230 W 500 South, 84101 (Downtown); tel 801/328-4466 or toll free 800/366-4466; fax 801/328-4072. 1 block N of I-15/I-80 exit 310. Built in April 1993, this property is conveniently located just three blocks south of Abravanel Hall and the Delta Center. Recommended for business travelers and tourists alike. Lobby has a working fireplace, TV, and a small snack room. **Rooms:** 175 rms and stes. CI 2pm/CO noon. Nonsmoking rms avail. Rooms are comfortable and attractively decorated; those on east side have view of the city with the Wasatch Mountains in the background. **Amenities:** A/C, cable TV w/movies, refrig, dataport, voice mail. Some units w/whirlpools. Coffeemaker available on request. **Services:** **Facilities:** 125 Sauna, whirlpool, washer/dryer. **Rates (BB):** $81–$101 S; $87–$101 D; $120–$150 ste. Extra person $10. Children under age 16 stay free. Parking: Outdoor, free. AE, DC, DISC, MC, V.

DoubleTree Hotel
215 W South Temple, 84101 (Temple Sq); tel 801/531-7500 or toll free 800/553-0075; fax 801/328-1289. Next to Salt Palace Convention Center. Very modern motel in heart of Salt Lake City. Southwestern-style lobby with large fireplace. **Rooms:** 381 rms and stes. Executive level. CI 4pm/CO noon. Nonsmoking rms avail. Attractive rooms have very large baths. Views are of city or mountains. Spacious hallways. **Amenities:** A/C, cable TV w/movies, voice mail. **Services:** VP Twice-daily maid svce, car-rental desk, children's program, babysitting. Guests receive two large chocolate chip cookies at check-in. **Facilities:** 500 1 restaurant, 1 bar, games rm, sauna, whirlpool, washer/dryer. Palm trees and tables surround the glassed-in pool. Top-floor restaurant has a commanding view of Temple Square and nearby mountains. **Rates:** Peak (Feb–Apr 15) $129–$169 S; $139–$179 D; $179–$325 ste. Extra person $10. Children under age 18 stay free. Lower rates off-season. AP rates avail. MAP rates avail. Parking: Indoor/outdoor, $5/day. AE, CB, DC, DISC, JCB, MC, V.

Embassy Suites Hotel
600 S West Temple, 84101; tel 801/359-7800 or toll free 800/EMBASSY; fax 801/359-3753. 6 blocks S of Temple Sq. Located in a commercial center, this all-suite hotel has an elegant lobby with comfortable seating areas, a beautiful white tile floor, and trees and other potted plants. **Rooms:** 241 stes and effic. CI 3pm/CO noon. Nonsmoking rms avail. Living rooms have pull-out couches and space for meals, games, relaxing. Rooms have city views. **Amenities:** A/C, cable TV w/movies, refrig, dataport, voice mail. **Services:** Complimentary beverages for two hours every morning; free cocktails in evening. **Facilities:** 60 1 restaurant, 1 bar (w/entertainment), sauna, whirlpool, washer/dryer. Pool area is stunningly landscaped with lots of greenery attractively arranged around seating areas. **Rates (BB):** Peak (Dec 15–Apr 15) $89–$159 ste; $89–$129 effic. Extra person $15. Children under age 12 stay free. Lower rates off-season. Parking: Indoor/outdoor, free. AE, CB, DC, DISC, ER, JCB, MC, V.

Inn at Temple Square
71 W South Temple, 84101; tel 801/531-1000 or toll free 800/843-4668; fax 801/536-7272. Across from SW corner of Temple Sq. This distinguished Edwardian-style building offers a delightful change from standard hotels. Spacious rooms are attractively furnished in 18th-century European elegance, yet with all the modern amenities you would expect in a top hotel. **Rooms:** 90 rms and stes. CI 3pm/CO noon. No smoking. **Amenities:** A/C, cable TV, refrig, dataport, VCR, bathrobes. 1 unit w/fireplace, some w/whirlpools. **Services:** VP Twice-daily maid svce, car-rental desk, babysitting. Complimentary local phone calls and newspapers. Free passes to nearby gym, pool, and spa. **Facilities:** 100 1 restaurant. Mezzanine library with wing chairs and piano. Carriage Court restaurant has outstanding menu, lovely table linens, and good service. **Rates (CP):** $113–$132 S or D; $155–$220 ste. Extra person $10. Children under age 18 stay free. MAP rates avail. Parking: Indoor/outdoor, free. AE, CB, DC, DISC, MC, V.

Little America Hotel & Towers
500 S Main St, 84101; tel 801/596-5785 or toll free 800/453-9450; fax 801/322-1610. An elegant hotel just a few blocks from Temple Square, this 17-story tower rises from a 10-acre oasis of foliage and fountains. Fresh flowers and plants in lobby. **Rooms:** 850 rms and stes. CI 1pm/CO 1pm. Nonsmoking rms avail. Rooms are very large and handsomely appointed; most have bird's-eye view of city and mountains beyond. **Amenities:** A/C, cable TV w/movies, refrig, dataport, VCR, bathrobes. Some units w/terraces, some w/whirlpools. **Services:** VP Twice-daily maid svce, car-rental desk, social director, babysitting. **Facilities:** 2100 2 restaurants (*see* "Restaurants" below), 1

bar, spa, sauna, steam rm, whirlpool, beauty salon. **Rates:** $63–$114 S; $73–$124 D; $114–$124 ste. Extra person $10. Parking: Indoor/outdoor, free. AE, CB, DC, DISC, EC, MC, V.

Peery Hotel

110 W 300 South, 84101; tel 801/521-4300 or toll free 800/331-0073; fax 801/575-5014. Downtown within 3 blocks of Temple Sq. This 1910 building was fully renovated in 1985 and makes a delightful base for exploring downtown Salt Lake City. **Rooms:** 77 rms. CI 2pm/CO noon. Nonsmoking rms avail. Tastefully decorated, with 19th-century period furniture in some rooms. **Amenities:** A/C, cable TV. **Services:** Car-rental desk, social director, babysitting. **Facilities:** 50 1 restaurant (lunch and dinner only). **Rates (CP):** $59–$99 S; $89–$99 D. Extra person $10. Children under age 18 stay free. Parking: Outdoor, free. AE, DC, DISC, MC, V.

Radisson Hotel Salt Lake City Airport

2177 W North Temple, 84116 (Salt Lake Int'l Airport); tel 801/364-5000 or toll free 800/333-3333; fax 801/364-5823. Just W of I-80 exit 117. Built in 1980, this rugged gray stone hotel is just three miles from downtown Salt Lake City. The lobby is elegantly furnished; a brass and wood staircase stands in front of a beautiful mural. **Rooms:** 127 rms and stes. CI 3pm/CO noon. Nonsmoking rms avail. Rooms are large and decorated in country French style with robust stained wood, rare marble, and rich fabrics. West-facing rooms have nice mountain views. **Amenities:** A/C, cable TV w/movies, refrig, dataport. Some units w/terraces, some w/fireplaces, 1 w/whirlpool. **Services:** Free daily newspapers. Complimentary coffee and fresh fruit in lobby. **Facilities:** 60 1 restaurant, spa, whirlpool. **Rates (CP):** $125–$135 S; $129–$139 D; $139 ste. Extra person $10. Children under age 16 stay free. Parking: Indoor/outdoor, free. AE, CB, DC, DISC, EC, ER, JCB, MC, V.

Red Lion Hotel

255 S West Temple, 84101; tel 801/328-2000 or toll free 800/RED-LION; fax 801/532-1953. 4 blocks N of exit 310 off I-15. Located adjacent to the downtown convention center, this impressive hotel has a spacious lobby accented by polished marble and rich warm woods. **Rooms:** 495 rms and stes. Executive level. CI 3pm/CO 1pm. Nonsmoking rms avail. Rooms are large and attractive, with large desks. North rooms have views of Capitol and Temple Square; west rooms look out at the Oquirrh Mountains; east rooms face towering Wasatch Mountains. **Amenities:** A/C, cable TV w/movies, dataport, voice mail. Some units w/whirlpools. Two-line phones. **Services:** VP Car-rental desk, masseur, babysitting. Multilingual staff. **Facilities:** 1200 2 restaurants, 2 bars (1 w/entertainment), spa, sauna, whirlpool. **Rates:** Peak (Sept 15–Mar 15) $149–$169 S; $164–$184 D; $225–$1,500 ste. Extra person $15. Children under age 17 stay free. Lower rates off-season. Parking: Indoor, $5/day. AE, CB, DC, DISC, JCB, MC, V.

Salt Lake Hilton

150 W 500 South, 84101 (Downtown); tel 801/532-3344 or toll free 800/421-7602; fax 801/531-0705. Exit 310 off I-15. Just five blocks south of Temple Square, this modern hotel is constantly upgrading its decor and facilities. **Rooms:** 351 rms and stes. Executive level. CI 3pm/CO noon. Nonsmoking rms avail. Rooms are spacious and well appointed. Some have mountain views, others overlook the city. Some baths have sunken tubs, some have showers only. **Amenities:** A/C, cable TV w/movies, dataport, voice mail. Some units w/terraces, 1 w/fireplace. **Services:** VP Car-rental desk, masseur, babysitting. **Facilities:** 1200 3 restaurants, 1 bar (w/entertainment), games rm, spa, sauna, whirlpool, beauty salon. Barber shop, state liquor store on premises. Laptop rentals available at business center. Ski Utah Center with rentals. **Rates:** $110–$155 S; $130–$175 D; $135–$350 ste. Extra person $20. Children under age 18 stay free. Parking: Indoor/outdoor, free. AE, CB, DC, DISC, ER, JCB, MC, V.

Shilo Inn

206 S West Temple, 84101 (Downtown); tel 801/521-9500 or toll free 800/222-2244; fax 801/359-6527. Exit 310 off I-15, 1 block S of Convention center. Newly remodeled hotel just minutes from downtown; a good choice for both business travelers and tourists. **Rooms:** 200 rms, stes, and effic. CI 2pm/CO noon. Nonsmoking rms avail. Attractive rooms with modern decor and views of Wasatch Mountains to the east and Temple Square to the north. **Amenities:** A/C, cable TV w/movies, refrig, VCR. **Services:** VP Complimentary *USA Today* delivered to door. **Facilities:** 125 2 restaurants, 1 bar (w/entertainment), games rm, sauna, whirlpool, washer/dryer. Bakery and espresso bar. **Rates (BB):** $95–$109 S or D; $199–$349 ste; $199–$349 effic. Extra person $12. Children under age 12 stay free. Parking: Indoor, $5/day. Special corporate membership includes free faxing and photocopying and discounts in restaurants and lounge. AE, CB, DC, DISC, JCB, MC, V.

MOTELS

Holiday Inn Airport

1659 W North Temple, 84116; tel 801/533-9000 or toll free 800/HOLIDAY; fax 801/364-0614. Exit 118 off I-80. Located just a few miles west of downtown near the airport, and on the city bus route. **Rooms:** 191 rms. CI 2pm/CO noon. Nonsmoking rms avail. Rooms are tastefully decorated; all have comfortable easy chair with ottoman and desk. Exterior rooms have parking at door and views of mountains and city, but may be noisy. Interior rooms overlook nicely landscaped pool in central courtyard. **Amenities:** A/C, cable TV w/movies, voice mail. **Services:** Babysitting. Cocktails and complimentary hors d'oeuvres 5–7pm weekdays in private club ($1 membership). Complimentary salt water taffy. **Facilities:** 1 restaurant, 1 bar, spa, whirlpool, washer/dryer. **Rates (CP):** Peak (June–Sept) $80–$99 S or D. Extra person $10. Children under age 19 stay free. Lower rates off-season. Parking: Outdoor, free. AE, CB, DC, DISC, JCB, MC, V.

Residence Inn by Marriott
765 E 400 South, 84102; tel 801/532-5511 or toll free 800/331-3131; fax 801/531-0416. 7 blocks E of downtown. Spacious lobby has two TVs and fireplaces. **Rooms:** 128 effic. CI 3pm/CO noon. Nonsmoking rms avail. **Amenities:** A/C, cable TV w/movies, refrig, dataport, voice mail, in-rm safe. Some units w/terraces, some w/fireplaces. **Services:** Babysitting. Bellman will shop for groceries. Complimentary wine, beer, soda, and snacks on weekdays. **Facilities:** Basketball, whirlpool, washer/dryer. **Rates (CP):** Peak (Jan–Apr/July–Sept) $120–$179 effic. Extra person $10. Children under age 12 stay free. Lower rates off-season. Parking: Outdoor, free. AE, DC, DISC, JCB, MC, V.

INNS

Anton Boxrud Bed & Breakfast Inn
57 S 600 East, 84102; tel 801/363-8035 or toll free 800/524-5511. 6 blocks E of Temple Sq. Located in a charming building in the historical area east of downtown, within walking distance of shopping and attractions. The large porch in front is a very pleasant place to relax. Good choice for business travelers and families. **Rooms:** 7 rms (3 w/shared bath). CI open/CO 11am. No smoking. Rooms are beautifully decorated, with lace window treatments. Some have nice views of the mountains. **Amenities:** A/C, cable TV, bathrobes. No phone. 1 unit w/whirlpool. Fresh flowers in rooms, as well as signature chocolates, tea, and evening snacks. **Services:** Social director, afternoon tea and wine/sherry served. Dinner can be arranged by special request. **Facilities:** Whirlpool, washer/dryer, guest lounge w/TV. **Rates (BB):** $59–$69 S w/shared bath, $89–$119 S or D w/private bath; $69–$79 D w/shared bath. Children under age 15 stay free. Parking: Outdoor, free. AE, DISC, MC, V.

The Armstrong Mansion Bed & Breakfast
667 E 100 South, 84102; tel 801/531-1333 or toll free 800/708-1333; fax 801/531-0282. 7 blocks E of Temple Sq. A romantic getaway in the historical area east of downtown. The home of the first mayor of Salt Lake City, the Armstrong dates from 1893 and is listed on the National Register of Historic Places. It retains the original chandeliers, fireplaces, stained glass, wallpaper, tile, and woodwork. Paintings and plants grace the rooms. Well suited for both business travelers and families. **Rooms:** 11 rms. CI 3pm/CO 11am. Nonsmoking rms avail. Each room has been tastefully decorated to reflect the motif of a particular month of the year. Most are Victorian style. Bridal suite has spiral staircase leading up to one of the two baths. **Amenities:** A/C, cable TV, dataport, bathrobes. Some units w/fireplaces, some w/whirlpools. **Services:** Car-rental desk, social director, masseur, babysitting, afternoon tea served. Complimentary beverages. Evening meal can be provided upon special request. **Facilities:** Whirlpool, washer/dryer, guest lounge w/TV. **Rates (BB):** $75–$82 S; $75–$184 D. Extra person $10. Children under age 18 stay free. Parking: Outdoor, free. AE, DISC, MC, V.

Brigham Street Inn
1135 E South Temple, 84102; tel 801/364-4461 or toll free 800/417-4461; fax 801/521-3201. 11 blocks E of Temple Sq. This graceful mansion, renovated in 1982, is attractively and comfortably decorated with antiques and many plants. Its living room features a piano, and the parlor and dining room have working fireplaces. A good choice for a quiet retreat. **Rooms:** 9 rms and stes. CI 2pm/CO noon. Nonsmoking rms avail. Each room has been beautifully furnished by a different interior decorator. **Amenities:** A/C, cable TV w/movies, VCR, bathrobes. 1 unit w/terrace, some w/fireplaces, 1 w/whirlpool. **Services:** Twice-daily maid svce, social director, afternoon tea served. **Facilities:** Guest lounge w/TV. **Rates (CP):** $75–$115 S; $115–$125 D; $175 ste. Extra person $10. Children under age 12 stay free. Parking: Outdoor, free. AE, CB, DC, MC, V.

Saltair Bed & Breakfast
164 S 900 East, 84102; tel 801/533-8184 or toll free 800/733-8184; fax 801/595-0332. 1 mi E of center of town. **Rooms:** 5 rms and stes (3 w/shared bath); 2 cottages/villas. CI 3:30pm/CO 11am. No smoking. **Amenities:** A/C, cable TV w/movies, voice mail, bathrobes. No phone. Some units w/terraces, some w/fireplaces, some w/whirlpools. **Services:** Masseur, babysitting, afternoon tea served. **Facilities:** Whirlpool, guest lounge. **Rates (BB):** $50–$69 S w/shared bath, $79–$95 S or D w/private bath; $79–$89 D w/shared bath; $95–$135 ste; $75–$149 cottage/villa. Extra person $15. Children under age 5 stay free. Min stay special events. Higher rates for special events/hols. Parking: Outdoor, free. AE, CB, DC, DISC, MC, V.

The Ute Hostel
21 E Kelsey Ave, 84111; tel 801/595-1645. 6 blocks S of Temple Sq about 1 mi E of I-15/I-80 exit 309. Typical hostel in an older renovated building, located in a small residential area sandwiched between commercial properties. Popular with young Europeans, particularly hikers and backpackers. **Rooms:** 5 rms (all w/shared bath). CI open/CO noon. Nonsmoking rms avail. Rooms are plain but clean. Two have five bunk beds each. **Amenities:** A/C, VCR. No phone or TV. **Services:** Social director, afternoon tea served. Complimentary tea, coffee, hot chocolate. **Facilities:** Guest lounge w/TV. Cooking facilities available for guests' use. Inexpensive bicycle, ski, skate, and golf rentals available.

Rates: Peak (May–Oct) $13–$15 S w/shared bath; $30–$35 D w/shared bath. Children under age 3 stay free. Lower rates off-season. Parking: Outdoor, free. No CC.

RESTAURANTS

Baci Trattoria

134 W Pierpont Ave (Downtown); tel 801/328-1500. 2½ blocks S of Temple Sq. **Italian/Seafood.** This friendly, comfortable restaurant occupies a historic building once used for railroad offices and later as a high school. It now has an Italian flair, with colorful flags and potted plants. The menu offers pizza, pasta, salads, fish, and, of course, Italian entrees. The fish is flown in fresh daily. In summer, outdoor patio dining is available. **FYI:** Reservations accepted. No smoking. **Open:** Lunch Mon–Fri 11:30am–2:30pm; dinner Mon–Thurs 5–10pm, Fri–Sat 5–11pm. **Prices:** Main courses $9–$24. AE, CB, DC, DISC, MC, V.

Cafe Trang

818 S Main St (Downtown); tel 801/539-1638. 2 blocks S of exit 310 off I-15. **Chinese/Vietnamese.** One of the top Chinese restaurants in Utah (and, for that matter, in the entire Rocky Mountain region), Cafe Trang boasts an extensive menu of 197 items, including Chinese and Vietnamese specialties and many vegetable dishes. Decor is casual and businesslike, with two large rooms and some large family-size tables. **FYI:** Reservations accepted. Beer only. No smoking. **Open:** Sun–Thurs 11:30am–9:30pm, Fri–Sat 11:30am–10pm. **Prices:** Main courses $5–$9. AE, MC, V.

Crown Burgers

3190 S Highland Dr; tel 801/467-6633. 2½ mi E of exit 306 off I-15 or 2½ mi S of exit 126 off I-80. **Burgers/Fast food.** Basically a fast food burger joint, this one is a lot better than the national chains. The building's exterior is of rugged stone; inside, comfortable seating fills the attractive, brightly colored dining area. Sandwiches feature chicken, steak, and ham, and there are gyros and the special pastrami burger; salads offer a light alternative. **FYI:** Reservations not accepted. No liquor license. No smoking. Additional locations: 377 E 200 South (tel 532-1155); 118 N 300 West (tel 532-5300). **Open:** Mon–Sat 10am–10pm. **Prices:** Main courses $3–$7. DISC, MC, V. VP

Diamond Lil's

1528 W North Temple; tel 801/533-0547. About 2 mi W of Temple Sq. **Steak.** On the west side of downtown, almost at the airport, this Salt Lake City landmark has been serving steak and prime rib to satisfied patrons for more than 20 years. Decor is 19th-century Wild West in a typical frontier building, with fake storefronts marked "Red Garter Saloon," "Wells Fargo," and "General Mercantile." The interior is made of logs salvaged from cabins, while lighting comes from wagon wheel chandeliers. The emphasis here is on beef—prime rib, T-bone and porterhouse steaks—but Alaskan crab and trout stuffed with shrimp round out the menu. **FYI:** Reservations accepted. No smoking. **Open:** Mon–Sat 11am–10pm. **Prices:** Main courses $9–$30. AE, DC, MC, V.

Ferrantelli

In Trolley Square Shopping Mall, 300 Trolley Sq; tel 801/531-8228. 7 blocks E and 5 blocks S of Temple Sq. **Italian.** Popular for its Northern Italian entrees and delicious desserts, this busy restaurant makes everything from scratch. The menu offers a wide selection of pasta dishes, usually with separate vegetarian and meat versions, plus seafood. **FYI:** Reservations accepted. Children's menu. No smoking. **Open:** Mon–Thurs 11:30am–10pm, Fri–Sat 11:30am–11pm, Sun 1–10pm. **Prices:** Main courses $7–$16; prix fixe $15. AE, CB, DC, DISC, MC, V.

★ Lamb's Restaurant

169 S Main St (Downtown); tel 801/364-7166. **American/Continental.** Utah's oldest restaurant, located just a block and a half from Temple Square, Lamb's has been serving the Who's Who of Salt Lake City since 1919. The quality of the food—everything is made from scratch, right down to the mayonnaise—and the service are unparalleled. The menu (printed on parchment) lists choices like corned beef and cabbage, chicken pot pie, braised tenderloin tips, rainbow trout, barbecued lamb shanks, and many Greek dishes. **FYI:** Reservations accepted. Guitar. No smoking. **Open:** Mon–Sat 7am–9pm. **Prices:** Main courses $13–$18. AE, CB, DC, DISC, MC, V.

Le Parisien

417 S 300 East (Downtown); tel 801/364-5223. At 400 South. **French/Italian.** Located near the city library and courthouse, this restaurant has been a local favorite for many years. Upstairs is an elegant dining room with fine views of the city. The decor is European, with old-world pictures on the walls, red Victorian-style upholstered chairs, and hanging lamps. The lounge has a full bar, and there's a patio for warm weather dining. Popular menu items include French onion soup, Dover sole, rack of lamb provençale, chateaubriand béarnaise, and fettuccine Alfredo. **FYI:** Reservations recommended. No smoking. **Open:** Peak (Oct–Jan 30) Mon–Thurs 11am–10:30pm, Fri–Sat 11am–11:30pm, Sun 4:30–9:30pm. **Prices:** Main courses $11–$20. AE, CB, DC, DISC, MC, V.

★ Little America Restaurant

In Little America Hotel & Towers, 500 S Main St; tel 801/596-5785. 5 blocks S of Temple Sq. **American/Steak.** Elegant, intimate dining in a setting softened by candlelight and warmed by a large fireplace. Specialties to savor include shrimp scampi, filet of chinook salmon, scaloppine of veal tenderloin, and Australian lobster. There are also nightly specials, plus a wide selection of vintage wines. **FYI:** Reservations accepted. Guitar/Keyboard. Children's menu. No smoking. **Open:** Breakfast Mon–Fri 7–10am, Sat 7–11am,

Sun 8am–2pm; lunch Mon–Fri 11am–2pm; dinner daily 5–11pm. **Prices:** Main courses $10–$23. AE, CB, DC, DISC, MC, V.

Marianne's Delicatessen
149 W 200 South (Downtown); tel 801/364-0486. **American/German.** A small deli downtown, Marianne's has been specializing in German foods since 1954. There are two German soups and lunch plates offered daily, and the specialty is a homemade European-style sausage. A selection from the long domestic and imported beer list will properly complement your authentic German meal. **FYI:** Reservations accepted. Beer only. No smoking. **Open:** Daily 11am–3pm. **Prices:** Lunch main courses $4–$8. AE, MC, V.

Market Street Broiler
260 S 1300 East; tel 801/583-8808. 13 blocks E of Temple Sq. **American/Seafood.** Located in the 1930 brick fire station #8 building, this sophisticated restaurant opened in 1983. Choices from the extensive menu include about a dozen seafood appetizers, chowder, sandwiches from the basic BLT or egg salad to baked chicken and ham with avocado, mesquite broiled steaks and seafood, barbecued ribs, and pasta. Recommended for seafood lovers and very popular with students. **FYI:** Reservations not accepted. Children's menu. No smoking. **Open:** Daily 11am–10pm. **Prices:** Main courses $7–$30. AE, DC, DISC, MC, V.

★ Market Street Grill
50 W Market St (Downtown); tel 801/322-4668. **American/Seafood.** One of Salt Lake City's most popular restaurants is just a few minutes from Temple Square and the convention center. Located in the historic 1906 New York Hotel Building, along with the Market Street Oyster Bar and New Yorker, the Grill has a high-tech atmosphere inside: light, bright, and colorful, with potted palms and a black and white tile floor. All meals are made from scratch, with fresh fish flown in daily. Choose from salads, chowder, sandwiches, and pasta for lunch; steaks, chops, and seafood are added for dinner. The appetizers are practically a meal in themselves. Sublime desserts include several fruit and cream pies and something called chocolate decadence—which lives up to its name. **FYI:** Reservations not accepted. Children's menu. No smoking. **Open:** Breakfast Mon–Fri 6:30–11:30am, Sat 7am–noon; lunch Mon–Fri 11:30am–3pm, Sat noon–3pm; dinner Mon–Thurs 5–10:30pm, Fri–Sat 5–11:30pm, Sun 4–9:30pm; brunch Sun 9:30am–3pm. **Prices:** Main courses $12–$24. AE, CB, DC, DISC, MC, V.

Market Street Oyster Bar
54 W Market St (Downtown); tel 801/531-6044. **American/Seafood.** Located in the historic 1906 New York Hotel Building, the Oyster Bar is a private club with two-week temporary memberships available for $5 (which allow patrons to purchase liquor by the drink). As the name implies, oysters are the mainstay of this restaurant, in particular, blue point oysters. They go through 300 pounds of shellfish here each day. In addition there are hot and cold seafood platters, chowders, stews, and pastas; landlubbers can choose from sandwiches, salads, steak, and chops. **FYI:** Reservations not accepted. Children's menu. **Open:** Daily 11:30am–12:30pm. **Prices:** Main courses $8–$34. AE, CB, DC, DISC, MC, V.

New Yorker
60 W Market St (Downtown); tel 801/363-0166. **American/Continental.** In the historic 1906 New York Hotel Building, along with the Market Street Grill and the Oyster Bar, the New Yorker has three dining rooms, two of which are very romantic. The cafe has the stained glass ceiling from the old Hotel Utah. Like the Oyster Bar, the New Yorker is a private club, but two-week temporary memberships available for $5 (which allow patrons to purchase liquor by the drink). But the food here is also a little more elegant than at its two neighbors. The dinner menu includes items like rack of lamb, dry aged steaks, sautéed sweetbreads and fresh foie gras, and grilled baby chicken with fresh thyme and polenta. **FYI:** Reservations recommended. Dress code. **Open:** Lunch Mon–Fri 11:30am–2:30pm; dinner Mon–Thurs 5:30–10pm, Fri–Sat 5:30–11pm. **Prices:** Main courses $20–$25. AE, CB, DC, DISC, MC, V.

Pierpont Cantina
122 W Pierpont Ave (Downtown); tel 801/364-1222. Near 6th St exit off I-15. **Mexican/Seafood.** This popular Mexican restaurant is a great stop while seeing the sights downtown. The kitchen prepares traditional Mexican dishes plus seafood flown in daily. Popular items include carnitos (slow-roasted pork with red pepper salsa, refried beans, and hot corn tortillas), snow crab enchiladas, and a combination of shrimp, crab, and halibut. The restaurant's own bakery provides fresh bread daily. **FYI:** Reservations accepted. Children's menu. No smoking. **Open:** Mon–Thurs 11:30am–10pm, Fri 11:30am–11pm, Sat 4–11pm, Sun 4–9:30pm. **Prices:** Main courses $7–$18. AE, CB, DC, DISC, MC, V.

ATTRACTIONS

The Beehive House
67 E South Temple; tel 801/240-2681. Brigham Young built this as a family home in 1894. The New England–style house includes a widow's walk for keeping an eye on the surrounding desert and has been restored and furnished with many original pieces. The second-floor Long Hall, for formal entertaining, was also used as a dormitory for visitors. Of Brigham Young's 27 wives, only one at a time lived in the Beehive House; the others, along with some of his children, would live next door in the Lion House (not open for tours). **Open:** Mon–Sat 9:30am–4:30pm, Sun 10am–1pm. **Free**

Geneology Research Center
35 N West Temple; tel 801/240-2331. Probably the world's largest collection of genealogical records under one roof. Most of the records, which date from about 1550 to about 1910, are from governments, many different church denomi-

nations, and other organizations and individuals. There is a substantial collection of records from the United States, Scotland, and England, and the collection is growing. Volunteers help visitors with researching their family origins. A 15-minute video explains procedures, while a booklet helps focus research. **Open:** Mon 7:30am–6pm, Tues–Fri 7:30am–10pm, Sat 7:30am–5pm. **Free**

Museum of Church History and Art
45 N West Temple; tel 801/240-3310. The collection of church artifacts, begun in 1869, includes the plow that cut the first furrows in Salt Lake Valley. The history of the LDS Church is described in the exhibits on each of the church presidents, from Joseph Smith to the present, and a theater presentation describes the museum's work and related topics. Puppet shows, costumed docents, audio tour. **Open:** Mon–Fri 9am–9pm, Sat–Sun 10am–7pm. **Free**

Pioneer Memorial Museum
300 N Main St; tel 801/538-1050. A four-story Grecian-style building housing an immense collection of pioneer portraits and memorabilia. The main floor includes theatrical exhibits, paintings, photos, and personal effects of church leaders Brigham Young and Heber C Kimball. There is also a manuscript room, household displays, and exhibits on spinning, weaving, railroading, mining, and guns. Guided tours available. **Open:** Peak (June–Aug) Mon–Sat 9am–5pm, Sun 1–5pm. Reduced hours off-season. **Free**

This Is the Place State Park
2601 E Sunnyside Ave; tel 801/584-8391. Here is where Brigham Young and the first group of pioneers got their first glimpse of the Salt Lake Valley. Old Deseret is a pioneer village made up of many original pioneer buildings from across the state. In summer it becomes a living history museum, with people in period garb, living and working the way their forefathers did. A visitor center contains exhibits depicting the Mormon pioneers' trek in 1847. The 1,600-acre park also offers hiking, cross-country skiing in winter, wildlife viewing, and a picnic area. **Open:** Mid-Apr–mid-Oct, daily 11am–7pm. **$$**

Council Hall
300 N State St; tel 801/538-1030 or toll free 800/200-1160. Completed in 1866, the Hall is a fine example of Greek revival architecture. Originally located downtown, it first served as City Hall and the meeting place for the Territorial Legislature. It was dismantled, coded, and reassembled in its present location. Today Council Hall houses the Utah Travel Council upstairs, and the Utah Tourism and Recreation Information Center on the ground floor. **Open:** Mon–Fri 8am–5pm, Sat–Sun 10am–3pm. **Free**

Utah Museum of Natural History
University of Utah Campus, jct 1340 E/200 S; tel 801/581-6927. More than 200 exhibits display fossils, gems, minerals, and plant species found in Utah. The collection takes visitors on a journey through time, describing the geologic and natural creation of Utah right up to the present. A museum field trip takes visitors to Utah's deserts, marshes, and paleontological sites. Also offered are classes and workshops for children and adults. **Open:** Mon–Fri 9:30am–5:30pm, Sun noon–5pm. **$**

Hansen Planetarium
15 S State St; tel 801/538-2104. Housed in the former city library, this planetarium presents multimedia star programs and 3-D laser shows on a 50-foot-diameter geodesic dome. On display are three floors of interactive exhibits ranging from the naming of the planets to an original Spitz star projector. Gift shop with science toys and books. **Open:** Sun–Thurs 10am–9pm, Fri–Sat 10am–midnight. **$$**

The Children's Museum of Utah
840 N 300 West; tel 801/328-3383. Activities and hands-on exhibits are the focus. Kids can try face painting and make-up, folk-dancing and art, or operate a telephone switchboard, uncover an animal skeleton on an archeological dig, or pilot a jet. Target ages are 2–12; children must be accompanied by an adult. **Open:** Mon–Thurs and Sat 9:30am–5pm, Fri 9:30am–9pm. **$**

Wheeler Historic Farm
6351 S 900 East; tel 801/264-2241. The restored Victorian farm house and working farm holds special events throughout the year: an ice cream social in late June, a brass band festival in August, a teddy bear Victorian tea in September, and breakfast with Santa in December. Hay rides in summer and a sleigh rides in winter; historic farming demonstrations. **Open:** Daily, call for schedule. **$**

Red Butte Garden
300 Wakara Way, University of Utah; tel 801/581-5322. Located in the foothills of the Wasatch Mountains, the garden covers 20 acres of display gardens and another 200 acres in their natural state. Visitors can hike the four miles of nature trails and tour the arboretum. **Open:** Daily sunrise–sunset. **Free**

Delta Center
301 W South Temple; tel 801/325-2000. Home of the NBA's Utah Jazz and the IHL's Utah Grizzlies. Star basketball players John Stockton and Karl Malone are both veterans of the US Olympic "Dream Team." The Jazz usually packs the house, so it's advised to get tickets early. **Open:** Call for schedule. **$$$$**

Brighton Ski Resort
Big Cottonwood Canyon, Brighton; tel 801/532-4731. Located 20 mi SE of Salt Lake City. Two high-speed quad lifts, two triples, and three double chairs servicing over 850 acres in the Wasatch-Cache National Forest with an average of 430 inches (36 feet) snowfall per year. The vertical drop is 1,745 feet, with a base elevation of 8,755 feet and summit of 10,500 feet. There are 64 runs, 21% of which are rated beginner, 40% intermediate, and 39% advanced. The Brighton Resort Center is a 20,000-square-foot day lodge with ticket windows,

restrooms, a common area, and a convenient depot for those using the bus. The Ski School offers a variety of workshops and clinics. **Open:** Peak (mid-Dec–mid-Mar) Mon–Sat 9am–9pm, Sun 9am–4pm. Reduced hours off-season. **$$$$**

Solitude Ski Resort
Cottonwood Canyon Rd; tel 801/534-1400. Located 28 mi from downtown Salt Lake City in Big Cottonwood Canyon. The resort operates one high speed quad lift, two triples, and four doubles to service 63 runs and three bowls. Runs are rated as 20% beginner, 50% intermediate, and 30% advanced/expert. With a summit elevation of 10,035 feet and a vertical drop of 2,047 feet, the resort receives an average snowfall of 430 inches (36 feet). **Open:** Mid-Nov–mid-Apr, daily, call for schedule. **$$$$**

Snowbird

See also Salt Lake City

Started in 1971, Snowbird is a full-service ski resort in Little Cottonwood Canyon, southeast of Salt Lake City. **Information:** Snowbird Ski & Summer Resort, PO Box 929000, Snowbird 84092 (tel 801/742-2222).

LODGE

The Lodge at Snowbird
UT 12, 84092; tel 801/742-2222 or toll free 800/882-4766; fax 801/742 3311. Across from Snowbird Plaza Ctr. Nestled in the mountains, the Lodge has panoramic views of the canyon and surrounding mountains, and a large stone fireplace in the lobby. **Rooms:** 120 rms, stes, and effic. CI 4pm/CO 11am. Nonsmoking rms avail. Spectacular room views of the mountains. Paneled walls hung with original artwork and lithographs. **Amenities:** A/C, cable TV w/movies, refrig, dataport, VCR. All units w/terraces, some w/fireplaces. **Services:** Car-rental desk, social director, children's program. In-room babysitting. Pizza delivered to room. **Facilities:** 13 10 2000 1 restaurant, 1 bar, volleyball, games rm, racquetball, squash, spa, sauna, steam rm, whirlpool, day-care ctr, washer/dryer. **Rates:** Peak (Dec 15–Mar 23) $169–$309 S or D; $509–$799 ste; $159–$532 effic. Children under age 18 stay free. Lower rates off-season. Parking: Outdoor, free. AE, CB, DC, DISC, JCB, MC, V.

RESORT

The Cliff Lodge
UT 210, 84092; tel 801/742-2222 or toll free 800/453-3000; fax 801/742-3204. E of Snowbird Plaza Ctr. 2,000 acres. The flagship of the Snowbird resort impresses with its spectacular architecture and breathtaking views of ski slopes, canyon, and mountains. A 10-story window wall is the dominant feature of the massive avalanche-proof structure. Floors are covered with magnificent Persian rugs. Ski-in/ski-out access. **Rooms:** 532 rms and stes. Executive level. CI 4pm/CO 11am. Nonsmoking rms avail. Wide variety of floor plans and luxury levels available. **Amenities:** Satel TV w/movies, dataport. No A/C. Some units w/terraces. **Services:** VP Car-rental desk, social director, masseur, children's program. In-room babysitting. **Facilities:** 2000 4 restaurants (*see* "Restaurants" below), 2 bars (1 w/entertainment), games rm, spa, sauna, steam rm, whirlpool, beauty salon, day-care ctr, washer/dryer. Penthouse Spa and Pool for adults only. Ski and snowboarding instruction for all ages. **Rates:** Peak (Dec 15–Mar 24) $189–$309 S or D; $509–$799 ste. Min stay peak. Lower rates off-season. Parking: Indoor/outdoor, free. AE, CB, DC, DISC, JCB, MC, V.

RESTAURANT

The Aerie Restaurant
In Snowbird Ski & Summer Resort, Cliff Lodge; tel 801/521-8040. **Eclectic/Pacific Rim.** The Aerie is a class act among resort restaurants. The spacious and elegant dining room atop the Cliff Lodge boasts magnificent mountain views through its expansive windows. Asian decor features black and gold screens for dividers, fresh flowers on the tables, ancient emperors' robes, and genuine Chinese horse sculptures. The menu features sushi, fresh fish, and tenderloin of beef, as well as some more exotic dishes. **FYI:** Reservations recommended. Guitar/harp/jazz/piano. Children's menu. Dress code. No smoking. **Open:** Breakfast daily 7–10:30am; dinner Tues–Thurs 6–9pm, Fri–Sat 6–10pm; brunch Sun 10am–2pm. **Prices:** Main courses $19–$29. AE, DC, DISC, MC, V. VP

ATTRACTION

Snowbird Ski and Summer Resort
UT 210; tel 801/521-6040 or toll free 800/453-3000. Visitors will find the same wonderful snow here as at nearby Alta, but with a wider range of upper-end amenities, including Snowbird's extremely popular spa and salon. Snowbird offers plenty for the expert skier, including Great Scott (one of the steepest runs in the country), plus beginner and intermediate trails and even some "family-only" ski zones. Snowbird also has a particularly good program for skiers with disabilities. **Open:** Mid-Nov–early May, daily 9am–4:30pm. **$$$$**

Springdale

See Zion National Park

Sundance

See Provo

Torrey

See Capitol Reef National Park

Tropic

See Bryce Canyon National Park

Zion National Park

So named by Mormon pioneers because it seemed to be a bit of heaven on earth, Zion National Park offers sheer multi-colored walls of sandstone, narrow canyons, hanging gardens of wildflowers, and the roar of the churning, tumbling Virgin River. Located in southwest Utah, at elevations ranging from 3,700 feet to 8,726 feet, the park has several sections: Zion Canyon, the main part of the park, and the less-visited Kolob Canyons. The main east–west road through Zion Canyon is UT 9, from which one can reach a 14-mile round-trip scenic drive/tram route that provides access to most scenic over-looks and trailheads.

Because of its extremes of elevation, Zion harbors a vast array of plants and animals. About 800 native species of plants have been found: cactus, yucca, and mesquite in the hot, dry desert areas; ponderosa pine trees on the high plateaus; and cottonwoods and box elders along rivers and streams. The red claret cup, one of the 14 varieties of cactus that grow in the park, has spectacular blooms in spring. **Bird watching** is plentiful in Zion. The rare peregrine falcon, among the world's fastest birds, sometimes nests in the Weeping Rock area, where the dipper, winter wren, and white-throated swift can also be seen. Golden eagles, several species of hummingbirds, ravens, and roadrunners also make their home in the park.

Zion offers a wide variety of hiking trails, ranging from easy half-hour walks on paved paths to grueling overnight hikes over rocky terrain along steep drop-offs. Several free brochures on hiking trails are available at the visitor centers, and the Zion Natural History Association publishes a 48-page booklet describing 18 trails. Hikers with a fear of heights should be especially careful when choosing trails; many include steep, dizzying drop-offs.

The park has two visitor centers. The more comprehensive **Zion Canyon Visitor Center** (tel 801/772-3256), near the south entrance to the park, has a museum with exhibits on the geology and history of the area and presents an introductory slide show on the park. Rangers answer questions and provide backcountry permits. The smaller **Kolob Canyon Visitor Center** (tel 801/586-9548), in the northwest corner of the park off I-15, provides information, permits, books, and maps. A variety of free programs and activities are presented by park rangers including evening amphitheater programs and ranger-guided hikes and walks.

For advance information on what to see in the park, hiking trails, camping, and lodging, contact: Superintendent, Zion National Park, Springdale, UT 84767 (tel 801/772-3256). It's best to write at least a month before a planned visit, and specify what type of information is needed.

HOTEL

Zion Park Inn

1215 Zion Park Blvd, PO Box 800, Springdale, 84767; tel 801/772-3200 or toll free 800/934-7275; fax 801/772-2449. 1½ mi S of park entrance. Lovely new hotel with terrific views of Watchman and Temple Mountains. Large lobby has high vaulted ceiling and south wall of glass. **Rooms:** 83 rms, stes, and effic. CI 3pm/CO 11am. Nonsmoking rms avail. **Amenities:** A/C, cable TV, voice mail. **Services:** **Facilities:** 150 1 restaurant, whirlpool, washer/dryer. Picnic tables nearby along river. State liquor store. **Rates:** Peak (Apr–Oct) $68–$88 S; $78–$88 D; $140 ste; $140 effic. Extra person $10. Children under age 12 stay free. Min stay special events. Lower rates off-season. Parking: Outdoor, free. AE, DC, DISC, MC, V.

MOTELS

Best Western Driftwood Lodge

1515 Zion Park Blvd, PO Box 98, Springdale, 84767; tel 801/772-3262 or toll free 800/528-1234; fax 801/772-3702. 2 mi S of park entrance. Lovely two-story brick and wood motel on seven acres of tree-shaded lawns in the shadow of Watchman Mountain. Art gallery is adjacent to lobby. **Rooms:** 47 rms. CI open/CO 11am. Nonsmoking rms avail. Great room views of Zion's majestic red cliffs. Rooms are large and are located in four separate buildings. Two-bed-room family suites available. **Amenities:** A/C, cable TV. Some units w/terraces. **Services:** Masseur, babysitting. **Facilities:** Whirlpool. **Rates (CP):** Peak (Apr–Oct) $64–$74 S; $74–$84 D. Extra person $4. Children under age 12 stay free. Lower rates off-season. Parking: Outdoor, free. AE, CB, DC, DISC, EC, MC, V.

Bumbleberry Inn

897 Zion Park Blvd, PO Box 346, Springdale, 84767; tel 801/772-3224 or toll free 800/828-1534. 1 mi S of park entrance. Set back from the highway, this 13-year-old motel has a great view of Watchman Mountain. **Rooms:** 23 rms. CI 2pm/CO 11am. No smoking. Mountain view from some rooms; others look out at pool and lawn. **Amenities:** A/C, cable TV, dataport. All units w/terraces, all w/whirlpools. **Services:** Social director. **Facilities:** 100 1 restaurant, playground. **Rates:** Peak (Apr–Oct) $54 S; $59 D. Children under age 18 stay free. Lower rates off-season. Parking: Outdoor, free. DISC, MC, V.

Canyon Ranch Motel

668 Zion Park Blvd, PO Box 175, Springdale, 84767; tel 801/772-3357; fax 801/772-3057. ¾ mi S of park entrance. Rustic motel reminiscent of the 1950s, with rooms in cottages

surrounding a lawn. Each holds one, two, or four units. **Rooms:** 22 rms and effic. CI 10am/CO 11am. Nonsmoking rms avail. Rooms are small but comfortable and newly remodeled. **Amenities:** A/C, cable TV w/movies. **Services:** **Facilities:** Whirlpool. Picnic tables and grills on central lawn. **Rates:** Peak (Mar–Oct) $54–$68 S or D; $54–$68 effic. Extra person $5. Lower rates off-season. Parking: Outdoor, free. AE, DISC, MC, V.

Cliffrose Lodge & Gardens
281 Zion Park Blvd, PO Box 510, Springdale, 84767; tel 801/772-3234 or toll free 800/243-8824; fax 801/772-3900. ¼ mi S of park entrance. This two-story motel sits on beautifully landscaped grounds, with flower beds and lawn stretching down to the river. **Rooms:** 36 rms, stes, and effic. CI 2pm/CO 11am. Nonsmoking rms avail. All rooms have excellent views of the rock cliffs or river; very comfortable and attractive. **Amenities:** A/C, cable TV. Some units w/terraces. **Services:** Masseur. **Facilities:** 20 Basketball, playground, washer/dryer. Picnic tables. **Rates:** Peak (Easter–Oct) $54–$64 S; $58–$68 D; $99–$145 ste; $48–$68 effic. Extra person $10. Children under age 18 stay free. Lower rates off-season. Parking: Outdoor, free. AE, DISC, MC, V.

Flanigan's Inn
428 Zion Park Blvd, PO Box 100, Springdale, 84767; tel 801/772-3244 or toll free 800/765-RSVP; fax 801/772-3926. ¼ mi S of park entrance. Set back from the road in a serene area among trees and flowers, plus a lily pond with frog statues. **Rooms:** 37 rms and stes. CI 2pm/CO 11am. Nonsmoking rms avail. Room views of lovely grounds. Attractive, coordinated decor with unusual twig art on walls. **Amenities:** A/C, cable TV w/movies. All units w/terraces, 1 w/fireplace, some w/whirlpools. Ceiling fan. **Services:** Babysitting. **Facilities:** 50 1 restaurant (dinner only; *see* "Restaurants" below), volleyball. State liquor store. Bicycle rentals across street. **Rates (CP):** Peak (Mar–Nov) $69–$89 S or D; $89 ste. Extra person $5. Children under age 2 stay free. Lower rates off-season. Parking: Outdoor, free. AE, DISC, MC, V.

INN

Dixie Hostel
73 S Main St, Hurricane, 84737; tel 801/635-8202; fax 801/635-9320. Clean, well-kept hostel 23 miles from Zion National Park. Large lounge has TV, VCR and videos, board games, some books. Kitchen facilities and four refrigerators for guest use. **Rooms:** 9 rms (all w/shared bath). CI open/CO noon. No smoking. Rooms very small but clean; some have chair and sink. Baths are down the hall. Dorm bunks also available. **Amenities:** A/C. No phone or TV. **Services:** Afternoon tea served. **Facilities:** Washer/dryer, guest lounge w/TV. Picnic tables and grills on tree-shaded lawn. Fishing, 18-hole golf course, bicycle rentals nearby. **Rates (CP):** $15 S w/shared bath; $30 D w/shared bath. Extra person $15. Children under age 12 stay free. Parking: Outdoor, free. No CC.

LODGE

Zion Lodge
UT 9, PO Box 400, 84720; tel 801/586-7686; fax 801/586-3157. 5 mi N of park entrance. The only lodging inside the national park offers a rustic elegance in keeping with its surroundings. Picture windows in the lobby frame view of the massive and towering rock for which the park is famous. **Rooms:** 121 rms and stes; 40 cottages/villas. CI 4pm/CO 11am. Nonsmoking rms avail. All units have great views. Motel rooms generally have two queen beds, cabins two double beds. **Amenities:** A/C. No TV. All units w/terraces, some w/fireplaces. Cabins have private porch, stone (gas-burning) fireplace. **Services:** Children's program, babysitting. **Facilities:** 100 1 restaurant (*see* "Restaurants" below). Open-air tram tours. **Rates:** Peak (Mar–Nov) $75–$80 S or D; $113–$120 ste; $79–$85 cottage/villa. Extra person $5. Children under age 16 stay free. Lower rates off-season. Parking: Outdoor, free. AE, MC, V.

RESTAURANTS

★ Bit & Spur Saloon
1212 Zion Park Blvd, Springdale; tel 801/772-3498. ¾ mi W of park entrance. **Southwestern.** This rustic, ivy-covered building features native rock and rough hewn wood inside and out. There are two indoor dining areas, a bar, and patio dining in warm weather. The kitchen prepares all the Mexican standards—burritos, flautas, chile rellenos, traditional chile stew with pork—but there are also more exotic creations like pollo relleno (grilled breast of chicken stuffed with cilantro pesto and goat cheese); smoked, charbroiled game hen with sourdough stuffing and chipotle sauce; and deep-dish chicken enchilada with scallions, green chiles, and cheese. **FYI:** Reservations accepted. No smoking. **Open:** Daily 5–10pm. Closed Dec. **Prices:** Main courses $6–$16. MC, V.

Flanigan's Restaurant
In Flanigan's Inn, 428 Zion Park Blvd, Springdale; tel 801/772-3244. ¼ mi W of park entrance. **Regional American.** Large picture windows offer diners panoramic views of the surrounding mountains in this dining room, which is further enhanced by beautiful paintings and prints of Zion National Park. Dinner choices include specials of fresh salmon and seafood, plus a variety of pasta dishes and beef and chicken entrees. **FYI:** Reservations not accepted. Children's menu. No smoking. **Open:** Dinner daily 5–9pm; brunch Sun 10am–2pm. **Prices:** Main courses $7–$20. AE, DISC, MC, V.

Index

Listings are arranged alphabetically, followed by a code indicating the type of establishment, and then by city, state, and page number. The codes for type of establishment are defined as follows: (H) = Hotel, (M) = Motel, (I) = Inn, (L) = Lodge, (RE) = Resort, (R) = Restaurant, (RS) = Refreshment Stop, (A) = Attraction.

A

B

C

D

E

F

G

M

N

O

P

Q

R

Y

Z

10 % OFF
TIME & MILEAGE

CRUISE AMERICA

RV RENTAL & SALES

For national reservations and information:

1-800-327-7799

The most comprehensive line of Recreational vehicles you'll find anywhere.

Save 10% at Thousands of Choice Hotels Worldwide!

Call 1-800-4-CHOICE and request the "America On Wheels Discount #00055607." You'll save 10% on each night's stay at participating Comfort, Quality, Clarion, Sleep, Econo Lodge & Rodeway Inns, Hotels and Suites!

UP TO $100.00 OFF

Save up to $100.00 off when you buy your airline ticket from Travel Discounters.

Call 1-800-355-1065 and give code AOW in order to receive the discount. See reverse side for discount prices.

May not be used in conjunction with any other discount or promotion. Offer expires 12/31/97.

$5.00 Off Per Night

With over 500 locations in the US, Canada and Mexico, Travelodge always offers a clean, comfortable room at a great rate. And you'll also enjoy all these services **free**: fresh brewed in-room coffee, a morning newspaper, cable TV and no long distance access charges.

And if you present this certificate upon check-in we'll take $5.00 off the regular room rate for each night of your stay at a Travelodge location. It just makes sense to stay with us and save

For reservations, call 1-800-578-7878 or your travel agent and ask for the 5CPN discount.

10 % OFF
TIME & MILEAGE

Terms and Conditions

- Offer includes 10% discount off all time and mileage charges on Cruise America or Cruise Canada vehicles only.
- Offer not available in conjunction with other discount offers or promotional rates.
- Excludes rental charges, deposits, sales tax, amd fuels.
- Normal rental conditions and customer qualification procedures apply.
- Members must reserve through Central Reservations only, at least one week in advance of pick up and mention membership affiliation at time of reservation.

  For reservations, call: 1-800-327-7799 US and Canada
- By acceptance and use of this offer, member agrees to the above conditions.
- Offer expires December 31, 1997.

Save 10% **Save 10%**

Offer expires December 31, 1997.

Savings are subject to certain restrictions and availability.
Valid for flights on most airlines.

Minimum Ticket Price	Save
$200.00	$25.00
$250.00	$50.00
$350.00	$75.00
$450.00	$100.00

Terms and Conditions

1. Advance reservations required.
2. Coupon must be presented at check-in.
3. Coupon cannot be combined with any other special offers, discounted rates.
4. Subject to availability.
5. Valid through December 31, 1997.
6. No photo copies allowed.

For reservations, call 1-800-578-7878 or your travel agent and ask for the 5CPN discount.

- 10% Discount off established rates at all motels
- 15 Discount with Alamo Rent A Car, I.D. #287272 and Rate Code SN (1-800-327-9633)
- Save $25-$75 off published airfares of $150.00 or more on preferred airlines with the Discount Air Travel Card. Call 1-800-752-9457 and mention Rate Code TPIS8-8704

CALL 1-800-8000 FOR RESERVATIONS *and use identification number 8800 167051*

Free One-Class Upgrade

(See Back For Details.)

Dollar® features quality products of the Chrysler Corporation like the Dodge Neon and other fine cars.

DOLLAR® RENT A CAR

For Worldwide Reservations, Call Your Professional Travel Agent Or:

800-800-4000

DOLLAR MAKES SENSE.℠

© 1996 Dollar Rent A Car Systems, Inc.

Valuable discount coupon good for 15% OFF your first order from

AMERICA'S LEADING SOURCE OF TRAVEL SUPPLIES

If it makes travel more comfortable, safe and rewarding, we have it!

Phone 1-800-962-4943 for a FREE CATALOG.

Mention code "afbg2"

10% OFF

Follow the Sun to Days Inn

Now you can save even more at any of more than 1,700 Days Inns throughout the United States and internationally. ust present this coupon upon check-in and Days Inn will take 10% off you regular room rate for your entire length of stay! Advance reservations required, so call now! 1-800-DAYS INN See details on back.

All reservations must be made by calling our toll free reservation system, Superline. Any reservation requiring a guarantee must be guaranteed with the corporate V.I.P. identification number and the individual traveler's major credit card. If a guaranteed reservation is made and subsequently neither used nor cancelled, the corporate traveler will be billed for the one night's room charge plus tax.

expires December 31, 1997

Redeemable at participating Dollar® locations only.

This coupon entitles you to a one class upgrade from a compact or economy car to the next higher car group at no extra charge. Simply make a reservation for a compact or economy class car, then present this coupon to any Dollar rental agent when you arrive. You'll receive an upgrade to the next car class at no additional charge. Upgrade subject to vehicle availability. Renter must meet Dollar age, driver and credit requirements. This coupon must be surrendered at time of rental and may not be used in conjunction with any other offer and has no cash value. **EXPIRES 12/15/97.**

For worldwide reservations, call your travel agent or
800-800-4000

DOLLAR MAKES SENSE.™

Mention code "afbg2" when you place your first order and receive 15% OFF

Offer expires December 31, 1997

PO Box 5485-AF2, Santa Barbara, CA 93150

Magellan's

10% OFF

- Available at participating properties.
- This coupon cannot be combined with any other special discount offer.
- Limit one coupon per room, per stay. Expires December 31, 1997.
- Not valid during blackout periods or special events.
- Void where prohibited.
- No reproductions accepted.

1-800-DAYS INN

2 FOR 1

4 Summer Locations
Steamboat, Grand Lake
Winterpark, Breckenridge
applies to Adult or Child maze
passport purchase.
Does not apply to reruns.
Coupon must be presented.
Expires December 31st, 1997.

50% OFF

1625
N. CENTRAL
AVENUE
PHOENIX
ARIZONA
85004-1685
TEL. (602) 257-1222

Coupon must be presented at time of purchase and may not be combined with any other offer.
Offer expires 12/31/97.

50% OFF

HOURS:
TUESDAY-
SUNDAY
10AM-5PM
THURSDAY &
FRIDAY
10AM-9PM

PRORODEO
HALL OF FAME
Colorado Springs, Colorado

Not valid with any other discount offer.
Valid anytime.

ARIZONA THEATRE COMPANY
THE STATE THEATRE OF ARIZONA
1996-97 30 THIRTIETH ANNIVERSARY SEASON

Receive 20% off the regular ticket price with this coupon. Please mention discount when ordering. Limit 4 tickets per order.

TUCSON

performances at the
Temple of Music and Art
330 S. Scott Ave.

BOX OFFICE
(520) 622-2823

GROUP SALES
(520) 884-8210

DILLARD'S
1-800-938-4253

PHOENIX

performances at the
Herberger Theater Center
222 E. Monroe

BOX OFFICE
(602) 252-8497

GROUP SALES
(602) 256-6899

DILLARD'S
(602) 678-2222

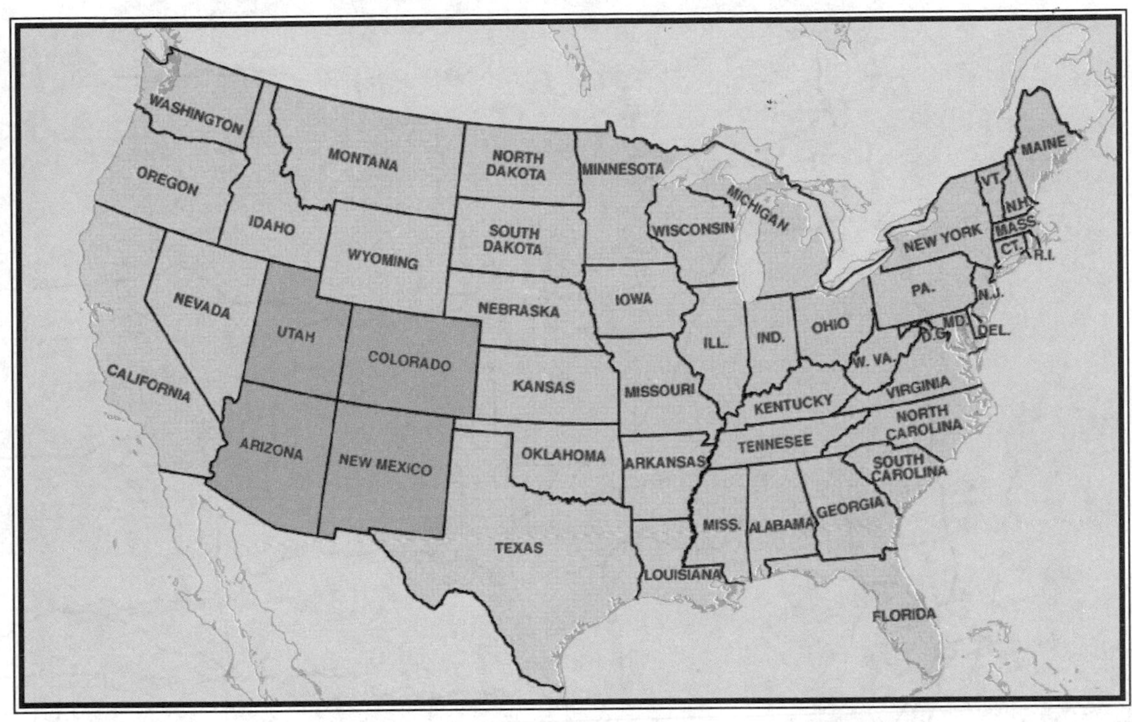
WASHINGTON
OREGON
IDAHO
MONTANA
WYOMING
NORTH DAKOTA
SOUTH DAKOTA
NEBRASKA
MINNESOTA
WISCONSIN
MICHIGAN
IOWA
NEVADA
UTAH
COLORADO
KANSAS
CALIFORNIA
ARIZONA
NEW MEXICO
OKLAHOMA
TEXAS
MISSOURI
ARKANSAS
LOUISIANA
MISS.
ALABAMA
GEORGIA
FLORIDA
ILL.
IND.
OHIO
KENTUCKY
TENNESEE
W. VA.
VIRGINIA
NORTH CAROLINA
SOUTH CAROLINA
PA.
NEW YORK
N.J.
MD.
D.C.
DEL.
VT.
N.H.
MAINE
MASS.
CT.
R.I.

CONTENTS

BRITISH COLUMBIA
ALBERTA
SASKATCHEWAN
MANITOBA
CANADA
UNITED STATES
Vancouver I.
Vancouver
Victoria
Calgary
Regina
Winnipeg
Moose Jaw
Lethbridge
Medicine Hat
PACIFIC
OCEAN
WASHINGTON
Seattle
Tacoma
Olympia
Spokane
Yakima
OREGON
Portland
Salem
Eugene
Columbia Plateau
IDAHO
Boise
Pocatello
Twin Falls
MONTANA
Missoula
Helena
Great Falls
Billings
Butte
NORTH DAKOTA
Bismarck
SOUTH DAKOTA
Rapid City
Pierre
WYOMING
Casper
Cheyenne
Laramie
Rock Springs
NEBRASKA
North Platte
Great Basin
NEVADA
Reno
Carson City
Las Vegas
UTAH
Salt Lake City
Ogden
Provo
COLORADO
Denver
Colorado Springs
Pueblo
Grand Jct.
CALIFORNIA
Sacramento
San Francisco
Oakland
San Jose
Fresno
Bakersfield
LOS ANGELES
San Bernardino
Long Beach
San Diego
Tijuana
Mojave Desert
ARIZONA
Phoenix
Tucson
Flagstaff
NEW MEXICO
Albuquerque
Santa Fe
El Paso
Ciudad Juárez
KANSAS
Wichita
OKLAHOMA
Oklahoma City
TEXAS
Amarillo
Lubbock
Dallas
Abilene
Midland
Odessa
San Angelo
San Antonio
Austin
Laredo
Edwards Plateau
MEXICO
BAJA CALIFORNIA
SONORA
Hermosillo
CHIHUAHUA
Chihuahua
COAHUILA
NUEVO LEON
Monterrey
DURANGO
Torreón
Mexicali
Ensenada
Sierra Madre Occidental
Gulf of California
PACIFIC
OCEAN

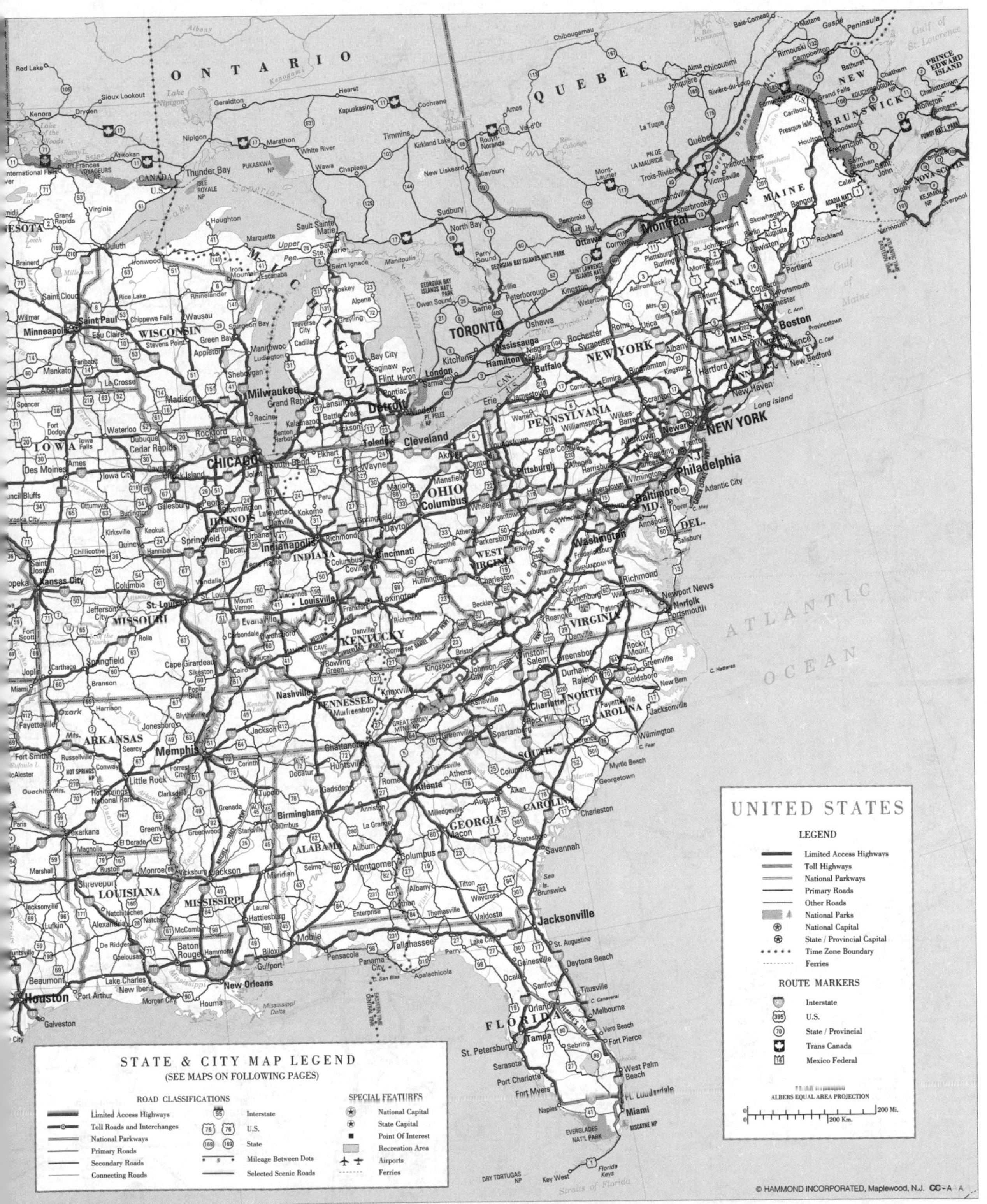
ONTARIO
QUEBEC
NEW BRUNSWICK
PRINCE EDWARD ISLAND
NOVA SCOTIA
Gulf of St. Lawrence
Gulf of Maine
ATLANTIC OCEAN
MAINE
N.H.
VT.
MASS.
NEW YORK
PENNSYLVANIA
OHIO
MICHIGAN
WISCONSIN
IOWA
ILLINOIS
INDIANA
MISSOURI
KENTUCKY
WEST VIRGINIA
VIRGINIA
MD.
DEL.
N.J.
NORTH CAROLINA
SOUTH CAROLINA
TENNESSEE
ARKANSAS
MISSISSIPPI
ALABAMA
GEORGIA
LOUISIANA
FLORIDA
TORONTO
Montreal
Ottawa
Québec
CHICAGO
Detroit
Cleveland
Pittsburgh
Philadelphia
NEW YORK
Boston
Baltimore
Washington
Indianapolis
Columbus
Cincinnati
Louisville
St. Louis
Kansas City
Minneapolis
Saint Paul
Milwaukee
Nashville
Memphis
Atlanta
Birmingham
Charlotte
Richmond
Norfolk
Jacksonville
Tampa
Orlando
Miami
New Orleans
Houston
UNITED STATES
LEGEND
Limited Access Highways
Toll Highways
National Parkways
Primary Roads
Other Roads
National Parks
National Capital
State / Provincial Capital
Time Zone Boundary
Ferries
ROUTE MARKERS
Interstate
U.S.
State / Provincial
Trans Canada
Mexico Federal
ALBERS EQUAL AREA PROJECTION
200 Mi.
200 Km.
STATE & CITY MAP LEGEND
(SEE MAPS ON FOLLOWING PAGES)
ROAD CLASSIFICATIONS
Limited Access Highways
Toll Roads and Interchanges
National Parkways
Primary Roads
Secondary Roads
Connecting Roads
Interstate
U.S.
State
Mileage Between Dots
Selected Scenic Roads
SPECIAL FEATURES
National Capital
State Capital
Point Of Interest
Recreation Area
Airports
Ferries
© HAMMOND INCORPORATED, Maplewood, N.J.

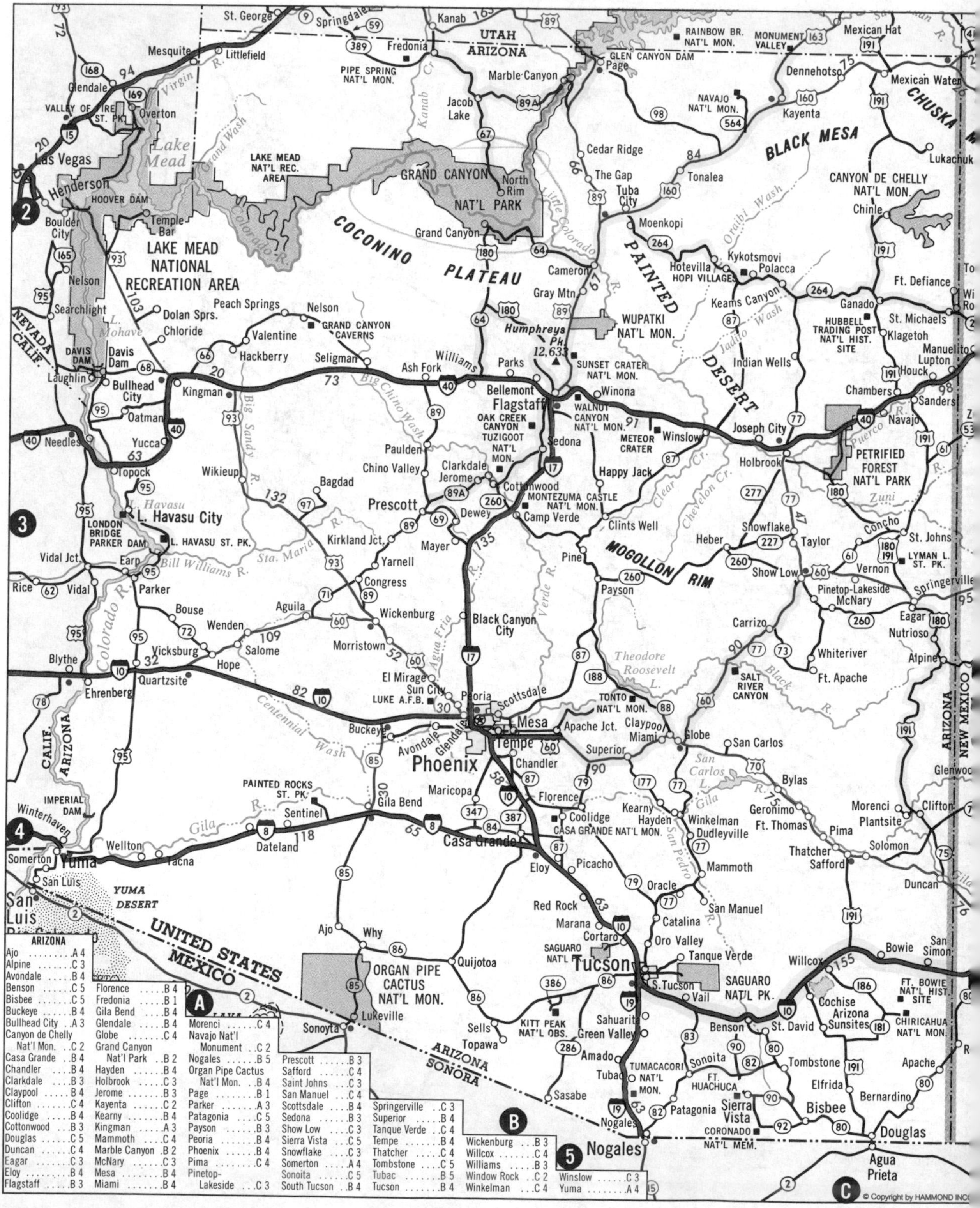

ARIZONA

Ajo .... A 4
Alpine .... C 3
Avondale ..... B 4
Benson .... C 5
Bisbee .... C 5
Buckeye ...... B 4
Bullhead City .. A 3
Canyon de Chelly Nat'l Mon. .. C 2
Casa Grande .. B 4
Chandler .... B 4
Clarkdale .... B 3
Claypool ..... B 4
Clifton .... C 4
Coolidge ..... B 4
Cottonwood ... B 3
Douglas ...... C 5
Duncan .... C 4
Eagar .... C 3
Eloy .... B 4
Flagstaff ..... B 3
Florence ..... B 4
Fredonia ..... B 1
Gila Bend .... B 4
Glendale ..... B 4
Globe .... C 4
Grand Canyon Nat'l Park .. B 2
Hayden ...... B 4
Holbrook ..... C 3
Jerome .... B 3
Kayenta ...... C 2
Kearny .... B 4
Kingman ..... A 3
Mammoth .... C 4
Marble Canyon . B 2
McNary ...... C 3
Mesa .... B 4
Miami .... B 4
Morenci ...... C 4
Navajo Nat'l Monument .. C 2
Nogales ...... B 5
Organ Pipe Cactus Nat'l Mon. .. B 4
Page .... B 1
Parker .... A 3
Patagonia .... C 5
Payson ...... B 3
Peoria .... B 4
Phoenix ..... B 4
Pima .... C 4
Pinetop-Lakeside ... C 3
Prescott ...... B 3
Safford ...... C 4
Saint Johns ... C 3
San Manuel ... C 4
Scottsdale .... B 4
Sedona .... B 3
Show Low .... C 3
Sierra Vista ... C 5
Snowflake .... C 3
Somerton ..... A 4
Sonoita ...... C 5
South Tucson .. B 4
Springerville .. C 3
Superior ..... B 4
Tanque Verde .. C 4
Tempe .... B 4
Thatcher ..... C 4
Tombstone .... C 5
Tubac .... B 5
Tucson .... B 4
Wickenburg ... B 3
Willcox .... C 4
Williams ..... B 3
Window Rock .. C 2
Winkelman ... C 4
Winslow ...... C 3
Yuma .... A 4

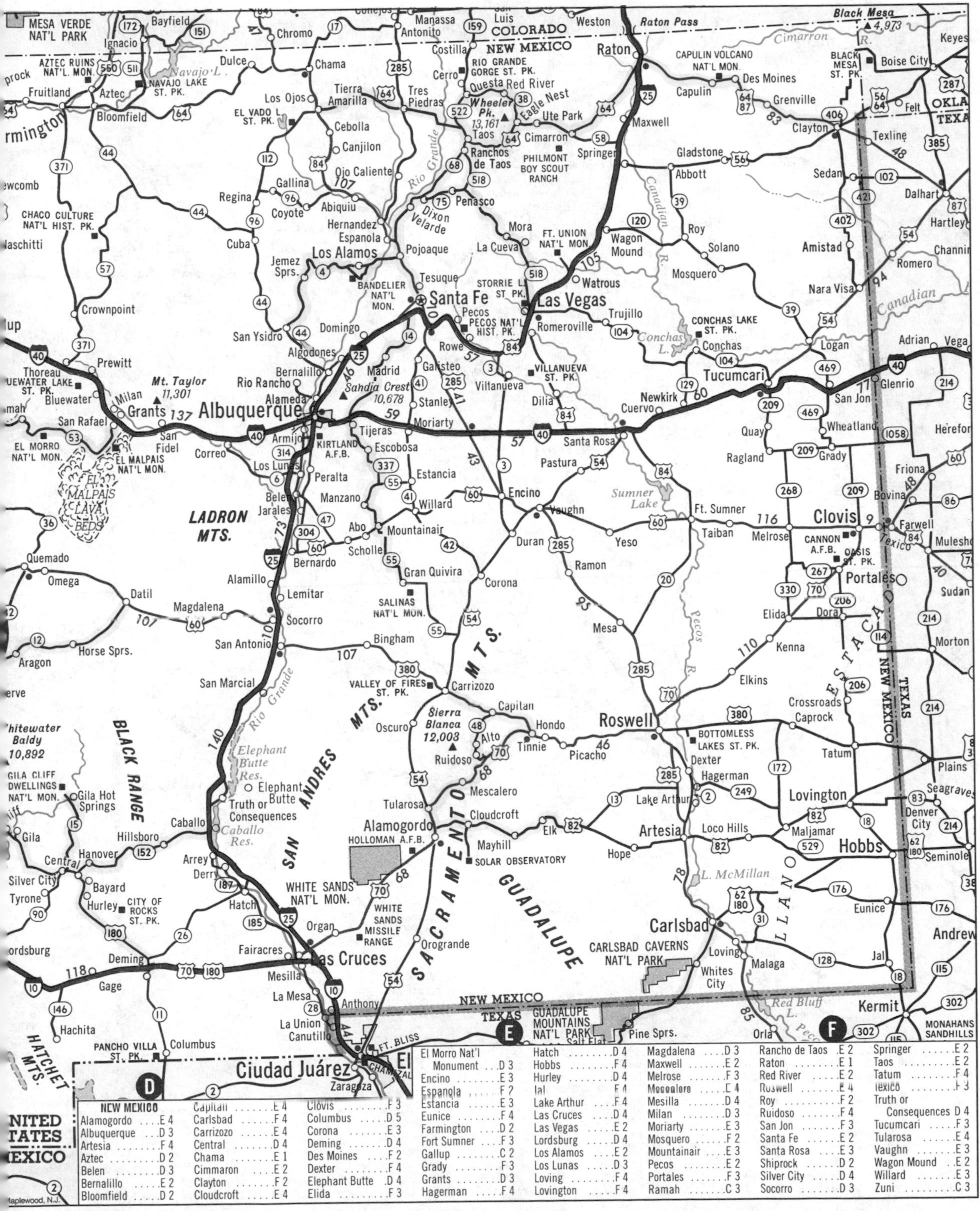

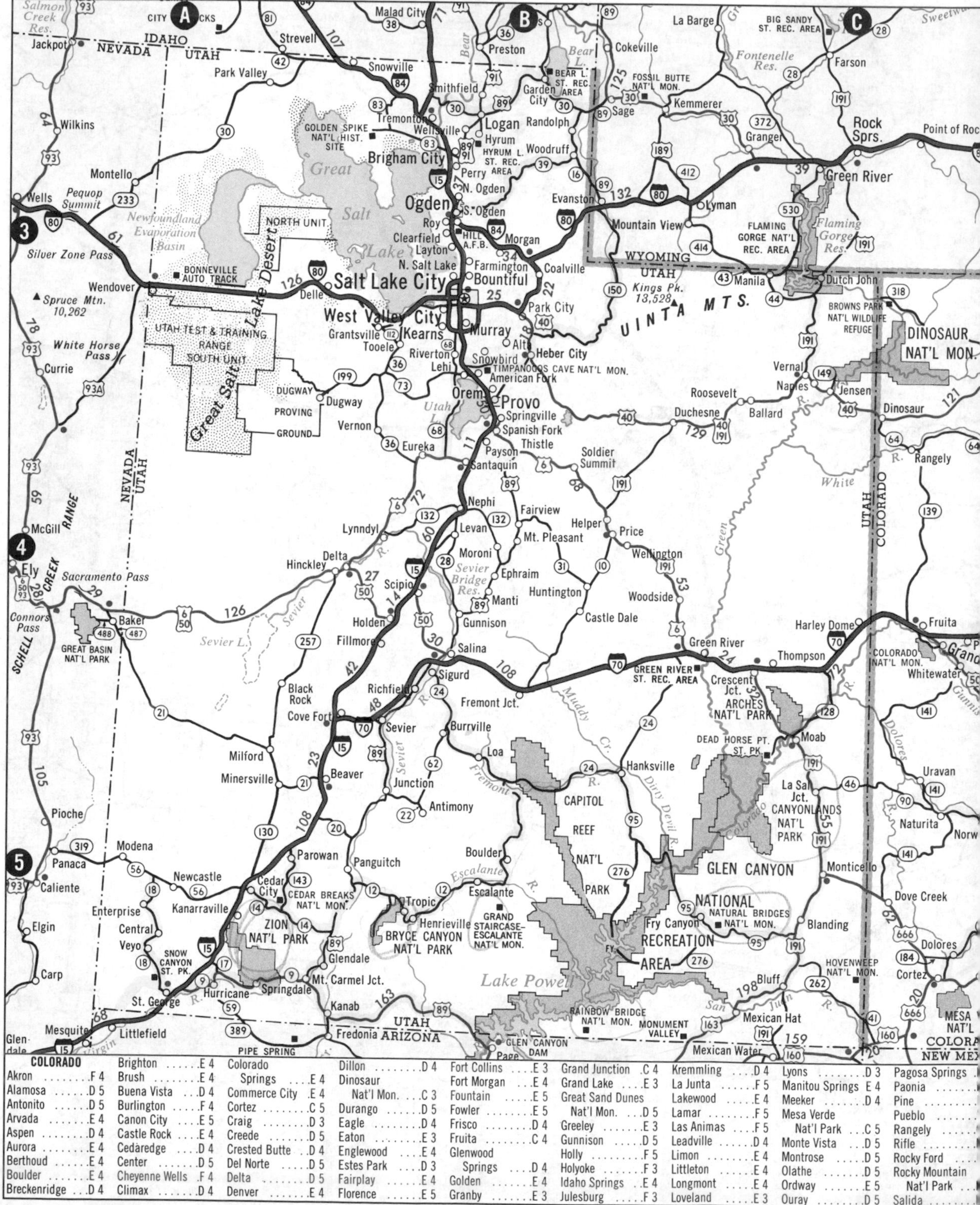

COLORADO

Akron . . . . F 4
Alamosa . . . . . D 5
Antonito . . . . . D 5
Arvada . . . . . . E 4
Aspen . . . . D 4
Aurora . . . . E 4
Berthoud . . . . . E 4
Boulder . . . . . . E 4
Breckenridge . . D 4
Brighton . . . . . E 4
Brush . . . . E 4
Buena Vista . . D 4
Burlington . . . . F 4
Canon City . . . E 5
Castle Rock . . . E 4
Cedaredge . . . D 4
Center . . . . . . D 5
Cheyenne Wells . F 4
Climax . . . . . . D 4
Colorado Springs . . . E 4
Commerce City . E 4
Cortez . . . . C 5
Craig . . . . D 3
Creede . . . . . . D 5
Crested Butte . D 4
Del Norte . . . . D 5
Delta . . . . D 5
Denver . . . . . . E 4
Dillon . . . . D 4
Dinosaur Nat'l Mon. . . . C 3
Durango . . . . . D 5
Eagle . . . . D 4
Eaton . . . . E 3
Englewood . . . . E 4
Estes Park . . . D 3
Fairplay . . . . . E 4
Florence . . . . . E 5
Fort Collins . . . E 3
Fort Morgan . . . E 4
Fountain . . . . . E 5
Fowler . . . . E 5
Frisco . . . . D 4
Fruita . . . . C 4
Glenwood Springs . . . D 4
Golden . . . . . . E 4
Granby . . . . . . E 3
Grand Junction . C 4
Grand Lake . . . E 3
Great Sand Dunes Nat'l Mon. . . D 5
Greeley . . . . . . E 3
Gunnison . . . . . D 5
Holly . . . . F 5
Holyoke . . . . . . F 3
Idaho Springs . . E 4
Julesburg . . . . F 3
Kremmling . . . . D 4
La Junta . . . . . F 5
Lakewood . . . . . E 4
Lamar . . . . F 5
Las Animas . . . F 5
Leadville . . . . . D 4
Limon . . . . E 4
Littleton . . . . . E 4
Longmont . . . . . E 4
Loveland . . . . . E 3
Lyons . . . . D 3
Manitou Springs E 4
Meeker . . . . . . D 4
Mesa Verde Nat'l Park . . C 5
Monte Vista . . . D 5
Montrose . . . . . D 5
Olathe . . . . D 5
Ordway . . . . . . E 5
Ouray . . . . D 5
Pagosa Springs . .
Paonia . . . .
Pine . . . .
Pueblo . . . .
Rangely . . . . . .
Rifle . . . .
Rocky Ford . . . .
Rocky Mountain Nat'l Park . .
Salida . . . .

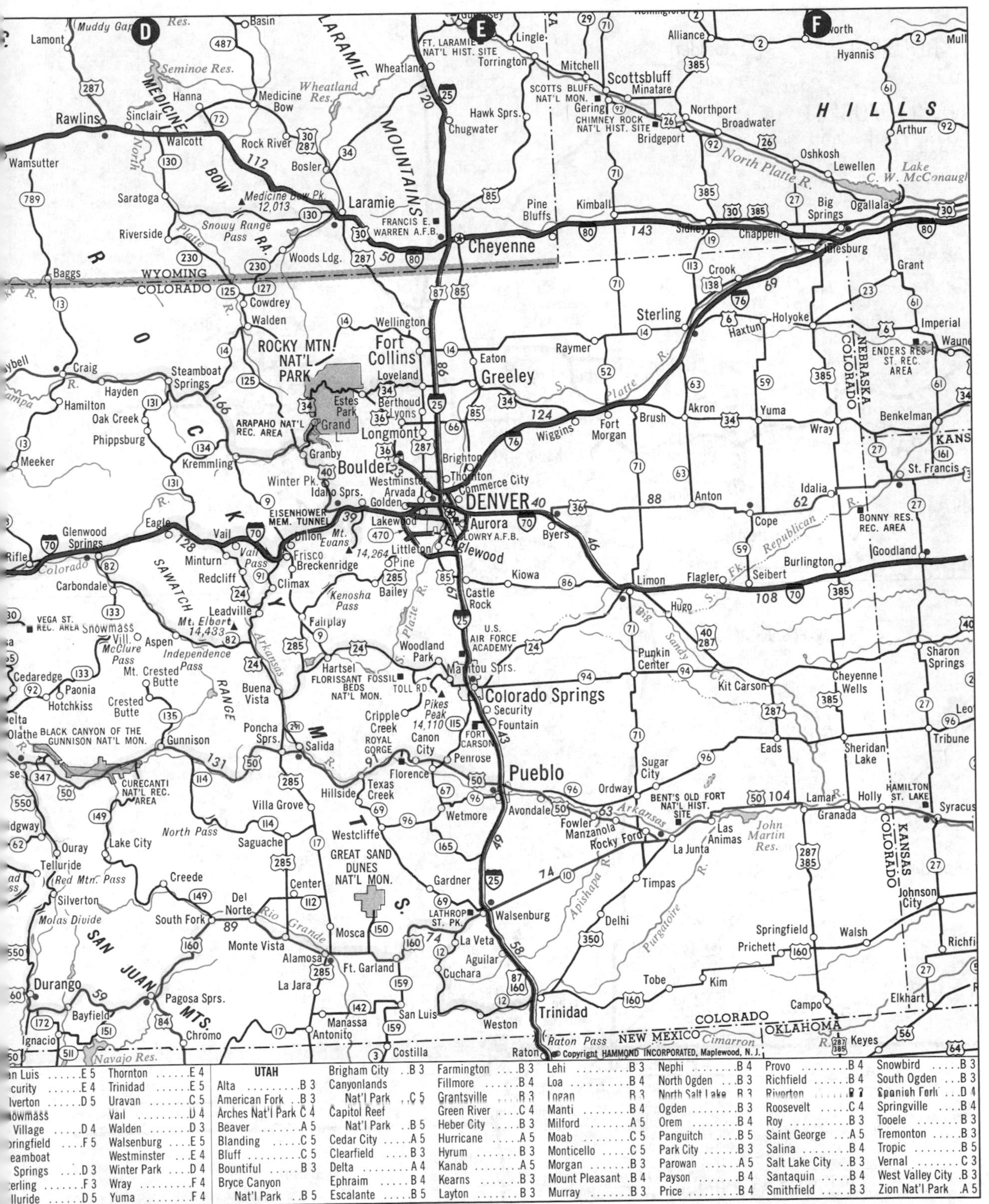

an Luis ......E 5
curity ......E 4
lverton ......D 5
owmass
Village .....D 4
ringfield ....F 5
eamboat
Springs ....D 3
erling ......F 3
lluride ......D 5
Thornton ......E 4
Trinidad ......E 5
Uravan ......C 5
Vail ......D 4
Walden ......D 3
Walsenburg ....E 5
Westminster ...E 4
Winter Park ....D 4
Wray ......F 4
Yuma ......F 4

UTAH

Alta ......B 3
American Fork ..B 3
Arches Nat'l Park C 4
Beaver ......A 5
Blanding .....C 5
Bluff ......C 5
Bountiful .....B 3
Bryce Canyon
Nat'l Park ..B 5
Brigham City ..B 3
Canyonlands
Nat'l Park ..C 5
Capitol Reef
Nat'l Park ..B 5
Cedar City ....A 5
Clearfield ....B 3
Delta ......A 4
Ephraim ....B 4
Escalante ....B 5
Farmington ....B 3
Fillmore ......B 4
Grantsville ....B 3
Green River ....C 4
Heber City ....B 3
Hurricane ....A 5
Hyrum ......B 3
Kanab ......A 5
Kearns ......B 3
Layton ......B 3
Lehi ......B 3
Loa ......B 4
Logan ......B 3
Manti ......B 4
Milford ......A 5
Moab ......C 5
Monticello .....C 5
Morgan ......B 3
Mount Pleasant .B 4
Murray ......B 3
Nephi ......B 4
North Ogden ...B 3
North Salt Lake B 3
Ogden ......B 3
Orem ......B 4
Panguitch ....B 5
Park City ......B 3
Parowan .....A 5
Payson ......B 4
Price ......B 4
Provo ......B 4
Richfield ......B 4
Riverton ......B 3
Roosevelt .....C 4
Roy ......B 3
Saint George ..A 5
Salina ......B 4
Salt Lake City ..B 3
Santaquin ....B 4
Smithfield ....B 3
Snowbird .....B 3
South Ogden ...B 3
Spanish Fork ...D 4
Springville ....B 4
Tooele ......B 3
Tremonton .....B 3
Tropic ......B 5
Vernal ......C 3
West Valley City .B 3
Zion Nat'l Park .A 5

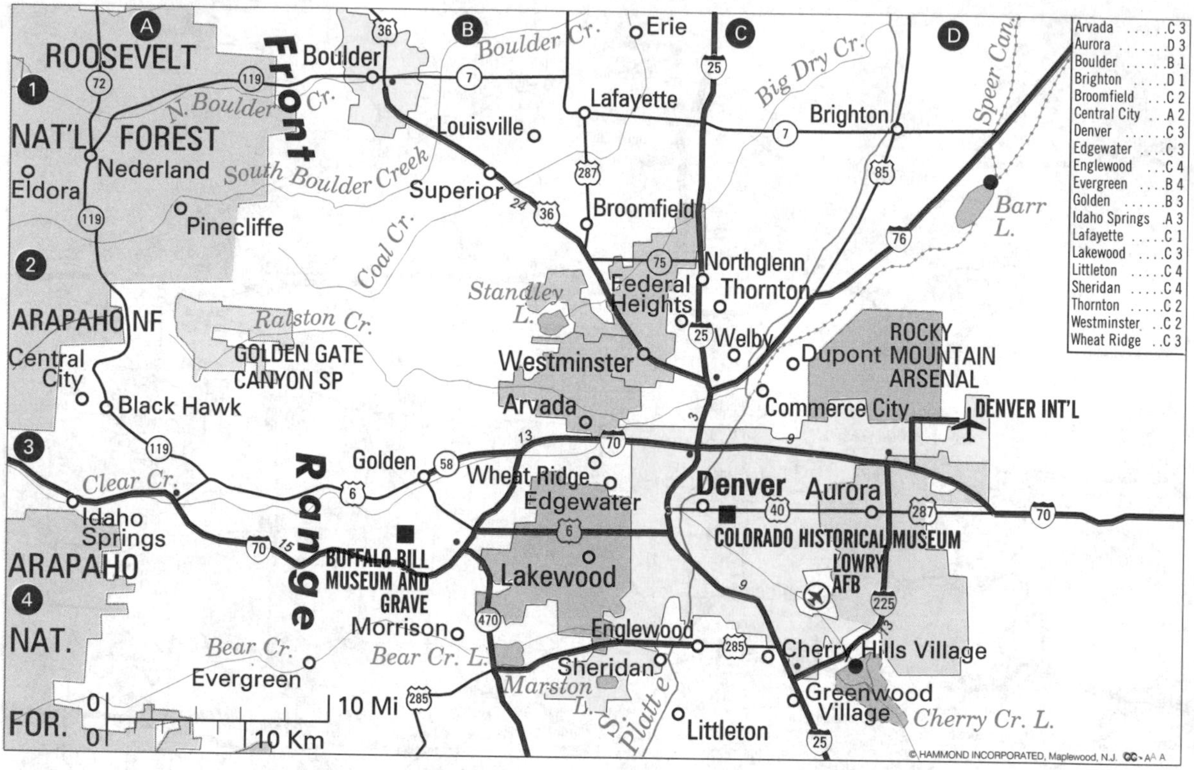

Arvada	C 3
Aurora	D 3
Boulder	B 1
Brighton	D 1
Broomfield	C 2
Central City	A 2
Denver	C 3
Edgewater	C 3
Englewood	C 4
Evergreen	B 4
Golden	B 3
Idaho Springs	A 3
Lafayette	C 1
Lakewood	C 3
Littleton	C 4
Sheridan	C 4
Thornton	C 2
Westminster	C 2
Wheat Ridge	C 3

ROOSEVELT NAT'L FOREST
Front Range
ARAPAHO NF
ARAPAHO NAT. FOR.
GOLDEN GATE CANYON SP
ROCKY MOUNTAIN ARSENAL
DENVER INT'L
COLORADO HISTORICAL MUSEUM
LOWRY AFB
BUFFALO BILL MUSEUM AND GRAVE
Boulder, Erie, Lafayette, Louisville, Superior, Broomfield, Brighton, Nederland, Eldora, Pinecliffe, Northglenn, Federal Heights, Thornton, Welby, Dupont, Westminster, Arvada, Commerce City, Central City, Black Hawk, Golden, Wheat Ridge, Edgewater, Denver, Aurora, Idaho Springs, Lakewood, Morrison, Englewood, Sheridan, Cherry Hills Village, Greenwood Village, Evergreen, Littleton
Boulder Cr., N. Boulder Cr., South Boulder Creek, Coal Cr., Big Dry Cr., Speer Can., Barr L., Standley L., Ralston Cr., Clear Cr., Bear Cr., Bear Cr. L., Marston L., S. Platte, Cherry Cr. L.

0 — 10 Mi
0 — 10 Km

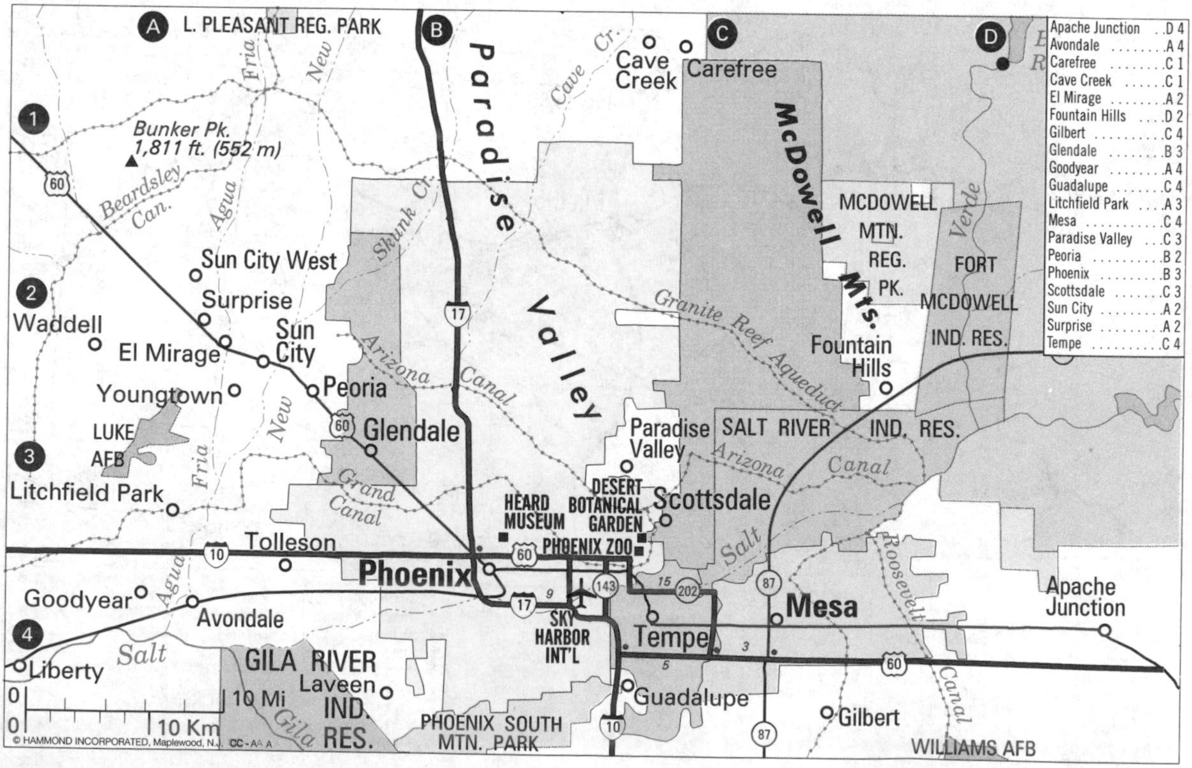

Apache Junction	D 4
Avondale	A 4
Carefree	C 1
Cave Creek	C 1
El Mirage	A 2
Fountain Hills	D 2
Gilbert	C 4
Glendale	B 3
Goodyear	A 4
Guadalupe	C 4
Litchfield Park	A 3
Mesa	C 4
Paradise Valley	C 3
Peoria	B 2
Phoenix	B 3
Scottsdale	C 3
Sun City	A 2
Surprise	A 2
Tempe	C 4

L. PLEASANT REG. PARK
Paradise Valley
McDowell Mts.
MCDOWELL MTN. REG. PK.
FORT MCDOWELL IND. RES.
SALT RIVER IND. RES.
GILA RIVER IND. RES.
PHOENIX SOUTH MTN. PARK
WILLIAMS AFB
LUKE AFB
HEARD MUSEUM
DESERT BOTANICAL GARDEN
PHOENIX ZOO
SKY HARBOR INT'L
Bunker Pk. 1,811 ft. (552 m)
Cave Creek, Carefree, Sun City West, Surprise, Waddell, El Mirage, Sun City, Youngtown, Peoria, Glendale, Fountain Hills, Paradise Valley, Scottsdale, Litchfield Park, Tolleson, Phoenix, Goodyear, Avondale, Tempe, Mesa, Apache Junction, Liberty, Laveen, Guadalupe, Gilbert
Cave Cr., Skunk Cr., New, Agua Fria, Beardsley Can., Arizona Canal, Granite Reef Aqueduct, Grand Canal, Verde, Salt, Gila, Roosevelt Canal

0 — 10 Mi
0 — 10 Km

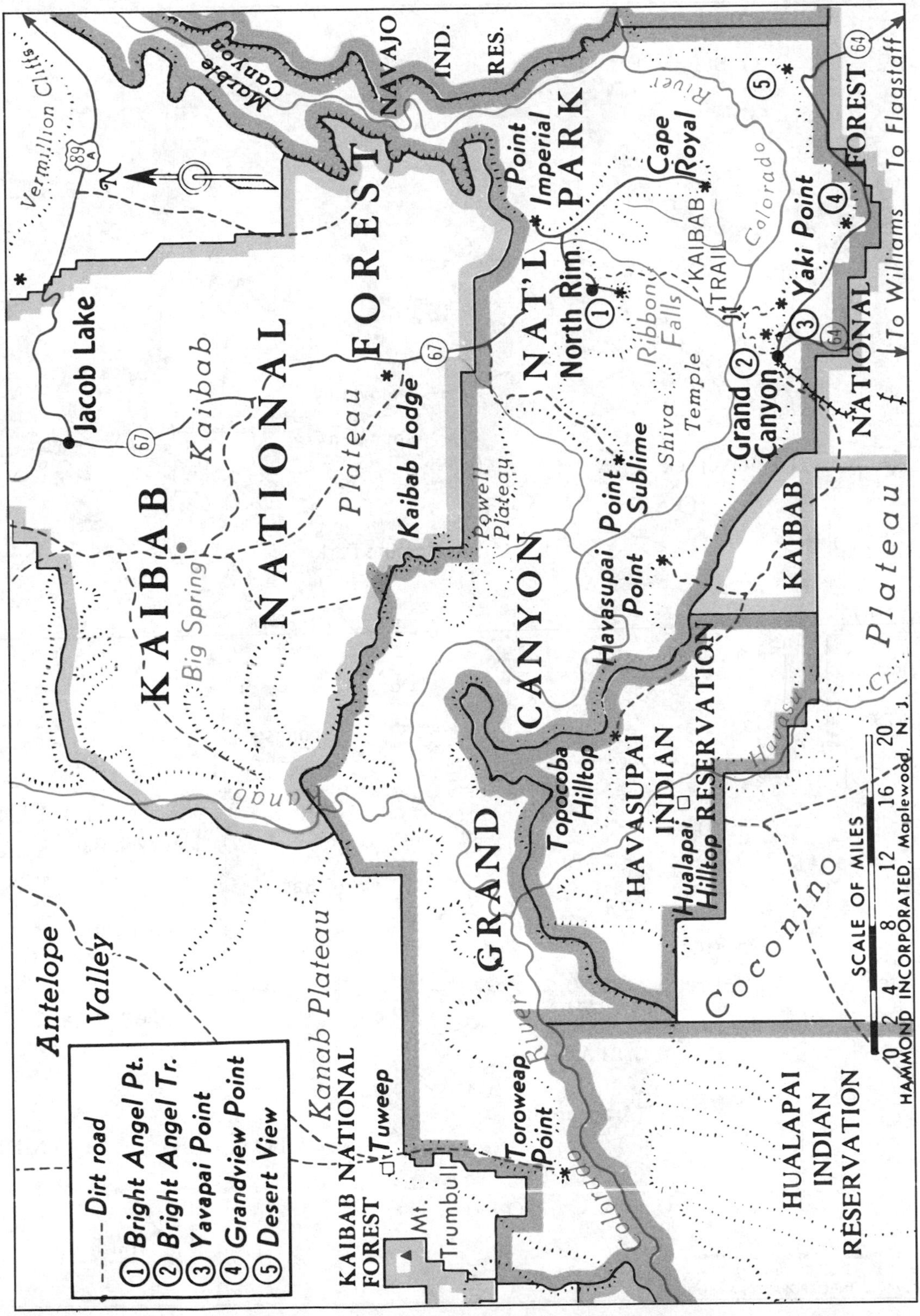

Dirt road
① Bright Angel Pt.
② Bright Angel Tr.
③ Yavapai Point
④ Grandview Point
⑤ Desert View
Antelope Valley
Vermillion Cliffs
Jacob Lake
89A
67
N
KAIBAB NATIONAL FOREST
Big Spring
Kaibab Plateau
Kanab
Kanab Plateau
Marble Canyon
NAVAJO IND. RES.
Kaibab Lodge
KAIBAB NATIONAL FOREST
Tuweep
Mt. Trumbull
GRAND CANYON NAT'L PARK
Powell Plateau
Toroweap Point
Colorado River
Point Imperial
North Rim
Topocoba Hilltop
Havasupai Point
Point Sublime
Shiva Temple
Ribbon Falls
Cape Royal
KAIBAB TRAIL
HAVASUPAI INDIAN RESERVATION
Hualapai Hilltop
Grand Canyon
Yaki Point
Colorado River
Coconino Plateau
Havasu Cr.
KAIBAB NATIONAL FOREST
HUALAPAI INDIAN RESERVATION
SCALE OF MILES
0 2 4 8 12 16 20
HAMMOND INCORPORATED, Maplewood, N. J.
64
To Williams
To Flagstaff

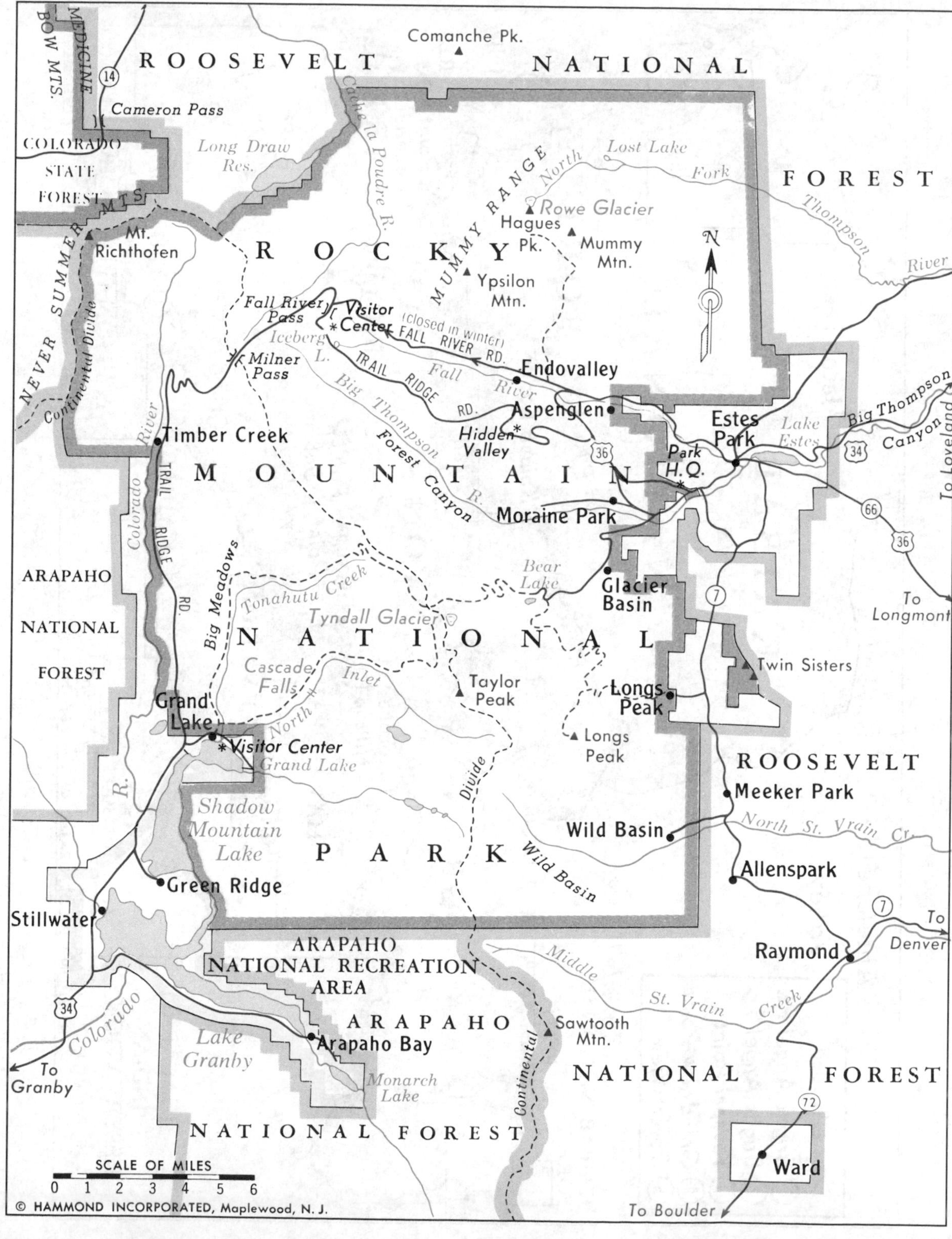

Comanche Pk.
ROOSEVELT NATIONAL FOREST
MEDICINE BOW MTS.
Cameron Pass
COLORADO STATE FOREST
Long Draw Res.
Cache la Poudre R.
NEVER SUMMER MTS.
Mt. Richthofen
Continental Divide
MUMMY RANGE
North Fork
Lost Lake
Thompson River
Rowe Glacier
Hagues Pk.
Mummy Mtn.
Ypsilon Mtn.
ROCKY MOUNTAIN NATIONAL PARK
Fall River Pass
Visitor Center
FALL RIVER RD. (closed in winter)
Iceberg L.
Milner Pass
TRAIL RIDGE RD.
Fall River
Endovalley
Big Thompson Forest Canyon R.
Aspenglen
Hidden Valley
Timber Creek
Colorado River
Estes Park
Lake Estes
Big Thompson Canyon
To Loveland
Park H.Q.
Moraine Park
ARAPAHO NATIONAL FOREST
Big Meadows
Tonahutu Creek
Tyndall Glacier
Bear Lake
Glacier Basin
To Longmont
Twin Sisters
Cascade Falls
North Inlet
Taylor Peak
Longs Peak
Grand Lake
Visitor Center
Grand Lake
Shadow Mountain Lake
Divide
ROOSEVELT
Meeker Park
North St. Vrain Cr.
Wild Basin
Allenspark
Green Ridge
Stillwater
To Denver
Raymond
ARAPAHO NATIONAL RECREATION AREA
Middle St. Vrain Creek
ARAPAHO NATIONAL FOREST
Sawtooth Mtn.
Arapaho Bay
Lake Granby
Monarch Lake
Colorado
To Granby
Continental
Ward
To Boulder
SCALE OF MILES
0 1 2 3 4 5 6
14 36 34 66 7 72

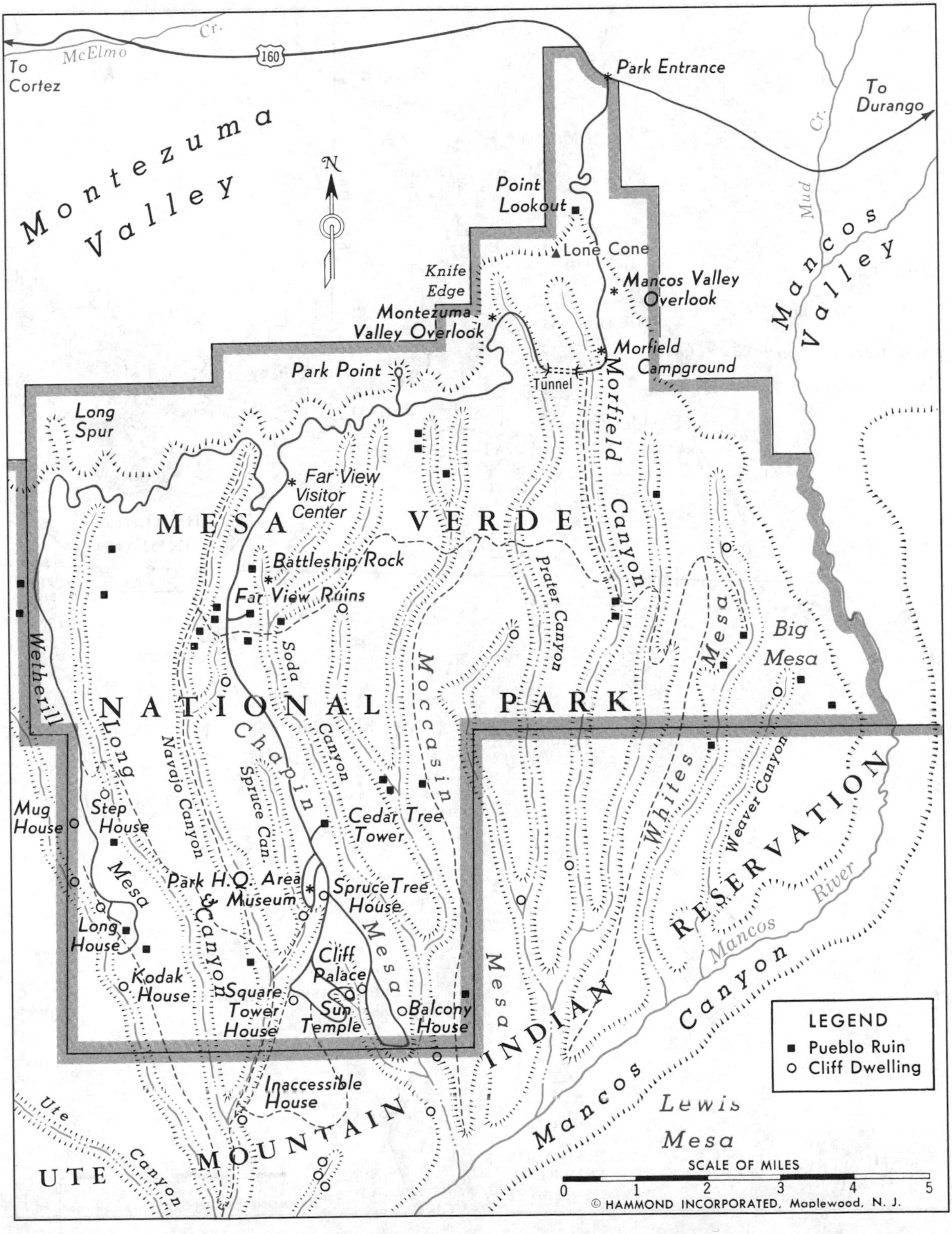

To Cortez
McElmo Cr.
160
Park Entrance
To Durango
Mud Cr.
Montezuma Valley
Mancos Valley
N
Point Lookout
Lone Cone
Knife Edge
Mancos Valley Overlook
Montezuma Valley Overlook
Morfield Campground
Park Point
Tunnel
Long Spur
Far View Visitor Center
MESA VERDE
NATIONAL PARK
Battleship Rock
Far View Ruins
Prater Canyon
Morfield Canyon
Wetherill
Soda Canyon
Moccasin Mesa
Big Mesa
Whites Mesa
Long Mesa
Navajo Canyon
Spruce Can.
Chapin Mesa
Mug House
Step House
Cedar Tree Tower
Weaver Canyon
Park H.Q. Area & Museum
Spruce Tree House
Long House
Kodak House
Square Tower House
Cliff Palace
Sun Temple
Balcony House
Mesa
Canyon
Inaccessible House
Mancos River
Mancos Canyon
Lewis Mesa
Ute Canyon
UTE MOUNTAIN INDIAN RESERVATION

LEGEND
■ Pueblo Ruin
○ Cliff Dwelling

SCALE OF MILES
0 1 2 3 4 5

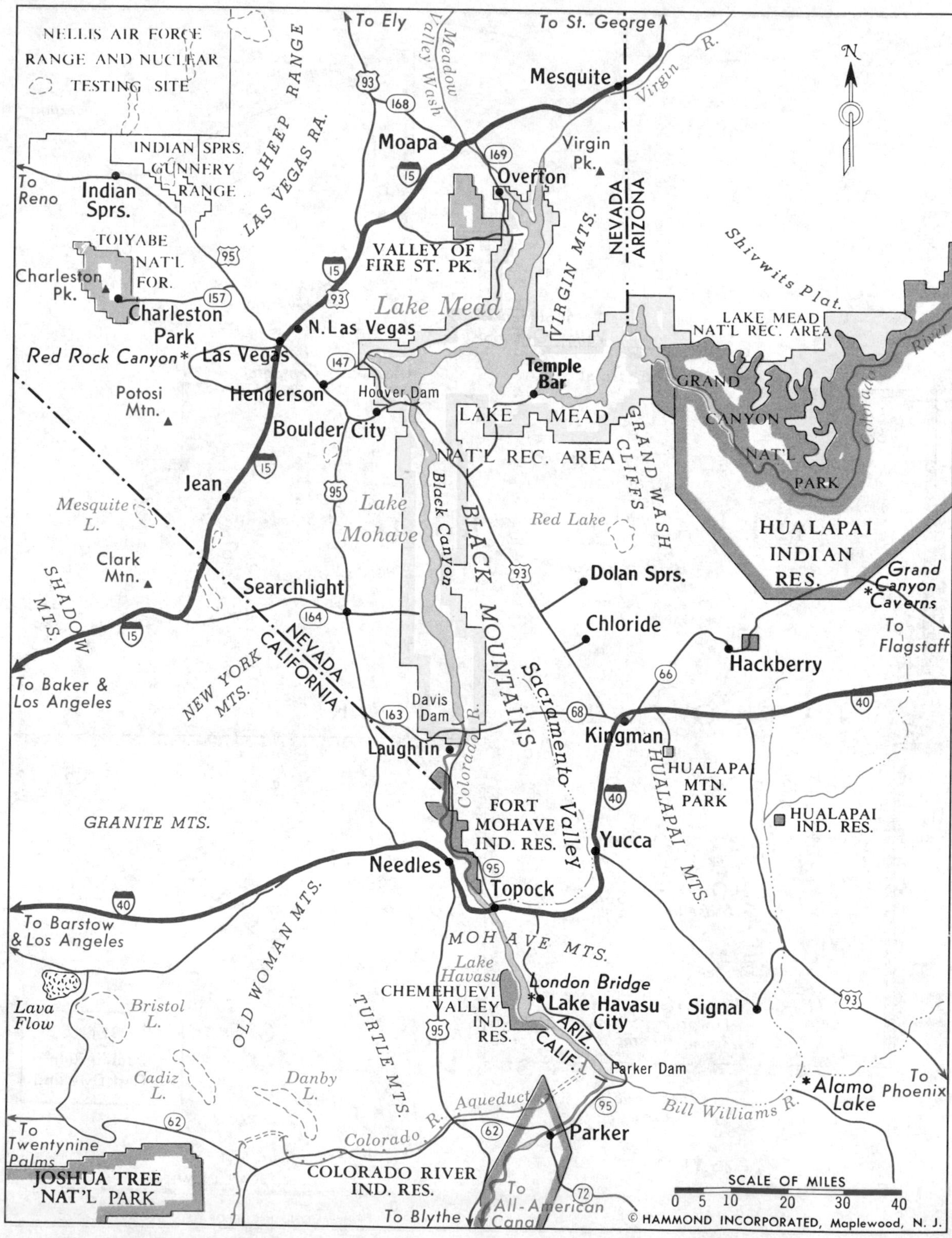

NELLIS AIR FORCE RANGE AND NUCLEAR TESTING SITE
To Ely
To St. George
Meadow Valley Wash
Mesquite
Virgin R.
SHEEP RANGE
LAS VEGAS RA.
Moapa
INDIAN SPRS. GUNNERY RANGE
To Reno
Indian Sprs.
Overton
Virgin Pk.
NEVADA
ARIZONA
VIRGIN MTS.
TOIYABE NAT'L FOR.
Charleston Pk.
Charleston Park
VALLEY OF FIRE ST. PK.
Shivwits Plat.
Lake Mead
N. Las Vegas
LAKE MEAD NAT'L REC. AREA
Red Rock Canyon
Las Vegas
Colorado River
Potosi Mtn.
Henderson
Hoover Dam
Temple Bar
GRAND CANYON NAT'L PARK
Boulder City
LAKE MEAD NAT'L REC. AREA
GRAND WASH CLIFFS
Jean
Mesquite L.
Lake Mohave
Black Canyon
BLACK MOUNTAINS
Red Lake
HUALAPAI INDIAN RES.
Clark Mtn.
Searchlight
Dolan Sprs.
Grand Canyon Caverns
SHADOW MTS.
Chloride
To Flagstaff
NEVADA
CALIFORNIA
Hackberry
To Baker & Los Angeles
NEW YORK MTS.
Davis Dam
Sacramento Valley
Kingman
Laughlin
Colorado R.
HUALAPAI MTN. PARK
HUALAPAI MTS.
FORT MOHAVE IND. RES.
HUALAPAI IND. RES.
GRANITE MTS.
Yucca
Needles
Topock
To Barstow & Los Angeles
MOHAVE MTS.
OLD WOMAN MTS.
Lake Havasu
London Bridge
CHEMEHUEVI VALLEY IND. RES.
Lake Havasu City
Signal
Lava Flow
Bristol L.
TURTLE MTS.
ARIZ.
CALIF.
Parker Dam
Cadiz L.
Danby L.
Aqueduct
Alamo Lake
To Phoenix
Bill Williams R.
To Twentynine Palms
Colorado R.
Parker
JOSHUA TREE NAT'L PARK
COLORADO RIVER IND. RES.
To All-American Canal
To Blythe
SCALE OF MILES
0 5 10 20 30 40
93 168 169 15 95 157 147 164 163 68 66 40 62 72